The Developing Person
Through Childhood and Adolescence

Christian Pierre, *My Friend,* **1995 (acrylic on canvas, 14″ × 18″).** The luminous colors and joyous figures in *My Friend* reflect the hope and discovery apparent in all Christian Pierre's paintings—of adults, animals, plants, landscapes, and, as shown here, children. Christian Pierre has lived in several cultures, under many life circumstances, but she has said that she could never make herself paint anything depressing. Instead, by combining colors, shapes, and composition in ways that simultaneously are fantasy and reality, she depicts a new perspective on what we might have actually seen—such as a child bareback on a horse. In the same way, life is a magical journey. Whenever you pick up this textbook, prepare to move ahead with hope, imagination, and a firm grip on reality.

The Developing Person

Through Childhood and Adolescence

Fifth Edition

KATHLEEN STASSEN BERGER

Bronx Community College

City University of New York

WORTH PUBLISHERS

The Developing Person Through Childhood and Adolescence

Fifth Edition

Copyright © 1980, 1986, 1991, 1995, 2000 by Worth Publishers

All rights reserved.

Printed in the United States of America.

ISBN: 1-57259-417-9

Printing: 5 4 3 2 1

Year: 04 03 02 01 00

Executive Editor: Catherine Woods

Developmental Editors: Marion Castellucci, Ed Millman

Project Director: Michael Kimball

Marketing Manager: Katherine Steinbacher

Design Director: Jennie Nichols

Associate Managing Editor: Tracey Kuehn

Production Manager: Sarah Segal

Senior Designer: Barbara Rusin

Photo Research Manager: Debbie Goodsite

Photo Researcher: Inge King

Composition: TSI Graphics, Inc.

Printing and binding: R. R. Donnelley & Sons Company

Cover Art: *front:* Christian Pierre, *My Friend,* 1995 (acrylic on canvas, 14″ × 18″)

　　　　　back: Christian Pierre, *The Stargazers,* 1995 (acrylic on canvas, 18″ × 24″)

Library of Congress Catalog Card Number: 99-64435

Photo and illustration acknowledgments begin on page IC-1 and constitute an
extension of the copyright page.

Worth Publishers

41 Madison Avenue

New York, New York 10010

www.worthpublishers.com

About the Author

Kathleen Stassen Berger received her undergraduate education at Stanford University and Radcliffe College, earned an M.A.T. from Harvard University and an M.S. and Ph.D. from Yeshiva University. Her broad experience as an educator includes directing a preschool, teaching philosophy and humanities at the United Nations International School, teaching child and adolescent development to graduate students at Fordham University, and teaching social psychology to inmates earning a paralegal degree at Sing Sing Prison.

For the past 26 years at Bronx Community College of the City University of New York, Berger has taught introduction to psychology, child and adolescent development, adulthood and aging, social psychology, abnormal psychology, and human motivation. Her students—who come from many ethnic, economic, and educational backgrounds, and who have a wide range of interests—consistently honor her with the highest teaching evaluations. She recently served as president of Community School Board Two in Manhattan.

Berger is also the author of *The Developing Person Through the Life Span*. Her three developmental texts are currently being used at over 600 colleges and universities worldwide. Her research interests include adolescent identity, sibling relationships, and employed mothers, and she has contributed articles on developmental topics to the *Wiley Encyclopedia of Psychology*. As the mother of four daughters, she brings to her teaching and writing ample firsthand experience with human development.

Contents in Brief

Contents

PART I The Beginnings   64

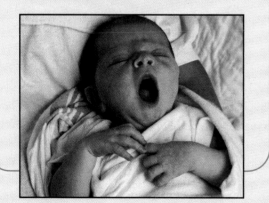

CHAPTER **3**   **Heredity and Environment**   67

The Beginning of Development   67

CHAPTER 6 The First 2 Years: Cognitive Development   173

PART III The Play Years   240

The Growth Spurt 445
Wider, Taller, Then Stronger 445
Proper Proportions 447
Organ Growth 447

Sexual Characteristics 448
Reproductive Possibilities 448
Sexual Appearance 450
  Breasts 450
  Voice and Hair 451

Health and Hazards 454
Sexual Abuse 454
  Special Vulnerability in Adolescence 454
  Gender Differences and Similarities 455
Nutrition 456
  Serious Problems 457
    Eating Disorders 457
Alcohol, Tobacco, and Other Drugs 458
  Disquieting Trends 459
    More Frequent Use 459
    Younger and Younger 459
  Health Impact of the Gateway Drugs 460
    Tobacco 461
    Alcohol 461
    Marijuana 461
  Solutions and Attitudes 463

Summary 466

CHILDREN UP CLOSE: Attitudes About
                    Sexual Maturity 448
RESEARCH REPORT: Body Image 452
CHANGING POLICY: Distinctions in Adolescent
                  Drug Use 462

CHAPTER 15 Adolescence:
           Cognitive Development 469

Adolescent Thought 469
New Intellectual Powers 470
  Hypothetical Thinking 470
  Deductive Reasoning 471
    Are Dolphins Fish? 472
Piaget's Balance Experiment 473

A Problem with the Theory 474
Thinking about Me 475
  Mistaken Assumptions 476

Schools, Learning, and the Adolescent Mind 477
The Adolescent Mind in the School Setting 477
Culture and Schools 478
  Competition and Individual Learning 480
  Standards and Group Learning 481
  Cooperative Learning and Cultural Diversity 483
Structuring Education 484
  School and Employment 485

Adolescent Decision Making 487
Deciding Their Future 487

Thinking About Sex 488
The Risks of Sex 488
  Sexually Transmitted Diseases 488
  Adolescent Pregnancy 488
  The Danger of Commitment 490
Making Decisions and Taking Action 491
  Reasoning About Sex 491
Better Sex Education 493
  Parents as Sex Educators 493
  The Latest Statistics 497

Summary 498

CHILDREN UP CLOSE: A Berger Teenager 478
RESEARCH REPORT: Uncaring and Careless
                  Students 482
CHANGING POLICY: Sex Classes in School 494

CHAPTER 16 Adolescence:
           Psychosocial Development 501

The Self and Identity 501
Multiple Selves 501
Identity 502
  Identity Status 503
    Research on Identity Status 505
    Variations in the Identity Search 506
  Society and Identity 507

Preface

High standards and clear expectations are required for excellent education. But effective learning does not occur unless the instructor follows through with enthusiasm, humor, and intellectual honesty, as I know from my own teaching. I try to apply this philosophy to textbook writing as well.

The best developmental textbooks integrate theory and practice with such powerful clarity that they make students think deeply about the long-term implications of the research and concepts, and simultaneously enable the students to master the specific facts and applied skills required of practiced professionals. There should be no gap between theory and practice; they need each other. This "best book" vision describes the high standards I hold; I hope these standards, as well as my enthusiasm for the field, my humor (especially about my own experiences), and my intellectual honesty are apparent on every page. If so, I thank my heroes and mentors. These include not only my own gifted professors who studied directly with Erikson, Piaget, and Skinner, but also researchers I admire from the cool distance of the printed page: Ainsworth, Bem, the Coles, Garbarino, Gardner, the Gibsons, Lightfoot, Olweus, Plomin, Rutter, Vygotsky, Wong Fillmore, Zigler—and many more (which explains why this text has more references than any comparable book).

As a result of these standards, concepts are clearly explained without condescension, and examples are plentiful and pertinent. Specific current issues, such as abortion, adoption, alcohol abuse, amniocentesis, anorexia, apprenticeship, assisted conception, attention deficit disorder, bilingual education, breast-feeding, birth abnormalities, bulimia, brain patterning, bullying, and so many more, are defined and delineated fairly, raising questions that have no easy answers. More importantly, controversies are put into context so that genetic, cultural, historical, ethnic, and economic influences are never ignored.

New Features

As for meeting expectations, this new edition has additional prompts to help students become scholars. Four new features are particularly designed to make learning interactive, which is the goal of the entire book.

Applications

Almost every topic leads to possible applications. Some of these are mentioned directly with a question or a comment in the text, others are left to the instructors and students to draw. However, several times in each chapter **Especially for . . .** followed by the name of one or another group (parents, social workers, educators, researchers and so on) appears in the margin,

❷ **Especially for Educators:** Suppose a particular school has 30 children in the second grade. Five of them have special problems. One speaks very little and seems autistic, one is very talkative but cannot read, one is almost blind, and two are ADHD (one of them aggressive). What are the advantages and disadvantages of creating a special class for these five, rather than mainstreaming them in the regular class? (See answer page 362.)

Now a Toddler As this very young lady begins to walk, she demonstrates why such children are called toddlers: They move unsteadily from side to side as well as forward.

❓ *Observational Quiz: What emotions and fine motor skills usually accompany early walking, as shown here? (See answer page 153.)*

with a question that can be answered deductively from the implications of the next few paragraphs. To show you how this works, an Especially For appears at the bottom of the previous page.

Observational Quizzes

The second new interactive feature accompanies several photographs in each chapter. Since well-honed observational skills are crucial for everyone who studies child development, an **Observational Quiz** appears after the caption. An example is in the margin. You can turn now to the answers, or wait until you reach that chapter of the book.

World Wide Web

The third new feature is the Berger Web site (www.worthpublishers.com), an online educational setting for students and instructors, featuring practice tests, annotated Web links, flashcard tutorials, charts and graphs from the book, and a topical table of contents. The site also offers a series of video clips and PowerPoint slides that professors can download for use in the classroom. Professors can also sign up to receive bimonthly updates from me on teaching ideas that can be incorporated in the classroom. I urge everyone to go to the site for this valuable supplementary information, and feel free to send me an e-mail with your opinions (kathleen.berger@bccc.cuny.edu).

Critical Thinking Exercises

Each chapter ends with a Critical Thinking Exercise, asking the student to answer a question that demands reflection and argument. Answers are in Appendix B.

Tried and True Features

As always, vocabulary is highlighted as a scaffold for learning, and cross-cultural examples, figures, photos, and charts draw each of us beyond the narrowness of our own experiences. The Changing Policy and Children Up Close boxes are more plentiful and more pointed and engaging for the reader than the Public Policy and A Closer Look boxes of the previous edition. Five characteristics of this text have been acclaimed since the first edition and, of course, I continue them in this edition and, here give credit to the sources of each.

- **Language That Communicates the Excitement and Challenge of the Field** To the extent that the writing is clear, I thank my loyal editor and friend, Peter Deane, as well as Marion Castellucci and the other editors at Worth Publishers.
- **Up-to-Date Coverage of Research, Policy, and Practice** Here I thank my students, who always keep me current with their questions and concerns.
- **Chronological Framework** As every researcher in human development knows, children develop chronologically, but science is organized topically. Teachers must find the right balance between these two. The topical within chronological structure that I use seems the best way to

help students remember the real child, while paying proper respect to the subdivisions of our field.

- **Topical Discussions**   The chapters that have common developmental foci have the same color-coded page numbers. Biosocial chapters are turquoise, cognitive chapters are blue, and psychosocial chapters are salmon. Check the index for specific coverage on various topics. As mentioned before, please visit the Berger Web site (www.worthpublishers.com) for a detailed topical table of contents.
- **Photographs, Tables, and Boxes That Are Integral to the Text** Sometimes such aspects of texts are add-ons, glitter and flash to woo the novice without aiding education. From the very beginning, Worth Publishers has allowed authors to choose photos, write captions, draft charts, and alter designs to better fit the words—not vice versa.

Content Changes for the Fifth Edition

This fifth edition marks a new era at Worth Publishers. The company has been reorganized, relocated, and reinvigorated since the fourth edition. This has meant a markedly better design for this book, with brighter colors, sharper photos, more graphs, and a stunning new cover by a contemporary artist.

As always, the main work of a textbook is in the words. The basic message of those words has been retained, for there are certain facts—stages and ages, dangers and diversities—that every student should know. After all, human development is a science, and scientists build on past discovery. However, life continues to unfold, so no page is exactly what it was, and every chapter includes innovative organization and content. Highlights of these <u>new</u> emphases and content appear below:

Chapter 1 (Introduction): There is now a nuanced exploration of the distinctions among ethnicity, race, and culture, with a research example of children's aggression after the 1992 Los Angeles riots.

Chapter 2 (Theories): The distinction between the "grand" theories (psychoanalytic, learning, cognitive) and "emergent" theories makes clear the value of both comprehensive and innovative thought. A completely new section on epigenetic systems theory shows how ethology, evolution, and genetics combine to form this ground-breaking theory.

Chapter 3 (Heredity and Environment): The text discussion and box on the causes of and solutions to infertility explore the ethical, economic, and epigenetic implications of alternative reproductive technology.

Chapter 4 (Prenatal Development and Birth): The prenatal and birth chapters are now combined into one, with new figures and charts to highlight the increase in low birthweight babies and in prenatal drug abuse—and controversial explanations for these trends.

Chapter 5 (The First 2 Years: Biosocial Development): Norms are described as the culturally influenced standards that they are, especially in a new Children Up Close that describes my own children as they began to walk. A completely new Research Report on otitis media emphasizes the importance of early experiences and the development of the brain.

Chapter 6 (The First 2 Years: Cognitive Development): The findings of all the key researchers—including the Gibsons, Piaget, Vygotsky, Rovee-Collier, and Bloom—are now more firmly connected to show infant cognitive development as the perceptual, cultural, and social experience that it is.

Chapter 7 (The First 2 Years: Psychosocial Development): The longitudinal ramifications during adulthood of early secure and insecure attachments are explained with alternative explanations of the research findings.

Chapter 8 (The Play Years: Biosocial Development): The connection between early experience and brain development is made, with reference to Romanian orphans, learning styles, and other applicable examples. The discussion of maltreatment now includes kin care, permanency planning, and the reasons to distinguish between the abuse cases that require immediate legal intervention and those that need ongoing family support.

Chapter 9 (The Play Years: Cognitive Development): New cross-cultural and contextual material shows the impact of family composition and community values on a child's theory of mind. A blind child's actual moment-by-moment experience in one preschool emphasizes the practical value of early education.

Chapter 10 (The Play Years: Psychosocial Development): Emotional regulation as a critical development during the early years is described, including prosocial and antisocial attitudes and behavior. All five theories regarding gender roles are explored with a new conclusion titled "Gender and Destiny."

Chapter 11 (The School Years: Biosocial Development): Four key ideas from the developmental psychopathology perspective—"abnormality is normal," "disability changes with time," "adulthood can be better or worse," and "diagnosis depends on social context" — are now explained, anchoring and structuring the entire special needs section.

Chapter 12 (The School Years: Cognitive Development): Actual transcripts from classrooms, new international data on math and science, and new historical data on how North American children spend their time all enliven the discussion of cognition.

Chapter 13 (The School Years: Psychosocial Development): Family structure is described internationally and historically and compared to a template of ideal family function. The major discussion on bullies includes long-term consequences for victim and bully. Sexual harassment, social rejection, and possible law-breaking are considered as part of this issue, with practical ideas about how to stop bullying at school.

Chapter 14 (Adolescence: Biosocial Development): The discussion of drug use is updated, and it now includes new material on the physical hazards of gateway drugs.

Chapter 15 (Adolescence: Cognitive Development): Data on fewer teen births, more condom use, and fewer abortions are presented, in part to explore the new methods of sex education. The idea that risk-taking is not only normative but also rational is presented.

Chapter 16 (Adolescence: Psychosocial Development): The myths of generation gap and peer pressure are exploded, since peers help adolescents explore identities, guide sexual interactions, and prevent parasuicide. The distinction between life-course persistent criminals and adolescent-limited delinquency is clarified to suggest effective crime prevention.

SUPPLEMENTS

As an instructor myself, I know the importance of good supplements. I have been known to reject a textbook adoption because the company had a bad record on ancillaries and service. Fortunately, Worth has a well-deserved reputation for the quality of such materials—for both professors and students. With this book, you will find:

Observational Video for Child Development

Bringing observational learning to the classroom, this new child development video allows students to watch and listen to real children as a way of supplementing and amplifying their reading of a text in child development. Designed both for in-class demonstration and at-home student viewing, this video will enable development students to observe children and their activities, responses, and behaviors in a variety of naturalistic environments, including school, home, and day-care and health-care settings. Each narrated, real-life segment of the video is accompanied by a "Focus on Research" portion, which is an interview with a noted researcher or child development expert who uses observations of the video just viewed to describe particular areas of research or discuss applied topics. The video will offer clips of children of various ages and ethnicities. This 60-minute video will be accompanied by a brief observational guide that can help students develop observational skills and, in addition, makes clear the linkages between segments.

The Scientific American Frontiers Video Collection

This valuable resource provides instructors with 17 video segments of approximately 15 minutes each, on topics ranging from language development to nature-nurture issues. The videos can be used to launch classroom lectures or to emphasize and clarify course material. The *Faculty Guide for Scientific American Frontiers Video Collection* by Richard O. Straub, University of Michigan, describes and relates each segment to specific topics in the text.

The Berger Web Site (www.worthpublishers.com)

See description on page xviii.

Study Guide

The *Study Guide,* by Richard O. Straub, helps students evaluate their understanding and retain their learning longer. Each chapter includes a review of key concepts, guided study questions, and section reviews that encourage students' active participation in the learning process; two practice tests and a challenge test help them assess their mastery of the material.

Instructor's Resources

The *Instructor's Resources,* by Richard O. Straub, features a chapter-by-chapter preview and lecture guide, learning objectives, springboard topics for discussion and debate, handouts for student projects, and supplementary readings from journal articles. Course planning suggestions, ideas for term projects, and a guide to audiovisual and software materials are also included, as are new Internet assignments that help students find better research sources on the Web.

Test Bank

A *Test Bank* by David E. Baskind, thoroughly revised, includes approximately 80 multiple-choice and 50 fill-in, true-false, and essay questions for each chapter. Each question is keyed to the textbook by topic, page number, type (factual or conceptual), and level of difficulty.

Computerized Test Bank

The *Computerized Test Bank* by David E. Baskind is available in an easy-to-use test-generation format for Windows and Macintosh, allowing instructors to select specific questions, generate a random assortment from one or more chapters, and even add questions to the system.

Transparencies

A set of 100 full-color transparencies of key illustrations, charts, graphs, and tables from the textbook, as well as additional material by Richard O. Straub, is available to instructors.

Thanks

I'd like to thank those academic reviewers who have read this book in every edition, and who have provided suggestions, criticisms, references, and encouragement. They have all made this a better book. I want to mention especially those who have reviewed this edition:

Marlene Adelman
Norwalk Community College

Kathy Brown
Southeastern Oklahoma State University

Mark A. Clement
Colby-Sawyer College

Donald R. Cusumano
St. Louis Community College

Sally Hill
Bakersfield College

Eric L. Johnson
Northwestern College

John A. Stefferud
Springfield Technical Community College College

Don Stephenson
College of Southern Idaho

Mark A. Stewart
American River College

Trish Vandiver
University of St. Thomas

In addition, I again want to thank those who reviewed the last edition:

Susan Barrett
Lehigh University

Judith Bernhard
Ryerson Polytechnic University

Lois Bloom
Columbia University, Teacher's College

Angela Pratts Buchanan
DeAnza College

Lily Chu
New Mexico State University

E. Mark Cummings
West Virginia University

Peggy A. DeCooke
State University of New York at Purchase

Judy DeLoache
University of Illinois at Urbana-Champaign

Nancy Eisenberg
Arizona State University

Gene V. Elliott
Rowan College of New Jersey

Jeffrey Fagen
St. John's University

Beverly I. Fagot
University of Oregon

Martin E. Ford
George Mason University

Hill Goldsmith
University of Wisconsin, Madison

Jan V. Goodsitt
Minnesota School of Professional Psychology

George W. Holden
University of Texas at Austin

Shelley Hymel
University of British Columbia

Russell A. Isabella
University of Utah

Philip Mohan
University of Idaho

David Moshman
University of Nebraska at Lincoln

Scott Paris
University of Michigan

Joseph M. Price
San Diego State University

Susan A. Rose
Albert Einstein College of Medicine

Anita Miller Sostek
National Institutes of Health

John Stefferud
Springfield Technical Community College

Linda A. Stoner
San Joaquin Delta College

Douglas Teti
University of Maryland

Laura A. Thompson
New Mexico State University

Mary Trepanier-Street
University of Michigan at Dearborn

Dedication

Textbooks don't have dedications, I was once told. Well, especially since my name is the only one on the cover, I have always included a dedication in the preface. This is my ninth dedication, this time to 21,000 children and to their parents, teachers, and principals in the public schools of District Two, New York City. All four of my children attended those schools and continue to benefit from them. For the past six years I have been elected to the School Board, humbled by the job but proud of the results. Our superintendent for most of those years, Anthony Alvarado (now Chancellor in San Diego) said, "Every child in every classroom must learn every day, no exceptions, no excuses," and that happens in our 45 schools. Although I am not running for a third term, the lessons I have learned from these children and their educators will continue to inspire me.

New York City
May 1999

The Developing Person

Through Childhood and Adolescence

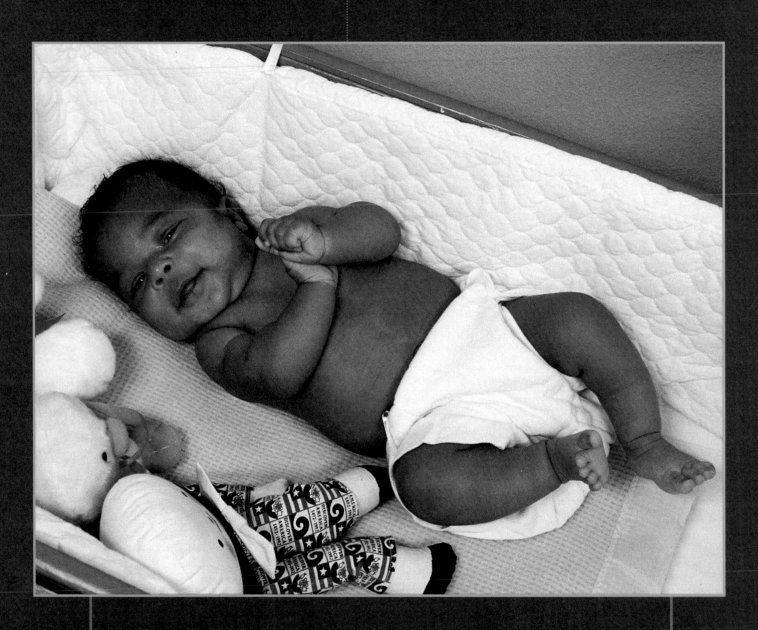

Introduction

You are about to begin a fascinating journey through childhood and adolescence. This chapter will serve as a kind of road map, outlining your route and familiarizing you with the general terrain. More specifically, it will introduce you to the goals and values that define the scientific study of human development and suggest the underlying assumptions, overarching themes, and practical applications of that science. But human development actually occurs not as a mass migration but on a one-by-one basis—one person and one step at a time. So, to begin our journey, I would like to introduce you to one developing person, my brother's son David.

THE STUDY OF HUMAN DEVELOPMENT

David has just celebrated his thirtieth birthday, which was itself a surprise, given the circumstances of his birth. Before describing the extraordinary, however, let me emphasize that, in many ways, David's childhood and adolescence were typical, marked by a family that cared for him from the moment he was born; schools and teachers that brought out his best, and sometimes his worst; and a social life with peers and the community that gave him both joy and pain. David is now 4 years out of college, and like many recent college graduates, he looks forward to someday raising a family and, more immediately, to having "a definite career, or at least a decent job."

One detail of his college years may seem familiar to some of you. As a sophomore, David struggled with his writing assignments, and he was regularly belittled by one professor. His reaction was to stop attending classes, flunk out, and spend more than a year at home doing odd jobs before deciding to return to college. With great effort, David finally earned his B.A. degree, completing his senior year with a 3.7 average. As he expressed it, "College itself was one of my adversities, but I rebounded big time."

The truth is that college was the least of his adversities. David began life with his very survival in doubt and with so many handicaps that a normal life seemed impossible. His infancy, childhood, and adolescence were filled with harsh, often heartbreaking obstacles.

Most of this book is, of course, about more typical development—that is, the usual patterns of growth and change that everyone follows to some degree and that no one follows exactly. But David's story is woven throughout this chapter for two reasons.

First, David's childhood struggles and triumphs offer a poignant illustration of the underlying goal of the study of human development: to help each person develop throughout life as fully as possible.

1

Second, David's example illuminates, with unusual vividness, the basic definitions and central questions that frame our study. Just as suddenly entering an unfamiliar culture makes us more aware of our own daily routines, habits, and assumptions—which we usually don't notice precisely because they are so familiar—so, too, can David's story highlight the major factors that influence more typical human development. Let us begin, therefore, with the ideas that delineate our work, and then return to David.

Definition and Scope

scientific study of human development A science that seeks to understand how and why people change, and how and why they remain the same, as they grow older.

Briefly defined, the **scientific study of human development** is the science that seeks to understand how and why people change, and how and why they remain the same, as they grow older. In pursuing this goal, we examine whatever kinds of change we find—simple growth, radical transformation, improvement, and decline—and whatever elements lead to continuity from day to day, year to year, or generation to generation. We consider factors ranging from the elaborate genetic codes that provide the foundations for human development to the countless particular experiences that shape and refine development, from the impact of prenatal life to the influences of the family, school, peer groups, and community over the life span. We examine all these factors, and many others, in light of the ever-changing social and cultural contexts that give them meaning and force. And always, we are aware of the possible implications and applications of our study. Indeed,

> developmental science originated from the need to solve practical problems and . . . from pressures to improve the education, health, welfare, and legal status of children and their families. [Hetherington, 1998]

The study of human development thus involves many academic disciplines—especially biology, education, and psychology, but also history, sociology, anthropology, medicine, economics, and dozens more. Because it is a science, it follows objective rules of evidence; but it is also laden with personal implications and applications. It originated with children, but because the same basic principles apply from the moment of conception to the last breath, it covers the entire life span.

This interplay of the objective and the subjective, of change and continuity, of the individual and the universal, of young and old, and of past, present, and future makes developmental science a dynamic, interactive, and even transformative study. Of all the sciences, the study of human development is the least static, least predictable, and least narrow. It also may have the most noble goal: "explaining, assessing, and promoting change and development" (Renninger & Amsel, 1997). In other words, developmental scientists seek not only to understand and measure human change over time but also to use their knowledge to help all people develop their full human potential.

The Three Domains

biosocial domain The part of human development that includes physical growth and development as well as the family, community, and cultural factors that affect that growth and development.

cognitive domain The part of human development that includes all the mental processes through which the individual thinks, learns, and communicates, plus the institutions involved in learning and communicating.

psychosocial domain The part of human development that includes emotions, personality characteristics, and relationships with other people, as well as cultural influences.

In an effort to somehow organize this vast interdisciplinary study, human development is often separated into three domains, or areas of study. The **biosocial domain** includes the brain and body, as well as changes in them and the social influences that direct them. The **cognitive domain** includes thought processes, perceptual abilities, and language mastery, as well as the educational institutions that encourage them. The **psychosocial domain** includes emotions, personality, and interpersonal relationships with family, friends, and the wider community. (See Figure 1.1.)

Figure 1.1 The Three Domains. The division of human development into three domains makes it easier to study, but remember that very few factors belong exclusively to one domain or another. Development is not piecemeal but holistic: Each aspect of development is related to all three domains.

DOMAINS OF HUMAN DEVELOPMENT

Biosocial Development	Cognitive Development	Psychosocial Development
Includes all the growth and change that occur in a person's body, and the genetic, nutritional, and health factors that affect that growth and change. Motor skills—everything from grasping a rattle to driving a car—are also part of the biosocial domain. Social and cultural factors that affect these areas, such as duration of breast-feeding, education of children with special needs, and attitudes about ideal body shape, are also part of biosocial development.	Includes all the mental processes that are used to obtain knowledge or to become aware of the environment. Cognition encompasses perception, imagination, judgment, memory, and language—the processes people use to think, decide, and learn. Education, including the formal curriculum within schools, informal tutoring by family and friends, and the results of individual curiosity and creativity, is also part of this domain.	Includes development of emotions, temperament, and social skills. The influences of family, friends, the community, the culture, and the larger society are particularly central to the psychosocial domain. Thus cultural differences in the value accorded children, or in ideas about "appropriate" sex roles, or in what is regarded as the ideal family structure are considered part of this domain.

Every Domain, Every Moment Every aspect of human behavior reflects all three domains. Obviously, biosocial factors—such as hormones and body strength—are at work here, but so are cognitive and psychosocial ones. For instance, each student's mental concentration or lack of it is critical to karate success. So is the culture's message about who should learn the martial arts—a message that seems to have made this an all-male class.

All three domains are important at every age. For instance, understanding an infant involves studying his or her health (biosocial), curiosity (cognitive), and temperament (psychosocial), as well as dozens of other aspects of development from all three domains. Similarly, understanding an adolescent requires studying the physical changes that mark the bodily transition from child to adult, the intellectual development that leads to efforts to think logically about such issues as sexual passion and future goals, and the emerging patterns of friendship and courtship that prepare the individual for the intimate relationships of adulthood.

How easy is it to determine which domain a particular topic belongs to? For example, in which domain would you place a baby's weight gain, a 5-year-old's idea that 3 + 3 = 33, and a 10-year-old's inclination to bully smaller children? If your answers were "biosocial," "cognitive," and "psychosocial," many developmentalists would agree with you. But you have probably already realized another fact: Each domain is affected by the other two. Whether or not an infant is well nourished, for instance, affects the baby's learning ability and social experiences. And those two domains not only are affected by a baby's nutrition but also affect it, in that a mother's knowledge (cognitive) or poverty (psychosocial) will influence her feeding of her infant (biosocial).

Discussion of any topic, from any domain, for any individual, thus requires reference to the other domains.

The school bully is a topic that belongs to the psychosocial domain and thus is discussed in Chapter 13 (The School Years: Psychosocial Development). But bullies also tend to be physically larger than their victims (biosocial domain) and ignorant of the implications of their actions (cognitive domain). Therefore, while the study of development is organized into domains and then segmented even further, the developmentalist is always aware that development is *holistic*. Each child is a person, growing as an integrated whole, but aspects of his or her development are studied separately by scientists in different academic disciplines. Similarly, each child is a whole person, but that person is seen quite differently by his or her pediatrician, teacher, and best friend.

THE MANY CONTEXTS OF DEVELOPMENT

We often think of development as originating *within* the person—the result of such internal factors as genetic programming, physical maturation, cognitive growth, and personal inclination. However, development is also greatly influenced by forces *outside* the person, by the physical surroundings and social interactions that provide incentives, opportunities, and pathways for growth. Taken together, groups of these external forces form the *contexts*, or *systems* or *environments*, in which development occurs.

Lonely or in Awe? Imagine yourself as the child on the left, spending much of your childhood following sheep near massive mountains, flowering meadows, running rivers. Would this childhood setting affect your skills, emotions, and attitudes as an adult? Research influenced by the ecological perspective has shown that it would. Depending on the values of the person describing them, the Indians shown here from the highlands of Peru are said to be more spiritual and poetic than most people or more fatalistic and passive. No one, however, sees their typical personality as just like that of residents of Chicago or Tokyo or Berlin.

❷ *Observational Quiz (answer on page 6): From the photo, what can you tell about the social relationships of the child in the left foreground?*

The Ecological Approach

Calling attention to these external influences more than 25 years ago, Urie Bronfenbrenner, a developmental researcher, began to emphasize an **ecological approach** to the study of human development (Bronfenbrenner, 1977, 1979, 1986). In essence, this approach regards human development as a "joint function of person and environment" (Bronfenbrenner, 1993). Thus, just as a naturalist studying a flower or a fish needs to examine the organism's supporting ecosystems, Bronfenbrenner argues, developmentalists need to study the ecological systems, or contexts, in which each human being seeks to thrive. In Bronfenbrenner's application of this concept, human ecosystems include both the *physical* environment (the climate, the

ecological approach A perspective on development that takes into account the various physical and social settings in which human development occurs.

Figure 1.2 The Ecological Model. According to Urie Bronfenbrenner, each person is significantly affected by interactions among a number of overlapping ecosystems. Microsystems are the systems that intimately and immediately shape human development. The primary microsystems for children include the family, peer group, classroom, neighborhood, and sometimes a church, temple, or mosque as well. Interactions among the microsystems, as when parents and teachers coordinate their efforts to educate the child, take place through the mesosystem. Surrounding the microsystems is the exosystem, which includes all the external networks, such as community structures and local educational, medical, employment, and communications systems, that influence the microsystems. And influencing all other systems is the macrosystem, which includes cultural values, political philosophies, economic patterns, and social conditions. Together, these systems are termed the context of human development.

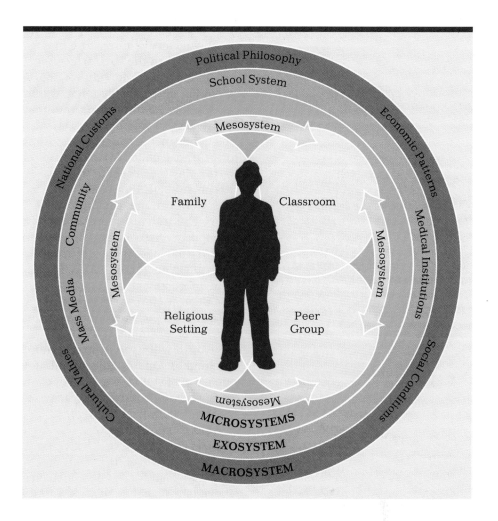

space per person, the arrangement of the dwelling) and the *social* environment (the people, the culture, the economy).

To depict the main ecosystems that support human development, Bronfenbrenner has devised an ecological model that organizes the broad contexts of development in terms of the relative immediacy of their impact on the individual. At the center of this model is the individual (see Figure 1.2). Each setting that directly surrounds and shapes that individual is called a *microsystem*. Examples of a child's microsystems include the family, the neighborhood play area, the peer group, and the classroom. The *mesosystem* is made up of connections among the various microsystems—such as parent-teacher conferences that link home and school. Next comes the *exosystem*, comprising the economic, political, educational, and cultural institutions and practices that directly affect the various microsystems and indirectly, but often powerfully, affect everyone in those microsystems. Surrounding and permeating all these other systems is the *macrosystem*, which consists of the overarching traditions, beliefs, and values of the society.

Reciprocal Influences

The influences within and between these systems are multidirectional and interactive. In fact, Bronfenbrenner and others use the word "system" to emphasize that, just as in any system, activity in one part will affect all the other parts. A change in ocean temperatures in the Pacific, for example, can cause a blizzard in New England. Or even, as the new perspective from physics, chaos theory, explains, the flap of a butterfly's wing on one continent can cause a hurricane in another. (A tiny change that leads to a major event is called the "butterfly effect.")

Interaction among these ecosystems means, for example, that the quality of life in the family microsystem directly affects a worker's productivity on the job. At the same time, the microsystem of the workplace—specifically, stresses and satisfactions at the office, store, factory, or farm—affects the quality of life at home, including how responsive people are to their children. Those children, in turn, can keep a family together or wedge it apart by the way they react to their parents (Barling & MacEwan, 1992; Loscocco & Roschlee, 1991; Parcel & Menaghan, 1997; Zedeck, 1992). The very presence of a child can make a difference: Couples with no children or with four or more children are more likely than other couples to separate and divorce. Obviously, these interactions are reciprocal. That is, children both affect and are affected by the nature of a marital relationship; family relationships both affect and are affected by job success; and similarly for other microsystem interactions.

Such reciprocal interactions within and among microsystems are also affected by the surrounding exosystem and macrosystem (Lerner et al., 1995). For example, if a culture expects couples to have many children, a new birth will usually strengthen the commitment of husband and wife to each other. On the other hand, if individual career success is an important measure of status in a society, then the time, energy, and sacrifice required to raise small children may lead to resentment, abuse, and depression. This is particularly true for wives if the macrosystem is such that women are expected to stay home with the children, and it is particularly true for husbands if wives expect them to share equally in household work.

Note, however, that while pressures from the ecosystem and macrosystem may lead to certain consequences for the family microsystem, it is not inevitable that they *will* lead to those consequences. In one case, a major problem, such as the birth of triplets, may seem to have little effect on a family ecosystem. In another case, a relatively minor problem, such as a baby's sleepless night just before one parent's major work deadline, may trigger harsh words, then alcohol abuse, then a fight, and then a divorce.

The Social Context

Bronfenbrenner's ecological approach to development is very useful in highlighting the complex influences, both immediate and distant, on any one person's development. However, Bronfenbrenner's terminology, and his depiction of spheres of influence, nested one inside the other, sometimes leads students to think of these ecosystems as discrete entities, with clear boundaries between them. This is not the case, because development is holistic in its contexts as well as in its domains. In fact, the various ecosystems are inextricably intermeshed, their effects dynamic, fluid, and overlapping.

To avoid this confusion, the term **social context** will be used in this book to encompass all the social ecosystems delineated by Bronfenbrenner. We will thus be able to focus on the various contexts in which development occurs, without worrying about where they lie within the ecological circles. Bear in mind, however, that whether we speak of a single social context or of many ecosystems, the core concept is the same. Always, every individual develops within, is influenced by, and in turn influences the dynamic relationships that exist among many interlocking settings.

---

❶ Answer to Observational Quiz (from page 4): *She is not close enough to converse with anyone, no males are present in her immediate group, and each child in the photo is quite distant from the others—because of the need to keep each herd of sheep separate from the other herds. If this is typical of her life, her social circumstances discourage language learning, encourage gender roles, and make play with peers impossible.*

social context All the means—including the people, the customs, the institutions, and the beliefs—by which society influences the developing person.

An Example: The Family in Social Context

The dynamic and reciprocal nature of the social context becomes evident when we look closely at its most basic unit, the family. Universally, the family is the primary setting for nurturing children to become competent and contributing members of society. In what manner, and how well, a given family does this depends on a wide array of factors. Some of these factors are rooted directly in the specific family setting—from the number and ages of children, parents, and other adults in the family to the emotional climate that the interactions of these individuals create. Each family relationship (such as that between husband and wife, parent and child, brother and sister, or grandparent and grandchild) affects all the other family members and all the other relationships.

For example, one hypothesis about intellectual development suggests that each new baby reduces the cognitive resources available to each child and thus a firstborn or only child is destined to be more intelligent than a middle child of a large family (Zajonc & Mullally, 1997). This may or may not be true: scientists have not reached firm conclusions about the impact of an additional child on previous children's intelligence. However, the idea that siblings can affect each other in such a way provides an example of how far-reaching family influences can be.

If You Lived Here . . . The social context includes not only the people who inhabit it but also the specific environments that people construct for themselves. The arrangement of rooms within a house, of houses within a neighborhood, of schools, businesses, and hospitals within a community—all create an environment that hinders, enhances, and directs each person's development. This deceptively ordinary backyard setting, for example, may be a good place for a multigenerational family picnic and may provide a secure place for children. At the same time, its high-fenced privacy and crowded space, especially for children, may limit play and even conversation with those outside the family. For example, where would these children play tag or hide-and-seek?

Many of the factors influencing family relationships occur outside the immediate home setting, in what Bronfenbrenner calls the macrosystem and the exosystem. The values of the community regarding gender roles; the ways in which neighborhood institutions affect family functioning; the past and current experiences of the grandparents, who, in turn, are influenced by the customs and core beliefs of earlier times—all these are part of the social context even though they are not directly part of the family microsystem within each home. The family is indeed the basic setting for intimacy and growth, but it is the complexity of contexts and histories impinging on each family that makes the family one of the most varied institutions on earth (Altergott, 1993).

Overlapping Systems: A "Difficult" Child

To sharpen our focus a bit, let us look at the contextual interactions that might be affecting a young boy who is "difficult"—disobedient, hostile, demanding, impulsive. In other words, let us take a *contextual approach* to this problem. A noncontextual analysis might point to the mother as the cause, finding her to be self-absorbed, or cold, or indulgent. Such an explanation would be flawed, however, because it is one-dimensional. As a leading family therapist explains:

> It may be relatively easy to discover that a little boy who misbehaves in school has a mother who doesn't make him behave at home. On closer examination we might see that she doesn't discipline the boy because she is overly involved with him. They're constantly together and interact more like playmates than parent and child. But why is the mother so close to the boy? Why does she need a playmate? Is it because she's emotionally

distant from her husband? . . . Perhaps she is deliberately lenient with the boy to counterbalance her husband's overly harsh control. The reason so many family dilemmas defeat us is that we fail to recognize that every family member's behavior is influencing and influenced by the behavior of the rest. [Minuchin & Nichols, 1993]

Increasingly, developmentalists recognize that the closeness of the marital relationship, the father's involvement in caregiving, and the rivalries and tensions of other siblings are implicated in each child's behavior. Even within the same family, different children experience the family context quite differently. In fact, one of the research surprises in recent years is that siblings, growing up in the same house with the same parents, usually experience quite distinct punishment and praise (Reiss et al., 1999; Rowe, 1994). A particular family might be dysfunctional for one child, adequate for another, and very supportive for a third, depending on each child's sex, birth order, and personality.

Of course, the child is a central player within the family system. In the case of the difficult child, the mother's apparent caregiving flaws might be the *result* of the child's intractable behavior more than the *cause* of it (Sanson & Rothbart, 1995). Thus, our contextual approach to development within the family setting requires that we consider the totality of family interactions. Each family member is likely to be both "a victim and an architect" of whatever problems the family might have (Patterson, 1982; Patterson & Capaldi, 1991).

A contextual approach does not stop there, however; just as each family member is affected by the interactions of all the family's members, so each family is influenced by (and influences) other contexts. As we already noted, the stresses and satisfactions of the workplace can have a significant impact on family interactions. Do the difficult child's parents feel secure and fulfilled in their work or anxious and frustrated? The answer can obviously affect the quality of the attention they give their son, as well as their tolerance for certain of his disruptive antics.

Other relevant influences can be found in the contexts of the peer group and the school. The difficult child's friends, for example, may admire and thus encourage his unruly behavior, or the school's demand for obedience and conformity may create tensions that spill out at home (Cairns & Cairns, 1994; Dishion et al., 1995; Patterson et al., 1992). Of course, the influences of these contexts could also be positive: the peer group might teach the child needed social skills, and the school might provide avenues of success in the classroom or on the playground that enhance self-esteem and reduce hostility.

Typically, the peer group and school affect the family only indirectly, through their influence on the behavior of the child. Sometimes, however, these other contexts have a direct impact on the family. Suppose the parents realize that their "difficult" son is actually less rowdy than most of his neighborhood friends, or they hear from a teacher that he is unusually creative, potentially a talented artist. As a consequence of such contact with the peer group or school, their perceptions may change. They may not only see their son in a new light but also treat him differently, and he, in turn, may begin to behave differently. In fact, many difficult children, through one influence or another, become admirable adults—rarely easygoing, perhaps, but with an independence and strength that leads them to success and love.

This same sort of multicontextual analysis can be applied to almost any specific behavior in almost any developing person. In every case, the individual's actions should be examined as both cause and consequence of the contexts in which development is occurring.

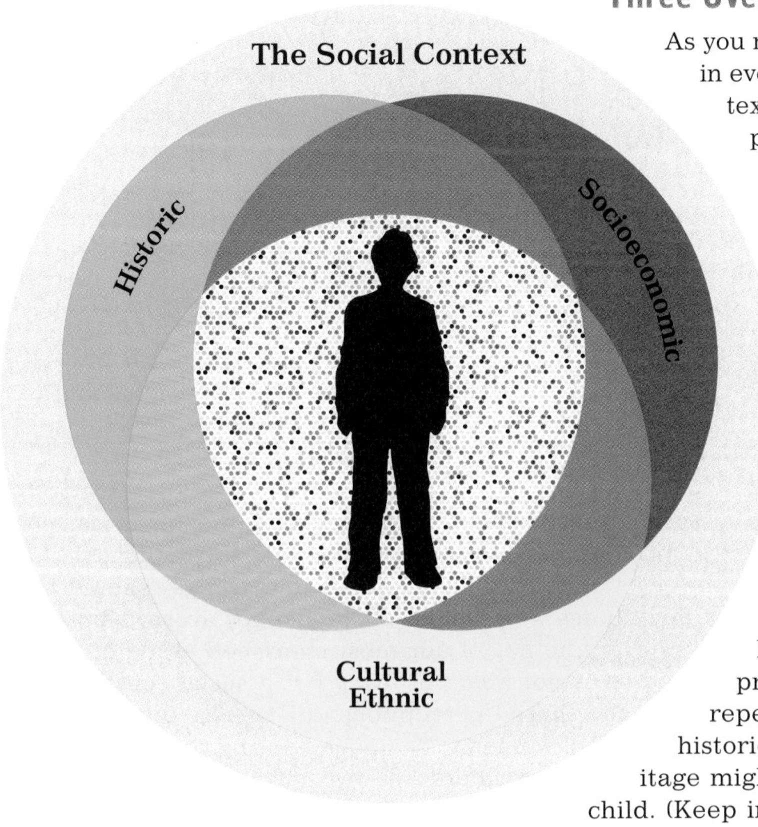

The Social Context

Historic

Socioeconomic

Cultural
Ethnic

Figure 1.3 Contexts Within Contexts. Three broad contexts within the social context—history, socioeconomic status, and culture—affect the development of children in many ways, sometimes distantly, sometimes directly, sometimes individually, sometimes in combination. Because these three contexts overlap, it is often impossible to determine whether a particular effect comes from cohort, social class, or ethnic heritage.

cohort A group of people who, because they were born within a few years of each other, experience many of the same historical and social conditions.

Three Overlapping Contexts

As you might imagine, it is impossible, in a single book or in everyday life, to consider simultaneously all the contextual factors that might bear on any particular aspect of development. Throughout this book, we will examine a great many such factors, exploring the ways in which specific contexts tend to push specific aspects of development in one direction or another. At the outset, however, we need to define and describe three contexts that affect the de-velopment of virtually every individual in every phase of development—the historical context, the socioeconomic context, and the cultural-ethnic context. Each of these is part of the overall social context (and each is also usually considered to be part of Bronfenbrenner's macrosystem).

Developmental researchers have found that these three contexts have a considerable impact which traditionally had been overlooked by child psychologists and misinterpreted by many students of development. To avoid repeating those errors, we need to understand how historical events, wealth or poverty, and family heritage might shape, guide, and limit the development of a child. (Keep in mind that, as Figure 1.3 suggests, these three contexts do not act in isolation.)

The Historical Context

All persons born within a few years of each other are said to be a **cohort,** which, defined loosely, is a group of people who travel through life together. The idea is that all the people in a particular cohort are subject to the same history—the same prevailing assumptions, important public events, technologies, and popular trends. How history affects the life and thoughts of a specific person depends partly on the age of the person when he or she experienced it. People in a specific cohort tend to be affected in the same way; those in different cohorts are generally affected differently.

For example, your attitudes about hard work and job security or about the relative importance of money, marriage, or personal privacy are likely not the same as those of your parents or grandparents. Your parents may value your college education considerably more or considerably less than you do. Such attitudes and values are affected by the economic and social environments that prevailed when one first reached adulthood—whether that was during the economically depressed 1930s, the affluent 1950s, or the financially unstable early 1990s.

One more example of the effect of history: Adults who were adolescents in the 1960s may be politically and personally more independent and less passive than older or younger adults. One possible explanation is that the historical circumstances of their youth (the freedom movement, the Vietnam war, women's liberation) promoted independence and assertiveness. Another explanation is that, since they were part of the baby boom, their sheer numbers enabled them to get used to having their own way (Alwin, 1997); that too is part of their historical context.

Changing Values To some extent, the experiences and values of late adolescence influence each cohort for a lifetime. Maturity does not usually change those values, but at least it can make each generation realize the limitations of its historical context.

"You'd better ask your grandparents about that, son—my generation is very uncomfortable talking about abstinence."

social construction An idea about the way things are, or should be, that is built more on the shared perceptions of members of a society than on objective reality.

Values as a Social Construction. Research into the historical context reveals that as profound economic, political, and technological changes occur over the years, basic concepts about how things "should be" are influenced by how things *were* before such changes arose. Moreover, we often find that one or another of our most cherished assumptions about how things should be is not a fact of living but a **social construction**—an idea built more on the shared perceptions of a society than on objective reality. The obligations of women to be docile housewives and of men to be strong and independent providers are two obvious examples of social constructions that, in many cultures and contexts, have lost their consensus in recent times. As changes occur, our basic ideas about things also tend to change. Right now, for example, we are in the midst of a change in our thinking about computers, and that change is occurring cohort by cohort. Older cohorts tend to consider computers as objects to be feared and mastered; younger cohorts see them as no more remarkable than toothbrushes or bicycles.

Even the most basic ideas about human development can change. For example, the very concept of childhood as we know it, as a precious and extended stage of life, is a social construction that was virtually nonexistent throughout much of history. In many historical contexts, children were nurtured only until they could care for themselves (at about age 7). Then they entered the adult world, working in the fields or at home and spending their leisure time engaged in the activities of grown-ups. Further, the social construction that children are born "little angels" would lead to quite different child rearing than would the idea that adults have to "beat the devil out of them" in order to make them proper, God-fearing adults (Hwang et al., 1996; Straus, 1994).

The historical context of development is thus a continually changing one because "differences in year of birth expose people to . . . different priorities, constraints, and options" (Elder et al., 1995). For instance, if you were a high school student in the United States in the late 1970s, you are three times more likely to have been a fairly regular user of marijuana than you would be if you reached age 18 in the United States in the early 1990s (Johnston et al., 1997). Each new generation defines its cohorts with distinctive clothes, hairstyles, slang, and values, among other things. Popular songs that once were considered risqué are now "golden oldies." A 15-year-old who rejects advice from a 30-year-old with "You don't understand; everything is different now" expresses more than a grain of truth.

The Socioeconomic Context

Another major contextual influence on development is **socioeconomic status,** abbreviated **SES** and sometimes called "social class" (as in "middle class" or "working class"). SES is an aspect of the social context because it influences many of the social interactions and opportunities a person might have.

Socioeconomic status is not simply a matter of how rich or poor a person is. Rather, SES is most accurately measured through a combination of several overlapping variables, including family income, education, place of residence, and occupation. The SES of a family consisting of, say, an infant, a nonemployed mother, and an employed father who earns $10,000 a year might be lower-class if the wage earner happens to be an illiterate dishwasher living in an urban slum or middle-class if he is a graduate student living on campus and teaching part-time. The point of this example is that SES is not just financial: it entails *all* the advantages and disadvantages, and *all* the opportunities and limitations, that may be associated with status. Social class is as much a product of the mind as of the wallet.

Why Not Put the Children to Work? The current view of childhood as a special period given over to formal education and play is a fairly recent one. As late as 1900, one out of every five children between the ages of 10 and 16 in the United States worked, often at dirty and dangerous jobs in factories, mills, and mines. These "breaker" boys, who usually started their work at age 10, had the task of picking out slate and rubble from crushed coal as it came down shutes from giant processors. Their hours were long; their environment was choked with coal dust; and their pay was less than a dollar a day.

Poverty. In official government statistics, SES is usually measured solely by family income (adjusted for inflation and family size), perhaps because it is difficult to include measures of education and occupation. For example, in 1998 in the contiguous United States, a family of four with an annual income of $16,450 or less was considered to be at the bottom of the SES scale. Their income was below a dollar amount called the *poverty level,* which is calculated as the minimum amount needed to pay for basic necessities. (In Alaska and Hawaii, the poverty level is set somewhat higher.)

Looking only at family income is simplistic yet sometimes useful, especially in regard to households with incomes below the poverty level. The reason is that inadequate family income both signals and creates a social context of limited opportunities and heightened pressures. These, in turn, make life much more difficult to manage than it is for families higher up on the socioeconomic ladder. For example, infant mortality, child neglect, inadequate schools, and adolescent violence are all much more common among the poor than among the affluent (Huston et al., 1994; McLoyd, 1998).

Considerable debate among social scientists concerns whether low income alone creates such developmental problems. Alternatively, there may be a "culture of poverty," a set of social values and practices that tends to perpetuate low SES and its problems from generation to generation. If so, there may also be a "culture of privilege" that tends to create other problems as well as widen the social distance between the rich and the poor.

Another debate concerning SES centers on which generation deserves the greatest portion of public financial support. Four decades ago, the old were the

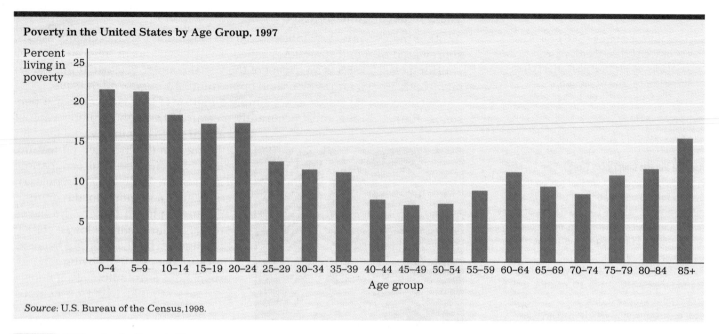

Poverty in the United States by Age Group, 1997

Source: U.S. Bureau of the Census,1998.

Figure 1.4 Children Are the Poorest. The American who sleeps hungry, in a crumbling house, in a crime-ridden community is more often a young child than an older adult and is rarely middle-aged. Is this fair? To those who study child development, it seems not, since children are the most vulnerable to the effects of deprivation. The more controversial question is, Who has an obligation to correct this imbalance—society as a whole or the older family members of those children?

poorest age group in the United States. Now, as you can see from Figure 1.4, the youngest are poorest, with more than one in five young children living in poverty. Some argue that this inequity is not only unfair but also foolish, because it creates problems in today's youth that will haunt society in years to come. Others contend that the older generations are more deserving of economic support and are more likely to spend it wisely—often to help younger generations. Indeed, when researchers examine money transfers within families, they find that persons over age 65 are more likely to give than to receive (Crystal, 1996).

A third poverty issue is how government policy affects poor children. In some nations, the United States among them, government social programs (such as Medicare, Headstart, food stamps, and public housing) rescue some of the poorest children from the worst consequences of poverty but leave children of the "near poor" as vulnerable as they were. For instance, in 1997, 55 percent of U.S. children whose family income was above the poverty level but below the nation's median income were uninsured for medical care. In other words, often the children in the very worst situations are helped, but other children in poor circumstances are not. Other nations put more or less government money into programs to care for more or fewer children. Some (Sweden, France) have universal education and child care beginning at age 1; others (Myanmar, Ethiopia) have no free public education for children of any age.

The Cultural Context

culture The set of shared values, assumptions, customs, and physical objects that are maintained by a group of people in a specific setting (a society) as a design for living daily life.

When social scientists use the term **culture,** they are referring to the set of values, assumptions, and customs, as well as the physical objects (clothing, dwellings, cuisine, technologies, works of art, and so on), that a group of people have developed over the years *as a design for living* that provides structure for their life together. The term "culture" is sometimes used rather loosely, as in the culture of poverty, or the culture of children, or the culture of America. However, whenever culture is considered as part of the social context, the emphasis is on values and attitudes, more than on the specific foods, clothes, and objects of daily life.

Cherish the Child Cultures vary tremendously in how much they value children. China's "one-child" policy urges every family to limit reproduction, which could be taken as a sign either that children are not as valuable as older people or that each child is destined to be precious.

❷ *Observational Quiz (answer on page 15):* *What three signs suggest that this community enjoys this boy?*

Cultural values and attitudes guide child development in a multitude of interrelated ways. Here is one example: In many developing agricultural communities, children are an economic asset because they work the family's farm and, later, perpetuate the family unit by remaining on the land, raising the young, and caring for the aged (LeVine, 1988). Thus, every newborn who survives to childhood benefits the entire family group. But in many poor rural communities, nutrition and medical care are scarce, leading to high infant mortality—a serious loss to the family unit. Therefore, infant care is designed to maximize survival and emphasize family cooperation. Typical features include intensive physical nurturance, feeding on demand, immediate response to crying, close body contact, keeping the baby close to the mother at night, and constant care by siblings and other relatives as well as by the mother. All these measures protect the fragile infant from an early death while establishing the value of interdependence among family members (LeVine et al., 1994).

By contrast, according to Robert LeVine, middle-class parents in postindustrial nations do not have to be so concerned about infant mortality. But they have other concerns, as each infant requires an enormous investment of time and money: there are cribs and strollers and diapers and toys to buy, and maternity leave, licensed day care, and food and shelter needs are far more costly in an urban than a rural community. The payoff comes not when the child begins herding the sheep but when the young adult lands a prestigious job. Therefore, hoping to ensure their children's future success in a technological and urbanized society, such families focus their child-rearing efforts on fostering cognitive growth and emotional independence. Middle-class parents in the United States typically engage their infants in activities to provide cognitive and social stimulation, talk to their babies more than touch them, put them to sleep by themselves in their own cribs in their own rooms, and often ignore their young children's whining, crying, and clinging so as not to "spoil" them. (See the Research Report on page 15.)

Not surprisingly, such contrasting parental strategies produce children with quite different capacities, goals, and expectations. But, in every culture, the children become relatively well prepared for the social group and economic setting in which they have been raised (Harkness & Super, 1995).

Closely Connected Even when she is all dressed up, this Masai woman is often in close physical contact with her young children. Her sleeping daughter, covered in a decorative blanket, remains cradled in her arms rather than beside her, and her son is also nearby—indeed (do you see it?) in touch.

ethnic group A collection of people who share certain background characteristics, such as national origin, religion, upbringing, and language, and who, as a result, tend to have similar beliefs, values, and cultural experiences.

❓**Especially for Health Professionals:** What do you think would be the biggest concern about their newborn for a family of recent immigrants from a developing country? For a family in which both native-born parents are well-paid professionals?

Give Your Baby the Best Touching only himself, but watching one of the best mobiles that money can buy, this 3-month-old North American baby wears his soft-snapped, unisex, right-size stretch suit as he rests alone in his adjustable wooden crib. Most infants of the world do not have their own carriage, crib, or playpen. Ironically, many of their parents wonder why westerners are so cruel as to put their babies behind bars.

Ethnicity and Culture.   An **ethnic group** is a collection of people who share certain attributes, such as ancestry, national origin, religion, and/or language. As a result, members of an ethnic group tend to recognize and identify with each other and have similar daily encounters with the social world. *Racial identity* can be considered an element of ethnicity. Indeed, sometimes outsiders assume that people of the same racial background are also from the same ethnic group. However, as social scientists emphatically point out, *biological traits* (such as hair or skin coloring, facial features, and body type) that distinguish one "race" from another are much less significant to development than are the *attitudes and experiences* that may arise from ethnic or racial consciousness, especially those resulting from minority or majority status.

Ethnic identity, then, is more than genetic; it is also a product of the social environment and the individual's consciousness. Two people may look like close relatives but may have quite different upbringings, heritages, and community settings and therefore quite different ethnic identities. Or two people may be very different in appearance but still share an ethnic identity. This is readily apparent in many Latin American ethnic groups. These groups include people of African, European, or Indian descent who are united by their common language and homeland as the key elements of their ethnicity.

Ethnicity is similar to culture in that it provides people with shared beliefs, values, and assumptions that can significantly affect their own development as well as how they raise their children. Indeed, sometimes ethnicity and culture overlap. However, people of many ethnic groups can all share one culture yet maintain their ethnic identities. Within multiethnic cultures, such as those of most large nations today, ethnic differences are most apparent in certain values and customs. Some examples of such values are whether children are raised in large, extended families or smaller, nuclear families; whether adolescents are encouraged toward independence, dependence, or interdependence; whether education is all-important or secondary to family responsibilities; and whether each generation defers to family elders or asserts its autonomy (Harrison et al., 1990).

The Individual and the Developmental Contexts

Since each child develops within many contexts, it is obviously important to understand the special impact that each context has. But it is also important not to try to explain any individual's personality traits, abilities, or actions in terms of a single context. No one is exactly like the statistically "average" person of his or her generation, socioeconomic status, or ethnic group. This is because each of us is pulled in divergent directions by the many contextual influences, whose power varies from individual to individual, situation to situation, and family to family.

Each of us differs in unexpected ways from any stereotypes or generalities that might seem pertinent, and our individual differences demand as much scientific respect and scrutiny as any of the commonalities that link us to a particular group. In fact, each of us is an active participant in our context. We contribute to the history of our cohort, help form our economic circumstances, and construct our own personal meanings from our cultural background (Rogoff, 1997; Valsiner, 1997). This power of the developing individual is well illustrated by David, whose story tells us of the many contexts that affected his development, yet it simultaneously reveals the uniqueness of each human being.

REACTIONS TO A CRYING BABY

To examine differences in infant care, one team of researchers arranged for trained observers to compare mothers' responses to their second and later-born babies in several communities; among them were a Gusii community in rural Kenya and a group of middle-class whites in suburban Boston (Richman et al., 1992). The observations, which spanned several months, were made in the subjects' homes, with the mothers going about their normal household activities and each observer taking the part of a visiting neighbor, trying to be as casual and unintrusive as possible while recording the mother's and child's behaviors as each responded to the other.

There were, of course, many cultural similarities in maternal responsiveness. When the infants cried, for example, mothers in both locations were attentive, usually responding to them with some form of social interaction—holding, touching, or talking. (As experienced caregivers, they did not assume that every cry signaled hunger; they offered a breast or bottle to their crying infants less than 10 percent of the time.) In both locations, mothers also took the baby's developmental stage into account: They were more likely to cradle their crying 4-month-olds than their crying 10-month-olds.

The researchers also found many cultural differences. One of the more intriguing was that the Boston mothers communicated much more with words and much less with physical contact than the Kenyan mothers did. This was apparent not only when the babies cried but also when they made other sounds, or played with objects, or merely looked at their mothers. Other research shows that babies respond in kind to this treatment: many North American children are far more talkative to adults than their African peers are.

The differences in mothers' responses are clearly related to cultural views of the mother's role, as the researchers explain:

Both groups of mothers are responsive to infant signals, but their different behaviors indicate divergent goals and styles. The responsiveness of the Gusii mothers is directed toward soothing and quieting infants rather than arousing them. . . . The responsiveness of the Boston mothers, especially as their infants become more communicative later in the first year, is designed to engage the infants in emotionally arousing conversational interaction. Gusii mothers see themselves as protecting their infants, not as playing with or educating them. [Richman et al., 1992]

Such cultural differences, far from being unusual, are found whenever child-rearing patterns are compared (Harkness & Super, 1995). Some cultures expect babies to cry loudly and forcefully; others shush them at the first whimper. Further, whether a child who interrupts an adult is rude or confident, whether a father who changes diapers is a henpecked husband or a liberated man, and whether spanking a child is abuse or discipline are matters of culture. This does not mean, of course, that there are no generalities that signify optimal child rearing for all humans. As one developmentalist explains:

It is still possible to find good reason for . . . searching out, beneath those cultural variations critical to us all, those developmental pathways that, at some deep level, work to ensure that we end up interestingly different things of the same general kind. [Chandler, 1997]

We are all the same general kind of creature, and some developmental pathways should be open to every wayfarer. Cultural differences do mean, however, that no one should assume that a particular response to children is best simply because their parents, their culture, or their ethnic group uses it.

❶ *Answer to Observational Quiz (from page 13):*
At least four adults are smiling at him; he is eating an apple that was brought to the market for sale; he is allowed to sit on the table with the food. If you noticed another sign—his new green sandals—give yourself bonus credit.

David's Story: Domains and Contexts

David's story begins in 1967, with an event that is straight out of the biosocial domain. In the spring of that year, in rural Kentucky, an epidemic of rubella (German measles) struck two particular victims—David's mother, who had a rash and a sore throat for a couple of days, and her 4-week-old embryo, who was damaged for life. David was born in November, with a life-threatening heart defect and thick cataracts covering both eyes. Other damage caused by the rubella virus became apparent as time went on, including minor malformations of the thumbs, feet, jaw, and teeth, as well as of the brain.

The historical context operative at the moment David entered the world was crucial. Had David been conceived a decade later, the development and

❗ **Response for Health Professionals (from page 14):** As you can see from the text, the immigrant family's biggest concern might be about physical survival; the professional family's might be about intellectual achievement. In thinking about this, you can derive additional expectations: that the immigrant parents would have more questions about nourishment, weight gain, illnesses, and crying; and the professional parents would have many questions about the possibility of mental retardation, finding good child care, language learning, and educational toys.

widespread use of the rubella vaccine would probably have prevented his mother's contracting the disease, and David would have been born un-scathed. On the other hand, had he been born a few years earlier, he would have died. The microsurgery that saved his life was, in 1967, a recent medical miracle, as were all the support services that made life possible. One recent discovery that specifically aided David was how to prepare a human weighing only 6 pounds for surgery. As former Surgeon General C. Everett Koop has noted, the medical profession was just discovering pediatric anesthesiology. Until the 1960s, "doctors knew they could put children to sleep, but they were not sure they could wake them up" (Koop, 1997).

The Early Years: Heartbreaking Handicaps, Slow Progress

At that place and time, heart surgery in the first days after birth did save David's life. However, surgery 6 months later to open a channel around one of the cataracts failed, completely destroying that eye. It was not obvious then that David's successful heart surgery was a blessing.

David's physical handicaps produced cognitive and psychosocial handicaps as well—an example of one domain affecting the other two. Not only did his near blindness make it impossible for him to learn by looking at his world, but his parents overprotected him to the point that he spent almost all his early months in their arms or in his crib, not learning about the world around him. An analysis of the family context would have revealed that David's impact on his family and their effect on him were harmful in many unintended ways. Like many relatives of seriously impaired infants, David's parents felt guilt, anger, and despair. During the first months they were, at times, less responsive to David's cries than they had been to those of their older sons.

Fortunately, however, David's parents came from a socioeconomic context that encouraged them to seek and obtain outside help. (David's father is a college professor, and his mother is a nurse.) Fortunately also, their community offered help. Their first step was to obtain advice from a teacher at the Kentucky School for the Blind, who told them to stop blaming themselves and to stop overprotecting David. If their son was going to learn about his world, he was going to have to explore it. For example, rather than confining David to a crib or playpen, they were to provide him with a large rug for a play area. Whenever he crawled off the rug, they were to say "No" and place him back in the middle of it. This would teach him to use his sense of touch to learn where he could explore safely without bumping into walls or furniture.

David's mother dedicated herself to a multitude of tasks that various specialists suggested, including exercising his twisted feet and cradling him frequently in her arms as she sang lullabies to provide extra tactile and auditory stimulation. His cries were more frequent and more grating than those of a normal infant, but his parents soon noticed that he quieted at his mother's touch and voice—an encouraging sign that he was capable of responding to human stimulation. The parent-child attachment became close and constructive.

David's responsiveness mobilized the entire family. His father took over much of the housework and the care of David's two older brothers, ages 2 and 4, old enough to begin talking and playing with David. When David's father was offered an opportunity to work in eastern Massachusetts, he took it, because the Perkins School for the Blind, in Boston, had just begun an experimental program for blind toddlers. At Perkins, David's mother learned specific methods for developing physical and language skills in children with multiple disabilities, and she, in turn, taught the techniques to David's

The Joy of Learning Multiple-handicapped but eager to learn: such is the condition of millions of children in the world today. Few, however, are as fortunate as this boy is: He has a teaching machine with individualized visual and audio response and, more important, a teacher with dedicated enthusiasm. My nephew David was born too soon for such educational technology. But he did benefit from medical advances and a new social understanding that severely handicapped children could learn—both absent everywhere in the world a mere 40 years ago.

father and brothers. Every day the family spent hours rolling balls, doing puzzles, and singing with David.

Thus, a smooth collaboration between home and school helped young David develop, aided by the cultural affinity between the experts' attitudes and the family's values. However, progress was slow. It became painfully apparent that rubella had damaged much more than his eyes and heart. At age 3, he could not yet talk, chew solid food, use the toilet, coordinate his fingers, or even walk normally. An IQ test showed him to be severely mentally retarded. Fortunately, although most children with rubella syndrome have hearing defects, David's hearing was normal. Yet his only intelligible vocalization mimicked the noises of the buses and trucks that passed by the family's house.

At age 4, David said his first word, "Dada." Open-heart surgery corrected the last of his heart damage. His mother, with tears in her eyes, said, "I am so grateful that he is alive, and yet I know that soon I will be angry at him when he spits out his food." At age 5, an operation brought partial vision to David's remaining eye. Vision in that eye was far from perfect, but he could now recognize his family by sight as well as by sound. Soon after, when the family returned to rural Kentucky, further progress became obvious: he no longer needed diapers or baby food.

David's fifth birthday occurred in 1972, just when the historical view that children with severe disabilities are unteachable was being seriously challenged. Many schools were beginning to open their doors to children with special needs. David's parents found four schools that would accept him. In accordance with the family's emphasis on education, they enrolled him in all four. He attended two schools for children with cerebral palsy: one had morning classes, and the other—40 miles away—afternoon classes. (David ate lunch in the car with his mother on the daily trip from one to the other.) On Fridays these schools were closed, so he attended a school for the mentally retarded. On Sundays he spent 2 hours in church school, which was his first experience with "mainstreaming"—the then-new idea that children with special needs should be educated with normal children. Particularly in the church community, the cultural-ethnic background of Appalachia benefited David's development, for a strong commitment to accepting and helping neighbors in need is one of the values that Appalachian people hold dear.

Childhood and Adolescence: Heartening Progress

By age 7, David's intellectual development had progressed to a point considered adequate for the regular educational system. In some skills, he was advanced; he could multiply and divide numbers in his head. He entered first grade in a public school, one of the first severely disabled children in the United States to be mainstreamed.

However, rubella continued to have an obvious impact on his biosocial, cognitive, and psychosocial development. His motor skills were poor (among other things, he had difficulty controlling a pencil); his efforts to learn to read were greatly hampered by the fact that he was legally blind even in his "good" eye; and his social skills were seriously deficient (he pinched people he didn't like, hugged girls too tightly, cried and laughed at inappropriate times). David's father became proficient at educating teachers whose initial response to David was impatience.

During the next several years, development in the cognitive domain proceeded rapidly. By age 10, David had skipped a year of school and was a fifth-grader. He could read—with a magnifying glass—at the eleventh-grade level and was labeled "intellectually gifted" according to tests of verbal and math

skills. At home he began to learn a second language, play the violin, and sing in the choir. He proved to have extraordinary auditory acuity and memory, although holding the violin bow correctly was difficult.

David's greatest remaining problem was in the psychosocial domain. Schools generally ignored the social skills of mainstreamed children, and no exception was made for David. For instance, he was required to sit on the sidelines during most physical-education classes and to stay inside during most recess periods. Without a chance to experience the normal give-and-take of schoolyard play, David remained more childish than his years. His classmates were not helped to understand his problems; some teased him because he still looked and acted "different."

Included in Life The efforts of these Special Olympians reflect not only the thrill of competition but also the satisfaction of having one's abilities and interests recognized and accepted. In a highly competitive society like the United States, being forced to the sidelines can be more devastating psychologically than the limitations imposed by disability.

Because of David's problems with outsiders and classmates, for high school his parents decided to send him to the Kentucky School for the Blind. There, his biosocial, cognitive, and psychosocial development all advanced: David learned to wrestle and swim, studied algebra with large-print books, and made friends with people whose vision was worse than his. He mastered not only the regular curriculum but also specialized skills, such as how to travel independently in the city and how to cook and clean for himself. In his senior year he was accepted for admission by a large university in his home state. As you may remember from page 1, David calls his college experience an adversity. But when he finally graduated, he did so with a double major in Russian and German. He has since received a master's degree in German. His current status, and some reflections on his development, are noted at the end of this chapter.

DEVELOPMENTAL STUDY AS A SCIENCE

As David's case makes abundantly clear, the study of development requires taking into account the interplay of the biosocial, cognitive, and psychosocial domains, within a particular historical period, under the influence of familial, socioeconomic, cultural, and other forces. Not surprisingly, assessing the relative impacts of all these factors is no simple matter. To help them proceed through this complexity, developmentalists have adopted scientific methodology. As scientists, developmentalists are willing to consider any issue and research any question but then to draw conclusions based only on the evidence—not on wishful thinking.

scientific method The principles and procedures used in the systematic pursuit of knowledge (formulating questions, testing hypotheses, and drawing conclusions) designed to reduce subjective reasoning, biased assumptions, and unfounded beliefs.

The Scientific Method

The **scientific method** is a general procedural model that is designed to promote objectivity. Social scientists apply it by asking pertinent questions and then systematically gathering and analyzing information that might answer them, while making every effort to let objective data, and not preconceived or biased ideas, lead to their conclusions.

The Steps

The scientific method, as it applies to developmental study, involves four basic steps, and sometimes a fifth:

1. *Formulate a research question.* On the basis of previous research, a particular developmental theory, or personal observation and reflection, pose a question that has relevance for the study of development.
2. *Develop a hypothesis.* Reformulate the question into a **hypothesis,** which is a specific prediction that can be tested.
3. *Test the hypothesis.* Design and conduct a research project that will provide evidence—in the form of data—about the truth or falsehood of the hypothesis.
4. *Draw conclusions.* Use the research data to determine whether the hypothesis is true or not. Make conclusions only from the evidence. Describe any limitations of the research and any alternative explanations for the results.
5. *Make the findings available.* Publishing the results of the research is often the fifth step in the scientific method. In this step, you describe the procedure and results in sufficient detail so that other scientists can evaluate the conclusions. If they wish to, other scientists can **replicate** the research—that is, repeat it and verify the results—or extend it, using a different but related set of subjects (people) or procedures. Replication and extension are the means by which new scientific studies provide more definitive and comprehensive knowledge.

hypothesis A specific prediction that is stated in such a way that it can be tested and either proved or disproved.

replicate To repeat a previous scientific study, at a different time and place but with the same research design and procedures, in order to verify that study's conclusions.

variable Any quantity, characteristic, or action that can take on different values within a group of individuals or a single individual.

Some Complications

In actual practice, scientific investigation is less straightforward than these five steps would suggest. The linkage between question, hypothesis, test, and conclusion is sometimes indirect, and the design and execution of research are influenced by (fallible) human judgment (Bauer, 1992; Howard, 1996). Human values tend to guide the choice of which topics to examine, which methods to use, and how to interpret the results. Minimizing the effects of such individual human values on research is always a challenge.

Further, there is always a question of whether researchers are aware of all the relevant **variables**—quantities that may differ or vary during an investigation. People vary in sex, age, education, ethnicity, economics, nationality, values, jobs, family background, personality—the list could go on and on. Moreover, developmental researchers must deal with both *intrapersonal variation,* by which a person varies within himself or herself from day to day, and *interpersonal variation,* which is variation between people or between groups of people, and the two are not always easily distinguished. Nonetheless, given all the complexities involved in human development, the scientific method—curious, conscientious, creative, rigorous, and open to unexpected or even unwanted findings—is a powerful tool.

RESEARCH METHODS

Between the questions developmental scientists ask and the answers they find lies their methodology, not only the steps of the scientific method but also the specific strategies used to gather and analyze data. These strategies are critical because "the ways that you attempt to clarify phenomena in large measure determine the worth of the solution" (Cairns & Cairns, 1994). In other words, *how* research is designed affects the *validity* (does it measure what it purports to measure?), *accuracy* (are the measurements correct?), *generalizability* (does it apply to other populations and situations?), and *usefulness* (can it solve real-life problems?) of the conclusions.

Some general strategies and cautions for making research valid are described in the Research Report (see pages 22–23). Now we turn to specific methods of testing hypotheses—observation, experiment, survey, and case study—as well as specific ways to measure developmental change.

Observation

scientific observation The unobtrusive watching and recording of subjects' behavior in a situation that is being studied, either in the laboratory or in a natural setting.

An excellent method of testing hypotheses regarding human development is **scientific observation,** that is, observing and recording, in a systematic and unbiased manner, what people do. Observations often occur in a *naturalistic* setting, such as at home, at school, or in a playground. Typically, the observing scientist tries to be as unobtrusive as possible so that the people being studied, the *research subjects,* will act as they normally do.

Observation can also occur in a *laboratory*. In this setting, the scientists sometimes are not visibly present at all; they may sit behind one-way windows that allow them to peer, unnoticed, into the experimental room, or they may record data with a video camera placed on the wall. In the laboratory, scientists study topics ranging, say, from the rate and duration of eye contact between infant and caregiver in specific situations, to the toys chosen by 4-year-olds in a well-equipped playroom, to the verbal aggression that occurs between boys and girls as they solve a math problem.

Example: Social Involvement of 4-Year-Olds

The value of observation becomes clear with an example: In one study, researchers examined 4-year-olds in various preschool settings in many cities and towns within the United States and Europe. They were concerned with the effect of the quality of child care, particularly on preschoolers' social and linguistic skills.

Generally, similar studies had found that day-care quality affects development but that the results depend not only on the quality of the care

Do Not Disturb: Science in Progress Does any 6-month-old understand that cups go on saucers, that circles are not squares, and that mothers know the answers when a child does not? In this laboratory observation, one scientist elicits the answers while another videotapes the results for later analysis.

but also on the economic and cultural background of the children (Scarr, 1998). Therefore, before the team of researchers could replicate and extend earlier research, they had to test another specific hypothesis—that the children's ethnic background would affect the way they got along with other children. The researchers needed to prove or disprove this hypothesis and then, if necessary, take ethnic differences into account before they could draw conclusions about the impact of, say, Headstart versus private preschools. Since more minority than majority children are enrolled in Headstart, the researchers would have to be careful not to attribute results to Headstart that really were the product of ethnic background.

This study is a continuing one that is investigating a number of issues using a variety of methods. We will look at one small part of it, which was focused on naturalistic observation of 96 European American and 96 Mexican American children (Farver & Frosch, 1996).

Remember that naturalistic observation must be systematic, performed by a trained observer who is as unobtrusive as possible. In this study, the researchers spent "considerable time in the classrooms familiarizing themselves and playing with the children before the data collection began." The children were observed during normal activities at their preschools. The data were recorded methodically: Each observer watched a single child for 30 seconds and then immediately took 30 seconds to record what that child had done. Each observer collected data on one child for 10 minutes (ten 30-second observations interspersed with ten 30-second written descriptions) and then shifted to another child, according to a predetermined schedule, until each targeted child was observed for eighty 30-second periods.

The social traits the scientists were looking for had been operationally defined. Specifically, their observations were coded as to whether, during each half minute, the watched child was *solitary*, defined as unoccupied or engaged in an activity alone; *social*, engaged in an activity with a partner or group of children; or *aggressive*, engaged in verbal aggression, such as name-calling, teasing, or quarreling, or engaged in physical aggression, such as pinching, hitting, pushing, poking, or grabbing another child, either for no reason or to obtain a toy.

Since one hypothesis to be tested was the impact of ethnicity, other variables such as age, SES, sex, type of preschool program, and location were accounted for in some way. To be specific, all the children were 4-year-olds from low-income families, half in each group were boys and half were girls, and the children attended many types of programs (Headstart, private day care, public preschool) in several cities (Newark, Detroit, San Jose, and Los Angeles).

Suppose you were one of the researchers connected with this project. Would you expect that, in this situation, the children would be mainly social, solitary, or aggressive? Would you hypothesize ethnic differences? As you can see in Table 1.1, most of the time these 4-year-olds socialized well, and ethnic differences were not significant in the statistical definition of the term.

However, you can also see that there is a trend toward ethnic differences. The Mexican Americans were slightly more likely to be solitary than the European Americans and less likely to be social. Although

Non-significant Ethnic Differences
The important finding of this data is that 4-year-olds in preschools were pretty much alike, spending most of their time socializing and one-fourth of their time alone. There were some cultural influences, but these were very small compared to the impact of witnessing a riot—as the text explains on page 25.

table **1.1**	**Time Spent in Social Behaviors**		
	Various Behaviors (percentage of time)		
Ethnic Group of Preschoolers	Social	Solitary	Aggressive
Mexican Americans	70	28	2
European Americans	77	22	1
Average (both groups)	73.5	25	1.5

Source: Farver & Frosch, 1996.

WAYS TO MAKE RESEARCH MORE VALID

Scientific investigation includes the possibility that researchers' procedures and/or biases may compromise the validity of their findings. Researchers can, however, use a number of techniques to increase the validity of their research. Six are explained here.

Sample Size

To make statements about people in general, called **populations,** scientists study groups of individuals chosen from populations. Each such group, called a **sample,** must be large enough to ensure that a few extreme cases within the sample do not distort the picture it gives of the population. Suppose, for instance, that researchers want to know the average age at which children begin to walk. Since they cannot include every infant in their study, they will choose a sample of infants, determine the age of walking for each member of the sample, and then calculate the sample average. If the sample is typical, the average walking age for the sample will be very close to the average for the entire infant population.

The importance of an adequate **sample size** can be seen if we assume, for the moment, that one of the infants in the sample had an undetected disability and did not walk until 24 months. Assume also that all the other infants walked at 12 months, the current norm. If the sample size was less than 10 infants, than one late walker would add more than a month to the age at which the "average" child is said to walk. However, if the sample contained 500 children, the one abnormally late walker would not change the results by even 1 day.

Representative Sample

Data collected from one group of individuals may not be valid for other people who are different in significant ways, such as in gender or ethnic background. Thus it is important that every sample be a **representative sample,** that is, consist of people who are typical of the general population the researchers wish to learn about. In a study of average walking age, for example, the sample should reflect—in terms of sex ratio, socioeconomic and ethnic background, and other characteristics—the entire population of children. Ideally, other factors would be taken into consideration as well. For instance, if there is some evidence that firstborn children walk earlier than later-born children, the sample should also be representative of birth order.

The importance of representative sampling is revealed by its absence in two classic studies of age of walking for infants in the United States (Gesell, 1926; Shirley, 1933). Both studies used a relatively small and unrepresentative sample (all the children were European American and most were

middle-class). Partly because the samples were not representative of the general population of infants, both studies arrived at an average walking age of 15 months. This is 3 months later than the current U.S. norm, which was obtained through research on a much larger, more representative sample including some low-SES children and some of African and Latino descent—groups known to have early-walking children. (Another reason why the earlier studies found babies walking 3 months later is that infants then were much more isolated from stimulation, and this slowed down their motor-skills development. In other words, infants actually did walk somewhat later then.)

"Blind" Experimenters

When experimenters have specific expectations about their research findings, those expectations can affect the research results. As much as possible, therefore, the people who actually gather the data should be **"blind,"** that is, unaware of the purpose of the research. Suppose we are testing the hypothesis that firstborn infants walk sooner than later-borns. Ideally, the examiner who measures the sample infants' walking ability should not know the hypothesis or the age or birth order of the infants. The subjects of the research should also be kept blind to its purpose, especially when the subjects are older children or adults who might be influenced by their own expectations.

Operational Definitions

When planning a study, researchers must establish *operational definitions* of whatever phenomena they will be examining. That is, they must define each variable in terms of specific, observable behavior that can be measured with precision. Even a simple variable, such as whether or not a toddler is walking, requires an operational definition. For example, does "walking" include steps taken while holding onto someone or something, or must it occur without support? Is one unsteady step enough to meet the definition, or must the infant be able to move a certain distance without faltering? For a study on age of first walking to be meaningful, the researchers would need to resolve questions like these in a clear and thorough definition. In fact, the usual definition of walking is "takes at least three steps without holding on," a good operational standard.

Understandably, operational definitions become much harder to establish when personality or intellectual variables are being studied. It is nonetheless essential that researchers who are investigating, say, "aggression" or "sharing" or "reading" define the trait in as precise and measurable terms as

"I'm walking."

Who Cares? Most parents actively teach their infants to walk, and then they telephone all their relatives to announce the first step. However, it may be the case that humans walk and talk when they are ready, no matter how little attention the parents provide. Careful research is the only way to test this hypothesis.

possible. Obviously, the more closely the operational definitions reflect the variables to be examined, the more objective and valid the results of the study will be.

Experimental and Control Groups

To test a hypothesis adequately in an experiment, researchers must gather data on two samples that are similar in every important way except one. They must compare an **experimental group,** which receives some special experimental treatment, and a **control group,** which does not receive the experimental treatment.

Suppose a researcher hypothesizes that infants who are provided with regular exercise to strengthen their legs walk earlier than babies who do not receive such exercise. To find out if this is true, the researcher would first select two representative samples of children and examine both groups to make sure they are equivalent in motor skills, such as the ability to roll over and sit up. Then one sample (the experimental group) would receive daily "workouts" devoted to leg-strengthening between, say, their sixth and twelfth months; the other sample (the control group) would have no special treatment. Results for the two groups would then be compared to test the hypothesis.

Statistical Significance

Whenever researchers find a difference between two groups, they have to consider the possibility that the difference oc-

curred purely by chance. For instance, in any group of infants, some will walk relatively early and some relatively late. If a number of infants are separated into an experimental group and a control group, it is possible that, by chance, most of the early walkers happen to end up in one group.

To determine whether or not the results of research are simply coincidence, researchers apply a test of **statistical significance.** The formula for computing significance takes into account many factors, including the sample sizes, the amount of variation within each group, and the difference between the averages of the two groups. Using the formula, the scientists calculate the *significance level,* a numerical indication of exactly how likely it is that the results occurred by chance. (Note that the word "significance" here means something quite different from its usual sense; it refers to the validity of specific results, not to the scientific value of the study.) Generally, results are statistically significant if there is less than 1 chance in 20 that they occurred by chance—that is, a significance level of 1/20 = .05. Some results are significant at the .01 level (only 1 chance in 100 of occurring by chance) or the .001 level (1 chance in 1,000).

population The entire group of individuals who are of particular concern in a scientific study, such as all the children of the world or all newborns who weigh less than 3 pounds.

sample A group of individuals drawn from a specified population. A sample might be the low-birthweight babies born in four particular hospitals that are representative of all hospitals.

sample size The number of individuals who are being studied in a single sample in a research project.

representative sample A group of research subjects who reflect the relevant characteristics of the larger population whose attributes are under study.

blind The "state" of researchers who are deliberately kept ignorant of the purpose of the research, or of relevant traits of the research subjects, to avoid biasing their data collection.

experimental group Research subjects who experience the special condition or treatment that is the crux of the research. (See also **control group.**)

control group Research subjects who are comparable to those in the experimental group in every relevant dimension except that they do not experience the special condition or treatment that is the key variable of the experiment.

statistical significance A mathematical measure of the likelihood that a particular research result occurred by chance.

❷ Especially for Social Scientists: There is a positive correlation between the number of storks living in certain towns of France and the birth rates of those towns. Does that prove that storks bring babies?

the rates of aggression were very low, Anglo children were less agggressive (1 percent) than Chicano children (2 percent). These ethnic trends were apparent in children from all the cities: the 64 children from Los Angeles (32 Chicano, 32 Anglo) acted very similarly to the 128 children from the other cities—an important detail that we will return to soon.

A Limitation of Observation

Naturalistic observation is an excellent research method, but it has one major limitation. It does not indicate what causes the behavior we see. Even if there were dramatic sociability differences between the two ethnic groups in the preschooler study, we could say only that one variable (ethnic heritage) is *correlated* with another variable (social play). Correlation is not causation. To understand this, we need to discuss correlation a bit.

correlation A relation between two variables such that one is likely (or unlikely) to occur when the other occurs or one is likely to increase (or decrease) in value when the other increases (or decreases).

Correlation.   We say there is a **correlation** between two variables if one of them is likely—or unlikely—to occur when the other variable occurs. For instance, there is a correlation between wealth and attending college and perhaps between springtime and falling in love. The fact that two variables are correlated does not mean they occur together in every instance. Some wealthy people never finish high school, and some people fall in love in the depths of winter. However, correlation does mean there is some sort of relation between two variables—generally, wealthier families are more likely than poor families to send their children to college, even though this does not occur in every case.

A correlation is *positive* if the occurrence of one variable makes it more likely that the other will occur. A correlation is *negative* if the occurrence of one makes it less likely that the other will occur.

Correlation does not prove cause. The correlation between education and wealth does not necessarily imply that having more money directly leads to more education. It may be, instead, that well-educated people are wealthier, in which case education might lead to wealth. Or there may be a third variable, perhaps intelligence or family values, that accounts for the level of both income and education.

Even when two variables are strongly (or highly) correlated, we cannot say that one variable causes the other. For example, there is a high correlation between the sex of a baby and the color of the trim on the baby's pacifier—blue for boys and pink for girls. But no one would suggest that pacifier color determines sex or that each sex has an inborn preference for a particular color. Instead, a cultural link between boys and blue, and between girls and pink—a link completely absent in some areas of the world—is the underlying explanation for the correlation. Many correlations found in research, and in everyday life, have no more bearing on cause than this one does, but often that fact is not obvious. Remember, always: Correlation is not causation.

In the preschool study, we can't tell what caused what. For example, did the children spend most of their time playing happily together because that is the nature of 4-year-olds or because preschool programs provide many opportunities for social interaction and manage to keep aggression to a minimum? What caused the slight ethnic differences? At least four variables could possibly explain those differences:

Fighting Over a Cat Naturalistic observation reveals that children are sometimes cruel to animals as well as to each other, but it does not explain why. Laboratory experiments, however, have shown that one factor is that children have observed cruelty and aggression in others. Chances are these children have seen someone else try to settle a dispute over a possession in a similar fashion.

- *Family* (Do Chicano parents encourage their children to be quiet and withdrawn, while Anglo parents encourage their children to be talkative and social?)
- *Culture* (Does Mexican-American culture value a distinct pattern of social interaction?)
- *Language* (Does being a Spanish-speaking person in an English-speaking nation affect personality?)
- *Neighborhood* (Do Chicano and Anglo children live in different kinds of neighborhoods that affect their socialization?)

To determine whether one of these variables is the cause, and not simply the correlate, of the observed behavior, scientists would perform an experiment.

The Experiment

experiment A research method in which the scientist deliberately causes changes in one variable (called the *independent variable*) and then observes and records the resulting changes in some other variable (called the *dependent variable*).

independent variable The variable that is manipulated in an experiment.

dependent variable The variable that is being studied in an experiment.

An **experiment** is an investigation designed to untangle cause and effect. In the social sciences, the experimenters typically expose a group of subjects to a particular treatment or condition; that is, they cause a change in an **independent variable.** They then note how that change affects some specific behavior they are studying, called the **dependent variable.** Thus the independent variable is the new, special treatment; the dependent variable is the response (which may or may not change because of the independent variable).

In the preschool study, the dependent variable is the children's social behavior. Among the possible independent variables are the four factors listed earlier: family, culture, language, and neighborhood. Neighborhood looks like a particularly promising variable that might cause children to be more shy or more aggressive than they otherwise would be. We already know that many Hispanic children in the United States live in violent neighborhoods, as defined by the number of serious personal-injury crimes that occur in those communities. Might that violence affect the sociability of young children? One way to answer this question through an experiment would be to make a community markedly more or less violent and then see if this affects its children's behavior. Would 4-year-olds even notice? Would they react?

Obviously, it would be unethical to add more violence to an urban community in order to perform this experiment; and efforts to make neighborhoods less violent are not undertaken in the dramatic and systematic ways necessary for good research. As it happened, though, unexpected external forces provided experimenters with their independent variable, violence.

The L.A. Riots This drawing depicts 9-year-old Abdullah Abbar's memories of the spring of 1992 in his Los Angeles neighborhood: flames, bullets, looting, and death. Anyone who thinks children ignore the conditions of their neighborhood needs to look closely.

Just as the researchers had completed the first part of their study, several Los Angeles police officers who had been videotaped beating suspect Rodney King were acquitted by a jury. Los Angeles erupted in riots lasting several days. Normal life stopped, stores were burned and looted, and innocent people were beaten; the streets were filled with gunfire while police patrolled overhead in helicopters. During the same time period, normal life

❶ Response for Social Scientists (from page 24): A correlation between two variables may be caused by something other than those variables. Towns with many storks are probably quieter, more spacious, more rural, with more farms; such towns are usually less wealthy and more religious. All these variables might affect their birth rates.

continued in the other cities in the preschool study. Fortuitously, the scientists in all the cities of the study were scheduled at that time to ask the children to tell make-believe stories about a set of toy figures:

> Children were taken individually to a familiar, private room where toys suggestive of imaginative play were placed on a large table. The toys included Smurf and Sesame Street characters, a car, four family figures, two horses, farm animals, and various sized Lego blocks. Children were told that they could play with the toys in any way they wished, but that they had to tell the experimenter what they were doing with the toys while they were playing. [Farver & Frosch, 1996]

Children who lived on a street that, according to police reports, had a high incidence of shooting, burning, and looting were assumed to have been directly exposed to the riots. Those children told much more aggressive stories than the children from other neighborhoods and cities, no matter what the ethnicity of the children. For example, the riot-exposed children were twice as likely to include unfriendly characters in their stories and four times as likely to include aggressive characters. There were some ethnic differences between the Mexican American and European American children in Los Angeles. But those differences were much smaller than the differences between the experimental, violence-exposed group, who were the 64 Los Angeles children (half Chicano and half Anglo), and the control group, who were the 128 children from other cities (again, half Chicano and half Anglo). Further, the teachers in Los Angeles reported that their children were much more fearful, withdrawn, or aggressive in the daily play in school than they had been before the riots, especially those children with the most intense exposure.

These results suggests an answer to at least one question we posed earlier: Four-year-olds *are* affected by violence in their communities. The experience of being in a riot-torn community made preschoolers more aggressive, as well as more fearful, in their thinking and their actions. This finding provides some clues about the cause of the ethnic differences found in the naturalistic schoolroom observations. At least some of the difference in social play found among children from different ethnic groups is the consequence of their specific neighborhoods. This conclusion is confirmed by other research on the relationship between neighborhood violence and children's temperament (Garbarino et al., 1992; Leavitt & Fox, 1993).

Limitations of Experimentation

By comparing the reactions of an experimental group and a control group, experimenters are often able to uncover the link between cause and effect. But ensuring that other variables do not intrude, even in experimental situations, is not usually a simple matter. And one question always remains: To what degree do the findings from an artificial experimental situation apply in the real world? A major problem with many experiments is that the controlled situation, with the scientist manipulating the independent variable, is different in important ways from normal, everyday life.

In addition, all experiments, except those with very young children, are hampered when the participants know they are research subjects; that knowledge leads them to behave differently than they normally would. Subjects may attempt to produce the results they believe the experimenter is looking for, or, especially if they are adolescents, they may try to undermine the study. Even if the subjects do not react in either of these ways, almost all experimental subjects are more nervous, more careful, or more conscientious than they otherwise would be. Yet it is difficult to keep subjects "blind" to the fact that they are in an experiment.

The last part of the preschool experiment avoided the pitfalls of being artificial because it was an "experiment in nature." By using young children, it also minimized the effect of subject awareness. However, it was limited in another way: the riot was over within a few days. This is an example of a third problem for developmental scientists: Most experiments are of very limited duration, even though actual human development takes years to form, change, and transform the person.

All these limitations add layers of potential artificiality to experimental research. For that reason, an experiment is most valuable in developmental study when it is combined with other methods rather than relied on exclusively. Indeed, the results of the preschool study were strengthened by other research, published and unpublished. Further, the scientists themselves re-examined the same children 3 years later and found (in research not yet published) that the pervasive patterns of the neighborhood affected the children's ongoing temperament, attitudes, and behavior patterns more than did one riot-filled week.

Other Research Methods

Wherever possible, researchers try to verify and extend the results of scientific study. As you have read, they may do so by replicating previous research with the same methods but other populations of subjects or by using different methods to investigate the same question. Two additional methods commonly used in developmental research are surveys and case studies.

The Survey

survey A research method in which information is collected from a large number of people, either through written questionnaires or through interviews.

In a scientific **survey,** information is collected from a number of people by personal interview, by written questionnaire, or by some other means. This seems to be an easy, quick, and direct way to obtain data. Surveys are especially useful when scientists want to learn about children, since an obvious way of doing so is to ask parents or teachers about the children. For example, in the preschool study we have discussed, the researchers asked the preschool teachers a series of questions about each child's social interactions. The teachers' responses confirmed the results of the naturalistic observation. Particularly significant (at the .001 level) were teachers' ratings of the children's hesitancy and shyness—traits that were more likely to be found in the Mexican American children than the European American children.

Unfortunately, getting valid data through an interview or questionnaire is more difficult than it seems, because these methods are vulnerable to bias on the part of the researcher and the respondents. To begin with, the very phrasing of the questions can influence the answers. A survey on the issue of abortion, for instance, will prompt different responses depending on whether it asks about "terminating an unwanted pregnancy" or "taking the life of an unborn child."

In addition, many people who are interviewed give answers that they think the researcher expects, or that express opinion rather than fact, or that they think will make them seem mature or "good." In one survey, parents were asked about their children's fears. They responded that their offspring were relatively fearless or were worried about such matters as quarreling with a friend or doing badly on a test. By contrast, the children themselves said they were more worried about global matters, such as starvation and pollution (Gottlieb & Bronstein, 1996). Why such a great difference? Do parents not know their children very well, or do they report what they hope is true? Do children think they will sound wiser if they express concern about world issues?

Simply asking questions and recording the answers does not guarantee that survey results are valid or accurate. Yet, despite the problems, a survey that is well designed and carefully administered can be extremely valuable; such a survey allows the collection of data from a large group of people much more quickly, and much less expensively, than does observation or an experiment. Before the results are considered valid, however, they should be confirmed through other means. In the preschool study, the teachers' responses, although highly significant, might not have been accurate. However, their value increased because they were in accord with the naturalistic observations, done over a period of months by trained observers.

The Case Study

case study A research method that focuses on the life history, attitudes, behavior, and emotions of a single individual.

A **case study** is an intensive study of one individual. Typically, the case study is based on interviews with the subject regarding his or her background, present thinking, and actions; it may also utilize interviews of others who know the individual. Additional case-study material may be obtained through observation, experiments, and standardized tests, such as personality inventories and intelligence tests.

Case studies can provide a wealth of detail, which makes them rich in possible insights. Many developmentalists prefer case studies precisely for that reason: the complexity of a human life is easier to comprehend through the rich *qualitative,* or descriptive, information of a case study than through a study involving sheer numbers, even though statistical significance depends on such *quantitative,* or numerical, data.

The interpretation of case-study information reflects the biases as well as the wisdom of the researcher; and, even when a case study is carefully interpreted, the conclusions apply with certainty to only one person. Nevertheless, the case study has three important uses: to provide a provocative starting point for other research; to understand a particular individual very well; and to illustrate general truths, as David's story does. Remember, however, that no confident conclusions about people in general can be drawn from a sample size of 1, or even 10 or 20, no matter how deep and detailed the study is.

Clearly, there are many ways to gather developmental data. Researchers can observe people in naturalistic or laboratory settings, or they can experimentally elicit reactions under controlled conditions or take advantage of unusual natural experiments. They can survey hundreds or even thousands of people, or interview a smaller number of people in great depth, or study one life in detail. Because each method has weaknesses, none of them provides data with ample scope and precision to merit broad conclusions. But each brings researchers closer to the issues and answers, and together they can prove or disprove theories and hypotheses.

Studying Changes Over Time

For research to be truly developmental, it must be able to deal with things that change and continue *over time.* Change is not always direct and linear; development might occur in fits and starts, zigzags, steps, or other ways as well (see Figure 1.5). Developmental scientists need to design their research so that it includes time, or age, as a factor. Usually they accomplish this with either of two basic research designs, cross-sectional and longitudinal.

Figure 1.5 Patterns of Developmental Growth. Many patterns of developmental growth have been discovered by careful research. Although linear (or near-linear) progress seems most common (people do get smarter as they get older, don't they?), scientists now find that almost no aspect of human change follows the linear pattern exactly.

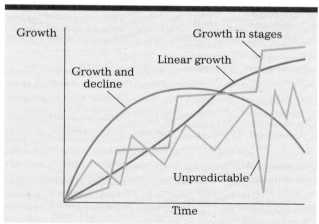

Cross-Sectional Research

cross-sectional research A research design in which groups of people, each group different from the others in age but similar to them in other important ways, are studied during the same time period.

The more convenient, and thus more common, way to include age in a developmental study is by using a **cross-sectional research** design. In a cross-sectional study, groups of people who differ in age but share other important characteristics (such as level of education, socioeconomic status, and ethnic background) are compared with regard to the variable under investigation. Any differences on this variable that exist between the people of one age group and the people of another are, presumably, the result of age-related developmental processes.

Cross-sectional design thus seems simple enough. However, it is very difficult to ensure that the various comparison groups are similar in every background variable except age. Yet this assurance is essential if researchers are to conclude that age, and not some other variable, is the explanation for whatever differences are found.

Compare These with Those The apparent similarity of these two groups in gender and ethnic composition makes them potential candidates for cross-sectional research. However, before we could be sure that any differences between the two groups are the result of age, we would have to be sure the groups are alike in other ways, such as socioeconomic background and religious upbringing.

As an example, suppose a group of 10-year-olds are found to be taller by about 12 inches (30 centimeters) than a comparable group of 6-year-olds. It seems reasonable to conclude that during the 4 years between ages 6 and 10, children gain a foot in height. However, even such an obvious conclusion might be wrong. It could be that the particular 10-year-olds in the study were better nourished than the 6-year-olds as babies or had some other relevant characteristic that was not accounted for. Certainly, if one group included more boys than girls, or more Asians than Africans, the height difference would reflect factors other than age.

Of course, good scientists try to make the groups similar in every relevant background variable. Nevertheless, even if two cross-sectional groups are identical except for age, they would still reflect cohort differences because of the particular historical experiences that affected each age group. Changes in medical care (today's children almost never get "childhood" diseases), in diet (less meat for today's toddlers), in housing conditions (play space is more scarce), and in other historical factors might skew cross-sectional results, even for such an obvious variable as height.

Longitudinal Research

To help discover if age, rather than some other background or historical variable, is really the reason for an apparent developmental change, researchers can study the *same individuals* over a long period of time. Because such a

longitudinal research A research design in which the same people are studied over time to measure both change and stability as they age.

longitudinal research design allows researchers to compare information about the same people at different ages, it eliminates the effects of background variables, even those that researchers are not aware of. If we know how tall a group of children are at 6 years old and at 10 years old, we can say definitively how much they grew, on average, during the 4 intervening years.

Longitudinal research is particularly useful in studying development over a long age span (Elder, 1998). It has yielded valuable and sometimes surprising findings on many topics, including the following:

- *Children's adjustment to divorce* (The negative effects linger, especially for school-age and older boys [Hetherington & Clingempeel, 1992].)
- *The long-term effects of serious birth problems* (Remarkable resiliency is often apparent [Werner & Smith, 1992].)
- *The role of fathers in child development* (Even 50 years ago, fathers were far more influential regarding their children's future happiness than the stereotype of the distant dad implies [Snarey, 1993].)
- *The consequences of an early delay in motor or language abilities* (Motor delays often disappear; language delays usually persist [Silva, 1996].)
- *The effects of enlisting in the military on juvenile delinquents* (Surprisingly positive achievement occurred [Sampson & Laub, 1996].)

Repeated longitudinal research can uncover not only the degree of change but also the process of change. Do children learn to read suddenly, by "breaking the code," or gradually? The answer could not be found by simply comparing preliterate 4-year-olds and fluent 8-year-olds. However, following children month by month revealed the answer: Reading is usually a gradual process, although certain aspects can be grasped quite suddenly (Adams, 1990).

Clearly, longitudinal research is "a design of choice from the developmental perspective" (Cairns & Cairns, 1994). You will see the results of many longitudinal studies throughout this book. Nevertheless, this design has some serious drawbacks. Over time, some subjects may withdraw, move far away, or die; their absence can skew the ultimate results because sometimes those who disappear are different (perhaps more rebellious, perhaps of lower SES) from those who stay. In addition, some people who remain may change because of their involvement in the research study ("improving" over a series of tests, for example, only because they become increasingly familiar with the tests); this makes the results of the study less applicable to the average person, who is not in such a study.

Perhaps the biggest problem of all is that longitudinal investigations are very time-consuming and expensive. They involve far more commitment from scientists and funding agencies than does cross-sectional research.

Cross-Sequential Research

cross-sequential research A research design in which groups of people of different ages are studied over time, to distinguish differences related to age from differences related to historical period. (Also called *cohort-sequential research* or *time-sequential research*.)

As you can see, both cross-sectional and longitudinal research designs allow scientists to look at development over time, but each design has flaws that are somewhat compensated for by the other. Because these two designs tend to make up for each other's disadvantages, scientists have devised various ways to use the two together. The simplest is **cross-sequential research** (also referred to as *cohort-sequential* or *time-sequential* research) (Schaie, 1996). With this design, researchers first study several groups of people of different ages (a cross-sectional approach) and then follow those groups longitudinally.

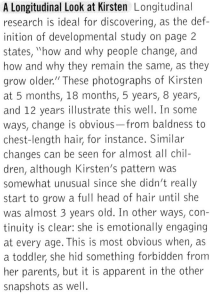

A Longitudinal Look at Kirsten Longitudinal research is ideal for discovering, as the definition of developmental study on page 2 states, "how and why people change, and how and why they remain the same, as they grow older." These photographs of Kirsten at 5 months, 18 months, 5 years, 8 years, and 12 years illustrate this well. In some ways, change is obvious—from baldness to chest-length hair, for instance. Similar changes can be seen for almost all children, although Kirsten's pattern was somewhat unusual since she didn't really start to grow a full head of hair until she was almost 3 years old. In other ways, continuity is clear: she is emotionally engaging at every age. This is most obvious when, as a toddler, she hid something forbidden from her parents, but it is apparent in the other snapshots as well.

Now, at age 13, it is not surprising that she is distinctive in predictable ways, such as her ballet, writing, social sensitivity, and cheerleading. She is also typical of her cohorts in other ways—she likes boys, computers, and television—as cross-sectional research would show as well. Longitudinal research (and, in this case, even longitudinal photos) also helps spot the impact of unusual events, which are not typical of either that child or children in general.

❓ Observational Quiz *(answer on page 32): Kirsten's parents got divorced. Can you spot when?*

Using cross-sequential design, we can compare findings for a group of, say, 10-year-olds with findings for the same individuals at age 6, as well as with findings for groups who were age 10 any number of years before. Cross-sequential research thus allows scientists to disentangle differences related to chronological age from those related to historical period.

ETHICS OF RESEARCH WITH CHILDREN

Every scientist must be concerned with the ethics of conducting and reporting research. At the most basic level, researchers who study human behavior and development must ensure that their research subjects are not harmed by the research process and that subjects' participation is voluntary and confidential. This is crucial when the subjects are children, as is reflected in the following precautions urged by the Society for Research in Child Development (1996):

> The investigator should use no research operation that may harm the child either physically or psychologically. . . . When in doubt about the possible harmful effects, consultation should be sought from others.
>
> Before seeking consent or assent from the child, the investigator should inform the child of all features of the research that may affect his or her willingness to participate and should answer the child's questions in terms appropriate to the child's comprehension. [The child is free to] discontinue participation at any time. . . . Investigators working with infants should take special effort to explain the research procedures to the parents and be especially sensitive to any indicators of discomfort in the infant.
>
> Informed consent requires that parents or other responsible adults be informed of all the features of the research that may affect their willingness to allow the child to participate.

When, in the course of research, information comes to the investigator's attention that may jeopardize the child's well-being, the investigator has a responsibility to discuss the information with the parents or guardians and with those expert in the field in order that they may arrange the necessary assistance for the child.

The investigators should keep in confidence all information obtained about research participants.

All these goals are endorsed by developmental researchers. However, it is easier to enunciate these ethical principles than it is to resolve some of the thorny dilemmas that they may entail (Fisher, 1993; Stanley & Sieber, 1992; Thompson, 1992). How can a developmentalist know, for example, that a child wishes to end his or her participation in a research project when many children are afraid to voice their reservations to an authority figure like a researcher? Does the confidentiality of research data include restricting parental access to this information? (This question may be of particular concern to adolescents who participate.) What is the best way to inform young children about the research and to make sure that they understand?

The most complex matter of all is ensuring that the benefits of research outweigh the risks. One complication is that the risks vary with the child's age: during research studies, a young child may be most vulnerable to stresses that stem from a separation from caregivers, while older children are more susceptible to loss of self-esteem and privacy violations. In addition, different children are affected by research procedures in different ways. And often, the studies with the greatest potential social benefit involve the children who are most vulnerable, such as children who have been maltreated or who have behavioral disorders. Balancing the risks and benefits in these cases can be extremely tricky.

Once an investigation has been completed, additional ethical issues arise concerning the use of research findings. The Society for Research in Child Development (1996) stipulates that "caution should be exercised in reporting results [and] making evaluative statements or giving advice" and that "the investigator should be mindful of the social, political, and human implications of his [or her] research."

David's Story Again

I wrestled with these very issues when I originally drafted David's story for an earlier edition of this book. I could see that his story would convey both the struggle and the hope of human development. But would publishing it hurt him in some way? I first asked my brother and sister-in-law. They said it might be okay, depending on what I wrote. I wrote the section, showed it to them, and they corrected it in minor ways.

Then I asked David, who was an adolescent at the time and was given to unexpected, contrary behavior. He took the draft of my manuscript to his room, read it with his magnifying glass, and told me, in a matter-of-fact voice, "It would be all right with me if you published it." Later I heard that he discussed with his parents some aspects of his infancy that they had never told him, including the extent of his many congenital disabilities.

Over the years, David has become more and more interested in his story in this book. He has been a guest speaker at my college to answer students' questions about his life, he has attended my publisher's sales meetings, he has learned about editing from my editors, and he is eager to answer my questions to update each edition.

❶ *Answer to Observational Quiz (from page 31):* *Kirsten's parents ended their marriage about when Kirsten was 8 (fourth picture). Signs of this disruption are that she is thoughtful, unsmiling, with arms held close.*

❷ Especially for Educators: Although one case study is never enough to make a generalization, what does David's story suggest about testing severely handicapped preschoolers?

One basic lesson in the ethics of research is to look very closely at the responses of particular subjects, rather than impose preconceptions and assumptions about the effects of research. In David's case, I am grateful to report, year after year he has been proud to be included. But the ethical role of the scientist goes far beyond simply doing no harm. It entails being mindful of the "social, political, and human implications" of the research. My obligation is step 5 of the scientific method: to publish the results so that others can learn. Accordingly, here is the latest update of David's story.

Looking Back and Looking Forward

Many of David's worst problems are behind him. In the biosocial domain, doctors have helped improve the quality of his life: an artificial eye has replaced the blind one; a back brace has helped his posture; and surgery has corrected a misaligned jaw, improving his appearance and his speech. In the cognitive domain, the once severely "retarded" preschooler is beginning a career as a translator (an interesting choice for someone who had to listen very carefully to what people said because he could not read their facial expressions). And in the psychosocial domain, the formerly self-absorbed child is now an outgoing young man, eager for friendship. Although he still lives at home with his parents, he looks forward to "breaking away" soon.

This is not to suggest that David's life is all smooth sailing. In fact, every day presents its struggles, and David, like everyone else, has his moments of self-doubt and depression. As he once confided to me:

> I sometimes have extremely pejorative thoughts . . . dreams of vivid symbolism. In one, I am playing on a pinball machine that is all broken—glass besmirched, legs tilted and wobbly, the plunger knob loose. I have to really work at it to get a decent score.

Yet David never loses heart, at least not for long. He continues to "really work" on his life, no matter what, and bit by bit his "score" improves.

In looking at David's life thus far, we can see how domains and contexts interact to affect development, both positively and negatively. We can also see the importance of science and application. For example, without research that demonstrated the crucial role of sensory stimulation in infant development, David's parents might not have been taught how to keep his young mind active. Without the efforts of hundreds of developmental scientists who proved that schools could provide effective teaching even for severely handicapped children, David might have never gone to school. He may have led a homebound and restricted life, as many children with his problems once did. Indeed, many children with David's initial level of disability have spent their entire lives in institutions that provide only custodial care, and some have died before reaching age 30.

David's story does more than illustrate domains and contexts. His life illustrates a universal truth: none of us is simply a product of our past history and present setting. Each person is an individual who uniquely reacts to, and acts upon, the constellation of contexts that impinges on his or her development. Thus the most important factor in David's past successes may have been David himself. His determination and stoic courage helped him weather the physical trauma of

Three Brothers Studying the development of other people is fascinating in many ways, not the least of which is that no human is untouched by understanding the personal story of another. I have learned many things from David, shown in this family photo with his two older brothers, Bill (left) and Michael (right). One is the role of siblings: Bill and Michael protected their younger brother, but David also taught them, making them more nurturant than most young men in their community. I know this firsthand—those boys are the closest thing my daughters had to big brothers, and they tolerated teasing that some older cousins would have put a stop to.

❶ Response for Educators (from page 33):
Tests, such as the IQ test that found David severely retarded, are a statement of the present, but not always predictive of the future. Effective teaching can have a decided impact, although it is unlikely teachers can ever erase the legacy of early neurological damage.

repeated surgery and the psychological devastation of social rejection. Of all those who should be proud of David's accomplishments—including the scientists, teachers, and family members who directly and indirectly contributed to his growth—the one who should be most proud is David himself. More than anyone else, in the final analysis, David, like each of us, directs his own development, within the boundaries set by his body and his context.

SUMMARY

THE STUDY OF HUMAN DEVELOPMENT

1. The study of human development explores how and why people change, and how and why they remain the same as they grow older. Development involves many academic and practical disciplines, especially biology, education, and psychology, and its subjects are people of every age and in every social group.

2. Development is often divided into three domains: the biosocial, the cognitive, and the psychosocial. While this division makes it easy to study the intricacies of development, researchers note that development in each domain is influenced by the other two, as body, mind, and emotion always affect one another; indeed, each aspect of development relates to each of the domains.

THE MANY CONTEXTS OF DEVELOPMENT

3. An ecological, or contextual, approach to development focuses on interactions between the individual and the various settings in which development occurs. Some of those settings involve the individual's physical surroundings—the layout of the neighborhood, the nature of the climate, and so on. Most, however, concern the people who create the social context for the individual's development.

4. Social contexts change over time, as changing historical events and conditions (the historical context) reshape the circumstances and perspectives surrounding development. There is quite a difference between being a child in an era when serious disease often meant death and being one when, except for accidents, almost every child is expected to reach old age.

5. Development is also strongly affected by a person's socioeconomic status, cultural values, and ethnicity. The influences of these social contexts often overlap, reinforcing and sometimes contradicting each other. Ultimately, however, each individual's path is unique, influenced but not determined by these contexts.

6. The interaction of domains is clearly seen in the example of David, whose problems originated in the biosocial domain but quickly affected the other domains. His example also shows how the individual is affected by, and affects, the contexts of family, society, and culture.

DEVELOPMENTAL STUDY AS A SCIENCE

7. The scientific method is used by developmental researchers. They first pose a research question; then they develop a hypothesis, collect data, and finally test the hypothesis and draw conclusions based on the data.

8. Often, the final step of the scientific method is to publish the research in sufficient detail so that others can evaluate the conclusions and, if they choose to, replicate the research or extend the findings with research of their own.

RESEARCH METHODS

9. One common method of gathering developmental research data is observation, which provides valid data but does not pinpoint cause and effect. The laboratory experiment indicates causes but is not necessarily applicable to daily life. Interviews, surveys, and case studies are also useful means of collecting data.

10. Researchers use a variety of methods to ensure the validity of their research. Among them are adequate sample sizes, selection of a representative sample, and use of "blind" experimenters, operational definitions, and control groups.

11. Developmental research is usually designed to detect change over time. A cross-sectional research design compares groups of people of different ages; a longitudinal design (which is preferable but more difficult to carry out) studies the same individuals over a long time period. Scientists combine both designs in cross-sequential research, which may provide more comprehensive findings.

ETHICS OF RESEARCH WITH CHILDREN

12. When studying children, scientists must take special care to ensure that participation is voluntary and no harm is done. The final obligation is to publicize findings in such a way that the social and political consequences are beneficial.

KEY TERMS

scientific study of human
   development (2)
biosocial domain (2)
cognitive domain (2)
psychosocial domain (2)
ecological approach (4)
social context (6)
cohort (9)
social construction (10)
socioeconomic status
   (SES) (11)
culture (12)
ethnic group (14)
scientific method (18)
hypothesis (19)
replicate (19)
variable (19)
scientific observation (20)
population (22)

sample (22)
sample size (22)
representative
   sample (22)
blind (22)
experimental group (23)
control group (23)
statistical significance (23)
correlation (24)
experiment (25)
independent variable (25)
dependent variable (25)
survey (27)
case study (28)
cross-sectional research
   (29)
longitudinal research (30)
cross-sequential research
   (30)

KEY QUESTIONS

1. What is the main focus of the study of human development?

2. Name and describe the three domains into which the study of human development is usually divided.

3. Give examples of interactions among the various microsystems that affect an individual's development.

4. Name and give examples of three social contextual factors that developmentalists recognize as powerful influences on human development.

5. Explain how the social context, as diagrammed in Figure 1.3, permeates the three domains of human development.

6. What are the advantages of the scientific method?

7. What are the steps of the scientific method?

8. What are the advantages and disadvantages of gathering research data by observation?

9. What are the advantages and disadvantages of gathering research data by experiment?

10. Compare the advantages and disadvantages of longitudinal research and cross-sectional research. Explain how the advantages of each method are combined in cross-sequential research.

11. *In Your Experience* Is any one of the three domains of development more important than the others? Explain.

CRITICAL THINKING EXERCISE

by Richard O. Straub

Take your study of Chapter 1 a step further by working this scientific-reasoning exercise.

Several studies suggest that breast-fed babies become more intelligent children than formula-fed babies. One such study (Lucas et al., 1992) involved 300 prematurely born babies whose mothers had decided, prior to the experiment, whether they would breast-feed their newborns or feed them formula. Infants in both the breast-milk and formula groups were fed first by tube and then by bottle for 18 months.

As 8-year-olds, the children who were fed breast milk as infants scored 8 points higher on a general IQ test than those who were fed formula. This difference was observed even after the researchers adjusted for differences in the social class and maternal education of the two groups. (This adjustment allowed the researchers to rule out any preexisting differences in the SESs of the mothers that might have contributed to IQ differences in their children.)

The researchers acknowledged that other differences between the groups, such as the children's genetic potential or their parents' caregiving skills or motivation to nurture, could explain the results. However, they believe that human milk contains hormones and other elements that enhance brain growth and maturation.

1. State the researchers' research hypothesis in your own words. Identify the independent and dependent variables and the experimental and control groups.

2. How do the researchers test their hypothesis? Is this a valid test of the hypothesis?

3. What explanation do the researchers offer for their findings? Does this explanation make sense based on the evidence?

4. What might be an alternative explanation for the results of this study? What could the researchers do in order to make a causal connection between the dependent and independent variables?

5. Are there any practical implications for this research?

Check your answers by comparing them to the sample answers in Appendix B.

Theories

CHAPTER 2

As we saw in Chapter 1, the scientific effort to understand human development usually begins with questions. One of the most basic is, How do children develop into the kind of people they ultimately become? Do early experiences—of breast-feeding, or bonding, or abuse—linger into adulthood, even if they seem to be forgotten? Can moral teachings produce an ethical person? How important are elementary school experiences in developing a child's mind? If a young boy is angry and aggressive, will he become a juvenile delinquent and then an adult criminal? What if that angry and aggressive child is a girl? If parents are depressed, schizophrenic, or alcoholic, will their children develop the same conditions—even if someone else raises them? For every answer there are more questions: Why or why not? When and how? So what?

WHAT THEORIES DO

To begin to answer such questions, we need some way to determine which facts about development are relevant, and then we need to organize those facts to lead us to deeper understanding. In short, we need a theory. A **developmental theory** is a systematic set of principles and generalizations that provides a coherent framework for studying and explaining development. A developmental theory is not a collection of facts; it connects facts and observations, putting the details of life into a meaningful whole.

Theories are also quite practical, in three ways:

- Theories offer insight and guidance for everyday concerns by providing a broad and coherent view of the complex influences on human development.
- Theories form the basis for hypotheses about behavior and development that can be tested by research and that add to developmental knowledge if confirmed. Thus theories "provide a point of departure," "a conceptual connection" for individual scientists who study according to their own particular research interests (Renninger & Amsel, 1997).
- Theories are constantly modified by new research findings and thus summarize our current knowledge about development, enabling us to communicate that knowledge in a way that makes sense (Meacham, 1997).

The study of development is never complete, because updated theories give rise to meaningful questions which lead to useful answers which lead to

What Is Happening Here? Every moment of development can be explained by many theories, but this moment is particularly intriguing. Is big sister Carly feeling unconscious hate or learned affection or some other emotion? Is baby brother William simply sensing the texture of dry leaves, or is he developing memories, concepts, or brain patterns that he is going to carry into adulthood? From a developmental perspective, one thing is certain: Carly and William are genetically and experientially linked in ways that will affect them both all their lives.

developmental theory   A systematic set of principles and generalizations that explains development, generates hypotheses, and provides a framework for future research.

grand theories   Comprehensive theories that have inspired and directed thinking about development for decades but no longer seem as adequate as they once did.

minitheories   Theories that explain some specific area of development, but that are not as general and comprehensive as grand theories.

emergent theories   Relatively new comprehensive theories formulated within the past 30 years, that bring together information from many disciplines but are not yet a coherent, comprehensive whole.

psychoanalytic theory   A grand theory of human development that holds that irrational, unconscious forces, many of them from childhood, underlie human behavior.

additional theory. For example, consider why most parents devote so much time and energy to caring for their children.

- Is it because parenting is a basic stage of adult development?
- Or because parental devotion arises from the rewards and reinforcement that children provide?
- Or because parenting impulses are rooted in the intellect and arise from an understanding of, and empathy for, children's needs?
- Or because cultural expectations, ingrained since childhood, lead most adults to assume that parenthood is a valued role?
- Or because there is a genetic impulse to protect and love one's own biological offspring as a self-perpetuating strategy?

Each of these hypotheses is suggested by one of the five theories discussed in this chapter. Those theories lead us to view parenting, in turn, as a stage, a reward, a decision, a cultural value, and a survival impulse. Each view has important practical applications, suggesting, for example, whether it is better to have children at the beginning of adulthood or closer to middle age, what can be done to prevent child abuse, or how fathers and mothers can best share the parental role.

In truth, hundreds of theories are relevant to the study of development. Some originated with extraordinary intellectual leaders, who fashioned what are called **grand theories,** "because each offered a powerful framework for interpreting and understanding change and development [and was] meant to apply to the change and development of all individuals, in all contexts, across all contents" (Renninger & Amsel, 1997). Some are called **minitheories,** because they are intended to explain only a part of development or to relate to only a particular group of people, rather than to explain everything, everywhere, for everyone (Parke et al., 1994). And some are called **emergent theories,** because they arise from the accumulated minitheories and may become the new systematic and comprehensive theories of the future. In this chapter we will focus on three grand theories—psychoanalytic, learning, and cognitive—and two emergent theories— sociocultural and epigenetic. These five theories, and several others, will also be described and applied as they become relevant later in this book.

GRAND THEORIES

In the first half of the twentieth century, two opposing theories dominated the child development scene: psychoanalytic theory and learning theory (originally called behaviorism). Both theories began as theories of psychology and later were applied to human development more broadly. By midcentury, they were joined by a third grand theory, cognitive theory. In regard to some ideas, proponents of each theory often scorned proponents of the other two; yet all of them agreed on many basic principles. Before we examine the points of disagreement and agreement, we will briefly describe each theory.

Psychoanalytic Theory

Psychoanalytic theory interprets human development in terms of intrinsic drives and motives, many of which are *irrational* and *unconscious*, hidden from awareness. These basic underlying forces are viewed as influencing every aspect of a person's thinking and behavior, from the smallest details of daily life to the crucial choices of a lifetime. Psychoanalytic theory also sees these drives and motives as providing the foundation for the universal stages of development that every human experiences. For everyone, each stage entails specific developmental tasks, from the formation of human attachments in infancy to the quest for emotional and sexual fulfillment in adulthood.

Freud's Ideas

Freud at Work In addition to being the world's first psychoanalyst, Sigmund Freud was a prolific writer whose many papers and case histories, primarily descriptions of his patients' bizarre symptoms and unconscious sexual urges, helped make the psychoanalytic perspective a dominant force for much of the twentieth century.

Psychoanalytic theory originated with Sigmund Freud (1856–1939), a physician who developed his theory as a result of his clinical work with patients suffering from mental illness. He listened to their accounts of dreams and fantasies, as well as to their "uncensored" streams of thought, and constructed an elaborate, multifaceted theory that includes an emphasis on unconscious conflicts originating in early childhood. According to this theory, development in the first 6 years occurs in three stages, each characterized by the focusing of sexual interest and pleasure on a particular part of the body. In infancy, it is the mouth (the *oral stage*); in early childhood, it is the anus (the *anal stage*); in the preschool years, it is the penis (the *phallic stage*). (See Table 2.1 on page 41 for descriptions of the stages in Freud's theory.)

Freud maintained that at each of these stages, the sensual satisfaction associated with the mouth, anus, or penis is linked to the major developmental needs and challenges that are associated with that stage. During the oral stage, for example, the baby not only gains physical nurturance through sucking but also experiences sensual pleasure and becomes emotionally attached to the mother—the provider of this oral gratification. During the anal stage, pleasures related to control and self-control— initially in connection with defecation and toilet training—are paramount. During the phallic stage, the young child's fascination with the physical differences between the sexes leads to gender identity, sexual orientation, and the development of moral standards. As you might imagine, this process differs for boys and girls, as is explained in Chapter 10. Emotions related to each stage remain powerful but disguised forces in adult personality, part of the unconscious legacy from childhood.

Childhood Sexuality? The girl's interest in the statue's anatomy may reflect simple curiosity, but Freudian theory would maintain that it is a clear manifestation of the phallic stage of psychosexual development, in which girls are said to feel deprived because they lack a penis.

The first three of Freud's stages are followed by a 5- or 6-year period of sexual *latency*, during which sexual forces are dormant. Then, at about age 12, the individual enters a final stage, the *genital stage*, characterized by mature sexual interests lasting throughout adulthood.

One of Freud's most influential ideas was that each stage arrives with its own potential conflicts between child and parent, as, for instance, when an adult tries to wean a child from the beloved bottle. According to Freud, how the child experiences and resolves the conflicts that occur in the oral, anal, and phallic stages—especially those related to weaning, toilet training, and childhood sexual curiosity—influences personality growth and determines the person's lifelong patterns of behavior. An adult may not know it, but the fact that he or she smokes cigarettes (oral), or keeps careful track of money (anal), or is romantically attracted to a much older partner (phallic), signifies unconscious problems at a childhood stage.

Erikson's Ideas

Freud had a number of students who became famous psychoanalytic theorists in their own right. Although they all acknowledged the importance

What's in a Name—Erik Erikson As a young man, this neo-Freudian changed his last name to the one we know him by. What do you think his choice means? (See caption to photo below.)

of unconscious, irrational forces (and of early childhood), each expanded and modified Freud's ideas. The most notable of these neo-Freudians was Erik Erikson (1902–1994), who formulated his own version of psychoanalytic theory.

Erikson spent his childhood in Germany, his adolescence wandering through Italy, and his young adulthood in Austria under the tutelage of Freud and Freud's daughter Anna. Just before World War II, he arrived in the United States, where he studied students at Harvard University, soldiers who had suffered emotional breakdowns, civil rights workers in the South, disturbed and normal children at play, and Native American tribes. Partly as a result of this diversity of experience, Erikson began to think of Freud's stages as too limited and too few. He proposed, instead, eight developmental stages covering the entire life span. Each of Erikson's stages is characterized by a particular challenge, or *developmental crisis,* which is central to that stage of life and which must be resolved.

As you can see from Table 2.1, Erikson's first five stages are closely related to Freud's stages. In addition, Erikson, like Freud, believed that the problems of adult life echo the unresolved conflicts of childhood; thus, for example, an adult who has difficulty establishing a secure, mutual relationship with a life partner might have never resolved the crisis of early infancy, *trust versus mistrust.* However, Erikson's stages differ significantly from Freud's in their emphasis on the person's relationship to the family and culture, not just to his or her own sexual urges.

In Erikson's theory, the resolution of each developmental crisis depends on the interaction between the individual's characteristics and whatever support is provided by the social environment. In the stage of *initiative versus guilt,* for example, children between ages 3 and 6 years often want to undertake activities that exceed their abilities and/or the

Who Are We? The most famous of Erikson's eight crises is the identity crisis, during adolescence, when young people find their own answer to the question, "Who am I?" Erikson did this for himself, by choosing a last name that, with his first name, implies "son of myself" (Erik, Erik's son). Although the identity crisis is universal, particulars vary from place to place and time to time—with each cohort distinguishing itself from the slightly older cohort in some way.

❷ *Observational Quiz (see answer page 42):* Where and when do you think this photograph was taken?

limits set by their parents. Their efforts to act independently leave them open to feelings of either pride or failure, depending partly on how they go about seeking independence, partly on the reactions of their parents, and partly on their culture's expectations regarding children's behavior. As an example of the last influence, we note that some cultures *encourage* assertive 5-year-olds as being creative spirits who know their own minds; other cultures *discourage* them as being rude or fresh children. The children internalize these reactions and thus later, as adults, some people are much bolder, and others are more self-critical, than their peers in other cultures—all because of what happened when they were ages 3 to 6.

table **2.1**	**Comparison of Freud's Psychosexual and Erikson's Psychosocial Stages**	
Approximate Age	Freud (Psychosexual)	Erikson* (Psychosocial)
Birth to 1 year	*Oral Stage* The mouth, tongue, and gums are the focus of pleasurable sensations in the baby's body, and sucking and feeding are the most stimulating activities.	*Trust vs. Mistrust* Babies learn either to trust that others will care for their basic needs, including nourishment, warmth, cleanliness, and physical contact, or to lack confidence in the care of others.
1–3 years	*Anal Stage* The anus is the focus of pleasurable sensations in the baby's body, and toilet training is the most important activity.	*Autonomy vs. Shame and Doubt* Children learn either to be self-sufficient in many activities, including toileting, feeding, walking, exploring, and talking, or to doubt their own abilities.
3–6 years	*Phallic Stage* The phallus, or penis, is the most important body part, and pleasure is derived from genital stimulation. Boys are proud of their penises, and girls wonder why they don't have one.	*Initiative vs. Guilt* Children want to undertake many adultlike activities, sometimes overstepping the limits set by parents and feeling guilty.
7–11 years	*Latency* This is not a stage but an interlude, during which sexual needs are quiet and children put psychic energy into conventional activities like schoolwork and sports.	*Industry vs. Inferiority* Children busily learn to be competent and productive in mastering new skills or feel inferior and unable to do anything well.
Adolescence	*Genital Stage* The genitals are the focus of pleasurable sensations, and the young person seeks sexual stimulation and sexual satisfaction in heterosexual relationships.	*Identity vs. Role Confusion* Adolescents try to figure out "Who Am I?" They establish sexual, political, and career identities or are confused about what roles to play.
Adulthood	Freud believed that the genital stage lasts throughout adulthood. He also said that the goal of a healthy life is "to love and to work well."	*Intimacy vs. Isolation* Young adults seek companionship and love with another person or become isolated from others by fearing rejection and disappointment. *Generativity vs. Stagnation* Middle-aged adults contribute to the next generation through meaningful work, creative activities, and/or raising a family, or they stagnate. *Integrity vs. Despair* Older adults try to make sense out of their lives, either seeing life as a meaningful whole or despairing at goals never reached.

*Although Erikson described two extreme resolutions to each crisis, he recognized that there is a wide range of outcomes between these extremes and that, for most people, the best resolution to a crisis is not either extreme but, rather, a middle course.

Learning Theory

Early in the twentieth century, John B. Watson (1878–1958) argued that if psychology was to be a true science, psychologists should study only what they could see and measure. He directly opposed Freud's emphasis on unconscious factors that patients might be able to recall only years later under psychoanalytic probing or might never remember at all, except via dreams or other disguised manifestations. In Watson's words:

> Why don't we make what we can *observe* the real field of psychology? Let us limit ourselves to things that can be observed, and formulate laws concerned only with those things. . . . We can observe behavior—what the organism does or says. [Watson, 1967]

! *Answer to Observational Quiz (from page 40):*
The signs suggest Asia, and the fact that overt rebellion is difficult in a small Asian town suggests a large city. If you guessed Tokyo, score one correct. A sharp eye on the T-shirt and an accurate memory of when Mohawk hairstyles were in fashion would give you another correct answer—probably 1992.

learning theory   A grand theory of development, built on behaviorism, that focuses on the sequences and processes by which behavior is learned.

stimulus   An action or event that elicits a behavioral response.

response   A behavior (either instinctual or learned) that is elicited by a certain stimulus.

conditioning   Any learning process that occurs according to the laws of behaviorism or learning theory. This can be classical conditioning, in which one stimulus is associated with another, or operant conditioning, in which a response is gradually learned via reinforcement.

According to Watson, anything can be learned. He said:

> Give me a dozen healthy infants, well-formed, and my own specified world to bring them up in and I'll guarantee to take any one at random and train him to become any type of specialist I might select—doctor, lawyer, artist, merchant, chief, and yes, even beggar-man and thief, regardless of his talents, penchants, tendencies, abilities, vocations, and race of his ancestors. [Watson, 1930]

Other psychologists agreed, partly because of the difficulty of trying to study the unconscious motives and drives identified in psychoanalytic theory. Actual behavior, by contrast, could be studied far more objectively and scientifically. Thus was developed the theory originally called behaviorism. Behaviorism gave rise to our second grand theory of development, **learning theory,** which focuses on the ways we learn specific behaviors—ways that can be described, analyzed, and predicted with far more scientific accuracy than the unconscious drives of the psychoanalysts (Horowitz, 1994).

Laws of Behavior

Learning theorists formulated laws of behavior that, they say, apply to every individual at every age, from newborn to octogenarian. These laws provide insights into how mature competencies are fashioned from simple actions and how environmental influences shape individual development. In the view of learning theorists, all development involves a process of learning and, therefore, does not occur in specific stages that are dependent only on age or maturation.

The basic laws of learning theory explore the relationship between a **stimulus,** that is, an action or event, and a **response,** that is the behavioral reaction with which the stimulus is associated. Some responses are automatic, such as reflexes. If someone suddenly waves a hand in your face, you blink; if a hungry dog smells food, it salivates. But most responses do not occur spontaneously; they are learned. Learning theorists emphasize that life is a continual learning process: new events and experiences evoke new behavior patterns, while old, unused, and unproductive responses tend to fade away. The learning occurs through **conditioning,** by which a particular response comes to be triggered by a particular stimulus. There are two types of conditioning: classical and operant.

Classical Conditioning.   A century ago, a Russian scientist named Ivan Pavlov (1849–1936) began to study the link between stimulus and response. While doing research on salivation in dogs, Pavlov noted that his experimental dogs began to salivate not only at the sight of food but, eventually, at the sound of the approaching attendants who brought the food. This observation led him to perform his famous experiment in which he taught a dog to salivate at the sound of a bell. Pavlov began by ringing the bell just before presenting food to the dog. After a number of repetitions of this bell-then-food sequence, the dog began salivating at the bell's sound even when there was no food nearby.

This simple experiment in learning was one of the first scientific demonstrations of *classical conditioning* (also called *respondent conditioning*). In classical conditioning, an organism (any type of living creature) comes to *associate* a neutral stimulus with a meaningful one and then responds to the former stimulus as if it were the latter. In Pavlov's original experiment, the dog associated the sound of the bell (the neutral stimulus) with food (the meaningful stimulus) and responded to the sound as though it were the food itself.

A Contemporary of Freud Ivan Pavlov was a physiologist who received the Nobel Prize in 1904 for his research on digestive processes. It was this line of study that led to his discovery of classical conditioning.

Many everyday examples suggest classical conditioning that you yourself have probably experienced: imagining a succulent pizza might make your mouth water; reading a final-exam schedule might make your palms sweat; seeing an erotic photograph might make your heart beat faster. In each instance, the previously neutral stimulus is associated, or connected, with another stimulus that directly produced the physiological response in the past. Classical conditioning is also apparent when a child who has been badly frightened by some event—say, an attack by a snarling dog—is returned to the scene of the incident and begins crying, because he or she now associates the location with previous feelings of terror. As Watson (1927) himself noted, emotional responses are especially susceptible to learning through classical conditioning, particularly in childhood.

Rats, Pigeons, and People B. F. Skinner is best known for his experiments with rats and pigeons, but he also applied his knowledge to human problems. For his daughter, he designed a glass-enclosed crib in which temperature, humidity, and perceptual stimulation could be controlled to make her time in the crib enjoyable and educational. He wrote about an ideal society based on principles of operant conditioning, where, for example, workers at the less desirable jobs would earn greater rewards.

Operant Conditioning. The most influential proponent of learning theory was B. F. Skinner (1904–1990), who not only researched and published hundreds of articles and books but also trained hundreds of graduate students who became influential scientists, testing and extending learning theory. Skinner agreed, with Watson, that psychology should focus on the scientific study of behavior and, with Pavlov, that classical conditioning explains some types of behavior. However, Skinner studied another type of conditioning—*operant conditioning*—that plays a much greater role in human behavior, especially in more complex learning. In operant conditioning, the organism learns that a particular behavior produces a particular consequence. If the consequence is useful or pleasurable, the organism will tend to repeat the behavior to achieve that consequence again. If the consequence is unpleasant, the organism will tend not to repeat the behavior. (Operant conditioning is also called *instrumental conditioning*.)

In operant conditioning, then, pleasurable consequences (such as rewards) might be used to train an animal to perform a new behavior. A simple example is training a dog to fetch newspapers or jump through a hoop by giving it a treat every time it performs the behavior. Or a behavior that the animal already sometimes performs can be operantly conditioned to occur more precisely or quickly. For example, early behaviorist experiments typically involved placing food at the end of a maze to condition rats to run the maze more efficiently.

Once a behavior has been conditioned (learned), animals (including humans) will continue to perform it even when the pleasurable consequences occur only occasionally rather than consistently. Almost all of a person's daily behavior, from socializing with others to earning a paycheck, can be understood as a result of operant conditioning. For instance, when a baby first gives a half smile in response to a full stomach, a mother might smile back. Soon the baby is conditioned to give a bigger smile, and the mother smiles more and picks the baby up or does something else to reinforce the smile. As time goes on, the baby becomes a smiling toddler, a cheerful child, an outgoing adolescent, and a friendly adult—all because of early operant conditioning and periodic reinforcing.

reinforcement The process whereby a particular behavior is strengthened, making it more likely that the behavior will be repeated.

In operant conditioning, the process of repeating a consequence to make it more likely that the behavior in question will recur is called **reinforcement** (Skinner, 1953). A consequence that increases the likelihood that a behavior will be repeated is therefore called a *reinforcer*. The mother's early reinforcement produces a socially responsive, smiling adult.

❷ **Especially for Parents:** Think of four specific suggestions for a parent who wants to teach a child to wash hands before every meal.

When parents and teachers apply the laws of conditioning with children, they need to be sure that the rewards they use are actually reinforcers for those children (some children are embarrassed or upset by social recognition, so putting their "A" papers on display might actually be punishment for them). Operant conditioning works best when the child's particular needs and past reinforcement history are taken into account. The timing and intensity of the reinforcement process must also be carefully planned to follow the various laws of conditioning. If the laws are followed, the child can be taught almost anything, even to become a "doctor, lawyer, begger-man, thief," as Watson bragged.

Social Learning

social learning   The theory that learning occurs through observation and imitation of other people.

modeling   Part of social learning theory; in particular, the process whereby a person tries to imitate the behavior of someone else. Modeling occurs with minor actions, such as how someone laughs or what shoes he or she wears, but it also occurs in powerful ways, as when a male child identifies with his father as a role model.

Originally, learning theorists sought to explain behavior primarily as arising from the organism's direct experience with classical or operant conditioning. More recent learning theorists also focus on less direct, though equally potent, forms of learning. They emphasize that humans can learn new behaviors merely by observing the behavior of others, without personally experiencing any conditioning. These theorists have developed an extension of learning theory called **social learning.**

An integral part of social learning is **modeling,** in which people observe behavior and then pattern their own after it. This is not simply a case of "monkey see, monkey do." People model only certain behaviors of certain individuals in certain contexts. Generally, modeling of a particular behavior is most likely to occur when the observer is uncertain or inexperienced and when the behavior has been enacted by someone considered admirable, powerful, or similar to the observer (Bandura, 1977).

Social learning involves much more than just observing a model and imitating behavior. The learner must be motivated to pay attention to the modeled behavior, to store information about it in memory (perhaps by mentally rehearsing it), and later to retrieve that information when opportunities to use the modeled behavior arise (Bandura, 1977, 1986, 1989). These cognitive and motivational processes help explain the fact that people's susceptibility to modeling changes as they mature. With increasing age, for example, children become more discriminating observers of other people; they also become better able to extract general rules from the specific behaviors they observe. Thus, young children tend to imitate the most obvious behaviors of a wide range of people, especially their parents, whereas adolescents and adults reproduce more subtle behaviors and general styles of conduct (such as a "laid-back air" or a more "scholarly" manner) observed in selected individuals.

Learning to Read One of the more controversial implications of social learning is that a boy needs a father to teach him how to be a man. Children learn from many people, and no doubt fathers, their behaviors, and their relationships are powerful models for young children.

Social learning is also affected by self-understanding, because the standards we set for ourselves, and our confidence in our ability to meet them, influence our motivation to learn from various sources—whether they be peers,

Social Learning in Action Social learning validates the old maxim "Examples speak louder than words." If the moments here are typical for each child, the girl in the left photo is likely to grow up with a ready sense of the importance of this particular chore of infant care. Unfortunately, the boy on the right may become a cigarette smoker like his father—even if his father warns him of the dangers of this habit.

❓ *Observational Quiz (see answer page 46): Beyond what they are doing, what else shows that these children model their parents?*

mentors, or media stars. In this emphasis on social and self-understanding, social learning theory incorporates insights from the next grand theory we will examine.

Cognitive Theory

Cognitive theory focuses primarily on the structure and development of the individual's thought processes and how those processes affect the person's understanding of the world. Cognitive researchers try to determine how this understanding, and the expectations it creates, affects the development of the individual's attitudes, beliefs, and behavior. In other words, to understand people, don't delve into what they forgot from childhood (psychoanalytic theory) or what has happened to them (behaviorism), but find out what they think.

cognitive theory   A theory that holds that the way people think and understand the world shapes their perceptions, attitudes, and actions.

Jean Piaget (1896–1980) was the major pioneer of cognitive theory. Although originally trained in the natural sciences, Piaget became interested in human thought processes when he was hired to field-test questions for a standard intelligence test for children. Piaget was supposed to find the age at which most children could answer each question right, but he found the children's wrong answers much more intriguing. He noted that children who were of the same age shared similar mistaken concepts, a fact suggesting a developmental sequence to intellectual growth. *How children think* is much more important, and more revealing of their mental ability, Piaget concluded, than *what they know*. Moreover, understanding how people think also reveals how they interpret their experiences, and thus explains how they construct their understanding of the world.

Would You Talk to this Man? Children loved talking to Jean Piaget, and he learned by listening carefully—especially to their incorrect explanations, which no one had paid much attention to before. All his life, Piaget was absorbed with studying the way children think. He called himself a "genetic epistemologist"—one who studies how children gain knowledge about the world as they grow up.

Periods of Cognitive Development

Piaget maintained that there are four major periods of cognitive development. These are age-related, and, as you will see in later chapters, each has features that permit certain types of knowing and understanding (Piaget, 1952, 1970).

Briefly, infants, in the first or *sensorimotor period,* know the world only through their senses and motor abilities; their understanding of the objects in their world is limited to their sensory experience of those objects and to the immediate actions they can perform on those objects. This is a very practical, experience-based kind of early intelligence. At about 1 year of age, babies become, in Piaget's words, "little scientists," tirelessly experimenting with objects to see how they work and to discover what new uses they can be put to. But the methods of the little scientist are limited to trial and error: to discover what happens when an egg is dropped on the floor, for instance, the little scientist has to drop one.

By contrast, preschool children, in the second or *preoperational period,* can begin to think symbolically; that is, they can think about and understand objects using mental processes that are independent of immediate experience. This is reflected in their ability to use language, to think of past and future events, to imagine, and to pretend—none of which requires the immediate presence of an object. However, they cannot think logically in a consistent way, and thus their reasoning processes are subjective and intuitive. They believe they are warriors and princesses; they fear tidal waves and monsters; they demand that their parents stop the rain, or the chicken pox, or their fighting—with no realization of the egocentrism such magic thinking entails.

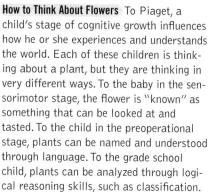

How to Think About Flowers To Piaget, a child's stage of cognitive growth influences how he or she experiences and understands the world. Each of these children is thinking about a plant, but they are thinking in very different ways. To the baby in the sensorimotor stage, the flower is "known" as something that can be looked at and tasted. To the child in the preoperational stage, plants can be named and understood through language. To the grade school child, plants can be analyzed through logical reasoning skills, such as classification.

School-age children, in the third or *concrete operational period,* begin to think logically in a consistent way, but only with regard to real and concrete features of their world. They cannot yet handle abstract situations. Nevertheless, logical reasoning abilities make the school-age child a more systematic, objective, and thus scientific kind of thinker.

In Piaget's final period, the *formal operational period,* adolescents and adults are able, in varying degrees, to think hypothetically and abstractly. They can think about thinking and speculate about the possible as well as the real. Table 2.2 summarizes Piaget's periods. Sometimes these are called stages, although Piaget called them "periods." In any case, they follow in sequence, and, as you will now see, each is preceded by a period of confusion.

How Cognitive Development Occurs

Underlying Piaget's theory is his basic view of cognitive development as a process that follows universal patterns. This process is guided, according to

table **2.2**	**Piaget's Periods of Cognitive Development**		
Approximate Age	Period	Characteristics	Major Gains During the Period
Birth to 2 years	Sensorimotor	Infant uses senses and motor abilities to understand the world. There is no conceptual or reflective thought; an object is "known" in terms of what an infant can *do* to it.	The infant learns that an object still exists when it is out of sight *(object permanence)* and begins to think through mental actions as well as physical actions.
2–6 years	Preoperational	The child uses *symbolic thinking*, including language, to understand the world. Sometimes the child's thinking is *egocentric*, causing the child to understand the world from only one perspective, his or her own.	The imagination flourishes, and language becomes a significant means of self-expression and of influence from others. Children gradually begin to *decenter*, that is, become less egocentric, and to understand and coordinate multiple points of view.
7–11 years	Concrete operational	The child understands and applies logical operations, or principles, to help interpret experiences objectively and rationally rather than intuitively.	By applying logical abilities, children learn to understand the basic concepts of conservation, number, classification, and many other scientific ideas.
12 years through adulthood	Formal operational	The adolescent or adult is able to think about abstractions and hypothetical concepts.	Ethics, politics, and social and moral issues become more interesting and involving as the adolescent becomes able to take a broader and more theoretical approach to experience.

cognitive equilibrium A state of mental balance, in which a person's thoughts and assumptions about the world seem (at least to that person) not to clash with each other or with that person's experiences.

Piaget, by the human need for **cognitive equilibrium,** that is, a state of mental balance. What Piaget meant is that each person needs to, and continually attempts to, make sense of new experiences by reconciling them with his or her existing understanding. Cognitive equilibrium is experienced when one's present understanding "fits" new experiences, whether this fitting involves a baby's discovery that new objects can be grasped in the same ways as familiar objects or an adult's being able to explain shifting world events in terms of his or her political philosophy.

When a new experience does not seem to fit existing understanding, the individual falls into a state of *cognitive disequilibrium.* Disequilibrium is a kind of imbalance that initially produces confusion and then leads to cognitive growth as the person modifies old concepts and constructs better ones to fit the new experience. In Piaget's terminology, there are two ways a person's understanding can adapt to new experiences: either by reinterpreting the new experiences so that they fit into, or *assimilate* with, the old ideas or by revamping the old ideas so that they can *accommodate* the new. Assimilation is easier, since it does not require much adjustment; but accommodation is sometimes necessary, and it produces significant intellectual growth.

You may experience cognitive disequilibrium, for example, when a friend's argument reveals logical inconsistencies in your views, when your favorite chess strategy fails against a skilled opponent, or when your mother does or says something you never expected her to. In the last example, you might assimilate your mother's unusual statement by deciding that it was just something she heard and she doesn't really mean it. Growth occurs if, instead, you adjust your previous conception of your mother to accommodate a new, expanded, and more comprehensive view of who she is.

Not What He Expected Water spraying out of a pipe that he can hold in his hand—a surprising event that is likely to trigger first cognitive disequilibrium and then cognitive growth.
❷ *Observational Quiz (see answer page 50):* *This boy is 14 months old, in the sensorimotor period, and at an age where he loves to experiment. What is he likely to do next?*

Not What He Expected Water spraying out of a pipe that he can hold in his hand—a surprising event that is likely to trigger first cognitive disequilibrium and then cognitive growth.
❷ *Observational Quiz (see answer page 50):* *This boy is 14 months old, in the sensorimotor period, and at an age where he loves to experiment. What is he likely to do next?*

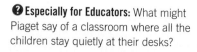

❷ **Especially for Educators:** What might Piaget say of a classroom where all the children stay quietly at their desks?

Periods of disequilibrium are disquieting to a child or an adult who suspects that accepted ideas no longer hold true. But they are also exciting periods of mental growth, which is one reason why people of all ages seek challenging experiences. According to cognitive theory, children are especially motivated to seek out novel experiences to put their current understanding to the test, and they grow as a result. Babies poke, pull, and taste everything they get their hands on; preschool children ask thousands of questions; school-age children become avid readers and information collectors; adolescents try out a wide variety of roles and experiences. Adults, too, continually increase their knowledge and expertise in areas that interest them—all because people at every age seek cognitive challenges.

Recognition of this active searching is the very essence of Piaget's theory of human cognitive development. Unlike psychoanalytic and learning theories, which depict children as buffeted and shaped by influences beyond their control, cognitive theory portrays a much more active child, who is seeking ways to comprehend the world.

As you will see in later chapters, many contemporary cognitive researchers go one step further, studying how various aspects of the social context or the neurological networks of the brain affect the child's active thinking processes. We will not describe those extensions here, because each of them is incorporated, to some extent, in the two emergent theories we shall discuss shortly.

Evaluation of Grand Theories

All three of the theories we have just described deserve to be called "grand." They are insightful and provocative, stimulating not only to researchers in human development but also to historians, educators, and particularly therapists. Thousands of psychiatrists, psychologists, and social workers still use techniques that originated from Freud, Skinner, or Piaget. However, as you will now see, none of these grand theories seems as relevant and comprehensive today as it did even 30 years ago.

Criticisms and Omissions

Both psychoanalytic theory and learning theory are quite focused on what adults did—or did not do—to the child. For example, if parents provide their infant with the proper oral gratification (according to Freud) or the appropriate reinforcement (according to Skinner), habits will develop that can benefit the child, the adolescent, and then the adult. These first two grand theories see the nature of the child in opposite ways—as a seething cauldron of unconscious desire, in psychoanalytic theory, and as a malleable organism that could become "doctor, lawyer . . . or thief" in learning theory. But the emphasis in both theories is on the parents' behavior, not on the child's innate temperament, cognitive capacity, or cultural context. In retrospect, that emphasis seems quite narrow to most developmentalists today (Cole, 1996; Dent-Read & Zukow-Goldring, 1997; Parke et al., 1994).

More specifically, learning theory is often criticized for being unable to explain complex cognitive, emotional, and perceptual dimensions of human development (Grusec, 1992). Critics point out that development is influenced not just by stimuli from the environment but also by genetic tendencies, biological maturation, internal thought processes, and the developing person's own efforts to comprehend new experiences. From this broader perspective, theories that focus primarily on learning from the environment seem to provide a very incomplete picture of developmental influences (Cairns, 1994). Similarly, the psychoanalytic emphasis on unconscious and uncontrollable sexual longings that plague adults lifelong seems quite culture-specific and time-bound—as it arose from Europe in the first half of the twentieth century—and much less applicable to modern life.

Cognitive theory escapes the primary criticism leveled at the psychoanalytic and learning theories: that the child is seen as responding only to instincts or reinforcement (Dent-Read & Zukow-Goldring, 1997). In fact, the active role of the child's intellectual curiosity is central to cognitive theory. However, critics complain that Piaget paid little attention to individual differences in ability, heredity, or motivation. Further, many people think Piaget was so absorbed by the individual's active search for knowledge that he underestimated the importance of instruction and, consequently, underestimated the role of society, school, and family in fostering cognitive development (Bjorklund, 1997; Gardner, 1987).

It was the universality of the grand theories that led to their downfall. The central idea that every child, in every culture, in every nation, passes through certain fixed stages (Freud, Erikson, Piaget), or can be conditioned according to the same laws of reinforcement (Watson, Pavlov, Skinner), does not square with the actual diversity of children worldwide. Listening to, and looking at, any living, breathing, growing child is bound to surprise any adult at some point, no matter what grand theory or basic assumptions he or she has.

In other words, all three grand theories seem much less comprehensive now than they did in previous decades. They focus too much on the individual child, focus too little on the social context, and seriously underestimate the role of biological and genetic influences.

Contributions of the Grand Theories

Nonetheless, each of these three theories has made significant contributions to developmental science. All developmentalists owe a debt of gratitude to Freud and to the neo-Freudians who extended and refined his concepts. Many psychoanalytic ideas are widely accepted today—for example, that unconscious motives affect our behavior, and that the early years are a formative period of personality development. And while much of Freud's thinking has come into question, many of today's developmentalists have learned from his insights (Emde, 1994). Indeed, the psychoanalytic approach laid the foundation for current minitheories about topics as diverse as mother-infant attachment, parental discipline, gender identity, moral development, and adolescent identity, as you will see in coming chapters.

The study of human development has benefited from learning theory too, in many ways. The theory's emphasis on the causes and consequences of observed behavior has led researchers to see that many behavior patterns that

The Founder of Sociocultural Theory Lev Vygotsky, now recognized as a seminal thinker whose ideas on the role of culture and history are revolutionizing education and the study of development, was a contemporary of Freud, Skinner, Pavlov, and Piaget. Vygotsky did not attain their eminence in his lifetime, partly because his work, conducted in Stalinist Russia, was largely inaccessible to the Western world and partly because he died prematurely, at age 38.

sociocultural theory   A theory which holds that human development results from the dynamic interaction between developing persons and the surrounding culture, primarily as expressed by the parents and teachers who transmit it.

❶ *Answer to Observational Quiz (from page 48):* *He will want to use all his senses and motor skills, so he might put the pipe to his mouth to taste it, rub it on his belly to feel the cold, shake it up and down to see and hear what happens, and—watch out—aim it at you to see your reaction.*

seem to be inborn, or seem to be the result of deeply rooted emotional problems, may actually be learned behaviors that can be "unlearned." This realization has encouraged many scientists to approach particular problem behaviors, such as temper tantrums, phobias, and harmful addictions, by analyzing and attempting to change the stimulus-response patterns they entail. In many cases, when parents and teachers use learning theory to analyze their reactions to children, they often discover that they have been reinforcing exactly the opposite of the behavior they want.

Cognitive theory has revolutionized developmental psychology by focusing attention on active mental processes (Beilin, 1992). Cognitive theorists' attempt to understand the thinking process and the search for intellectual accommodation when disequilibrium occurs has led to a new understanding of human behavior. Thanks to the ideas of cognitive theory, we now understand the types of thinking that are possible at various ages.

Thus, the grand theories have provided powerful insights into child behavior. They have taken developmental science quite far and have done so fairly quickly (see Changing Policy, pages 52–53). Now, though, it is time for new ideas to carry us further (Greene, 1997; Kessen, 1990).

EMERGENT THEORIES

The three grand theories are primarily theories of psychology originally set forth by one person (Freud, Skinner, Piaget), whereas the two emerging theories include observations, minitheories, and hypotheses from many sciences that currently study human development. Sociolcultural theory draws on research from education, sociology, history, and anthropology; epigenetic theory, on research from biology, genetics, ethology, and neuroscience. In part because of their scope, and in part because of their recency, neither theory has become a comprehensive, coherent whole. However, as you will now see, both provide significant frameworks for the study of human development.

Sociocultural Theory

This emergent theory arises from a recognition of the importance of the social context, as is apparent in Erikson's elaboration of Freud's theory, as is characteristic of the social learning extension of behaviorism, and as is also evident in the newer versions of cognitive theory. **Sociocultural theory** seeks to explain individual knowledge, development, and competencies in terms of the guidance, support, and structure provided by the society and to explain social change over time in terms of the cumulative effect of individual choices. Note the bidirectional influence of culture and person. People are affected by society, but people also change society.

The central thesis of sociocultural theory is thus that human development is the result of *dynamic interaction* between developing persons and their surrounding culture. According to this theory, culture is not simply an external variable that impinges on the developing person; it is integral to development (Cole, 1996). As such, its effect cannot be understood simply by comparing the developmental patterns of different cultures (as did the "cross-cultural" research of the past) or by simply recognizing that there is such an effect.

Sociocultural theorists recognize the importance of children learning from parents, teachers, and peers in their homes, schools, and neighborhoods. But they also look beyond that, to the ways in which instruction and learning are shaped by the beliefs and goals of the community. And they look even beyond that, to the ways in which such learning affects all later development—for the individual, the family, and the ethnic group.

! **Response for Educators (from page 48):**
That not much new learning is going on. According to Piaget, learning experiences need to include cognitive disequilibrium—challenging, surprising, or unexpected events that provoke questions, discussion, debate, investigation.

guided participation   A learning process in which an individual learns through social interaction with a "tutor" (a parent, a teacher, a more skilled peer) who offers assistance, structures opportunities, models strategies, and provides explicit instruction as needed.

Learning the Language In Bali, elegant ritualized body movement is a key element in many facets of religious life. Through guided participation, these young girls are acquiring their culture's language of ritualized dance—a language unknown in most cultures where the skills of rollerblading or video games are valued.

Guided Participation

A major pioneer of the sociocultural perspective was Lev Vygotsky (1896–1934), a psychologist from the former Soviet Union. As his writings and those of his student A. R. Luria have become widely available, they have attracted a large audience (Luria, 1976, 1979; Vygotsky, 1978, 1987). Many current researchers in developmental psychology take a sociocultural view that is deeply influenced by Vygotsky's ideas.

Vygotsky was particularly interested in cognitive competencies that developed among the culturally diverse people of the then-new Soviet Union, including such skills as the proper use of tools in an agricultural community and the use of abstract words among people who had never been to school. In the sociocultural view, these competencies develop from interactions between novices and more skilled members of the society, acting as tutors or mentors, in a process called an "apprenticeship in thinking" (Rogoff, 1990). The implicit goal of this apprenticeship is to provide the instruction and support that novices need for acquiring the knowledge and capabilities that are valued by the culture. The best way to accomplish this goal is through **guided participation,** in which the tutor engages the learner in joint activities, offering the learner not only instruction but also direct involvement in the learning process.

In every culture, children learn practical skills such as casting a fishing net, sewing a button on a shirt, or using a TV remote control; social skills such as shaking hands, showing deference to elders, or expressing one's wishes in an acceptable manner; and intellectual skills such as writing in one's native language, learning tribal history by consulting a village elder, or researching population statistics by visiting a specific Web site. Children develop these competencies during a "social apprenticeship": either formally, through explicit instruction, or informally, as they observe older friends or family members carry out the activities of everyday life.

According to sociocultural theory, social interaction between teacher and learner not only imparts specific skills; it also provides the context for mastering the culture's tools for further learning, whether those tools include an alphabet, Roman or Arabic numerals, an abacus, the telephone, or a computer. Vygotsky believed that, universally, language is the most important learning tool, because language provides a powerful means of learning through exchange of ideas and facts between one person and another. As people master their community's language, they can express thoughts and ideas to social partners and, in turn, absorb the ideas of others—and of the culture at large—into their thinking (Vygotsky, 1978, 1987).

Note that this apprenticeship depends on social interaction, not on a learner discovering knowledge on his or her own or on a teacher writing down what he or she knows. Instead, one person learns from another, through the words and activities that they engage in *together* (Karpov & Haywood, 1998). This is one crucial difference between sociocultural theory and the grand theories of the past: Together, child and adult actively shape the knowledge in their culture, by participating in the learning process rather than receiving or transmitting existing knowledge (Rogoff, 1997).

NATURE VERSUS NURTURE

The very practical implications of the grand theories are highlighted by the central controversy of human development—the debate over the relative influence of heredity and environment in shaping personal traits and characteristics. This debate is often called the *nature-nurture controversy*.

Nature refers to the traits, capacities, and limitations that each person inherits genetically from his or her parents at the moment of conception. Body type, sex, and genetic diseases are obvious examples. Nature also includes a host of intellectual and personality characteristics, such as facility with numbers, attraction to novelty, sociability, and tendency to depression, that are powerfully influenced by genes.

Nurture refers to all the environmental influences that come into play after conception, beginning with the mother's health during pregnancy and including all the individual's experiences in the outside world—in the family, the school, the community, and the culture at large.

The nature-nurture controversy has taken on many names, among them *heredity versus environment* and *maturation versus learning*. Under whatever name, however, the basic question remains: How much of any given characteristic, behavior, or pattern of development is the result of genetic influences, and how much is the result of the myriad experiences that occur after conception?

Note that the question asks "How much?"—implying that for all characteristics, behaviors, and patterns of development, both nature *and* nurture are influential. All developmentalists agree that it is neither nature nor nurture alone but, rather, the *interaction* between the two that is the crucial factor. They note, for example, that intelligence is determined both by heredity and by schooling. Despite their acknowledgment that the interaction between nature and nurture is what matters, however, developmentalists can get into heated arguments about the relative importance of each (Baumrind, 1993; Jackson, 1993; Scarr, 1992).

Nature and Nurture in Math Aptitude

The main reason the nature-nurture controversy is very much alive is that its practical implications are enormous. Consider one example: In elementary school, boys and girls show similar mathematics aptitude; but for teenagers the mathematical achievement of the average boy is higher than that of the average girl. Furthermore, high school students who are gifted in math are usually boys, by a 4-to-1 ratio according to one North American study (Benbow & Lubinski, 1996). A closer analysis of the male advantage reveals that, beginning at about age 10, boys are better at spatial skills—the kind required for geometry—and this accounts for much of the difference in math achievement (Johnson & Meade, 1987). In addition, boys are better prepared in math, in that they take more geometry and calculus classes than girls do, and they show an advantage in science as well (Beal, 1994; Beller & Gafni, 1996).

Is nature responsible for these differences? Perhaps some difference in the sex hormones causes early specialization of brain structures in such a way that, at puberty, males have an advantage (Gaulin, 1993; Jacklin et al., 1988). Psychoanalytic theory, especially Erikson's, notes that little boys build block towers and little girls create family groups, a sex difference that is inborn (Erikson, 1963). Cognitive theory also offers an explanation for how this might occur: Since humans seek challenges that are intriguing to them, boys might find calculus a challenge, whereas girls might not—in both cases because biological inclinations lead the children down increasingly divergent intellectual paths.

Or is nurture the key factor, as learning theory would suggest? Perhaps girls observe that math ability is not considered feminine, and perhaps their parents, teachers, or boyfriends, sharing this view, subtly (or not so subtly) discourage their interest in math while reinforcing their brothers' interest. Added to this subtle pressure is social learning: engineers are almost always men—a fact not lost on observant young teenagers searching for role models.

Finally, sex-related differences in math aptitude could result from both nature and nurture. Worldwide research about women scientists shows that the percentage of physics faculty members who are women ranges from about 1 percent in Japan to 47 percent in Hungary (see Figure 2.1). Such diversity suggests that, in this particular example at least, the cultural context is much more influential than biology. However, note also that no nation has more women physicists than men physicists (Barinaga, 1994).

Whatever the answer, the policy and human implications are profound. If boys are naturally better at math than girls, it may be neither wise nor desirable to push girls to study mathematics and related subjects such as physics and engineering. On the other hand, if such gender differences are the result of nurture, we are wasting a major portion of our mathematical potential, as well as limiting the career options for many women, by discouraging girls from developing their mathematical abilities.

Nature and Nurture in Homosexuality

Another of the many controversial issues that pivots on the nature-nurture debate is sexual orientation. Most psychiatrists and psychologists once assumed that adult homosexuality resulted from unusual patterns in the mother-father-child relationship, a belief strongly endorsed by psychoanalytic theory. Other psychologists felt that a person learned to be homosexual, through reinforcement and modeling. The cognitive perspective held that a person's concept of appropriate sexual interaction influenced his or her orientation—that the idea itself led to the action. Each of these explanations clearly emphasized nurture.

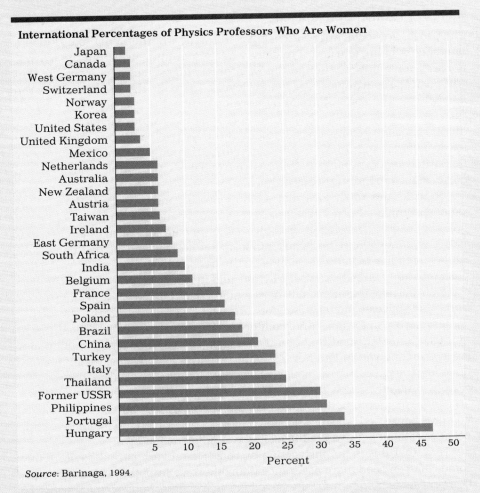

International Percentages of Physics Professors Who Are Women

Source: Barinaga, 1994.

Figure 2.1 Nature and Nurture in Physics. Nations differ dramatically in how many of their university instructors are women, particularly in the natural sciences and math. The data in this chart show the percentage of female physics professors in 31 nations. Notice that even within continents the rates vary by nation. Compare, for example, Spain and Portugal, Taiwan and China, or Austria and Hungary. Obviously, nurture—especially the political and economic patterns of each country—is more at work here than nature.

their simplest versions, are inadequate for explaining why some people are homosexual.

But the evidence for a genetic influence on homosexuality may not be conclusive, and culture may play a role (Bailey et al., 1993; Maddox, 1993). And once again, the policy and human implications are profound. If homosexuality is primarily the result of culture, those who are concerned about the future sexual orientation of the young should look to the influence of school curriculum, television programming, and laws about marriage, because these all reflect culture. On the other hand, if the primary influences on a person's sexual orientation are genetic, different issues should be debated—and perhaps the debate itself is unnecessary.

Finally, both positions may be too extreme for those who take "a developmental perspective." It may be that:

Those who dichotomize sexual orientation into pure biological or social causation fall into a dangerous quagmire. To deny any role for biology affirms an untenable scientific view of human development. Equally harsh and deterministic would be to deny the significance of the environment. [Savin-Williams & Diamond, 1997]

Theories about nature and nurture are implicit in many public policies, not just those involving the mathematics education of young girls and the laws about homosexuality. They are interwoven into public-policy controversies concerning the effects of alcohol exposure on fetal development, the placement of maltreated children, the impact of class size on school learning, and the causes and consequences of teenage pregnancy. On a more personal level, all prospective parents wonder whether their children will inherit their best or worst qualities, whether genetics can be overcome by upbringing, whether the influence of the dominant culture can be modified. Probably all young adults look critically at their older relatives, wondering if the family problems they observe are genetic or a matter of life choices or cultural values.

As we noted at the start of this chapter, theories do not provide all the answers, but they do provide a framework for study and/or research that may yield the answers. Obviously, the impact of culture and that of genes needs further study. The emergent theories are now setting the framework for such research.

New research suggests that homosexuality is at least partly genetic (Bailey, 1998). For example, researchers have found that a man is more likely to be gay if his mother's brother or his own brother—especially his identical twin—is homosexual (Hamer et al., 1993; Pool, 1993; Whitam et al., 1993). Further evidence that nature, more than nurture, affects sexual orientation comes from children raised by lesbian mothers. Most of these children are heterosexual, in similar proportions to children raised by heterosexual parents; this implies that whatever they learned at home did not change their inborn orientation (Golombok & Tasker, 1996).

In fact, virtually no contemporary social scientist believes that a warped mother-son relationship causes homosexuality (as psychoanalytic theory might hold); or that homosexuality is somehow rewarded by society (learning theory); or that homosexuality is logically chosen after intellectual reflection (cognitive theory). Thus all three grand theories, at least in

Zone of Proximal Development

The process of social apprenticeship is the same whether a manual skill or a language is being learned. Typically, when a mentor senses that the learner is ready for a new challenge the mentor arranges social interactions that will push the learner's skills to new levels. To do so, the mentor draws the learner into the **zone of proximal development,** which is the range of skills that the learner can exercise with assistance but cannot perform independently. Through sensitive assessment of the learner's abilities and capacity for growth, the mentor then offers guidance that engages the learner's participation and gradually facilitates the learner's transition from assisted performance to independent performance.

To make this rather abstract-seeming process more concrete, let's take a simple example—a father teaching his 5-year-old daughter to ride a bicycle. He probably begins by helping his daughter to get the feel of the bicycle as he slowly rolls her along; he firmly supports her weight and holds her upright while telling her to keep her hands on the bars and her feet on the pedals, to push the right and left pedals in rhythm, and to look straight ahead. If she says she feels that she is going to fall, he reassures her, "I'm here, I won't let you get hurt," and suggests that she lean forward a bit and relax her arms. As she becomes more comfortable and confident, he begins to roll her along more quickly, noting out loud that she is now able to keep her legs pumping in a steady rhythm. Within another lesson or two he is jogging beside her, holding on to just the handlebar, as he feels her control gradually go from dangerously wobbly to slightly shaky. Then comes the moment when he senses that, with a little more momentum, she could maintain her balance by herself. Accordingly, he urges her to pedal faster and slowly loosens his grip on the handlebar until, perhaps without her even realizing it, she is riding on her own.

Note that this is not instruction by rote: First, every parent realizes that some children need more assurance than others, so from the start the instruction process is modified for the particular learner. Second, even knowing the child, a parent needs to listen and sense exactly whether more support or more freedom is needed at each moment, so the process is constantly modified to fit as it is used. And third, such skills are almost impossible to transmit unless the teacher has mastered them: The father who does not know how to ride might intellectually understand the general principles of bicycle riding, but he is best advised to let his bike-riding wife do the instructing.

Such excursions into and through the zone of proximal development are commonplace, not only in childhood but throughout life. Ideally, the learning process follows the same general pattern in all instances: The mentor, sensitively attuned to the learner's ever-shifting abilities and motivation, continually urges the learner on to new levels of competence, while the learner asks questions and shows signs of progress that guide and inspire the mentor.

Cultural Variations

Although the basic principles of sociocultural theory are universal, its major emphasis on culture has helped developmentalists recognize how the skills, challenges, and opportunities involved in human development vary, depending on the values and structures of the society in question. In order to understand the developmental process in a specific culture, researchers study how values affect the individuals and shape the specific cultural context in a systematic way, with each component affecting the whole. If a particular competency is not meaningful to both mentor and apprentice, who both become convinced it is needed within their society, it will probably not be perpetuated. Certainly every adult knows things that he or she will not attempt to pass on, and every student is exposed to skills that he or she will

zone of proximal development   The skills, knowledge, and understanding that an individual cannot yet perform or comprehend on his or her own but could master with guidance; this is the arena where learning occurs.

Learning to Ride Although they are usually not aware of it, children learn most of their skills because adults guide them carefully. What would happen if this father let go?

resist learning. Further, teachers and students together refine the competencies that are part of the culture. The World Wide Web, now a part of global culture, is one recent example.

The importance of beliefs as a prerequisite for learning various skills was discovered by a team of researchers who were trying to assess the logical abilities of people in western Africa (Cole et al., 1971; Glick, 1968). At first the Africans seemed unable to arrange a set of items in abstract logical categories, rather than in practical clusters, even when they were explicitly told to do so. They responded that a wise person would always do as they did. However, their seeming ignorance disappeared when, "in total exasperation, the researchers finally said 'How would a fool do it?'" (Greenfield, 1997). Then they could, and did, achieve competence in the logical skills that American scientists hoped to measure.

In traditional societies, where decades come and go with little social change, most lessons learned in childhood are good for a lifetime. But in modern technological societies, especially those with strong multicultural influences, the tools, skills, customs, and values through which the culture functions are under continual pressure to change. In such societies, the older generations often find themselves having to learn from the innovations of a younger cohort. For everyone, development and change occur lifelong.

Sociocultural theorists have been criticized, however, for overlooking developmental processes that are not primarily social. Vygotsky's theory, in particular, has been viewed as neglecting the role of genes in guiding development, especially with regard to neurological maturation in mental processes (Wertsch, 1985; Wertsch & Tulviste, 1992). The final theory we will now discuss begins with the influence of genetics.

Epigenetic Systems Theory

Epigenetic systems theory emphasizes the interaction between genes and the environment, an interaction that is seen by proponents as dynamic and reciprocal. This is the newest of the developmental theories, but it builds on several established bodies of research and theory, particularly those originating from the natural sciences including ethology (see Children Up Close, pages 56–57). (Dent-Read & Zukow-Goldring, 1997; Goldsmith et al., 1997). To understand what is involved in this theory, let us first examine the root word "genetic," the prefix "epi," and the idea of "systems."

Before and After the Genes

The word "genetic" refers both to the genes that make each person (except monozygotic twins) unique and to the genes that humans have shared with all other humans for hundreds of thousands of years, as well as to the genes that humans share with other primates, about 98 percent of the total (Gibbons, 1998). In emphasizing this genetic foundation, the epigenetic systems theory stresses that we have powerful instincts and abilities that arise from our biological heritage. At conception, diverse genetic instructions combine into a complex set that influences every aspect of development, affecting not only obvious characteristics such as sex, coloring, and body shape but also less visible traits, psychological as well as physical—from blood type to bashfulness, from metabolic rate to moodiness, from voice tone to vocational aptitude. Even the timing and pace of certain developmental changes are genetically guided, a fact no less true for the octogenarian than for the embryo, or for the human than for the butterfly.

❓ Especially for Health Professionals: How might sociocultural theory guide a school nurse who discovers that a child is fed too many fried foods at home and has high cholesterol?

epigenetic systems theory   The developmental theory that emphasizes the genetic origins of behavior but also stresses that genes, over time, are directly and systematically affected by many environmental forces.

The Epigenetic Perspective Although these parents may not realize it, their words echo the essence of epigenetic thought, that each human is born with genetic possibilities that must be nurtured in order to grow.

"Isn't she marvelous? Our own little bundle of untapped potential."

ETHOLOGY OF INFANT CARE

As we have emphasized, the epigenetic systems approach focuses on both the "micro" interactions of genes at the individual level and the "macro" genetic systems that have developed within the species over time. In the latter respect, epigenetic theory builds on a well-established theory called ethology or ethological theory (Hinde, 1983). **Ethology** is the study of patterns of animal behavior, particularly as that behavior relates to evolutionary origins and species survival.

Typically, ethologists study such phenomena as the behaviors that trigger aggression, the particular rituals that precede mating, the means by which animals or birds communicate that food or danger is nearby, and the behaviors involved in the care and raising of young. After collecting detailed data on such behaviors, ethologists attempt to determine how those behaviors evolved to contribute to the perpetuation of the species. Ethologists hold that to understand the typical behaviors of any species, including *Homo sapiens*, we must understand what role those behaviors have played in the species' evolutionary heritage and survival (Hinde, 1989).

Infant Instincts

The ethological perspective has particular relevance for infancy, not just of rat pups but of human babies as well. Many of the instinctive behaviors of young infants and their caregivers tend to promote survival (Marvin, 1997).

Newborns are genetically programmed for social contact, as a means of survival. To be specific, throughout the long evolution of our species, babies have depended on close social contact with those who feed, clothe, clean, and otherwise care for them. Nurturance depends on social interaction. Consequently, infants come into the world "preequipped" with social predispositions and social skills that can help ensure their nurturance and development. For example, they can distinguish the sounds and rhythms of speech, recognize the facial expressions of fear and pleasure, distinguish one person from another by smell as well as by touch and sight, and do all of this much more readily than they can notice similar sensations from an inanimate source.

In addition, human infants, despite being so obviously immobile and helpless, are nonetheless genetically programmed to display reflexes, including the grasping, clinging, crying, and grunting that summon adults or keep them nearby. In the beginning, infants accept help from anyone—a good survival strategy in the centuries when women regularly died in childbirth. By the time they are able to crawl, however, infants become emotionally attached to their specific caregivers, as well as fearful of unfamiliar situations that might represent potential dangers.

By the time infants are able to crawl or toddle away, their attachment and fear have triggered a new set of dependent behaviors (such as regularly glancing in the caregiver's direction while moving away, to confirm his or her presence) and increased the babies' motivation to stay close to their caregiving adults (Lieberman, 1993). In short, over the course of human history, infants who stayed near nurturing and protecting adults were more likely to survive; hence, selective adaptation produced this broad repertoire of actions and emotions in the human genetic makeup to keep infants near their caregivers.

Adult Impulses

Caregiving adults are similarly equipped. Logically, no reasonable adult would ever put up with the sleepless nights, dirty diapers, and frequent cries of a baby, the rebellion of a teenager, and all the years in between simply to raise the child to the point where he or she leaves home but occasionally returns to request emotional and financial support. Fortunately, however, our genetic impulses are not logical. We are programmed to cherish and protect our children. As the mother of four, the power of this programming has surprised me many times. With my firstborn, I remember asking my pediatrician if she wasn't one of the most beautiful, perfect babies he had ever seen.

"Yes," he said, with a twinkle in his eyes, "and my patients are better looking than the patients of any other pediatrician in the city."

With my second newborn, the hospital offered to sell me a photo of her at 1 day old; I glanced at it and said no, because it didn't look at all like her—it was almost ugly. I was similarly enamored of my third and fourth. For the fourth, however, a new thought came to me: I am not only a woman who loves her children; I am a woman who loves her sleep.

Even if you are not a parent, you are irrational in the same way because your genes make you react emotionally. Imagine that you hear an infant crying, for example. No matter where you are, no matter what you are doing, you are likely to feel distracted, sympathetic, and troubled. Such a reaction occurs because, universally, on some deep, primordial level, adults recognize the infant cry as a signal that a vulnerable, defenseless human may be cold, hungry, or otherwise in danger, and we are compelled to respond. Surprisingly, even adults who have never cared for a baby become physiologically aroused, with focused attention and more rapid heart beat, on hearing the sound of a baby's cry (Thompson & Frodi, 1984). Caregivers generally respond with greater urgency the more distressed the baby sounds (Corter & Fleming, 1995).

The emotions aroused by an infant cry are among the most powerful a parent feels, and the frustration at not being able to console a baby leads to even stronger feelings:

> I don't just hate it when my baby cries—I sometimes hate my crying baby. Often she cries for no reason I can understand: howls when I am washing her as if I put soap in her eyes and goes on as if I was just ignoring her even though I'm doing everything I can think of. . . . Sometimes I think I must be totally a hopeless, unfit mother; sometimes I think she's the crossest, worst-natured child in the world. It's probably both. [Quoted in Leach, 1997]

In fact, both parents and infants are reacting to deep urges that signal and respond, in a system that sometimes seems overwhelming in the early months but is much better than the opposite. If newborns never signal their needs or parents are indifferent to their signals, the species would not survive.

In addition to responding to infants' cries, adults become emotionally and physiologically aroused by the sight of a baby's smile or by the sound of an infant's laughter and by the round-faced, chinless, hairless head or even the tiny feet of a newborn. (This truth leads advertisers to use images of babies to sell everything from toilet paper to political candidates.) Adults seem particularly mesmerized by their own children's simplest actions, doting on their every move, watching them sleep, and listening to them breathe. This is, beyond doubt, an example from epigenetic theory, for parental attention serves a survival function: It increases the likelihood that adults will notice when something is amiss with a child. Thus adults and infants are part of an epigenetic *system*, with interactive genetic actions and reactions that ensure survival of the next generation. Fortunately, these irrational responses include joy. As the expert who reported on the hateful parent wrote: "The same baby who right now ruins all your evenings by crying may one day make all your mornings feel like Christmas" (Leach, 1997).

Open Wide Caregivers and babies elicit responses in each other that ensure survival of the next generation. The caregiver's role in this vital interaction is obvious, but ethology has shown that infants starve if they themselves do not chirp, meow, whine, bleat, squeak, cry, or do whatever it is that they do to signal hunger, and then open their mouths wide when dinner comes. (Have you ever tried to feed a baby who refuses to "open"?)

❓ *Observational Quiz (see answer page 58): Infant feeding is universal among all species. However, at least three aspects of the bottom photo signify that the creatures there are human. What are these aspects?*

ethology The study of behavior as it is related to the evolution and survival of a species.

❶ Response for Health Professionals (from page 55): Family eating habits are embedded in culture, but all cultures seek to protect their children. Thus, the nurse would not suggest that the family abandon their culinary traditions. Instead, he or she would explain the health hazards of animal fat and make culturally respectful suggestions, such as serving fried foods only on special occasions or in smaller portions or frying them in another type of fat. Peers mentor learning as well, so the nurse might enlist the child's friends in producing nutritional change.

selective adaptation   An aspect of evolution in which, over generations, genes for the traits that are most useful will become more frequent within individuals, making the survival of the species more likely.

❶ Answer to Observational Quiz (from page 57): *(1) The caregiver's age. Edwin is actually being fed by his grandmother—rare in birds, but common in humans. (2) Grandma's mouth and eyes. Most infant animals depend on smell, not vision, but humans use vision as their main source of communication. Therefore, human caregivers rely on elaborate facial expressions to communicate with babies. (3) Tool use. Unlike other animals, humans construct permanent tools for eating; here, the spoon and highchair are dedicated exclusively to this infant.*

The fact that genes affect every aspect of human behavior—substantially—was at first unknown and then disputed for most of the twentieth century. (That explains why the earlier grand theories did not give heredity a substantial role in explaining human development.) Now genetic research has shown that instructions from the genes affect everything, and molecular genetics is beginning to explain exactly which genes interact with which factors to produce which traits.

Unfortunately, instead of being ignored, the power of genes is now sometimes exaggerated as determining human behavior, rather than affecting it. That is an error that epigenetic systems theory seeks to avoid.

The prefix "epi" means (among other things) "before," "after," "on," and "near"; thus *epigenetic* refers to all the factors that affect the expression of the genetic instructions. Some of these factors are chemical, such as the presence, absence, or various possible concentrations of nutrients, hormones, and toxins. Some are stress factors, such as injury, temperature, or crowding. All these epigenetic factors are part of, or arise from, the environment in which the organism develops, from the first cell of the complete organism. They influence how cells form the body and the active brain, particularly in the early months of life but also throughout life (Gilbert & Borish, 1997).

Adaptation of the Genes

Some epigenetic factors are the consequence of the evolutionary adaptation of the species, which, over generations, increases the frequency of some genes in a population and makes others increasingly rare, a process called **selective adaptation.** For example, some species of animals develop abnormal facial features, or change the color of their fur or even their sex (all genetic traits), depending on environmental conditions. Some birds develop specific plumage or rituals or songs with a decided genetic origin, because over the years those traits led to improved mating and reproduction. Experimental research has shown, for example, that deafening a baby bird temporarily so that it cannot learn the melody of local birdsong results in an impaired ability to mate later on. Indeed, an estimated 90 percent of all species that have existed at one time or another have become extinct because their genes did not adapt to environmental change and their reproduction fell below the replacement rate until eventually the species died out (Buss et al., 1998).

Humans, of course, have adapted well thus far, so their numbers rise. Specific epigenetic factors within humans are harder to pin down by experiments, partly because both human genes and the human context are more diverse than those of nonhuman animals and partly because ethical research on human epigenetic factors is difficult to perform. However, for humans as well as other animals, epigenetic theory stresses that "organisms adapt and environments surround" (Dent-Read & Zukow-Goldring, 1997).

Consequently, humans follow one or another pathway from their genetic base, depending on conditions. This is most obvious in psychopathology (Goldsmith et al., 1997; Rutter et al., 1997). For instance, a person may genetically be at risk for schizophrenia, but the schizoid-tending genes will not be expressed unless, sometime during prenatal development or early childhood, an environmental insult occurs to permit expression of these genes. Once a person becomes schizophrenic, the disease does not disappear (although it can be controlled and treated) because the genes have worked their effects; but if that same person, with the same genes, manages to reach adulthood without the insult, his or her schizophrenic genes will probably never result in mental illness (Gottesman, 1991).

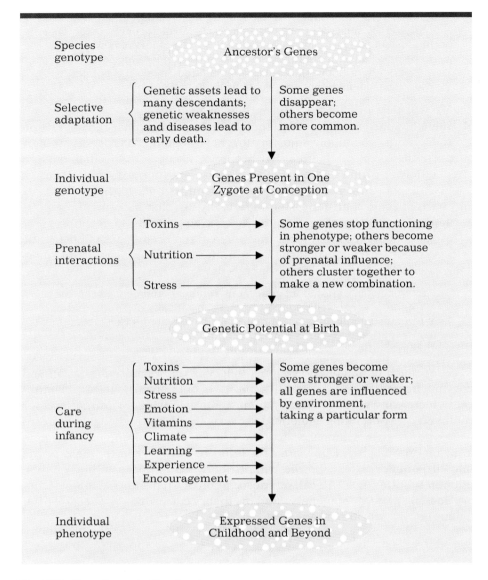

Figure 2.2 Always Human, but Everchanging.
The genes inherited from our ancestors still echo throughout the centuries and affect every member of the human species today. However, the particulars are always influenced by ongoing experiences that can increase, decrease, or stop the expression of genes, a process epigenetic theory emphasizes.

A more common example is height. Each person is genetically programmed to grow to a certain height, and most of us in developed nations have sufficient nourishment as children to grow to that height. As adults, we could undereat to the point of extreme thinness, but we will never shrink, because the genetic expression of our height genes has already occurred.

Research on genes finds that no genetic instruction—including instructions for basic traits such as physical structure and intellectual potential—is unaffected by environment. Each person's genetic inheritance is so intertwined with his or her individual experiences that it is virtually impossible to isolate the specific effects of genes without considering the context; everything that seems to be genetic is actually epigenetic. The point in all these examples is that environmental factors make genetic influences stronger, weaker, or nonexistent over time, within individuals, within populations, and within the human race (see Figure 2.2) (Buss et al., 1998).

Systems That Support Development

Finally, this theory also emphasizes *systems*. The critical aspect of a system, as scientists use the term, is that change in one part of the system causes corresponding adjustments and changes in every other part. This is true for the biological systems that foster the development of an individual (e.g., the cardiovascular system), the systems that support an entire species (in an ecosystem), and the systems that govern all nature (Masterpasqua, 1997).

One example of the environment's causing a systemic change is the effect of human handling of rat pups. It has long been realized that such handling makes the rats smarter as adults, and some scientists thought that the rats learned from their early human involvement. More recent research shows specifically how handling produces systemic change: Handling increases the mother's licking and grooming of her pup, which leads to decreases in the release of stress hormones, which leads to increased tolerance of potentially stressful conditions, which, in adulthood, leads to less brain degeneration than in unhandled rats (Sapolsky, 1997).

This example raises important questions for humans, of course, which the researcher wryly addressed. He wrote:

> It is a rare parent of a newborn who does not feel panic built around the consequences that her or his actions now have. Developmental studies have indicated that the quality, quantity, and timing of infant stimulation

can have long-lasting effects—and soon the anxious parent is convinced that one lullaby sung off-key ensures that a child will not only one day be a sociopath, but will also never use dental floss. If mothers of newborn rats harbor similar anxieties, a report by Liu and colleagues affirms their worries: The authors show that subtle stimulation in a rat's infancy has marked consequences that are probably life-long (Sapolosky, 1997).

We will soon discuss the implications of such research for humans. We already know, however, that each individual is (among other things) an epigenetic system, continually adjusting to a never-ending flux of proteins, hormones, and electrical charges that occur in response to biochemical and physical forces within and outside the body. Genes form the foundation of that system, but they never act alone (Goldsmith et al., 1997). Each society and each species is also a system, gradually shaping its common genetic heritage in such a way as to adapt to the changing world.

We should make it very clear that some of the predictions of epigenetic systems theory are not established certainties but remain parts of an emergent theory. As one psychologist reminds us:

> The attempt at integration (of genes, environment, and behavior) faces a daunting task—genes only make proteins, specifically enzymes, and the leap from the simple alphabet of molecular biology to the rich tapestry of human experience requires a combination of up-to-date scientific information in addition to some fast footwork. (Anderson, 1998)

How much of epigenetic systems theory is up-to-date information and how much is fancy footwork is still a matter of opinion, to be tested scientifically. Increasingly, epigenetic systems theory provides a framework for combining fast-breaking genetic discoveries and methodologies with intriguing speculations about exactly how genes and environments combine to propel development. A team of leading researchers in the field warns that "it is difficult to strike the balance between enthusiasm and caution (Plomin & Rutter, 1998). Recall our description of what a developmental theory does, on page 37: epigenetic systems theory can frame the questions, but it does not yet provide the answers.

THE THEORIES COMPARED

Each of the theories presented in this chapter has contributed a great deal to the study of human development (see Table 2.3):

- *Psychoanalytic theory* has made us aware of the importance of early childhood experiences and of the impact of the "hidden dramas" that influence daily life.
- *Learning theory* has shown us the effect that the immediate environment can have on behavior.
- *Cognitive theory* has brought us to a greater understanding of how intellectual processes and thinking affect actions.
- *Sociocultural theory* has reminded us that development is embedded in a rich and multifaceted cultural context.
- *Epigenetic systems theory* emphasizes the biological forces that affect each person and all humankind.

In order, these five theories present us with the unconscious processes; the environment; the intellect, the culture, and the genes. No comprehensive view of development can ignore any one of these factors.

table **2.3**	**Major Theories and Major Controversies**			
	Basic Focus	Fundamental Depiction of the Individual	Emphasis on early experiences?	Relative Emphasis on Nature and Nurture
Psychoanalytic	Psychosexual (Freud) or psychosocial (Erikson) stages	Battling unconscious impulses and overcoming major crises	Yes (especially in Freudian theory)	More nature (biological, sexual impulses are very important, as are parent-child bonds and memories)
Learning	Conditioning through stimulus and response	Responding to stimuli, reinforcement, and models in the environment	No (conditioning and reconditioning are lifelong)	More nurture (direct environment influences produce various behaviors)
Cognitive	Thinking, remembering, analyzing	Actively seeking to understand experiences, forming concepts and cognitive strategies	No (new concepts and control processes are developed lifelong)	More nature (person's own mental activity and motivation are key)
Sociocultural	Social context, expressed through people, language, customs	Learning the tools, skills, and values of society through apprenticeships	Yes (family and school acculturation are critical)	More nurture (specific interaction between mentor and learner, within cultural context, is pivotal)
Epigenetic	Genes and their expression, in individuals and species	Living out the impulses, interests, and patterns inherited from ancestors and developed from childhood	Yes (early biochemical forces alter the manifestation of genes)	Nature begins the process; nurture affects it directly, through hormones, enzymes, toxins, and selective adaptation

Each theory has been criticized. Psychoanalytic theory has been faulted for being too subjective; learning theory, for being too mechanistic; cognitive theory, for undervaluing genetic differences; sociocultural theory, for neglecting individuals; and epigenetic theory, for neglecting society.

Many developmentalists hope that "a new integration may be emerging in the form of a systems approach that will bring together biological, social, cognitive, and emotional theories into a more coherent framework" (Parke et al., 1994). Both sociocultural theory and epigenetic systems theory are moving in that direction, and both attempt to incorporate significant forces—cultural on the one hand and biochemical on the other—that traditional developmental science undervalued. However, both may stretch too far, losing the actual developing child amid diverse cultures or multifactorial genetic interactions. Further, sociocultural theory may overestimate the potential for human change throughout life in response to cultural and historical changes, while epigenetic systems theory may overestimate the impact of evolutionary adaptation or of early experiences, from conception through infancy.

Until a new grand theory is tested and established, most developmentalists still take an **eclectic perspective.** That is, rather than adopt any one of these theories exclusively, they make selective use of many or all of them. When 45 leaders in the field were asked to identify their approach to developmental studies, "clear theoretical labels were hard to come by," with many describing themselves through some combination of terms, such as "cognitive social learning," "social interactive behaviorist," and even "social evolutionary cognitive behaviorism" (Horowitz, 1994).

eclectic perspective Perspective choosing what seem to be the best, or most useful, elements from the various theories, instead of adhering to only a single perspective.

In later chapters, as you encounter elaborations and echoes of the five major theories and various minitheories, you will no doubt form your own opinion of the validity and usefulness of each. Probably you will also take an eclectic view—one that chooses the best from each theory to guide your exploration of development. You may even begin to devise a coherent, comprehensive, systematic approach of your own.

SUMMARY

WHAT THEORIES DO

1. A theory provides a framework of general principles that can be used to guide research and explain observations. Each developmental theory interprets human development from a somewhat different perspective, but all developmental theories attempt to provide a context for understanding how individual experiences and behavior change over time. Theories are practical in that they provide a framework for interpretation and research, as well as a coherent set of assumptions that aids inquiry.

GRAND THEORIES

2. Psychoanalytic theory emphasizes that human actions and thoughts originate from powerful impulses and conflicts that often are not part of our conscious awareness. Freud, the founder of psychoanalytic theory, explained how sexual urges arise during the oral, anal, phallic, and genital stages of development. Parents' reactions to conflicts associated with these urges have a lasting impact on the child's personality.

3. Erikson's version of psychoanalytic theory emphasizes psychosocial contexts, with individuals shaped by the interaction of personal characteristics and social forces. Erikson describes eight successive stages of psychosocial development, from infancy through old age, each of which involves a developmental crisis that must be resolved.

4. Behaviorists, or learning theorists, believe that the focus of psychologists' study should be behavior, which can be observed and measured. This theory seeks to discover the laws that govern the relationship between events and the reactions they produce, that is, between stimulus and response.

5. Learning theory emphasizes various forms of conditioning—a learning process by which particular stimuli become linked with particular responses. In classical conditioning, a neutral stimulus becomes associated with a meaningful stimulus, and eventually the neutral stimulus alone produces the response normally associated with the meaningful stimulus. In operant conditioning, certain responses, called reinforcers, are used to make it more likely that certain behaviors will recur.

6. Social learning theory recognizes that much of human behavior is learned by observing the behavior of others. The basic process is modeling, in which we first observe a behavior and then repeat it. Generally, the person being observed is admirable in some way, or the behavior is one that the observer is motivated to repeat.

7. Cognitive theorists believe that a person's thought processes have an important effect on his or her understanding of the world, and thus on the person's development. Piaget proposed that an individual's thinking develops through four age-related periods, with sensorimotor intelligence in infancy, preoperational intelligence during the preschool years, concrete operational intelligence during the school years, and formal operational intelligence beginning in adolescence and continuing lifelong.

8. Piaget believed that cognitive development is an active and universal process. Curiosity is guided by the search for cognitive equilibrium, which is a person's ability to explain a new situation with existing understanding. When disequilibrium occurs, the person develops cognitively by modifying his or her understanding to cover the new situation.

9. The nature-nurture controversy centers on how much influence heredity has on development, as compared to how much influence environment has. Every researcher agrees, however, that both factors influence human development.

EMERGENT THEORIES

10. Sociocultural theory explains human development in terms of the guidance, support, and structure provided by one's culture. For Vygotsky, learning occurs through the social interactions learners share with more knowledgeable members of the society. They guide learners through the zone of proximal development.

Learning, in theory, occurs as a result of collaboration between society, represented by a mentor, and learner. And both learner and society develop as a result of that collaboration.

11. Epigenetic systems theory begins by noting that genes are powerful and omnipresent, potentially affecting every aspect of development. This theory also stresses an ongoing interaction between the genes and environmental forces, which can range from prenatal toxins to lifelong stresses. This interaction can halt, modify, or strengthen the effects of the genes, both within the person and, over time, within the species.

12. Epigenetic systems theory also focuses on the systems, within the individual as well as the species, that support development. In one such system, infants are born with various drives and reflexes that help ensure their survival, while adults are normally also equipped with innate predispositions to nurture babies, no matter what sacrifices might be required.

THE THEORIES COMPARED

13. Psychoanalytic, learning, cognitive, sociocultural, and epigenetic systems theories have each contributed to the understanding of human development, yet no one theory is broad enough to describe the full complexity and diversity of human experience. Most developmentalists, well aware of the criticisms of these perspectives, selectively incorporate ideas and generate hypotheses from all of them. In addition, many find various minitheories, related to specific age groups or topics, useful for formulating research questions.

KEY TERMS

developmental theory (37)
grand theories (38)
minitheories (38)
emergent theories (38)
psychoanalytic theory (38)
learning theory (42)
stimulus (42)
response (42)
conditioning (42)
reinforcement (43)
social learning (44)
modeling (44)

cognitive theory (45)
cognitive equilibrium (47)
sociocultural theory (50)
guided participation (51)
zone of proximal
  development (54)
epigenetic systems theory
  (55)
ethology (56)
selective adaptation (58)
eclectic perspective (61)

KEY QUESTIONS

1. What functions does a good theory perform?

2. What is the major assumption of psychoanalytic theory?

3. What are the key differences between Freud's and Erikson's ideas concerning development?

4. What is the major focus of learning theory?

5. How are stimulus and response related in classical conditioning? In operant conditioning?

6. According to Piaget, how do periods of disequilibrium lead to mental growth?

7. According to sociocultural theory, how does development occur?

8. Give an example of guided participation that is not in the text.

9. According to epigenetic theorists, how can genetic instructions change?

10. What is the ethological view of behavior? How does it relate to epigenetic systems theory?

11. What are the main differences among the grand theories and between the two emergent theories we have discussed?

12. *In Your Experience* Does the behavior of children at about age 4 or 5 years appear to be more the result of nature or nurture? Why?

CRITICAL THINKING EXERCISE

Take your study of Chapter 2 a step further by working this perspective-taking exercise.

Today, more teenagers are becoming sexually active, and at younger ages, than ever before. This is true throughout the world, but especially in the United States, where the rate is 16 times that of Japan, which has the lowest rate among the developed countries (United Nations Population Division, 1994). Although the rate of teen pregnancy is much lower than it was 30 years ago, developmentalists consider it to be a major problem because most teen births now occur to unmarried women. At the very least, newborns tend to make life, and development, difficult for those teens.

1. To test your understanding of the five theories outlined in this chapter, try your hand at using them to explain why the teenage birth rate is as high as it is. Answer in this order: **(a)** psychoanalytic theory; **(b)** learning theory; **(c)** cognitive theory; **(d)** sociocultural theory; and **(e)** epigenetic systems theory.

2. Which theoretical perspective most closely represents your own belief? Why?

Check your answers by comparing them to the sample answers in Appendix B.

PART I

The Beginnings

When considering the human life span, most people ignore or take for granted the time from conception through birth. Indeed, among all the cultures of the world, China seems to have been the only one to have ever included the prenatal period when reckoning age. Yet these 266 or so days could not be more crucial. On the very first day, for instance, our entire genetic heritage is set, affecting not only what we see when we look in the mirror but also many of the abilities, talents, and disabilities that characterize each of us. Survival is much more doubtful and growth much more rapid during the prenatal period than at any other time in our lives. At the end of this period, the day of birth usually provides the occasion for more anticipation, worry, excitement, and joy on the part of parents than any other day of childhood. Indeed, the impact of the physiological and emotional events of that day can be felt for weeks, months, even years.

These early days, usually uncounted and underemphasized, are the focus of the next two chapters.

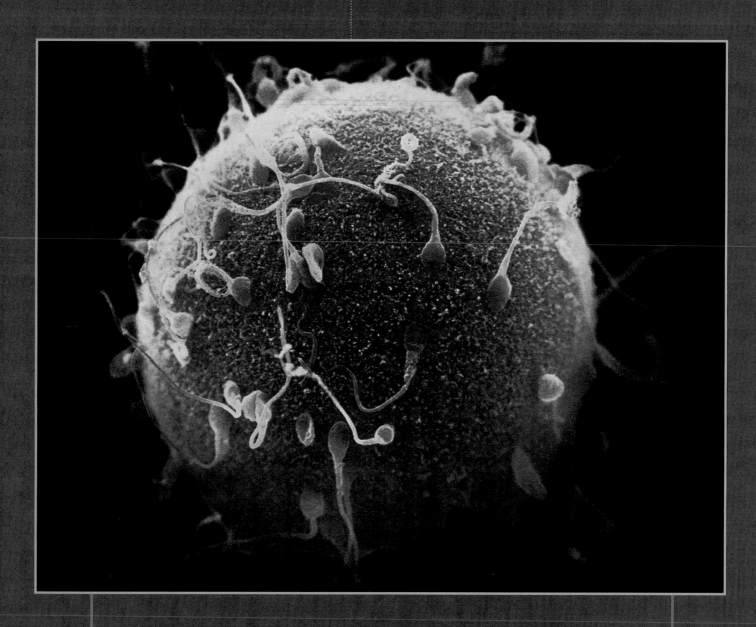

Heredity and Environment

From the very beginning, individual development arises from the interaction of two prime forces: genetic instructions inherited at conception, and environmental factors that allow those instructions to be expressed, shaped, deflected, or silenced. The interaction between heredity and environment in each person is intimate, dynamic, and lifelong. Also lifelong are influences that never directly touch the developing organism but nonetheless have a decided impact: Decisions made by the parents, guidelines set by the community, and directions provided by the culture all restrict or expand each developing person's life. In this chapter we will look at the interaction of these factors—a heredity and environment within the social context. Understanding them provides insight into how we became who we are and what else we can become.

THE BEGINNING OF DEVELOPMENT

Human development begins very simply, when a male reproductive cell, or **sperm** (plural: sperm), penetrates the membrane of a female reproductive cell, or **ovum** (plural: ova). Each human **gamete,** which is the name for any reproductive cell whether it comes from a male or a female, contains more than a billion chemically coded genetic instructions. These instructions represent half of a rough blueprint for human development. At conception, when the sperm and ovum combine, the two blueprint halves form a complete set of instructions for creating a person.

From One Cell to Trillions

For the first hour or so after the sperm enters the ovum, the two cells maintain their separate identities, side by side, enclosed within the ovum's membrane. Suddenly they fuse, and a living cell called a **zygote** is formed: two reproductive cells have literally become one.

Within hours after its formation, the zygote begins the first stages of growth through a process of *duplication* and *division*. First, the combined genetic material from both gametes duplicates itself, forming two complete sets of genetic instructions. Then these two sets move toward opposite sides of the zygote; the zygote then divides neatly down the middle, and thus the one-celled zygote has become two cells, each containing a complete set of the original genetic instructions. These two cells duplicate and divide to become four; these four, in turn, duplicate and divide to

The Moment of Conception The ovum shown here is about to become a zygote. It has been penetrated by a single sperm, whose nucleus now lies next to the nucleus of the ovum. Shortly, the two nuclei will fuse, bringing together about a hundred thousand genes that will guide future development.

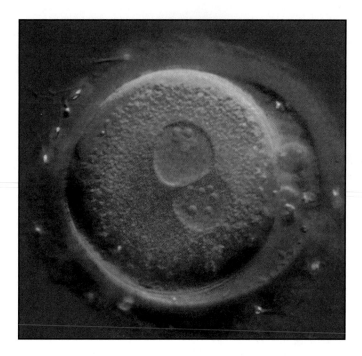

sperm A male gamete, or reproductive cell (plural: sperm).

ovum A female gamete, or reproductive cell (plural: ova).

gamete A reproductive cell; that is, a cell that can reproduce a new individual if it combines with a gamete from the other sex.

zygote The single cell formed from the fusing of a sperm and an ovum.

Figure 3.1 What One Human Cell Contains

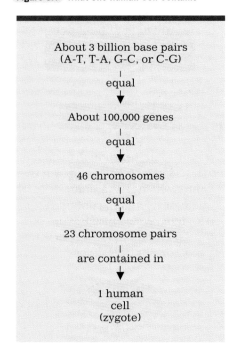

About 3 billion base pairs
(A-T, T-A, G-C, or C-G)
|
equal
↓

About 100,000 genes
|
equal
↓

46 chromosomes
|
equal
↓

23 chromosome pairs
|
are contained in
↓

1 human
cell
(zygote)

gene The basic unit for the transmission of heredity instructions.

chromosome A carrier of genes; one of forty-six segments of DNA that together contains all human genes.

genetic code The sequence of chemical compounds (called bases) that is held within DNA molecules and directs development, behavior, and form.

become eight; and so on. At about the eight-cell stage, a third process, *differentiation,* is added to duplication and division. Cells begin to specialize, taking different forms and reproducing at various rates, according to the functions they have been genetically programmed to perform in the developing person.

When you (or I, or any other person) were newborn, your body had about 10 trillion cells. By adulthood, the number of cells in your body had increased to between 300 and 500 trillion. But no matter how many cells you may have, and no matter how much division and duplication, differentiation, and specialization has occurred, each body cell carries a copy of the complete genetic instructions inherited by the one-celled zygote that you were at the moment of conception.

The Genetic Code

The basic unit of genetic instruction is the **gene.** A gene is a discrete segment of a **chromosome,** which in turn is a molecule of *DNA (deoxyribonucleic acid).* Except for sperm and ova, every normal human cell has 23 pairs of chromosomes (46 chromosomes in all), which collectively carry about 100,000 distinct genes (see Figure 3.1).

The instructions on each gene are "written" in a chemical code made up of pairs of only four chemical *bases*—adenine, guanine, cytosine, and thymine, abbreviated A, G, C, and T. These chemical bases normally combine in only four pairings, A-T, T-A, G-C, and C-G, which might seem to provide a very limited genetic vocabulary. In fact, there are approximately 3 billion base pairs in the DNA of every human, and thousands of base pairs in every gene, which means there are many, many possible sequences.

The precise nature of a gene's instructions is determined by this **genetic code,** that is, the sequence in which base pairs appear along each segment of the DNA molecule. Scientists now engaged in deciphering the complete genetic code estimate that, when fully transcribed, it will cover at least as many pages as 13 full sets of the *Encyclopædia Britannica* (Lee, 1993).

What this multitude of genetic instructions does is provide the body's cells with directions for the synthesis of hundreds of different kinds of proteins, including enzymes, that serve as the body's building blocks and regulators. Following these instructions, certain cells become neurons (brain cells); others become the lens of the eye; others become the valves of the heart; and so on throughout the body. In short, "genes determine each organism's size, shape and structure—all the features that distinguish, say, humans from honeybees" (Pennisi & Roush, 1997).

The influence of genes doesn't stop there. Through some sort of on-off switching mechanism that is not yet understood, genes control life itself, instructing cells to grow, to repair damage, to take in nourishment, to multiply, to atrophy, to die (Finch & Tanzi, 1997). Even certain kinds of cognitive development involve genes that switch on at particular ages, propelling maturation in specific areas of the brain (Gottesman & Goldsmith, 1993; Plomin et al., 1997). And all this activity occurs in collaboration with other genes and with the environment. The gene that grows the legs of a butterfly, for example, is exactly the same gene that shapes the four legs of a cat, the many legs of a centipede, and the two legs of a person. The differences between your legs and those of other creatures are governed by additional genes that advise the leg gene as to the particular shape and number of legs to make (Pennisi & Roush, 1997).

Chromosomes

As we have noted, each normal human has 46 chromosomes, duplicated in every body cell except gametes. The chromosomes are arranged in 23 distinct pairs, one member of each pair being inherited from the mother and the other from the father.

This very specific genetic and chromosomal pairing continues lifelong, in every cell—with one important exception. When the human body makes sperm or ova, cell division occurs in such a way that each gamete receives only one member of each chromosome pair. This is why sperm and ova each have only 23 chromosomes; and that ensures that when they combine, the new organism will have a total of 46 chromosomes. In other words, genetically we are whatever we are: Every cell of your body, from the soles of your feet to the lining of your gut to the dancing neurons of your brain, contains the distinct code that makes you you, and every cell of my body contains the unique code that makes me me. The one exception occurs if you and I reproduce. Our children are neither yours nor mine but ours—half me, half you.

Sex Determination

Of the 23 pairs of human chromosomes, 22 are closely matched pairs, with the two chromosomes of each pair containing similar genes in almost identical positions and sequence. The **twenty-third pair,** which is the pair that determines the individual's sex (among other things), is a different case. In the female, the twenty-third pair of chromosomes is composed of two large X-shaped chromosomes. Accordingly, it is designated XX. In the male, the twenty-third pair is composed of one large X-shaped chromosome and one much smaller Y-shaped chromosome. It is designated XY.

Obviously, since a female's twenty-third chromosome pair is XX, every ovum her body creates will contain either one X or the other—but always an X. And since a male's twenty-third pair is XY, half his sperm will contain an X chromosome, and half will contain a Y. That Y chromosome (and not the X) contains a gene that directs a developing fetus to make male organs, so

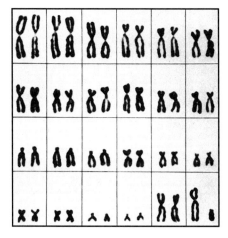

Mapping the Karyotype A *karyotype* portrays a person's chromosomes. To create a karyotype, a cell is grown in a laboratory, magnified, and then usually photographed. The photo is cut into pieces and rearranged, matching the pairs of chromosomes, from pair 1, the largest pair *(top left)* to pair 23, here the *XY* of a normal male *(bottom right)*.
❓ *Observational Quiz (see answer page 70): Is this the karyotype of a normal human?*

twenty-third pair The chromosome pair that, in humans, determines the zygote's (and hence the person's) sex, among other things.

Figure 3.2 Determining Zygote Sex. As you can see, any given couple can produce four possible combinations of sex chromosomes; two lead to female children, and two to male. In terms of the future person's sex, it does not matter at all which of the mother's *X*s the zygote inherited. All that matters is whether the father's *Y* sperm or *X* sperm fertilized the ovum. However, for *X*-linked conditions it matters a great deal, since typically one, but not both, of the mother's *X*s carries the trait.

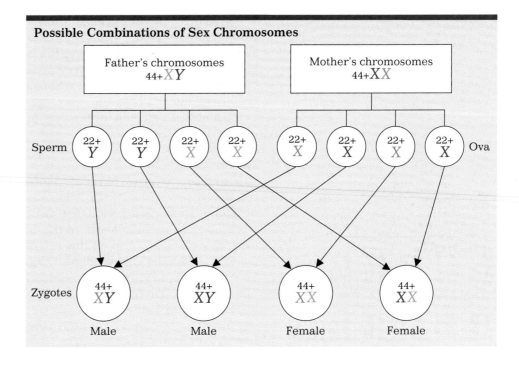

Possible Combinations of Sex Chromosomes

eventually a baby boy is born. Thus the critical factor in the determination of a zygote's sex is which sperm reaches the ovum first—a *Y* sperm, creating a male (*XY*), or an *X* sperm, creating a female (*XX*) (see Figure 3.2).

Continuity and Diversity

The vast majority of each person's genes are identical to those of every other person, related or not (Plomin et al., 1997). As a result of the instructions carried by these genes, each new member of the human race shares certain characteristics with every other person, alive or dead or not yet born:

- Common physical structures (such as the pelvic alignment that allows us to walk upright)
- Common behavioral tendencies (such as the urge to communicate through language)
- Common reproductive potential (allowing any male and female to produce a new member of the species)

These species-specific characteristics, and thousands of others, have been fashioned through our long evolutionary history, promoting our survival by enabling humans to live successfully on Earth.

The remainder of each person's genes differ in various ways from those of other individuals. The diversity that these genes provide, over generations, is essential for human adaptation to new environments and needs. Thus the fact that each human differs from the others genetically means that our species survives as conditions and circumstances change. Our diversity benefits the entire community through specialization and cooperation as well. Because each of us inherits specific talents and abilities, each of us is better at some tasks or activities than at others. By specializing on those particular tasks, performing them for others as well as ourselves, we can together achieve more than we could if each of us had to be his or her own priest, artist, carpenter, farmer, cook, doctor, teacher, and so on. We gain intellectually as well, by exchanging and combining ideas and perspectives. Both our commonalities and our diversities allow our survival.

❶ Answer to Observational Quiz (from page 69):
No, there are 24 pairs here. This photo shows the two different possibilities for the twenty-third pair. (The normal female XX is just to the left of the normal male XY.)

Any Monozygotic Twins Here? Sometimes twins are obviously dizygotic, as when they are of different sexes or, like the girls on the bottom, differ notably in coloring, size, and perhaps visual acuity. However, sometimes dizygotic twins can look a lot alike, just as two siblings born a year or two apart can share many physical characteristics.

❓ *Observational Quiz (see answer page 74): What do the similarities and differences of the boys in the top photo suggest of their zygosity?*

monozygotic twins Twins who have identical genes because they were formed from one zygote that split into two identical organisms very early in development.

dizygotic twins Twins formed when two separate ova were fertilized by two separate sperm at roughly the same time. Such twins share about half their genes, like any other siblings.

The Mechanisms of Diversity

Given that each sperm or ovum from a particular parent contains only 23 chromosomes, how can every conception be genetically unique? The answer is that when the chromosome pairs divide during the formation of gametes, chance alone determines which one of each pair will wind up in one gamete and which in the other. A vast number of chromosome combinations are possible. According to the laws of probability, there are, in fact, 2^{23}—that is, about 8 million—possible combinations. In other words, approximately 8 million chromosomally different ova or sperm can be produced by a single individual.

In addition, just before a chromosome pair in a man's or woman's body divides to form sperm or ova, corresponding segments of the pair are sometimes broken off and exchanged, altering the genetic composition of both pair members. Through the new combinations it produces, this *crossing-over* of genes adds greatly to genetic diversity. And finally, when a sperm and ovum unite, the interactions of their genes create DNA sequences not present in either parent.

All things considered, then, a given mother and father can form over 64 trillion genetically distinct offspring, all full brothers and sisters but each quite different from the others. Outsiders might see strong family resemblances in siblings (once a neighbor said my four children were "like four peas in a pod"). But every parent knows that each child is unlike the others. It is no exaggeration to say that every zygote is unique, with the potential of becoming a genetically unique individual.

Twins

Although every zygote is genetically unique, not every newborn is. In some pregnancies, the growing cluster of cells splits apart in the early stages of duplication and division, creating two identical, independent clusters (Gall, 1996). These cell clusters become **monozygotic twins** (identical twins), so named because they originated from one *(mono)* zygote. Since they originated from the same zygote, they share identical genetic instructions for physical appearance, psychological traits, vulnerability to diseases, and almost everything else. The incidence of monozygotic twins may soon be increased by fertility measures, for it is technically possible to split a human organism at the two- or four-cell stage and create monozygotic twins or quadruplets. At the moment, such cloning is considered unethical and illegal, and the incidence of monozygotic twins (about 1 in every 270 births) is holding steady for every ethnic group, in every nation.

Not all twins are monozygotic. **Dizygotic twins** (fraternal twins) begin life as two separate zygotes created by the fertilization of two ova at roughly the same time. Dizygotic conceptions may occur as frequently as one in every six pregnancies, but usually only one twin develops past the embryo stage. Hence dizygotic births occur naturally only about once in every 60 births, and there is considerable variation in incidence among racial and ethnic groups. (Women from Nigeria, for example, spontaneously produce dizygotic newborns about once in every 25 pregnancies; women from England, once in 100; and women from Japan, once in 700 [Gall, 1996].) Dizygotic twins share no more genes than do any other offspring of the same parents; that is, they share about 50 percent of the genes governing individual differences. They may be of different sexes and be very different in appearance, or they may look a great deal alike, just as nontwin brothers and sisters sometimes do.

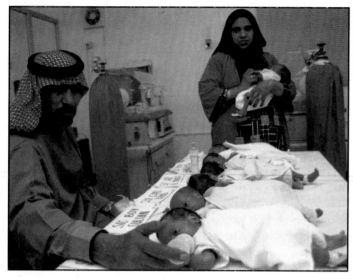

Septuplets! Within weeks after seven healthy babies were born to Bobbi McCaughey in Des Moines, Iowa, two other women carrying septuplet pregnancies made international news. In England, a woman, like McCaughey, refused to undergo selective abortion (aborting of some so that the rest could live); but unlike the McCaughey outcome, this time the expected outcome occurred—all seven died. In Saudi Arabia, a woman gave birth to seven survivors. Her problem soon became one familiar to many new parents—not enough time and space. When this photo was taken, the hospital was threatening to call the police unless the parents took their 8-week-old septuplets home, but the mother refused—unless she got round-the-clock aides at public expense.

❷ **Especially for Health Professionals:** Suppose you are developing specific, numerical standards regarding which women should attempt in vitro fertilization, how many times each should attempt it, and with how many embryos. What would your standards be?

infertile Unable to conceive a child despite a year of trying to do so.

in vitro fertilization (IVF) Fertilization of ova by sperm in the laboratory, usually followed by insertion of the resulting cell mass into the uterus in the hope that it will implant and develop as a normal pregnancy and birth.

Other multiple births, such as triplets and quadruplets, can likewise be monozygotic, dizygotic, trizygotic, quadrazygotic, and so on (or even some combination of these). Over the past decade, the incidence of multiple births (but not monozygotic multiples) has doubled in most medically advanced nations, because of the increased use of fertility drugs and other methods of helping infertile couples have children. Indeed, the rate of quadrazygotic births has increased by 2,000 percent (Gall, 1996). Generally, the greater the number of embryos that develop together in one uterus, the smaller, less mature, and more vulnerable each one is. This means that the increase in multiple births, which has produced many happy couples, has increased medical costs, infant mortality, and the incidence of children with special needs.

Fertility and Genes

We have discussed the genetic beginnings of human life but not the sexual beginnings. In fact, genes, sex, and fertility are intertwined. For almost all of human history, people did not know that men and women produced gametes and that putting those gametes together could produce children. However, high infant mortality made it imperative for couples to "be fruitful and multiply," lest populations become extinct (as some of our humanlike predecessors did). Accordingly, adaptation favored powerful genes that awaken at puberty to provoke first the signals of sexual attraction, then falling in love, and then passionate longing for the intimacy that leads to biological reproduction and to the social bonding needed for babies to thrive.

A Brief History of Fertility

The actual timing of puberty, and hence the onset of fertility, is partly genetic but also partly nutritional. Generally a couple cannot produce children, nor are the partners romantically interested in each other, until the woman is sufficiently well nourished to support a fetus and then nurse an infant and the man is strong enough to protect her and the child. In earlier centuries, this meant parenthood could not begin until about age 17. But, as a result of centuries of effective adaptation, genes now cause peak fertility at lower ages, a year or two after the human body reaches adult size. This has created a problem, as nutrition and medical care make teenagers biologically and genetically eager to have sexual relations years before they are ready emotionally and financially for parenthood.

Genes also reduce fertility with age, making reproduction more difficult for both sexes beginning at about age 30, reducing sperm count in men and impeding ovulation and implantation in women. For this and many other reasons, about one couple in six is considered **infertile,** which is defined as not conceiving a child after a year of trying to do so. Through most of history reduced fertility was a blessing, not a problem. Now, however, we live longer, and many couples marry later, have more intense work lives, and so postpone parenthood; as a result, many couples in their thirties and forties want children but are unable to conceive within a year. Technically, they are infertile. Often they turn to alternative conception.

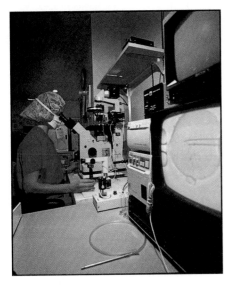

From Pipette to Party Usually conception begins deep within the fallopian tubes, but this laboratory technician is about to release one sperm into this ovum. If all goes well, she will begin another life like those of the "miracle babies" at the fertility clinic reunion on the right.

❷ *Observational Quiz (see answer page 77):* *Can you spot three demographic differences between these U.S. families and a typical cross section of U.S. families whose children were conceived in the traditional way?*

Our Changing World As reproductive technology advances, couples have more choices, including donor sperm, donor wombs, or, as shown here, donor eggs. The economic aspects of those donations depend on the individuals involved. More than 200 students answered this ad that they read in the college newspapers at the most select universities of North America.

Alternative Conception

Sometimes changing one's personal habits (diet, cigarettes, other drugs, stress) brings fertility. If not, medical measures often help. A man with a low sperm count can have his sperm collected and stored in a laboratory until there is a sufficient amount for conception and his partner can be artificially inseminated (a process in which the sperm are inserted into the uterus through a tube, rather than during intercourse). In women, an inability to ovulate can usually be treated with drugs, and blocked fallopian tubes can often be opened surgically.

If obstructions to conception cannot be removed, **in vitro fertilization (IVF)** may help. In this procedure, ova are surgically removed from the ovaries, fertilized by sperm in the laboratory, and allowed to divide until the 16- or 32-cell stage. The resulting cells are then inserted into the uterus, where about one cell cluster in seven successfully implants, develops, and becomes a healthy baby. Other techniques include gamete intrafallopian transfer (GIFT) and zygote intrafallopian transfer (ZIFT), which involve inserting either sperm and unfertilized ova (gametes) or fertilized ova (zygotes) into the fallopian tube; under optimal conditions these techniques have even better success rates than IVF—about one birth in five attempts (Hodder, 1997).

These innovations make possible a variety of third-party contributions to fertility—donor sperm, donor ova, even donor wombs. Sperm donation is the easiest, since it requires only that a man produce semen which is then saved and eventually inserted into the uterus—a method that has been used for decades. In the United States, twice as many babies are conceived through this *artificial insemination by donor (AID)* process than are adopted each year.

Ovum donation is more complicated. In one version a woman volunteers to become a *surrogate mother* (temporary or substitute mother); usually, she is artificially inseminated with sperm from an infertile woman's husband. She then carries the pregnancy to term, giving the newborn immediately to the father and his wife. In another version of ovum donation, some of a donor woman's ova are removed and artificially inseminated with a man's sperm (as in IVF); then the cluster of forming cells is inserted into his own wife's uterus. She carries the pregnancy and gives birth, thereby eliminating the emotional complications that sometimes affect a birth (surrogate) mother who must relinquish her newborn.

ISSUES SURROUNDING INFERTILITY

The alternative paths to reproduction raise profound personal and ethical questions that must be addressed, not only by the individuals directly involved but also by society as a whole. At the broadest level are questions regarding rights and obligations.

- Should third-party donors, whether of sperm, ova, or womb, have any parental rights?
- Should access to alternative reproduction be equally available to everyone, no matter what their marital status, sexual orientation, lifestyle, age, or motives for wanting a baby?
- Does an embryo conceived in vitro have a right to be implanted rather than kept frozen indefinitely or destroyed after some set time limit?
- If a woman, through alternative reproduction that was too successful, carries so many embryos that they probably cannot survive, is she obligated to abort some of them to save the others?
- Do children have the right to know if the parents who raise them are not their biological parents?

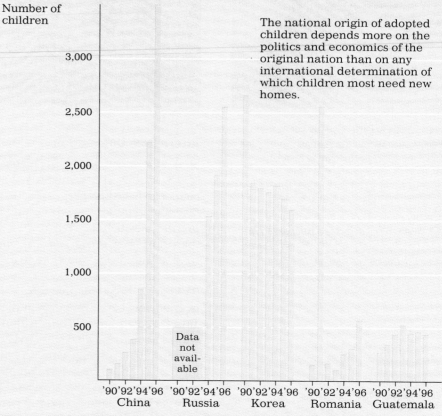

Children Entering the U.S. for Adoption, by Country of Origin*

Number of children

The national origin of adopted children depends more on the politics and economics of the original nation than on any international determination of which children most need new homes.

Data not available

'90'92'94'96 '90'92'94'96 '90'92'94'96 '90'92'94'96 '90'92'94'96
China   Russia   Korea   Romania   Guatemala

*Top five countries of origin, ranked by 1996 numbers.
Source: The New York Times, August 19, 1997.

Answers do not come easily; compassionate, thoughtful people—including developmentalists—differ widely on these issues.

Another set of questions involves the economics of alternative reproduction. Infertility is actually more common among poorer adults, but fertility options become more available as in-

❶ *Answer to Observational Quiz (from page 71):*
They are almost certainly monozygotic. Their similarities include every obvious genetic trait—coloring, timing of tooth loss, thickness of lips, and shape of the ears and chin. Their differences include exactly the kinds that might be imposed by parents who have trouble distinguishing one child from the other—the color of their eyeglass frames and the length of their hair.

To give you an idea of the relative use of these methods, we note that in the United States about 1,000 babies are born through surrogacy each year, about 15,000 through in vitro fertilization, and about 60,000 through artificial insemination by donor (ISLAT Working Group, 1998). For comparison, about 30,000 healthy infants are available for adoption. Each year 4 million are born who were conceived in the usual way, perhaps half a million of them after some concern on the part of the parents that fertility was delayed. (Ethical issues related to alternative conception are discussed in Children Up Close, above.)

come rises. The average cost of one baby resulting from IVF, ZIFT, or GIFT is more than $30,000, which puts those procedures beyond the reach of many couples. Should babies, to any degree, be a possession that some can afford and some cannot?

Similar economic issues can be raised about becoming a surrogate mother or relinquishing a newborn for adoption. It is usually low-income, unmarried women who carry a fetus for someone else, in exchange for expenses and a fee. And when adoption takes place across national borders, almost always children from poor, politically unstable regions are transferred to families in wealthier, more powerful communities. International adoptions cost between $15,000 and $50,000, with almost all of that money going to lawyers, adoption agencies, temporary guardians, government officials, airfare, and other expenses, and almost none to birth parents (Rosenthal, 1996). Of course, both sets of parents usually believe that children adopted from poor nations and raised in wealthy ones are much better off, and this may be true. However, if the money spent on international adoptions were instead made available to support adoptive or biological child rearing in the children's own culture, would the overall welfare of the children be improved?

One final question: Should laws, medical ethics, and contemporary culture encourage infertile individuals to willingly, even obsessively, incur great financial cost, psychic stress, and sometimes physical pain in attempting to have their own biological children? An example of the kind of case that medical ethics might forbid involved a woman who, after eight failed IVF attempts, insisted that it was still her "right" to try one more time, even though her health was at risk and the chance of success was very slim (Seibel, 1993). Managing such cases is made more complicated by the numerous fertility centers, private and public, that depend on fees from clients. The costs to the infertile person are emotional as well as financial and medical. As another woman said:

> Infertility takes the whole person. I used to feel attractive; I used to feel like I had a wonderful personality; I used to feel like I was smart; I used to feel like I could have a child if I wanted a child. And now all those things are shattered. [quoted in Sandelowski, 1993]

Should a doctor (or a counselor) have convinced this woman that reproduction was neither possible nor desirable, instead of letting her infertility "take the whole person"?

The obsessive quest for offspring is given a sharper edge by largely overlooked statistics: about one-third of all *untreated* infertile couples eventually produce their own biological babies, and about half of all treated couples remain barren. Fertility treatments often carry substantial psychological costs—marriages stressed by months or years of scheduled, monitored sexual relations as part of the attempt at pregnancy; egos damaged from feeling betrayed by one's body; friendships strained by resentment of other people's parenthood. The statistics mean that these costs may never be offset by the birth of a child.

However, before criticizing all those who pursue their unconventional, irrational, and perhaps selfish quest for parenthood, we need to recognize that every species has a powerful biological impulse to pass genes on to the next generation. So far we have examined this issue only from sociocultural and cognitive perspectives, questioning the cultural assumptions and reasoning processes that allow contemporary couples and physicians to seek alternative conception. However, recall the genetic instinct that underlies the reproductive drive. As one infertile woman explained,

> When you take away being able to have a child biologically, it is like having to face death—almost like having half of you die. Having kids is the main way that people deal with the fact that they are mortal. [Fry, quoted in Hodder, 1997]

Many social scientists agree that there is a genetic imperative to procreate, an urge that is integral to species survival (Barkow et al., 1992; Buss, 1994). As epigenetic systems theory would explain, not everyone feels this biological need, nor should everyone have children. But, especially in this chapter, which is primarily about biology, we need to remember a truth sometimes ignored by those who become pregnant easily: Conception is not just the mechanics of sperm meeting egg; it is the beginning of a process that has a profound emotional impact on all concerned.

FROM GENOTYPE TO PHENOTYPE

polygenic traits Characteristics produced by the interaction of many genes (rather than a single gene).

multifactorial traits Characteristics produced by the interaction of genetic and environmental (or other) influences (rather than by genetic influences alone).

As we have seen, conception brings together, from both parents, genetic instructions concerning every human characteristic. Exactly how do these instructions influence the specific traits that a given offspring inherits? The answer is usually quite complex, because most traits are both **polygenic**—that is, affected by many genes—and **multifactorial**—that is, influenced by many factors, including factors in the environment.

genotype A person's entire genetic inheritance, including genes that are not expressed in the person.

phenotype All the genetic traits, including physical characteristics and behavioral tendencies, that are expressed in a person.

carrier A person who has a gene in his or her genotype that is not evident as part of the phenotype. Carriers can pass such a gene on to their offspring.

Skin Color Is Inherited But ... Using "black," "white," "red," and "yellow" to denote human skin color is misleading, because humans actually have thousands of skin tones, each resulting from the combination of many genes, and none of them are these four colors. Depending on which half of each parent's skin-color genes children happen to inherit, each child can be paler, ruddier, lighter, darker, more sallow, more olive, or more freckled than either parent. This is particularly apparent in many African-American families, like this one, whose ancestors came from at least three continents.

additive pattern A common pattern of genetic inheritance in which each gene affecting a specific trait makes an active contribution to that trait. Skin color and height are determined by an additive pattern.

nonadditive pattern A pattern of genetic inheritance in which a trait is influenced much more by one gene than by other genes that could also influence the trait.

dominant-recessive pattern A pattern of genetic inheritance in which one member of a gene pair (referred to as *dominant*) hides the influence of the other (*recessive*) gene. Eye color is determined via a dominant-recessive pattern.

To grasp the complexity of genetic influences, we must first distinguish between a person's genetic inheritance—his or her genetic *potential*—and the actual *expression* of that inheritance in the person's physiology, physical appearance, and behavioral tendencies. The sum total of all the genes a person inherits is the **genotype** (the genetic potential). The sum total of all the actual, expressed traits that result from the genes—including physical traits such as bushy eyebrows and nonphysical traits such as a hunger for excitement—is the person's **phenotype** (the genetic expression).

Clearly, we all have many genes in our genotypes that are not apparent in our phenotypes. In genetic terms, we are **carriers** of these unexpressed genes; that is, we "carry" them in our DNA and can pass them on to our sperm or ova and thus to our offspring. When a zygote inherits a gene that was only carried (not expressed) in one parent, the zygote will, at least, have that gene in the genotype. That gene may be expressed in the phenotype or may simply be carried again, with a chance of affecting the next generation.

Gene-Gene Interaction

Whether or not a genetic trait becomes expressed in the phenotype is determined by two levels of interaction: (1) interaction among the proteins synthesized according to the specific genes that affect the trait, and (2) ongoing interaction between the genotype and the environment. We will look first at interactions among the genes themselves.

Additive Genes

One common pattern of interaction among genes is the **additive pattern.** When genes interact additively, the phenotype reflects the contributions of all the genes that are involved. The many genes that affect height, hair curliness, and skin color, for instance, usually interact in an additive fashion.

Consider the simplified situation in which a tall man whose parents and grandparents were all very tall marries a short woman whose parents and grandparents were all very short. Let us assume that every one of his height genes is for tallness, and hers are all for shortness. The couple's children will inherit tall genes via the father's sperm and short genes via the mother's ovum. Because the genes affecting height interact additively, the children will be of middling height (assuming that their nutrition and physical health are adequate). None of them will likely be as tall as their father or as short as their mother, because the contributions of all their genes for tallness and all their genes for shortness, somehow "averaged" together, will put them about halfway between the two.

In actuality, most people have both kinds of ancestors—relatively tall ones and relatively short ones—so we often see children who are notably taller or shorter than both their parents. How any additive trait turns out depends on all the contributions of whichever genes (half from each parent's varied genotype) a child happens to inherit. Every additive gene has some impact on the phenotype.

Dominant and Recessive Genes

Less common are **nonadditive patterns** of genetic interaction, in which the phenotype shows the influence of one gene much more than that of others. One kind of nonadditive pattern is the **dominant-recessive pattern,** which refers specifically to the interaction of gene pairs—one gene from the mother and one from the father, both influencing a particular trait. When a gene pair interacts according to this pattern, the phenotype reveals the

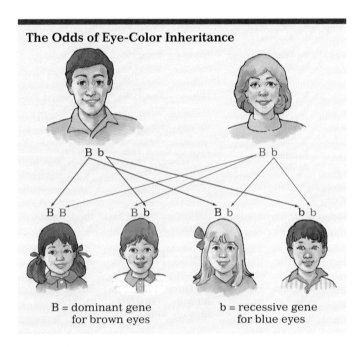

The Odds of Eye-Color Inheritance

B = dominant gene for brown eyes   b = recessive gene for blue eyes

Figure 3.3 Brown Eyes and Blue Genes. Two brown-eyed parents who are carriers for blue eyes can donate eye-color genes to their offspring only in the four ways that are shown here. So there is a 1-in-4 chance that a child will inherit brown-eye genes from both parents (and have brown eyes), a 2-in-4 chance that a child will inherit one brown-eye and one blue-eye gene (and again have brown eyes because brown is dominant), and a 1-in-4 chance that a child will inherit two recessive blue-eye genes (and have blue eyes).

❶ *Answer to Observational Quiz (from page 73):* *The parents are older than average, none seem to be African-American, and a high proportion have twins, including at least three sets in the front row.*

***X*-linked genes** Genes that are carried on the *X* chromosome.

influence of one powerful gene, called the *dominant gene.* The other, weaker gene, the *recessive gene,* is not expressed in any obvious way. Sometimes the dominant gene completely controls the characteristic in question, and the recessive gene is merely carried, with its influence not evident at all in the phenotype. In other instances, the outcome reflects *incomplete dominance,* with the phenotype influenced primarily, but not exclusively, by the dominant gene.

Hundreds of physical characteristics are determined according to the dominant-recessive pattern (with some modification due to environmental factors and the influence of other genes). A classic example of dominant-recessive interaction is eye color.

For the sake of illustration, let us simplify and say that a person inherits only two eye-color genes, one from each parent. Further, let us say that an eye-color gene is coded for only one of two possible instructions, brown eyes and blue eyes, and that no other factors interfere in eye-color determination. We know that the gene for brown eyes is dominant, and the gene for blue eyes is recessive. (Following traditional practice, we indicate the dominant gene with an uppercase letter, here "B" for dominant brown, and the recessive gene with a lowercase letter, here "b" for recessive blue). If both inherited genes in a person are for brown eyes, the person is BB, and the person's eyes will be brown. If one gene is for brown eyes and the other for blue (Bb), the person's eyes will also be brown, because the brown-eye gene is dominant. If both genes are for blue eyes (bb), the person will have blue eyes.

When we try to predict eye color in as-yet-unborn offspring, the possibilities become more complicated. Only when both parents have blue eyes is the prediction simple: their children will *always* have blue eyes. Since the parents must both be bb to have blue eyes, their gametes will each have one b; consequently, every child of theirs will inherit one b from the mother and one b from the father, becoming a bb and thus having blue eyes.

If either parent (or both) has brown eyes, his or her genotype is either BB or Bb. The difference is important. For example, if even one parent is BB (double-dominant brown), every gamete from that parent will have one B; because one dominant gene is sufficient to determine a phenotype, all the children will have brown eyes. If one parent has blue eyes and the other has brown eyes but carries the blue-eye gene (thus making the parents bb + Bb), each of their children will have a 50–50 chance of being Bb, and brown-eyed, or bb, and blue-eyed.

Surprisingly, a blue-eyed child may also be born to two brown-eyed parents if both parents are carriers of the blue-eye gene. With any such couple (Bb + Bb), the chances are 1 in 4 that a child will inherit bb and have blue eyes (see Figure 3.3). In actuality, eye-color genes come in more shades than simply brown or blue, which further complicates the picture.

X-Linked Genes

Some genes are called ***X*-linked** because they are located only on the X chromosome. If an X-linked gene is recessive—as are the genes for most forms of color blindness, many allergies, several diseases, and some learning disabilities—the fact that it is on the X chromosome is critical. Recall that males have only one X chromosome. Thus, whatever recessive genes a male happens to inherit on that X chromosome cannot be counterbalanced or dominated by genes on a second X chromosome—there is no second X. So those recessive genes will be expressed in his phenotype. This explains why some traits can be passed from mother to son (via the X) but not from father to son (since the Y does not carry the trait). (See Figure 3.4.)

Figure 3.4 The Twenty-Third Pair and X-Linked Color Blindness. The phenotypes on lines 1 and 2 are normal because their genes are normal. Those on lines 3 and 4 are normal because the abnormal X-linked gene is recessive and the normal gene is dominant. Those on lines 5 and 6 are color-blind because they have only defective X-linked genes and no dominant, normal X.

The 23rd Pair and X-linked Color Blindness
X indicates an X chromosome with the X-linked gene for color blindness

23rd Pair		Phenotype	Genotype	Next Generation
1.	XX	Normal woman	Not a carrier	No color blindness from mother.
2.	XY	Normal man	Normal X from mother	No color blindness from father.
3.	XX	Normal woman	Carrier from father	Half her children will inherit her X. The girls with her X will be carriers, the boys with her X will be color-blind.
4.	XX	Normal woman	Carrier from mother	Half her children will inherit her X. The girls with her X will be carriers, the boys with her X will be color-blind.
5.	XY	Color-blind man	Inherited from mother	All his daughters will have his X. None of his sons will have his X.
6.	XX	Color-blind woman	Inherited from both parents	Every child will have one X from her. Therefore, every son will be color-blind. Daughters will be only carriers, unless they also inherit an X from the father, as their mother did.

❷ **Especially for Educators:** Teaching genetic probabilities is sometimes hard. How could you illustrate the odds of dominant-recessive inheritance, if both parents are carriers, using a deck of ordinary playing cards?

genetic imprinting The tendency of certain genes to be expressed differently when they are inherited from the mother than when they are inherited from the father.

More Complications

As complex as the preceding descriptions of gene interaction patterns may seem, they make gene-gene interaction appear much simpler than it actually is. That is because, to be able to discuss interaction at all, we are forced to treat genes as though they were discretely functioning "control devices." But, as we have noted, what genes actually do is direct the synthesis of hundreds of kinds of proteins, which then form the body's structures and direct its biochemical functions. In a sense, each body cell is "nothing more than a sea of chemicals" that is continually affected by other chemicals (proteins, enzymes, nutrients, and toxins) that direct the cell's functioning (Lee, 1993).

In regard to the dominant-recessive pattern, for example, no single gene pair directly determines even simple traits, such as eye color or height. And in the additive pattern, some genes contribute substantially more than others, either because they are naturally partially dominant or because their influence is amplified by the presence of certain other genes.

In addition, certain genes behave differently depending on whether they are inherited from the mother or from the father (Hoffman, 1991). The full scope of this parental **genetic imprinting**, or tagging, of certain genes has yet to be determined. However, it is known that some of the genes that influence height, insulin production, and several forms of mental retardation affect a child in different ways—even in opposite ways—depending on which parent they came from.

Such polygenic complexity is particularly apparent in psychological characteristics, from personality traits such as sociability, assertiveness, moodiness, and fearfulness to cognitive traits such as memory for numbers, spatial perception, and fluency of expression. One example comes from the genetics of mental retardation, which has been studied in great depth and detail because of its role in limiting human potential. Scientists now know that virtually every type of inheritance pattern, including additive, dominant-recessive, X-linked, polygenic, multifactorial, and imprinting, is evident in at least one of the major types of mental retardation (Simonoff et al., 1996). The same is probably true for all aspects of personality and intellect, with every behavioral tendency affected by many pairs of genes, some interacting in the dominant-recessive mode, some additive, and some creating new combinations of epigenetic functioning, not yet cataloged or understood. And it is likely that every behavior pattern can sometimes be caused by a different set of genes (Yeung-Courchesne & Courchesne, 1997).

Finally, many genetic traits become more apparent as children mature and change and, at the same time, parental restrictions and influence wane (Caspi & Moffitt, 1991; McGue et al., 1993). This is especially the case with adopted children. When they are very young, such children reflect many of their adoptive parents' interests, behaviors, and personality traits. However, with maturity, they often choose friends, hobbies, and habits that express their biological, more than their familial, heritage. Sometimes adoptive parents are slow to spot a potential problem, or to encourage a potential talent, because they do not recognize it from their past personal experience. Of course, nonadoptive parents can make the same mistake, especially if the trait is recessive and therefore not familiar to them. In either case, caregivers need to understand the vast variety of genetic inclinations and abilities so that each child is seen as an individual and not necessarily as "a chip off the old block."

Gene-Environment Interaction

The environment adds another level of complexity to the relationship between genotype and phenotype. To understand the wide-ranging impact of nurture on genetic inheritance, you need to know that when social scientists discuss the effects of the environment, they are referring to a multitude of variables. As they use the term, **environment** includes everything that can interact with the person's genetic inheritance at any point of life, from the first stages to the last heartbeat; such environmental influences range from the impact of uterine acidity on prenatal cell duplication to all the ways that the external world impinges on the developing child or adult. Some of these external elements affect the genes and brain cells directly, as do nutrition, climate, medical care, and family interaction, and some affect them indirectly, as do the broad economic, political, and cultural contexts.

The impact of the environment also involves varying degrees of permanence. Some effects are irreversible, such as the lifelong toll that severe brain injury has on cognitive ability. Others are transitory, such as the impact that a moment of stress has on an individual's mood. Thus, the influence of the environment is lifelong, multifaceted, and of varied force and duration—just as the influence of heredity is.

Distinguishing Heredity and Environment

In order to examine the complex interplay of heredity and the environment, researchers would like to separate the impacts of these two forces. This is difficult because, within any given trait, nature and nurture are intertwined

environment All the nongenetic factors that can affect development—everything from the impact of the immediate cell environment on the genes themselves to the broader effects of nutrition, medical care, socioeconomic status, family dynamics, and the economic, political, and cultural contexts.

"I don't know anything about the bell curve, but I say heredity is everything."

The Inheritance of the Throne   Some people have much more to gain than others from the notion that genes are more influential than environment.

🛈 **Response for Educators (from page 78):** Dominant could be the black cards, and recessive the red. Divide the 52 cards into two half decks, each with 13 red cards and 13 black. Shuffle each half deck, and then pick pairs of cards, one from each deck. Odds are that both cards in three pairs will be black (not even a carrier of the recessive gene), the cards in pairs will be mixed (hence, carriers), and both cards in three pairs will be red (the double recessive.). Of course, reality doesn't always follow the odds—a lesson that can be taught if the pairs don't match what you expect.

at every moment. When the trait in question is an obvious physical one, the impact of genes on the phenotype seems fairly obvious. Family resemblances in facial features, coloring, or body shape can make it easy to say, "He has his mother's nose," meaning "That's hereditary."

But when a trait is a psychological one, especially a trait that changes over time, the fact that it runs in families could be explained by nurture just as easily as by nature. If children of highly intelligent parents excel in school, their school performance could, theoretically, be attributed entirely to their genetic inheritance, entirely to the family environment (which is likely to encourage reading, intellectual curiosity, and high academic standards), or to any combination of the two. How, then, do scientists distinguish genetic from environmental influences on psychological characteristics?

Comparing Twins.   One solution to this puzzle has been to study twins raised in the same families and presumably sharing the same nurture. As we have seen, monozygotic twins have all the same genes, whereas dizygotic twins, like any other two siblings from the same parents, share only half their genes. Thus, if monozygotic twins are found to be much more similar to each other on a particular trait than dizygotic twins are, it seems likely that genes play a significant role in the development of that trait. On the other hand, if both kinds of twins are equally likely to express or not express a characteristic, family environment is the likely source of whatever similarities are found.

Such twin comparisons have revealed that many *psychological traits* are strongly influenced genetically. There is, however, one problem with this approach: It assumes, among other things, that twins growing up in a particular family share the same environment. In fact, however, twins in the same family sometimes have quite separate experiences—both in obvious ways, such as when one twin but not the other suffers a serious illness or learns from an extraordinary teacher, and in more subtle, ongoing ways, such as when parents punish one twin more harshly or when one twin defers to the other (Reiss, 1997).

Comparing Adoptees.   An alternative approach to distinguishing the impact of genes from that of upbringing is to compare the traits of large numbers of adopted children with the traits of both their biological and their adoptive parents. Traits that show a strong correlation between adopted children and their biological parents would seem to have a genetic basis; traits that show a strong correlation between adopted children and their adoptive parents would suggest environmental influence. This approach has flaws as well. One difficulty is that adopted children are often placed in families whose socioeconomic, educational, and religious backgrounds are similar to those of their birth families. As a consequence, some of the strong similarities typically found between adopted children and their biological parents may be the result of shared culture rather than of shared genes. Another difficulty is that adoption itself may be an unsettling experience, diminishing or increasing the effects of either genes or upbringing.

Advanced Research.   The most telling way to try to separate the effects of genes and environment is to combine both approaches, studying identical twins who have been separated at birth and raised in different families (see the Research Report on page 81). Finding enough separated monozygotic

TWINS REARED IN SEPARATE HOMES

One of the most extensive investigations of twins raised in separate homes is the Minnesota Study of Twins Reared Apart, which over the past 20 years has studied hundreds of twin pairs who were separated early in life (Bouchard, 1994; Bouchard et al., 1990; Finkel et al., 1995). This study, like others of its kind, has consistently found such striking psychological and behavioral similarities between monozygotic twins that the important role of genes in personality development can no longer be denied.

Typical is the case of Oskar Stohr and Jack Yufe, identical twins born of a Jewish father and Christian mother in Trinidad in the 1930s. Soon after their birth, Oskar was taken to Nazi Germany by his mother to be raised as a Catholic in a household consisting mostly of women. Jack was raised as a Jew by his father, spending his childhood in the Caribbean and some of his adolescence in Israel.

On the face of it, it would be difficult to imagine two more disparate cultural backgrounds. And when the twins were re-united in middle age, they certainly had their differences. Oskar was married and a devoted union member; Jack was divorced and the owner of a store in southern California. But when the brothers met for the first time in Minnesota,

Long-Lost Brother Since Oskar Stoher *(left)* and Jack Yufe *(right)* are monozygotic twins, it is not surprising that they are the same height, both are balding, and both need glasses. And since Oskar has always lived in Germany, and Jack spent most of his life in southern California, it is also not surprising that their clothes are quite distinct and that Jack is more willing to smile for the camera. ❷ *Observational Quiz (see answer page 82): In this photo Jack and Oskar both exhibit at least four traits that are usually thought of as resulting from individual choice, not genes, until their circumstances—being monozygotic twins reared apart—suggest otherwise. What are those traits?*

similarities started cropping up as soon as Oskar arrived at the airport. Both were wearing wire-rimmed glasses and mustaches, both sported two-pocket shirts with epaulets. They share idiosyncrasies galore: they like spicy foods and sweet liqueurs, are absentminded, have a habit of falling asleep in front of the television, think it's funny to sneeze in a crowd of strangers, flush the toilet before using it, store rubber bands on their wrists, read magazines from back to front, dip buttered toast in their coffee. Oskar is domineering toward women and yells at his wife, which Jack did before he was separated. [Holden, 1980]

Their scores on several psychological tests were very similar, and they struck the investigator as remarkably similar in temperament and tempo.

Other pairs of monozygotic twins in this study likewise startled the observers with their similarities, not only in appearance and on test scores but also in mannerisms and dress. One pair of twins, raised in rather serious homes, giggled at almost everything. In fact, when they were interviewed, it was hard to gather information because every comment triggered peals of laughter. Another set of female twins, separated since infancy, arrived in Minnesota each wearing seven rings (on the same fingers) and three bracelets, a coincidence that likely was partly genetic. How could this be? No doubt, their genes endowed both women with beauti-

ful hands. But more than that, it is quite possible that they both also have a genetic interest in attractive objects and in self-decoration. Indeed, some people like the feel of rings, bracelets, and such against their skin, while others do not—for reasons that could be related to the sense of touch, itself genetically influenced.

Case after case in this study has produced similar findings of surprising "coincidences," suggesting that genes affect a much greater number of characteristics than was previously suspected by most psychologists, including the leader of the Minnesota study, Thomas Bouchard. Bouchard now concludes that genetic variation is significant for "almost every behavioral trait so far investigated, from reaction time to religiosity" (Bouchard et al., 1990).

Many researchers are astonished at the similarities they find in monozygotic twins raised separately (Lykken et al., 1992). Their findings make us wonder anew about the sources of our own individuality. Are our life choices—large and small—mostly an outgrowth of experience and cultural background, or do they come from much deeper roots? Could many of our distinctive habits, behavior patterns, and values result not so much from personal choice as from genetic push?

By the way, how many rings do you have on your fingers, and why?

twin pairs to yield statistically significant conclusions is, however, a painstaking process. Nonetheless, several groups of researchers in the United States, Sweden, England, Denmark, Finland, and Australia have done just that, discovering altogether more than a thousand twins reared in separate homes. The results of these researchers' investigations provide dramatic confirmation of the general conclusion reached by the study methods described above. And that conclusion is that virtually every psychological characteristic and personal trait is genetically influenced. At the same time, these studies reinforce another, equally important conclusion: Virtually every psychological characteristic and personal trait is affected, throughout the life span, by the person's environment.

The next step is to deduce exactly how genetic and environmental influences combine, especially for behavioral traits; these are the most fascinating traits, but they are also the most likely traits to be polygenic and multifactorial, with each impinging factor having so small and variable an influence that its effect is hard to detect. Here, detailed analytic and statistical techniques developed in conjunction with the mapping of the genetic code have been very helpful. Particularly promising is a locating technique called *quantitative trait loci (QTL)* (Plomin, 1995). Instead of simply using the family connection (such as mother-child, or uncle-niece) as a measure of genetic closeness, researchers can now look directly at a pattern of genes two individuals share, that pattern's location on a particular chromosome. Then, if two people with the same genetic locus (location for a particular gene pattern) are also more similar in some aspect of their phenotypes than are people without that gene pattern at that location, researchers can conclude that the particular gene contributes something to that trait.

QTL has already found a gene that contributes to reading disability (Cardon et al., 1994) and one that contributes to high intelligence (Chorney et al., 1998). As we learn more about the impact of genes, it becomes increasingly important to realize that when we say something is "genetic," we do not mean that its genetic origins are substantial, fixed, or unalterable. We mean that it is part of a person's basic foundation, affecting many aspects of life while determining none.

Height, Shyness, and Schizophrenia

Environment, as we have defined it, affects every human characteristic. Even traits that show a strong genetic influence are also influenced by environment.

Physical Traits.   Height is a good example of a physical trait that is influenced by environment as well as heritage. An individual's height potential is genetically directed, yet adults in developed countries are, *on average,* taller than their ancestors were but about the same height as their own full-grown children. Why? Because to reach his or her genetically based height, a person must have good nutrition and health—the proper environment.

In previous centuries, nutrition and health were not nearly as good as they are now. Consequently, Europeans and North Americans averaged about 6 inches shorter a century ago than today (Tanner, 1971). Throughout the twentieth century, as nutrition and medical care improved, each generation grew slightly taller than the previous one. This trend has ended during the past several decades, because prevailing levels of health and nutrition have permitted the vast majority of the population's members to reach their full genetic height.

❶ *Answer to Observational Quiz (from page 81):*
Both men eat too much, have small mustaches, prefer their top shirt button open, and wear lightly tinted glasses with rectangular frames.

Of course, in individual cases, environmental factors such as malnutrition, chronic illness, and stress can make a child considerably shorter than the upper limit set by his or her heredity. And in many developing nations, a generational trend of increasing height is still very obvious, as many a teenager towers over all four of his or her grandparents—even though genetically they are the same.

Inhibition. The role of the environment in the genetic expression of physical traits such as height is fairly simple to understand. More varied, hidden, and intriguing are gene-environment interactions for psychological traits. Let us look at shyness as an example.

Being fearful of talking in public, of making new friends, of expressing emotions—in short, being shy—is a personality trait that scientists refer to as *inhibition*. Study after study has found that levels of inhibition (or its opposite, *extroversion* or *sociability*) are more similar in monozygotic twins than in dizygotic twins—a result which proves that genes affect this trait. Further evidence of genetic roots for shyness comes from studies that have found many early biological differences between inhibited and extroverted children. Compared to other infants, babies who will later be shy show quicker *startle reactions* (when they are suddenly surprised by a loud noise, for instance), with more motor activity and crying. Then, as toddlers, they are less active overall but more fearful (as you would expect an inhibited child to be) (Calkins et al., 1996; Kagen, 1994).

However, inhibition is also affected by the social atmosphere provided by parents and the culture. If the parents are able to encourage their shy children without shaming or embarrassing them, initial hesitancy and withdrawal in social encounters might gradually give way as the children learn to relax in social settings and become less observably shy. A child with a genetic disposition to shyness who is raised by outgoing parents would have many contacts with other people and would observe his or her parents socializing freely, even with strangers. Alternatively, of course, if a shy child's parents are themselves very shy and socially isolated, but nonetheless blame their child for being fearful, the child might grow up much more timid socially than would be the case with outgoing parents—and he or she would be dramatically more inhibited than most other children.

The point here is *not* that as life experiences accumulate, genetically based tendencies disappear: shy people always feel a twinge of inhibition when entering a new school, for instance, or arriving at a party full of strangers. And these tendencies affect their life course. For example, on average, shy people marry later than nonshy people (Caspi et al., 1988; Kerr et al., 1996). But life experiences do make a difference. As an example, a longitudinal study in the United States found that shyness slowed down young men's career advancement, but this was not found in longitudinal research in Sweden. The researchers speculated on one reason for the difference:

> Swedish culture values shy, reserved behavior . . . and support systems of various sorts made it possible for Swedish boys to enter universities and careers without being assertive (Kerr et al., 1996).

The same conclusion applies to other psychological traits that have been found to have strong genetic influences, including intelligence, emotionality, activity level, aggression, and even religiosity (Bronfenbrenner & Ceci, 1994; Caspi & Silva, 1995; Loehlin, 1992; Plomin et al., 1997). In each case, various dimensions of an individual's environment can enhance, inhibit, or alter the phenotypic expression of that person's heredity.

Shyness Is Universal Inhibition is more common at some ages (late infancy and early adolescence) and in some gene pools (natives of northern Europe and East Asia) than others. But every community includes some individuals who are unmistakably shy, such as this toddler in Woleai, over 3,000 miles west of Hawaii.

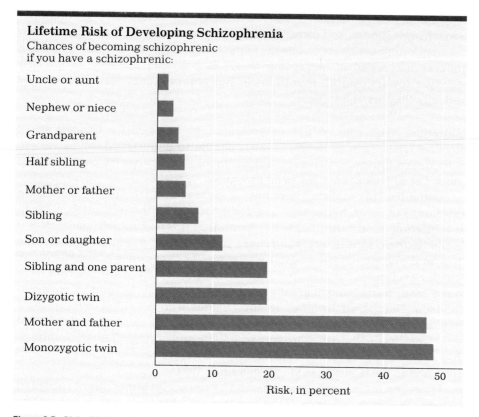

Lifetime Risk of Developing Schizophrenia

Chances of becoming schizophrenic
if you have a schizophrenic:

- Uncle or aunt
- Nephew or niece
- Grandparent
- Half sibling
- Mother or father
- Sibling
- Son or daughter
- Sibling and one parent
- Dizygotic twin
- Mother and father
- Monozygotic twin

0   10   20   30   40   50

Risk, in percent

Figure 3.5 Risk of Schizophrenia. If a person has a relative who has schizophrenia, that person's lifetime risk of being diagnosed with schizophrenia is greater than the 1 percent chance overall, depending on how genetically close he or she is to the afflicted relative. The highest risk occurs for monozygotic twins: when one twin is diagnosed with schizophrenia, the other has almost a 50 percent chance of eventually being so diagnosed. Note, however, that while this chart shows a clear genetic influence on schizophrenia, the odds also show the effects of environment. Over half the monozygotic siblings whose twin has schizophrenia do *not* have schizophrenia themselves.

Mental Illness. Psychopathologies such as depression, antisocial behavior, phobias, and compulsions, as well as virtually every other neurotic or psychotic disorder are again genetic with strong environmental influence (Caspi & Silva, 1995; Goldsmith et al., 1997; Plomin et al., 1997; Rutter et al., 1997). For example, relatives of people with schizophrenia have a higher-than-normal risk of developing the illness themselves (Gottesman, 1991) (see Figure 3.5).

Most striking is the fact that if one monozygotic twin develops schizophrenia, about half the time the other twin does too. Viewed another way, however, the same statistic reveals the importance of the environment: half of the monozygotic twins whose twin has schizophrenia are not themselves afflicted. Moreover, many people diagnosed with schizophrenia have no close relatives with the illness (Cromwell, 1993). Obviously, schizophrenia is multifactorial, with environmental elements—possibly a slow-acting virus, head injury, or other physical insult—playing a pivotal role.

Alcoholism: From Genotype to Phenotype and Back

One particularly clear example of the way the environment moderates genetic potential can be seen with alcoholism. At various times, alcoholism was thought to be a moral weakness, a personality flaw, and a sign of psychopathology. It is now obvious, however, that some people's inherited biochemistry makes them highly susceptible to alcohol addiction. Of course, anyone can abuse alcohol, but each person's genetic makeup creates an addictive pull that can be overpowering, or minuscule, or something in between.

Evidence for "alcoholic genes" is found in the fact that some ethnic groups (such as those from the British Isles and from northern Russia) have a much higher proportion of alcoholics than others. Biochemistry may be the difference. For instance, among many East Asians, sweating and becoming red-faced is a common biochemical reaction to drinking alcohol, a response that, particularly for women, provides an incentive to stop drinking (McGue, 1995). Among Europeans, some become sleepy, others nauseous, others aggressive, and others euphoric when alcohol hits their brains, and each person's reaction increases or decreases the eagerness to have another drink.

Given that alcoholism is a destructive trait, one might ask why alcoholic genes have been passed on from generation to generation in certain groups. Part of the answer is that, in some regions, beer and wine were, at one time, actually healthier for people than water—since the distillation process killed many of the destructive bacteria that thrived in drinking water. Thus, being able to drink beer or wine in quantity was adaptive for those groups. East Asians had a different solution to the problem of bacteria: they boiled their water and drank it as tea. This explains why about half of all Asians lack the gene for an enzyme necessary to fully metabolize alcohol: their ancestors didn't need it. Such a lack might have been life-threatening in a European, who had to drink alcohol to avoid polluted water; it was not a problem for tea-drinking East Asians (Vallee, 1998).

No single gene, recessive or dominant, produces either the physical or the psychological traits that lead to alcoholism. But genes are at least partly involved in certain temperamental characteristics that are correlated with abusive drinking. Among these are a quick temper, a readiness to take risks, and a high level of anxiety. Thus alcoholism is polygenic, with almost every alcoholic inheriting a particular combination of biochemistry-affecting and temperament-affecting genes that push him or her toward abusive drinking (Bower, 1996).

But alcoholism is not just genetic (McGue, 1993). If a person with a strong genetic tendency toward alcoholism spends a lifetime in an environment where alcohol is unavailable (in a devout Islamic family in Saudi Arabia, for example), the tendency of the genotype will never be expressed in the phenotype. On the other hand, if the same person is allowed to drink frequently at an early age, the power of the genes will increase. Further, if that person is raised in a culture that promotes the use of alcohol and is exposed to peer pressures that lead to alcohol abuse, he or she is likely to become an active alcoholic. Even for such unfortunates, wherever they live, social influences and personal choices can dramatically alter the eventual outcome. Some alcoholics die of the disease before they are 30; others spend decades alternating between periods of abuse, periods of controlled drinking, and periods of abstinence; still others recognize the problem, get help, and are sober and productive throughout a long life.

In sum, it is quite clear that genes, the immediate biochemical environment, and the more distant social environment are all powerful influences, and that their complex interaction is involved in every aspect of development at every age and era. On a practical level, this means we should not ignore the genetic component in any given trait—whether it be something wonderful, such as a wacky sense of humor, something fearful, such as a violent temper, or something quite ordinary, such as the tendency to tire of the same routine. At the same time, we must always recognize that the environment affects every trait, in every individual, in ways that change as maturational, cultural, and historical processes unfold. Genes are always part of the tale, influential on every page, but they never determine the plot or the final paragraph.

GENETIC AND CHROMOSOMAL ABNORMALITIES

In studying human development, we give particular attention to genetic and chromosomal abnormalities for three reasons:

- By investigating genetic and chromosomal disruptions of normal development, we gain a fuller appreciation of the complexities of genetic interactions like those described above.
- The more we know about the origins of genetic and chromosomal abnormalities, the better we understand how to reduce or limit their harmful consequences.
- An understanding of genetic and chromosomal abnormalities and those who inherit them is essential to everyone concerned about fostering human development. Without it, misinformation and prejudice compound the problems of those affected.

syndrome A cluster of distinct characteristics that tend to occur together in a given disorder.

trisomy-21 (Down syndrome) A syndrome that includes such symptoms as a rounded head, thick tongue, unusual eyes, heart abnormalities, and mental retardation. It results when there is an extra chromosome at the site of the twenty-first pair.

Chromosomal Abnormalities

Sometimes when gametes are formed, the 46 chromosomes divide unevenly, producing a sperm or an ovum that does not have the normal complement of exactly 23 chromosomes. If such a gamete fuses with a normal gamete, the result is a zygote with more or fewer than 46 chromosomes. This is not unusual. An estimated half of all zygotes have an odd number of chromosomes. Most such zygotes do not even begin to develop, and most of the rest never come to term—usually because a spontaneous abortion occurs (Snijders & Nicolaides, 1996).

Once in about every 200 births, however, a baby is born with 45, 47, or, rarely, even more chromosomes. In every case, the chromosomal abnormalities lead to a recognizable **syndrome**—a cluster of distinct characteristics that tend to occur together.

Down Syndrome

The most common of the extra-chromosome syndromes is **trisomy-21**, or **Down syndrome**, in which the individual has three chromosomes at site 21. Some 300 distinct characteristics can result from the presence of that extra chromosome, but no individual with Down syndrome is quite like another, either in the particular symptoms he or she has or in their severity (Cicchetti & Beeghly, 1990; Lott & McCoy, 1992). Despite this variability, almost all people with trisomy-21 have certain specific facial characteristics—a thick tongue, round face, slanted eyes—as well as distinctive hands, feet, and fingerprints. Many also have hearing problems, heart abnormalities, muscle weakness, and short stature.

In terms of neurological development, almost all individuals with Down syndrome experience mental slowness, but their eventual intellectual attainment varies: some are severely retarded; others are of average or even above-average intellect. Usually—but not always—those who are raised at home and given appropriate cognitive stimulation progress to the point of being able to read and write and care for themselves (and often much more), while those who are institutionalized tend to be, and to remain, much more retarded (Carr, 1995).

Many children with trisomy-21 are unusually sweet-tempered; they are less likely to cry or complain than most other children. By middle adulthood, however, individuals with Down syndrome are likely to develop a form of dementia similar to Alzheimer's disease, severely impairing their limited communication skills and making them much less compliant (Rasmussen & Sobsey, 1994). They are also prone to a host of other problems more commonly found in older persons, including cataracts and certain forms of cancer. Consequently, their mortality rate begins to rise at about age 35, and their life expectancy is lower than that of other mentally retarded adults as well as that of average people (Strauss & Eyman, 1996).

Abnormalities at the Twenty-Third Location

Every newborn infant has at least one X chromosome in the twenty-third pair. About 1 in every 500 infants, however, either is missing a sex chromosome, and thus the X stands alone, or has an X chromosome complemented

Pretending to Give Her Baby a Bottle This is a perfect example of normal cognitive and social development at age 22 months. In fact, Syvonne is fortunate that she lives at home and was enrolled in a special intervention program when she was a few months old, because her development thus far is just like that of other toddlers. The only hint of her Down syndrome is that her head might be bigger and rounder, and her eyes wider and more oval, than is usual. Also her mouth is open, not remarkable for a child with a cold, or an ear infection, or a large tongue because she has an extra chromosome at site 21.

by two or more other sex chromosomes. As you can see from Table 3.1, these abnormalities impair cognitive and psychosocial development as well as sexual maturation, with each particular syndrome having a specific set of effects. In many cases, treatment with hormone supplements can alleviate some of the physical problems, and special education may remedy some of the deficits related to psychological functioning.

The specific features of any syndrome vary considerably from one individual to another. In fact, in many cases, the presence of abnormal sex chromosomes goes undetected until a seemingly normal childhood is followed by an abnormally delayed puberty. This is particularly likely for a boy who has *Klinefelter syndrome, XXY.* Such a boy will be a little slow in elementary school; but it is usually not until puberty—when his penis does not grow and fat begins to accumulate around his breasts—that his parents will wonder if something is seriously wrong.

The Fragile *X*. One of the most common syndromes associated with the sex chromosomes is **fragile-*X* syndrome,** which is actually genetic in origin. In some individuals, part of the X chromosome is attached to the rest by such a thin string of molecules that it seems about to break off (hence the name of the syndrome). This abnormality in the chromosome is caused by the mutation of a single gene. Unlike most other known mutations, the mutation involved in fragile X intensifies as it is passed from one generation to the next (Dykens et al., 1994; Hagerman, 1996).

Of the females who carry it, most are normal (perhaps because they also carry one normal X chromosome), but one-third show some mental deficiency. Among the males who inherit a fragile-X chromosome, about 20

fragile-*X* syndrome A disorder in which part of the *X* chromosome is attached to the rest by a very slim string of molecules; it is caused by a genetic abnormality and often produces mental deficiency.

table **3.1**	**Common Abnormalities Involving the Sex Chromosomes**			
Name	Chromosomal Pattern	Physical Appearance*	Physchological Characteristics*	Incidence
Klinefelter syndrome	*XXY*	Male. Secondary sex characteristics do not develop. For example, the penis does not grow, the voice does not change. Breasts may develop.	Learning-disabled, especially in language skills.	1 in 900 males
(No name)	*XYY*	Male. Prone to acne. Unusually tall.	Tend to be more aggressive than most males. Mildly retarded, especially in language skills.	1 in 1,000 males
Fragile X	Usually *XY*	Male or female. Often, large head, prominent ears. Occasionally, enlarged testicles in males.	Variable. Some individuals apparently normal; others severely retarded, with impaired social skills.	1 in 1,000 males 1 in 2,500 females
(No name)	*XXX, XXX*	Female. Normal appearance.	Retarded in almost all intellectual skills.	1 in 500 females
Turner syndrome	*XO* (only one sex chromosome)	Female. Short in stature, often "webbed" neck. Secondary sex characteristics (breasts, menstruation) do not develop.	Learning-disabled, especially in abilities related to math and science and in recognition of facial expressions of emotion.	1 in 2,000 females

*There is some variation in the physical appearance of the individuals and considerable variation in their intellectual and temperamental characteristics. With regard to psychological characteristics, much depends on the family environment of the child.
Sources: Borgaonkar, 1994; Dykens et al., 1994; Lee, 1993; McCauley et al., 1987; Rovet et al., 1996.

percent are apparently completely normal, about 33 percent are somewhat retarded, and the rest are severely retarded. The last group is relatively large: the cognitive deficits caused by fragile-X syndrome represent the most common form of inherited mental retardation. In addition to cognitive problems, fragile X often causes inadequate social skills and extreme shyness (Dykens et al., 1994; Hagerman, 1996).

The wide range of effects produced by this disorder is somewhat unusual. However, some geneticists believe that the more we learn about other abnormal genes, chromosomes, and syndromes, the more diversity we will find in their effects (McKusick, 1994).

Causes of Chromosomal Abnormalities

Chromosomal abnormalities are caused by many factors, some genetic and some environmental (such as viruses contracted by the mother during pregnancy). However, the variable that most often correlates with chromosomal abnormalities is maternal age. According to one detailed estimate, a 20-year-old woman has about 1 chance in 800 of carrying a fetus with Down syndrome; a 39-year-old woman has 1 chance in 67; and a 44-year-old woman has 1 chance in 16 (see Appendix A for the month-by-month, age-specific incidence). Other chromosomal abnormalities are less common, but virtually all follow an age-related pattern (Snijders & Nicolaides, 1996). Since about half of all fetuses with these abnormalities are aborted spontaneously, and some others are aborted by choice, the actual birth rate of infants with chromosomal abnormalities is lower than these statistics suggest.

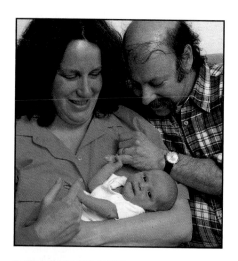

Not Too Old to Have a Baby The fact that older parents have a higher risk of conceiving an embryo with chromosomal abnormalities should not obscure another reality: With modern medical care and prenatal testing, pregnancies that occur when the parents are in their forties can, and almost always do, result in healthy babies.

Harmful Genes

While relatively few people are born with abnormal chromosomes, everyone has at least 20 genes (usually additive or recessive) that could produce serious diseases or handicaps in one's offspring and, in some cases, in oneself. Relatively few of these diseases or handicaps have been traced to a person's particular genetic code. Nonetheless, to date, close to 7,000 genetic disorders have already been named and described, many of them exceedingly rare (McKusick, 1994).

Most of the *known* genetic disorders are dominant, since whenever the gene for such a disorder is inherited, it is apparent in the person's phenotype. With a few exceptions, dominant disorders are not seriously disabling because people with disabling dominant disorders are unlikely to have children, and thus unlikely to pass their genes on. One exception is *Huntington's chorea,* a central nervous system disease caused by a gene that remains inactive until adulthood, by which time a person could have had many children (as the original Mr. Huntington did).

Another dominant disorder that can be serious is *Tourette syndrome,* which is quite common—perhaps because its severity varies widely. About 30 percent of those who inherit the gene exhibit recurrent uncontrollable tics and explosive outbursts of verbal obscenities. The remaining 70 percent experience milder symptoms, such as an occasional twitch that is barely noticeable and a postponable impulse to speak inappropriately. In much the same way as we all resist the impulse to publicly scratch a private spot, a person who has the dominant Tourette syndrome gene but not the full manifestation might go to an empty room, close the door, and only then yell profanities.

Although fewer in number than dominant genetic disorders, recessive and multifactorial disorders claim many more victims, largely because such disorders can pass unchecked (and unnoticed) from carrier to carrier for generations. As a result, carrier status can easily become widespread in a population. Among the more common recessive disorders are cystic fibrosis, thalassemia, and sickle-cell anemia, with as many as 1 in 12 North Americans being a carrier for one or another of the three. (See Table 3.2 on pages 90–91.)

CHOICES TO MAKE

Until recently, the parents of a child with a serious or even fatal genetic disease or a serious chromosomal disorder did not know the cause. They continued to have children, who were also likely to have the problem or be carriers of it. Today, many prospective parents worry about their genes, partly because almost every adult knows a relative with a serious disease that may well be genetic. **Genetic counseling** can help relieve such worries. At the same time, it can prepare families and physicians in cases where a genetic disorder is likely to occur.

genetic counseling Consultation and testing that enables individuals to learn about their genetic heritage, including conditions that might affect future children.

Genetic Counseling

In general, prenatal, preconceptual, or even prenuptial genetic counseling and testing are recommended for:

- Individuals who have a parent, sibling, or child with a serious genetic condition
- Couples who have a history of early spontaneous abortions, stillbirths, or infertility
- Couples who are from the same ethnic group or subgroup—especially if the group is a small one with a high rate of intermarriage, and most particularly if the couple are relatives
- Women over age 34

When a couple begins counseling, the counselor constructs a family history, charting patterns of health and sickness over the generations, particularly with regard to early deaths and unexplained symptoms. The counselor

Genetic Counseling in Action Early in genetic counseling the prospective parents typically view a chart, such as the one held by the female counselor, that helps them understand inheritance patterns and risks. The counselors also look for signs that the two individuals will be able to understand and mutually decide on their next steps.

❓ *Observational Quiz (see answer page 92): At least one sign is evident that these two prospective parents will face their dilemma together. What is it?*

| table **3.2** | **Common Genetic Diseases and Conditions** |

Name	Description	Prognosis	Methods of Inheritance	Incidence*	Carrier Detection†	Prenatal Detection?
Alzheimer's disease	Loss of memory and increasing mental impairment.	Eventual death, often after years of dependency.	Some forms are definitely genetic; others are not.	Fewer than 1 in 100 middle-aged adults; 20 percent of all adults over age 80.	No	No
Cleft palate, cleft lip	The two sides of the upper lip or palate are not joined.	Correctable by surgery.	Multifactorial. Drugs taken during pregnancy or stress may be involved.	1 baby in every 700. More common in Asian Americans and Native Americans; rare in African Americans.	No	Yes
Club foot	The foot and ankle are twisted, making it impossible to walk normally.	Correctable by surgery.	Multifactorial.	1 baby in every 200. More common in boys.	No	Yes
Cystic fibrosis	Mucous obstructions, especially in lungs and digestive organs, due to a missing enzyme.	Most live to middle adulthood.	Recessive gene. Also spontaneous mutations.	1 European American baby in every 2,500. 1 in 20 European Americans is a carrier.	Usually (some are mutations.)	Yes, in some cases
Diabetes	Abnormal metabolism of sugar because body does not produce enough insulin.	Early onset is fatal unless controlled by insulin. Late onset (in adulthood) increases the risk of other diseases.	Multifactorial. Exact pattern hard to predict because environment is crucial.	1 child in 500 is born diabetic. More common in Native Americans. 1 elderly adult in 10 is diabetic.	No	No
Hemophilia	Absence of clotting factor in blood.	Crippling and death from internal bleeding. Blood transfusions can reduce or prevent damage.	X-linked recessive. Also spontaneous mutations.	1 in 10,000 males. Royal families of England, Russia, and Germany had it.	Yes	Yes
Hydro-cephalus	Obstruction causes excess water in the brain.	Can produce brain damage and death. Surgery sometimes makes normal life possible.	Multifactorial.	1 baby in every 100.	No	Yes
Muscular dystrophy (13 separate diseases)	Weakening of muscles. Some forms begin in childhood, others in adulthood.	Inability to walk, move; wasting away and sometimes death.	Duchenne's is X-linked; other forms are recessive or multifactorial.	1 in every 3,500 males will develop Duchenne's; about 10,000 Americans have a form of MD.	Yes, for some forms	Yes, for some forms

*Incidence statistics vary from country to country; those given here are for the United States. All these diseases can occur in any ethnic group. When certain groups have a high incidence, it is noted here.
†Studying the family tree can help geneticists spot a possible carrier of many genetic diseases or, in some cases, a definite carrier. However, here "Yes" means that a carrier can be detected even without knowledge of family history.

Name	Description	Prognosis	Methods of Inheritance	Incidence*	Carrier Detection†	Prenatal Detection?
Neural tube defects (open spine)	Two main forms: *anencephaly* (parts of the brain are missing) and *spina bifida* (the lower portion of the spine is not closed).	Often, early death. Anencephalic children are severely retarded; children with spina bifida have difficulties with lower body control.	Multifactorial; defect occurs in first weeks of pregnancy.	Anencephaly: 1 in 1,000 births; spina bifida: 3 in 1,000. More common in those of Welsh and Scottish descent.	No	Yes
Phenylketonuria (PKU)	Abnormal digestion of protein.	Mental retardation, hyperactivity. Preventable by diet.	Recessive gene.	1 in 15,000 births. 1 in 100 European Americans is a carrier. More common in those of Norwegian and Irish descent.	Yes	Yes
Pyloric stenosis	Overgrowth of muscle in intestine.	Vomiting, loss of weight, eventual death. Correctable by surgery.	Multifactorial.	1 male in 200; 1 female in 1,000. Less common in African Americans.	No	No
Sickle-cell anemia	Abnormal blood cells.	Possible painful "crisis"; heart and kidney failure. Treatable with drugs.	Recessive gene.	1 in 500 African-American babies is affected. 1 in 10 African Americans is a carrier, as is 1 in 20 Latinos.	Yes	Yes
Spina bifida: see *Neural tube defects.*						
Tay-Sachs disease	Enzyme disease.	Apparently healthy infant becomes progressively weaker, usually dying by age 5.	Recessive gene.	1 in 4,000 births. 1 in 30 American Jews and 1 in 20 French Canadians are carriers.	Yes	Yes
Thalassemia	Abnormal blood cells.	Paleness and listlessness, low resistance to infections.	Recessive gene.	1 in 10 Greek, Italian, Thai, and Indian Americans is a carrier.	Yes	Yes
Tourette syndrome	Uncontrollable tics, body jerking, verbal obscenities.	Often imperceptible in children; worsens with age.	Dominant gene.	1 in 500 births.	Sometimes	No

Sources: Bowman & Murray, 1990; Brunn & Brunn, 1994; Caskey, 1992; Connor & Ferguson-Smith, 1991; Lee, 1993; McKusick, 1994; National Academy of Sciences, 1994.

then explains the specific conditions and risks for couples of the clients' age, ethnicity, and genetic history and discusses what the options will be if testing reveals that the risk of genetic disorders is high.

The couple then decides whether to proceed with genetic testing. Some may prefer not to know their specific risks if the only way to prevent the birth of a child with a serious genetic disorder is surgical sterility or abortion—options some couples will not consider. Others want to know all the possibilities and options, believing they will make the best decision only after learning all they can. At this point, the couple learns more about the reliability of the various tests, which are never 100 percent accurate. There is always a possibility of *false negatives* (the disorder is present, but the test does not indicate it) or *false positives* (the disorder is not present, but the test indicates it is).

If a couple chooses to be tested, what is involved?

Testing

Sometimes searching the parents' genotype for signs of a particular disorder is quite simple. Blood tests, for example, detect carriers of the genes for sickle-cell anemia, Tay-Sachs disease, PKU, hemophilia, thalassemia, and many less common diseases. These tests pose no risk and are quite accurate, especially if unexpected or ambiguous results are confirmed by further testing. Chromosomal analysis of the parents can indicate fragile *X*, as well as the inherited form of Down syndrome.

Detection of other disorders is more difficult because the culprit genes have not yet been precisely identified. In many cases, research has identified only roughly where on a particular chromosome the troublesome gene is likely to be located. This enables scientists to identify **markers,** which are specific gene sequences or genetic traits, harmless in themselves, that typically occur when the disorder in question is present (Plomin et al., 1997).

markers Particular genetic traits, physiological characteristics, or gene clusters that suggest the presence of a genetic disorder.

A Six-Fingered Dwarf? Being born with six fingers is a rare, minor genetic abnormality, of no consequence if it occurs alone. However, it sometimes is a marker for more serious recessive problems, including dwarfism.
❓ *Observational Quiz (see answer page 95):*
Although six fingers is a marker for a genetic abnormality that includes short stature, large head, and learning difficulties, something here indicates that this boy will be of normal size. What is it?

Some markers can be detected through QTL analysis, either of the individual or, for some disorders, of several family members over at least three generations. Sometimes, markers appear in the phenotype as well as in the genotype. An oddly shaped earlobe or finger, or a particular pattern of eye movement, or a peculiar formation of the toes may signal the presence of a certain problematic gene.

The information gathered about the genotypes of prospective parents can, in many cases, lead to a fairly precise calculation of the odds of their having a child with a specific genetic disorder. For example, if *one* parent has a gene for a dominant disorder, each child has a 50 percent chance of inheriting that gene and, thus, the disorder. If *both* parents are carriers of a certain recessive disorder, each of their offspring has a 25 percent chance of inheriting the recessive gene from both parents and therefore of hav-

❓ Especially for Parents: Which do you
believe you would find harder: coping with
the fact that you might carry a genetic disorder, undergoing tests for the disorder, or
making a decision about what to do after
the tests?

Figure 3.6 At-Risk Decision Making. With the
help of a genetic counselor, even couples who
know they run a risk of having a baby with a
genetic defect might decide to have a child.
Although the process of making that decision
is more complicated for them than it is for
couples with no family genetic illness and no
positive tests for harmful recessive genes, the
outcome is usually a healthy baby. Genetic
counselors provide facts and alternatives;
couples make decisions.

ing the disorder. (The probability is the same as that in the case [Figure 3.3] of two brown-eyed parents who both have the recessive gene for blue eyes and thus have a one-in-four chance of having a blue-eyed offspring.) If only one parent is a carrier of a recessive gene, there is no chance that the child will have the disorder.

In considering such odds, one must realize that *chance has no memory,* which means that the odds apply afresh to each child the couple has. If both partners have the recessive gene for sickle-cell anemia, for instance, and the couple has several children, then all of them, some of them, or none of them could have the disease. Probability laws tell us that one child in four will be afflicted, two in four will be carriers, and one in four will not even be a carrier. But gametes do not consult probability laws; nor do they remember the fate of earlier pregnancies before deciding which sperm and ovum should fuse.

Of course, genetic counseling does not eliminate all problems. Even when a couple has been counseled and tested for genetic conditions and found to be at low risk, the couple may still have a child with genetic disease, either because of a spontaneous mutation or because certain tests are not yet accurate or even available. In some cases, prenatal testing can provide further information (see Changing Policy, page 94).

Many Alternatives

Most couples who undergo genetic counseling and testing have a relatively easy decision to make, discovering perhaps that only one partner carries a harmful recessive trait and that therefore none of their children will have the disease. Or perhaps they learn that their odds of bearing a child with a serious illness are not much higher than those for any other couple, and thus the childbearing decision rests on psychological or financial factors more than genetic ones. Similarly, prenatal testing usually reveals that all is okay or that special treatment during birth and infancy will remedy the problem.

Even if couples learn that both partners are carriers of a serious condition or that they are at high risk in other ways, they still have many alternatives, as Figure 3.6 indicates. Some may avoid pregnancy and, perhaps, plan adoption. Some might choose a reproductive alternative such as artificial insemination with donor sperm, in vitro fertilization with a donor ovum, or in vitro fertilization using the parents' own gametes but then testing the cell mass to determine the genetic

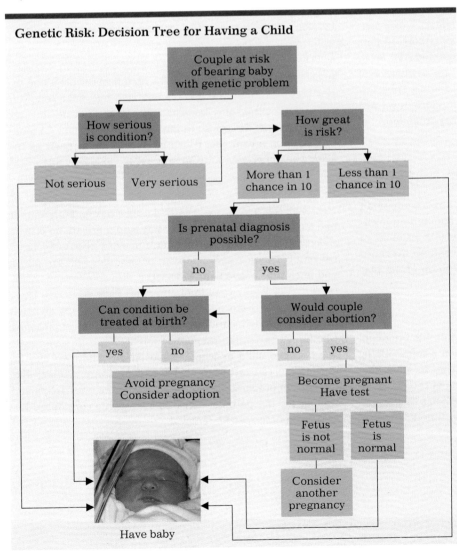
Genetic Risk: Decision Tree for Having a Child

PRENATAL DIAGNOSIS

Within the past 20 years, researchers have refined dozens of tests to determine if a fetus is developing well. Many of these are now routine, recommended for every pregnancy. For example, blood tests are used to reveal whether the mother has had diseases that might harm the fetus; various measurements are taken to tell whether fetal growth and development are occurring on schedule; urine analysis and blood-pressure readings are used to indicate how well the mother's system is coping with her pregnancy.

Many other tests are not routine. They are used selectively—especially when there is some likelihood of genetic or chromosomal difficulty or prenatal damage. The five tests we describe below demonstrate the amazing sophistication and awesome implications of prenatal diagnosis today.

Alphafetoprotein Assay

Analyzing the level of alphafetoprotein (AFP) in the mother's blood is useful for indicating neural-tube defects, Down syndrome, or the presence of multiple embryos. About 10 percent of all pregnant women exhibit an unexpected AFP level, but most of these are false alarms, caused by miscalculation of the age of the fetus or some other normal variation. Thus, unexpected AFP levels indicate mainly that more tests are needed; usually, the new tests reveal a normal pregnancy.

Sonogram

The sonogram, or ultrasound image, uses high-frequency sound waves (like sonar) to produce a "picture" of the fetus. Sonograms can reveal problems such as an abnormally small head or other body malformations, excess spinal fluid accumulating on the brain, and several diseases (for instance, of the kidney). In addition, sonograms are used to diagnose twins, estimate fetal age, determine the position of the placenta, and reveal the rate of fetal growth.

Fetoscopy

In fetoscopy, a very narrow tube is inserted into the pregnant woman's abdomen, piercing the uterus. Then a fetoscope (a viewing instrument) is inserted into the tube, to allow the physician to observe the fetus and the inside of the placenta directly. Fetoscopy is most often performed when a malformation is suspected. With a slightly different instrument, it is also used to take a blood sample from the placenta or the umbilicus or to take a blood, skin, or liver sample directly from the fetus to diagnose a suspected abnormality of the blood, immune, or organ system.

Amniocentesis

In amniocentesis, about half an ounce of the fluid surrounding the fetus, inside the placenta, is withdrawn through the mother's abdominal wall with a syringe. The fluid contains sloughed-off fetal cells that can be analyzed to detect chromosomal abnormalities as well as many other genetic and prenatal problems. The amniotic fluid also reveals the sex of the fetus (useful knowledge if an X-linked disorder is likely) and provides clues about fetal age and health. Amniocentesis has been the "mainstay" of prenatal diagnosis since 1973 (Evans et al., 1989). However, it has one decided disadvantage: It cannot be performed until midpregnancy, about 14 weeks after conception, when there is sufficient fluid available for sampling.

Chorionic Villi Sampling

In chorionic villi sampling (CVS), a sample of the placental tissue that surrounds the fetus is obtained and analyzed. This test provides the same information as that obtained through amniocentesis, with close to the same accuracy, but CVS has one decided advantage: It can be performed as early as the sixth week of pregnancy (Carlson, 1994).

Risks and Benefits

Nearly all these tests are regarded as low risk for both mother and fetus. The AFP is completely safe, and there are no proven risks with the sonogram. However, 1 in every 200 amniocenteses and between 1 and 2 percent of chorionic villi samplings and fetoscopies have been associated with spontaneous abortions that probably would not otherwise have occurred. Thus, before any of these tests, the risk of spontaneous abortion must be weighed carefully against the benefit of knowing whether a particular pregnancy might result in a seriously handicapped child or whether special prenatal care may be needed (Serra-Pratt et al., 1998). As with every medical test, the risks of prenatal diagnosis—including the uncertainty and waiting for the parents—must be thoroughly considered before the benefits can be realized.

❶ *Answer to Observational Quiz (from page 92):*
He shares the six-finger abnormality with his
grandfather, who is fully grown.

❶ **Response for Parents (from page 93):** Since
every family has some genetic disorders,
you have probably already come to terms
with the fact that you might carry one. As
the text explains, the tests are usually quite
simple. Thus, the hardest part, usually, is
making the decision—many people find
themselves stressed, confused, and
ambivalent about what to do.

situation before inserting it into the uterus. If testing during pregnancy shows serious problems, a couple can consider abortion or, alternatively, begin gathering information that will help the partners deal with the child-care problems that may lie ahead.

Some may decide to postpone pregnancy until promising treatments—either prenatal or postnatal—are further developed. Genetic engineering is the most innovative of these; but many other, more conventional, treatments have already made a dramatic difference for those with sickle-cell anemia, cystic fibrosis, and various other conditions.

Genetic engineering is the altering of an organism's genetic instructions through the insertion of additional genes (or, sometimes with lower animals such as mice, through the removal of certain genes in the early stages of development). In humans, genetic engineering involves adding normal genes, either indirectly via a blood transfusion or bone marrow transplant or directly into a particular cluster of cells, thereby enabling the body to replace ailing cells with healthy ones (Anderson, 1995; Lyon & Gorner, 1995). The technique is being used experimentally for hemophilia, cystic fibrosis, rheumatoid arthritis, several types of cancer, and dozens of rarer diseases, and some encouraging results have been obtained.

In the most celebrated use of genetic engineering to date, a dying 4-year-old, Ashanti De Silva, received the very first human genetic transfusion, in 1990, to remedy a severe immune deficiency known as SCID. One gene on the pair of chromosomes at site 20 causes SCID when it fails to instruct for a particular enzyme. Deficiency of this enzyme had left Ashanti defenseless against any form of infection, requiring her to live in near isolation. Now, as a result of her treatment, Ashanti not only survives but thrives, experiencing all the scrapes and sniffles of a normal child with no adverse effects. However, while Ashanti's case is a sign of hope for millions of people with inherited and acquired diseases, many experts caution against overoptimism. So far, the successes of genetic engineering have been rare and partial (Crystal, 1995).

Obviously, decisions about conception are not based simply on genetic analysis. Two couples with identical odds of conceiving zygotes with the same condition might make quite different choices—depending on their age, ethnicity, religion, finances, ethics, and personal relationship and on the number and health status of any other children they may have—or two couples with the same amniocentesis results might make opposite decisions (Asch et al., 1996). Thus, counseling begins with objective facts but ends with a very personal decision. Indeed, throughout this chapter, it is apparent that conception is not only a biological event. Personal decisions and social values affect every aspect of development, beginning at conception and continuing through prenatal development and birth (the topics of the next chapter) and beyond.

Survivors Ashanti De Silva (right) was the first human recipient of a genetic transfusion. She is shown with Cynthia Cutshall, another girl with SCID who would have died if she had been born 2 years earlier. In Cynthia's case, advanced genetic analysis discovered her genetic defect just as advanced biotechnology transformed an enzyme from cows into a drug that would help humans with SCID. As you can see, both girls are alive and well, able to do something their parents would otherwise never let them do: visit a public place that contains living plants.

SUMMARY

THE BEGINNING OF DEVELOPMENT

1. Conception occurs when a sperm penetrates and fuses with an ovum, creating a single cell called a zygote. The zygote contains all the genetic material—half from each of the two gametes—needed to create a unique developing person.

2. Genes contain the chemically coded instructions that cells need to become specialized and to perform specific functions in the body. Genes are arranged on chromosomes. With the exception of gametes, every human cell contains 23 pairs of chromosomes, with one member of each pair contributed by each parent. Every cell contains a duplicate of the genetic information in the first cell, the zygote.

3. Twenty-two pairs of chromosomes control the development of most of the body. The twenty-third pair determines, among other things, the individual's sex: zygotes with an XY combination will become males; those with an XX combination will become females.

4. Genes provide genetic continuity across the human species, ensuring that we all share common physical structures, behavioral tendencies, and reproductive potential. Genes also ensure the genetic diversity that allows our species to continue to evolve through adaptation and natural selection.

5. Each person has a unique combination of genes, with one important exception. Sometimes a zygote separates completely into two or more genetically identical organisms, creating monozygotic (identical) twins, triplets, and so on, all with the same genes.

FROM GENOTYPE TO PHENOTYPE

6. The sum total of all the genes a person inherits is the person's genotype. The expression of those genes, in combination with the many influences of the environment, is the person's phenotype, or observable traits.

7. The various genes in the genotype interact in many ways to influence the phenotype. Most often, genes from both parents contribute to a trait in an additive fashion, both having an influence on the trait. Sometimes genes act in a nonadditive pattern. The dominant-recessive pattern is one such case: the phenotype reflects the influence of the dominant gene for the trait, while the recessive gene's effects are obscured.

8. Some genes are located only on the X chromosome. Traits controlled by such genes are passed from mother to son but not from father to son, because a male inherits his only X chromosome from his mother. Females inherit two X chromosomes, one from each parent. Thus, males are likely to express recessive traits, such as color blindness, that are X-linked. Females are likely to be carriers of X-linked disorders but not to express them.

9. Genes affect almost every human trait, including intellectual abilities, personality patterns, and mental illnesses. Similarly, from the moment of conception and throughout life, the environment influences genetic tendencies. Gene-environment interaction is thus ongoing and complex. Twin studies are often used to separate genetic and environmental influences.

GENETIC AND CHROMOSOMAL ABNORMALITIES

10. Chromosomal abnormalities occur when the zygote has too few or too many chromosomes or when a chromosome has a missing, a nonfunctioning, or an extra piece of genetic material. Most embryos with chromosomal abnormalities are spontaneously aborted early in pregnancy.

11. Babies who survive with chromosomal defects usually have extra, or missing, sex chromosomes. One of the most common abnormalities of the sex chromosomes is fragile-X syndrome, which actually has a genetic origin; it is often accompanied by some mental deficiency, particularly in males.

12. The most common chromosomal abnormality that does not involve the sex chromosomes occurs when an extra chromosome is attached to the twenty-first pair. This causes trisomy-21, or Down syndrome, a varying cluster of problems in physical and intellectual functioning.

13. Every individual carries some genes for genetic handicaps and diseases. However, most of the dominant disorders are not seriously disabling. Recessive disorders claim more victims and can be disabling or lethal, but they remain common because carriers are unaware that they can pass on a destructive gene—until their offspring express the disorder.

CHOICES TO MAKE

14. Genetic testing and an evaluation of family background can help predict whether a couple will have a child with a genetic problem. If there is a high probability that they will, they have several options, such as adopting a child, remaining childless, or obtaining prenatal diagnosis and, if the diagnosis confirms a serious problem, considering abortion.

KEY TERMS

sperm (67)
ovum (67)
gamete (67)
zygote (67)
gene (68)
chromosome (68)
genetic code (68)
twenty-third pair (69)
monozygotic twins (71)
dizygotic twins (71)
infertile (72)
in vitro fertilization (IVF) (73)
polygenic traits (75)
multifactorial traits (75)
genotype (76)

phenotype (76)
carrier (76)
additive pattern (76)
nonadditive pattern (76)
dominant-recessive pattern (76)
X-linked genes (77)
genetic imprinting (78)
environment (79)
syndrome (86)
trisomy-21 (Down syndrome) (86)
fragile-X syndrome (87)
genetic counseling (89)
markers (92)

KEY QUESTIONS

1. How is genetic diversity among people ensured, and why is this important?

2. In what ways does genetics affect fertility and infertility?

3. What is the difference between phenotype and genotype?

4. What are the differences between the additive pattern of gene-gene interaction and the dominant-recessive pattern?

5. Why is the expression of a recessive X-linked gene affected by whether a male or a female inherits it?

6. What research strategies are used to separate genetic influences on psychological characteristics from environmental influences?

7. How can environment influence genetic physical traits, such as height, and psychological traits, such as shyness?

8. Which is more serious and which is more common: dominant genetic disorders or recessive genetic disorders?

9. What factors determine whether a couple is at risk for having a child with genetic abnormalities?

10. How can genetic counseling help parents who are at risk for having a child with genetic problems?

11. *In Your Experience* What would you do if you knew you were the carrier of a gene for a serious disease?

CRITICAL THINKING EXERCISE

by Richard O. Straub

Take your study of Chapter 3 a step further by working this practical problem-solving exercise.

Conception brings together genetic instructions from both parents for every human characteristic. How these genetic instructions work to influence the specific characteristics of an offspring is usually quite complex, because most traits are both polygenic and multifactorial, and gene-gene interaction can occur in several different patterns. Based on what you studied in this chapter, however, you should be able to answer the following questions. (*Hint:* You might find it helpful to diagram some of the situations as in Figure 3.3, using uppercase letters to indicate dominant genes and lowercase letters to indicate recessive genes.)

1. A dark-skinned woman, whose parents and grandparents all had very dark skin, marries a light-skinned man, whose parents and grandparents were all very light-skinned. What is the probable skin tone of their offspring?

2. A man with red hair (recessive) marries a woman with black hair (dominant) whose mother had red hair. What are the chances that their first child will have red hair? Black hair?

3. A woman and a man both have brown eyes, but their first child has blue eyes. What are the chances that their second child will have blue eyes?

4. An apparently healthy couple has one normal daughter and then a son, who later develops Duchenne's dystrophy, an X-linked recessive disease. What are the chances that the boy's sister is a carrier of the disability? What chance is there that the sister will develop the disability herself?

Check your answers by comparing them to the sample answers in Appendix B.

Prenatal Development and Birth

CHAPTER 4

As we saw in Chapter 1, every moment of development results from continuing interaction among all three domains, influenced by contexts of many kinds. This is as true in the first 9 months of life as it is in the 900 or so that follow.

Our primary focus now is on the astounding biological transformation from a single-cell zygote to a fully formed baby. However, the specifics and later impact of this growth are deeply influenced by the mother-to-be's health habits and activities, the community's laws and practices affecting toxins and diseases, and the culture's customs regarding birth itself. These are just some of the myriad contextual factors that make some newborns—those fortunate enough to be born to certain mothers in certain communities and cultures—much better prepared for a long and happy life than others. And that is the underlying theme of this chapter: How adult perceptions and actions affect what is arguably the most important developmental period, and then the most significant day, of a human life.

FROM ZYGOTE TO NEWBORN

The process of human growth before birth is generally discussed in terms of three main periods. The first 2 weeks of development are called the **germinal period;** from the third week through the eighth week is the **period of the embryo;** and from the ninth week until birth is the **period of the fetus.**

The Germinal Period: The First 14 Days

Within hours after conception, the one-cell zygote, traveling slowly down the fallopian tube toward the uterus, begins the process of cell division and growth. The zygote first divides into two cells, which soon become four, then eight, then sixteen, and so on. As explained in Chapter 3, at least through the third doubling, each of these cells is identical, and any one of them could (and sometimes does) become a complete human being.

As you also saw in Chapter 3, at about the eight-cell stage the process of differentiation begins, in which the cells take on distinct characteristics and gravitate toward particular locations that foreshadow the types of cells they will become. One unmistakable sign of differentiation occurs about a week after conception, when the multiplying cells (now numbering more than a hundred) separate into two distinct masses. The outer cells form a protective circle that will become the *placenta* (which is discussed shortly), and the inner cells form a nucleus that will become the embryo.

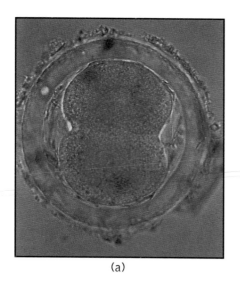

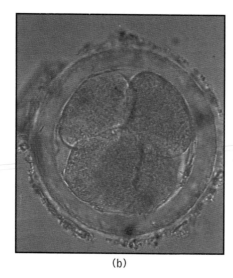

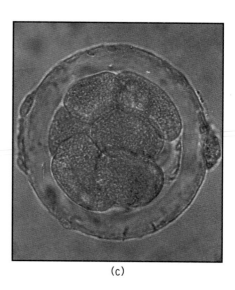

(a)   (b)   (c)

First Stages of the Germinal Period The original zygote as it divides into *(a)* two cells, *(b)* four cells, and *(c)* eight cells. Occasionally at this early stage, the cells separate completely, forming the beginning of monozygotic twins, quadruplets, or octuplets.

germinal period The first 2 weeks of development after conception; characterized by rapid cell division and the beginning of cell differentiation.

period of the embryo From approximately the third through the eighth weeks after conception, the period during which the rudimentary forms of all anatomical structures develop.

period of the fetus From the ninth week after conception until birth, the period during which the organs grow in size and complexity.

implantation Beginning about a week after conception, the burrowing of the organism into the lining of the uterus, where it can be nourished and protected during growth.

❷ **Especially for Fathers:** When does a man's nongenetic influence on his children begin?

Implantation

The first task of the outer cells is to achieve **implantation,** that is, to embed themselves in the nurturant environment of the uterus. This is accomplished as the cells nestle into the uterine lining, rupturing tiny blood vessels in order to obtain nourishment from them and to build a connective web of membranes and blood vessels that links the mother and the developing organism. It is this connective web that will allow the organism to grow over the next 9 months or so. Implantation is far from automatic, however. An estimated 58 percent of all natural conceptions fail to become properly implanted (Gilbert et al., 1987) (see Table 4.1), so the new life ends even before the embryo begins to form or the woman suspects she is pregnant.

If accomplished, implantation triggers hormonal changes that halt the woman's usual menstrual cycle, elevate her body temperature slightly, make her tired, increase the supply of blood to her breasts, and cause many other body changes that nurture the new life. For many women, cigarette smoke becomes nauseating, coffee tastes bitter, and many other substances are less palatable, which may be nature's way of protecting the future baby before the mother knows she is pregnant. Even heavy drinkers and drug abusers sometimes moderate their habits.

A woman who hopes and plans for a baby usually notices these first hints of body change and then makes an effort to live a more healthy life. But these same early signs may produce the opposite reaction in women who dread pregnancy but nonetheless conceive; their unhealthy reactions lead to a high rate of spontaneous abortions, stillbirths, and low-birthweight newborns (Bustan & Coker, 1994).

Of course, the distinction between wanted and unwanted pregnancies is a rather complex issue. For example, couples who use "natural" contraception, abstaining from sex when the woman ovulates, conceive far more often than those who use a contraceptive pill or spermicide and condom. However, when miscalculations of the woman's rhythm lead to an unplanned pregnancy, the rate of complications is low, not high—no higher, in fact, than that with planned pregnancies (Bitto et al., 1997). The probable reason is that many couples who choose this form of contraception do so for religious reasons. If they conceive anyway, they are likely to believe that God wanted this particular conception to occur, and so they nurture the unplanned embryo just as if they had planned it.

table **4.1**	**The Vulnerability of Prenatal Development**

The Germinal Period

From the moment of conception until 14 days later. Fifty-eight percent of all developing organisms fail to grow or implant properly, and thus do not survive the germinal period. Most of these organisms were grossly abnormal.

The Period of the Embryo

From 14 days until 56 days after conception. During this time all the major external and internal body structures begin to form. About 20 percent of all embryos are aborted spontaneously, most often because of chromosomal abnormalities.

The Period of the Fetus

From the ninth week after conception until birth. About 5 percent of all fetuses are aborted spontaneously before viability at 22 weeks or are stillborn after 22 weeks.

Birth

Only 31 percent of all conceptions survive prenatal development to become living newborn babies.

Sources: Carlson, 1994; Gilbert et al., 1987; Moore & Persaud, 1998.

The expectant mother's activities are affected by her social contexts as well as her own cognition. For example, one California study focused on 545 low-income women, about half of them teenagers, pregnant with their first child. Many did not begin prenatal care until after the first 3 months. For all these reasons (income, age, lack of medical attention), their rate of birth complications should have been higher than the U.S. average, but it was not. In fact, only 2.6 percent of their births were low-birthweight infants, a rate far lower than the U.S. average of more than 7 percent. The probable reason is that these women had more encouragement from their babies' fathers and from their culture than the average pregnant woman has, and underlying this is the fact that these women had been born in Mexico.

Even compared to similar women of Mexican ancestry but born in California, more were living with the father (72 percent) and overall they experienced less stress, used fewer substances before and during pregnancy, and, as noted, had fewer birth complications (Zambrana et al., 1997). Similar trends, in which low-income immigrants have fewer underweight newborns than expected, have been found in other nations (Israel, Spain, and Belgium)—and again the trends are explained by more support from the father and the culture and less drug use (Buekens et al., 1998).

The Period of the Embryo: The Third Through Eighth Weeks

The start of the third week after conception initiates the *period of the embryo,* during which the formless mass of cells becomes a distinct being. First the developing organism begins differentiating into three layers, each of which eventually forms key body systems. Then a perceptible sign of body formation appears, a fold in the outer layer of cells. At 22 days after conception this fold becomes the **neural tube,** which will later develop into the central nervous system, including the brain and spinal column (Larsen, 1998).

Throughout prenatal development, growth proceeds in two directions: from the head downward, called **cephalo-caudal development** (literally, "from head to tail"), and from the center (that is, the spine) outward, called **proximo-distal development** (literally, "from near to far"). Thus the most vital organs and body parts form first, before the extremities.

The head starts to take shape in the fourth week after conception. It begins as a featureless protrusion. Within days, eyes, ears, nose, and mouth start to form. Also in the fourth week, a blood vessel that will become the heart begins to pulsate, making the cardiovascular system the first to show any sign of activity. By the fifth week, in the cephalo-caudal sequence, the parts of the body that are downward and more distant from the head and heart begin to develop: buds that will become arms and legs appear, and a

neural tube A fold of outer embryonic cells that appears about 3 weeks after conception and later develops into the central nervous system.

cephalo-caudal development Growth and maturation of the human body that progresses from the head downward. This sequence is obvious in prenatal development; it continues throughout childhood.

proximo-distal development Growth and maturation of the human body that progresses from the spine outward.

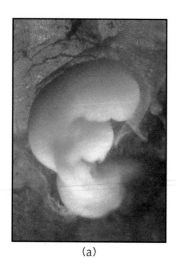
(a)

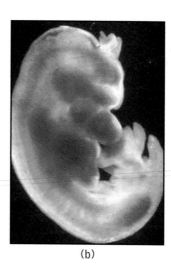
(b)

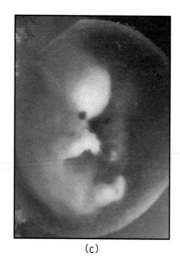
(c)

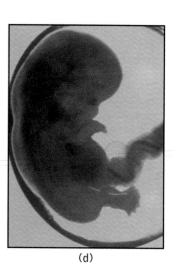
(d)

The Embryonic Period *(a)* At 4 weeks past conception, the embryo is only about ⅛ inch (3 millimeters) long, but already the head *(top right)* has taken shape. *(b)* At 5 weeks past conception, the embryo has grown to twice the size it was at 4 weeks. Its primitive heart, which has been pulsing for a week now, is visible, as is what appears to be a primitive tail, which will soon be enclosed by skin and protective tissue at the tip of the backbone (the coccyx). *(c)* By 7 weeks, the organism is somewhat less than an inch (2½ centimeters) long. Eyes, nose, the digestive system, and even the first stage of toe formation can be seen. *(d)* At 8 weeks, the 1-inch-long organism is clearly recognizable as a human fetus.

tail-like appendage extends from the spine. The embryo at 5 weeks is about ¼ inch (6 millimeters) long—about 7,000 times the size of the zygote it was a month before.

In the proximo-distal sequence, the upper arms and then the forearms, the palms, and webbed fingers appear about 5 weeks after conception. Legs, feet, and webbed toes, in that order, emerge a few days later, each having the beginning of a skeletal structure (Larsen, 1998).

At 8 weeks after conception, the embryo weighs about ⅓₀ ounce (1 gram) and is about 1 inch (2½ centimeters) long. The head has become more rounded than the narrow protrusion it was, and the features of the face are formed. The embryo has all the basic organs and body parts (except sex organs) of a human being, including elbows and knees. The fingers and toes have become distinct and separate (at 52 and 54 days after conception, respectively), and the "tail" is no longer visible, having been incorporated into the lower spine at about 55 days. The organism is now ready for another name: *fetus.*

The Period of the Fetus: The Ninth Week Until Birth

The future baby is called a fetus until it is born. That one name covers tremendous change, from a tiny, sexless creature smaller than the final joint of your thumb to a boy or girl who could nest comfortably in your arms. We will now describe some of the details of this transformation.

The Third Month

During the third month, the sex organs take discernible shape. The first stage of their development actually occurs at the sixth week, with the appearance of the *indifferent gonad,* a cluster of cells that can develop into male or female sex organs. Through the seventh week, males and females are virtually identical (Larsen, 1998). Then, if the embryo is male *(XY),* a gene on the *Y* chromosome sends a biochemical signal that initiates the development of male sexual organs. If the embryo is female *(XX),* no such signal is sent and the indifferent gonad soon begins to develop female sex organs, first the vagina and uterus and then the external structures (Koopman et al., 1991).

Sex organs take several weeks to develop, but by the twelfth week after conception the external genital organs are fully formed. At the end of the

⚠ **Response for Fathers (from page 100):**
Before conception, through his influence on the mother's attitudes and health.

placenta The organ that connects the circulatory system of a mother with that of her growing embryo. It allows nourishment to flow to the embryo and wastes to flow away but maintains the separation of the two circulatory systems.

third month, the fetus has all its body parts, weighs approximately 3 ounces (87 grams), and is about 3 inches (7.5 centimeters) long. You should be aware, though, that early prenatal growth is very rapid, so there is considerable variation from fetus to fetus, especially in body weight. The numbers given above—3 months, 3 ounces, 3 inches—have been rounded off for easy recollection. (For those on the metric system, "100 days, 100 millimeters, 100 grams" is similarly useful.) Actually, at 12 weeks after conception, the average fetus weighs about 1½ ounces (45 grams), while at 14 weeks the average weight is about 4 ounces (110 grams) (Moore & Persaud, 1998). So you can see that the 3-ounce (100-gram) point is just a moment in a period of rapid change.

The first 3 months, which include the entire germinal and embryonic periods and the beginning of the fetal period, are sometimes called the *first trimester of pregnancy*. "Trimester" literally means "3 months," so a normal 9-month pregnancy is three trimesters long. By the end of the third month, the fetus can and does move almost every part of its body—kicking its legs, sucking its thumb, even squinting and frowning—and changes position easily within the placenta. The 3-month-old fetus also swallows amniotic fluid, digests it, and urinates, providing its tiny organs with practice for the day when it will take in nourishment and excrete wastes on its own.

The Placenta

During these early weeks of life, rapid growth is also occurring in the **placenta,** which contains the growing embryo. This organ is made up primarily of blood vessels that lead to the circulatory systems of both the mother (through the blood vessels that line the uterus) and the embryo (through the umbilical cord, which connects the embryo to the placenta).

The placenta also contains an elaborate network of membranes that prevents the mixing of the two blood supplies. These membranes act as a very fine mesh, like cheesecloth or a fabric that is water-resistant but not waterproof. They enable the developing organism to have its own independent bloodstream and, at the same time, to obtain nourishment from the mother and excrete wastes to the mother. Oxygen, carbohydrates, and vitamins diffuse from the mother's blood vessels, through the placental membranes, and into the embryo's bloodstream, while carbon dioxide and other waste products from the developing organism similarly diffuse into the mother's bloodstream and then are removed through her lungs and kidneys. A pregnant woman is literally breathing, eating, and urinating for two.

The placenta contains not only the developing organism but also the liquid surrounding it, called *amniotic fluid*. The amniotic fluid cushions the embryo and then the fetus, allowing room for activity while absorbing the impact of any sudden blow. By midpregnancy, the fetus expels urine and other material into the fluid (as well as through the umbilical cord). If the fetus does not urinate (because of some abnormality), the resulting insufficiency of amniotic fluid will cause serious defects (Larsen, 1998).

The Second Trimester: Preparing to Survive

In the *middle trimester* (the fourth, fifth, and sixth months), the heartbeat becomes stronger and the digestive and excretory systems develop more fully. Fingernails, toenails, and buds for teeth form, and hair (including eyelashes) grows. Amazing as all that is, the most impressive growth is in the brain, which increases about six times in size and begins to react to stimuli (Carlson, 1994). In fact, in the second trimester, the entire central nervous system first becomes responsive and sentient.

age of viability The age (about 22 weeks after conception) at which a fetus can survive outside the mother's uterus if specialized medical care is available.

These advances in brain functioning may be the critical factor in the fetus's attaining the **age of viability,** that is, the age at which a preterm newborn can survive, because it is the brain that regulates basic body functions, such as breathing and sucking. Viability begins at about 22 weeks after conception (Moore & Persaud, 1998). Babies born before 22 weeks gestational age rarely survive more than a few days, because even the most sophisticated respirators and heart regulators cannot maintain life in a fetus whose brain has not yet begun to function. Even those born at 22 weeks who do survive are nearly always severely brain-damaged.

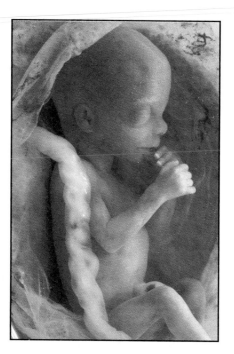

The Fetus At the end of 4 months, this fetus, now 6 inches long, looks fully formed but out of proportion—the distance from the top of the skull to the neck is almost as large as that from the neck to the rump. For many more weeks, the fetus must depend on the translucent membranes of the placenta and umbilical cord (the long white object in the foreground) for survival.

❷ *Observational Quiz (see answer page 107):* Can you see eyebrows, fingernails, and genitals?

At about 28 weeks after conception, brain maturation takes a "striking" leap forward (Carlson, 1994); at that time the brain-wave pattern of the fetus shifts from a flat pattern to one with occasional bursts of activity, resembling the sleep-wake cycles of a newborn. Similarly, because of ongoing brain maturation, at some time between 28 and 32 weeks after conception, the heart rate becomes regulated by body movement (speeding up during activity, slowing during rest) (DiPietro et al., 1996). Largely because of this neurological awakening, the odds of survival are much better for a preterm infant who is at least 28 weeks old. With multiple births, gestational age is particularly important.

Weight is also crucial to viability: a 24-week-old single-born fetus typically weighs about 22 ounces (600 grams) and, even with excellent medical care, is as likely to die as to live (Allen et al., 1993; Reuss & Gordon, 1995). By 28 weeks, the typical fetus weighs about 3 pounds (1,300 grams), and its chances of survival have increased to more than 90 percent. The Nigerian American octuplets, born in December 1998 to the Chukwu family in Houston, Texas, would probably all have survived if they had each weighed at least 2 pounds. The first to die was also the smallest. Even though her gestational age was 28 weeks, her birthweight was only 10.3 ounces (300 grams).

The Third Trimester: From Viability to Full Term

Attaining the age of viability simply means that life outside the womb is *possible.* Each day of the *third trimester* of prenatal growth improves the odds, not only of survival but also of a healthy and happy first few months for baby and parents. A viable preterm infant born in the seventh month is a tiny creature requiring intensive hospital care, dependent on life-support systems for each gram of nourishment and for every shallow breath. By contrast, after 9 months or so (the "due date" is exactly 266 days, or 38 weeks, after conception), the typical full-term infant is a vigorous person, ready to thrive at home on mother's milk—no expert help, oxygenated air, special food, or technical assistance required.

The critical difference between the fragile preterm infant and the robust full-term newborn is maturation of the respiratory and cardiovascular

table **4.2**	Average Prenatal Weights*			
Period of Development	Time After Conception	Weight (Nonmetric)	Metric Weight	Notes
End of embryo period	8 wk	⅟₃₀ oz	1 g	A birthweight below 2 lb (1,000 g) is considered extremely low birthweight (ELBW).
End of first trimester	13 wk	3 oz	100 g	
At viability (50-50) chance of survival	24 wk	22 oz	600 g	
End of second trimester	26–28 wk	2–3 lb	1,000 – 1,300 g	One below 3½ lb (1,500 g) is very low birthweight (VLBW).
End of preterm period	35 wk	5½ lb	2,500 g	One below 5½ lb (2,500 g) is low birthweight (LBW).
Full term	38 wk	7½ lb	3,400 g	

*To make them easier to remember, the weights are rounded off (which accounts for the inexact correspondence between metric and nonmetric measures). Actual weights vary. For instance, a normal full-term infant can weigh between 5½ and 9 pounds (2.5 and 4 kilograms); a viable infant, especially one of several born at 26 or more weeks, can weigh less than shown here.

systems, which occurs in the last trimester of prenatal life. During that period, the lungs begin to expand and contract, exercising the muscles that are involved in breathing and using the amniotic fluid surrounding the fetus as a substitute for air. The fetus takes in fluid through mouth and nose and then exhales it, much as a fish would. At the same time, the valves of the heart go through a final maturation that, at birth, enables the circulatory system to function independently.

In addition, the fetus usually gains more than 4.5 pounds (2,000 grams) of critical weight in the last 10 weeks, increasing, on average, to 7½ pounds (3,400 grams) at birth (see Table 4.2). This weight gain is in the form of fat, which not only insulates the developing person when the mother's body warmth no longer surrounds him or her but also provides calories that will be burned in the early days after birth, before the mother's breast milk is fully established. (The special hazards of the low-birthweight infant are described later in this chapter.)

In many ways, the final trimester is also the beginning of the relationship between mother and child, for during this time the size and movements of the fetus make her very aware of it, and her sounds, smells, and behavior become part of fetal consciousness (see Children Up Close, pages 106–107).

RISK REDUCTION

The 9 months that transform a single-cell zygote into a viable human newborn are a time of miraculous growth, but also of considerable vulnerability. Lest the future parents reading this book become needlessly frightened as we examine a number of potential prenatal hazards, keep two facts in mind:

- Despite the complexity of prenatal development and the many dangers to the developing organism, the large majority of babies are born healthy and capable.
- Most hazards can be avoided, or their effects ameliorated, through care taken by an expectant woman, her family, and the community.

Thus, prenatal development should be thought of not as a dangerous period to be feared but as a natural process to be protected, increasing the odds that every newborn will have a healthy start in life. This is the goal of **teratology,** the study of birth defects.

Scientists now understand a great deal about **teratogens,** the broad range of substances (such as drugs and pollutants) and conditions (such as severe malnutrition and extreme stress) that increase the risk of prenatal abnormalities. These abnormalities include obvious physical problems

teratology The scientific study of birth defects caused by genetic or prenatal problems or by birth complications.
teratogens Agents and conditions, including viruses, drugs, chemicals, stessors, and malnutrition, that can impair prenatal development and lead to birth defects or even death.

SOCIAL INTERACTION

The fetus is no passive passenger in the womb, nor is the woman simply "carrying" the fetus. Development is interactive, even before birth (Kisilevsky & Low, 1998). Biologically, of course, fetal growth is closely linked to the mother-to-be's nutrition and physiology. This means not only that the fetus is affected by every aspect of her lifestyle but also that the expectant woman is affected by the development of the fetus—with nausea, increased urination, and digestive upsets being fairly routine, and perhaps gestational diabetes, high blood pressure, and even toxemia occurring as well. The fetus reacts to the specifics of the woman's body, and the woman experiences each pregnancy differently because the idiosyncracies of the fetus make her adjust to that particular developing person (Haig, 1995).

Beyond this physiological interdependence, fetus and adult have a much more intellectual, brain-based interaction. Beginning at about 9 weeks, the fetus moves its body in response to shifts in the woman's body position, with imperceptible movements of tiny heels, fists, elbows, and buttocks. Soon the woman notices flutters, at first so faint she wonders if gas or imagination, instead of a developing person, is the cause. Then movements become easier to detect and more predictable, and she learns to expect a reaction when sitting, stretching, or, especially, changing position while lying down. As the due date approaches, a sudden fetal kick or somersault can turn delight into dismay over a sore rib or interrupted sleep.

Such momentary discomfort aside, the perception of fetal movements usually evokes feelings of wonder. Indeed, many parents-to-be, fathers as well as mothers, enjoy rubbing the woman's rippling belly. The fetus feels and responds to such stimulation, beginning what may become a lifelong pattern of communication by touch (Ronca & Alberts, 1995). Interestingly, a busy woman's daily rhythms of running, bending, and resting affect fetal movement schedules, and infants who are quite active were often unusually active in the womb (DiPietro et al., 1996). Thus both parties adjust to each other's particular movement habits before birth.

Toward the end of prenatal development, other fetal sensory systems begin to function, and again interaction between fetus and mother-to-be is apparent. For example, how much amniotic fluid the fetus swallows depends partly on the taste of that fluid: fetuses swallow sweetened fluid more rapidly than noxious fluid, and thus their lungs, digestion, and nutrition are intimately related to the particulars of their mother's diet (Carlson, 1994). Immediately after birth, the smell of amniotic fluid is more soothing than other smells or than no smell at all, again indicating sensory adaptation before birth (Porter et al., 1998). Further, at about the twenty-seventh week, the eyelids open, and the fetus perceives the reddish glow of sunlight or other bright illumination that diffuses through the woman's belly (Kitzinger, 1989).

The most remarkable fetal learning involves hearing. Most mothers-to-be are well aware that their fetus can hear, having felt the developing person quiet down when they sing a lullaby or startle with a kick when a door slams. But many people do not realize that newborns remember certain sounds heard before birth. The most obvious example is that infants typically stop crying when they are held with an ear close to the mother's heart, comforted by the familiar rhythm they have heard for months. Few mothers know this explicitly, but most instinctively cradle their infants on their left side rather than their heartless right.

behavioral teratogens Teratogens that tend to harm the prenatal brain, affecting the future child's intellectual and emotional functioning.

risk analysis The process of weighing the potential outcomes of a particular event, substance, or experience to determine the likelihood of harm. In teratology, the attempt to evaluate all the factors that can increase or decrease the likelihood that a particular teratogen will cause harm.

(such as missing limbs) and more subtle impairments, such as brain damage that first appears in elementary school. A specific teratogen may damage the body structures, the growth rate, the neurological networks, or all three. Teratogens that can harm the brain, and therefore make a child hyperactive, antisocial, retarded, and so on, are called **behavioral teratogens;** their effects can be far more damaging over the life of the person than physical defects.

Determinants of Risk

Teratology is a science of **risk analysis,** of weighing the factors that change the likelihood that a particular teratogen will cause harm. Although all teratogens increase the risk of harm, none *always* causes damage. The ulti-

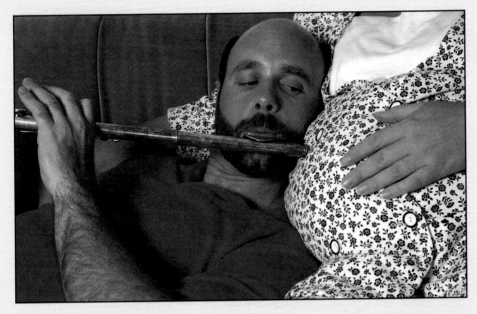

Sensory Stimulation An expectant father serenades his future child.

❓ Observational Quiz (see answer page 109): *Is this weird, irrational, or other? What three senses are involved in this early family interaction?*

Newborns remember voices heard in the womb (Fifer & Moon, 1995). In a series of experiments, pregnant women read the same children's book aloud daily during the ninth month. Three days after birth, their infants listened to recordings of the story read either by the infant's own mother or by another baby's mother. Laboratory monitoring indicated that the newborns paid greater attention to the recordings of their own mothers. What's more, the newborns responded more when their mothers read a familiar story than when they read an unfamiliar one.

In other words, the newborns remembered both who talked to them before birth and what was said—or, to be accurate, they recognized the voice and the speech patterns. Not surprisingly, then, infants born to monolingual English or Spanish mothers—when listening to the taped speech of a stranger speaking English or Spanish—preferred to listen to their native language (Moon et al., 1993).

Such results suggest that, at least in some ways, fetuses prepare more than just their reflexes and organ systems for physiological functioning after birth; they also begin to accustom themselves to the particulars of the social world that they soon will join. Meanwhile, mothers begin to identify features of their future offspring: almost all pregnant women, by the last trimester, are talking to, patting, and dreaming about their long-awaited child.

mate impact depends on the complex interplay of many factors, both destructive and protective. This means that exposure to a particular teratogen might be of low risk for one embryo, causing no harm at all, and of high risk for another, almost certainly causing damage. Obviously, analysis needs to pinpoint exactly what separates these two outcomes.

Timing of Exposure

One crucial factor is when the developing organism is exposed to which teratogen. Some teratogens cause damage only during specific days or weeks early in pregnancy, when a particular part of the body is undergoing formation. Others can be harmful at any time, but how severe the damage is depends on when the exposure occurred.

❶ Answer to Observational Quiz (from page 104): Yes, yes, and no. Genitals are formed, but they are not visible in this photo. That object growing from the lower belly is the umbilical cord.

critical period In prenatal development, the time when a particular organ or other body part is most susceptible to teratogenic damage.

The time of greatest susceptibility is called the **critical period.** As you can see in Figure 4.1, each body structure has its own critical period: it begins for the ears, limbs, and eyes at about 4 weeks after conception, for the lip at about 5 weeks, and for the teeth and palate at about 7 weeks. As a general rule, for physical defects the critical period is the entire period of the embryo (Moore & Persaud, 1998).

For conditions (such as severe malnutrition) and substances (such as heroin) that disrupt and destabilize the overall functioning of the woman's body, there are two critical periods. The first is at the very beginning of pregnancy, when stress during the germinal period, can impede implantation. The second is toward the end of pregnancy, when the fetus most needs to gain weight and when the cortex of the brain is developing, making the fetus particularly vulnerable to damage that can cause learning disabilities. Further, near the end of pregnancy, instability of the mother's body systems (for instance, if she has chills or the shakes) can loosen the placenta or cause hormonal changes to precipitate birth.

Note, however, that there is no safe period for behavioral teratogens. The brain and nervous system can be harmed throughout prenatal development.

Figure 4.1 Critical Periods in Human Development. The most serious damage from teratogens is likely to occur in the first 8 weeks after conception (dark shading). However, significant damage to many vital parts of the body, including the brain, eyes, and genitals, can occur during the last months of pregnancy as well (lighter shading).

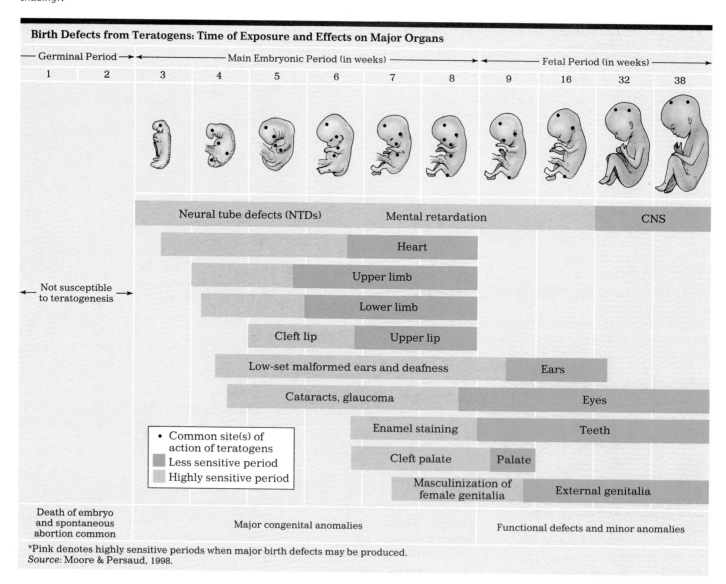

Birth Defects from Teratogens: Time of Exposure and Effects on Major Organs

*Pink denotes highly sensitive periods when major birth defects may be produced.
Source: Moore & Persaud, 1998.

threshold effect The phenomenon in which a particular teratogen is relatively harmless in small doses but becomes harmful when exposure reaches a certain level (the threshold).

interaction effect The phenomenon in which a teratogen's potential for causing harm increases when it is combined with another teratogen or another risk factor.

Amount of Exposure

A second important factor is the dose and/or frequency of exposure to a teratogen. Some teratogens have a **threshold effect;** that is, they are virtually harmless until a certain level, at which point they "cross the threshold" from being innocent to being damaging. Indeed, a few substances (vitamin A is one) are actually beneficial in small amounts but fiercely teratogenic in large quantities (Kraft & Willhite, 1997).

For most teratogens, experts are reluctant to specify a threshold below which the substance is safe. One reason is that many teratogens have an

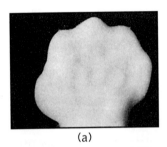

(a)

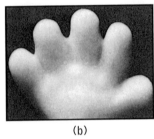

(b)

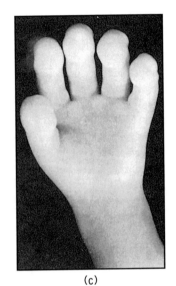

(c)

interaction effect; that is, one poison intensifies the effects of another. For example, both marijuana and alcohol are probably threshold-type teratogens, harmful at a certain level or over a sustained period of use but not teratogenic in smaller, occasional doses (Waterson & Murray-Lyon, 1990). However, when taken together, their thresholds drop, making them behavioral teratogens at an amount that, for each drug taken separately, would be inconsequential. Similar interaction effects are likely to occur with all other drugs that affect the central nervous system, from nicotine to cocaine (Robins & Mills, 1993).

Genetic Vulnerability

A third factor that determines whether a specific teratogen will be harmful, and to what extent, is the developing organism's genes. When a woman carrying dizygotic twins drinks alcohol, for example, the twins' blood alcohol levels are exactly equal; yet one may be more severely affected than the other (Maier et al., 1996). This difference probably

A Week for Fingers The impact of a potential teratogen partially depends on when the developing organism is exposed to it. This is because there is a critical period in the formation of every body part during which the part is especially vulnerable. Shown here are three stages in finger development that define the critical period: *(a)* notches appear in the hand at day 44; *(b)* fingers are separated and lengthened by day 50; *(c)* fingers are completely formed by day 55, and the critical period for hand development is over. Other parts of the body, including the eyes, heart, and central nervous system, take much longer to complete development, so the critical period during which they are vulnerable to teratogens lasts for months rather than days.

involves a gene affecting a specific enzyme (alcohol dehydrogenase) that is crucial to the breakdown of alcohol. Similar genetic susceptibilities are suspected in other birth disorders, including cleft palate. Indeed, one expert believes that "ultimately every teratogen is going to involve a genetic susceptibility" (Holmes, quoted in Kolata, 1995).

Genes are also implicated in the teratogenic effect of a deficiency of folic acid (a B-complex vitamin) in the mother-to-be's diet. Researchers have known for several years that folic-acid deficiency can produce neural-tube defects, either spina bifida, in which the spine does not close properly, or anencephaly, in which part of the brain does not form (see Table 3.2, page 90). Neural-tube defects occur more commonly in certain families and ethnic groups (specifically, Irish and English), and that fact led to research that found the source: A defective gene produces an enzyme that prevents the normal utilization of folic acid (Mills et al., 1995).

Even without this gene, severe folic-acid deficiency may cause a neural-tube defect; however, pregnancies that are burdened by this particular genetic defect are vulnerable even if the mothers' diets are nourishing. The worst combination is genetic vulnerability and inadequate diet. That double jeopardy is one possible cause of the higher rate of neural-tube defects in California newborns whose mothers were born in Mexico, compared to newborns of U.S.-born women of Mexican descent (whose current diets are more likely to include adequate orange juice, green leafy vegetables, and other sources of folic acid), and especially compared to newborns not of Mexican heritage (who may be less genetically susceptible) (Shaw et al., 1997).

In some cases, genetic vulnerability is related to the sex of the developing organism. Generally, male *(XY)* embryos and fetuses are at greater risk

❶ **Answer to Observational Quiz (from page 107):** The auditory, tactile, and visual senses. The fetus can hear the father's flute, and both parents can see and feel the movement of the fetus. This scene may be weird in that it is unusual, but it is actually quite rational: early communication is not only possible but also beneficial to mother, father, and offspring.

than female *(XX)*, in that male fetuses are more often aborted spontaneously. In addition, newborn boys have more birth defects, and older boys have more learning disabilities and other problems caused by behavioral teratogens. A strong suggestion that this sex difference is related to teratogens (not solely to the sex chromosomes) comes from couples who lived near an Italian chemical plant that exploded in 1976, releasing a cloud of dioxin. The adults most highly exposed (as indicated by dioxin levels in their blood) had 74 children between 1977 and 1984—48 daughters and only 26 sons. Obviously, many potential boys never survived to be born. No one is certain why male embryos and fetuses are more vulnerable, but the reason could well be genetic: since *X* chromosomes carry far more genes than *Y* chromosomes, males have many genes on their one *X* chromosome that are not paired with (and strengthened or tempered by) a corresponding gene on their *Y* chromosome. This may make them more vulnerable, when a harmful substance reaches the placenta.

Specific Teratogens and Preventive Measures

Because of the many variables involved, risk analysis cannot precisely predict the results of teratogenic exposure in individual cases (Jacobson & Jacobson, 1996). However, decades of research have revealed the possible effects of some of the most common and damaging teratogens. More important, much has been learned about how individuals and society can reduce the risks.

Diseases

Many diseases, including many viruses and virtually all sexually transmitted diseases, can harm a fetus. Here we will focus on only two, rubella and HIV, that clearly illustrate the potential for public health measures to prevent birth defects.

rubella A viral disease that, if contracted early during pregnancy, can harm the fetus, causing blindness, deafness, and damage to the central nervous system. (Sometimes called *German measles*.)

Rubella.   One of the first teratogens to be recognized was **rubella** (sometimes called *German measles*). Rubella was long considered a harmless childhood disease. But 50 years ago doctors discovered that if a woman contracts rubella early in pregnancy, her embryo might suffer blindness, deafness, heart abnormalities, and brain damage. (Some of these problems and their effects were apparent in David's story in Chapter 1.)

The seriousness of this teratogen became all too evident in a worldwide rubella epidemic in the mid-1960s. In the United States alone, 20,000 infants had obvious rubella-caused impairments, including hundreds who were born both deaf and blind (Franklin, 1984). Thousands more showed no immediate effects (because damage was done only to the brain), but behavioral or learning problems appeared years later (Enkin et al., 1989).

Since that epidemic, widespread immunization—either of preschool children (as in the United States) or of all adolescent girls who are not already immune (as in England)—has reduced the rubella threat. As a consequence, between 1990 and 1995 in the United States, an average of only 15 rubella-syndrome infants were born per year, half of them to immigrants from nations without childhood rubella vaccinations. Even fewer such infants were born annually in England and Canada. Immunization rates continue to improve. Consequently, only two rubella-syndrome infants were born in the United States in 1996 (*MMWR*, April 25, 1997). Other teratogenic diseases (for example, chicken pox) likewise have been diminished by immunization and now rarely cause damage to fetuses.

❓ Especially for Social Workers: When is it most important to convince women to be tested for HIV—a month before pregnancy, a month after conception, or immediately after birth?

human immunodeficiency virus (HIV) A virus that gradually overwhelms the body's immune responses, leaving the individual defenseless against a host of pathologies that eventually manifest themselves as AIDS.

acquired immune deficiency syndrome (AIDS) The diseases and infections, many of them fatal, that result from the degradation of the immune system by HIV.

Pediatric AIDS.   No widespread immunization is yet available for the most devastating viral teratogen of all: **human immunodeficiency virus (HIV).** HIV gradually overwhelms the body's natural immune responses, leaving the individual vulnerable to a host of diseases and infections that together constitute **acquired immune deficiency syndrome (AIDS).**

In Africa and Asia, AIDS occurs virtually equally among men and women. In the Western world, by contrast, AIDS first appeared predominantly among gay men. As a result, its transmission to women of childbearing age was quite slow. In fact, nearly all the first American children with AIDS were hemophiliacs, infected via blood transfusions. Now the blood supply is safe, but women are not: heterosexual women of childbearing age are the fastest-growing HIV-positive group, outranking men in some regions of the world. In the United States the proportion of AIDS cases that involved heterosexual women rose from 7 percent in 1985 to 20 percent in 1996 (*MMWR*, February 28, 1997). Worldwide, more than 1 million children are now infected (Wilfert & McKinney, 1998).

Normally, about one in every four newborns whose mother is HIV-positive has the deadly virus and not just the *antibody* that the body produces in response to the virus and that, like the virus, is acquired from the mother. The virus is acquired during pregnancy or birth. Within months or years, an infant with the virus always develops pediatric AIDS, partly because drugs that reverse the course of HIV have not even been tested on children (much less proven successful) and partly because the virus overwhelms a very young body faster than a fully grown one (Wilfert & McKinney, 1998). About one-third of the infected children die during infancy, another third before kindergarten, and the remaining third by age 20 (Grubman et al., 1995).

The best way to prevent pediatric AIDS is to prevent adult AIDS. The second best way is to prevent pregnancy in HIV-positive women. Both strategies are complicated by the disease's long incubation period in adults—up to 10 years or more—during which people can transmit the virus without knowing that they are infected.

This long incubation period makes it clear that early detection of the virus is critical to reducing pediatric AIDS, not only by preventing HIV-positive pregnancy

Fighting AIDS, One Child at a Time These children, all born to HIV-positive mothers, do not all have the deadly virus, but they suffer from the disease nonetheless. Although those who are HIV-negative will survive, their mothers are unable to care for them because they are dying, or already dead, of the disease. Nonetheless, these children are more fortunate than many others in their condition: they are residents of Hale House, founded by a grandmother in Harlem who opened her home and heart to children with AIDS.

but also by reducing prenatal transmission of HIV—because now there is a third prevention strategy. Women with the HIV virus who take the drug AZT during pregnancy and at birth have far fewer HIV-positive newborns: 8 percent of births with AZT versus 26 percent without (*MMWR*, April 29, 1994). Obviously, testing women for HIV when they give birth (as some U.S. states require) is testing at least 6 months too late; every woman needs confidential prenatal care, including an HIV test if warranted, in the first trimester.

Many other maternal conditions, including RH-negative blood (a recessive genetic trait, not a disease), syphilis and other sexually transmitted diseases, and drug use, also need to be recognized months before birth to protect the fetus. But unless all women obtain early prenatal testing and good care, another million of the world's children will contract AIDS from their mothers—in just the next 3 years (Wilfert & McKinney, 1998).

Medicines

Once physicians believed that the placenta was a natural barrier that protected the embryo from any damaging toxins. Then, in 1960, a drug recommended for pregnant women, *thalidomide,* caused more than 10,000 babies to be born missing arms, legs, or ears. This sudden rise in birth deformities alerted the medical community to the dangers of teratogenic drugs.

Now virtually everyone realizes that many widely used *medicinal drugs*—drugs that remedy some real or potential problem in a person's body—are teratogenic in some cases. The list includes tetracycline, anticoagulants, bromides, anticonvulsants, phenobarbital, retinoic acid (a common treatment for acne, as in Accutane), and most hormones. Other prescription drugs and nonprescription drugs (such as aspirin, antacids, and diet pills) may be teratogenic. Obviously, then, women who might become pregnant, or who are pregnant, should avoid any medication unless recommended by a doctor who is both well versed in teratology *and* aware of the possible pregnancy.

Ironically, thalidomide has reappeared—first on the underground market in Brazil and now in the United States, where it was recently approved for use against the deforming disease leprosy—but only with ongoing physician approval and very severe restrictions. Among the restrictions, women of childbearing age must provide proof of contraceptive use and must read a booklet with color photographs of thalidomide-affected children. The hope is that, once thalidomide and other teratogenic drugs are understood and dispensed according to strict regulations, no more infants with drug-caused deformities will be born (Stolberg, 1997). This hope is becoming reality, at least as regards medicinal drugs.

Psychoactive Drugs

By contrast, prenatal damage caused by *psychoactive drugs*—that is, drugs that affect the psyche, which include beer and wine, liquor, cigarettes and smokeless tobacco, heroin and methadone, LSD, marijuana, cocaine in any form, inhalants, antidepressant pills, and many other substances—is far too common. All psychoactive drugs slow down growth and increase the risk of premature labor. And all can affect the developing brain, producing both short-term and long-term deficits. For days or weeks after birth, infants who were prenatally addicted to any of these drugs sleep fitfully, startle easily, cry unhappily, suck voraciously, eat erratically, and show other signs of drug withdrawal.

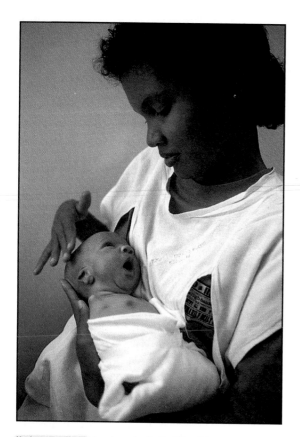

No Leprosy Here Luciene took thalidomide to control leprosy symptoms—unaware that she was halting the growth of arms, legs, and the outer ear in the fetus she was carrying. Two items of good news about this tragedy: The government of Brazil has taken steps to halt black-market sales of thalidomide to childbearing women, and Luciene's maternal expression is quite appropriate. Thalidomide does not damage the brain, so Rafael may well become a bright, socially responsive, successful young adult, as have many of the early victims of thalidomide, who are now approaching middle age.

Differences and Similarities The differences between these two children are obvious at a glance: One is an African-American teenager, the other a Swedish toddler. One similarity is obvious too: Both are girls. However, the most important similarity— fetal alcohol syndrome—is apparent only on closer observation.

❷ *Observational Quiz (see answer page 114): How many of the five visible facial characteristics of fetal alcohol syndrome can you see in both girls?*

fetal alcohol syndrome (FAS) A cluster of birth defects, including abnormal facial characteristics, slow physical growth, and retarded mental development, that is caused by the mother's drinking excessive quantities of alcohol when pregnant.

As they develop, children who were exposed prenatally to psychoactive drugs may exhibit ongoing learning difficulties, impaired self-control, poor concentration, and overall irritability. Beyond these general effects, each drug varies in its specific effects; thus, tobacco causes low birthweight, and alcohol causes **fetal alcohol syndrome (FAS)**, the leading teratogenic cause of mental retardation (see Table 4.3).

table **4.3**	**Effects of Certain Drugs**	
Drug	Usage	Effects
Alcohol	3 or more drinks daily, or binge drinking of 5 or more drinks on one occasion early in pregnancy	Causes *fetal alcohol syndrome (FAS)*. Symptoms include abnormal facial characteristics (small head, wide spacing between the eyes, a flattened nose, and a narrow upper lip, unusual eyelids, and missing skin indent between nose and upper lip), overall growth retardation, learning disabilities, and behavior problems (including poor concentration and impaired social skills).
	More than ½ oz of absolute alcohol a day	Causes *fetal alcohol effects (FAE)*. FAE does not obviously affect facial appearance or physical growth, but it affects brain functioning. The first sign is noisy, higher-frequency cries at birth. Later signs, on cognitive tests, include lower IQ (by about 5 points).
	Moderate drinking: less than 1 or 2 servings of beer or wine or 1 mixed drink on a few days per week	Probably has no negative effects on prenatal development, although this is controversial.
Tobacco	Maternal smoking early in pregnancy	Increases risk of abnormalities, including malformations of the limbs and the urinary tract.
	Maternal smoking late in pregnancy	Reduces birthweight and size. Babies born to habitual smokers weigh, on average, about 9 oz (250 g) less than would otherwise be expected, and they are shorter, both at birth and in the years to come. They may have childhood problems, particularly with respiration and, in adulthood, increased risk of becoming smokers themselves.
	Paternal smoking	Reduces birthweight by about 2 oz (45 g) on average.
Marijuana	Heavy use	Affects the central nervous system, as evidenced by the tendency of affected newborns to emit a high-pitched cry that denotes brain damage.
	Light use	Has no proven long-term effects.
Heroin		Because of the physiological "highs" and "crashes" of the addiction (such as the reduction of oxygen, irregular heartbeat, and sweating and chills that occur during withdrawal), it causes slower fetal growth and premature labor. (See also *methadone effects*.)
Methadone	Later in pregnancy	Moderates the effects of heroin withdrawal during pregnancy but is as addictive as heroin. Heavily addicted newborns require regulated drug doses in the first days of life to prevent the pain and convulsions associated with sudden opiate withdrawal.
Cocaine		Causes overall growth retardation, problems with the placenta, and specific learning problems in the first months of life. Research on long-lasting effects is confounded by the effects of poverty and the ongoing addiction of the mother. The major concern is in language development (Lester et al., 1998).
Solvents	Especially early in pregnancy	Causes smaller heads, crossed eyes, and other abnormalities.

Overall Sources: Larsen, 1998; Lyons & Rittner, 1998.

Alcohol (Manteuffel, 1996; Nugent el al., 1996; Streissguth et al., 1993); *Tobacco* (Eskenazi et al., 1995; Kallen, 1997; Kandel et al., 1994; Li et al., 1996; Tisi, 1988; *Marijuana* (Lester & Dreher, 1989); *Methadone* (Schneider & Hans, 1996); *Cocaine* (including crack) (Hurt et al., 1996); *Solvents* (glue, other inhalants) (Arnold, 1997).

● Response for Social Workers (from page 110): Voluntary testing and then treatment can be useful at any time, since those who learn they are HIV-positive are more likely to get treatment, to reduce the likelihood of transmission, and to avoid pregnancy. If pregnancy does occur, diagnosis early in pregnancy is best, since abortion is one option and taking AZT is another—one that prevents many cases of pediatric AIDS.

● Answer to Observational Quiz (from page 112): All five: wide-set eyes, large and unusual eyelids, flat nose bridge, narrow upper lip, missing indentation in the skin between the nose and the lips.

Little or no longitudinal research on the effects of prenatal exposure to specific illegal drugs is available, because it is virtually impossible to locate a sizable representative sample of newly pregnant women who use one, and only one, illicit drug at a steady and measurable dose. Even if such a group could be found, researchers would then need to locate a control group of women of similar age, health status, and ethnic, religious, and socioeconomic background who differ from the experimental group in just one way—they are completely drug-free during pregnancy.

The problem is that illicit drug users almost always use several legal and illegal drugs—not just their drug of choice. One study of infants who were prenatally exposed to cocaine found, for example, that 83 percent were also exposed to tobacco and 43 percent to heavy doses of alcohol. Further, 29 percent of their mothers received no prenatal care of any kind, and 7.5 percent had syphilis (Batemen et al., 1993). Another study found that most cocaine-exposed infants were also exposed to tobacco and had high blood levels of lead—a known teratogen (Neuspiel et al., 1994).

When a mother-to-be is *addicted* to an illicit drug, the fetal hazards are compounded by her erratic sleeping and eating habits; her bouts of anxiety, stress, and depression; and her increased risk of accidents, violence, and sexual abuse. One study of more than 3,000 women found that, fortunately, most of those who used psychoactive drugs quit during pregnancy. The unfortunate exceptions were the hundred or so who were physically abused by their partners; they were more likely to continue drug abuse (Martin et al., 1996). Finally, severely addicted women are often malnourished and sick, unsupported by concerned family members, and without medical care. After the baby is born, all these problems typically surround the child for years, along with additional stresses from the father and the neighborhood.

Prevention of Drug Damage

Despite the ambiguity of much of the longitudinal research on drug use, the evidence leads to a strong recommendation: Pregnant women should avoid drugs entirely. Nothing is risk-free. Unfortunately, many women in their prime reproductive years drink alcohol, smoke cigarettes, and/or use illicit drugs. Most continue their drug use in the first weeks before they realize that they are pregnant (Robins & Mills, 1993). If they then stop, it is already late, after the early formation of the embryo. To make matters worse, those who are addicts, alcoholics, or heavy users of multiple drugs are least likely to be able to stop their drug use on their own, and they are also least likely to recognize their condition in the first few weeks and obtain early medical care.

General education helps, but it is not enough. For example, the dangers of alcohol during pregnancy are widely known. Yet in a 1995 U.S. survey, 15 percent of pregnant women admitted drinking, at least a little, and 3.5 percent said that they drank a lot within the previous month—at least one drink per day or five or more drinks on one occasion. Although there is some debate about moderate drinking, the 3.5 percent drank at a level everyone recognizes as risky. Moreover, 4 years earlier in a similar survey, only .9 percent admitted drinking a lot. This suggests an alarming increase of 400 percent in the number of pregnant heavy drinkers between 1991 and 1995 (Ebrahim et al., 1998). Worse, the actual amount and prevalence of drinking is undoubtedly higher than these numbers indicate, because many alcoholics hide the extent of their drinking. A careful assessment in Seattle, Washington, of babies born in 1981 found that 3 in 1,000 had FAS and another 6 in 1,000 had less obvious brain damage (Sampson et al., 1997). The overall rate, about 1 in 100, shows that while not every drinker harms her fetus, far too many do—and every measure to reduce the harm should be tried.

Beyond detailing the harm of psychoactive drugs, the research suggests five protective steps:

1. *Abstinence even before pregnancy.* The best course is to avoid drugs altogether. This can make a dramatic difference, as is shown by data on babies born to women who have recently emigrated to the United States. For many reasons, including poverty and lack of medical care, such women are at higher risk for prenatal and birth complications of every kind. However, their newborns weigh more, and are born with fewer defects, than those of native-born women of the same ethnicity (Singh & Yu, 1996; Zambrana et al., 1997). One reason is that immigrants are more often drug-free, not only because of cultural patterns but also because their husbands and parents discourage any substance use in pregnancy.

2. *Abstinence after the first trimester.* The teratogenic effects of psychoactive drugs accumulate throughout pregnancy. Thus early prenatal care, with routine testing for drug use and effective treatment toward abstinence, would reduce fetal brain damage substantially. In fact, because the last trimester of pregnancy is critical for brain development, a drug-free second half of pregnancy *may* be enough to prevent brain damage if drug use during the first half was moderate (Maier et al., 1996). Note that since alcohol and tobacco are at least as teratogenic as illegal drugs, they need to be tested for and targeted just as much as cocaine, heroin, marijuana, and the like.

3. *Moderation throughout pregnancy* (if abstinence from before conception until after birth is impossible). Since the prenatal effects of psychoactive drugs are dose-related, interactive, and cumulative, each dose that is reduced, each drug that is eliminated, and each day that is drug-free, represents a reduction in the damage that can be caused.

4. *Social support.* Maternal stress, psychological problems, loneliness, and poor housing correlate with prenatal complications as well as with drug use (Nordentoft et al., 1996; Shiono et al., 1997). In fact, the correlation between psychoactive drugs and prenatal problems may be due, in part, to a hidden factor—psychological difficulties (Robert, 1996). If this is true, then befriending, encouraging, and assisting pregnant drug users may not only reduce their use of teratogens but also, even without directly affecting drug use, aid fetal development. In contrast, punitive measures that bring shame, stress, and isolation may make matters even worse.

5. *Postnatal care.* Newborns with alcohol, cocaine, or even heroin in their systems sometimes become quite normal, intelligent children if they receive optimal care (Mayes et al., 1992; Richardson & Day, 1994). Thus another way to protect children from suffering the consequences of their mothers' prenatal drug abuse is to ensure sensitive nurturance after birth (as through parenting education, preventive medicine, home visits, early day care, and, if necessary, foster care). Note that social prejudices tend to work against these children; for instance, the assumption that "crack babies" are destined to have serious learning problems might reduce educational outreach to children of crack-using, shabbily dressed mothers (Lyons & Rittner, 1998). The most recent research continues to suggest that cocaine alone does no more damage than alcohol alone and that environmental factors after birth (such as a highly stressed mother and multiple caregivers) are the primary cause of the so-called crack-baby syndrome (Alessandri et al., 1998; Brown et al., 1998).

One preventive measure that does *not* seem to help is prosecuting pregnant women who use drugs. Jailing such women does lead to abstinence,

Drug Abuse Smoking and drinking are an essential part of daily life for millions of young women, many of whom find them impossible to give up when they become pregnant. If you met this woman at a party and you thought complete abstinence was too much to ask, temperance might be a reasonable suggestion. Taking a few puffs and a few sips, or using just one drug and not the other, might prevent damage to the developing body and brain.

❷ **Especially for Women:** If you have already decided to become pregnant soon, you obviously cannot change your genes, your age, or your economic status. But you can do three things in a month or two that can markedly reduce the chance of having a low-birthweight baby a year from now. What are they?

low birthweight (LBW) A birthweight of less than 5½ pounds (2,500 grams).

preterm birth Birth that occurs 3 weeks or more before the full term of pregnancy has elapsed, that is, at 35 or fewer weeks past conception rather than at the full term of about 38 weeks.

and, ironically, imprisoned pregnant women have healthier babies than their peers outside the walls (Martin et al., 1997); but such measures, in effect, keep thousands of pregnant women, attempting to avoid arrest, away from prenatal care and, hence, increase fetal damage that might have been prevented (Lyons & Rittner, 1998). (See Changing Policy, page 118).

LOW BIRTHWEIGHT AND ITS CAUSES

The final complication we will discuss here is **low birthweight (LBW)**, defined by the World Health Organization as a weight of less than 5½ pounds (2,500 grams) at birth. LBW babies are further grouped into *very low birthweight (VLBW)* babies, weighing less than 3 pounds (1,500 grams), and *extremely low birthweight (ELBW)* babies, weighing less than about 2 pounds (1,000 grams). The rate of LBW varies enormously from nation to nation (see Figure 4.2); the United States' 1996 rate of 7.4 percent was twice that of some other developed nations (see Figure 4.3).

Causes of Low Birthweight

Many factors can cause low birthweight, including malnutrition and poverty. As you will see, the worst problems occur when several factors combine.

Preterm Birth

Remember that the fetal body weight doubles in the last months of pregnancy, with a typical gain of almost 2 pounds (about 900 grams) occurring in the final 3 weeks. Thus if a baby is born **preterm**, defined as 3 or more weeks

Figure 4.2   Low Birthweight Around the World, 1990s. Poverty and policy interact to affect the rate of infants born weighing under 5½ pounds (2,500 grams), as shown in a sample of 24 nations (among the 148 reported by the United Nations). Generally, the nations of Europe do best on this indicator of national health, and those of southern Asia, worst. However, income alone does not result in excellent medical and social care. For example, although the U.S. gross national product (at more than $7 trillion a year) is larger than that of any other nation, 33 nations do better than the United States on LBW, 20 nations are tied at 7 percent, and 95 nations do worse. Except for the last four nations shown here, none have more than 20 percent LBW, a worldwide improvement over the rate 20 years ago.

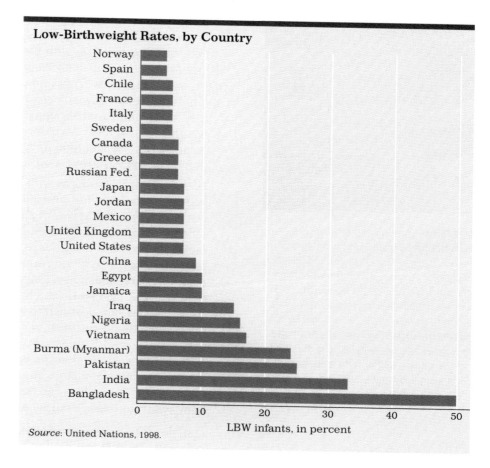

Low-Birthweight Rates, by Country

Source: United Nations, 1998.

Figure 4.3 Not Improving. The rate of LBW infants is often taken to be a measure of a nation's overall health. In the United States, the rise and fall of this rate is related to many factors, among them the availability of good prenatal care, maternal use of drugs, and overall nutrition.

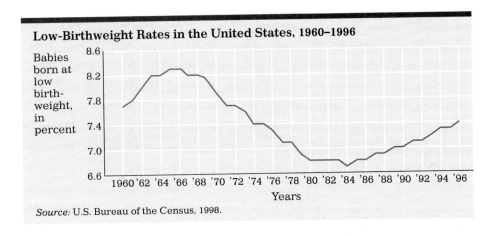

Low-Birthweight Rates in the United States, 1960–1996

Babies born at low birthweight, in percent

Source: U.S. Bureau of the Census, 1998.

before the usual 38 weeks, he or she is usually of low birthweight. Not always, however. Babies born even a month early may not be LBW if they were well nourished throughout prenatal development. They may weigh 6½ pounds (3,000 grams) or so, well above the 5½-pound (2,500-gram) cutoff. Most preterm infants, however, are not so fortunate.

Why would pregnancy end prematurely? Conditions that disrupt the physiological equilibrium of the mother, such as a high dose of psychoactive drugs, extreme stress, and chronic exhaustion, can precipitate preterm birth. Physiological factors specific to the pregnancy, such as a placenta that becomes detached from the uterine wall or a uterus that cannot accommodate further fetal growth, also trigger early birth. This last factor helps explain why small women and women bearing multiple fetuses often go into labor weeks before the due date. Similarly, women with an unusually short cervix are more likely than other women to begin labor early (Goldenberg et al., 1998).

A Hand or a Handout? A number of factors—including maternal malnutrition and infection—are potential contributors to low birthweight, and often they occur in combination. Frequently these factors are related to poverty. Preventing them by giving a supportive hand, not a handout after the fact, would reduce the rate of LBW considerably.

Another key factor in preterm birth is infection, which stimulates the mother's body to produce inflammatory chemicals that interfere with fetal development and trigger uterine contractions. A minor vaginal infection recently linked to early birth is *bacterial vaginosis,* easily cured with standard antibiotics. In the United States, this infection alone is responsible for an estimated 8 percent of all preterm births (Meis et al., 1995). Even a pregnant woman's untreated gum disease leads to a sevenfold increase in the rate of low birthweight (Offenbacher et al., 1996).

Growth Retardation

Not all low-birthweight babies are preterm babies. Some fetuses simply gain weight more slowly than they should and are born with LBW. They are called *small-for-dates,* or **small for (their) gestational age (SGA).**

small for gestational age (SGA) A term applied to newborns who weigh substantially less than they should, given how much time has passed since conception.

Why would a fetus grow abnormally slowly? Every psychoactive drug slows growth, but tobacco is the worst, as well as the most prevalent, culprit. Cigarettes are implicated in 25 percent of all low-birthweight births in the United States (Chomitz et al., 1995); they are involved in about 50 percent of LBW births in many European nations, where more women smoke cigarettes and fewer women experience infections or other causes of low birthweight. Evidence for a connection between smoking and low birthweight comes from

WHEN DOES A DEVELOPING EMBRYO BECOME A PERSON?

The controversy over whether or not abortion should be legal is, in a sense, a controversy about prenatal development. On one hand, pro-life (antiabortion) advocates maintain that life begins at conception, that the first pulses of blood vessels at 4 weeks are heartbeat, and thus that the embryo is already a person. On the other hand, pro-choice advocates argue that a one-cell zygote is obviously not a human being and cite 6-month brain waves and viability as the first sign of personhood. The settlement of this controversy probably depends on interpretations of religious values and constitutional precedents, and thus is not a topic for this text.

However, a relevant practical and ideological issue concerns medical and legal protection (Daniels, 1993). Doctors and judges, as well as the public at large, are now granting the fetus some rights previously reserved for a fully formed, independently breathing newborn. Health professionals treat the fetus itself as a patient, with medical needs distinct from those of the mother. If the fetus is ailing, drugs can be prescribed and surgery can be performed within the uterus. A *fetoscope* allows outsiders to view the fetus within the amniotic sac, so surgeons can diagnose and repair heart or kidney defects, transfuse blood through the wall of the uterus and placenta (if antibodies are destroying the fetal blood supply), or implant a tube into the fetal skull to drain abnormal collections of fluid—all a month or two before birth.

At the moment, such procedures are, unquestionably, miraculous. But as routine diagnostic techniques reveal more and more fetuses that might benefit from them, the question arises as to whether expectant women should be legally required to go through such procedures—to experience pain and medical risk if doing so might save the life of a fetus. Already, judges have compelled pregnant women close to term to have blood transfusions and surgical births, even when those procedures were contrary to the women's religion or personal desire. If you agree with the judges in such cases, would your opinion be different in cases where the fetus is not yet viable or the fetal risk is not death but only possible disability?

A related problem involves the requirement, in some states, that doctors, nurses, and social workers report drug use during pregnancy to legal authorities. In at least 24 states, women have been arrested for drug abuse during pregnancy with no evidence that their fetuses had been harmed (Lyons & Rittner, 1998). One result is that some pregnant drug addicts—the very women who most need prenatal care—avoid every doctor or clinic, fearing they will be tested against their will and then arrested or forced to give up the baby after it is born (Robins & Mills, 1993). In fact, one of the best predictors of late, or completely absent, prenatal care is illegal drug use (Brown et al, 1998; McCalla et al., 1995).

To take this one step further, should every pregnant woman be prohibited from smoking, required to eat nutritious foods, and forced to abstain from alcohol altogether? Is possible harm to a developing person sufficient to negate a developed person's right to privacy and self-determination? Who should decide—a judge, a doctor, a priest, a scientist, a public prosecutor? As one woman, protesting her treatment after she was *voluntarily* hospitalized to protect her developing fetus, complained, "I'm a person, too, not just something that happens to be wrapped around a baby" (quoted in Snyder, 1985).

The idea of prenatal "protective custody" to safeguard a fetus need not, of course, be limited to mothers-to-be. Should men be required to curtail their freedoms when anticipating fatherhood? Men who work with pesticides somehow produce more children with birth defects (Savitz et al., 1989). Should they, or their employers, be prosecuted if they do not quit such work before conceiving a child?

Logically, violence by anyone toward a pregnant woman can be considered an attack on a child, even if the woman is unwilling to bring charges. Already, a Texas driver who caused a crash that precipitated labor, leading to the birth and then death of a preterm infant, has been convicted of manslaughter (*Associated Press*, 1996). How about those who sell or give a pregnant woman drugs, cigarettes, or alcohol: should they be prosecuted (like a bartender who sells liquor to a customer who obviously can't handle it)?

If the fetus is as much a person as a pregnant woman is, does this imply that women must be subservient to the wishes and values of others? If so, the idea runs against a central tenet of human development: to value each individual person. On the other hand, if pregnant women can do as they wish, then untold numbers of future children may be disabled. That is against basic developmental goals as well. At what point is a mother fully responsible for her child—at conception, as some argue; at viability, as others believe; or weeks or even months *after* birth, as was the case in some traditional societies where newborn infanticide was acceptable? We could begin our answer with education and health policy: Every pregnant woman should understand prenatal development, have free and excellent prenatal care, and be encouraged and supported by her community. Beyond that, only the issues—and not the answers—are clear.

Response for Women (from page 116):
Avoid all drugs, check your weight and gain some if your are under the norm, and receive diagnosis and treatment for any infections—not just sexual ones but infections anywhere in your body, including your teeth.

table **4.4**	**Factors of Maternal Nutrition Correlated with Low Birthweight**

Weight

Low prepregnancy weight
Low body fat
Low total weight gain
Low weight gain during any month, especially in the third trimester
Inadequate late weight gain (after 24 weeks)

Lack of Specific Nutrients

Fasting or starvation, even for 1 day
Inadequate vitamin A, folic acid, iron, magnesium, calcium, zinc, essential fatty acids, essential amino acids

Substances That Decrease Nutrient Absorption

Tobacco, alcohol, and diuretics, among others

Source: Luke, 1993.

Figure 4.4 Effects of Smoking, Obesity, and Weight Gain on the Rate of Small for Gestational Age (SGA) Births. As you can see, smokers' babies are more often SGA than non-smokers' babies, especially if the mother does not gain enough weight during pregnancy. Even women who are obese before pregnancy should gain, but not as much as smaller women. Not shown here are the consequences that can occur when mothers gain *more* than recommended. Especially if the mothers are already obese, their babies are likely to weigh over 9 pounds at birth, a risk factor for gestational diabetes and other birth complications.

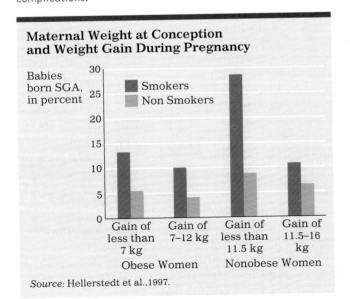

Maternal Weight at Conception and Weight Gain During Pregnancy

Source: Hellerstedt et al.,1997.

Sweden, where good nutrition and medical care make LBW less than half as common as in the United States. Between the mid-1980s and the mid-1990s, smoking in Sweden declined 24 percent (from 29 to 22 percent of the population), and correspondingly the total rate of SGA births declined 18 percent (from 3.4 to 2.8 percent of all births) (Cnattingius & Haglund, 1997).

Malnutrition

Another common reason for slow fetal growth—and hence for low birthweight—is maternal malnutrition, a problem that has many specific causes (see Table 4.4). Women who begin pregnancy underweight, eat poorly during pregnancy, and consequently do not gain at least 3 pounds (1½ kilograms) per month in the second and third trimesters run a much higher risk than others of having a low-birthweight infant. Indeed, women who gain less than 15 pounds (7 kilograms), even if they are nonsmokers who begin pregnancy overweight, still have a higher risk of preterm and SGA babies than those who gain at least 15 pounds (7 kilograms) (see Figure 4.4).

Research indicates that obese women should gain 15 to 25 pounds (7 to 11½ kilograms) during pregnancy; normal-weight women, 25 to 35 pounds (11½ to 16 kilograms); and underweight women, even more, with the specifics dependent on how underweight they are (Hellerstedt et al., 1997). Unfortunately, the three risk factors—being underweight, undereating, and smoking—tend to occur together.

Beyond overall weight, certain nutrients defend against low birthweight, including zinc, iron, and folic acid. As an example, women who consume less than 240 micrograms of folic acid a day—about half the recommended amount—are two to three times more likely than others to have a low-birthweight infant (Scholl et al., 1996). Indeed, malnutrition (not age) is the primary reason young teenagers tend to have small babies: they tend to eat sporadically and unhealthily, and because their own bodies are still developing, their diet is inadequate to support the growth of two.

Enough or Too Much? A balanced diet is important throughout pregnancy and especially toward the end, when, among other special requirements, calcium is needed to build bones and teeth.

❷ *Observational Quiz (see answer page 122): Beyond the healthy meal on the plate, do you see any signs that this woman's fetus will develop well?*

Poverty

Low birthweight can result from a single risk factor or from several. Of particular concern is that many of these risks are related to poverty (Hughes & Simpson, 1995). Compared with women of higher socioeconomic status, pregnant women at the bottom of the economic ladder are more likely to be ill, malnourished, teenaged, and stressed. If they are employed, their jobs often require long hours of physically stressful work, exactly the kind of work that correlates with preterm and SGA birth (Ceron-Mireles, et al., 1996). They often receive late or inadequate prenatal care, breathe polluted air, live in overcrowded conditions, move from place to place, and ingest unhealthy substances, from psychoactive drugs to spoiled foods—all of which can have deleterious effects on the developing fetus (Shiono et al., 1997).

Physical difficulty like malfunction of the placenta or the umbilical cord is more likely when pregnancies are closely spaced, and close spacing correlates with poverty for at least two reasons: Poor women have less access to family planning services, and they live in communities that encourage higher birth rates, partly because these communities have higher death rates (see Figure 4.5). In this way, the social context may underlie many of the biological causes of low birthweight.

Poverty helps explain the wide national and international variations in the following statistics:

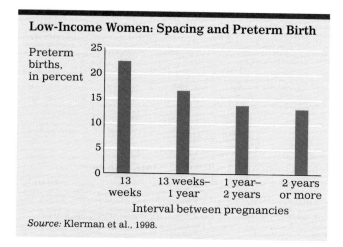

Source: Klerman et al., 1998.

Figure 4.5 Time to Prepare. In many ways, a woman's body needs to be ready to sustain a full-term pregnancy. This is evidenced in the higher rate of preterm pregnancies in women who are very young or old, who are undernourished or small, or—as shown here—who have a second child soon after their body has experienced a previous pregnancy. Many of the women conceiving too quickly were slow to realize they were pregnant, and therefore were slow to obtain prenatal care.

- Of the more than 25 million low-birthweight infants born worldwide each year, the overwhelming majority are in developing countries.
- Developing countries in the same general region, with similar ethnic populations, have markedly different LBW rates when they have different average incomes. For example, Nicaragua's LBW rate (15 percent) is more than twice that of neighboring Costa Rica (6 percent), where per capita income is five times greater (UNICEF, 1995).

■ Within nations, differences in LBW rates among ethnic groups follow socioeconomic differences among those groups. The most telling example in the United States is that the African-American LBW rate was 13 percent in 1995, more than twice the rates for European or Asian Americans, and African Americans have the lowest per capita income of the three groups. That these differences are socioeconomic and not ethnic is underscored by the fact that wealthier African Americans have heavier babies, on average, than poorer African Americans (Starfield et al., 1991). Similarly, the rate among Hispanic Americans of Puerto Rican heritage is 9.2 percent, whereas the rate among those of Cuban descent, who tend to be more affluent, is 6.1 percent (U.S. Bureau of the Census, 1996).

■ Within the United States, LBW rates in the poorest states (e.g., in Louisiana and Mississippi, greater than 9 percent) are almost twice those in some richer states (e.g., in Alaska and Oregon, about 5 percent). Such differences cannot be attributed solely to the greater proportions of African Americans in the South, for similar state-by-state disparities are seen within ethnic groups. For example, the rate of low-birthweight births among white newborns in Mississippi is significantly higher than that among white newborns in Alaska (7 percent compared to 5 percent) (Children's Defense Fund, 1998).

Of course, socioeconomic status is only a rough gauge, and other factors sometimes have more effect in some cases. This is apparent with another Hispanic group—Americans of Mexican descent. Their LBW rate is only 5.6 percent, much lower than the rates of other groups with similar levels of income and education (U.S. Bureau of the Census, 1996). As you have already seen, cultural values and paternal support are among the probable reasons for this relatively low rate (Singh & Yu, 1996; Zambrana et al., 1997).

This raises a question: Can cultural practices and public policies change to reduce the LBW rate? Recent statistics suggest that the opposite is occurring in the United States (see Table 4.5). Other data show that the VLBW and ELBW rates are rising even more rapidly. At the same time, the median birthweight has actually been increasing (from 7 pounds 4 ounces in 1970 to 7 pounds 8 ounces in 1997) and neonatal deaths have plummeted, from 15 to 5 per 1,000. Thus most newborns are healthier, but there are far more tiny newborns who survive for years than ever before. This raises a new choice among three desirable goals:

table **4.5**	**Percent of Low-Birthweight Infants in U.S. by Census Category**			
	1985	1990	1993	1996
White	5.6	5.7	6.0	6.3
Black	12.4	13.3	13.3	13.0
Hispanic	6.2	6.1	6.2	6.3
Native American	5.9	6.1	6.4	not available
Overall	6.8	7.0	7.2	7.4

Source: United States Bureau of the Census, 1992, 1996, 1998.

Why? Some reasons for the unwanted increase in low-birthweight babies are known: more multiple births because of fertility drugs and better prenatal care, which means fewer stillbirths. However, this explains only part of the increase, especially since several other nations continue to decrease the number of infants born below 5½ pounds (2,500 grams).

■ Better support for women throughout pregnancy so that fewer LBW infants are born
■ Better intensive care so that more tiny infants survive
■ Better long-term family support so that children who were low-birthweight reach their full potential

❶ **Answer to Observational Quiz (from page 120):** The woman is probably married (see the ring) and probably practices good hygiene (even her fingernails are very clean), and both correlate with healthier pregnancies. However, the four bottles of pills are troubling: unless she has some special deficiency, one multivitamin with folic acid should be enough.

All three are obviously important, but currently the most costly and intensive effort is devoted to saving the lives of the tiniest babies; fewer resources are given to prevention, and almost no public or private insurance provides adequate at-home care during the early years or specialized education until preschool age. Without such help few parents are prepared to cope with the special needs of a very tiny baby, who typically is more demanding and less responsive than a full-term, full-size infant. Perhaps as a result, the rates of child abuse and neglect are elevated for children who were LBW, especially if they are disabled as well (Giardino et al., 1997). To make matters worse, although more LBW infants are born to impoverished families than to middle-class families, LBW infants raised in low-income homes are particularly likely to develop long-term intellectual disabilities (Doussard-Roosevelt et al., 1997; Ross et al., 1996; Sansavini et al., 1996).

Taken as a whole, these statistics provide sobering evidence of the need for a developmental perspective on the LBW rate that looks at each stage of life: The best medicine may be preventive medicine; the best treatment may not involve highly specialized monitors, respirators, or microsurgery but may involve ongoing efforts to help families and communities provide the care that all children deserve.

Figure 4.6 A Normal, Uncomplicated Birth.
(a) The baby's position as the birth process begins. *(b)* The first stage of labor: The cervix dilates to allow passage of the baby's head. *(c)* Transition: The baby's head moves into the "birth canal," the vagina. *(d)* The second stage of labor: The baby's head moves through the opening of the vagina (crowns) and *(e)* emerges completely. The head is turned, and the rest of the body emerges.

THE NORMAL BIRTH

For a full-term fetus and a healthy mother, birth can be simple and quick. At some time during the last month of pregnancy, most fetuses change position for the final time, turning upside down so that the head is low in the mother's pelvic cavity. They are now in position to be born in the usual way, head first. (About 1 in 20 does not turn and is born "breech," buttocks first.)

Then, at about the 266th day after conception, the fetal brain signals the release of certain hormones that pass into the mother's bloodstream. These hormones trigger her uterine muscles to contract and relax, at first irregularly.

Regular contractions then gradually push the fetus downward, putting pressure on the cervix and causing it to dilate until it is open about 4 inches (10 centimeters), enough to allow the fetus's head to squeeze through (see Figure 4.6). This process, called the *first stage of labor,* typically lasts 6 hours in first births and 3 hours in subsequent births, although there is much variation—from a few minutes to a few days (Nichols & Zwelling, 1997). In a few minutes of transition, the head descends from the uterus and "crowns" (that is, the first bit of scalp becomes visible at the opening of the vagina). Then the *second stage of labor* begins. The skin surrounding the vagina stretches with each second-stage contraction until the head emerges, usually less

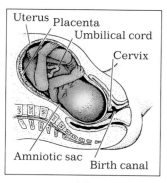

Uterus
Placenta
Umbilical cord
Cervix
Amniotic sac
Birth canal

(a)

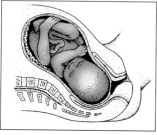

(b)

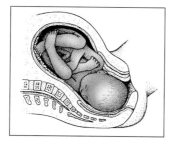

(c)

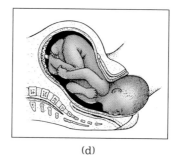

(d)

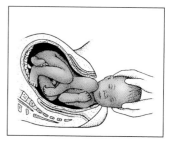

(e)

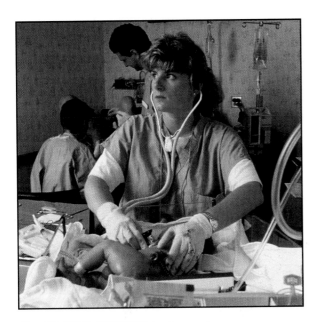

One Hundred Plus per Minute A minute after birth, this newborn is undergoing his first exam, the Apgar. From the newborn's ruddy color and obvious muscle tone, it looks as if he will pass with a score of 7 or higher.

Apgar scale A means of quickly assessing a newborn's body functioning. The baby's color, heart rate, reflexes, muscle tone, and respiratory effort are scored (from 0 to 2) 1 minute and 5 minutes after birth and compared with a standard for healthy babies (a perfect 10).

than an hour after crowning. Since the head is by far the biggest part of the newborn, once the head is born, the rest is easy. Within a few seconds of the next contraction, the baby is fully born.

The Newborn's First Minutes

People who have never witnessed a birth often picture the newborn being held upside down and spanked by the attending doctor or midwife, to make the baby start crying and therefore breathing. Actually, newborns usually breathe and cry on their own as soon as they are born. In fact, they sometimes cry as their heads emerge from the birth canal, even before their shoulders—one by one—appear. As the first spontaneous cries occur, the newborn's circulatory system begins to function; soon the infant's color changes from a bluish tinge to pink, because oxygen circulates throughout the system. The eyes open wide; the tiny fingers grab anything they can; the even tinier toes stretch and retract. The newborn is instantly, zestfully, ready for life.

Checking for Problems

Nevertheless, there is much for those attending the birth to do. Any mucus that might be in the baby's throat is removed, especially if the first breaths seem shallow or strained. The umbilical cord is cut to detach the placenta, leaving the "belly button" to signify the first 9 months of life. The infant is wiped dry of fluid and blood, weighed, and wrapped to preserve body heat. If the birth is assisted by a trained health worker (as are 98 percent of the births in industrialized nations and 51 percent of the births worldwide [United Nations, 1994]), the newborn is immediately checked for body functioning.

One common means of assessing the newborn's condition is a measure called the **Apgar scale** (see Table 4.6). From a brief examination, the examiner assigns a score of 0, 1, or 2 to the heart rate, breathing, muscle tone, color, and reflexes at 1 minute after birth and again at 5 minutes. A low score at 1 minute is a warning, but usually newborns quickly improve. If the 5-minute total score is 7 or better, there is no danger. If the 5-minute total score is below 7, the infant needs help establishing normal breathing; if the score is below 4, the baby is in critical condition and needs immediate medical attention to prevent respiratory distress and death. Few newborns score a perfect 10, but most readily adjust to life outside the womb.

table **4.6**	**Criteria and Scoring of the Apgar Scale**				
Score	Color	Heartbeat	Reflex Irritability	Muscle Tone	Respiratory Effort
0	Blue, pale	Absent	No response	Flaccid, limp	Absent
1	Body pink, extremities blue	Slow (below 100)	Grimace	Weak, inactive	Irregular, slow
2	Entirely pink	Rapid (over 100)	Coughing, sneezing, crying	Strong, active	Good, baby is crying

Source: Apgar, 1953.

The Parents' Reaction

The moments right after birth are very special: the newborn is usually quiet and alert, and the parents are usually relieved and joyful. In one father's words:

> Christopher was placed in my wife's arms even before the umbilicus was cut; shortly after it was cut, he was wrapped (still dripping and wonderfully new like a chick out of an egg) and given to me to hold while my wife got her strength back. He was very alert, apparently able to focus his attention on me and on other objects in the room; as I held him he blossomed into pink, the various parts of his body turning from deep purple and almost blue, to pink, to rose. I was fascinated by the colors: time stopped. [quoted in Tanzer & Block, 1976]

Often, the mother soon cradles the newborn against her skin, perhaps offering the breast for the first time. Some infants are too dazed or drugged (from birth anesthesia) to react, but most begin sucking vigorously. Fortunately, they have flat noses and virtually no chins, which make it easier to latch on to the nipple.

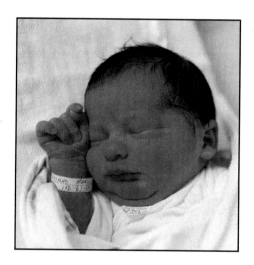

Picture Perfect One-day-old James looks bruised, scraped, and squashed—a perfectly normal, beautiful newborn.

But here is a warning for those who have never seen a newborn until their own is handed to them. Newborns look strange. Especially if they are born a bit early, their skin may be covered with a waxy white substance called *vernix*; if they are a bit late, their skin is often red and wrinkled. Whatever color their complexion will eventually take on, at birth their skin is usually lighter, is often uneven in color (with whitish, bluish, or reddish patches), and sometimes shows visible bruises and birthmarks. The body looks strange too. Not only is the baby chinless and the hair merely fuzz, but the skull is sometimes misshapen, a result of the bones' pushing together to squeeze through the birth canal. A pulse is visible in the top of the head, where the skull has not yet fused. And the tiny legs and arms flail out, or tuck in, instead of extending quietly and straight.

All these characteristics are temporary. The Apgar score and the birthweight are the critical measures of early health—not the newborn's appearance. Every day that passes makes the newborn look more normal (advertisements involving "newborns" typically feature babies several weeks old) and behave more predictably. The particulars of their early physical development are described in Chapter 5.

Medical Attention

How closely any given birth approaches the foregoing description depends on many factors. Among them are the mother's preparation for birth (gained through prenatal classes, conversations with women friends and relatives, or personal experience); the physical and emotional support provided by birth attendants (both professional and familial); the position and size of the fetus; and the cultural context (Creasy, 1997). An additional and sometimes very important factor affecting the birth experience is the nature and degree of medical intervention.

Almost every birth in every developed nation now occurs amid ongoing medical activity, typically including medication to dull pain or speed contractions; sterile procedures that involve special gowns, gloves, and washing; and electronic monitoring of both the mother and the fetus. Often surgery is performed, typically an *episiotomy* (a minor incision of the tissue at the opening of the vagina to speed the last moments before birth) or, in about 22 percent of births in the United States, a **Cesarean section** to remove the fetus from the uterus through the mother's abdomen.

Cesarean section A means of childbirth in which the fetus is taken from the mother surgically, through an incision that extends from the mother's abdomen through the uterus.

Worldwide, the actions of doctors, midwives, and nurses save millions of lives each year—the lives of mothers as well as of infants. Indeed, a lack of medical attention during childbirth is a major reason why motherhood is still hazardous in the least developed nations. "An African woman has a one in 21 lifetime risk of dying from birth complications, a woman in Asia has a one in 54 lifetime risk, and a woman in Northern Europe has an almost negligible one in 10,000 lifetime risk" (Nowak, 1995).

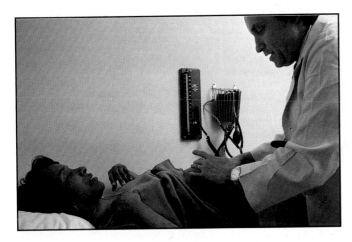 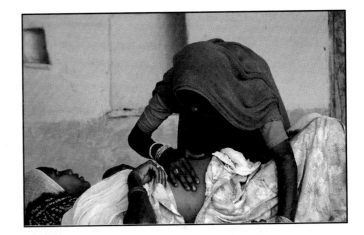

Same Event, Thousands of Miles Away Both these birth attendants—the obstetrician in New York City and the midwife in Rajastan, India—are assessing the size, position, and heartbeat of a developing fetus. Which pregnancy is more likely to result in a healthy baby? If the birth is of high risk, the high-tech equipment on the left might be critical. However, if the pregnancy is a normal one, as most pregnancies are, the experience and empathy of the trained attendant is more important than the diagnostic tools he or she uses.

Medical attention makes delivery faster, easier, and safer for mother and child alike. In many nations (including some of the most advanced), increasing numbers of trained midwives fill the gap between the busy, highly trained obstetrician, who specializes in serious complications, and the neighborhood "granny nurse," whose ministrations are most welcome in uncomplicated births but whose expertise is limited. In developed countries, trained and licensed midwives not only know how to deal with medical aspects of most births but also understand the psychic impact of birth on the new mother. As one midwife stresses, "Let's not leave any woman holding her baby without having conveyed to her our complete respect and belief in her ability to think clearly, to make decisions, and to be a good parent (Walton & Hamilton, 1998).

From several perspectives, there seems little to fault in a medicalized, technological approach to birth. Most women decide to give birth in a hospital rather than at home, want relief of pain instead of a drug-free birth, and prefer receiving medical attention to being left alone. In some nations, such as England, about half of all births occurred at home in 1970; now almost all women choose to give birth in a hospital. Indeed, the Netherlands is unique among developed nations in its high rate of home births: about 35 percent (Ferguson, 1997). However, many specific aspects of hospital births, including the routine use of medication, intravenous fluids, electronic monitoring, and episiotomy, have been criticized as being more rooted in medical tradition than in medical necessity (Emory et al., 1996; Ferguson, 1997).

As a result of these criticisms, by the early 1990s only 41 percent of all U.S. hospital births occurred in delivery rooms with high-tech equipment, whereas 53 percent occurred in the *labor room*—typically a smaller, friendlier room where a woman stays, with her husband or other familiar person, from the time she enters the hospital until she and her baby are recovered from birth (Nichols & Zwelling, 1997). In this setting, doctors and nurses intervene when needed, but the woman has much more control. The fact that it is *her* room, and she is with *her* husband, makes it *her* birth—and that itself reduces anxiety, pain, and complications. Even if there are complications, they seem to cause less stress.

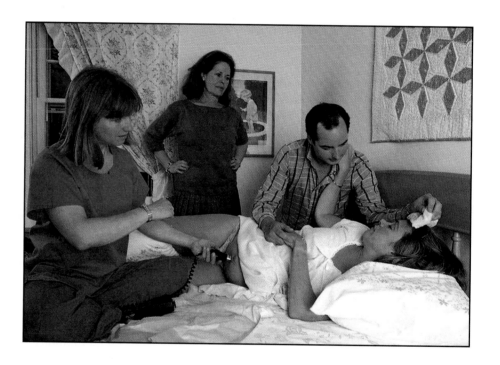

Eight Hands, One Focus While the birth attendant checks the fetal heartbeat, the husband wipes the brow of the laboring woman and her mother looks on. This is a cultural switch: in earlier generations of home births, the mother was the main caregiver during labor, while the future father waited anxiously in another room.

Another 5 percent of U.S. births occur in freestanding *birthing centers*, which are even more family-centered. As one women recounts:

When we arrived at the Birthing Center to have the baby, we were told to go right to the room we had chosen ahead of time. There weren't any strong hospital odors, no people rushing around, no papers for Gary to fill out while I was wheeled off down a long hall without him. We just walked together to our room.

There is always some amount of anxiety in starting labor; but the atmosphere at the Birthing Center was so relaxing that it had a calming effect on me. The thing that meant the most to my husband was his feeling that he belonged there. No one made him feel that he was in the way. (The comfortable recliner in our room helped, too.)

I can remember how great it felt to be able to get up and shower to relieve my back labor and to take a walk out in the hall when I felt the need to walk. I wasn't confined to bed; I was in control.

Several hours later, our third daughter was born. She never left us to go to the nursery with harsh lights and lots of other crying babies. She remained in our quiet room with us. We could hold her when she wanted to be held and feed her when she wanted to be fed. Gary and I both were there when the pediatrician checked her.

Even though it was my most difficult labor and delivery, it was our happiest. [La Leche, 1997]

Only 1 percent of U.S. births occur at home—about half of these by choice and attended by a midwife, and half due to unexpectedly rapid birth (Nichols & Zwelling, 1997).

The Question of Medical Intervention

One question not usually asked by the medical personnel directly involved with the birth, but very important for those interested in human development as an ongoing process, is: How will the mother, father, and child be affected by various procedures in the hours and days after birth? Some negative effects can arise directly from the use of medications, which inevitably remain in the bloodstreams of both mother and child and slow down their ability to focus on each other and enjoy their early interaction (Adams, 1989; Brackbill et al., 1988; Emory et al., 1996). Further, the postdelivery pain from an episiotomy or a Cesarean section, the aftereffects of anesthesia on the mother's emotions, and the separations imposed on the new family by medical procedures and hospital protocol can add to the difficulty of the early family relationship.

One review of Cesarean sections found that they do more than produce pain and require longer recovery times; they also make it less likely that a mother will hold her baby in the hours after birth, or breast-feed the infant, or even, 6 weeks later, feel satisfied with the newborn or the birth (DiMatteo et al., 1996).

We do know that social context, not medical need, dictates many obstetrical practices. As regards Cesarean sections, three studies together make this crucial point:

"I suppose this puts my new bike on the back burner?"

Bike Versus Baby? Often neglected in the medicalization of birth are the new baby's older siblings. Few are as sophisticated as this boy making the connection between the cost of the new baby and his own material condition, but most miss the absent mother. If the mother is gone for several days, because she is recovering from surgery or other complications, and if she comes home tired, depressed, distracted, or in pain, many siblings develop deep resentments against the innocent cause of it all.

1. In the United States and Canada, after a Cesarean section, only 8 percent of women who become pregnant again have a normal vaginal birth. But in Norway and Scotland, 40 percent do so (Goldman et al., 1993).

2. In the state of Washington, the rate of Cesarean sections in church and military hospitals is only half of that in private hospitals, even though the private-hospital patients are generally in good health. The explanation seems to be that American doctors have a "financial disincentive" to perform Cesarean sections on poorer patients (such as those in church and military hospitals), because the doctors and hospitals will not be reimbursed as well for the surgery or the longer hospitalization. Is there sometimes a financial incentive to perform Cesareans (McKenzie & Stephenson, 1993)?

3. In Shanghai, the rate of Cesarean sections increased from about 5 percent in 1970 to 10 percent in 1985 to 23 percent in the early 1990s. The primary reason: Government insurance paid for it (Cai et al., 1998).

Obviously, the costs and benefits of medicalized childbirth vary from birth to birth. However, from a developmental perspective, the cost-benefit equation often seems biased in favor of immediate action, without considering the impact on the new family in the days and months to come. The issues are particularly salient when the birth is a high-risk one.

BIRTH COMPLICATIONS

If a fetus is already at risk because of low weight, preterm birth, genetic abnormality, or teratogenic exposure, or because the mother is unusually young, old, or small or has other medical problems, birth complications are much more likely. The crucial concept to emphasize is that birth complications are part of a continuum, beginning long before the first contractions and continuing in the months and years thereafter.

As an example, **cerebral palsy** (difficulties with movement control resulting from brain damage) was once thought to be solely caused by birth procedures such as excessive analgesia, slow breech birth, or misapplied forceps. (Forceps are sometimes used to pull the fetal head through the birth canal.) Now we realize, however, that cerebral palsy often results from genetic vulnerability, worsened by teratogens and a birthing process that includes **anoxia**—a temporary lack of oxygen that can cause brain damage. We also realize that the quality of life of the cerebral palsy child depends a great deal on the education of parents and child.

Similarly, low-birthweight infants are at risk for many problems before, during, and immediately after birth, especially when they are very early or very small. These problems sometimes affect them lifelong.

cerebral palsy A disorder that results from damage to the brain's motor centers, usually as a result of events during or before birth. People with cerebral palsy have difficulty with muscle control, which can affect speech or other body movements.

anoxia A lack of oxygen that, if prolonged, can cause brain damage or death.

First the Intensive-Care Nursery

Vulnerable infants are typically placed in intensive-care nurseries where they are confined to enclosed *isolettes* (so that their environment can be monitored and controlled), hooked up to one or another piece of medical machinery, and surrounded by bright lights and noise. Although these measures are often medically warranted, they also deprive the neonate of certain kinds of stimulation, such as the gentle rocking they would have experienced if they still were in the womb or the regular handling involved in feeding and bathing if they were at low risk. To overcome this deprivation, many hospitals provide high-risk infants with regular massage and soothing stimulation, which aid weight gain and increase overall alertness (Scafidi et al., 1993). Ideally, parents share in this early caregiving, in recognition of the fact that they too are deprived and stressed (Goldberg & Divitto, 1995). Not only must they cope with uncertainty about their baby's future, but they must struggle with feelings of inadequacy and perhaps with sorrow, guilt, and anger. Such emotions are relieved somewhat if they can cradle and care for their vulnerable newborn. Anything that strengthens the family may forestall difficulties later on.

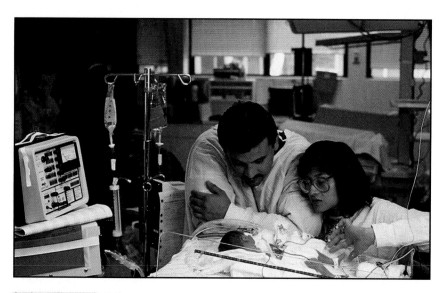

Getting to Know You If these new parents were kept at a distance, they might be troubled by the intravenous drips, the beeping monitor, and the protective plastic of the intensive-care nursery. Through the intimacy of closeness and touch, the LBW patient becomes, to the parents, simply "our baby."

Then Home

For high-risk infants who survive, complications await, including unexpected minor medical problems and slow development. Preterm infants often are late to smile, to hold a bottle, and to communicate. As the

❓ Especially for Social Scientists: When is animal research used too quickly to support conclusions about people?

months go by, short- and long-term cognitive difficulties emerge. Cerebral palsy, evident weeks after birth, affects 20 percent of those who weighed less than 35 ounces (1,000 grams) at birth, 15 percent of those who weighed between 2 and 3½ pounds (1,000 and 1,500 grams), and 7 percent of those who weighed between 3½ and 5½ pounds (1,500 and 2,500 grams) (Hack et al., 1995). High-risk infants who escape such obvious impairments are often more distractible and slower to talk (Byrne et al., 1993; Lukeman & Melvin, 1993).

Fortunately, long-term handicaps are not inevitable. Some newborns who had heart defects or other serious abnormalities, or were very small, can and do develop quite normally (Bigsby et al., 1996). Thus, parents of high-risk infants should not assume either that birth was the child's last major challenge or, conversely, that severe intellectual and medical problems will soon emerge.

Risks increase when the infant is very, very tiny—less than 3½ pounds (1,500 grams)—or when medical complications affect brain development for days or weeks, or when the infant is raised in a home already burdened by low socioeconomic status (Bendersky & Lewis, 1995; Brooks-Gunn et al., 1993; Kalmar, 1996; Rieck et al., 1996). Preterm babies are always "more work and less fun," but even when mothers are young and poor, intervention—including parent-support programs and intensive high-quality day care beginning at age 1—can result in substantial intellectual gains for the child and notable benefits for the mother-child relationship (Goldberg & Divitto, 1995; Ramey et al., 1992). Let us look, then, at that relationship.

parent-newborn bond The strong feelings of attachment that arise between parents and their newborn infants.

Expressions of Love Smell and touch are essential components for mother-infant bonding for many animals, including the nuzzling lions seen here. Fortunately, bonding between humans can occur in varied ways, with early contact not at all essential—although physical intimacy, from breast-feeding at infancy to hugs at adolescence, sustains close attachment between parent and child.

THE BEGINNING OF BONDING

Popular attention has been captured by the concept of the **parent-newborn bond,** an almost instant connection between parents and newborns as they touch each other in the first hours after birth. Over the past decade, hundreds of newspaper and magazine articles have waxed rhapsodic over the joy and the necessity of forming this special bond. Without immediate physical contact, according to some, the long-term love between parent and child will be diminished and the child will suffer. Many people have come to believe that bonding is a critically important "magical social glue." As one mother who was deprived of early contact said, "It made me feel like a rotten mother when I didn't get to bond with my first two children. Made me feel they were going to go out and rob a bank" (Eyer, 1992). Research, however, has failed to support the concept as most people understand it (see the Research Report, page 130).

That raises an interesting query: Why was the notion of essential bonding so quickly accepted, when the research evidence was so sparse? Diane Eyer, a social scientist who has studied this topic, concluded that bonding is a *social construction,* an idea formed as a rallying cry against the medicalization, depersonalization, and patriarchy of the traditional hospital birth. Eyer argues that women and developmental experts were ready to believe that newborns and mothers need to be together from the start, and therefore that it took only a tiny nudge from scientific research for the mystique of early bonding to spring forth into general acceptance. She fears that this

BONDING IN GOATS, RATS, AND HUMANS

The best evidence for a parent-newborn bond comes from studies of a quite specific and powerful bond between mother and newborn in various species of mammals (Fleming & Corter, 1995). Many female animals, for instance, nourish and nurture their own young and ignore, reject, or mistreat the young of others. And many male animals kill newborns that seem abnormal or that do not seem to be theirs.

At least three factors have been identified as contributing to the mother-infant bond:

- *Hormones* released during and after birth that trigger maternal behavior
- The mother's *recognition* of her particular infant by its smell
- The *timing* of the first physical contact between mother and newborn

The third of these factors can be remarkably precise: in some species, contact must occur within a critical period in order for bonding to take place. For example, if a baby goat is removed from its mother immediately after birth and returned a few hours later, the mother sometimes rejects it, kicking and butting it away no matter how pitifully it bleats or how persistently it tries to nurse. However, if a newborn goat remains with the mother who nuzzles and suckles it for the critical first 5 minutes and then is separated from her, the mother goat welcomes its return (Klopfer, 1971). Sheep and cows react in like fashion, with contact in the first hours after birth leading to the mother's strong urge to unite with the infant. Other species display a less pronounced form, with touching in the "sensitive" period soon after birth helpful but not essential (Rosenblith, 1992).

It is not only the mother who searches for her missing newborn. On their part, newborn animals are primed to seek out their mothers. Even baby rats have multiple pathways for bonding, including an acute sense of smell and taste that begins to identify their particular mother before birth and thus lead the blind newborns to nuzzle up to her. Newborn rats also signal severe distress with a high-pitched cry that is inaudible to humans but piercing to mother rats, who typically respond with signs of mother-rat love, licking and nuzzling. This mutual mother-newborn bond is crucial for metabolism, temperature regulation, heart rate, and cognition and hence allows the newborn rats to thrive (Hofer, 1995).

Does a corresponding sensitive time period exist for bonding in humans? Some early research (with a few dozen mothers) suggested that it does. In those studies, the benefits of both immediate contact in the moments after birth and extended contact during the first days of life were apparent over the entire first year. This was especially true for first-time mothers who were very young, poor, or otherwise stressed or who had preterm infants who might have been deemed too frail, or too dependent on life support, to be touched. The mothers who had held their infants soon after birth were more attentive and attached to them 1 year later than were the mothers who had barely seen their infants in the early days (Grossman et al., 1981; Klaus & Kennell, 1976; Leifer et al., 1972).

This research is credited with ending several *postpartum* (after-birth) hospital practices that were once routine. These include whisking newborns away to the nursery, preventing mothers from holding their newborns for the first 24 hours, and barring parents even from setting foot in intensive-care units. All these practices were originally thought to protect mother and child from infection; all are now seen as unnecessary.

Today almost no one questions the wisdom of early contact between mother and child. It can provide a wondrous beginning to the parent-child relationship, as suggested by this mother's account:

> The second he came out, they put him on my skin and I reached down and I felt him and it was something about having that sticky stuff on my fingers . . . it was really important to feel that waxy stuff [vernix] and he was crying and I made soothing sounds to him. . . . And he started calming down and somehow that makes you feel—like he already knows you, he knows who you are—like animals or something, perhaps the smell of each other . . . it was marvelous to hold him and I just touched him for a really long time and then they took him over but something had already happened. Just instant love. [quoted in Davis-Floyd, 1992]

But is this early contact, as has been claimed, essential for formation of the mother-child bond? Absolutely not. Extensive later research found that immediate or extended early skin-to-skin togetherness made no measurable long-term differences in the mother-child relationship (Lamb, 1982; Myers, 1987). In retrospect, this makes sense. All human children need parental nurturance, through a steady stream of the infant's nighttime feeding, the toddler's temper, the preschooler's incessant questioning, the schoolchild's self-absorption, and the adolescent's rebellion—punctuated by illness, disappointment, and other unhappiness—that requires devoted parents to sacrifice some of their own wishes and plans for at least 20 years. Surely, the relationship between parent and child could not hinge on a critical episode of bonding at birth—nature is not so foolhardy as to create one, and only one, pathway for survival.

zealous acceptance came at a high price: the setting of a standard of instant affection and "active love right after birth . . . that many women find impossible to meet" (Eyer, 1992).

Depression and Love

Indeed, too rigidly applying the idea of bonding may be no better than not promoting it at all. If a medicated mother, exhausted from the birth process, is handed her infant for 10 minutes or so while the episiotomy is stitched, and then the baby is removed because "bonding" has supposedly occurred, she may well feel guilty for not experiencing the surge of emotion that the mystique prescribes. Even worse, if an inexperienced mother is, for any reason, not allowed to hold her infant in the minutes after birth, all her fears about her own ability to be a good mother may overwhelm her. One possible consequence is **postpartum depression,** the feeling of inadequacy and sadness that between 10 and 20 percent of women feel in the days and weeks after birth (called *baby blues* in the mild version, *postpartum psychosis* in the most severe form). There are many possible causes of this reaction, but the mother's perception of her own inability to care for her infant is one of them (O'Hara, 1997). Thus, we must ensure that the mystique of bonding does not boomerang, undermining the very relationship it is supposed to protect.

If the mystique of early bonding were taken too far, the experts might end up emphasizing the first few minutes and ignoring the day-to-day support that beleaguered mothers need. Fortunately, the evidence now confirms that immediate contact is neither necessary nor sufficient for bonding, as evidenced by the millions of very affectionate and dedicated biological, adoptive, or foster parents who never touched their children when they were newborns.

Does this mean that hospital routines can go back to the old ways, separating mother and newborn? Never. As one leading developmentalist states:

> I hope that the weakness of the findings for bonding will not be used as an excuse to keep mothers and their infants separated in the hospital. Although such separation may do no permanent harm for most mother-infant pairs, providing contact in a way that is acceptable to the mother surely does not harm and gives much pleasure to many. It is my belief that anything that may make the postpartum period more pleasurable surely is worthwhile. [Rosenblith, 1992]

In general, the mother's hormonal and physiological condition during the hours and days right after birth "is clearly a state of intense affect" (Corter & Fleming, 1995). In this emotional period, everything possible should be done to help the mother cherish her infant's touch, smell, and appearance. But care should be taken not to overwhelm the mother with a cultural ideal she cannot reach—lest the "bonding" between a crying, scrawny newborn and an exhausted mother lead to anger, rejection, and depression. Love between a parent and a child is affected by their *ongoing interactions* throughout infancy and childhood and beyond, as well as by the manifold social contexts in which their relationship flourishes. As the next 12 chapters will reveal, the nature of the parent-infant relationship is critical for healthy development, but the specifics of its formation are not.

postpartum depression The profound feeling of sadness and inadequacy that sometimes is experienced by new mothers, leading to an inability to eat, sleep, or care normally for their newborns.

❶ **Response for Social Scientists (from page 129):** When it supports a point of view that is popular but not yet substantiated by research data, as in the social construction about bonding.

SUMMARY

FROM ZYGOTE TO NEWBORN

1. The first 2 weeks of prenatal growth are called the germinal period. During this period, the single-cell zygote develops into an organism more than a hundred cells in size, travels down the fallopian tube, and implants itself in the uterine lining, where it continues to grow.

2. The period from the third through the eighth week after conception is called the period of the embryo. The development of the embryo is cephalo-caudal (from the head downward) and proximo-distal (from the inner organs outward). During this period the heart begins to beat and the eyes, ears, nose, and mouth begin to form.

3. At 8 weeks after conception, the future baby is only about 1 inch (2½ centimeters) long. Yet it already has the basic organs and features of a human baby, with the exception of the sex organs. The behaviors of the mother, father, and community have already affected the embryo.

4. The fetal period extends from the ninth week until birth. By the twelfth week all the organs and body structures have formed. The fetus attains viability when the brain is sufficiently mature to regulate basic body functions, around the twenty-fourth week after conception.

5. The average fetus weighs approximately 2 pounds at the beginning of the third trimester and 7½ pounds at the end. The additional weight, plus maturation of brain, lungs, and heart, ensures survival for more than 99 percent of all full-term babies.

RISK REDUCTION

6. Many teratogens can harm the embryo and fetus. Diseases, drugs, and pollutants can all cause birth defects. Some cause explicit physical impairment. Others, called behavioral teratogens, harm the brain and therefore impair the child's intellect and actions.

7. Teratogens are risks, not inevitable destroyers. Whether a particular teratogen will harm a particular embryo or fetus depends on the timing and amount of exposure and the developing organism's genetic vulnerability.

8. To protect against prenatal complications, a woman can avoid or limit exposure to teratogens, maintain good nutrition, and seek early and competent prenatal care. Social support from family and the community is also important.

9. In developed countries, many serious teratogens, including rubella and some prescription drugs, now rarely reach a fetus. However, psychoactive drugs remain common hazards. How and when the community should intervene when a woman uses drugs or alcohol is a controversial topic.

LOW BIRTHWEIGHT AND ITS CAUSES

10. Low birthweight arises from a variety of causes, which often occur in combination. They include the mother's poor health or nutrition, smoking, drinking, drug use, and age. Many of these factors are associated with poverty.

11. Preterm or small-for-gestational-age babies are more likely than full-term babies to suffer from stress during the birth process and to experience medical difficulties, especially breathing problems, in the days after birth. Long-term cognitive difficulties may occur as well, depending on whether the newborn was of very low birthweight, had serious medical problems, or is raised in an impoverished home.

THE NORMAL BIRTH

12. Birth typically begins with contractions that push the fetus, head first, out from the uterus and then through the vagina. The Apgar scale, which rates the neonate's vital signs at 1 minute after birth and again at 5 minutes after birth, provides a quick evaluation of the infant's health.

13. Medical intervention in the birth process can speed contractions, dull pain, and save lives. However, many aspects of the medicalized birth have been faulted as having a negative emotional impact, with the high rate of cesarean sections (22 percent in the United States) a source of particular concern. Many contemporary birthing practices try to find a balance between these results.

BIRTH COMPLICATIONS

14. Birth complications, such as unusually long and stressful birth that includes anoxia, a lack of oxygen to the fetus, have many causes. Vulnerable newborns are placed in an intensive-care unit for monitoring and treatment. Long-term handicaps are not inevitable for such children, but careful nurturing is required once they are taken home by parents.

THE BEGINNING OF BONDING

15. Ideally, both parents spend time with their baby in the hours and days after birth. However, most developmentalists believe that early, skin-to-skin contact between mother and child is much less important for humans than for some animals. The human parent-infant bond develops continuously over a long period of time, with the moments after birth contributing to, but not determining, the success of the parent-infant relationship.

KEY TERMS

germinal period (99)
period of the embryo (99)
period of the fetus (99)
implantation (100)
neural tube (101)
cephalo-caudal development (101)
proximo-distal development (101)
placenta (103)
age of viability (104)
teratology (105)
teratogens (105)
behavioral teratogens (106)
risk analysis (106)
critical period (108)
threshold effect (109)
interaction effect (109)
rubella (110)

human immunodeficiency virus (HIV) (111)
acquired immune deficiency syndrome (AIDS) (111)
fetal alcohol syndrome (FAS) (113)
low birthweight (LBW) (116)
preterm birth (116)
small for gestational age (SGA) (117)
Apgar scale (123)
Cesarean section (125)
cerebral palsy (128)
anoxia (128)
parent-newborn bond (129)
postpartum depression (131)

KEY QUESTIONS

1. What developments occur during the germinal period?

2. What major developments occur during the period of the embryo?

3. What major developments occur during the period of the fetus?

4. How and when does a fetus respond to the outside world?

5. What are the factors that make a fetus more likely to survive if born at 38 weeks rather than at 24?

6. What factors determine how likely a fetus is to be harmed by teratogens?

7. What public health measures can prevent many cases of rubella and pediatric AIDS?

8. What are some effects of drug abuse on the fetus?

9. What can be done to reduce the damage done by prenatal use of psychoactive drugs?

10. What are the causes and consequences of low birthweight?

11. What is the relationship among the newborn's appearance, the Apgar scale, and health?

12. What are the advantages and disadvantages of the intensive-care nursery?

13. How is the formation of the parent-infant bond different in animals than it is in humans?

14. *In Your Experience* How do the preparation for birth, the actual birth process, and the newborn's appearance affect parent's attitudes toward their baby?

CRITICAL THINKING EXERCISE

by Richard O. Straub

Take your study of Chapter 4 a step further by working this perspective-taking exercise.

Our increasing knowledge about the developing fetus brings with it legal, medical, and ethical questions. For example, doctors are increasingly able to treat the fetus within the womb, as an individual patient with distinct medical needs. This gives rise to the question of whether women should be expected, and even legally required, to submit to medical intervention—including surgery—that might save a fetus but risk their own lives.

Assume that you are an attorney arguing a test case under a new prenatal protective-custody law. The case involves an ailing 24-week-old fetus, for whom surgery within the uterus can be performed. Without surgery, the fetus will die before birth; with surgery, the odds of survival are about 50-50. With surgery, there is also 1 chance in 10 that the mother will not be able to have any more children, and 1 chance in 1,000 that she will die of complications. She is not willing to give permission for the operation, and the father supports his wife.

1. If you are the attorney defending the fetus, what basic arguments and strategies would you use to persuade that surgery *should* be performed?

2. If you are the attorney defending the mother, what basic arguments and strategies would you use? What basic concept would you use to support the position that the surgery *should not* be performed?

Check your answers by comparing them to the sample answers in Appendix B.

PART II

The First 2 Years:
Infants and Toddlers

Adults usually don't change much in a year or two.

Sometimes their hair gets longer or grows thinner, or they gain or lose a few pounds, or they become a little wiser. But if you were to be reunited with friends not seen for several years, you would recognize them immediately.

If, on the other hand, you were to care for a newborn twenty-four hours a day for the first month, and then did not see the baby until a year later, you probably would not recognize him or her. After all, would you recognize a best friend who had quadrupled in weight, grown 14 inches, and sprouted a new head of hair? Nor would you find the toddler's behavior familiar. A hungry newborn just cries; a hungry toddler says "more food" or climbs up on the kitchen counter to reach the cookies.

A year or two is not much time compared to the almost eighty years of the average life span. However, children in their first 2 years reach half their adult height, develop cognitive abilities that have surprised even researchers, and learn to express almost every emotion, not just joy and fear, but also many others, including jealousy and shame. And two of the most important human abilities, talking and loving, are already apparent.

The next three chapters describe these radical and wonderful changes.

The First 2 Years:
Biosocial Development

CHAPTER 5

In the first 2 years of life, the forces of biosocial growth and development are very powerful. Proof of this is visible to any observer, as infants quickly outgrow one set of clothes after another, attempt new behaviors almost daily, and display a rapidly increasing mastery of emerging skills: Sit . . . stand . . . walk . . . run! Reach . . . touch . . . grab . . . throw! Point . . . poke . . . pinch! And every object becomes something to explore with every sense and limb.

Proof is also available from laboratory data on brain development. Small infant brains not only become larger overall but also show the increasing density and complexity that are vital to the maturing of physical and mental capacities.

All these changes are, of course, biologically rooted. But they are also facilitated by the social context, as parents and others nourish, protect, and encourage the infant's development. This is not easy. Infants develop so quickly that, as one expert explains, "Parenting an infant is akin to trying to hit a moving target" (Bornstein, 1995). In this chapter we will look at both the physical development of the child's body and brain and the social environment—particularly as it involves health and nutrition—which can either enhance or inhibit that development.

PHYSICAL GROWTH AND HEALTH

Monitoring growth and protecting health are critical from birth throughout the growing years. During most of childhood, annual visits to the doctor for preventive care are sufficient. In early infancy, by contrast, growth is so fast and vulnerability so great that medical checkups should occur monthly—not only to spot signs of trouble as soon as possible but also to guide parents in their new, pivotal role as the first, and best, defense against illness and injury.

Size and Shape

Every medical checkup in infancy begins with weighing and measuring, for good reason. Except for prenatal development, infancy is the period of the most notable changes in size and proportion, when any slowdown is a cause for immediate concern.

Exactly how rapidly does normal growth occur? Recall that at birth, the average North American weighs a little more than 7 pounds (3.2 kilograms)

immunization A process that stimulates the body's own defensive (immune) system to defend against attack by a particular infectious disease.

and measures about 20 inches (51 centimeters). This means that the typical newborn is lighter than a gallon of milk and about as long as the distance from a man's elbow to the tips of his fingers. In the first days of life, most newborns lose between 5 and 10 percent of their birthweight because they eliminate more substances as body wastes than they take in as nourishment. Then they make up that loss and begin to gain, doubling their birthweight by the fourth month and tripling it by the end of the first year. Much of the weight increase in the early months of life is fat, which provides insulation for warmth and a store of nourishment. After 8 months or so, weight gain derives more from growth in bone, muscle, and body organs.

Infants get taller or, more accurately, longer as well. In each of the first 12 months they grow almost an inch (2.5 centimeters) in length. By age 1, the typical baby weighs about 22 pounds (10 kilograms) and measures almost 30 inches (75 centimeters) (Behrman, 1992).

Physical growth is slower in the second year, but it still is quite rapid. By 24 months most children weigh almost 30 pounds (13 kilograms) and measure between 32 and 36 inches (81 and 91 centimeters), with boys being slightly taller and heavier than girls. In other words, typical 2-year-olds have attained almost one-fifth of their adult weight and half their adult height (see Figure A.4 in Appendix A for details).

As infants grow, their body proportions change. Most newborns seem top-heavy because their heads are about one-fourth of their total length, compared to one-fifth at 1 year and one-eighth in adulthood. Their legs, by contrast, represent only about a quarter of their total body length, whereas for adults, legs account for about half the total height. Thus, while every part of a child's body grows, some parts grow more than others. Those parts that grew most slowly in prenatal development now grow fastest. By adulthood, a person's feet, for example, will be about five times as long as they were at birth, whereas the head will have only doubled in size.

Preventive Medicine

Nowadays, the growth pattern just outlined is taken for granted. However, a century ago in developed nations and a mere decade or two ago in less developed ones, not only growth but even survival were very much in doubt. About 35 percent of all newborns died before age 7 (Bogin, 1996). At any time an infectious disease—smallpox, whooping cough, polio, diphtheria, measles, or any of several others—might suddenly and rapidly spread from child to child, putting them all at risk for stunted growth, serious complications, and death.

Every Child in the World Measles can be a deadly disease for undernourished children and infirm adults in developing nations. This boy's immunization will not only protect him but will also help to protect those in his village in northern India who are too young, too enfeebled, or too frightened to obtain their own shots.

Today, deadly childhood epidemics are rare. An infant's chance of dying from infectious disease in North America, western Europe, Japan, or Australia is less than 1 in 500, down from 1 in 20 in the first half of the twentieth century. This dramatic reduction in early death, not the extension of life in old age, is the primary reason for the almost 20 years added to the average life span worldwide since 1950 (see Figure 5.1).

Many factors have reduced disease-related deaths among young children, from improved sanitation to high-tech treatment for high-risk newborns. However, the single most important cause of the dramatic improvement in child survival is **immunization,** a process that stimulates the body's immune system to defend against a particular infectious disease. Immunization

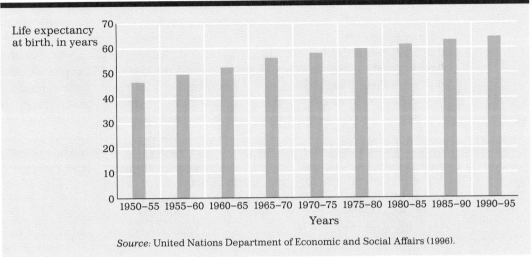

Life expectancy at birth, in years

Source: United Nations Department of Economic and Social Affairs (1996).

Figure 5.1 World Life Expectancy at Birth. The average life expectancy worldwide today is about 20 years longer than it was 40 years ago. The reason is not primarily because older people are living longer (if a person reaches age 30, his or her life expectancy is now only about 5 years longer than it was 50 years ago) but because fewer infants and children die. A century ago almost every family mourned the death of a young child. Now, of all the children who reach age 1, fewer than 1 in 1,000 dies before age 5.

can occur in many ways, through injection (as when a person is vaccinated in the arm or leg), ingestion (as when a child eats a sugar cube that has oral vaccine), inhalation (as when a substance is breathed through the nostrils), or naturally, by actually catching the disease and surviving. The required timing and dosage of the immunization, as well as the incidence and success of immunization programs, vary from illness to illness. In the less developed nations, the rate of immunization against the deadliest childhood diseases improved from about 20 to 80 percent during the 1980s, reducing deaths from these diseases by three-fourths (UNICEF, 1990).

Smallpox, the most lethal disease of all for children, has been completely eradicated worldwide. Consequently, immunization against smallpox is no longer necessary. In 1955, Jonas Salk developed a vaccine against polio, a crippling disease that still affects many older adults with "post-polio syndrome." Now, new cases of polio are very rare (there have been none in the past 10 years in the United States) because no one can catch it or transmit it, and soon the polio vaccination will also be unnecessary (Hull & Aylward, 1997). Measles (which can be fatal in the early months of life, when it causes dehydration) is disappearing too. In the United States, only 138 cases of measles were reported in 1997, a marked contrast to the peak of 770,000 in 1958, and the lowest number since 1911, when disease statistics were first recorded (*MMWR*, April 17, 1998).

Worldwide, both the quality and the scope of immunization have improved every decade. Now, more than 90 percent of all infants are immunized against the childhood diseases of diphtheria, pertussis, tetanus, measles, polio, and mumps (UNICEF, 1995). In developed nations, many infants are immunized against hepatitis B, hemophilus influenza type B (HIB), rubella, and chicken pox as well. (See Appendix A, Table A.1, for a recommended immunization schedule.) Some developed countries also immunize children against tuberculosis, whereas others, including the United States, test children for exposure and then follow up with further testing and treatment if needed.

Obviously, lack of complete immunization puts the child at risk; childhood illnesses are usually mild, but not always. In addition to the problems already mentioned, mumps can produce nerve deafness, and HIB is the leading cause of meningitis. Less obviously, lack of immunization jeopardizes the well-being of others: infants too young to be immunized may die if they catch a disease from an older child; pregnant women who contract rubella may transmit the virus to their fetuses, causing blindness, deafness, and brain damage; healthy adults who contract mumps or measles suffer much worse consequences than a child might; and those who are particularly vulnerable, such as the elderly, the HIV-positive, or cancer patients, can be killed by any number of "childhood" diseases.

Chicken pox, for instance, can be fatal, especially to those whose immune systems are depleted by chemotherapy or AIDS, and sometimes to healthy adults as well. Before the chicken pox vaccine was approved in 1995, about 100 people, mostly adults, died of that disease each year. Now the rate is falling, but not fast enough, as you can see from the case of two preschool children who, unvaccinated, came down with chicken pox in early January 1997. Their 23-year-old mother caught it from them, was hospitalized on January 23, and died on February 2 (*MMWR*, May 16, 1997).

Individual tragedies such as this one highlight the need for large-scale immunization programs. It is not possible for every person, from newborn to centenarian, to be immunized, and in some cases immunization would jeopardize an individual's health more than protect it. Fortunately, 100 percent immunization is not necessary. For most diseases, if 90 percent or more of all children under age 6 are immunized, a disease is unlikely to spread. Note that even in the case of the 23-year-old mother, and even though her particular circumstances (perhaps poverty, poor public health outreach, or recent immigration) left her two children unprotected, she would not have died if they had not gotten the disease from someone else, who got it from someone else, and so on. Thus, although most unimmunized children would not be seriously ill if they contracted a childhood disease, every unimmunized child is a potential carrier of a lethal dose.

Sudden Infant Death Syndrome

Because widespread immunization has now made contagious fatal diseases rare in infancy, more than half of all deaths that occur in a child's first year actually occur in the first month. They are the direct or indirect outcome of congenital abnormalities (such as heart defects), of very low birthweight, or of similar problems obvious in the first days of life (see Figure 5.2). Prevention of such complications was discussed in Chapter 4.

However, one common cause of infant death does not occur in the first few weeks and is not related to any obvious infirmity: **sudden infant death syndrome**, or **SIDS**. SIDS typically kills infants who are at least 2 months old and seemingly completely healthy—already gaining weight, learning to shake a rattle, starting to roll over, and smiling at their caregivers. In the United States, SIDS is now the third leading cause of infant death. Each year more than 3,000 babies in the United States go to sleep and never wake up, victims of a sudden failure to breathe.

sudden infant death syndrome (SIDS)
Death of a seemingly healthy baby who, without apparent cause, stops breathing during sleep.

Figure 5.2 Leading Causes of Infant Death in the United States. Three causes of infant mortality have taken a marked downturn over the past 15 years. In two of them (congenital abnormalities and respiratory distress), intense research and medical technology have made a difference, with advanced genetic testing and counseling, neonatal intensive care, and new drugs given to newborns. However, in the third case, SIDS, the decrease involves no technology or medicine at all. A simple cross-cultural discovery now leads parents to do the direct opposite of what their parents did. Babies are put "back to sleep," (literally, on their backs to sleep) and thousands survive who would have died.

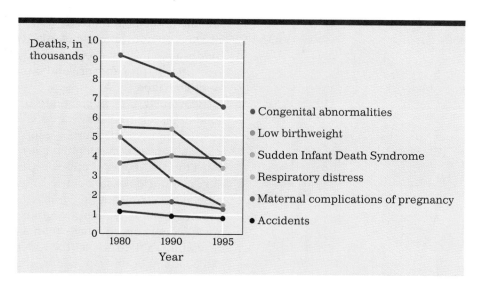

The term "sudden infant death" (also called *crib death* or *cot death*) is more a description after the fact than a diagnosis of cause. Despite decades of research, the root cause of SIDS is still unknown. The designation "sudden infant death" is assigned when an autopsy finds that an infant unexpectedly stopped breathing, and other possible causes, such as deliberate or accidental suffocation, are ruled out. Crib deaths sometimes provoke unfounded suspicions in neighbors and police, who mistakenly assume that the parents have done something wrong. On the other hand, cases of fatal child abuse and even murder have been misdiagnosed as SIDS. For both reasons, immediate and expert investigation and determination of the cause of every sudden infant death are needed.

In recent years, as the diagnosis of SIDS has become more definitive, scientists have intensified their search for a cause—perhaps a subtle neurological or physiological abnormality, or some disease agent that is particularly harmful to young infants. Several potential culprits have been identified in different cases; they range from a bacterium that is occasionally found in raw honey to cardiac instability, to a brain-stem defect that impairs the infant's arousal response (not awakening an infant when oxygen in the lungs falls below a certain level), to an excessive intake of carbon dioxide (as from rebreathing exhaled gases trapped under a blanket) (Kinney et al., 1995; Schwartz et al., 1998).

None of these factors seems to be present in every case, and researchers are becoming increasingly convinced that there is no single cause of SIDS. In all probability, SIDS results from a combination of factors (see Table 5.1), and each factor adds slightly to the overall risk for *certain* infants who, for unknown genetic reasons, are vulnerable. Drawing a profile from the table of risk factors, for example, we can say that a particular (but unidentifiable) 4-month-old boy who was born in September weighing only 5 pounds, whose mother decided not to breast-feed him because she wanted to keep smoking cigarettes, who lives with several siblings in an old overheated dwelling in a low-income neighborhood is much more likely to die of SIDS than an older or younger baby girl who has none of these characteristics. Of course, as with all risk analysis, scientists can spot vulnerability but cannot predict outcomes of actual cases. Indeed, most 4-month-old boys who have all the above characteristics survive with no problems, and some infants with no known risk factors succumb to SIDS.

"Back to Sleep"

Recently, one critical factor in SIDS has been discovered: the infant's sleeping position. All controlled research finds SIDS less likely to occur when healthy infants sleep on their backs than when they

> ❓ **Especially for Police Officers and Social Workers:** If an infant dies suddenly, what would you look for to distinguish SIDS from homicide?

table **5.1**	**SIDS Risk Factors**	
	SIDS More Likely	SIDS Less Likely
Characteristics of the Mother		
Age	Under 20	Over 25
Blood type	O, B, or AB	A
Personal habits	Smoker	Nonsmoker
Income	Poverty level	Middle class
Education	Grade school only	College or higher
Ethnic background	African descent	Asian descent
Characteristics at Birth		
Sex	Male	Female
Birth order	Later-born	First born
Multiple birth?	Yes (twin or triplet)	No (single born)
Apgar score at 5 min.	7 or lower	8 or higher
Heartbeat	Some irregularity	Normal
Situation at Death		
Time of year	Winter	Summer
Age in months	1 to 3	Under 1, over 4
Health	Has a stuffy nose	No cold, no runny nose
Feeding	Bottle-fed	Breast-fed
Sleeping Conditions		
Position	Sleeps on stomach	Sleeps on back
Mattress	Soft, natural fibers	Firm, synthetic
Blankets, nightclothes	Swaddled, tight	Allow free movement
Bedroom temperature	Heated	Cool

Sources: Guilleminault et al., 1982; Haas et al., 1993; Meny et al., 1994; Mitchell et al., 1993; *MMWR*, October 11, 1996; Ponsoby et al., 1993.

sleep on their stomachs. Indeed, one comparison study found that an infant's risk of SIDS quadruples if the baby is put to sleep in a prone rather than a supine position (Ponsoby et al., 1993). Ironically, putting infants to sleep on their stomachs had been recommended by Western pediatricians for decades, assuming that, when babies spit up (as all sometimes do), they might choke if they are lying on their backs (Spock, 1976). While this idea makes sense and may occasionally be borne out, it is now accepted that putting babies on their "back to sleep" is the safer course (Willinger et al., 1994). One possible exception is very young and preterm babies, for whom the best sleeping position *might* sometimes be on their stomachs.

Unfortunately, many parents have not yet gotten the message. In a survey of parents of infants in the United States, 24 percent said their infants sleep on their stomachs; thus, one-fourth of the nation's babies are still at a higher risk of SIDS than need be (Willinger et al., 1998).

Practices Among the Maya Every culture has some traditional practices that are protective of infants and some that are dangerous.

❷ *Observational Quiz (see answer page 145): Can you spot at least one of each here?*

❶ Response for Police Officers and Social Workers (from page 141): An autopsy, or at least a speedy examination by a medical pathologist, is needed, because any suspicions of foul play need to be substantiated with evidence or firmly rejected so that the parents can grieve. However, your careful notes about the immediate circumstances, such as the position of the infant when he or she was discovered, the mattress and blankets nearby, the warmth and humidity of the room, and the baby's health (any evidence of a cold) can be indicative. Further, while SIDS victims sometimes turn blue overall, and thus might seem bruised, they rarely display signs of specific injury or neglect, such as a broken limb, a scarred face, an angry rash, or a skinny body. Especially if maltreatment is evident and the dead baby is not between 2 and 4 months of age, something other than SIDS may have occurred.

Ethnic Differences

A key risk factor in SIDS is ethnic background (see Table 5.1). Generally, within ethnically diverse nations such as the United States, Canada, Great Britain, Australia, and New Zealand, babies of African descent are more likely, and babies of Asian descent less likely, to succumb to SIDS than are babies of European descent. For decades, pediatricians thought the reasons for this difference were either genetic or related to background variables that correlate with ethnicity but are not caused by it (such as the rate of teenage pregnancy). Not much could be done by an individual pediatrician to change an infant's genes or background, so doctors were as helpless to prevent SIDS as parents were.

Fortunately, new attention to ethnicity, not race, led to a closer look at specific infant-care routines that may be widespread in one culture and rare in others. For example, Bangladeshi infants in England tend to be low in both birthweight and socioeconomic status; yet surprisingly they have *lower* rates of SIDS than white British infants, who are more often of normal birthweight and middle-class. If not genes, then what? Bangladeshi infants, even when they sleep, are usually surrounded by many family members in a rich sensory environment, continually hearing noises and feeling the gentle touch of their caregivers. Therefore they do not sleep deeply for very long. By contrast, their native British age-mates tend to sleep in their own private spaces in an environment of enforced quiet, and these "long periods of lone sleep may contribute to the higher rates of SIDS among white infants" (Gantley et al., 1993).

Similarly, Chinese infants, born either in China or elsewhere, have a low rate of SIDS (Beal & Porter, 1991). Why? First, Chinese parents place their babies to sleep on their backs; second, they tend to their babies periodically as they sleep, caressing a cheek or repositioning a limb; and third, most Chinese infants are breast-fed, which makes them sleep less soundly. Therefore Chinese infants are unlikely to fall into a deep, nonbreathing sleep.

It is easy to imagine that many other specifics—perhaps in frequency of feeding, or in sleeping garments, or in crib mattresses, or even in the parents' reaction to thumb-sucking—may likewise have an impact on SIDS (Davies & Gantley, 1994; Farooqi et al., 1993). Already, just from looking at cultural patterns that differ from one group to another, we know we can decrease the prevalence of SIDS by limiting risk—by encouraging breast-feeding, creating smoke-free environments, putting infants to sleep on their backs, and so on. In fact, the last two measures alone are considered largely responsible for a 37 percent decrease in the rate of SIDS in the United States between 1990 and 1995.

BRAIN GROWTH AND DEVELOPMENT

Of all the aspects of growth in the infant, none is more critical than the rapid growth of the brain, which has been called "by far the most complex structure in the known universe" (Thompson, 1993). Recall that the newborn's skull is disproportionately large. In fact, it must be big enough to hold the brain, which at birth has already attained 25 percent of its adult weight. (The neonate's body weight, by comparison, is typically less than 5 percent of adult weight.)

The brain develops most rapidly not only during the prenatal period but also during infancy. By age 2, the brain has attained about 75 percent of its adult weight, while the 2-year-old's body weight is only about 20 percent of what it will eventually be. It is, actually, imperative that the brain grow and develop *ahead of* the rest of the body, for it is the brain that makes all other development possible.

Connections in the Brain

Weight, of course, provides only a crude index of brain development. More significant are changes that occur in the brain's communication systems and that greatly advance the brain's functioning. These communication systems consist primarily of nerve cells, called **neurons,** connected by intricate networks of nerve fibers called **axons** and **dendrites.** Each neuron has a single axon and numerous dendrites; the axon of one neuron meets the dendrites of other neurons at intersections called **synapses** (see Figure 5.3).

---

neuron A nerve cell of the central nervous system. Most neurons are in the brain.

axon The single nerve fiber that extends from a neuron and transmits impulses from that neuron to the dendrites of other neurons.

dendrites Nerve fibers that extend from a neuron and receive the impulses transmitted from other neurons via their axons.

synapse The point at which the axon of one neuron meets the dendrites of another neuron. At that point, brain chemicals called neurotransmitters carry the impulse from axon to dendrites.

Cell nucleus

Dendrites (receive messages from other cells)

Myelin sheath (speeds neural impulses)

Axon

Cell body

Neural impulse (signal traveling down the axon)

Axon terminals (form junctions with other cells)

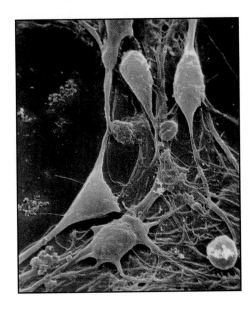

Figure 5.3 An Isolated Neuron. Each neuron includes a cell body, dendrites that bring messages, and an axon that sends messages.

A neuron communicates by sending an electrical impulse through its axon to the dendrites of other neurons. However, axon and dendrites do not actually touch at synapses. Instead, the electrical impulse triggers brain chemicals called neurotransmitters to carry information about the impulse from the axon of the "sending" neuron, across the *synaptic gap*, to the dendrites of the "receiving" neurons.

At birth, the brain contains over 100 billion neurons, far more than any developing person will ever need. However, the networks composed of their axons and dendrites are fairly rudimentary, with relatively few connections (synapses). During the first months and years, there are major spurts of growth and refinement in the networks (see Figure 5.4). These changes are particularly notable in the **cortex,** the brain's eighth-of-an-inch-thick outer layer (the so-called gray matter), which controls perception and thinking.

An estimated fivefold increase in the density of dendrites in the cortex occurs from birth to about age 2 (Diamond, 1990). As a result, in some cases, as many as 15,000 new connections may be established *per neuron* in the first 2 years; the total number of connections has been estimated at a quadrillion (a million billion). This proliferation enables neurons to become connected to (and communicate with) a greatly expanding variety of other neurons within the brain. The establishment of dendrites continues, less rapidly, throughout life (Thompson, 1993).

The phenomenal increase in neural connections over the first 2 years has been called **transient exuberance** (Nowakowski, 1987), a label that actually highlights two key aspects of early brain development. "Exuberance," of course, refers to the sheer magnitude of the growth in neural connections. "Transient," on the other hand, means transitory or temporary. This refers to the fact that the rate of growth of neural connections slows down as the child grows older. Perhaps more important, it also refers to the fact that connections which are not used shrink, atrophy, and then disappear, in a kind of pruning action that is particularly evident in the first years of life.

Indeed, because of this pruning action, many areas of the human brain have more neural connections at age 2 than at any later age. In effect, during infancy the human brain is prepared to process every type of experience a baby might have. Then, through the early years, neural pathways that are exercised become stronger and larger, developing more connections; those that are not used die. Together, proliferation and pruning enhance the efficiency of neural communication while simplifying the brain's overall organization (Thompson, 1993).

The functioning of the brain's communication networks is also enhanced by a process in which axons become coated with *myelin,* a fatty insulating substance that speeds the transmission of neural impulses. This process, called **myelination,** proceeds most rapidly from birth to age 4 and continues through adolescence. Myelination allows children to gain increasing neurological control over their motor functions and sensory abilities, and this control facilitates their intellectual functioning. Further, speed underlies most intellectual functions; it is no accident that we often praise individuals for being quick thinkers or for being able to hold many ideas in their heads at once.

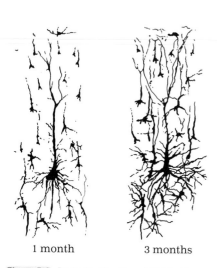

1 month   3 months   15 months

Figure 5.4 Brain Proliferation. Within the brain, nerve fibers increase in size and number over the first 2 years of life, increasing the number of neuronal connections greatly and enabling impressive advances in cognition and the control of actions.

cortex The outer layer of the brain, about an eighth of an inch thick. This area is involved in the voluntary, cognitive aspects of the mind.

transient exuberance The great increase in neurons, dendrites, and synapses that occurs in an infant's brain over the first 2 years of life.

myelination The process in which axons are coated with myelin, a fatty substance that speeds communication between neurons.

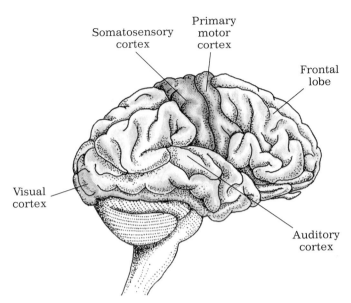

Somatosensory cortex

Primary motor cortex

Frontal lobe

Visual cortex

Auditory cortex

Figure 5.5 Brain Specialization. Areas of the brain are specialized for the reception and transmission of different types of information. Research has shown that both experience and maturation play important roles in brain development. For example, myelination of the nerve fibers leading from the visual cortex of the brain will not proceed normally unless the infant has had sufficient visual experience in a lighted environment.

❶ *Answer to Observational Quiz (from page 142):* *The infant sleeps on her back, near the mother, and thus her risk of SIDS is lower than it would be if she slept on her stomach alone. However, the spaces within the crib walls appear large and flexible enough for a small head or limb to get stuck. After some tragic deaths, the United States regulates the distance between the slats of a crib—no more than 3 inches.*

binocular vision The ability to use both eyes together to focus on a single object.

Brain Growth and Brain Function

Different areas of the brain mature at different times and at different rates, affecting the child's behaviors and abilities accordingly. For example, the frontal area of the cortex (located right behind the forehead; see Figure 5.5) assists in self-control and self-regulation. This area is immature in the newborn—with the result that a young infant cannot stifle a cry of pain or stay awake when drowsiness hits. As the neurons of the frontal area become more interconnected and their axons more myelinated during the first year, the baby becomes better able to regulate everything from reflexive responses to sleep-wake patterns.

With continued development in the frontal area, cognitive skills requiring deliberation begin to emerge, along with a basic capacity for emotional self-control (Bell & Fox, 1992; Dawson, 1994; Fox, 1991). As a result, by age 1 the child's emotions are already much more nuanced and predictable than at birth, responsive as much to the external world (such as a frightening stranger) as to internal states such as hunger. We shall see the results of these developments in more detail in Chapter 6, when we discuss cognition and memory, and in Chapter 7, when we discuss emotions and social interaction. At the moment, the crucial fact to remember is that early brain growth is rapid and widespread. The specifics of which neurons become connected to which other neurons depend on genes, degree of maturation, and—of critical importance lifelong—the infant's experiences (Nelson & Bloom, 1997).

The Role of Experience in Brain Development

As is suggested by our discussion of transient exuberance, brain development in the early years does not stem solely from biological maturation. At least a minimal amount of experience is essential for neural pathways to develop and become permanent. This is true not only for the development of particular learned abilities but even for the full development of the brain structures that make seeing, hearing, touching, and other functions possible. A part of the cortex is dedicated to each such function (hence we speak of the visual cortex, the auditory cortex, and such); and each such function depends on experience to develop.

A Cat's Eye

The role of experience in the development of neural pathways is demonstrated clearly by experiments with animals who are temporarily prevented from using one sensory system or another in infancy. They can become permanently handicapped in that sensory system. For example, if kittens are blindfolded for the first several weeks of life, they never acquire normal vision, even though the anatomy of their eyes appears to be normal. This handicap develops because, without visual experience, the neural pathways that transmit signals from the eyes to the visual cortex of the brain will atrophy, or fail to develop. If only one eye is temporarily blinded and the other remains normal, the kitten will be able to see well with one eye but will never acquire **binocular vision,** the ability to focus two eyes together on a single object. Binocular vision plays a role in depth perception; thus a one-eyed adult cat seems to see normally until, unexpectedly, it falls while jumping onto a table or leaping from one chair to another.

Surprisingly, the visual pathways dedicated to a particular eye disappear faster if only that eye is blindfolded than if both are. Apparently, the increase in brain connections for the one seeing eye somehow signals the brain that the neural pathways waiting for input from the other eye are superfluous. The imbalance between activity in one eye and inactivity in the other eye speeds the demise of the unused neurons (Hubel, 1988). When similar experiments are performed with older cats, their sight is not affected. Once early experiences have formed and strengthened neural connections, those connections remain in place.

Fine-Tuning the Brain's Networks

In general, abnormalities occur whenever a deprivation of basic experiences in infancy prevents the development of the normal neural pathways that transmit sensory information. Once the animal's infancy is over, the brain does not readily build new basic pathways, but pathways already in place stay in place.

Researchers sometimes explain the neural development process metaphorically: The "hard-wiring" of the brain—that is, the basic structures in every living mammal's brain that allow the development of specific capabilities—is genetically programmed and present at birth (Thompson, 1993). What is required, beginning in the final weeks of prenatal life and continuing through the first months after birth, is that these hard-wired structures be "fine-tuned" through the development and integration of the connective neural networks. Fine-tuning is affected by the animal's experience or lack of it; without the proper experience the hard-wiring may remain "untuned" and become forever disconnected.

Connections in the Brain Does experience affect the infant brain? Close observation of this 3-month-old expressing her perceptions with wide-open eyes, closed hands, and probably a noise or two answers this question with an enthusiastic yes. The same answer, in more measured scientific terms, comes from researchers' measurements of infants' brain waves.

Recent research has proved that lack of experience (not some biochemical reaction), especially for cats at about 4 weeks after birth, is indeed the catalyst for the observed visual loss (Hensch & Stryker, 1996). This is an example straight out of epigenetic systems theory: the cat's genetic basis for normal vision is in place at birth, but the experiences of early kittenhood are needed to make the genetic possibilities operative.

As best we know, the human brain, like that of kittens and other animals, becomes fine-tuned through experiences in the first months and years. The main difference is that the process is more gradual in humans than in most other mammals. In the case of vision, for example, it can last up to 6 years (Thompson, 1993).

What does this fine-tuning process imply for human development? *Not* that an infant would benefit from a multimedia blitz of stimulation during infancy (indeed, overstimulated babies typically cry and then go to sleep). Rather, that a certain minimal level of stimulation for each of the senses helps neural connections to develop optimally. In addition, the areas of the brain dedicated to language and emotion mature rapidly in the first 2 years. Hence, it seems likely that the cognitive and emotional experiences a child has during this "time window" will foster and shape the brain connections involved in later language learning and emotional expression (Rovee-Collier, 1995).

Some of the specifics of this phenomenon, particularly what might happen if an infant were deprived cognitively or socially, have far-reaching implications (Schore, 1994; Serbin, 1997). An adult might be mentally retarded or emotionally stunted—perhaps never able to understand poetry or sustain a loving relationship—because of deprivation in the early years. But that is speculation. For the moment, our understanding of brain maturation leads us to conclude that talking to a preverbal infant and showing affection toward a person too immature to love in return may be essential first steps toward developing that small person's full human potential.

Regulation of Physiological States

An important function of the brain throughout life is the regulation of **physiological states,** or conditions of body functioning. Just like an older child or adult, a full-term infant normally exhibits several regularly occurring states (Thoman & Whitney, 1990). The four most distinct are:

- *Quiet sleep*, in which breathing is regular and relatively slow (about 36 breaths per minute) and muscles seem relaxed
- *Active sleep*, in which the facial muscles move and breathing is less regular and more rapid (46 or more breaths per minute)
- *Alert wakefulness*, in which the eyes are bright and breathing is relatively regular and rapid
- *Active crying*, in which the infant produces a long, loud exhaling noise, then pauses for a deep gasping breath, and then produces a loud exhaling noise again

Each state produces a particular pattern of electrical activity in the brain that can be measured and recorded as an **electroencephalogram (EEG),** a graphic readout of the electrical impulses, or *brain waves*, produced by neurons. As the EEGs in Figure 5.6 make clear, brain waves change rapidly from about 3 months before term to about 3 months after, reflecting the maturation that is taking place.

As the brain develops, physiological states become more cyclical and distinct. With each passing week, infants are asleep and awake for longer, more regular periods, as brain maturation allows deeper sleep, more definite wakefulness, and greater self-regulation of alertness. (This is a gradual process, however; it is a mistake for new, sleep-deprived parents to hope for too much too soon.)

Between birth and age 1, the infant's *total* daily sleep is reduced by only 3 hours or so—from about 16 hours a day for the newborn to 13 hours for the 1-year-old. However, although older infants still sleep a lot, the length and timing of their sleep gradually become more closely matched to the day-night activities of the family. No newborns but about one-third of all North American 3-month-olds and 80 percent of all 1-year-olds "sleep through the night" (defined as sleeping for at least 6 straight hours beginning some time in the evening). The remaining two-thirds of young infants and 20 percent of 1-year-olds continue to wake up at some time during the night wanting food and attention (Bamford et al., 1990; Michelsson et al., 1990). As one might expect, preterm newborns sleep more than full-term babies, but less regularly, throughout the first year.

Infants' sleep cycles are influenced by their parents' caregiving practices as well as by brain maturation. Thus, even older infants whose parents respond to their predawn cries with food and playtime are likely to wake up night after night. For the same reason, firstborns often exhibit more sleep problems, as in this report from one mother:

> I have strong opinions, having raised my first taking him wherever I went, when I went, confident he would adapt. While he was always happy, he was never a good sleeper and his first 4 years were very hard on me (I claim he didn't sleep through the night until he was 4, but I could be wrong, I was so sleep-deprived).
>
> The second came along 15 months after Sam, and forced to do less, he had more of a schedule and was a better sleeper.
>
> Bryn came along 18 months ago: 8 years after Sam. I was determined to give her a schedule. . . . I did and little interferes with it. I don't want it to. She is a good sleeper . . . no, she is a GREAT sleeper, happy to go to bed. I am convinced, anecdotally, that schedules are the most important part of

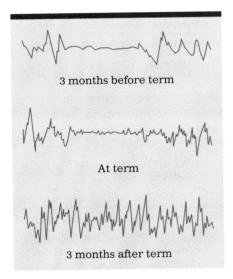

Figure 5.6 Fetal and Infant EEGs. The more mature brain-wave recordings show many more bursts of electrical activity (individual peaks) and greater overall intensity (measured by peak height). All three recordings were made during sleep.

3 months before term

At term

3 months after term

this. When I talk to new mothers, I give them this advice: Let the baby determine the schedule, then let nothing interfere with it. [Freda, personal communication, 1997]

That is good advice. Developmentalists agree that insisting that an infant conform to the parents' busy schedule, rather than vice versa, can be frustrating to the parents and, in some cases, detrimental to the infant.

MOTOR SKILLS

We now come to the most visible and dramatic body changes of infancy, those that ultimately allow the child to "stand tall and walk proud." Thanks to their ongoing changes in size and proportion and increasing brain maturation, infants markedly improve in their abilities to move and control their bodies. Compare, as an example, the reactions of a 2-month-old and a 6-month-old to a toy that is dangling within reach. Typically, a 2-month-old displays excited, undirected flapping of arms. In contrast, a 6-month-old exhibits a smooth, efficient movement of the arm and shoulder muscles to intercept the toy, together with hand and finger movements that effectively close the hand around the object. In the additional 4 months of development, the older infant has learned to:

- Balance muscle movement against gravity to reach a desired object and not overshoot it
- Compensate for the inertial forces that are transmitted from one muscle group to other muscles (from the shoulder to the arm, for example)
- Anticipate the paths of the arm in motion and the dangling toy to enable the hand to intercept the object
- Coordinate moving and braking forces in different hand-muscle groups
- Organize these various components into a smooth motor action

developmental biodynamics Maturation of the developing person's ability to move through, and with, the environment, by means of crawling, running, grasping, and throwing.

And all this learning has occurred while the infant's body has been changing in size and strength! Researchers who have studied **developmental biodynamics,** as the maturation of movement skills is called, see a seemingly simple act like grabbing a toy as a remarkable achievement—one that evolves through a painstaking trial-and-error process which gradually assembles and fine-tunes the proper sequence of smooth motor actions (Goldfield et al., 1993; Lockman & Thelen, 1993; Thelen et al., 1993). Thus developmental biodynamics—whether it involves learning to take a step or learning to grasp small objects with the fingers—is not simply a matter of waiting for a maturational timetable to unfold. It also requires the infant's active efforts to master and coordinate the several components of each complex skill.

Because of the growing independence they afford the child, motor skills become a "catalyst for developmental change" (Thelen, 1987), as they open new possibilities for the child's discovery of the world. For this reason especially, it is important to study the development of these skills—including the usual sequence and timing of their emergence—and the various factors that might cause one child to develop certain skills "behind" or "ahead of" schedule.

Reflexes

reflexes Involuntary physical responses to stimuli.

Strictly speaking, the infant's first motor skills are not skills at all but **reflexes,** that is, involuntary responses to particular stimuli. Newborns have dozens of reflexes. Some are essential to life itself; others disappear completely

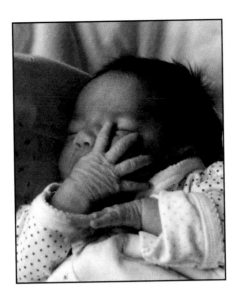

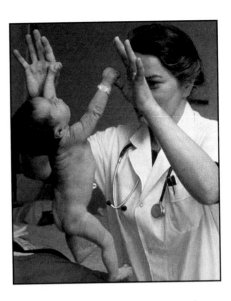

Never Underestimate the Power of a Reflex
For developmentalists, newborn reflexes are mechanisms for survival, indicators of brain maturation, and vestiges of evolutionary history. For parents, they are mostly delightful and sometimes amazing. This is demonstrated by three star performers: a 2½-week-old infant stepping eagerly forward on legs too tiny to support her body; a 3-day-old infant, still wrinkled from being immersed in amniotic fluid, contentedly sucking his thumb; and a newborn grasping so tightly that his legs dangle in space.

breathing reflex A reflex that ensures an adequate supply of oxygen and the discharge of carbon dioxide by causing the individual to inhale and exhale.

sucking reflex A reflex that causes newborns to suck anything that touches their lips.

rooting reflex A reflex that helps babies find a nipple by causing them to turn their heads toward anything that brushes against their cheeks and to attempt to suck on it.

in the months after birth; still others provide the foundation for later motor skills.

Three sets of reflexes that are *critical for survival* and become stronger as the baby matures are:

- *Reflexes that maintain oxygen supply*. The **breathing reflex** begins in normal newborns even before the umbilical cord, with its supply of oxygen, is cut. Additional reflexes that maintain oxygen are reflexive *hiccups* and *sneezes*, as well as *thrashing* (moving the arms and legs about) to escape something that covers the face.
- *Reflexes that maintain constant body temperature*. When infants are cold, they *cry, shiver,* and *tuck in their legs* close to their bodies, thereby helping to keep themselves warm. When they are hot, they try to *push away* blankets and then stay still, as well as drink plain water if it's offered. To what extent these are reflexes is debatable, but they do seem universal to all infants.
- *Reflexes that manage feeding*. The **sucking reflex,** which is crucial to their taking in nourishment, causes newborns to suck anything that touches their lips—fingers, toes, blankets, and rattles, as well as natural and artificial nipples of various textures and shapes. The **rooting reflex** causes babies to turn their mouths toward anything that brushes against their cheeks—a reflexive search for a nipple—and start to suck. Even if a mother does nothing but put a newborn within striking distance of the nipple, the neonate instinctively grasps and sucks with sufficient skill to feed (Koepke & Bigelow, 1997). *Swallowing* is another important reflex that aids feeding, as are *crying* when the stomach is empty and *spitting up* when too much has been swallowed too quickly.

Other reflexes are not necessary for survival but are important signs of normal brain and body functioning. Among them are the following:

- *Babinski reflex*. When infants' feet are stroked, their toes fan upward.
- *Stepping reflex*. When infants are held upright with their feet touching a flat surface, they move their legs as if to walk.
- *Swimming reflex*. When they are held horizontally on their stomachs, infants stretch out their arms and legs.
- *Palmar grasping reflex*. When something touches infants' palms, they grip it tightly.

■ *Moro reflex.* When someone bangs on the table they are lying on, infants fling their arms outward and then bring them together on their chests, as if to hold onto something, while crying with wide open eyes.

None of these five remain as reflexes after the first few months of life. Why, then, do they exist at all? Some may be vestiges of earlier evolutionary development. The Moro reflex and palmar grasping reflex, for example, may have been crucial ways for the young primate infant to remain close to the mother, especially during startling or unexpected events, when it was important to grab tightly onto her. Others are the precursors of voluntary movements, of motor skills. The stepping reflex, for instance, if practiced daily, probably leads to earlier walking.

Gross Motor Skills

gross motor skills Physical skills involving large body movements such as waving the arms, walking, and jumping.

Gross motor skills, which involve large body movements, emerge directly from reflexes. As you just saw, newborns placed on their stomachs move their arms and legs as if they were swimming and attempt to lift their heads to look around. As they gain muscle strength, they start to wiggle, attempting to move forward by pushing their arms, shoulders, and upper bodies against the surface they are on. Although these initial efforts usually get them nowhere (or even move them backward), infants persist in these motions whenever they have the opportunity. Usually by the age of 5 months or so, they become able to use their arms, and then legs, to inch forward on their bellies.

By the age of 6 months, most infants have succeeded at this belly-crawl (Chandler, 1990). A few months later, usually between 8 and 10 months after birth, most infants can lift their midsections and crawl (or *creep*) on "all fours," coordinating the movements of their hands and knees in a smooth, balanced manner. Within the next couple of months, most infants also learn to climb up onto couches and chairs—as well as ledges, windowsills, and down other dangerous places, including into pools and lakes.

Some 10-month-old babies do not crawl or creep at all, but instead achieve mobility by either scooting along on their buttocks, rolling over and over, doing the "bear walk" (on all four "paws," without letting their knees or elbows touch the ground), or even cruising unsteadily on two feet, moving

(a)

(b)

(c)

(d)

More Than Brothers Nicholas and Daniel are monozygotic twins, and consequently reach various stages of motor skills virtually together. The abilities shown here are **(a)** lifting the head and shoulders at 4 months, **(b)** preparing to crawl at 6 months, **(c)** standing with one supporting hand at 8 months, and **(d)** finally walking at 12 months—right on time.

from place to place by holding onto tables, chairs, or bystanders. There may be some genetic or neurological reasons for this apparent resistance to crawling, but often the reason is more practical—a cold, hard, or scratchy floor.

Walking shows a similar progression: from reflexive, hesitant, newborn stepping to a smooth, speedy, coordinated gait (Thelen & Ulrich, 1991). On average, a child can walk while holding a hand at 9 months, can stand alone momentarily at 10 months, and can walk well, unassisted, at 12 months. In recognition of their accomplishment of walking, infants at this stage are given the additional name **toddler,** for the characteristic way they move their bodies, toddling from side to side. Since their heads and stomachs are relatively heavy and large, they spread out their short little legs for stability, which makes them seem bowlegged, flat-footed, and unbalanced.

Interestingly, once an infant can take steps, walking becomes the preferred mode of movement—except when speed is an issue; then many new walkers quickly drop to their hands and knees to crawl. Two-year-olds are proficient walkers and almost never crawl except when, with a mocking grin on the face, they pretend to be babies. Within a short time, mastery of walking leads to mastery of running, and then watchful caregivers need to be ready to dash to the rescue if an attractive hazard gets a toddler's attention.

Self-Mobility Changes the World

Any form of mobility opens new opportunities and challenges for infants. Once they can locomote on their own, they can propel themselves toward intriguing objects, whether nearby or across the room. They can even leave the room, exploring new areas and gaining a sense of their own independent actions. New dangers are also within reach, from the stairs they might tumble down to the floor polish they might taste. (The prudent parent seals off all forbidden places and poisons by the time the child reaches 6 months, if not sooner.)

Fortunately, the advent of crawling usually coincides with an emerging wariness about unfamiliar things, producing a new caution that tempers infants' curiosity. Infants investigate a novel situation tentatively; they frequently interrupt their explorations to glance back at a parent for signs of encouragement or disapproval (this new caution is described at the beginning of Chapter 7). Thus, a combination of motor skills, cognitive awareness, social interaction, and access to new surroundings makes the crawling—and then the walking—infant a quite different baby from the precrawler (Bertenthal & Campos, 1990).

In addition to allowing freedom of movement, crawling and walking aid development in many other ways (Lockman & Thelen, 1993). Upright mobility raises the child's vistas, literally as well as figuratively, giving him or her a new viewpoint on the world. It also frees up the child's hands, fostering the development of fine motor skills, of perceptual understanding, and of new challenges to parental control. It is no coincidence that a forward leap in infants' cognitive awareness (detailed in Chapter 6) and new dimensions in parent-infant interaction follow on the heels of increased mobility and independence.

Fine Motor Skills

Fine motor skills, which are skills that involve small body movements (usually of the hands and fingers), are more difficult to master than gross motor skills because they require the precise coordination of complex muscle groups. These skills develop step-by-step, unlike some gross motor skills, such as standing up, which seem to emerge quite suddenly.

toddler A child, usually between the ages of 1 and 2, who has just begun to master the art of walking.

Now a Toddler As this very young lady begins to walk, she demonstrates why such children are called toddlers: they move unsteadily from side to side as well as forward.

❓ *Observational Quiz (see answer page 153): What emotions and fine motor skills usually accompany early walking, as shown here?*

fine motor skills Physical skills involving small body movements, especially with the hands and fingers, such as picking up a coin or drawing.

Exercise Equipment for the Hand All babies, including 8-month-old Edwin, reach and finger any object that challenges their hand skills. Paper is generally safe, so an old book or newspaper to tear, a roll of toilet paper to unravel, or a box of tissues to empty out one by one is much better than any of the glass, metal, or plastic objects that are equally attractive to the infant.

Successful Grabbing

The best example of an early fine motor skill is grabbing. As we have seen, infants are born with a reflexive grasp, but they seem to have no control of it. During their first 2 months, babies excitedly stare and wave their arms at an object dangling within reach; by 3 months of age, they can usually touch it. But they cannot yet grab and hold on unless the object is placed in their hands, partly because their eye-hand coordination is so limited.

By 4 months of age they sometimes grab, but their timing is off: they close their hands too early or too late, and their grasp tends to be of short duration. Finally, by 6 months of age, with a concentrated stare and deliberation, most babies can reach for, grab at, and hold onto (usually successfully) almost any object that is of the right size. They can hold a bottle, shake a rattle, and yank a sister's braids. Moreover, they no longer need to see their hands in order to grab; they can grasp a moving object that is illuminated in an otherwise dark room (Robin et al., 1996).

Fingering and Holding

Once grabbing is possible, infants explore everything within reach, mastering other fine motor skills while learning about the physical properties of their immediate world. Eleanor Gibson, a leading researcher in infant perception, describes the infant at 6 months of age as having "a wonderful eye-hand-mouth exploratory system." Several weeks before age 1 year, this system becomes sufficiently developed that the infant can "hold an object in one hand and finger it with the other, and turn it around while examining it. This is an ideal way to learn about the distinctive features of an object" and, bit by bit, about the tangible world (Gibson, 1988). (Some of the specifics of this learning are described in Chapter 6.)

Other developing hand skills contribute to the child's ability to explore. By the time they are 4 to 8 months of age, most infants can transfer objects from one hand to the other. By 8 or 9 months, they can adjust their reach in

Maturation and Patience Almost the only thing that might prevent a child from growing up as fast as possible is pressure to speed up the process.

"All right. Time to grow up."

① Answer to Observational Quiz (from page 151): *Walking is thrilling to most toddlers, a source of pride and joy (see the infant's face)—and perhaps disobedience, if the seated woman is unwilling to follow along and so asks her to stop. Finger skills take a leap forward too: Notice the dirt in the baby's right hand and the extended finger pointing on the left.*

pincer grasp The skill of using the thumb and forefinger together, usually mastered between the ages of 9 and 14 months.

an effort to catch objects that are tossed toward them, even when the object is thrown fairly fast and from an unusual angle (von Hofsten, 1983). And by 11 or 12 months, they can coordinate both hands to enclose an object that is too big for one hand alone (de Róiste & Bushnell, 1996).

At the same time, the skill of picking up and manipulating tiny objects develops. At first, infants use the whole hand, especially the palm and the fourth and fifth fingers, to grasp. Later they use the middle fingers and the center of the palm, or the index finger and the side of the palm. Finally, they use thumb and forefinger together, a skill called the **pincer grasp**, mastered sometime between the ages of 9 and 14 months. At this point, infants delight in picking up every little object within sight, including bits of fuzz from the carpet and bugs from the lawn.

Development of these fine motor skills is enhanced by the development of gross motor skills and vice versa. The floor-bound creature who has learned how to sit steadily suddenly becomes more adept at reaching and manipulating objects (Rochat & Bullinger, 1994; Rochat & Goubet, 1995). Then, once the child is able to grab, he or she can hold onto chair legs, table-tops, and crib rails. This makes standing and even walking possible, strengthening leg muscles in the process. Once walking is possible, toddlers can move to and poke, pick, and pull at hundreds of tiny things that previously were beyond their reach. They can even move out of sight, or run away, if they choose. Now, more than ever, careful attention to "babyproofing" the home is needed, especially with regard to poisons and breakables.

Variations in Timing

Although all healthy infants develop the same motor skills in the same sequence, the age at which these skills are acquired varies greatly from infant to infant. Table 5.2 shows the age at which half of all infants in the United States master each major motor skill and the age at which 90 percent master each skill.

table **5.2**	**Age Norms (in Months) for Motor Skills**	
Skill	When 50% of All Babies Master the Skill	When 90% of All Babies Master the Skill
Lifts head 90° when lying on stomach	2.2	3.2
Rolls over	2.8	4.7
Sits propped up (head steady)	2.9	4.2
Sits without support	5.5	7.8
Stands holding on	5.8	10.0
Walks holding on	9.2	12.7
Stands momentarily	9.8	13.0
Stands alone well	11.5	13.9
Walks well	12.1	14.3
Walks backward	14.3	21.5
Walks up steps (with help)	17.0	22.0
Kicks ball forward	20.0	24.0

Source: The Denver Developmental Screening Test (Frankenburg et al., 1981).

norm A standard or average, derived or developed for a specified group population. What is "normal" may not be what is ideal.

Ethnic Differences

These averages, or **norms**, are based on a large representative sample of infants from a wide range of ethnic groups. Representative sampling is necessary because norms vary from group to group and place to place, as explained in Chapter 1. For example, throughout infancy, African Americans are more advanced in motor skills than Americans of European ancestry (Rosser & Randolph, 1989). Internationally, the earliest walkers in the world seem to be in Uganda, where, if well nourished and healthy, the typical baby walks at 10 months. Some of the latest walkers are in France, where taking one's first unaided steps at 15 months is not unusual.

What factors account for this variation in the acquisition of motor skills? Of primary importance are inherited factors, such as how active, how physically mature, and how fat a particular child might be. The power of the genetic component is suggested by the fact that identical twins are far more likely to sit up, and to walk, on the same day than fraternal twins are. Moreover, there are striking individual differences in the strategies, effort, and concentration that infants apply to the mastering of motor actions. These differences too may be genetic, and they certainly affect the timing of motor-skill achievements (Thelen et al., 1993).

Patterns of infant care are also influential. For example, in many African cultures, infants are held next to an adult's body, usually in the upright position, virtually all day long; they are cradled and rocked as the adult works. Being able to continually feel the rhythm and changes of an adult's gait tends to stimulate the infant to practice movement. This may well give African babies an advantage in gross motor skills over European infants who spend much of each day lying in a crib or sitting in a playpen (Bril, 1986).

In short, the age at which a *particular* baby first displays a *particular* skill depends on the interaction between inherited and environmental factors. Each infant has a genetic timetable for maturation, which can be faster or slower than that of other infants from other ethnic groups, from the same ethnic group, and even from the same family (see Children Up Close on page 155). Each infant also has a family and culture that provide varying amounts of encouragement, nutrition, and opportunity to practice these skills.

Safe and Secure Many Navaho infants still spend hours each day on a cradle board, to the distress of some nonnative adults, until they see that most Navaho babies are quite happy that way. The discovery in the 1950s that Navaho children walked at about the same age as European American children suggested that maturation, not practice, led to motor skills. Later research found that most Navaho infants also received special exercise sessions each day, implying that practice plays a larger role than most psychologists once thought.

THE NORMAL BERGER DAUGHTERS

The study of human development is a science and, as such, deals with and accepts both norms of development and normal variations from those norms. But when one's own child is involved, it is difficult to remain scientific and not become at least a bit subjective about the norms.

When I had my first baby, Bethany, I was a graduate student, so I had already memorized such norms as "sitting by 6 months, walking by 12." During her first year, Bethany reached all the developmental milestones pretty much on time. However, at 14 months, she was still not walking. I became a little anxious. I then began to read about developmental norms with a sharper eye and learned three comforting facts. First, variation is normal. Second, when late walking is a sign of a problem, it is accompanied by other signs, and Bethany showed no other signs of delayed development: she was growing normally, using two hands to grab, and beginning to talk. Third, norms for motor skill development vary among cultures. Remembering that my grandmother was Alsatian, I decided that Bethany's late walking was an expression of her French genes.

Two months later, Bethany was walking and my second child, Rachel, was born. Motivated by my experience with Bethany's late walking, I began marshaling evidence that motor skills followed a genetic timetable, taught that truth to my students, and received from them additional testimony as to the power of genes. Among my students who were immigrants, those from Jamaica, Cuba, and Barbados expected babies to walk earlier than did students emigrating from Russia, China, and Korea. Among my students who were born in North America, both expectations as to walking norms and personal experience followed racial lines. Many of my African American students proudly cited their sons, daughters, or younger siblings who walked at 10 months, or even 8 months, to the chagrin of their European American classmates.

Believing now in a genetic timetable for walking, I was not surprised when Rachel took her first steps at 15 months—over Christmas vacation at Grandma's house. Our third child, Elissa, also walked "late," just on schedule for a Berger child with some French ancestry. By then I was not worried at all about her late motor-skill development, partly because her older sister Bethany had become the fastest runner in her class. I taught all my students about genetic variation in developmental norms and told them they could start worrying when a child didn't sit up by 8 months or walk by 16 months, but not before that.

By the time our fourth child, Sarah, was born, I was an established professor and author, able to afford a full-time caregiver, Mrs. Todd, who was from Jamaica. Mrs. Todd thought Sarah was the brightest, most advanced baby she had ever seen, except, perhaps, her own daughter Gillian. I agreed, of course, but I cautioned Mrs. Todd that Berger children walk late.

"She'll be walking by a year," Mrs. Todd told me. "Maybe sooner. Gillian walked at 10 months."

"We'll see," I replied, confident in my genetic interpretation.

However, I had not anticipated Mrs. Todd's dedication to seeing her prediction come true. She bounced baby Sarah on her lap, day after day. Sarah loved it. By the time Sarah was 8 months old, Mrs. Todd was already spending a good amount of time bent over, holding Sarah by both hands, and practicing walking—to Sarah's great delight. And lo and behold, with Mrs. Todd's urging and guidance, Sarah took her first step at exactly 1 year—late for a Todd baby, but amazingly early for a Berger.

As a scientist, I know that a single case proves nothing. It could be that the genetic influences on Sarah's walking were different from those on her sisters. She is only one-eighth French, after all, a fraction I had ignored when I was explaining Bethany's late walking to myself. But in my heart I think it was much more likely practice, fostered by a caregiver with a different cultural tradition than mine, that made the difference. From that day forward, as I teach, I always emphasize both nature and nurture in describing motor skills. I also am more open and accepting when my students tell me of even large variations and discrepancies from the "norms" of development.

My Youngest at 8 Months When I look at this photo of Sarah, I see evidence of Mrs. Todd's devotion. Sarah's hair is washed and carefully brushed, her dress and blouse are cleaned and pressed, and the carpet and footstool are perfect equipment for standing practice. Sarah's legs—chubby and far apart—indicate that she is not about to walk early, but given all these signs of Mrs. Todd's attention to caregiving, it is not surprising, in hindsight, that my fourth daughter was my earliest walker.

Although variation in the timing of the development of motor skills is normal, an infant who shows a pattern of slow development—that is, development several months behind the norms for babies of the same culture and ethnicity—should be checked to ensure that no problem impedes the child's progress. Slow infants may be mentally retarded, physically ill, or seriously neglected, or they may be perfectly fine.

SENSORY AND PERCEPTUAL CAPACITIES

sensation The response of a sensory system when it detects a stimulus. People are not necessarily aware of sensations.

perception The mental processing of sensory information.

Psychologists draw an important distinction between sensation and perception. **Sensation** occurs when a sensory system detects a stimulus, as when the inner ear reverberates with sound, or the pupil and retina intercept light. **Perception** occurs when the brain tries to make sense out of that stimulus, when the individual becomes aware of it.

This distinction between sensation and perception may be clarified with an example. Have you ever done homework while playing your stereo and realized that you had worked through an entire recording but had actually "heard" only snatches of it? During the gaps in your "hearing," your auditory system was *sensing* the music—your tympanic membranes, hammers, anvils, and stirrups were vibrating in response to the sound waves coming from the speakers—but you were not *perceiving* the music; that is, you were not consciously aware of it. Similarly, if you have ever walked past a friend without recognizing him or her, or walked into a utility pole without noticing it in daylight, the problem was not sensation—your eyes could still see—but perception.

Both sensation and perception are apparent at birth, in all our senses, according to recent research. Newborns see, hear, smell, and taste; they respond to pressure, motion, temperature, and pain. Most of these sensory abilities are immature and somewhat selective; they are activated by only a narrow range of stimuli. Thus the newborn's perceived world is limited, not at all the "great, blooming, buzzing confusion" psychologists once believed it to be (James, 1950; Mehler & Fox, 1985). Further, the stimuli newborns do respond to—such as visual patterns, the sound of a human voice, and sweet and sour tastes—reveal much about their comprehension of the surrounding world.

Here, we will briefly consider the infant's sensory capacities and basic perceptual abilities. The fuller cognitive dimensions of infant perception will be examined in Chapter 6.

Research on Infant Senses

Over the past 20 years, there has been an explosion of research into infant sensory and perceptual skills. New technology—from brain scans to computer measurement of the eyes' ability to focus—has enabled researchers to detect the precise capabilities of infants' senses and to gain a greater understanding of the relationship between perception and physiology.

The foundation for this research is the fact that, for all of us, the perception of an unfamiliar stimulus usually elicits physiological responses—for example, changed heart rate, faster brain waves, concentrated gazing, and, for infants who have pacifiers in their mouths, intensified sucking. However, eventually **habituation** occurs, in which the stimulus becomes so familiar and uninteresting that these responses slow down. Habituation, then, is like boredom: an indication that a particular stimulus is no longer interesting.

Employing habituation, researchers have been able to assess infants'

habituation The process of becoming so familiar with a particular stimulus that it no longer elicits the physiological responses it did when it was originally experienced.

ability to discriminate between very similar stimuli. Typically, they present an infant with a stimulus—say, a plain circle—until habituation occurs. Then they present another stimulus similar to the first but different in some detail—say, a circle with a dot in the middle. If the infant reacts in some measurable way to the new stimulus (a change of heart rate, a refocusing of gaze), that reaction indicates that the difference in the stimuli has been perceived.

An alternative research strategy depends not on habituation but on signs of perception. Researchers measure the infant's focused attention as indicated by, say, a fixed gaze, slow and steady heart rate, active brain waves, or reduced body movement. Such fixation signifies that the infant has noticed, and perceived, a particular stimulus. As you might imagine, the interpretation of such simple reactions in very young infants sometimes requires a very creative scientist. Nonetheless, decades of research, patiently undertaken and conscientiously replicated, reveals that newborn infants can see, hear, taste, touch, and smell far more than scientists or parents once believed.

Vision

At birth, vision is the least developed of the senses, with distance vision particularly blurry. Newborns focus most readily on objects between 4 and 30 inches (10 and 75 centimeters) away. Their distance vision is about 20/400, which means a baby sees an object that is 20 feet (6.1 meters) away no better than an adult with 20/20 vision sees the same object at 400 feet (122 meters)

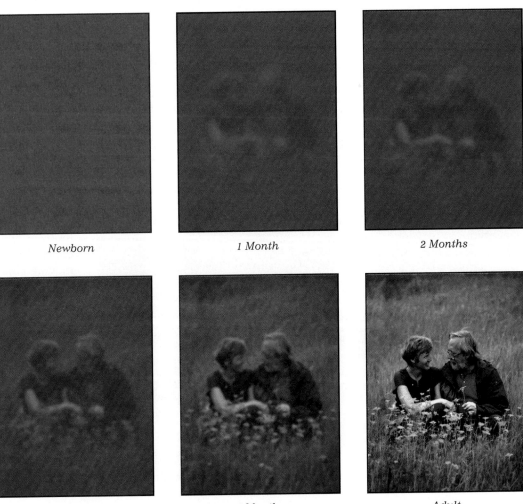

What a Baby Sees Very young infants stare at objects within their reach and not much else for a very good reason—that's all they can see. Five stages of infant distance vision are here illustrated by artist Tony Young, working with Davida Teller, a noted researcher. Teller warns that these images (actually photos) may overestimate infant perception, because we see them "with the adult visual system, with all of the higher level perceptual capacities brought to bear." We see a middle-aged couple, perhaps in love. Since a 6-month-old, but not a 3-month-old, can see yellow, an older baby might be excited to see some amazing yellow flowers, hidden somewhat by two human shapes.

Newborn   *1 Month*   *2 Months*

3 Months   *4 Months*   *Adult*

away. Distance vision develops rapidly, however, reaching 20/40 by the age of 6 months and 20/20 by 12 months (Haith, 1990, 1993).

This visual improvement results more from changes in the brain than from changes in the eye. That is, the newborn's eyes are actually capable of focusing on distant objects, but the immaturity of the brain's neural networks makes such focusing slow and difficult and makes distance vision blurry (Braddick & Atkinson, 1988). Focusing improves as neurological maturation and myelination allow better coordination of eye movements and more efficient transmission of information from the eyes to the brain. By the age of 6 months, the visual system more closely approximates adult visual capabilities. (However, vision does not become fully mature until the school years.)

Increasing maturation of the visual cortex accounts for other improvements in infant visual abilities. When 1-month-olds look at an object, their gaze often wanders; their ability to *scan the object* (examine it completely, side to side and top to bottom) and *attend to the critical areas* (peruse the most prominent features) is quite imperfect. When looking at a face, for example, they stare at peripheral features, such as the hairline, and then stare into space. However, by 3 months of age, scanning is more organized, more efficient, and centered on important aspects of a visual stimulus. Thus, when 3-month-olds look at a face, they look more closely at the eye and mouth regions, which contain the most information (Aslin, 1988; Braddick & Atkinson, 1988).

Binocular vision also develops in the early months, occurring quite suddenly at about 14 weeks, on average (Held, 1995). Binocular vision is required for depth perception (as you saw in our discussion of cats' eyes), so babies can see the edges of beds and such long before they can use vision to guide their crawling.

Color vision is probably absent at birth, but it rapidly becomes refined during the early months (Teller, 1997). One-month-old infants can distinguish among red, green, and white, but their ability to detect other colors is limited. By 3 to 4 months of age, however, infants can distinguish many more colors and can also differentiate them more acutely, perceiving aqua, for example, as a shade of blue rather than green (Bornstein & Lamb, 1992; Haith, 1990). Color nuances are perceived better as time goes on, according to individual timetables that are influenced by cultural emphases on certain colors as well as by visual experience.

All Four People, Staring Intently Scientists, aided by Donald Duck, monitor a 7-month-old girl's responses to visual stimuli. As various pictures flash on the screen, the infant's brain activity is recorded by means of the headband device she is wearing. From the recording, researchers can tell not only what she sees and how well she sees it but also which parts of her developing brain are processing visual stimuli.

As a result of all these achievements, depth and motion perception improve dramatically. Evidence of this comes from infants' ability to *track* a moving object, that is, to visually follow its movement. Some instances of tracking are apparent in the first days of life—newborns are more interested in objects that move and lights that flicker than in static, dull displays—but newborns' ability to track and focus is very unstable (Teller, 1997). Most very young babies lose sight of an object that moves slowly right in front of the face. One reason is that newborns' eyes do not remain focused for long even on stationary objects; another is that newborns do not pay special attention to the edges of moving objects (Bronson, 1990). Thus they likely are not aware of the basic indicators of object motion.

In the months after birth, however, tracking improves week by week, with large, slow-moving, high-contrast objects being tracked more readily than small, fast-moving, low-contrast objects. Tracking continues to improve—gradually—through infancy, and then through childhood and adolescence, to the point at which a skilled adult can track a baseball traveling 90 miles per hour or faster. The crack of the bat is evidence of fully developed tracking skill.

Infant Visual Preferences

So far we have described sensation, what young infants are *able* to see. But what do they *prefer* to see when given a choice? One clear conclusion from the research on infant visual preferences is that babies seek visual stimulation that offers complexity within their range of perceptual ability. They prefer to look, for example, at new images rather than at familiar ones, at complex visual patterns rather than at solid colors, and at stimuli with contrast and contour density (like a three-dimensional mask of a face) rather than at something two-dimensional (like a picture of a face).

In addition, as their perception improves, infants increasingly enjoy visual images that are incongruous with, or diverge from, the usual—such as seeing a familiar crib toy turned upside down (Haith, 1980, 1990). This preference for visual stimulation over visual blandness may arise from the fact that visual stimulation is necessary for the full development of the visual cortex in the early months of life. It may also arise because visual complexity contains more information that will provoke the baby's interest—and, thereby, stimulate cognitive growth. Research on other infant senses shows similar preferences for stimulation over blandness.

These findings have led to a new appreciation of the young infant as a stimulus seeker who strives to make sense out of his or her surroundings. Infants do not simply look at things more astutely as they mature. Research on what parts of a face, or what movements of an object, or what elements of a scene capture attention reveals that infants prefer to examine those sights that will teach them something. As Marshall Haith (1990), who has studied infant visual perception for more than 30 years, comments,

> This creature is actively processing whatever lies within its visual province and even looks for more, rather than simply choosing one stimulus or another. It is important for investigators to appreciate the infant as an active processor rather than a selector and to try to figure out what the baby is trying to accomplish rather than how dimensions of the world control its activity.

Hearing

Relative to vision, hearing at birth is already quite sensitive. Sudden noises startle newborns, making them cry; rhythmic sounds, such as a lullaby or a heartbeat, soothe them and put them to sleep. When they are awake, they turn their heads in an effort to locate the source of a noise, and they are particularly attentive to the sound of conversation. Indeed, as we saw in Chapter 4, newborns can distinguish their mothers' voices from the voices of other mothers soon after birth, because even in the womb they listen. Interestingly, while their hearing is sufficiently sensitive to detect a whisper, newborns do not prefer the mother's whisper over that of another woman, presumably because they could not hear whispers before birth (Spence &

(a)

(b)

The Baby Can Hear The procedure pictured here tests an infant's ability to detect changes in speech sounds. While the child is focused on a toy held by the experimenter (a), a single speech sound is played repetitively through a loudspeaker. At random intervals the speech sound changes, and then toys on the infant's right become illuminated and begin to move (b). After this routine is repeated a number of times, the infant learns that a change in speech sounds signals a delightful sideshow. Then researchers can tell whether the infant discriminates between similar speech sounds by whether or not the child looks expectantly over to the toys after a particular sound.

❷ *Observational Quiz (see answer page 163): Can you guess why both the mother and the experimenters are wearing headphones but the baby is not?*

Freeman, 1996). Sensation after birth does include whispers, but perception takes time to form, so whispers are not meaningful at first.

By the age of 1 month, infants can perceive differences between very similar speech sounds, as was first shown in an experiment that astonished scientists almost 30 years ago. The experiment was set up so that the subject babies activated a recording of the "bah" sound whenever they sucked on a nipple. Even 1-month-olds quickly appreciated that their sucking reflex produced the sound. At first they sucked diligently, but as habituation took place, their rate of sucking decreased. At this point, the experimenters changed the sound from "bah" to "pah." Immediately the babies sucked more, indicating by this sign of interest that they perceived the difference (Eimas et al., 1971). Later research finds that very young infants may have some ability to discriminate between vowels (a much harder task) and to sense stress differences in spoken two- and three-syllable words (Sansavini et al., 1997).

Young infants can also distinguish between speech sounds that are *not* used in their native languages—and that are indistinguishable to adult speakers of their native languages. For example, whereas English-speaking adults cannot tell the difference between different "t" sounds that are used in Hindi speech, or between various glottal consonants used in some Native American dialects, their infants are able to differentiate these sounds; Japanese adults have trouble hearing the distinction between the English "l" and "r," but Japanese babies know the difference; English-speaking adults have trouble with sounds in Thai and Czech that their babies can discriminate (Jusczyk, 1995).

This suggests that there is another kind of transient exuberance involved in early speech perception—an exuberance of hard-wiring, in the language areas of the infant's brain, that will allow any of the world's thousands of languages to be learned (Werker, 1989). Significantly, as infants' early language skills emerge, they gradually lose this capability. By late childhood, many children can no longer perceive nuances of pronunciation that are irrelevant to their mother tongue. Thus, the exuberance of early speech perception is transient, lost as perception becomes fine-tuned to the sounds of the family's home language. The child's sensory experience has changed his or her capacity to perceive speech.

❷ Especially for Educators: Suppose you are the director of a day care center for infants. Should you do anything special to overcome the effects of otitis media? If so, what?

otitis media A middle-ear infection that can impair hearing temporarily and therefore can impede language development and socialization if it continues too long in the first years of life.

Early Hearing Loss (Otitis Media)

Since hearing is the most acute sense of the newborn, deafness is usually obvious to the parents and pediatrician in the first few months. Newborn hearing can be tested, and testing is mandated by some states; it finds that 1 in 1,000 infants is profoundly deaf (Mason & Herrmann, 1998). In many cases, hearing aids or surgery can ameliorate the deafness. If not, the caregiver needs to learn sign language, because the neurons and dendrites that apply to language develop rapidly.

However, many normal babies have mild to moderate hearing losses for a period of weeks or months. How does this happen, and does it make any difference? The answer to the first question is easy. Middle-ear infections, called **otitis media,** are common in infancy, with almost every child having at least one bout. Indeed, between birth and age 3 years, one-third of all children have three or more episodes of otitis media—and these are only the diagnosed and recorded episodes (Behrman, 1992). Otitis media often begins with the sniffles and then leads not only to inflamed ears but also to acute pain—with crying that propels parents to the doctor for diagnosis and the antibiotics that can clear up the problem.

Sometimes otitis media is less obvious and goes untreated, or is not fully treated, if parents, pressed for money or time, avoid or postpone a doctor visit, stint on prescribed antibiotics, or fail to have the child reexamined to be sure that the infection is completely gone. In such cases, the original infection can develop into *chronic otitis media*, a condition in which the inner ear becomes filled with fluid. As a result of that condition, which may last for weeks or months, the infant's hearing is usually impaired in one or both ears (Werner & Ward, 1997).

What are the consequences? Repeated or long-term episodes of chronic otitis media can become a developmental problem. If the family does not provide a rich and steady flow of linguistic input—so that the remaining hearing ability is well exercised—this reduction in hearing sensation can have an effect similar to blindfolding a kitten: the child's language pronunciation and fluency will be reduced (Vernon-Feagens & Manlove, 1996; Wallace et al., 1996). Whether this can become a lifelong handicap is controversial, with evidence on both sides (Roberts et al., 1986). However, as the Research Report (page 162) describes, caregivers should prevent chronic otitus media if they can.

Normal Impediments to Hearing

Very young infants can, then, discriminate among a wide variety of *phonemes* (speech sounds), as long as their ears are healthy. However, infant hearing is not as good as that of older children, especially for deeper-voiced (lower-pitched) sounds (Olsho et al., 1988; Trehub et al., 1991). Undoubtedly this is one reason most adults use a higher pitch as well as a louder voice when talking to babies than when talking to other people. ("Baby talk" is discussed in more detail in Chapter 6.)

Compared to older people, infants are also less capable of locating sounds in space (say, off to the right or left). Most older children can intuitively perceive sound location on the basis of which ear receives the auditory signal first. But because infants' ears are closer together, and infants have little experience noticing that a voice or an ambulance siren came from a particular direction, their sound localization ability is far from perfect (Morrongiello & Rocca, 1990). With experience, this perceptual skill improves; by age 1 year, a baby will squeal with delight and toddle toward the sound of familiar footsteps coming down the hall.

CHRONIC OTITIS MEDIA

An intensive study on the effects of hearing loss (Vernon-Feagens & Manlove, 1996) included weekly medical checkups of infants who spent 30 hours or more per week in day care, beginning at 3 or 4 months of age. Researchers found that almost half the children had chronic otitis media. The 36 infants in this study were at "very low risk" for serious intellectual or cognitive problems. All were healthy, with no significant history of birth complications or medical problems. They lived in middle-class communities with middle-class parents—all high school–educated and native English-speaking, more than half of them college-educated with family incomes over $45,000 per year. Perhaps the most striking indicator of the privileged status of these babies was that 33 of the 36 had both parents living at home. Indeed, for 2 of the 3 infants who lived in single-parent homes, the missing parent was serving in the armed forces. Further, the day care centers in the study were well staffed and designed to be cognitively stimulating as well as medically sound. Thus, if any cognitive or health problems were found, they could not be blamed on the quality of these infants' home life or day care.

On the basis of careful weekly checks by a nurse and a doctor, infants were divided into 2 groups: those with chronic otitus media (findings of infection more than 20 percent of the time) and those with less frequent disease. Seventeen children were found to be in the chronic group; on average, they spent 5 months per year with otitis media. The 19 less affected children averaged 1 month of otitis media per year.

The two groups were tested on several cognitive and social variables. No differences in language ability—either in expressing themselves or in understanding simple words—were found between them. However, the children with chronic otitis media were more likely to play alone and were less likely to talk with their peers, either positively or negatively (see Figure 5.7). Such findings suggest that ear problems, an experience in the physical domain, affect socialization, a behavior in the psychosocial domain.

This study suggests that chronic otitis media is widespread but not typically noticed, with the potential of causing developmental lags in the ability to learn, make friends, solve social problems, deflect aggression, and such. As the researchers noted:

> Children in day care must continually negotiate the noisy verbal environment with other children and adults in close proximity. Children with a hearing loss for even part of the time may learn to withdraw as much as possible from a verbal environment because it is more difficult for them than for other children. Over time this pattern of behavior may persist even when they are not experiencing otitis media and the accompanying hearing loss. [Vernon-Feagens & Manlove, 1996]

Note, however, that this study included only 36 children.

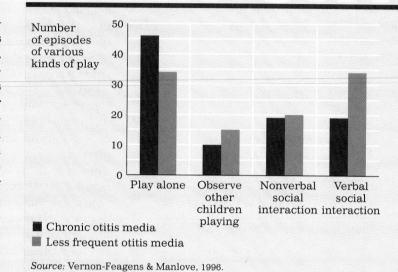

Source: Vernon-Feagens & Manlove, 1996.

Figure 5.7 With and Without Ear Infections. Toddlers with a history of frequent ear infections are much more likely to play alone rather than talk and play with others. If this pattern persists, it may affect the development of social skills.

The results provide a reason for concern, not for jumping to conclusions.

Research to date suggests that ear infections need prompt and repeated attention, and caregivers should do what they can to prevent them. Prevention might include taking precautions such as ensuring frequent hand washing (among children and caregivers alike), preventing toddlers from sharing food with one another, and extending breast-feeding at least until the age of 1 year (since breast-fed babies get sick less often). Because infections spread quickly among infants and toddlers, precautions might also include limiting a child's exposure to groups of other children until age 2 or so, especially if that child is particularly susceptible. Precautions should not only be medical but also linguistic: toddlers with possible hearing loss should hear language frequently and clearly, without the continual background noise of some day care centers and even some homes.

Finally, there are two treatments for chronic otitis media—repeated antibiotics and placement of a tube in the inner ear to drain the fluid. Both are controversial, as each has negative side effects. Each is warranted in certain cases, but some research finds that the best treatment for chronic, but mild, cases is time, since maturation of the ear makes infection less likely.

In sum, ear infections are common in infancy. They *can* lead to hearing problems, which, in turn, *can* lead to interpersonal and cognitive difficulties. Every parent, teacher, and health professional needs to help prevent, diagnose, treat, and cure such problems—not only for health reasons, but for social and intellectual ones as well.

● Response for Educators (from page 161):
You must do what you can, because even moderate hearing loss over a long period might impair language and social skills. Begin by doing what you can to prevent infections, particularly colds. You could mandate hand washing, eliminate food sharing, take the children outside as much as possible, and insist that sick babies stay home. Further, your language-learning and social-skill activities should be planned as if you had several hard-of-hearing children (because probably you do). For instance, play areas and settings should include relatively quiet and intimate areas, so that the child with a hearing loss is not disadvantaged, and soundproofing should minimize outside and inside background noises.

● *Answer to Observational Quiz (from page 160):* *The headphones keep the adults from hearing what the baby can hear. Without such masking, the adults would notice the new sound and unintentionally signal the baby with facial or body movements. With it, researchers can be sure, as here, that the infant noticed the switch on his or her own.*

❷ Especially for Parents: Is it likely that your next newborn will be breast-fed for 2 years, as WHO recommends? Why or why not?

Other Senses

Although less developed than their hearing, neonates' sense of taste is clearly functioning. This was vividly shown in a demonstration with a dozen 2-hour-old infants who were each given tastes of sweet, sour, salty, and bitter water (Rosenstein & Oster, 1988). Careful analysis of their videotaped facial expressions revealed distinctive reactions to all the samples except the salty one, with the infants preferring sweet tastes. Indeed, the sense of taste may be particularly significant for the very young. One study found that sugar calmed 2-week-olds but had no effect on 4-week-olds—unless accompanied by eye contact (Zeifman et al., 1996).

Infant sense of smell is even more acute, especially for odors that are particularly meaningful to them—like those associated with feeding (Porter et al., 1992). In a number of experiments, breast-fed infants a few days old were positioned in a crib between two gauze pads, one worn by the infant's mother in her bra for several hours, the other similarly worn by another breast-feeding mother. In trial after trial, infants tended to turn their heads toward the mother's pad, preferring her smell to that of another woman (Schaal, 1986).

Together, taste and smell continue to develop during the early months, and they become quite acute by age 1. By late infancy, these senses are probably sharper than at any other time in the entire life span. Experts recommend giving infants a wide variety of foods, not because nutrition demands it but because taste preferences develop so rapidly that the introduction of new foods becomes more difficult with each passing year (Birch, 1990). Tastes and smells of early childhood probably are remembered for a lifetime: many an adult will catch the scent of a flowering tree, burning leaves, or baking bread and suddenly identify it as a childhood smell. The brain records and collects the sensations of infancy, creating the template for a lifetime of later perceptions.

Finally, the sense of touch is remarkably acute during the first year (Bushnell & Boudreau, 1993). Even in the early months, long before their limited visual skills permit careful visual inspection, babies manipulate objects to examine them (and often transfer them to their mouths for exploration with their tongues, gums, cheeks, and lips, which are very sensitive to touch). By 6 months of age, infants distinguish objects on the basis of their temperature, size, hardness, and texture; somewhat later, they are able to differentiate weight.

Sometimes the sense of motion is considered a sixth sense, and if this is the case, it is obviously strong at birth. Many a crying infant will not hush unless carried, cradled, or cuddled in a parent's arms, a moving car, or a pushed carriage.

You may have noticed that our focus here has been primarily on early sensation and perception—in the first 6 months or so. As time goes on, the role of cognition increases in significance. Accordingly, we discuss perception among older babies at length in Chapter 6, including the question of how early memories of perceptions are preserved.

NUTRITION

Good nutrition is the foundation for all development. As you saw, newborns usually double their birthweight in the first 4 months, a growth that requires feeding at least every 3 or 4 hours, day and night. The actual feeding "schedule" varies considerably from child to child and culture to culture. Some experts in some regions advocate a rigid pattern of feeding every 4 hours at birth, soon increasing to every 6 hours; others recommend feeding at first whimper, which can sometimes mean every half hour or so.

Preferred feeding schedules also vary from generation to generation. One developmental researcher writes:

> It is easy to forget how rapidly ideas about parenting have changed. I was brought up as a Truby King baby. Influenced by this New Zealand pediatrician, my father, also a physician, believed that babies should be fed on a strict 6-hour schedule. Whenever we visited my father after our first child was born, at 6 p.m. he would start to fidget in his chair and say, "Isn't it time he was nursed?" [Hinde, 1995]

This researcher was influenced by the attitudes of his own era, not his father's era, so his son was fed whenever the son cried, rarely at precisely 6 o'clock because, usually, he had been fed an hour or two before and hunger had not yet reappeared. Culture also influences—powerfully—what the baby eats and when it is weaned to more adult foods.

Timing is not the critical factor in feeding, however. What matters is the overall quality and quantity of the infant's nutritional intake. Good quality and sufficient quantity are vital not only for physical growth and health but also for brain development and skill mastery.

The Ideal Diet

At first, infants are unable to eat or digest solid food, but their rooting, sucking, swallowing, and breathing reflexes are designed to ensure that they consume large quantities of liquid nourishment. In fact, when you consider how much eating you would have to do to double your own weight in 4 months, it becomes clear that the new infant must be a dedicated eating machine. The inevitable stomach upsets are also easy to understand.

A Day in the Park In the 1990s, breast-feeding in public has become more common in the United States. One reason is that mothers are more aware of the importance of nursing when the baby is hungry rather than adhering to a fixed feeding schedule. Another reason is that, in some parts of the country, pioneering women who have been arrested for indecent exposure because they breast-fed their infants in public have challenged the law and won.

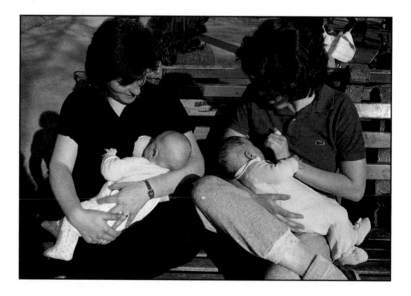

What should that small human eat? Something easy to swallow and digest that provides everything essential for growth. Given these requirements, the ideal infant food is obvious (Lawrence, 1998). Breast milk.

Breast milk is always sterile and at body temperature; it contains more iron, vitamin C, and vitamin A than cow's or goat's milk; it provides antibodies to protect against any disease that the mother is immunized against, either through vaccine or through having had the illness herself. The specific fats and sugars in breast milk make it more digestible than any prepared baby formula, which means that breast-fed babies have fewer allergies and stomachaches than bottle-fed babies. And even beyond protecting against contagious diseases and digestive upsets, breast-feeding decreases the frequency of almost every other common infant ailment (Beaudry et al., 1995; Dewey et al., 1995; Isolauri et al., 1998).

Breast milk probably contains numerous other crucial substances. As one scientist explained, "It's a cocktail of potent hormones and growth factors, most of which we are just beginning to understand" (Frawley, quoted in Angier, 1994). Among the newly discovered ingredients in breast milk are various hormones believed to regulate growth, encourage attachment between mother and baby, reduce pain, and aid in the development of the brain, liver, intestines, and pancreas by providing nutrients that cannot be found in vitamin pills. There is even one hormone in breast milk that may affect the timing of sexual maturation, about a dozen years later.

Given all the benefits of breast milk, doctors worldwide recommend breast-feeding for almost all babies, unless the mother is an active drug user (including alcohol and tobacco), HIV-positive, or severely malnourished. More precisely, the World Health Organization recommends that infants should be fed *exclusively* on breast milk at least for the first 4 to 6 months of life. At that point, other foods should be added—cereals and fruits particularly because breast milk does not have adequate iron, vitamin D, or vitamin K—but breast-feeding should continue until age 2 or later (UNICEF, 1990; Wharton, 1996).

Nutritional Problems

Nutritional problems of every sort, including obesity and life-threatening vitamin deficiencies, can occur throughout the life span. Young adolescents undertake crazy fad diets, senior citizens try to subsist on toast and tea, and people of all ages eat too much fat, salt, and sugar. In the first 2 years, however, there is usually only one simple nutritional problem—not enough nourishing food. The consequences can be devastating to body, brain, and life itself.

● **Response for Parents (from page 163):** The arguments for and against breast-feeding fall neatly into two camps, with the baby's well-being in favor of breast-feeding and cultural customs against it. The physiological advantages are numerous; you can cite 10 or more listed in the text. The cultural arguments against breast-feeding are not listed, but you can read between the lines; they include inconvenience for the mother, jealousy of the father and siblings, disapproval by outsiders, and the difficulty of breast-feeding at the workplace.

Long-Term Consequences Many people hope that breast-fed babies become smarter, healthier, and more loving adults. However, research finds no such guarantees. Hiring a worker on the basis of his infant experiences would be like using a laundry detergent because your grandmother once used that brand. There might be something to it, but the cleanliness of last week's wash (or how the worker did at his last job) is a better guide.

"I forgot to say I was breast-fed."

Malnutrition: At a Glance, and with a Closer Look New photos of children near death from starvation are published almost every year. The photo on the right, from the Sudan, is similar to photos from Chile, Somalia, Brazil, India, Biafra, Indonesia, and Ethiopia published in earlier editions of this text. The photo below is equally sad, but more subtle. It shows child victims of a continuing famine in North Korea.
❷ *Observational Quiz (see answer page 169): What signs of undernutrition can you see in the North Korean children? (Consider body size, clothes, hair, and behavior.)*

Severe Malnutrition

protein-calorie malnutrition A nutritional problem that results when a person does not consume enough nourishment to thrive.

marasmus A disease that afflicts young infants suffering from severe malnutrition. Growth stops, body tissues waste away, and death may eventually occur.

kwashiorkor A disease resulting from a protein deficiency in children. The symptoms include thinning hair and bloating of the legs, face, and abdomen.

In infancy, the most serious nourishment problem is **protein-calorie malnutrition,** which occurs when a child does not consume sufficient nourishment (of any kind) to thrive. Roughly 7 percent of the world's children are severely protein-calorie malnourished during their early years, with rates running above 50 percent in impoverished nations (including Peru, the Sudan, and the Philippines) (United Nations, 1994).

In the first year of life, severe protein-calorie malnutrition can cause **marasmus,** a condition in which growth stops, body tissues waste away, and the infant eventually dies. During toddlerhood, malnourished children are more likely to suffer **kwashiorkor,** a condition that is caused by a deficiency of protein, and in which the child's face, legs, and abdomen swell with water; this swelling sometimes makes the child appear well fed to anyone who doesn't know the real cause of the bloating. In children with kwashiorkor, the essential organs claim whatever nutrients are available, so other parts of the body become degraded. This includes the children's hair, which usually becomes thin, brittle, and colorless—a telltale sign of systemic malnutrition.

Kwashiorkor is usually not fatal in itself, but it makes the child vulnerable to death from almost any other disease, including measles, diarrhea, and even the flu. One cause of kwashiorkor is having babies too close together, which prevents the mother from breast-feeding each child exclusively for at least 2 years. (Indeed, the word "kwashiorkor" means the disease of the firstborn when a second baby arrives.) One consequence of kwashiorkor is reduced organ size, which makes the person, even as an adult, have reduced caloric needs but also reduced energy (Henry, 1996).

More broadly, the primary cause of malnutrition in developing countries is early cessation of breast-feeding for any reason. In many countries, breast-feeding used to continue for at least 2 years, as WHO recommends. Now it is often stopped much earlier in favor of bottle-feeding, usually with powdered formulas. Under normal circumstances, such formulas are adequate and safe. However,

undernutrition Inadequate nutrition, but not as severe as in malnutrition. Sometimes called failure-to-thrive. Undernutrition in children is indicated by a child who is notably underweight (called *wasted*) or short (called *stunted*) compared to the norms.

failure-to-thrive Undernutrition; usually applied to a child who lives in an adequately nourished community but is not exhibiting normal childhood weight gain.

For many people in the developing world . . . the hygienic conditions for the proper use of infant formula just do not exist. Their water is unclean, the bottles are dirty, the formula is diluted to make a tin of powdered milk last longer than it should. What happens? The baby is fed a contaminated mixture and soon becomes ill, with diarrhea, which leads to dehydration, malnutrition, and, very often, death. [Relucio-Clavano, quoted in Grant, 1986]

In developed countries, severe infant malnutrition is unusual, even when babies are not breast-fed. This is because social programs, whether they are adequate in other ways or not, tend to meet infant nourishment needs. Even when impoverished families cannot obtain welfare, food supplements, or other governmental assistance, enough help is usually available from their communities, churches, or nearby relatives to prevent the extremes of marasmus or kwashiorkor.

However, even in wealthy nations, isolated cases of severe protein-calorie malnutrition during infancy do occur. Usually it is because emotional and physical stress, or the devastating effects of drug addiction, are so overwhelming that the parents ignore the infant's feeding needs or prepare food improperly, *and* the larger community does not notice the resulting malnutrition. This is one reason New Zealand, among other countries, requires well-baby checkups for every registered birth, at home by visiting nurses as well as at a doctor's office. Such home visits yield multiple health benefits for babies, with longer-term breast-feeding and better nutrition among them (Moffitt, 1997).

Undernutrition

Less apparent, but far more prevalent than malnutrition, is **undernutrition,** also called **failure-to-thrive.** Actually, the distinctions among malnutrition, undernutrition, and failure-to-thrive are not clear-cut; even experts find them somewhat arbitrary. Generally, *malnutrition* is used for severe, obvious lack of food, while *undernutrition* is less severe and less obvious. Both are most often used in situations where an entire community is underfed.

Figure 5.8 Underweight Children. A standard deviation is a measure of the difference between an item of statistical data and the median (or norm or average) of a group of similar data. In a well-fed community, about 2 percent of all children would weigh below 2 standard deviations less than the norm, simply because they are genetically destined to be small. As you can see here, however, many children worldwide are underweight by this measure. Given the pervasive consequences of even undernutrition, public health officials contend that relief efforts should center as much on undernourished children as on the emaciated, listless, severely malnourished children who easily capture public sympathy.

The term *failure-to-thrive* is most often used when a particular infant or child lives in an adequately nourished community but, nonetheless, is not gaining weight. Twenty years ago "failure-to-thrive" was thought to stem from psychological causes, and undernutrition from biological causes. Now, however, experts recognize that both stem from inadequate consumption of food for a variety of reasons, psychological as well as biological. Therefore, here undernutrition and failure-to-thrive are used interchangeably.

Worldwide, according to United Nations statistics, 188 million children are undernourished, including 56 percent of the children in the least developed countries (UNICEF, 1994). For developing countries, estimates vary from about 3 percent to about 15 percent (see Figure 5.8).

In general, whenever an infant gains weight more slowly than would be expected for his or her age, sex, and genetic background, undernutrition should be suspected. Two other warning signs are an infant's being sick often

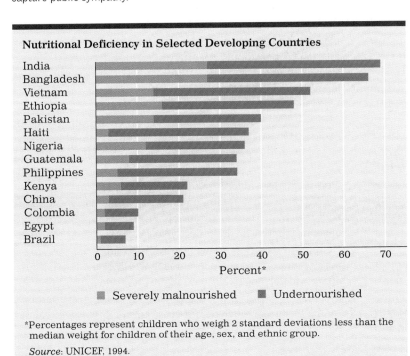

Nutritional Deficiency in Selected Developing Countries

India
Bangladesh
Vietnam
Ethiopia
Pakistan
Haiti
Nigeria
Guatemala
Philippines
Kenya
China
Colombia
Egypt
Brazil

0   10   20   30   40   50   60   70
Percent*

■ Severely malnourished   ■ Undernourished

*Percentages represent children who weigh 2 standard deviations less than the median weight for children of their age, sex, and ethnic group.
Source: UNICEF, 1994.

PREVENTING UNDERNUTRITION

Undernutrition is caused by a complex interaction of factors, with political and familial problems being of prime importance (Pollitt et al., 1996; Wright & Talbot, 1996). That importance is most obvious in those less developed nations where almost everyone is undernourished. Typically, in those nations, socioeconomic policies do not reflect the importance of infant nutrition; political conflicts such as civil war make the problem worse; and parents may not even realize that their somewhat thin offspring are undernourished. But the fact that undernutrition is occurring becomes evident when the height of the upper and lower classes within those countries is contrasted and the poor children are found to be notably shorter, or when families emigrate to well-nourished nations and teenagers born in the new country grow to tower over their immigrant grandparents. One recent example occurred in Guatemala, where civil war between 1979 and 1982 fostered a generation of undernourished children who are now stunted adults. Some families escaped by emigrating to Florida or California. Their children are significantly taller, heavier, and more muscular than children that were left behind (Bogin, 1995).

In developed countries, failure-to-thrive generally originates in the home and generally does not manifest itself as a national problem. Mothers who are depressed, for example, tend to feed their children erratically. They are also highly arbitrary in deciding when an infant has had enough to eat, perhaps judging by the clock and the amount consumed rather than by the baby's behavior (Drotar et al., 1990). A different problem occurs in families that are inflexible: They may have great trouble adjusting to an infant's feeding pattern if it is irregular (Drotar et al., 1994). The result, again, is undernutrition.

Because a variety of factors may be involved, programs that assume undernutrition is always a problem of poverty, and that seek to provide poor families with free food, are too narrowly focused (Brown & Sherman, 1995; Ricciuti, 1991). To be successful in staving off the harm of inadequate nutrition, social policy must deal with the entire context. This includes raising "nutritional consciousness" in every nation and, particularly in developing nations, making sure leaders realize that the intellectual potential of the next generation is jeopardized when small children are underfed.

In one program, free nutritional supplements were fed to children in impoverished rural communities of Guatemala. This resulted in better nutrition, which led to better performance, years later, on tests of reading, vocabulary, arithmetic, and general knowledge. The difference was particularly apparent for the poorest children who received extra food as infants and toddlers, but it also was evident for older, less impoverished children (Pollitt et al., 1993). However, close analysis of the data reveals that not all the children who could have benefited actually did—primarily because not all the mothers faithfully brought their children to be fed the supplements. Mothers who lived farther away did not usually make the trek unless they themselves had some school education (Carmichael et al., 1994). Thus, this program makes the point again: To reduce the effects of undernutrition, at least two things must be done together:

- Provide supplements, nearby and nourishing, for all children
- Improve maternal education so that every mother will participate

Simply providing free food, without careful attention to the cultural and family contexts, might not help at all (McGuire & Bundy, 1996).

These basic themes are no less true in developed countries. It is not enough to simply make food available, if access is difficult and if most mothers do not realize the critical importance of proper nutrition.

As an example, one common nutritional deficiency in the United States is *milk anemia*—a deficiency of iron—so named because it arises from parents' giving their toddler a bottle of milk (which has no iron) before every nap and with every meal, inadvertently destroying the child's appetite for other foods that are iron-rich. A bottle of juice is equally harmful in this regard; so is a diet that consists mostly of rice and vegetables. One careful survey in Massachusetts found 15 percent of all 6- to 12-month-olds are iron-deficient, with the rate among Hispanics about 50 percent higher and that among Asians about 300 percent higher than the rates among those of European or African ancestry (Sargent et al., 1996). Such deficiencies may become obvious only when the child's teeth show early signs of decay—a result of the continual presence of sugar on the gums, called "milk mouth." The permanent teeth, fortunately, replace the rotted baby teeth, but the effects of an early nutritional deficiency can remain lifelong.

Another fairly common deficiency in the early years is of zinc, which is essential for normal growth. Many children who become stunted in their first years as a result of this deficiency will catch up if they are well fed later on, but only if they get enough zinc (Golden, 1996). Worldwide, in both developing and developed nations, public attention to good preventive care for every infant, and education for every mother, would produce a much healthier and more intelligent population in another decade or two.

❶ Answer to Observational Quiz (from page 166): *The most obvious signs of malnutrition are the large heads and skinny arms and legs on most of the children—the human body sacrifices overall fat and growth to protect the brain, if possible. Another sign is the clothes—most children of this age have outgrown their baby clothes, but these children actually have lost weight because of the famine. Did you note the shaved heads on all but the two best-fed children? Here we can speculate that kwashiorkor made their hair so dull and sparce that shaving seemed best or that lice appeared and the parents had no energy or medicine to remove them. Finally, the children's behavior—docile, sad, immobile—may reflect their diminished energy. Sometimes a child who is unusually quiet and "good" is actually chronically hungry.*

(since illness is both a consequence and a cause of undernutrition) and a caregiver's being inattentive, depressed, or inflexible (since adequate feeding requires frequent, patient, and responsive care) (Drotar et al., 1990, Drotar et al., 1994).

The final proof of undernutrition or failure-to-thrive is *stunting*, in which a child's height is significantly below the norm for well-nourished children of the same genetic background. This proof, however, comes too late for many infants and toddlers, for it is not obvious that a child is too short for his or her genetic potential until years after the damage is done. Consequently, whenever an infant grows slowly (for example, not doubling his or her birthweight by age 4 months) or is late to reach for and grab objects (past 6 months of age) or is not standing at 10 months, careful attention should be given to the daily diet.

Long-Term Effects

The consequences of infant nutritional problems extend far beyond the obvious threats to life and health, and even beyond the shorter stature of the adult who went hungry as a child. Because the brain is developing rapidly during the early years, an inadequate supply of nutrients can stunt intellectual growth for decades. Only in extreme cases does malnutrition directly starve brain development, but undernutrition can indirectly impair neurological networks, with similar results. The process is as follows: Undernourished infants and toddlers are less likely than normal infants to be interested in the sensory, intellectual, and social events that surround them, and their lack of interest limits their experiences. With only limited experience, their brains may not develop as many neural connections as they ordinarily might. In addition, an undernourished infant crawls and walks later, thus postponing experience and limiting perceptual growth. Too, parents of relatively docile, small, immobile (that is, undernourished) toddlers treat them as "good babies" and thus tend to give them fewer of the language and intellectual challenges they need (Lozoff et al., 1998; Pollitt et al., 1996). Finally, when they are hungry, such infants fuss impatiently—not the best stimulus for storytelling, song singing and other language-rich experiences.

For all these reasons, it should not be surprising that longitudinal research on children in Mexico, Kenya, Egypt, Jamaica, Indonesia, and Barbados, as well as in Europe and North America, reveals that children who are underfed in infancy tend to show impaired learning—especially in their ability to concentrate and in their language skills—throughout childhood and adolescence (Pollitt et al., 1996; Ricciuti, 1993; Wachs, 1995). However, the same research also shows that if a severely malnourished infant later receives good caregiving as a toddler and young child—with adequate food, balanced nutrients, cognitive stimulation, and caring social support—many of the deficits caused by the early hunger will disappear.

This research echoes one of the themes of biosocial growth illustrated throughout this chapter: The remarkable unfolding of brain maturation, physical growth, and perceptual development is guided by a genetic plan but requires a supportive social environment to reach full inherited potential. Try to keep this theme in mind as we proceed to the next chapter, because the equally remarkable unfolding of cognitive development also reflects the dual influences of biological endowment and social support.

SUMMARY

PHYSICAL GROWTH AND HEALTH

1. In their first 2 years, most babies gain about 22 pounds (10 kilograms) and grow about 15 inches (38 centimeters), with growth particularly rapid in the first year. Proportions change: the head is relatively large at birth, and fat accumulates quickly at first and then more slowly after age 1.

2. Improved immunization programs have almost wiped out many of the diseases that once sickened almost every child and killed many. However, although infants rarely die of disease (unless they were born with life-threatening problems), they still sometimes die of sudden infant death syndrome. While the precise cause and ultimate cure of SIDS are yet to be discovered, various measures reduce its risk. One of the simplest is putting the infant to sleep on his or her back.

BRAIN GROWTH AND DEVELOPMENT

3. At birth the brain contains over 100 billion nerve cells, or neurons, but the networks of nerve fibers that interconnect them are relatively rudimentary. During the first few years of an infant's life, there are major spurts of growth in these networks, enabling the emergence of new capabilities, including self-regulation and certain cognitive skills.

4. Over the course of the early years, neural pathways in the brain that are used become strengthened and further developed, and those that are not used die.

5. Brain maturation alters the infant's physiological states, bringing deeper sleep, more definitive wakefulness, greater self-regulation of alertness, and increasingly regular sleep patterns.

MOTOR SKILLS

6. At first, the newborn's motor abilities consist only of reflexes — involuntary responses to stimuli. Some reflexes are essential for survival; some provide the foundation for later motor skills; others simply disappear in the first months. However, all reflexes index brain development.

7. Gross motor skills involve large movements, such as running and jumping; fine motor skills involve small, precise movements, such as picking up a penny. The development of both kinds of motor abilities during the first 2 years allows the infant new possibilities in discovering the world. Thus motor-skill development becomes a catalyst for cognitive and social skills.

8. Although the sequence of motor-skill development is the same for all healthy infants, variations — for hereditary, developmental, and environmental reasons — are normal in the ages at which infants master specific skills. Unusual slowness, however, is a cause for concern, as it might be a symptom of a deeper problem.

SENSORY AND PERCEPTUAL CAPACITIES

9. Both sensation and perception are apparent at birth, and both become more developed with time. Newborns show evidence of all five senses, although their sensory abilities are limited. Newborns and toddlers tend to seek new and more complex stimuli, part of the active role that infants play in their sensory development.

10. At birth, vision is the least developed of the senses, but during the first months of life, distance and binocular vision, focusing skills, and color perception improve considerably. Tracking, the ability to follow a moving object, develops rapidly.

11. Hearing is very sensitive, even at birth. Infants listen particularly to speech sounds, quickly distinguishing the necessary distinctions and accents of their native languages. Hence, moderate hearing loss is a cause for concern.

NUTRITION

12. Physical growth, brain development, and the mastery of motor skills all depend on adequate nutrition. Doctors worldwide recommend breast milk as the ideal food for most babies.

13. Although breast-feeding on demand may be best throughout infancy, the crucial question is whether an infant gets sufficient food or is undernourished. Marasmus, which is caused by long-term protein-calorie deficiency, results in a cessation of growth, the wasting away of body tissue, and eventual death. Kwashiorkor, which is caused by long-term protein deficiency, results in bloating and degradation of various parts of the body. Long-term cognitive deficits may occur.

14. Undernutrition is quite common in developing countries and is often apparent in developed countries as well. The consequences vary, depending in part on how long the child was underfed. Nationwide political and social factors influence infant nutrition in developing countries, whereas parental inadequacy and community neglect are more often responsible for malnutrition in developed countries.

KEY TERMS

immunization (138)
sudden infant death
   syndrome (SIDS) (140)
neurons (143)
axons (143)
dendrites (143)
synapses (143)
cortex (144)
transient exuberance
   (144)
myelination (144)
binocular vision (145)
physiological states (147)

electroencephalogram
   (EEG) (147)
developmental
   biodynamics (148)
reflexes (148)
breathing reflex (149)
sucking reflex (149)
rooting reflex (149)
gross motor skills (150)
toddler (151)
fine motor skills (151)
pincer grasp (153)
norms (154)

sensation (156)

perception (156)

habituation (156)

otitis media (161)

protein-calorie
  malnutrition (166)

marasmus (166)

kwashiorkor (166)

undernutrition (167)

failure-to-thrive (167)

KEY QUESTIONS

1. How do the weight, length, and proportions of the infant's body change during the first 2 years?

2. How does immunizing infants protect the entire community?

3. What are the leading risk factors for sudden infant death syndrome?

4. What specific changes occur in the brain's communication system during infancy?

5. How does experience affect the development of the brain's neural pathways?

6. Which reflexes are critical to an infant's survival?

7. What is the general sequence of the development of gross motor and fine motor skills?

8. How does the development of motor skills affect the development of cognitive and social skills?

9. What factors account for individual differences in the timing of motor achievements?

10. What are some ways researchers determine whether an infant perceives a stimulus, such as a specific sound or visual detail?

11. How do the sensory capabilities of a newborn infant change over the first year of life?

12. What kinds of sensory experiences do babies typically prefer in early infancy, and why?

13. What are the advantages of breast-feeding?

14. What are some of the consequences of serious, long-term malnutrition?

15. What are the major causes of undernutrition?

16. *In Your Experience* What are the factors that determine what, and when, a young infant is fed?

CRITICAL THINKING EXERCISE

by Richard O. Straub

Take your study of Chapter 5 a step further by working this problem-solving exercise:

This exercise is concerned with the effect that experiences in one domain of development might have on development in other domains. Imagine that a 6-month-old infant named Samantha has a vision disorder which can be completely corrected only through surgery. The disorder involves uneven curvature of the lenses of both eyes. Unless it is corrected, Samantha's vision will be slightly out of focus, even if she wears corrective eyeglasses or contact lenses.

Samantha's parents, who are understandably concerned about the dangers of performing an operation on so young a child and about being away from her for any period, have asked for your advice. In essence, they need answers to the following:

1. Is there any evidence suggesting that Samantha's vision problem should be corrected sooner, rather than later, in life? Why not wait until Samantha is older, stronger, better able to understand?

2. If her parents postpone the surgery, will Samantha's physical development lag behind that of other children?

3. What about Samantha's cognitive and social development? Could her visual problem affect these areas of her life?

4. Finally, if the parents are of a philosophical bent, they might ask why "Mother Nature" would permit early sensory experiences to influence neural development. Wouldn't it be more adaptive to our species to leave such an important process entirely to biological maturation?

Check your answers by comparing them to the sample answers in Appendix B.

The First 2 Years:
Cognitive Development

CHAPTER 6

This chapter is about infant *cognition,* by which we mean thinking in a very broad sense. Cognition involves intelligence and learning, memory and language, facts and concepts, and every mental process concerned in intellect. You might think that a chapter on mental processes during the first 2 years of life would be quite short, but you can see that this is not the case. Why?

Imagine, for a moment, that you are a newborn. Consider what you need to learn: New and constantly changing images, sounds, smells, and physical sensations swirl around you, and you must make sense of them all, connecting smells with visual images, tastes with feelings. You need to develop perceptions of objects, people, and even the parts of your own body and to figure out which are enduring and which change from moment to moment, in what sequence, and how they relate to you. Then you need to put it all together: sensations, sequences, objects, people, significant characteristics, permanent and transient features, causes and effects. And this is just the beginning.

Consider another task, one that has left developmental psychologists in awe: By the end of the first year—and often much sooner—infants grasp the fundamental attributes of the objects and people around them (such as their boundaries, their permanence over time and in space, and their relation to the infant). They also have a concept of number, demonstrate simple problem-solving capacities, and have begun to talk. It is as if newborn infants are biologically endowed with the motivational and intellectual tools necessary to understand the world in all its great complexity. And those tools continue to be used, so that, by the end of their second year, toddlers talk in short sentences, think before acting, and can pretend to be someone or something (a mother, an airplane) that they know they are not. No wonder, then, there is much to describe about infant cognition.

PERCEPTION AND COGNITION

As you learned in Chapter 5, infants possess remarkably acute sensory abilities from their very first days. They also develop early *preferences* for what they experience, showing a hunger for novelty and stimulation. But how do infants make sense of what they experience? Our examination of this side of perception—which is closely related to cognitive growth—will reveal that infants are active and eager interpreters of the world.

The first major theorist to stress that infants are active learners and that early learning is based on sensory abilities was Jean Piaget, whose depiction of infants' *sensorimotor intelligence* is presented later in this chapter.

We begin, however, with the work of Eleanor and James Gibson, a husband-and-wife team of researchers. Their understanding of the links between perception and cognition has inspired much of the current research on infants' cognitive growth (Gibson, 1969; Gibson, 1979).

The Gibsons' Affordances

Perception, remember, is the mental processing of information that arrives from sensory organs. The Gibsons' central insight regarding perception is that it is not an automatic phenomenon that everyone, everywhere, experiences in the same way. Rather, perception is, essentially, an active cognitive process which requires that each individual selectively interact with a vast array of perceptual possibilities.

In the Gibsons' view, "the environment *affords* opportunities"; that is, every event, object, or place affords, or offers, the potential to be perceived and interacted with in a variety of ways (Gibson, 1997). Each of those opportunities for perception and interaction is called an **affordance.** Which particular affordance (of the many available) an individual perceives and acts on depends on that person's:

affordance   Each of the various opportunities for perception, action, and interaction that an object or place offers to any individual.

- Past experiences
- Current developmental or maturational level
- Sensory awareness of the opportunities
- Immediate needs and motivation

As a simple example, a lemon may be perceived as something that affords smelling, tasting, touching, viewing, throwing, squeezing, and biting (among other things). Which affordance a particular person perceives and acts on depends on the four factors above: a lemon might elicit quite different perceptions from an artist about to paint a still life, a thirsty adult in need of a refreshing drink, and a teething baby wanting something to gnaw on. This example implies (correctly) that affordances require an ecological fit between the individual and his or her environment. Hence, affordances arise both from specific qualities of an object and from how the individual subjectively perceives the object. As one psychologist explains:

A Hole Is to Dig As for any scientist, discovery and application are the motivating forces for infant activity. Clamshells have many uses, one for clams, one for hungry people, and another—shown here—for toddlers on the beach.

> If I want to sit down in a sparsely furnished bus station, a floor or a stack of books or a not-too-hot radiator might afford sitting. None of these are chairs, and thus their affordance of "sit-ability" is in relationship to my perception. [Gauvain, 1990]

Affordances are not limited just to objects but also are perceived in the physical characteristics of a setting and the living creatures in it (Reed, 1993). A toddler's idea of what affords running might be any unobstructed surface—a meadow, a long hallway floor in an apartment building, or an empty road. To an adult eye, the degree to which these places afford running may be restricted by such factors as a bull grazing in the meadow, neighbors in the building, or traffic patterns on the road.

Graspability

graspability   The perception of whether or not an object is of the proper shape, size, texture, and distance to afford grasping or grabbing.

One of the first affordances that infants perceive from their environment is **graspability**—whether an object is the right size, shape, and texture for grasping and whether it is within reach. This is vital information, since infants learn about their world by handling objects (Palmer, 1989; Rochat,

It's OK to Grasp Daddy's Nose Infants quickly learn what objects are of the right size and proximity for grasping. If the adults in their life allow it, graspability affords sociability also, an impulse that requires one to distinguish appropriate objects from inappropriate ones.

1989). Extensive research has shown that infants perceive graspability long before their manual dexterity enables them to actually grasp successfully. For instance, when 3-month-olds view objects, some graspable and some not, they move their arms excitedly in the direction of those that are of the right size and distance for grasping but they merely follow ungraspable objects with their eyes (Bower, 1989).

The fact that babies perceive graspability so early helps explain how they explore a face. Once they have some control over their arm and hand movements, they will grab at any face that comes within their reach. But their grabbing is not haphazard: they do not grab at the eyes or mouth (although they might poke at them), for they already perceive that these objects are embedded and thus do not afford grasping. A tug at the nose or ears is more likely, because these features do afford grasping. Even better, however, are eyeglasses, earrings, and long mustaches—all of which are quickly yanked by most babies, who perceive at a glance the graspability these objects afford.

Other Affordances

One of the more difficult affordances for babies to learn is *digestibility*. The typical baby tastes and, if possible, swallows everything available to discover if it affords nourishment. Such behavior is a sign of active cognition—just what an infant should do. However, it is also dangerous behavior, and the caregiver must ensure that nothing within the infant's reach will afford poisoning or choking. By routinely offering certain foods, caregivers teach babies and children what is delicious and what is not, thereby building preferences that linger long past toddlerhood. In some cases the preferences are healthy habits that endure lifelong; in other cases they are culture-specific; in still other cases they are quite unhealthy. An example of the latter is salt, butter, or sugar that caregivers add to baby food—condiments that infants may not want but that they learn to expect.

Similarly, from very early on, an infant begins to understand which objects afford *suckability,* which afford *noisemaking,* which afford *movability,* and which afford other interesting opportunities. An impressive feature of this understanding is the infant's ability to find similar affordances in dissimilar objects (rattles, flowers, and pacifiers do not look alike, but they are all graspable) and to distinguish different affordances in similar objects (among objects of the same color, size, and shape, furry ones are more likely to be patted and rubber ones more likely to be squeezed) (Palmer, 1989). Once again, caregivers and culture help make some affordances easier to learn than others, a fact that explains why the pickled foods of Korea, Norway, or Mexico may be delicious or disgusting to you—depending on what you ate as a child.

Sudden Drops and Sloping Surfaces

The affordances that an infant perceives in common objects evolve as the infant gains experience with those objects. An example is provided by the **visual cliff,** a firm surface that seemingly (but not actually) ends with a sudden drop (see photograph, page 176). Perception of a visual cliff was once thought to be purely a matter of visual maturity: 8-month-olds could see the difference; younger babies, because of their inadequate depth perception, could not. "Proof" came when 6-month-olds could be enticed to wiggle forward over the supposed edge of the visual cliff, in contrast to 10-month-olds who fearfully refused to budge, even when their mothers called them (Gibson & Walk, 1960).

❷ **Especially for Parents:** At which age—4 months, 8 months, or 12 months—is an infant most likely to fall off a bed or a table if you put him or her there for a moment?

visual cliff An apparent (but not actual) drop between one surface and another. The illusion of the cliff is created by connecting a transparent glass surface to an opaque patterned one, with the floor below the same pattern as the surface.

Depth Perception Like thousands of crawling babies before him, this infant refuses to crawl to his mother.

❷ *Observational Quiz (see answer page 179): What does he see when he looks down?*

Affordances for Locomotion *(a)* Like the other 14-month-olds in Karen Adolph's study, Lauren perceives that a gently sloping ramp affords walking and she confidently descends it. *(b)* When later confronted with a steep slope, Lauren, like the other experienced walkers in the study, perceives the affordance of falling; consequently, she descends the slope by sliding down it. *(c)* This is in marked contrast to the inexperienced 8-month-olds, who, like Jack, try to descend every slope, no matter how steep, by crawling, and who sometimes end up in a nosedive.

Later research found, however, that this hypothesis was wrong. In fact, even 3-month-olds notice the difference between a solid surface and an apparent cliff, as evidenced by their speeding heart rates and wide open eyes when they are placed over the "edge." But they do not realize that one affordance of the cliff is falling. That realization comes when they start crawling, and their memories of caregiver fear (and perhaps their own tumble off a bed) teach them what cliffs afford to crawling infants (Campos et al., 1978).

A more subtle example comes from research with a sloping ramp—which may afford ascent and descent but may also afford falling. The research showed that which affordances an infant perceives in the ramp depend in part on prior experience. In one experiment, Karen Adolph and her colleagues observed two groups of infants as they moved up and down ramps pitched at different inclines (Adolph & Gibson, 1993). One group consisted of 14-month-olds with plenty of walking experience; the other consisted of 8½-month-olds with crawling (but not walking) experience. The researchers expected that the older infants would respond more cautiously to the inclines since they could better perceive the affordance of falling because of their prior experience of walking—and falling—over various surfaces.

And this time the researchers' hypothesis was correct: The 14-month-olds confidently walked down gentle slopes; but when the slopes were made steeper, they negotiated the descent by sliding down in a sitting position, often after much hesitation and much searching for the best position. By contrast, the 8½-month-olds, regardless of the steepness of the slope, tried to descend by crawling rather than sliding, often falling headlong (their mothers were nearby to catch them). Thus, although infants of both ages could perceive the ramp's affordance of descent, only the older infants (with prior walking experience) could perceive its affordance of falling. They re-

(a)

(b)

(c)

sponded more cautiously as a result. In longitudinal follow-up research, Adolph (1997) found that experience with walking made the infants less reckless and also more astute in their preliminary exploration (looking, swaying, touching, thinking) before they descended the slope.

The Gibsons' contextual view emphasizes, therefore, that early perceptual development involves a growing knowledge of affordances, acquired through infants' active interactions with the objects, events, and people around them. Each infant, in each social context, will learn somewhat different affordances than other infants learn.

Object Constancy

object constancy The concept that each object is whatever it is, despite changes in appearance or movement caused by shifts in the observer, the object, or the context.

Essential to the infant's overall cognitive growth, including the perception of affordances, is an understanding of the constancy of objects. The essence of **object constancy** is the realization that things remain what they are despite changes in the perspective of the viewer or the appearance of the object. This is a surprisingly complex accomplishment, as illustrated in this example:

> Consider what we see when we gaze at the family cat stretched out before the fireplace. We see a single, solid, three-dimensional object, located in a particular region of space and separate from both the objects it touches (e.g., the rug on which it lies) and the object it occludes (e.g., the fireplace behind it). We see an object of a particular size, shape, and color, and do so regardless of the distance between us and the cat, the angle of viewing, or the lighting in the room (all factors that change the image in our retina). If an object comes between the cat and us, blocking all except head and tail, we do not perceive the cat as being bisected; rather, our perception is still of a continuous, indivisible object. . . . If the cat stirs itself and strolls from the room we do not expect its [tail] or any other part to remain behind; instead, we realize that the parts of an animate object move together in predictable unison. If the movement takes the cat away from us we correctly perceive that it is receding from us (but not changing size, despite changes in the size of the retinal image); on the other hand, if the cat suddenly makes a run for our lap we perceive not only that it is approaching but that its course guarantees contact within a very short time. (Of course, how we feel about such contact depends more on our attitude toward cats than on perception per se.) [Flavell et al., 1993]

● Response for Parents (from page 175):
Don't do it! The 4-month-old cannot move much and can see depth, so you might think he or she is safe. But 4-month-olds have no understanding of the danger, so any wiggle might produce a fall. The 12-month-old has a firm grasp of depth and of the dangers of a headlong drop, but might try to get down feet first. In the most danger of all is the 8-month-old, because at that age babies have only the beginning of awareness of the dangers of depth but are quite able to move.

How long does it take a newborn infant to master these complex interpretations of the sensory world? Not long. Even though vision is the least developed sense at birth, by the age of 3 months infants are able to distinguish the boundaries of separate three-dimensional objects; a few months later, they can do so even when one object partly overlaps another. This ability persists even when the objects are in motion, as they typically are in everyday life. In fact, motion makes it easier for infants to perceive the constancy of objects; they are more likely to understand where the cat begins and ends than they are to have the same understanding about the rug on the floor.

perceptual constancy The fact that the size and shape of an object remain the same despite changes in the object's appearance due to changes in its location.

Further, infants understand **perceptual constancy**; that is, they become aware that the size and shape of an object remain the same despite changes in the object's appearance due to changes in its location. Thus, even though an object (like a cat) looks smaller when seen from a greater distance, and looks different when perceived from different viewpoints, infants quickly grasp that it is the same object nevertheless.

Dynamic Perception

Movement plays a key role in infants' perception of the properties of objects and in the development of their perceptual and cognitive skills generally (Bornstein & Lamb, 1992; Flavell et al., 1993). Babies prefer to look at things in motion, whether those things are a mobile rotating overhead, their own flexing fingers, or their favorite bobbing, talking, human face. Beginning in the first days of life, they attend to movement cues to discern not only the boundaries of objects but also their rigidity, wholeness, shape, and size. Infants soon form simple expectations of the path that a moving object will follow (Haith et al., 1993; Nelson & Horowitz, 1987).

dynamic perception   Perception that arises from the movement of objects and changes in their positions.

The fact that infants have **dynamic perception,** that is, perception primed to focus on movement and change of position, works well in a world in which stimuli are constantly moving within an infant's field of vision. Movement captures the baby's attention, highlights certain attributes of the moving object (like its boundaries), and advances the infant's perception of the object, enabling him or her to attend to learning about its other qualities.

The baby's own movements also enhance sensory and perceptual skills (Bertenthal & Campos, 1990). As babies scoot, crawl, creep, walk, and climb, they are able to perceive and explore many new and old objects from many different perspectives, thereby gaining important information about the world around them. Indeed, once infants are able to move from one place to another, the way their eyes scan the environment changes to adapt to their movement (Higgins et al., 1996).

One Constant, Multisensual Perception From the angle of her arm and the bend of her hand, it appears that this infant recognizes the constancy of the furry mass, perceiving it as a single entity whether it is standing still, rolling in the sand, or walking along the beach.

Information gained from movement is fascinating and highly motivating to infants. Parents show they have learned this when they shake a rattle and then put it in a 3-month-old's hand to distract the infant from the discomfort of diapering or when they put an unhappy 6-month-old in a stroller and take a walk to quiet fussing. They learn it again when they try to restrain a 9-month-old who is crawling down from the lap (say, in a busy restaurant) and elicit such loud wails of protest that all the other customers look for signs of abuse. Infants want to move and watch, because that helps them think, and thinking is the most compelling thing they do.

Coordination of Sensory Systems

Once researchers were alerted to the early development of the infant's perceptual skills, they also began to look closely at the infant's ability to combine perceptual information from two or more sensory systems.

Simultaneous Awareness

intermodal perception   The ability to connect, simultaneously, information from one sensory mode (such as vision) with information from another (such as hearing).

Intermodal perception is the ability to associate information from one sensory mode (say, vision) with information from another (say, hearing). For example, when we sit near a lighted fireplace, it is through intermodal perception that we realize that the heat we feel, the crackling we hear, the smoky odor we smell, and the flickering light we see all come from the same source.

Even newborns exhibit some intermodal perception, as when they look for the source of a sound—though not always in the right direction. As early as 3 months of age, however, they have a notion not only of where to locate sounds but of which sounds are likely to accompany what events. This has been demonstrated in various experiments that test whether infants can "match up" a film they are watching with an appropriate sound track. The results show that they can, whether the sound track is of music, a voice, or

● **Answer to Observational Quiz (from page 176):** He sees a visual cliff. It has the same attractive pattern as the surface on which he rests, but he perceives a 1-meter drop (that's why he hesitates).

simply noises—such as squishing sounds (matched with a film of a sponge being squeezed) or clacking sounds (matched with a film of wooden blocks hitting one another) (Bahrick, 1983).

In one experiment, infants about 6 months old simultaneously viewed two screens, each showing a film of a person talking. One person seemed happy, the other sad. At the same time, the infants heard the sound track of one of the films, which conveyed either a happy mood or a sad mood. Although the infants at first looked equally at both films, they soon began looking more intently at the one that matched the mood of the sound track (Walker, 1982).

Infants make similar discriminations based on a speaker's sex: When one screen showed a talking man and the other a talking woman, infants looked more at the screen with a man when the sound track was of a male voice and more at the screen with a woman when the sound track was of a female voice (Walker-Andrews et al., 1991). Amazingly, in another experiment, infants looked more at speakers whose lip movements matched the speech sounds the infants were hearing (Kuhl & Meltzoff, 1988). Basically, they were "reading lips" before they understood words!

The fact that infants 6 months old and younger are able to match moving pictures with sounds in so many different ways suggests that the babies are not simply making a primitive match between visual and auditory rhythms. Rather, they seem to be doing something more complex and cerebral: turning information from one sensory mode into an expectancy and simultaneously matching that expectancy with information from another sensory mode. This requires coordinating information from the visual cortex to the auditory cortex of the brain, and this means that the network of axons and dendrites is beginning to build. As infancy progresses, infants become much quicker and more skilled at intermodal perception—a sign that myelination is also occurring.

From Actual Sense to Imagined Sense

cross-modal perception The mental ability to translate (or transfer) information obtained through one sensory mode (say, touch) to another (say, vision).

Cross-modal perception is the ability to translate information from one sensory system to another, not simply to match sensory information that arrives in the brain simultaneously from two sources. The main difference between intermodal perception and cross-modal perception is in timing, which makes cross-modal perception a more difficult intellectual accomplishment. The first evidence of cross-modal perception in very young infants involves the sense of touch. To test this ability, experimenters might allow infants to touch and hold an object that is hidden from view and then show them two objects, one of which is the object they have just touched. By analyzing the infants' gaze, researchers can tell whether the infants are able to distinguish the object they previously manipulated from the one they didn't. In one example, 2½-month-olds touched either a plastic ring or a flat disk without seeing it and then were shown both objects. The duration of their gazing revealed that most of the infants "recognized" the object they had just manipulated (Streri, 1987).

Intermodal and cross-modal perceptual skills improve significantly during the first year, because infants can deduce the qualities of objects more quickly and sensitively with increasing age (Rose & Ruff, 1987). By the age of 9 months, if a fussy baby hears mother's voice, "I'm coming, I'm coming," and then big sister walks into the room, the infant might wail in dismay—even though big sister ordinarily is greeted with smiles of delight. Cross-modal perception is more advanced than intermodal perception because the infant must transfer the stimulus from one sense to another cognitively and remember it before the next cue is presented. Amazingly, a

All Five Senses With great concentration, Eleanor brushes the leaf against her palm, feeling the odd combination of crispness and flexibility of dry leaves.

❓ *Observational Quiz (see answer page 183, top): How is this an example of intermodal perception, and what would be necessary for this to become cross-modal perception?*

longitudinal study found that 1-year-olds' skill at cross-modal perception predicted, ten years later, not only their cross-modal skill but also their overall intelligence (Rose et al., 1998).

The remarkable speed and apparent ease with which infants attain all the perceptual skills have led some researchers to conclude either that basic perceptual skills are innate or that newborns are biologically endowed with powerful capabilities and the motivation to quickly acquire these skills (Spelke, 1991). It is quite clear that very young infants do not absorb sights, sounds, and other sensory impressions passively. In a simple way, they analyze, interpret, and integrate their perceptions to learn about the world around them. Their early skill in doing so provides the foundation for the equally impressive emergence of early cognitive abilities.

KEY ELEMENTS OF COGNITIVE GROWTH

From our discussion so far, it is clear that a considerable portion of infants' knowledge of the world is built upon their developing perceptual skills. These skills form the basic tools infants use to structure the data they receive through their daily experiences. This enables them to build for themselves a coherent intellectual map to predict the territory they inhabit. Essential to this structuring are several key cognitive abilities. We will look at four of them: the abilities to develop categories, to understand object permanence, to understand cause and effect, and—most important—to remember.

Categories

From a very early age, infants coordinate and organize their perceptions into categories such as soft, hard, flat, round, rigid, and flexible. For the preverbal infant, of course, these categories do not have labels such as "soft" and "hard," yet they provide a useful and important way of organizing the world. For example, once an object is mentally placed into a category (say, "soft"), the infant has a ready set of expectations about what that object affords (perhaps "nice to touch" and "graspable") and can distinguish it from objects that belong to other categories.

How do researchers study the ability to categorize in an infant far too young to name the categories? Often they measure *habituation*, which (as you learned in Chapter 5) occurs when a stimulus becomes familiar. A young infant usually stares wide-eyed at a new object, for example, but if the object doesn't move or change, the baby eventually becomes uninterested and looks away. The infant's interest is reignited if an object that is perceived as different then appears. Using habituation to signify perception is actually complicated by an alternative reaction: At some point babies begin to prefer sensations that are *familiar*—especially a particular smell, or blanket, or voice that reminds them of mother—and then they prefer the old object and ignore new ones. Researchers can, nonetheless, use these two indicators to determine infants' preferences for new or familiar categories, not just new or familiar objects.

Infants Under 6 Months

The results of such research, carefully interpreted, are astonishing. Infants younger than 6 months can categorize objects on the basis of their shape, color, angularity, density, relative size, and number (up to three objects) (Caron & Caron, 1981; van Loosbroek & Smitsman, 1990; Wynn, 1992).

Taken as a whole, the evidence suggests that young infants do not merely perceive the difference between shapes like circles versus squares or relative sizes like larger and smaller; they also apply organizing principles that enable them to develop a concept of what is, or is not, relevant for inclusion in each category. Many researchers believe that a rudimentary understanding of certain categories in the natural world may be biologically based ("hard-wired" in the brain) but that experience with different objects and events is also essential for developing the innate ability to sort things into categories.

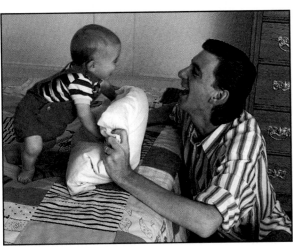

Peek-a-Boo Edwin's father ducks down behind the pillow and then reappears, time after time, to his son's delight.
❷ *Observational Quiz (see answer page 183, middle): How old is Edwin?*

Older Infants

Experience becomes especially significant when we observe that as infants get older, they categorize in increasing complexity. For example, infants as young as 3 months old seem to understand "above" and "below." At least, after seeing several depictions of a small diamond-shaped dot above a line, their longer stares suggest they notice when the diamond is below the line. However, the above-below distinction escapes them if the target object varies from trial to trial—from the diamond to, say, a tiny arrow, to the letter "E," a plus sign, and then a triangle. By the age of 6 months, though, the concepts of "above" and "below" are more firmly established. Then, varying the object does not distract babies from paying attention to an object below a line after seeing various objects above it (Quinn et al., 1996).

Other experiments have shown that by the end of the first year, babies can categorize and discriminate between photographs, all the same size, of:

- Faces, categorizing them on the basis of features such as hair length and nose size (Sherman, 1985)
- Animals, distinguishing them according to tail width or leg length (Younger, 1990, 1993)
- Birds (as a group different from animals), by perceiving pictures of parakeets as similar to hawks but distinct from horses (Roberts, 1988)

The categories that infants construct and use to recognize the subjects of photos, as in these examples, are quite simple; they have little of the complexity of the verbally labeled, and often highly ordered, categories that older children construct. Nevertheless, they form a foundation for later cognitive accomplishments, and they enable young infants to conceptualize their world in increasingly more meaningful ways.

Object Permanence

One of the most important cognitive accomplishments of infancy is the ability to understand that objects and people exist independently of one's perception of them. With this understanding, referred to as **object permanence**, infants realize that even when objects (like a familiar toy, the family cat, or Mommy) cannot be seen or heard, they exist somewhere else in the world. Objects do not cease to exist simply because they are not immediately apparent.

Although object permanence no doubt seems obvious to you, it is not obvious to very young infants; their early awareness of reality is strictly limited to what they can see, hear, and otherwise sense at any given moment. Consequently, the development of object permanence has been the subject of much developmental research.

object permanence   The realization that objects (including people) still exist even when they cannot be seen, touched, or heard.

Where's Rosa? At 18 months, Rosa knows all about object permanence and hiding. Her only problem here is distinguishing between "self" and "other."

Piaget's Test

One way to test for awareness of object permanence is to observe whether an infant searches for a hidden object. In an experiment devised by Piaget, an adult shows an infant an interesting toy and then covers it up with a blanket or cloth. If the infant searches under the covering for the toy, he or she realizes the toy still exists even though the object cannot be seen at the moment.

Various forms of Piaget's basic experiment have been carried out in virtually every university, every city, and every nation of the world, with fairly consistent results: Infants do not search for hidden objects until about 8 months of age. Even then, their search abilities are limited; they cannot find an object that they see concealed in one hiding place and then moved to a second hiding place (until they are about 12 months old, they tend to look for the object in the first hiding place, not where they just saw it hidden). If 8-month-olds are made to wait even a few seconds between the time they see an object disappear and the time they are allowed to search, they seem to lose all interest in searching. Thus a firm understanding of object permanence develops rather slowly, over the first 2 years of life. In fact, even 3-year-olds playing hide-and-seek sometimes become fearful that someone has really disappeared or sometimes hide themselves in very obvious places—signs that some aspects of object permanence are not entirely understood.

But does a 6-month-old's failure to search necessarily mean that the infant does not have any concept at all of object permanence? After all, many skills are needed to search competently (Harris, 1987). Removing a cover to reveal a familiar toy requires at least two abilities: setting a goal and knowing how to achieve it. However, such understanding of the connection between goals and actions is quite advanced, beyond the 6-month-old. In addition, searching depends on prior experience and on motivation. How can an experimenter be sure an infant wants to find the toy and is not distracted by some other event? Finally, the nature of the hiding place, the length of the delay between hiding and searching, the specifics of the cover used, and other details can all discourage searching. Is it possible, then, that younger babies have some understanding of object permanence but that other factors included in Piaget's classic test mask that understanding?

Baillargeon's Test

This possibility was explored by Renée Baillargeon and her colleagues in a series of experiments. In one, Baillargeon (1987) placed 3½- and 4½-month-old infants directly in front of a large screen that was hinged along its base to the center of a tabletop. The screen was then repeatedly rotated back and forth through a 180-degree arc (see Figure 6.1) until, as

Figure 6.1 The Old Screen-and-Box Game. The basic steps of Renée Baillargeon's test of object permanence—a test that doesn't depend on the infant's searching abilities or motivation to search. (*a*) First the infant is habituated to the movement of a hinged screen that rotates through a 180-degree arc toward and (as shown) away from the infant. (*b*) Next, with the infant observing, a box is placed in the backward path of the screen. Then the infant witnesses two events: (*c*) the "possible event," in which the screen's movement through the arc is stopped by the box, and (*d*) the "impossible event," in which the screen completes its movement through the arc as though the box did not exist. Infants as young as 4½ months old stare longer at the impossible event, indicating they are aware that the box does exist even though they cannot see it behind the screen.

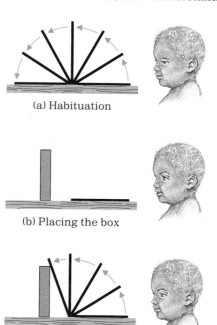

(a) Habituation

(b) Placing the box

(c) Possible event

(d) Impossible event

● Answer to Observational Quiz (from page 180): *Distinguishing the types of early perception is difficult, so be proud of yourself if Eleanor's concentration implied to you that she is associating (intermodally) the look and the feel of the leaf (and probably its sound, too). Be even prouder if you also knew that this leaf could remind her (cross-modally) of another sensation, perhaps the smell of a pile of leaves or the taste of a leaf (yes, she probably did or will bite one), or that (still cross-modally) she might later smell burning leaves and remember the feel of this leaf on her hand.*

● Answer to Observational Quiz (from page 181): *Look at his legs—he is trying to stand, a milestone normally attained at 10 months, but variable. Edwin could be as young as 7 months or as old as 1 year. The better clue is cognitive. Unless he is mentally retarded, object permanence in this manifestation begins at 8 months and is no longer so much fun at 12 months (unless the hiding is less obvious). In fact, Edwin is 10 months old.*

❓ Especially for Social Workers: Suppose you suspect that an infant, not yet talking, has been mistreated, but no bruises or other signs are present. Is there any way you can confirm your suspicions?

habituation occurred, the infants began to look away. At that point, a box was placed directly in the path of the screen's backward descent. Then the screen was rotated again, rising until it reached its full vertical height, which concealed the box from view. Thereafter, two experimental conditions followed. In the first, named the "possible event," the screen continued to move until it was intercepted by the box and stopped, as one would expect. In the second, named the "impossible event," the screen moved through its entire 180-degree arc, as if no box were in the way. (In fact, although the babies didn't see it happen, the box had dropped through a trapdoor before the screen could hit it.)

Even 4½-month-old infants stared longer at the impossible event than at the possible event, as if they were curious and surprised. Their longer stares mean that the babies had three expectations (Baillargeon & DeVos, 1992):

- The box continued to exist behind the screen.
- The screen could not rotate through the space occupied by the box.
- The screen would stop short.

When the screen did not stop short (in the impossible event), the infants' reactions proved that they have some concept of object permanence, as well as dynamic perception, long before they uncover attractive toys at 8 months.

Many other procedures also prove that infants understand object permanence months before they demonstrate it on Piaget's hidden-object task (Baillargeon, 1991; Baillargeon & DeVos, 1992; Wilcox et al., 1996). In each case, young infants have looked significantly longer at "impossible events" in which objects appeared to move through other, hidden, solid objects. These experiments also reveal that infants expect hidden objects to retain their original size, rigidity, and location and that even hidden objects can support other, visible, objects. All told, young infants have an impressive understanding of object permanence long before they can uncover a hidden toy.

This series of experiments proves something about adult concepts as well. Piaget's experiment proved to him that infants do not understand object permanence, because he failed to realize that the experiment itself kept babies from showing what they know. Piaget's mistake is not so unusual; probably anyone might notice a bit of ignorance in someone else and assume it represents much more incompetence than it really does. The surprising part is that Piaget's basic finding was accepted by the scientific community for almost 50 years, from about 1940 to 1990—until finally some iconoclastic young researchers began to prove him wrong.

Memory

Central to the development of all cognitive ability is memory. You have already seen evidence of infant memory in habituation studies (remembering certain objects as familiar), in cross-modal perception (remembering and translating sensory stimuli), and in object permanence (keeping in mind an object that has disappeared from view). But these involve memory over a few minutes at most. What about *long-term memory*—the ability to store information in memory and then retrieve it after days, weeks, and months? The conventional consensus, from both common sense and research, has been that infants' long-term memory is very poor.

However, here again, researchers have recently revised their assessment. To be sure, in their first 6 months babies have great difficulty storing new memories. But they can show that they remember provided that (1) the situations used by researchers are similar to real life, (2) motivation is high, and (3) special measures aid memory retrieval.

Memory Span and Reminder Sessions

Notable in memory research is a series of innovative experiments that taught 3-month-olds to make a mobile move by kicking their legs (Rovee-Collier, 1987, 1990; Rovee-Collier & Hayne, 1987). The infants lay on their backs, in their own cribs, and were connected to a brightly colored mobile by means of a ribbon tied to one foot. Virtually all the infants began making some occasional kicks (as well as random arm movements and noise) and realized after a while that kicking made the mobile move. They then kicked more vigorously and often, sometimes laughing at their accomplishment. So far, this is no surprise—we know that such control of movement is highly reinforcing to infants. But would the infants remember this experience?

reminder session An experience that includes some aspect (a sight, a smell, a sound) of something to be remembered, and thus serves to trigger the entire memory.

When infants had the mobile-and-ribbon apparatus reinstalled in their cribs *1 week later*, most started immediately to kick—indicating that they did remember. But when other infants were retested 2 *weeks later*, they did not kick more than they had before they were hooked up to the mobile. Apparently they forgot what they had learned.

However, a further experiment demonstrated a remarkable effect: The infants could remember after 2 weeks *if* they were given a brief reminder session prior to the retesting (Rovee-Collier & Hayne, 1987). A **reminder session** is any perceptual experience that might make a person recollect an idea or thing but that does not test the actual memory. In this particular reminder session, 2 weeks after the initial training the infants were not tied to the ribbon and could not kick, but they watched the mobile move. The next day, when they were again connected to the mobile and positioned so that they could move their legs, they kicked as they had learned to do 2 weeks earlier. In effect, their faded memory had been reactivated by watching the mobile move on the previous day.

He Remembers! In this demonstration of Rovee-Collier's experiment, a young infant immediately remembers how to make the familiar mobile move. (Unfamiliar mobiles don't provoke the same reaction.) He kicks both legs and flails both arms, just as he learned to do so successfully several weeks ago.

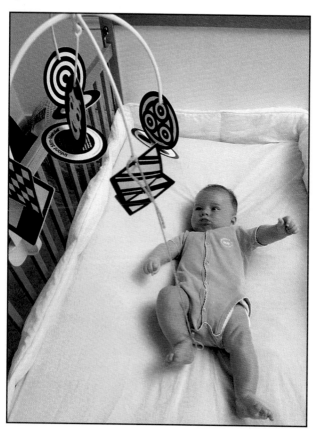

Similar experiments have been performed with younger infants (as young as 8 weeks) after a longer interval (up to 18 days) with the same result: a brief reminder session evokes and prolongs young infants' memory of an earlier event. Researchers have also found that memory improves when there is extra training, there is less time separating training and recall, or there are familiar cues (such as a distinctive crib bumper) to help bring to mind the earlier training or when distinctive background music (such as classical or jazz) aids the memory. The specific timing and context of reminder sessions are critical factors, and some reminders (such as a stationary mobile) have no effect (Borovsky & Rovee-Collier, 1990; Butler & Rovee-Collier, 1989; Fagen et al., 1997; Hayne & Rovee-Collier, 1995).

Carolyn Rovee-Collier, the lead researcher in this series of experiments, believes natural reminder sessions are part of every infant's daily experience, because the same events and circumstances occur to an infant day after day. For example, parents regularly shake a rattle and then put it in the baby's hand. If one day they simply show the rattle, the infant might reach out to grab and shake it, remembering what the rattle does. Such events are common, and if adults are alert, they will notice that very young infants remember. However, it still is true that infants do not remember much. Under the age of 6 months, they recall only for a limited period of time, only under specific conditions, and probably only events that include their own activities (Rovee-Collier & Gerhardstein, 1997).

Deferred Imitation

deferred imitation The ability to witness, remember, and later copy a particular behavior.

After they are 6 months old, infants become capable of retaining information for longer periods of time, and they can do so with less training and less reminding. (See the Research Report on pages 186–187.) Toward the end of the first year, a new memory ability is apparent: **deferred imitation,** the ability to remember and imitate behaviors that have been witnessed but never personally performed. For example, suppose a 9-month-old watches someone playing with a toy the baby has never seen before. The next day, if given the toy, the 9-month-old is likely to play with it in the same way as the person he or she observed had played. (Younger infants do not usually do this.)

Over the next few months, deferred imitation becomes more elaborate (Barr et al., 1996; Heimann & Meltzoff, 1996). Infants retain more details, including the sequence of events, and they can duplicate those details days later, prompted by only minimal clues associated with the experience—such as a sound or a part of the setting (Bauer & Mandler, 1992). A 1-year-old, for instance, might stare intently as an adult opens the refrigerator, takes out an egg carton, and cracks a few eggs into a bowl. The next day (perhaps when the adult has left the refrigerator open while answering the phone), the child might take out the egg carton and crack all the remaining eggs—in a bowl, if it happens to be visible and within reach, or in the sink or the garbage pail or even on the floor, if not.

Play It Again, Sam This probably is deferred imitation, if this toddler saw someone else playing the piano and now has a chance to try it.

By the middle of the second year, toddlers are capable of remembering and reenacting even more complex sequences. They can also *generalize* their memories, moving from the particular details to the general concept just as they did with affordances and categories several months earlier.

In one experiment, 16- and 20-month-olds first watched an experimenter perform various activities, such as putting a doll to bed, making a party hat, or cleaning a table. For each activity, the experimenter used particular props and gave a brief "instruction" for performing each step. For instance, to clean the table, the experimenter wet it with water from a white spray bottle, saying "Put on the water"; wiped it with a paper towel, saying "Wipe it"; and placed the towel in a wooden trash basket, saying "Toss it." A week later, most toddlers remembered how to carry out the sequence just from hearing "Put on the water. Wipe it. Toss it." They could do this not only when given the same props the experimenter had used but also when given quite different props (for instance, a clear spray bottle, a sponge, and a plastic lidded garbage can). Thus, they had obviously formed and remembered a general scheme of the activity; they were not just reenacting a memorized sequence, triggered by visual props. To make sure the toddlers were remembering the sequence and not merely playing imaginatively, the experimenters presented the instructions and the props to toddlers of the same ages who had *not* seen the demonstration. Those youngsters played with the objects but did not perform the specific actions in order (Bauer & Dow, 1994).

❷ Especially for Researchers: How could you assess implicit memory for a second language in adults who heard a language in infancy (perhaps from a grandmother) but who now say they have no knowledge (explicit memory) of it?

Cause and Effect

Another major cognitive accomplishment is recognizing the causes of events and the effects they produce. Infants' ability to understand and even anticipate events (e.g., shoving one toy into another to send the second toy flying), as well as to act effectively in the world (e.g., kicking their legs to

LONG-TERM MEMORY IN INFANCY?

Most adults cannot remember specific events from their very early years. (The experiences they think they recall are often ones that they were later told about by relatives or friends or that have been memorialized in family photographs, home movies, and the like.) Freud specifically described *infantile amnesia*, a hypothesis he thought was a fact—that no one could remember anything that happened before the age of 2 years or much of any importance that occurred before the age of 5. Piaget likewise emphasized the absence of early memories and the pure fantasy of what we "recollect" from early childhood.

More recent theorists disagree, suggesting that earlier scientists may have been misled because they did not realize that there are critical differences between memory processes in infancy and those in later years (Nelson, 1993; Siegler, 1991). In infancy, memories are probably stored and retrieved according to the sensations (smells, sights, sounds) and motor skills that are associated with the remembered events or objects. In later childhood and beyond, however, memories are usually tied to more complex language-based concepts for storage and retrieval.

The distinction between implicit memory and explicit memory helps explain which memories can be retrieved and how that happens (Nelson, 1997). **Implicit memory** is memory of events, objects, or experiences that can be recognized but not necessarily recalled; that is, implicit memories are evoked when certain cues are present, but they cannot be brought to mind independent of any reminder cues. Implicit memory is most likely involved when something suddenly triggers a memory, when we learn something so fast that we must have known some aspect of it earlier, or when something seems vaguely, inexplicably familiar. **Explicit memory** is memory that is available for instant recall; that is, a person can demonstrate it on demand. Often, explicit memory involves material that was deliberately learned. Evidence of explicit memory might be performance on a memory test, either a straightforward one such as a history quiz or an informal one, such as the question "When is your mother's birthday?"

For example, you may know that among your childhood memories is your *explicit memory* of an early address (because your parents, worried that you might get lost, taught it to you until you could repeat it on demand); you may not realize, however, that you also *implicitly remember* the color and texture of your first bedspread—until you see it again and a flood of memories return. Virtually all current researchers agree that different parts of the brain are involved in implicit and explicit memories and that some kinds of memory are stored and retrieved better in early childhood than others (Parkin, 1993).

Let us now return to the very basic issue we discussed at the start of this Research Report: Can any memory that is stored in the first year or two of life endure for more than a few weeks? The answer is yes, under very specific conditions.

In one study, conducted in a university laboratory, 6-month-olds were trained during a single 20-minute session to reach for a dangling Big Bird toy when it made a noise, first in normal lighting and then in the dark (Perris et al., 1990). Two years later, the same children were brought back to the lab and retested on this reaching task, as were a control group of 2½-year-olds who had received no training. Prior to the retesting, the trained children were interviewed to see if they had any explicit memory of the laboratory setting or the training experience. They did not. Then, 30 minutes before testing, half of all the children who were to participate were randomly selected and given a 3-second exposure to the sound of the toy in the dark—intended as a possible reminder session for those in the trained group.

In the retesting that followed, the conditions of the original test were repeated: Each child sat in his or her mother's

❶ Response for Social Workers (from page 183): Infants do remember what has happened to them, and they show it by emotional expressions (crying or pulling away when they see someone) or deferred imitation (slapping a doll, putting a stuffed animal in a dark closet). However, lack of such evidence is not proof that nothing occurred, and it is impossible to prove all the details based on an infant's actions.

make a mobile move or lifting a blanket to find a concealed toy), hinges on the capacity to identify cause and effect.

One way to study cause-and-effect understanding is to observe whether a child intentionally repeats some action that has produced an interesting result. For example, an infant may squeeze a rubber duck, producing a squeak. If the child, delighted by the noise, squeezes the duck again, he or she has connected squeeze and squeak. But this method of study requires certain motor skills. (Even deliberately squeezing a rubber duck demands strength and hand control that are beyond the youngest infants.) For this reason, to examine early awareness of cause and effect, researchers again turn to habituation.

lap and was told the lights would go out. Then, in the dark, the experimenter dangled the noisemaking toy in front of the child. Compared with the untrained children, those who had been trained at 6 months were more likely to reach for and grab the toy—just as they had done long ago! In fact, among those who experienced the 3-second reminder session, the trained children reached for the toy almost four times as often as the untrained children. Moreover, their reaction to suddenly being in the dark was "an almost global emotional acceptance," in marked contrast to the discomfort and fussiness exhibited by many children from the control group (and, indeed, by most 2½-year-olds who suddenly find themselves in a dark, unfamiliar room!). Thus, not only the specific behaviors of a single training experience at age 6 months but also the emotional tone of that experience can remain in the memory of a young child for 2 full years.

It is important to remember that long-term recall was facilitated in many ways in this study—by the children's return to a distinctive testing room, by their reacquaintance with unique procedures and materials, and, ultimately, by a reminder session for some of the children. Nevertheless, findings like these, which have been reported by other researchers as well (Myers et al., 1987), put to rest the idea that all infant memories inevitably disappear. In one such experiment, 11-month-olds were shown how to feed a teddy bear with a "bottle" that did not look like a bottle (a plastic cylinder with an attached plunger) and were then brought back the next day so that they could repeat the feeding by themselves. A year later these babies remembered how to do the feeding after simply seeing the objects involved—something no untrained 23-month-old did spontaneously. One toddler even verbalized "bottle," perhaps an indication of explicit memory (McDonough & Mandler, 1994).

Developmentalists are now reexamining many aspects of infant memory to discover exactly how it functions. So far, they have concluded the following:

- Early in life, even under the best of conditions, long-term-memory storage and retrieval appear to be fragile and uncertain, facilitated by repetition, reminders, and active involvement of the infant.
- Improvement in memory ability seems tied to brain maturation and language development, with notable increases in memory capacity and duration occurring at about 8 months of age and again at around 18 months. Early memories are usually implicit; explicit memory improves with language development.

That raises another question: When a familiar setting or reminder object triggers an implicit memory in an older child or adult, can that implicit memory be expressed without distortion in the words and logic that define explicit memory? Probably not. Indeed, as we will see in Chapter 9, even preschoolers have fragile memories, sometimes distorted, sometimes irretrievable, sometimes quite accurate. And even when adults, in all honesty, believe something happened in childhood, it might or might not have occurred (Loftus, 1997).

More research in this area is now under way. We have found one surprise: Early memories are "highly enduring, and become even more so after repeated encounters with reminders" (Rovee-Collier & Gerhardstein, 1997). Infantile amnesia is much more selective than psychologists once assumed.

implicit memory   Memory that a person is not able to recall verbally on demand but nonetheless has some recollection of—such as seeing a face and recognizing that it is familiar or being able to ride a bicycle by knowing, in the abstract, what the process is.

explicit memory   Memory that can be recalled and thus demonstrated verbally, such as in response to a written test or an oral question.

launching event   Something that seems to start, or trigger, a particular happening. Launching events are used to study understanding of cause-and-effect relationships.

One technique uses a **launching event,** in which one action produces, or seems to produce, another. In this technique, the infant sees an object, such as a square, move in one direction across a table until it bumps into another object, such as a circle. The square stops, and the circle immediately begins moving in the same direction. Most adults would view such an event as indicating cause and effect: The square appears to push, or "launch," the circle into motion. By contrast, if the circle begins to move before the square bumps it, or a second or two after it is hit, most adults would conclude that the square was not the cause of the circle's movement.

● **Response for Researchers (from page 185):**
You could not simply test them, because
that would be explicit memory. You would
need to try to teach them something, perhaps a poem, in the original language, to
see how quickly they would learn it. To
make it scientifically valid, you would need
to teach the same poem to a control group
who never knew that language and then
compare learning time for the two groups.

Do young babies draw similar inferences? In some studies, infants were
first habituated to the bump-and-move launching event as described above
and were then shown variations of it (such as the circle moving before contact or after a delay). These studies revealed that 6-month-olds seem to have
only a very rudimentary understanding of cause-and-effect relations; they
don't seem surprised or even particularly interested when movement occurs without a bump or much after it. However, 10-month-olds can properly
interpret the cause-and-effect nature of simple launching events like this,
and they are surprised when the effect doesn't happen as it should (Cohen &
Oakes, 1993; Leslie & Keeble, 1987; Oakes & Cohen, 1990).

An understanding of cause-and-effect relationships is basic to problem-
solving ability, which explains why infants first demonstrate simple deductive skills as their cause-effect awareness is blossoming. In one study, Peter
Willatts (1989) presented 9-month-olds with a formidable challenge: to obtain an attractive toy that was beyond reach on a table. Fortunately, the toy
was resting on a cloth that was within reach. Unfortunately, a foam block
prevented the infants from grabbing the cloth. Infants as young as 9 months
old skillfully removed the block and then deliberately pulled the cloth to obtain the toy. Their strategic behavior contrasts with the actions of a comparison group of infants who were presented with the same three
objects—block, cloth, and toy—except that the out-of-reach toy was *not* resting on the cloth. These infants tended to play with the foam block but
showed no interest in the cloth because they could not use it to get the toy.
This ability to solve problems becomes much better every month from 9
months on (Chen et al., 1997; Siegler, 1991).

The surprising competencies we have surveyed—intermodal perception, categorizing, object permanence, memory skills, expectation, delayed
imitation, cause-effect understanding, and even simple problem solving—
can all be considered indications of intelligence in infancy. Clearly, this kind
of thinking is not the symbolic, language-based intelligence used by older
children and adults. Nonetheless, research on infant cognition reflects astonishing abilities in very young beings, far beyond what most people assume possible and beyond what even the experts recently believed.

Actually, these abilities are evidence not only of infant intelligence but
also of scientific imagination—the imagination of teams of researchers who,
over the past two decades, have devised increasingly creative ways to test
and measure infant ability. Before undertaking this difficult work, researchers had to believe they might find something. Specifically, they approached their research with the notion that infants had active, curious
minds. For that belief, if for nothing else, developmental scientists are in-
debted to Piaget.

ACTIVE INTELLIGENCE: PIAGET'S THEORY

So far, our account of infant cognitive development relies heavily on laboratory research. It may, therefore, seem to depict infants as unable to demonstrate any cognition except under very unusual conditions. Do not be
misled. Such an image omits one of the most important characteristics of
young babies: their *active intelligence*. This aspect of intelligence is central
to Jean Piaget's theory of infants' cognitive development.

Over 60 years ago, starting with the study of his own three children,
Piaget discovered that infants are indeed active learners. Piaget believed that
humans of every age actively seek to comprehend their world and that their
understanding of it reflects specific, age-related cognitive stages. This seek-

sensorimotor intelligence Piaget's term for the intelligence of infants during the first (sensorimotor) period of cognitive development, when babies think by using the senses and motor skills.

ing, he said, begins at birth and accelerates rapidly in the early months of life. To Piaget, infants might lack words, concepts, and ideas, but they are nevertheless intelligent; and that intelligence functions exclusively through the senses and motor skills (Gratch & Schatz, 1987). Consequently, Piaget called the intelligence of infants **sensorimotor intelligence** and the first period of cognitive development the *sensorimotor period* (as we saw in Chapter 2).

What did Piaget mean by saying that infants think exclusively with their senses and motor skills? As Flavell (1985) expresses it, the infant "exhibits a wholly practical, perceiving-and-doing, action-bound kind of intellectual functioning: he does not exhibit the more contemplative, reflective, symbol-manipulating kind we usually think of in connection with cognition." Piaget was actually incorrect in his belief that infants do not develop concepts—as we have seen, infants have a fairly rich set of conceptual categories and assumptions—and some of his other proposals have also been revised by recent findings. Nonetheless, his portrayal of the "practical, perceiving-and-doing" side of early intelligence remains valid.

The Six Stages of Sensorimotor Intelligence

According to Piaget, sensorimotor intelligence develops through six successive stages, each characterized by a somewhat different way of understanding the world. Taken together, they provide a vivid description of the ways in which infants demonstrate their growing cognitive abilities. We shall follow the arrangement in Table 6.1 as we briefly examine these stages. We shall also be highlighting the progression of infants' cognitive growth—from reflexes to deliberate responses to the beginning of symbolic understanding.

table **6.1**	**The Six Stages of Sensorimotor Intelligence**
For an overview of the stages of sensorimotor thought, it helps to group the six stages into pairs.	
The first two stages involve the infant's responses to its own body (sometimes called *primary circular reactions*):	
Stage One (birth to 1 month)	*Reflexes*—sucking, grasping, staring, listening.
Stage Two (1–4 months)	*The first acquired adaptations*—assimilation and coordination of reflexes—sucking a pacifier differently from a nipple; grabbing a bottle to suck it.
The next two stages involve the infant's responses to objects and people (sometimes called *secondary circular reactions*):	
Stage Three (4–8 months)	*An awareness of things*—responding to people and objects.
Stage Four (8–12 months)	*New adaptation and anticipation*—becoming more deliberate and purposeful in responding to people and objects.
The last two stages are the most creative, first with action and then with ideas (sometimes called *tertiary circular reactions*):	
Stage Five (12–18 months)	*New means through active experimentation*—experimentation and creativity in the actions of the "little scientist."
Stage Six (18–24 months)	*New means through mental combinations*—considering before doing provides the child with new ways of achieving a goal without resorting to trial-and-error experiments.

Stages One and Two: Reflexes and First Adaptations

Sensorimotor intelligence begins with newborns' *reflexes,* such as sucking and grasping, and with sensory responses that are so automatic they seem like reflexes, such as looking and listening. Through the repeated exercise of these reflexes over the first month, newborns gain important information about the world—information that allows them to begin stage two, the *adaptation* of their reflexes to the specifics of the environment.

Adaptation occurs in two complimentary ways: by assimilation and by coordination (as you learned in Chapter 2). *Assimilation* means taking new information into the mind by incorporating it into previously developed mental categories, or action patterns, or, in Piaget's terminology, "schemas." *Accommodation* means taking new information into the mind in such a way that the person readjusts, refines, or expands previous schemas.

Adaptation of the Sucking Reflex.   Consider sucking, for example. Newborns suck anything that touches their lips—a reflex that shows assimilation. Then, at about the age of 1 month, according to Piaget, infants start to adapt their sucking to specific objects. Some items, such as the nipple of a bottle (for a breast-fed infant) require merely assimilation: suck it reflexively and get nourishment. Others require more accommodation: Pacifiers need to be sucked without the suction, tongue-pushing, and swallowing, since they do not provide food. By 3 months, infants have organized their world into objects to be sucked for nourishment (breasts or bottles), objects to be sucked for pleasure (fingers or pacifiers), and objects not to be sucked at all (fuzzy blankets and large balls). The particulars of the sucking reflex (intensity, suction, frequency, and such) have been accommodated to these various types of objects.

In addition, once infants learn that some objects satisfy hunger and others do not, they will suck contentedly on a pacifier when their stomachs are full but will usually spit one out when they are hungry, again adapting a reflex.

This rapid accommodation of the sucking reflex between the ages of 1 and 4 months, which involves adjustment to particular objects, contains a practical tip for parents of newborns. Many parents want their babies to be exclusively breast-fed—no bottles or pacifiers ever. (That is a fine decision, one many pediatricians would applaud.) But suppose that after 6 months the breast-feeding mother wants to go back to work full-time, and her employer refuses to let her bring her baby to the workplace; or suppose the baby begins thumb-sucking and both grandmothers say this is an unsanitary habit that will deform the teeth.

The logical solution is to switch to bottles and/or pacifiers. But many babies do not follow such logic and will not cooperate, because stage two has produced a powerful accommodation of the sucking reflex. The infant spits out the bottle or pacifier and cries pitifully, searching for the breast and the thumb. Only a particular kind of nipple (mother's own) will now satisfy his or her hunger, and only a particular thumb (usually the right, not the left) will soothe distress. If the parents had had the foresight to offer an occasional bottle earlier, the baby would have assimilated breast and rubber nipple; if they had given the pacifier much earlier (making sure it is of a type they will be able to replace immediately if it gets lost or damaged), the thumb would not have been needed. After 6 months, though, it is very hard to break a pattern of accommodation.

In other words, adaptation in the beginning weeks relied on assimilation—everything suckable was assimilated as a worthy object, unless other accommodation was required. After several months, however, patterns are set: Only familiar nourishment nipples will do, and all others are to be re-

Stage Two Sucking everything is a mere reflex in the first month of life, but by 3 months Katie has already learned that some objects afford better sucking than others. Many infants her age have learned not to suck on people's faces, but with this mother, that adaptation is not necessary.

jected. Similarly, most babies want something to suck for comfort; if a pacifier has not been offered, they begin sucking their thumbs, fingers, or knuckles (a choice that depends on the baby). Obviously, parents need to decide in the first—reflexes—stage whether they want to use a pacifier, and even which particular brand to use. By the age of 6 months, it is difficult to introduce a pacifier to a thumb-sucking baby, because babies of this age are already past the stage when they can "understand" it.

Another feature of early sensorimotor intelligence is that infants spend a good deal of time playing with their bodies, seemingly for the pleasure of doing so. They chew their fingers, kick their legs, wave their arms, and stare at their hands again and again. In the process, they gain valuable information. They learn, for instance, that those wiggly little things that regularly come into view and often wind up in their mouths are actually attached to them—and that those things, which they will later know as fingers and toes, are within their control. Information such as this is basic to developing an awareness of *body integrity*—that is, an awareness of one's body as a whole. The emergence of this awareness at stage two is one of the first steps in understanding the world of other people and objects.

Stage Three: An Awareness of Things

During stage three (age 4 to 8 months), babies interact diligently with people and objects to produce exciting experiences. Realizing that rattles make noise, for example, they shake their arms and laugh whenever someone puts a rattle in their hand. Even the sight of something that normally delights an infant—a favorite toy, a favorite food, a smiling parent—can trigger an active attempt at interaction.

Stage Three This 7½-month-old knows that a squeal of delight is one way to make the interesting experience of a tickle from Daddy last.

Vocalization of all sorts increases a great deal at this time, and not just in a chorus (as with younger infants—when one newborn in the nursery cries, they all tend to cry). Now that babies realize that other people can and will respond, they love to make a noise, listen for a response, and answer back. Interestingly, by the age of 3 or 4 months, babies are already unlikely to make sounds at the same moment that someone else is talking to them. They prefer to wait for silence, then vocalize, and then wait for a response. This behavior pattern becomes more pronounced as time goes on, continuing throughout stages four and five until it peaks at age 18 months, when—just as they are about to add many words to their vocabulary— babies listen most intently (Elias & Broerse, 1996).

Overall, in the third stage infants become more aware of objects and other people; they recognize some of the specific characteristics of the things in their environment, and they develop ways to interact in order to continue whatever sensations they seek. One way in which infants show this new awareness is by repeating a specific action that has just elicited a pleasing response from some person or thing. As you saw earlier, a baby might accidentally squeeze a rubber duck, hear a squeak, and squeeze the duck again. If the squeak is repeated, the infant will probably laugh and give another squeeze, delighted to be able to control the toy's actions.

Another example, already described, is kicking a leg tied to a ribbon to make a mobile move. That behavior not only reveals early memory but also exhibits stage-three cognition. (You might remember that the research showed that infants younger than 4 months deliberately kicked to make the mobile move, and you might note that stage three begins at 4 months. Don't worry about the seeming contradiction: Piaget's ages are approximate, and many current babies, encouraged by contemporary researchers, demonstrate competence slightly before Piaget's stages. Nonetheless, even when Piaget's ages are off, his sequence of stages is correct.)

Stage Four: New Adaptation and Anticipation

In stage four (age 8 to 12 months), babies adapt in new, more deliberate ways. They anticipate events that will fulfill their needs and wishes, and they try to make such events occur. A 10-month-old girl who enjoys playing in the tub might see a bar of soap, crawl over to her mother with it as a signal to start her bath, and then remove all her clothes to make her wishes crystal clear—finally squealing with delight when she hears the bath water being turned on. Similarly, if a 10-month-old boy sees his mother putting on her coat to go out without him, he might begin tugging at it to stop her or he might drag over his jacket to signal that he wants to come along.

goal-directed behavior   Purposeful action initiated by infants in anticipation of events that will fulfill their needs and wishes.

Both these examples reveal anticipation and, even more noteworthy, **goal-directed behavior**—that is, purposeful action. The baby's obvious goal-directedness at this age stems from the development of an enhanced awareness of cause and effect during this phase (as you already saw in the discussion of cognitive growth). And that cognitive awareness coincides with the emergence of the motor skills needed to achieve the infant's goals. Thus a stage-four baby might see something from across the room, be attracted to it, and crawl toward it, ignoring many interesting distractions along the way. Or he or she might grab a forbidden object—a box of matches, a thumbtack, a cigarette—and cry with rage when it is taken away, even after being offered a substitute that he or she normally finds fascinating.

As we noted earlier, Piaget thought that the concept of object permanence begins to emerge during stage four, because at this point—and usually not before—infants actively search for objects that are no longer in view. Researchers have since shown that the concept of object permanence actually begins to emerge much earlier. However, the *goal-directed* search for toys that have fallen from the baby's crib, rolled under a couch, or disappeared under a blanket does not begin to emerge until the age of about 8 months, just as Piaget indicated.

Intellectual Ability in Evidence   Brandon has a goal firmly in mind and is wielding the tools to attain it—an achievement beyond most younger babies. At age 12 months he is about to enter a more elaborate stage of goal-directedness, one in which he might deliberately drop a few peas on the floor, or smash a few noodles on his head, or turn his plate upside down—all as "experiments in order to see."

Stage Five: Experimentation

Stage five (12 to 18 months) builds directly on the accomplishments of stage four, as infants' goal-directed and purposeful activities become more expansive and creative after the first birthday. Toddlerhood is a time of active exploration and experimentation, a time when babies "get into everything," as though trying to discover all the possibilities their world has

little scientist Piaget's term for the stage-five toddler (age 12 to 18 months), who actively experiments to learn about the properties of objects.

mental combinations Sequences of actions developed intellectually, before they are actively performed. Mental combinations are a characteristic of the toddlers at Piaget's stage six of sensorimotor intelligence.

to offer. Because of the experimentation that characterizes this stage, Piaget referred to the stage-five toddler as the **little scientist** who "experiments in order to see." Having discovered some action or set of actions that is possible with a given object, stage-five infants seem to ask, "What else can I do with this? What happens if I take the nipple off the bottle, or turn over the trash basket, or pour water on the cat?" Their scientific method is one of trial and error, but their devotion to discovery sounds familiar to every adult researcher.

Stage Six: Mental Combinations

In the final stage of sensorimotor intelligence (18 to 24 months), toddlers begin to anticipate and solve simple problems by using **mental combinations.** That is, they try out various actions mentally, before actually performing them, to test what consequences the actions might bring. Thus stage-six children can invent new ways to achieve a goal without resorting to physical trial-and-error experiments. Consider how Piaget's daughter Jacqueline solved a problem she encountered at the age of 20 months:

> Jacqueline arrives at a closed door with a blade of grass in each hand. She stretches out her right hand toward the knob but sees that she cannot turn it without letting go of the grass. She puts the grass on the floor, opens the door, picks up the grass again and enters. But when she wants to leave the room, things become complicated. She puts the grass on the floor and grasps the doorknob. But then she perceives that in pulling the door toward her she will simultaneously chase away the grass which she placed between the door and the threshold. She therefore picks it up in order to put it outside the door's zone of movement. [Piaget, 1952]

The ability to construct mental combinations leads the toddler beyond better problem-solving skills. It enables the child to think more flexibly about past and future events and to anticipate what can occur in a particular situation. Some children will walk toward an alluring piece of bric-a-brac, say "no" to themselves, and then walk away without touching it, because they expect punishment if they follow their first impulse.

Being able to use mental combinations also makes it possible for the child to pretend. A toddler might lie down on the floor, pretend to go to sleep, and then jump up laughing. Or a child might sing to a doll before tucking it into bed. This is in marked contrast to the behavior of the younger infant, who might treat a doll like any other toy, throwing it, biting it, or banging it on the floor. Piaget believed that deferred imitation also begins at stage six, although (as you saw earlier) under proper conditions deferred imitation (and many other abilities indicating Piaget's stages of sensorimotor intelligence) can begin much earlier.

Nonetheless, Piaget was not completely wrong about deferred imitation or anything else. Deferred imitation comes to full flower at stage six, as children then act out entire sequences of actions that they have earlier observed. This is one of many reasons why everyone needs to mind their behavior when a toddler is present—lest embarrassing actions be revealed to other people a few days later.

Stage-six behaviors all share an important characteristic. They are a step beyond the simple motor responses of sensorimotor thought and a step closer to "the more contemplative, reflective, symbol-manipulating activity" that we usually associate with cognition (Flavell, 1985). As you will see in Chapter 9, the ability to devise mental combinations soon blossoms into the symbolic thought typical of the next period of cognitive development.

table **6.2**	The Development of Spoken Language: The First 2 Years

Age*	Means of Communication
Newborn	Reflexive communication—cries, movements, facial expressions.
2 months	A range of meaningful noises—cooing, fussing, crying, laughing.
3–6 months	New sounds, including squeals, growls, croons, trills, vowel sounds.
6–10 months	Babbling, including both consonant and vowel sounds repeated in syllables.
10–12 months	Comprehension of simple words; simple intonations; specific vocalizations that have meaning to those who know the infant well. Deaf babies express their first signs; hearing babies use specific gestures (e.g., pointing) to communicate.
13 months	First spoken words that are recognizably part of the native language.
13–18 months	Slow growth of vocabulary, up to about 50 words.
18 months	Vocabulary spurt—three or more words learned per day.
21 months	First two-word sentence.
24 months	Multiword sentences. Half the infant's utterances are two or more words long.

*The ages of accomplishment in this table reflect norms. Many healthy and intelligent children attain these steps in language development earlier or later than indicated here.
Sources: Bloom, 1993; Lenneberg, 1967.

LANGUAGE DEVELOPMENT

Mastering the sounds and meanings of one's first language is "doubtless the greatest intellectual feat any one of us is ever required to perform," according to one early developmental scholar (Bloomfield, 1933). Children the world over follow the same sequence of early language development, although the timing of their accomplishments may vary considerably (see Table 6.2). Indeed, about 10 percent of 24-month-olds have a vocabulary of over 550 words, but another 10 percent speak fewer than 100 words—more than a fivefold difference (Merriman, 1998). Long before using words, very young infants communicate their emotions, preferences, and ideas through cries, laughs, body movements, gestures, and facial expressions. These early communication skills serve the primary role of **language function:** to understand, and be understood by, others. Within the first 2 years of life, this rudimentary ability to communicate evolves into **language structure,** that is, the particular words and rules of the infant's native tongue. Now we will look at the sequence of language function and structure in detail, to better understand this "greatest intellectual feat" of humankind.

First Noises and Gestures

Infants are equipped to learn language from birth, partly due to brain readiness and partly due to their auditory experiences during the final prenatal months. Newborns prefer hearing speech over hearing other sounds, prefer

language function The primary purpose of language—communication, allowing people to understand, and be understood by, others.

language structure The body of sounds, words, and rules (including grammar, usage, inflection) of a particular language.

"baby talk" over normal speech, and, as you saw in Chapter 4, listen more readily to their mothers' voices than to voices of other adults (Fifer & Moon, 1995). Moreover, infants as young as 1 month can distinguish among many different speech sounds, including sounds that adults no longer can differentiate (Sansavini et al., 1997; Werker, 1989). To every young infant, the sound of human speech—whether it comes from Mommy or Daddy, another child, or a stranger speaking a language no one understands—evokes special interest and curiosity.

Very young babies do much more than listen. They are noisy creatures—crying, cooing, and making a variety of other sounds even in the first weeks of life. These noises gradually become more varied over the first months, and by the age of 4 months, most babies have verbal repertoires that include squeals, growls, gurgles, grunts, croons, and yells, as well as some speech-like sounds. The first sounds are actually reflexes, uttered whether or not someone is talking, but by 4 months they are more deliberate, uttered now as conversation. If caregivers have been attentive in the early weeks, a whimper now means "I'm awake and hungry," and the response "Oh, I'm coming" is usually sufficient to preclude escalation to a demanding cry (perhaps meaning "Get me food now!").

Babbling with Noises and Gestures

babbling The extended repetition of certain syllables, such as "ba, ba, ba," that begins at about 6 or 7 months of age.

By 6 or 7 months of age, babies begin to repeat certain syllables ("ma-ma-ma," "da-da-da," "ba-ba-ba"), a phenomenon referred to as **babbling** because of the way it sounds. In some respects, babbling is universal—all babies do it, and the sounds they make are similar no matter what language their parents speak. However, over the next few months, babbling begins to vary and to incorporate more and more sounds from the native language, perhaps as infants imitate the sounds they hear (Boysson-Bardies et al., 1989; Masataka, 1992). Many cultures assign important meanings to some of these sounds, with "ma-ma-ma," "da-da-da," and "pa-pa-pa" usually taken to apply to significant people in the infant's life (Bornstein, 1995). (See Table 6.3.)

table **6.3**	**First Sounds and First Words: Cross-Linguistic Similarities**	
	Baby's Word for:	
Language	Mother	Father
English	mama, mommy	dada, daddy
Spanish	mama	papa
French	maman, mama	papa
Italian	mamma	babbo, papa
Latvian	mama	tēte
Syrian Arabic	mama	baba
Bantu	ba-mama	taata
Swahili	mama	baba
Sanskrit	nana	tata
Hebrew	ema	abba
Korean	oma	apa

Too Young for Language? No. The early stages of language are communication through noise, gestures, and facial expressions, very evident here between this Kung grandmother and granddaughter.

Deaf babies begin to make babbling sounds several months later than hearing infants, and they make the sounds less frequently (Oller & Eilers, 1988). However, recent research suggests that deaf infants may actually begin a type of babbling—manually—at about the same time hearing infants begin babbling orally (Petitto & Marentette, 1991). Analysis of videotapes of deaf children whose parents communicate via sign language reveals that before their tenth month, these infants use about a dozen distinct hand gestures—most of which resemble basic elements of the American Sign Language used by their parents—in a rhythmic, repetitive manner analogous to oral babbling.

Actually, both hearing and deaf babies communicate with gestures, such as lifting their hands to be picked up, at about 10 months of age. And both hearing and deaf babies do some spontaneous manual babbling as well as oral babbling. For obvious reasons, however, deaf infants reduce their oral babbling and increase their gesturing just when hearing babies do the opposite (Petitto & Marentette, 1991).

The similar timing, but different manifestation, of babbling among hearing babies who will speak and deaf babies who will sign suggests that brain maturation, more than maturation of the vocal apparatus, underlies the human ability to develop language. Further evidence that language is innate to the human brain comes from studies of brain damage in adulthood. The motor skills underlying hand gestures are controlled in one part of the brain, and those underlying speech in another part. Brain injury to one or the other of those areas, as we would expect, makes a person incapable of the movements needed for gestures or for vocalization. However, if brain damage occurs not in those motor areas but in the *language* area of the brain, a hearing person will lose facility in talking and a deaf person will lose facility in signing (Hickok et al., 1996). They will usually retain the ability to make gestures that are not linguistic, such as pointing to an object, or sounds that are not language, such as a cry.

Comprehension

At every point of language development, including the preverbal stage, all humans understand more than they express. In fact, according to reports from parents, most children understand more than 25 words by the age of 10 months, among them "mommy," "daddy," "no," "hi," "bye," "bath," "book," "car," "kitty," "kiss," and "uh-oh" (Fenson et al., 1994). When asked "Where's Mommy?" for instance, many 10-month-olds will look in her direction, and many will reach out their arms when asked "Do you want Daddy to pick you up?"

Motherese Infants' verbal understanding advances well ahead of their abilities at verbal production. "Fishee" is probably one of dozens of words that this child readily recognizes even though he has yet to say them himself.

Context and tone help supply meaning to these first understood words (Fernald, 1993). For example, when parents see their crawling infant about to touch an electric outlet, they will likely shout "No!" sharply, to startle and halt the explorer. Typically, they will then move the child away, pointing to the danger and repeating "No, no." Given the frequency with which the mobile infant's behavior produces this response, and the tone in which it is rendered, there is little wonder that many infants understand "no" months before they can talk.

In addition, infants as young as 8 months listen attentively to all language and start to sort out the words. This was shown in an experiment in

Cultural Values If his infancy is like that of most babies raised in the relatively taciturn Ottavado culture of Ecuador, this 2-month-old will hear significantly less conversation than infants from most other regions of the world. Is that child neglect? According to many learning theorists, a lack of reinforcement will result in a child who is much less verbal, and in most Western cultures that might be called educational neglect. However, each culture tends to encourage the qualities it most needs and values, and verbal fluency is not a priority in this community. In fact, people who talk too much are ostracized, and those who keep secrets are valued, so encouragement of language may itself be maltreatment.

underextension The use of a word to refer only to certain things, even though the word generally means much more to most people.

overextension The application of a newly learned word to a variety of objects that may share a particular characteristic but are not in the general category described by that word.

which 8-month-olds listened to a recording of children's stories for 10 days over a 2-week period. Then, after a 2-week rest period, they listened to a taped list of words—both words that had been in the stories and words that were similar in linguistic complexity but that the infants had probably not heard repeatedly. The infants listened significantly longer to the words they had heard, indicating "that 8- to 9-month-olds engage in long-term encoding and retention of information about the sound patterns of words" (Jusczyk & Hohue, 1997). This is months before infants are speaking themselves.

First Spoken Words

Finally, at about 1 year of age, the average baby speaks a few words, not pronounced clearly or used precisely. Usually, caregivers hear and understand the first word before strangers do, which makes it hard for researchers to pinpoint exactly what a 12-month-old can say (Bloom, 1993). For example, at 13 months, Kyle knew "da," "ba," "tam," "opma," and "daes," which his parents knew to be "downstairs," "bottle," "tummy," "oatmeal," and "starfish" (yes, that's what "daes" meant) (Lewis et al., 1999).

No matter who measures it, all agree that vocabulary increases gradually at first, perhaps by 10 words per month. By 16 months of age, the average baby speaks about 40 words and comprehends many more (Fensen et al., 1994). For English-speaking babies, most of these early words are names of people and objects in the child's daily world, although some "action" words are included as well (Barrett, 1986; Kuczaj, 1986). By contrast, Mandarin-speaking infants express more verbs than nouns, an indication that culture and experience shape the universal urge to speak (Tardif, 1996).

The Vocabulary Spurt

Once the vocabulary reaches about 50 words, it begins to build more rapidly—in some children by 100 or more words per month (Fensen et al., 1994). Toddlers differ in how their vocabularies grow: some children (called *referential*) primarily learn naming words (such as "dog," "cup," and "ball"), whereas others (called *expressive*) acquire mainly words that can be used in social interaction (such as "please," "want," and "stop") (Nelson, 1981). Such differences no doubt reflect individual personality and family emphases (Dixon & Shore, 1997). Culture also shapes early language acquisition. North American infants, for example, tend to be more referential than Japanese infants, partly because playing with toys and labeling objects are more central in North American families (Fernald & Morikawa, 1993).

At first, toddlers are quite imprecise in the way they connect the words they know to the people, objects, and events around them. One common inaccuracy is **underextension,** applying a word more narrowly than it usually is applied. The word "cat" may be used to name only the family cat, for example, and no other feline. Another inaccuracy is that a toddler might learn one name for something and then resist alternative names—insisting, for example, that the little fuzzy, yellow, winged thing the toddler calls a "bird" is not a "chick," as Grandpa keeps calling it (Shatz, 1994). This is called the *mutual exclusivity bias* (Merriman, 1998).

A bit later the opposite tendency appears, with words being applied beyond their meaning. This characteristic, known as **overextension,** or *over-*

generalization, might lead one child to call anything round "ball" and another to call every four-legged creature "doggie."

As their vocabularies expand, toddlers seem to "experiment in order to see" with words just as they do with objects. Little scientists become "little linguists." It is not unusual for 18-month-olds to walk down the street pointing to every animal, asking "Doggie?" or "Horsie?" or "Kitty?"—perhaps to confirm their hypotheses about which words go with which animals.

One-Word Sentences

holophrase   A single word that expresses a complete thought.

As children learn their first words, they become adept at expressing intention, using intonation and gestures and a single word that expresses a complete thought; such a word is called a **holophrase.** When a toddler pushes at a closed door and says "bye-bye!" in a demanding tone, it is clear that the child wishes to go out. When a toddler, upon the arrival of the baby-sitter, holds on to Mommy's legs and plaintively says "bye-bye," it is equally clear that the child is pleading with Mommy not to leave. In the early stages of language development, almost every single-word utterance is a holophrase; that makes toddlers much more proficient linguists than their limited vocabulary would suggest.

Indeed, it is important to note that vocabulary size is not the only—or the best—measure of early language learning. The goal of early language is *communication,* not vocabulary. If parents are concerned because, say, their 1-year-old son has not yet said even a few words, they should look at his ability and willingness to understand what others say and to make his needs known in other ways, perhaps with gestures and facial expressions. If those skills seem to be normal, if the child has no history of repeated ear infections, and if the child hears enough simple language addressed to him every day (through someone's reading to him, singing to him, or talking to him about the sights he sees), he will probably be speaking in sentences before age 2.

In fact, an in-depth study of infant language development found that the infants who were most adept at expressing their emotions nonverbally (through frowns, smiles, cries, and laughter, for example) were generally slower to talk. However, once those infants began to talk, they progressed to multiword sentences just as rapidly as early talkers did (Bloom, 1993). On the other hand, infants who show signs of early language delay (for example, not babbling back when parents babble to them, or not responding to any specific words by the age of 10 months) should have their hearing examined as soon as possible. Even a moderate early hearing loss can delay speech acquisition or, as you saw in Chapter 5, can slow socialization.

Combining Words

Within about 6 months of speaking their first words, children begin to learn new words more rapidly. Soon after that spurt, they start to put words together. As a general rule, the first two-word sentence occurs at about 21 months of age, with some normal infants achieving this milestone at 15 months and others not reaching it until 24 months.

Combining words demands considerable linguistic understanding because, in every language, word order affects the meaning of a sentence. However, even in their first sentences, toddlers demonstrate that they have figured out the basics of subject-predicate order. They declare "Baby cry" or ask "More juice" rather than the reverse. And, by the time they get to three-word sentences at age 2, they will say, properly, "Kitty jumping down," as Sarah does in Children Up Close (see page 199).

LISTEN TO YOUR OWN

It is easy to undervalue children's language learning, since it seems to occur quite effortlessly. But, as with sunrise and sunset, just because it happens often, we should not take it for granted. Imagine yourself as a tourist in a foreign land, surrounded by natives chattering rapidly in a language quite different from your own. Without extensive experience in that language, you could not even tell where one word stops and another begins; or which nuances of tone and pronunciation are significant and which are merely variations in individual speech; or how the string of sounds works together to make statements or questions; or, most important, whether the content of the conversation should make you embarrassed, frightened, or delighted. And yet, lost as you might be, at least you would know that spoken sounds have specific meanings and that you are capable of learning those meanings. The newborn, of course, does not know even this, yet typically by age 2 "children, bright and dull, pampered or neglected, exposed to Tlingit or to English" all learn language (Wanner & Gleitman, 1982).

Consider, for example, the words, grammar, and conversational skill of one 24-month-old named Sarah who was determined to distract her silent mother from intently revising an earlier edition of this textbook:

"Uh, oh. Kitty jumping down."

"What drawing? Numbers?" [said as her words were being transcribed]

"Want it, paper."

"Wipe it, pencil."

"What time it is?" [said about her mother's watch]

These sentences show that Sarah had a varied vocabulary and a basic understanding of word order. For example, Sarah said "Kitty jumping down" (noun, verb, adverb) rather than "Down jumping kitty" or any of the four other, less conventional combinations of these three words. Sarah's speech also shows that she had much to learn, for she incorrectly used the pronoun "it" and its referent together ("it, paper," "it, pencil"), omitted personal pronouns, and used declarative rather than inquisitive word order in asking a question ("What time it is?").

But beyond demonstrating specifics of English vocabulary and grammar, Sarah's words show something even more critical. By the time she reached age 2, Sarah had learned the universal function of language—to express one's thoughts and wishes to another using accepted signals, codes, and cues. Despite my preoccupation and nonresponsiveness, Sarah produced seven successive sentences crafted to entice me into a dialogue. The final question—"What time it is?"—reveals considerable sophistication about the rules of polite conversation: Sarah must have noticed that almost any adult, even a stranger on the street, usually answers that particular question.

Sarah's impressive but imperfect language is quite similar to that of 2-year-olds in many families and cultures. Much of the research on early language over the past 30 years began with a researcher writing down the words of his or her own child and then testing various hypotheses by studying many other children. You can do the same with your own children, your relatives, or even strangers at the supermarket. Writing down exactly what a 24-month-old says and then noting the communication skill embedded in the simple words may astonish you—just as a sunrise might.

❷ Especially for Educators: How would you instruct caregivers to interact with infants to help language development proceed as well as possible?

Adults and Babies Teach Each Other to Talk

How do babies learn to talk? Early researchers on language development tended to choose one of two positions. They focused either on the ways parents teach language to their infants or on the emergence of the infant's innate language abilities.

Two Theories: Learned Versus Innate

The focus on parents' teaching arose from B. F. Skinner's learning theory, which held that conditioning (learning) could explain verbal behavior just as well as it could explain other types of behavior (Skinner, 1957). According to this theory, for example, if a baby's babbling is reinforced with food and attention from the very first time it occurs, the baby will soon be calling "mama," "dada," or "baba" whenever the baby wants his or her mother, father, or bottle. Similarly, many learning theorists believe that the quantity and quality of parents' talking to their child affect the child's rate of language development, from the early words through complex sentences.

The opposite focus, on innate language ability, came from the theories of Noam Chomsky (1968, 1980) and his followers, who believe that language is too complex to be mastered so early and so easily through conditioning. Chomsky noted that all young children worldwide master the rudiments of grammar and that all do so at approximately the same age. This, he said, implies that the human brain is uniquely equipped with some sort of structure or organization that facilitates language development. Somewhat boldly, Chomsky labeled this theoretical facilitator the **language acquisition device,** abbreviated **LAD.** The LAD enables children to quickly and efficiently derive rules of grammar from the speech they hear every day, regardless of whether their native language is English, Chinese, or Urdu. Other theorists have proposed other innate structures to facilitate other features of language learning

Research in recent years has suggested that both Skinner's and Chomsky's theories have some validity but that both miss the mark (Bates & Carnevale, 1994; Bloom, 1991; Golinkoff & Hirsh-Pasek, 1990; Jusczyk, 1997).

One reason is that both theories overlook the social context in which the actual language-learning process occurs, a social context framed by the adult's teaching sensitivity as well as the child's learning ability. Every infant makes expressive noises, but if caregivers are too intrusive (interrupting with a lesson, demanding responses) or too negligent (ignoring various preverbal noises), the infant will learn more slowly (Baumwell et al., 1997). The crucial factor seems to be catching the infant's mood and attention and responding with simple language as if the exchange were a conversation (Tomasello, 1996). Infants are genetically primed to pick up language (Chomsky was right), and, on the whole, caregivers are surprisingly skilled at facilitating infants' language learning (Skinner was right). However, it is this *combination* of learner and teacher and context that achieves the language explosion we see in children (Messer, 1994; Moerk, 1996).

Evidence for the interactive nature of early language is apparent to anyone who observes babies. Infants have a "deep biological need to interact emotionally with the people that love and care for them," and this pushes them to talk (Locke, 1993). The need of adults to communicate with infants is no less strong. Even strangers on the street feel compelled to smile and talk to a baby, as they never would to an unfamiliar adult.

language acquisition device (LAD)
Chomsky's term to denote the innate ability to acquire language, including the basic aspects of grammar.

Lots of Communication Mother-toddler conversations that are rich with facial expressions, gestures, and the dramatic intonation of an occasional word are universal, as is illustrated by this winning pair in a Mexican market.

Baby Talk

Typically, the type of speech adults use to talk with babies is a special form of language that developmentalists call **baby talk** or, sometimes, *motherese.* Baby talk differs from normal speech in a number of features that are consistent throughout all language communities (Ferguson, 1977). It is distinct in its pitch (higher than normal language), its intonation (more low-to-high fluctuations), its vocabulary (simpler and more concrete), and its sentence length (shorter). It also employs more questions, commands, and repetitions and fewer past tenses, pronouns, and complex sentences than adult talk does.

baby talk The special form of language that adults use when they talk to babies, with shorter, more emphatic sentences and higher, more melodious pitch.

❶ Response for Educators (from page 199):
Encourage communication of all sorts—with facial expressions, gestures, and words. Talk should be responsive, simple, and repetitious. "Baby talk" is fine, as long as infants also hear some talk at a level slightly above their expressed ability.

People of all ages, from preschoolers to elders, speak baby talk with infants, and almost everyone is fluent without ever having to be taught. Preverbal infants prefer listening to motherese over normal speech (Cooper, 1993; Fernald, 1985), even if the motherese is in a language the infants have never heard (Fernald, 1993). Indeed, 5-month-old deaf infants prefer to look at a film of an unfamiliar deaf mother signing to her baby (only the mother can be seen in the movie) than a film of the same mother signing the identical message to her adult friend (Masataka, 1996).

Part of the appeal, and the impact, of baby talk is thought to arise from its energy and exaggerated expressiveness. This idea is supported by research showing that the baby talk of *depressed* mothers is too flat in intonation and too slow in its conversational responses to hold babies' interest (Bettes, 1988).

Many parents have learned that singing captures their babies' attention; the melody, repetition, and rhythm all facilitate learning, just as baby talk does, and for the same reasons—because babies enjoy learning language and will take every opportunity to do so. No wonder mothers and fathers, even those with far-from-perfect singing voices, croon to their infants—usually more slowly and emotionally than they do when singing the same song in their infants' absence. They also sing more imaginatively, as is exemplified by one father's favorite song for his baby, "It's bath time in Canada" (Trehub et al., 1997).

The function of baby talk is clearly to facilitate language learning, for the sounds and words are those that infants attend to, and speak, most readily. Difficult sounds are avoided: consonants like "l" and "r" are regularly omitted, and hard-to-say words are given simple forms, often with a "-y" ending. Thus, "father" becomes "daddy," "stomach" becomes "tummy," and "rabbit" becomes "bunny," because if they didn't, infants and parents would have difficulty talking about them. Moreover, the intonations and special emphases of baby talk help infants make connections between specific words and the objects or events to which they refer (Fernald & Mazzie, 1991). Imagine a man telling a baby girl, in a higher-than-normal voice, "Daddy's going to kiss your tum-tum-tummy," and then doing so with a loud, wet smooch. Wouldn't the baby remember who Daddy is, and where the tummy is, better than she would if the man said "Your father will now kiss your stomach"—especially if he said it in a low-voiced monotone?

The One-Sided Conversation

In the earliest stages of baby talk, the conversation is, of course, rather one-sided: adults speak and babies listen. Nevertheless, this provides a foundation for the infants' language learning. Babies who are spoken to, sung to, and even read to months before they themselves begin to talk learn language sooner and faster, with a more extensive and elaborate vocabulary, than babies whose caregivers are taciturn or inattentive. Most caregivers also emphasize the word they are trying to teach—by making it louder and higher-pitched, repeating it, and placing it at the beginning or end of the sentence (Messer, 1994).

Caregivers promote early language learning by acting as if the child is communicating, and then responding accordingly. That is, they adopt the child's focus of attention and speak the proper words for that focus. If a child is looking at his or her hands, the speaker will make a comment using the word "hand"; if the child's focus shifts suddenly to a nearby toy, the speaker is likely to comment on the toy. Talking to a child about whatever the child is looking at, listening to, or touching at a given moment contributes to vocabulary growth (Akhtar et al., 1991; Bloom, 1993; Tomasello, 1995).

It is also useful to pause, as if the baby were part of the conversation. For example, instead of simply dressing a child quietly, a mother might develop this "dialogue":

Mother: Where is your *foot?*
(Pause, just long enough for the baby to have said, "Here is my foot.")
Mother: Yes, there's your foot *(gently squeezing the foot).* Now, where is your *sock?"*
(Another pause; then the mother waves the sock in the air.)
Mother: OK. Now *sock* on the *foot.*
(Another squeeze, on the stockinged foot.)
(Baby smiles.)
Mother: Where is your other *foot?*
(Baby offers the other foot, for squeezing.)

Tactile stimulation, as in this example, is another way for caregivers to promote early language, which is why "This little piggie went to market" and many other equally ridiculous rhymes persist across the generations.

The Two-Sided Conversation

Once the child begins to talk, observations of exchanges between parent and child show the adult interpreting the child's imperfect speech and then responding by using short, repeated, clear sentences the child can understand and by placing special emphasis on important words. Naturalistic observation is the best way to study such interactions, for facial expression and intonation are as much a part of baby talk as the words that are spoken. However, recorded dialogues like the following one between a mother and her toddler son at bedtime do convey the flavor of these exchanges, showing how attentive a good caregiver can be (Halliday, 1979):

Mother: And when you get up in the morning, you'll go for a walk.
Nigel: Tik.
Mother: And you'll see some sticks, yes.
Nigel: Hoo.
Mother: And some holes, yes.
Nigel: Da.
Mother: Yes, now it's getting dark.
Nigel: I wa. *(Repeats this 12 times.)*
Mother: What?
Nigel: I wa. *(Repeats this 6 times.)* Peaz.
Mother: What do you want in bed? Jamie? *(his doll)*
Nigel: No!
Mother: You want your eiderdown? *(his quilt)*
Nigel: (Grins.) Yeah!
Mother: Why didn't you say so? Your eiderdown.
Nigel: Ella. *(Repeats 2 times.)*

In most episodes of two-way baby talk, the toddler is an active participant, responding to the speaker and making his or her needs known. In this one, Nigel asked for his quilt a total of 18 times, persisting until his mother got the point. An analysis of toddlers' speech shows that, especially after the vocabulary spurt begins, early speech is almost never idle conversation. Babies seem intent on communicating their needs and desires, as well as commenting on their own actions.

Language Acquisition as Guided Participation

Adults have many ways to support infants in their acquisition of language. We have discussed four:

- Holding prelinguistic "conversations" with the infant
- Engaging in baby talk
- Persistently naming objects and events that capture the child's attention
- Expanding the child's sounds and words into meaningful communications

A Family in Nairobi This baby's intellectual development is well nourished.

❓ *Observational Quiz (see answer page 204): Can you spot four signs of this?*

As you should recall from Chapter 2, Lev Vygotsky and his followers maintained that a child's intellectual competencies emerge through an "apprenticeship in thinking," in which skilled mentors instruct and guide the learner through shared activities that facilitate the development of skills. The four activities listed above are very much in keeping with this theory. In fact, in many ways, early language development provides an almost perfect example of how an important feature of intellectual growth—mastery of a child's native tongue—is structured, guided, and nurtured under the sensitive tutelage of the adults in the child's world.

Of course, this does not mean that adults should "talk down" to children, using baby talk when children are capable of understanding more advanced language. Remember that Vygotsky emphasized teaching to the *potential* of the child. The 1-year-old needs "tummy," "kitty," and "bunny;" the 3-year-old can already understand "stomach," "cat," and "rabbit."

A Social Interaction

As you have seen repeatedly in this chapter on early cognition, infants are motivated to understand the world. Very young babies look, listen, and grab whatever they can, developing a knowledge of affordances and concepts as they do so. And the same motivation that makes toddlers resemble little scientists makes infants seek to understand the noises, gestures, words, and grammatical systems that describe the world in which they live, as well as to use words to engage in social relationships. One researcher writes:

> Language . . . could not emerge in any species, and would not develop in any individual, without a special kind of fit between adult behavior and infant behavior. That fit is pre-adapted: It comes to each child as a birthright, both as a result of biological propensities and as a result of social processes learned and transmitted by each new generation. [Kaye, 1982]

The idea that language develops as the outcome of "biological propensities" and "a special kind of fit" highlights the fact that both innate processes and the social context are prerequisites. Humans are biologically destined to communicate, and their brains are primed to develop language. At the same time, verbal interaction between adult and infant is essential, for unless a child has a sensitive and responsive conversational partner, his or her language learning will not flourish. Thus, parent and baby together accomplish what neither could do alone: they teach a person to talk.

❶ *Answer to Observational Quiz (from page 203):* *The delight on both parents' faces, the "breast is best" shirt, the variety of surrounding objects that stimulate exploration and conceptualization, and the language of gesture that obviously communicates to all three.*

This mutuality is equally true of all the cognitive accomplishments discussed in this chapter. Affordances are tied to experience and motivation, concepts and categories rely on expectancies, cognitive growth of every kind is based on sensorimotor stimuli—all provided by the people and events of each infant's social setting. And as you will see in the next chapter, the underlying caregiver-child interaction, within a cultural context that guides and supports their relationship, is at the core of the infant's psychosocial development as well.

SUMMARY

PERCEPTION AND COGNITION

1. Infants quickly begin to grasp the affordances of things, that is, the opportunities that objects, people, and circumstances allow for interaction. New affordances are discovered and old ones are expanded as an infant's experience and repertoire of skills and abilities increase.

2. Infants' perceptual skills contribute to such early cognitive understanding as their grasp of the boundaries of objects and of perceptual constancy—that boundaries and objects do not change when things move or are out of sight.

3. Both intermodal perception (such as associating the look of an object with its feel) and cross-modal perception (such as touching an object and imagining how it might look) are evident in the first months of life.

KEY ELEMENTS OF COGNITIVE GROWTH

4. Habituation research has provided important insights into infants' early skill at categorization—the ability to mentally sort objects by their properties. With increasing experience, both the categories and the properties used for categorizing grow in complexity.

5. Young infants have a basic appreciation for the permanence of objects at the age of 5 months, even though they will not search for a hidden object until later in their first year, at about 8 or 9 months.

6. Early memory is fragile yet surprisingly capable. Infants easily forget, but their memory can also be reactivated, with reminder sessions, to help them remember past events. There is also intriguing evidence for long-term-memory capacity in infancy, especially when implicit, not explicit, memory is involved.

7. The ability to understand cause-and-effect relationships develops slowly in the first few months of life. Toward the end of the first year, this understanding leads to early problem-solving abilities.

ACTIVE INTELLIGENCE: PIAGET'S THEORY

8. From birth to age 2, during what Piaget called the sensorimotor stage, infants use their senses and motor skills to understand their environment. They begin by using and then adapting their reflexes; soon they become aware of their own and others' actions and reactions, and this awareness guides their cognition. By the end of the first year, they can, and do, set simple goals and have the knowledge and ability to achieve those goals.

9. In the second year, toddlers find new ways to achieve their goals, first by actively experimenting with objects and actions and then, toward the end of the second year, by manipulating mental images of objects and behaviors. They can pretend; they can play; they can remember what they saw days before and then repeat it.

LANGUAGE DEVELOPMENT

10. Language skills begin to develop as babies communicate through noises and gestures and then practice babbling. Infants typically say a few words at the end of the first year and, thereafter, gradually add a few words to their vocabulary each month. At about 18 months, rapid vocabulary acquisition begins.

11. At every age, children understand more words and phrases than they use. Even those who verbalize relatively little communicate in other ways. By age 2, if not earlier, most toddlers can combine two or three words to make sentences.

12. Children vary in how rapidly they learn vocabulary, as well as in the ways they use words. In the first two years, a child's comprehension of simple words and gestures and his or her willingness and ability to communicate are more significant than the size of the child's vocabulary.

13. Language learning occurs so rapidly in part because infants are primed to listen to speech sounds (or, for deaf babies, to see linguistic gestures) and to try to repeat them. On their part, most caregivers are amazingly attuned to early language teaching.

14. The obvious example of infant-adult language interaction is baby talk, a simplified and melodious form of language that caregivers speak in response to infant actions. The specifics of infant language learning depend on infant temperament, caregiver sensitivity, and cultural guidelines, but universally human babies are predisposed to learn, and caregivers to teach, linguistic skills.

KEY TERMS

affordance (174)
graspability (174)
visual cliff (175)
object constancy (177)
perceptual constancy (177)
dynamic perception (178)
intermodal perception (178)
cross-modal perception (179)
object permanence (181)
reminder session (184)
deferred imitation (185)
implicit memory (186)
explicit memory (186)
launching event (187)

sensorimotor intelligence (189)
goal-directed behavior (192)
little scientist (193)
mental combinations (193)
language function (194)
language structure (194)
babbling (195)
underextension (197)
overextension (197)
holophrase (198)
language acquisition device (LAD) (200)
baby talk (200)

KEY QUESTIONS

1. What is an affordance, and how does an affordance depend on the individual and on the individual's environment?

2. Distinguish between perceptual constancy and object permanence.

3. In what ways can infants coordinate their perceptions of the same object through different senses?

4. Give an example of the early growth of categorization skills.

5. How can a scientist show that infants have object permanence even before they are capable of searching for a hidden object?

6. How good is the long-term memory of young infants, and what specifics strengthen their memory?

7. Explain the link between an understanding of cause-and-effect relations and the beginning of problem-solving ability.

8. What emphasis did Piaget bring to the study of cognitive development in infancy?

9. Describe how changes in a baby's actions and behaviors over the first 2 years of life reveal the growth of sensorimotor intelligence.

10. What are the major milestones in the growth of language ability in infancy, and when, typically, are these milestones reached?

11. What are the major factors that promote language acquisition?

12. How does baby talk differ from adult speech, and why do the differences exist?

13. *In Your Experience* What is the most surprising cognitive ability that a toddler (one you know or know of) has exhibited, and, from what you know of the context, how was that ability acquired?

CRITICAL THINKING EXERCISE

by Richard O. Straub

Take your study of Chapter 6 a step further by working this perspective-taking exercise.

As you saw in this chapter, behaviorist B. F. Skinner believed that language development could be explained by the principles of *learning,* particularly how parents teach language to their children. Linguist Noam Chomsky maintained, however, that language is far too complex to be mastered so early and so easily through learning alone and thus that our language capacity must be inborn—that is, biological. More recently, developmentalists have come to the view that both Skinner and Chomsky have some validity: it is the *interaction* of biology and learning, within the child's social context, that accounts for the ease with which children acquire language.

Below are four examples of language use by infants. For each, first decide whether it provides evidence for biology or learning or their interaction in language development; then explain your reasoning.

1. Whenever 8-month-old Juwan calls out "ma-ma-ma," his mother comes to him. Consequently, Juwan utters those syllables much more frequently and clearly now than he did a month ago.

2. Even in her very first sentences, it is obvious that 21-month-old Melissa has figured out the basics of subject-predicate word order. Seeing her mother returning from work, for example, she says "Mommy home" rather than "home Mommy."

3. Seven-month-old Tara, who is deaf, has begun to babble manually but still coos verbally.

4. Michelle was born and grew up in Ottawa, Canada; as a child, she was exposed to the French language in her home, English in school, and both languages among her peers. Now a teenager, Michelle speaks English and French fluently, but she is having trouble with pronunciation in her high-school Chinese class.

Check your answers by comparing them to the sample answers in Appendix B.

The First 2 Years:
Psychosocial Development

CHAPTER 7

Psychosocial development, by definition, involves interaction between the *psyche* (from the Greek word meaning "soul," "spirit," "feelings") and the *social context* (family, community, culture). Every infant obviously gets a great deal of social attention, as people tend to the young person day and night. As a result, the infant's social context can easily be observed, and it has been examined and debated extensively over the years. But it has not been obvious whether, or how, the baby's (internal) psyche should be studied. Consequently, scientists examining infant psychosocial development first studied social events—and mainly the actions of the mother. They believed that babies themselves brought little to the interaction, other than a need for food and physical protection, and that the mother was the crucial parent.

As you will learn, however, developmentalists now realize that even newborns are innately predisposed to sociability—capable, in the very first month of life, of expressing their own spirited emotions and of responding to the moods, feelings, and actions of others. And mothers are just one part of the social context; they are joined by fathers, other children, and even the entire community, all of whom affect each infant. Thus, we begin this chapter with the infant's own contribution to psychosocial growth, and we end it with the widening circles of social influence.

EARLY EMOTIONS

Examining infant emotional development reveals how young infants begin to perceive, understand, and respond to their surroundings. It also shows that infant emotions contribute to social interactions: a baby's cry, frown, grimace, and smile are significant signals. And, as you learned in Chapter 2, caregivers react to such social signs with precisely the responses necessary to protect and nurture the youngest members of the human family.

The First Half Year

The first emotion we can discern in newborns is *distress,* most obviously signaled by cries of hunger or pain. In addition to such physical discomfort, a loud noise, a sudden loss of support, or an object looming toward them can distress very young infants—and once again their cries are a call for help, alerting caregivers that protection, or at least reassurance, is needed.

Sadness, or at least a sensitivity to it, is also apparent early in infancy. In one experiment, mothers of infants between 1 and 3 months old were asked to look sad and appear downcast; their infants responded by looking away and fussing (Cohn & Tronick, 1983; Tronick et al., 1986). Moreover, expressions of sadness are prominent and significant in the infants of chronically depressed mothers, even by age 1 to 3 months. This continues throughout infancy (Field, 1995; Jones et al., 1997).

On the positive side, newborns show wide-eyed looks of *interest* when something catches their attention. *Pleasure* also begins early. A fleeting smile in response to a soothing noise or a full stomach appears in the first days of life. The **social smile**—a smile in response to a face or voice—appears at about the age of 6 weeks. At first the social smile is a hesitant half-smile, exhibited when a moving, smiling, talking object, directly in front of the infant, is perceived as a human face. The social smile then becomes a more reliable grin of recognition, with the quickest and broadest smiles evoked by the most familiar, most playful people. By 3 or 4 months babies begin to laugh rather than grin if something is particularly pleasing, especially during play with a caregiver (Malatesta et al., 1989). These smile patterns are universal; they are as evident among, say, the hunter-gatherers of the Kalahari as among the upper class of Boston or Paris, as evident among Canadians as among Chinese (Bakeman et al., 1990; Kisilevsky et al., 1998). Interestingly, the social smile is far from the only early sign of happiness. Some of the most potent smiles and laughs erupt when young infants can control events (such as shaking a rattle to make a noise) (Ellsworth et al., 1993; Lewis et al., 1990).

Conversely, loss of control is frustrating. By age 4 to 7 months, infants express *anger* when circumstances end their ability to make things happen (such as when big brother takes a rattle away) or when they are prevented from moving (Stenberg & Campos, 1983). The joy of active mastery of one's life, and the frustration when that mastery is abruptly interrupted, are among the earliest and most universal of human feelings.

social smile An infant's smile of pleasure in response to a human face or voice.

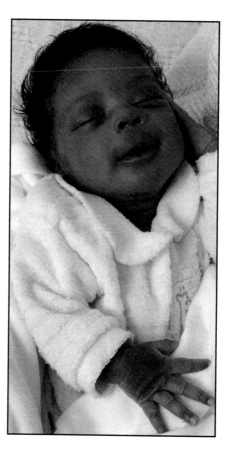

Weeks Before the Social Smile At 1 month of age, Toni smiles in her sleep, as many very young babies do, in response to the inner satisfaction of a full belly and a comfortable bed. However, not until about 6 weeks of age do babies smile in response to outside stimuli, such as a caregiver's face. Since Toni was born a month preterm, her first social smile is likely to occur at 10 weeks of age, since neurological maturation rather than experience outside the womb seems to be the main prerequisite for the appearance of the social smile.

The Older Infant

Infant emotions become more differentiated and distinct sometime between the ages of 6 and 9 months. For example, the baby begins to direct anger at particular people, and his or her expressions of anger reveal variations from mere annoyance to red-hot fury. Thus the 7-month-old's anger when a father moves his magazine out of reach is not as loudly expressed as when big sister takes the baby's own Raggedy Ann and dangles it an arm's length away. Marked differences among individual infants also become apparent in the intensity of emotions and in how quickly they appear (Kochanska et al., 1998). Physical maturation, growing cognitive skills, and more varied experiences make the emotions of the older baby more selective and diverse, and this differentiation of emotions continues into the second year.

Fear

The developmental change in emotions is evident with *fear* and anxiety. Most infants become much more fearful as they mature, with a peak between 9 and 15 months. For example, **stranger wariness,** or fear of strangers, is first noticeable at about 6 months of age and is full-blown by 10 to 14 months. You may have observed this fear yourself if you offered a 1-year-old a friendly greeting in, say, a supermarket—and the child erupted in loud wailing! Contrary to popular belief, however, not all infants experience wariness with every stranger, and those who do vary considerably in the intensity of their reactions. Indeed, some infants respond positively to unfamiliar adults. Others mingle wary and friendly reactions in an unmistakably "coy" demeanor.

How a baby responds to a stranger depends on aspects of the infant (including temperament and the security of the mother-infant relationship), the stranger (including gender and behavior toward the baby), and the situation (including the mother's proximity and the infant's current mood) (Thompson & Limber, 1990). Here is a tip: Approach cautiously, watching the infant's face and body position. A baby may be friendly toward a person who keeps at a comfortable distance but may react fearfully if the same stranger looms suddenly and noisily.

A related reaction is **separation anxiety,** the fear of being left by the mother or other caregiver. Separation anxiety emerges at about 8 or 9 months, peaks at about 14 months, and then gradually subsides; thus, it is best to introduce a new baby-sitter when the infant is either under 6 months or over 18 months. Whether or not infants are distressed by separation also depends on the baby's past experiences and the manner in which the caregiver departs—leaving abruptly, for example, or in a relaxed fashion with good-byes and reassurance. At its peak, however, separation anxiety makes a 1-year-old wail when mother goes to the store, to the shower, or even under the blankets in bed.

Both stranger wariness and separation anxiety reveal that the older infant's emotions are not based on any single event (such as the approach of an unfamiliar person). After the age of about 8 or 9 months, emotions arise from the interplay of past experience and the various features of the current situation. For this reason, as they approach 2 years of age, some unfortunate infants become even more fearful, because their personal experiences have been frightening and their caregivers are not reassuring. However, most infants become less fearful, of strangers and other scary objects, by age 2.

Frustration

As every parent knows, anger intensifies in toddlerhood because infants become more aware of the significance of events that frustrate them. In one study, videotapes of 2- to 19-month-olds being inoculated were categorized as to emotional intensity by "blind" raters who could see only the infants' facial expressions. The raters noted dramatic increases in anger between ages 7 and 19 months. In addition, the duration of the anger also increased,

stranger wariness A fear of unfamiliar people, exhibited (if at all) by infants over the age of about 6 months.

separation anxiety An infant's fear of being left by his or her caregiver.

From Wariness to Fear to Terror For most toddlers, the approach of a stranger with a buzzing razor triggers a full-blown case of stranger wariness—one that even reassurances and kisses from Mom can't quiet. Had the boy here encountered the stranger in a different context—say, in a friendly conversation with Mom on the street—his reaction might have been a bit different.

from a fleeting expression in early infancy to a lengthy demonstration at 19 months (Izard et al., 1987). Since the actual inoculation is similarly painful at all ages, the reason anger increased with age is that the older infants increasingly anticipated the event, realized that somebody's action caused the pain, and struggled unsuccessfully to avoid it. Given this role of awareness, and what you learned about cognition, it is no surprise that frustration and anger first appear at about 7 months and that both increase as cognition regarding goal-directed actions increases.

Although infants experience frustration more intensely as they mature, they also become better at handling their emotions. Instead of simply crying in helpless protest, as a 6-month-old might, toddlers take action (climb out of a playpen, grab for a toy), or get help (cry *at* someone, gesture toward what they want), or comfort themselves (look away from the source of distress, suck their fingers) (Gustafson & Green, 1991; Stifter & Braungart, 1995). Which specific actions they take seems to depend on their stage of cognitive development: 12-month-olds are more likely to cling to mother and suck their fingers; 18-month-olds are much more likely to attack the problem (Parritz, 1996). By age 2, some children have learned that a full temper tantrum (shrieking, limbs flailing, and visible tears) is likely to bring results; others have learned just the opposite.

Social Referencing Is it dangerous or joyous to ride in a bicycle basket through the streets of Osaka? Check with Mom to find out.

social referencing   Looking to trusted adults for cues on how to interpret unfamiliar or ambiguous events.

EMOTIONS AS A SOCIAL WINDOW

In many ways, expressions of emotion become the vital code that enables one person to connect with another, the transparent glass that allows outsiders to look into a person's thoughts and allows the person inside to reflect outward. As the infant becomes older, both processes are at work: the infant's emotions are becoming easier for others to read, just as the infant is becoming better able to read the emotional expressions of others.

Social Referencing

As early as 5 months of age, infants associate emotional meanings with specific facial expressions, such as smiles of happiness or frowns of anger, and with different tones of voice, such as encouraging or disapproving intonations. Not only in their daily interactions but even when the emotions are expressed in a photograph of a stranger, or in a voice that speaks a language the infant has never heard, infants interpret emotions correctly (Balaban, 1995; Fernald, 1993).

At about 6 months of age, infants begin to use **social referencing**—searching the expressions of others for emotional cues. A mother's glance of calm reassurance or voiced caution, a father's expression of alarm or dismay—each can become a guide to action, telling an infant how to react to an unfamiliar or ambiguous event. Social referencing becomes increasingly important when crawling (at about 9 months) and walking (at about 12 months) make infants independently mobile, and the active exploration of the "little scientist" begins (Derochers et al., 1994). As a result, seemingly self-assured, free-roaming toddlers regularly glance back at their caregivers, checking for a signal regarding a new toy, a new playmate, or a new activity.

Social referencing is particularly important at mealtime: as the menu expands because milk is no longer the primary food, infants look to caregivers for cues about new foods. This explains why caregivers the world over smack their lips, pretend to taste, and say "yum-yum" (or the equivalent) as they feed toddlers beets, liver, spinach, or whatever. They are trying to lead the infants to like whatever is offered. On their part, toddlers become quite astute at reading expressions, insisting on the table food that the adults *really* like.

An infant uses father for social reference as much as mother, if both are present. In fact, fathers tend to be more encouraging and mothers more protective, so when toddlers are about to explore, they wisely seek a man's opinion to spur their curiosity (Parke, 1995).

Referring to Dad

❷ **Especially for Fathers:** What are the implications of the current research on fathers' role in caregiving?

As researchers looked closely at mothers, fathers, and infants, they discovered a curious difference: Although fathers provide less basic care, they play more. Infants look to fathers for fun and to mothers for comfort. Compared to mothers' play, fathers' play is more noisy, emotional, boisterous, physical, and idiosyncratic (as fathers tend to make up active and exciting games on the spur of the moment) (Fagot, 1997; MacDonald & Parke, 1986).

For instance, even in the first months of a baby's life, fathers are more likely to move the baby's legs and arms in imitation of walking, kicking, or climbing, to zoom the baby through the air (playing "airplane"), or to tap and tickle the baby's stomach. Mothers, on the other hand, are more likely to caress, murmur, or sing soothingly, to combine play with caretaking routines such as diapering and bathing, or to use standard sequences that involve only one part of the body, such as peek-a-boo and patty-cake. As a result, young infants typically laugh more, and cry more, when playing with Daddy.

Once a baby starts to crawl and walk, fathers usually spend more time in physical play, swinging their toddlers around, tumbling with them on the floor, or crawling after them in a "chase." They also are apt to tease their children (scaring them with a noise, pretending to take away a favorite toy, saying "I'm the baby now"), often to the mother's disapproval, and to play more creatively. For example, in one study in France, parents were given a set of objects including sponges, Styrofoam chips, plastic containers, and a toy bear and were asked to play with their 1-year-olds. Mothers were fairly staid in their play, putting the chips into the containers, using the sponge to clean the bear, and so on. Fathers, on the other hand, were more likely to use the objects in unconventional ways, putting chips down the bear's sweater, using the chips as falling snow, playfully tossing sponges at the child, and the like (Pecheux & Labrell, 1994).

What do infants gain from playing with their fathers, in addition to having fun? In all probability, the more physical play of fathers helps the children master motor skills and develop muscle control (Pellegrini & Smith, 1998). In addition, play with father may contribute to the growth of social skills and emotional expressions. In one study, 18-month-olds met a stranger while either parent sat passively nearby. The father's presence made the toddlers more likely to smile and play with the new person than the mother's presence did, a difference especially apparent for the boys. The authors of the study speculated that the toddlers' past boisterous, idiosyncratic play with Dad made his presence a signal to be bold and playful (Kromelow et al., 1990).

Similar speculations have been raised about fathers' teasing, which requires the baby's social response to an unpredictable game—and thereby

FATHERS AND INFANTS

Traditional views of infant development focused almost exclusively on mothers. Partly, this was because the belief in most cultures was that fathers are naturally "remote and authoritarian," too busy with other matters to have time for an intimate relationship with young children (Poussaint, 1990). Further, in industrialized nations fathers were removed from most caregiving activities, in response to the cultural expectations and practical necessities of working long hours away from home while mothers tended the house, the children, and the garden (Pleck & Pleck, 1997).

Nowadays, however, as family size shrinks and mothers work outside the home, fathers take on a "significant share of the nurturing responsibilities" for their offspring (Poussaint, 1990). This shift is apparent worldwide, including countries such as Ireland and Mexico, where the stereotype used to be that fathers are above changing diapers or spooning baby food (Bronstein, 1984; Lamb, 1987; Nugent, 1991). Virtually all developmentalists applaud this trend, for fathers who share child-care responsibilities enhance the development of their children much more than the remote fathers of earlier generations did (Pleck, 1997; Snarey, 1993). In fact, some developmentalists make the case that, throughout the world, active father-child relationships benefit the mothers, the fathers, and the entire society—in that involved fathers become active in their communities and are less likely to become self-absorbed, self-destructive, or violent (Mackey, 1996).

On a practical level, can men provide adequate care for newborns and infants? Scientists asked this question, did the research, and found that babies drank just as much formula, emerged from the bath just as clean, and seemed just as content with the caregiving of fathers as with the caregiving of mothers. It was further determined that fathers can provide the necessary emotional and cognitive nurturing, speaking motherese like a native and forming secure relationships both as secondary caregivers and as primary ones (Geiger, 1996; Lamb,

1997; Parke, 1995). If the mother was sick, suffered from postpartum depression, or simply went back to a demanding job immediately after birth, many fathers did an excellent job of "mothering." In short, "There is perhaps no mystique of motherhood that a man cannot master except for the physical realities of pregnancy, delivery, and breast feeding" (Poussaint, 1990).

Given that fathers *can* master caregiving, the next question is, Why don't more fathers develop this skill? Worldwide, women spend far more time at child care than men do, especially in the child's first few months, and particularly if the child is a girl. In some cultures, women still provide almost all child care until middle childhood. Even in contemporary Western marriages, even when both parents work outside the home on weekdays, even when both earn the same amount of money, and even when both agree that child care is a shared responsibility, the reality is that fathers do some basic caregiving in the evenings and on weekends but mothers do a great deal more (Bailey, 1994; Thompson & Walker, 1989). African American fathers are somewhat more involved, especially with older boys, but, like other fathers, they talk about equal involvement but they play more than they diaper (Hossain & Roopnarine, 1994). Thus contemporary fathers are more actively engaged with their children than fathers were in 1970, but mothers still spend twice as much time in child care as fathers do (Pleck, 1997).

These generalities apply to residential fathers married to the mothers. Divorced or never-married fathers (which is the situation for about one-third of all infants born in the United States in the 1990s) spend even less time in infant care than married fathers. A sizable minority are not involved at all.

Surprisingly, although the media—and many mothers—tend to blame the fathers, women may be as responsible for this unequal distribution of labor as men are. Many mothers assume the status of the family child-care authority: they serve as a kind of gatekeeper and judge of the father's performance,

may increase not only excitement but also emotional regulation and social understanding (Pecheux & Labrell, 1994). Another study, this one of very low birthweight infants in Japan, found they were much more likely to develop normal social skills if their fathers were actively involved with them (Itoigawa et al., 1996). And in Israel, father-infant involvement led to an increase in exploratory play (Feldman et al., 1997). Throughout today's changing world, mothers and fathers together are more likely to meet all their infants' needs—biological, cognitive, and psychosocial—than can either parent alone. (See Changing Policy, above.)

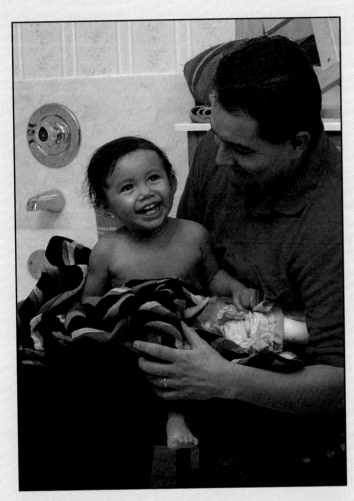

Dads Are Fun Of all the caregiving tasks fathers might do, bathing is one of the ones most frequently chosen and most often turned into good clean fun. This is true in every culture worldwide, including the one shown here—in Texas, with a Mexican American dad.

forbidding or criticizing certain behaviors and permitting and praising others (Kranichfeld, 1987; Pollack & Grossman, 1985). This is particularly true if the parents are not married. Then mothers and maternal grandmothers either open the door to involvement or slam it shut (Wattenberg, 1993).

Cross-culturally, when mothers are not present and fathers are alone with their children, fathers tend to be as actively involved as mothers are; but mothers usually are present, and then fathers usually let them be the caregivers (Mackey 1996). It seems that fathers' limited involvement with babies is partly their own choice, a choice often encouraged by mothers.

Added to such role preferences within families are social pressures and assumptions, with nations and employers likely to expect mothers to do more child care than fathers. Sweden, alone among the nations, grants 15 months of paid parental leave per child that can be divided between the two parents in any way they choose. Still, Swedish mothers usually take much more than half the total time (Geiger, 1996). Overall, fathering is more a result of personal choice and culture than mothering is, because a father's role seems to depend much more than a mother's on his financial contributions, on his past experiences, on his relationship to his partner, and on the cultural context (LaRossa, 1997). As one study explains, if a man does not get along with his wife, "he may be present as a father, but the quality of his relationship with his children is apt to suffer" (Doherty et al., 1998). Mothers, by contrast, are likely to become *more* involved with their children if their relationships with their husbands weaken (Owen & Cox, 1997).

Many factors, then—not just the man's reluctance to be a caregiver but also his wife, his marriage, his work, and his culture—make a father's involvement with day-to-day infant care much more fragile than it need be. Policy and practice are changing, and children are the beneficiaries.

⏺ Response for Fathers (from page 211): Fathers are much more capable than some women think, and paternal caregiving makes the infant happier and braver. This means that fathers should be active parents, even when work schedules, personal preferences, or maternal criticism pushes them in the other direction.

Shaping Later Emotions

In many ways, lessons learned from social referencing become a guide to later activity. This was shown in one experiment that began as a straightforward demonstration of social referencing. In the presence of their mothers, 12-month-olds were presented with a toy robot or a moving, cymbal-clapping monkey. Their mothers were instructed to express either disgust or delight with the toy. As expected, the infants' willingness to play with the toys was affected by their mothers' reactions. In a later extension of the experiment, the mothers were told not to provide any emotional cues when the same toys were presented again to their children. Nevertheless, the infants welcomed or spurned the robot or monkey, depending on the social guidance they remembered (Hornick et al., 1987).

Other research proves that infants look to caregivers for specific messages, rather than for overall attitudes of approval or disapproval. By 12 months, infant responses to a specific toy already reflect their mothers' positive or negative words and facial expressions about the toy much more than their mothers' general happy or unhappy facial expressions. With a toy that elicited positive messages, they played more and happily. When the messages about the toy were negative, they avoided the toy and were more anxious and more active (Stenberg & Hagekull, 1997).

Over time, lessons learned from many social-referencing episodes have a general shaping effect on infant behavior. For example, all toddlers experience frequent bumps and tumbles in their first attempts to walk—sometimes with no hurt at all, and at other times with scrapes or bruises that bring worried attention from caregivers. As a result, when a fall occurs at, say, 18 months, most toddlers look first to their caregivers to see if it was a serious one, and then they burst into tears or laughter accordingly. (Lessons about "hurt" that are learned early in childhood may explain why some adults seem to attend to every little ache they might have while other adults seem to ignore even obvious injury.)

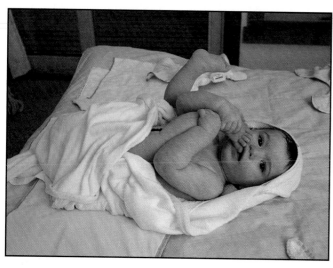

Tasty Toes Most of us (including the photographer) are amazed at this toes-in-mouth demonstration, but such is not the concern of the baby. Instead, at 6 months she is very interested in and not too comfortable with the stranger taking the photograph. Body awareness, including the realization that those toes are her own, will take months to appear, propelled not only by cognitive maturation but perhaps by the emergence of top and bottom teeth at about 1 year of age.

Generally, if toddlers receive more signals of interest and encouragement than of fear and prohibition as they explore their universe, they are likely to be more friendly, and less aggressive, than they would be if the opposite messages had been received (Calkins, 1994). If an infant or toddler sees few signals of any kind (as might happen if the primary caregiver is depressed, neglectful, or overtired), the child becomes relatively emotionless and passive (Field, 1995).

The social signals a young child receives can have lifelong impact (Schore, 1994). If an infant is overwhelmed by fear or frustration, this might make it difficult for that child to experience positive encounters, and thus might have an effect on future brain development as well as cognition. This is certainly true for vulnerable infants and for animals; it probably is true for normal infants as well (Courchesne et al., 1994; Fox et al., 1994).

Self-Awareness

self-awareness A person's sense of himself or herself as being distinct from other people.

A pivotal accomplishment of later infancy is the onset of **self-awareness,** a person's realization that he or she is a distinct individual whose body, mind, and actions are separate from those of other people. This emerging sense of "me" and "mine" fosters the growth of many self-conscious emotions—from pride and confidence to guilt, shame, and embarrassment. Simultaneously, self-awareness leads to new consciousness of others. That, in turn, fosters other-directed emotions, such as defiance and jealousy, as well as empathy and affection.

The onset of self-awareness is strikingly evident when infants of various ages are compared. Very young infants have no sense of self; in fact, they do not even have an awareness of their bodies as theirs (Lewis, 1990). To them, for example, their hands are interesting objects that appear and disappear. In effect, 2-month-olds discover their hands each time they catch sight of them, become fascinated with the movements, and then lose interest as the hands slip out of view. Even 8-month-olds often don't seem to know where their bodies end and someone else's body begins. An 8- or 9-month-old might grab a toy that is in another child's hand and then react with surprise when the toy "resists." By 1 year, however, most infants are aware that another child is a distinct person, and they might show this awareness with a smile or a shove if the coveted toy is not immediately forthcoming.

Who's in the Mirror

The emerging sense of self was demonstrated in a classic experiment in which babies looked in a mirror after a dot of rouge had been surreptitiously put on their noses (Lewis & Brooks, 1978). If the babies reacted to the mirror image by touching their own noses, they knew they were seeing their own faces. By trying this experiment with 96 babies between the ages of 9 and 24 months, the experimenters found a distinct age-related developmental shift. None of the babies under 1 year old reacted to the mark as if it were on their own faces (they sometimes smiled at the baby in the mirror and touched the dot on the mirror baby). However, most of those between ages 15 and 24 months did react with self-awareness, perhaps by touching their own faces with an expression of curiosity and puzzlement.

The link between self-awareness and self-conscious emotions was shown in a later extension of the rouge-and-mirror experiment (Lewis et al., 1989). In this study, 15- to 24-month-olds who showed self-recognition in the mirror also looked *embarrassed* when they were effusively praised by an adult; that is, they smiled and looked away, covered their faces with their hands, and so on. Infants without self-recognition, in that they had not recognized that the rouge was on their own noses, were not embarrassed. This connection between self-awareness and self-conscious emotions is exhibited at about the same age among toddlers from various backgrounds (Schneider-Rosen & Cicchetti, 1991). Before their second birthday, most children point to themselves when asked "Where's [child's name]?" and can use their own names appropriately when pointed at and asked "Who's that?" (Pipp et al., 1987).

A Beautiful Bonnet At 18 months, Austin recognizes himself, obviously delighted by his colander hat. Once self-recognition begins at about this age, many children spend years admiring themselves with various hats, makeup, and other accessories. Almost every view of themselves is a joy; children are not yet worried about looking stupid or ugly.

Pride and Shame

Developing self-awareness enables toddlers to be self-critical and to have emotional responses such as guilt (Emde et al., 1991). By age 2, for example, most children are aware of the basic do's and don'ts they should follow, and they sometimes show distress or anxiety when they have misbehaved—even when no adult is present. In one experimental demonstration of this behavior, 2-year-olds were "set up" to experience two mild mishaps: They were left alone in a playroom with (1) a doll whose leg was rigged to fall off when the doll was picked up, and (2) a juice drink in a trick cup that dribbled when drunk from. Many of the children responded to their "accidents" with expressions of sadness or tension, along with efforts to repair the damage (Cole et al., 1992).

The link between self-awareness and emotions is evident at home as well as in the laboratory: Mothers report that toddlers' sense of *shame* and *guilt* appears for the first time only after self-awareness develops (Stipek et al., 1992). At that point, being angry over an injustice (such as another child's getting the first slice of pie), as well as being "sorry" for a misdeed, become part of the child's developing moral sense (Zahn-Waxler et al., 1992).

Interestingly, self-awareness seems to be a prerequisite for one of the most difficult grammatical lessons for children: the proper use of "you" and "me." Most children will confuse these terms until they are at least 2 years old. The fact that this confusion is a matter of self-awareness, and not simply of grammatical complexity, is shown by deaf toddlers. The signs for "me" and "you" are simple—pointing to oneself and to the other person—but deaf toddlers have the same confusion as hearing toddlers, presumably because the underlying concept is hard for them to grasp (Petitto & Marentette, 1991).

Self-awareness also permits a child to react in an entirely new way to his or her misdeeds—with pride at going against another's wishes. Shortly before his second birthday, for example, a certain toddler named Ricky teased his mother by deliberately pouring a cup of juice onto a rug. Evidence that Ricky knew he was being naughty was in his reaction to his mother's scolding: he was unsurprised and unfazed by her angry words and was quite willing to help his mother clean up the mess. Only when his mother sent him to his room did he protest angrily, apparently not anticipating such punishment. Later that day he told his grandmother, "Juice on a floor." Her response was "Juice doesn't go on the floor," delivered somewhat sternly. "Yes, juice on a floor, juice on a floor," Ricky laughingly repeated several times, pretending to turn an imaginary cup upside down. As Ricky's grandmother, a noted psychologist, comments:

> The boy's pleasure at watching the juice spill and anger at being sent to his room are emotions that are typical at all periods of infancy, but his obvious pride at his ability to act counter to convention or his mother's wishes is possible only when self-awareness is firmly established. [Shatz, 1994]

THE ORIGINS OF PERSONALITY

personality   The emotions, behaviors, and attitudes that make an individual unique.

By **personality** we mean the myriad of emotions, behaviors, and attitudes that characterize each person, distinguishing one from another. Once we know (more or less) the timetable for emotional development during infancy, the next question seems to be: Does something happen to the infant's responses to evoke or create the traits and social habits that become the patterns that form personality?

The Traditional View: The Importance of Nurture

In the first half of the twentieth century, the prevailing view among psychologists was that personality is permanently molded by the actions of the parents—most especially the mother—in the early years of childhood. There were two major theoretical versions of how this comes about.

Learning Theory

From the perspective of traditional learning theory (discussed in Chapter 2), personality is molded as parents reinforce or punish their child's spontaneous behaviors. Behaviorists proposed, for example, that if parents smile and pick up their baby at every glimmer of an infant grin, the baby will become a child—and later an adult—with a sunny disposition. Similarly, if parents continually tease their infant by, say, removing the nipple as the baby is contentedly sucking or by playfully pulling at a favorite toy that a toddler is clutching, that child will develop a suspicious, possessive nature.

"I get along fine with people my age and I get along fine with people your age—it's the ones in the middle who give me all kinds of problems."

Parents Are the Problem According to psychoanalytic theory, the inevitable conflicts between parents and young children create the need for personality quirks and defensive measures.

oral stage Freud's term for the first stage of psychosexual development, in which the infant gains pleasure through sucking and biting.

anal stage Freud's second stage of psychosexual development, in which the anus becomes the main source of bodily pleasure, and control of defecation and toilet training are therefore important activities.

❓ Especially for Mothers: What are the implications of Freud's perspective that mothers are crucial?

The strongest statement of this early view came from John Watson, the leading behaviorist of the time, who cautioned:

> Failure to bring up a happy child, a well-adjusted child—assuming bodily health—falls squarely upon the parents' shoulders. [By the time the child is 3] parents have already determined . . . whether . . . [the child] is to grow into a happy person, wholesome and good-natured, whether he is to be a whining, complaining, neurotic, an anger-driven, vindictive, over-bearing slave driver, or one whose every move in life is definitely controlled by fear. [Watson, 1928]

Later theorists in the behaviorist tradition incorporated social learning into personality formation; they found that infants observe and then imitate personality traits of their parents, even if they are not directly reinforced for doing so. A child might develop a quick temper, for instance, if a parent regularly displays anger and in return gets respect—or at least obedience—from other family members. Although not all personality traits are directly reinforced in babyhood, "the guiding belief of these social learning theorists was that personality is learned" (Miller, 1993).

Psychoanalytic Theory

Beginning with a different set of assumptions about human nature, psychoanalytic theorists (also discussed in Chapter 2) similarly concluded that the individual's personality is first formed and then permanently fixed in early childhood. Sigmund Freud, who established the framework for this view, felt that the experiences of the first 4 years "play a decisive part in determining whether and at what point the individual shall fail to master the real problems of life" (Freud, 1918/1963). He thought that the mother was "unique, without parallel, established unalterably for a whole lifetime as the first and strongest love-object and as the prototype of all later love relations" (Freud, 1940/1964). Other psychoanalytic theorists agreed: mother-child relationships in the first months and years are pivotal.

Freud: Oral and Anal Stages. As we noted in Chapter 2, Freud viewed human development in terms of psychosexual stages that occur at specific ages. According to Freud (1935), psychological development begins in the first year of life, with an **oral stage**, so named because the mouth is the young infant's prime source of gratification. In the second year, the infant's prime focus of gratification shifts to the anus—particularly the sensual pleasure taken in bowel movements and, eventually, the psychological pleasure in controlling them. Accordingly, Freud referred to this period as the **anal stage.**

The shift from oral to anal gratification is more than a simple change of body focus; it is a shift in the mode of interaction with the environment—from a passive, dependent mode to a more active, controlling mode in which the child has some power. In the anal stage, mothers strive to foster the toddler's self-control through potty training as well as in other ways. And the toddler has the self-awareness and self-control to resist. The situation is thus prime for a power struggle between adult and child. More than one toddler has spent time sitting unhappily on the potty, with no outcome, only to get off, get diapered, and poop. The mother's subsequent exasperation is not just about the cleanup but also about the loss of her power to "train" the child.

Indeed, according to Freud, both oral and anal stages are fraught with potential conflicts that can have long-term consequences. If a mother frustrates her infant's urge to suck—by, say, weaning the infant from the nipple too early or preventing the child from sucking on fingers or toes—the child

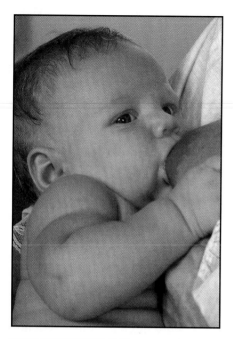

More Than a Balanced Meal To psychoanalytic theorists, breast-feeding is important not just because it is a source of nourishment but also because the pleasurable, intimate contact it affords strengthens the infant's attachment to the mother and fosters a feeling of "basic trust" in the world.
❷ *Observational Quiz (see answer page 220): What is the infant receiving in this important process?*

trust versus mistrust Erikson's first stage of psychosocial development, in which the infant experiences the world either as secure and comfortable or as unpredictable and uncomfortable.

autonomy versus shame and doubt Erikson's second stage of psychosocial development, in which the toddler struggles for self-control but feels shame and doubt about his or her abilities if it is not achieved.

may become distressed and anxious and eventually be an adult with an oral fixation. Such a person is stuck (fixated) at the oral stage and therefore eats, drinks, chews, bites, or talks excessively, in quest of mouthy pleasures that were denied in infancy.

Similarly, if toilet training is overly strict or if it occurs before the child is mature enough to participate (before age 18 to 24 months), interaction between parents and child may become locked into a conflict over the toddler's resistance or inability to comply. This conflict, too, may have important consequences for the child's future personality. The child becomes fixated and develops an anal personality; as an adult, he or she may seek control of self and others and demonstrate an unusual need for regularity in all aspects of life.

Freud's ideas concerning orality and anality have been extremely influential. However, research has failed to link specific oral- and anal-stage conflicts with later personality traits. Rather, the overall pattern of parental warmth and sensitivity, or coldness and domination, affects the child's emotional development much more than the particulars of either feeding or toilet training. This broader perspective is reflected in the theory of Erik Erikson.

Erikson: Trust and Autonomy.   As you should remember from Chapter 2, Erik Erikson believed that development proceeds through a series of developmental crises, or challenges, that occur throughout the life span. The first crisis of infancy, in Erikson's view, is **trust versus mistrust.** In this crisis, the infant learns whether the world is essentially a secure place, where basic needs will be readily satisfied, or the opposite, an unpredictable arena where needs are met only after much crying—and sometimes not even then. Erikson (1963) contended that babies begin to develop a sense of security when their mothers provide food and comfort with "consistency, continuity, and sameness of experience." When interaction with the mother inspires trust and security, the child (and later the adult), experiences confidence in engaging and exploring the world.

The next crisis, which occurs in toddlerhood, is **autonomy versus shame and doubt.** Toddlers want autonomy, or self-rule, over their own actions and bodies. If they fail in their effort to gain it, either because they are incapable or because their caregivers are too restrictive and forbidding, they feel ashamed of their actions and doubtful of their abilities. According to Erikson, the key to meeting this crisis and gaining a sense of autonomy is parental guidance and protection:

> Firmness must protect him [the toddler] against the potential anarchy of his as yet untrained sense of discrimination, his inability to hold on and let go with discretion. As his environment encourages him to "stand on his own feet," it must protect him against meaningless and arbitrary experiences of shame and of early doubt. [Erikson, 1963]

If parents accomplish this, the child will become increasingly self-confident when encountering new challenges.

Like Freud, Erikson believed that problems arising in early infancy can last a lifetime. He maintained that the adult who is suspicious and pessimistic or who always seems burdened by shame may have been an infant who did not develop sufficient trust or a toddler who did not achieve sufficient autonomy. However, Erikson also emphasized that experiences later in life can alter or transform the effects of early experiences and that earlier developmental crises can be revisited and resolved later in life.

Overall, then, traditional psychological theories maintained that personality is shaped primarily by early nurture, particularly the mother's

Just Looking or About to Pull? If the girl's explorations result in smashed dinnerware, will her parents react with anger, as though her goal were destruction, or with a firm but understanding caution, as though her goal were discovery? According to Erikson, how parents react to their children's efforts at autonomy can shape how young children resolve the psychosocial crisis of autonomy versus shame and doubt.

temperament The set of innate tendencies, or dispositions, that underlie and affect each person's interactions with people, situations, and events.

① Response for Mothers (from page 217): If mothers are crucial, they must devote themselves exclusively to infant care, keeping baby-sitters, day-care teachers, and even fathers at a distance. For better or worse, children will be strongly identified with their mothers, who can take pride in their accomplishments and blame for their failures. Fortunately for today's women, Freud's theories are unproven.

caregiving. This view has serious challengers who say the basic elements of temperament emerge so early that caregiving influences cannot be credited or blamed for personality.

Temperament: The Importance of Nature

Every individual is born with a distinct, genetically based set of psychological tendencies, or dispositions. These tendencies, which together are called **temperament,** affect and shape virtually every aspect of the person's developing personality. Temperament has been defined as the "relatively consistent, basic dispositions inherent in the person that underlie and modulate the expression of activity, reactivity, emotionality, and sociability" (McCall, in Goldsmith et al., 1987). As an example of temperamental tendencies, we might note that one person is a *cautious* individual whereas another is a *risk taker.*

The distinction between temperament and personality is a matter of time and complexity. Temperament is composed of basic tendencies, apparent early in life, that are the foundation ("underlie and modulate") for *later* personality dimensions ("the expression of activity, reactivity, emotionality, and sociability"). Thus, if risk taking is a temperamental tendency, the personality of an individual with that tendency might include a propensity to gamble, to speak bluntly, to seek physical challenges (like mountain climbing), to be sexually promiscuous, and/or to change jobs often. Probably each risk taker develops a distinct set of personality traits, all connected to his or her basic temperament but not dictated in every detail by it. Moreover, temperament and personality tend to overlap; it is sometimes difficult to distinguish one from the other.

Temperament (and therefore personality) is epigenetic, not merely genetic: it begins in the multitude of genetic instructions that guide the development of the brain and then is affected by the prenatal environment, especially the nutrition and health of the mother, and probably by postnatal experiences as well. Signs of temperament are evident from birth, and temperamental individuality is clearly established within the first months. As the person develops, the social context and the individual's experiences continue to influence the nature and expression of temperament.

Twins They were born on the same day and now are experiencing a wading pool for the first time.

❷ Observational Quiz (see answer page 223): *Are these monozygotic or dizygotic twins?*

❶ Answer to Observational Quiz (from page 218): *Breast milk, of course, with nutrients, antibodies, and hormones, as explained in Chapter 5. But this baby may also be gaining an outgoing and generous personality, a confident and easygoing attitude toward humanity, and a lifelong affection for Mother.*

Dimensions of Temperament

Because temperament is fundamental in determining the kind of individuals we become and how we interact with others, many researchers have set out to describe and measure the various dimensions of temperament (Buss, 1991; Lemery et al., 1999; Rothbart & Bates, 1998). The most famous, most comprehensive, and longest ongoing study of children's temperament remains the classic New York Longitudinal Study (NYLS), begun over four decades ago (Thomas & Chess, 1977; Thomas et al., 1963). For this study parents of very young infants were interviewed repeatedly and extensively. The researchers detailed the various aspects of the infants' behavior, and they described the approach they used to reduce the possibility of parental bias:

> For example, if a mother said that her child did not like his first solid food, we asked her to describe his actual behavior. We were satisfied only when she gave a description such as, "When I put the food into his mouth he cried loudly, twisted his head away, and let it drool out."
>
> If we asked what a six-month-old baby did when his father came home in the evening, and his mother said, "He was happy to see him," we pressed for a detailed description: "As soon as he saw his father he smiled and reached out his arms." [Chess et al., 1965]

According to the researchers' initial findings, in the first days and months of life babies differ in nine characteristics:

- *Activity level.* Some babies are active. They kick a lot in the uterus before they are born, they move around a great deal in their bassinets, and, as toddlers, they are nearly always running. Other babies are much less active.
- *Rhythmicity.* Some babies have regular cycles of activity. They eat, sleep, and defecate on schedule almost from birth. Other babies are much less predictable.
- *Approach-withdrawal.* Some babies delight in everything new; others withdraw from every new situation. The first bath makes some babies react in wide-eyed wonder and others tense up and scream; the first playtime with another child makes some crawl toward their new playmate with excitement and makes others try to hide.
- *Adaptability.* Some babies adjust quickly to change. Others are unhappy at every disruption of their normal routine.
- *Intensity of reaction.* Some babies chortle when they laugh and howl when they cry. Others are much calmer, responding with a smile or a whimper.
- *Threshold of responsiveness.* Some babies seem to sense every sight, sound, and touch. For instance, they waken at a slight noise or turn away from a distant light. Others seem blissfully unaware, even of bright lights, loud street noises, or wet diapers.
- *Quality of mood.* Some babies seem constantly happy, smiling at almost everything. Others seem chronically unhappy; they are ready to protest at any moment.
- *Distractibility.* All babies fuss when they are hungry, but some will stop if someone gives them a pacifier or sings them a song. Others will keep fussing. Similarly, some babies can easily be distracted from a fascinating but dangerous object and diverted to a safer plaything. Others are more single-minded, refusing to be distracted.
- *Attention span.* Some babies play happily with one toy for a long time. Others quickly drop one activity for another.

The lead NYLS researchers, Alexander Thomas and Stella Chess (1977), believe that "temperamental individuality is well established by the time the infant is two to three months old." In terms of combinations of the above characteristics, most young infants can be described as being one of three types: about 40 percent are *easy*, about 15 percent are *slow to warm up*, and about 10 percent are *difficult*. (Difficult babies are irregular, intense, disturbed by every noise, unhappy, and hard to distract for very long—quite a handful, even for the experienced parent. Easy babies are the opposite of difficult, and slow-to-warm-up babies are distinguished by their initial unwillingness to approach, adapt, and be distracted. They do, however, adjust with time.)

Most parents can personally validate these categories, in that they readily describe their infants as good (meaning easy), shy (meaning slow to warm up), or difficult. But notice that about 35 percent of normal infants do not fit into any of these specific types. If your mother says you were a good baby, consider her assessment a compliment but remain skeptical: your actual behavior may have been more ambiguous. You might ask her, just as the researchers did, to describe your "good" behavior by giving specific behavioral examples.

Stability and Change in Temperament

A series of NYLS follow-up studies that were carried into adolescence and adulthood (Carey & McDevitt, 1978; Chess & Thomas, 1990; Thomas et al., 1968), and other research on the same characteristics as those in the NYLS (Cowen et al., 1992; Guerin & Gottfried, 1994), indicate that easy babies usually remain easy children while difficult ones continue to give their parents problems. Similarly, slow-to-warm-up infants, who at 8 months cried on seeing strangers, may well hide behind Mother's skirt on arriving at nursery school and avoid crowds in the halls of middle school. Indeed, some researchers of adult personality see temperament types as lifelong patterns.

But research results remind us that human development is never simple, straightforward, or predetermined. Temperament evolves over time and can change in many ways. Even some of the NYLS characteristics are not stable. Rhythmicity and quality of mood are particularly variable: a young infant who takes naps on schedule might not do so a few months later, and a baby who seems consistently happy might become a malcontent if life circumstances change for the worse. Change itself follows genetic timetables, and that includes change in temperament. Shifts in temperament are particularly likely in the first 2 years, but they can occur at any time (Lemery et al., 1999). Moreover, inborn tendencies may be more or less apparent during certain developmental periods and under certain conditions. For example, a particular tendency, such as a long attention span, may be very obvious in the first grade when a child works on his or her penmanship for hours, but it may seem to disappear at puberty when a rush of hormones turns the studious child into an easily distracted adolescent (Chess & Thomas, 1990; Plomin et al., 1993).

Researchers who study adult personality have also searched for the basic temperamental dimensions that underlie personality in humans everywhere (Digman, 1990; McDonald, 1995; McCrea et al., 1999). Through a series of statistical calculations they have found what are called the **"big five"** dimensions of temperament:

big five   The five main clusters of personality, found in adults to be extroversion, agreeableness, conscientiousness, neuroticism, and openness.

- *Extroversion:* the tendency to be outgoing, assertive, and active
- *Agreeableness:* the tendency to be kind, helpful, and easygoing
- *Conscientiousness:* the tendency to be organized, deliberate, and conforming
- *Neuroticism:* the tendency to be anxious, moody, and self-punishing
- *Openness:* the tendency to be imaginative, curious, and artistic, welcoming new experiences

As you can see, these five tendencies are not identical to the nine characteristics of the NYLS, but there are many similarities. The big five are found in international studies of adult personality, as well as in descriptions of children's traits by parents from many nations (Kohnstamm et al., 1996). This confirms that temperament is probably innate to the human race and that at least some patterns that distinguish one infant, child, or adult from another transcend culture or child-rearing specifics. Other research finds that temperament is linked to biological and neurological patterns (in heartbeat, crying, activity, and such) that appear in the first months of life, so parents cannot be blamed or credited for all their infants' actions (Huffman et al., 1998; Rothbart et al., 1994).

The Match Between Parent and Child

goodness of fit The degree to which a child's temperament matches the demands of his or her environment.

The environment can affect a child's temperamental tendencies in several ways. One way is through the **goodness of fit,** or "match," between the child's temperamental pattern and the demands of his or her social context—mainly through parenting. When parents adapt their child-rearing expectations to their offspring's temperament, the result is a harmonious fit, with good outcomes for both child and family. This might involve setting up a spacious, childproof play area where a high-activity-level child can use up excess energy without safety risk, or it might require allowing extra time for a slow-to-warm-up child to adjust to new situations.

Crucial here are not only the actual parenting behaviors but also the parents' expectations. If a highly active boy's parents learn to accept and appreciate him, they will enroll him in the soccer league and cheer from the sidelines, rather than nag their son for not sitting quietly or not completing hours of neatly written homework. The same applies, perhaps even more so, to the parents of an active girl. The result of a proper match will be a developing person with skills, talents, self-esteem, and a proud set of parents.

By contrast, when there is a poor match between the child's temperamental pattern and the caregiving expectations, parents and offspring experience greater conflict. Suppose an irregular infant, who is sometimes hungry 1 hour after a meal and sometimes 6 hours later, happens to be born to a busy mother who makes schedules and follows routines to cope with her own anxieties and insecurities. That's a volatile combination, leading to mutual resentment and conflict unless one or the other adjusts. Even as grown-ups, temperamentally irregular people who have learned to fight their mothers' rules might resist any attempt to become organized and predictable. Such people might undermine their own potential by procrastinating, arriving late for appointments, or losing things.

The importance of goodness of fit is illustrated by one of the original subjects of the NYLS:

> Carl was one of our most extreme cases of difficult temperament from the first months of life through 5 years of age. However, he did not develop a behavior disorder, primarily due to optimal handling by his parents and stability of his environment. His father, who himself had an easy temperament, took delight in his son's "lusty" characteristics, recognized on his own Carl's tendencies to have intense negative reactions to the new, and had the patience to wait for eventual adaptability to occur. He was clear, without any orientation by us, that these

Which Sister Has a Personality Problem?
Culture always affects the expression of temperament. In Mongolia and many other Asian countries, females are expected to display shyness as a sign of respect to elders and strangers. Consequently, if the younger of these sisters is truly as shy as she seems, her parents are less likely to be distressed about her withdrawn behavior than the typical North American parent would be. On the other hand, they may consider the relative boldness of her older sister to be a serious problem.

❶ Answer to Observational Quiz (from page 220): *True tests of zygosity involve analysis of blood type, although physical appearance often provides some clues. Here such clues are minimal: we cannot see differences in sex, coloring, or hand formation— although the shape of the skulls seems different. The best clue from this photo is personality. Confronting their first experience in a wading pool, these twins are showing such a difference on the approach-withdrawal dimension of temperament that one would have to guess they are dizygotic.*

characteristics were in no way due to his or his wife's influences. His wife tended to be anxious and self-accusatory over Carl's tempestuous course. However, her husband was supportive and reassuring and this enabled her to take an appropriately objective and patient approach to her son's development.

By [Carl's] middle childhood and early adolescent years, few new situations arose which provoked the difficult temperament responses. The family, school, and social environment was stable and Carl flourished and appeared to be temperamentally easy rather than difficult. . . .

When Carl went off to college, however, he was faced simultaneously with a host of new situations and demands—an unfamiliar locale, a different living arrangement, new academic subjects and expectations, and a totally new peer group. Within a few weeks his temperamentally difficult characteristics reappeared in full force. He felt negative about the school, his courses, the other students, couldn't motivate himself to study, and was constantly irritable. Carl knew something was wrong, and discussed the situation with his family and us and developed an appropriate strategy to cope with his problem. He limited the new demands by dropping several extracurricular activities, limited his social contact, and policed his studying. Gradually he adapted, his distress disappeared, and he was able to expand his activities and social contacts. . . . [In] the most recent follow-up at age 29 . . . his intensity remains but is now an asset rather than a liability. [Chess & Thomas, 1990]

INTERACTION AGAIN

As our discussion of temperament makes clear, the traditional psychological view of the mother as the sole shaper of the child's personality was in error. A more inclusive view, involving the father, siblings, and other family members, still gives too little credence to inborn tendencies. Yet we also see that personality is not determined solely by the individual's temperamental tendencies. Not just genetics, the mother, or others, but the *interaction* between caregiver and child is crucial to all psychosocial growth. This interaction is affected by the personality of the parent, the temperament of the child, the surrounding culture, and the child's stage of development. Synergy between caregiver and infant is the spark that ignites development.

Becoming Social Partners

As you saw earlier, even very young infants communicate emotionally, through sounds, movements, and facial expressions. And they are interested in social interaction virtually from birth: voices and faces are among the first stimuli to capture a newborn's attention. But although tiny babies are social, they are not equal partners. First-time parents who eagerly anticipate joyous exchanges are disappointed to discover that their newborn spends most of the day sleeping, awakening mainly to cry and suck and rarely responding to a caregiver. A fixed stare is typically the best that parents can expect from an attentive newborn; managing to soothe a crying infant is a major success.

Even this success eludes some parents. Certain colicky infants engage in prolonged, aversive bouts of crying—typically after the evening feeding and due to intestinal discomfort. Such crying makes parents feel helpless and angry, worried that they are failures or that their baby already hates them. The cry of such a baby is, in fact, a very unpleasant sound, as upsetting as the scratching of a blackboard might be (Zeskind & Barr, 1997). Even if they are not colicky, immature infants (under 3 months of age) often become upset for reasons that have little to do with the care they receive. Boys, for instance, tend to be fussier than girls, even though their parents try harder to comfort them

(a)

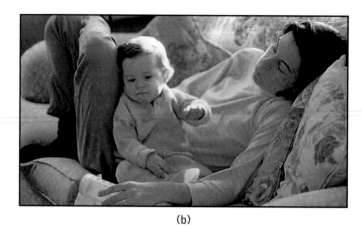

(b)

Personality of Caregiver Both nature and nurture may be in evidence here, in that the mother's personality obviously affects the quality of interaction with her offspring. Adults typically use special social behaviors (a) with their young infants—leaning in close, opening their eyes and mouths wide in exaggerated expressions of surprise or delight, maintaining eye contact—because those behaviors elicit the baby's attention and pleasure. But such behaviors are subdued or absent when the adult is depressed or stressed (b), and this makes social interaction much less enjoyable for each partner.

synchrony   Coordinated interaction between infant and parent (or other caregiver) in which each individual responds to and influences the other.

(Weinberg et al., 1999). When babies are between 3 and 9 months old, their parents are much more influential, making some fussy young infants more placid and others more irritable as they mature (Scher & Mayseless, 1997).

Synchrony

By the age of 2 to 3 months, changes occur that make parents rejoice: their baby begins to respond to them in special ways. To be sure, any face elicits smiles, but the mother, the father, or another familiar caregiver now provokes widened grins, lilting cooing, and other reactions that signify special status in that infant's world. Many parents report that their own affection for their baby deepens at this time. In a sense the parents are proceeding from a newborn phase of caregiving, when they perceive the child as a delicate guest requiring careful treatment, to a family phase in which they perceive the child as a social partner who reciprocates their love. Instead of merely gazing intently over the crib rails, trying to decipher what the baby's needs might be, caregivers begin to initiate focused episodes of *face-to-face social play*, eliciting unmistakable responses from the infant.

One of the goals of face-to-face play is to develop and maintain **synchrony,** or coordinated interaction between infant and caregiver. Synchrony has been variously described by researchers as the meshing of a finely tuned machine (Snow, 1984), an emotional "attunement" of an improvised musical duet (Stern, 1985), and a smoothly flowing "waltz" that is mutually adaptive (Barnard & Martell, 1995). The critical factor is the split-second timing of the interaction, such that each responds to the other. Synchrony helps infants learn to express and read emotions (Bremner, 1988). Through synchrony they begin to develop some of the basic skills of social interaction, such as taking turns, that they will use throughout life.

These play episodes occur in almost any context—during a feeding, a diaper change, or a bath, for example. After a while, they can be initiated by either the adult or the infant: the caregiver might notice the baby's expression or vocalization and echo it (such as cooing when the baby coos), or the baby might notice the adult's wide-eyed beaming and break into a grin.

What really distinguishes episodes of synchrony from routine caregiving are the moment-by-moment actions and reactions of both partners. To complement the infant's animated but quite limited repertoire, as well as to elicit new or increased reactions, caregivers perform dozens of actions that seem to be reserved exclusively for babies. Typically, they may open their eyes and mouths wide in exaggerated expressions of mock delight or surprise; make rapid clucking noises or repeat one-syllable sounds ("ba-ba-ba-ba-ba," "di-di-

A Moment of Synchrony Much of synchrony is impossible to photograph, since noises and movements—a split second apart—are a big part of the dance. But facial expressions and body positions are also part of it.

❓ *Observational Quiz (see answer page 228):* Can you see three examples of synchrony here?

di-di," "bo-bo-bo-bo"); raise and lower the pitch of their voices; change the pace of their movements (gradually speeding up or slowing down); imitate the infant's actions; bring their faces close to the baby's and then pull back; tickle, pat, poke, lift, rock, stroke, and do many other simple things. (You may well recognize some of these behaviors as your own natural reaction to a baby—sometimes surprising yourself and amusing those around you!) Infants' responses complement the actions of adults: they may stare at their partners or look away, vocalize, widen their eyes, smile, move their heads forward or back, or turn aside. (See Children Up Close, pages 226–227.)

Cross-Cultural Variation

It appears that episodes of face-to-face play are a universal feature of the early interaction between caregivers and infants. However, the frequency and duration of these episodes, as well as the goals of the adults who initiate them, differ in different cultures. Here are the results of three studies contrasting mother-infant play:

- North American mothers often direct their infants' attention to a nearby toy, object, or event, while Japanese mothers typically focus on establishing mutual intimacy by maintaining eye contact with their infants as well as kissing, hugging, and such (Bornstein et al., 1992).
- Whereas mothers in an urban New England city employed social overtures that stimulated and excited their babies (such as tickling the baby), mothers from the Gusii community in rural Kenya were more soothing and quieting in their initiatives (LeVine et al., 1994).
- Among three French-speaking cultures in Quebec, Canada—Vietnamese, Haitian, and native-born Quebecois—mothers responded to their infants' active curiosity in different ways. The Vietnamese mothers tended to guide and restrict many of their infants' exploratory activities, limiting the infants' individual initiative. By contrast, the Haitian mothers encouraged their infants, particularly to interact socially with anyone nearby. The Quebecois mothers were also encouraging, particularly with toys—including allowing their infants to mouth objects that the Vietnamese or Haitian mothers would have immediately taken away (Sabatier, 1994).

Mothers are not the only ones who engage infants in face-to-face play. Fathers are also active partners and, as you have seen, sometimes are better playmates than mothers. In many non-Western cultures, older siblings and other adults also assume an active role in infant care and participate in social play with babies (Tronick et al., 1992; Zukow-Goldring, 1995).

Attachment

The relationship between parent and child is lifelong, and even adult children and their parents can have episodes of quick-response interaction, with mutual glances and laughter. The term "synchrony" is, however, usually reserved for the first year, when preverbal play predominates. Another term, **attachment,** is used particularly to describe the relationship between parents and slightly older infants. Attachment, according to Mary Ainsworth (1973), "may be defined as an affectional tie that one person or animal forms between himself and another specific one—a tie that binds them together in space and endures over time."

attachment   An enduring emotional connection between people that produces a desire for continual contact as well as feelings of distress during separation.

REPAIRING BROKEN BONDS

Synchrony can be observed even in the early months of an infant's life. Adults tend to modify the timing and pace of their "invitations" to play in accordance with their babies' readiness to respond, and infants modify their social and emotional expressiveness (smiling, looking, cooing) to match their caregivers' overtures. But synchrony is not necessarily common or constant. In fact, true synchrony occurs less than one-third of the time in normal adult-infant play. Gradually, however, infants and caregivers learn how to socialize smoothly and how to remedy or "repair" social awkwardness and lapses—a process that is an invaluable life lesson (Biringen et al, 1997).

Generally, repair is not difficult. The signs of dyssynchrony are obvious—the baby's averted eyes, stiffening or abrupt shifting of the body, an unhappy noise—and the alert caregiver can quickly make adjustments, allowing the infant to "recover" and return to synchrony. Depending on their temperament and maturity, of course, some infants take longer than others to recover. Because development of the central nervous system improves awareness and timing, 5-month-olds are able to lead the "dance" notably better than 3-month-olds (Lester et al., 1985). Throughout the first year, the main choreographer, of course, is the caregiver (Feldman et al., 1999).

There are two main impediments to the initiation and repair of synchrony:

- *Either* the caregiver ignores the infant's invitation to interact,
- *Or* the caregiver overstimulates a baby who wants to pause and rest (Isabella & Belsky, 1991).

If infants are repeatedly ignored, they do not try as much to respond. Offspring of depressed mothers, for example, are less likely than others to smile and vocalize, not only when interacting with their mothers but also when responding to a nondepressed adult (Field, 1995). At the other extreme, infants whose caregivers are intrusive and overstimulating are more obvious in their self-defense: they turn away or even "shut down" completely—perhaps crying inconsolably or

going to sleep. Unfortunately, some caregivers miss all the cues, as Jenny's mother did in what follows:

> Whenever a moment of mutual gaze occurred, the mother went immediately into high-gear stimulating behaviors, producing a profusion of fully displayed, high-intensity, facial and vocal . . . social behavior. Jenny invariably broke gaze rapidly. Her mother never interpreted this temporary face and gaze aversion as a cue to lower her level of behavior, nor would she let Jenny self-control the level by gaining distance. Instead she would swing her head around following Jenny's to reestablish the full-face position. Jenny again turned away, pushing her face further into the pillow to try to break all visual contact. Again, instead of holding back, the mother continued to chase Jenny. . . . She also escalated the level of her stimulation more by adding touching and tickling to the unabated flow of vocal and facial behavior. . . . Jenny closed her eyes to avoid any mutual visual contact and only reopened them after [she had moved her head to the other side]. All of these behaviors on Jenny's part were performed with a sober face or at times a grimace. [Stern, 1977]

This example clearly shows the mother's insensitivity, but an infant's personality and predispositions also affect the ease of synchrony. In particular, infants who are oversensitive to stimulation have problems with an intrusive caregiver like Jenny's mother. Fortunately, even with such a mismatch, repair is achievable. Sometimes a helpful outsider can teach the caregiver how to read the baby's signals, and sometimes the baby and caregiver begin to adjust to each other spontaneously. Jenny, for example, eventually became more able to adjust to her mother's episodes of overstimulation. Then her mother, finding Jenny more responsive, no longer felt the need to bombard her with stimulation as she had earlier. With time, Jenny and her mother established a mutually rewarding relationship.

Not every difficult relationship finds repair on its own, however. One example involves a boy who was welcomed, but

proximity-seeking behaviors Behaviors that are intended to place a person close to another person to whom he or she is attached.

contact-maintaining behaviors Behaviors that are intended to keep a person near another person to whom he or she is attached.

Not surprisingly, when people are attached to each other, they try to be near one another and they interact with each other often. Thus children show attachment through **proximity-seeking behaviors**—such as approaching, following, and climbing onto the caregiver's lap—and through **contact-maintaining behaviors**—such as clinging, resisting being put down, and using social referencing once they are moving around on their own. Parents show their attachment by keeping a watchful eye, even when safety does not require it, and by responding affectionately and sensitively to vocalizations, perhaps somewhat ignored, in infancy. Here is his father's description of the situation:

> Reuben is Hebrew for "look, a boy," which is just how we felt when Jacob was born. We were convinced that we were set. We had surpassed our quota of 2.6 children and were ready to engage parental auto-pilot. I had just begun a prestigious job and was working 10–11 hours a day. The children would be fine. We hired a nanny to watch Jacob during the day.
>
> As each of Jacob's early milestones passed we felt that we had taken another step toward our goal of having three normal children. We were on our way to the perfect American family. Yet, somewhere back in our minds we had some doubts. Jacob seemed different than the girls. He had some unusual attributes. There were times when we would be holding him and he would arch his back and scream so loud that it was painful for us. [Jacob's Father, 1997]

Jacob was unable to relate to his parents (or to anyone else) for the first two years of his life, although his parents were not really aware of the problem. They already had two older daughters, so they noticed that something was odd, but they told themselves "boys are different," and they blamed his inability to talk on a nanny who did not speak English well. His father explains:

> Jacob had become increasingly isolated [by age 2]. I'm not a psychologist, but I believe that he just stopped trying. It was too hard, perhaps too scary. He couldn't figure out what was expected of him. The world had become too confusing, and so he withdrew from it. He would seek out the comfort of quiet, dark places and sit by himself. He would lose himself in the bright colorful images of cartoons and animated movies. [Jacob's Father, 1997]

When Jacob was finally diagnosed with a "pervasive development disorder" at age 3, his parents felt despair and were advised to consider residential placement. Then, luckily, they found a psychologist who taught them about "floor time," 4 hours a day when the parents were supposed to get on their son's level and do anything to interact with the child, imitating him, acting as if they were part of the game, putting their faces and bodies in front of his, creating synchrony even though Jacob did nothing to initiate it. The father continues:

> We rebuilt Jacob's connection to us and to the world—but on his terms. We were drilled to always follow his lead, to always build on his initiative. In a sense, we could only ask Jacob to join our world if we were willing to enter his. . . . He would drop rocks and we would catch them. He would want to put pennies in a bank and we would block the slot. He would want to run in a circle and we would get in his way. I remember a cold fall day when I was putting lime on our lawn. He dipped his hand in the powder and let it slip through his fingers. He loved the way it felt. I took the lawn spreader and ran to the other part of our yard. He ran after me. I let him have one dip and ran across the yard again. He dipped, I ran, he dipped, I ran. We did this until I could no longer move my arms. [Jacob's Father, 1997]

Jacob's case is obviously extreme, but many infants and parents have difficulty establishing synchronistic interaction. From the perspective of early psychosocial development, nothing could be more important.

> In Jacob's case it worked. He said his first word at age 3, and by age 5 [as his father notes], . . . he speaks for days at a time. He talks from the moment he wakes up to the moment he falls asleep, as if he is making up for lost time. He wants to know everything. "How does a live chicken become an eating chicken? Why are microbes so small? Why do policemen wear badges? Why are dinosaurs extinct? What is French? (A question I often ask myself.) Why do ghosts glow in the dark?" He is not satisfied with answers that do not ring true or that do not satisfy his standards of clarity. He will keep on asking until he gets it. Rebecca and I have become expert definition providers. Just last week, we were faced with the ultimate challenge: "Dad," he asked: "Is God real or not?" And then, just to make it a bit more challenging, he added: "How do miracles happen?" [Jacob's Father, 1997]

expressions, and gestures. Many parents enjoy tiptoeing to the crib to gaze at the sleeping infant, and many like to smooth the toddler's hair or pat a hand or a cheek—examples of proximity seeking and contact maintaining, respectively. Attachment not only deepens the parent-child relationship but, over our long evolutionary history, may also have contributed to human survival by keeping infants near their caregivers and keeping caregivers vigilant.

John Bowlby, a psychologist influenced by ethology (the study of animal behavior) as well as psychoanalytic theory, was the first researcher to

❶ *Answer to Observational Quiz (from page 225):* *The positioning of the mouths and lips, the half-closed eyes, and the tilt of the heads of both father and son.*

describe attachment (Bretherton, 1995). From observations of primates, Bowlby and many others recognized that infant monkeys, chimpanzees, and baboons have a need for physical contact (as in the grooming and touching that mother monkeys do with their offspring) which balances their need for independence (the curiosity and exploration that are familiar to readers of the Curious George books). Bowlby's work influenced Mary Ainsworth, the researcher who developed a way to measure attachment in humans.

Measuring Attachment

Ainsworth found, as many other scientists have, that universal human characteristics are most easily observed in a place where one's usual cultural blindness is removed. She therefore went to Central Africa to observe mothers and infants in a culture different from her own. There she found that, while the specifics of mother-infant interaction were different from those in England or the United States (for example, there was more physical contact but no kissing), the bonds of affection were still visible in various proximity-seeking and contact-maintaining behaviors (Ainsworth, 1967). Ainsworth discovered that virtually all normal infants develop special attachments to the people who care for them and that some infants are much more secure in those attachments than others—a fact later confirmed by hundreds of other researchers (Bretherton, 1992; Colin, 1996).

secure attachment A caregiver-infant relationship from which the infant derives enough comfort and confidence to begin exploration of the environment on his or her own.

A **secure attachment** is one in which an infant derives comfort and confidence from a caregiver, as evidenced first by the infant's attempts to be close to the caregiver and then, equally important, by the infant's readiness to explore the environment. In such a relationship the caregiver acts as a *secure base for exploration,* from which the child is willing to venture forth. The child might, for example, scramble down from the caregiver's lap to play with a toy but periodically look back, vocalize a few syllables, or return for a hug. This is a step beyond social referencing; it is reestablishing contact.

insecure attachment A caregiver-infant relationship characterized by the child's overdependence on or lack of interest in the caregiver and by a lack of confidence on the part of the child.

By contrast, **insecure attachment** is characterized by an infant's fear, anxiety, anger, or seeming indifference toward a caregiver. Compared with the securely attached infant, the insecurely attached child has much less confidence, perhaps being unwilling to let go of the caregiver's arms or perhaps playing aimlessly without trying to maintain contact with the caregiver.

Strange Situation An experimental condition devised by Mary Ainsworth to assess an infant's attachment to a caregiver. The infant's behavior is observed in an unfamiliar room while the caregiver (usually the mother) and a stranger move in and out of the room.

Ainsworth developed a classic laboratory procedure, called the **Strange Situation,** to measure attachment. The Strange Situation is designed to evoke an infant's reactions to the caregiver (usually the mother) under somewhat stressful conditions. In a well-equipped playroom, the subject infant is closely observed in eight 3-minute-long episodes, in each of which the infant is either with the caregiver, with a stranger, with both, or alone. The first episode has caregiver and child together, and then each successive planned segment begins when one or the other of the two adults (stranger or caregiver) enters or leaves the playroom.

The infant's reactions to the eight episodes indicate motivation to be near the caregiver (proximity and contact) and whether the caregiver's presence is a secure base (confidence to venture forth). The key observational aspects of the Strange Situation are:

1. *Exploration of the toys.* A securely attached toddler plays happily when the caregiver is present.
2. *Reaction to the caregiver's departure.* A secure attached toddler shows some sign that the caregiver is missed—a loud cry, or perhaps only a pause and a woeful look.

The Attachment Experiment In this episode of the Strange Situation, Brian shows every sign of secure attachment. *(a)* He explores the playroom happily when his mother is present; *(b)* he cries when she leaves; and *(c)* he is readily comforted when she returns.

(a)

(b)

(c)

3. *Reaction to the caregiver's return.* A securely attached toddler exhibits a welcoming response when the caregiver returns to the room after leaving—especially when this occurs for a second time.

Almost two-thirds of all normal infants tested in the Strange Situation demonstrate secure attachment. The mother's presence in the playroom is enough to give them courage to explore the room and investigate the toys; her departure may cause some distress (usually expressed through verbal protest and a pause in playing); and her return is a signal to reestablish positive social contact (with a smile or by climbing into the mother's arms) and then resume playing. This balanced reaction—concerned about the mother's departure but not overwhelmed by it—is called type-B attachment.

The remaining one-third of infants show one of three types of insecure attachment (see Table 7.1 on page 230). Some are *insecure-avoidant:* they engage in little interaction with the mother; they may show no apparent distress when she leaves; they may be overly friendly to the stranger; and on the mother's return, they avoid reestablishing contact, sometimes even turning their backs. Others are anxious and *insecure-resistant:* they cling nervously to the mother even before her initial departure from the playroom, are unwilling to explore the playroom, and are frightened by the appearance of a stranger; they cry loudly each time the mother leaves; and they refuse to be comforted when she returns, perhaps continuing to sob angrily even when they are back in her arms. Others are *insecure-disorganized,* or *disoriented and ambivalent:* they show an inconsistent mixture of behavior toward the mother, such as avoiding her just after seeking to be close to her. This last group is the most worrisome. While the avoidant and resistant infants have at least developed a strategy to deal with a neglectful or overly intrusive parent, the disorganized infants are unable to do so and therefore are overwhelmed, often unable to cope later on with peers, school, and many other situations (Crittenden, 1995). The three kinds of insecure attachment are referred to as types A, C, and D: avoidant, clingy, and disorganized.

Attachment and Context

Ainsworth's Strange Situation has been used in thousands of studies, and her seminal concepts regarding attachment have been the basis for additional thousands of studies. From them we have learned that attachment is powerfully affected by the quality of care in early infancy, as well as by the caregiver's past experiences and the infant's temperament (Ainsworth, 1993; Belsky & Cassidy, 1995; DeWolff & van Ijzendoorn, 1997; Isabella, 1993). Among the caregiving features that have been shown to increase the quality of attachment are:

■ General sensitivity to the infant's needs
■ Responsiveness to the infant's specific signals
■ Infant-caregiver play that actively encourages the child's growth and development

❓ **Especially for Social Workers:** Suppose you are sent to investigate an accusation of child maltreatment of a 1-year-old. What will you look for?

table **7.1**	**Patterns of Attachment in Infancy**
Type of Attachment	**Characteristics of Infant**
Secure (type B)	Uses caregiver as a "secure base," explores freely when the caregiver is available, may or may not be distressed at separation but greets caregiver positively on reunion, seeks contact if distressed, settles down, returns to exploration. Includes 55 to 65% of infant population.
Insecure-avoidant (type A)	Appears minimally interested in caregiver, explores busily, shows minimal distress at separation, ignores or avoids caregiver on reunion. Includes 15 to 25% of infant population.
Insecure-resistant (type C)	Does minimal exploration, is preoccupied with caregiver, has difficulty settling down, both seeks and resists contact on reunion, may be angry or very passive. Includes 10 to 15% of infant population.
Insecure-disorganized (disoriented and ambivalent) (type D)	Exhibits disorganized and/or disoriented behavior in the caregiver's presence (e.g., approaches with head averted, engages in trancelike freezing, adopts anomalous postures). Infants placed in this category are also "forced" into the best fit of the preceding categories. Includes 10 to 20% of infant population.
Other (cannot classify)	Some children may not fit any of the four patterns. This is rare, except in combination with insecure-disorganized classification.

Source: Adapted from Goldberg et al., 1995.

Not surprisingly, greater synchrony in early interactions between a mother and a young infant tends to produce more secure attachment between mother and toddler.

Attachment is also influenced by the broader family context, including the extent and quality of the father's involvement in the child's care and the nature of the marital relationship, and by the overall social context (Belsky, 1996; Colin, 1996; van Ijzendoorn & DeWolff, 1997). Attachment can be affected by any change in family circumstances—such as a parent losing his or her job—that alters established patterns of family interaction. Partly for this reason, changes in attachment status are not uncommon during toddlerhood. Further, an infant can be attached to one caregiver but not another—to the father or grandmother but not the mother, for instance. Or the infant can be attached, quite securely, to two or three caregivers or to none.

The infant's temperament is also part of the story, again within the family context. As you saw earlier, the *goodness of fit* between infant temperament and parenting style is a key developmental factor. This goodness of fit may also be a key influence on the type of attachment—secure or insecure—that develops (Belsky, 1997; Mangelsdorf et al., 1990).

Finally, the macrosystem of the general cultural context can affect attachment. In cross-cultural comparisons using the Strange Situation, for example, Japanese and Israeli children show a higher rate of insecure-resistant (type-C) attachment than American infants do. Infants from Germany show higher rates of insecure-avoidant (type-A) attachment.

In spite of such differences, extensive analysis of cross-cultural data on attachment reveals that the majority of infants worldwide are securely attached (van Ijzendoorn & Kroonenberg, 1988). Most infants in most cultures consider their mothers' presence a reassuring sign that it is safe to explore the environment, and most infants come back to their mothers for comfort under stress (Sagi et al., 1991). Most infants also exhibit secure attachment to other caregivers—fathers, siblings, day-care providers—although this varies from culture to culture, with some cultures much less mother-focused than others.

No One Cares This Romanian boy had been abandoned by both parents and put in an orphanage, developed under the Ceausescu regime, where personal attention, any sort of attachment, and toys were absent. This photo was taken in 1990, shortly after the rest of the world became aware of these conditions and sent clothes and toys to the orphanages (which explains the doll's head). If he is still alive, this boy is now an adolescent, and he probably still shows many signs of his early deprivation.

❶ **Response for Social Workers (from page 229):** Of course, you will look for injuries and malnutrition, but even more important might be the quality of attachment between parent and child. If the toddler plays happily but tries to stay in contact, neither clinging to nor avoiding the parent, the relationship is likely okay. If not, and if no other mistreatment is obvious, weekly visits designed to teach caregiver responsiveness might be in order.

The Importance of Attachment

An infant's attachment pattern may be a preview of the child's social and personality development in the years to come. Securely attached infants tend to become children who interact with teachers in friendly and appropriate ways, who seek help when needed, and who are competent in a wide array of social and cognitive skills (Belsky & Cassidy, 1995; Fagot, 1997; Turner, 1993). By contrast, insecure infants are more likely to display problems later on. One study of 4-year-olds who had been rated insecurely attached as infants found that the boys tended to be aggressive and the girls to be overly dependent (Turner, 1991).

Does this mean that whether attachment is secure or insecure in infancy *determines* whether the child will grow up to be sociable or aggressive, self-directed or dependent, curious or withdrawing? Probably not. However, attachment often indicates the nature of the relationship between child and caregiver, and that usually continues through childhood (Crittenden, 1995). A sensitive caregiver who fosters secure attachment is likely to maintain this approach as the child matures, encouraging the development of sociability, curiosity, and independence. And, unfortunately, insensitive care that contributes to insecure attachment is also likely to be maintained, pushing the child toward caution, aggressiveness, or dependence.

Remember, however, that attachment relationships sometimes change. As we noted, shifts in family circumstances (a divorce, a new job, better day care, a new baby) often alter patterns of family interaction and, thus, of attachment. And, as attachment patterns change, so do their long-term effects. Thus, a child who is insecurely attached at age 1 might become securely attached by age 2, and this considerably brightens any long-term predictions of personality.

Family circumstances are not the only reason for changes in pattern. As children mature, they face new developmental challenges and experience new social settings, any of which may modify the long-term effects of early attachment patterns. Thus, although insecure-resistant attachment may lead a young child to approach relationships skeptically and cautiously, later secure relationships (perhaps with another relative or a teacher) may encourage trust and confidence. The opposite can also happen: a child who seemed securely attached at age 1 year can edge toward avoidance, becoming aggressive and detached by age 3.

The idea that early relationships do not inevitably determine later social relationships is important; it provides a basis for helpful intervention. In one study with Spanish-speaking immigrant families in the United States, for example, three groups of 1-year-olds were compared: a securely attached group, an insecurely attached control group, and an insecurely attached experimental group. The mothers of the experimental-group infants were visited weekly at home by an empathic bilingual and bicultural adviser. Within a year, these mothers and infants were relating to each other almost as well as the mothers and group of infants who were originally securely attached—and far better than the control-group infants and their mothers—as indicated by infant anger, maternal responsiveness, and similar measures (Lieberman et al., 1991).

Another study involved 100 Dutch infants who were at risk of insecure attachment because of their own difficult temperaments and their mothers' stressful low-income status. Half of them received three home visits designed to foster synchrony—advisers taught the mothers when and how to play with, feed, and soothe their babies. Four months later, in the Strange Situation, 72 percent of these infants qualified as securely attached, compared to only 32 percent of the remaining 50 infants (the control group), who had had no such home visits (Van den Boom, 1995). Happy outcomes like these tell us that although early stresses and temperament may provide a fragile foundation for later growth, that foundation can usually be strengthened (see the Research Report, pages 232–233).

THE PARENTS' SIDE OF ATTACHMENT

Each of us has a long history of attachment experiences with our parents, best friends, and romantic partners. As you know from your own experience, every new relationship can inspire trust or, instead, anxiety and thereby influence expectations about future attachments. Recently, researchers have begun to see whether the security or insecurity of a parent's past relationships affects attachment with the next generation.

To explore the parents' side of attachment, Mary Main and her colleagues created the Adult Attachment Interview (AAI), an hour-long series of questions about childhood attachment experiences, perceptions of early trust and security, and current relationships with parents and adult partners (Main, 1995). On the basis of the responses, adults are classified into four categories:

■ *Autonomous.* Autonomous adults value close relationships and regard them as influential. However, they are not overwhelmed by emotions concerning their childhood attachments; they can discuss them with some objectivity, including negative as well as positive aspects.
■ *Dismissing.* Dismissing adults tend to devalue the importance and influence of their attachment relationships. Sometimes they idealize their early relationships with their parents without being able to provide specific examples to support their view.
■ *Preoccupied.* Preoccupied adults are very involved with their childhood experiences. They are unable to discuss early attachment relationships objectively, and they often show considerable emotion when asked about their relationships with their parents.
■ *Unresolved.* Unresolved adults have not yet reconciled their past attachments with their current ones. They are still trying to understand parental rejection, death, or other early experiences.

Researchers have discovered that mothers' AAI ratings closely parallel the kinds of attachment their children form with them (Crowell et al., 1996; Fonagy et al., 1995; Zeanah et al., 1993). Autonomous mothers tend to have securely attached infants; dismissing mothers tend to have insecure-avoidant babies; and preoccupied mothers tend to have insecure-resistant infants. (The parallel is less clear for unresolved mothers, partly because "unresolved" is often a transitional status for adults.)

These findings were extended by researchers who administered the AAI first to pregnant women and then to their mothers. About a year after the women gave birth, the researchers used the Strange Situation with the toddlers (Benoit & Parker, 1994). As you can see from the accompanying figure, attachment patterns tended to be passed down

Three Generations of Smiling The woman in the middle is the mother, watching happily as her mother plays with 1-year-old Jonathon. Not every adult child is as fortunate as this mother; some who had insecure attachments may avoid contact with their mothers as much as possible throughout their lives or may resist every opportunity to break free and become caregivers for their own children.

from one generation to the next, with 64 percent of the families having the exact same status in all three generations.

In tracing the impact of early experiences on adult relationships, researchers have found that especially when childhood attachments were insecure and when current life is stressful, a parent's ability to be reflective is crucial. If adults realize that their parents may have intended one thing but had done another, and if they acknowledge that ambivalence, complexity, and change permeate human relationships, they are much more likely to develop secure relationships with their own children. Indeed, one group of researchers found that, even under stressful conditions, highly reflective mothers had securely attached infants but mothers who were unable to reflect on past experiences almost always had insecurely attached infants (one such woman said, "My mother loved all us children; I don't remember any more") (Fonagy et al., 1995).

Mary Main, the researcher who devised the AAI, has spent years documenting the enduring effects of early insecure attachments. She has concluded that "the most striking results of these studies is that, even when the early history is unfavorable, individuals who are coherent, consistent, and plausible have infants whose response to them in the Strange Situation is judged secure" (Main, 1995).

As you may remember from Chapters 1 and 2, scientists look for the connections between theory and observation and simultaneously develop alternative hypotheses for the research results that are found. The conclusion of this re-

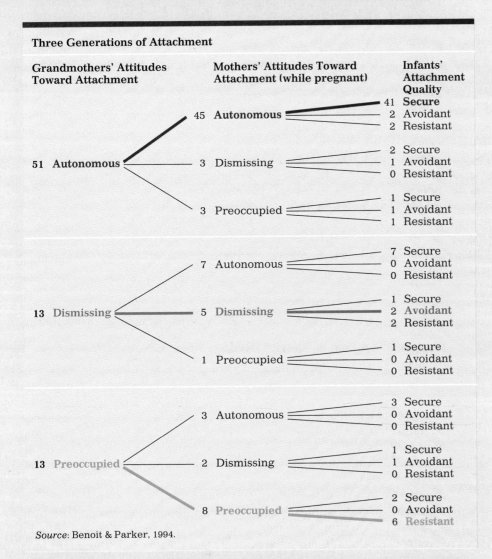

Three Generations of Attachment

Grandmothers' Attitudes Toward Attachment	Mothers' Attitudes Toward Attachment (while pregnant)	Infants' Attachment Quality	
51 Autonomous	45 Autonomous	41	Secure
		2	Avoidant
		2	Resistant
	3 Dismissing	2	Secure
		1	Avoidant
		0	Resistant
	3 Preoccupied	1	Secure
		1	Avoidant
		1	Resistant
13 Dismissing	7 Autonomous	7	Secure
		0	Avoidant
		0	Resistant
	5 Dismissing	1	Secure
		2	Avoidant
		2	Resistant
	1 Preoccupied	1	Secure
		0	Avoidant
		0	Resistant
13 Preoccupied	3 Autonomous	3	Secure
		0	Avoidant
		0	Resistant
	2 Dismissing	1	Secure
		1	Avoidant
		0	Resistant
	8 Preoccupied	2	Secure
		0	Avoidant
		6	Resistant

Source: Benoit & Parker, 1994.

Figure 7.1 Attitudes and Attachment. Using the Adult Attachment Interview, researchers rated the attachment attitudes of pregnant women and those of their mothers. The ratings comprised three categories: autonomous (valuing attachment objectively), dismissing (tending to devalue attachment), and preoccupied (emotional about attachment). More than a year later, blind observers (researchers who know nothing of the subjects' previous ratings) rated the attachment quality of the formerly pregnant women and their infants by using the Strange Situation. The results show that attachment attitudes tend to be transmitted intergenerationally (e.g., of the 51 autonomous grandmothers, 45 had autonomous daughters). Further, the attitudes of the mothers seem to be reflected in the quality of their infants' attachment (e.g., of the 55 autonomous mothers, 51 had securely attached infants).

search—that early mother-child relationships have long-term effects that can be influenced by adult insights—tends to confirm the central tenets of psychoanalytic and cognitive theories: First, childhood experiences, even those of early infancy, affect adult attitudes and behavior, and, second, understanding those experiences (as might happen in therapy) can overcome some of the damage that may have occurred. However, such conclusions are controversial, especially for those who believe that childhood experiences are much less powerful than psychoanalytic theorists believed. Let us raise several alternative explanations for the results reported by this research.

It may be that adults who value attachment and can reflect objectively on their own experiences (i.e., autonomous adults) are naturally more sensitive to their offspring and therefore inspire secure attachment as a result. This explanation suggests that it is not past attachment experiences that are passed down over the years but, rather, current attitudes that are crucial. Or perhaps inherited temperament predis-

poses individuals to reciprocate certain attachment patterns, so what seems like a generational legacy of learned mother-infant patterns is actually a genetic transmission. Or it may be that parents' current attachment with their own children affects their memories of first attachments, and thus that the AAI is a snapshot of the present, disguised as a mirror of the past. Or, finally, it may be that some cultural contexts encourage attachments and others do not, so what appears to be a correlation within families is actually a cultural influence that each generation of a family reflects (Grossmann, 1995).

Whatever the explanation for the connections that are found, it does seem useful for each of us to look back to our attachments with our early caregivers and try to understand how those attachments might influence our current actions and attitudes with partners, parents, and children. Indeed, if Ainsworth is correct and attachment provides a secure base for exploration, our approach to learning, to study, and to intellectual inquiry may be the result of our playfulness at our mothers' knees!

Optimal Infant Care

For many children today, day-care providers have become important care-givers. (By *day care* we mean nonmaternal care during the daytime hours, typically while the mother is working at a part-time or full-time job). Until recently, developmentalists in the United States were engaged in a heated debate over the possible detrimental effects of day care, especially during the first year of infancy. The first to sound the alarm was Jay Belsky, who reported that infants who experience early and extended day care are 10 percent more likely than other infants to avoid and ignore their mothers in the Strange Situation. On that basis, he warned that more than 20 hours of nonmaternal care per week in the first year of life represents a "risk factor" for insecure attachment with parents (Belsky, 1986).

Developmentalists on the opposing side rejected this warning on several grounds. First, they called attention to a number of weaknesses in the research, including a failure to take into account the parents' early relationship with the child at home. Second, they emphasized the infants' past experiences. If attachment is measured by the Strange Situation, day-care infants may seem to be insecure merely because they are less upset by separation from or reunion with their mothers. Finally, Belsky's critics asserted that if any attachment problems at all are associated with extended day care, the crucial variable is the *quality* of caregiving, not the fact of day care (Clarke-Stewart, 1989; Fox & Fein, 1990; Lamb & Sternberg, 1990; Thompson, 1997).

Nowadays most researchers, including Belsky, agree that when infant day care is "of high quality, there should be little reason to anticipate negative developmental outcomes" (Belsky, 1990). In fact, there is strong evidence that, for some children, high-quality day care is more beneficial to the development of cognitive and social skills than is exclusive home care (Aureli & Colecchia, 1996; National Institute of Child Health and Development, 1997; Roggman et al., 1994).

Trained caregivers in well-designed settings foster healthy development by means of toys, games, and social stimulation that few homes can surpass. When the mother is severely depressed, the home is conflict-filled, or the family is neglectful, day care not only is a lifesaver for the infant but also may help repair a family context that is destructive. Even without these special circumstances, high-quality day care offers something that no home provides—a wide assortment of potential playmates and friends.

What, then, are the signs of "high-quality" day care that parents should look for? Researchers have identified four factors that seem essential:

- *Adequate attention to each infant.* This means a low caregiver-to-infant ratio and a small group of infants. The ideal situation might be two reliable caregivers for a group of five infants.

- *Encouragement of sensorimotor exploration and language development.* Infants should be provided with a variety of easily manipulated toys and should have a great deal of language exposure through games, songs, and conversation.

- *Attention to health and safety.* Cleanliness routines (such as hand washing before meals), accident prevention (such as the absence of small objects that could be swallowed), and safe areas for exploration (such as a clean, soft-surfaced area for crawling and climbing) are all good signs.

- *Well-trained and professional caregivers.* Ideally, every caregiver should have a degree and certification in early-childhood education and should have worked in this field for several years. Turnover should be low, morale high, enthusiasm evident. Indeed, if the caregivers are knowledgeable and committed, the first three items on this list will follow automatically.

Who Should Pay for Day Care?

Beyond the specifics that a particular parent might seek in a day-care setting, however, are broader public-policy issues. In some nations, including the United States, parents must find and finance infant care on their own. That typically results in a patchwork arrangement of baby-sitters, relatives, and neighbors—some excellent, some dangerous, many mediocre, and almost all untrained, underpaid, and unregulated. Few working mothers in the United States can find, much less afford, a small day-care setting with two college-educated caregivers for every group of five babies.

How bad is poor-quality care? The answer, of course, depends on exactly how inadequate the supervision is (Is it dangerous?); how unstimulating the cognitive setting is (Do the babies play?); and, if intellectual stimulation is sparse, how many hours per day the infant is in day care. A large-scale study of infant day care throughout the United States found that even mediocre care was generally harmless. Infants were likely to become insecurely attached only if their own mothers were insensitive, if the day-care quality was poor, *and* if they were in day care more than 20 hours per week. Even under these circumstances, girls were less likely to have problems than boys, and steady care was better than care from a patchwork of caregivers (National Institute of Child Health and Development, 1997). However, given the potential benefit of quality infant care, to judge some care as simply harmless is faint praise indeed.

Developmentalists contend that any nation committed to the future of its youngest citizens must develop high-quality care, especially for the children of parents who are too young, too stressed, or too unaware to provide intellectual stimulation and responsive caregiving. As Sandra Scarr, past president of the Society for Research in Child Development, writes:

> For children from middle- and upper-income families—especially stable, two-parent families in nondangerous neighborhoods—day care merely

Infant Day Care In Grenoble, France, infant day care is subsidized by the government. Consequently, many children are in day-care centers like this one.

❷ *Observational Quiz (see answer page 236): If you were grading this center on quality of care, what grade would you give it, and why?*

❶ *Answer to Observational Quiz (from page 235):* *This clearly is not an F or an A. Perhaps a C, for average. Most signs indicate a fairly good setting, in that the infants all seem active, the caregivers are attentive, the toys are appropriate, children's artwork is displayed, and the setting seems clean. On the other hand, eight 1-year-olds may be a handful for two adults, and the toys and the activities seem scattered. Is there a curriculum or just individual play? Obviously a more accurate rating would require more than a snapshot, with attention given to peer interactions and to the relationship between each caregiver and each child.*

supplements what parents can offer. For children from disturbed and seriously disadvantaged families—especially unstable, one-parent families who live in dangerous neighborhoods—good day care is the most powerful, positive intervention we now have. . . . Most low-income, working families cannot afford to buy decent child care, not to mention good quality care. Federally funded child care assistance is insufficient to meet even present needs, which will expand with welfare reform. Do we in the United States have the political will to provide quality care for poor children? [Scarr, 1996]

This final question will become more urgent as state and federal welfare reforms result in many more infants needing care outside the home. Since high-quality day care reduces the incidence of many major hazards—from accidental injury to academic failure—it is imperative that the answer to Scarr's question be a resounding *yes.*

Another theme emerges from this and the other two chapters on early infancy, however. Tremendous growth—physical, cognitive, linguistic, emotional, and social—occurs in the first 2 years of life. That growth may be hampered, guided, or encouraged by both the immediate family and the cultural context. The questions "Is maternal care, paternal care, or day care best for infants?" and "Who should pay for infant care?" are the wrong questions. Every infant should experience high-quality care from all three sources, as an expression of commitment to infants from parents and from the entire community. Sadly, some infants have only one good caregiver or even none. The proper question is "How can excellent maternal care, paternal care, and day care be made available to every infant?" Chapters 5, 6, and 7 describe many signs of excellent care, in everything from early eye-hand coordination to responsive vocalization, as detailed by thousands of researchers. The task for all of us, scientists and practitioners alike, is to make sure that somehow, somewhere, somebody provides every infant with such care.

SUMMARY

EARLY EMOTIONS

1. From birth onward infants express distress, sadness, and contentment. Pleasure is expressed in a first social smile at about 6 weeks and the first laughter at about 3 months.

2. Fear also begins early, and stranger wariness and other clear signs of fear are evident at about 6 months, when cognitive advances allow differentiation between the familiar and the unexpected. Typically, fearful behavior peaks at about 14 months.

3. Anger builds in the first 2 years, particularly in response to frustration. All the emotions become more selective and individualized in their expression, and all are influenced by culture.

EMOTIONS AS A SOCIAL WINDOW

4. The social context teaches infants when and how to express their emotions. Social referencing—to fathers as well as mothers—begins at about 8 months.

5. Self-awareness develops in the second year of life and allows a new set of emotions, including pride, embarrassment,

and jealousy. At this time the infant becomes less predictable and less compliant—and more interesting as well.

THE ORIGINS OF PERSONALITY

6. Learning theorists believe that personality is the product of early reinforcement and punishment that mold the infant traits. Young children also observe their parents' personality traits and try to copy them, according to social learning theory.

7. Freud believed that an infant's early experiences with feeding and toilet training could set certain lifelong personality traits. This is an influential hypothesis, but one that has not been proved by research. Psychoanalytic theory also emphasized the central role of the mother, the child's first and most enduring love object.

8. Erikson believed that an infant's early experiences, first in trusting that basic needs will be met and then in developing self-expression (autonomy), create personality traits. He also felt that a person can, later in life, resolve developmental crises that appear during these early stages.

9. Personality is often thought to be an expression of temperament, which is a set of inborn tendencies. Researchers who stress temperament contend that personality is not primarily the product of early mothering, as Freud and others believed. Instead, the crucial factor is the fit between the social context (especially the family setting) and the innate tendencies.

INTERACTION AGAIN

10. The interaction between caregiver and child, or, more specifically, between the social context and the innate temperament of the young infant, is crucial to the shaping of personality. Ideally, in the early months this interaction becomes synchrony, a coordinated series of actions and reactions between infant and caregiver.

11. The attachment between caregiver and infant can be secure or insecure, depending on many factors, including the responsiveness of parents to the child. If an infant is securely attached, he or she will be willing to explore and play in the caregiver's presence, will react to the caregiver's absence, and will welcome the caregiver's return.

12. Attachment patterns in infancy can change as circumstances change. However, many psychologists believe that habits and attitudes of early social relationships, including those formed from infant attachment, influence development lifelong.

13. The hypothesis that mothers, and only mothers, provide the best care in the first 2 years of life has been disproved by research on infant day care and care by fathers. However, research still finds that quality care, including responsive interaction between at least one caregiver and the individual infant, is important for later intellectual, emotional, and social development.

KEY QUESTIONS

1. What is the first notable emotion of a newborn, and how does that emotion benefit the newborn?

2. How do emotions develop (change) over the first 2 years of life?

3. What does an infant get from social referencing—both when the infant engages in it (at, say, 8 months of age and older) and later in life?

4. What are some consequences of the toddler's developing sense of self?

5. What are the similarities and differences between mother-infant and father-infant interactions?

6. In the classical view, who and what determine personality?

7. What is temperament, and how is it related to personality?

8. Describe and contrast the three most common temperamental patterns in infancy.

9. What temperamental factors tend to change over time, and how much change occurs?

10. How does synchrony help in the development of the infant?

11. What are the four main types of attachment?

12. How does early attachment affect later psychosocial growth?

13. *In Your Experience* How do infants under age 2 react to you? What is it about your actions, the infant's age and cognitive development, and the parents' presence that affect these reactions?

KEY TERMS

social smile (208)
stranger wariness (209)
separation anxiety (209)
social referencing (210)
self-awareness (214)
personality (216)
oral stage (217)
anal stage (217)
trust versus mistrust (218)
autonomy versus shame
  and doubt (218)
temperament (219)

big five (221)
goodness of fit (222)
synchrony (224)
attachment (225)
proximity-seeking
  behaviors (226)
contact-maintaining
  behaviors (226)
secure attachment (228)
insecure attachment (228)
Strange Situation (228)

CRITICAL THINKING EXERCISE

by Richard O. Straub

Take your study of Chapter 7 a step further by working this scientific reasoning exercise.

A recent study revealed that temperamental style in early childhood might be linked to adjustment problems during adolescence. The study involved a cohort of 1,037 children born between April 1, 1972, and March 31, 1973, in Dunedin, New Zealand (Caspi et al., 1997).

At ages 3, 5, 7, and 9 years, the behavior of each child was rated in terms of 22 aspects of temperament. To assess later behavior problems, teachers and parents rated the children at ages 9, 11, 13, and 15 on two widely used behavior-problem checklists. These checklists include measures of anxiety/withdrawal, which represents feelings of inferiority and failure; attention problems, which reflect difficulty in concentration skills; conduct disorder, which reflects aggressiveness and alienation; and socialized delinquency, which reflects norm-violating tendencies.

Among both boys and girls, there was a significant positive correlation between lack of control at ages 3 and 5 and teacher and parent reports of antisocial behavior and conduct disorder at ages 9 and 11. In addition, boys and girls who were rated as lacking in control in early childhood were less likely than others to be rated as mature and confident in adolescence.

One possible explanation the researchers offer for these intriguing results is that certain temperamental characteristics in young children are actually mild, early manifestations of more extreme behavior disorders. Whatever the correct explanation, the results of this study suggest that early temperament may be a predictor of behavior problems during adolescence.

1. What type of research design was used in this study (e.g., cross-sectional, longitudinal, experimental, correlational, naturalistic observational)? Is the design appropriate?

2. Given the results of this study, why can't the researchers say definitely that there is a causal connection between behavior disorders and temperament?

3. Devise an alternative explanation for the results of this study.

Check your answers by comparing them to the sample answers in Appendix B.

BIOSOCIAL

Body, Brain, and Nervous System

Over the first 2 years, the body quadruples in weight and the brain triples in weight. Connections between brain cells grow into increasingly dense and complex neural networks of dendrites and axons. As neurons become coated with an insulating layer of myelin, they send messages faster and more efficiently. The infant's experiences are essential in "fine-tuning" the brain's ability to respond to stimulation.

Motor Abilities

Brain maturation allows the development of motor skills from reflexes to coordinated voluntary actions, including grasping and walking. At birth, the infant's senses of smell and hearing are quite acute; although vision at first is sharp only for objects that are about 10 inches away, visual acuity approaches 20/20 by age 1 year.

Health

The health of the infant depends on nutrition (ideally, breast milk), immunization, and parental practices. Survival rates are much higher today than they were even a few decades ago.

COGNITIVE

Perceptual Skills

The infant's senses are linked by both intermodal and cross-modal perception, allowing information to be transferred among senses. The infant is most interested in affordances, that is, what various experiences and events offer to the infant. Movement and personal sensory experiences contribute to the perception of affordances.

Cognitive Skills

The infant's active curiosity and inborn abilities interact with various experiences to develop early categories, such as object size, shape, texture, and even number, as well as an understanding of object permanence. Memory capacity, while fragile, grows during the first years. The infant progresses from knowing his or her world through immediate sensorimotor experiences to being able to "experiment" on that world through the use of mental images.

Language

Babies' cries are their first communication; they then progress through cooing and babbling. Interaction with adults through "baby talk" teaches them the surface structure of language. By age 1, an infant can usually speak a word or two, and by age 2 is talking in short sentences.

PSYCHOSOCIAL

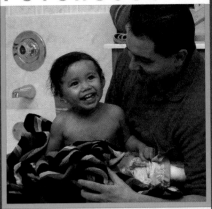

Emotions and Personality Development

Emotions change from quite basic reactions to complex, self-conscious responses. Infants become increasingly independent, a transition explained by Freud in terms of the oral and anal stages, by Erikson in terms of the crises of trust versus mistrust and autonomy versus shame and doubt. While these theories emphasize the parents' role, research finds that much of basic temperament—and therefore personality—is inborn and apparent lifelong.

Parent-Infant Interaction

Early on, parents and infants respond to each other by synchronizing their behavior in social play. Toward the end of the first year, secure attachment between child and parent sets the stage for the child's increasingly independent exploration of the world. The infant becomes an active participant in this social interaction, first in directly reacting to others and then in seeking out opinions through social referencing. By age 2, toddlers have definite personalities, the product of the interaction of nature and nurture.

PART III

The Play Years

The period from ages 2 to 6 is usually called early childhood, or the preschool period. Here we shall call it the "play years" as well, to underscore the importance of play during that time. Play occurs at every age, of course. But the years of early childhood are the most playful of all, for it is then that young children spend most of their waking hours at play, acquiring the skills, ideas, and values that are crucial for growing up. They chase each other and dare themselves to attempt new tasks, developing their bodies; they play with words and ideas, developing their minds; they invent games and dramatize fantasies, learning social skills and moral rules.

The playfulness of young children can cause them to be delightful or exasperating. To them growing up is a game, and their enthusiasm for it seems unlimited—whether they are quietly tracking a beetle through the grass or riotously turning their play area into a shambles. Their minds seem playful too, for the immaturity of their thinking enables them to explain that "a bald man has a barefoot head" or that "the sun shines so children can go outside to play."

If you expect them to sit quietly, think logically, or act realistically, you are bound to be disappointed. But if you enjoy playfulness, you might enjoy caring for, listening to, and even reading about children between 2 and 6 years old.

The Play Years:
Biosocial Development

CHAPTER 8

Between ages 2 and 6, significant biosocial development occurs on several fronts. The most obvious changes are in size and shape, as chubby toddlers seem to stretch up and become thinner as well as taller. Less obvious but more crucial changes occur in the brain and central nervous system. There, maturation turns the clumsy toddler into an accomplished and deft 6-year-old.

Together, these changes in body and brain allow children's exploration and mastery of their world to proceed by leaps and bounds, both literally and figuratively. That exploration typically occurs with joy and imagination, which is one reason this period is called "the play years." But playfulness is not the opposite of productivity, and in these years the two coincide. Unfortunately, the combination of growth and play makes the preschool child vulnerable to many biosocial hazards, including accidental injury and, for some children, abuse.

We begin our examination of the play years by looking at the way the child's body proportions change.

SIZE AND SHAPE

During early childhood, children generally become slimmer as the lower body lengthens and some baby fat melts away. The kindergarten child no longer has the protruding belly, round face, short limbs, and large head that characterize the toddler. By age 6, a child's body proportions are similar to those of an adult, although muscles, curves, and stature are obviously quite different.

Steady increases in height and weight accompany these changing proportions. From ages 2 through 6, well-nourished children add almost 3 inches (about 7 centimeters) in height and gain about 4½ pounds (2 kilograms) in weight per year. By age 6, the average child in a developed nation weighs about 46 pounds (21 kilograms) and measures 46 inches (117 centimeters).

The range of normal development is quite broad. Many children are notably taller or shorter than average, and the spread among age-mates becomes greater with every passing preschool year. Weight is especially variable. For example, by age 6, about 5 percent of North American children weigh less than 36 pounds (16 kilograms) and another 5 percent weigh more than 57 pounds (26 kilograms). This means that, among a typical class of first-graders in a developed nation, the heaviest child weighs almost twice as much as the lightest (Behrman, 1992). (See the growth tables in Appendix A for details.)

table **8.1**	**Factors Affecting the Height of Preschoolers**
Taller than Average If	**Shorter than Average If**
Well nourished	Malnourished
Rarely sick	Frequently or chronically sick
Of African or northern European ancestry	Of Asian ancestry
Mother is nonsmoker	Mother smoked during pregnancy
In upper socioeconomic status	In lower socioeconomic status
Live in urban area	Live in rural area
Live at sea level	Live high above sea level
Firstborn in a small family	Third- or later-born in a large family
Male	Female

Sources: Eveleth & Tanner, 1976; Lowrey, 1986; Meredith, 1978.

Several factors that influence growth are listed in Table 8.1. Of these, the three most influential are genetic background, health care, and nutrition. The last factor—nutrition—is largely responsible for dramatic differences between children in developed and underdeveloped nations. In the Netherlands, for example, typical 4-year-olds are taller than the average 6-year-old in India, Nepal, or Bangladesh, where 65 percent of children experience stunted growth due to poor nutrition (Eveleth & Tanner, 1991; United Nations, 1994). Similar height disparities occur when children living in Africa or South America are compared to children of the same African or Latino descent who are born and raised in Europe or North America. Genetically, such children are quite similar, but marked differences in food supply cause dramatic contrasts in height.

Within developed nations, where food in most families is adequate, height and weight variation among preschoolers is usually due to genes and chromosomes, not health and nutrition. In general, boys are more muscular, less fat, and slightly taller and heavier than girls. (This changes temporarily at puberty.)

When many ethnic groups live together in one developed nation, such as England, France, Canada, Australia, or the United States, children of African descent tend to be tallest, followed by Europeans, then Asians, and then Latinos. However, these are very broad generalities; many ethnic groups and individual families exhibit quite different inherited height patterns (Eveleth & Tanner, 1990). Even in developed nations, height is particularly variable among children of African descent, because various groups living in Africa over many centuries developed more genetic diversity than humans from any other region.

Cultural patterns can also have an impact. Traditionally, in the Indian subcontinent and in many South Asian families today, males are more highly valued and, consequently, better fed when food is scarce than are females, so girls are much smaller. On the other hand, if a particular North American family has ample food but requires that children be polite and quiet at meals, and the parents bestow love and praise in the form of extra dessert, it is more often the boys of the family who are skinny.

Eating Habits

For all children, even in the richest families and nations, annual height and weight gains are much lower between ages 2 and 6 years than they were during the first 2 years of life (Eveleth & Tanner, 1990). Growth gradually speeds up again, especially at puberty, until it slows once more at about age 16 (for girls) or 18 (for boys). With their growth slowed, children need fewer calories per pound of body weight during the preschool years than they did from birth through toddlerhood—especially if they are modern, sedentary children who spend most of their time indoors. As a result, their appetites become markedly smaller, a fact that causes many parents to fret, threaten, and cajole to get their children to eat more. ("If you eat your dinner, you can have your cake.") However, reduced appetite is not a medical problem unless a child is unusually thin or is not gaining any weight at all.

Of course, the food consumed during the preschool years should be nutritious. The most common diet deficiency in developed countries during early childhood is *iron-deficiency anemia,* and one of its main symptoms is chronic fatigue. Anemia, which stems from an insufficiency of quality meats, whole grains, eggs, and dark-green vegetables, is three times more common among low-income families than among others, because less expensive foods tend to contain less iron. Adding to this problem among families of every social class is the tendency to give young children candy, sugary drinks (soda, fruit-flavored punch, chocolate milk), sweetened cereals, and other sweets. Because these items spoil a small appetite very quickly, they can keep a child from consuming foods that contain essential vitamins and minerals. Since some essential nutrients have not yet been identified, foods (usually high in sugar) that are advertised as containing a day's worth of added vitamins nonetheless lack crucial nourishment. Such advertisements are particularly misleading for parents of preschoolers, because the child who eats these foods ends up eating fewer healthy foods and thus is more likely to be vitamin-deficient.

Each to His Own Lifelong food preferences are formed during early childhood, which may be one reason why the two children on the right seem dubious about the contents of the pink lunchbox, broccoli and all. Nevertheless, each of these children appears to be a model of healthful eating.

Too much sugar also is the main cause of early tooth decay, the most prevalent disease of young children in developed nations (Lewit & Kerrebrock, 1998). Many cultures promote children's eating of sweets, in the form of birthday cake, holiday sweets, Halloween treats, and such; the specifics depend on family ethnicity and religion, but the general trend is pervasive and hard to resist.

A related problem is that many children, like most adults, eat too few fruits and vegetables and consume too much fat. No more than 30 percent of daily calories should come from fat, but six out of seven preschoolers in the United States exceed that limit. Interestingly, one North American study found that both children whose family income is below the poverty level and children whose family income is three times above it are more likely to exceed the 30 percent fat limit, compared to those whose income lies somewhere in between (Thompson & Dennison, 1994).

Adding to the complications of feeding a 4-year-old well is the fact that many preschoolers are quite compulsive about daily routines, including meals. For example:

> Whereas parents may insist that the child eat his vegetables at dinner, the child may insist that the potatoes be placed only in a certain part of the plate and must not touch any other food; should the potatoes land outside of this area, the child may seem to experience a sense of near-contamination, setting off a tirade of fussiness for which many 2- and 3-year-olds are notorious. [Evans et al., 1997]

Most preschoolers' food preferences and rituals are far from nutritionally ideal. (One preschooler I know of wanted to eat only cream cheese sandwiches on white bread; another, only fast-food chicken nuggets.) But when parents eventually lose patience and either let their child eat what he or she wishes or send the child to bed hungry, nutrition suffers.

BRAIN GROWTH AND DEVELOPMENT

As you saw in Chapter 5, during childhood the brain develops faster than any other part of the body. The brain already weighs 75 percent of its eventual adult weight by age 2. By age 5 it has grown to 90 percent, and by 7, it is full grown. By comparison, the total body weight of the average 7-year-old is only about one-third that of the average adult.

Part of the increase in brain weight is due to continued proliferation of communication pathways (via the growth of dendrites and axons) among the brain's various specialized areas, in response to the child's specific experiences (Huttenlocher, 1994). Another part of brain growth is due to ongoing *myelination*—the insulating process that speeds up the transmission of neural impulses. Finally, several areas of the brain undergo notable expansion—in particular those areas dedicated to control and coordination of the body, the emotions, and thinking processes.

As a result of all these changes, during the play years children not only react more quickly to stimuli but also become better at controlling their reactions. For instance, compared to 2-year-olds, 5-year-olds more readily notice when another child begins playing with their favorite toy, but they are less likely to have a stomping-screaming-throwing tantrum over the misappropriation. Instead, they might think of a better tactic, perhaps offering another toy as a distraction, explaining the rules of ownership, or even offering to compromise, take turns, or share, as 2-year-olds almost never do unless guided or coerced by an adult.

Again owing to brain maturation, older preschool-age children are better at games that require quick thinking followed by deliberate action, such as musical chairs, Simon says, steal the bacon, and duck-duck-goose. If older preschoolers let a little one join in any of these games, a 2-year-old perhaps, he or she is likely still thinking about what to do long after the moment to act has passed. Then, if the 2-year-old is, say, bumped from a game of musical chairs, his or her lack of emotional control might produce bawling, sulking, or the knocking over of furniture. This might not be so for a 5-year-old, who can sometimes (but not always) take minor disappointments in stride.

New Connections

corpus callosum   A network of nerves connecting the left and right hemispheres of the brain.

At about age 5, children show important gains as a result of growth in the **corpus callosum,** a band of nerve fibers that connects the right and left sides of the brain (see Figure 8.1). The corpus callosum becomes notably thicker due to dendrite growth and myelination. As a result, communication between the two sides of the brain becomes more efficient, allowing children to coordinate functions that involve both sides of the brain and body. A simple example of such coordination is hopping on one foot while using both arms for balance, something few children under age 4 can do.

A more complex illustration of coordination of the right and left sides of the brain is the older child's increased ability to process information from several parts of the brain all at once and, simultaneously, connect and interweave sensory observations, emotions, thoughts, and reactions. Gradually, children learn to think before they leap, or, in a practical lesson taught to school-age children, "cross at the green and not in between." Such ability to monitor their behavior and sensations is one reason older children are less likely to suffer from serious injury than younger children.

Accidents and the Brain

In all but the most disease-ridden or war-torn countries of the world, accidents are by far the major cause of childhood death. In the United States, a child has about 1 chance in 500 of dying due to an accident before age 15—four times the risk of dying from cancer, the second-leading cause of childhood death. Roughly two-thirds of accidental deaths among children involve nonvehicular causes, such as falling, drowning, choking, and poisoning. These kinds of accidents are particularly prevalent among preschool children.

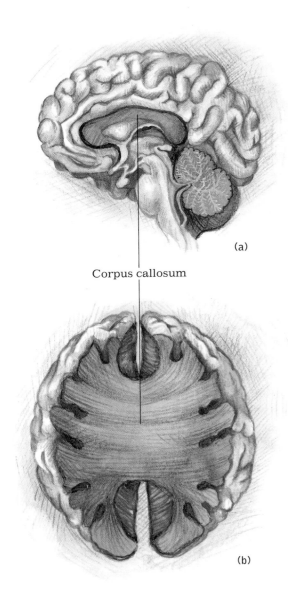

Of course, injuries are far more common than deaths. In the United States, a child has at least one chance in four *each year* of having an injury that needs medical attention (U.S. Bureau of the Census, 1996). Virtually every child needs stitches or a cast sometime before adolescence, and 44 percent of all patients hospitalized for serious injuries, including a high proportion of those with severe brain injuries, are children under age 15.

Accidents do not occur randomly. Rather, some children, because of their sex, socioeconomic status, and community are at much higher risk than others (Rivara, 1994). Boys, as a group, suffer more injuries and accidental deaths than girls—about one-third more between ages 1 and 5, and twice as many between ages 5 and 14. Sex differences are particularly salient when the neighborhood is filled with attractive hazards, as is the case in crowded cities and rural areas. Farm equipment—especially corn augers, tractors, and gravity boxes—injures 20,000 children and kills 300 each year. Most of these children are boys, with deaths more likely during harvest time, when equipment use is heavy and supervision light (Salmi et al., 1989).

The strongest risk factor of all is socioeconomic status (SES). One study of childhood deaths in North Carolina found that low-SES children were three times more likely to die accidentally than other children (Nelson, 1992). Overall, the impact of SES was most evident during infancy and the play years, when brain immaturity makes children least able to understand danger and coordinate their responses.

Figure 8.1 Connections. Two views of the corpus callosum, a band of nerve fibers (axons) that conveys information between the two hemispheres of the brain. When developed, this "connector" allows the person to coordinate functions that are performed mainly by one hemisphere or the other. *(a)* A view from between the hemispheres, looking toward the right side of the brain. *(b)* A view from above, with the gray matter not shown in order to expose the corpus callosum.

Corpus callosum

(a)

(b)

injury control   The practice of limiting the extent of injuries by planning ahead, controlling the circumstances, preventing certain dangerous activities, and adding safety features to others.

Indeed, because of their brain immaturity, preschool children of all SES groups dart into the street, swallow pieces of toys, climb on the ledge of a window, or play carelessly with fire more often than school-age children. But low-SES preschool children are especially likely to be harmed because they live in homes where hazards are more prevalent. As a result, in the North Carolina study, 1- to 4-year-olds whose families were on welfare were found to be four times more likely to be fatally hit by a car, four times more likely to die by choking, and nine times more likely to burn to death, compared to children of less impoverished families (Nelson, 1992). Obviously, young children need the protection of adults. **Injury control,** as the various measures to reduce harm are called, is everyone's responsibility (see Changing Policy, pages 250–251).

Eyes, Brain, and Reading

Researchers have studied visual pathways in the brain extensively. They have discovered that the areas of the brain associated with the control of eye movements and visual focusing undergo measurable myelination and growth throughout the preschool years. As a result, 4-year-olds are much better at looking at—and recognizing—letters and other small shapes than are younger children. As 4-year-olds move their eyes across a printed page, they can usually track the small variations from word to word, in sequence; younger children's eyes dart around a page much more randomly (Aslin, 1987; Borsting, 1994).

This development of the visual pathways combines with improved communication between the left and right sides of the brain to enhance eye-hand coordination, enabling older preschoolers to draw people, button sweaters, and—most important for later reading—copy familiar letters and numbers. By age 5, eye-hand coordination becomes fairly well attuned to left-right distinctions; children then are first able to successfully copy a diamond (which measures the ability to draw diagonals) and to write letters such as "b" and "d" facing in the proper direction (Borsting, 1994). Children who are left-handed might take longer to write a language such as English that is designed for right-handed individuals (as will be discussed on pages 349–350), but handedness seems largely inborn and genetic. As a result, few educators would try to switch a preschooler who wants to write left-handed.

Brain growth is not necessarily linear. Sometimes it occurs in spurts and plateaus (Fischer & Rose, 1994). And neuroscientists are starting to draw connections between growth spurts in specific brain areas and forward leaps in cognitive ability. For example, the left hemisphere of a child's brain, where the primary language abilities are usually located, undergoes a growth spurt at around age 2, and the right hemisphere, where the primary area for recognition of visual shapes is usually located, undergoes a growth spurt between ages 4 and 5 (Thatcher, 1994)—as does the brain overall. Beginning at around age 5, expansion of the corpus callosum, development of the frontal lobe of the brain, and other qualitative (not just quantitative) changes in the brain allow most children to link spoken and written language, remembering what sounds go with what symbols (Janowsky & Carper, 1996).

It is for this reason that formal instruction in reading, writing, and arithmetic begins in earnest all around the world at about age 6. By that age, children's brains are usually mature enough to forge ahead on these basic literacy skills. Of course, the social and intellectual preparation for literacy—reading picture books, memorizing rhymes, identifying signs such as EXIT in a theater and OFF on a computer, and writing one's name—begins years before, at home. But the sudden acceleration of reading skill must wait until brain maturation occurs (Bialystok, 1997).

MASTERING MOTOR SKILLS

As their bodies grow slimmer, stronger, and less top-heavy, and as their brain maturation permits greater control and coordination of their extremities, children between 2 and 6 years move with greater speed and grace and become more capable of directing and refining their own activity. The result is impressive improvement in motor skills.

Gross Motor Skills

Gross motor skills, involving large body movements such as running, climbing, jumping, and throwing, improve dramatically. This is apparent to anyone who watches a group of children at play. Two-year-olds are quite clumsy, falling down frequently and sometimes bumping into stationary objects. But by age 5, many children are both skilled and graceful. Most North American 5-year-olds can ride a tricycle, climb a ladder, pump a swing, and throw, catch, and kick a ball. Some of them can even ice-skate, ski, roller-blade, and ride a bicycle, activities that demand balance as well as coordination. Skills vary by culture, of course; in certain nations, some 5-year-olds swim in waves or climb cliffs that few adults in other nations would attempt. Underlying the development of such skills is a combination of the brain maturation we have just discussed and, obviously, guided practice.

Most young children practice their gross motor skills wherever they are, whether in a well-equipped nursery school with climbing ladders, balance boards, and sandboxes or at home, with furniture for climbing, sidewalk curbs for balancing, and gardens or empty lots for digging. (Indeed, as we have seen, their active exploration and curiosity, combined with their developing brain and motor skills, can lead to serious injury.)

Generally, children learn basic motor skills by teaching themselves and learning from other children, rather than through adult instruction. According to sociocultural theory, this is no problem, as learning from peers is probably the ideal way for children to master skills needed for the future.

More Curiosity than Caution As they master their gross motor skills, children of every social group, in every setting, seem to obey a universal command: "If it can be climbed, climb it." That command is usually heard louder than any words of caution—one reason direct supervision is needed during the play years.

INJURY CONTROL IS NO ACCIDENT

Although it is true that, everywhere and always, impoverished younger boys are more at risk of injury than older, wealthier girls, it is also true that the risk of serious injury could be much rarer for all children, everywhere and always. With forethought, many accidents can be avoided completely. Moreover, although some scrapes and bruises are inevitable in a normal childhood, proper precautions reduce the seriousness of injury when accidents do occur.

Forethought

The first step in reducing childhood injury, many believe, is to approach the problem in terms of "injury control" instead of "accident prevention." The word "accident" misleadingly implies that no one was at fault, whereas most serious childhood injuries involve someone's lack of forethought. *Injury control* means using forethought and precautions to prevent as many injuries as we can and to reduce the harm of those that do occur.

Often, forethought involves little more than providing adequate adult supervision. But what is "adequate" for controlling injury? There are no absolutes and no guarantees: sometimes children get hurt even when they are closely watched in their own homes; sometimes children play alone in dangerous places without incident; and sometimes children are overprotected to the point of losing their opportunity to develop the independence, judgment, and self-confidence they need.

Nonetheless, research finds some consensus. Pediatricians, child-protection workers, and most parents agree that a crawling baby cannot be safely left alone anywhere, even for a minute, and that children between the ages of 4 and 8 should never be left unsupervised in an area that contains an attrac-

(a)

(b)

(c)

Protective Settings In order for parents to safeguard their children from injury, they first need to be aware of safety hazards and then need to take whatever action is necessary to prevent accidents. In two of these photos, the parents are to be commended: The parents of the child in *(b)* not only put a helmet on their skater but protected his knees, wrists, elbows, and hands as well. The mother in *(c)* probably has been securing her child in a safety seat from infancy. However, the boy in *(a)* may be in trouble. What is immediately below him? We hope it is a "safety surface" designed to prevent serious injury, or an adult ready to catch him. Such forethought is essential for injury control.

tive danger, such as a pond, swimming pool, or other accessible body of water (Peterson et al., 1993). For older children, temperament, cognitive maturity, and past history are important indicators of how long a particular child can safely go unsupervised in an area that poses any kind of risk.

Forethought also involves instituting safety measures *in advance* to reduce the need for vigilant supervision and to prevent serious injury if an accident does occur. For instance, compared to adults, children are more likely to drown, choke on a nonfood object, tumble from a bicycle, suffocate in a fire, and fall out a window. Advance precautions, such as teaching children to swim, removing swallowable objects from reach, requiring a helmet for bicycling, and installing smoke alarms and window guards, would prevent many deaths. The goal is not to change the nature of the child but to change the nature of the condition. Many laws have already accomplished some of this. For instance, in the United States an active, curious preschooler can never swallow a lethal dose of baby aspirin because the bottle doesn't contain enough pills to cause death.

Other Measures

Note that the responsibility for injury control does not fall on the parents alone. Not until accurate nationwide data became available did parents even realize the extent of the hazards associated with, for example, poisons in the medicine cabinet, cribs with widely spaced slats, playgrounds surfaced with concrete, balloons that can pop, and roller-blading without headgear and protective pads. Research is thus needed to identify hazards, and then risks must be publicized so that parents, community leaders, and legislators can take action. What action should they take?

General, broad-based television announcements and poster campaigns do not have a direct impact on children's risk taking. Such educational broadsides may, however, foster a safety-consciousness that reduces resistance to specific safety programs. Similarly, educational programs in schools and preschools teach children to verbalize safety rules, but unless parents become involved, classroom education appears to have little effect on children's actual behavior (Garbarino, 1988; Rivara, 1993).

More effective than educational measures are safety laws that include penalties. Among such measures that have led to significant reductions in accidental death rates for children in the United States are laws requiring:

- That childproof safety caps be on medicine bottles (resulting in an 80 percent reduction in poisoning deaths of 1- to 4-year-olds)
- That children's sleepwear be flame-retardant (decreasing deaths from burning pajamas and nightgowns by 97 percent)
- That fencing be placed around swimming pools (reducing childhood drowning in Arizona and southern California by 51 percent)

- That car safety seats be used for children (bringing passenger deaths down by 70 percent for children under age 5, between 1980 and 1991)
- That helmets be worn by bicyclists (credited for reducing serious bicycle head injuries by 88 percent)

(National Center for Injury Prevention and Control, 1992, 1993; Rivara, 1994)

Largely as a result of laws like these, accidental deaths of 1- to 5-year-olds in the United States decreased by 50 percent between 1980 and 1986. Downward trends are apparent in most other nations as well, although the specifics vary from nation to nation. The leading nation for injury control is Sweden. Over a 45-year period, annual childhood deaths in Sweden decreased to one-fifth of what they were, from 450 to 88 (Bergman & Rivara, 1991).

Think, Think Again, Analyze, and Advocate

It is increasingly apparent that the child who escapes serious injury in childhood is not "just lucky" and that no accident is "just an accident." Every parent can practice injury control on a small scale. First, parents must *think prevention* and *protection*, locking away poisons, checking the smoke detector, always using a child safety seat, and so on. Then they must *analyze actual injuries*. Repeated scrapes on the knees, for instance, suggest that a better play surface or protective gear is called for—not because scraped knees themselves are a problem but because a brain concussion or broken limb may result if the next tumble occurs under slightly different circumstances.

On a broader scale, prevention and protection can become part of a community pattern, as adults teach each other about the hazards facing children. Then, together, the community can analyze and modify the conditions whenever a child is hurt, so that more children survive their early years with only tiny scars and no serious traumas.

This leads to the final step: *Advocate safety.* Children need to be protected until they are wise enough to protect themselves—a fact that places everyone, not only the parents, at fault when a serious childhood injury occurs. We all must work to insure that research and practice keep every child safe.

Steps to Injury Control	
Step	Example
Think prevention	Lock up guns.
Think protection	Require safety helmets.
Analyze injuries	Consider scraped knees as a warning.
Advocate safety	Work for laws that prevent speeding near schools.

❶ Response for Parents (from page 248): In general, age, sex, and family income are the demographic indicators of injury vulnerability, with 2-year-old lower-income boys most at risk. However, these generalities are less useful when analyzing risk for a specific child. Even if your child is a 5-year-old girl in a middle-class family, if her particular history includes many bruises, scrapes, stitches, and so on, or if your neighborhood is filled with "attractive hazards" that have injured other children, it is wise to increase prevention and protection.

What Is She Accomplishing? The papier-mâché animals produced by this girl and her preschool classmates are more likely to be mushy and misshapen than artistic. However, the real product is development of eye-hand coordination. With intensive, dedicated practice, fine motor skills are mastered by the school years, when children's artwork is sometimes truly remarkable.

❶ Response for Educators (from page 248): You might explain that the brain maturation required for reading and writing small print does not occur in most children until age 5 or so and that you don't want to create anxiety about skills that should be a joy. However, you might also explain that the curriculum of a good school for 3-year-olds includes extensive spoken language, reading from picture books, and other activities that prepare the children for learning to read and write when their brains are ready.

As long as a child has the opportunity to play in an adequate space and has suitable playmates and play structures, gross motor skills develop as rapidly as maturation, body size, and innate ability allow. Unfortunately, neither opportunity nor play space can be taken for granted—especially in large cities.

Fine Motor Skills

Fine motor skills, involving small body movements (especially those of the hands and fingers), are much harder to master than gross motor skills. Such things as pouring juice from a pitcher into a glass, cutting food with a knife and fork, and achieving anything more artful than a scribble with a pencil are difficult for young children, even with great concentration and effort. Preschoolers can spend hours trying to tie a bow with their shoelaces, often producing knot upon knot instead.

The chief reason many children experience difficulty with fine motor skills is simply that they have not yet developed the necessary muscular

control, patience, and judgment—in part because the central nervous system is not yet sufficiently myelinated. For many, this deficit is compounded by short, stubby fingers. Unless caregivers keep these limitations in mind when selecting utensils, toys, and clothes, frustration and destruction can result: preschool children may burst into tears when they cannot zip their pants, or may mash a puzzle piece into place when they are unable to position it correctly, or may tear up the paper when they cannot cut it with their blunt "safety" scissors.

Fortunately, such frustrations usually fade as a child's persistence at practicing fine motor skills gradually leads to mastery. Adults can certainly help by offering tools, time, and encouragement. One fine motor skill that seems particularly linked to later success in school is also one that is easy for parents and teachers to encourage—the skill of making meaningful marks on paper.

Children's Art

Drawing is an important form of play. On the simplest level, "the child who first wields a marker is learning in many areas of his young life about tool use" (Gardner, 1980). In addition, drawing requires that the child think about what to draw, manipulate the pencil, crayon, or brush to execute the thought, and then view, and perhaps explain, the end product. A developmental study of children's painting found that 3-year-olds usually just plunked their brushes into the paint, pulled them out dripping wet, and then pushed them across the paper without much forethought or skill. However, by age 5 most children took care to get just enough paint on their brushes, planned just where to put each stroke, and stood back from their work to examine the final result (Allison, 1985). By doing so, 5-year-olds experience a sequence that not only provides practice with fine motor skills

(a)

(b)

(c)

(d)

Artists in Progress The maturation of fine motor skills is evident in this progression, from the two-handed overlapping vertical lines (circles and horizontals are more advanced) in *(a)* to the left-handed artistic control, combining imagination and representation, in *(d)*. Steps along the way include *(b)* the imaginative use of color and design but no representation of reality and *(c)* the careful observation of conventions (five fingers on each hand, a triangle nose, a line of grass at the bottom) with little imagination. All four of these artists are mastering the skills appropriate for their ages, and all show the strong concentration that signals that intense brain activity accompanies motor skill advancement.

but also involves coordination of action and thought and, in the end, enhances their sense of accomplishment.

Children's artwork provides a testing ground for another important skill: self-correction. Older preschool children are eager to practice their skills, drawing essentially the same picture again and again, with the later versions usually having more details and better proportions.

Such mastery of drawing skills is related to overall intellectual growth. In general, as children become more skilled and detailed in their drawing, their level of cognitive development rises as well (Bensur & Eliot, 1993; Chappell & Steitz, 1993). There is no sure way of distinguishing correlation from causation here—of knowing how much the mastery of drawing skills *contributes* to cognitive advances and how much it is a *consequence* of them. But it is quite possible that a sketch pad and a box of markers are no less an "educational toy" than traditional alphabet blocks or counting games.

Forgive Us The name is misspelled, and the flowers and gorilla arrived too late to help—testimony to the truth that "we were not there" until 6-year-old Elisa was killed by her mother. Sadly, whenever a child is severely maltreated, dozens of people—relatives, neighbors, teachers, social workers—notice that something is wrong but fail to act to prevent further abuse.

CHILD MALTREATMENT

Throughout this chapter and elsewhere in this text, we have assumed that parents naturally want to foster their children's development and protect them from every danger. Yet daily, it seems, reporters describe parents who harm their offspring. When the harm takes the form of horrific abuse or results in death, the story makes national news, as when the mother of a 6-year-old

> confessed to killing Elisa by throwing her against a concrete wall. She confessed that she had made Elisa eat her own feces and that she had mopped the floor with her head . . . there was no part of the six-year-old's body that was not cut or bruised. Thirty circular marks that at first appeared to be cigarette burns turned out to be impressions left by the stone in someone's ring. [Van Biema, 1995]

We are shocked by the brutality and senselessness of cases like Elisa's and appalled at the pathological perpetrators, indifferent neighbors, and overworked professionals (in education, medicine, and especially child welfare) who share the blame. Yet sensational cases like Elisa's represent only a small portion of all maltreatment cases. And, as experts in child-maltreatment research point out, "journalism is an impatient enterprise and the tragic, bungled case will always be more newsworthy . . . than the small successes of family reunification or the incremental process of reform" (Larner et al., 1998). Not only do sensational cases distract attention from other, far more typical and common, incidents, but the emotional reaction to the extremes dwarfs the lessons we need to learn. Such lessons begin with an understanding of what typical abuse is, and then lead to knowledge of its causes and consequences, and finally teach us what works to treat and, even better, prevent maltreatment of every sort. If we could only remember those lessons and apply them, all children would benefit.

Typical Abuse

The irrational rage of Elisa's mother is rare; the ignorance of caregivers who do not understand how to love and guide a child is common. Some parents might, for example, not realize that children need to be patiently shown how to "do things right." Typical is the mother whose 3-year-old was having trouble carrying an umbrella:

> "Carry that umbrella right or I'll slap the [expletive] out of you," she screamed at him. "Carry it right, I said . . . " and then she slapped him in the face, knocking him off balance. [Dash, 1986]

Another example is the father who has set ideas of how children should behave and believes that his son should be "kept on his toes":

> So his dad teases him a lot . . . [and] plays games with him. If Jon wins, his dad makes fun of him for being an egghead; if he loses, he makes fun of him for being a dummy. It is the same with affection. Jon's dad will call him over for a hug; when Jon responds, his dad pushes him away, telling him not to be a sissy. . . . Jon is tense, sucks his thumb, and is tongue-tied (which his dad teases him about). [Garbarino et al., 1986]

Changing Definitions of Maltreatment

Neither of the above-described incidents would have been recognized as maltreatment a few decades ago. Until about 1960, child maltreatment was thought of mostly as instances of obvious physical assault, assumed to result from a rare outburst of a mentally disturbed person who was typically *not* a member of the

child maltreatment Any intentional harm to anyone under age 18.

abuse Any action that is harmful (either physically or psychologically) to an individual's well-being. The severity of abuse depends on how much and how often it occurs and on the vulnerability of the victim.

neglect Any inaction that harms or endangers a person. Neglect can involve physical needs (food, warmth) or psychological needs (love, language).

child's family. However, we now recognize that maltreatment is neither rare nor sudden, and that 80 percent of the time its perpetrators are not deranged and not strangers but the child's own parents (Cicchetti & Carlson, 1989; National Child Abuse and Neglect Data System, 1997; Wang & Daro, 1998).

With this recognition has come a broader definition: **Child maltreatment** includes all intentional harm to, or avoidable endangerment of, anyone under 18 years of age. Thus, child maltreatment includes both **abuse**—deliberate action that is harmful to a child's well-being—and **neglect**—failure to appropriately meet a child's basic needs. Abuse and neglect are further subdivided into more specific categories, with abuse including physical, emotional, and sexual abuse, and neglect including inattention to the child's emotional as well as physical needs. Neglect is twice as common, and at least as damaging, as abuse.

Reported and Substantiated Maltreatment

Obviously, historical and cultural norms influence our ideas about what constitutes child maltreatment: behaviors that would be considered abusive in some eras or cultural settings may be regarded as legitimate and acceptable in other times and places.

However, no one can deny that in many nations, the rate of child maltreatment has been, and continues to be, alarmingly high. Since 1993, in the United States, the number of *reported* cases is about 3 million per year, and the number of *substantiated* cases has been about 1 million, a rate that represents roughly 1 child in every 70 (Wang & Daro, 1998). These are official statistics, in which "reported" cases are those the authorities have been informed of and "substantiated" cases are those which the authorities have investigated and then verified as maltreatment.

The gap between the 3 million reported cases and the 1 million substantiated cases is attributable mainly to two factors. First, a case may be reported many times but will be tallied as only one substantiated case. Second, before a case is substantiated, investigators must find some proof—usually visible, unmistakable signs or credible witnesses (such as the other parent and the maltreated child). And standards of proof vary from state to state, with neither high nor low ratios of reported to substantiated maltreatment being necessarily better. As an example, the highest 1997 substantiation rate was in Kentucky (56 percent) and the lowest was in Kansas (10 percent), but the two states probably have similar rates of severe maltreatment, at least as indicated by the rate of maltreatment deaths (about 1 death for every 60,000 children in both states).

Failure to Protect Self-centered parents neglect their children's basic needs in a pattern of maltreatment that may be even more harmful than abuse.

❓ **Especially for Social Workers:** Which would be most helpful in figuring out if a specific child is mistreated: the particular child-discipline practices used, signs of injury on the child's body, the relationship between the child and the parent, or the overall social and intellectual patterns of the child?

Causes

It is hard to imagine why someone would hurt a child entrusted to his or her care. However, research has shown that a very wide variety of factors—from community values to the caregiver's history, from the family culture to the child's temperament—contribute to child maltreatment.

The Cultural and Community Context

Each culture, over the generations, develops a particular ecosystem—a combination of customs, values, and ideals that creates a climate for growth. Some ecosystems are much more conducive to maltreatment than others

Consequences of Maltreatment In many nations of the world, abused and neglected children are not runaways but throwaways, pushed out onto the streets by their parents and communities.

❷ *Observational Quiz (see answer page 258): Can you guess where these boys are, and can you see two activities they use for comfort?*

❶ **Response for Social Workers (from page 255):** All of these indicators are useful, and none by itself indicates abuse. However, the most important are probably the latter two: if the child seems afraid of or indifferent to the parent, or if the child does not play well with other children or communicate and explore as most preschoolers do, something is amiss. Your job is to find out if that "something" is in the family or if it is a serious inborn problem in the child.

(just like the temperature and humidity in some ecosystems nurtures harmful bacteria, bugs, or weeds).

According to the United Nations, overall concern and protection for the well-being of children varies markedly worldwide. Obviously, extreme poverty within a nation makes it more likely that children will be neglected or abused—they may be forced to sacrifice for the survival and welfare of their elders. However, even countries in the same region of the world, with similar per capita incomes, differ markedly in how much they cherish children, as is evident in their children's general health, education, and overall well-being (United Nations, 1994). Day-to-day caregiving varies tremendously by region, by nation, by area within a nation, by culture within an area, and by cohort within a culture (Buchanan, 1996; Korbin, 1994; Sigler, 1989).

Therefore, before a particular practice can be considered abusive, community standards must be taken into account. One set of examples comes from the numerous customs that give children pain: pierced ears, circumcisions, caster oil, forced feeding of hated foods, ceremonial facial scars, permed or tightly braided hair, encouragement of sports that bring exhaustion and bruises, forced sleeping alone despite tears of protest, harsh words designed to shame a child into proper behavior, and many other such examples are commonplace in some cultures and criticized in others. In some neighborhoods, not letting children play outside for hours every day is considered maltreatment; in others, letting a child play outside unsupervised for even 10 minutes is considered neglectful. The Japanese say "Before seven, among the Gods" to advise parents that young children are not pure and not to be punished; but that saying promotes "the Western view that Japanese adults are indulgent with their children . . . not playing their roles as socializing agents properly" (Chen, 1996).

Despite such variation, two aspects of the overall context seem universally conducive to maltreatment: poverty and social isolation. No matter how maltreatment is defined or counted, it occurs more frequently as family

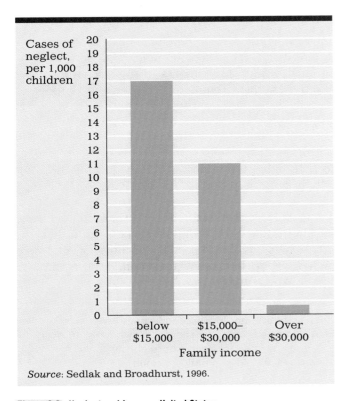

Source: Sedlak and Broadhurst, 1996.

Figure 8.2 Neglect and Income, United States. Rates of neglect skyrocket as family income falls, with single mothers of families with either four or more children or a single child most likely to be neglectful. Abuse also shows dramatic income differences, but here fathers are more likely than mothers to be perpetrators. Interestingly, neither age nor race correlates with maltreatment.

income falls (see Figure 8.2) (Drake & Zuravin, 1998; Pelton, 1994). This is particularly true for neglect and physical abuse, which fall most heavily on children under age 6 who live in families with an income below the poverty line, an unemployed father, and four or more children. In such families, children obviously add to the financial pressures and are likely to become victims because of it (Wolfner & Gelles, 1993).

The second major risk factor that stems from the culture is social isolation. Every society has certain "family values"—beliefs that encourage parents to care for their children. The human species could not have survived if communities had not developed such values. One of these values is the belief that each family should decide how to raise its own children—a useful principle in nations with many ethnic and religious groups, such as the United States. However, this value can boomerang when children need intervention: because it encourages privacy and social isolation, signs of maltreatment become "not my business," and this abuse can continue and spread. Even among neighborhoods with low-income and similar ethnicity, those with less social isolation have markedly lower rates of abuse (Korbin et al., 1998).

A word of caution here: Although some cultures and societies condone or even encourage abuse more than others, we must always guard against the cultural arrogance that says that one way is best for all children. For example, is it better for a child to grow up on a farm or in a city? Throughout the nineteenth century, in England and the United States, children of the "unworthy poor" living in the cities were sent without their families to distant farms where they would experience fresh air and hard work. At the time, such a move was thought to be kindness, but it is now seen as cruelty caused by cultural myopia (Schene, 1998). It is not a simple matter to judge whether a culture's practices and assumptions are abusive—although that judgment sometimes must be made to protect the world's most vulnerable citizens.

Watching the World Go By How can passersby ignore the impoverished families in front of them, knowing that poverty multiplies the incidence of maltreatment? One way is to blame the parents. Did you protect your conscience by asking why this couple had four children so close together, or whether the husband can get a job, or if this mother got welfare payments for each child? Whatever the answers to the first two questions, we know that these children sit on the boardwalk of Atlantic City, New Jersey, a state that now subsidizes only the first two children per mother.

Intergenerational Bonding Devoted grandfathers, such as this one in Su Zhou, China, prevent the social isolation that is a prerequisite for serious abuse. Can you imagine this man's response if he thought his granddaughter was underfed, overdisciplined, or unloved?

❶ *Answer to Observational Quiz (from page 256):* They're in Rio de Janeiro. You might have guessed that they were somewhere in South America from the wide gap between rich and poor, the warm climate (the only shoes are sandals), and the contrasting facial features of the mannequin and the boys. The two comforting actions are less ambiguous and more universal: The boys buddy up (note the pairs who choose to sit right next to each other), and they sniff glue through soda cans (the cheapest high).

The Family Context

Each family has its own private culture, including habits and routines, coping styles, and values. The daily routine of most families is somewhat flexible; adults and children make minor adjustments in their schedules and their established roles as the occasion requires. However, the routines of maltreating families are typically at one of two extremes. Either the family is so rigid in its schedules and role demands that no one can measure up to them or the family is so chaotic and disorganized that no one knows what is expected or when appreciation, encouragement, protection—or even food and a clean bed—are forthcoming. In families at either extreme, hostility and neglect are inevitable (Dickerson & Nadelson, 1989; Panel on Research on Child Abuse and Neglect, 1993).

Maltreatment is especially likely to develop if the family's code also includes isolation and distrust of outsiders. A child's parents might, for example, be unusually suspicious of all preschool teachers or of every athletic coach. For them, it is easier to "protect" their child by keeping him or her at home than to realize their own limitations. Thus, the child is stuck within

> a family system in which exploitation, loyalty, secrecy and self-sacrifice form the core of the family's value system. In a sense, the victim's survival is dependent on adjusting to a psychotic world where abusive behavior is acceptable but telling the truth about it is sinful. [Carmen, 1989]

Another family-system element that holds the potential for child maltreatment is abuse or neglect between the adults, especially when the relationship between the mother and the father or between the grandparents and the parents is either extremely hostile, emotionally cold, or both. That hostile or cold climate exacerbates the child's vulnerability, intensifying the impact of any direct attack; moreover, if the child must witness domestic violence, that climate alone can constitute abuse, even if the child is not touched (Cummings et al., 1994; Fantuzzo et al., 1991).

An additional factor is alcohol or drug dependency. According to caseworkers, substance abuse is the most frequent major problem interfering with effective child care. The second most common problem is lack of parental capacity and skill (Wang & Daro, 1998). Both problems are hard to admit, but if a parent complains about a child, the complaining may be a clue that help is needed. As one study found, caregivers

> may be unable to separate their children's behavior from their own stress and may attribute problems to their children. Thus when parents describe behavior problems in their children they may be asking for assistance for themselves, particularly with child-rearing and family functioning. [Harrington et al., 1998]

Consequences

The more we learn about child maltreatment, the more we see that its causes are many and its consequences extend far beyond any immediate injury or deprivation. Compared to well-cared-for children, chronically abused and neglected children tend to be underweight, slower to talk, less able to concentrate, and delayed in academic growth (Cicchetti et al., 1993; Eckenrode et al., 1993). Deficits are even more apparent in social skills: maltreated children tend to regard other children and adults as hostile and exploitative, and hence they are less friendly, more aggressive, and more isolated than other children (Dodge et al., 1994; Egeland, 1991). The longer their abuse continues, and the earlier it started, the worse their relationships with peers are (Bolger et al., 1998). As adolescents and adults, those who were severely maltreated in childhood (either physically or emotionally) often use drugs or alcohol to numb their emotions, choose unsupportive relationships, sabotage their own careers, eat too much or too little, and generally engage in self-destructive behavior (Crittenden et al., 1994).

Those are some of the human costs. The financial costs of child maltreatment, both to the victim and to society, are virtually impossible to measure. One estimate puts the average cost at $813 per investigation (whether substantiated or not), $2,702 for providing in-home services such as homemaker assistance, and $21,902 annually per child for providing foster care (Courtney, 1998). These costs all include administration and paperwork as well as direct charges. To those costs must be added, when maltreatment is unreported or unsubstantiated, or when intervention is too late or too little, special education for learning disabilities, institutionalization for emotional problems, and, in some cases, imprisonment for acts of misdirected anger.

From Generation to Generation?

The human costs of maltreatment are paid not only by the victim and by persons who interact with the victim but perhaps by members of the next generation who will experience maltreatment as well. But in assessing those costs over the years, we must neither minimize nor exaggerate. It is sadly true that virtually every child who experiences serious, ongoing maltreatment will bear some lifelong scars, including depression, fear of intimacy, difficulty controlling emotions, or low self-esteem. Yet it is also true that many adults who were victims of childhood abuse or neglect live normal law-abiding lives, working, marrying, and raising healthy children.

Many people erroneously believe that the **intergenerational transmission** of maltreatment—that is, maltreated children becoming adults who abuse or neglect their own children—is automatic and unalterable. This assumption is not only false but destructive. As one review of research explains:

> Uncritical acceptance of the intergenerational hypothesis has caused undue anxiety in many victims of abuse, led to biased response by mental health workers, and influenced the outcome of court decisions, even in routine divorce child custody cases. In one such case . . . a judge refused a mother custody rights because it was discovered during the trial that the mother had been abused as a child. Despite the fact that much of the evidence supported the children's placement with their mother, the judge concluded that the mother was an unfit guardian, since everyone "knows" abused children become abusive parents. [Kaufman & Zigler, 1989]

Retrospective analyses, which ask maltreating parents to recall their own childhoods, invariably show high rates of intergenerational transmission; almost all adults who seriously mistreat their children remember a painful, neglectful, and abusive childhood. But to determine the actual rate of intergenerational transmission, researchers must study the problem longitudinally, not retrospectively, because retrospective analyses omit victims who do not themselves become abusers (Buchanan, 1996). And there are many, many such people.

On the basis of longitudinal studies that begin before abused individuals become parents, experts estimate that between 30 and 40 percent of abused children actually become child abusers themselves. This rate is

intergenerational transmission The assumption that mistreated children grow up to become abusive or neglectful parents themselves. This is less common than is generally supposed.

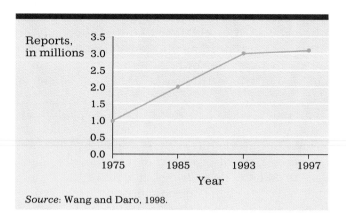

Source: Wang and Daro, 1998.

Figure 8.3 Reports of Maltreatment in the United States. The great increase in reports of maltreatment since 1975 is attributed primarily to increased awareness on the part of the public and mandated reporting for professionals. No expert believes that the actual rate of maltreatment tripled over two decades.

many times that of the general population, but it shows that more than half of all severely mistreated children do not become abusive or neglectful parents (Egeland, 1993; Kaufman & Zigler, 1993). Least likely to transmit abuse are those who have been loved and cared for by someone—perhaps by the other parent or a foster caregiver in childhood or by their spouses in adulthood. In addition, adults who remember their maltreatment and understand its effects are much less likely to harm their own children than are adults who do not even recall or recognize that something was seriously wrong with the care they received.

These findings about intergenerational transmission should not be surprising, given what you learned about attachment in Chapter 7—specifically, that attachment status influences, but does not completely determine, later social relationships. An adult who was insecurely attached but remembers and understands why may form a secure relationship with his or her own children (Main, 1995). On the other hand, parents who deny the abuse they suffered as children, especially if they think they might have deserved it, are likely to maltreat their offspring (Egeland, 1993).

Treatment

As we finally grasp the broad spectrum and devastating consequences of child maltreatment, efforts to treat it are intensifying. As you will see, such efforts are still clumsy and piecemeal.

Linking Reports to Action

In many countries worldwide, laws now require that any teacher, health professional, police officer, or social worker who becomes aware of possible maltreatment must report it. These laws have made a difference. Reporting has increased, and in the United States more than half of all reports of maltreatment come from professionals. With better awareness, many public and private organizations now tally reports of abuse and neglect, monitor treatment, and fund research (see Figure 8.3).

Some people wonder whether alerting the police or social workers might harm rather than help a maltreated child (Finkelhor, 1993). There are two reasons for concern. The first is that reporting does not create enough protection (Levine & Doueck, 1995). The second reason, related to the first, is that the sheer number of reports sometimes overwhelms the ability of public workers to investigate properly, as well as to provide appropriate protection and treatment.

differential response The idea that child maltreatment reports should be separated into those that require immediate investigation, possibly leading to foster care and legal prosecution, and those requiring supportive measures to encourage better parental care.

One solution is to institute a policy of **differential response**, that is, responding in either of two ways depending on the particular situation. Some high-risk cases may require complete investigation, perhaps with removal of the child—which should be done quickly and legally. Low-risk cases may require only an offer of help (such as providing child care, income supplementation, or health care) that the family can accept or reject (Waldfogel, 1998). The acceptance of such help might prevent a later incident of serious neglect while freeing caseworkers' time for more difficult cases. It would not, however, protect a child from a family that already is locked in a pattern of serious abuse. In situations of the latter type, a differential-response policy would give child-care workers both the mandate and the focused time to proceed with full legal force (not the

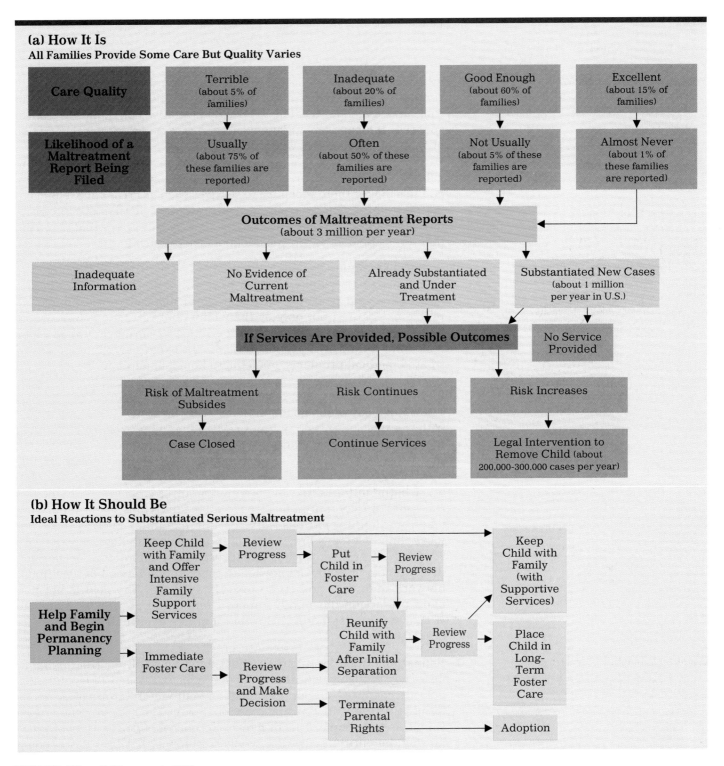

(a) How It Is
All Families Provide Some Care But Quality Varies

Care Quality	Terrible (about 5% of families)	Inadequate (about 20% of families)	Good Enough (about 60% of families)	Excellent (about 15% of families)
Likelihood of a Maltreatment Report Being Filed	Usually (about 75% of these families are reported)	Often (about 50% of these families are reported)	Not Usually (about 5% of these families are reported)	Almost Never (about 1% of these families are reported)

Outcomes of Maltreatment Reports
(about 3 million per year)

Inadequate Information	No Evidence of Current Maltreatment	Already Substantiated and Under Treatment	Substantiated New Cases (about 1 million per year in U.S.)

If Services Are Provided, Possible Outcomes — No Service Provided

Risk of Maltreatment Subsides	Risk Continues	Risk Increases
Case Closed	Continue Services	Legal Intervention to Remove Child (about 200,000–300,000 cases per year)

(b) How It Should Be
Ideal Reactions to Substantiated Serious Maltreatment

Help Family and Begin Permanency Planning

- Keep Child with Family and Offer Intensive Family Support Services → Review Progress → Put Child in Foster Care → Review Progress → Keep Child with Family (with Supportive Services)
- Reunify Child with Family After Initial Separation → Review Progress → Place Child in Long-Term Foster Care
- Immediate Foster Care → Review Progress and Make Decision → Terminate Parental Rights → Adoption

Figure 8.4 Differential Response to Child Maltreatment. One goal of differential response is to move more effectively when a case is deemed serious. Immediate and intensive help is provided to the family, often with temporary removal of the child. Permanency planning begins immediately, so all options are considered. Then the decision is made either to begin long-term, extensive support to the family or to place the child permanently in a foster or adoptive home. Ideally, progress review is frequent, and decisions serve the child.

superficial, hasty response necessitated by a caseload of hundreds per week), thereby providing more effective protection and assistance to the child than they could if they were required to investigate all reports with equal attention.

Differential response to high-risk and low-risk situations is only the beginning of a more careful response. A further step is to categorize each high-risk maltreating family as either vulnerable to crisis, restorable, supportable, or inadequate (Crittenden, 1992) and to treat such families accordingly (see Figure 8.4):

1. **Vulnerable-to-crisis families** are generally adequate-caregiving families that are pushed over the edge by immediate stressful problems. The

vulnerable-to-crisis families Families that are experiencing unusual problems and need temporary help to resolve them.

loss of a job, for example, or the birth of a handicapped infant can severely strain most parents' ability to cope with the normal demands and frustrations of child rearing. Especially if relatives or friends are unresponsive, the children might become the target of their parents and be blamed for problems they never created.

About one-fourth of all substantiated maltreatment occurs in vulnerable-to-crisis families. Usually they realize they have a problem, and this makes them receptive to services such as crisis counseling and parent training. Once the parents learn to cope with their specific problem more effectively—a process that usually takes less than a year—they are again able to provide adequate child rearing.

restorable families Families that have the potential to provide adequate care but are experiencing a combination of current stresses and past deficits that seriously impairs their parenting abilities.

2. **Restorable families** make up about half of all maltreating families. The caregivers in restorable families have the potential to provide adequate care, and perhaps have done so in the past, but a number of problems—caused not only by their immediate situations but also by their past histories and their temperaments—seriously impair their parenting abilities. A single mother, for example, might have untreated medical problems, inadequate housing, and poor job skills, all of which fray her quick temper and cause her to explode just as her father did when she was a disobedient child. Or a binge-drinking husband with a battered ego might periodically beat his children, perhaps with the tacit permission of an overly dependent, isolated wife. Or a teenage couple might both be immature and addicted to drugs, with the result that they disregard their infant's basic needs or seriously overestimate his or her abilities.

Treatment for restorable families requires a caseworker who has the time and commitment to become a family advocate, mediating and coordinating various services (for example, making sure the local clinic provides low-cost and appropriate medical care, as well as securing transportation and prescription medicine, or helping drug addicts not only acknowledge their dependence but also find a network of former addicts to provide support). The goal is not just child protection but family support, emotional as well as material. With such intense help, restorable families eventually become successful ones.

supportable families Families that can meet their children's needs only with the help of an extensive array of social services.

3. **Supportable families** make up about one-fifth of all maltreating families. They probably will never function adequately and independently, but with continual support they might meet their children's basic needs for physical, educational, and emotional care. The support might be as simple as daily home visits by a nurse or housekeeper or as involved as moving the entire family to a special residence that provides ongoing medical attention, day care, recreation, social work, and group therapy. Unfortunately, such intense support services are rarely available to the families that need them most, although some residential programs for battered women or for recovering addicts come close. Unless support is forthcoming, the children of a supportable family will need to be placed in another home.

inadequate families Families that are so impaired by emotional problems and/or cognitive deficiencies that they can never meet their children's needs.

4. **Inadequate families** constitute nearly 10 percent of maltreating families. They are so impaired by deep emotional problems or serious cognitive deficiencies that the parents or other caregivers will never be able to meet the needs of their children. For children born into these families, long-term adoption, beginning with foster care in infancy, is the best solution.

Foster Care

foster care A legally sanctioned, publicly supported arrangement in which children are cared for by someone other than their biological parents.

Over the years, many children have been raised by "foster parents"—usually relatives or neighbors—because their biological parents died or were too poor or too ill to care for them. Even today, such informal foster care is common. One study of severely alcoholic mothers found that more than one-third of them placed their children informally in foster care (Goldberg et al., 1996). However, in contemporary society, **foster care** generally means a legally sanctioned, publicly supported arrangement in which children are officially removed from their parents and entrusted to another adult or family who is paid to nurture them. Ideally, such fostering is the result of *permanency planning,* that is, devising a plan for a child's long-term care that does not remove the child from the parents unless doing so is necessary, in which case the child is placed in a home where he or she can stay until adulthood.

Foster care has long been stereotyped as inadequate. This stereotype arises partly from the notion that children are *always* better off with their biological parents. That notion is false. The stereotype also arises from the generality that foster children do worse in school than other children, have fewer friends, and are more likely to become criminals. That is, unfortunately, true. However, the comparison is unfair. When foster children are compared only with children who stay with severely abusive or neglectful biological parents, they come out way ahead.

Even though foster children usually bring behavioral problems, learning disabilities, or traumatic memories to foster families, their foster families usually treat them well. (Foster parents cause only 1 in 200 cases of substantiated abuse. Foster children often do quite well as parents themselves, eventually becoming good, nonmaltreating caregivers.) A positive outcome is especially likely when the foster parents are committed to the child and when they have the resources to address whatever emotional, physical, and social problems the child might have (Barth et al., 1994; Klee et al., 1997). These problems most often require extensive special educational and medical care; because few states provide such help whenever needed, many foster parents find their role much more difficult than they anticipated.

About half a million children in the United States were in foster care in 1996, with the number increasing each year (Children's Defense Fund, 1998; Kools, 1997). It is not surprising, then, that there is a lack of approved foster families, trained and willing to take in troubled children. Measures to increase their number include providing ongoing psychological and economic support and using permanency planning that allows foster parents to adopt their foster children or to care for them as long as they can. However, as the stay in foster care has decreased (on average, it is now only 2 to 3 years) and the numbers of children needing foster placement has risen (by about 200,000 per year), the number of families willing to foster unrelated children has declined.

Kinship Care

kinship care A form of foster care in which a relative of a maltreated child takes over from the abusive or neglectful parents.

Fortunately, the use of another form of foster care, called **kinship care,** has increased. In kinship care, a relative of the maltreated child becomes the approved caregiver. It is estimated that 40 percent of all foster children are staying with relatives, who receive some financial support for doing what, traditionally, they might have done on their own.

Many experts have raised concerns about the quality of kinship care, since the available kin are usually the grandparents who raised the abusive parents in the first place and who are older, poorer, less healthy, and less educated than traditional foster parents. Indeed, some states and cities have policies that make it very difficult for any kin to be officially sanctioned and reimbursed to care for their mistreated relatives. Other communities find that since many relatives could not afford to take in additional family members without financial support, subsidizing kinship care seems the best plan—especially since kin are more likely to help restorable or supportable families, allowing the biological parents to see their children, and hence have them reunited eventually.

That there are diverse opinions about kinship care is indicated by noting that in Baltimore 2 of every 3 foster-care children are with kin whereas in Norfolk, Virginia, a mere hundred miles away, only 2 of every 100 foster children are in kinship care (Curtis et al., 1995). The most recent research finds that children fare as well in kinship homes as in the homes of strangers and that kinship care is often better than conventional foster care if the kin receive the same screening, supervision, and support as other foster parents (Berrick, 1998).

Adoption and Other Outcomes

Adoption is the final option, ideal when families are inadequate and children are young. However, primarily because judges and parents are reluctant to release children for adoption, this ideal solution is actually the least likely to occur. For example, Elisa, whose death was described in the beginning of this section, had five siblings who witnessed her torture and death when they were 2, 3, 4, 9, and 10 years old. They entered the foster-care system, stayed in more than four foster homes, and 3 years later had still not been released for adoption (Swarns, 1998). The three youngest children are now together in one foster family, where they may be adopted once the courts have severed the parental rights of their mother, who has been convicted for Elisa's death and now is in prison. Elisa's two oldest siblings will probably never be adopted.

Sadly, the children who fare worst in foster care are children like these, who have witnessed and endured years of maltreatment in their biological family—and therefore are likely to hate themselves, distrust others, and feel so angry at life that they suffer no matter where they are raised. Per-

The Chosen Family Two of these three children are adopted, and adoption is probably the best solution for children whose birth parents are unable to care for them. The third child, the 6-week-old girl, is a foster child who could be returned to her mother—which might protect the legal rights of the original family but likely not the emotional needs of the child.

manency planning for them is difficult, because they are older and harder to place. Their kin are either woefully inadequate or reluctant to take them in because they fear any connection to the original parents. Such children are often sent to group homes—which are better for children than living on the street but sometimes create new problems faster than they solve old ones.

Each state and each nation has its own mix of treatment options, and particular mixes can often do harm to the child. One U.S. child says:

> My parents didn't want me. I lived in three foster homes. My foster parents didn't want me. Now, I live in a group home, and I'm a loner. Probably for what's happened to me in my life, I'll never fit in. [Kools, 1997]

In fact, no nation has a good record of permanency planning. About one-third of all British children removed from their homes are placed in group homes, with sometimes abusive results (Buchanan, 1996). Thousands of mistreated children in Brazil, India, Romania (and many other nations) simply leave home for the streets, probably with even worse consequences for themselves and their future. And in Germany, where reporting of maltreatment is not required, constructive intervention on the part of professionals or the public is generally too little and too late: when child-abuse cases reach official attention, the reaction is more often punitive toward the parents than helpful for the child, partly because by that time the parents are past helping and the child has become unmanageable (Frehsee, 1996).

Experiments in Iowa, Kentucky, and Florida with differential response have thus far produced mixed success (Waldfogal, 1998). There are also programs to develop culturally sensitive care, especially for groups such as Native Americans and African Americans—groups for whom foster placement often was almost automatically chosen over support for families. Such culturally sensitive programs make sense in theory, but research has not yet documented their success.

This spotty record is discouraging. But when we realize that even the definition of child maltreatment was murky and off the mark only 40 years ago and that public recognition of the problem is only a decade or two old, we can agree with one expert that "the real culprit is wishful thinking about parents and the efficiency of treatment" (Besharov, 1998). In other words, this expert believes current policy places too much trust in the family and in treatment for neglectful or abusive parents. He advocates more good group homes. Others advocate more attention to prevention within the society, to combat "the erroneous notion that the most widespread threats to the safety and well-being of children stem from the misbehavior of their parents" (Pelton, 1998).

Prevention

primary prevention An approach to child maltreatment that is designed to prevent maltreatment (or other harm) from ever occurring.

The ultimate goal of child-care policy is to keep maltreatment from happening at all. The effort to attain this goal is called **primary prevention** because it must occur early in the sequence that can lead to maltreatment, before the problems start. Three research findings point the way:

- Some neighborhoods are much better than others at preventing child abuse, even if the families are poor. Factors such as stability of the residents, home ownership rather than renting, and support of churches and community centers are among the elements that make such a neighborhood (Korbin et al., 1998).
- Some basic values, such as two-parent families with planned and wanted children, or children raised by an ethnic, religious, and

educational community that cherishes the next generation, make serious abuse or life-threatening neglect less likely.

■ Since neglect is related to income, nations where the gap between rich and poor is greatest are those that have the highest numbers of children who suffer from neglect in early childhood and become runaways or throwaways in adolescence.

Public-policy measures aimed at attaining stable neighborhoods, basic values, and greater income equality tend to be controversial, and some would argue that they are beyond the mandate, the obligation, or even the power of public policy. Nonetheless, primary prevention is the first step toward reducing maltreatment.

secondary prevention An approach to child maltreatment that focuses on responding to the first symptoms of maltreatment or risk of maltreatment. Secondary prevention can, and should, begin before the problem becomes severe.

The next step is **secondary prevention,** which involves preventing serious problems by spotting and treating the early warning signs that indicate maltreatment might develop. One specific secondary-prevention measure is home visiting. As part of their national health-care systems, many developed countries, England and New Zealand among them, provide a network of nurses and social workers who visit all families with infants and young children at home, encourage good health practices, screen for potential problems, and provide referrals as necessary (Kamerman & Kahn, 1993). In an ambitious state-funded effort in Hawaii called Healthy Start, similar home visitation is available to the majority of the state's civilian population (Breakey & Pratt, 1991; Hawaii Department of Health, 1992). Although high-risk families are especially encouraged to join, parents participate voluntarily. At regular intervals in the child's early years (from birth to age 5), trained visitors come to the home to provide emotional support, model positive parent-infant interaction, and help the mother find health-care providers and other community agencies for further assistance.

Cultural Differences This baby waits outside alone while his mother eats sweets in the café.

❓ *Observational Quiz (see answer page 269): What signs indicate that this is maltreatment?*

The preliminary results of Hawaii's program were astonishing. Among the 1,204 high-risk families that participated in Healthy Start between 1987 and 1989, only three cases of abuse and six cases of neglect were reported to child-protection caseworkers—a less-than-1-percent rate of substantiated maltreatment in a high-risk segment of the population where the average had been 18 to 20 percent (Hawaii Department of Health, 1992). Thirty-one other states also provide some home-based case services for families with children (Child Welfare League, 1996).

Many other nations and states provide less comprehensive programs that specifically focus on situations where signs of trouble are apparent but the problem is not yet full-blown. Parent-newborn bonding sessions for high-risk families, classes in parent education for teen parents, crisis hotlines, respite care, drop-in centers, special training for teachers and police officers on recognizing abuse and neglect, and programs that educate children about sexual abuse are examples of secondary-prevention measures (Willis et al., 1992).

Secondary prevention is tricky. Sometimes efforts to target groups that might be incubating problems actually make the problem worse. As one reviewer of early-intervention programs notes, "The world of public policy is crowded with results that are unexpected and [with] unwanted by-products of well-meaning legislative or administrative initiatives" (Gallagher, 1990). Among these unwanted by-products are:

- Wrongfully stigmatizing certain families as inadequate
- Undermining family or cultural patterns that, contrary to conventional wisdom, do nurture children
- Creating a sense of helplessness in the family instead of strengthening its self-confidence, skills, and resourcefulness

tertiary prevention   An approach to child maltreatment that is aimed at halting maltreatment after it occurs and treating the victim. Removing a child from the home, providing needed hospitalization or psychological counseling, and jailing the perpetrator are all examples of tertiary-prevention measures.

However, the dangers of waiting until there is a need for **tertiary prevention,** which occurs after the problem is obvious, are all too familiar. Consider, as an analogy, the efforts we all make to prevent serious illness: Some important primary-prevention efforts are obvious—eat nutritious, low-fat, high-fiber foods, get ample exercise, avoid drug addiction—but it is controversial how much of this should be impelled by law. Secondary prevention must be sensitively undertaken: Should everyone with high blood pressure, or low self-esteem, or asthma symptoms take medication? Tertiary prevention—when serious illness strikes—must be done to prevent death or lifelong disability, but it can occur too late or too thoughtlessly.

Now let us look specifically at tertiary prevention of child maltreatment. Sometimes authorities wait too long before removing a child from a family, as with Elisa. Other times, the need for ongoing family support without removal is clear, but again only in retrospect. An example is the case of Lia, a preschooler in California whose parents were immigrants from Cambodia. The child had epilepsy and was given many medications, which the parents eventually discarded as worthless. Fearful that Lia would die of medical neglect and impatient with the parents' religious rituals that were supposed to cure the problem, a caseworker removed the child to foster care and then to the hospital. With medication but without the comfort of her parents, Lia had a massive seizure that left her brain-dead (Fadiman, 1997). For both Lia and Elisa, good secondary prevention could have avoided the severe maltreatment that occurred, and better tertiary prevention could have prevented the death of brain or body. Best of all, of course, would have been primary prevention—education and community support that would have prevented the strain on the parents in the first place.

One final thought regarding policy: Effective prevention programs are sometimes criticized as being too expensive, but their costs are small in comparison with the costs that arise when nothing is done. The cost of Hawaii's Healthy Start program averaged out to an estimated $1,600 per year per family in 1993. For comparison, hospitalization for severe physical abuse costs $33,641 on average (Irazuzta et al., 1997), and a year of prison costs $22,000. And the psychological costs of maltreatment far exceed the monetary ones, especially when we consider the consequences of turning a well-functioning and loving family into an abusive, violent, victimized set of blood relatives.

Although primary-prevention policies are understandably controversial, both theories and research in human development suggest that prevention programs should be broad enough to involve the entire social context. Since poverty, youth, isolation, and ignorance tend to correlate with unwanted births, inadequate parenting, and then mistreated children, we should not reject measures to raise the lowest family incomes, discourage teenage pregnancies, encourage community involvement, and increase the level of education of prospective parents merely because they are expensive. They may provide the most cost-effective prevention of all.

SUMMARY

SIZE AND SHAPE

1. During early childhood, children grow about 3 inches (7 centimeters) and gain about 4½ pounds (2 kilograms) a year. Normal variation in growth is caused primarily by genes, health care, and nutrition, with genes most important in developed nations but nutrition most important in developing nations worldwide. Generally, appetite decreases by age 5, especially for children who do not exercise much, and the decrease can lead to nutritional imbalance and/or parental concern.

BRAIN GROWTH AND DEVELOPMENT

2. Brain maturation, including increased myelination and improved coordination between the two halves of the brain, brings important gains in children's physical abilities and emotional self-regulation. As they get older, preschool children develop quicker reactions to stimuli and are more able to control those reactions.

3. Brain maturation helps make older children safer than younger ones, even though younger ones are more closely supervised. Although boys and low-income children are more at risk, injury control can substantially reduce accidental deaths and serious harm.

4. Better control of eye movements and improved focusing are associated with brain maturation. Development of the visual pathways also enhances eye-hand coordination. These improvements enable children to begin mastery of basic literacy skills at around age 6.

MASTERING MOTOR SKILLS

5. Gross motor skills improve dramatically during early childhood, making it possible for the average 5-year-old to perform many physical activities with grace and skill. Safe play space, maturation, and guided practice help to move this process along.

6. Fine motor skills, such as holding a pencil or tying a shoelace, improve more gradually during early childhood, with guidance much more essential. Mastery of drawing skills develops steadily and is correlated with intellectual growth.

CHILD MALTREATMENT

7. Child maltreatment takes many forms, including physical, emotional, or sexual abuse and emotional or physical neglect. In the United States, about 3 million cases of child maltreatment are reported and 1 million are confirmed each year. Although certain cultural conditions and values—poverty and social isolation among them—are almost universally harmful, some practices that are considered abusive in one culture in one time period are acceptable in others.

8. The consequences of child maltreatment are far-reaching; in general, it tends to impair the child's learning, self-esteem, social relationships, and emotional control. Some of its effects can scar the person lifelong. However, it is not inevitable that maltreated children become maltreating adults.

9. Once maltreatment is reported, the response should depend on the particular situation. Intervention should support and restore families that can be helped and should provide permanent placement, with foster parents, kin, or adoptive families, for the minority of families where the pattern of maltreatment cannot be halted.

10. The most effective primary- and secondary-prevention strategies for maltreatment are those that enhance community support and address the material and emotional needs of troubled families. One specific measure is home-visitation programs that offer support and assistance to families at risk.

KEY TERMS

corpus callosum (246)
injury control (248)
child maltreatment (255)
abuse (255)
neglect (255)
intergenerational
  transmission (259)
differential response (260)
vulnerable-to-crisis
  families (261)

restorable families (262)
supportable families (262)
inadequate families (262)
foster care (263)
kinship care (263)
primary prevention (265)
secondary prevention
  (266)
tertiary prevention (267)

KEY QUESTIONS

1. How do the size, shape, and proportions of the child's body change between ages 2 and 6?

2. What causes variations in height and weight during childhood, in developed and developing countries?

3. What effect does maturation of the corpus callosum have in older preschoolers?

4. In what ways do the gross and fine motor skills develop differently?

5. What measures are most effective in reducing the rate of injuries in children?

6. What are the similarities and differences between abuse and neglect?

7. What factors in the culture, the community, and the family increase the risk of child maltreatment?

8. What are the long-term consequences of childhood abuse and neglect?

9. What are the advantages and disadvantages of foster care, including kinship care?

10. Give an example of effective primary, secondary, and tertiary prevention of child abuse.

11. *In Your Experience* What child-rearing practice do you know that one culture or family considered necessary but that you considered maltreatment? Explain both viewpoints.

CRITICAL THINKING EXERCISE

by Richard O. Straub

Take your study of Chapter 8 a step further by working this creative problem-solving exercise:

Developmental psychologists view play as the major means through which physical, cognitive, and social skills are mastered—especially during the preschool years. Unfortunately, many adults are so imbued with the work ethic that they tend to denigrate children's play. Some even punish their children for "horsing around," criticize preschool teachers for letting children "play too much," or schedule their children's lives so heavily with lessons and chores that there is little time for play.

Your task is to mentally design a toy, suitable for a 2- to 6-year-old child, that will enhance the physical, cognitive, and/or social development of the preschool child.* Then answer the questions below.

1. What is the name of your toy? How does the child play with it or use it?

2. How old is the child for whom this toy is intended? What features of the toy make it developmentally appropriate?

3. What domain or domains of development is your toy designed to stimulate? How are they stimulated?

4. What are some of the specific features of the toy (for example, size, shape, color) that enhance its attractiveness and play value?

5. What considerations should be given to injury control when this toy is used?

Evaluate your answers—and your toy—in light of the information provided in Appendix B.

*Based on an idea from Neysmith-Roy (1994).

❶ *Answer to Observational Quiz (from page 266):* None! The baby is obviously well-cared-for, with a hat to protect him from the sun, warm and colorful socks, and a chance to experience the fresh air and the view. If you thought this was neglect, you need to note from the sign that this café is in Germany, where toddlers are often parked in carriages or strollers outside restaurants without injury, kidnapping, or any other distress. (A Danish mother did the same thing in New York City in 1997. She was arrested and jailed, and her baby was put in temporary foster care. Which was maltreatment?)

The Play Years:
Cognitive Development

The cognitive development that begins even before birth continues through the play years. As you now know, developmentalists underestimated the thinking skills of infants—until new research strategies allowed them to probe more closely into infants' capacities for memory and thought. Recent research has also led to an appreciative acknowledgment of cognitive abilities during early childhood, which include mathematics, language, and social understanding. Indeed, research on intellectual development before age 7 has inspired a completely new understanding of preschool education, once thought of as merely "day care" and now considered an important learning experience. One developmental psychologist explains:

> People often call this the "preschool period," but that's not only a mundane name for a magic time, it's also a misnomer. These three-ish and five-ish years are not a waiting time before school or even a time of preparation for school, but an age stage properly called "early childhood" that has a developmental agenda of its own. (Leach, 1997)

We begin our examination of cognitive growth during the play years by seeing how Piaget and Vygotsky interpreted the development of cognitive skills in preschoolers. We then discuss basic intellectual skills such as number sense, problem solving, memory, and something called "theory of mind." Next, we consider preschoolers' remarkable accomplishments in language development. We conclude with a description of the long-term benefits of preschool education.

HOW YOUNG CHILDREN THINK

One of the delights of observing young children is seeing them express a growing, but often fanciful and subjective, understanding of their lives. They beguile us with their imaginative, even magical, thinking when they chatter away with an invisible playmate, or wonder where the sun sleeps, or confidently claim that they themselves always sleep with their eyes open. At the same time, they startle us when they are confused by metaphors (as in "Mommy is tied up at the office," or "The car's engine just died") and when they are illogical about common occurrences (for instance, that the moon follows them when they walk at night). Clearly, their thinking is often dictated more by their own subjective views than by reality.

For many years, the magical and self-absorbed nature of young children's thinking dominated developmental conceptions of preschooler cognition, guided by Piaget. More recent research has highlighted another side of preschool thought. That side is suggested by the following episode between a 2-year-old child and his mother, who has been trying to hold his sweet tooth in check:

> (Child sees chocolate cake on table.)
> Child: Bibby on.
> Mother: You don't want your bibby on. You're not eating.
> Child: Chocolate cake. Chocolate cake.
> Mother: You're not having any more chocolate cake, either.
> Child: Why?
> Mother: (No answer)
> Child: (Whines) Tired.
> Mother: You tired? Ooh! (Sympathetically)
> Child: Chocolate cake.
> Mother: No chance.
> (adapted from Dunn et al., 1987)

The young child in this episode is definitely *not* being illogical or oblivious to the constraints of the real world. He is showing strategic skill in pursuing his goal—from asking for his bib (a noncontroversial request) to eliciting sympathy by feigning fatigue. He is, as Vygotsky would recognize, thinking beyond the bounds of egocentrism.

Piaget's Theory of Preoperational Thought

symbolic thought Thinking that involves the use of words, gestures, pictures, or actions to represent ideas, things, or behaviors.

According to Piaget, the striking difference between cognition during infancy and cognition during the preschool years is **symbolic thought,** the use of words or objects to signify other objects, behaviors, or experiences. The idea of a cat is not contained solely in the furry creature that a sensorimotor infant sees and touches; it is also what a preschooler signifies when sounding out the word "cat," or when pointing at a picture of a cat, or when crawling on the floor and saying "meow."

preoperational thought Piaget's term for the cognition of children between the ages of about 2 and 6 years, implying that such children have not yet learned to use logical principles in their thinking.

Humans are freed from the narrow restrictions of their immediate senses and actions once they can think symbolically. As monumental as symbolic thought may be, however, Piaget chose to refer to cognitive development between the ages of about 2 and 6 years as **preoperational thought;** in doing so, he was referring to what preschool children *cannot* do, rather than the symbolic thinking they can now use. And what they cannot yet do is think *operationally.* That is, they cannot develop a thought or an idea step-by-step according to some set of logical principles.

Obstacles to Logical Operations

The observation that young children are not logical (or, to Piaget, that they are prelogical) does not mean that they are stupid or ignorant. Rather, it means their thinking reflects certain characteristics that we associate with preoperational thought (Flavell et al., 1993). One such characteristic is **centration,** which is a tendency to focus thought on one aspect of a situation, to the exclusion of all others. Young children may, for example, insist that lions and tigers are not cats because the children center on the house-pet aspect of the cats they know. Or they may insist that Father is a *daddy* and not a son or brother or uncle because children center on each family member exclusively in the role that person plays for them.

centration The tendency to focus on one way of thinking and perceiving, without acknowledging any alternatives.

egocentrism The tendency to perceive events and interpret experiences exclusively from one's own, self-centered, perspective.

One particular type of centration is ego-centration, better known as **egocentrism,** in which the child contemplates the world exclusively from his or her personal perspective. In the daddy example above, the fact that the man's relationship to the child is the only role the child sees is an example of egocentrism, which severely limits cognitive development until about age

7. As Piaget described it, preschoolers are not necessarily selfish; they would, for example, rush to comfort a tearful parent. But the comfort would come in a decidedly egocentric form, such as a teddy bear or a lollipop.

A second characteristic of preoperational thought is its focus on *appearance* to the exclusion of other attributes. A girl given a short haircut might worry that she has turned into a boy; a boy might refuse to wear a pink shirt because he is not a girl. Or upon meeting, say, a tall 4-year-old and a shorter 5-year-old, a child might explain that the 4-year-old is actually older because "bigger is older."

Further, preschoolers tend to be *static* in their reasoning, assuming the world is unchanging, always in the state in which they currently encounter it. If anything does change, it changes totally and suddenly. When she awakened on her fifth birthday, my daughter Rachel asked, "Am I 5 yet?" Told yes, she grinned, stretched out her arms, and said, "Look at my 5-year-old hands."

A closely related characteristic of preoperational thought is **irreversibility.** Being irreversible in their thinking means that preschoolers fail to recognize that reversing a transformation brings about the conditions that existed before the transformation process began. A preschooler who cries because his mother put lettuce on his hamburger might not think to suggest removing the lettuce and might refuse to eat the hamburger even after the lettuce is removed.

irreversibility   The inability to review the prior steps to whatever the current situation might be, leading to an inability to change things by reversing the process.

Conservation and Logic

Piaget devised a number of experiments to test and illustrate the ways in which preoperational characteristics (centration, irreversibility, and focus on static appearance) limit young children's ability to reason logically. For example, he studied children's understanding of **conservation,** the principle that the amount of a substance present is unaffected by changes in its appearance. Piaget found that conservation, taken for granted by older children and adults, is not at all obvious to preschoolers. Rather, preschoolers tend to focus exclusively on one facet of shape or placement and to use that as a measure of amount.

conservation   The concept that the total quantity, number, or amount of something is the same (preserved) no matter what the shape or configuration.

As one example, suppose some young children are shown two identical glasses containing the same amount of liquid. Then the liquid from one of the glasses is poured into a taller, narrower glass. If the children are asked whether one glass contains more liquid than the other, they will insist that the narrower glass, now with the higher liquid level, contains more. They make that mistake because they center on liquid height, noticing only the static appearance and ignoring the idea that they could reverse the process and re-create what they saw a moment earlier.

Demonstration of Conservation   Professor Berger's daughter Sarah, here at age 5¾, demonstrates Piaget's conservation-of-liquids experiment. First, she examines both short glasses to be sure they contain the same amount of milk. Then, after the contents of one are poured into the tall glass and she is asked "Which has more?" she points to the tall glass, just as Piaget would have expected. Later she added, "It looks like it has more because it is taller," indicating that some direct instruction might change her mind.

Similarly, if an experimenter lines up, say, seven pairs of checkers in two rows of equal length and asks a 4-year-old whether both rows have the

Tests of Various Types of Conservation

Type of conservation	Initial presentation	Transformation	Question	Preoperational child's answer
Liquids	Two equal glasses of liquid.	Pour one into a taller, narrower glass.	Which glass contains more?	The taller one.
Number	Two equal lines of checkers.	Increase spacing of checkers in one line.	Which line has more checkers?	The longer one.
Matter	Two equal balls of clay.	Squeeze one ball into a long, thin shape.	Which piece has more clay?	The long one.
Length	Two sticks of equal length.	Move one stick.	Which stick is longer?	The one that is farther to the right.

Figure 9.1 Conservation, Please. According to Piaget, until children grasp the concept of conservation at (he believed) about age 6 or 7 years, they cannot understand that the transformations shown here do not change the total amount of liquid, checkers, clay, and wood.

same number of checkers, the child will usually say yes. But suppose that, while the child watches, the experimenter elongates one of the rows by spacing its checkers farther apart. If the experimenter then asks again whether the rows have the same number of checkers, the child will most likely reply no. The child seems compelled by appearance to conclude that the row with the greater length contains the greater number of checkers. Other conservation tests, shown in Figure 9.1, produce similar results.

In such tests of conservation, Piaget believed, preschoolers center on appearances and ignore or discount the transformation—even though they watched as it occurred. They are not yet able to understand simple, logical transformations.

Vygotsky's Theory: Children as Apprentices

Every developmentalist, every preschool teacher, and every parent knows that young children strive for understanding in a world that fascinates and sometimes confuses them. They are active learners, as Piaget emphasized. Lev Vygotsky would certainly agree.

But Vygotsky also emphasized another point: Children do not strive alone; their efforts are embedded in a social context. They notice things and they ask "Why?" with the assumption that others know why. They want to know how machines work, why weather changes, where the sky ends—and they expect answers.

Meanwhile, parents, as well as older children, preschool teachers, and many others, do more than just answer questions. They try to guide a young child's cognitive growth by:

- Presenting challenges for new learning,
- Offering assistance with tasks that may be too difficult,

- Providing instruction,
- Encouraging the child's interest and motivation

In many ways, then, a young child is an *apprentice in thinking* whose intellectual growth is stimulated and directed by older and more skilled members of society. Children learn to think through their **guided participation** in social experiences and in explorations of their universe (Rogoff, 1990; Rogoff et al., 1993).

If this social (apprenticeship) aspect of cognitive development seems familiar, that's because it is given particular emphasis in the sociocultural perspective discussed in Chapter 2. As you read on pages 51 to 55, Vygotsky's ideas have become the basis for much research that emphasizes the cultural foundations of growth and development. In contrast to many developmentalists (including Piaget) who tend to regard cognitive growth as a process of *individual* discovery propelled by personal experience and biological maturation, Vygotsky believed that cognitive growth is driven by cultural processes that shape the child's experiences, incentives, and goals. More specifically, Vygotsky saw cognition not as a process of private discovery but as a social activity, advanced through the guidance of parents and other teachers who motivate, channel, and construct children's learning.

How to Solve a Puzzle

To see how Vygotsky's approach works in practical terms, let's look at an example. Suppose a child tries to assemble a jigsaw puzzle, fails, and stops trying. Does that mean the task is beyond the child's ability? Not necessarily. The child may do better if he or she is given guidance that provides motivation to solve the puzzle, that focuses attention on the important steps, and that restructures the task to make its solution more attainable.

An adult or older child might begin such guidance by encouraging the child to look for a missing puzzle piece for a particular section ("Does it need to be a big piece or a little piece?" "Do you see any blue pieces with a line of red?"). Suppose the child finds some pieces of the right size, and then some blue pieces with a red line, but again seems stymied. The tutor might then be more directive, selecting a piece to be tried next, or rotating a piece so that its proper location is more obvious, or actually putting a piece in place with a smile of satisfaction. Throughout, the teacher would praise momentary successes, maintain enthusiasm, and help the child see their joint progress toward the goal of finishing the puzzle.

The critical element in guided participation is that the mentor and child *interact* to accomplish the task, with the teacher sensitive and responsive to the precise needs of the child. Eventually, as the result of such mutuality, the child will be able to succeed independently.

In our example, once the child puts the puzzle together with the tutor's help, he or she might try it again soon—this time needing less assistance or perhaps none at all. The tutor gradually guides the child to do more on his or her own, encouraging each step toward independence. If puzzle solving is a valued skill in the culture, the adult might find a new puzzle for the child. Then, skills mastered with the first puzzle—such as locating pieces with the proper coloring or finding and connecting all the edge pieces first—will be transferred to the next puzzle, and, eventually, generalized to all possible puzzles. In families that value and encourage puzzle solving, the children all learn to perform and enjoy that activity, just as in other families children all learn to play musical instruments, to bake bread, to catch balls, or whatever.

Guided Participation Through shared social activity, adults in every culture guide the development of their children's cognition, values, and skills. Typically, the child's curiosity and interests, rather than the adult's planning for some future need, motivate the process. That seems to be the case as this Guatamalan girl eagerly tries to learn her mother's sewing skills.

Such interactive apprenticeships are commonplace and continual. In every culture of the world, adults provide guidance and assistance to teach various skills; soon, children who are given such guided practice learn to perform the skills on their own (Rogoff, 1990; Rogoff et al., 1993; Tharp & Gallimore, 1988). Eventually, they become the tutors.

Scaffolding

Key to the success of apprenticeship is the tutor's sensitivity to the child's abilities and his or her readiness to learn new skills. According to Vygotsky (1934/1986),

> The only good kind of instruction is that which marches ahead of development and leads it. It must be aimed not so much at the ripe as at the ripening functions. It remains necessary to determine the lowest threshold at which instruction may begin, since a certain ripeness of functions is required. But we must consider the upper threshold as well: instruction must be oriented toward the future, not the past.

As you saw in Chapter 2, Vygotsky believed that for each developing individual at each skill level, there is a **zone of proximal development (ZPD)**, that is, a range of skills that the person can exercise with assistance but is not yet quite able to perform independently. How and when children master potential skills depends, in part, on the willingness of others to **scaffold,** or sensitively structure, participation in learning encounters (Bruner, 1982; Wood et al., 1976).

Developmentalists who have observed how parents scaffold their child's emergent capabilities have identified a number of steps that contribute to effective scaffolding. They emphasize that adults cannot simply build a scaffold and expect the child to climb it alone; they must construct it with the child and help the child through it (Bruner, 1982; Rogoff, 1990; Stone, 1993). The steps are these:

1. *Arouse* interest in a new task, or build on an activity that already captures the child's interest.
2. *Simplify* the task, helping the child think about the best strategy or completing certain steps for the child.
3. *Scaffold* the task itself, so that it is within the child's ability, perhaps by doing some steps jointly or by arranging the materials and the setting to make success possible.
4. *Interpret* the activity, so that cognitive understanding will facilitate skill mastery.
5. *Solve* problems, anticipating mistakes, and guide the child to avoid or correct them.
6. *Teach* enthusiasm by encouraging the desire to achieve and by reducing boredom and self-doubt.

These six steps reveal once again that cognitive development is essentially a social process, for interaction is called for at each step. Note the need for emotional involvement—sparking motivation, maintaining enthusiasm, dealing with frustration—which is at least as important as the specific, task-based activities. Finally, to make them easier to remember, think of the six steps as the acronym "Assist"—itself a scaffold for learning about apprenticeship.

Talking to Learn

Vygotsky believed that verbal interaction is a cognitive tool, essential to intellectual growth in two crucial ways. The first way is through

zone of proximal development (ZPD) The skills or knowledge that are within the potential of the learner but are not yet mastered.

scaffold To structure participation in learning encounters in order to foster a child's emerging capabilities. Scaffolds can be provided in many ways: by a mentor, by the objects or experiences of a culture, or by the child's past learning.

ZPD The best way to learn almost any practical or intellectual skill is with the help of a "mentor" who guides one's entry into the zone of proximal development, the area between what one can do alone and what one might do with help.

❓ *Observational Quiz (see answer page 278): In social apprenticeship, three elements—the teacher, the context, and the learner—each make a unique contribution. What evidence of such contributions can you see here?*

private speech   The dialogue that occurs when one talks to oneself, either silently or out loud, to form thoughts and analyze ideas.

private speech, the internal dialogue that occurs when people talk to themselves (Vygotsky, 1987). In adults private speech is usually silent, but in children, especially preschoolers, it is likely to be uttered out loud. With time, children's loud self-talk becomes first soft-voiced and then inner, silent speech. During the play years, however, most children are not aware that they—or anyone else—can ever talk to themselves without talking out loud (Flavell et al., 1997).

Researchers studying private speech have found that preschoolers use it to help them think and learn—to review what they know, decide what to do, and explain events to themselves and, incidentally, to anyone else within earshot. Children who have learning difficulties tend to develop private speech more slowly and to use it less (Diaz, 1987). Training children to say things to themselves to focus their thoughts sometimes helps them learn—another sign that private speech aids the learning process.

The second way in which language advances thinking, according to Vygotsky, is as the *mediator of the social interaction* that, as you have seen, is vital to learning. Whether this **social mediation** function of speech occurs during explicit instruction or only casual conversation, whether it is intellectual interpretation or simply enthusiastic comments, language as a tool of verbal interaction refines and extends a person's skills. Language allows a person to enter and traverse the zone of proximal development, because words provide a bridge from the child's current understanding to what is almost understood.

social mediation   In regard to language, the use of speech as a tool to bridge the gap in understanding or knowledge between learner and tutor.

Comparing Piaget and Vygotsky

As is evident in Table 9.1, the theories of Piaget and Vygotsky are similar in a number of ways. However, each perspective suggests limitations of the other, as you will now see with a contextual view of Piaget's classic experiments in conservation.

table 9.1   Concepts from the Theories of Piaget and Vygotsky

Piaget	Vygotsky
Active Learning The child's own search for understanding, motivated by the child's inborn curiosity.	**Guided Participation** The adult or other mentor's aid in guiding the next step of learning, motivated by the learner's need for social interaction.
Egocentrism The preschooler's tendency to perceive everything from his or her own perspective and to be limited by that viewpoint.	**Apprenticeship in Thinking** The preschooler's tendency to look to others for insight and guidance, particularly in the cognitive realm.
Structure The mental assumptions and modalities (schema) the child creates to help him or her organize an understanding of the world. Structures are torn down and rebuilt when disequilibrium makes new structures necessary.	**Scaffold** The building blocks for learning put in place by a "teacher" (a more knowledgeable child or adult) or a culture. Learners use scaffolds and then discard them when they are no longer needed.
Symbolic Thought The ability to think using symbols, including language. This ability emerges spontaneously at about age 2 and continues lifelong.	**Proximal Development** The next step in cognition, the ideas and skills a child can grasp with assistance but not alone; influenced not only by the child's own abilities and interests, but also by the social context.

Both theories emphasize that learning is not passive, but is affected by the learner. The two theories share concepts and sometimes terminology; the differences are in emphasis.

❷ **Especially for Social Scientists:** For 50 years Piaget's conservation experiments were the standard that indicated the nature of preschool thought. Children almost always answered as predicted. Can you think of any reasons, other than lack of logic, why preschoolers would not demonstrate conservation?

Eliciting Conservation

Piaget believed that cognitive immaturity makes it impossible for preoperational children to grasp the idea of conservation (as well as other principles of concrete operational thought), no matter how carefully adults explain such thinking to them. But some later researchers wondered if perhaps the specific nature of Piaget's conservation experiments—including their formal or testlike features—might affect children's performance. And, in fact, in playful, gamelike situations (rather than the formal experimental situations described above), preschoolers have revealed an accurate grasp of conservation.

For example, in one variation of the checkers test of conservation of number, the elongation of one row of checkers was caused by the action of a "naughty" teddy bear rather than by the deliberate manipulation of an adult (Donaldson, 1978). In this context, preschoolers were more likely to recognize that both rows still contained the same number of checkers. The researchers hypothesized that in the formal experimental situation, young children assume that if an adult repositions a row of checkers, then something significant, like the total number of checkers, is being changed. In the gamelike situation, however, the teddy's "messing up" the rows does not lead to this distracting assumption.

Children are particularly likely to grasp the concept of conservation if they are given special training, including explicit verbal instructions to focus their attention and memory, with demonstrations. In other words, good scaffolding in the zone of proximal development nurtures cognitive abilities. One particularly successful experiment with liquid conservation began with both pretend play (in which the children themselves poured liquids from one container to another as part of a game) and step-by-step explanations of why the amount of liquid is the same no matter what the shape of the containers. When they were later given the classic Piagetian test, some of them did much better than is typical for their age group.

As a follow-up, the experimenters asked very explicit questions of the successful trainees to determine the depth of their understanding. For instance, they asked, "How can the water in this one be so much taller and still have the same amount as this one?" The preschoolers were quick and confident in correctly explaining the rationale for conservation (Golumb & McLean, 1984).

In a variety of experiments that include training, most preschool children are able to follow the examiner's guided instructions and then, apparently, grasp the idea of conservation. Several weeks after such training, many 4- and 5-year-olds (but almost no 3-year-olds) still understand the concept. Indeed, older preschoolers not only grasp the type of conservation taught to them (such as for liquids) but also other types of conservation (such as for number or matter) (Field, 1987). Nevertheless, their capacity to exercise reasoning skill is limited and fragile: When they are faced with tasks that are more complex or challenging, their tendencies toward centration, egocentrism, and irreversibility reemerge. As Piaget would explain it, they have not yet restructured their thinking to include the basic structures of concrete operational thought.

Without a Scaffold

Vygotsky would suggest another explanation for the fragility of older preschoolers' ability to master conservation or the other principles of operational thought. He would say that the scaffold was not sufficiently steady and enduring to keep the more advanced thinking in place.

❶ *Answer to Observational Quiz (from page 276):* First, the teacher's work is most obvious. She is using both hands, and very watchful eyes, to guide the process. Without her, the nail would never be safely pounded, and the child might be hurt and frustrated. Second, note the table, and the model already done right in front of them, which suggests a woodworking activity within an educational program—not something offered in most cultures to most students. Finally, the child provides something only he can—concentrated, dedicated effort. Evidence for that: his tongue.

Calvin and Hobbes

by Bill Watterson

Language as Mediation One of the problems with cultural transmission of knowledge is that children are ready to learn whatever they are told—as myths about storks or cabbage patches, boogiemen or witches, will attest.

This highlights a criticism of Vygotsky's ideas: Parents are not always willing and able to tune in to their children's emotions and thoughts—an essential aspect of scaffolding. Some parents do not see their role as one of imparting knowledge, and some children do not want to learn what their parents want them to learn (Goodnow, 1993). Does this mean that some children, those without parental guidance, will not learn? Or can someone else become their escort through the zone of proximal development? Can such children teach themselves, as Piaget would contend, or is guidance of some sort essential?

According to sociocultural theory, many experiences with various adults or other children, either at home or in preschool, can provide the incentives and skills needed for social understanding and cognitive competence. Further, many of the tools provided by the culture, such as educational toys or television programs or the experience of caring for a pet or walking through a supermarket, are scaffolds for participatory learning. In other words, if the parents do not tutor the child, society or the culture may. And if the child's interest in learning is not aroused by his or her parents, it may be aroused—and powerfully—when the child begins to compare his or her skills with those of other children of the same age.

Evidence that culture influences the development of cognitive abilities comes from a process that seems to be universal: In every culture, children become more adept at precisely those cognitive skills that are most valued by that culture, while other interests and skills atrophy. Thus, for example, children in the Micronesian islands are much better at interpreting weather and navigation signs than are, say, children growing up in Dallas or Detroit, who may have no awareness of the significance of various phases of the moon, types of cloud formation, or shifts in the wind. On their part, children of educated parents acquire skills that are well suited to abstract and scientific reasoning, and their parents enjoy answering "why" questions that another parent might consider rude.

An example of "striking cultural differences" is that mothers in Salt Lake City talked more than twice as much to their preschoolers as did mothers in Guatemala, who engaged their children with touch or visual demonstration instead of words (Rogoff et al., 1993). Verbal fluency is

After Ten Comes Eleven The day, the date, the season, and the weather are all concepts that are part of the curriculum of a good preschool. Young children's ability to grasp these concepts—as well as to develop an understanding of number—is a good deal stronger than researchers or educators once imagined.

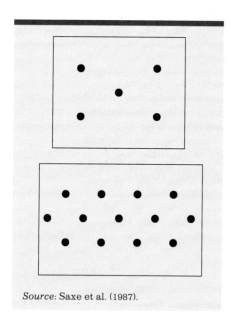

Source: Saxe et al. (1987).

Figure 9.2 Up for the Count. In the experimental game of "count the dots," 2½- and 4-year-olds were asked to count and touch each dot in these two different displays. Most 2½-year-olds made several errors, even on the 5-dot display. But some 4-year-olds did both tasks perfectly. They had already learned the most basic of counting rules: Count each object once, and only once.

much more valued in Utah than in Guatemala, so parents nurture language accordingly.

Such cultural variation was anticipated by Vygotsky, who believed each society has its own lessons and skills, as well as ways to teach them. However, the variation makes children, and all learners, highly dependent on their teachers and cultures. To what extent cognitive development comes from within the child, as Piaget would say, and to what extent from outside the child, is still a topic for debate.

WHAT PRESCHOOLERS CAN DO

As you have seen, developmentalists can—and do—debate how much a preschooler's cognitive accomplishments are the result of maturation, and how much the result of culture. However, while this nature-nurture debate continues, there is no doubt that preschoolers demonstrate amazing competency in several areas, three of which—number, memory, and theory of mind—we will now describe.

Number

Even infants have some perceptual awareness of quantity (such as noticing the difference between two and three objects), and by age 2 they sometimes can answer "How old are you?" correctly. However, the connection between numbers and objects is quite tenuous in the early stages of symbolic thought. When asked to count a group of objects, younger preschoolers are likely to delete numbers from the number sequence, counting "one, two, four, seven, . . . ," or to count the same item more than once, or to omit some items from the count. It takes time to master the key counting principles, which include:

- The *stable-order principle:*
  In counting, numbers must be said in a fixed order.
- The *one-to-one principle:*
  Each item being counted gets one number, and only one.
- The *cardinal principle:*
  The last number in a count represents the total.

The fact that counting ability improves progressively was illustrated by a study in which 2½- and 4-year-olds were presented with two displays of dots, one of 5 dots and the other of 13, and were asked to "count the dots and touch each dot as you count it" (see Figure 9.2). The younger children seemed to understand what they had been asked to do, but their performance was poor. In other words, they had some comprehension of symbolic thought, but they could not demonstrate it without help. Typically, they failed to touch at least 2 dots of the 5-dot display, and an average of 8 dots in the 13-dot display. They also miscounted, some saying only "one, two, three" for both displays.

By contrast, most of the 4-year-olds performed perfectly on the 5-dot display and averaged only two counting mistakes and two pointing errors on the 13-dot display. Indeed, many 4-year-olds did the 13-dot task with no errors (Saxe et al., 1987). Presumably, in 18 preschool months these children had learned the necessary principles of counting.

❶ Response for Social Scientists (from page 278): We now know that preschoolers want to please adults, and if they think an adult expects a particular answer, they will try to give it. In playful situations, or after careful instruction, preschoolers sometimes do demonstrate conservation.

How Number Skills Develop

What contributes to the child's developing understanding of number? One factor is simple maturation, of three different kinds:

- Brain development that continues throughout childhood
- Maturation of language, enabling the preschooler to conceptualize and express number
- Maturation in the sense emphasized by Piaget—that is, the flowering of the child's innate curiosity and exploration of the world of objects

In addition, the overall cultural context and specific family guidance play a role. In many societies the child's mathematical flowering has a rich environment to sustain it. Preschoolers typically

> accompany their parents on shopping trips; hear numbers used in talk about time, birthdays, and how many presents they will or will not get; and ride elevators in buildings with many floors. . . . They watch the Count on the television program "Sesame Street" talk about his passion for counting different size sets, or Señor Zero looking for nothing so he can count zero things, or even a puppet dressed up in a black leather jacket singing "Born to Add" set to the tune of a popular rock and roll song. (Gelman & Massey, 1987)

In some cultures, another factor that promotes preschoolers' number competence is the particular language they speak. One hypothesis about the general math superiority of East Asian children over European and American youngsters is that Japanese, Korean, and Chinese are much more logical in their labeling of numbers. For instance "eleven, twelve, thirteen," and so on, are called "ten-one, ten-two, ten-three," and so on, in the Asian languages (Fuson & Kwon, 1992). This linguistic ordering advances young Asian children's intuitive grasp of the number system as soon as they begin to talk.

Another way in which the Chinese language, in particular, fosters number learning is that its names for the numbers are short, one-syllable words. Because all children's brains have limited storage and processing capacity, a child's brain can process more one-syllable Chinese numbers than one- and two-syllable English ones (such as "seven, twenty, one hundred")—and, for that matter, more English numbers than even longer Welsh ones. The more numbers memory can contain, the easier it is to count, add, and perform other arithmetic operations (Schneider & Pressley, 1997).

A final factor in building number competence—a factor we will emphasize in connection with other cognitive abilities as well—is the structure and scaffolding support provided by parents, other adults, and older children. "Structure" and "scaffolding" in this case do not mean a formal curriculum, but just natural interaction, as Vygotsky particularly would emphasize. In many families, parents and offspring frequently use numbers together—counting small quantities, playing number games ("one, two, button my shoe . . ."), pushing television-channel buttons, sorting coins, and measuring (as in putting the allotted spoonfuls of cocoa mix into a glass of milk). Through such shared activities, number concepts become attractive and come within the children's capabilities.

Memory

Preschoolers are notorious for having poor memory, even when compared with children only a few years older. Ask a school-age child "What did you do today?" and you may get a detailed accounting, complete with reflections about why people acted as they did and how their current behavior relates to their past actions. Ask that older child what happened in a television sit-com, and again you might hear a lengthy, blow-by-blow sequence, with more specifics than you ever wanted to know. Ask a preschooler the same questions, and you are likely to hear "I don't remember" or "I liked it" or a string of seemingly irrelevant details.

Even with skilled help from a patient mother who knows her child and understands the basics of early memory, preschool children's memory is far from fluent. This example is typical:

Mother: Did you like the apartment at the beach?
Rachel: Yeah, and I have fun in the, in the, water.
Mother: You had fun in the water?
Rachel: Yeah, I come to the ocean.
Mother: You went to the ocean?
Rachel: Yeah.
Mother: Did you play in the ocean?
Rachel: And my sandals off.
Mother: You took your sandals off?
Rachel: And my jamas off.
Mother: And your jamas off. And what did you wear to the beach?
Rachel: I wear hot cocoa shirt.
Mother: Oh, your cocoa shirt, yeah. And your bathing suit.
Rachel: Yeah, and my cocoa shirt.
Mother: And did you go in the water?
Rachel: (No response)
Mother: Who went in the water with you?
Rachel: Daddy and Mommy.
Mother: Right. Did the big waves splash you?
Rachel: Yeah.
[Hudson, 1990]

The Script: Birthday Child Blows Out Candles
The fact that preschoolers have scripts for events such as birthdays is especially evident when someone "violates" the script. If this birthday-boy's sister (on his right) had blown out the last candle rather than merely pointing at it, he might have exploded in angry tears.

The difficulty is not primarily that preschoolers have deficient *memory* circuits in their brains. Sometimes they remember particular events or details very well, as Rachel remembered the "hot cocoa shirt." But they have not yet acquired the strategies they need for deliberately *storing* memories of events and later *retrieving* them. Preschoolers rarely *try* to retain an experience or a bit of information in memory, and they seldom know precisely how to recall some hard-to-retrieve bit of past experience (Kail, 1990). As a result, they sometimes appear strangely incapable of remembering what older children can recall with ease. Rachel seemed to forget that she wore a bathing suit and played in the waves, surely the most important detail of a trip to the beach.

Script Creation

This does not, however, tell the whole story about memory in young children. In some ways, young children are remarkably capable of storing in their minds useful representations of past events that they can later retrieve. One way they do

scripts Skeletal outlines of the usual sequence of events during certain common, recurring experiences.

so is by retaining **scripts** of familiar, recurring experiences. Each script acts as a kind of self-made scaffold, or skeletal outline. By age 3, for example, children can tell you what happens in a restaurant (you order food, eat it, and then pay for it); at a birthday party (you arrive, give presents, play games, have cake and ice cream, and sing "Happy Birthday"); at bedtime (first a bath, then a story, and then lights out); and during other everyday events. Here is one 5-year-old's description of what happens during grocery shopping:

> Um, we get a cart, uh, and we look for some onions and plums and cookies and tomato sauce, onions, and all that kind of stuff, and when we're finished we go to the paying booth, and um, then we, um, then the lady puts all our food in a bag, then we put it in the cart, walk out to our car, put the bags in the trunk, then leave. [quoted in Nelson, 1986]

This is a typical script in two key respects. First, it has a beginning and an end; and second, it recognizes the causal flow of events—reflecting an awareness that some events (like putting food in the cart) must precede other events (like going to the "paying booth") (Bauer & Mandler, 1990; Ratner et al., 1990). Preschoolers use scripts not only when recounting familiar routines but also when, in pretend play, they enact everyday events such as eating dinner, shopping, and going to work.

Scripts aid early memory development because they provide a general framework within which memories of specific experiences can be recalled (Nelson, 1993). However, when a child relies on a routine script to recall a particular experience, the child's account may reflect knowledge of the script much more than it reflects accurate remembrance—especially if the experience was unusual, complex, or difficult to understand (Farrar & Goodman, 1992; Fivush & Shukat, 1995). A 2½-year-old's recollection of a recent camping trip, for example, might typically begin with mention of some notable event, such as sleeping in a tent, and then revert to a familiar domestic script, such as "First we eat dinner, then go to bed, and then wake up and eat breakfast" (Fivush & Hamond, 1990). Thus, scripts are an aid to memory, but they can also impair recall of particular experiences. And without the past experiences needed to build a script, children seem lost, as Rachel did in remembering that she took her "jamas" off at the beach but forgetting that she put her bathing suit on.

Following the Script Preschoolers remember what routinely happens in their lives by following a script in their play. This young lady has learned something about tea parties, and she has a dog who follows her script. Other preschoolers act out scripts one wishes they had never experienced.

Young children sometimes appear more forgetful than they are because they often do not focus attention on the specific features of a situation that an older person would consider most pertinent (Bjorklund & Bjorklund, 1992). Every parent has had the experience of taking a preschooler to a memorable event (a circus, a baseball game, a play), only to find that the child's later account of that experience focused on the ticket taker, the person sitting in the next row, or the refreshments!

Memories of Special Experiences

Under certain circumstances, however, children show surprising long-term memory. As you saw above, this is particularly so for experiences that happen so many times that a script is formed—especially when parents aid in the development of the script. Children also can remember distinctive experiences—including natural disasters, family changes, or traumatic events—that occur only once (Howe, 1997).  (See Changing Policy box on pages 284–285.)

WITNESS TO A CRIME

Until quite recently, most countries prohibited young children from testifying in court. It was assumed that children are egocentric, suggestible, likely to confuse fact and fiction, and therefore unable to "provide a truthful and accurate account" (as the witness's oath requires) of stressful events. It is also feared that adults might manipulate child witnesses for their own ends. Parents in custody battles, or overzealous authorities handling alleged abuse in day-care centers (where abuse is actually far less common than in homes), or prosecutors hoping for some publicity, or drug addicts seeking sympathy might misuse an innocent, confused, imaginative child who may not be able to remember.

However, sometimes a child is the only witness who can testify against an accused suspect. As the text discussion points out, young children often retain accurate memories of happy past events. If they could also recount stressful events truthfully, more of the guilty and fewer of the innocent would be convicted.

Of course, ethics forbid stressing children merely to test their memories of emotionally traumatic events. Therefore, researchers use events that normally occur in every child's life, such as a medical inoculation or a dental exam, as the basis for experiments.

Recall of Stressful Experiences

In one series of such studies, children between the ages of 3 and 6 were videotaped during a medical examination that included a DPT inoculation administered by a nurse they had never seen before (Goodman et al., 1990). The children's reactions varied widely. Most looked frightened, but some were quite stoic, unfazed. Indeed, some claimed, "It didn't hurt." A few, at the other extreme, became nearly hysterical. They had to be physically restrained, often by two or three people, so that they could get the inoculation. They cried, screamed, yelled for help, tried to run out of the room, and sobbed afterward while complaining about the pain—they reacted as if they had been attacked.

Several days later, the children were asked to tell about the experience, then to answer specific questions about it, and finally to identify the nurse who administered the shot from a lineup of photos. None of the children offered any false information during the free recall. Contrary to the hypothesis that emotional arousal might scramble a child's memory, those who showed the most distress during the exam were the ones who provided the most detailed, accurate accounts.

When asked specific questions, all the children were quite good witnesses. Notably, none of them answered yes to "Did she hit you?" "Did she kiss you?" "Did she put anything in your mouth?" and "Did she touch you anyplace other than your arm?" However, although the children were very clear about what had and had not been done to them, they were less sure about who did it. In the photo lineup, only half picked the right nurse's photograph, 41 percent picked other photos, and 9 percent said they couldn't remember.

To test the durability of these children's memories, they were interviewed again a year later. Their overall recall had diminished, but they reported virtually no significant false memories. However, most of the children again failed the photo-identification task, with only 14 percent correctly identifying the nurse this time around. Most of the rest said they didn't remember, but 32 percent picked the wrong photo.

Effects of Misleading Questions

Can children's memories be deliberately distorted? In another series of experiments, the initial interview after a medical checkup included purposely misleading questions. Questions such as "She touched your bottom, didn't she?" and "How many times did she kiss you?" were asked, either in a friendly, encouraging manner or in an intimidatingly stern one.

Older children (ages 5 to 7) were rarely misled by such questions; they affirmed false occurrences less than 9 percent of the time, whether the questioning was friendly or stern. Of the 3- and 4-year-olds, 10 percent responded untruthfully to the friendly questions, and 23 percent were misled by the stern questions.

These results accord with other research that finds that, particularly for young children, the social context (including the relationship of the child to the questioner, the age of the questioner, and whether the atmosphere of the interview is intense or relaxed) has a substantial influence on children's answers to memory questions (Baker-Ward et al., 1993; Ceci & Huffman, 1997; Rogoff & Mistry, 1990).

What happens if a child is deliberately given false information? This was the topic of another study that employed a

Would You Believe Her? As the only eyewitness to the slaying of a playmate, 4-year-old Jennifer Royal was allowed to testify in open court. Her forthright answers, and the fact that she herself had been wounded, helped convict the accused gunman. While most developmentalists agree that, when questioned properly, children can provide reliable testimony about events they have experienced or witnessed, many advocate arranging a more sheltered way for young children to give testimony.

medical-exam format, this time with 5-year-olds (Bruck et al., 1995). Immediately after each child was examined and inoculated by a pediatrician, he or she met Laurie, a research assistant who had simply observed the medical exam.

About a year later, the same children were given misleading information (in such questions as "When Laurie gave you the shot, was your mom or dad with you?"). When interviewed yet again, many of the children had accepted the inaccuracies. For example, more than one-third reported, *on their own*, that Laurie had given them the shot. Even more troubling, children who had incorporated misinformation into their accounts altered other details to make their accounts consistent. For instance, many of the children who reported that Laurie herself had administered the inoculation also added that she had performed other parts of the medical examination, such as checking eyes and nose.

Some Conclusions

What can we conclude from all this research? As one pair of researchers explains:

> Children are neither as hyper-suggestible and coachable as some pro-defense advocates have alleged, nor as resistant to suggestions about their own bodies as some pro-prosecution advocates have claimed. They can be led, under certain conditions, to incorporate false suggestions into their accounts of even intimate bodily touching, but they can also be amazingly resistant to false suggestions and able to provide highly detailed and accurate reports of events that transpired weeks or months ago. [Ceci & Bruck, 1993]

The research provides five useful guidelines.

- When children are required to give eyewitness testimony, they should be provided a structured sequence (as in the Disney World questioning) that enhances their ability to remember accurately.
- Children should be interviewed by a neutral professional who asks specific but not misleading questions in a friendly—not stern or shocked—manner.
- The interview of a child should occur only once, as soon as possible after the event, and be videotaped for later trial use.
- Although quite young children can provide accurate details concerning what happened, remembering who was involved may be more difficult.
- Children sometimes add false information to compose an account that follows a script that makes sense to them.

(Cassel et al., 1996; Bruck et al., 1997; Schneider & Pressley, 1997)

Many nations and courts, including the U.S. Supreme Court, now permit videotaped child testimony. However, many other nations and many state courts do not. This policy needs changing: Children are not necessarily worse witnesses than adults, as long as their vulnerability to intimidation is fully taken into account. Indeed, the more we learn about *adult* memory, the more we realize that the truth is rarely remembered and retold, with 100 percent accuracy, by anyone of any age (Loftus, 1997).

Structured-Interview Questions

1. *Open-Ended Questions:*

   I know that you remember a lot about your trip to Disney World. I've never gone there before. Can you tell me about Disney World? What was the very first thing that happened? And then what?

2. *Directive Questions:*

   How did you get to Disney World?
   Who went with you?
   Where did you stay?
   What did you see at Disney World?
      What did you think about that?
   Who did you see there?
      What was that like?
   What rides did you go on at Disney World?
      Which one did you like the most?
      What did that feel like?
      What did you like/dislike about it?
   What rides did "X" (other people there) go on?
      What did "X" think of it?
      Did "X" like it?
      What did "X" like about it?
   Did you eat anything there?
      What did you eat?
   Did you buy anything at Disney World?
      What did you buy?
   Did anything bad happen at Disney World?
      What happened?
      Was there anything you didn't like?
      What didn't you like?
   What was your favorite fun thing at Disney World?
      What did you like about it?
   If you got to go to Disney World again, what would you want to do the most?

   Source: Hamond and Fivush, 1991.

Figure 9.3 Where's Mickey? This structured interview elicited amazingly accurate memories, even from 4-year-olds who had visited Disney World when they were about 3 years old. In general, preschool children can remember in much more specific detail when asked directive questions than when asked open-ended ones. In this case, the children produced, on average, four times more information in response to directive questions than to open-ended ones.

Memories of Disneyland One particularly revealing study began with 48 children who had visited Disney World at about their third or fourth birthday. The children were interviewed in their homes, either 6 months or 18 months after their Disney World visit.

An experimenter first asked an open-ended question: "Can you tell me about Disney World?" Then the experimenter posed a series of directive (leading) questions (see Figure 9.3), soliciting information about anything the child had not already mentioned, such as rides taken, sights seen, food eaten, presents bought, and—perhaps most important in evoking the memories—how the child felt about the trip. These questions were followed with nondirective prompts ("And what else?" or "And then what?" or "Tell me more about that") designed to elicit further information, unless the child, on his or her own, told the entire tale (as some nonstop talkers did).

The children provided much more information in response to directive questions than they did spontaneously. Across both age groups and both retention intervals, nearly 80 percent of the information elicited from the children came in response to directive questions (Hamond & Fivush, 1991).

Every child recalled an impressive amount of information, confirmed as accurate by their parents. The older children remembered slightly more information than the younger ones, but age-related differences in the amount of recall were minimal. Even more surprisingly, the length of time between the Disney World visit and the interview didn't matter much. In other words, memories endured, irrespective of how old the children were when they visited Disney World, how much time had passed since their visit, and how old they were when they were interviewed.

Overall, this study confirms and amplifies other recent research that strongly suggests that when they are recollecting *personally meaningful material*, "even quite young preschoolers can recall a great deal of information if given appropriate cues and prompts" (Hamond & Fivush, 1991).

The study is particularly helpful in understanding why preschoolers' memory abilities often appear inadequate. Sometimes they may be asked to remember experiences that had little meaning for them. Other times seemingly vague memories may merely be the result of vague questioning. The question at the beginning of this "Memory" section, "What did you do today?" is an example of a question that is much too general. Preschool children do not necessarily tell everything they know, especially when the questioner does not know what specifically to ask (MacDonald & Hayne, 1996).

Theory of Mind

Human emotions, motives, thoughts, and intentions are among the most complicated and thought-provoking phenomena in a young person's world, whether that young person is trying to understand a playmate's

Brotherly Love At age 2, Robert is not yet supposed to have much theory of mind. That means he is not yet supposed to know what his baby brother might think about having a rubber frog put on his head. If the same scenario occurred 2 years later, however, brother Peter might consider this a hostile act, and Robert would have enough theory of mind to anticipate his brother's reaction, as well as that of his parents. Indeed, the same advances that would allow him to imagine other people's reactions might also enable him to claim, in his most aggrieved voice, "I thought he would like it." Siblings learn not only how to read emotions but also how to try to fool each other and how to convince their parents that they are the innocent ones.

theory of mind An understanding of human mental processes, that is, of one's own and others' emotions, perceptions, intentions, and thoughts.

unexpected anger, or determine when a sibling will be generous or selfish, or avoid an aunt's too-wet kiss, or persuade a parent to purchase a toy. Children want to understand this complexity. Guided by Piaget, most developmentalists assumed that children were unable to do so. It was thought that until children were 6 or 7 years old, egocentrism limited their perspective, making them unable to think beyond their own emotions and points of view. We now know, however, that using their experiences with others as data, preschoolers develop informal theories about human psychology to answer basic questions about mental phenomena. They try to figure out how a particular person's knowledge and emotions affect that person's actions and why people differ so markedly from each other in thoughts, feelings, and intentions, even in the same situations. In other words, young children develop a **theory of mind,** an understanding of human mental processes (Frye & Moore, 1991; Mitchell, 1997; Wellman, 1990).

By age 3 or 4 years, some children have sufficiently advanced in theory of mind to be able to:

- Clearly distinguish between mental phenomena and the physical events to which they refer (for example, you can pet a dog that is in front of you but not one that is in your thoughts)
- Appreciate how mental phenomena (like beliefs, expectations, and desires) can arise from experiences in the real world
- Understand that mental phenomena are subjective (others cannot "see" what you are imagining)
- Recognize that people have differing opinions and preferences (someone might like a game that you dislike)
- Realize that beliefs and desires can form the basis for human action (Dad is driving the car fast because he doesn't want to be late for Grandma's dinner)
- Realize that emotion arises not only from physical events but also from one's goals, expectations, and other mental phenomena (a 4-year-old might eat lunch by himself at day care to avoid his friends' envy of and request to share his dessert)
(Flavell et al., 1993; Stein & Levine, 1989; Wellman & Gelman, 1992)

All six of these abilities signify something parents and psychologists did not appreciate until recently: Children commit as much effort to understanding their social surroundings as they do to understanding their physical world, and sometimes they succeed.

The growth of children's theory of mind during the play years has broad implications. As an older preschooler begins to grasp how people's thinking is affected by past experiences and by other people's opinions, he or she

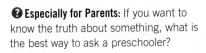

② Especially for Parents: If you want to know the truth about something, what is the best way to ask a preschooler?

IT'S JUST PRETEND

Even 1-year-olds sometimes pretend that something is true that is not, but under age 4 few children know that their pretending might not be understood by everyone. In fact, younger preschoolers can get quite angry if someone else doesn't share their fantasies, such as when an adult sits on top of an imaginary friend or a playmate ignores the conventions of a make-believe game.

An important advance in theory of mind occurs sometime between the ages of 3 and 6, when children realize that mental phenomena may not reflect reality. This idea leads to the concept that individuals can believe various things and, therefore, that people can be deliberately deceived or fooled—an idea beyond most younger preschoolers, even when they have themselves been deceived. Consider the following experiment involving a child who does not understand pretense.

An adult shows a 3-year-old a candy box and asks, "What is inside?" The child says, naturally, "Candy." But, in fact, the child has been tricked:

> *Adult:* Let's open it and look inside.
> *Child:* Oh . . . holy moly . . . pencils!
> *Adult:* Now I'm going to put them back and close it up again. (Does so) Now . . . when you first saw the box, before we opened it, what did you think was inside it?
> *Child:* Pencils.
> *Adult:* Nicky (friend of the child) hasn't seen inside this box. When Nicky comes in and sees it . . . when Nicky sees the box, what will he think is inside it?
> *Child:* Pencils.

(adapted from Astington & Gopnik, 1988)

Like this child, most 3-year-olds have considerable difficulty realizing that a belief can be false or that subjective understanding can be wrong. Since false belief is not possible to them, when children learn that they have the wrong mental image, they not only correct the mistake but also believe that they have *always* held the correct view. They even think that others (like Nicky) will intuitively know what they now know is correct (that pencils are in the candy box). In other words, they fail to understand how someone would be fooled by appearance; their theory of mind is inadequate to explain this difference between a person's thinking and the actual case.

But 3-year-olds are not always naive about whether other people can be deceived. In some studies 3-year-olds have provided false leads to an experimenter, or to a nasty puppet, whom they wanted to mislead. For instance, in one experiment, as part of a game to fool someone else, children painted a set of footprints leading *away* from a treasure rather than to it, realizing this might lead another astray (Chandler et al., 1989). Similarly, in repetitions of the candy-box experiment, some 3-year-olds who personally replaced candies with pencils to trick someone then correctly guessed that the trick would be successful (Sullivan & Winner, 1993). However, in other studies, researchers experimenting with very similar tasks found that children younger than 4 years old could *not* reliably produce false leads (such as the deceptive footprints) (Sodain, 1991), or interpret why they had been fooled when a false lead was successful (Ruffman et al., 1993).

The general conclusion of all this research is that the ability of a 3- or 4-year-old to understand pretense is fragile and vulnerable to nuances of the situation and of the child's particular cognition. Theory of mind seems, like so much of play-years cognition, sophisticated yet simple, fragile and fleeting, apparent in some conditions and not in others (Mitchell, 1997).

Generally, between ages 4 and 5, when the brain undergoes the general growth spurt described in Chapter 8, theory of mind takes a leap forward (Fischer & Rose, 1994). Then preschoolers gain a much firmer grasp of the distinction between objective reality and subjective understanding. When most 4- and 5-year-olds discover that the candy box is filled with pencils, for example, not only do they acknowledge that they were earlier mistaken, but they take considerable delight in the prospect of their friends' being similarly fooled. However, a 5-year-old's theory of mind is still not as developed as it will be at, say, age 8 or 18, as research cited in later chapters will show.

Meeting Barney A preschooler might be told that a person is actually inside this Barney costume, but nonetheless believe that Barney himself is there. During the play years, the relationship between appearance and reality is a tenuous, tricky one.
❷ Observational Quiz *(see answer page 291): What would happen if the preschooler saw Barney take his costume off?*

becomes far more capable of anticipating and influencing the thoughts, emotions, and intentions of others (Astington, 1993; Flavell et al., 1995). Not surprisingly, this conceptual growth quickly becomes enlisted for various practical purposes, such as persuasion ("If you buy me a TV for my room, Mom, then I won't always fight with Susie over what to watch!"), sympathy (consoling a sad friend by reminding her of an upcoming birthday party), teasing (telling an older brother, who is a Shaquille O'Neal fan, that "Shaq would never wear such a stupid-looking T-shirt!"), and pretending. (See the Research Report on page 288.)

Culture and Context

Recently, developmentalists have asked what, precisely, strengthens theory of mind at about age 4. Is it brain maturation alone, or does experience play a role? Consider one study, in which 68 children aged 2½ to 5½ were presented with four standard theory-of-mind situations, including a Band-Aid box that really contained pencils (Jenkins & Astington, 1996). More than one-third of the children succeeded at all four tasks (for example, they understood that someone else might initially believe, as they did, that the Band-Aid box would contain Band-Aids); more than one-third failed on three or four tasks; and the remaining 26 percent were in between, succeeding at two or three tasks. Not surprisingly, age had a powerful effect: the 5-year-olds were most likely to succeed on all four tasks, and the 3-year-olds most likely to fail every time. This result suggests that maturation is a powerful influence.

Interestingly, however, as a predictive variable, general language ability was as significant as maturation: the greater a child's verbal proficiency (at any age), the better he or she did. Other research also finds that language ability, particularly the ability to use the words "think" and "know," correlates with theory-of-mind development (Moore et al., 1990).

In the Jenkins & Astington (1996) study, when the effects of both age and language ability were accounted for, a third important factor emerged: having at least one brother or sister. Having a sibling particularly aided younger children whose language ability was not quite up to the norm for children of their age. The researchers suggest that the "familiarity and intimacy of the sibling relationship facilitates the learning process"—especially the understanding of false belief.

Before we conclude that brain maturation, with a little help from language and siblings, always produces theory of mind by age 5, consider one more study: All the 4- to 8-year-olds in a certain Peruvian village were tested on a culturally appropriate version of the candy-box situation, in this case with a sugar bowl that contained tiny potatoes. Of course, the children at first thought the bowl contained sugar, as anyone from that village would. But surprisingly, even up to age 8, these children often answered questions about the bowl's contents incorrectly: they could not explain why someone would initially expect sugar to be in a sugar bowl and then be surprised to discover potatoes. They also had difficulty with other theory-of-mind experiments and questions that most North American 5-year-olds could answer.

Culture is probably the key difference between the Peruvian and the North American children. In the Peruvians' mountainous, isolated homeland, "there is no reason or time for elaborate deception . . . where subsistence farmers, working from dawn to dusk just to survive. . . . live mostly on the landscape of action, and not on the landscape of consciousness" (Vinden, 1996). Neither their language nor their culture describes false

❶ Response for Parents (from page 287): Ask very specific questions, but not leading questions, in a nonthreatening manner—not "Did you break the plate?" but "Did you hear when the plate fell? Did you see it?" all expressed in a friendly, interested manner. Never punish a child for telling the truth or for being afraid to tell the truth.

belief or "how people's thoughts might affect their actions." Thus, culture is a fourth crucial factor in the development of theory of mind (Vinden, 1996).

LANGUAGE LEARNING

As we noted in Chapter 6, humans normally begin talking at about 1 year, with new vocabulary and expressions added slowly at first. Toddlers typically master new spoken words relatively slowly, talking mostly in one-word sentences about immediate experiences. They do not yet think, or talk, symbolically. They tend to frustrate themselves, and even the most patient caregiver, as they seek to communicate.

During the preschool years, however, the pace and scope of language learning increase dramatically, and language becomes a pivotal part of cognition. We sometimes say that a *language explosion* occurs, with words and sentences bursting forth.

Vocabulary

The typical child's vocabulary more than doubles between 18 and 21 months of age and then doubles again over the next 3 months. In the preschool period, vocabulary explodes, increasing exponentially. By age 6, the average child has a lexicon containing more than 10,000 words (Anglin, 1993). According to one source, "Children typically produce their first 30 words at a rate of three to five new words per month. The same children learn their next 30,000 words at a rate of 10 to 20 new words per day" (Jones et al., 1991).

How does this rapid learning happen? One explanation is that after a year or so of painstakingly learning one word at a time, the human mind develops an interconnected set of categories for vocabulary, a kind of grid or mental map on which to chart the meanings of various words. Here is an analogy: If you want to find a certain town, it is useful if someone tells you its

A One-to-One Ratio of Teachers to Learners One of the key features of any good preschool program is the frequent opportunity it affords children to hear and express new vocabulary. Of course, adults should read to young children and engage them in conversation, but the best language teachers for children are sometimes other children.

fast mapping Used by children to add words to their vocabulary, the process of hearing a word once or twice and then quickly defining it by categorizing it with other words.

❗ *Answer to Observational Quiz (from page 288):* *She might be upset and think Barney had gone away, because her thinking is still static and irreversible, and current appearance is taken as reality. She might cry "Bring Barney back," but not know how to do it.*

direction and distance from a known city within a named country and then gives you a map so that you can locate it. In the same way, if you want to define a certain word, it is helpful to know other similar words and its general category (such as "animal," "emotion," or "mode of transportation") and to have your mind organized in such a way that you can then put the new word in its proper place.

This speedy and not very precise process of acquiring vocabulary by "charting" new words is called **fast mapping.** Thus children quickly learn new animal names, for instance, because they can be mapped in the brain close to old animal names. "Tiger" is easy if you already know "lion." Similarly, children learn new color names by connecting them with those they already know. The process is called fast mapping because, rather than stopping to figure out an exact definition and waiting until a word has been understood in several contexts, the child simply hears a word once or twice and sticks it on a mental language map. (Something similar occurs when someone is asked, for instance, where Nepal is. Most people can locate it approximately ["near India"] in their mental map of the world, but few can locate it precisely, citing each border.)

Evidence for the underlying aptness of this mapping concept (specifically, that people spontaneously organize their language into categories) comes from adults who suffer a stroke or other brain damage. They sometimes lose or confuse whole categories of words. For instance, they may remember the names of fruits very well but forget the names of most vegetables. Or they may mix up words that are conceptually related but not synonymous: a tunnel may be called a bridge, or a skunk may be called a zebra.

Apparently, we all store words according to categories, although this organizational map does not usually become obvious until it is damaged. Linguists now realize that, during language acquisition, children do the same thing; they categorize words with a speed that sometimes leads to notable and telling mistakes (Golinkoff et al., 1992; Wilkinson et al., 1996). On hearing a new word, a child uses clues from the immediate context to create a quick, partial understanding and then categorizes the word on the basis of that partial understanding. (See Children Up Close, page 292.)

Young children's fast mapping is aided by the way adults label new things for them. A helpful parent might point at an animal the child is watching at the zoo and say, "See the *lion* resting by the water. It's a *lion!* A very big cat." In less than a minute, "lion" enters the child's vocabulary. Zoos and children's first picture books do the same thing, organizing animals and objects into categories. In addition, children make some basic assumptions that help them learn. They assume, for example, that words refer to whole objects (rather than to their parts) and that each object has only one label (Clark, 1990; de Villiers & de Villiers, 1992; Markman, 1991). These assumptions usually lead to good provisional definitions, although they sometimes prove misleading—as is obvious when we hear a child say, "That's not an animal, it's a *dog!*" or "I have two sisters, big sister Susan and kitty-cat Fluffy."

Building Vocabulary

The learning of new words tends to proceed predictably according to parts of speech. In English and many other languages, nouns are generally mastered more readily than verbs, which in turn are learned more easily than adjectives, adverbs, conjunctions, and interrogatives. Within a particular part of speech, the order is predictable as well. For instance, basic categories, such as "dog," are learned before specific nouns, such as "collie," or

FAST MAPPING

Fast mapping has an obvious advantage, in that it fosters quick vocabulary acquisition. However, it also means that children *seem* to know words because they use them, when in fact their understanding is quite limited. One very simple common example is the word "big," a word even 2-year-olds use and seem to understand. In fact, however, young preschoolers often use "big" when they mean "tall" or "old" or "great" ("My love is so big!") and only gradually come to use "big" correctly (Sena & Smith, 1990).

A more amusing example involves a 3-year-old who told her father that her preschool group had visited a farm, where she saw some Dalmatian cows. Luckily her father (my student) remembered that, a week before, the girl had met her uncle's Dalmatian dog, so he understood his daughter's fast-mapping mistake.

When adults realize that children often do not fully comprehend the meanings of words they use, it becomes easier to understand—and forgive—the mistakes children make. I still vividly recall an incident that stemmed from fast mapping

and that occurred when my youngest daughter, then 4, was furious at me.

Sarah had apparently fast mapped several insulting words into her vocabulary. However, her fast mapping did not provide precise definitions or reflect nuances. In her anger, she called me first a "mean witch" and then a "brat." I smiled at her innocent imprecisions, knowing the first was garnered from fairy tales and the second from comments she got from her older sisters. Neither invective bothered me, as I don't believe in witches and my brother is the only person who can appropriately call me a brat.

But then Sarah let loose an X-rated epithet that sent me reeling. Struggling to contain my anger, I tried to convince myself that fast mapping had probably left her with no real idea of what she had just said. "That word is never to be used in this family!" I sputtered. My appreciation of the speed of fast mapping was deepened by her response: "Then how come Rachel [her sister] called me that this morning?"

more general nouns, such as "animal." If the child's family has their own pet dog, its name is learned first, before the categorization of words begins. The first interrogatives children typically learn are "Where?" and "What?" and then "Who?" and "How?" and "Why?" (Bloom et al., 1982).

The vocabulary-building process occurs so quickly that, by age 5, some children seem to be able to understand and use almost any term they hear. In fact, 5-year-olds *can* learn almost any word or phrase, as long as it is explained to them with specific examples and used in context. At age 5, my colleague's son Scott surprised his kindergarten teacher by stating that he was ambidextrous. When queried, he explained, "That means I can use my left or my right hand just the same." In fact, preschoolers soak up language like a sponge, an ability that causes most researchers to regard early childhood as a crucial period for language learning and causes many educators to believe that every child deserves a good preschool education.

The vocabulary acquisition that occurs between ages 2 and 6 is so impressive that we need occasionally to remind ourselves that young children cannot comprehend *every* word they hear. Abstract nouns, such as "justice" and "government," are difficult for them because there is no referent in their experience. Metaphors and analogies are also difficult, because the fast-mapping process is quite literal, allowing only one meaning per word. When a mother, exasperated by her son's frequent inability to find his belongings, told him that someday he would lose his head, he calmly replied, "I'll never lose my head. If I feel it coming off, I'll

Hi, Grandma This boy has been having telephone conversations with his grandmother since he was 1 year old. At first, he mostly listened and then cried when the phone was taken away. Now, almost 3 years old, he chatters away unstoppably, revealing an extensive grasp of vocabulary and grammar. However, he still doesn't necessarily provide all the details that would let his grandmother follow the conversation: he may sometimes refer to events she has no knowledge of and people she does not know or tell the ending of a story without a beginning.

find it and pick it up." Another mother warned her child who was jumping on the bed:

> *Mother:* Stop. You'll hurt yourself.
> *Child:* No I won't. *(Still jumping)*
> *Mother:* You'll break the bed.
> *Child:* No I won't. *(Still jumping)*
> *Mother:* OK. You'll just have to live with the consequences.
> *Child: (Stops jumping).* I'm not going to live with the consequences. I don't even know them.
> [adapted from *The New York Times,* November 2, 1998]

Young children can most easily grasp nouns because nouns have objective meanings; they name things. Most verbs and adjectives are also relatively easy. Children have greater difficulty with words expressing comparisons, such as "tall" and "short," "near" and "far," "high" and "low," "deep" and "shallow," because they do not understand the *relative* nature of these words. Once preschoolers know which end of the swimming pool is the deep end, for instance, its depth becomes their definition of "deep." They might obey parental instructions to stay out of deep puddles by splashing through every puddle they see, insisting that none of those is "deep." Words expressing relationships of place and time, such as "here," "there," "yesterday," and "tomorrow," are difficult as well. More than one pajama-clad child has awakened on Christmas morning and asked, "Is it tomorrow yet?"

Grammar

The *grammar* of a language includes the structures, techniques, and rules that are used to communicate meaning. Word order and word repetition, prefixes and suffixes, intonation and pronunciation—all are part of this element of language. Grammar is apparent in toddlers' two-word sentences, since youngsters always put the subject before the verb, and even in most holophrases, since one-word thoughts are expressed differently depending on whether they are questions, statements, or commands.

By the time children are 3 years old, their grammar is quite impressive: Children not only place the subject before the verb but also put the verb before the object and the adjective before the noun. They say "I eat red apple" and not any of the 23 other possible combinations of those four words. They can form the plurals of nouns, the past, present, and future tenses of verbs, and the subjective, objective, and possessive forms of pronouns. They rearrange word order to create questions and can use auxiliary verbs ("I *can* do that"). They are well on their way to mastering the negative, having progressed past the simple "no" of the 2-year-old ("No sleepy" or "I no want it") to more complex negatives such as "I am not sleepy" or "I want nothing."

Children's understanding of grammar is revealed when they create original phrases and expressions like those in Table 9.2. The words in the table show both children's mastery of grammatical rules and their ability to apply the rules—in these cases, to create expressions that they have never heard before but that convey their thoughts clearly and accurately to others.

How do preschoolers master the basic rules of language so quickly and easily? There is no doubt that the human brain is wired to learn language very early in life (Jusczyk, 1995). This innate mental program provides children with a set of intuitive guidelines for quickly deducing the rules of their native language, whether they are learning English, Russian, Swahili, or Mandarin Chinese.

table **9.2**	**Children's Knowledge of Grammar in Creating Words**	
Rule Followed	Word	Context
Add "un" to show reversal.	"unhate"	Child tells mother: "I hate you. And I'll never unhate you."
Use a limiting characteristic as an adjective before a noun to distinguish a particular example.	"plate-egg," "cup-egg" "sliverest seat"	Fried eggs, boiled eggs. A wooden bench.
Add "er" to form comparative.	"salter"	Food needs to be more salty.
Create noun by saying what it does.	"tell-wind"	Child pointing to a weather vane.
Add "er" to mean something or someone who does something.	"lessoner" "shorthander"	A teacher who gives lessons. Someone who writes shorthand.
Add "ed" to make a past verb out of a noun (as in "punched," "dressed").	"nippled"	"Mommy nippled Anna." Reporting that Mother nursed the baby.
	"needled"	"Is it all needled yet?" Asking if Mother has finished mending the pants.
Add "s" to make a noun out of an adjective.	"plumps"	Buttocks.
Add "ing" to make a participle out of a noun.	"crackering"	Child is putting crumbled crackers into soup, thereby crackering it.

Source: Examples come from Bowerman, 1982; Clark, 1982; Reich, 1986; and the Berger children.

Children's understanding of grammar is also facilitated by hearing conversations at home that are models of good grammar and by receiving helpful feedback about their language use (Tomasello, 1992). Reflecting this fact was a study that followed the language development of two groups of 2-year-olds (Hoff-Ginsberg, 1986). The mothers of one group frequently asked questions (such as "Where does the duck live?") and then repeated their child's answers, rephrased correctly (changing "Duck, water," for example, into "Yes, the duck lives on the water"). The mothers of the other group rarely used such strategies. After 6 months, the children who had received "lessons" in grammar as part of normal dialogue with their mothers advanced in their use of grammar compared to the children in the other group.

Cultural and social context profoundly influences the acquisition of both vocabulary and grammar: The child learns what he or she is exposed to. Thus, young Mandarin-speaking children have more verbs than nouns in their vocabulary, because their mothers are more likely to emphasize actions than objects (Tardif, 1996). With regard to grammar, most North American children have difficulty with the passive voice; even at age 6 a child may think that "The dog was bitten by the boy" means the dog did the biting. For some time experts considered this difficulty to be developmentally based; they assumed that a certain amount of brain maturation has to occur before children could understand the unusual word order (object, verb, subject). However, we now know that Inuit children in Alaska acquire the passive voice as early as age 2. From other evidence such as this, it seems that context, more than maturation, is the engine that drives grammar (Allen & Crago, 1996).

Difficulties with Grammar

Young children learn their grammar lessons well—so well that they often tend to apply the rules of grammar even when they should not. This tendency, called **overregularization,** creates trouble when a child's language includes many exceptions to the rules. As an example, one of the first rules that English-speaking children apply is to add "s" to form the plural. Overregularization leads many preschoolers to talk about foots, tooths, sheeps, and mouses. They may even put the "s" on adjectives when the adjectives are acting as nouns, as in this dinner-table exchange between my 3-year-old and her father:

> *Sarah:* I want somes.
> *Father:* You want some what?
> *Sarah:* I want some mores.
> *Father:* Some more what?
> *Sarah:* I want some more chickens.

Once preschool children learn a rule, they can be surprisingly stubborn in applying it. One developmentalist reports the following conversation between herself and a 4-year-old:

> *She said:* "My teacher *holded* the baby rabbits and we *patted* them."
> *I asked:* "Did you say your teacher *held* the baby rabbits?"
> *She answered:* "Yes."
> *I then asked:* "What did you say she did?"
> *She answered again:* "She *holded* the baby rabbits and we *patted* them."
> "Did you say she *held* them tightly?" I asked.
> "No," she answered, "she *holded* them loosely." (Gleason, 1967)

Although technically wrong, such overregularization is actually a sign of verbal sophistication; it shows that children are applying the rules. Indeed, as preschoolers become more conscious of grammatical usages, they exhibit increasingly sophisticated misapplications of them. A child who at age 2 correctly says she "broke" a glass may at age 4 say she "braked" one and then at age 5 say she "did broked" another. After children hear the correct form often enough, they spontaneously correct their own speech, so parents can probably best help a child's development of grammar by example rather than by explanation or criticism. In this case, for example, a parent might simply respond, "You mean you broke it?" While few children will immediately correct their grammar, continual exposure to good grammar speeds language mastery (Farrar, 1992).

During the preschool years, children comprehend more complex grammar, and more difficult vocabulary, than they produce. Thus, although it is a mistake to expect proper grammar, it is also an error to always mirror preschoolers' speech, "talking down" to their level. Surely some grammatical forms (the future subjunctive, the past perfect) are beyond preschoolers, but most other forms are potentially within their comprehension. The zone of proximal development is a useful concept here, suggesting that between the simple grammatical forms that are well understood and those that are as yet incomprehensible lies a zone of potential improvement, where social mediation facilitates language learning. Similarly, given children's spongelike ability to fast map vocabulary, several new words should be used and explained every day.

overregularization The tendency to make a language more logical and "regular" than it actually is, which leads to mistaken application of the rules of grammar.

Drawing by Glenn Bernhardt

No, Timmy, not "I sawed the chair." It's "I saw the chair" or "I have seen the chair."

Correct Grammar This mother has obviously become too accustomed to her son's overregularization.

PRESCHOOL EDUCATION

The most dramatic cohort change that has occurred in the life of the preschool child in the past 30 years is that he or she is now very likely to be "in school." Indeed, the word "preschool" once meant before school begins;

now it often means a school for younger children, complete with curriculum, homework, and graduation. In the United States in 1970, only 30 percent of married mothers with children under age 6 were in the labor force, and only 20 percent of all 3- and 4-year-olds were in an organized program of some type (including day-care centers, which used to provide simply "care" and now provide education as well). In 1996, the figures were 60 percent of mothers working and 49 percent of 3- and 4-year-olds in a program. Further, almost all 5-year-olds are in preschool now, often called kindergarten, usually all day (see Figure 9.4). In most other developed countries, preschool attendance for 3- and 4-year-olds is even higher than it is in the United States, because their governments sponsor education in early childhood.

Over the past 30 years, scientists have shown that young children learn a great deal through formal as well as informal preschool education. This is apparent particularly in verbal skills and social understanding. The preschools that consistently provide the most extensive benefits are characterized by:

- A low teacher-child ratio
- Staff with training and credentials in early-childhood education
- Curriculum geared toward cognitive development
- Learning spaces organized for creative and constructive play

Cultural Values

In every culture, preschool education not only includes but goes beyond cognitive preparation for later schooling (Mallory & New, 1994). As an example, Japanese culture places great emphasis on social consensus and con-

❷ **Especially for Teachers:** In helping plan a new preschool with limited resources, you need to rank the four characteristics of preschools from most to least important. How would you do that?

Figure 9.4 Changing Times. As research increasingly finds that preschool education provides a foundation for later learning, more and more young children are in educational programs. Currently, almost half of all 3- and 4-year-olds are in school. Those numbers are expected to rise even higher in the twenty-first century.

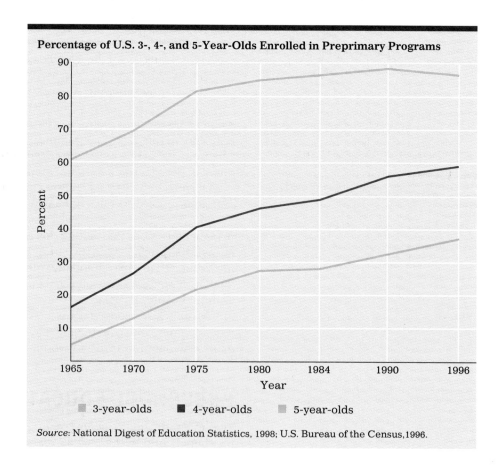

Percentage of U.S. 3-, 4-, and 5-Year-Olds Enrolled in Preprimary Programs

■ 3-year-olds   ■ 4-year-olds   ■ 5-year-olds

Source: National Digest of Education Statistics, 1998; U.S. Bureau of the Census, 1996.

Happy Kindergartners These photos show happy kindergartners in teacher-directed exercise in two settings, southern California and Tokyo.

❓ *Observational Quiz (see answer page 299): If you were a stranger to both cultures, with no data other than what you see in the photos, what would you conclude about the values, habits, and attitudes adults hope to foster in these two groups of children?*

Project Headstart A massive preschool education program, developed in the United States in the early 1960s, for children from low-SES families.

formity. Therefore, Japan's preschools provide training in the behavior and attitudes appropriate for group activity: children are encouraged to show concern for others and to contribute cooperatively in group activities (Rohlen & LeTendre, 1996). These social attitudes and habits prepare young children for both the formal school system and later work settings (Peak, 1991). In China, similarly, learning how to be part of the group is combined with creativity in self-expression, both drawn from the culture's Confucian ethic of disciplined study.

In the United States, by contrast, preschools are often designed to foster self-confidence and self-reliance and to give children a good academic start through emphasis on language skills (Tobin et al., 1989). Since most North American preschools are privately or parochially sponsored, they vary a great deal in rules, curriculum, and values. (See Children Up Close, page 298).

Headstart: A Longitudinal Look

Project Headstart, a federally funded program, was inaugurated in 1965 to give children who were thought to be disadvantaged by poverty a "head start" on the skills required in elementary school (Zigler & Berman, 1983; Zigler et al., 1993). Accordingly, thousands of preschools were organized within 2 months to provide a half-day program of education and health checkups for children whose family income was below the poverty line. Many schools also included a limited number of middle-class children, especially if they were disabled in some way.

Headstart continues to this day, stressing parental involvement and preparation for formal learning. The ongoing survival of Headstart, decades after the "War on Poverty" rhetoric has ended, is a victory for social science research. The outcome of this battle was in doubt because, although the first evaluation of Headstart found that children advanced in IQ scores from September to June of the initial year, longitudinal research found that those advances faded by second grade (Westinghouse, 1969). When Headstart advocates explained that IQ scores were not the best measure of effectiveness and that good preschool education was needed for all children, many members of congress were dubious, especially since the costs of the Vietnam War had begun to mount.

PETER'S PRESCHOOL EDUCATION

Some adults, whose childhood ended long before the expansion of early-childhood education in the 1970s, may still equate "school" (and hence "preschool") with sitting at desks in rows, memorizing times tables, and practicing penmanship—skills beyond the zone of proximal development for even the brightest 4-year-old. For them, a "preschool" child is literally what the word says, a child before school age. If such an adult were asked whether massive public money should underwrite schools for young children, where one goal is to encourage children's play (Jones & Reynolds, 1992), they might ask, "Why pay for play?" Perhaps the following account would convince them. It surely would give them a better idea of what preschool is like. It also illustrates how a preschool setting offers experiences, facilitates social interaction, and expands language as few families do, or even can.

The children were settling in for a videotaped movie and a little boy offered Peter the empty chair beside his own. . . . Peter's thumb went into his mouth. . . . Miss Murray put a stuffed teddy bear in Peter's lap and whispered, "You need to hold onto Mr. Bear and don't let him get away until the story is over. Help him listen too, by holding him in your lap with both hands." Peter held Mr. Bear in a death grip with both arms. The little boy who had offered Peter the chair asked if he could have an animal and Miss Murray pulled one out of the basket on the shelf. The movie was Jack and the Beanstalk, a favorite of many of the children. The two boys held their stuffed animals and echoed the giant's "Fee, fie, foe, fum" in their best and deepest "giant" voices.

The last activity of the day was a watermelon party. The class went out on the grass near the classroom door to begin the festivities. The teacher placed the watermelon in the middle of the circle of children and they all admired it and talked about how it grew. The teacher encouraged the children to touch it and allowed them to try and pick up the "Monster Melon."

Peter was fascinated. "Boy, this is real, real, big!" he exclaimed, trying to lift up one end of the melon. "I bet my Dad could pick it up though. He's real strong." He ran his hands along the sides and ends of the melon and then commented, "It's like a ball . . . but not really . . . just sorta like a ball."

The teacher made the first cut, lengthwise, and then she and Miss Murray (another teacher) each took a group of children to cut the two halves into smaller pieces. One at a time, the children were allowed to help cut their own slice of watermelon. The children were soon busy biting, chewing, spitting seeds, and enjoying the sloppy affair. But Peter stood immobile. He was holding his watermelon in front of him with the pink juice running down his arms. He looked forlorn and helpless, seeming not to know what to do with the slice of watermelon. It then dawned on Miss Murray that Peter may have never experienced watermelon before

or perhaps he couldn't relate this cold slab of wetness to the neat chunks he may have been given at home.

She took Peter's index finger and poked it into the pink part of the melon and then into the firmer rind. She explained that the soft part was for eating, but there were small, hard bits called "seeds" all mixed up in it. She helped Peter find a seed and feel how hard and slippery it was. She then encouraged him to take a bite and asked him if his teeth or tongue had found any seeds yet. Perplexed, he nodded his head "yes," but he didn't know how to spit them out. They just slid down his chin. Miss Murray coaxed Peter to blow the seeds out, but he was only minimally successful. Even so, he managed to get a few seeds into the air instead of on his chin. From the look on Peter's face, it was safe to say that he did not especially enjoy this new experience. This was confirmed when Peter announced sheepishly, "I like my mom's watermelon better—hers doesn't have seeds."

The buckets of water available for clean up were the source of as much fun as the watermelon itself. The splashing of water and giggling that accompanied it were much more to Peter's liking. In the midst of the fun, a taller version of Peter strode into view and said, "Hey there, Buddy . . . whatcha doin'?"

Peter turned and hugged his dad's knees. "Guess what, Dad? We had watermelon today, and guess what? Their watermelon has a lot of seeds. And guess what? I know how to spit now! I can show you how to spit. Wanna see me spit? I can show Mommy how to spit too. What d'ya think of that, huh?"

Peter's father smiled, patted his son on the back, and said, "Okay, Buddy, we'll go home and show Mommy how to spit. Find my pocket and let's go." Peter put his fingers in his dad's back pocket and followed him toward the gate. [Bishop, 1993]

The most obvious benefit of school as compared to home is friendship, as the two boys in the excerpt illustrate. Same-sex and same-age playmates are preferred by children, but this is difficult to arrange in most at-home settings. Likewise, the facilitated sharing (here, of the chair, the stuffed animal, and the giant voices) are common in preschool but virtually impossible at home. Varied experiences are also more likely to happen at preschool. Peter was probably not the only child who, for the first time that day, wielded a knife to slice a large fruit, spit out watermelon seeds, or tried to lift a "monster melon." Such new experiences teach words as well as motor skills—here, "spit," "slippery," "oval," and "monster" became better understood.

Social skills also develop as children share—here, the carrying and cutting, eating and spitting, washing and drying. In this instance, the preschool children learned an additional lesson: that disabilities need not prevent a person from taking part in normal activities. Did you guess? Peter is blind.

sleeper effect Any outcome of a program or experience that is hidden for a while (asleep) but later becomes apparent (awake).

❶ Response for Teachers (from page 296):
Obviously, the ranking of the four characteristics in a particular case depends on the specifics of the audience—the ages and background of the children, for example. However, experts generally find that a good, detailed, well-executed curriculum is the most important element and that the adult-child ratio is least important—provided that training, skill, curriculum, and space organization are reasonable.

❶ *Answer to Observational Quiz (from page 297):* *The most obvious difference is the greater emphasis on individualism in California—no uniforms, diverse ethnicity, smaller group size. Evaluation of this contrast depends on the values of the beholder. In addition, three other differences might have caught your attention (you are an excellent observer if you saw all three): The Japanese head teacher is male (virtually never the case in a U.S. early-childhood classroom); the Japanese children are segregated by gender (indicated by hats as well as position), whereas the U.S. children are not; and the wall decorations are creative in the U.S. classroom and serious in the Tokyo classroom.*

Fortunately, just before the Headstart program was about to be scrapped, new social science research over a still longer time period proved that the fading was temporary, a **sleeper effect.** The learning advances from Headstart were indeed quiescent, and were unobservable at around age 7, but they were awakened after a few more years of maturation.

Over the decades, various longitudinal studies of former Headstart students have found that they score higher on achievement tests and have more positive school report cards by age 10 than non-Headstart children from the same backgrounds and neighborhoods. By junior high, they are significantly less likely to be placed in special classes for slow or disruptive children or to repeat a year of school. In adolescence, Headstart graduates have higher aspirations and a greater sense of achievement than their non-Headstart peers. And as they enter adulthood, Headstart graduates are more likely to be in college, are less likely to be in jail, and have fewer dependent children (Haskins, 1989).

Longitudinal research on similar programs, some also begun in the 1960s, yields similar findings. The most notable concerns the Perry Preschool program, a well-financed preschool education project in Ypsilanti, Michigan. The latest survey of Perry students, now adults, indicates that compared to the study's control group, they have more education, greater earning power, and greater family stability and require fewer social services (Schweinhart & Weikart, 1993).

Education for All

Do the same conclusions that we can draw about Headstart children hold for children who are not poor? Yes, to a degree. Longitudinal research on more advantaged children in the United States and elsewhere finds that all children benefit from a quality preschool setting. The more months and years a child spends in preschool, the more apparent the benefits are (Field, 1991). There is one caution, however, and one proviso. The caution is that poor preschools (crowded, unsafe, focused on discipline and not cognition) can be worse than an average home. The proviso is that the better the home environment, the less pronounced the influence of the preschool is likely to be.

Considering all the research we've discussed about cognitive development between the ages of 2 and 6, you probably are not surprised at the benefits of a well-run preschool. Piaget described young children as being capable of symbolic thought. Vygotsky stressed that actual learning requires guided participation and opportunities to manipulate objects, use language, and interact with other children. When all goes well, children can learn everything from mathematics to grammar to social insight.

In the ongoing debate described near the beginning of this chapter, developmentalists are now tilting toward Vygotsky. The influence of culture and scaffolding on various cognitive abilities and the discovery of the benefits of quality preschool education are evidence for sociocultural theory. Few developmentalists are content to follow Piaget, merely letting time lead to cognitive development. Past history, however, teaches that new research will find additional abilities in the minds of 2- to 6-year-olds and additional strategies to develop that potential. Although our view of young children has changed, it probably will change again. What will the new discoveries be? Some readers of this book will likely be among the scientists who find out.

SUMMARY

HOW YOUNG CHILDREN THINK

1. Preschoolers are active and eager thinkers, at times showing the effects of egocentrism, in which their cognitive development is limited by their own narrow perspective, and at times grasping the basic concepts of their world.

2. Piaget described preschoolers as able to think symbolically, a major advance over sensorimotor thought. However, this preoperational thought is, essentially, also prelogical. This is because preschoolers are distracted by appearances and irreversible in their thought processes. They center on one aspect of a situation to the exclusion of others, and they reason in a static rather than a dynamic fashion.

3. Vygotsky viewed cognitive development as an apprenticeship in which children acquire cognitive skills through guided participation in social experiences that stimulate intellectual growth. He and other sociocultural theorists contend that how well children master potential skills depends in great part on how willing and able other people and the culture are to scaffold participation in learning.

4. According to Vygotsky, there exists, for each child, a range of potential development, called the zone of proximal development, that foreshadows new cognitive accomplishments. Social guidance needs to move children forward through the zone, from what they can already do to what they are ready to learn to do next.

5. Also according to Vygotsky, language fosters cognitive growth as an intermediary between learner and tutor, facilitating the social interaction that teaches new skills. In addition, children use private speech to guide and direct their own actions.

6. Although preschoolers do not possess the well-established, systematic, logical reasoning skills of older children, they are not as illogical as Piaget believed them to be. In particular, young children can understand the concept of conservation in certain situations. On the other hand, parents and culture may not always be as helpful in teaching young children as sociocultural theory contends.

WHAT PRESCHOOLERS CAN DO

7. Although young children cannot count large amounts and cannot easily add or subtract, by about age 4 they understand basic counting principles. Parents, through the many number activities they engage in with their children, play an important role in the development of early number skills.

8. Young children are not skilled at deliberately storing or retrieving memories, but they can devise and use scripts, or outlines of familiar, recurring events. Children sometimes display surprising long-term-memory ability when adults use directive questions to help them focus their attention on specific aspects of meaningful past events.

9. Children develop elementary theories about mental processes—theirs and others. A preschooler's theory of mind reflects developing concepts about human mental phenomena and their relation to the real world, as well as the difference between the two. A strengthened theory of mind at about age 4 allows preschoolers to see that subjective understanding may not always accurately reflect reality.

LANGUAGE LEARNING

10. Language accomplishments during the play years include learning 10,000 words or more. Preschool children increase their vocabulary almost explosively. They seem to do so by quickly inferring an approximate meaning for each new word and mentally categorizing it with similar familiar words.

11. Preschoolers also show marked growth in their understanding of basic grammatical forms. Children of this age, however, often overregularize, or apply grammatical rules where they do not fit. Again, in the acquisition of language, parental guidance and support are invaluable.

PRESCHOOL EDUCATION

12. Over the past 30 years, insights from developmental psychology and changes in family composition and work patterns have resulted in great increases in early-childhood education throughout the world. Programs, whether called day care, preschool, or kindergarten, that emphasize cognitive development tend to benefit children. To a great extent, each nation's preschools reflect its cultural values.

13. Project Headstart was initiated to bring the skills of disadvantaged preschoolers up to those of other students entering elementary school. Longitudinal studies have shown that Headstart provides long-lasting educational and social benefits.

14. The learning potential for all children during early childhood is remarkable. Organized education before age 6 helps develop the young mind although the specifics depend on the values of the culture.

KEY TERMS

symbolic thought (272)
preoperational thought (272)
centration (272)
egocentrism (272)
irreversibility (273)
conservation (273)
guided participation (275)
zone of proximal development (ZPD) (276)

scaffold (276)
private speech (277)
social mediation (277)
scripts (283)
theory of mind (287)
fast mapping (291)
overregularization (295)
Project Headstart (297)
sleeper effect (299)

KEY QUESTIONS

1. In what ways does preoperational thought limit a child's ability to think logically?

2. What sets Vygotsky's ideas apart from those of Piaget?

3. Give a hypothetical illustration (not the one in the book) of how a parent can foster cognitive accomplishments in the zone of proximal development.

4. How does the ability to count show that a child is capable of symbolic thinking?

5. How do young children's scripts aid recall of specific past experiences, and how do they distort recollections?

6. How can caregivers aid in the development of memory during the preschool years?

7. What advice might you give to a police officer who was planning to interview a preschool child who had witnessed a crime?

8. How do 2-year-olds differ from 6-year-olds in theory of mind?

9. What four factors influence whether a young child will understand a false belief?

10. How does the rapid acquisition of new words occur during the preschool years?

11. What limitations are to be expected in a young child's accurate use of words and grammar?

12. What social change and what research discovery combined to increase the numbers of children in preschool programs?

13. What findings indicate that preschool education programs such as Project Headstart succeed?

14. *In Your Experience* What misunderstanding did you have as a preschool child, because of your limited theory of mind or because of your magical or egocentric perspective?

CRITICAL THINKING EXERCISE

Take your study of Chapter 9 a step further by working this pattern recognition exercise.

When we progress to higher levels of cognitive functioning, we do not spend all our time at those higher levels. Piaget himself once observed that he spent only a fraction of each day in formal operational thought processes. This suggests that even as adults, we do not entirely leave preoperational thought behind.

To better understand preoperational thought processes in children, see if you can identify the characteristic of preoperational thought that "you" illustrates in each of the following adult behaviors:

1. Following an especially heated argument with an elderly relative, you shout that you would like nothing better than to have him get out of your life for good. Several days later your relative dies, leaving you feeling intensely guilty.

2. According to your roommate, you are a sucker for deceptive packaging when you buy groceries because you always choose taller bottles and cans over shorter, wider ones.

3. A classmate from high school started an Internet business several years ago and has become one of the wealthiest, most successful entrepreneurs in the nation. Whenever you see her, you think about her business ventures and fantasize about her material success, imagining her house, her car, her hired help. ("What must it be like to live in such luxury?" is the way you put it.)

4. One day you learn that this same wealthy friend has become active in a community organization that serves the mentally retarded. You are told that her work with children consumes most of her weekends and a substantial part of her income and that she lives in modest circumstances. You find this hard to believe, and you suspect that somehow she is profiting from her involvement.

Check your answers by comparing them to the sample answers in Appendix B.

The Play Years:
Psychosocial Development

CHAPTER 10

Picture a typical 2-year-old and a typical 6-year-old, and consider how emotionally and socially different they are. Chances are the 2-year-old still has many moments of clinging, of tantrums, and of stubbornness, vacillating between dependence and self-determination. Further, the 2-year-old cannot be left alone, even for a few moments, in any place where curiosity might lead to danger or destruction.

The 6-year-old, by contrast, has both the confidence and the competence to be relatively independent. A typical child at that age can be trusted to do many things alone and is proud to do them—perhaps fixing breakfast before school and even helping to feed and dress a younger sibling. This child shows affection toward family members without the obvious clinging, exasperating demands or exaggerated self-assertion of the 2-year-old. The 6-year-old might say good-bye to Mom or Dad at the door of the first-grade classroom and then take care of business: following classroom routines, befriending certain classmates and ignoring others, respecting and learning from teachers.

If you have been able to imagine these two children, you can see that self-confidence, social skills, and social understanding all develop markedly during the play years. These psychosocial advances are partly the result of cognitive growth—notably in the *theory of mind* that produces an appreciation of psychological roles, motives, and feelings, thereby deepening preschoolers' understanding of themselves and of others. Simultaneously, the preschooler's social world grows in complexity and breadth, providing richer interactions with familiar people and new relationships with a wider circle. The impetus for psychosocial development thus comes from inside and outside the child, from a maturing mind and from an expanded environment. This chapter reflects both parts of that duality, to complete our description of child development between ages 2 and 6 years.

THE SELF AND THE SOCIAL WORLD

Self-concept, self-esteem, and self-understanding, as well as social attitudes, social skills, and social roles, are familiar topics for psychologists who study adults. Increasingly, the same topics intrigue researchers studying children, especially those looking at the early years (Campos et al., 1989; Eisenberg & Fabes, 1992; Schore, 1994; Sroufe, 1996; Tangney & Fischer, 1995). They find that, between ages 1 and 6, children progress from a dawning awareness that they are independent individuals to a firm understanding of who they are, what they like to do, and how their selfhood relates to their social environment.

Cooperation Six hands and one bowl of ingredients to mix—it could be a recipe for disaster. Here it seems just fine, because these Headstart children have learned to coordinate their efforts, in an advanced form of social play.

Self-Concept and Social Awareness

The play years are filled with examples of a blossoming self-concept, as preschoolers repeatedly assert their identity ("I'm a big girl"; "I am not a baby"), their ownership of possessions (everything from "My teacher" to "My mudpie"), and the reason things are important to them ("I saw it first"). This emerging self-concept can also be seen when two preschoolers meet for the first time. After initial staring, they often show off any interesting toy, garment, or skill they may have and then invite interaction ("Want to play with my ball?").

During the play years, children gradually begin to perceive themselves in terms of their physical attributes ("I'm bigger than Natalie!"), their abilities ("I can run fast!"), and their dispositions and traits—seeing themselves, for example, as friendly, shy, happy, or hardworking (Eder, 1989, 1990). They also become quite involved in their relationships with other people and their emotions about them (Feeny et al., 1996). By the late preschool years, self-concept includes recognition of some psychological tendencies, as is revealed in this exchange between a 5-year-old and two puppets (manipulated by an experimenter):

Puppet 1: My friends tell me what to do.
Child: Mine don't.
Puppet 2: I tell my friends what to do.
Child: I do too. I like to boss them around.

[Eder, 1990]

The growth of preschoolers' social awareness is nowhere more apparent than in their negotiations with others. Just prior to the preschool years, parents typically find themselves dealing with a demanding, stubborn toddler whose primary negotiating skills seem to be whining and throwing tantrums. A parent's attempt to negotiate with a 2-year-old might be met with a defiant command of "No talk!" But as children's theory of mind expands, giving them a better grasp of how other people think and feel, their negotiations—over what they will wear, what they will eat, when they will go to bed, and such—gradually evolve. From obstinate demands and defiance they shift to bargaining, compromising, and rationalizing (Crockenberg & Litman, 1990; Kuczynski & Kochanska, 1990).

One of the most important aspects of preschoolers' self-definition is that they feel older, stronger, and more skilled than younger children. The significance of this feeling, as well as their skill in negotiations, is shown in this episode of play involving three 4-year-old girls:

Beth: How about this. Pretend he married two of us and you were the sister. OK? You were the sister of us—OK? Of both of us, cause you were the littler one.
Celia: No, I don't want to be a little one.
Beth: No, you're both, you're big. Um, let's pretend.
Annie: But we were a little bigger.
Beth: You're 20.
Celia: Yeah.
Beth: And both of us are 21.
Celia: OK, so that means . . .
Annie: So, we're one month older than you.

[Furth, 1996]

ONE BIG HAPPY
By RICK DETORIE

© 1997 by Creators Syndicate, Inc.

Know-It-Alls Have Something to Learn Like many preschoolers, Ruthie thinks her art is worth money and she would love to be the rescuer of another child, an animal, or even a bird. In the real world, however, that self-concept will need some modification.

phobia An irrational fear that is strong enough to make a person try to avoid the fearful object or experience.

The young ladies' chronological understanding clearly is immature, but their social skills are not. All three want to maintain their self-esteem as big girls without giving up their social interaction, and they have combined self-assertion and social compromise to achieve that end.

One last change that occurs during the preschool years is that children become less ritualistic and superstitious; such behaviors seem to increase during the first 2 years, peak at about age 2½, and then exhibit a marked decrease (Evans et al., 1997). This does not necessarily mean, of course, that 5-year-olds will readily let someone else sit in their seat at the dinner table or that they will walk by a cemetery without holding their breath and saying a prayer to keep the ghosts away. In fact, many preschoolers develop fears, and some become so afraid of certain things that the fear could be called a **phobia:** an irrational and exaggerated fear that terrifies the person.

Phobias are particularly likely if a child's parents are also somewhat phobic, because children by age 3 or 4 become quite astute at sensing their parents' feelings. Even when a worried parent says, "Let's pet the nice doggie," children will notice the hesitant hand, the fast breathing, or the sudden startle if the dog moves. Nightmares also increase during the preschool years, because enhanced imagination is not yet held in check by emerging rationalization, especially when the child is half asleep. Parents can help their children by telling stories in which the child masters the feared experience. For example, if the dream is about being chased by tigers, the story can involve dreaming about a hole the tigers fall into, a stick to beat the tigers, Superman to stop them, wings to escape them, or a gift that turns them into surprised and grateful friends (Brett, 1988).

Children gradually learn to assert themselves and use objects, people, imagination, mantras, or rituals to combat their disconcerting emotions. Routines help control the many fears that can overwhelm young children, whose imagination far outdistances their reason. The important point is that during the play years children can and do begin to take control of their fears and desires, becoming themselves despite their confusing social world.

And It Was Good During the play years, pride in the final accomplishment generally overshadows any reasons for self-doubt or self-criticism—such as whether the skyscraper this child just built is recognizable to anyone else.

Self-Evaluation

For children of all ages, psychologists emphasize the importance of developing a positive self-concept. (In fact, more than a little self-criticism is one sign of psychosocial problems in a preschooler.) Normally, preschoolers have no problem with this; typical 2- to 6-year-olds form quite optimistic impressions of themselves. They regularly overestimate their own abilities, believing that they can win any race, skip perfectly, count accurately, and make up beautiful songs. They enjoy undertaking various tasks, and they expect all others—grandparents, playmates, stuffed animals—to be a patient audience for their showing-off and to applaud when it is over. The next day, they might gather the identical audience for a repeat performance. Self-confidence is tied to competence, and competence demands repeated demonstration of mastery.

Mastery Play

Children who repeatedly act out the same drama, read the same book, draw the same picture, and such, are using repetition to understand themselves and their world and are developing their skills. Practicing a skill until one is proficient at it, and gaining self-esteem in the process, is called **mastery play**; it is one of many forms of play that developmentalists have learned to respect in young children. Most researchers, teachers, and other professionals who specialize in understanding young children believe that *play is the work of childhood*. As you will see throughout this chapter, during the preschool years play is productive as well as fun—an avenue for motor development, intellectual growth, and self-discovery.

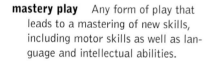

mastery play Any form of play that leads to a mastering of new skills, including motor skills as well as language and intellectual abilities.

A child's simple walk down the street can quickly become a series of mastery-play episodes as the child balances along the edge of the curb, jumps over every crack in the sidewalk (so as not to "step on a crack and break your mother's back"), and then skips, walks backward, or races ahead. Along the way, there may be ice patches to slide across, or wind to run against, or puddles to leap over (or into). Hand skills are also developed in mastery play, as when children intentionally tie knots in their shoelaces, put pegs in pegboards, or use a pair of scissors to make snippets of paper out of a single sheet. Similarly, making a snack, getting dressed, and singing along with music all are instances of mastery play.

Mastery play is most obvious when it involves physical skills, but it can be used for almost any skill the child feels motivated to learn. For instance, as children grow older, mastery play increasingly includes activities that are clearly intellectual, such as play with words or ideas.

Initiative Versus Guilt

The impulse to engage in mastery play comes naturally to preschool children, who normally believe they can do almost anything. This positive enthusiasm, effort, and self-evaluation is as it should be, according to Erikson's

Practice Versus Perfection Often the best way to recognize mastery play is not from the task or the result but from the child's facial expression while doing it. For these children, using their fine motor skills to make a collage is obviously mastery play.

initiative versus guilt The third of Erikson's eight "crises" of psychosocial development, in which the preschool child eagerly begins new projects and activities—and feels guilt when his or her efforts result in failure or criticism.

psychosocial theory (first discussed in Chapter 2). During the developmental stage that Erikson calls **initiative versus guilt,** between ages 3 and 6 years, young children's self-esteem is largely defined by the skills and competencies that demonstrate their independence and initiative. Most preschoolers leap at almost any opportunity to show "I can do it!" According to Erikson, children's developing sense of themselves and of the larger society motivates them to eagerly take on new activities, but they feel guilty when their efforts result in failure or criticism.

Preschoolers' readiness to take the initiative stems from their desire for mastery, not simply for autonomy as in toddlerhood. Thus, in nursery school, for example, older preschoolers build impressive block towers (expressing initiative), whereas toddlers (in the *autonomy versus shame* stage) try to knock them down. Such a transgression might make toddlers feel shame (an emotion that comes directly from social disapproval) but not guilt (an emotion that comes from one's internal standards). Likewise, preschoolers would rather complete a difficult task themselves, because they have internal standards, whereas toddlers will readily accept help if that seems the best way to reach a desired goal (Stipek et al., 1992). Preschoolers express pride in their accomplishments and guilt over their misdeeds, both indicative of their growing self-esteem.

This high self-esteem was demonstrated in a laboratory test in which 4- to 6-year-olds were given 2 minutes to solve an impossible puzzle. When they failed, they were asked to guess how many of two additional puzzles they could solve if they tried. Almost all the children, despite having just failed, answered "both." When the same children were asked to indicate how smart they were by awarding themselves one, two, three, four, or five stars (representing the range from "not smart at all" to "very smart"), more than 90 percent confidently chose five stars (Stipek et al., 1995). In this study, confidence was affected by the style of school the child attended (those in nurturing, child-centered preschools were more likely to be proud of themselves and rate themselves highly than were those in more critical, work-centered preschools), but all the children were quite self-assured. Interestingly, the older children were decidedly *more* competent (on other, skill-based tests) but slightly *less* confident of their abilities than the younger children.

As this example suggests, the fact that preschoolers evaluate themselves highly does not mean they are impervious to the judgments of others. Over early childhood, children become increasingly aware of, and concerned with, what others think. They begin to appraise their own behavior, using standards they have heard from others (Butler, 1998). Children in the laboratory study described above admitted they were somewhat anxious about their performance at school—especially those children in the more demanding preschools, where they actually learned more but were frequently made aware of how they were doing (Stipek et al., 1995).

Preschoolers' self-evaluation and initiative derive, in part, from their *social awareness*. This leads to a desire to acquire for themselves the skills that they observe in community members, especially those who have obvious, visible, and essential roles to play. They want to be "grown up"; they enjoy dressing in costumes of the police officer, the firefighter, the store owner; they even willingly undertake tasks that adults would rather avoid, such as pulling weeds, sweeping the floor, and washing the dishes—if they have seen their favorite grown-ups doing these jobs and if they are sufficiently encouraged in their efforts. When enthusiastic exploration and proud initiative lead to a broken toy, a crying playmate, or a criticizing adult, the healthy preschooler's reaction is guilt—but usually a momentary guilt that is soon relieved by saying "I'm sorry" and replaced by a new burst of energy. Such guilt is beyond the scope of the toddler because it requires social awareness, an internalized conscience, and a sense of self that toddlers have not yet developed (Tangney & Fischer, 1995).

Indeed, children as young as 2 or 3 years of age begin to respond with disappointment or guilt when they fail at a task (perhaps knotting instead of tying their shoelaces) or when they cause some mishap (such as spilling a cup of juice), even when no adult is present. Many older preschoolers take this one step further, trying to make reparations and spontaneously confessing that they caused a problem. Sometimes they feel much more guilty at their inadequacies than is warranted (Cole et al., 1992; Lewis et al., 1992). When my daughter Sarah was 4, she asked me:

"Can God see everything I do?"
"Yes," I reassured her. But worry rather than relief crossed her face.
"Oh no," she said, "then God knows that I pick my nose."

Emotional Regulation

The most important emotional development during early childhood, however, is not the emergence of new emotions, such as pride and guilt, but the growing "ability to inhibit, enhance, maintain, and modulate emotional arousal to accomplish one's goals" (Eisenberg et al., 1997). Thus pride is tempered by guilt (and vice versa); joy by sadness; anger by fear; fear by rituals. All are regulated and controlled by the 3- or 4-year-old in ways unknown to the exuberant, expressive, and often-overwhelmed toddler.

emotional regulation   The ability to direct or modify one's feelings, particularly feelings of fear, frustration, and anger. Because of brain maturation, emotional regulation becomes more possible during the preschool years.

This ability, called **emotional regulation,** is developed in response to society's expectations that preschoolers "manage frustration" and "modulate emotional expression" (Sroufe, 1996). And most preschoolers become quite successful at this difficult task. As one expert explains, preschoolers must:

delay, defer, and accept substitutions without becoming aggressive or disorganized . . . cope well with high arousal, whether due to environmental challenge or fatigue. At the same time they are to be spontaneous and exuberant when circumstances permit. . . . Occasional breakdowns in emotional control, especially when taxed, fatigued, or ill, are an expected part of healthy emotional development. Still, progress is remarkable during this period. [Sroufe, 1996]

❷ Especially for Social Workers: Suppose a 3-year-old is unable to control his or her emotions, crying and attacking, for example, when that is not the appropriate response. Should you blame the way the parents treat the child, take some sort of action, or expect that the child will grow out of it in a few years?

How does emotional regulation develop? Part of it is neurological (Schore, 1994). The ability to regulate one's emotions, to think before acting, is related to a specific part of the brain in the frontal cortex. This area is immature in toddlers but develops and matures during the preschool years. If a child was damaged prenatally or stunted in infancy (by stress or poor nutrition), the child may be intellectually intact in most ways but unable to regulate his or her emotions (Casey, 1996; Diamond et al., 1997). Unfortunately, evidence from lower animals finds that extremely stressful experiences in infancy permanently alter brain structures; it is feared that the same applies to humans (Zahn-Waxler et al., 1996).

Learning is also crucial to emotional regulation. During infancy, caregivers guide children in the "appropriate" expression of emotion. For example, parents teach their infant to keep fear at bay because the parents repeatedly respond to the infant's anxiety with reassurance. Then, in the "terrible twos," parents teach their children to moderate anger. The best teacher is example, so ideally the parents never lose their own tempers when the child erupts in protest, and they never react with irrational fear when a dog approaches, thunder roars, or a mouse scampers across the floor. The circuits of the child's developing brain respond to such experiences, and gradually innate emotional triggers are connected to intellectual responses, allowing the 4-year-old girl to stand her ground when a circus clown approaches or the 4-year-old boy to restrain himself when another child bumps into him.

According to Daniel Goleman, the ability to modulate and direct emotions is crucial to *emotional intelligence*. This is learned during early childhood when the reflective, intellectual areas of the cortex gradually come to govern the rush of fear, anger, and other passions from the amygdala, an area deep within the brain. If infants become attached to their caregivers, and if the caregivers then use their relationships to teach the children how and when to express their feelings, the children will become balanced and empathetic human beings, neither overwhelmed by nor unresponsive to their own emotions. The proper childhood learning might prevent, years later, such negative emotional responses as addiction, delinquency, teenage motherhood, or suicide (Goleman, 1998).

Just What He Should Do? This 3-year-old might like either to slap his baby brother or to lift him and hold him, but his emotional regulation yields an appropriate gesture and expression. He avoids both emotional extremes, being neither too worried and solicitous nor too angry and upset at the crying.

Attachment and Emotional Regulation

The results of past caregiving are clearly exhibited by children's reactions when another child cries in pain. Children who have been well nurtured and have formed secure attachments are able to regulate their own emotions and can express empathy, comforting the hurting child, reassuring the frightened child, or getting help if need be. (Attachment is described in Chapter 7.)

Longitudinal research finds that those with insecure attachments respond abnormally to other children's distress. Some might do whatever

would precisely further distress the child (e.g., scaring a child with the very mask that had been frightening, taunting a crying child and calling him or her a "cry baby," or punching a child with a stomach ache in the stomach). . . . [Others] would often become upset themselves when another was distressed (e.g., holding their own lip and seeking a teacher's lap when another child had fallen). [Sroufe, 1996]

❶ **Response for Social Workers (from page 309):** A lack of emotional regulation is a potentially serious sign in a 3-year-old, since the child may become unhappy and uncontrollable later on, and there is a risk he or she will end up as a criminal. Often the problem began earlier, either in brain damage or in poor attachment relationships. At this point, blaming the parents is no help. However, emotional control is not beyond the child, who can still learn to regulate his or her emotions if the parents now provide the proper guidance and if a structured setting with other children—such as a good preschool with a skilled teacher—is available.

Most preschoolers, however, are quite sympathetic to those who are hurt or sick, although they don't always know how to express their sympathy (Zahn-Waxler et al., 1995). Many a parent, with a small cut, has been told to sit patiently while his or her child solicitously cleans the wound and then kisses and Band-Aids it, or a parent, with a minor cold, has been sent to bed, tucked in, and given lemonade.

Another example of emotional regulation is appropriate expression of friendliness. Toddlers sometimes take shyness or sociability to an extreme, perhaps literally hiding behind a mother's skirt when a stranger offers ice cream or not only taking the ice cream but also the stranger's hand and asking to go with the stranger to play at his or her house. Preschoolers learn to moderate these extremes. However, children with damaged attachment in the first year of life are sometimes excessively friendly at age 4 or 5, seeking out strangers and sitting on their laps, for instance.

In one study, researchers examined a group of adopted Canadian children who had spent their first year or so in a Romanian orphanage and the next 3 years with their adoptive families. Most of the children still showed insecure attachments (Chisholm, 1998). Compared to Romanian orphans who had been adopted in the first 4 months of life, and to a control group of Canadian-born, nonadopted, never-institutionalized children, more of those with a year of orphanage experience were characterized by strongly insecure attachment together with very poor emotional regulation.

According to their adoptive parents, 71 percent were "overly friendly," a characterization rare in the early-adopted Romanians or in the nonadopted children. The researcher points out that many of these children did form some kind of attachment but states that "when the attachment process does go wrong in previously institutionalized children it may go very wrong.... On a practical level this may mean that parents need to be more than merely adequate parents to deal with children from orphanages" (Chisholm, 1998). Emotional regulation requires a balance between friendliness and fear that was hard for these children to attain.

ANTISOCIAL AND PROSOCIAL BEHAVIOR

prosocial behavior   An action, such as sharing, cooperating, or sympathizing, that is performed to benefit other people without the expectation of reward for oneself.

Some of the emotions that mature during the preschool years lead to **prosocial behavior,** actions that are voluntarily performed to help another person without obvious benefit to oneself (Eisenberg & Murphy, 1995). Expressions of sympathy, offers to share, and the inclusion of a shy child in a game or conversation are all examples of prosocial behavior. Such behavior is indicative of social competence and appears during the later play years, continues to develop during the school years, and is correlated with emotional regulation (Eisenberg et al., 1997). It also correlates with the making of new friends. Normally,

> after about age 3–4 years, episodes of strong negative affect begin to diminish, and the capacity for self-control is more evident; social skills and relationships are developing as networks widen to include peers as well as family members. [Zahn-Waxler et al., 1996]

antisocial behavior   An action, such as hitting, insulting, lying about, or taking from another person, that is intended to harm someone else.

Of more concern is **antisocial behavior**—deliberately hurtful or destructive actions. Antisocial behavior that may be exhibited during childhood and adolescence is usually preceded (or accompanied in some cases) by a lack of emotional regulation during the preschool years (Eisenberg et al., 1997).

How is it that children develop these social and antisocial attributes? The answers range from genetic and prenatal influences to school and society. Here we look at two influences that are particularly powerful in developing social skills during the preschool years: playing with peers and watching television.

Learning Social Skills Through Play

Compare the peer interactions of a 2-year-old, which consist mainly of simple games (such as bouncing and trying to catch a ball and becoming angry or upset if the other child does not cooperate), to the more sophisticated interactions of a 5-year-old, who has learned how to gain entry to a play group, to manage conflict through the use of humor, and to select and keep friends and playmates. Many of these new social skills are learned from play with peers, because only with age-mates do children themselves assume responsibility for initiating and maintaining harmonious social interaction. Whether learning how to share crayons or sand toys, or how to include everybody in the construction of a spaceship, or how to respond to a friend's accusation that "it's not fair," children must deal with playmates who are not always understanding and self-sacrificing (as a mother might be).

For example, when coloring with a child, most adults would readily let the child use a coveted color first. But another child might say, "I'm using the blue; you can't have it." At this point the preschooler needs to learn to allow the other child to have the blue, at least for a while. Of course, if the other child never gives up the blue, the tactics change—get adult help, switch color schemes, threaten "I'll never be your friend," or simply try to grab the crayon. Each one of these choices has consequences that teach the child about social interaction.

The progression of social skills in young children's play was described almost 70 years ago by a researcher named Mildred Parten (1932):

- *Solitary play*. A child plays alone, seemingly unaware of any other children playing nearby.
- *Onlooker play*. A child watches other children play.
- *Parallel play*. Children play with similar toys in similar ways, but they don't interact with each other.
- *Associative play*. Children interact, including sharing materials, but they don't seem to be playing the same game.
- *Cooperative play*. Children play together, either helping to create and elaborate a game or else taking turns.

Originally Parten thought these skills developed in sequence, perhaps one stage per year. For example, a 1-year-old might be at the first stage, and a 5-year-old at the fifth stage. Now we know that, especially with the advent of preschool, the progression of social play is more rapid and variable, so a 4-year-old might have a stretch of solitary play as well as an episode of cooperative play. Still, these categories are useful, in part because they emphasize that the social skills involved in associative and cooperative play take time and practice to develop. How does this occur? With physical activity and with shared imagination.

Rough-and-Tumble Play

rough-and-tumble play Play such as wrestling, chasing, and hitting that mimics aggression but actually occurs purely in fun, with no intent to harm.

One beneficial form of social play is called **rough-and-tumble play.** The aptness of its name is made clear by the following example:

> Jimmy, a preschooler, stands observing three of his male classmates building a sand castle. After a few moments he climbs on a tricycle and, smiling, makes a beeline for the same area, ravaging the structure in a single

sweep. The builders immediately take off in hot pursuit of the hit-and-run phantom, yelling menacing threats of "come back here, you." Soon the tricycle halts and they pounce on him. The four of them tumble in the grass amid shouts of glee, wrestling and punching until a teacher intervenes. The four wander off together toward the swings. [cited in Maccoby, 1980]

One distinguishing characteristic of rough-and-tumble play is its mimicry of aggression, but rough-and-tumble play is clearly prosocial, not antisocial. This was first observed by ethologists studying the wrestling, chasing, and mutual pummeling engaged in by young monkeys (Jones, 1976). The observers discovered that the key to the true nature of this seemingly hostile behavior was the monkeys' **play face,** that is, a mildly positive facial expression that seemed to suggest that the monkeys were having fun. The play face was an accurate clue; only rarely, and then apparently by accident, did the monkeys actually hurt each other. (The same behaviors accompanied by a threatening expression usually meant that a serious conflict was taking place.)

play face   A smiling or relaxed facial expression that indicates that a child (or other animal) does not intend to be aggressive; used, for example, during rough-and-tumble play.

In human children, too, rough-and-tumble play (unlike aggression) is both fun and constructive; it teaches children how to enter a relationship, assert themselves, and respond to the actions of someone else while exercising gross motor skills, all without hurting the other person (Pellegrini & Smith, 1998). Adults who are unsure whether they are observing a fight that should be broken up or a social activity that should be allowed to continue may be helped by knowing that the play face is as telltale in children as it is in monkeys: children almost always smile, and often laugh, in rough-and-tumble play, whereas they frown and scowl in real fighting.

Rough-and-tumble play is universal. It has been observed in Japan, Kenya, and Mexico as well as in every income and ethnic group in North America, Europe, and Australia (Boulton & Smith, 1989). There are some cultural and situational differences, however. One of the most important is space and supervision: children are much more likely to instigate rough-and-tumble play when they have room to run and chase and when adults are not directly nearby. This is one reason the ideal physical environment for children includes ample safe space for gross motor activities, with adults within earshot but not underfoot (Bradley, 1995).

A Sign of Social Maturity For many young children, especially boys who know each other well, rough-and-tumble play brings the most pleasure. Many developmentalists believe that this kind of play teaches social skills—such as how to compete without destroying a friendship—that are hard to learn any other way.

In addition, rough-and-tumble play usually occurs among children who have had considerable social experience, often with each other. Not surprisingly, then, older preschoolers are more likely to engage in rough-and-tumble play than younger ones. In fact, the incidence of rough-and-tumble play increases with age, peaking at about age 8 to 10, and then decreasing (Pellegrini & Smith, 1998). Finally, boys are much more likely to engage in rough-and-tumble play than girls are. Indeed, preschool girls typically withdraw from boys' rough-and-tumble play (Fabes, 1994).

Sociodramatic Play

sociodramatic play   Pretend play in which children act out various roles and themes in stories of their own creation.

In the type of social play called **sociodramatic play,** children act out various roles and themes in stories they themselves have created. Typically, children create family dramas, scenarios involving sickness or death, or stories that include monsters and superheroes. From simple plots at age 2 (a mother-baby script that consists mainly of eating, sleeping, and waking) to elaborate ones by age 5 (such as a trip through the jungle confronting various challenging animals, people, and geological barriers), sociodramatic play provides a way for children to:

- Explore and rehearse the social roles they see being enacted around them
- Test their own ability to explain and convince others of their ideas
- Regulate their emotions through imagination
- Examine personal concerns in a nonthreatening manner

The beginnings of dramatic play can be seen in solitary or parallel play, when a toddler "feeds" or "cuddles" or "punishes" a doll or stuffed animal. However, the frequency and complexity of dramatic play greatly increase between the ages of 2 and 6, as such play becomes a much more social event. As young children develop their theory of mind and their emotional regulation, they practice what they learn (Goncu, 1993; Harris & Kavanaugh, 1993; Lillard, 1993a, 1993b, 1994). They can, for instance, use sociodramatic play to try out various means of managing their emotions, as in a scary situation in the dark (in a tent made of blankets, quickly opened if the "dark" becomes too much), or providing nurturance to an injured playmate (who falls down dead, and needs to be miraculously revived), or exhibiting courage when the bad guys attack (with machine guns, bombs, or poison gas—but the defenders always prevail). In this sense, then, sociodramatic play is a testing ground for early psychological knowledge, always protecting the self-esteem of the players.

The increase in this form of play during the preschool years is also related to the development of self-understanding. In sociodramatic play, a child can assume and then discard roles with ease, because of the confidence the child derives from knowing who he or she is—and is not. Interestingly, girls tend to engage in sociodramatic play more often than boys do, just as boys initiate more rough-and-tumble play. Both sexes learn important prosocial lessons in the process.

Sociodramatic Play Just like the boys in the previous photograph, these girls are developing their social skills—in this case, as store owner and grocery shopper.

❓ *Observational Quiz (see answer page 315): Which specifics of the girls' fantasy play are similar to the real thing, and which are not?*

The Role of Television

According to Neilson Media Research, in 1996 children between the ages of 2 and 5 in the United States watched 23 hours and 21 minutes of television each week (see Table 10.1). This is more than 3 hours per day, and it is at least 3 hours more a week than the viewing time of any other age group (Neilson, 1997). It's easy to understand why: parents of preschoolers soon learn how good a baby-sitter the "idiot box" is; it can keep children relatively quiet and in place for hours at a time.

Among the criticisms of television are the time it takes away from active, interactive, and imaginative play; the faulty nutritional messages it sends; and the sexist, racist, and ageist stereotypes it provides that are particularly harmful for inexperienced, vulnerable viewers. The snap visual stereotypes that are reinforced by television are the opposite of an understanding of what people are really feeling—and that understanding underlies prosocial behavior. Prosocial behavior also depends on emotional

table **10.1**	**Television Watching, by Age and Sex**		
	Viewing Time per Week		
Age/Sex	November, 1994	November, 1995	November, 1996
Children:			
Age 2 to 5 years	24 h 42 min	24 h 52 min	23 h 21 min
Age 6 to 11 years	21 h 30 min	21 h 40 min	19 h 59 min
Teenagers:			
Girls	20 h 20 min	19 h 59 min	18 h 19 min
Boys	21 h 59 min	20 h 38 min	19 h 59 min

Source: Neilson Media Research, 1997.

Wrong Lessons Learned Preschoolers are eager for knowledge, and these boys are learning to shoot the bad guys whenever they appear. The most frightening aspect of television watching at this age is that children absorb it totally, without a firm understanding of the difference between real and pretend.
❓ *Observational Quiz (see answer page 318): Is this a usual activity for these boys, or just an occasional, rainy-day event?*

regulation, which is best learned through active social relationships, not through passive observation. In other words, television undercuts the very attributes, skills, and values that lead to prosocial activity.

However, the most compelling and convincing criticism of television concerns the antisocial behavior it encourages, especially in children. The effect is interactive and cumulative: children who watch a lot of television are likely to be more aggressive than children who do not, and children who are already inclined to be aggressive are likely to watch a lot of violence (Huston et al., 1989).

In television cartoons designed primarily for young children, physical violence occurs an average of 25 times an hour (National Coalition on Television Violence, 1993). The good guys (Mighty Morphin Power Rangers, Teenage Mutant Ninja Turtles, Batman, and other "heroes") do as much hitting, shooting, and kicking as the bad guys, yet the consequences of *their* violence are made comic or are sanitized; they are never portrayed as bloody or evil. In cartoonland, demolition—whether of people or of things—is just plain fun.

Television desensitizes children to violence in real life, making physical aggression seem normal. Moreover, prosocial emotions and emotional regulation are hard to portray on the screen, where quick dramatic action captures the eye much better than a thoughtful monologue of self-reflection. For all these reasons, children who watch substantial quantities of violent television are more likely than others to be bullies, more likely to retaliate physically for any perceived attack, more likely to be passive victims, and more likely to be onlookers rather than mediators when other children fight (Slaby & Eron, 1994).

Obviously, not every child who watches television aggression becomes a bully or victim as a result. Humans, even at age 3, are not so mindless as to copy everything they see. However, summing up the evidence for the relationship between television violence and aggression in children, Leonard Eron, head of the American Psychological Association's Commission on Violence and Youth, observes, "The evidence is overwhelming and longitudinal. The strength of the relationship is the same as for cigarettes causing lung cancer" (quoted in Mortimer, 1994).

Aggression

As we have seen, prosocial behavior and antisocial behavior take many forms. However, aggression is of particular concern; it begins with inadequate self-concept and emotional regulation during the early preschool years, and it can become a serious social problem as time goes on. As one group of researchers reports:

> Children with [emotional] control problems observed by home visitors at ages 3 and 4 years were seen by teachers as more hostile and hyperactive in the classroom at age 5 years. . . . Early onset aggression, in particular, is likely to become entrenched and linked to multiple problems late in development. [Zahn-Waxler et al., 1996]

In other words, a child who is angry and hurtful at age 3 is a child headed for trouble at age 5, 10, or even at 15 or 25. Here we will look at the forms, causes, and consequences of aggression that are specific to children of ages 2 to 6. The consequences are not always dire: Every normal preschool child sometimes hurts another child or an adult with unexpected and deliberate hitting, kicking, biting, hair pulling, name-calling, arm twisting, or such. Normally, children are more aggressive at age 4 than age 2, because as children become more aware of themselves and their needs, they become more likely to defend their interests. In fact, the 4-year-old who internalizes every insult and never lashes out is at risk for serious anxiety and depression later on (Eisenberg et al., 1997).

Therefore, in looking at aggression, developmentalists distinguish between aggression that is quite normal and innocuous and aggression that is more unusual and ominous. Researchers recognize three forms:

instrumental aggression   Aggressive behavior whose purpose is to obtain or retain an object desired by another.

reactive aggression   Aggressive behavior that is an angry retaliation for some intentional or accidental act by another.

bullying aggression   Aggressive behavior in the form of an unprovoked physical or verbal attack on another person.

- **Instrumental aggression:** engaged in to obtain or retain a toy or other object
- **Reactive aggression:** angry retaliation for an intentional or accidental act
- **Bullying aggression:** an unprovoked attack

The first type, instrumental aggression, is the most normal and the most likely to increase from age 2 to 6 years. Although it should be discouraged as a strategy, instrumental aggression involves objects more than people and is quite normal, and therefore is not of serious concern. The last type, bullying, is most worrisome overall. (Bullies and victims are discussed in more detail in Chapter 13.) Particularly during the preschool years, the middle type, reactive aggression is of special concern because it indicates poor emotional regulation.

All three of these forms of aggression are usually *physical* in nature, and physical aggression is much more common in boys than in girls. Recently, however, social scientists have identified another manifestation of aggression, called **relational aggression,** or social aggression, which involves insults or social rejection. The aim of relational aggression is not to produce physical pain through a show of force but to cause psychic pain through a social attack. Among older children, especially girls, relational aggression (e.g., during class, a classmate passes you a note that says, "No one wants to be your friend") is considered even more hurtful than physical aggression (e.g., four children are talking in a group in the hallway; as you walk by them, they push and trip you) (Galen & Underwood, 1997).

relational aggression   Aggressive behavior that takes the form of insults or social rejection. (Also called *social aggression.*)

Children of both sexes and all ages engage in relational aggression, but girls do so more often than boys and older children more often than younger. However, although the problem is more obvious later on, preschool relational aggression is a precursor of later problems if it goes unchecked. Therefore, parents and teachers need to pay as much attention to relational aggression as to reactive or bullying physical aggression.

Indeed, children who use relational aggression tend to later be considered unpopular or problematic by peers and teachers, even more than those who use physical aggression (Crick et al., 1997; Rys & Bear, 1997). You have seen that peers learn how to interact with each other in rough-and-tumble or sociodramatic play. However, for the proper development of social skills as well as the cognitive skills described in the previous chapter, sometimes adults need to intervene to make sure the appropriate lessons are learned (see Children Up Close, pages 316–317).

❶ *Answer to Observational Quiz (from page 313):* The particular hats, necklaces, and shoes are all quite different from those their mothers would likely wear to the store, and the stock, the money holder, and the grocery bag are quite different. However, the essence of shopping is here: money is exchanged for goods, and both participants politely play their roles.

PARENTING PATTERNS

During the preschool years, as children are able to do more and hence need more guidance, the range of decisions that parents must make expands as well. From big decisions (such as what neighborhood the family lives in or

LEARNING FROM PLAYMATES

Whereas it was once typical for young children to spend most of their time at home, today many attend a preschool program or day-care center. You saw in Chapter 9 that high-quality day-care or preschool programs benefit cognitive growth. They do the same for psychosocial development. Children in well-run programs acquire a wide range of social skills and become more competent socially as a result of their frequent interactions with other children of the same age (Hayes et al., 1990; Zaslow, 1991; Zigler & Lang, 1990).

They also make many friends. Indeed, friendships are remarkably consistent during the play years: young children choose regular playmates, and then their ongoing rough-and-tumble or sociodramatic play together becomes obviously different from play with casual acquaintances in its complexity, self-disclosure, and reciprocity (Hinde et al., 1985; Howes, 1983; Park et al., 1993).

Adults sometimes consider peer relationships a mixed blessing: children in group day programs learn how to be more helpful and cooperative, but they also become more assertive and aggressive than children without extensive group-care experience. Not every parent is thrilled with that result. However, peer encounters in day care typically teach children to defend their interests, whether the goal is holding on to their favorite toy, keeping their place in line, or exercising their right to use their own imagination in a dramatic episode—all instances of self-defense that may involve some instrumental aggression. The topics we have just discussed—the self within the social world, prosocial and antisocial behavior, peer play, and relational aggression—are illustrated by this extensive example of sociodramatic play, part of a detailed year-long study of social interaction in one preschool:

(Jenny and Regina prepare something together in the housekeeping area, while Tina brings the honey jar out of the area and pretends to pour things in it; there is some talk that cannot be heard.)

Regina: What is you doing up all night? Now get to bed!
Tina: I'm not up *(pause)* for nothin' . . .
Regina: Get to bed, now! Get to bed!
Tina: I'm doing something!
Regina: Get to bed now!
Tina: I am. I AM. Golly! *(continues to pour into the jar)*
Regina: We're gonna have a thousand people and all— and everybody in this house is gonna take a nap! *(Tina continues "doing something.")*
Regina: Get to bed!
Tina: But Mom, I'm finished. Don't you ha-happy at me?
Regina: No, but I'm very mad at you, now get to bed, cause there's gonna be a millions of people over!

(Ilana and Esther enter after watching from the entrance-way. A number of players [in the pretend episode] speak at once. Tina makes coffee; Esther makes apple-spice lemon cake; Jenny spins salad. There is a great deal of commotion and noise. Most of what is said cannot be heard, with the notable exception of Regina's barking orders. The following phrases can be discerned from Regina's running lecture: "I am so mad that I can even turn my face to red"; "Now get to bed"; "And you need a boyfriend"; "Now get to bed everybody, you too, and you and me and you and you." When her co-players stop paying attention to her, Regina begins to bark orders at a picture on the wall of a monkey: "If you don't behave little monkey . . ." Finally, exhausted, Regina leans against the trunk and moans in a worn out tone: "Just would you please go to bed, will you please go to bed.")

Tina: No, you go to bed.
Regina: I don't have to.
Tina: Well you're tired, you're going like: "Ohhh, please go to bed."
Regina: It's not me that's tired, so go to bed, and you and you and you.
Tina: Not me. I'm making the coffee. I have to make—. We have all the jobs we need, right?
Esther: Right.
Tina: And we don't wanna go to, uh, uh, go to bed, cause it's not time to, and her's spinning her thing, and her's— We're not gonna do it. *(pointing to Regina)* Her's bad, right?
Ilana: Yeah right, she's a liar.
Tina: Yeah, her's a liar.
Regina: I am not, I am the mother in this house!
Tina: So what? We don't care. We—it's not bedtime, uh, today, cause we don't—Cause we're not going to bed, cause we're big, uh, sisters, right?
Ilana: Right.
Regina: I'm big too.
Tina: You, you're a mom and we're big sisters so ha, ha, ha, ha, ha, ha, ha, ha.
(Regina leaves the housekeeping area.)
Tina: I'm glad we said that. Right guys?
Ilana: Right.
Tina: Just laugh at her. Let her go. Ha ha ha.
(They all laugh at Regina.)
Tina: Her is a cry-baby, her is a cry-baby, aha.

(Esther proposes to put "Mom's" [i.e., Regina's] silver-ware in the salad spinner where she cannot find them. Ilana collaborates. Tina pantomimes washing her hands and sings something about having the house to herself.

Ilana suggests throwing the contents of a mixing bowl on Regina's head. They laugh at Regina again.)

[Furth, 1996]

Regina is learning an important lesson here, about playing with others: at a certain point, even in the high-status role of mother, when a person is too demanding, others are going to rebel. Regina is also learning that shouting doesn't always work as a social strategy. Evidence that she is actually, not just hypothetically, learning from this experience comes from reports from the researchers: in subsequent play episodes Regina often played a sister or baby role, and when she was the mother, she was a much more nurturant one.

Tina is learning social skills as well. She finally realized that sometimes she can say no, a lesson in effective instrumental aggression. She is also experiencing the thrill of leadership, heading a rebellion against Regina, who had been one of the most popular children up to this point.

On her own, Tina might not have learned any prosocial lessons here. Fortunately, this episode occurred in a preschool, where the adults understood the need to develop prosocial behavior. Relational aggression ("her is a cry-baby, aha") was not allowed to escalate.

(Wen [the teacher] approaches the entrance to housekeeping.)
Wen: Can Regina come in and play?
Ilana: She's an ugly mom.
Wen: Why don't you tell Regina how you feel about having that kind of mom?
Tina: We don't want that mom. That's not the kind of mom we picked out.
Wen: Aha, what kind of mom did you pick out?
Tina: We picked out a different mom. Then her came along and her played that kind of mom.
Wen: Well, what kind of mom would you like?
Esther: Short, skinny,—
Wen: Oh, skinny! That's Regina!
Tina: Not that skinny, short and fat.
Wen: She can pretend to be short and fat, right Regina? Regina is terrific at pretending.
Ilana: No, no, she—
Tina: Well, we don't want that one.
Wen: Well, Regina would really like to play with you. Can she be—
Tina: (stirring a spoon around a bowl) We don't want her to play with the—us? We don't want her to play—
Wen: Tina, Regina is your friend. It hurts her feelings when you say that.
Tina: Well, I just don't want to play with her.
Wen: Look at her face. Do you want her to feel like that?
Ilana: Regina, well, we don't want you—Tomorrow you can play in here because, 'cause maybe Esther and me are gonna play, maybe color or something, so you can play here the whole day 'til it's meeting.

Wen: She wants to play in there now. *(to Regina)* Is that right, Regina?
Tina: Well, we don't want her to, because we decide that one, because we're only—We just don't decide that one.
Wen: Well, Tina, look at Regina's face. Do you think that's hurting her feelings when you say that?
Tina: I know that, but I don't want, I don't want to play with her.
Wen: Well, she would really like to play in here.
Tina: We're staying in here because we started that game.
Wen: Well, she would really like to be in here with you.
Tina: No-o-o. We don't want to.
Wen: Well, Tina, it really hurts her feelings.
Tina: We don't want her to. 'Cause she, 'cause we, we do things and her's, uh, her's getting angry at us and we don't want her and get her angry at us.
Wen: Oh is that the problem?
Tina: Yeah, but we're—and I'm try—trying to get her to say—I wanna play with, and no, I wanna get her to play—
Wen: Tina, if she promises not to get angry with you, can she play in here?
Tina: Yes!
Wen: Regina, did you hear that? The problem is that Tina doesn't like it when you get angry with her. Would you promise not to get—
(Tina takes Regina's hand and pulls her gently into the housekeeping area)

[Furth, 1996]

Thus, with the teacher's help, Tina is made to feel some sympathy for Regina and finally to articulate what made her so mad in the first place. Ilana's solution, allowing Regina to play in the housekeeping area by herself tomorrow, is clearly seen as unacceptable. The conflict ends with the children not only playing together again but being wiser for it.

The researchers found that, over the course of the year, as the children became older and more familiar with each other, they became more skilled at social interaction and they established their own guidelines for that interaction. For example, as a means of settling conflicts, arguments based on personal wishes ("Esther's putting me in jail and I don't want her to") declined, from 43 percent of all the disputes to 16 percent over the year, while arguments based on fairness ("Friends don't do that to friends") and protocol ("I started the game") increasingly prevailed. More often than not, throughout the year, the boys as well as the girls settled their disputes without the intervention of a teacher. However, as in the example above, teachers were there when needed.

As experience accumulated, the types of sociodramatic play changed as well, from predominantly family dramas to more sophisticated and imaginative play that required ongoing communication and mutual agreement (Furth, 1996). From this and many other studies, it is apparent that peer encounters in early childhood afford important experiences that teach reciprocity, cooperation, and justice.

❷ **Especially for Parents:** Although it might be hard on the adult, wouldn't children be happier if their parents let them do almost anything they wanted, as long as they didn't do anything really dangerous?

whether the child should attend preschool) to small ones (such as how to respond to a child's requests for more playtime or more dessert), parents' child-rearing choices affect everything we have just described—self-concept, emotional regulation, prosocial or antisocial behavior.

Which specific parental practices help children develop well? This question has no simple, universal answer partly because there is no guaranteed cause-and-effect relationship between how parents rear a child and how the child turns out. There are a number of effective parenting styles—ranging from quite strict to very permissive, and from intensely involved to rather relaxed—and a child reared in one style may be surprisingly similar to a child reared in another. Conversely, sometimes children raised in the same household differ quite notably, even when their parents have tried to treat all the children the same. Clearly, parental practices alone do not shape personality. Nevertheless, nearly 40 years of careful research have led to suggestive conclusions about parenting styles—including that some styles are more likely than others to produce confident and competent children.

Three Classic Parenting Styles

❶ *Answer to Observational Quiz (from page 314): The signs are not good. Note the sun on the plant, the drawn blinds, and the two well-used, child-size chairs—all suggesting that this scene substitutes for outside play, day after day.*

The seminal work on parenting styles began in the early 1960s, when Diana Baumrind set out to study 100 preschool children, all from California and almost all European-American and middle-class (Baumrind, 1967, 1971). As a careful researcher, she used many measures of behavior, several of them involving naturalistic observation. First, she observed the children in their preschool activities and, on the basis of their actions, rated their self-control, independence, self-confidence, and other attributes. She then interviewed both parents of each child and observed parent-child interaction in two settings, at home and in the laboratory, in search of possible relationships between the parents' behavior at home and the child's behavior at preschool.

Baumrind found that parents differed in four important parenting dimensions:

- Their expressions of *warmth,* or nurturance, which ranged from very affectionate to quite cold
- Their strategies for *discipline,* which might involve explanation, persuasion, and/or punishment
- The quality of their *communication,* which ranged from extensive listening to demands for silence
- Their expectations for *maturity,* evident in how much responsibility and self-control they demanded

On the basis of these four dimensions, Baumrind concluded that most of the parenting she had observed was of three basic styles:

authoritarian parenting A style of child rearing in which standards for proper behavior are high, misconduct is strictly punished, and parent-child communication is low.

permissive parenting A style of child rearing in which the parents rarely punish, guide, or control their children but are nurturant and communicate well with their children.

1. **Authoritarian parenting.** The parents' word is law, not to be questioned. Misconduct brings strict punishment, usually physical, although authoritarian parents do not cross the line into physical abuse. Maturity demands are high, and parent-child communication, especially about emotions, is low. Authoritarian parents seem aloof from their children, showing little affection or nurturance.
2. **Permissive parenting.** The parents make few demands on their children, hiding any impatience they feel. Discipline is lax because maturity demands are low. Permissive parents are nurturant, accepting, and communicate well with their offspring. They view themselves as available to help their children but not as responsible for shaping how their children turn out.

authoritative parenting A style of child rearing in which the parents set limits and provide guidance but are willing to listen to the child's ideas and make compromises.

3. **Authoritative parenting.** Authoritative parents are similar in some ways to authoritarian parents, in that they set limits and enforce rules. However, they also listen to their children's requests and questions and discuss feelings and problems. Family rule is more democratic than dictatorial. The parents make maturity demands on their offspring, but they also are nurturant and readily understanding, forgiving (rather than punishing) a child when maturity demands are not met.

The characteristics of these styles are summarized in Table 10.2.

Baumrind and others have continued this research, following the original 100 children as they grew into adulthood and studying thousands of other children of various backgrounds and ages (Baumrind, 1989, 1991; Lamborn et al., 1991; Steinberg et al., 1989). Their basic conclusions are that *authoritarian* parents raise children who are likely to be conscientious, obedient, and quiet but not happy; *permissive* parents raise children who are even less happy and who lack self-control; and *authoritative* parents raise children who are more likely to be successful, articulate, intelligent, happy with themselves, and generous with others (Darling & Steinberg, 1993; Maccoby, 1992). Follow-up research has also found that, at least for middle-class families of European-American ancestry, the initial advantages of the authoritative approach are likely to grow even stronger over time (Steinberg et al., 1994). Authoritative parents, for example, "are remarkably successful in protecting their adolescents from problem drug use and in generating competence" (Baumrind, 1991).

Given the number of people who are parents, it seems likely that parenting ranges over a wide spectrum of styles, rather than three—or even five or ten—separate and distinct styles. Often the two parents in one family differ as to parenting style, and they may combine their parenting in many different ways. For instance, if the mother tends toward permissive and the father toward authoritarian, cooperation between the two might keep both from the destructive extremes so that their children grow up quite well. This results in a style called "traditional," which in fact leads to good outcomes (Baumrind, 1989). On the other hand, if the parents argue over each occurrence, the conflict itself might make both styles worse. Children need consistency, a theme we emphasize further in Chapter 13.

Punishment

How a parent disciplines a child is an integral part of parenting style. No one suggests that preschoolers should be allowed to do as they please, but given what we have learned about preschool cognition, it should be obvious

table **10.2**	**Characteristics of Baumrind's Parenting Styles**				
			Characteristics		
			Communication		
Style	Warmth	Discipline	Parent to Child	Child to Parent	Maturity Expectations
Authoritarian	Low	Strict, often physical	High	Low	High
Permissive	High	Low	Low	High	Low
Authoritative	High	Moderate, with much talk	High	High	Moderate

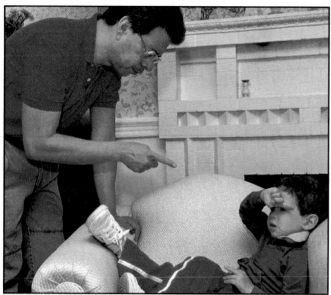

Certainly Not Permissive It's hard to tell what kind of parenting is occurring here, but this is not permissive. Both authoritarian and authoritative parents might sometimes scold a child. The difference is that the authoritarian parent tolerates no back talk and is likely to use physical punishment in response to a display of disrespect. The authoritative parent, however, might listen to a child's response, paying close attention not only to the child's words but also to his or her gestures and body language.

① Response for Parents (from page 318): No! Perhaps surprisingly, children are quite unhappy if their parents don't set limits and guidelines. Further, their lack of self-control gets them into trouble with peers and teachers.

to you that discipline can be much more proactive than punitive. Four specific suggestions are listed in Table 10.3.

No disciplinary technique works quickly and automatically. Instead, over the years from 2 to 6, children gradually learn to reflect on the consequences of their actions, and their actions become more in line with the expectations of their families and cultures. Indeed, culture is a strong influence on actions and disciplinary techniques. Japanese mothers, for example, use reasoning, involve empathy, and express disappointment as techniques to control their preschoolers' social behavior more than North American mothers do. By contrast, parents in the United States are more likely than Japanese parents to encourage emotional expressions of all sorts, including anger. Perhaps as a result, in a series of experimental situations designed to elicit distress and conflict, American 4- to 5-year-olds were more aggressive than their Japanese counterparts (Zahn-Waxler et al., 1996).

What about physical punishment? It is popular, and it seems to work. At least, most children stop doing whatever they are doing if they are spanked or even threatened with spanking. More than 90 percent of today's American adults were spanked when they were young, and most consider themselves none the worse for it. Indeed, most parents, not only in North America but also throughout Asia, Africa, and South America, still believe that spanking is acceptable, legitimate, and necessary at times (Durrant, 1996; Levinson, 1989). They are especially likely to spank their children during the preschool years, when children are considered "old enough to know better" but not "old enough to listen to reason." Spanking is so common that parents of all types resort to it: permissive types in exasperation; authoritative types as a last resort, after extensive warning; and authoritarian types as a legitimate consequence of breaking a rule.

However, many developmentalists wonder if spanking has a boomerang effect—if children who are physically punished learn to be more aggressive. The answer probably is yes. Domestic violence of any type, from spanking a child to letting siblings "fight it out" to exposing children to mutual insults or hitting between the parents, makes children likely to be aggressive with peers and, later on, with their own families (Straus, 1994) (see the Research Report, pages 322–323).

Reasons for Parenting Variations

What might account for differences in parenting style? Stop and make a short list before you read on.

You probably listed culture, religion, ethnicity or national origin, and perhaps sex of the parent. All these factors affect a person's goals for child rearing and his or her beliefs about the nature of children, the best way to raise children, and the proper role of parents. These, in turn, have a proven influence on parental style (Coll et al., 1995; Goodnow & Collins, 1990; Murphey, 1992; Sigel et al., 1992). In addition, a person's own upbringing affects his or her parenting style. This factor sometimes reveals itself when parents use a certain admonishing phrase, affectionate gesture, or mode of discipline and suddenly recognize it from their own childhood.

One parenting influence that might not be on your list is the family's economic well-being. Parents who are stressed by poverty and poverty-related problems are not very likely to expend the energy needed to be authoritative parents. More often they demand obedience, use physical pun-

| table **10.3** | **Relating Discipline to Developmental Characteristics of Preschool Children** |

- *Remember theory of mind.* Preschool children are becoming able to understand things from other viewpoints. Hence involving empathy ("How would you feel if . . . ") will increase prosocial and decrease antisocial behavior.

- *Remember emerging self-concept.* Preschool children are developing a sense of who they are and what they want, sometimes egocentrically. Hence adults should protect that emerging self: they should not force 3-year-olds to share their favorite toys, nor should they tell them, "Words will never hurt me."

- *Remember language explosion and fast mapping.* Preschool children are eager to talk and think, but they are not always accurate in their verbal understanding. Hence it may be inaccurate to say a child doesn't "listen," because a command might be misunderstood. However, conversation before and after the event might be productive.

- *Remember that preschoolers are still illogical.* The connection between the misdeed and the punishment needs to be immediate and transparent. A child might learn nothing from waiting several hours to be spanked for breaking a dish but might learn a lot from having to pick up the pieces, mop the floor, and perhaps contribute some saved pennies toward a replacement.

ishment to maintain control, and express little affection—all signs of authoritarian parenting (Carter & Middlemiss, 1992; Hoff-Ginsberg & Tardif, 1995).

Another influence that has surprising power is the parent's personality, including his or her quickness to anger, capacity for empathy, and even tendency toward optimism (Dix, 1991). In one study, researchers compared attitudes and approaches toward parenting in three types of siblings—monozygotic twins, dyzygotic twins, and people who were biologically unrelated but became siblings by adoption. All the subjects had children under age 8.

The researchers found no differences in parenting style by type of sibling (twins overall were quite similar to nontwins), but they did find several interesting correlations related to genetics. For example, in their responses to the statement "I threaten punishment more than I actually give it," biologically unrelated parents who had been adopted and raised in the same household showed a quite small correlation (actually, .20 compared to a "perfect correlation" of 1.0). In other words, the responses of these siblings were quite often disparate from those of their adoptive brother or sister. Dyzygotic twins, who have half their genes in common, showed a somewhat higher correlation of .28. However, genetically identical twins had a correlation of .45, about as high as monozygotic twins show on many other measures of personality or mental ability. Similar correlations between types of siblings on other parenting questions suggest that inborn temperament has a notable effect on parenting style (Losoya et al., 1997).

Family Pattern and Family Size

Parents often seem to adopt different styles for different children, depending on the age, birth order, and sex of the particular child. This is called **differential treatment** (Furman, 1995). An easy example is that many parents continually make more maturity demands on the oldest child. A single parent of a 2-year-old and a 5-year-old, might regularly send the older child to the corner store to buy milk (trusting, of course, in the safety of the neighborhood). Three years later, that parent might still be sending the older child for milk rather than the now 5-year-old and might have been stricter with the older child all the while (McGuire et al., 1995). Especially if such differential treatment also includes numerous instances in which the older child is assigned to keep the younger from harm ("Make sure he doesn't fall while I get something from the bedroom"), and if it is the older child who is punished when the two

differential treatment The practice of responding to individuals on the basis of their own real or presumed characteristics. In families, differential treatment means that the parents give praise, permission, and punishment to each of their children in a distinct way.

ANY HARM IN SPANKING?

One research team (Strassberg et al., 1994) tracked 273 children—4- to 6-year olds—and their parents to study the relationship between punishment at home and aggression at school. The families were from a full range of socioeconomic and cultural backgrounds. For example, roughly one-third were single parents, about three-fourths were European-American, and about one-fourth were African-American.

Before their children entered kindergarten, the parents were asked how frequently they had spanked, hit, or beaten their children over the past year. If the parents asked the difference between spanking and hitting, *spanking* was defined as "an open hand or an object on the child's buttocks in a controlled manner," whereas *hitting* was "the impulsive or spontaneous use of a fist or closed hand (or object) to strike the child more strongly than one would while spanking." Beating, apparently, did not need to be defined. Of the 408 parents surveyed, 9 percent never used physical punishment, 72 percent spanked but did not use more violent punishment, and 19 percent hit and/or beat, as well as spanked, their preschool children.

Six months later, observers, blind to the children's punishment history, recorded their behavior in kindergarten, taking particular note of acts of aggression. For an accurate snapshot of behavior, the observation phase was divided into twelve 5-minute segments per child, occurring over several days. Within each segment, the observers recorded how many times each child engaged in instrumental, reactive, or bullying aggression. Every child was watched by two observers

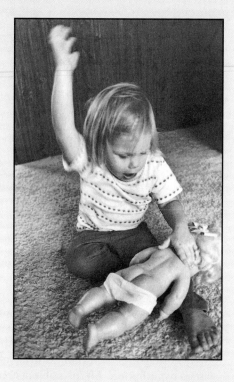

Angela at Play Research suggests that being spanked is a salient and memorable experience for young children, not because of the pain but because of the emotions. Children seek to do what they have learned; they know not only how to place their hands but also that an angry person is able to do the hitting. The only part of the lesson they usually forget is what particular misdeed precipitated the punishment. Asked why she is spanking her doll, Angela will likely explain "She was bad."

overall. The pairs of observers agreed 96 percent of the time about whether aggression had occurred and 90 percent of the time about what type of aggression it was. (This level of agreement is especially important in naturalistic observation that requires some subjective judgment. This study would have been much less valid if, say, one observer was likely to see bullying where another saw reactive aggression.)

Analysis of the data (see the accompanying figure) revealed that family punishment affected the types of aggression differently:

- *Instrumental aggression* by the children seemed unrelated to the punishment they had experienced in the home. In other words, a kindergarten child was just as likely to fight over a toy whether he or she was spanked, hit, beaten, or not physically punished at all.
- *Reactive aggression* in the preschool was powerfully affected by spanking at home. Compared to children who

fight ("You are bigger, you should know better"), the relationship between the two siblings is likely to be one of dominance and dependence, or perhaps that of a boss and a "baby," long after they are fully grown (Cicirelli, 1995).

Many parents believe there is good reason to treat their children differently, but the children themselves typically do not see it that way. By their school years, children's complaints of unfairness abound in almost every family; the older children usually feel that the younger ones are spoiled, and the younger ones believe that the older ones get special privileges.

In fact, many parents do tailor their child-rearing practices to fit each child's unique personality, as they learn what works, what is ineffective, and

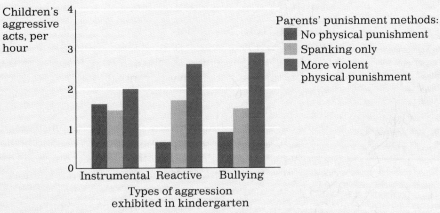

Effect of Punishment Method on Children's Aggression

Children's aggressive acts, per hour

Parents' punishment methods:
- No physical punishment
- Spanking only
- More violent physical punishment

Types of aggression exhibited in kindergarten

Source: Strassberg et al.,1994.

Punishment and Aggression All the children, regardless of how their parents punished them, were about equally likely to exhibit instrumental aggression—fighting to get or retain something, such as a toy. The typical child did so once or twice an hour. By contrast, children who were severely punished by their parents were most often the bullies. The most interesting result involves reactive aggression—children's retaliation for intentional or accidental actions by another child. Children who were spanked were more than twice as likely as those who were not punished physically to consider such actions as hostile and requiring an aggressive response.

were not spanked, children who were spanked were *almost three times more likely* to retaliate for any wrong, real or imagined, via reactive aggression. They angrily shoved, punched, and kicked at any provocation, rather than, say, moving away, asking for an explanation, telling the other child that that child had transgressed, or apologizing themselves.

- *Bullying aggression,* as expected, was clearly associated with being violently punished, particularly in the case of "a few extremely aggressive children," mostly boys who were frequently hit or beaten as well as spanked by both parents.

The researchers point out that while violent punishment (hitting or beating) seems to lead a child to be aggressive under all circumstances (to be a bully), spanking does not produce that blatant result. Rather, it seems to create a specific emotional-response pattern—a quick physical reaction to a perceived attack. Because the "anger accompanying the spanking is highly salient to the child," the child models "the emotional behavior pattern and not the form of aggression, per se" (Strassberg et al., 1994). Interestingly, frequency of spanking and which parent did the spanking (in the 29 percent of two-parent families in which one parent punished differently than the other) were not particularly influential, with one exception: boys who were spanked by their fathers were more likely to react as if they had been hit as well as spanked; that is, they tended to become bullies.

In general, however, spanking even a few times a year by only one of the parents was still likely to make the child higher in reactive aggression. Close analysis of all their data led the researchers to conclude that "in spite of parents' goals, spanking fails to promote prosocial development and, instead, is associated with higher rates of aggression toward peers" (Strassberg et al., 1994).

what is overkill. A parent's pointed criticism, for example, may be taken in stride by a child who is assertive and outgoing but may wither a child who is temperamentally fearful or inhibited (Kochanska, 1991, 1993). Children themselves influence parenting style; in particular, pleasant, self-reliant children make it easy to be an authoritative parent.

Such tailoring to fit each child makes logical sense but has one decided disadvantage: Siblings who notice that their parents treat them differently tend to strongly resent it, and they get along less well with their brothers and sisters as a result (Furman, 1995). This fact alone is an example of the influence children have on parenting styles: parents with many children tend

Should You Become the Judge? "Why can't you get along?" I once asked my two oldest children. "Because we are sisters," they replied. The two siblings in this photo might cite their blood relationship to explain why they both urgently need the same plastic toy at this exact moment. If a parent tries to intervene, perhaps with "He's younger, so let him have it" or "She's older, so she knows how to use it," the result of such differential treatment is likely to be resentment and—reading from their faces—an angry attack from the boy or tearful protests from the girl.

to slide toward a parenting extreme—authoritarian or permissive—because more responsive styles are more complicated when the family is large. As more families have "only" children, more children are being raised in authoritative homes (see Changing Policy, page 325.)

Ethnicity and Culture

Throughout this discussion, we have implicitly assumed that children should be happy, sociable, and successful in school, and therefore that the parenting style that seems to promote that—authoritative parenting—is best. However, you may have noticed that these conclusions depend primarily on studies of European American families. When we include other ethnicities, the picture gets complicated.

Within the same community, the impact of a particular parenting style may depend on the child's ethnicity. A recent study of more than 6,000 adolescents from California found that, as expected, the European American youths who fared best—in regard to both academic achievement and self-concept—came from authoritative homes. However, unexpectedly, the African American youths who fared best came from authoritarian homes (Lamborn et al., 1996).

One possible reason for this finding has to do with neighborhood: Families living in chaotic or dangerous communities may need to be more strict and structured to protect their children. And, in fact, many African American families do live in dangerous urban ghettos. However, in this study the correlation between authoritarian parenting and adolescent accomplishment seemed stronger for *middle-class* African American youths—particularly those living in predominantly white neighborhoods—than for poor youths (Lamborn et al., 1996).

Other research, with younger children, found that physical punishment obviously promotes aggressiveness in European American children but not necessarily in African American children (Deater-Deckard et al., 1996). Several researchers have suggested that children in some minority groups interpret parental strictness as supportive and protective, while children from the majority group see it as rejection (Chao, 1994; Taylor et al., 1993). Thus parental warmth may be open to subjective judgment, with children experiencing nurturance even when an outsider doesn't see it.

It is also possible that if minority parents anticipate that their children will experience prejudice, they may fear that the personality style encouraged by authoritative parenting—happy, creative, talkative, confident, self-assertive—is maladaptive for children who must make their way in a hostile world. Instead, they might push their children to high standards of accomplishment but discourage them from freely expressing their feelings—especially from arguing with an authority figure. Evidence for this hypothesis comes from a study comparing the values of Anglo and Puerto Rican parents; the former tend to encourage self-expression in their children, and the latter self-control. "Be all you can be" would be an Anglo parent's advice; "Be well mannered and respectful" would be a Puerto Rican family's goal (Harwood et al., 1996).

What, then, can we conclude about choice of parenting style? In truth, few parents analyze their parenting style to determine which they prefer or what the long-term impact might be. Instead, they operate mainly on automatic. Most justify whatever they do as best for the child; many are very critical of other parents, whom they find to be too lenient or too harsh, too accepting or too demanding, and who "let their child tell them what to do"

THE ONLY CHILD

Worldwide, the number of both lifelong and temporary only children is clearly rising. For example, in the United States, among all the families that included at least one child under age 18 years, the percentage with only one such child rose from 33 percent in 1970 to 41 percent in 1994. Spending at least several years with no brothers or sisters at home is now a common experience for young American children: in 1994, half of all children under age 6 years were the only such child in their families (U.S. Bureau of the Census, 1996).

Some of these children are only temporary "onlies"; another older child has gone before, or a younger child will soon be born. The latter experience may be difficult. It is called *dethronement*, implying that the older child is no longer treated royally. However, according to traditional wisdom, it may be even more difficult to stay on that throne, to be a lifelong only.

Family composition in many nations of the world is shifting from many children to only one or two. Italian women once had large families, for instance; now the average Italian woman has only 1.3 children, which means that many families have only one. Similar low rates are found in several European nations—Spain, Germany, and Portugal among them. The most dramatic shift has occurred in China, where the government enacted and enforces a strict "one-child policy" to combat overpopulation. In 1991, 95 percent of the student body of most primary schools in Beijing consisted of only children (Bakken, 1993). Even without government policies, the economics of modern life have markedly reduced family size in every continent except Africa (United Nations, 1994).

Is it actually difficult to be an only child? It used to be, and many people still believe that children are handicapped if they have no brothers or sisters, because then their parents are not sufficiently authoritarian. In China, among the older generations, there is widespread prejudice against only children, especially boys. They are stereotyped as lonely, spoiled, and overly dependent on their parents, as disrespectful "little emperors" and potential delinquents.

The truth, however, is usually otherwise: only children typically gain more from increased parental attention than they lose from lack of siblings (Falbo & Poston, 1993; Mellor, 1990). Single-child status is particularly beneficial intellectually; only children are generally more verbal, more creative, and more likely to attend a college than children who have one or more siblings. The contrast is most marked when one-child families are compared to families with four or more children. All the experiences known to develop the child's mind, such as "conversations" at age 1, reading books together at age 2, quality day care at age 3 to 5, and homework help

And Baby Makes Three Chinese couples, like this one in Shanghai, typically marry late, live in cramped quarters, and have only one child, who benefits from paternal and maternal devotion.

throughout the school years, are much harder for parents of several children to provide than for parents with only one child. Further, parenting styles at both extremes are particularly rare in a family that chooses to have only one child. No wonder only children are smarter and more successful—a result found in China, in Europe, and in North America (Bakken, 1993; Blake, 1989; Yang et al., 1995).

The only disadvantage for only children might be in social skills, particularly in the development of cooperative play, theory of mind, negotiation strategies, and self-assertion, all of which are usually enhanced through sibling interaction (Falbo & Poston, 1993). However, preschool education and public day care, which are becoming the rule rather than the exception in industrialized nations, tend to make up for some of the lack of sibling interaction. Most only children today develop social skills that are comparable to those of their peers.

Prejudice about only children arose when almost every "normal" family had two or three children. Forty years ago, onlies were singled out as odd, and sometimes the reason they had no siblings was that their parents didn't like sex, or each other, or children. Obviously the lone child from such a family might have difficulty with self-confidence (too much or too little) or with social development. However, many quite happy couples now choose to have only one child, and consequently today's only children seem to develop as well as, or better than, other children.

What Kind of Parenting? The relationship between these two Botswana bushmen suggests authoritative, not authoritarian, parenting and serves as a reminder that parenting practices follow cultural and ethnic lines, not racial ones. In the largely democratic communities in the open areas of the Kalahari Desert, unlike urban neighborhoods, parents do not have to be strict.

or "don't try to understand their child" (Darling & Steinberg, 1993; Maccoby, 1992). But can we really say that one parenting style is best for all children in all cultures?

This much is certain: Culture, ethnicity, and community affect not only parental goals and values but also the appropriateness and effectiveness of the various parenting styles. Communication skills and academic achievement are highly valued in technologically advanced nations, but quite different traits may be needed in developing nations. In a dangerous area, such as a crowded neighborhood, responsible parenthood for a particular family might well require a high level of parental control; however, in a more secure, spacious, and stable setting the same family might find a more permissive style to be preferable. Thus, because parenting takes place within a broad network of practices, beliefs, and forces from outside the family, the goals and effects of parental style must always be examined within the context of culture and community.

BOY OR GIRL: SO WHAT?

sex differences   Biological differences between males and females.

gender differences   Cultural differences in the roles and behavior of the two sexes.

Male or female identity is an important feature of self-understanding during the play years, as well as a particular concern of many parents. Social scientists distinguish between **sex differences,** which are the biological differences between males and females, and **gender differences,** which are cultural differences in the roles and behaviors of the two sexes. Curiously, true sex differences are far less apparent in childhood (when boys and girls are about the same size and shape) than in adulthood (when physical differences become more visible and anatomy becomes critical in sexual intercourse, pregnancy, and birth). However, *gender* differentiation seems more significant to children than to adults.

Developmental Progression of Gender Awareness

Even at age 2, gender-related preferences and play patterns are apparent. Children already know whether they are boys or girls, can identify adult strangers as mommies or daddies, and apply gender labels (Mrs., Mr., lady, man) consistently. That simple cognitive awareness becomes, by age 3, a rudimentary understanding that male and female distinctions are lifelong (although some pretend, hope, or imagine otherwise). By age 4, children are convinced that certain toys (such as dolls and trucks) and certain roles (such as nurses and soldiers) are appropriate for one gender but not the other (Fagot et al., 1992; Levy, 1994; Martin & Little, 1990). When given a choice, chil-

Two Sets of Cousins Same day, same trampoline, and similar genes and culture, because these eight children are cousins. But sex or gender differences are quite apparent in the later preschool years. Of course, no one should read too much into a photograph. Nonetheless, this group, like any group of preschoolers, offers suggestive evidence of boy-girl differences—here including one specific aspect of their wearing apparel.

❷ *Observational Quiz (see answer page 329): What sex or gender differences can you see?*

dren play with children of their own sex, a tendency apparent at age 2 and clear-cut by age 5 (Moller & Serbin, 1996). As one kindergarten teacher noted:

> Kindergarten is a triumph of sexual self-stereotyping. No amount of adult subterfuge or propaganda deflects the five-year-old's passion for segregation by sex. Children of this age think they have invented the differences between boys and girls and, as with any new invention, must prove that it works. [Paley, 1984]

Of course, following boy-girl play patterns and understanding biological sex differences are not the same thing. A leading researcher of gender identity, Sandra Bem, described the day her young son Jeremy

> naively decided to wear barrettes to nursery school. Several times that day, another little boy insisted that Jeremy must be a girl because "only girls wear barrettes." After repeatedly asserting that "wearing barrettes doesn't matter; being a boy means having a penis and testicles," Jeremy finally pulled down his pants as a way of making his point more convincingly. The boy was not impressed. He simply said, "Everybody has a penis; only girls wear barrettes."[Bem, 1989]

As in this example, a child's awareness of differences is soon associated with what is good, bad, or simply wrong, even though children confuse gender and sex through the preschool years (Fagot & Leinbach, 1993). By age 4, children criticize peers who choose toys that are not appropriate for their gender (Lobel & Menashri, 1993) and are proud of themselves when they act in gender-typical ways (Cramer & Skidd, 1992).

By age 6, children have well-formed ideas (and prejudices) about sex differences and also know which sex is better (their own) and which sex is stupid (the other one) (Huston, 1993). Young children also insist on dressing in stereotypic ways: shoes for preschoolers are often designed with symbols such as pink ribbons or blue footballs, and no child would dare wear the shoes meant for the other sex. Such dress codes become rigidly enforced by first grade, with some of the cruelest barbs of relational aggression used against children who dress oddly. When they reach school age, a few children still may have a good friend of the other sex, but they rarely play with that friend when other children are around (Kovacs et al., 1996).

Stereotypes and taboos are also evident in fantasy play, where most of the other restrictions of daily life disappear. For instance, costumes for Halloween allow children to become animals, or grown-ups, or even giants; nonetheless, the fairy princesses and witches are almost always girls, and the superheroes almost always boys, with rarely a gender-neutral (and almost never a cross-gender) exception (Ogletree et al., 1993). Similarly, when children play house, the girls are the mothers and babies, and the

Boy Will Be Boys Even in today's world, preschool boys and girls tend to engage in play that is gender-stereotyped, especially with a good friend of the same sex. While some gender barriers have fallen, they have related more to girls than to boys. These girls might sword fight, for example, but the boys would probably not play patty-cake, especially for the camera. The question, still not answered with certainty, is "Why?"

boys—if they play the game at all—are the fathers who go off to work and come home to demand that dinner be on the table. You read on page 304 of a trio of preschool girls who created a game in which "he married two of us and you were the sister." In their game, polygamy is readily accepted, the age of the sister becomes a topic for compromise, but no one suggests letting any girl become the groom.

Stereotypes such as these are often soundly criticized by adults, especially feminists, who realize how limiting they can be. In the past few decades, more and more women have entered traditionally male occupations, such as police officer, physician, and construction worker, and more fathers have become involved and nurturant caregivers (Mackay, 1996; Snarey, 1993). But preschoolers still maintain their sex and gender stereotypes, despite the efforts of some adults to deemphasize gender distinctions. Consider the following examples cited by Beal (1994):

> A mother who had struggled through medical school, in part so that she would be a strong role model for her daughter, was startled when the little girl told her that she must be a nurse because only men could be doctors. Another little girl said, "Mommy cleans the living room," even though she had seen only her father doing the vacuuming and dusting. When another girl was given a truck to play with, she said, "My Mommy would want me to play with this, but I don't want to." [Bussey & Bandura, 1992]

Why?

Theories of Gender-Role Development

Experts disagree about what proportion of observed gender differences is biological—perhaps a matter of hormones, of brain structure, or of body size and musculature—and what proportion is environmental—perhaps embedded in centuries of cultural history or in the immediate, explicit home training each child receives (Beal, 1994). One reason for their disagreement is that the topic is so vast, individual experiences so varied, and the research so various that clear conclusions are difficult to reach. To develop a framework for analyzing the conflicting evidence, we need a theory. Fortunately, we have five theories, first described in Chapter 2.

Psychoanalytic Theory

Freud (1938) called the period from about age 3 to 6 the **phallic stage,** because he believed its center of focus is the *phallus,* which is an ancient word for penis. At about 3 or 4 years of age, said Freud, the process of maturation

phallic stage The third stage of psycho-sexual development, occurring in early childhood, in which the penis becomes the focus of psychological concerns as well as physiological pleasure.

Oedipus complex   In the phallic stage of psychosexual development, the sexual desire that boys have for their mothers and the related hostility they have toward their fathers.

identification   A defense mechanism that makes a person take on the role and attitudes of someone more powerful than himself or herself.

superego   The part of the personality that is self-critical and judgmental and that internalizes the moral standards set by parents and society.

Electra complex   In the phallic stage of psychosexual development, the female version of the Oedipus complex: girls have sexual feelings for their fathers and accompanying hostility toward their mothers.

❶ *Answer to Observational Quiz (from page 327): The most obvious ones are in appearance. The girls have longer hair, and the colors and styles of their clothes are different. Did you notice the wearing-apparel difference—that the soles of all four boys' shoes are black, whereas the girls' are white or pink? Now let's get more speculative. The girl on the left, who may need to establish her alliance with the group since she is the only one in colors a boy might wear, is looking at and talking with her cousins—a very female thing to do. In addition, the girls' facial and body expressions suggest they are much more comfortable with this close contact. In fact, the two boys on the left seem about to relieve their tension with a bout of rough-and-tumble play.*

makes a boy aware of his male organ. He begins to masturbate, to fear castration, and to develop sexual feelings toward his mother. These feelings make him jealous of his father—so jealous, according to Freud, that every son secretly wants to replace his dad. Freud called this the **Oedipus complex,** after Oedipus, son of a king in Greek mythology. Abandoned as an infant and raised in a distant kingdom, Oedipus later returned to his birthplace and, not realizing who they were, killed his own father and married his mother. When he discovered what he had done (after disaster struck the entire kingdom), he blinded himself in a spasm of guilt.

Freud believed this bizarre, ancient story still echoes through history because every boy feels horribly guilty for his incestuous and murderous emotions. He fears that his father will inflict terrible punishment on him if his evil secret is ever discovered. Boys cope with their guilt and fear through **identification,** a defense mechanism that allows a person to ally himself or herself with another person. In a sense, since they cannot replace their fathers, young boys strive to become them, copying their fathers' masculine mannerisms, opinions, and actions. Boys also develop, again in self-defense, a powerful conscience called the **superego** that is quick to judge and punish "the bad guys." According to Freud's theory, a young boy's fascination with superheroes, guns, karate chops, and the like, comes directly from his patricidal urges, and an adult man's obsession with crime and punishment might be a product of an imperfectly resolved phallic stage. Homosexuality, either overt or latent, is also evidence of a poorly managed phallic stage, as is homophobia.

Freud offered two overlapping descriptions of the phallic stage in girls. One form, the **Electra complex** (also named after a figure in classical mythology), is similar to the Oedipus complex: the little girl wants to eliminate her mother and become intimate with her father. In the other version, the little girl becomes jealous of boys because they have penises, an emotion called *penis envy*. The girl blames her mother for this "incompleteness" and decides the next best thing to having a penis is to become sexually attractive so that someone with a penis—preferably her father—will love her (Freud, 1933/1965). Her *identification* is with women her father finds attractive; her *superego* strives to avoid his disapproval.

Thus, the origins and consequences of the phallic stage are basically the same for girls as they are for boys. Biological impulses within a family context produce, first, lust and anger and, then, guilt and fear. By the end of the preschool years these emotions have caused the development of a strict superego that mandates gender-appropriate behavior and harsh punishment for those who do not abide by the code. No wonder, then, that 5-year-olds seem obsessed by sex roles; this is their best defense against unconscious urges.

Other psychoanalytic theorists agree that male-female distinctions are important to the young child's psychic development, although, as you might imagine and as the Children Up Close discussion (page 330) makes clear, many disagree about the specifics.

Learning Theory

In contrast with psychoanalytic theorists, learning theorists believe that virtually all roles are learned and hence are the result of nurture, not nature. Therefore, to learning theorists, the gender distinctions that are so obvious by age 5 are evidence of years of ongoing reinforcement and punishment, rather than the product of any specific stage.

What evidence supports learning theory? Parents, peers, and teachers all reward "gender-appropriate" more than "gender-inappropriate" behavior (Etaugh & Liss, 1992; Fagot, 1995; Fagot et al., 1992; Lytton & Romney,

BERGER AND FREUD

As a woman, and as a mother of four daughters, I have always regarded Freud's theory of sexual development as ridiculous, not to mention antifemale. I am not alone. Psychologists generally agree that Freud's explanation of sexual and moral development is one of the weaker parts of his theory, reflecting the values of middle-class Victorian society at the end of the nineteenth century more than any universal developmental pattern. Many female psychoanalysts (e.g., Horney, 1967; Klein, 1957; Lerner, 1978) are particularly critical of Freud's idea of penis envy. They believe that girls envy not the male sex organ but the higher status males are generally accorded. They also suggest that boys may experience "womb envy," wishing that they could have babies and suckle them. Virtually no contemporary psychologist or psychiatrist believes that homosexual urges are caused by problems during the phallic stage.

However, my own view of Freud's theory as utter nonsense has been modified somewhat by my four daughters. Our first "Electra episode" occurred in a conversation with my eldest, Bethany, when she was about 4 years old:

Bethany: When I grow up, I'm going to marry Daddy.
Mother: But Daddy's married to me.
Bethany: That's all right. When I grow up, you'll probably be dead.
Mother: (Determined to stick up for myself) Daddy's older than me, so when I'm dead, he'll probably be dead, too.
Bethany: That's OK. I'll marry him when he gets born again.

At this point, I couldn't think of a good reply, especially since I had no idea where she got the concept of reincarnation. Bethany saw my face fall, and she took pity on me:

Bethany: Don't worry, Mommy. After you get born again, you can be our baby.

Our second episode was also in conversation, this time with my daughter Rachel, when she was about 5:

Rachel: When I get married, I'm going to marry Daddy.
Mother: Daddy's already married to me.
Rachel: (With the joy of having discovered a wonderful solution) Then we can have a double wedding!

The third episode was considerably more graphic. It took the form of a "valentine" left on my husband's pillow by my daughter Elissa, who was about 8 years old at the time. It is reproduced here.

Finally, when Sarah turned 5, she also expressed the desire to marry my husband. When I told her she couldn't, because he was married to me, her response revealed one of the disadvantages of not being able to ban TV: "Oh yes, a man can have two wives. I saw it on television."

Pillow Talk Elissa placed this artwork on my husband's pillow. My pillow, beside it, had a less colorful, less elaborate note—an afterthought. It read "Dear Mom, I love you too."

I am not the only feminist developmentalist to be taken aback by her own children's words. Nancy Datan (1986) wrote about the oedipal conflict: "I have a son who was once five years old. From that day to this, I have never thought Freud mistaken." Obviously, these bits of "evidence" do not prove that Freud was correct. I still think he was wrong on many counts. But Freud's description of the phallic stage now seems less bizarre than it once appeared to be.

Theodore Lidz (1976), a respected developmental psychiatrist, offers a plausible explanation. Lidz believes that all children must go through an oedipal "transition," overcoming "the intense bonds to their mothers that were essential to their satisfactory pre-Oedipal development." As part of this process, children imagine becoming an adult and, quite logically, taking the place of the adult of their own sex whom they know best, the father or the mother. This idea must be dispelled before the sexual awakening of early adolescence; otherwise, an "incestuous bond" will threaten the nuclear family, prevent the child's extrafamilial socialization, and block his or her emergence as a well-adjusted adult. According to Lidz, the details of the oedipal transition vary from family to family, but successful desexualization of parent-child love is essential for healthy maturity. That this happens toward the end of the preschool years, when children become less dependent on their mothers' nurturance, is as it should be.

Modeling Much of gender-role learning happens without adult realization or intention. This father did not ask his son to pretend to fix his toy lawnmower, just as no mother asks her daughter to pretend to iron the clothes, set the table, or wear high heels. The impulse to copy obviously comes from the children—which is one of the reasons the lessons are learned so well, even when we would rather teach something else.

1991). Parents praise their sons for not crying when hurt, for example, but caution their daughters about the hazards of rough play. Interestingly, males seem to be caught in the learned-gender curriculum more than females. Researchers have found that boys are criticized for being "sissies" more than girls are criticized for being "tomboys" and that fathers, more than mothers, expect their daughters to be feminine and their sons to be tough. If a 3-year-old boy asks his father for either a doll or a truck for his birthday, you can be quite sure which present he will get; if a girl gives her mother the same choice, there is at least a chance she'll get the truck.

Social learning theorists remind us that children learn about behavior not only through reinforcement (such as a gift or a word of praise) but also by observation, especially of people seen as nurturing, powerful, and yet similar to themselves. Parents are, therefore, important models of gender behavior. Fifty years ago in North America, young children saw their mothers as primary caregivers and housewives and their fathers as workers exempt from daily housework—a pair of role models that was perfect for learning sexual stereotypes. Today, although most mothers are employed (70 percent of all married mothers were in the labor market in the United States in 1995), social learning theorists point out that the earlier sexual division of labor still remains strong. Mothers of small children still do most of the cooking, cleaning, and child care, and fathers "help out" or, in about one-third of all households, are absent altogether (Barnett & Rivers, 1996; Hochschild, 1989).

Thus, gender-role conformity is still rewarded, punished, and modeled, especially for preschool children and especially for boys, according to research inspired by learning theory. This can explain why girls and women sometimes wear pants and aspire to male occupations but boys cannot wear skirts or aspire to female roles without experiencing massive disapproval, especially from other males. Note again that this gender prejudice is strongest during the preschool years. If a college man aspires to be a nurse or a preschool teacher, most of his classmates will respect his choice. If a 4-year-old boy wants the same thing, his peers will probably soon set him straight. As one professor reports:

> My son came home after 2 days of preschool to announce that he could not grow up to teach seminars (previously his lifelong ambition, because he knew from personal observation that everyone at seminars got to eat cookies) because only women could be teachers. [Fagot, 1995]

Cognitive Theory

In explaining gender identity and gender-role development, cognitive theorists focus on children's understanding—the way a child intellectually grasps a specific matter at hand. Preschool children, they point out, have many gender-related experiences but not much cognitive complexity. They tend to see the world in intellectually simple terms. For example, in the classic demonstration of conservation, preschoolers see a glass as containing more or less water than another glass only on the basis of its appearance at the moment, not the quantity it held a moment ago. Similarly, they see male and female as complete opposites, on the basis of appearance at the moment, even when past evidence (such as the father who cleaned the living room) contradicts such a sexist assumption.

Remember that the basic tenet of cognitive theory is that a person's thinking determines how the world is perceived and how that perception

gender-schema theory   The theory that children's ideas about gender are based on simple and somewhat stereotyped generalities (scripts) developed from their experience.

is acted on. Preschoolers' thinking about gender follows preschoolers' cognitive patterns, which are static and egocentric. From this generality, **gender-schema theory** explains that young children develop a simplified concept of male-female distinctions and then apply it universally (Bem, 1989, 1993). For example, if they see that women *usually* are the ones who care for babies and that men *usually* are the ones who do the heavy lifting, preschoolers "remember" that male and female are *always* opposites, and thus they might conclude that women *always* care for babies and men *always* do the lifting. Then, if a man tries to feed a crying infant, children are likely to note the discrepancy between what is observed and what is in their baby-care schema, and therefore tell the man to give the baby to its mother. Essentially, according to gender schema theory, children form a script describing what the various gender roles should be and then intellectually follow that script (Levy & Fivush, 1993; Martin, 1993). When personal experience is ambiguous or contradictory, preschoolers search for the script. For example, when researchers gave children unfamiliar, gender-neutral toys, the children first tried to figure out if the toys were for boys or for girls and then decided whether they personally would like to play with the toys or not (Martin et al., 1995).

Given what we know about children's thinking, we should not be too surprised when children leap to stereotyped conclusions, not only about gender differences but about racial, ethnic, and national differences as well—as many children do (Aboud, 1988). Children try to sort out a complex world, and given their cognitive immaturity, they must simplify what they see. Stereotypes provide one kind of simplification. Of course, adults need not accept a child's biased thinking, as the next theory makes clear.

Sociocultural Theory

Proponents of the sociocultural perspective note that many traditional cultures emphasize gender distinctions, and these are quickly evidenced in the gender patterns adopted by children. In societies where adults have quite distinct sex roles, girls and boys attend sex-segregated schools beginning in kindergarten, and they virtually never play together (Beal, 1994). They are also taught different skills. For instance, in rural communities throughout the world, girls tend the chickens and the younger children, while boys tend the larger animals, such as sheep, pigs, and cattle (Whiting & Edwards, 1988). As a result, gender distinctions are clear and inflexible in the mind and behavior of both children and adults.

When immigrants from such traditional societies come to less segregated societies, they tend to maintain their gender values strenuously. For example, among Khmer refugees in the United States, the boys are urged to continue their education, and the girls are urged to become wives and mothers before graduating from high school so that they will be protected from the sexual permissiveness that the Khmer see as corrupting American daughters (Smith-Hefner, 1993). Similar gender distinctions can be found worldwide. Almost every study of preschool children finds that boys are encouraged by their culture to take on different roles than girls.

Socioculturalists point out that the particulars of gender education—such as which activities are promoted for which sex—vary by region, socioeconomic status, and historical period. But every society has values and attitudes regarding preferred behavior for men and women, and every culture teaches these to the young.

In this way sociocultural theory provides an explanation for the findings of the three previous theories. For instance, Freud's emphasis on a link between sex organs and gender development seems, to socioculturalists, to be the

? Especially for Teachers: Suppose you want children to fulfill all their potential, and therefore you plan to structure your preschool to counter the gender training children might have had at home. For instance, you encourage the girls to engage in rough-and-tumble play and the boys to dress up, and you make sure each play group has children of both sexes. Is androgyny going to appear in your classroom?

product of Viennese society at the turn of the century, not contemporary society. As for learning theory, since preschool children are wide open to learning whatever they experience, they are sponges not just for language and emotions but for societal values as well. Similarly, if a culture adheres to a particular cognitive perspective (say, on gender), its children will follow that intellectual framework as well. Hence, sociocultural theorists are not surprised (as learning or cognitive theorists might be) that 5-year-olds mirror whatever gender distinctions their society endorses, even if their parents strive to be gender-neutral. Learning, they maintain, is *culturally* fostered, and cognition is *culturally* based. Children aspire to gender-linked occupations even if their parents don't, because children notice that teachers are almost always women and doctors are almost always men and that books and television portray the leaders of the nation as men and the housewives (of course) as women (Barnett, 1986; Beal, 1994; Crabb & Bielawski, 1994; Huston, 1983). Children could become less gender-conscious, but only if their entire culture were so.

This possibility of cultural change leads to another idea: **androgyny.** As a biological term, "androgyny" is defined as the presence of both male and female sexual characteristics in an organism. As developmentalists use the term, *androgyny* means a balance, within a person, of what are commonly regarded as male and female psychological characteristics. The idea is to break through the restrictiveness of cultural gender roles and to encourage the individual to define himself or herself primarily as a human being, rather than as male or female. Boys should be encouraged to be nurturant, and girls to be assertive, according to the goals of androgyny, so that with maturity and patience they will develop less restrictive rule-bound gender patterns.

Sociocultural theory stresses, however, that androgyny (or any other gender concept) cannot be taught to children simply through cognition or parental reinforcement. The only way children will be truly androgynous is if their entire culture promulgates the ideas and practices—something no culture has yet done. Why not? The reasons may be far deeper than the political forces or social values of the moment, as our final theory suggests.

androgyny A balance, within an individual, of male and female gender characteristics such that the individual feels comfortable in breaking through gender stereotypes; thus, for example, an androgynous male will feel comfortable being nurturant as well as being assertive.

Nature or Nurture? At first glance, the boy-girl differences seen here seem entirely cultural. The boy must have seen a fireman, and the girl a fancy lady, if not in person then on television. However, epigenetic theory urges us to go deeper, to see if something innate is also portrayed in this photo.

❷ *Observational Quiz (see answer page 334): Can you see it?*

Epigenetic Systems Theory

Epigenetic systems theory contends that every aspect of human behavior, including gender attitudes and behavior roles, is the result of interaction between genes and early experience—not just for the individual but also for the species. The idea that *many* gender differences are genetically based is supported by recent research in neurobiology, which finds biological differences between male and female brains. In females, for example, the corpus callosum tends to be thicker, and overall brain maturation seems to occur more quickly than in males. This could account for the fact that girls tend to be slightly more advanced than boys in skills such as reading and writing, which demand simultaneous coordination of various areas of the brain (Dudek et al., 1994). In males, neural activity and dendrite formation in the right hemisphere tend to be more pronounced than in females. The right hemisphere is concerned with logic, spatial skills, and mathematical processes, so this could account for the typical superiority of boys in these areas, a superiority that eventually leads to more men than women among engineers, physicists, and pilots.

These brain differences are probably not the result of any single gene occurring more frequently in one sex than the other. More likely, they appear because differing sex hormones produced by *XX* and *XY* chromosomes begin to circulate in the fetal stage, affecting the development of male and female brains differently. Those hormones continue to influence brain development through childhood (Gaulin, 1993; Hines, 1993). The social context,

❶ Response for Teachers (from page 332):
The goal of androgyny may be a good one, and you can decrease the worst of sexism, but children have powerful reasons of their own to stick to male and female patterns. These may be biological, or they may be cultural, but they are not easy for one teacher to change. If you don't want to have a room full of frustrated children, and perhaps angry parents, you need to be selective when you cross the gender boundaries. For example, to get the boys to engage in sociodramatic play, you might stock the room with dress-up clothes that boys would like and encourage games that are best played with both sexes—playing a family that has a father and a big brother, for instance.

❶ Answer to Observational Quiz (from page 333): *Universally, boys and men seem more intrigued by moving gadgets and manipulated tools, and women seem attracted to frills, lace, and fuzzy shoes. Of course, many individuals are involved in activities dominated by the other sex: women use machines to accomplish many things, and men wear expensive tuxedos and gold cufflinks to indicate status. But in both those examples, the behavior is a means to an end. In more usual cases, males tend to be fascinated with machines, and women with wearing sheer fabrics—just for the fun of it.*

then, may enter by affecting the pruning of the brain's transient exuberance in ways that program proper male and female behavior.

Of course, this programming is not inevitable. Remember: Although epigenetic systems theory stresses the biological and genetic origins of behavior, it also stresses that manifestation of those origins are shaped, enhanced, or halted by environmental factors. Here is one example: Infant girls seem to be genetically inclined to talk earlier than boys. However, the language parts of an infant's brain do not develop fully unless someone talks to the infant. Suppose an only child who is a boy is raised in a household with several adult women; he might be talked to, sung to, and read to quite often by his devoted caregivers. He will develop superior verbal ability in his brain, because of the interaction between his genetic potential (which might be slightly less than that of the typical girl) and his social environment (which is much richer than it is for most children of either sex). Enviromental factors will have enhanced his genetic capabilities greatly.

Of course, this is not the usual scenario. In a typical family that includes one man, one woman, and several children of both sexes, language stimulation will differ by sex. Since girls are more responsive to language and since mothers are usually more verbal than fathers, mother-daughter pairs will typically talk most, and father-son pairs least. This will likely turn the females' slight linguistic advantage in their brain circuitry into a notably higher level of language proficiency (Leaper et al., 1998).

There is evidence for the suggestion (above) that hormones affecting the brain, and not solely familial training or cultural responses, are the source of many of the sex or gender differences we observe. The best evidence comes from girls (XX children with female organs) who have congenital adrenal hyperplasia, a disorder that causes their hormone balance to be more like a boy's than a girl's. Even in their preschool years, such girls tend to prefer boys' toys and boys' play activities (Berenbaum & Snyder, 1995).

Epigenetic systems theory emphasizes the interaction between the genetic potential and the environmental actuality. If boys' brains are already primed to be attracted to, say, spatial relationships, and if young boys then are provided with experiences that enhance right-hemisphere development (for example, building structures with Legos or playing catch with their fathers), by the end of their preschool years this combination of nature and nurture will surely make boys much more interested in "masculine" play activities, school subjects, and future careers than are girls who were given dolls and coloring books to play with.

Conclusion: Gender and Destiny

The first and last of our five theories emphasize the power of biology as regards gender development. A reader who is quick to form opinions might decide that the gender roles and stereotypes exhibited by preschoolers are unchangeable. This conclusion might be reinforced by the fact that gender awareness emerges very early, by age 2, or that play patterns and social interactions of young boys and girls differ. But the three middle theories all present persuasive evidence for the influence of family and culture in guiding and shaping the powerful gender patterns we see by age 5. Actually, psychoanalytic theory and epigenetic systems theory both acknowledge some learning in gender development as well. Boy-girl differences are partly innate, a matter of sex, but much is taught.

Thus our five theories, collectively, have led to at least one conclusion and one critical question. The conclusion is that gender differences are not simply cultural or learned; the biological foundation for gender differences is far more pervasive than the minor anatomical differences between boys and girls. At the same time, biology is not destiny; children are shaped by their experiences.

This raises the question: What gender patterns should children learn, ideally? Answers vary. In those cultures and families that encourage each child to develop his or her own inclinations, many children grow up to choose gender roles, express emotions, and develop talents that would be taboo—or even punished—in cultures that adhere to strict gender guidelines. On the other hand, some societies and families encourage gender differences, widening whatever innate sex distinctions there may be. In these societies, adults fall naturally into two quite separate worlds, one designed for men and one for women.

To what extent would you want your children to follow gender roles, and to what extent would you want them to be androgynous? Is harm done to a person's development by requiring him or her to adhere to certain social guidelines and thereby changing that person's natural orientation—making the person either more or less gender-bound than he or she might otherwise be?

If you agree that the theories we have examined have at least some merit, you must conclude that both nature and nurture influence the gender behaviors you see. But the theories don't answer value questions about the relative merits of the various gender patterns. Perhaps that is why various cultures and individuals—and the theories themselves—come to such different conclusions about gender.

Of course, the same can be said about the proper expression of aggression, or the preferred parenting style, or the degree of emotional regulation that should be evident in a person. The research describes what is, and what can develop, during early childhood. It is up to you to decide what should be.

SUMMARY

THE SELF AND THE SOCIAL WORLD

1. An increasing self-understanding helps preschoolers increase their social understanding and become more skilled in their relationships with others. Confidence is quite high, as these children do not focus on their failures but on their new successes, developed through mastery play, initiative, and the efforts of appreciative adults.

2. Learning to regulate emotions is one key aspect of emotional intelligence during the preschool years. Normally, children modulate their fear and anger, becoming quite sympathetic and outgoing (but not overly solicitous or excessively friendly) to others.

ANTISOCIAL AND PROSOCIAL BEHAVIOR

3. Children's social understanding can be either positive or negative. Play with friends teaches responsiveness and caring. Boys are more likely to engage in rough-and tumble play, and girls more likely to become involved in sociodramatic play.

4. Usually early attachments, as well as brain maturation, encourage prosocial behavior. Antisocial behavior, particularly aggression, is encouraged by television and is modeled by parental actions. Some aggression is normal; other types are a matter of concern.

PARENTING PATTERNS

5. Parent-child interaction is complex. Many factors other than parenting affect child outcomes, and research offers no simple answers about the best way to raise a child. However, in general, authoritative parents, who are warm and loving but are willing to set and enforce reasonable limits, have children who are happy, self-confident, and capable. Highly authoritarian parents tend to raise unhappy and aggressive children, whereas children with very permissive parents often lack self-control.

6. Parents do not necessarily analyze their patterns and choose the best one. Instead, many factors influence the adults, including their marital relationship, their personality, and their own childhood experiences. The cultural and community context is also influential. In fact, although authoritative parenting is generally beneficial, in some contexts and cultures more authoritarian parenting may be better.

7. Family size affects parenting patterns, with large families easier to manage via authoritarian parenting. Differential treatment of siblings, almost inevitably in authoritative or permissive families, can lead to resentments in large families, which is one reason why "only" children are more likely to be reared in authoritative homes.

BOY OR GIRL: SO WHAT?

8. Developmentalists agree that children begin to display gender role and gender identity during early childhood, with consciousness of male-female differences apparent as early as age 2. However, psychologists disagree about why sex differences are so important during the preschool years. Boys and girls become quite distinct in their behavior and attitudes by age 5.

9. Each of the major theories has a somewhat different explanation for sex or gender differences. Psychoanalytic theorists describe fears and fantasies that motivate children to adore their opposite-sex parent and then identify with their same-sex parent. Learning theorists emphasize reinforcement, punishment, and modeling, which are particularly strong for males. Cognitive theory begins by noting preschool children's simplified, stereotypic understanding overall.

10. Two emerging theories note the influence of the wider society, both currently and in earlier times. Sociocultural theory notes the pervasive influence of cultural patterns. Epigenetic systems theory points out the biological tendencies that are inherited through genetic transmission and explains how these tendencies may affect the child's brain patterns as well as other aspects of behavior.

11. These theories together suggest that biology and society (sex and gender) are both powerful influences on children. They do not, however, specify how parents and cultures should attempt to mold children. Although children have innate tendencies, those tendencies can be strengthened, directed, or overcome by the child's upbringing.

KEY TERMS

phobia (305)
mastery play (306)
initiative versus guilt (307)
emotional regulation (308)
prosocial behavior (310)
antisocial behavior (310)
rough-and-tumble play (311)
play face (312)
sociodramatic play (312)
instrumental aggression (315)
reactive aggression (315)
bullying aggression (315)
relational aggression (315)

authoritarian parenting (318)
permissive parenting (318)
authoritative parenting (319)
differential treatment (321)
sex differences (326)
gender differences (326)
phallic stage (328)
Oedipus complex (329)
identification (329)
superego (329)
Electra complex (329)
gender-schema theory (332)
androgyny (333)

KEY QUESTIONS

1. How would you describe preschoolers' evaluations of themselves?

2. How do children learn emotional regulation?

3. What are the types of aggression, and which are most troubling?

4. What are the similarities between rough-and-tumble play and sociodramatic play?

5. What can children learn from peers that they are unlikely to learn from adults?

6. What behaviors in preschool children might be the result of a disturbed early attachment?

7. How do the three classic parenting styles differ?

8. What factors influence a parent to follow one or another of the parenting styles?

9. How does punishment of young children influence their behavior?

10. What evidence do you know of that implies preschool children are aware of sex differences?

11. Which theory of development seems to offer the best explanation of gender roles, and why?

12. *In Your Experience* Can you describe a parenting style that was influenced by the ethnic background of the parents?

CRITICAL THINKING EXERCISE

by Richard O. Straub

Take your study of Chapter 10 a step further by working this reasoning exercise:

The minor theories of development disagree about the origins of gender roles and stereotypes. Two of the theories (psychoanalytic and epigenetic systems) emphasize the power of genetic and biological forces on development. The remaining three theories (learning, cognitive, and sociocultural) emphasize the influence of family and culture in children's learning of gender patterns.

In this exercise you will evaluate evidence relative to the following question: *Is gender development the result of biological forces or cultural learning?* First, decide whether each of the three research findings listed below *more directly* provides evidence in support of the biological argument or the cultural-learning argument, and explain your reasoning. Then use the same research finding to develop a counterargument that supports the *other* side of the controversy.

1. There are more male than female engineers, physicists, and airplane pilots.

2. Girls tend to play in small groups, with one or two friends, whereas boys tend to play in larger, less intimate groups.

3. In their play, 5-year-olds aspire to sex-linked occupations even if their parents' behavior tends to counter such stereotyping.

Check your answers by comparing them to the sample answers in Appendix B.

BIOSOCIAL

Brain and Nervous System

The brain continues to develop, attaining 90 percent of its adult weight by the time the child is 5 years old. Both the proliferation of neural pathways and myelination continue. Coordination between the two halves and the various areas of the brain increase, allowing the child to settle down and concentrate when necessary, and to use various parts of the body in harmony. Gross motor skills, such as running and jumping, improve dramatically. Fine motor skills, such as writing and drawing, develop more slowly.

Maltreatment

Child abuse and neglect, potential problems at every age, are particularly likely in homes with many children and few personal or community resources. During early childhood, home-visitation programs can be an effective preventive measure. Recognition of the problem has improved, but treatment is still uneven. Distinguishing the ongoing problems of a family that needs support, and the immediate danger for a child who needs to be removed and placed in foster care, is critical for long-term development.

COGNITIVE

Cognitive Skills

Many cognitive abilities, including some related to number, memory, and problem solving, become more mature, if the social context is supportive. Children begin to develop a theory of mind, in which they take into account the ideas and emotions of others. Social interaction, particularly in the form of guided participation, is of help in this cognitive advancement. At the same time, however, children's thinking can be quite illogical and egocentric.

Language

Language abilities develop rapidly; by the age of 6, the average child knows 10,000 words and demonstrates extensive grammatical knowledge. Children also learn to adjust their communication to their audience, and use language to help themselves learn. Preschool education helps children develop language and express themselves, as well as prepare them for later education and adult life.

PSYCHOSOCIAL

Emotions and Personality Development

Self-concept emerges, as does the ability to regulate emotions. Children boldly initiate new activities, especially if they are praised for their endeavors.

Parent-Child Interaction

Some parenting styles are more effective than others in encouraging the child to develop autonomy and self-control; those that are most responsive to the child, with much communication, seem to do best. Parenting styles are influenced by cultural and community standards, the parents' economic situation, upbringing and personality, and the characteristics of the child.

Gender Roles

Increasingly, children develop stereotypic concepts of sex differences in appearance and gender differences in behavior. The precise roles of nature and nurture in this process are unclear, but both are obviously involved.

Play

Children engage in play that helps them master physical and intellectual skills and that teaches or enhances social roles. As their social and cognitive skills develop, children engage in ever more complex and imaginative types of play, sometimes by themselves and, increasingly, with others.

PART IV

The School Years

If someone asked you to pick the best years of the entire life span, you might choose the years from about 6 to 11 and defend your choice persuasively. Physical development is usually almost problem-free, making it easy to master dozens of new skills. With regard to cognitive development, most children are able to learn quickly and think logically, providing the topic is not too abstract. Moreover, they are usually eager to learn, mastering new concepts, new vocabulary, and new skills with a combination of enthusiasm, perseverance, and curiosity that makes them a joy to teach. Indeed, we call these the "school years" because every culture worldwide takes advantage of the fact that these children are ready and eager to learn.

Finally, the social world of middle childhood seems perfect, for most school-age children think their parents are helpful, their teachers fair, and their friends loyal. The child's moral reasoning and behavior have reached that state where right seems clearly distinguished from wrong, without the ambiguities and conflicts that complicate morality during adolescence. As you will see, however, not every child escapes middle childhood unscathed.

The next three chapters celebrate the joys, and commemorate the occasional tragedies, of middle childhood.

The School Years:
Biosocial Development

Compared with other periods of the life span, the period comprising age 7 to 11 is relatively uneventful in terms of biosocial development. Most school-age children easily master new physical skills, from tree climbing to hammer pounding to in-line skating, without extensive adult instruction. Disease and death are rare, sex-related differences in physical development and ability are minimal, and sexual urges are quiescent. Certainly when growth in these years is compared with the rapid and dramatic growth that occurs during infancy and adolescence, middle childhood seems a period of smooth progress and tranquility.

For some children, however, the school years are particularly challenging, because their disabilities become more evident and disturbing. In this chapter, we will examine the body changes and variations that characterize middle childhood, as well as several biosocial difficulties that sometimes occur.

SIZE AND SHAPE

Children grow more slowly from age 7 to 11 than they did earlier or than they will later, in adolescence. Although the actual pounds or kilograms gained per year are more than those gained between ages 2 and 6, the rate of increase is slower during the school years. Each year, the typical well-nourished child gains about 5 pounds (2¼ kilograms) and grows about 2½ inches (6 centimeters); by age 10, he or she weighs about 70 pounds (32 kilograms) and measures 54 inches (137 centimeters) (Lowrey, 1986). (See Appendix A.)

Children generally seem to become slimmer as their height increases, their limbs lengthen, and their body proportions change. Muscles become stronger as well. Thus, the average 10-year-old, for instance, throws a ball twice as far as the average 6-year-old. Lung capacity expands as well, so with each passing year children can run faster and exercise longer.

Variations in Physique

In the poorer nations, most variation in children's height and weight is caused by differences in nutrition. Wealthier children are generally several inches taller than their impoverished classmates from the other side of town—whether the town is Nairobi, Rio de Janeiro, or New Delhi (Eveleth & Tanner, 1991). In more affluent countries, heredity is the main source of variation, since most children get enough food during middle childhood to grow as tall as their genes allow.

All Healthy, All Different During the school years, variations in children's size and rate of physical maturation are the result of genetic inheritance and nutrition, as well as of chronological age.

Among North American children, nutrition is usually more than adequate. Consequently, genes affect height in obvious ways, not only for individuals but also for ethnic groups. American children of African descent tend to mature earlier (as measured by bone growth and loss of baby teeth) and to have longer legs than those of European descent, who, in turn, tend to mature ahead of those with Asian ancestors (Eveleth & Tanner, 1991). Of course, within each of these ethnic groups, genes (and hence physical growth) vary: children with ancestors from northern China tend to be taller than those with ancestors from southern China; those of East African descent are often taller than those of Southwest African descent; and so on. Such variations are quite normal and healthy; only if a child is surprisingly short should a pediatrician or social worker be consulted.

Body shape is also affected by genes, but here family habits have obvious impact, and medical advice may be needed. Parents of children who are too thin, or too fat, need to understand how they influence their children's weight, and teachers, medical professionals, and other members of the community who deal with children need to understand the serious consequences of being an underweight or overweight child.

❷ **Especially for Parents:** Suppose your 6-year-old is quite chubby and also quite happy. Should you upset the child by imposing a diet?

Childhood Obesity

Although every difference, from having freckles to wearing the wrong shoes, can become a source of embarrassment during the sensitive years from 7 to 17, being overweight is the most common "real" problem. Being overweight to the point that it affects emotional and physical well-being is called *obesity,* and it is not precisely determined. The point at which a particular child is considered not just chubby but truly obese varies, depending partly on the child's body type, partly on the child's proportion of fat to muscle, and partly on the culture's standards. One measure is the **body mass index (BMI),** which is the weight in kilograms divided by the square of the height in meters. At age 8, obesity begins at about 18 BMI. At age 12, if the BMI is over 23, the child is probably obese (Hubbard, 1995).

body mass index A measure of obesity determined by dividing weight in kilograms by height squared in meters.

Experts believe that between 20 and 30 percent of American children are obese, a rate that has been steadily increasing since 1960 (Dietz, 1995) and that parallels the increase in adult obesity. The causes are many, but the marked increase over a few decades must be primarily caused by nurture, not nature, since genes do not change much from one generation to the next. The various social causes and consequences of obesity are

How to Calculate Body Mass Index

Many current studies of the relationship between body size and overall health focus on the ratio of body weight to height, referred to as the *body mass index*, or *BMI*. The formula for calculating body mass index is

$$BMI = w/h^2$$

w = weight in kilograms (pounds divided by 2.2)
h = height in meters (inches divided by 39.4)

Thus if a 12-year-old measures 1.47 meters (about 58 inches), his or her height squared is 2.06. BMI reaches 23 if that child weighs 46 kilograms (90 pounds) or more. For younger school-age children, obesity begins between 18 and 21 BMI, depending on the child's age; for adults, overweight begins at 25 BMI and obesity begins at about 28 BMI.

discussed further in the Research Report (pages 344–345).

Obese children are especially prone to orthopedic and respiratory problems and are at risk for a number of other illnesses. In fact, "overnutrition in children is as important a risk factor as is malnutrition" (Eveleth & Tanner, 1991), with the risks eventually including heart disease, diabetes, and strokes.

Being overweight as a child is often a psychological problem as well. Indeed, compared to overweight adults who were normal-weight children, overweight adults who were obese as children tend to be more distressed and to have more psychophysiological problems (Mills & Adrianopoulos, 1993).

Variations in Health

In general, in developed nations, children age 7 to 11 are the healthiest humans of all—least likely to die or become seriously ill or injured (see Figure 11.1). Even accidents and serious abuse, which are the leading causes of mortality and morbidity during these years, occur more often in the preschool or adolescent years. (These topics were first discussed in the chapters on the play years).

However, for two reasons, differences in physique and health between one child and another become important. First, as we have said, children are more aware of each other's and their own physical imperfections during

Figure 11.1 Death at an Early Age? Never!
Schoolchildren are remarkably hardy, as measured in many ways. These charts show that death rates for 7- to 11-year-olds are lower than those for younger or older children, 15 times as low as their parents' rates, and 1,000 times lower than their grandparents' rates.

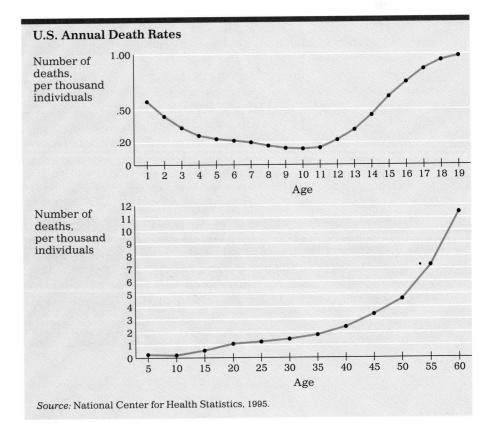

Source: National Center for Health Statistics, 1995.

CHILDHOOD OBESITY: CAUSES AND REMEDIES

How do children become obese? Obesity usually results from the interaction of a number of factors. Here are the most important of them:

- *Heredity.* Body type, including height, bone structure, and the amount and distribution of fat on the body, is inherited. So are individual differences in metabolic rate and activity level. Certain combinations of body type and metabolism result in excessive storage of fat on the body and higher-than-average BMI. Indeed, research on adopted children shows that heredity is at least as strong as family context in predisposing a person toward being overweight (Bray, 1989). However, changes in population genetics occur slowly, over generations, so the recent increase in obesity is not genetic.

- *Exercise.* Inactive people burn fewer calories and are more likely to be overweight than active people, especially in infancy and childhood, when many children seem to be on the move all day. A child's activity level is influenced not only by heredity but also by a willingness to engage in strenuous play, the availability of safe play areas, the parents' example, and weight itself, which slows down precisely those children who need more exercise.

- *Television.* While watching television, children eat more and burn fewer calories than they would if they were actively playing. In fact, they burn fewer calories when watching television than they would if they were doing *nothing.* One study found that when children are "glued to the tube," they fall into a deeply relaxed state, akin to semiconsciousness, that lowers their metabolism below its normal at-rest rate—on average, 12 percent lower in children of normal weight and 16 percent lower in obese children (Klesges, 1993). Further, 60 percent of the commercials shown during Saturday morning cartoons on U.S. television are for food products—almost all of them with high fat and sugar content. The foods are usually shown being consumed by slim children who seem to be having a wonderful time because of what they are eating (Ogletree et al., 1990).

- *Cultural attitudes toward food.* In some cultures, overeating is a sign of wealth and happiness, so parents urge their offspring to have a second helping. The implied message seems to be that a father's love is measured by how much food he can provide; a mother's love,

For Once, the Leader Tug-of-war is one of the few competitive events in which this fifth-grader is likely to be the first one chosen for the team.

by how well she can cook; and a child's love, by how much he or she can eat. This attitude is especially evident in families whose parents or grandparents grew up in places where starvation was a real possibility; the cultural values that once protected against disease have now become a cause of disease.

- *Precipitating event.* For many children, the onset of obesity is associated with a critical event or traumatic experience—a hospitalization, a move to a new neighborhood, a parental divorce or death. Generally, such an event or experience creates a sense of loss or diminished self-image, along with a corresponding need for an alternative source of gratification. When the new source of gratification is food, obesity can result (Neumann, 1983).

Dealing with Childhood Obesity

What is a parent to do? It is a mistake to use ultimatums ("You can't play until you eat your broccoli") or bribes ("Eat all your spinach and you can have dessert") or critiques ("You're getting fat"). Those strategies usually backfire, reinforcing the child's dislike of healthy foods, enhancing the attractiveness of sweets, or making the child crave the solace of food.

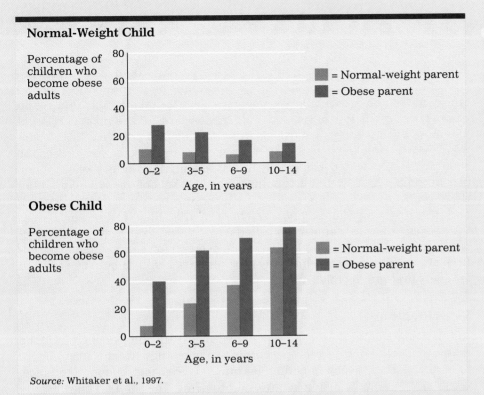

Normal-Weight Child

Percentage of children who become obese adults

80
60
40
20
0

■ = Normal-weight parent
■ = Obese parent

0–2   3–5   6–9   10–14
Age, in years

Obese Child

Percentage of children who become obese adults

80
60
40
20
0

■ = Normal-weight parent
■ = Obese parent

0–2   3–5   6–9   10–14
Age, in years

Source: Whitaker et al., 1997.

A Reason to Slim Down As you can see, a child's chance of becoming an obese adult is increased by having an obese parent. By middle childhood, however, the child's own obesity is a better predictor. Only 15 percent of normal-weight 10-year-olds with an obese parent become obese adults, but 64 percent of obese 10-year-olds without an obese parent do so.

It is also a mistake to put children on a crash diet, because they become irritable and, ironically, fatter. Why? Centuries ago, humans developed an automatic, physiological defense against starvation. Specifically, in periods of "famine," metabolism slows down to enable the body to maintain its weight with fewer calories. Thus, after rapid initial weight loss, additional pounds become more difficult to lose (Wing, 1992), and a few days of overeating quickly produces fat. This is one reason crash diets are inadvisable; they don't work. The other is that, in childhood, severe reduction of basic nourishment can hinder important brain and bone growth.

The best way to get obese children to slim down is to increase their physical activity (Dietz, 1995). However, since overweight children tend to move more slowly and with less coordination than other children (Hills, 1992), obese children are not often selected for teams, invited to join backyard games, or inclined to exercise on their own. Adults can encourage children to do exercises in which size is no disadvantage: walking to school, bicycling, swimming. Parents can also exercise with their children to provide a good model, bolster the children's self-confidence, and make physical exercise more enjoyable. In fact, one of the strongest influences on childhood weight is the parents' own exercise habits, whether or not a parent exercises with the child (Ross et al., 1987).

Proper health habits can counter even the genetic tendency toward obesity. As the accompanying figure indicates, among normal-weight children under age 3, the risk of becoming an obese adult is about 30 percent for those with an obese parent but only about 10 percent for those with normal-weight parents—strong evidence of heredity. However, by age 10, the child's own weight is much more critical than his or her genes (Whitaker et al., 1997). This seems to indicate that a child's biological inclination may be to overeat, but if the family can rechannel that urge until at least age 10, the child has a good chance of being a normal-weight adult. Given the culture, this is difficult to achieve. But given the burden on the overweight child, it is worth the work.

⚠ **Response for Parents (from page 342):**
Unless they slim down, chubby, happy 6-year-olds tend to become unhappy 10-year-olds and unhealthy adults, so you should not simply let nature take its course. However, imposing a diet is probably not the best solution. Better would be to change the entire family's eating habits and begin regular exercise for both you and your 6-year-old.

these years, so minor health problems can take on major importance. Second, the requirements of regular school attendance and steady performance, enabling every child to master the same basic curriculum, mean that any impediment can become a notable educational handicap.

Vision

Vision is the best example of a minor problem that can make a major difference. Between ages 7 and 11 humans see more clearly than at any other period of life. Focusing on small print for hour after hour—impossible for the typical farsighted preschooler—usually poses no visual difficulty. Almost no one begins serious loss of vision during these years; for the most part, legal blindness begins either at birth or in middle or late adulthood. However, minor vision problems, such as with near vision, muscle weaknesses, or steady scanning, which are usually inconsequential in the preschool years, can become seriously handicapping when the school years begin. Often these problems are not noticed until after a year or two of academic work and then are compounded because children are reluctant to wear glasses ("four-eyes," they are sometimes called) or do visual exercises. A careful vision exam (not just the standard, 2-minute screen for nearsightedness), followed by sensitive counseling if any problems are found, should be required for every first-grade child.

Figure 11.2 Bed-Wetting. Although most children are dry at night by age 3, about 15 percent of 5-year-olds still sometimes wet their beds at night. Maturation processes make their sleep less sound and their bladders bigger, so by age 9 only 5 percent are still wetting the bed. By adolescence almost every child has been dry for several years, but some experience emotional problems that make them become bed-wetters again.

Sleep Problems

Another common problem is sleep disturbances, affecting 18 percent of the lowest-achieving first-graders, according to one study (Gozal, 1998). These interrupt sleep, thereby impeding learning, decreasing school attendance, and causing behavioral problems. The solution may include medical intervention to improve breathing.

In contrast to children with sleep disturbances, some children sleep *too* soundly. Instead of waking up when their bladders are full, they wet their beds. As Figure 11.2 shows, *primary enuresis* (bed-wetting that has continued, at least once a month, since infancy) decreases with maturation. Other data show that by age 13, it has virtually disappeared. *Secondary enuresis* (bed-wetting that has ceased for at least a year and then begins again) is about equally likely to appear at any age from 7 to 13, affecting about 1 child in 25 each year.

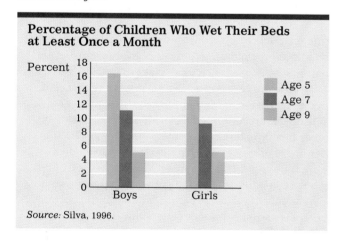

Percentage of Children Who Wet Their Beds at Least Once a Month

Age 5
Age 7
Age 9

Source: Silva, 1996.

Primary enuresis is probably more closely related to sleep patterns than to any emotional or neurological problems, but it affects children by making them reluctant to sleep over at a friend's or relative's house or to go to sleepaway camp. Secondary enuresis may be a sign of emotional troubles at school or at home that are affecting the child, and thus it should alert caregivers that a child may need help with the stresses of life (Silva, 1996).

Asthma

asthma A disorder characterized by chronic inflammation of the airways.

Finally, let us look closely at a more serious health problem that is becoming increasingly prevalent in developing nations. **Asthma,** defined as a "chronic inflammatory disorder of the airways," affects between 10 and 20 percent of school-age children. For almost half the children, it disappears by late adolescence (Clark & Rees, 1996).

The origin of this repeated narrowing of the path of air through the lungs is genetic—but, like every other characteristic, not solely genetic. In fact, the

❷ Especially for Health Professionals: Since a predispositon for asthma is genetic, should medical advice be limited to controlling the severity of asthma rather than preventing it?

epidemiology of asthma suggests that environmental factors are crucial. First, the rate of asthma has at least doubled since 1980 in virtually every developed nation in the world, a far greater increase than can be accounted for by any change in the gene pool. Second, asthma patients tend to be those least susceptible to other childhood diseases. Children who are onlies or the oldest in their families, who have not had many serious childhood infections, and who live relatively easy lives are also the children most likely to visit the hospital time after time with asthma attacks (Cookson & Moffatt, 1997). Indeed, asthma is at least 10 times more common in the urban areas of developed nations than in the rural areas of developing nations. It was rare in any nation 100 years ago. Obviously, something contextual, not genetic, is the reason.

Causes and Triggers.   Because asthma interferes with school attendance for so many children, and because an untreated asthma attack may lead to death, many researchers are studying its causes. Genes on chromosomes 2, 11, 12, 13, and 21; infections that once protected against asthma but now rarely occur; exposure to allergens early in life that predispose toward asthma; current exposure to allergens that trigger attacks (including pet hair, dust mites, cockroaches, and air pollution); exercise; and emotional outbursts are among the causes. Current exposure to allergens, exercise, and emotional outbursts require further explanation, because they are really triggers, not causes. We know this because the heavily polluted areas of eastern Europe have fewer cases of asthma than the comparable areas of western Europe, because some forms of exercise (such as swimming) are actually good for asthmatics, and because some children with extreme emotional stress never develop asthma (Cookson & Moffat, 1997; Vogel, 1997).

Several aspects of modern life—carpeted floors, more bedding, dogs and cats living inside the house, airtight windows, less outdoor play for children, and urbanization, which crowds people together in buildings where cockroaches multiply—all increase the risk. The last of these may be the worst. Not all asthmatic children are sensitive to cockroach particles in dust, of course, but those who are, and who are exposed to them, are more likely to wake up in the middle of the night, go to the hospital, and miss school than are asthmatic children who are allergic, and exposed, to pet hair or dust mites.

Medical and Ecological Treatments.   Medical measures now treat acute asthma fairly effectively, either controlling asthma before it gets past the nighttime coughing and occasional wheezing stage or relieving serious attacks when they occur (Vogel, 1997).

However, from a developmental point of view, the medical focus is too narrow and too late, because it ignores the overall ecological setting and the earliest symptoms. Asthma begins when a certain level of sensitivity is reached, so a parent who notices a young child coughing at night could first determine if this is an early warning and could then rid the house of animals, rugs, down comforters, and dust, as well as get the children to play outside. That might forestall or delay the increase in the level of sensitivity that makes a child vulnerable to a full-scale attack. Prevention could begin even sooner than that, undertaken by the entire community before the first symptoms appear. Fresh air could circulate in schools and homes, pollution could be decreased, cockroaches could be eradicated, and safe outdoor play spaces could be maintained. These measures would make life and health better for every school-age child and would particularly protect vulnerable children.

MOTOR SKILLS

At least partly because children grow slowly during middle childhood, many become quite skilled at controlling their own bodies. This is in contrast to the sudden changes in body shape and size that occur during toddlerhood and puberty, which are typically accompanied by an obvious clumsiness. School-age children can master almost any motor skill, as long as it doesn't require too much strength or split-second judgment of speed and distance. With practice, their mastery of both gross and fine motor skills can be impressive.

However, the maxim "Practice makes perfect" does not always hold true. Every motor skill involves several abilities, some requiring practice alone (for those, practice *does* lead to mastery), others requiring a certain body size, brain maturation, or inherited talent—as well as practice—to be perfected. For instance, **reaction time,** the length of time it takes a person to respond to a particular stimulus, is a component of several athletic skills, but quick reactions require brain maturation that is attained only with adolescence. Hand-eye coordination, balance, and judgment of movement (in-

reaction time The time it takes to respond to a particular stimulus.

Mastery of Motor Skills The impressive gross motor skills of school-age children are well illustrated in these two photos: many adults could neither climb a rope nor jump one with the skill shown here. What is not clear from these photos is that whatever notable gender gaps there may be in motor ability usually arise from influences in the social context.

Boys are admired for taking risks, so they practice climbing, not just up ropes high above the gym floor but up trees, cliffs, and almost anything else that offers a challenge and a bit of danger. Girls are encouraged to be verbal and cooperative, so they develop variations of rope jumping, hand clapping, and rhythmic stepping, while singing "Tell me the name of your sweetheart," "Miss Mary had a baby," and so on.
❓ *Observational Quiz (see answer page 350):*
What sex differences and similarities do you see, and how do you explain them?

cluding time, distance, and trajectory) are other key abilities that are still developing during the school years, and thus 12-year-olds are better than 9-year-olds who are better than 6-year-olds in all of these.

Gender, Culture, and Genetics

Boys and girls are just about equal in their physical abilities during the school years, although boys tend to have greater upper-arm strength and girls to have greater overall flexibility. Consequently, boys have the advantage in sports such as baseball, whereas girls have the edge in sports such as gymnastics. However, for most physical activities during middle childhood, biological sex differences are minimal: boys can do cartwheels, and girls can hit home runs. Usually they don't, of course, not because they are unable to but because the social setting discourages them from doing so. Expertise in many areas, athletic prowess among them, depends primarily on three elements: motivation, guidance, and many hours of practice. These three are rarely equal for both sexes in any particular area.

Thus every skill depends not only on personal choice but also on gender, culture, and national policy. Many North American 8- and 9-year-olds can

Soccer for 8-Year-Olds Many children around the world play soccer, with some nations much more involved than others.

❓ *Observational Quiz (see answer page 351): What nation is this?*

❗ **Response for Health Professionals (from page 347):** Since the rate of asthma is so much higher in modern cities than it was anywhere a few decades ago, genetics is not the only cause. Every parent of a young child should be counseled on the benefits of fresh air, lung-strengthening exercise, and dust and cockroach-free homes. If a child comes from an allergic or asthmatic family, or has early episodes of night coughing or wheezing, the preventive measures can escalate to excluding down pillows, carpets, curtains, and cats.

pound a nail, saw wood, use garden tools, sew, knit, draw in good proportion, write or print neatly, polish their fingernails, cut their toenails, ride bicycles, scale fences, swim, dive, roller-skate, ice-skate, jump rope, and play baseball, football, jacks, and dozens of other games that require specialized body movements. Halfway around the world, Indonesian school-age children master many of the same skills—though for environmental reasons, they do not learn to ice-skate; for cultural reasons, they do not learn to play baseball or football; and on Bali (one of the islands that make up Indonesia) they do not learn to swim (water is considered to harbor evil) (Lansing, 1983). Also from ages 7 to 11, Indonesian children learn skills not common among North American children, such as whittling wood with sharp knives and weaving intricate baskets.

National policy affects motor-skill development. For example, the average schoolchild in France or Switzerland gets 3 hours a week of physical education, compared to 1½ hours for a child in the United States and only 1 hour for a child in England or Ireland. During such classes, or during recess, boys tend to be much more active than girls (Armstrong & Welsman, 1997).

Unfortunately, many sports that American adults value (and often push their children into) demand precisely those skills that are hardest for children. Softball and baseball, for example, are difficult, because throwing, catching, and batting all involve more distance judgment, better eye-hand coordination, and shorter reaction time than many elementary school children possess. Younger children are therefore apt to drop the ball even if it lands in their mitts, since they are slow to enclose the ball once it lands. They are similarly likely to strike out, because they swing too late to hit a pitched ball.

Hereditary differences also can be pivotal. Some children, no matter how hard they try, never can throw or kick a ball with as much strength and accuracy as others—a fact that parents, teachers, coaches, and teammates sometimes forget, not only in encouraging a particular child but in designing sports or exercise programs to include everyone, talented or not. Whether the "program" is part of a school curriculum, or a children's sports league, or simply a group of neighborhood children playing together, it should provide fun and activity for all, boys and girls, fat and thin, gifted or clumsy (Armstrong & Welsman, 1997). Programs are counterproductive when they:

- Are too competitive (especially if certain less skilled children continually sit on the sidelines)
- Foster disparaging comparisons (as when skillful children laugh at another's clumsiness and weakness)
- Lack excitement (such as substantial time spent waiting for a turn, resting, or repeating the same routine)

The same is true for fine motor skills. Some children naturally write more neatly than others, and these are the children who are more likely to practice their penmanship, refining the curve of the "s" or the slant of the "t," for instance. Adults need to provide extra motivation and time for the children with less natural skill. This may be particularly true for left-handed children, for whom writing a right-handed language such as English runs against the natural direction

Figure 11.3 Write It Right.

Left-handed children naturally draw from right to left and clockwise, a preference apparent in their early scribbles with crayons as well as their first attempts to write words. This natural inclination requires some readjustment not only when they need to read from left to right but even when they learn to form their letters, since most languages are biased against them (Hebrew is the only major language that is written from right to left, with books starting at the "back" and pages turned toward the "front"). Look at the alphabet in capital letters, as a left-handed and right-handed child would be inclined to draw them:

Right: A B C D E F G H I L K L M N O P Q R S T U V W X Y Z

Left: Z Y X W V U T S R Q P O N M L K J I H G F E D C B A

All children naturally draw the dominant line from top to bottom, but then right-handed children put the "add-ons" to the right and begin their curves counter-clockwise—which gets them into trouble only once, with the rarely used "J." Left-handed children's directional sense makes them write 12 letters wrong, until they work against nature to do it "right." Incidentally, why is right called *right*? Are some children *left* back or *left* out or *left* over?

of their hands and brains. (See Figure 11.3.) Patience at teaching, rather than forced hand-switching or competitive ranking, seems to be the best strategy.

Most children age 7 to 11 develop well, physically, unless their families and cultures fail them. Before leaving this chapter, however, we need to consider school-age children with special needs. Some developmentalists think that almost every child has special needs of one sort or another. Others disagree. All, however, believe that understanding "special" children helps us to understand childhood.

❶ *Answer to Observational Quiz (from page 348):* Differences are that boys are slightly advantaged in upper-arm strength, and girls in quick rhythmic reactions—assets that these two children have developed into skills. Similarities are that both children are similarly dressed, similarly active, and similarly pleased with their accomplishments. Score one for equal opportunity and one for sex differences.

CHILDREN WITH SPECIAL NEEDS

All parents watch with pride and satisfaction as their offspring become taller and more skilled. For many parents, however, these feelings mingle with worry and uncertainty when their children manifest unexpected difficulties in one area of development or another. Although the origin of many problems is biological, the observable symptoms are often more psychological and cognitive than physical, and thus more apparent in the classroom or playground (when a child is compared to others the same age) than at home or in the pediatrician's office. Consider the experience of this mother:

Except for the fact that my daughter has always been a physically active and strong-willed child, it was not until she entered the first grade that the problems seemed to start. She became very reluctant to attend school, which was very different from her excitement over kindergarten. The stomach aches that she had complained of since age 2 became more frequent and necessitated her going to the nurse's office at school at least once per day if not more often. She could not seem to complete her assignments—sometimes taking an hour to complete just one sentence. She did not seem to willfully refuse to do assignments but seemed preoccupied with daydreams and other, more interesting activities. She was not disruptive in class but did seem to go through a bout of pushing in line, and there were some reports of aggressiveness. At home, I could not seem to get her moving in the morning—even to the point where I took her to the babysitter's home in her pajamas because she would not get up and get dressed. Kimberly also began to appear angry and frustrated, having more problems getting along with parents and peers. She had always had best friends, been very sociable, and friendly. She then started to verbalize that people didn't like her and no one wanted to play with her. She would often get very angry at the neighborhood children she played with. As a parent, I found myself constantly yelling and totally frustrated with how to handle my child. [quoted in Thompson, 1995]

What is a parent to do in such a situation? In this case, Kimberly's mother sought the advice of her daughter's teachers and school counselors, who also had been perplexed when Kimberly, an intelligent child, had such difficulty paying attention and socializing. They contacted developmental experts at a local child-guidance clinic, who interviewed the mother and tested and observed Kimberly at school. They diagnosed Kimberly's problem as attention-deficit hyperactivity disorder (ADHD), which you will read about later in this chapter. Treatment included medication, parent-child therapy sessions, and structured school activities. With treatment, Kimberly became a much happier and more capable child—although some emotional difficulties and attention-focusing problems remained.

Kimberly is one of a great many **children with special needs,** defined as children who require particular accommodations (physical, intellectual, or social) in order to learn. For these children, the development of new skills, closer friendships, and more mature ways of thinking is impaired by psychological disorders and symptoms—including aggression, anxiety, autism, conduct disorder, depression, developmental delay, hyperactivity, learning disabilities, mutism, and mental slowness—or as a direct consequence of physical disabilities such as blindness, deafness, or paralysis.

children with special needs Children for whom learning new skills and developing friendships are hampered by a psychological or physical disorder.

The Developmental Psychopathology Perspective

In recent years, psychologists who study childhood disorders have joined with psychologists who study normal development to create the new field of **developmental psychopathology.** In developmental psychopathology, knowledge about normal development is applied to the study and treatment of childhood disorders, and vice versa, because "we can learn more about an organism's normal functioning by studying its pathology and, likewise, more about its pathology by studying its normal condition" (Cicchetti, 1990).

developmental psychopathology A field of psychology that applies the insights from studies of normal development to the study and treatment of childhood disorders, and vice versa.

Research from this perspective has already provided four developmental lessons:

1. *Abnormality is normal.* The distinction between normal and abnormal children can become quite blurry and even disappear. Most normal children sometimes act in ways that are decidedly unusual, and most children with psychological disorders are, in many respects, quite normal. If we ignore this complexity, we may "seriously distort the variability of development" for all children (Fischer et al., 1997). Children with psychological disorders should be viewed as children first—with the many developmental needs that all children share—and only secondarily as children with special challenges.

2. *Disability changes over time.* The behaviors associated with almost any special problem change as the child grows older. A child who seems severely handicapped by a disability at one stage of development may seem much less handicapped at the next stage, or vice versa. Such changes are not simply due to the passage of time; they result from the interplay of developmental changes within the individual, treatment regimens, and forces in the ecological setting (Berkson, 1993; Eyberg et al., 1998).

3. *Adulthood can be better or worse.* Many children with seemingly serious disabilities, from blindness to mental retardation, become happy and productive adults once they find a vocational setting in which they can perform well. On the other hand, any disability that makes a child unusually aggressive and socially inept becomes more serious during adolescence and adulthood, when physical maturity and social demands make self-control and social interaction particularly important (Davidson et al., 1994; Lahey & Loeber, 1994).

❶ Answer to Observational Quiz (from page 349): *Surprise – it's the United States. Soccer evokes life-and-death national passions in many nations, but not in the United States, so if you guessed Argentina or France, for instance, you had good reason. However, there are two clues here that would have led to the right answer. The first is the girls' involvement. For sports that are highly competitive in a given nation, teams of young children are usually segregated by sex. The second clue—hard to spot but a giveaway if you noticed—is the map of Texas on the children's jerseys.*

DSM-IV   The fourth edition of the *Diagnostic and Statistical Manual of Mental Disorders,* developed by the American Psychiatric Association, which describes and distinguishes the symptoms of various emotional and behavioral disorders.

4. *Diagnosis depends on the social context.* The social context must be considered as part of the diagnosis. As a direct outgrowth of the developmental psychopathology perspective, the official fourth edition of the diagnostic guide of the American Psychiatric Association, the ***Diagnostic and Statistical Manual of Mental Disorders,*** or ***DSM-IV,*** now explicitly recognizes that the "nuances of an individual's cultural frame of reference" need to be understood before any disorder can be diagnosed (American Psychiatric Association, 1994). Nonetheless, according to many researchers, DSM-IV does not go far enough in this direction, because disorders may not reside "inside the skin of an individual" but "between the individual and the environment" (Jensen & Hoagwood, 1997).

Because the disorders that developmental psychopathologists study are too great in number to discuss here, we will focus on only three: autism, learning disabilities, and attention-deficit hyperactivity disorder. Each originates in the biosocial domain, and each is a typical example of many disorders. By applying our knowledge of these three, we can begin to understand the development of all children, no matter what special needs they might have.

Autism

autism   A disorder characterized by an inability or unwillingness to communicate with others, poor social skills, and diminished imagination.

One of the most severe disturbances of childhood is called **autism.** The label "autism" was chosen in 1943 by an American physician, Leo Kanner, to describe children who seemed to be totally self-absorbed. According to Kanner (1943), an autistic child has an "inability to relate in an ordinary way to people . . . an extreme aloneness that, whenever possible, disregards, ignores, shuts out anything that comes to the child from the outside." Kanner's choice of terminology was apt. "Auto-" means "self," and autistic individuals seem unusually restricted by their own perspective and by their need for predictable routines. They seem unable or unwilling to be interested in anyone else. Autism was described by Kanner as extreme asocial and uncommunicative behavior, to the extent that the autistic person never learns normal speech or forms normal human relationships. This severe form of the disorder is quite rare; it occurs in about 1 of every 2,000 children, according to DSM-IV (American Psychiatric Association, 1994).

However, the first lesson from the developmental psychopathological perspective is to look for the similarities between people diagnosed as "abnormal" (in this case, as autistic) and people considered "normal." Many children have autistic symptoms that are less severe than Kanner's classic syndrome. They are sometimes diagnosed as *high-functioning autistic,* or as having **Asperger syndrome,** named after a German psychiatrist who described a disorder in 1944 that he also called autism. (World War II prevented Kanner and Asperger from realizing that they were reaching similar conclusions and using similar terminology.) Asperger's definition of autism, like Kanner's, emphasized self-absorption, but Asperger included some individuals who were quite intelligent and verbal. His portrayal of autism was less extreme than the classic type described by Kanner.

Asperger syndrome   A disorder in which a person masters verbal communication (sometimes very well) but has unusual difficulty with social perceptions and skills. (Also called *high-functioning autism.*)

Exactly how impaired must a child be before being diagnosed as autistic? Even today, there is no firm consensus. Experts do agree, though, that Kanner's original definition is too narrow and that, when the entire spectrum of autistic disorders is taken into account, as many as 1 child in 100 shows autistic traits (Szatmari, 1992). Both the severe and the less severe instances of the disorder are much more common in boys than in girls, at least by two to one. Indeed, one careful study done in Sweden found the ratio was six to one, suggesting that whatever genetic, prenatal, or infancy precursors to autism there might be, boys suffer them more severely (Steffenburg, 1991).

The Early Developmental Path of Autism

Autism is truly a *developmental* disorder (as the second "lesson" emphasizes), because its manifestations change markedly with age. As babies, many autistic children seem quite normal and sometimes unusually "good" (that is, undemanding), although they are often hypersensitive to stimulation, and the way they roll over, sit up, crawl, and walk may be less coordinated than the norm (Teitelbaum et al., 1998). Soon, however, severe deficiencies appear in three areas:

- Communication ability
- Social skills
- Imaginative play

Deficiencies in the first two areas become apparent at age 1 or 2, as autistic children lack spoken language or normal response to others. During the preschool years, many autistic children continue to be mute, not talking at all, while others engage exclusively in a type of speech called *echolalia,* in which they repeat, word for word, such things as advertising jingles or questions that are put to them. "Good morning, John" is echoed with "Good morning, John." Autistic preschoolers also avoid eye contact with others and prefer to be by themselves.

Also during the preschool years, the third deficit, in play, suddenly becomes obvious, because most normal children at this age are quite playful. Autistic preschoolers avoid spontaneous imaginative interaction with peers, such as the rough-and-tumble play and sociodramatic play described in Chapter 10. Instead, they engage in repetitive movements (such as spinning a top over and over) or compulsive play (assembling a puzzle in a particular order time after time). One autistic adult, who has unusual verbal ability, remembers her childhood in the following manner:

> When left alone, I would often space out and become hypnotized. I could sit for hours on the beach watching sand dribbling through my fingers. I'd study each individual grain of sand as it flowed between my fingers. Each grain was different, and I was like a scientist studying the grains under a microscope. As I scrutinized their shapes and contours, I went into a trance which cut me off from the sights and sounds around me.
>
> Rocking and spinning were other ways to shut out the world when I became overloaded with too much noise. Rocking made me feel calm. It was like taking an addictive drug. The more I did it, the more I wanted to do it. My mother and my teachers would stop me so I would get back in touch with the rest of the world. I also loved to spin, and I seldom got dizzy. When I stopped spinning, I enjoyed the sensation of watching the room spin. [Grandin, 1996]

Later Childhood and Beyond

Deficiencies in communication, social skills, and play remain pronounced from the preschool years on, but in childhood and adolescence the lack of social understanding often proves to be the most devastating because human relationships are the usual path toward learning and self-concept. Autistic children appear to lack a theory of mind—an awareness of the thoughts, feelings, and intentions of other people (Holroyd & Baron-Cohen, 1993; Leslie & Frith, 1988). People seem of no greater interest than objects, because these children develop no theories about the internal processes that make people unique and provocative.

Unaffected by the opinions of others, autistic children also lack emotional regulation. Many seem cold, aloof, and uninvolved until something triggers an outburst of laughter or, worse, fury. Then other people are frustrated and bewildered, surprised by the unexpected explosion and unable to respond in a way that satisfies the child, because they do not know what triggered the behavior in the first place.

As children with autism grow older, their symptoms vary widely. Most score in the mentally retarded range on intelligence tests, but a closer look at their intellectual performance shows isolated areas of remarkable skill (such as memory for numbers or for putting together puzzles). In general their strongest cognitive skills are in abstract reasoning; their weakest, in social cognition (Scott & Baron-Cohen, 1996). For example, on a trip to the grocery store, a child might be able to calculate that each apple in a bag of a dozen costs exactly 10½ cents but might not understand why certain shoppers refuse to buy such a bargain.

Some autistic children never speak or have only minimal verbal ability, but many who were diagnosed as autistic at age 2 or 3 learn to express themselves in language by age 6. They may demonstrate exceptional academic skills during the school years, eventually becoming self-supporting adults, although less imaginative and communicative and more ritualistic and socially isolated than most people. Occasionally, Asperger individuals may be quite successful (as the third lesson, that remarkable success or failure can occur in adulthood, suggests), especially in professions in which their attention to routine, concentration on detail, and relative indifference to sentiment are an asset. One study of individuals with Asperger traits found a dentist, a financial lawyer, a military historian, and a university professor among them (Gillberg, 1991). Temple Grandin, quoted above remembering the flow of sand, is an international expert in the design of slaughtering facilities for animals. Her ability to envision things from the animal's perspective makes her able to reduce pain and panic for cows, sheep, pigs, and so on (Grandin, 1995).

Remember, finally, the fourth lesson, that diagnosis depends on social context. Probably there are many adults with autistic tendencies who were never diagnosed because they functioned adequately within their ecological niche.

Hope for Autism The prime prerequisite in breaking through the language barrier in a nonverbal autistic child, such as this 4-year-old, is to get the child to pay attention to another person's speech. Note that this teacher is sitting in a low chair to facilitate eye contact and is getting the child to focus on her mouth movements—a matter of little interest to most children but intriguing to many autistic ones. Sadly, even such efforts were not enough: at age 13 this child was still mute.

Causes and Treatment of Autism

Twin studies make it clear that genetic factors play a role in autism (Rutter et al., 1997). The same studies also make it clear that genes are not the whole story. Autism probably results from a genetic vulnerability in combination with some sort of damage—occurring either prenatally or soon after birth. Whatever the causes, quite specific brain abnormalities seem to underlie autistic symptoms (Waterhouse et al., 1996).

Because of the nature of autism and the way it progresses, a developmental view is essential to treatment of the severe forms of the disorder. Since language skills normally develop most rapidly between ages 1 and 4, these are crucial years, with successful treatment usually including individualized behavioral therapy to shape particular skills. For example, the child may be asked (in any of various ways) to make eye contact, name a particular part of the face, or use a pronoun appropriately and then will be rewarded immediately for doing so.

With intensive therapy—usually over several years—many autistic children can learn to talk, show appropriate social behaviors, and improve in other ways; some make sufficient progress to enter normal schools. In fact, the Early Intervention Project (developed by a noted behaviorist named Ivar Lovaas) is said to be so effective with young autistic children that half of them live normal lives by the time they are school-age and most of the rest make substantial progress (McEachin et al., 1993). Whether these recovery rates are realistic is disputed, but all agree that the key seems to be early and very intensive treatment, with the goal of breaking through the autistic communication barrier by age 6 (Bristol et al., 1996; Gresham & MacMillan, 1998).

Learning Disabilities

Children vary a great deal in how quickly and how well they learn to read, to write, and to do arithmetic. Among those who have obvious difficulty, some seem slow in almost every aspect of intellectual development. Their thinking is like that of a much younger child—sometimes several years younger than their actual age. These children are considered to suffer **mental retardation**, that is, a notable delay in their overall cognitive development. Some of these children eventually catch up to normal levels, in which case they are said to have experienced a *pervasive developmental delay*.

Other children are slow learners only in certain areas. They show remarkable "scatter" in their abilities, and they are generally quite competent except in particular skills. Such a child is said to have a **learning disability**, that is, a failing in a specific cognitive skill that is not due to overall intellectual slowness, to a physical handicap such as hearing loss, to severely stressful living conditions, or to a lack of basic education (Silver, 1991). As you can see, the diagnosis of learning disability is based on *disparity* and *exclusion*. First, there must be a disparity, or surprising difference, between expected performance on a given skill (based on age and intelligence) and actual performance; second, all the obvious reasons (such as abuse, inadequate teachers, or biological disability) must be ruled out. This again illustrates the fourth lesson, that the social context must be considered before the diagnosis is made.

mental retardation   Slow learning in all, or almost all, intellectual abilities. The degree of retardation is usually measured by an intelligence test. In young children, mental retardation is often called pervasive developmental delay, allowing the possibility that the child will catch up to normal, age-appropriate development.

learning disability   Difficulty in mastering a specific cognitive skill that is *not* attributable to intellectual slowness, obvious impairment of the senses, lack of education, or family dysfunction.

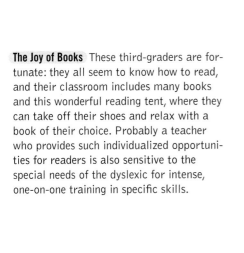

The Joy of Books These third-graders are fortunate: they all seem to know how to read, and their classroom includes many books and this wonderful reading tent, where they can take off their shoes and relax with a book of their choice. Probably a teacher who provides such individualized opportunities for readers is also sensitive to the special needs of the dyslexic for intense, one-on-one training in specific skills.

dyslexia A specific learning disability involving unusual difficulty with reading.

dyscalcula A specific learning disability involving unusual difficulty with math.

Types of Learning Disabilities

The most commonly diagnosed learning disability is **dyslexia,** unusual difficulty with reading. Dyslexic children seem bright and happy in the early years of school, volunteering answers to sometimes difficult questions, diligently completing their worksheets, sitting quietly and looking at their books in class. However, as time goes on, it becomes clear that they are reading only with great difficulty or not at all. They guess at even simple words (occasionally making surprising mistakes) and explain what they have just "read" by talking about the pictures. In fact, one of the signs of dyslexia is a child who is advanced in comprehension, using contextual clues, and behind in ability to match letters to sounds (Nation & Snowling, 1998) (See Figure 11.4).

Another fairly common learning disability is **dyscalcula,** difficulty with math. Dyscalcula usually becomes apparent somewhat later in childhood, at about age 8, when even simple number facts, such as 3 + 3 = 6, are memorized one day and forgotten the next. It soon becomes clear—especially with word problems—that the child is guessing at whether numbers should be added, subtracted, multiplied, or ignored to solve a problem, and that almost everything the child knows about arithmetic is a matter of rote memory rather than understanding.

Other specific academic subjects that may reveal a learning disability are spelling and handwriting. A child might read at the fifth-grade level but repeatedly make simple spelling mistakes ("kum accros the rode"), or a child might take three times as long as any other child to copy something from the chalkboard, and then produce only a large, illegible scrawl. In addition, although they are not usually said to be learning-disabled or given special help, some children have great difficulty with a mental ability that affects all intellectual areas—such as with spatial relations, sequential processing, memory, or abstract reasoning (Rourke, 1989). Problems in these most basic abilities are especially difficult to spot and treat.

Because of various cutoff levels (how much disparity between actual and expected scores is disabled?) and the fact that many children are not even tested, the percentage of children who are "learning-disabled" varies from place to place. For example, all the 6-year-olds in Bergen, Sweden, were given a battery of tests (Gjessing & Karlsen, 1989). Seven percent were rated dyslexic. This incidence is greater than that found by the usual method, which is counting only children whose learning problems are noticed in school and who are then tested and diagnosed as learning-disabled. Using that method, DSM-IV finds dyslexia at 4 percent and dyscalcula at 1 percent, and it states that the prevalences of other learning disabilities are "difficult to establish" (American Psychiatric Association, 1994).

Incidence rates are confounded not only by schools but by parents. Some parents are reluctant to have their children identified as different, because they fear the child will be stuck in special education forever; other parents want smaller classes and untimed tests for their children, and thus try to qualify them for some special category. Obviously, if the first two lessons from developmental psychopathology are accepted—that every child is both normal and abnormal, and that every disability changes with time—parents will have less to fear from either special or regular education.

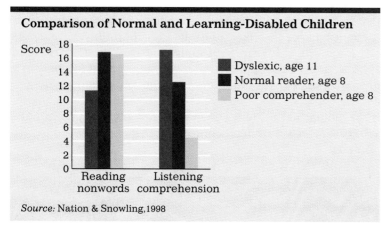

Comparison of Normal and Learning-Disabled Children

Dyslexic, age 11
Normal reader, age 8
Poor comprehender, age 8

Source: Nation & Snowling, 1998

Figure 11.4 Reading and Comprehension. In this study, three groups of children were compared, all reading at the third-grade level. The children in one group were dyslexic, and they were age 11, on average. The children in the other two groups were 8 years old, but half of them were normal readers and the other half had problems with reading comprehension. As you can see, the ability of the groups to pronounce a nonword (letters combined to make a possible word that does not mean anything, such as "wug" or "tedork") or to comprehend a passage read to them differed markedly. Each group would require a different pattern of reading instruction.

Causes of Learning Disabilities

The precise cause of any particular learning disability is hard to pinpoint (Chalfant, 1989; Gerber, 1993). In some cases, there may be no separate, identifiable cause. Instead, the child might happen to be at the low end of the normal range of abilities in, say, reading or math, just as another child might happen to be at the low end of the normal range of some other trait, such as height (Shaywitz et al., 1992). In most cases, however, some particular part of the child's brain does not seem to process a certain type of information.

For instance, if some aspect of visual processing, such as the neurons that enable the eye to scan from left to right or to rapidly perceive small differences in the shapes of letters, is amiss, this may cause reading difficulties (Adams, 1990). It is quite logical that deficiencies in the visual part of the brain are the primary cause of dyslexia, and certainly, as already stressed, every 5-year-old should have a thorough vision exam.

Nonetheless, according to recent theory, dyslexia may originate in certain *auditory* areas of the brain. For example, one area detects differences between sounds spoken very rapidly—such as *p* and *b,* which both take less than one-twentieth of a second to say. These quick sounds are much harder to hear and process than longer sounds—such as *a,* which lasts a full one-tenth of a second. Poor functioning in this area of the brain might affect language comprehension and the development of spoken language. This would not be noticed at first, because helpful cues from the social context and the environment would advise a young child whether to pick up the "pill" or the "bill" and whether someone wants a "bat" or a "pat." But reading requires distinguishing sounds with few contextual clues. Teaching phonics might not solve the problem, because the dyslexic child could not hear the differences between certain sounds. Thus the child would suddenly and unexpectedly fall behind.

This theory has received support (Blachman, 1997; Gerber, 1993). For example, detailed studies show that many dyslexic individuals have different activity in the auditory region of their brains than normal readers do. In addition, they have fewer large neurons in the brain area that controls the timing of auditory signals (Tallal et al., 1993). Such differences could account for their inadequacy in processing sounds. A possible clue to treatment emerges: Teachers and parents can slow down their speech and take care with pronunciation. This might help dyslexic children hear subtle differences in sounds, which they could then translate into comprehension of the written word.

Attention-Deficit Hyperactivity Disorder

attention-deficit hyperactivity disorder (ADHD) A behavior problem characterized by excessive activity, an inability to concentrate, and impulsive, sometimes aggressive, behavior.

One of the most puzzling and exasperating of childhood problems is **attention-deficit hyperactivity disorder (ADHD)**, in which the child has great difficulty concentrating for more than a few moments at a time and, indeed, is almost constantly in motion (Barabasz & Barabasz, 1996; Weiss, 1991). After sitting down to do homework, for instance, an ADHD child might repeatedly look up, ask irrelevant questions, think about playing outside, get up to get a drink of water, sit down, fidget, squirm, tap the table, jiggle his or her legs, and then get up again to get a snack or—if an adult says "no food"—insist that a trip to the bathroom is urgent. Often this need for distraction and diversion is accompanied by excitability and impulsivity.

The crucial factor in attention-deficit disorder seems to be neurological (Aman et al., 1998): a brain deficit that results in great difficulty in "paying

Normal or Not? It's impossible to judge just from this photo. In some children, actions like this may be an isolated instance of showing off or of outrageous mischief. In children with ADHD, they are common-place. When such behavior is accompanied by aggression, the child may be at risk of developing a conduct disorder—possibly becoming the kind of stubborn, disobedient daredevil who is constantly in trouble at home, at school, and in the neighborhood.

attention," the result of genetic vulnerability, prenatal teratogens, or postnatal damage such as lead poisoning. This makes it hard for the child to focus on any one thought or experience long enough to process it (Oosterlaan et al., 1998). In the classroom, the child might not have the concentration to read and remember a passage in a school textbook and might impulsively blurt out the wrong answer to a teacher's question.

Teachers notice such disruptive children, but often a formal diagnosis is never made. In one study, a checklist of DSM-IV symptoms was given to all teachers in every elementary school in one Tennessee county. Although the percentage of ADHD children who had already been diagnosed was less than 5 percent (the usual number), actually 16 percent of the children met the criteria for the disorder (Wolraich et al., 1998). In this study, as well as generally, about four boys are diagnosed with ADHD for every girl (Bhatia et al., 1991; Lahey & Loeber, 1994).

Related Problems

Many children with ADHD are also prone to aggression, suddenly attacking a playmate or an adult, a fact that has led some researchers to propose ADHDA—*attention-deficit hyperactivity disorder with aggression*—as a subtype of this problem. Children who exhibit aggression with ADHD appear to be at increased risk for developing oppositional and conduct disorders, as you will soon see (Dykman & Ackerman, 1993). Attention-deficit disorder can also occur with neither hyperactivity nor aggression. Children with this form of the problem, sometimes called ADD, appear to be prone to anxiety and depression.

DSM-IV describes several forms of ADHD, as well as oppositional disorder and conduct disorder, as distinct disabilities (see details in Appendix A). One critical factor in all these disorders is the context (the fourth lesson from developmental psychopathology). For instance, DSM-IV states that in threatening, impoverished, high-crime, or war-ravaged situations, *conduct disorder behaviors* (aggression, destructiveness, and stealing) may be protective and that the clinician should "consider the social and economic context" before diagnosing such actions as pathological (American Psychiatric Association, 1994). More detail from DSM-IV is in Appendix A.

There may be a developmental sequence in problems with attention, activity, opposition, and aggression (Stormshak et al., 1998). The toddler who cannot pay attention may be especially unresponsive when parents demand that the child be quiet and stay put (something every parent of a 2-year-old has tried, with limited success). Further, an attention-deficit child soon learns that one way to increase mental concentration is to move around (just as some adults think better when walking than when standing still). Thus the child may begin as ADD but become ADHD by age 4 or 5.

Then, if others try to force quiet or to demand concentration from a child unable to comply, the child may become oppositional, that is, may refuse to comply with authority. If that opposition ("I won't do it") is met with aggression ("Do it or I'll spank you"), the child might become aggressive and be likely to create disruptions in the classroom once formal schooling begins. Aggression is especially likely to develop if the teacher demands that every child concentrate quietly at his or her desk (an impossible goal for an ADHD child).

Such a developmental sequence, as well as contextual considerations, would explain why these conceptually distinct disorders often occur in the same child (Stormshak et al., 1998). They also help explain cultural differences in the frequency of these disorders. Children in Britain, for instance, are less likely to be diagnosed as having ADHD than are children in the United States, but they are more likely to be diagnosed with conduct disorder (Epstein et al., 1991; MacArdle et al., 1995). In any case, parents and teachers need to do whatever they can to keep the disorder at the simplest level, ADD or ADHD, because once the child becomes oppositional and aggressive, it is much harder to prevent serious antisocial activities later on. A disproportionate number of ADHD children are eventually arrested for major felonies, a sad example of the third lesson, that adulthood can be better or, in this case, worse (Patterson et al., 1989).

Help for Children with ADHD

Not surprisingly, children with ADHD are usually annoying to adults and rejected by their peers. Medication, psychological therapy, and changes in the family and school environments can all help some children. Ideally, all three forms of treatment are at least considered (Hinshaw, 1994).

For reasons not yet determined, certain drugs that stimulate adults have the *reverse* effect on many—but not all—children with attention-deficit problems, whether or not they are hyperactive and/or aggressive (de Quirós et al., 1994; Krusch et al., 1996). Among these psychoactive drugs are amphetamines and methylphenidate (Ritalin). For many children, the results are remarkable; taking the drug allows them to sit still and concentrate for the first time. However, while the new ability to pay attention is a welcome relief to many teachers, parents, and children, it does not necessarily produce gains in intelligence scores or achievement (Swanson et al., 1993).

Moreover, despite the remarkable results that psychoactive drugs provide for some children with ADHD, drug therapy is not a cure. Further, if drugs are prescribed without proper diagnosis or follow-up, an overmedicated child can become lethargic, too quiet to participate in class or play with peers. The actual effects of any drug cannot be predicted merely by diagnosis: some children are finally able to learn with medication, others are not helped at all.

❷ Especially for Educators: Suppose a particular school has 30 children in the second grade. Five of them have special problems. One speaks very little and seems autistic, one is very talkative but cannot read, one is almost blind, and two are ADHD (one of them aggressive). What are the advantages and disadvantages of creating a special class for these five, rather than mainstreaming them in the regular class?

Out of Control The use of psychoactive drugs to control mental disorders is controversial as well as complicated. However, those who assert that children should never be medicated to quiet their hyperactivity have not met Dusty Nash, age 7, or his mother. Without his daily Benzedrine, Dusty cannot concentrate or even sit quietly for a moment.

WHERE TO PUT THE "SPECIAL" CHILDREN?

All types of special problems need to be recognized early, before first grade if possible. Although some "developmentally delayed" children catch up on their own, most do not. For example, reading disabilities do not usually correct themselves, and ADHD children become more problematic, to themselves and others, the older they are (Fergusson et al., 1996).

After a problem is recognized, what is the best educational setting in which to solve that problem? The earliest answer was special classes, segregated from other children, where all the special-needs children were taught together by a special-education teacher. However, this approach made the children feel as though a spotlight were being focused on their problem. Often they were right: all sorts of disabled children were being educated together—including those with overall retardation and delay—with no recognition of an individual child's strengths and abilities. Further, segregated classrooms impaired the development of normal social skills, as well as slowed advancement in areas in which a child was not disabled, a violation of all four lessons from the developmental psychopathology perspective (see page 351).

In response, **mainstreaming** emerged about 30 years ago. Mainstreaming is a way to organize students and teachers in which children with special educational needs are taught with children in the general (main) classroom. The regular teacher is asked to be particularly sensitive to the special children, perhaps using alternative methods to teach them or allowing extra time for them to complete assignments and tests.

Unfortunately, mainstreaming tended to become a "sink-or-swim" situation for special-needs students. Many teachers were untrained, unwilling, or simply unable to cope with the special needs of a few children—especially in a classroom of 30 or so students. As one teacher complained:

I do not have the training that you people [speech-language pathologists] have. However, I've been in the business for a long time, and I think I know when I see a child with a language problem. So I make all the referrals. Now I don't know what happens in the 1:1 session, or what kinds of tests you give the kids, but my speech person keeps sending these children back to me saying they don't have a language problem. Finally I just said to her, "Then you get in the classroom and see what is wrong." [quote in Constable, 1987]

Accordingly, some schools set aside a **resource room,** where special-needs children would spend part of each day with a teacher trained and equipped to remedy whatever disability they might have. But pulling the child out of regular class once again undermined classroom social relationships and left the regular teacher unaccountable for the progress of the child. Further, scheduling resource-room time meant the child missed out on vital parts of the day, either play periods or academic-skill practice.

One recent solution is called **inclusion.** In this approach, children with disabilities are included in the regular class, as in mainstreaming, but the burden does not rest on the regular teacher; a specially trained teacher or paraprofessional assists with the included children, for all or part of the day. This solution may be the most expensive, and it necessitates adjustment on the part of classroom teachers, who are not used to working side-by-side with other teachers. Nonetheless, children who need both social interaction with their schoolmates and special remediation for their learning difficulties may be well-served (Banerji & Dailey, 1995). To take the idea of inclusion one logical step further, many teachers and parents now emphasize *integration,* the idea that each child within the classroom, learning-disabled or not, is a vital part of that social and educational group.

Unfortunately, for children with special needs, none of these solutions necessarily solves their academic or social problems (Siperstein et al., 1997). From a developmental perspective, this is not surprising: all manner of special needs, from severe physical impairment to subtle learning disabilities, are real, long-standing, often brain-based problems. This makes them quite likely to be helped by the proper educational context but quite unlikely to disappear.

The key seems to be to help the child understand what the problem is and how he or she might be helped. This did

By the time an ADHD child has become a candidate for psychoactive drugs, the child's behavior has usually created problems that drugs alone cannot reverse. Children diagnosed with ADHD need help overcoming their confused perception of their social world and their low opinion of themselves, while the family members need help with their own management techniques and interaction. That help must come from the other two crucial components of ADHD treatment: individual and family psychological therapy, plus contextual changes within the home and school (Pelham et al., 1998).

What Are These Children Learning? This deaf boy is fortunate—he is with his hearing peers and his teacher knows how to sign to him. Are the other children doing their work? One hopes, over the course of the year, they will learn more from the inclusion of the special child than they miss from the teacher's targeted attention.

not happen with Sally Osbourne, but it did happen with Ennis Cosby, as the following two excerpts reveal:

> I was in the seventh grade when my teacher asked me to stand up and read. I stood up, but couldn't recognize even one word on the page. After what seemed an eternity, the teacher got angry and told me to go into another classroom where I was to write again and again, "I am stupid because I cannot read."
>
> I didn't say a word. But I couldn't do what the teacher wanted, because I couldn't spell. So I just sat and waited until a friend came in at the end of the day to collect the assignment. After she had spelled it out for me, I wrote it over and over again. Then I gave it to the teacher and went home.
>
> That was the end of it. The teacher never helped me with my reading or writing before or after that time. [Levine & Osbourne, 1989]

> The happiest day of my life occurred when I found out I was dyslexic. I believe that life is finding solutions, and the worst feeling to me is confusion. [Cosby, 1997]

mainstreaming An approach to educating children with special needs by putting them in the same "stream"—the general-education classroom—as all the other children, rather than segregating them.

resource room A designated room, equipped with special material and staffed by a trained teacher, where children with special needs spend part of their school day getting help with basic skills.

inclusion An approach to educating children with special needs whereby they are included in the regular classroom while also receiving special individualized instruction, typically from a teacher or paraprofessional trained in special education.

Teacher behavior at either extreme—too rigid or too permissive—is most likely to exacerbate ADHD, because these children cannot follow strict guidelines exactly, nor can such children set their own limits when guidelines do not exist, as some children can. Thus some teachers unwittingly make the problem worse, creating the symptoms that qualify the child to be diagnosed as disruptive, oppositional, and aggressive. The treatment may be placement in a special class, a solution that creates problems of its own. (See Children Up Close, above.)

❶ **Response for Educators (from page 359):**
Ideally, your answer considers the benefits to the 5 children as well as the 25 and the challenge for the teachers involved. From the special children's perspective, being segregated and educated in such a disparate group would hurt their learning. Unless the aggressive child could be controlled, the others might learn only self-defense. For the regular teacher, however, it would be easier to teach 25 children who could all achieve at grade level. Simple mainstreaming is clearly unworkable—no one would learn much, and the teacher might quit. The unanswered question is whether the regular teacher and the 25 ordinary children could team up with the special teacher and the 5 children with disabilities so that they all could learn in one classroom. Inclusion, especially inclusion with integration, should be attempted.

Conclusion

What happens if a problem is not diagnosed, as was the case for three-fourths of the ADHD children in the Tennessee study, probably half the learning-disabled children in the United States (if the prevalence found in the Swedish study is accurate), more than half of the high-functioning autistic children, and a large number of children who have disorders? Life-span developmental research finds that childhood problems rarely disappear but that their lifelong legacy depends on the specifics of the home and school contexts. These contexts affect a person's fortune, ability, or misfortune in finding a vocation, a partner, and a community who guide him or her. For example, as you have seen, children with ADHD who have become aggressive by fourth grade are likely to become delinquents and then adult criminals, especially if family disruptions continue within a community of marked social disadvantage (Patterson et al., 1989). On the other hand, ADHD children who avoid serious difficulties in childhood can find careers in which their high energy, ability to deal with interruptions, and impatience with sitting still are all assets. Even some autistic children, surely among the most severely impaired, can become happy and successful adults.

Ideally, children with special needs are spotted and their teachers and parents provide the necessary educational and emotional support. If not, the children may still find ways to compensate for, overcome, or circumscribe their difficulties in the larger social context. On this all researchers agree: development during the school years is a multifaceted mixture of risks and assets, with the particular educational and familial contexts usually able to prevent serious problems from growing worse as development continues.

SUMMARY

SIZE AND SHAPE

1. Children grow more slowly during middle childhood than at any other time until the end of adolescence. Variation in size, shape, and rate of maturation is caused by genes, nutrition, family, and national policy.

2. Childhood obesity is caused by the interaction of genes, inactivity (including excessive TV viewing), family habits, and the child's own psychological stress. More exercise, rather than severe dieting, is the best solution.

3. Most school-age children are quite healthy, but problems with vision and sleep may need special attention. In addition, asthma, which is aggravated by modern life (including more indoor pollutants and less outdoor play), affects children's school attendance and overall well-being.

MOTOR SKILLS

4. School-age children can master almost any motor skill as long as it doesn't require adult strength, size, or judgment. Boys and girls are about equal in motor-skill potential, with differences between one child and another more a matter of genes, practice, culture, and maturation than of sex.

5. All children should be physically active, with specific activities geared to the gross motor skills that children of this age

are physically prepared to master. Fine motor skills are as important to practice as gross motor skills are.

CHILDREN WITH SPECIAL NEEDS

6. The developmental psychopathology perspective applies research regarding normal development to an understanding of childhood psychological disorders, and vice versa. It emphasizes that "special-needs" youngsters are children first—with the developmental needs that all children share.

7. The developmental psychopathology perspective also stresses that the manifestations of any disorder change as the child grows older and that the social context has an impact on the diagnosis of a problem. Two contexts—family interactions and school structure—are pivotal in treatment and prognosis.

8. Autism is characterized by a lack of interest in people, delays in language acquisition and communication, and extreme self-preoccupation. It is caused by an interaction of genetic vulnerability and neurological damage. The development of children with autism varies enormously, depending on initial severity, early treatment, and the success of behavioral techniques.

9. Specific learning disabilities can impair any of several particular abilities, such as learning to read (dyslexia) or do math (dyscalcula), or an underlying ability, such as abstract reasoning or spatial organization. Learning disabilities have many causes, including genes, prenatal teratogens, and postnatal brain damage.

10. Children who have unusual difficulty with concentration are often unusually active as well and may be diagnosed as hyperactive, or as having ADHD. It is important to treat this problem, both in school and at home, and often with drugs, to prevent low achievement, antisocial behavior, and outright aggression.

11. A developmental perspective suggests that all special-needs children can benefit from early diagnosis and appropriate schooling techniques. Targeted education, interaction with "normal" children, and adjustments at home can often remedy the problem sufficiently so that the child eventually becomes a normal functioning adult.

KEY TERMS

body mass index (342)
asthma (346)
reaction time (348)
children with special
    needs (351)
developmental
    psychopathology (351)
DSM-IV (352)
autism (352)
Asperger syndrome (352)

mental retardation (355)
learning disability (355)
dyslexia (356)
dyscalcula (356)
attention-deficit
    hyperactivity disorder
    (ADHD) (357)
mainstreaming (360)
resource room (360)
inclusion (360)

KEY QUESTIONS

1. How do nutrition and heredity affect stature and physique in middle childhood?

2. What are the causes of obesity?

3. How is asthma sometimes caused by modern life?

4. What factors affect which specific motor skills a child masters during the school years?

5. What gender differences and similarities are apparent in motor skills between ages 7 and 11?

6. How does the developmental psychopathology perspective view children with psychological disorders relative to "normal" children?

7. What are the three major characteristics of autism?

8. What are the signs of at least two specific learning disabilities?

9. How might the symptoms of ADHD in a specific child change with age?

10. What are the arguments for and against the use of psychoactive drugs to control ADHD?

11. What are the advantages and disadvantages of inclusion for learning-disabled students?

12. *In Your Experience* What aspects of your physical appearance or behavior made you different from other children during the school years? Were you teased because of them?

CRITICAL THINKING EXERCISE

by Richard O. Straub

Take your study of Chapter 11 a step further by working this practical problem-solving exercise:

Celine's parents are concerned about their daughter's weight.

Although neither of her parents is overweight, 9-year-old Celine, whom they adopted 2 years ago, weighs about 30 percent more than the average girl of her age and height. "We just can't understand it," they lament. "She's tried several diets and still can't lose weight! And she's starting to have problems at school. What can we do to help our daughter?"

To advise Celine's parents, you obviously need more information. Your task in this exercise is twofold. First, generate a list of at least four questions you might ask to help pinpoint the causes of Celine's weight problem. Each question should focus on a specific biological, social, or behavioral influence that might cause obesity. Then, for each question, explain how the answer will help you determine the cause of Celine's weight problem and what you might recommend as a result. To help you get started, one question is provided.

Question 1: How many hours of television does Celine watch each day?

Reason for asking:
Recommendation:

Question 2:

Reason for asking:
Recommendation:

Question 3:

Reason for asking:
Recommendation:

Question 4:

Reason for asking:
Recommendation:

Check your answers by comparing them to the sample answers in Appendix B.

The School Years:
Cognitive Development

CHAPTER 12

As you saw in Chapters 6 and 9, parents, teachers, and researchers have tended to underestimate the cognitive competency of the infant and young child. No such error occurs with middle childhood, age 7 to 11.

We are well aware of the cognitive skills of school-age children; we see them in action every day. Many 7- to 11-year-olds not only learn rapidly in school but can also outscore their elders on computer games, repeat the rapid-fire lyrics of a rap song, and recognize out-of-towners by the clothes they wear—accomplishments beyond some people twice their age, and beyond almost everyone six times their age.

To understand the development of cognition, we will first turn to the insights of current research, then to the overview provided by Piaget and by language learning, and finally to school itself—obviously a powerful influence that can channel, fortify, or hinder cognition during middle childhood.

REMEMBERING, KNOWING, AND PROCESSING

A 9- or 10-year-old child is a very different kind of thinker than, say, a 4- or 5-year-old preschooler. Not only do older children know more; they also use their minds much better when they must solve a problem or remember a piece of information. By middle childhood, most children have acquired a sense of "the game of thinking," and they enjoy an intellectual challenge as much as an athletic one. They begin to realize that good thinking involves considering evidence, planning ahead, thinking logically, formulating alternative hypotheses, and being consistent; they try to incorporate these qualities into their own reasoning and use them to evaluate the thinking of others (Flavell et al., 1993).

Information-Processing Theory

One way to understand this advance in thinking is to consider each component of the intellectual process (Kuhn et al., 1995). **Information-processing theory** likens many aspects of human thinking to the way computers analyze and process data. Of course, no computer can match the mind's capacity for reflection, creativity, and intuition. However, information-processing theorists suggest that by focusing on the step-by-step mechanics of human thinking, we can derive a more precise understanding of cognitive development (Klahr, 1989, 1992; Siegler, 1983, 1991). Like computers, humans must store large amounts of information, get access to that information when it is needed, and analyze situations in terms of the particular problem-solving strategies that are likely to yield correct solutions.

Steps in the Thinking Process

One example of how researchers portray the information-processing system is shown in Figure 12.1. The **sensory register** stores incoming stimulus information for a split second after it is received, to allow it to be processed. Most information that comes into the sensory register is lost or discarded, but what is meaningful is transferred to working memory for further analysis. It is in **working memory** (sometimes called *short-term memory*) that your current, conscious mental activity occurs. This includes, at this moment, your understanding of this paragraph, any previous knowledge you recall that is related to it, and also, perhaps, distracting thoughts about your weekend plans or the interesting person who sat next to you in class today. Working memory is constantly replenished with new information, so thoughts and memories are usually not retained for very long. Some are discarded, while a few are transferred to long-term memory.

Long-term memory stores information for days, months, or years. The capacity of long-term memory—how much information can be crammed into one brain—is virtually limitless. Together with the sensory register and working memory, long-term memory assists in organizing your reactions to environmental stimuli, with certain information more readily retrievable (you remember your birthdate more easily than your phone number) but with all of the information stored somehow, unless something (like a stroke) destroys it.

Putting it all together are **control processes**, which regulate the analysis and flow of information within the system. Control processes are involved when you try to retrieve specific information from your long-term memory or ignore distractions. When you want to concentrate on only one part of all the material in your sensory register, or summon a rule of thumb from long-term memory to working memory to solve a problem, control processes assume an executive role in the information-processing system, regulating the analysis and transfer of information.

information-processing theory   A theory of learning that focuses on the steps of thinking—such as sorting, categorizing, storing, and retrieving—that are similar to the functions of a computer.

sensory register   A memory system that functions for only a fraction of a second, retaining a fleeting impression of a stimulus on a particular sense organ.

working memory   The part of memory that handles current, conscious mental activity. (Also called *short-term memory*.)

long-term memory   The part of memory that stores information for days, months, or years.

control processes   That part of the information-processing system that regulates the analysis and flow of information, including memory and retrieval strategies, selective attention, and rules or strategies for problem solving.

Figure 12.1 Information Processing. From stimulus to response, input to output, much goes on in the human mind that makes thinking analogous to a computer. The solid arrows indicate the transfer of information, and the broken arrows indicate control processes that govern how and when the transfers occur. As with a computer, innate speed and capacity are important, but the crucial factor is the program. This is what is developed most in middle childhood.

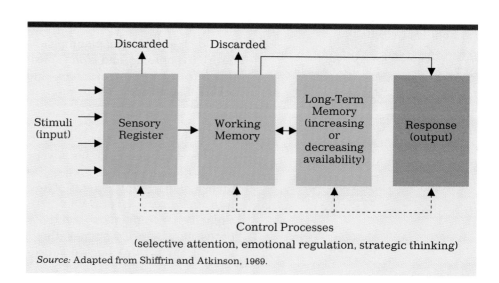

Source: Adapted from Shiffrin and Atkinson, 1969.

Information-processing theorists believe that advances in school-agers' thinking occur because of basic changes in the way children process and analyze information (Bjorklund, 1990; Klahr, 1992; Kuhn et al., 1995; Schneider & Pressley, 1997). As you will see, these changes are directly related to the growth of three elements: memory, knowledge base, and, finally, control processes.

Improvements in Memory

A marked improvement in memory occurs between ages 7 and 11, particularly apparent in older children's ability to remember essential facts over a period of days or longer, with almost no forgetting (Brainerd & Reyna, 1995). Selective attention, increases in processing speed, and the development of thinking patterns are all factors behind the improvement (Schneider & Pressley, 1997).

Selective Attention

If you were to observe children learning in a kindergarten classroom and a fifth-grade classroom, you would see many differences. Kindergartners are easily distracted, whether they are listening to a story or printing letters of the alphabet. While they are working, they chatter to each other, look around, fidget, call out to the teacher, and sometimes get up to visit friends or just wander around. Their curriculum is designed to be highly motivating, with plenty of changes of activity, because the teachers know the nature of their 5-year-old charges.

By contrast, fifth-graders might work independently at desks or in groups around a table, managing to read, write, discuss, and seek assistance without distracting, or being distracted by, other students. Or, they might all quietly follow a demonstration at the chalkboard, raising their hands to be called on rather than shouting out. Their academic tasks are more difficult, of course, and take longer to complete, but their teachers rightly expect them to persist in the face of that challenge, because it is within their intellectual capacity to do so.

Selective attention, the ability to screen out distractions and concentrate on relevant information, is the critical difference between these two scenarios. Indeed, memory and thought depend on the ability to ignore most of the information that bombards the senses and to focus on details that will help in later recall—perhaps using an already-memorized address to remember a historical date, rather than allowing a conversation across the room to interfere with concentration. Focusing on what should be remembered and ignoring what should be forgotten are equally important components of selective attention (Cowan, 1997).

Processing Speed and Capacity

Older children are much quicker thinkers than younger children, and this benefits memory and a host of other cognitive skills (Schneider & Pressley, 1997). Speed directly increases mental capacity, because faster thinking makes it possible to hold and process more thoughts in one's conscious mind (working memory) at once. A sixth-grader can listen to the dinner-table conversation of her parents, respond to the interruptions of her younger siblings, think about her weekend plans, and still remember to ask for her allowance. In school, increased processing capacity means that she can answer a teacher's question with several relevant ideas rather than just

Concentration This girl's ability to ignore her classmates and her own nail-bitten fingers, in order to push the right keys in proper sequence, is an impressive example of selective attention. Fortunately, the human brain becomes better at selective attention with maturation and experience, so this girl is not necessarily an extraordinary student.

selective attention The ability to concentrate on relevant information and ignore distractions.

one and, at the same time, monitor her words for accuracy and note her classmates' reactions to her answer.

Why do thinking speed and capacity increase during middle childhood? Of course neurological maturation, especially the ongoing myelination of neural axons and the development of the frontal cortex, partly accounts for these changes (Bjorklund & Harnishfeger, 1990; Dempster, 1993; Kail, 1991). But the advances seem more a matter of learning than maturation. Indeed, there is no evidence that the critical parts of the brain literally grow bigger during middle childhood. Instead, speed and capacity increase because as children learn to use the brain more efficiently, myelination increases and dendrites become more dense (Schneider & Pressley, 1997).

Patterns and Habits

automatization   The process by which familiar and well-rehearsed mental activities become routine and automatic.

Automatization is the process in which familiar, well-practiced mental activities become routine and automatic. As children use their intellectual skills, many processes that at first required hard mental labor now become automatized. This increases processing speed, frees up capacity, allows more to be remembered, and thus advances thinking in every way (Schneider & Pressley, 1997).

Eye on the Ball This boy's concentration while heading the ball and simultaneously preparing to fall is a sign that he has practiced this maneuver enough times that he can perform it automatically. Not having to think about what to do on the way down, he can think about what to do when he gets up, such as pursuing the ball or getting back to cover his position.

Can you remember how much time and effort you spent on reading your first words, completing your first arithmetic worksheets, or hitting the ball when you first tried to play tennis or baseball? As such activities become more familiar, well practiced, and routine, less mental work is required to carry them out. They become instantaneous and automatic, "no-brainers," and that makes it easier to devote mental energy to other tasks. Consequently, you can now (most likely) comment mentally to yourself about what you are reading while you are reading it—even in a foreign language—or plot your batting strategy while preparing to hit the ball, because you no longer need to devote your full attention to deciphering the letters on the page or adjusting your grip on the bat.

Progress from initial effort to automatization often takes years, however. Many children lose cognitive skills over the summer because the halt in daily schooling erases earlier learning (Huttenlocher et al., 1998). Not until something is overlearned does it become automatic.

The Growth of Knowledge

"What the head knows has an enormous effect on what the head learns and remembers" explains a leading cognitive researcher (Flavell, 1985). In other words, the more you know, the more you can learn. Having an extensive **knowledge base**, a broad body of knowledge in a particular subject, makes it easier to master new learning in that area. In fact, it makes it very much easier. (See the Research Report on page 369.)

knowledge base   A body of knowledge in a particular area that has been learned and on which additional learning can be based.

THE EXPERT AND THE NOVICE

That expansion of the knowledge base aids learning, at least a little, is obvious. However, developmental scientists are amazed at *how much* difference the knowledge base can make—independently of remembering, thinking, and reasoning. For example, as you might expect, chess experts remember the board locations of chess pieces better than novices do, because they know more. But does knowledge base make a substantial difference even when the experts are children, with all their immature information-processing skills, and the novices are adults?

In a classic study of young (grade 3 to 8) chess experts, recruited from a local chess tournament, Michelene Chi (1978) compared children's recall of complex chess positions with that of a group of adults who knew the game but were not experts. The children were strikingly more accurate and more efficient: they organized their memory of the chess positions into logical, interrelated memory "chunks."

This impressive performance led the researchers to wonder whether these particular children might be little geniuses, with minds that were simply sharper than those of most people of any age. To test this hypothesis, the researchers compared the same children and adults on a standard test of number recall—and the adults scored better (see the accompanying figure). Thus the children's memory was advanced only when they had the advantage of a greater knowledge base, and that made a dramatic difference.

A related study compared fourth-graders of varied intelligence, some expert soccer players and some novices, on the ability to understand and remember a written passage about soccer. As expected, high-IQ children did somewhat better than low-IQ children—but this was true only for children at the same level of soccer expertise. When an expert soccer player with low intelligence was compared to a highly intelligent novice, the expert did better: a larger knowledge base was sufficient to overcome slower thinking overall (Schneider et al., 1996). Further research on this topic emphasizes that it is the connections between bits of information that improve as the knowledge base expands. As a person learns more about a particular topic, that person learns how the new knowledge relates to the previous knowledge. This explains why learning by rote is fragile, while learning by comprehension endures.

This is obvious to any good teacher, who realizes that the best way to teach a child about the principles of biology or the nations of the earth, for instnace, is to make it comprehensible in a personal way. For example, children collect stream water and look at it through a microscope in order to learn about the living organisms that make up life, or they read a personal story of a child living in Siberia or Somalia in order to grasp life in another culture.

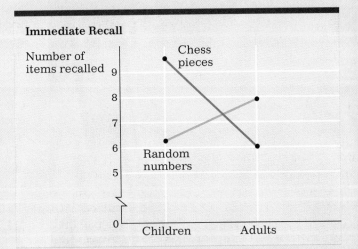

Immediate Recall

Checkmate. The graph shows the results of Michelene Chi's (1978) classic test of memory for chess positions. Children who were expert at chess remembered the location of chess pieces (red line) better than adults who were novices—even though they did less well than adults at remembering a series of random numbers (blue line). This suggests that knowledge base has an important role in memory.

Most of the experimental research has focused on recreational themes—chess and soccer, as described above, or basketball, tennis, and playing a musical instrument. Again and again, practice and motivation are key. Chess-playing children were better than novice adults in a replication of Chi's initial research, but then, three years later, those children who became experts did much better on the memory task than they had done earlier while those who lost interest and no longer played much chess were not as good (Gruber et al., 1993).

The finding that school-age children can become experts in a given field is no surprise to any parent who has been corrected by a 7-year-old dinosaur buff for mistaking a diplodocus for a brontosaurus. But it implies something few adults realize: Children might be able to think as clearly, deeply, and completely as adults if they were not handicapped by their limited knowledge and experience. As a child's knowledge base increases, concepts become more detailed and interconnected, and the young learner becomes able to ask better questions and hence to learn more (Chi et al., 1989). A corollary to this finding is that teaching a child additional information about anything—international politics, automobile repair, clothes design, musical scores, or whatever—will enable the child to become more expert in that area in the future.

They've Read the Book Acting in a play based on *The Lion, the Witch and the Wardrobe* suggests that these children have metacognitive abilities beyond almost any preschooler. Indeed, the book itself requires a grasp of the boundary between reality (the wardrobe) and fantasy (the witch), which demands "thinking about thinking" in order to appreciate the allegory.

❷ *Observational Quiz (see answer page 373): Beyond the book, what are three examples of metacognition implied here? Specifically, how does the ability to memorize lines, play a part, and focus on the play illustrate metacognition?*

metacognition   The ability to evaluate a cognitive task to determine how best to accomplish it, and then to monitor one's performance—"thinking about thinking."

This concept has important ramifications for parents and teachers of children who are unusually gifted or talented. If the talent can be nurtured by encouraging the child to spend hours each day developing his or her knowledge and skills, the child can become truly extraordinary. It is *not* true that talent always emerges. Many gifted young children never develop their abilities, because their social context does not provide the necessary motivation, instruction, or knowledge base (Csikszentmihalyi et al., 1993; Winner, 1996).

In the past, children who became geniuses often had lost one parent while they were young, as if the parent's absence encouraged the child to focus on a talent (Simonton, 1988). But today, fewer children are so lonely and distressed that they are driven on their own to focus all their efforts on one particular talent. Instead, "sustained, coordinated, and effective support from family and others for at least 10 years" seems necessary for a talented child to acquire the knowledge and expertise to become an exceptional adult (Feldman & Piirto, 1996). Of course, since the child is the one who must actually do the intellectual work, parents cannot simply impose their ideas of what the child must learn.

In other words, the family genius needs family support. If, instead of cultivating unusual talents or intellectual achievement, adults allow their children to spend hours baby-sitting, watching television, or playing with friends, those hours are likely to bring expertise in those domains. If a child knows all the character names and mannerisms on various TV shows, and can relate the plot of an episode with impressive detail, that achievement signifies not only expertise but also family and peer-group values. Our children learn where to put their intellectual energies, for good or ill.

Improvements in Control Processes

The ability to control one's mental processes begins during the preschool years, as children show signs of emotional regulation—holding their anger instead of hitting their friends, distracting themselves instead of crying at the dentist, and so on. However, during the school years, control processes become markedly better, especially in regard to intellectual, not just emotional, efforts. Children become aware that the content of their thinking is partly under their conscious control (Flavell et al., 1995). They develop **metacognition,** which means "thinking about thinking," the ability to evaluate a cognitive task to determine how best to accomplish it, and then to monitor and adjust their performance on that task. Metacognition leads to the development of effective cognitive strategies—ways to think—which are practiced so often that they become automatic.

There are many indicators of school-agers' development of metacognition (Flavell et al., 1993; Schneider & Pressley, 1997; Siegler, 1991). As one example, preschoolers have difficulty judging whether a problem is easy or difficult, and thus they devote equal effort to both kinds of problems. In contrast, children in the school years know how to identify challenging tasks, and they devote greater effort to these challenges—with greater success. They know how to evaluate their learning progress, judging whether they have learned a set of spelling words or science principles, rather than simply asserting (as many younger children do) that they know it all. In short, older children approach cognitive tasks in a more strategic and analytic manner.

Storage and Retrieval Strategies

storage strategies Procedures for placing and holding information in memory.

retrieval strategies Procedures for recalling previously memorized information.

Indeed, a major reason memory improves between ages 7 and 11 is that children become much more strategic. Older children use both **storage strategies** for putting material in long-term memory and **retrieval strategies** for pulling it from long-term memory.

From preschool through adolescence, a child's repertoire of storage strategies continually increases (Kail, 1990). Preschoolers might just stare at a group of objects to be remembered; 5- or 6-year-olds might repeat the names of the objects over and over (a strategy called *rehearsal*), and 9- and 10-year-olds are likely to mentally *reorganize* the objects to make them easier to memorize. Imagine asking a young child to memorize a list of the 30 most populous nations of the world. Staring at the list would be of no help at all, and rehearsing would probably help for the first few items on the list but not all 30. A 10-year-old, by contrast, might cluster them by region, sort them alphabetically, or create a rhyme or a sentence that uses the first letter of each country.

Research finds that such advances in memory storage skills are the result of learning by doing, not just maturation. By about age 9, if a child spontaneously uses reorganization to complete a simple memory task, usually he or she will use the same strategy if immediately given a more difficult memory problem (Best, 1993). However, at that age, if the researchers present the more difficult problem first, children usually do not spontaneously use the effective strategy of reorganization. In other words, children can apply what they have just learned, but the learning and application process must proceed step by step.

Teamwork How best to remember the names and locations of countries around the world? These boys know that any of a variety of memory strategies would be helpful—including simple rehearsal, grouping countries by region or in alphabetical order, or color-coding them on maps according to their location or other features.

Retrieval strategies also develop in middle childhood and improve steadily thereafter (Ackerman, 1996; Kail, 1990). By fifth grade, children usually have learned that if something can't be recalled immediately, then "taking a walk down memory lane"—that is, systematically searching one's recollections of other relevant events or information—can prove helpful (Flavell et al., 1993). They may try to jog their memory by thinking of clues to stimulate their recall (perhaps the first letter of a name or key term) or by attempting to visualize an experience they are trying to remember. By the seventh grade (just past middle childhood), many students would not panic during a geography test if they could not immediately remember the exact location of Bolivia or Bulgaria. Unlike a typical third-grader, who might immediately give up in frustration, a seventh-grader is likely to begin a systematic effort at recall, mentally picturing a map of the world or reconstructing the context of the relevant geography lesson.

The best example of metacognition may be that older children are likely to devise their own learning aids—by making lists, drawing diagrams, or planning their approach to learning new material. In such devices, they use the knowledge base more than younger children do, because they know how to connect bits of information. When such metacognition efforts involve memory techniques, they are called *metamemory*. An example of the use of metamemory is using the rhyme "*I* before *E* except after *C*" to remember how to spell. Older children are capable of devising their own memory techniques.

Of course, not every school-age child is an effective learner, just as not every adult is an effective worker. The school-age child who experiences repeated and guided practice in learning develops knowledge of metacognition strategies. The fact that metacognition is *possible* at this age makes it clear that adults can foster it; the fact that metacognition is *not automatic* makes it clear that social values, practices, and priorities all affect it (Perkins et al., 1994), a topic we will return to when we discuss school and culture. But first let us look at the descriptions developed by Piaget, who tried to provide an overview of school-age thought that would hold true in every culture.

CONCRETE OPERATIONAL THOUGHT

concrete operational thought   In Piaget's theory, the third period of cognitive development, in which a child can reason logically about concrete events and problems but cannot reason about abstract ideas and possibilities.

In Piaget's view, the most important cognitive achievement of middle childhood is the attainment of **concrete operational thought,** whereby children can reason logically about the things and events they perceive. According to Piaget, at about age 5 many children begin the shift to concrete operational thought, the *5-to-7 shift* that occurs in every domain of thinking. Then, between ages 7 and 11 years, children understand logical principles, and they apply them in *concrete* situations, that is, situations that deal with visible, tangible, real things. They thereby become more systematic, objective, scientific—and educable—thinkers.

Here is an example of this change: Preschoolers tend to use intuition and subjective insights to understand the results of a science experiment ("Maybe the caterpillar just felt like becoming a butterfly!"), but school-age children seek explanations that are rational, consistent, and generalizable ("Does the caterpillar use the air temperature to know when it's time to begin a cocoon?"). Preschoolers ask "Why" but reject answers not to their liking; school-age children ask "Why" and then want to know more.

The Scientific Method   During middle childhood, as Piaget described it, children become able to transcend their subjective and egocentric notions and objectively observe the world around them. This is an ideal age for budding scientists to undertake the steps of the scientific method. These girls not only have asked which food cats prefer but are gathering evidence before they reach their conclusion. Given the position of their pencils, they may even reach the ultimate step, "Publish the results."

Similarly, out on the playground, first-graders may argue over the rules of a game by using increasingly loud and assertive protests ("Is!" "Is not!" "Is!" "Is not!"), whereas fifth-graders temper their arguments with reason and justification ("That *can't* be right, because if it was, we'd have to score points differently!"). In both academic and nonacademic contexts, school-agers' logical thinking is crucial to understanding, to acquiring knowledge, and to communicating clearly and persuasively with others.

Three Logical Principles

identity   The logical principle that certain characteristics of an object remain the same when other characteristics are changed.

reversibility   The logical principle that something that has been changed can be returned to its original state by reversing the process of change.

reciprocity   The logical principle that two objects, quantities, or actions can be mutually related, such that a change in one can be compensated for by a corresponding or opposite change in another.

To understand the place of logic in concrete operational thought, we will consider three of the many logical structures that Piaget describes: identity, reversibility, and reciprocity. **Identity** is the idea that certain characteristics of an object remain the same even when other characteristics change. Children who understand identity realize that superficial changes in an object's appearance do not alter its underlying substance or quantity. In conservation tests (see page 271), for example, identity tells us that pouring a liquid from one container into a different container does not change the amount of liquid present. "It's still the same milk," a 9-year-old might say; "you haven't changed that."

Two other logical principles, **reversibility** and **reciprocity,** are also important to concrete operational thought. School-age children come to understand that sometimes a thing that has been changed can be returned to its original state by reversing the process of change (reversibility) and that some changes have the effect of undoing other characteristics (reciprocity). Applying these two principles to our conservation test, a school-age child

Learning by Doing This science teacher and student are demonstrating the effects of static electricity. Such demonstrations bring out the logical abilities of concrete operational children much better than do abstract descriptions in textbooks.

might prove that the amount of liquid has not changed by pouring it back into the first container (reversibility) or might point out that the height of the liquid changed when it was poured into the second container because that container has a different width (reciprocity).

Identity is relevant to mathematical understanding. Children need a firm grasp of identity to realize, for example, that the number 24 is always 24, whether it is obtained by adding 14 and 10, or adding 23 and 1, or adding $6 + 6 + 6 + 6$. This logical principle also enhances scientific understanding, whether that means grasping the underlying oneness of the tadpole and the frog or seeing that frozen water is still H_2O.

Identity shows up in nonacademic areas as well, particularly in everyday social encounters. A school-age child understands—as most preschoolers cannot—that his mother was once a child and that her baby picture is, in fact, a picture of his mother (even though she looks quite changed). School-agers are even able to imagine their parents growing old—and to promise, as one child did, always to be around to push their wheelchairs.

Reversibility and reciprocity are also essential to a school-ager's understanding of math. For example, subtraction is the *reverse* of addition (if $5 + 9 = 14$, then $14 - 9 =$ the original 5) and 2 is the *reciprocal* of ½ (if $8 \times ½ = 4$, then $4 \times 2 =$ the original 8). Reversibility and reciprocity have everyday relevance as well. They are often applied to social problem solving, as in "Let's start over and be friends again, OK?" or "Mom didn't like my C in geography, but I got an A in spelling, so she's not too unhappy." Note that, for Piaget as well as for information-processing theorists, the distinguishing feature of school-age children is the ability to apply certain logical principles, or general strategies, or metacognitive insights, to a variety of specific situations. The difference is that information-processing theorists emphasize experience; Piaget emphasizes maturation.

A Case Study: Selling Lemonade

The shift toward logical thinking during middle childhood was highlighted by researchers who asked children to predict how various circumstances would affect sales at a child's lemonade stand (Siegler & Thompson, 1998). Specifically, the researchers manipulated five variables: demand ("A lot of

Figure 12.2 Understanding Supply and Demand. When children age 4 to 10 were asked to explain which factors might affect lemonade sales, and how that might happen, dramatic improvement occurred at about age 7.

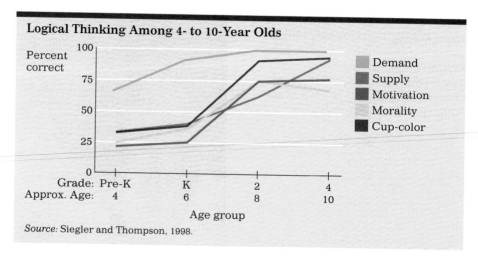

Logical Thinking Among 4- to 10-Year Olds

Source: Siegler and Thompson, 1998.

❓ Especially for Parents: Many parents object to the clutter created by their children's passion for collecting, especially when the objects are of little material value. When adults feel like storing or discarding the assortment of shells, pencils, advertisements, stickers, gum wrappers, cards, or whatever, what should they remember?

people were out of town"), supply ("Both kids next door decided to run lemonade stands too"), motivation (the child running the stand "really wanted to earn a lot of money"), morality (the child mistreated a sibling that morning), and appearance (the child switched from red to green cups).

As you can see from Figure 12.2, even the prekindergartners had a pretty good understanding of the effect of demand: fewer customers mean fewer sales. However, understanding the effect (or lack of effect) of changes in supply, motivation, morality, and cup color were hard for the youngest children and quite easy for the older children. The most dramatic increase in the use of logic to analyze those variables occurred between ages 5 and 7 years, just when Piaget said the shift to concrete operational thought occurs.

Note that to understand the effect of supply, one must understand reciprocity (more lemonade stands mean fewer lemonade sales per stand). To understand the effect of cup color, one must understand identity (it's still the same drink). To understand all the effects of motivation and morality, one must grasp the logical connection, or lack of it, between those variables and sales.

Answers to questions about cup color, motivation, and morality were considered correct either if the child said "no effect" or if the child thought of some plausible explanation. Most of the youngest children lost track of the issue, and many gave irrelevant, wrong answers, (e.g., "because people had electricity"). However, the young children (about 30 percent) who were considered correct on those problems usually said "no effect." By contrast, some of the older children were scored correct because they hypothesized a plausible connection. For example, in explaining how motivation could lead to an increase in sales, one child said, "He probably jumped out and said to every person he saw, 'Hey, would you like a nice cold cup of lemonade today?'" (Siegler & Thompson, 1998).

Classifying Objects, Ideas, and People

classification The process of organizing objects into groups on the basis of some common property; also, the result of that process and the understanding that such a process is possible.

class inclusion The idea that an object may be classified into more than one group, depending on its properties and how the groups are defined.

Classification is the process of organizing things into groups (or *categories* or *classes*) according to some common property. For example, a child's parents and siblings belong to the class called "family." "Toys," "animals," "people," and "food" are other everyday classes.

A related but more complicated concept is **class inclusion,** the idea that a particular object or person may belong to more than one class. For example, a baseball may be included in the class of round objects, of sports equipment, and of small things, as well as in many other classes. Until school age, few children really understand class inclusion.

Classification These two children illustrate the dramatic advances in classification skills between age 4 *(left)* and 12 *(right)*. Daphne puts her animals in family groups and uses her own voice to have them talk to each other. By contrast, John is quietly reorganizing his stamp collection, sorted by a combination of nation, value, and size. In fact, he lives on an isolated farm in New Zealand, which makes his absorption in international affairs all the more impressive. As with many children his age, intellectual challenges beyond his personal experience are not only possible to think about but also fascinating to explore.

Consider the following experiment, similar to experiments conducted by Piaget. An examiner shows children nine plastic dogs. Five of the dogs are collies, and the others are a poodle, a Labrador retriever, and two German shepherds. First, the examiner makes sure that the child knows all the plastic toys are types of dogs and that the child can name each breed. Then comes the crucial question: "Are there more collies or more dogs?" Until the concept of class inclusion is firmly established (at about age 7), most children say "More collies." They do not understand that "dog" is the general category here and "collie" the subcategory, and that the general category includes (and so is greater than) the subcategory. So when they hear "collies" and realize that there are more collies than all the other breeds put together, they jump to the conclusion that there are more collies than dogs.

When children finally understand the relation between a category and its subcategories, they can understand the wide variety of relationships among people, objects, and events—all of which can, and usually do, belong to more than one class. They understand that categories or subcategories can be:

■ *Hierarchical* (a child is simultaneously a human, primate, mammal, animal, and living creature), with each category belonging to the higher categories, and each higher category including more members than the lower categories include. For example, all humans are primates, but not all primates are human.
■ *Overlapping* (a child, within a family, can be an offspring, a sibling, one of the girls, and one of those with curly hair, and other family members are in some of those categories but not all of them).
■ *Separate* (a child may be a member of the Lee family and simultaneously a member of Mr. Smith's fourth-grade class, but the other members of Mr. Smith's class are not members of the Lee family).

Obviously, a child who can consistently and thoughtfully apply logical principles is better equipped to analyze problems, derive correct solutions, and ask follow-up questions than an intuitive, haphazard thinker would be. The ability to think logically also makes older children more objective, enabling them to think analytically, not only to react emotionally.

❶ Response for Parents (from page 374):
During the concrete operational period, children learn through active manipulation. Counting and classifying those collections, and comparing and trading them with each other, are fuel for the intellectual fire.

Critical Thinking

Many criticisms have been leveled at Piaget, whose ideas do not always stand the test of evidence. Some of Piaget's writings imply that children progress from one stage to the next rather suddenly, in every cognitive area, in social activities as well as in schoolwork, in geography as well as in language arts. The very idea of "stage" implies a steplike progression.

However, current studies have found that the movement to a new level of thinking is much more erratic. A certain type of logic (say, reversibility) might be evident in one domain of a school-ager's thought—say, math or biology—but not in another, such as social understanding or economics. Moreover, whether the shift to concrete operational thought is evident between ages 5 and 7 years or at some other time (even earlier, as you saw in Chapter 9) seems to depend on the specific child and the contexts in which the shift occurs. Education and practice are the forces behind many aspects of cognitive maturation (Siegler, 1996).

In other words, cognitive development seems to be considerably more affected by sociocultural factors than Piaget's descriptions imply. In fact, because knowledge base and educational guidance are pivotal during the school years, the 5-to-7 shift itself may be the result of first-grade curriculum rather than brain maturation. Keep these issues in mind as we look at the major intellectual tool of childhood, language.

LANGUAGE

How do these advances in memory, knowledge, control processes, and logic affect the language skills of the school-age child? Instead of using dozens of imprecisely understood words, as occurred during the preschool years, school-age children acquire a deeper and stronger ability to use language. Children are now strategic, which means they come to understand the ways in which language is structured, the ways in which words are connected, and, ultimately, the way oral and written communication can occur.

The Growth of Vocabulary

During middle childhood, children really enjoy words, as demonstrated in the poems they write, the secret languages they create, and the jokes they tell. Joke telling actually demands several skills not usually apparent in younger children: the ability to listen carefully; the ability to know what someone else will think is funny; and, hardest of all, the ability to remember the right way to tell a joke. Vocabulary is often key, with puns a mainstay of school-age humor.

The child's delight with words makes middle childhood a good time for adults to work with children to expand their vocabularies. By some estimates, the rate of school-age vocabulary growth exceeds that of the preschool years; school-age children acquire as many as 20 words daily to achieve a vocabulary of nearly 40,000 words by the fifth grade (Anglin, 1993).

But this vocabulary increase does not qualify as an "explosion" (with the implication of sudden, scattershot, eruption), as it did in earlier years. During middle childhood, children become more analytic and logical in their comprehension of vocabulary. Suppose we ask children to say the first thing that comes to mind on hearing, say, "apple." A preschooler is likely to respond with a word about perceptions or appearance ("red" or "round") or egocentric action ("eat" or "cook"). An older child, however, might respond

PEANUTS

Drawing by Charles Schultz © 1980 by United Features Syndicate

Are Kids Goats? With a language as irregular as English, it should be no surprise that many children (as well as adults) sometimes generate grammatical errors by applying logic to their language constructions. By school age, at least they understand that the same word can mean several things. Only one meaning per word is allowed in early childhood, but by age 9, "kid" can mean "child," "baby goat," and "deceive," and "behooves" does not mean "bee-hooves."

to "apple" by referring to an appropriate category ("fruit" or "snack") or to other objects that logically extend the apple context ("pie" or "tree"). Moreover, the older child could, if asked, deduce the meanings of new words that have "apple" as their root (such as "apple butter" and "apple-cart"). This ability to see logical word connections is a major reason vocabulary expands rapidly in middle childhood: in "applesauce," "applecart," "apple butter," "applewood," and "apple polisher," five separate words are connected to the word "apple" and are acquired through that connection.

The exact meaning of each word also becomes better understood. One study found that most 4-year-olds consider something "forgotten" if it is an unfilled desire or if it was never known. ("I forgot the cheesecake" can mean "I did not get any cheesecake" or "I do not know what cheesecake is"). By age 8, however, most children use "forgot" to mean "failed to remember" (Hill et al., 1997).

Mastery of Grammar

The school-age child's ability to think logically is also of help in understanding the complexities of grammar, including comparatives ("longer," "deeper," "wider"), the subjunctive ("If you were a millionaire . . ."), and metaphors (how a person could be a "dirty dog" or a "rotten egg") (Waggoner & Palermo, 1989). The fact that logical thinking helps in mastering such grammatical constructions is shown by comparing children's language acquisition across the world.

For instance, the subjunctive form is much simpler in Russian than in English, yet Russian-speaking children master the subjunctive only slightly earlier than English-speaking children. The problem is that the subjunctive form expresses the concept of *if things were other than they are,* and that concept must be understood before it can be expressed via the subjunctive case (de Villiers & de Villiers, 1978, 1992).

School-age children have another advantage over younger children when it comes to mastering grammar. Preschool children are quite stubborn in clinging to their grammatical mistakes (remember the child in Chapter 9 whose teacher "holded" the baby bunnies?), but school-age children are more teachable. They no longer judge correctness solely on the basis of their own speech patterns. If they have had ample opportunity to learn, by the end of middle childhood they will apply grammatical rules when they need to—even if they don't use them in their own everyday speech. Thus, a 10-year-old might say "Me and Suzy argued" but still understand that "Suzy and I argued" is correct.

Further evidence of school-agers' skill with grammar is their understanding of polite speech. School-age children soon come to realize that when a teacher says, "I would like you to put away your books now," the statement is not a wish but a command. Similarly, they realize that when they make requests of persons of higher status—particularly a person who

❓ **Especially for Educators:** Imagine that you are a teacher of fourth-graders and you notice a cluster of children who use accented speech with incorrect grammar. What do you do?

seems unlikely to grant the request—they should use more polite grammatical constructions ("May I please . . . ?") and more indirect phrases ("It would be nice if . . . ") than they use when they are negotiating with their peers (Axia & Baroni, 1985).

The Development of Code Switching

By elementary school, children also become sensitive to variations in the speech and tone of others—realizing, for example, that a father's clipped speech is an indication of growing anger or that the whole range of linguistic conventions may be changed to suit particular audiences. The latter concept is apparent in this example:

> A brand-new black teacher is delivering her first reading lesson to a group of first-grade students in inner-city Philadelphia. She has almost memorized the entire basal-provided lesson dialogue [the introduction provided in the teacher's edition of the textbook] while practicing in front of a mirror the night before.
>
> *"Good morning, boys and girls. Today we're going to read a story about where we live, in the city."*
>
> A small brown hand rises.
>
> *"Yes, Marti."*
>
> Marti and this teacher are special friends, for she was a kindergartner in the classroom where her new teacher student-taught.
>
> *"Teacher, how come you talkin' like a white person? You talkin' just like my momma talk when she get on the phone."*
>
> I was that first-year teacher many years ago, and Marti was among the first to teach me the role of language diversity in the classroom. Marti let me know that children, even young children, are often aware of the different codes we all use in our everyday lives. They may not yet have learned how to produce those codes or what social purposes they serve, but children often have a remarkable ability to discern and identify different codes in different settings. [Delpit, 1995]

In addition to recognizing codes, children can change from one form of speech to another, a process called **code switching**. Children in middle childhood censor profanity when they talk to adults, use picturesque slang and drama on the playground, and even switch back and forth from one language to another. All these are changes in code.

● Response for Educators (from page 377): Avoid either extreme of total acceptance or complete rejection. Respect the children's informal language, but explain that they must learn and use standard language in the classroom. If necessary, split them up by pairing each with a partner who already speaks standard English well—but make sure that mutual respect, not superiority, characterizes the relationship.

code switching A pragmatic communication skill that involves a person's switching from one form of language, such as dialect or slang, to another.

Recitation The formal code is appropriate in the classroom, as this girl demonstrates.
● Observational Quiz (see answer page 380): *What signs suggest that she is trying to avoid the informal code?*

formal code A form of speech used by children in school and in other formal situations; characterized by extensive vocabulary, complex syntax, lengthy sentences, and conformity to other middle-class norms for correct language. (Sometimes called *elaborated code*.)

informal code A form of speech characterized by limited use of vocabulary and syntax. Meaning is communicated by gestures, intonation, and shared understanding. (Sometimes called *restricted code*.)

Formal and Informal Codes

The universal example of code switching occurs when children shift from formal communication in the classroom to informal communication with friends outside of school. In general, the **formal code** is characterized by extensive vocabulary, complex syntax, and lengthy sentences. The **informal code,** by comparison, uses fewer words and simpler syntax; it relies more on gestures and intonation to convey meaning. The formal code is relatively *context-free;* that is, the meaning is clear regardless of the immediate context. The informal code tends to be *context-bound;* that is, the meaning relies on the shared understandings and experiences of speaker and listener, as well as on the immediate subject at hand. A dispirited student might tell a teacher, in formal code, "I'm depressed today because [a detailed excuse that the teacher is likely to accept] and I don't want to read out loud or write my book response," and later confide to a friend informally, "I'm down. School ---s" [the particular word depends on the specific local code].

Research has shown that children of all backgrounds engage in some code switching, changing pronunciation, grammar, and vocabulary in certain situations. Black English, southern dialect, patois, valley talk, cockney, mountain speech, Newyorican, pidgin, street language, broken English, and slang all refer to informal codes that are maintained by adults (especially when speaking with other adults who had similar childhood origins) as well as children. Even children who do not know a designated, regionalized informal code tend to speak to their friends informally, with less crisp enunciation and nontextbook grammar (Romaine, 1984; Yoon, 1992).

Formal language is sometimes called *correct, proper, high,* or *standard* (as in "Standard English" or "High German/*Hoch Deutsch*"). Such adjectives imply that the formal code is best, but actually both codes have their place. It is important to be able to speak in formal terms, partly because standard language is considered educated speech and its vocabulary is more precise. The two pivotal skills learned during middle childhood—reading and writing—depend on understanding and employing formal language without the use of informal gestures, intonations, and immediate context. At the same time, peer communication via informal code is vital, not only for social acceptance but also for more direct, emotional dialogue. While many adults rightly stress their children's mastery of proper language ("Say precisely what you mean in complete sentences, and no slang"), the code that is used with peers is also evidence of the child's ability (Goodwin, 1990).

Secrets In many ways, the informal speech of 7- to 11-year-olds reflects their overall desire to distinguish themselves from adult culture.

❓ *Observational Quiz (see answer page 381): Beyond the whispered words, what three characteristics do you see here that run contrary to formal adult standards?*

Second-Language Learners

Almost every nation has a sizable minority who speak a nonmajority language; for them, learning the majority language is a necessity. It also behooves those speaking the majority language to learn the minority one. A second or third language is useful, even required, as multinational business, finance, and travel become more common. An added intellectual benefit is that learning another language enhances children's overall linguistic and cognitive development, especially if it occurs before puberty (Baker, 1993; Edwards, 1994; Romaine, 1995).

The best time to *teach* a second language seems to be during early or middle childhood, although the best time to *learn* a second language on one's own through exposure is during early childhood. Because of their

❶ *Answer to Observational Quiz (from page 378):* *Her clasped hands, touching feet, and serious expression suggest that she will not use the gestures, body movements, and humor that characterize the informal code. Note that her audience is equally serious, even stiff. On the playground, this same group would be much more active, relaxed, smiling, and informal.*

readiness to engage in code switching, their eagerness to communicate, their grasp of logic, and their ear for nuances of pronunciation, children age 7 to 11 are at their prime for being taught a second language.

According to the 1990 census, about 3 million U.S. children between the ages of 5 and 11 (14 percent of the total age group) had a first language other than English, with more than 1 million of them speaking English "less than very well" (U.S. Bureau of the Census, 1997). That number has undoubtedly increased since 1990, because the U.S. immigration rate was twice as high between 1988 and 1998 as it had been over the previous decade. Many other countries, including Australia, England, and most of the nations of Europe, face the same challenge: A sizable minority of immigrant children enter school without knowing the usual language of instruction.

In Canada the question is even more complex, since bilingualism is part of a cultural and political struggle that goes to the heart of Canadian identity. About 40 percent of Canadian children are English-speaking, 30 percent are French-speaking, and 30 percent speak other first languages. Beginning in kindergarten, children who speak English at home are required to learn French, French-speaking children are required to learn English, and children knowing neither language must learn both, thus becoming trilingual.

Maintaining Tradition Some would say that these Vietnamese children in Texas are fortunate. They are instructed in two languages by a teacher who knows their culture, including the use of red pens for self-correction as well as teacher correction. Others would say that these children would be better off in an "English only" classroom.

Strategies for Teaching Another Language

The question of how to teach the majority language to nonnative speakers has been one of intense concern and emotion, but no educational approach has yet been recognized as best. Strategies include both extremes—from total **immersion,** in which the child's instruction occurs entirely in the second (majority) language, to *reverse immersion,* in which the child is taught in his or her first (native) language for several years, until the second language can be taught as a "foreign" language. Variations between these extremes include presenting some topics of instruction in one language and other topics in the other language or presenting every topic in both languages.

immersion An approach to learning a second language in which the learner is placed in an environment where only the second language is spoken.

English as a second language (ESL)
An approach to teaching English in which English is the only language of instruction for students who speak many other native languages.

bilingual education An approach to teaching a second language that also advances knowledge in the first language. Instruction occurs, side by side, in two languages.

bilingual-bicultural education An approach to teaching a second language that adds preservation of nonnative cultural symbols and strategies (such as in the way teaching occurs) to a bilingual program.

In the United States, three approaches attempt to avoid the shock of complete immersion but still teach English eventually:

- **English as a second language,** or **ESL,** requires that all non-English-speaking children go through an intensive instructional period together, with the goal of mastering the basics of English in 6 months or so, before joining regular classes with all the other children. In classes using ESL, the teacher does not speak the child's native language (indeed, the teacher may not even understand all the languages spoken by the children); but at least the teacher and the other children have a common goal and understand the shared dilemma of helping every child master an alien tongue. A total of 43 percent of all public schools in the United States provided ESL classes in 1994, up from 34 percent in 1988 (Henke et al., 1996).
- **Bilingual education** requires that the teacher instruct the children in school subjects using their native language as well as English. In the early years, children are greeted, instructed, and (when necessary) disciplined in two languages, in the hope that they will progress in both. Informal talk between one child and another is almost always in the native language, as is much of the teacher's informal conversation. In 1994, 18 percent of U.S. public schools provided bilingual education, down from 20 percent in 1988 (Henke et al., 1996).
- **Bilingual-bicultural education** recognizes that non-English-speaking children come to school with non-Anglo values, traditions, and perceptions that may need to be preserved within the larger American culture. Implementation of the strategy may be as simple as celebrating special holidays (such as, for Mexican-American children, Three Kings Day, Cinco de Mayo, and the Day of the Dead), or it may be as complex as instituting new classroom strategies (such as more or less cooperative learning or special punishment tactics). Bilingual-bicultural education preserves a child's native language and heritage.

Practically as well as politically, both bilingual and bilingual-bicultural education require a large concentration of children with the same linguistic and ethnic background in one school system or in an after-school program that parents, cultural groups, or religious bodies organize. In the United States, bilingual-bicultural in-school programs usually involve Hispanic children, and bilingual-bicultural after-school programs are more common with Asian children.

Success and Failure

Which teaching strategy is best? In Canada, immersion has succeeded with more than 300,000 English-speaking children who were initially placed in French-only classrooms. These children showed no declines in English skills (learned at home) or in other academic achievement (Edwards, 1994; Lambert et al., 1993).

Immersion programs do not always work well, however. Immersion tends to fail if the child feels shy, stupid, or socially isolated or if the attitude of the school is that the child is deficient because he or she doesn't speak the majority language. In such cases, this educational approach might more aptly be called "submersion," because the child is more likely to sink than swim (Edwards, 1994). In the United States, many school systems used none of the three approaches described above. Consequently, many Spanish-speaking children who were instructed only in English became slow learners who repeated a grade or two until they were old enough to drop out of school.

❶ *Answer to Observational Quiz (from page 379):* Actually, distinctions between child and adult culture are apparent in every part of this photo. Any three of the following would be correct: mismatched shoes, men's boxers, cotton "bracelet," over-large shirts, missing sock on the right, braces on the left, and, finally, physical touching, from knees up to foreheads.

Figure 12.3 Que Pasa? Dropping out of school is both the result and the cause of trouble. Most dropouts are alienated from school years before, and are unemployed years after, they drop out. Rates among whites and blacks are improving—a very good sign. However, rates over the past 25 years among Hispanics show little change and may even be worse than they were in the early 1980s. Obviously, much more needs to be done to change the schooling of such children.

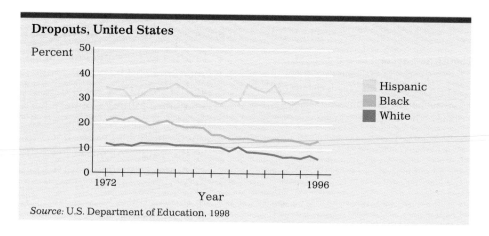

Dropouts, United States

Source: U.S. Department of Education, 1998

Friendly Immersion The poster is in English, because this Toronto teacher is explaining a sign in the city, but all the instruction occurs in French, even though none of these children are French-speaking natives. Their parents chose it not only because French immersion works successfully in Canada but also because such programs have a reputation for academic rigor, including high standards for conduct and achievement. Attitudes, not just instruction, facilitate learning a second language.

(See Figure 12.3.) Typically, their poor performance was blamed on their deficit in English, rather than on the teachers and educational programs that failed to take into account the special needs of such children (Romo & Falbo, 1996).

In most Canadian instances of successful immersion, parents voluntarily place their children in the program. In the United States, parents usually have little choice as to the specific type of education their children get, and entire school systems, or even states, mandate one form of education or another. Given the successes and failures of immersion programs, it is apparent that attitudes within cultures, families, and communities are often transmitted to the classroom. In some cases, these adult attitudes cause the child to cling steadfastly to the first language and then drop out; in others, they cause the child to forget the mother tongue; and in still others, they cause the child to readily learn the second language and, perhaps, to become truly bilingual and bicultural.

One critical classroom factor is the teacher's ability to create a social milieu that encourages all the children to make friends, to join conversations, and to feel free to make mistakes. The presence of this factor alone allows children in some classes to pick up a second language much more quickly than children in other classes.

Another critical factor is the age of the children. As children grow older and more self-conscious about making friends, it becomes harder simply to immerse them in a classroom and expect them to learn. One boy recalled his early experiences in a Toronto classroom:

I did not know what to do when the other students spoke to me because I did not understand them. I was forced to use signs with my hands to communicate with people, just as if I were deaf and dumb. I hated the students who spoke with me. . . . Sometimes there was a joke, and I had to laugh with the others even though I did not know what the joke was, because I was afraid of being laughed at. [quoted in Coelho, 1991]

A Case Study: Gains and Losses of Immersion

Mexican-American Richard Rodriguez entered an all-English school in the first grade. He eventually learned English so well that he studied English literature in graduate school at Berkeley and Columbia and became a well-regarded writer (Lucas et al., 1990).

At the start, Rodriguez and his family were determined that he would learn English, no matter

what the cost. When his teacher advised his parents to stop speaking Spanish to their children, even though their understanding of English was minimal, they did so. Rodriguez (1983) explained the consequences:

> As we children learned more and more English, we shared fewer and fewer words with our parents. Sentences needed to be spoken slowly when a child addressed his mother or father. (Often the parent wouldn't understand.) The child would need to repeat himself. (Still the parent misunderstood.) The young voice, frustrated, would end up saying "Never mind"—the subject was closed. Dinners would be noisy with the clinking of knives and forks against dishes. My mother would smile softly between her remarks; my father at the other end of the table would chew and chew his food, while he stared over the heads of his children.

Despite such drawbacks, in retrospect Rodriguez (1983) approves of his immersion:

> Without question, it would have pleased me to hear my teachers address me in Spanish when I entered the classroom. I would have felt much less afraid. I would have trusted them and responded with ease. But I would have delayed—for how long postponed?—having to learn the language of the public society.

Rodriguez never learned to write Spanish, and as he grew older, he lost his ability to speak it as well. He also found himself increasingly distanced from his parents and their culture, which is not uncommon for immigrant children who succeed in the majority school. The latest wave of immigrants to suffer these consequences are from Southeast Asia. Many of the children in this group eventually become quite successful in school, but they pay a high price—the loss of their ability to communicate with their parents (Wong Fillmore, 1991).

Goals and Limitations

Rodriguez's experience raises a basic question: What is the goal of second-language education? Almost all evaluations of such programs focus on one measure of success: proficiency in the new language. Other measures—school success, personal success, family disruption, cultural alienation—are often ignored (Hakuta & Garcia, 1989; McKeon, 1994). But can a program be called successful when it teaches one language at the expense of another?

Obviously, school-age children need to learn the language of their society, but they also need to develop their understanding of themselves and of others. Educational practices, including attitudes regarding children's native languages, can be instrumental in determining whether "the linguistic, cognitive, and sociocultural resources children bring to school" are used to achieve the larger goal—seeing that "the developing child becomes a fully functioning and valued member of the community" (Genesee, 1994). They should always work toward that goal.

To reach that goal, developmental research emphasizes four findings:

- Children learn a first and second spoken language best early in life, ideally under age 5, otherwise under age 11.
- Peers are the best teachers, with the encouragement and guidance of adults who understand the school-age eagerness to learn new structures, strategies, and vocabulary.
- Each combination of child, family, and culture is unique, and goals and attitudes vary tremendously. No single language-teaching approach is best for everyone, everywhere, but attitudes are an important gateway or barrier for language learning.
- Immigrant children are great learners—if given the opportunity.

The last fact above was made clear in a research study that compared immigrant children with children of their own racial-ethnic group who were born in North America (Fuligni, 1997). (For example, Latin American immigrants were compared with children of Hispanic heritage, children from the Caribbean and Africa were compared with African Americans, European immigrants were compared with white, non-Hispanic Americans.)

By high school, the immigrant children had higher motivation and spent more time studying. They outperformed the native-born Americans of the same heritage in grade-point average, not only in math and science but also in English (although their standardized English test scores were lower.) Two expected factors correlated with their success: SES, and whether or not the family spoke English at home. However, even without controlling for these factors, immigrant children were better students than nonimmigrants. Thus children born in Mexico or China did better in high school than their U.S.-born classmates whose parents or grandparents were born in those countries. The authors of this study concluded:

> The increased presence of the children from immigrant families in American schools has recently become a subject of great public concern. The results of this study suggest that the vast majority of these students who possess a working knowledge of English actually perform just as well as if not better than their counterparts from native-born families. These students possess an academic eagerness and initiative that would be welcomed by most teachers and schools. [Fuligni, 1997]

Thus speaking a language other than the majority language, or using a code other than the standard one, is not a cognitive problem during middle childhood, unless this somehow impedes mastering the majority, standard language—something 7- to 11-year-olds are intellectually and socially primed to do. However, they do not master this skill in isolation, spontaneously. They need to be taught, informally through positive cultural and familial attitudes and formally through school.

THINKING, LEARNING, AND SCHOOLING

The school-age child described thus far is thoughtful and eager to learn, able to focus attention, to remember interrelated facts, to master logical operations, and to use several linguistic codes. That description is universal: it

Learning to Learn These two classes, in India *(left)* and Somalia *(right),* are different from each other in many ways. However, they both share several characteristics that are rare in most nations where this textbook is used.

❓ *Observational Quiz (see answer page 388): What are some differences between these classes and European- or American-style classes?*

holds for children age 7 to 11 the world over, and it evokes numerous adult efforts to train, teach, and educate.

Consequently, schooling of some sort during middle childhood is available in every nation. But the specifics—who receives instruction, in what subjects, and how—vary enormously. In the past, boys and wealthier children were much more likely to receive formal education than girls and poor children, and some of that inequality is still apparent today. In developing countries, more boys than girls attend elementary school (58 and 42 percent, respectively). Indeed, girls are more likely to drop out of school before sixth grade, with the percent of boys and girls ages 6–11 in school ranging from 99% to 90% in Algeria to 42% to 14% in Afghanistan. In developed countries, less is generally demanded of girls and poor children, particularly in mathematics and science (UNICEF, 1996; U.S. Department of Education, 1997). Teaching techniques also vary widely, from the *strict lecture method*, in which students are forbidden to talk, whisper, or even move during class, to *open education*, in which students are encouraged to interact and make use of all classroom resources—with the teacher serving as an adviser, guide, and friend more than as a subject-matter authority and disciplinarian.

Until recently, such variations did not usually trouble the communities involved, because each culture's methods reflected traditions and values that its people took for granted. Now, however, international economic competition has intensified public concern about education, particularly about the outcomes. Measuring those outcomes is no simple matter. (See Changing Policy, pages 386–387.)

Evaluating Differences in Cognitive Growth

Simply asking a parent or a teacher how well a child is learning is considered very imprecise, since personal biases may cloud accurate perceptions. Even school report cards typically reflect the teacher's judgment of the child's behavior, as well as the teacher's personal standards, rather than something more objective. To remedy this problem, educators and psychologists have turned to tests that measure intellectual progress.

Basically, there are two kinds of tests. **Aptitude tests** are designed to measure potential—what the person could learn and how capable the person is of learning. In childhood the most commonly used aptitude tests are tests of general intelligence. In adulthood, aptitude testing might also include clerical quickness, or abstract reasoning, and college-admission exams, such as the SAT (Scholastic Assessment Test).

② Especially for Social Workers: What would you do if a child who had an IQ of 65 was referred to you?

aptitude tests Tests designed to measure potential, rather than actual, accomplishment.

Performance IQ This puzzle, part of a performance subtest on the Wechsler IQ test, seems simple until you try to do it. Actually the limbs are difficult to align correctly and time is of the essence, with a bonus for speed and failure after a minute and a half. However, this boy has at least one advantage over most African-American boys who are tested. Especially during middle childhood, boys tend to do better when their examiner is of the same sex and race.

EDUCATION IN THE UNITED STATES, JAPAN, AND THE REPUBLIC OF CHINA

An international team of researchers headed by Harold Stevenson spent 20 years comparing the school achievement, leisure-time use, and academic attitudes of more than 5,000 children and their parents at 64 schools in three comparable cities: Minneapolis (United States), Taipei (Republic of China, or Taiwan), and Sendai (Japan) (Stevenson & Stigler, 1992; Stevenson et al., 1993). They found that children in the three cities were similar in aptitude, as measured by intelligence tests. However, the Chinese and Japanese students outperformed the Americans in mathematics and science at every grade level and across every level of ability. Indeed, the achievement of the top 10 percent of U.S. students was only at the level of the average Chinese or Japanese student.

If it was not a matter of ability (aptitude), why did these differences occur? One reason is the hours the children in the three countries spent at schoolwork. In Japan and Taiwan, children attend school 5½ days a week, the average school year is one-third longer, and the average school day is an hour or two longer than that in the United States.

Even more important is classroom activity: schoolchildren in Minneapolis more frequently engaged in nonacademic activities (chatting with friends, lining up for lunch, taking trips, and such). By fifth grade, they were spending 64 percent of the school day on academic work, whereas Sendai students were academically engaged 87 percent of the time. One notable result was that the American children spent an average of only 3 hours per week on math, whereas the Japanese children spent an average of 7 hours.

Also, compared with Japanese and Chinese children, American children were more inclined to work alone than in groups, and their teachers worked more frequently with individual children or with small groups than with the class as a whole. Teachers in Japan and the Republic of China, on the other hand, strongly emphasized group instruction, with every child actively participating and every teacher following a curriculum designed to motivate as well as provide specific learning. As a consequence, children from the Asian nations had more opportunity to learn directly from their teachers in class.

Added to this was a notable difference in homework. In grade 5, the U.S. children averaged less than 4 hours per week studying at home, compared with 13 hours for the Chinese children and 6 hours for the Japanese (Stevenson & Lee, 1990). One reason for this difference is that homework for the Asians was carefully constructed and used as practice and introduction for the next classroom lesson. As Harold Stevenson says,

In East Asia meticulous care is given to the construction of homework assignments. It's a great contrast to the routine assignments given in the U.S. Here we don't recognize that changing a child's mind is as complex as open-heart surgery. [quoted in Tovey, 1997]

The Individual and the Group Japanese primary schools typically group children by age, not ability, and encourage cooperation among members at each table. The underlying belief is that all children can succeed at mastering quite complex material, as these sixth-graders in Tokyo seem to be doing. Note that even ideographs reflect individual thought, not mindless copying, as shown by the different messages on the two visible pages.

Education also involves parents, of course. According to Stevenson and his colleagues, academic achievement was much more central to the Japanese and Chinese parents, who had higher academic expectations for their offspring and were more involved in fostering their children's success (Stevenson & Stigler, 1992; Stevenson et al., 1993). Asian parents encouraged and supervised homework (91 percent of the Japanese children had their own desks at home), maintained high standards for academic work, and emphasized the value and importance of hard work as the primary determinant of success. By contrast, the Minneapolis mothers, according to these researchers, believed that "it is better for children to be bright than to be good students." Parents in the United States were far more satisfied with their children's progress and achievement than were parents in Japan and the Republic of China. Perhaps because of their parents' contentment, the U.S. children spent more time engaged in nonschool activities (socializing, working part-time, participating in sports) than did their Asian peers.

In fact, parents in the United States were concerned with home instruction before age 6, but

they abdicated this responsibility to the teacher once the child entered school. This trend is opposite from that which occurs in Chinese and Japanese families, who tend

A Week in the Life of a Child
Time Spent on Activity, per Week

Activity	6- to 8-Year-Olds		9- to 11-Year-Olds*		Average Time Change (1981–1997)
	1981	1997	1981	1997	
School	24:20	33:54	26:15	33:50	8h 34 min more
Sports	3:00	4:38	3:09	5:14	1h 52 min more
Studying	0:44	2:03	2:49	3:37	1h 3 min more
Art	0:28	0:45	0:23	0:56	25 min more
Reading	0:49	1:14	1:05	1:16	18 min more
Being outdoors	0:36	0:32	1:58	0:47	37 min less
Playing	15:15	11:26	8:29	8:44	1h 47 min less
Watching TV	12:47	12:38	18:20	13:36	2h 27 min less

*The 1997 figures are for children age 9 to 12.
Source: Institute for Social Research, 1997.

A Trade-Off? When international comparisons revealed that children in the United States were not first in academic achievement, parents and schools demanded more homework, longer school years, and less television. The results include advances in math and reading, and less time for play, especially for the youngest children.

to be quite indulgent of the youngest children but . . . from the time that the child enters school, life for the Chinese and Japanese child becomes purposeful; the child, the parents, and the teachers begin the serious task of education. [Stevenson & Lee, 1990]

Critics of the Asian emphasis on schooling have long maintained that Asian children, worn down by the constant grind and pressure to excel, are depressed and even suicidal. In fact, the comparison works the opposite way: students in the United States are more likely to feel stressed, depressed, and aggressive, as well as to be anxious about school (Stevenson et al., 1993).

There is also evidence that the entire Japanese society values education. For example, Japanese teachers are better trained, and almost half the elementary schoolteachers in Japan are men, versus less than 20 percent in the United States. Japanese schools are clean and very well equipped, having libraries, music rooms, science laboratories, and large gyms. Indeed, 75 percent of them have swimming pools, a luxury enjoyed by only 1 percent of U.S. schools. The Japanese are generally proud of their schools and teachers, although not always of their children.

Here is an interesting cultural contrast: Given extra money, few Americans would put swimming pools in schools. Their main concerns are discipline and drugs, so they might hire more deans, counselors, or security officers instead. They tend not to be proud of education overall, although they grade their own schools with a B–, on average better than schools in general, which they grade C. In contrast, the Japanese believe that quality instruction is crucial. They probably would use any extra money to hire another master teacher whose job would be to instruct and inspire all the others.

It is tempting to pick one or two features of Asian education and consider them as solutions to educational problems in the United States. However, because of the importance of cultural context, it is very unlikely that parts of one nation's educational system can be made to work in another nation. Even the solutions that seem easiest, such as extending the school day, may contain hidden risks when lifted out of their overall context (see the accompanying table). As the researchers in the comparison study warn,

Increasing the amount of time spent in academic activities without modifying the content of the curriculum and the manner of instruction might further depress American children's interest in school and increase their dislike of homework. Greater time on task is not the primary basis for the high achievement of Chinese and Japanese children. The answer lies instead in the high quality of experiences that fill this time. . . . Chinese and Japanese elementary school classrooms, contrary to common stereotypes, are characterized by frequent interchange between teacher and students, enthusiastic participation by the students, and the frequent use of problems and innovative solutions. [Stevenson & Lee, 1990]

This is precisely the direction suggested by developmental theory—a direction that more and more educators in the United States, Canada, and elsewhere are pursuing. More time on task and better instructional methods may be responsible for the recent upsurge in U.S. math and science scores. The question is always, At what cost? To pick a dramatic example: As you saw in the previous chapter, over the past decade children in the United States have become fatter, even as they have become better at math. Perhaps swimming pools are not all wet.

achievement tests   Tests designed to measure how much a person has learned in a specific subject area.

Achievement tests are designed to measure what the child has actually learned. Usually achievement is tested in each particular curriculum area, perhaps reading or math or, more specifically, European history or graph-reading skill. There are serious problems with, as well as effective uses of, both kinds of tests.

Tests of Potential

For schoolchildren, aptitude tests are used to predict school success and to diagnose children with special learning needs, such as gifted children or children with learning disabilities.

The most commonly used aptitude tests are *intelligence tests*, often called **IQ tests** (*IQ* being an abbreviation for "intelligence quotient"). Originally, a score on an IQ test was actually calculated as a quotient—the child's mental age (that is, the age at which most children attain the score that this particular child did) divided by the child's chronological age, times 100:

IQ tests   Aptitude tests designed to measure a person's intelligence (which at one time was defined as mental age divided by chronological age, times 100—hence, intelligence quotient, or IQ).

> Actual age of three children: 12
> Mental ages of the same children: 15, 12, 8
>
> IQ of each child:
> = 15/12 = 1.25 × 100 = 125 (superior)
> = 12/12 = 1   × 100 = 100 (average)
> = 8/12 = .75 × 100 = 75 (slow learner)

The calculation currently used to determine IQ scores is more complex than the original formula and is designed to ensure that the score variation follows the bell curve (see Figure 12.4), but the underlying concept is the same.

Two highly regarded IQ tests are the *Stanford-Binet* and *Wechsler* intelligence scales. Both test general knowledge, reasoning ability, mathematical skill, memory, vocabulary, and spatial perception. The Stanford-Binet can be used to test individuals from 2 to 18 years of age, although obviously test items vary depending on the child's age and ability. The Wechsler has special versions for preschoolers (the WPPSI), schoolchildren (the WISC-R), and adults (the WAIS-R) (see Figure 12.5). Both tests are administered orally by a trained examiner to an individual. Many school systems also use paper-and-pencil aptitude tests, given to groups of students, but these are less accurate.

❶ *Answer to Observational Quiz (from page 384): Barefoot children, outdoor classes, and sex segregation. If you look closely, you can also see more age variation than in a typical European- or American-style classroom, where almost all the children are born in the same calendar year.*

Studies have found that IQ tests are quite reliable in predicting school achievement (Neisser et al., 1996). When there is a mismatch between IQ score and achievement, something is amiss, either in the child, the home, or the school. In fact, as you probably remember from the previous chapter, a 2-year discrepancy between aptitude and achievement is the usual indicator of a learning disability.

Figure 12.4 In Theory, Most People Are Average. IQ scores between 85 and 115 are considered average, and almost 70 percent of the scores fall in that range. Note, however, that this is a norm-referenced test. In fact, actual IQ scores have risen in many nations; 100 is no longer exactly the midpoint. Further, in practice, scores below 50 are slightly more frequent than indicated by the normal curve shown here, because severe retardation is the result, not of the normal distribution, but of genetic and prenatal causes.

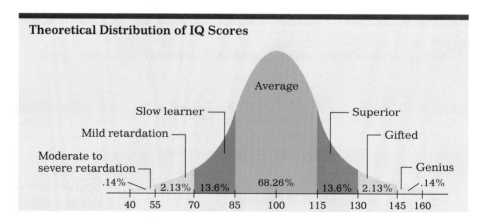

Theoretical Distribution of IQ Scores

Average

Slow learner

Superior

Mild retardation

Gifted

Moderate to severe retardation

Genius

.14%   2.13%   13.6%   68.26%   13.6%   2.13%   .14%

40   55   70   85   100   115   130   145   160

Figure 12.5 The Wechsler Intelligence Scale for Children.

❶ Response for Social Workers (from page 385): You would realize that this low score is in the mentally retarded range and that the child might need special education in school and special help at home. But before you would act on your knowledge, you would find out if anything (health, abuse, anxiety, language barriers) might have interfered with the child's best performance on the test. Even if none of these factors was evident, you would still have the child retested by a conscientious trained examiner with a background similar to that of the child's.

Questions Similar to Those on the WISC

Half of the items on the WISC are designed to measure five aspects of *verbal intelligence:*

- Knowledge ("How many thumbs do you have?")
- Reasoning ("How are an elephant and a whale alike?")
- Arithmetic ("If a train traveling at 32 miles per hour takes 3 days to get from one place to another, how fast must a train go to travel the same distance in half a day?")
- Vocabulary ("What is a stanza?")
- Memory ("Say these numbers backward: 8, 6, 3, 7, 1, 9.")

The other half includes various tasks that assess performance intelligence, such as putting together a puzzle, organizing pictures into a sequence that tells a story, and arranging colored blocks to match a specific design.

Problems with IQ Tests. Using a single test score to designate a child's level of intelligence seems contrary to everything we have discussed about development. We know that children develop at different rates, depending on their genes, family, school, and cultural contexts. Thus IQ scores should be used with caution: they are only black-and-white snapshots of a rapidly moving, multicolored subject.

Further, IQ tests are intended to measure intellectual potential, but it is impossible to measure potential without also measuring achievement. Scores reflect knowledge of vocabulary, understanding of basic math, and familiarity with cultural ideas and artifacts—all of which are learned. Performance on an IQ test also reflects the ability to pay attention and concentrate, to express thoughts verbally, and to ask questions if the instructions are unclear. In addition, a child's performance can be affected by emotional stress, health, test-taking anxiety, and similar factors.

In comparing IQ scores—especially the scores of individuals from significantly different cultural backgrounds—or in evaluating the scores of children from troubled families, all these factors must be considered. Otherwise, an IQ score may seriously underestimate the intellectual potential of a disadvantaged child or overestimate that of a child from an advantaged background (Laosa, 1996). An aptitude score may indeed be more objective than the subjective and biased opinion of a parent or teacher, but, despite efforts to make tests culture-free and accurate, problems with interpretation cannot be entirely eliminated. Especially when a low score leads to lower expectations, and therefore inferior education (as sometimes happens), the results may be a self-fulfilling prophecy (Rosenthal, 1996).

Our final criticism, however, is even more devastating, because if true, it applies to every child, from retarded to genius. We may have many intelligences, not just one, which would mean that the very idea of one test to measure intelligence is based on a false, and narrow, assumption.

Multiple Intelligences. A number of researchers stress that there are many kinds of abilities and many ways to demonstrate potential. Robert Sternberg (1996) describes three distinct types of intelligence: *academic* (measured by IQ and achievement tests), *creative* (evidenced by imaginative endeavors), and *practical* (seen in everyday interactions). In the usual academic test setting, according to Sternberg, the highly creative or practical child not only might fail to shine but might also become stressed and distracted.

Similarly, Howard Gardner (1983) describes seven distinct intelligences: linguistic, logical-mathematical, musical, spatial, body-kinesthetic, interpersonal (social-understanding), and intrapersonal (self-understanding).

Gardner's Seven Intelligences
- Linguistic
- Logical-Mathematical
- Musical
- Spatial
- Body-Kinesthetic
- Interpersonal (social-understanding)
- Intrapersonal (self-understanding)

Demonstration of High IQ? If North American intelligence tests truly reflect all the aspects of the mind, children would be considered mentally slow if they could not replicate the proper hand, arm, torso, and facial positions of a traditional dance, as this young Indonesian girl does brilliantly. She is obviously adept in kinesthetic and interpersonal intelligence. Given her culture, it would not be surprising if she were deficient in the logical mathematical intelligence required to use the Internet effectively or to surpass an American peer on a video game.

Gardner believes every normal person has at least a basic aptitude for all seven, but each of us is stronger in some than in others. For example, a person may be an able writer because of strong linguistic intelligence but may get lost easily when driving a car because spatial intelligence is fairly weak. Another person may paint extraordinarily revealing portraits because his or her spatial, body-kinesthetic, and social-understanding intelligences are strong but may have difficulty talking about the creative process owing to weaker language and self-understanding. If there are indeed many kinds of intelligence, the common assumption that children who are gifted in one area are gifted in all areas is likely to be false (Winner, 1996).

One implication of multiple intelligences is that when aptitude tests measure only linguistic and logical-mathematical ability, scores do not reflect the actual potential or skills that children possess. Ideally, children should develop all their intelligences and then demonstrate achievement in many ways (Gardner, 1991). Note that schools traditionally emphasize language and math, and this may explain why IQ tests are predictive of school achievement. However, such validation is circular. If intelligence is seen as the multifaceted jewel that Gardner believes it to be, schools will develop a broader curriculum so that every child can shine.

Tests of Accomplishment

Achievement tests are designed to measure actual learning—for example, how well a child reads, adds, or understands science concepts. To be effective, an achievement test must include questions of varying difficulty so that test scores differentiate among high-, average-, and low-achieving students. Achievement tests can be **norm-referenced,** in which scores are compared to the normal or typical score of a child with the same amount of schooling or the same background, or they can be **standards-based,** that is, measured against some objective benchmark of what should be learned.

For instance, the reading achievement of a fourth-grade boy in Denver, Colorado, might be compared to that of other fourth-graders in Denver, to that of other fourth-graders in the United States, or to that of other male schoolchildren of the same SES, age, or ethnicity. In all three cases, this is norm-referenced scoring, the first two with a norm based on school grade and the third with a norm based on sex and background. Alternatively, his score may be compared to a general standard, such as being able to read and understand a basic vocabulary of 20,000 words.

Most nationally used achievement tests are norm-referenced. By contrast, international comparisons usually are standards-based, measuring children against what a child that age "should" know. Ideally, achievement tests reveal not only what children have learned in a particular subject area

norm-referenced   A test or procedure that is assessed relative to a particular average or norm based on a group already tested. The norm is the average, but soon after a norm is set, performance tends to surpass it.

standards-based   A test or procedure that is assessed relative to a particular criterion or standard set in advance. For example, if the standard for keyboarding speed is set at 100 words a minute, the standard does not change even if everyone, or no one, achieves it.

❓ **Especially for Social Scientists:** Measuring all variables that comprise a good education is complex. Which research designs (from Chapter 1) would indicate whether a particular school provides a good education?

What Is Being Measured? The fourth-graders taking this standardized achievement test in Walnut Creek, Texas, are being tested on more than their reading ability and vocabulary. Also being tested, indirectly, are their reading vision at 20 inches, their hand-eye coordination for filling in the proper circle with a dark-enough mark, their ability to concentrate and keep from looking out the window or at their neighbors, and their ability to control their anxiety. Another important factor that is being unintentionally tested is the children's motivation to do well.

❷ *Observational Quiz (see answer page 392):* Looking at this photo, can you see any differences between the children who seem to be performing well on this achievement test and those who do not?

"Big deal, an A in math. That would be a D in any other country."

International Comparisons No nation can be first in everything, because national performance reflects cultural values. Recently, math and science achievement have become the standard of academic excellence.

Wobegon effect The tendency to view oneself, one's children, and one's culture as "above-average." Tests that are designed with norms for average scores quickly become ways to prove that some children are better than others.

but also what their specific weaknesses are so that the teachers can help the learners. Thus, a mathematics achievement test might show that a certain child has good computation skills but a poor understanding of graphs. Such information, compiled for an entire class, could guide the teacher in planning instruction as well as in providing individualized help to students.

This ideal is rarely met, however. More often, achievement tests are used to determine whether students will be promoted and how they are to be grouped into performance-based classes (perhaps one class each for high, average, and low achievers). Such tests are also sometimes used to evaluate the performance of individual teachers, schools, or school systems. This occurred in 1991, when an International Assessment of Educational Progress found that U.S. students tested in the 1980s scored substantially lower than students in Korea, Taiwan, Japan, the Soviet Union, Hungary, France, Canada, Switzerland, and Israel in both math and science (LaPointe et al., 1992). These results propelled many educators, parents, and political leaders to invest more effort and money in math and science. At the same time, the National Council of Teachers of Mathematics revamped the curriculum to fit the development potential of children. This meant the teachers taught strategies and teamwork, not rote memory. The results were dramatic, with U.S. achievement rising, especially at the fourth-grade level (see Figure 12.6).

This use of tests raises another concern, however. Teachers or school systems may narrow their instructional goals to focus only on the tasks measured by the tests (Armistead et al., 1992; Toch, 1991). As you now know, the mind of the school-age child is primed to learn whatever is emphasized within the school, family, and culture. Consequently, on norm-referenced tests, the score set as "average" quickly becomes surpassed by most of the children (a phenomenon called the **Wobegon effect,** named after the mythical Minnesota town where "all the women are strong, all the men are good-looking, and all the children are above-average").

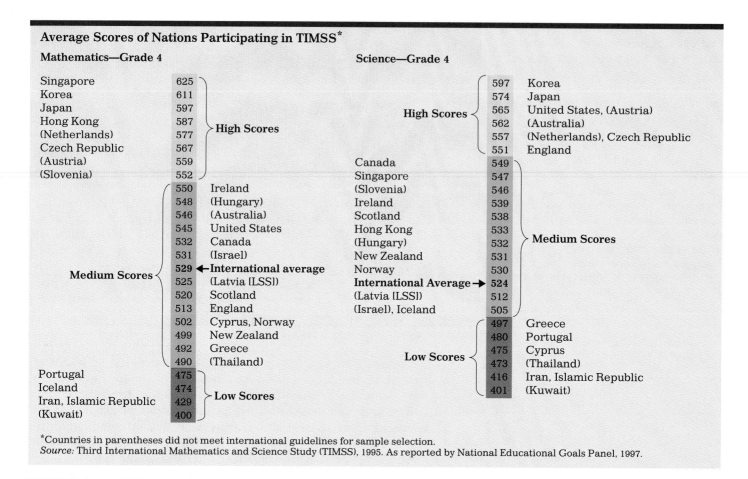

Average Scores of Nations Participating in TIMSS*

Mathematics—Grade 4

Singapore	625	
Korea	611	
Japan	597	
Hong Kong	587	High Scores
(Netherlands)	577	
Czech Republic	567	
(Austria)	559	
(Slovenia)	552	
	550	Ireland
	548	(Hungary)
	546	(Australia)
	545	United States
	532	Canada
	531	(Israel)
Medium Scores	529	←International average
	525	(Latvia [LSS])
	520	Scotland
	513	England
	502	Cyprus, Norway
	499	New Zealand
	492	Greece
	490	(Thailand)
Portugal	475	
Iceland	474	Low Scores
Iran, Islamic Republic	429	
(Kuwait)	400	

Science—Grade 4

High Scores	597	Korea
	574	Japan
	565	United States, (Austria)
	562	(Australia)
	557	(Netherlands), Czech Republic
	551	England
Canada	549	
Singapore	547	
(Slovenia)	546	
Ireland	539	
Scotland	538	
Hong Kong	533	Medium Scores
(Hungary)	532	
New Zealand	531	
Norway	530	
International Average →	524	
(Latvia [LSS])	512	
(Israel), Iceland	505	
	497	Greece
	480	Portugal
Low Scores	475	Cyprus
	473	(Thailand)
	416	Iran, Islamic Republic
	401	(Kuwait)

*Countries in parentheses did not meet international guidelines for sample selection.
Source: Third International Mathematics and Science Study (TIMSS), 1995. As reported by National Educational Goals Panel, 1997.

Figure 12.6 Math and Science Around the World: 1995. International exams are given every few years to a representative sample of children. The most recent series shows a marked improvement for the United States in math and science, especially at the fourth-grade level (shown here). Not shown are eighth- and twelfth-grade results, which are lower for the United States but higher for Canada and New Zealand.

❶ *Answer to Observational Quiz (from page 391):* The boys taking the test don't seem to be applying themselves as diligently as the girls. In fact, on national achievement tests, most of the lowest scoring children are boys. This has consequences later on: fewer boys enjoy school and go on to college—even though on aptitude tests they do as well as or better than girls.

Similar problems appear when a standards-based test is used, because whoever sets the standards affects the curriculum. When the need "to ensure a competitive workforce . . . to fill the jobs of the future and compete in a global economy" led the United States to set the goal of being first worldwide in math and science by the year 2000, most Americans probably agreed that this was a desirable achievement. But as math and science have become priorities, and scores continue to rise, what will happen in literacy and creativity, areas in which the United States has traditionally excelled? Already historians are bemoaning children's ignorance, such that only 32 percent of fourth-graders can name even one of the original 13 colonies (Hitchens, 1998). Music, art, and physical education have been cut back in almost every school.

School-age children, as the research shows, are able and eager to learn almost anything, but they cannot learn everything at once. Comparing nations, comparing schools, and comparing children on achievement tests helps show which educational strategies and curricula are successful, but another set of criteria is needed to suggest which should be emphasized.

Developmental Theory in the Classroom

As you have seen, school-age children are active learners, eager to master logical principles and learning strategies, as well as to develop academic

● **Response for Social Scientists (from page 390):** There are many right answers as long as you realize that single impressions are likely to be simplistic and that context is critical. You would use several methods, including naturalistic observation, multi-faceted testing, and some controlled experimentation in order to compare and evaluate the impact of several variables. A survey might not be appropriate, since cultural values, rather than objective analysis, affect students' opinions about the quality of their education. You certainly would want to study long-term results, ideally with a longitudinal study of outcomes.

skills and accumulate knowledge. Further, skills are most readily mastered through guided instruction and personal involvement. All this means that passive learning (such as sitting quietly and copying work from the chalkboard) and piecemeal learning (such as repetition and rote memorization of the sounds of the alphabet, the sums of simple numbers, or the names of the continents) are *not* the most appropriate means of instruction. Educators influenced by developmental theorists, particularly Piaget and Vygotsky, have concluded that the classroom should always be a busy place in which children's curiosity is met with the materials of discovery—coins to count, objects to measure, books to read.

More recently, the information-processing perspective has led to a reemphasis on explicit teacher-centered instruction. Such instruction was sometimes ignored in the excitement, generated by Piaget, of treating the child as a self-motivated explorer-scientist. However, with its emphasis on skills and the child's knowledge base, the information-processing viewpoint not only steers clear of Piaget's discovery methods but also avoids the workbooks and memorization of passive learning. Information-processing theorists stress the need for explicit, highly motivated instruction that gets students to use their selective attention and develop control processes.

An even more recent insight has been the recognition of the importance, as highlighted by Vygotsky, of social interaction in the classroom—not only between teacher and student but also among the children themselves (Karpov & Haywood, 1998). Numerous studies have shown that if classroom cooperation is encouraged classmates can draw each other into the zone of proximal development, expanding each other's knowledge

Who Is the Smart One Here? Research on child street vendors in Brazil, such as this boy in São Paulo, reveals that few have attended school but that most have quite advanced arithmetic skills, allowing them to divide per-item cost, subtract to determine change, and even convert currency of another nation into the Brazilian equivalent—adjusted for inflation. Other research confirms that school-age children use their cognitive capacities to master whatever their culture values or requires, including the social skills needed, in this case, to convince tourists to buy lemons.

as well as, and more often than, any one teacher can (Rogoff, 1990). An illustration of this is provided in Children Up Close, pages 394–395.

Schooling and Cultural Values

We will close this chapter with an example that again stresses the strong intellectual capacity of the school-age child, if experience and motivation are in place. Young Brazilian street vendors—all in middle childhood, with little formal education—did very poorly when given standard problems presented the way achievement tests usually present them (such as 420 + 80). When instead given oral problems involving fruit purchases and making change for a customer ("I'll take two coconuts that cost 40 cents apiece. Here's a five-dollar bill. What do I get back?"), they solved the problems far more quickly and successfully, often using unconventional but effective math strategies (Carraher et al., 1985,

INTERACTIVE TEACHING

Good teachers differ greatly in how they teach, what they teach, and what their educational goals are. Yet, worldwide, as classroom practice comes closer to developmental theory, teachers have become much more encouraging of children's efforts. Look for the similarities and differences in the two examples extracted below:

In a first grade classroom in central Tokyo, 6-year-old Shoji Itoh repeatedly jumped up from his seat during the reading lesson. Each time he shouted "baka yaro" (you're a jerk) at the teacher so loudly that it could be heard several classrooms away. Each time little Itoh yelled, Ms. Nakanishi went over to his seat, put her arm around him and pointed to the sentence currently being read out loud. The class read aloud, with intermittent outbursts from Itoh, for about 15 minutes. Then they began an activity called "collecting words." Up and down the rows, each of the 35 students named a favorite object in a picture projected on the front wall: Mrs. Nakanishi wrote each named object on the board.

When Itoh's turn came, he named "electric rice cooker." Ms. Nakanishi asked him to come to the front of the class, put her arm around him, and praised him extravagantly. "You are very smart . . . let's all clap for him. . . ." Itoh gave a theatrical bow to the class's applause and took his seat, beaming. [Lewis, 1996]

Halfway around the world, an American teacher uses some of the same techniques. It is the beginning of the school year, and there is a math problem to be solved. Specifically, "There are six runners on each team. There are two teams in the race. How many runners altogether?" The children have already worked in pairs to come up with the process for answering, called the "answer solution."

Teacher: Jack, what answer solution did you come up with?
Jack: Fourteen.

Teacher: Fourteen. How did you get that answer?
Jack: Because 6 plus 6 is 12. Two runners on two teams . . .

(Jack stops talking, puts his hands to the side of his face and looks down at the floor. Then he looks at the teacher and at his partner, Ann. He turns and faces the front of the room with his back to the teacher and mumbles inaudibly.)

Teacher: Would you please say that again. I didn't quite get the whole thing. You had—say it again please.
Jack: (Softly, still facing the front of the room) It's six runners on each team.
Teacher: Right.
Jack: (Turns to look at the teacher) I made a mistake. It's wrong. It should be twelve. *(He turns and faces the front of the room again.)*

(Jack's acute embarrassment . . . confounded the teacher's intention that the children should publicly express their thinking and, more generally, engage in mathematical practice characterized by conjecture, argument, and justification.)

Teacher: (Softly) Oh, okay. Is it okay to make a mistake?
Andrew: Yes.
Teacher: Is it okay to make a mistake, Jack?

1988). In other words, though seeming to lack the cognitive strategies necessary to solve arithmetic problems, these children had developed sophisticated math abilities. In fact, the price of the fruit they sold had to be recalculated daily, as wholesale prices varied with supply. These unschooled children mastered that math very well: their survival depended on it.

Further research in Brazil, on 4- to 14-year-olds with a broad range of living situations, confirms the special relationship of thinking and experience during middle childhood. The cognitive advantage of actually having

Jack: Yea.

Teacher: You bet it is. As long as you're in my class it is okay to make a mistake. Because I make them all the time, and we learn from our mistakes—a lot. Jack already figured out, "Ooops, I didn't have the right answer the first time" *(Jack turns and looks at the teacher and smiles),* but he kept working at it and he got it. [Cobb et al., 1993]

Educators have been criticized for swinging from harsh, dull, standards-based lessons to a warm, lax, nondirectional approach. These excerpts, different as they are, avoid both extremes. In both cases, the teacher saw something wrong and worked to correct it—getting one boy to conform to the group discipline and the other boy to find and correct an error. In both cases, the teacher used the other students as allies, rather than allowing antagonism. And finally, in both cases, the child's ego was protected, so, hopefully, he will want to learn again.

The first example was cited by an American educator who observed many Japanese classrooms. He was struck by the cultural emphasis on cooperation—not only in this instance but overall.

Teachers explained that disruptive children needed to strengthen their bonds to other children. What I saw as issues of control and misbehavior, teachers talked about as issues of community; they transformed any questions about discipline into discussions of the teacher-child bond and the bonds among children. [Lewis, 1996]

It is easy to ask if these teachers were misguided. Is the Japanese teacher rewarding disruption instead of controlling it? Is the American teacher downplaying accurate computation by not only allowing the student's mistake but emphasizing that she makes mistakes as well?

In both cases, the proof is in the results—not just in the apparent success for these two boys but also in careful research that finds that this interactive approach works well. For instance, in an extensive experiment on the development of reading skills, the teachers of 3,345 children in Hawaii were trained to follow a Vygotskian model that emphasized social interaction within the zone of proximal development. Instead of the usual practice of having students read silently to themselves, with the teacher then asking the entire class some simple comprehension questions, these teachers had groups of children read a paragraph aloud together, and then the children in each group discussed questions designed to deepen their comprehension (just as in the excerpts above, all the children were asked to name a favorite object or work in pairs to answer a math problem). Compared to a control group who received more conventional teaching within the same schools, the experimental children scored significantly higher on standard reading tests (Klein, 1988). A similar approach is being taken in many math classes, as workbooks, rote learning, and pure memorization are being replaced by instruction that involves hands-on materials, cooperative problem solving, and active discussion.

dealt with money was greatest for children age 6 to 11. Those who were younger were less able to understand the arithmetic problems as presented to them, and those who were older could do just as well without using their experience as a prop (Guberman, 1996). This is exactly what we might have predicted, based on the research in this chapter as well as on the theories of Piaget (remember, *concrete* operational thought) and Vygotsky (who emphasized the tools of culture that help children learn). The years of middle childhood are especially well suited for both teaching and learning.

SUMMARY

REMEMBERING, KNOWING, AND PROCESSING

1. Thinking processes of school-age children are quite different from those of younger children. An understanding of "the game of thinking" gives school-agers the ability to direct their thinking and to become more effective learners in formal settings such as a school classroom.

2. The information-processing approach looks specifically at how the person takes in, remembers, and processes new material. This approach, inspired by the computer, finds that working memory and control processes in particular advance in middle childhood.

3. A marked improvement occurs in children's ability to concentrate on the task at hand and ignore distractions. Cognitive improvement is also apparent in the strategies school-agers use for memorization and in their increased capacity for, and speed of, thinking. In addition, the knowledge base increases with each year of school, making it easier for new information to be assimilated.

4. Some of the advances in school-age thinking are the result of brain maturation For the most part, however, accumulated experience, motivated practice, and explicit instruction aid children to develop metacognitive skills.

CONCRETE OPERATIONAL THOUGHT

5. According to Piaget, after the 5-to-7 shift, children use the logical operations of concrete operational thought. They apply logical principles such as identity, reversibility, reciprocity, and classification to problems of conservation, mathematics, science, and social understanding.

6. While Piaget's theory captures some essential qualities of the development of 7- to 11-year-old children's reasoning, most developmentalists believe that older children are not as consistently logical or objective as his theory portrays. Further, sociocultural factors may have a considerable effect on cognitive development.

LANGUAGE

7. Language abilities continue to improve during middle childhood, partly because increased cognitive development makes it easier to acquire new vocabulary, understand difficult grammatical constructions, and use language appropriately in various everyday situations. Children successfully learn to switch codes, depending on the context and audience.

8. Teaching children a second language can be accomplished by a number of different methods, from total immersion in the new language to gradually increasing exposure over time. However, the most important factors seem to be a positive attitude, at home and in school, toward both the original language and the acquisition of the new one.

THINKING, LEARNING, AND SCHOOLING

9. A growing interest in individual and international differences in intellectual achievement in the school years accounts for the use of achievement and aptitude tests, including intelligence tests, for school-age children. Achievement tests index how much a child has learned, whereas aptitude tests measure cognitive potential.

10. Although tests of cognitive development are useful, and often less biased than evaluation by teacher and parents, many factors other than inherent ability are reflected in performance on aptitude and achievement tests. Researchers such as Howard Gardner argue that there are many more kinds of intelligence and ways to assess achievement than traditional tests reflect.

11. School-age children are active learners, which means that passive instruction is not the most appropriate means of teaching. Recent developmental research has shown the pedagogical benefits of greater classroom interaction, both between teachers and students and among the students themselves.

12. International comparisons reflect substantial variation in what and how school systems teach their children. Universally, however, children are eager and able to learn whatever their community considers important.

KEY TERMS

information-processing theory (365)
sensory register (366)
working memory (366)
long-term memory (366)
control processes (366)
selective attention (367)
automatization (368)
knowledge base (368)
metacognition (370)
storage strategies (371)
retrieval strategies (371)
concrete operational thought (372)
identity (372)
reversibility (372)
reciprocity (372)

classification (374)
class inclusion (374)
code-switching (378)
formal code (379)
informal code (379)
immersion (380)
English as a second language (ESL) (381)
bilingual education (381)
bilingual-bicultural education (381)
aptitude tests (385)
achievement tests (388)
IQ tests (388)
norm-referenced (390)
standards-based (390)
Wobegon effect (391)

KEY QUESTIONS

1. How does the information-processing approach analyze cognitive development?

2. What accounts for the better working memory of school-age children compared to that of younger children?

3. What factors account for the increase in cognitive processing speed and capacity during the school years?

4. How does an expanded knowledge base affect thinking and memorization?

5. How does metacognition enhance school-agers' thinking?

6. Describe several of Piaget's logical operations, or principles, that enhance reasoning during middle childhood.

7. How does vocabulary increase in middle childhood?

8. What are the chief characteristics of formal and informal language codes, and when is each type of code used?

9. Describe four strategies that are used in teaching a second language.

10. What does an IQ test measure?

11. What are some of the benefits and problems involved in the use of standardized achievement tests?

12. What do international comparisons reveal about the relative scholastic achievement of children?

13. What changes in teaching practices have resulted from the application of cognitive theory regarding middle childhood?

14. *In Your Experience* What was the best measure of your intellectual ability in childhood: your parents' and teachers' opinions, your scores on tests, or the evaluation of your peers? Why?

CRITICAL THINKING EXERCISE

by Richard O. Straub

Now that you have read and reviewed Chapter 12, take your learning a step further by testing your critical thinking skills on this perspective-taking exercise:

Few controversies have so divided educators and parents as the controversy concerning international variations in the academic performance of schoolchildren. Until recently, such variations were not troubling, because each culture's educational system reflected deeply seated traditions and values. In recent years, however, concerns among American educators, developmentalists, and parents have intensified, with some suggesting that lengthening the school year would improve the performance of American students.

There are two opposing viewpoints on whether the school year should be lengthened. Those who advocate this position point to the gap in standardized test scores between American students and those from Pacific Rim countries. Others dispute the argument that equalizing the amount of time in school will solve the problem, claiming that greater time in school is not the primary basis of the high achievement of Asian children.

Before answering the questions below, review the material in the chapter under the heading "Thinking, Learning, and Schooling," starting on page 384.

LENGTHENING THE SCHOOL YEAR

1. Find two pieces of evidence *supporting* the argument that the school year should be lengthened.

a. _____

_____

b. _____

_____

2. Find two pieces of evidence *challenging* the viewpoint that the school year should be lengthened.

a. _____

_____

b. _____

_____

3. Which side of the argument do *you* find more convincing? Explain your reasoning.

_____

_____

_____

Check your progress on becoming a critical thinker by comparing your answers to the sample answers in Appendix B.

The School Years:
Psychosocial Development

At age 6 or so, children break free from the closely supervised and limited arena of the younger child. Usually with their parents' blessing, school-age children explore the wider world of neighborhood, community, and school. They experience new vulnerability, increasing competence, ongoing friendships, troubling rivalries, and deeper social understanding.

However, although they often are unobserved by adults, their lives are still shaped by family structures and community values. Our goal in this chapter is to examine the interplay between expanding freedom and guiding forces. First we will look at emotional and moral growth, then at the peer and family configurations that direct and propel that growth, and, finally, at the coping strategies and personal strengths that enable most children to move forward, ready for the adolescence.

AN EXPANDING SOCIAL WORLD

Throughout the world, school-age children are noticeably more independent, more responsible, and more capable than younger children. This increased competence is recognized by parents and schools, in research results, and in every developmental theory.

Theories of School-Age Development

Freud describes middle childhood as the period of *latency*, during which children's emotional drives are quieter, their psychosexual needs are repressed, and their unconscious conflicts are submerged. This makes latency "a time for acquiring cognitive skills and assimilating cultural values as children expand their world to include teachers, neighbors, peers, club leaders, and coaches" (Miller, 1993).

Erikson (1963) agrees with Freud that middle childhood is a quiet period emotionally, a period in which the child "becomes ready to apply himself to given skills and tasks." During Erikson's crisis of **industry versus inferiority,** children busily try to master whatever their culture values. On the basis of their degree of success, they judge themselves as either industrious or inferior or, in other words, competent or incompetent, productive or failing, winners or losers.

Developmentalists influenced by learning theory, by the cognitive perspective, or by the sociocultural perspective are concerned with the step-by-step acquisition of new skills (learning theory), self-understanding (cognitive

Celebrating Spring No matter where they live, 7- to 11-year-olds seek to understand and develop whatever skills are valued by their culture. They do so in active, industrious ways, as described in cognitive, learning, sociocultural, and psychoanalytic theories. This universal truth is illustrated here, as four friends in Assam, northeastern India, usher in spring with a Bihu celebration. Soon they will be given sweets and tea, which is the sociocultural validation of their energy, independence, and skill.

industry versus inferiority The fourth of Erikson's eight crises of psychosocial development, in which school-age children attempt to master many skills and develop a sense of themselves as either industrious and competent or incompetent and inferior.

5-to-7 shift The rapid change in intellectual and social competence that many children experience between ages 5 and 7.

social cognition A person's awareness and understanding of human personality, motives, emotions, intentions, and interactions.

perspective), or social awareness (sociocultural perspective). The overview from these three theories is quite similar to that from psychoanalytic theory: during middle childhood children meet the challenges of the outside world with an openness, insight, and confidence that few younger children possess. The abilities to learn, to analyze, to express emotions, and to make friends now come together, forming a stronger, unified, and more self-assured personality. Children now have the potential to master many social and practical skills.

From an epigenetic systems perspective, the school-agers' new independence is the result of the need, within the species, to free parental efforts so that they may be focused on the younger children and to accustom school-age children to their peers and the adults in the wider community. Responding to genetic mechanisms, the brain and body of the child reach a level of maturation that allows much greater intellectual focus (what we called selective attention in Chapter 12), rationality (concrete operational thought), physical hardiness (slowed growth and increased strength), and motor skill. Developmentalists, noting the leap forward at the beginning of the school years, consider it part of the **5-to-7 shift,** the rapid change that enables the child to participate in the wider social world with a safety not previously possible (Sameroff & Haith, 1996). Accordingly, cultures throughout history have selected about age 6 as the time for more independence and responsibility, from attending first grade to having first communion, from doing significant chores at home to facing major challenges at school. (See Chapter 12 for more on the 5-to-7 shift and cognitive development.)

Understanding Others

The emotional development of school-age children depends on advances in **social cognition,** that is, in understanding the social world. In their simple theory of mind, children younger than 5 begin to realize that other people are motivated by thoughts and emotions that differ from their own. But the preschoolers' early theorizing is prone to error, because their grasp of other viewpoints is quite limited and fragile.

In contrast, during the school years theory of mind evolves into a complex, multifaceted perspective. Cognitive advances allow children to understand that human behavior is not simply a response to specific thoughts or desires. Instead, they see behavior as actions that are influenced—simultaneously—by a variety of needs, emotions, relationships, and motives (Arsenio & Kramer, 1992; McKeough, 1992).

For example, a preschooler who was told to stop getting into fights with his friends said he couldn't help it because sometimes the fight "just crawled out of me." By contrast, school-age children know what leads to the fights—and what might follow if they choose to fight back. They judge where, when, why, and with whom to fight, according to this new, deeper understanding.

The development of social understanding was demonstrated in a simple study in which children between the ages of 4 and 10 were shown pictures of various domestic situations and asked how the mother might respond and why (Goldberg-Reitman, 1992). In one picture, for example, a child curses while playing with blocks. As you can see in the following typical responses, the 4-year-olds focused only on the immediate behavior, whereas the older children recognized the implications and possible consequences:

> *4-year-old:* "The mother spanks her because she said a naughty word."
> *6-year-old:* "The mother says 'Don't say that again' because it's not nice to say a bad word."
> *10-year-old:* "The mother maybe hits her or something because she's trying to teach her . . . because if she grew up like that she'd get into a lot of trouble . . . she might get a bad reputation."   (Goldberg-Reitman, 1992)

Similar research studies and everyday experience tell us that younger children are likely to focus solely on observable behavior—not on motives, feelings, or social consequences. They know when an adult might protect, nurture, scold, or teach a child, but not why. Older children add three more elements:

- They understand the motivation and origin of various behaviors.
- They can analyze the future impact of whatever action a person might take.
- They recognize personality traits and use them to predict a person's future reactions. (Gnepp & Chilamkurti, 1988)

During the school years, moreover, children realize that someone can feel several emotions simultaneously (and can thus have conflicting or ambivalent feelings). They also realize that people sometimes disguise their emotions to comply with social rules (such as looking delighted after opening a disappointing gift) (Thompson, 1994).

Read Their Expressions This girl seems hesitant to proceed, perhaps in anticipation of getting a cold shock. However, because of the expanded emotional understanding that is typical of school-age children, she probably realizes that if she stalls much longer, she is bound to get teased. This greater emotional understanding may also help her to control her anxiety long enough for her to take the plunge.

❓ *Observational Quiz (see answer page 402): What gender differences do you see?*

Understanding Themselves

As a result of their new social cognition, children can better manage their own emotions. They can mentally distract themselves to avoid becoming fidgety during a boring concert, for example, or can look attentive in class even when they are not paying attention.

They can even mask or alter inborn tendencies. For example, a group of 7-year-olds looked at videotapes of themselves being shy at age 2. Most were distressed to see how timid they had once been, but few still acted shy. Many said they had learned to understand themselves and adjust their timidity. As one explained, "I was a total idiot then [but] I learned a lot of new stuff, so now I'm not as scared as I was when I was a baby . . . I've gotten older and I don't want to be embarrassed" (Fox et al., 1996).

The Rising Tide of Self-Doubt

School-age children begin to measure themselves in terms of a variety of competencies. They might, for example, realize they are weak at playing sports, okay at playing a musical instrument, and a whiz at playing Nintendo. Similarly, they might feel that they are basically good at making friends but that they have a quick temper that sometimes jeopardizes their friendships.

Increased self-understanding comes at a price. Self-criticism rises and self-esteem dips. Children evaluate themselves through **social comparison,** comparing their skills and achievements with those of others (Pomerantz et al., 1995). They accept and use the standards set by parents, teachers, and peers and then look at their own actual behavior (not at imaginary, rosy self-evaluation as preschoolers do) (Grolnick et al., 1997). This means that older

social comparison The tendency to assess one's abilities, achievements, social status, and the like, by measuring them against those of others, especially those of one's peers.

What Is She Saying? An outsider, or even an elder of this tribe, might see all these girls as dressed magnificently, in appropriate style. But knowing schoolchildren, we can surmise that the girl on the left, with the red and yellow vest, may be criticizing the blue dress of the girl beside her. Almost every schoolgirl worries about her attire and sometimes tells her mother, in tears or anger, "I'm never wearing this again."

children are more likely to feel personally at fault for their shortcomings and less likely to blame luck or someone else. Further, as they compare themselves to others, "children become increasingly concerned about self-presentation" (Merrell & Gimpel, 1998), with other children becoming more important critics than parents or teachers.

The age changes are illustrated by these two self-descriptions:

Four-year-old. My name is Jason and I live in a big house with my mother and father and sister, Lisa. I have a kitty that's orange and a television in my own room. I know all of my A B C's, listen: A, B, C, D, E, F, G, H, J, L, K, O, M, P, Q, X, Z. I can run faster than anyone! I like pizza and I have a nice teacher. I can count up to 100, want to hear me? I love my dog, Skipper. I can climb to the top of the jungle gym, I'm no scared! Just happy. You can't be happy *and* scared, no way! I have brown hair and I go to preschool. I'm really strong. I can lift this chair, watch me! [Harter, 1996]

Eight-year-old. I'm in third grade this year, and pretty popular, at least with the girls. That's because I'm nice and helpful and can keep secrets. Most of the boys at school are pretty yukky. I don't feel that way about my little brother Jason, although he does get on my nerves. I love him but at the same time, he also does things that make me mad. But I control my temper, I'd be ashamed of myself if I didn't. At school, I'm feeling pretty smart in certain subjects: Language Arts and Social Studies. I got A's in these subjects on my last report card and was really proud of myself. But I'm feeling pretty dumb in Arithmetic and Science, particularly when I see how well the other kids are doing. Even though I'm not doing well in those subjects, I still like myself as a person, because Arithmetic and Science just aren't that important to me. How I look and how popular I am are more important. [Harter, 1996]

It is obvious that younger children identify with their preferences, possessions, and family members, whereas older children can look at themselves, including their self-control, moral values, emotional traits, strengths, and weaknesses.

❶ *Answer to Observational Quiz (from page 401): All the girls look distressed, but the boys do not. The girls also seem more likely to cover their bodies, a recognition of their problems with social comparison, self-esteem, and gender norms that often accompany middle childhood. The boys may be unaffected by such problems or may have already learned to appear tough.*

MORAL DEVELOPMENT

Awareness of other people's standards and opinions leads to advances in moral development. Of course, the development of moral values begins early and continues throughout the life span. Childhood, however, is the time when moral values are taught, ethical principals are tested, and religious beliefs are laid down. It also is a time when the various parts of the brain—emotional and intellectual—become better connected, enabling children to think through their instinctive reactions, setting moral values and then acting on them:

> It's a real passion for them. . . . In elementary school, maybe as never before or afterward, given favorable family and neighborhood circumstances, the child becomes an intensely moral creature, quite interested in figuring out the reasons of this world: how and why things work, but also, how and why he or she should behave in various situations. [Coles, 1997]

These two aspects of moral development, thinking and acting, are intertwined. To analyze them we will separate them, looking first at cognition, then at behavior.

Kohlberg's Stages of Moral Thinking

Building on Piaget's theories and research, Lawrence Kohlberg (1963, 1981) studied moral reasoning by presenting subjects with a set of ethical dilemmas. Responses to several scenarios allowed Kohlberg to describe how people reasoned about situations that demanded moral judgments. The most famous story involves the conflict between private property and human life as experienced by Heinz, a poor man whose wife is dying of cancer. A local pharmacist has developed the only cure, a drug sold for thousands of dollars—far more than Heinz can pay and 10 times what the drug costs to make:

> Heinz went to everyone he knew to borrow the money, but he could only get together about half of what it cost. He told the druggist that his wife was dying and asked him to sell it cheaper or let him pay later. But the druggist said "no." The husband got desperate and broke into the man's store to steal the drug for his wife. Should the husband have done that? Why? [Kohlberg, 1963]

In people's responses to such dilemmas, Kohlberg found three levels of moral reasoning—**preconventional**, **conventional**, and **postconventional**—with two stages at each level (see Table 13.1 on page 404).

According to Kohlberg, *how* people reason, rather than what specific moral conclusions they reach, determines their stage of moral development. For example, reasoning that seeks social approval (stage 3) might produce opposite conclusions: either Heinz should steal the drug (because people will blame him for not saving his wife) or he should not steal it (because people would call him a thief if he stole). But in both cases, the underlying moral precept is the same—that people should behave in ways that earn the praise of others.

In every stage, what counts for Kohlberg is the thinking that results in the person's responses. Children, adolescents, and adults gradually move up the hierarchy, reasoning at a more advanced stage as time goes on. Generally, during middle childhood, children's answers are at the first two levels—primarily preconventional for younger children and conventional for older ones—although much depends on the specific context and on the child's opportunity to discuss moral issues.

Kohlberg's Critics

Kohlberg's moral-stages theory was welcomed by many developmentalists who sought to understand and measure moral thinking. Over the past two decades, however, his theory has met with substantial criticism. For example, some critics suggest that Kohlberg's dilemmas and hierarchy, with their

preconventional moral reasoning
Kohlberg's term for the first level (stages one and two) of moral thinking, in which the individual reasons in terms of his or her own welfare.

conventional moral reasoning
Kohlberg's term for the second level (stages three and four) of moral thinking, in which the individual considers social standards and laws to be the primary arbiters of moral values.

postconventional moral reasoning
Kohlberg's term for the third and highest level (stages five and six) of moral thinking, in which the individual follows moral principles that may supersede the standards of society or the wishes of the individual.

table **13.1**	**Kohlberg's Three Levels and Six Stages of Moral Reasoning**

Level I: Preconventional Moral Reasoning
Emphasis is placed on getting rewards and avoiding punishments; this is a self-centered level.

- *Stage One: Might makes right* (a punishment and obedience orientation). The most important value is obedience to authority, so as to avoid punishment while still advancing self-interest.
- *Stage Two: Look out for number one* (an instrumental and relativist orientation). Each person tries to take care of his or her own needs. The reason to be nice to other people is so that they will be nice to you.

Level II: Conventional Moral Reasoning
Emphasis is placed on social rules; this is a community-centered level.

- *Stage Three: "Good girl" and "nice boy."* Proper behavior is now behavior that pleases other people. Social approval is more important than any specific reward.
- *Stage Four: "Law and order."* Proper behavior means being a dutiful citizen and obeying the laws set down by society.

Level III: Postconventional Moral Reasoning
Emphasis is now on moral principles; this level is centered on ideals.

- *Stage Five: Social contract.* One should obey the rules of society because they exist for the benefit of all and are established by mutual agreement. If the rules become destructive, however, or if one party doesn't live up to the agreement, the contract is no longer binding.
- *Stage Six: Universal ethical principles.* General universal principles, and not individual situations or community practices, determine right and wrong. Ethical values (such as "Life is sacred") are established by individual reflection and may contradict the egocentric or legal values of earlier stages.

"philosophical emphasis on justice and psychological emphasis on reasoning," are too narrow and restrictive (Walker et al., 1995).

Others believe that Kohlberg's level III (stages 5 and 6) reflects only liberal, Western intellectual values. In many non-Western nations and among many non-Western ethnic groups within Western cultures, the good of the family, the well-being of the community, and/or adherence to religious tradition takes moral precedence over all other considerations (Wainryb & Turiel, 1995). This makes it harder for non-Westerners to score at Kohlberg's postconventional level.

Gender Differences in Moral Thinking.   Carol Gilligan (1982) has raised the most telling criticism. She contends that Kohlberg overlooks significant differences in the way males and females view moral dilemmas, in part because his original research used only boys as subjects. Gilligan explains that females develop a **morality of care** more than a **morality of justice.** The morality of care makes girls and women reluctant to judge right and wrong in absolute terms (justice) because they are socialized to be nurturant, compassionate, and nonjudgmental (caring).

As an example, Gilligan cites the responses of two bright 11-year-olds, Jake and Amy, to the Heinz story. Jake considered the dilemma "sort of like a math problem with humans," and he set up an equation that showed that life is more important than property. Amy, on the other hand, seemed to sidestep the issue, arguing that Heinz "really shouldn't steal the drug—but his wife shouldn't die either." She tried to find an alternative solution (a bank loan, perhaps) and then explained that stealing wouldn't be right because Heinz "might have to go to jail, and then his wife might get sicker again, and he couldn't get more of the drug."

morality of care   Moral thought and behavior based on comparison, nurturance, and concern for the well-being of other people. This morality is said to be more common among girls and women.

morality of justice   Moral thought and behavior based on depersonalized standards of right and wrong, with judgments based on abstractions, not relationships. This morality is said to be more common among boys and men.

Amy's response may seem just as ethical as Jake's, but Kohlberg would score it lower. Gilligan argues that this is unfair, because what appears to be females' moral weakness—their hesitancy to take a definitive position based on abstract moral premises—is, in fact,

> inseparable from women's moral strength, an overriding concern with relationships and responsibilities. The reluctance to judge may itself be indicative of the care and concern that infuse the psychology of women's development. [Gilligan, 1982]

Many researchers have tested Gilligan's ideas with children, by looking for a morality of care or a morality of justice. Some have found that school-age children (both boys and girls) are more likely to seek justice, whereas more mature subjects tend to show caring (Walker, 1988). Others have found just the opposite (Garrod & Beal, 1993).

In one study, the moral dilemma presented was not Kohlberg's but a fable about a family of moles who invite a lonely and cold porcupine to share their underground home for the winter. He accepts, but then the moles realize that the porcupine's size and quills make them very uncomfortable. They politely ask him to leave, but he refuses. What to do? One 8-year-old was very caring:

> They should all go on an expedition for marshmallows and stick the marshmallows on the porcupine's quills and then the moles will really, really, really not get pricked. Then the porcupine would be happy because he could live in the moles' house that suited him just fine and the moles could have tasty tidbits as well as a warm home because of the porcupine's body heat . . . and all would be happy. [Garrod, 1993]

By contrast, law and order were evident in another response:

> The central problem, as I see it, is that the moles want the porcupine to leave and he's refusing. I think that they should kick him out. They were nice to let him in in the first place. And it's not their fault that he has quills. They have a right to be comfortable in their own home . . . they can do what they want in their cave. It's like if a homeless man moved into my home while my family was vacationing in Florida. We'd definitely call the police. [Garrod, 1993]

Both these respondents were boys. Thus, in this research (and in other research involving the actual responses and actions of school-age children) there is no clear gender distinction regarding the morality of justice or the morality of care. However, all the researchers agree that moral dilemmas

Prosocial Behavior: Two Versions School-age children, such as this Girl Scout and these Habitat builders, are able to perform many useful prosocial tasks. Although prosocial acts are performed without expectation of rewards, they can result in a very important benefit: a sense of connection. The adults' role is to find suitable prosocial activities—not always an easy task because children don't always feel comfortable "helping." These boys, for instance, might not enjoy wearing a uniform and chatting with the elderly, but they certainly take pride in pounding nails with their friends.

are provocative issues for school-age children: these children have opinions, and they like to express them. Almost all researchers also agree that abstract reasoning about the justice of hypothetical situations is not the only, or necessarily the best, way to measure moral judgment. What children actually do when they personally care about an issue is crucial.

Moral Behavior

How do children learn to act morally, choosing what to do and then actually doing it? As we have seen, during middle childhood children are passionately concerned with issues of right and wrong. Overall, these are the

> years of eager, lively searching on the part of children, whose parents and teachers are often hard put to keep up with them as they try to understand things, to figure them out, but also to weigh the rights and wrongs of this life. This is the time for growth of the moral imagination, fueled constantly by the willingness, the eagerness of children to put themselves in the shoes of others. [Coles, 1997]

prosocial behavior Any act, such as sharing, cooperating, or sympathizing, performed to benefit other people without the expectations of reward for oneself.

If a family and culture are conscientious about providing children with guided participation in their set of values, with both adult and child undertaking moral actions, school-age children learn and, eventually, behave accordingly (Goodnow, 1997). **Prosocial behavior**—acts of sharing, helping, and caring—is learned in much the same way that antisocial behavior is, from parents, schools, and peers (Eisenberg et al., 1996).

Cultural Variations and Children's Choices

Few children *always* follow their parents' moral standards, their culture's conventions, or their own best moral thinking; yet moral thought has a decided influence on children's actions (Eisenberg, 1986; Rest, 1983). (See Children Up Close, page 407.) Increasingly, as they grow older, children try to figure out their own standards of what is the "right" thing to do, and they feel guilt and ashamed when they do "wrong," even if no one else knows (Harter, 1996).

For example, when children were asked whether they would break a law to help their siblings or peers, the answer was almost always "yes." In general, school-age children considered loyalty to siblings or peers—especially to a close friend—a compelling reason to ignore community standards of proper action. Many children said they would cheat, lie, or steal to help a needy friend (Smetana et al., 1991; Turiel et al., 1991).

And, indeed, many children do so. Lying to a teacher to cover for a friend's misdeeds not only is common but is admired as prosocial by the society of children. That such actions are not thoughtless but involve moral decisions is underscored by research that shows that children are quite aware of the laws of the land, family rules, and personal choices and know when they choose one over the other (Turiel et al., 1991).

In one study, 10-year-olds (but not 6-year-olds) were convinced that stealing an eraser is a more serious transgression than wearing pajamas to school; stealing is wrong, they said, while clothing is simply a custom. However, the 10-year-olds also admitted that, personally, they would be more likely to steal than to dress inappropriately (Turiel, 1983)!

In another study, school-age children from India and the United States were asked about the seriousness of various behaviors. Children from both

Give Peace a Chance The setting is Israel; the sheep washers include Jews and Muslims. In all probability, these boys are aware that their cooperative efforts are in accord with moral values and contrary to the social customs prevailing around them. The school years are a good time to teach children about other races and cultures, a lesson best learned through personal experience.

CHALLENGING THE ADULTS

As a mother of four, teaching moral thinking and behavior is very important to me. I have often said that I would rather have my children become loving and caring adults than become successful and rich—although I take great pride in their successes. It is not surprising, then, that they also pay attention to moral issues, sometimes taking actions that are not the ones I would choose.

For example, my daughter Sarah regularly gives her pocket money to homeless people and is quick to criticize me for rudely (her word) passing them by. The strength of her conviction was illustrated years ago when her fourth-grade class visited the local police precinct in New York City to hear an officer instruct them on street safety. Most of his talk was accepted without protest, until:

Officer: "Never take money out of your pocket while you are on the street—

(At this point, according to the mother who helped chaperone the school trip, Sarah raised her hand insistently, "the way children do who have to go to the bathroom right away.")

Officer: (Interrupting his speech) Yes?

Sarah: But what if a homeless man wants money?
Officer: Your parents give you money for lunch, not to give away.
Sarah: But what if you decide you don't need lunch?
Officer: You should not give money to beggars; you don't know how they will spend it.
Sarah: But what if you decide he really really needs it?
Officer: Don't give it. Adults are taking care of the homeless people who really need help.
Sarah: (Shaking her head) Well, you aren't doing a very good job.

That incident made me proud, as the mother who telephoned me to report it knew it would.

Although I still disagree about the most moral response to street beggars, I appreciate at least one aspect of this incident. Sarah's active sense of morality bodes well. Children who engage in moral discussion and feel personally responsible for their ethical behavior tend to be more accomplished than others, socially as well as academically (Bandura et al., 1996). Active reflection is much more likely to lead to moral action than is merely accepting social conventions and laws.

cultures agreed that it was wrong to break a promise, destroy another's picture, or kick harmless animals, and said that they themselves did not do these things. However, consistent with their cultural and religious beliefs, children from India believed that eating beef, addressing one's father by his first name, and cutting one's hair or eating chicken after a father's death were far worse violations than did American children. By contrast, American children believed that inflicting serious corporal punishment and eating dinner with one's hands were more serious offenses than did children in India (Schweder et al., 1990).

Because cultural and religious values shape moral perception, what is merely conventional in a particular culture may take on moral significance for children (Gabennesch, 1990; Schweder, 1990). Children behave in accordance with their moral beliefs, nurtured by family, school, and especially the society formed by their own friends, and they continue those patterns when they are grown. Many middle-aged and older adults obey conventions they learned when young, finding it hard to readjust moral behavior.

THE PEER GROUP

peer group A group of individuals of roughly the same age and social status who play, work, or learn together.

Perhaps the most influential system in which the school-age child develops his or her self-concept is the **peer group**—a group of individuals of roughly the same age and social status who play, work, or learn together. The increasing contact with peers leads to an increasing sense of self-competence

❓ **Especially for Parents:** Suppose you are the parent of an 8-year-old, wondering if you should make your child come home immediately after school and socialize only with family members because you are worried that peer pressure might lead your child into trouble. What should you do?

(Feiring & Lewis, 1989; Vandell & Hembree, 1994). Most developmental researchers consider getting along with peers to be a crucial social skill during middle childhood (although parents and teachers do not always agree) (Merrell & Gimpel, 1998). Indeed, some think peers are the deciding influence on children (Harris, 1998).

There is an important developmental progression here. Preschool children have friends and learn from playmates, of course, but they are more egocentric and hence slower to use social comparison. At the other end of childhood, teenagers typically identify with the opinions of one group and reject those of another. In middle childhood, however, children tend to be concerned with the judgment of the entire group of classmates. They become more dependent on each other, not only for companionship but also for self-validation and advice. One reason is that peer relationships, unlike adult-child relationships, involve partners who must learn to negotiate, compromise, share, and defend themselves as equals (Hartup, 1996).

The Society of Children

society of children The social culture of children, including the games, vocabulary, dress codes, and rules of behavior that characterize their interactions.

When school-age children play together, they develop patterns of interaction that are distinct from those of adult society and culture. Accordingly, some social scientists call the peer group the **society of children,** highlighting the fact that children create their own subculture, which is firmly in place by age 10 or so.

Children's Games One expression of the society of children is its play behavior, including the rules, rituals, and chants of hide-and-seek, kick the can, and, as shown here, jump-rope and stickball. Double-dutch skills and jumping rhymes, as well as rules for choosing teams and leaders, are passed down from slightly older children to younger ones, with each new cohort likely to put its own distinctive twist on both. Sex segregation is typical during the school years, with "No boys [girls] allowed" a common rule.

The society of children typically has special norms, vocabulary, rituals, and rules of behavior that flourish without the approval, or even the knowledge, of adults. Its slang words and nicknames are often ones adults would frown on (if they understood them), and its activities—such as hanging out at the mall, playing games in the meadow, or long, meandering phone conversations—do not invite adult participation (Zarbatany et al., 1990). Its dress codes become known to parents only when they try to get their son or daughter to wear something that violates those codes—as when a perfectly fine pair of hand-me-down jeans is rejected because, by the norms of the society of children, they are an unfashionable color, with the wrong label, unusual zipper, legs that are too loose, too tight, too short, too long, too flared, too baggy, and so on.

Many of the norms and rules of the peer group implicitly encourage independence from adults, and some go even further, requiring distance from adult society. By age 10, if not before, children (especially boys) whose parents kiss them in public are pitied ("momma's boy"), whose teachers favor them are teased (teacher's pet"), and who betray other children to adults are despised ("tattle-tale," "snitch," "rat").

Friendship

While acceptance by the entire peer group is valued, personal friendship is even more important. Indeed, if they had to choose "popular but friendless," or "close friends, but unpopular," most children would take the friends. Such a choice is consistent with developmentalists' view of the importance of friendship to children's overall psychosocial development and self-esteem (Hartup, 1996; Parker & Asher, 1993).

No One Sleeps at a Slumber Party Between the preschool and teenage years children use friendship groups to share secrets, learn skills, and build self-esteem. While most of these girls still have hair ribbons, stuffed animals, and the pajamas of children, all attention is focused on the hallmarks of adolescence—new hairstyles and junk food (popcorn with butter and salt, and soda with sugar and caffeine).

Because friendship is so important to them, children spend a good deal of time thinking about it (Bukowski et al., 1996). As a result, their understanding of friendship becomes increasingly abstract and complex. Children learn to balance self-revelation with self-protectiveness, mutual dependence with a respect for independence, competition with cooperation, and shared conversation with joint activities (Berndt, 1989; Rawlins, 1992). At the same time, school-agers perceive their friends in psychologically richer ways, partly because they now understand their own personalities better (Parker & Gottman, 1989).

People of all ages believe that friends are people who do things together and can be counted on for help. However, younger children will say that their friends helped *them*, whereas older children and adults stress the *mutuality* of friendship, with trust and loyalty as key components. This difference implies "a major change in friendship values" during middle childhood (Merrell & Gimpel, 1998). For example, in one study children were asked, "How do you know your best friend?" A typical kindergartner answered:

> I sleep over at his house sometimes. When he's playing ball with his friends he'll let me play. When I sleep over, he lets me get in front of him in 4-squares [a playground game]. He likes me. [Berndt, 1981]

By contrast, a typical sixth-grader said:

> If you can tell each other things that you don't like about each other. If you get in a fight with someone else, they'd stick up for you. If you can tell them your phone number and they don't give you crank calls. If they don't act mean to you when other kids are around. [Berndt, 1981]

As suggested by the sixth-grader's account, older children increasingly regard friendship as a forum for self-disclosure and expect that their intimacy will be reciprocated and protected (Rotenberg & Sliz, 1988). Partly because friendships become intense and more intimate, older children demand more of their friends, change friends less often, find it harder to make new friends, and are more upset when a friendship breaks up. They also are more picky: they tend to choose best friends whose interests, values, and backgrounds are similar to their own. In fact, from ages 3 to 13, close friendships increasingly involve children of the same sex, age, ethnicity, and socioeconomic status. When friendships across age, sex, ethnic, or

⚠ **Response for Parents (from page 408):**
Children need friends at school, to develop social skills and self-esteem. Accordingly, you need to let your child play with classmates, either in after-school activities or by inviting friends to your house. If you are really concerned about bad influences from school, you might want to encourage some friendships more than others, network with other parents, or, if necessary, find another school. But don't disallow friendship.

SES lines flourish, they are based on a common need, interest, or personality trait (Hartup, 1996). Generally, however, having a best friend who is not the same age or sex correlates with being rejected or ignored by one's classmates and being unhappy (Kovacs et al., 1996). Having no friend at all, of course, is worse (Bukowski et al., 1996).

As children become more choosy, they have fewer friends. Whereas most 4-year-olds say they have many friends (perhaps everyone in their nursery school class, with one or two specific exceptions), most 8-year-olds have a small circle of friends. And by age 10, children often have one "best" friend to whom they are quite loyal. This trend toward fewer but closer friends is followed by both sexes, but it is more apparent among girls. Boys tend to emphasize group identity and loyalty, "using the group in their quest for recognition and self-esteem while they jockey for position within the group." By contrast, girls form smaller networks and then are more concerned about being excluded from the small circle (Bukowski et al., 1996). By the end of middle childhood, many girls have one, and only one, best friend on whom they depend (Gilligan et al., 1990).

Aggression

Among the most important norms of the peer group are those that govern playful and nonplayful aggression—the teasing, insulting, and physical threatening that are at the edge of many episodes of children's social interaction. The social norms of the school years require that children deftly anticipate and defend themselves against sarcastic comments, implied insults, or direct verbal or physical attacks. If they do not, they risk isolation from their peers, especially if they rely on adult intervention. "Tell the teacher" is good advice for the 4-year-old; it may not be for the 8-year-old.

Following Social Rules This argument in a school yard is not just a fight between two boys but a sociocultural event.

⚠ *Observational Quiz (see answer page 412):* *What can you see in the behavior of these four boys that suggests that they are aware of the rules of such confrontations?*

The specifics regarding when aggression is appropriate, in what forms, and to what degree depend on the particular society of children (DeRosier et al., 1994; Foster et al., 1996). A study in England, for example, found that the children who were most accepted "gave as much as they got," sometimes teasing and mocking each other and—girls as well as boys—coming to blows. In fact, reciprocity of aggression was such an important element of peer-group popularity that those who suffered attack without retaliating were rejected as "piss weak." Limits on aggression are also important. In this study, most school-age children were quite critical of "getting the snobs, getting the cranks, . . . lying, showing off, getting too full of yourself, posing . . . wanting everything your way, being spoilt." (Davies, 1982).

Additional research indicates that many boys, especially those from minority groups in the United States, view quick response as necessary to deter future threats. However, retaliation must be deftly done; if it is ineffectual, it leads to continued victimization (Kochenderfer & Ladd, 1997; Perry et al., 1993).

Variation in the norms for aggression occur by age, by ethnic and socioeconomic group, by neighborhood, by gender, and by the specific social situation. Customs vary about which types of contact (being bumped up against, being shoved, having one's shoe stepped on) require retaliation, which types of insult (directed at one's relatives, one's physical appearance, one's intellect) should be ignored, and which children (friends, enemies, bystanders, the other sex, the physically impaired, smaller or younger ones) are fair targets and which are exempt.

Generally, physical aggression declines with age—except for those children who are headed toward more serious violence and criminal activity (Stanger et al., 1997). Relational aggression—verbal insults and social isolation—does not decline. In girls as well as boys, relational aggression becomes more hurtful, more isolating, and more important to deflect—with humor, a shrug, or a counterattack when possible (Crick & Grotpeter, 1996).

The Rejected Child

All children occasionally feel left out or unwelcome among their peers, but a small minority are unpopular most of the time. Some are merely ignored; others are actively *rejected*. Children in the latter category tend to be either **aggressive-rejected**—disliked because of their antagonistic, confrontational behavior—or **withdrawn-rejected**—disliked because of their timid, anxious demeanor (Bierman et al., 1993; Cillessen et al., 1992; Graham & Hoehn, 1995; Hymel et al., 1993).

Most withdrawn-rejected children are aware of their social isolation, which makes them lonely, anxious, and unhappy (Graham & Juvonen, 1998). Their low self-esteem reduces academic achievement, disrupts family relationships, and makes them vulnerable to bullying.

Aggressive-rejected children, by contrast, remain oblivious to their lack of acceptance and tend to overestimate their social competence (Hymel et al., 1993; Parkhurst & Asher, 1992). However, their peers perceive them as argumentative, disruptive, and uncooperative—a perception that is confirmed by teachers' ratings and direct observations (Bierman et al., 1993; Dodge et al., 1990; Patterson et al., 1990). Ironically, "their veneer of self-satisfaction and invulnerability may further decrease the likelihood that others will offer encouragement, warmth, and support" (Hughes et al., 1997).

Aggressive-rejected children are impulsive, immature, and likely to misinterpret social situations, interpreting a compliment as sarcastic, or regarding a request for a bite of candy as a demand, or assuming that someone's inadvertent touch was intended to hurt. To make matters worse, their reaction is to get even—especially when the act is interpreted as hostile, but even when they believe it probably was not intentional (Erdley & Asher, 1996). In contrast, children at the opposite extreme, those who are withdrawn-rejected, are more likely to ignore such an affront, even if they think it was aggressive.

Both types of rejected children are a contrast to school-agers who are well liked. Well-liked children assume that social slights are usually accidental and not intended to harm. Given an ambiguous situation, they try to solve the problem, perhaps asking the other child what happened (Erdley & Asher, 1996). (See Table 13.2 on page 412.)

Note that since most children develop social cognition from the normal give-and-take with peers, rejected children are excluded from the very learning situations they need most. As the years go by, their problems worsen, partly because their peers become more critical of social ineptness and partly because their own behavior becomes more self-defeating. They become the victims, disliking themselves and being repeatedly vulnerable to children who are temporarily accepted, even encouraged, in their aggression.

aggressive-rejected children Children who are actively rejected by their peer group because of their aggressive, confrontational behavior.

withdrawn-rejected children Children who are actively rejected by their peer group because of their withdrawn, anxious behavior.

Can I Play? If she dares to ask, she is likely to be rejected, because the rules of bonding at this age tend to exclude as well as include. Learning how to deal with such situations is one of the most difficult skills taught by the society of children.

table **13.2**	**An Example: Perceptions and Reactions of Three Types of Children**		
Situation	Child B's Type	Typical Interpretation	Typical Response
Child A spills a glass of milk on child B during lunch.	Aggressive-rejected	It was on purpose.	Pour milk on child A, or say something mean.
	Withdrawn-rejected	It was on purpose or it was accidental.	Ignore it, or leave the table.
	Well liked	It was accidental.	Get a towel, or ask how it happened.

Bullies

bullying   Repeated efforts to inflict harm on a particular child through physical, verbal, or social attacks.

Researchers define **bullying** as *repeated,* systematic efforts to inflict harm through physical attack (such as hitting, punching, pinching, or kicking), verbal attack (such as teasing, taunting, or name-calling), or social attack (such as deliberate social exclusion or public mocking). Implicit in this definition is an imbalance of power. Boys who are bullies are often above average in size, whereas girls who are bullies are often above average in verbal assertiveness. Bullies' victims tend to be less assertive and physically weaker (boys) and more shy (girls).

These gender differences are reflected in bullying tactics: boys typically use force or the threat of force; girls often mock or ridicule their victims, making fun of their clothes, behavior, or appearance or revealing their most embarrassing secrets (Lagerspetz & Bjorkquist, 1994). In many cases, the strength differential is multiplied by the fact that the bullying is done by a group of children. In one ongoing study, at least 60 percent of bullying incidents involved group attacks (Olweus, 1992, 1993, 1994).

Bullying was once thought to be an unpleasant but normal part of child's play—not to be encouraged, of course, but of little consequence in the long run. However, developmental researchers who have looked closely at the society of children now realize that bullying is a serious problem, harming both the victim and the aggressor (Garrity & Baris, 1996).

The leading researcher in this area is Dan Olweus (1992, 1993, 1994), who has studied bullying for 25 years. The cruelty, pain, and suffering that he has documented are typified by the details he provided for two cases:

Bully and Victim? Several signs indicate this is not an incident of typical bullying: there is only a single aggressor; his victim is actively resisting; and both aggressor and victim seem close to the same size and strength. In advanced bullying, typically a much larger boy or group of children humiliates another child to the point that resistance is either obviously inadequate or completely absent.

> Linda was systematically isolated by a small group of girls, who pressured the rest of the class, including Linda's only friend, to shun her. Then the ringleader of the group persuaded Linda to give a party and invite everyone. She did. Everyone accepted, but, following the ringleader's instructions, no one came. Linda was devastated, her self-confidence "completely destroyed."

Figure 13.1 Every Country Has Bullies. The rates of being bullied in the various grades as reported by Norwegian schoolchildren are typical of the rates in many other countries. This chart shows physical bullying only; relational bullying may increase with age. Although physical bullying is less common among older children, it is more devastating, because older children depend much more on peers for self-esteem.

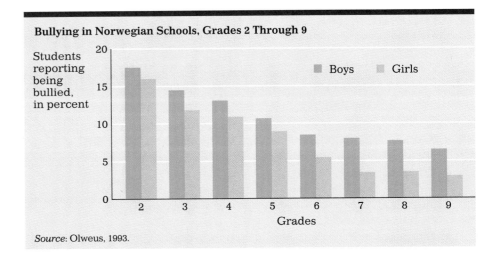

Bullying in Norwegian Schools, Grades 2 Through 9

Source: Olweus, 1993.

Henry's experience was worse. Daily, his classmates called him "Worm," broke his pencils, spilled his books on the floor, and mocked him whenever he answered a teacher's questions. Finally, a few boys took him to the bathroom and made him lie, face down, in the urinal drain. After school that day he tried to kill himself. His parents found him unconscious, and only then learned about his torment.

Bullying Around the World. Following the suicidal deaths of three victims of bullying, the Norwegian government asked Olweus to determine the extent and severity of the problem. After concluding a confidential survey of nearly all of Norway's 90,000 school-age children, Olweus reported that bullying was widespread and serious (see Figure 13.1); that teachers and parents were "relatively unaware" of specific incidents; and that even when adults noticed, they rarely intervened. Of all the children Olweus surveyed, 9 percent were bullied "now and then"; 3 percent were victims once a week or more; and 7 percent admitted that they themselves sometimes deliberately hurt other children, verbally or physically.

As high as these numbers may seem, they are equaled and even exceeded in research done in other countries. For instance, a British study of 8- and 9-year-olds found that 17 percent were victims of regular bullying and that 13 percent were bullies (Boulton & Underwood, 1992). A study of middle-class children in Florida found that 10 percent were "extremely victimized" (Perry et al., 1988). And a study of a multiethnic group of Los Angeles children of diverse SESs found that 10 percent (three-quarters of them boys) were teased and picked on and another 17 percent (57 percent of them girls) were probably socially rejected (Graham & Juvonen, 1998).

Recently, American researchers have looked particularly at sexual harassment, an aspect of childhood bullying too often ignored. Fully one-third of all 9- to 15-year-old girls say they have experienced sexual teasing and touching sufficiently troubling that they wanted to avoid school (American Association of University Women Foundation, 1993). Among boys who are approaching puberty, almost every one who is perceived as homosexual by his peers is bullied, sometimes mercilessly (Savin-Williams, 1995).

Thus, bullying during middle childhood seems to be pervasive. It occurs in every nation, is present in small rural schools and in large urban ones, and is as prevalent among well-to-do majority children as among poor immigrant children. Contrary to popular belief, victims are no more likely to be fat or homely or to speak with an accent than nonvictims are. But they

❷ Especially for Educators: Imagine you are the principal of a school that is about to change from assigning children with special needs in a specialized class to including them in the regular classroom. Based on the lessons learned from the program to eliminate school bullying, what would you do to prepare for the change?

STOPPING A BULLY

Each bullying event requires at least two participants: the bully and the victim. Efforts to reeducate both participants have involved:

- *Teaching social problem-solving skills* (such as how to use humor or negotiation to reduce a conflict)
- *Changing negative assumptions* (such as the view of many rejected children that nothing can protect them, or the bully's assumption that accidental slights are deliberate threats)
- *Improving academic skills* (hoping to improve confidence and raise low self-esteem)
(Crick & Grotpeter, 1996; Merrell & Gimpel, 1998; Ogilvy, 1994)

These approaches sometimes help individuals. However, because they target one child at a time, they are piecemeal, time-consuming, and late in the sequence—an example of tertiary rather than primary prevention. Further, they are up against habits that have been learned and reinforced and are resistant to change. After all, why should bullies learn new social skills when their current attitudes and actions bring them status and pleasure (Patterson et al., 1992)? And "even if rejected children change their behavior, they still face a difficult time recovering accepted positions in the peer group," gaining friends who will support and defend them (Coie & Cillessen, 1993).

Not only do both bullies and victims have established behavior patterns, but they also share a firm cognitive assumption: adults will not intervene. Robert Coles (1997) describes a 9-year-old boy who reported that one of his classmates, a girl, was cheating. The boy was then victimized, not only by the girl and her friends but more subtly by the teacher and the principal, who made excuses for the girl (her grandfather had died several months earlier). Coles believes the overall moral climate taught this boy what it teaches many children: that they

can, and should, ignore the actions, feelings, and needs of their classmates.

The best solution begins with the recognition that bullies and their victims are both caught within a particular social dynamic (Pierce & Cohen, 1995). Accordingly, intervention must change the social climate so that bully-victim cycles no longer spiral out of control. This intervention was attempted by a government-funded campaign for every school in Norway (Olweus, 1992, 1993, 1994).

First, the bullying problem was explained at community-wide meetings. All parents received pamphlets that described signs of victimization (such as a child's having bad dreams, no real friends, damaged clothes, torn books, or unexplained bruises). Videotapes were shown to all students to evoke sympathy for victims. Teachers were given special training on intervention.

The second phase was more direct. In every classroom, students discussed reasons to stop bullying, ways to mediate peer conflicts, and how to befriend lonely children. The last action is particularly crucial: having at least one peer who loyally protects and defends you, "watching your back," not only prevents the escalation of bullying but reduces the emotional sting (Hodges et al., 1999). Teachers organized cooperative learning groups so that no child could be isolated and then bullied, and they halted each incident of name-calling or minor assault as soon as they noticed it, recognizing the undercurrent of the bully's excuses and understanding the victim's fear. Principals learned that schools where bullying was rare were characterized by adequate supervision in the lunchroom, bathroom, and playground, and they redeployed personnel.

If bullying occurred despite these preventive steps, counselors were ready to try a third set of measures, which included conducting intensive therapy with the bully and his or her parents to restructure discipline; reassigning the bully to

usually are rejected-withdrawn children, anxious and insecure, unable or unwilling to defend themselves, without friends who will take their side.

Children themselves are quite aware of bullying even when they do not experience it. One 8-year-old explains:

He sits across the aisle from me, and he doesn't give me any trouble, because I'm able to defend myself, and he knows it, but he's a bully, that's what he is, a real meanie. He tries to get his way by picking on kids who he's decided are weaker than him. They help him with his homework—they give him answers. They give him candy from their lunches. They take orders from him. He cheats—I see him. I think the teacher knows, but the kid's father is a lawyer, and my dad says the teacher is probably afraid—she's got to be careful, or he'll sue her. [Coles, 1997]

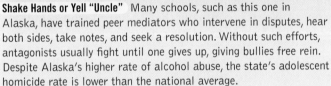

Shake Hands or Yell "Uncle" Many schools, such as this one in Alaska, have trained peer mediators who intervene in disputes, hear both sides, take notes, and seek a resolution. Without such efforts, antagonists usually fight until one gives up, giving bullies free rein. Despite Alaska's higher rate of alcohol abuse, the state's adolescent homicide rate is lower than the national average.

❷ *Observational Quiz (see answer page 418): Could this be one reason?*

a different class, grade, or even school; and helping the victim strengthen social and academic skills. (Note that the bully and his or her family bore the major burden. If the victim changed schools and the bully stayed, the wrong child had been punished.)

Twenty months after this campaign began, Olweus resurveyed the children in 42 schools. He found that bullying had been reduced overall by more than 50 percent, with dramatic improvement for both boys and girls at every grade level (Olweus, 1992). These results are thrilling to developmentalists because they show that research can lead to an inexpensive, widespread intervention that effectively reduces a serious problem. This research and intervention program provides a model approach to other problems that might be tackled in the future.

Olweus (1993) concludes, "It is no longer possible to avoid taking action about bullying problems at school using lack of awareness as an excuse . . . it all boils down to a matter of will and involvement on the part of adults." Unfortunately, at the moment, Norway is the only nation to have mounted a nationwide attack on bullying. Many other school systems, in many other nations, have not even acknowledged the harm caused by this problem, much less shown the "will and involvement" to stop it.

As in this example, children usually do not intervene to stop bullying unless a close friend is the victim or the adults encourage intervention (see the Research Report above).

The Consequences of Bullying. A key word in the definition of bullying is "repeated." Most children experience isolated attacks or social slights from other children and come through unscathed. But when a child endures such shameful experiences again and again—being forced to hand over lunch money, or to drink milk mixed with detergent, or to lick someone's boots, or to be the butt of insults and practical jokes, with everyone watching and no one ever coming to his or her defense—the effects can be

Jimmy, Sixth-Generation Pain in the Ass

Like Father, Like Son If parents and grandparents use their greater physical power to punish and criticize their offspring, the children (especially the boys) are often hostile to everyone they know.

deep and long-lasting. Bullied children are anxious, depressed, and underachieving during the months and years of their torment. Even years later, they still have damaged self-esteem as well as painful memories.

The picture is more ominous for bullies. Contrary to the public perception that bullies are actually insecure and lonely, at the peak of their bullying they usually have friends who abet, fear, and admire them. They seem brashly unapologetic about the pain they have inflicted "all in fun." Their parents do nothing to stop them. In fact, their parents often seem indifferent to what their children do *outside the home* but use "power-assertive" discipline on them *at home,* with physical punishment, verbal criticism, and displays of dominance meant to control and demean them (Olweus, 1993).

But the popularity and school success of bullies fades over the years, as their peers become increasingly critical. Bullies become more hostile, challenging everyone who tries to stop them, getting into trouble not only with peers but also with the police. In one longitudinal study, by age 24 two-thirds of boys who had been bullies in the second grade were convicted of at least one felony, and one-third of those who were bullies in the sixth through ninth grades were convicted of three or more crimes, often violent ones, and already had done prison time (Olweus, 1993). This particular study came from Norway, but international research confirms that children who regularly victimize other children often become violent criminals later on (Junger-Tas et al., 1994).

FAMILIES IN SCHOOL YEARS

Children need families. Worldwide, all societies share the belief that children are best raised in families, nurtured and guided by their parents and other relatives. Families differ greatly, however, in both structure and function.

Structure and Function

A family that functions well nurtures its children to develop their full potential. Although the details obviously vary, a functional family nurtures school-age children in five essential ways:

- *Meets basic needs by providing food, clothes, and shelter.* In middle childhood, children are old enough to dress, wash, and put themselves to bed, but they cannot yet obtain the basic necessities of life without their families' help.
- *Encourages learning.* A critical task during middle childhood is to master academic skills. Families must get their children to school and then guide and motivate their learning.
- *Develops self-esteem.* As they become more cognitively aware, children become more self-critical. Families need to make their children feel competent, loved, and appreciated.
- *Nurtures peer friendship.* Families can provide the time, space, opportunity, and skills needed to develop peer relationships.
- *Provides harmony and stability.* Children need to feel safe and secure at home, confident that family routines are protective and predictable.

Family Styles

Thus, a family that functions well provides material and cognitive resources, as well as emotional security, so that the children grow in body and mind. Of course, no family functions perfectly for every child. Furthermore, families have various styles, and some children are more comfortable with, and develop better with, one style than another (Constantine, 1986, 1993). Especially when older children are adopted into families, matching the family style with the child's temperament may be crucial (Ward, 1997).

As an example, families with an *open* style value contributions from every family member, including children. This style tends to develop a child's confidence and self-esteem. But an open family might emphasize family cooperation and conversation so much that a defiant or demanding child, who needs structured guidance and carefully set limits, might founder. Or a family with a *closed* style (in which one parent, usually the father, sets strict guidelines, limits, and rules) might function well if scarce family resources need to be carefully shared or if the school and neighborhood are so chaotic that the parents must monitor the child's homework, peer group, and so on. But for some creative children, closed families may be stifling, and the result may be depression or rebellion—both of which are destructive to children.

There are many other ways to categorize family styles, as you know from reading Chapter 10. In a well-functioning family of any style, a mutual adjustment process between child and parents begins at birth; it enables the family to become flexible enough to serve the child well, while the child becomes used to the family style. Flexibility and mutual adjustment may very well be the keys to a proper balance between the family's nurturance and the child's need for independence (Maccoby, 1992). Obviously, the danger comes at either extreme—a family so closed that the family becomes enmeshed, tangling the child with family intimacy, or so open as to be disconnected, letting the child drift alone.

Diverse Structures

All five nurturing elements can occur in any form of family. Structure does not determine function or dysfunction. Nonetheless, all five elements, especially the harmony and stability that school-agers particularly need, are af-

Happily Ever After Traditions, especially religious ones, help keep families together, as shown by this Christmas dinner with three generations in Florida. Note, however, that the only couple sitting together are the grandparents, who were married decades ago, when the nuclear family was strong. Their children and grandchildren are experiencing several variations of family structure.

family structure   The legal and genetic relationships between members of a particular family.

extended family   A family that includes other relatives in addition to parents (or a parent) and their children. Extended families usually include grandparents and may include aunts, uncles, and cousins as well.

nuclear family   A family consisting of two parents and their mutual biological children.

single-parent family   A family consisting of a single parent and his or her children—usually the parent's biological children.

blended family   A family consisting of two parents, at least one with biological children from another union; thus, at least one adult is a stepparent. Blended families may include children of several prior unions as well as children of the current union.

❶ Answer to Observational Quiz (from page 415): *Yes. Children learn their conflict-resolution patterns in elementary school and then tend to use them in adolescence.*

fected by the **family structure,** defined as the legal and genetic relationships between the adults and children in a household. The four most common family structures are:

- The **extended family,** which includes several relatives, usually of three or more generations, along with parents and children.
- The **nuclear family,** which consists of the father, the mother, and their biological children.
- The **single-parent family,** which usually is one parent with his or her biological children.
- The **blended family,** which includes two parents, one or both of whom have biological children from an earlier union, so each child is also a stepchild to one parent. Such families might also include children from the new relationship, who then live with their half-siblings.
- Other family structures involve grandparents, without the parent generation, or adoptive or foster parents, or many other combinations.

Is any structure always best? The answer is "probably not." (See Changing Policy, page 419.) Phrases like "broken home," "fatherless household," and "illegitimate child" mistakenly imply that every family structure not headed by married biological parents is deviant and destructive. That isn't so. Longitudinal research confirms what history and cultural comparisons tell us: Children can thrive in almost any family structure. In each generation and each culture, tax policies, housing design, divorce laws, and so on, sometimes mistakenly assume one type of family structure is universally best. This assumption is false, but not totally misguided. Although any structure might provide the five basic requirements for children, some structures are more likely to do so than others, as you will now see.

Two Parents Together

According to large-scale surveys, children living with both biological parents (either in nuclear or extended families) tend to fare best. From infancy through childhood, they experience fewer physical, emotional, and learning difficulties than children in other family structures. At adolescence, they are more likely to avoid drug abuse, delinquency, and school failure. In adulthood, they are more likely to graduate from college and to develop self-confidence, social acceptance, and career success (Acock & Demo, 1994; McLanahan, 1997; Simons, 1996).

Three reasons for this advantage seem clear.

- First, the most apparent is that two adults, both of whom have known and loved a child since birth, can provide more complete caregiving and an extra measure of warmth, discipline, and attention. They can also support each other, compensate for each other's personal shortcomings, and encourage each other's parental strengths.
- Second, all mammals, including humans, have a genetic impulse to protect and nurture their own progeny, perhaps for genetic continuity or perhaps simply in recognition of the fact that a child is literally part of themselves. Sometimes parents neglect, abuse, or even kill their own biological children, but this is shocking partly because it is contrary to biological impulses. Centuries of fairy tales, and data on child homicide, make it clear that children have much more to fear from household members who are not their biological parents (Daly et al., 1993).
- Third, the advantage of two married parents is financial. Married couples are generally better able to provide for their children, for reasons that predate the child's arrival:

OVER THE CENTURIES, ACROSS THE CONTINENTS

In various periods of history and various cultures, children have thrived in diverse family structures. The preferred structure in most developing countries in Asia and Latin America has been the large extended family, with many relatives—grandparents and even great-grandparents, cousins, aunts, and uncles—living within the same large household. In many African and Arab nations, in addition to being raised in extended families, children are often raised in polygamous households, with men having several wives and most children growing up in the company of a dozen or more siblings and half-siblings.

Both extended families and polygamous families existed in the United States a hundred years ago, but they were relatively rare. More common were nuclear families, especially if the parents had left their childhood home and settled in a distant place, as immigrants and pioneers had done. In some regions, even more common were various alternative family forms, usually necessitated by death (especially of women during childbirth) or desertion (especially by fathers seeking a better life). These included single-parent and blended families, as well as many households in which children were informally raised by relatives or neighbors or were adopted by nonrelatives. When parents divorced or separated, fathers were given custody, since women were considered too weak to raise a family properly on their own. Such fathers usually immediately remarried, or found a live-in housekeeper, because men were not considered capable of child care.

By the mid-twentieth century in North America, a family of two parents living with their two or three biological offspring had become the norm. Such nuclear families were glorified on early television (such as in *Ozzie and Harriet*) and are still idealized by many Americans (Coontz, 1992).

Family Structure Today

The classic nuclear family of the 1950s is less common today. Fewer children are being born, women are now more likely to choose to raise children without men, and divorce is more frequent. Worldwide, the extended family is also becoming less common, as urbanization and mobility undermine traditional

Husband and Wives Polygamy is encouraged in some communities as for this Muslim family in western China. When war or sickness reduces the supply of adult men, this ensures that most women marry, bear children, and have help with the household. The alternative is many unmarried women—and more divorce, extramarital affairs, and out-of-wedlock births.

rural family structures. The trend everywhere is toward smaller families and more varied family structures (Taylor, 1997).

In the United States, if current trends continue, only a minority—about 37 percent—of children born in the 1990s will live with both biological parents from birth to age 18. On birth certificates in the United States, in 1996, 32.5 percent of all infants were born to unwed mothers (Monthly Vital Statistics Report, 1998). Almost half of the other two-thirds are likely to live in a single-parent household before age 18—usually because of divorce or, less often, parental death. Many of these children will experience several changes in household composition—spending part of their childhood living with a grandparent, a step-parent, or a parent's live-in lover—and will witness several marital transitions, from marriage to divorce to remarriage to divorce again (Bumpass & Raley, 1995).

1. Individuals who are financially secure are more desirable marriage partners.
2. Couples who have good economic prospects are more likely to decide to marry and to have children.
3. Couples who are financially secure are more likely to avoid divorce.
4. Most contemporary two-parent families have two wage earners, so they tend to be more financially secure than other families.

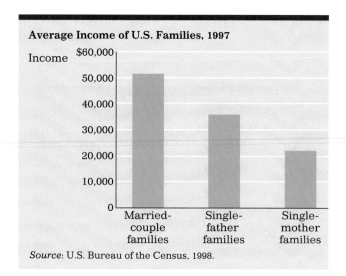

Average Income of U.S. Families, 1997

Source: U.S. Bureau of the Census, 1998.

Figure 13.2 No Father, No Money. Although some single mothers are quite wealthy (3 percent of families headed by a single woman have an income of more than $75,000 a year), most are poor. This may affect children as much as or more than the father's absence does.

❷ Especially For Social Workers and Psychotherapists: Imagine you are counseling one or both members of a married couple who are furious at each other and report frequent episodes of verbal and even physical abuse. They have two children, ages 5 and 9. What do you advise?

Once a child is born, two-parent households in which only one parent works save money on household and child-care services for which a single parent might have to pay, and so two-parent households—even those with only one wage earner—have more money for housing, food, health care, and education. Thus the general stability of their home and work situations tends to enhance the financial security of nuclear families. Consequently, the median income for two-parent homes in the United States is two to three times that for one-parent homes (see Figure 13.2). Similar advantages are found in other nations.

When Are Two Biological Parents Not Best?

However, two-parent homes are not always best for children. To begin with, some two-parent homes are, contrary to the general trend, very low income. Poverty erodes the competence, self-esteem, and achievement of school-age children more than any family structure does (Bolger et al., 1995; Montgomery et al., 1996).

We also need to note that the *correlation* between two-parent families and healthy children does not prove that this family structure is the *cause* of the benefit. Several powerful factors, including race, ethnic background, and religion, also correlate with family structure. Advantages that at first seem to stem from the two-parent family may actually result from some other influence.

For example, the children of Mormons, Mennonites, and Orthodox Jews are almost always raised in two-parent households *and* almost never abuse drugs—at least while they live at home. But it would be a mistake to say that their resistance to drugs is due primarily to their parents' marital status, for that would ignore the powerful influence of their religious upbringing. Similarly, characteristics of some adults—hostility, impatience, and antisocial behavior—make it more likely that those adults will be single parents and less likely that they will be adequate parents. Thus parental personality (which is partly inherited) may be the underlying reason their children suffer. Correlation is not causation.

Finally, when we say that such homes are generally best for children, we should bear in mind two important qualifications: (1) Not every biological father or mother is a fit parent, and (2) not every marriage creates a nurturant household. Some parents are so disturbed, addicted, or self-absorbed that they mistreat their children or, at the least, interfere with their partners' child-rearing efforts; the harm they do ruins the benefits usually associated with the two-parent household, and the children would be better off without them. Many others are adequate parents by themselves, but they fight with their spouses. As a result, their children suffer—much more than they would in a tranquil one-parent home. One review of cross-sectional and longitudinal research has found that while all children are "harmed by intense conflict, whether or not their parents live together . . . children who live in intact families with persistently high levels of conflict are the most distressed of all" (Furstenberg & Cherlin, 1991).

In openly hostile families like these, the parents often fight for years before separating or getting help. And all the while, their children must live in a home where blame and anger, attack and counterattack, destroy the emotional stability that would allow them healthy growth (Cummings & Davies, 1994).

Experts disagree as to how bad a marriage must become before divorce is the best alternative. A certain amount of marital coldness—but not open warfare—may be better for the children than the disruption of divorce (Simons et al., 1996). However, unless the parents find a way to disagree without involving the children in their hostility, or unless the parent who functions well can protect the children from the direct attacks of an addicted, disturbed, or violent spouse, separating "for the sake of the kids" may be best.

Divorce

The disruption and discord of divorce almost always adversely affect the children for at least a year or two. Immediately before and after a divorce, the children show signs of emotional pain, such as depression or rebellion, and symptoms of stress, such as having lower school achievement, poorer health, and fewer friends. Whether this distress is relatively mild and short-lived, or serious and long-lasting, depends primarily on the stability of the child's life and the adequacy of caregiving (Amato, 1993).

As we have noted, harmony and stability are crucial to a well-functioning family. Both are jeopardized by divorce. For instance, the feeling of being abandoned by a trusted adult (parent, grandparent, baby-sitter)—even if that is not actually the case—is devastating to a child. Moving to a less desirable neighborhood and attending a different school can be particularly disruptive for children who are old enough to have best friends. Divorce also reduces the attention that parents give their children, partly because financial needs require that they work more hours or take a second job and partly because emotional needs make them resume their own social lives, dating and socializing with other adults.

For all these reasons, divorce increases the risks of childhood. Yet divorce does not have to be disastrous. An extensive study comparing children of divorce with similar children in both happy and unhappy marriages found that most parents of every family structure were adequate and, consequently, that most children seemed to develop well enough. However, if a mother who was the primary caregiver was financially stressed, emotionally depressed, or inadequate as a parent (all at least twice as common among divorced than among married mothers) then the children were likely to suffer (Simons, 1996).

Nonresidential fathers are also part of the problem. After divorce, they typically visit their offspring less frequently and more inconsistently over time, gradually feeling less affectionate toward them than they did during the marriage (Amato & Booth, 1996; Seltzer, 1991). Moreover, fathers who visit only as a playmate (the "Disneyland Dad") do not necessarily foster healthy development. Children need involved fathers who attend parent-teacher meetings, guide moral development, and generally take part in their children's life. Without such involvement, mere visiting by noncustodial fathers may not benefit the children at all (Amato, 1993).

As you can surmise, divorce may not harm the children if the family income remains stable, if conflict between the parents decreases, and if caregiving by both parents is as good as or better than it was before the divorce (Amato & Rezac, 1994; King, 1994). However, even if all that is in place, simply scheduling and organizing visitations can be a source of conflict between the parents. On their part, children sometimes become stressed or even sick when they must shuttle back and forth between homes that have different rules, expectations, and emotional settings. These problems are compounded when the animosity of former spouses leads them—deliberately or not—to put the child in the middle of their continuing battles.

"*Must I pick one of my parents? I'd rather live with Bill Cosby.*"

Custody Decisions Such determinations are never easy, especially when decided primarily by a judge and a child.

Custody Decisions

Custody means having caregiving responsibility. In two-parent families, both parents are involved in custody, allocating the particular tasks (e.g., who puts the children to bed, who takes them to the doctor, who decides about school or vacations) and sharing the responsibility. No such simple flexibility is available for separated or divorced parents. Typically, one parent is on the scene and the other is distant. In most divorces, one parent (often the mother) is granted primary custody, and the other parent is granted visitation rights.

Theoretically, the best decision is "joint custody," in which the divorced parents share legal custody and work out an equitable division of physical custody, deciding who the child lives with. Unfortunately, joint custody is not easy to carry out in practice, and it is especially hard when the parents are fighting. Thus the custody solution that at first appears best for the children may actually be the worst.

When custody and visitation disputes arise, what should the solution be, on the basis of developmental research? There are no easy answers, for two reasons. First, whichever parent is "better" (more competent and more involved) should have primary custody, but that parent is not necessarily the mother. Custodial fathers sometimes do as well as mothers, partly because they usually choose to maintain active parenthood, and adults generally perform better when they have chosen a role compared to when it is forced upon them. Research finds that in some ways custodial fathers can be better than custodial mothers: typically, they have more income, more authority over the boys, and greater willingness to accept caregiving help from relatives of the other sex, including the child's mother. The last point is particularly important, since children ideally should have good ties with both parents. Children whose fathers have custody have close relationships with their mothers more often than vice versa (Hetherington et al., 1998). However, individual differences and personal relationships are so complex that any gender guidelines regarding custody need to be applied gingerly, if at all.

Second, the needs of children and the lives of their parents change continually. Custody requirements change as well. It is quite possible that a young child would thrive best in the custody of her mother, having weekend outings with her father, and then, by the end of middle childhood, do best spending all summer with one parent and all the school year with the other—without the interruptions of weekend visits. During adolescence, some children of divorce (especially boys) do well with their fathers, and others (especially girls) benefit particularly from the involvement of maternal grandparents. No one pattern is best for all children at all ages (Hetherington & Stanley-Hagen, 1999; Simons, 1996). An added factor is remarriage, which often disturbs children and requires reconsideration of the best custody arrangement.

Developmental psychologists can, however, offer one bit of advice to almost every couple who cannot agree on custody: Try mediation. A trained and authoritative outsider can often help feuding parents find the best outcome for the children (Maccoby & Mnookin, 1992).

Family Dinner At one time, the entire family—parents and several children—ate together each night. This has become rare even in nuclear families but especially in single-parent families such as this one. A home-cooked, sit-down, no-TV dinner (as shown here) is not always received appreciatively by the children, so many single parents give up trying, as do many married parents if both parents are not willing to insist on a traditional family meal.

Single-Parent Households

The number of single-parent households has increased markedly over the past two decades in virtually every major industrialized nation, in large part because births to unmarried mothers are increasing but also

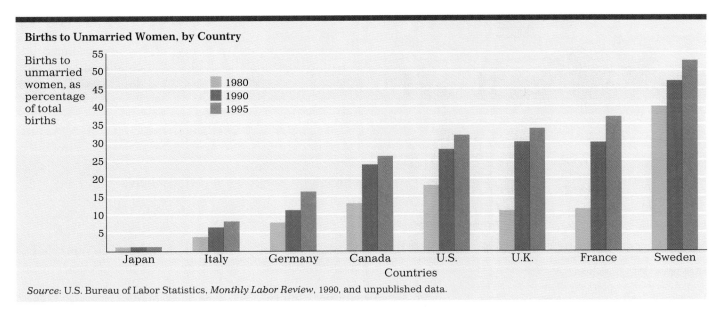

Births to Unmarried Women, by Country

Births to unmarried women, as percentage of total births

Legend: 1980, 1990, 1995

Source: U.S. Bureau of Labor Statistics, *Monthly Labor Review*, 1990, and unpublished data.

Figure 13.3 No Wedding?

First comes love,
Then comes marriage,
Then comes baby in the baby carriage.

This rhyme from the 1950s seems quaint today.

"Wait a minute! When we decided to separate, I thought I was leaving home!"

The Joy of Single Parenthood More and more men are becoming custodial fathers, not always out of choice.

because divorce and death (especially due to homicide and AIDS) are increasing as well (Burns & Scott, 1994) (see Figure 13.3). This family structure is typically blamed for all manner of developmental problems, from sickness to academic failure (Blankenhorn, 1995; U.S. Department of Education, 1991). Such blanket condemnation often is linked to a grossly distorted stereotype—that of a single mother with little education, many neglected children, few conventional morals, and no ambition, who spends her time collecting government checks and watching television day and night.

However, this stereotype is false. In the United States, most single mothers are in the labor force, including both a large majority (77 percent) of those with children age 6 to 17 and most (60 percent) of those with younger children (U.S. Bureau of the Census, 1996). Even before the federal welfare reform of 1996 cut benefits for many single mothers, fewer than half received government assistance of any kind, not even food stamps or medical care. And unmarried mothers from every racial group have fewer children and are less likely to want more children than married mothers of the same age, education, and ethnicity. Similar nationwide statistics are not available on single-father households, but all evidence suggests that custodial fathers are even more likely to be in the labor force than are single mothers (Greif, 1995; Greif et al., 1993). We do know that the number of single fathers in the United States has quadrupled over the past 25 years, to more than 1.7 million in 1994 (see Figure 13.4).

Overall, then, no matter what their sex, nationality, ethnicity, or education, single parents are likely to work hard to fill the dual role of major

Number of Single Fathers in the United States				
	1970	1980	1990	1997
Male householder, with no spouse but with children under age 18	393,000	616,000	1,158,000	1,709,000

Figure 13.4 More Single Fathers

A Well-Loved Child More than half of all black American newborns had unmarried mothers in 1998. However, a sizable percentage of the children, like this boy, will do as well as or better than their two-parented peers in school. The reason is partly that their community has a tradition of support for unmarried mothers. Relatives (often including the child's father and his parents), neighbors, and other single mothers usually provide caregiving help.

provider and major caregiver—usually surrendering personal recreation, social life, and sleep to do so. Single parents are also more likely to have experienced adverse life circumstances, either in childhood or as parents, and hence to be stressed and depressed (Davies et al., 1997; Simons, 1996). And, despite their hard work, in the United States more than half have incomes below the poverty line (McLanahan, 1997). Nonetheless, they carry on.

Children in Single-Parent Households

How do children actually develop in single-parent households? With the exception of children whose parents are recently divorced, children from single-parent families usually do as well as other children from the same neighborhood, school, socioeconomic group, and ethnic group in three crucial areas: school achievement, emotional stability, and protection from serious physical injury. This generality holds for preschoolers, school-age children, and adolescents (Dawson, 1991; Entwisle & Alexander, 1996; Hawkins & Eggebeen, 1991; Pong, 1997). They do not do as well, however, in behavioral problems, being more likely to challenge authority and act out in school or at home (McLanahan, 1997).

One important factor that does affect children in single-parent households is the maturity of the single parent (Weinraub & Gringlas, 1995). In

table **13.3**	**The Impact of Single Parenthood on Child Development**
Likely to Be Harmful If	Likely to Be Beneficial If
Low-income home	Middle-income home
Conflict-filled home	Peaceful home
Parent under age 25	Parent over age 30
Parent not high school graduate	Parent has college education
More than two siblings	Only child, or one sibling
Several changes (e.g., divorce, remarriage, divorce)	Stable family structure (no change ever or none within past 5 years)
No help from relatives	Grandparents actively helpful
Conflict with other parent	Cordial relations with other parent
Parent has live-in lover	Parent not romantically involved
Parent socially isolated	Parent active with friends, church, etc.
Community hostile to single parents	Community supportive of single parents
If child is under age 5 More than four caregivers	Two or three caregivers
No steady day care	High-quality preschool
Parent employed 60+ hours a week	Parent has part-time job
If child is over age 5 Frequent change of school	Child stays in one school
Frequent change of neighborhood	Child stays in one neighborhood
Parent unemployed	Parent employed, flexible hours
Child hostile or friendless	Child has several friends

Source: Compiled from several sources, among them Angel & Angel, 1994; McLanahan & Sandefur, 1994.

⚊ **Response for Social Workers and Psychotherapists (from page 420):** This is an untenable situation that has to stop. But the obvious solution, divorce, might actually create more problems, particularly for the children, given their ages. Your first task is to stop the open conflict, getting both parents to see that they are seriously damaging some innocent bystanders (their own children). If they cannot stop, a temporary truce and separation must lead to finding the best solution for the children. If they choose divorce, you must get them to understand that their commitment to the children not only is material but also entails protecting their education, friendship networks, self-esteem, and stable living situation.

1995 in the United States, 31 percent of the births to unmarried mothers were to teenagers, who are not likely to have either the emotional maturity or the financial resources to be good parents. It would not necessarily help the children if teenage mothers were married, because teenage marriages are more likely to be abusive and end in divorce. Unless the grandparents become major caregivers, as many do, children of young parents may suffer. On the other hand, the fastest-growing category of single parents today is educated women in their thirties, who choose to be mothers even though they are not planning to be wives. This trend is too new for any extensive longitudinal research, but evidence so far suggests that they usually have the emotional and financial resources to make child rearing go well (Weinraub & Gringlas, 1995).

Thus, the mere fact of growing up in a single-parent family does not always hurt a child's development (see Table 13.3). If a child's family is poor, that has a greater impact on child development than whether the parents are married, were never married, or were married and divorced (Miller & Davis, 1997). Indeed, some of the correlation between single parenthood and child problems is actually a correlation between poverty and problems. Such correlations are particularly strong in nations that do not provide much government support for children in poor families (see Figure 13.5).

Blended Families

Most divorced parents remarry within a few years, and many unmarried parents marry eventually. When such a marriage ends loneliness, improves finances, reduces conflict with a former spouse, and creates a more stable household organization, it may benefit the children. There is, however, a complication. Most new partners are initially happy, but that is almost never the case for the children, who are likely to show stress due to the marriage or remarriage (Cherlin, 1992; Mott et al., 1997). They must suddenly negotiate a new set of family relationships, sharing the parent not

Figure 13.5 Millions of Poor Children. For many reasons, including the high rate of single parenthood, the rate of child poverty is higher in the United States than in any other developed country, except Ireland and the United Kingdom. (Poverty is defined here as living in a family whose income is less than half the national median.) The other contrast occurs for political and historical reasons: children in the United States are least likely to be helped substantially by government assistance.

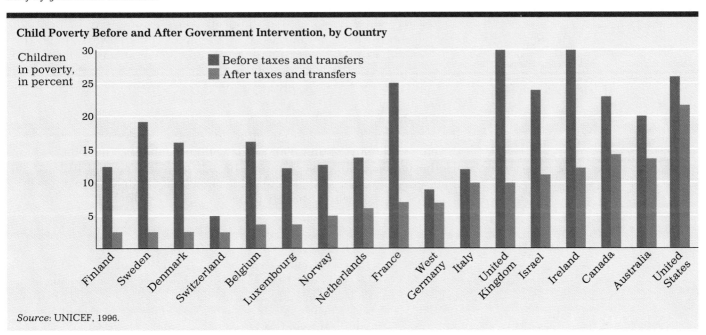

Child Poverty Before and After Government Intervention, by Country

Children in poverty, in percent

- ■ Before taxes and transfers
- ▨ After taxes and transfers

Source: UNICEF, 1996.

Who Belongs to Whom? Only two members of this newly formed blended family chose each other. The success of their relationship, like that of all parents in blended families, will largely depend on how well the other family members work out their relationships with stepparents, step-siblings, and other "acquired" relatives. Generally, the younger the children, and the more years that pass, the more likely it is that stepparents and even half-siblings will be accepted as one's own.

only with a stepparent but often with half-siblings, step-grandparents, and others, most of whom they would never select as relatives if they had a choice (Ganong & Coleman, 1994).

The same functions that are important to children in all other families—meeting basic needs, encouraging academic learning, enhancing self-esteem, fostering friendship, and providing harmony and stability—also are important to children in stepfamilies (Arendell, 1997). Even in the best of circumstances, however, adequate family functioning in these five areas takes time to achieve. The blended family must develop a style and culture, one that all members can live with. Doing so requires that each family member make certain accommodations to the others. In the process, some children are likely to benefit—especially young boys from single-mother families, because they gain a male figure as well as much needed independence. Others are more likely to suffer: adolescent girls typically resent a new stepfather; only children suddenly lose privacy; and many children become targets of the non-remarried parent's jealousy (Allison & Furstenberg, 1989; Buchanan, 1996; Hetherington & Jodl, 1994; Vuchinich et al., 1991).

Eventually, many remarriages work out well. However, the divorce rate is higher for second than for first marriages, especially if children about 9 to 15 years old are involved, because children undergoing emotional and sexual transitions need stable and patient families and are more likely to become volatile when a parent remarries. The child's reaction adds to the new couple's stress, and often something must suffer—either the child's well-being, or the household tranquillity, or the marriage itself (Hetherington et al., 1998).

A second divorce disrupts the children's lives even more than the first. However, it is hard to predict the eventual impact of any change in family structure. One recent study obtained a surprising result. Children born to unmarried mothers who later got married and then divorced scored higher in reading and math than children from any other type of family, including those whose parents were always married or always single. The authors of the study were puzzled by this result, but suggest that the critical variable may be the mother's investment in her child—if she has tried and rejected marriage in order to focus on motherhood, the child may benefit from her choice (Cooksey, 1997).

This hypothesis is also suggested by other research. Quality of parenting is the crucial variable that determines which children of divorce will develop well (most of them) and which will not (about 25 percent of them) (Hetherington et al., 1998; Simons, 1996). Again we see that it is not the family structure per se that determines how well children develop; rather, it is what goes on within that structure.

Other Family Structures

The same general rule applies to other family arrangements, such as those in which grandparents are responsible for child rearing, an arrangement that is increasing (see Appendix A). If the family is relatively free of conflict and the caregivers provide stability as well as ongoing love and guidance, the children are likely to thrive. However, when grandparents feel stressed by the obligation to care for grandchildren, the result is more likely to be added emotional problems for the children and health problems for the elders (Shore & Hayslip, 1994). As one 53-year-old great-grandmother laments:

> I have been taking care of all these kids for a mighty long time. Sandy [her daughter] needs so much help with her children. LaShawn [her granddaughter] I raised from a baby. Now she got two kids and I'm doing it again. I bathe, feed them, and everything. Three generations I raised. Lord Almighty! I'm tired, tired, tired. Sick too. [quoted in Burton, 1995]

Children growing up in gay or lesbian families also develop quite well, again depending on the particulars of how the family functions and not on the nature of the parents' sexual relationship (Patterson, 1995). This highlights the critical role of the broader social context: If a particular family type is accepted and supported by ethnic, cultural, or community values, the chances are good that the adults will be able to nurture the children entrusted to them. In fact, over the past 30 years, as social acceptance of nontraditional families in the United States has been increasing, the negative effects of nonnuclear families on children have been decreasing (Acock & Demo, 1994).

Among African Americans, single-mother families have become the norm, with 64 percent of all black households in 1997 headed by a single parent, compared to 26 percent of white families and 36 percent of Hispanic families (U.S. Bureau of the Census, 1998). Perhaps as a result, fathers and both maternal and paternal grandparents tend to be more involved with the children than is typical for European American single-mother families. Consequently, many African American children develop as well with single parents as they would in two-parent families (Tucker et al., 1996; Zimmerman et al., 1995). Such ethnic variations make it difficult to find easy answers to questions about family structure and that means that the actual experiences of a particular child in a particular community must be viewed with sensitivity. Remember, however, that every child needs a family that functions well, no matter what the structure.

COPING WITH PROBLEMS

As you have seen in the three chapters on middle childhood, the expansion of a child's social world sometimes brings new and disturbing problems. The beginning of formal education forces learning disabilities to the surface, making them an obvious handicap. Speaking another language in school may hinder learning and provoke prejudice. The peer group may bring rejection and attack. Living in a family that is angry, impoverished, or unstable is destructive.

These problems of middle childhood are often exacerbated by longstanding problems that harm children of every age, such as having a parent who is emotionally disturbed, drug addicted, or imprisoned, or growing up in a community that is crumbling, violent, and crime-filled. Because of a combination of problems, some children fail at school, fight with their friends, fear the future, or cry themselves to sleep. Indeed, every academic and psychiatric difficulty that school-age children suffer can be traced, at least in part, to psychosocial stresses (DeFries et al., 1994; Luthar & Zigler, 1991; Rutter, 1987).

The stresses and hassles of middle childhood are so common that almost every child experiences some of them. Fortunately, the coping measures that school-age children develop are common as well. As a result, between ages 7 and 11, the overall frequency of psychological problems

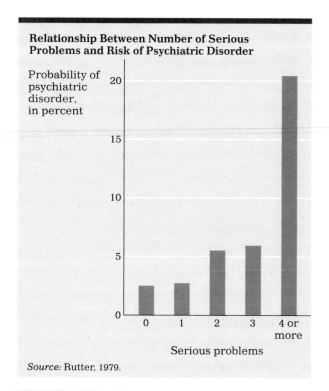

Relationship Between Number of Serious Problems and Risk of Psychiatric Disorder

Probability of psychiatric disorder, in percent

Serious problems

Source: Rutter, 1979.

Figure 13.6 Childhood Stresses. Michael Rutter found that children who had to cope with one serious problem ran virtually as low a risk of suffering a psychiatric disorder as did children who faced no serious problem. However, when the child had two problems, the chances more than doubled. Four or more problems produced about 10 times the likelihood of a psychiatric disorder as one problem did. About one child in five who experienced four or more serious stresses became emotionally disturbed, according to the judgment of British psychiatrists.

decreases while the number of evident competencies—at school, at home, and on the playground—increases (Achenbach et al., 1991). Two factors described in this chapter—the development of social cognition and an expanding social world—combine to protect school-age children against many of the stresses they encounter (Ackerman et al., 1999). According to some observers, many school-agers seem "stress-resistant," or even "invulnerable" and "invincible" (Garmezy, 1985; Werner & Smith, 1992). Let us look more closely at how some children rise above problems that might seem potentially devastating.

Assessing Stress

The likelihood that a given problem will affect a child depends on how many other stresses the child is already experiencing and how much these stresses affect the daily patterns of the child's life (Fergusson & Lynskey, 1997; Luthar & Zigler, 1991).

Typical of research in this area is a classic study that found that children coping with one—and only one—serious, ongoing stress (such as poverty, large family size, a criminal father, an emotionally disturbed mother, or frequent fighting between the parents) were no more likely to develop serious psychiatric problems than children with none of these stresses. However, as is illustrated in Figure 13.6, when more than one such risk factor was present, the stresses made each other much more potent: the effect of the combined stresses was very much greater than the sum of the effects of the individual stresses (Rutter, 1979). Other studies have found that, in general, a single chronic problem creates vulnerability in a child without causing obvious harm. However, if that vulnerability is added to other burdens—even mild ones that might be called "daily hassles" rather than "stressful events"—the child can suffer evident damage (Luthar & Zigler, 1991; Shaw et al., 1994).

Remember that the crucial question is, "How much does the stress affect the child's daily life?" For example, living with an emotionally dysfunctional parent may mean that a child (1) has to assume many of the responsibilities for his or her own daily care and school attendance; (2) has to contend with an adult's confused, depressed, or irrational thinking; and (3) has to supervise and discipline younger siblings. Nevertheless, some children are able to cope with this stress with only minimal difficulty.

However, additional stress may cause the same circumstances to become overwhelming because ordinary daily life becomes impossible. For example, if the dysfunctional parent is the only adult in the household, it is likely that he or she cannot provide a steady place to live. For school-age children especially, frequent changes of address are strongly correlated with low self-esteem, school failure, and parental neglect. The worst situation occurs when the child has *no* address—except, perhaps, that of a shelter for the homeless (see Changing Policy, page 429).

On the brighter side, we should note that even multiple stresses need not be devastating. In our example, living with a dysfunctional parent may not irreparably damage the child if other family adults give the child stability and nurturance; or if the school recognizes, praises, and encourages the child's competencies; or if the neighborhood cares for all its children. Community influences can counteract the effects of poverty, family stress, and even abuse (Garbarino et al., 1997).

POOR AND HOMELESS

Poverty itself is a risk factor for children's development, because it triggers a cascade of stresses that affect children: their parents' stress about money leads to ineffective caregiving; overcrowded schools in low-income areas give children little competence; violent neighborhoods make friendship difficult (Duncan & Brooks-Gunn, 1997). Every problem of poverty, however, is magnified if a child is homeless. Unfortunately, children are the segment of the homeless population that is increasing most rapidly in the United States (Nunez, 1996) and in many other nations as well.

An estimated 50,000 to 100,000 U.S. children are homeless each night, about half of them school-age (Jencks, 1994; Masten, 1992). Those literally without a roof over their heads are most often adolescents, either runaways whose parents have abused them or "throw-aways" whose parents have disowned them. Those under age 12 usually live with their families in shelters. Although these children have, for the moment, the assurance of a bed and meals, they are troubled in many ways. As one report explains:

> By the time they arrive in a shelter, children may have experienced many chronic adversities and traumatic events. More immediately, children may have gone hungry and lost friends, possessions, and the security of familiar places and people at home, at school, or in the neighborhood. . . . Locations [of shelters] are usually undesirable, particularly with respect to children playing outside. Moreover, necessary shelter rules may strain a child and family life. For example, it is typical for no visitors to be allowed, and for children to be . . . accompanied at all times by a parent. [Masten, 1992]

Further, the parents are caught in a situation in which their autonomy and competence is always compromised (Seltser & Miller, 1993). Hence, they cannot really be parents—caregivers and tutors—to their school-age children. Moreover, a shelter is only a temporary solution to homelessness, requiring periodic upheaval as children move to alternative locations with a parent who is humiliated, depressed, and emotionally exhausted. Sometimes the child is sent to foster care or to some institution while the parent is treated separately. Thus three major risk factors—conflict, instability of relationships, and poverty—are glaringly present for homeless children.

Compared to their nonhomeless peers of similar economic and ethnic status, homeless children have fewer friends, more fears, more fights, more chronic illnesses, more changes of school, lower school attendance, and less academic achievement (Buckner et al., 1999; Huth, 1997; Nunez, 1996). During middle childhood, when school and friends become so important, about one-third of all homeless children are absent from school on any given day. Those in school are likely to be

Fighting Homelessness Despite the anxiety evident in these children, this is a hopeful scene. The woman on the left, formerly homeless, is now living with her children in a stable community residence and is also studying for her high school degree, with the help of a college student. With secure housing and education or job training, many homeless families can become functional again.

in special education or to be held back. The net result is that "many homeless youth are cut off forever from achievement in traditional school programs" (Huth, 1997).

In terms of long-term development, the most chilling result may be a loss of faith in life's possibilities. Compared even with other impoverished children, homeless children have lower aspirations, less hope, and more suspicion, expressing doubt that anyone will ever help them. And often they are right, especially regarding the most important support during childhood—that of other children. Virtually no homeless child can make school friends. The lack of continuity in their lives and their low self-esteem keep them from developing mutually supportive friendships. Even practical considerations, such as shelter rules about visiting and curfews, tend to make friendships impossible. Perhaps because of a lack of such support, clinical depression is common, striking almost one homeless child in every three (Bassuk & Rosenberg, 1990).

While the public may debate the root causes of, and the best solutions to, homelessness, it is apparent from a developmental perspective that something must be done immediately for every homeless child. Every month of education that a homeless child loses, and every blow to self-esteem that he or she suffers, may take years—or perhaps a lifetime—to overcome. For those who are interested in establishing public policies that can provide a better future, education of homeless children is a good issue to start with (Nunez, 1996).

table **13.4**	**Strengths and Relationships That Help Children Under Stress**
Source	Strength
Individual child	Good intellectual functioning Appealing, sociable, easygoing disposition Self-efficacy, self-confidence, high self-esteem Talents (artistic, athletic, academic) Religious faith
Child's family	Close relationship to a caring parent figure Authoritative parenting: warmth, structure, high expectations Socioeconomic advantages Connections to extended supportive family networks
Other	Bonds to prosocial adults outside the family Connections to prosocial organizations (e.g., a church, temple, mosque, or settlement house) Attendance at an effective school with understanding teachers

Focus on Competency

If a child has several crucial strengths (see Table 13.4), he or she can "sustain reasonably good development" even in the face of serious problems (Masten & Coatsworth, 1998). Particularly important are various competencies—especially social, academic, and creative skills—which can help the child deflect or avoid many of the problems he or she may encounter at home or in the community (Conrad & Hammen, 1993).

There are several ways in which competence can make up for disabling factors. One is through self-esteem. If children feel confident in at least one area of their lives, they become able to see the rest of their lives in perspective. They can believe, for example, that despite how others might reject or belittle them, they are not worthless failures.

More practically, children with better-developed cognitive and social skills are able to employ coping strategies against their problems—perhaps by changing the conditions that brought about a problem in the first place or by restructuring their own reaction to the problem (Masten & Coatsworth, 1998). You learned from Chapter 12 that, during middle childhood, children develop metacognition and become more logical, an advance that allows them to think rationally about thinking. They can use this ability to convince themselves that "it's not my fault," or "when I am older, I will escape."

Because their cognitive abilities and, hence, their coping repertoires "increase and become more differentiated in middle childhood," older children may deal with the stresses of life better than children who are just beginning middle childhood (Aldwin, 1994). Thus, when a peer is suddenly antagonistic, a 6-year-old is likely to dissolve into tears or to launch a clumsy counterattack that merely brings further rejection. Older children, on the other hand, are more adept at finding ways to disguise their hurt, keep a bully at bay, repair a broken friendship, or even make new friends to replace old ones (Compas et al., 1991).

Schools and teachers can play a significant role in the development of such competencies. School achievement can help all children, including those from seriously deprived backgrounds, to aspire beyond the limited horizons they may encounter in their daily lives.

Active Listening What every boy needs—a father who is physically close, listening carefully (note the cocked head), and not afraid to get his feet wet.

Social Support

Another important element that helps children deal with problems—one we have already touched on—is the social support they receive (Garmezy, 1993). Ideally, a strong bond with a loving and firm parent can help see a child through many difficulties. Even in war-torn or deeply impoverished neighborhoods, when a child is strongly attached to a parent, who in turn has been present consistently since the child's infancy, the child tends to be resilient (Masten & Coatsworth, 1998). If such a parent is not available, the companionship and comfort provided by a steadfast grandparent, sibling, or even family pet can remove some tension from a child's life (Furman & Buhrmester, 1992; Werner & Smith, 1992).

One of the benefits of the expanding social world of middle childhood is the possibility of seeking out many more potential sources of social support. For example, a child whose parents are fighting bitterly on their way to divorce may spend hours on the phone with a friend whose parents have successfully separated; may often be invited to dinner at a neighbor's house where family harmony still prevails; or may devote himself or herself to helping a teacher or a coach or to working with a community group. One specific example comes from Jonathan Kozol's study of children in the South Bronx (Kozol, 1991). A young fatherless boy, whose mother had AIDS, found himself intrigued by a neighborhood man who was a poet. The boy often heard quotations from great literature; learned to read, especially admiring Edgar Allen Poe ("Did you know he grew up in the Bronx?"); and aspired to become a writer himself. Such hope for the future can sustain many a deprived young person.

An additional source of support is religion. Especially for children in difficult circumstances, religious faith itself can be psychologically protective. The South Bronx boy wrote to Kozol:

> No violence will there be in heaven. There will be no guns or drugs or IRS. You won't have to pay taxes. You'll recognize all the children who have died when they were little. Jesus will be good to them and play with them. At night he'll come and visit at your house. God will be fond of you. [quoted in Kozol, 1991]

School-age children, almost universally, develop their own theology, influenced by whatever formal religious education they might receive, but by no means identical to it. This personal religion helps them structure life and deal with worldly problems (Coles, 1990; Hyde, 1990). An 8-year-old African-American girl who, in the 1960s, was one of the first to enter a previously all-white school, remembers walking past a gauntlet of adults yelling insults:

> I was all alone, and those people were screaming, and suddenly I saw God smiling, and I smiled. A woman was standing there, and she shouted at me

"Hey you little nigger, what are you smiling at?" I looked right up at her face, and I said "At God." Then she looked up at the sky, and then she looked at me, and she didn't call me any more names. [quoted in Coles, 1990]

In a way, this example illustrates many aspects of children's coping abilities, for it was not only faith but also a measure of self-confidence, social understanding, and skill at deflecting her own emotional reactions that enabled this child to overcome a very real threat.

Conclusion

We wish that all children could have an idyllic childhood, but that is never the case. Nor is it necessary. Research on coping in middle childhood clearly suggests that as they grow older, most children develop ways to deal with all varieties of stress, from minor hassles to major traumatic events.

This realization can guide adults who seek to be of help. If the home situation is difficult, for instance, any adult, from a caring teacher to a loving grandparent, can step in and make a critical difference. If parents want to divorce, they should first figure out how to ensure that their children will receive the necessary material and emotional resources. Or if a child has a severe reading difficulty, developing the child's talents in some other area—math or baseball or music—may be as important to the child's overall well-being as immediately overcoming the learning disability.

Within neighborhoods, the attitude that everyone is responsible for all the children's behavior can also improve life for individuals (Sampson et al., 1997). More broadly, measures designed to enhance the social context, perhaps by making violent neighborhoods safer or improving job opportunities in impoverished communities, can benefit school-age children substantially:

> Successful children remind us that children grow up in multiple contexts in families, schools, peer groups, baseball teams, religious organizations, and many other groups—and each context is a potential source of protective factors as well as risks. These children demonstrate that children are protected not only by the self-righting nature of development, but also by the actions of adults, by their own actions by the nurturing of their assets, by opportunities to succeed, and by the experience of success. The behavior of adults often plays a critical role in children's risks, resources, opportunities, and resilience. Development is biased toward competence, but there is no such thing as an invulnerable child. If we allow the prevalence of known risk factors for development to rise while resources for children fall, we can expect the competent individual children and the human capital of the nation to suffer. [Masten & Coatsworth, 1998]

As you will see in the next three chapters, adolescence is a continuation of middle childhood, as well as a radical departure from it. Stresses and strains continue to accumulate, and "known risk factors," including drug availability and sexual urges, become more prevalent. Fortunately, for many young people protective resources and constructive coping also increase. Personal competencies, family support, and close friends get most children not only through childhood but also through adolescence undamaged. Indeed, the same factors help each of us throughout our development, as we overcome the problems, and build on the strengths, that characterized the first decade of our lives.

SUMMARY

AN EXPANDING SOCIAL WORLD

1. In middle childhood, children move away from their narrow social sphere and their unswerving self-satisfaction and enter a wide arena, as described by all developmental theories. Erikson, for example, calls this the time of industry, and Freud says that sexual concerns are latent.

2. School-age children develop a multifaceted view of social interactions, becoming increasingly aware of the complex personalities, motives, and emotions that underlie others' behavior. At the same time, they become better able to adjust their own behavior to interact appropriately with others.

3. Children also develop more sophisticated conceptions of themselves and their own behavior. As they become more knowledgeable about their personalities, emotions, abilities, and shortcomings, they evaluate themselves by comparing themselves with others. This contributes to greater focus on competence, more self-criticism, and diminished self-esteem.

MORAL DEVELOPMENT

4. Moral reasoning becomes more significant during middle childhood. Kohlberg proposed that this reasoning develops through six stages of increasing complexity, from the elemental "might makes right" to the recognition of universal ethical principles. Kohlberg's theory seems generally valid, although it has been criticized for being biased toward males and toward liberal Western values.

5. School-age children think about moral values—about what is right and what actions are ethical. Their actual behavior is powerfully influenced by their loyalty to their peers as well as by their culture.

THE PEER GROUP

6. Peer relationships provide opportunities for social growth because peers are on an equal footing with each other and must learn to adjust to each other accordingly. During the school years, children create their own subculture, with its own language, values, and codes of behavior. Quite specific norms for conflict and aggression are developed by each society of children.

7. Friendships become more selective and exclusive as children grow older. Psychologists, and children themselves, consider having a few close friends, or at least one best friend, an important indicator of psychosocial health.

8. Rejected and accepted children differ in many ways. One of the most important is how they interpret an ambiguous social situation—as a threat, an attack, an innocent mistake, or a friendly overture.

9. Bullying—repeated efforts by children to inflict harm on a particular child—seems to be universal. Among girls, victims tend to be shy, and bullies overassertive; among boys, victims are physically weaker, and bullies of above-average size. Over the years, victims may develop low self-esteem and bullies may become socially rejected and eventually criminal.

FAMILIES IN SCHOOL YEARS

10. Family functioning is far more crucial to children's well-being than family structure is. Families should provide five things in middle childhood: basic sustenance, education, self-esteem, peer friendship, and harmony within a stable setting. Families structured with various legal or biological connections among their members or with various numbers of adults and children can function well.

11. While family functioning is key, certain family structures—especially those characterized by conflict, low income, or family arrangements that change unpredictably from year to year—tend to be more stressful for children. Divorce and remarriage are not easy on children. Support from the extended family, friends, and the community can ease the difficulty of such transitions.

COPING WITH PROBLEMS

12. Almost every child has some difficulties at home, at school, or in the community. Most children cope quite well, as long as the problems are limited in duration and degree and do not stress daily life too much. Homelessness is particularly devastating in middle childhood.

13. How well particular children cope with the problems in their lives depends on the number and nature of the stresses they experience, the strengths of their various competencies, and the social support they receive.

KEY TERMS

industry versus
  inferiority (399)
5-to-7 shift (400)
social cognition (400)
social comparison (401)
preconventional moral
  reasoning (403)
conventional moral
  reasoning (403)
postconventional moral
  reasoning (403)
morality of care (404)
morality of justice (404)

prosocial behavior (406)
peer group (407)
society of children (408)
aggressive-rejected
  children (411)
withdrawn-rejected
  children (411)
bullying (412)
family structure (418)
extended family (418)
nuclear family (418)
single-parent family (418)
blended family (418)

KEY QUESTIONS

1. How does a child's understanding of other people change during the school years, and what difference does this make for the child?

2. How does a child's self-understanding change from the preschool years through middle childhood?

3. What is the basic difference between each of the three levels of moral development, according to Kohlberg?

4. How do children learn to apply their moral thinking to their behavior?

5. Why are peer relationships particularly important during the school years?

6. What characteristics distinguish the society of children from the larger adult society?

7. How are the two types of rejected children different?

8. What are some of the consequences of bullying, for the victims and for the bullies?

9. What were the particulars, and the effects, of the antibullying program that was implemented in Norway?

10. What are the most important aspects of family functioning?

11. What are the advantages and possible disadvantages of a two-parent home?

12. When is divorce particularly difficult for children, and what advantages might it bring?

13. What are some of the problems that are experienced in single-parent, blended, or other "nontraditional" households?

14. How can school-age children be helped to cope with the stresses they encounter as they develop?

15. *In Your Experience* What were your specific individual and family characteristics? What cultural and community factors helped you cope during middle childhood? What factors tended to have the opposite effect?

CRITICAL THINKING EXERCISE

by Richard O. Straub

Take your study of Chapter 13 a step further by working this perspective-taking exercise.

Here is a situation that is somewhat similar to Kohlberg's dilemmas for moral reasoning. Three weeks before their history term papers are due, Jennifer, Blake, and Sharon meet at the campus library to conduct on-line literature searches on their topics. After 30 minutes of surfing the Web, Blake announces that he's found a Web site that offers inexpensive term papers on a variety of subjects, including the topic of his paper. Jennifer, who has never cheated in her academic career, says nothing and maintains her concentration on her own research. Sharon, who is appalled by Blake's intention to cheat, vows that she will report Blake to their professor.

In choosing their selected courses of action, Blake, Sharon, and Jennifer each made a moral decision. Behavior alone does not indicate moral thinking, however. Your job is to write a justification that each of these three students might use at each of Kohlberg's three levels of moral reasoning—preconventional, conventional, and postconventional. All together, then, you are being asked for nine justifications. As an example, at the preconventional level, Blake might reason: "There's no way I'll be caught; I don't think the teacher even knows there are term papers on the Web."

After you have devised the remaining eight justifications, you can check your answers by comparing them to the sample answers in Appendix B.

Then decide which course of action would be most like your own, and which justification you would use.

BIOSOCIAL

Growth and Skills

During middle childhood, children grow more slowly than they did during infancy and toddlerhood or than they will during adolescence. Increased strength and lung capacity give children the endurance to improve their performance in skills such as swimming and running. Slower growth contributes to children's increasing bodily control, and children enjoying exercising their developing skills of coordination and balance. Which specific skills they master depends largely on culture, gender, and inherited ability.

Special Needs

Many children have special learning needs that may originate in brain patterns but that express themselves in educational problems. Early recognition, targeted education, and psychological support help all children, from those with autism to the much milder instance of a specific learning disability.

COGNITIVE

Thinking

During middle childhood, children become better able to understand and learn, in part because of growth in their processing capacity, knowledge base, and memory capacity. At the same time, metacognition techniques enable children to organize their learning. Beginning at about age 7 or 8, children also develop the ability to understand logical principles, including the concepts of identity, reciprocity, and reversibility.

Language

Children's increasing ability to understand the structures and possibilities of language enables them to extend the range of their cognitive powers and to become more analytical in their use of vocabulary. Most children develop proficiency in several language codes, and some become bilingual.

Education

Formal schooling begins worldwide, with the specifics of the curriculum depending on economic and societal factors. An individual child's learning success depends on the time allotted to each task, specific guided instruction from teachers and parents, and the overall values of the culture.

PSYCHOSOCIAL

Emotions and Personality Development

School-age children come to understand themselves and others, as well as what is right in their relations with others. Morality arises as a social construct, dependent on the example of parents and peers. The peer group becomes increasingly important as children become less dependent on their parents and more dependent on friends for help, loyalty, and sharing of mutual interests.

Parents and Problems

Parents continue to influence children, especially as they exacerbate or buffer problems in school and the community. During these years, families need to meet basic needs, encourage learning, develop self-esteem, nurture friendship, and—most important—provide harmony and stability. Parents in the midst of divorce may be deficient in all of these. Most single-parent, foster, or grandparent families are better than families in open conflict, but a family with two biological parents, both of whom are cooperative with each other and loving to the child, is generally best. Low family income, and particularly homelessness, add substantial stress in middle childhood. Fortunately, school-age children often develop competencies and skills that protect them somewhat against the stresses that almost all experience. Friends, family, school, and community can all be helpful in encouraging the resilience that many children manifest.

435

PART V

Adolescence

Adolescence is the period of transition from childhood to adulthood. It is probably the most challenging and complicated period of life to describe, to study, or to experience. The biological changes of puberty, which is considered to begin adolescence, are universal, but their expression, timing, and extent show enormous variety, depending on gender, genes, and nutrition. Cognitive development varies as well: many adolescents are egocentric, while others think logically, hypothetically, and theoretically. Psychosocial changes during this second decade of life show even greater diversity, as adolescents develop their own identities—choosing from a vast number of sexual, moral, political, and educational paths. Most of this diversity simply reflects differences in social and cultural contexts. But for about one adolescent in four, fateful choices are made that handicap, and sometimes destroy, the future.

Yet there is also a commonality to the adolescent experience. All adolescents are confronted with the same developmental tasks: they must adjust to their changing body sizes and shapes, to their awakening sexuality, and to new ways of thinking. They all strive for the emotional maturity and economic independence that characterize adulthood. As we will see in the next three chapters, the adolescent's efforts to come to grips with these tasks is often touched with confusion and poignancy.

Adolescence:
Biosocial Development

CHAPTER 14

During **adolescence,** roughly age 11 to 21, humans everywhere cross a great divide between childhood and adulthood—biosocially, cognitively, and socio-culturally. No one would call this process easy. The biological aspect is uneven but occurs fairly quickly; the cognitive and psychosocial aspects typically take longer, lasting at least until age 18 and often until age 22, 25, or even 30. Adjusting to all of the changes of adolescence can be difficult and stressful.

This does not mean that adolescence is defined by its problems. However, all adolescents experience moments of awkwardness, confusion, anger, and depression; many make serious missteps on the path toward maturity; and some encounter obstacles that halt their progress completely. This chapter and the two that follow examine some of these problems, putting them into perspective.

However, the same developmental changes that cause difficulty also create excitement, challenge, and growth: "Adolescence in all industrial societies, and at all times during this century, constitutes a period of life that is full of [both] opportunity and risk" (Leffert & Petersen, 1995). The risk is real, but most adolescents seize the opportunity instead. Seriously troubled adolescents are in the minority, and many of the so-called problems of adolescence are actually more problematic for parents and society than for teenagers themselves. For instance, the same music that makes adults shake their heads in disbelief makes young people jump with joy; the incessant telephoning that exasperates parents is a social lifeline for teenagers; the sexual awakening that many adults in our culture fear is, for many individuals, the beginning of thrilling intimacy. Any generalizations about the nature of adolescence, and especially about its turbulence, must be applied with care.

PUBERTY BEGINS

Puberty is a period of rapid physical growth and sexual maturation that ends childhood and begins adolescence, producing a person of adult size, shape, and sexual potential. Puberty is triggered by a chain of hormonal effects that bring on visible physical changes (see Table 14.1).

For girls, these visible changes include, in sequence, the onset of breast growth, the initial pubic hair, a peak growth spurt, widening of the hips, the first menstrual period, the completion of pubic-hair growth, and final breast development. For boys, the visible physical changes of puberty include, in approximate order, the initial pubic hair, growth of the testes, growth of the penis, the first ejaculation, a peak growth spurt, voice changes, beard development, and the completion of pubic-hair growth (Malina, 1990; Rutter, 1980).

table **14.1**	**Sequence of Puberty**		
Girls	Approximate Average Age*		Boys
Ovaries increase production of estrogen and progesterone†	9	10	Testes increase production of testosterone†
Uterus and vagina begin to grow larger	9½	11	Testes and scrotum grow larger
Breast "bud" stage	10	12	Pubic hair begins to appear
Pubic hair begins to appear	11	12½	Penis growth begins
Weight spurt begins	11½	13	Spermarche (first ejaculation)
Peak height spurt	12	13	Weight spurt begins
Peak muscle and organ growth (also, hips become noticeably wider)	12½	14	Peak height spurt
Menarche (first menstrual period)	12½	14½	Peak muscle and organ growth (also, shoulders become noticeably broader)
First ovulation	13½	15	Voice lowers
Final pubic-hair pattern	15	16	Readily visible facial hair
Full breast growth	16	18	Final pubic-hair pattern

*Average ages are rough approximations, with many perfectly normal, healthy adolescents as much as 3 years ahead of or behind these ages. In addition, the sequence is somewhat variable.

†Estrogen, progesterone, and testosterone are hormones that influence sexual characteristics, including reproductive function. All three are also provided, in small amounts, by the adrenal glands in both sexes. Major production, however, occurs in the gonads, with marked male-female differences.

adolescence The period of biological, cognitive, and psychosocial transition from childhood to adulthood, usually lasting a decade or so.

puberty A period of rapid growth and sexual change that occurs in early adolescence and produces a person of adult size, shape, and sexual potential.

gonads The pair of sex glands in humans. In girls, these are called ovaries; in boys, these are called testes or testicles.

Typically, the major events of growth and sexual maturation are finished 3 or 4 years after puberty begins, although some individuals gain an additional inch or two of height, and most gain additional fat and muscle, in early adulthood. Before further detailing the growth spurt and sexual maturation, we will look at the factors that precede those visible changes.

Hormones and Puberty

The biology of puberty begins with a hormonal signal from the *hypothalamus*, located at the base of the brain. This signal stimulates the *pituitary gland* (located next to the hypothalamus) to produce hormones that then stimulate the *adrenal glands* (two small glands near the kidneys at both sides of the torso) and the **gonads**, or sex glands (the *ovaries* and *testes* or *testicles*). One hormone in particular, *GnRH (gonad releasing hormone)*, causes the gonads to dramatically increase the production of sex hormones, chiefly *estrogen* in girls and *testosterone* in boys. This increase, in turn, loops back to the hypothalamus and pituitary gland, causing them to produce more GH (growth hormone) as well as more GnRH, and this, in turn, causes the adrenal glands and gonads to produce more sex hormones (see Figure 14.1).

Although testosterone is considered the male hormone and estrogen the female hormone, levels of both hormones increase in boys and girls at puberty. However, the rate of increase is sex-specific: testosterone production skyrockets in boys, up to 18 times the level in childhood, but increases much less in girls; estrogen production increases up to 8 times in girls, but

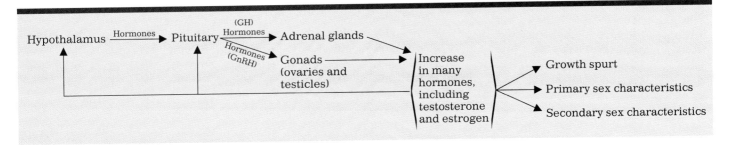

Figure 14.1 Biological Sequence of Puberty.
Puberty begins with a hormonal signal from the hypothalamus, which signals the pituitary gland. The pituitary, in turn, signals the adrenal glands and the ovaries or testes.

not nearly as much in boys (Malina & Bouchard, 1991). You will later see that changes in facial hair, voice quality, and breast size also occur in both sexes—and again, the difference is in degree.

Body and Mind

It is a popular notion that hormonal changes are responsible for the emotional changes of puberty, as well as for the physical changes. To some extent this is true (Golub, 1992; Richards, 1996; Susman, 1997):

- Rapidly increasing hormone levels, especially of testosterone, cause the more rapid arousal of emotions seen in teenagers.
- Hormones affect the quick shifts in the extremes of emotions—from feeling great to suddenly feeling lousy—that seem typical.
- For boys, hormonal increases lead to more thoughts about sex, as well as more masturbation.
- For many girls, the ebb and flow of hormones during the menstrual cycle produce specific mood changes, from a positive mood at midcycle to sadness or anger a day or two before the next period.

All these hormonal shifts are lifelong, but they are more erratic and powerful, and less familiar and controllable, in puberty.

Nonetheless, detailed studies suggest that hormonal levels make a relatively small *direct* contribution to the daily emotional changes of puberty. A much more potent hormonal influence on the overall emotional tone of adolescence, both positive and negative, is indirect, via the *psychological impact of the visible changes.* And that impact, in turn, is powerfully influenced by the values and expectations of the developing person's family, peer group, and culture (Brooks-Gunn & Reiter, 1990; Nottelman et al., 1990).

In other words, hormones directly cause moods and emotions to change more quickly than before, but hormones have their greatest emotional impact indirectly, by causing visible signs such as the growth of breasts or beards. It is these signs, and the reactions they produce in other people, that cause most adolescent emotional reactions and counterreactions. The strength of all these reactions depends on the social context. Even the one change that is linked most directly to hormones, specifically thinking about sex, is powerfully affected by culture, which can shape such thoughts into enjoyable fantasies, shameful preoccupations, or an impetus to action.

Raging Hormones? At this age, testosterone is suddenly flooding teenagers' bloodstreams, and sex is on their minds—a bawdy locker room joke will seem hilarious. For the most part, however, hormones await social triggers, and until something happens, these boys will remain emotionally neutral and socially detached. An unexpected team victory or defeat, or, for the boy on the left, the visible eruption of a pimple or a beard hair, could lead to an emotional explosion—sudden, exaggerated, and then gone a few hours later.

❷ **Especially for Immigrants:** Improved nutrition is an obvious benefit of leaving an impoverished nation and raising children in a developed one. However, can you see any problems this nutritional advantage might bring during adolescence?

When Do Changes Begin?

The visible changes of puberty, as you just read, are themselves triggered by an invisible sequence of hormone production, which typically begins a year or more before the first pubic hairs appear. But what is it that starts the hormones? We know that the age at which puberty starts is highly variable: normal children begin to notice body changes at any time between the ages of 8 and 14, with the hormonal changes beginning a year or two earlier for girls than for boys. Beyond gender, three other factors play a role in timing: genes, nutrition, and stress.

Genes

menarche   A female's first menstrual period.

Genetic influence is clearly seen in **menarche**, a girl's first menstrual period. The "normal" age of menarche varies widely, from 9 to 18 years. However, sisters reach menarche, on average, only 13 months apart, and monozygotic twins typically differ by a mere 2.8 months. A daughter's age of menarche also is correlated with her mother's age of menarche, which (of course) occurred under quite different historical and familial circumstances (Golub, 1992). Other pubertal changes, for boys as well as for girls, also follow familial patterns (Brooks-Gunn, 1991).

Perhaps for genetic reasons, the average age of puberty varies somewhat from nation to nation and from ethnic group to ethnic group. Within Europe, for example, the onset of puberty tends to be relatively late for Belgians and relatively early for Poles (Malina et al., 1988). Within the United States, African Americans often begin puberty earlier, and Asian Americans later, than Americans of European ancestry.

An Awkward Age The normal variation in age of puberty is readily apparent in this junior high gym class in Texas.

❷ *Observational Quiz (see answer page 445): What three signs can you see that the boy in the foreground wants to be taller and the girl beside him wishes she were less conspicuous?*

Nutrition

In general, stocky individuals experience puberty earlier than those with taller, thinner builds. Menarche, in particular, seems related to the accumulation of a certain amount of body fat; it does not usually occur until a girl weighs about 100 pounds (about 45 kilograms). Females who have little body fat (either because they are seriously malnourished or because they are gymnasts, runners, or similar athletes) menstruate later and more irregularly than the average girl, and those who are generally inactive (and thus have less muscle) menstruate earlier (Richards, 1996).

In times of famine, puberty is typically delayed by several years (Golub, 1992). For instance, among teenagers in Kenya, those in impoverished rural communities experience puberty later than their urban age-mates, by 3 years for boys and 2 years for girls (Kulin, 1993).

secular trend   The tendency of successive generations to develop differently as a result of social changes—mainly improved nutrition and medical care. As related to adolescence, the secular trend results in earlier puberty than in previous centuries.

The effects of nutrition are more broadly seen in the **secular trend,** which is the tendency of successive cohorts to develop differently because of historical conditions, especially more food and better medicine. One manifestation of the secular trend has been that each new generation has experienced puberty earlier than the previous generation did (Tanner, 1991). A century ago, for example, the first visible signs of puberty were typically apparent in females at about age 15 and in males at about age 16, not at ages 10 and 11 as they now are.

As best we can determine, the current average age of puberty in developed nations is close to the genetic minimum for our species, since most children are well fed (Leffert & Peterson, 1995). Thus, most of today's middle-aged Western adults reached puberty at an earlier age than their own parents

A Proud Papa Why has this father decided to capture this moment? Perhaps his eldest daughter is the first in the family to graduate from high school, much less to attend her senior prom with an elegant costume and a handsome escort. That is speculation. But one thing is obvious: These parents are much shorter and stockier than their high school child, suggesting that their childhood diet was less than adequate. The secular trend is apparent in body growth. The secular trend also affects educational attainment, although this is not captured in a snapshot.

and grandparents did, but most of today's children will experience puberty at approximately the same age as their parents did.

In developing countries, however, the secular trend may continue as diet and health care improve. Or it may fluctuate, depending on the overall quality of life. This possibility was dramatically illustrated in Japan: There, the average age of puberty became slightly younger from 1900 to 1935, as we would expect with the secular trend. However, it then rose from 1935 to 1950, when economic depression, World War II, and the devastation of defeat severely compromised the Japanese quality of life, making young bodies too thin to begin puberty early. As conditions improved after 1950, the secular trend took hold again and the age of puberty fell until recently; now, apparently having reached its genetic minimum, it has leveled off (Tanner, 1991).

Stress

A third factor may also influence the onset of puberty: the stress of the child's life, particularly conflict in the parent-child relationship. Many studies have found a correlation between early puberty and parent-adolescent strife. The traditional explanation always was that puberty caused the strife—more specifically, that the combination of the young person's "raging hormones" and emotional immaturity provoked anger and rejection from the parents.

Surprisingly, longitudinal research suggests that cause and effect may be reversed—that family conflict and stress may precede the early onset of puberty (Steinberg, 1988; Surbey, 1990; Wierson et al., 1993), with the particulars that cause stress varying from culture to culture. For example, a New Zealand study found that girls experience earlier puberty when their parents are divorced (Moffitt et al., 1992); this was not found to be true in England (Richards, 1996). A Swedish study found that adopted girls from India typically began puberty at age 11½ years, which was earlier than the onset for girls in India (age 12½ for privileged girls and age 13½ for impoverished girls) and for native Swedish girls (age 13) (Proos et al., 1991). Again, family or community stress could be the underlying reason. Confirmation comes from research on animals, which shows that stress causes increased production of the hormones that initiate puberty.

None of this proves that the correlation between puberty and family conflict is caused solely by stress; more likely, the biogenetic and the psychosocial factors interact. Overall, as Figures 14.2 (below) and 14.3 (on page 444) depict, biological events and psychological stresses are intertwined in the causes and consequences of puberty.

Figure 14.2 From Hormones in the Brain to Changes in the Body. Even this chart is a simplification of a complex interaction that includes genes, biological events, and psychological conditions every step of the way.

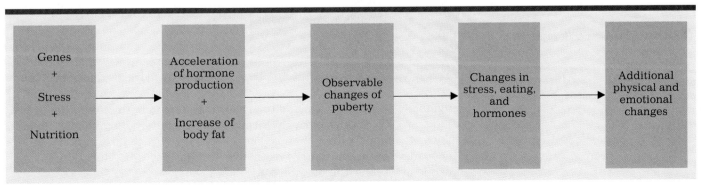

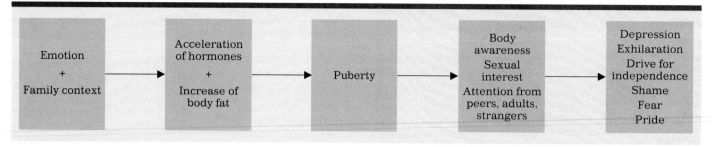

Figure 14.3 Biosocial Causes and Consequences of Puberty. The emotions caused by puberty are part of a chain of events that begin with genes and social context and end with a teenager who is proud or ashamed. At every step, the interplay of biological and psychological factors determines the emotions of the person.

Early and Late Maturation

Young people who reach puberty "on time" (when their friends do) view the changes more positively than those who reach it earlier or later (Dubas et al., 1991). Usually, the specific effects of early and late maturation differ for the two sexes. Early maturation is harder on girls; later maturation, on boys.

Too Soon a Woman

Early-maturing girls, who are taller and more developed than their classmates, discover added pressures and expectations but find few peers who share their interests or problems. Prepubescent girls call them "boy crazy," and boys tease them about their big feet or developing breasts. Almost every sixth-grade class has at least one early-maturing 11-year-old who slouches so she won't look so tall, wears loose shirts so no one will notice her breasts, and buys her shoes too small. Her body image is worse and her risk of developing eating disorders is greater than they are among girls who reach puberty later (Graber et al., 1994).

The Same Age, but Years Apart Both 14-year-olds pictured here experienced puberty "off-time." Probably the early maturer suffered considerable stress at around age 11, when her feet, hips, and breasts provoked unwanted attention. By this point, however, she may already have learned to cope with her body image, and the late-maturing girl may be wishing her body would "hurry up."

If an early-maturing girl begins dating, her boyfriends are usually older. They typically encourage her to smoke, drink, and engage in other "adult activities" long before her intellectual judgment can cope with them (Brooks-Gunn, 1991). She may feel constantly scrutinized by her parents, who suspect she is up to no good, criticized by her girlfriends for not spending time with them, and pressured by her dates to be sexually active. Such difficulties for early-maturing girls may be compounded by ongoing family tensions, since, as you have seen, family conflict correlates with early puberty in girls.

In many communities in the United States, early maturation increases the risk of teen pregnancy. This does not seem to be true in England, although it does lead to earlier coupling in both sexes (Richards & Elliott, 1993). Nor does early maturing seem to hinder German girls; in fact, they have higher, rather than lower, self-esteem. These international differences may originate in more extensive and positive sex education in some European nations (Silbereisen & Kracke, 1993).

❶ Response for Immigrants (from page 442): A nutritional improvement means the new generation will reach puberty sooner and grow taller than the previous one. Unless this is anticipated, cultural traditions regarding sexual information may come too late to be helpful, and authoritarian discipline may be difficult when teenagers are taller and stronger than their parents.

Is He Okay? The small, skinny boy seems overwhelmed by the horde towering around him, and he seems to be a target. However, his very presence suggests that, perhaps with humor or friendship skills, he may be holding his own. Many similarly built boys his age have already beat a shameful exit, to the library, the TV, or their own private retreats.

growth spurt The period of relatively sudden and rapid physical growth of every part of the body that occurs during puberty.

❶ *Answer to Observational Quiz (from page 442): He is on his tip-toes, his arms stretch their longest, and even his hairstyle adds an inch or two. The girl beside him has her feet flat and wide apart, her T-shirt big and loose, and her hair as short and unfeminine as she can make it. If you noticed that his #23 Bulls shirt is Michael Jordan's, give yourself extra credit.*

Too Late a Man

Late-maturing boys must watch themselves be outdistanced, first by the girls in their class and then by most of the boys—all the while enduring the patronizing scorn of those who only recently were immature. Beyond that, generalizations are more difficult to make for boys than for girls. A review of the relevant research finds that although the effects of early male puberty are generally positive, the effects of late puberty are not necessarily negative. They depend on the boy's particular personality traits, the population under study, and cultural pressures (Downs, 1990).

Generally, boys who are unusually short, who are not athletic, who appear physically weak or unattractive, and/or who are slow to become sexually involved tend to have lower self-esteem. They also create more problems during adolescence, such as disrupting class or challenging a police officer. This is true no matter what the timing of a boy's development. However, the later puberty begins, the more likely it is that each of these liabilities will occur and will be noticed by peers. Obviously, these characteristics do not always coexist: some late developers may be quite handsome and athletic. This would counteract the negative impact of later maturation, especially if the school is small enough and the sports varied enough so that a gifted small boy can excel.

Further, if a boy is smart, creative, and witty, he will be admired no matter how "behind" he is in beard growth or muscle size, as long as his social skills are adequate. An added factor is how much the culture emphasizes male size and strength, because when these are highly valued, late-maturing boys suffer. Thus, the extent of the late developer's problems will vary, from person to person, peer group to peer group, and culture to culture. Probably the worst context for a late-developing boy is to be in a large high school, where homecoming dances, cheerleading squads, and public approval all focus on the captain and quarterback of the football (U.S.-style) team.

THE GROWTH SPURT

The **growth spurt** is just what the term suggests—a sudden, uneven, and somewhat unpredictable jump in the size of almost every part of the body. The first sign of the pubertal growth spurt is increased bone length and density, beginning at the tips of the extremities and working toward the center of the body. Adolescents' fingers and toes lengthen before their hands and feet, and their hands and feet lengthen before their arms and legs. The torso is the last part to grow, so many pubescent children are temporarily bigfooted, long-legged, and short-waisted, appearing to be "all legs and arms" (Hofmann, 1997).

Wider, Taller, Then Stronger

While the bones begin to lengthen, the child eats more and gains weight more rapidly than before, to provide energy for the many changes taking place. As a result, fat accumulates (Malina, 1991). In fact, parents typically notice that their children are emptying their plates, cleaning out the refrigerator, and

He's Outgrown His Shoes The typical body proportions of the young adolescent are particularly noticeable in this runner: long legs, long feet, and a relatively short torso.

straining the seams of their clothes even before they notice that their children are growing taller. By the end of middle childhood, usually between the ages of 10 and 12, all children become noticeably heavier, although exactly when, where, and how much fat accumulates depends partly on heredity, partly on diet and exercise, and partly on gender. Females gain more fat overall, especially on their legs and hips, because evolution designed young adult females to have extra body fat to sustain pregnancy and lactation and designed young adult males to move swiftly in the hunt.

A height spurt follows soon after the start of the weight increase, burning up some of the stored fat and redistributing some of the rest. About a year or two later, a period of muscle increase occurs (Hofmann, 1997). As a consequence, the pudginess and clumsiness exhibited by the typical child in early puberty generally disappears a few years later. Overall, boys increase in muscle strength by at least 150 percent (Armstrong & Welsman, 1997). This is particularly notable in boys' upper bodies: between ages 13 and 18 years, male arm strength more than doubles (Beunen et al., 1988).

The typical girl gains about 38 pounds (17 kilograms) and 9⅝ inches (24 centimeters) between the ages of 10 and 14; the typical boy gains about 42 pounds (19 kilograms) and about 10 inches (25 centimeters) between the ages of 12 and 16. Girls typically gain the most weight in their thirteenth year, and boys in their fourteenth year (Malina & Bouchard, 1991). (See Appendix A.)

Note, however, that all these "typical" data are deceptive, because they are the average of many individual growth spurts, which occur at widely different ages for different children. Any year between ages 10 and 16, we can find some individuals who do not grow much at all because their major growth spurt has not begun, some who do not grow much because their spurt is already over, and some who are growing very rapidly. Thus, individual growth spurts are obviously much more rapid than the overall average: during the 12-month period of their greatest growth, many girls gain as much as 20 pounds (9 kilograms) and 3½ inches (9 centimeters), and many boys gain up to 26 pounds (12 kilograms) and 4 inches (10 centimeters) (Tanner, 1991).

Transitions These four adolescents, close in age, illustrate the discrepancy in timing that is typical at this age. No two people reach adult size and activity in every way simultaneously. Compare each of these pubescent individuals to a child or an adult, and you can see that each of them is in transition.

❷ *Observational Quiz (see answer page 450): What aspects of each person are ahead or behind in development?*

Proper Proportions

One of the last parts of the body to take final form is the head, which reaches adult size and shape several years after final adult shoe size is attained. To the embarrassment of many teenagers, their facial features—especially the ears, lips, and nose, which are markedly larger in adults than in children—grow before the skull itself takes on the larger, more oval shape typical of adults. Next time you see a 14-year-old covering his or her ears with a hat, or nose and mouth with a hand, remember that shame may be part of the reason.

At least as disturbing to some young people can be the fact that the two halves of the body do not always mature at the same rate; one foot, breast, testicle, or ear can be notably larger than the other. Fortunately, none of these anomalies persists very long. Once the growth process starts, every part of the anatomy reaches close to adult size, shape, and proportion in 3 or 4 years. (Of course, for an adolescent, a year or two spent waiting for one's body to take on normal proportions can seem like an eternity.)

Organ Growth

While the torso grows, internal organs also grow. Over the course of adolescence, the lungs increase in size and capacity, actually tripling in weight, so the adolescent breathes more deeply and slowly than a child (a 10-year-old breathes about 22 times a minute, while an 18-year-old breathes about 18 times). The heart doubles in size, and the heart rate decreases, slowing from an average of 92 beats per minute at age 10 to 82 at age 18. In addition, the total volume of blood increases (Malina & Bouchard, 1991).

These changes increase physical endurance, making it possible for many teenagers to run for miles or dance for hours without stopping to rest. Note, however, that the more visible spurts of weight and height precede the less visible spurts of muscles and organs. This means that athletic training and weight lifting for an adolescent should be designed to match the young person's size of a year or so earlier. Exhaustion and injury, as a result of overuse, occurs when demands on a young person's body do not take this muscle and organ growth lag into account (Armstrong & Welsman, 1997). These organic changes also increase the child's need for sleep, as well as change the day-night cycles. Because of hormonal shifts (especially the growth hormones) many teenagers crave sleep in the mornings and are wide awake late at night (Greydanus, 1997; Wolfson & Carskadon, 1998).

One organ system, the *lymphoid system,* which includes the tonsils and adenoids, actually decreases in size at adolescence. Having smaller tonsils and adenoids makes teenagers less susceptible to respiratory ailments. Mild asthma, for example, often switches off at puberty (Clark & Rees, 1996).

Finally, the hormones of puberty cause many relatively minor physical changes that, despite their insignificance in the grand scheme of development, have substantial psychic impact. For instance, the oil, sweat, and odor glands of the skin become much more active. One result is acne, which occurs to some degree in about 90 percent of all boys and 80 percent of all girls (Greydanus, 1997). Another result is oilier hair and smellier bodies, which is one reason adolescents spend more money on shampoo and deodorants than does any other age group. The eyes also undergo a change: the eyeballs elongate, making many teenagers sufficiently nearsighted to require corrective lenses. All told, no part of the older adolescent's body functions or appears quite the same as it did a few years before.

"Yes, when I was your age, all my friends used drugs, but they were all acne medications."

Cohort Differences The biological changes of puberty are universal, apparent in every culture and century. How individuals react, however, varies tremendously, from pride to shame, celebration to treatment.

CHILDREN UP CLOSE

ATTITUDES ABOUT SEXUAL MATURITY

Obviously, how a particular adolescent responds to the changes in his or her body depends on many things, including the teenager's understanding of what is happening; the conversations he or she has had with parents and peers about puberty; the timing of his or her sexual maturity in relation to that of others in the peer group; and the broader cultural values concerning the meaning of sexual maturation.

In some cultures, for example, menstruation is heralded, with elaborate rituals, as a young woman's entry into adult status. Similar "rites of passage" occur to celebrate entry into manhood (Brooks-Gunn & Reiter, 1991). In the United States, reactions are more mixed. Newly menstruating girls report a combination of positive and negative feelings about menarche, including feelings of fear and distress mingled with a sense of maturity (Brooks-Gunn & Reiter, 1991; Kaplan, 1997). Those who reach menarche earlier than their friends or who have relatively little information about it tend to be most upset; those who are well-informed and "on time" are more proud. The same may be true for boys reaching spermarche, with the latecomers most upset.

No matter what their personal attitudes about the sexual changes of puberty, almost all adolescents have a strong sense of privacy about them. Very few discuss their specific experiences of menarche or spermarche with friends or with their parent of the other sex until months later, if at all. Indeed, although most boys are proud to reach this point, few tell other boys the personal details of masturbation or ejaculation. They rarely confess unexpected or unwanted sexual arousal, (caused by a photo, for instance) to another boy or a relative, even though such arousal is quite common (Gaddis & Brooks-Gunn, 1985). On their part, girls typically promise to tell all their close friends when menarche arrives, but become

A Rite of Passage Cultures and families teach their youths whether puberty is shameful, prideful, or neither. Traditional religious celebrations to mark the passage from childhood to adulthood are now rare in mainstream culture, although the Sweet Sixteen, the gang initiation, and even the high school graduation have elements of it. However, many traditional groups still follow practices, such as that shown here among the Apache people, to guide the young person into new status, with expectations for spiritual, intellectual, and social maturity.

reticent when the actual event happens (Brooks-Gunn et al., 1986). Most girls want their mothers to provide practical advice—not generalities about "becoming a woman"—and they

SEXUAL CHARACTERISTICS

The growth spurt, as you have just seen, alters every body part somewhat. Meanwhile, another set of changes is not just an alteration but a revolution, transforming boys and girls into men and women.

Reproductive Possibilities

primary sex characteristics   The sex organs—those parts of the body that are directly involved in reproduction, including the vagina, uterus, ovaries, testicles, and penis.

The **primary sex characteristics** are those parts of the body that are directly involved in reproduction. During puberty, every primary sex organ becomes much larger. In girls, the uterus begins to grow and the vaginal lining thickens, even before any outward signs of puberty appear. In boys, the testes would prefer that their fathers not be informed at all. If the father is told, they hope he makes no comments, even congratulatory ones (Koff & Rierdan, 1995).

Given this variability and secrecy, some of the best information about the particular thoughts and reactions to sexual maturity, in earlier decades and today, comes from popular literature. An autobiographical account is provided in *Angela's Ashes:*

> I know about the excitement and I know it's a sin but how can it be a sin if it comes to me in a dream where American girls pose in swimming suits on the screen at the Lyric Cinema and I wake up pushing and pumping? It's a sin when you're wide awake and going at yourself the way the boys talked about it in Leamy's schoolyard after Mr. O'Dea roared the Sixth Commandment at us, Thou Shalt Not Commit Adultery, which means impure thoughts, impure words, impure deeds, and that's what adultery is, Dirty Things in General. . . .
>
> Oh, boys, the devil wants your souls. He wants you with him in hell and know this, that every time you interfere with yourself, every time you succumb to the vile sin of self-abuse you not only nail Christ to the cross you take another step closer to hell itself. Retreat from the abyss, boys. Resist the devil and keep your hands to yourself.
>
> I can't stop interfering with myself. I pray . . . I'll never do it again but I can't help myself and swear I'll go to confession and after that, surely after that, I'll never never do it again. I don't want to go to hell with devils chasing me for eternity jabbing me with hot pitchforks.
>
> [McCourt, 1996]

A fictional version of menarche appears in *She's Come Undone.* After a fight between her parents, the protagonist goes bike riding for hours. When she comes back home, she sees her mother in the kitchen:

> She told me she didn't want to talk about anything right now . . .
> Something about my pink shorts made her stop.
> "What?" I said.
> She was staring down there at me.
> I saw and felt it at the same time: the dark red blotch of blood.
> "That's great, Dolores. Thanks a lot," Ma said, her face crumpling in tears. "That's just what I need right now."
> [Lamb, 1993]

Fortunately, in the United States and elsewhere, attitudes toward spermarche and menarche have changed over the past decades, and accounts like these are less likely today.

As best we can determine, young people face these events with much less anxiety, embarrassment, or guilt than their parents did. This fact is illustrated by a recent example involving a 13-year-old who, happening to be away from home at menarche, called her mother in tears to announce the event. Her mother, remembering her own experience and mindful of the shame and misunderstanding that generations of women have experienced regarding menstruation, immediately reassured her about the glory of womanhood, the joy of fertility, the renewal of the monthly cycle, the evidence of health (since menstruation prevents disease and prepares the uterus for pregnancy), and so on. "I know all that," her daughter protested impatiently. "I'm glad I got my period. I'm crying because this means I won't grow much more, and I want to be tall!"

begin to grow and, about a year later, the penis lengthens and the scrotum enlarges and becomes pendulous.

The specific event that is usually taken to indicate sexual maturity and fertility in girls is *menarche,* the first menstrual period. For boys, the comparable indicator is **spermarche,** the first ejaculation of seminal fluid containing sperm. Ejaculation can occur during sleep in a nocturnal emission (a "wet dream"), through masturbation, or through sexual intercourse. Today, masturbation is the most frequent precipitator of the first ejaculation; a few generations ago masturbation was considered so depraved that the dire warnings against it meant most young boys first ejaculated when they were asleep and dreaming. (Adolescents' reactions to sexual maturity are discussed in Children Up Close, above.)

spermarche A male's first ejaculation of live sperm.

Wanting to Be a Woman Soon after their bodies begin to differentiate into male or female shapes, most young people become intent on adding secondary sex characteristics from the culture to those nature provides. Boys practice walking, talking, and looking tough, and girls beautify each other's hair, nails, and faces—often only to remove the evidence and start over before letting any boy see it.

❷ *Observational Quiz (see answer page 454): This photo shows another sign of puberty experienced by both sexes. What is it?*

❶ *Answer to Observational Quiz (from page 446): The boy on the right is the easiest—his hands, arms, and height are growing rapidly—even though his head and facial features are still boyish in size and shape. The girl sitting has similar discrepancies, with long legs and arms but short torso and relatively girlish head. The other two are still child-size overall, and what we can see of their faces would be quite appropriate at age 8, not the 12 or so that they are. However, their behavior suggests that their sexual hormones are already active, as you would expect at their age. Very few 8-year-old boys would happily toss a large ball back and forth for girls to admire, and very few 8-year-old girls would stand in the water, keeping their curls dry, simply watching, as these young adolescents are doing.*

secondary sex characteristics Body characteristics that are not directly involved in reproduction but that indicate sexual maturity, such as a man's beard or a woman's breasts.

Actually, neither menarche or spermarche signifies full reproductive maturity, which is reached several years later. A girl's first menstrual cycles are usually *anovulatory,* that is, without ovulation. Even a year after menarche, most teens are still relatively infertile: ovulation is irregular, occurring only occasionally rather than every 28 days (as in most adult women). And if fertilization does occur, all the risks of pregnancy—from spontaneous abortion to preterm birth—are greater than they are for older adolescents, whose primary sex organs have reached adult size (Golub, 1992). For boys, the concentration of sperm necessary to fertilize an ovum is not reached until months or even years after spermarche (Muller et al., 1989). (As many young teenagers discover too late, unfortunately, this relative infertility does not preclude pregnancy. It simply makes reproduction less likely and more hazardous—to both mother and child—than it would be at the ripe old age of 16 or so.)

Sexual Appearance

Along with maturation of the reproductive organs come changes that yield **secondary sex characteristics,** which are parts of the body that are not directly involved in reproduction but that signify sexual development. Most obviously, body shape is virtually unisex in childhood but differentiates at puberty. Males grow taller than females (by 5 inches, on average) and become wider at the shoulders (because historically they needed to do the heavy lifting and throwing). Females take on more fat all over and become wider at the hips (in preparation for childbearing). In addition, other specific parts of the body change to indicate sexual maturity.

Breasts

Probably the secondary sex characteristic that receives the least welcome attention is breast development. For most girls, the first sign of puberty is the "bud" stage, when a small accumulation of fat causes a slight rise around the nipples. From then on, breasts develop gradually for about 4 years, with full breast growth reached when almost all the other changes of puberty are completed (Malina, 1990). Because our culture misguidedly takes breast development to be symbolic of womanhood, girls whose breasts are very small or very large are often distressed. Small-breasted

A Cultural Ideal At age 15, figure skater Michelle Kwan, from California, won the American Ladies National and World Championship titles. At 17 she won the Olympic silver medal but lost the gold to teammate Tara Lipinski, then 15. The combination of grace, strength, and slimness that she and other young female skaters and gymnasts exemplify is admired even more than the accomplishments of medalists in other Olympic events. This idealization may, however, be the downfall of many normally developing adolescent girls.

Why Shave? Facial hair is often considered a sign of virility, which explains why many young men shave regularly before doing so seems warranted. However, since the act of shaving may signal the young male's adult interests and urges, parents should not ridicule it, even when it involves little more than fuzz.

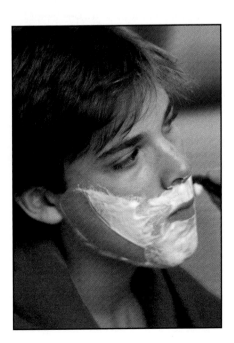

girls often feel "cheated," even disfigured; large-breasted girls become extremely self-conscious when they attract unwanted stares and remarks. No wonder some bras are padded to enlarge, others advertised as "minimizers," and the most common major cosmetic surgery is that which increases or decreases breast size.

In boys, as well as girls, the diameter of the areola (the dark area around the nipple) increases during puberty. Much to their consternation, about 65 percent of all adolescent boys experience some breast enlargement (typically in midpuberty) (Behrman, 1992). However, their worry is usually short-lived, since this enlargement normally disappears by age 16.

Voice and Hair

Another secondary sex characteristic that changes markedly is the voice, which becomes lower as the larynx grows, a change most noticeable in boys. (Even more noticeable, much to the chagrin of the young adolescent male, is an occasional loss of voice control that throws his newly acquired baritone into a high squeak.) Girls also develop somewhat lower voices, a fact that most people do not realize but that is the underlying reason people think a low, throaty female voice is "sexy."

During puberty, existing hair on the head, arms, and legs becomes coarser and darker, and new hair grows under the arms, on the face, and in the groin area. Visible facial hair and body hair are generally considered distinct signs of manliness in American society. This notion is mistaken, because hairiness is inherited. How often a man needs to shave, or how hairy his chest is, is determined primarily by his genes, not his virility. Further, during puberty all girls develop some light facial hair, as well as more noticeable hair on their arms and legs, with the specifics of color and density more genetic than hormonal.

Of course, sex hormones do have some influence on the growth of body hair at puberty. But each hormone has a number of other functions throughout the body, so taking artificial hormones to increase or decrease hair (as some people do) forces a major change on the entire body in order to achieve a minor and superficial goal.

In general, adolescents' concern about their appearance can seem exaggerated, even pathological. However, as the Research Report on pages 452–453 makes clear, concerns about body image arise from peers, family, and society as much as, or more than, from the individual. Such realization should make us all more sympathetic to the young person's worries about appearing attractive.

BODY IMAGE

The physiological changes of puberty necessitate a drastic revision of adolescents' **body image,** that is, their mental conception of, and attitude toward, their physical appearance. According to many psychologists, developing a healthy body image is an integral part of becoming an adult (Erikson, 1968; Simmons & Blythe, 1987). Indeed, one researcher states that "body image lies at the heart of adolescence" (Ferron, 1997). Adolescents need to appreciate their bodies "not simply as an object, but as a lived-in subject which is perceived as part of their being" (Richards, 1996). However, few adolescents are satisfied with their physiques; most imagine that their bodies are far less attractive than they actually are.

This negative self-appraisal can have a major impact on self-esteem. Although self-esteem is obviously influenced by success in athletics, academics, friendship, or other areas that the adolescent considers significant, a teenager's assessment of his or her appearance is the most important determinant. In explaining why, for teenagers, "self-esteem is only skin deep," one researcher notes that

> the domain of physical appearance ... is an omnipresent feature of the self, always on display for others and for the self to observe. In contrast, one's adequacy in such domains as scholastic or athletic competence, peer social acceptance, conduct, or morality is not constantly open to evaluation, but rather is more context specific. Moreover, one has more control over whether, when, and how such characteristics [such as having good grades] will be revealed. [Harter, 1993]

As a result of this intense focus on physical appearance, many adolescents spend hours examining themselves in front of a mirror—worrying about their complexions, about how their hairstyles affect the shape of their faces, about whether the fit of their clothes makes them look alluring or cool. Some teenagers exercise or diet with obsessive intensity (perhaps lifting weights to build specific muscles or weighing food to the gram to better calculate calories).

At one time or another, almost every American girl undereats, sometimes drastically, to be thinner. In one study, girls age 14 to 18 typically wanted to be about 12 pounds lighter than they were (Brooks-Gunn et al., 1989). Amazingly, this held true across the board—regardless of the girls' maturation status, height, or exercise level (see the table). For example, girls who matured late, and thus had relatively thin, girlish bodies, wanted to lose almost as many pounds as girls with more womanly shapes who had matured on time. Similarly, competitive swimmers, whose bodies were quite muscular and who needed some fat to help them with buoyancy and endurance, wanted to lose weight just as much as nonathletes, who had somewhat more fat on their bodies and less reason to need it. Even the thinnest group, late-maturing girls who practiced daily in professional dance schools, wished they weighed 10 pounds less.

Far from Perfect Many teenagers sacrifice time, money, and health to attain the lean look of the female model or the muscled physique of the macho movie star. Even teenagers who already have attractive bodies are often highly self-critical, while those who inherit a shape or size that is far from the cultural ideal are likely to be excessively self-conscious and depressed.

Boys are also vulnerable. Roughly 5 percent of male high school seniors use steroids to build up their muscles (Johnston et al., 1998), ranging from about 9 percent of those in West Virginia to 2 percent in Hawaii (MMWR, 1998, August 4). These young men risk a variety of serious health problems, especially if they obtain the drugs illegally and "stack" one drug with another, as many do. One misguided motivation for taking steroids may be to excel at sports, but a survey found that one-third of steroid users did not participate at all in interscholastic athletics; they were apparently taking steroids solely for the sake of appearance (Johnston et al., 1989). Boys who do not take drugs are nonetheless concerned, lifting weights, doing push-ups, and so on, in an attempt to change their physiques.

Before dismissing adolescents' preoccupation with their looks as narcissistic, we should recognize that their concern is, in part, a response to the reactions of other people. Parents and siblings sometimes make memorable and mortifying comments about the growing child's appearance: "You look like a cow" (or bear or gorilla) or "You're flat as a board" or "What's that peach fuzz on your face?" These are comments that they would not dare make to anyone else.

Strangers, too, target young people with remarks that are unwanted and disconcerting. Pubescent girls suddenly hear whistles, catcalls, and lewd suggestions; boys, depending on their level of maturation, often find themselves labeled as studs or wimps. Adolescents even get subtle messages about their appearance from their teachers. In junior high school, at least, teachers tend to judge new students who are physically attractive as academically more competent than their less comely classmates (Lerner et al., 1990).

The concern with physique dominates the peer culture, particularly during early adolescence (Harter, 1993). Unattractive teenagers tend to have fewer friends—of either sex. And attractiveness is a sexual lure, especially during adolescence. In one study, close to 200 ninth-graders were asked to rank 10 possible qualities of an ideal man or woman, and physical appearance was high on the list for both sexes (Stiles et al., 1987). In fact, for the boys, "good looks" was the most important quality in the ideal woman, followed by being "sexy" and then "fun," with "kind and honest" a distant fourth. For the girls, "kind and honest" and "fun" were tied for first, with "good looks" second.

Adolescents also receive powerful messages from the broader social environment. Media images of handsome faces and beautiful bodies are used to sell almost everything, from clothes and cosmetics to luncheon meats and auto parts. These images reinforce the cultural stereotype that men should be tall and muscular, that women should be thin and shapely, and—at least in North America—that both should have facial features that suggest Anglo ancestors.

Obviously, few real bodies fit this model. Not only many individuals but also entire ethnic groups are genetically endowed with shorter stature, broader hips, or chunkier bodies than this cultural ideal projects. Often these genetic differences are latent during childhood, before hormones produce the adult body type the person is destined to have. This means that many young adolescents are suddenly required to come to terms with a body form, inherited from their ancestors, quite unlike that of the fashion models, sports heroes, and movie stars they idolize. They stare at their emerging selves, with fascination and horror, in the mirror every morning (posing, turning, wetting an unruly lock of hair, changing clothes again just when it is time to leave) and again whenever they have a chance. As one father complained, "Whenever they talk to us, they won't even look at us if a mirror is close by, or even if a window is nearby. They will invariably look right by us at whatever might project an image of themselves" (Garvin, 1994).

With time, this intense self-preoccupation lessens, and adolescents gradually become more satisfied with their physical selves (Rauste-von Wright, 1989). By adulthood, most have learned to accept the gap between the cultural ideal and their own natural appearance; acceptance becomes easier when they have been assured, over the years, that they and their bodies are loved "just as they are."

Meanwhile, however, teenagers' concern over their body image should not be taken lightly. For most adolescents, *thinking* that they look terrible makes them feel terrible—even depressed. Instead of ignoring or belittling an adolescent's self-preoccupation, adults might provide whatever practical help seems warranted—such as new clothing, encouragement to exercise, and medical treatment for acne—even while assuring the adolescent that other characteristics are more important. Understanding and compliments, instead of criticism and derision, could have far-reaching benefits, not only for the adolescent's body image but also for his or her self-esteem, social acceptance, and overall enjoyment of life.

body image A person's mental concept of how his or her body appears.

Adolescent Girls' Actual and Desired Weights*

	Girls Who Matured On Time		Girls Who Matured Late	
	Actual	Desired	Actual	Desired
Dancers	116	102	108	98
Swimmers	130	117	128	114
Nonathletes	125	114	121	111

*For all six groups, average height was between 5'4" and 5'5½".
Source: Brooks-Gunn et al., 1989.

❶ *Answer to Observational Quiz (from page 450):* Braces. When faces reach adult size, jaws do too, and few early adolescents have perfectly aligned teeth. Whether or not to do anything about this, of course, is cultural, not biological.

HEALTH AND HAZARDS

In many ways, adolescence is a healthy time. The minor illnesses of childhood (such as flu, colds, earaches, and high fevers) become much less common, because inoculations and years of exposure have increased immunity. The two main killers of adults, heart disease and cancer, are rare: a 15-year-old's chance of dying from them is only one-third that of a 30-year-old and one-hundredth that of a 60-year-old.

However, while diseases are relatively uncommon, adolescents are at risk for health hazards of a different kind—especially as they gain increasing independence and make more of their own decisions. Several such hazards are discussed in the next chapters. Here, we will look at three of them: sexual abuse, eating disorders, and drug abuse.

Sexual Abuse

The definition of *sexual abuse* is quite comprehensive: any situation in which one person engages another person in a sexual activity, whether verbal or physical, without that person's freely given consent. Since children and younger adolescents are vulnerable to the power of adults and have little (if any) understanding of the implications of sexual activity, they are legally incapable of freely consenting to sexual acts. (The "age of consent" was only 10 in the nineteenth-century United States; today it varies from 14 to 18, depending on state law) (Donovan, 1997). Under that age, even voluntary sexual intercourse between, say, a 15-year-old girl and a 19-year-old man can be considered statutory rape.)

childhood sexual abuse   Any activity in which an adult uses a child for his or her own sexual stimulation or pleasure—even if the use does not involve physical contact. For purposes of defining sexual abuse, childhood ends between ages 14 and 18, depending on state laws.

Thus, **childhood sexual abuse** is defined as any erotic activity that arouses an adult and excites, shames, or confuses a young person—whether or not the victim protests and whether or not genital contact is involved. Using this definition, we find that sexual abuse is very common. Teasing a child in a sexualized manner, photographing a young person in erotic poses, intrusively questioning a young adolescent about his or her developing body, and invading the privacy of a child's bathing, dressing, or sleeping routines—especially once puberty begins—can all be sexually abusive. Even when the definition is more narrow—"forced to touch an adult or older child or forcibly touched by an older adult or older child in a sexual way"—30 percent of mothers and 9 percent of fathers polled nationwide had been abused as children (Gallup, 1995).

As with other forms of maltreatment, any particular act of sexual abuse becomes more damaging the more it is repeated, the more it distorts adult-child relationships, and the more it impairs the child's ability to develop normally. The immediate and obvious impact is less significant than the long-term harm. In particular, repeated childhood sexual abuse has the potential for permanently damaging the person's ability, years later, to establish a warm, trusting, and intimate relationship with another adult.

Special Vulnerability in Adolescence

❷ **Especially for Social Workers:** What signs might indicate that a young person is sexually abused?

Sexual victimization in adolescence is often the continuation of less blatant childhood abuse. It may begin with fondling, explicit nudity, or suggestive comments—all of which tend to confuse a preschooler or young school-age child. Then, in late childhood or early adolescence, such sexualized adult-child interaction may escalate, with onset typically between ages 8 and 12 (Stewart, 1997). Overt force is seldom involved, because the perpetrator usually can easily dominate the child. The victim is especially powerless when she is a pubescent girl and the perpetrator is her own father. Although the victim may have confused feelings about the sexual contact, and may believe the reassurances or accusations she receives from the perpetrator ("You know you like it"), there is no question that a sexual father-daughter relationship is victimization. With other men, even slightly older partners, sexual relations are least likely to be voluntary if the girl is under age 15 and her partner is age 18 or older (Elo et al., 1999).

The *meaning* of being sexually victimized may be especially disturbing for older children and adolescents compared to younger children. At a time when they want to take pride in changes in their bodies, as they become increasingly self-aware and attracted to peers, sexual victimization can turn a pubescent child's world upside down. Indeed, adolescents often react to such maltreatment in ways that younger children rarely do—with self-destruction (such as suicide, drug abuse, or running away) or with counter-attack (such as vandalism or violence, aimed at society or directly at the perpetrator) (Ewing, 1990).

Virtually every physical or psychological health problem is more common among sexually abused adolescents than among other teens. Consider teenage pregnancy as one example: In a group of 535 pregnant teenagers, nearly two-thirds said they were sexually abused *before* they themselves became sexually active, with 44 percent reporting having been raped. Compared with the one-third who had not been sexually abused, those who had been maltreated reported greater use of drugs and alcohol, earlier sexual activity, and higher rates of school suspension, expulsion, or dropping out. They were also more likely to have experienced physical and emotional abuse (Boyer & Fine, 1992). The sample in this study is not representative of all teens, or even all pregnant teens. But it is a stark example of a generality found from many studies: When a teenager has serious problems, sexual abuse may be part of the reason.

Gender Differences and Similarities

Most sexual abuse is committed by men known to the victim, rather than by women or strangers (Finkelhor, 1994). Girls are the most commonly victimized, typically by family members at home. Boys are also often abused, either at home by a parent or outside the home by someone from the community (Cappelleri et al., 1993; Finkelhor, 1994).

When boys are sexually abused, problems abound. In addition to bearing the stigma of unwelcome sexual activity, a molested boy is likely to feel shame at being weak and unable to defend himself and is also likely to worry that he is homosexual—all contrary to the macho image that many young adolescent boys strive to attain (Bolton et al., 1989). The male perpetrator of sexual abuse of boys does not necessarily consider himself homosexual, nor is a boy's involvement a true indication of his sexual orientation. However, when the boy is, in fact, gay and is abused for it, the shame escalates. And when the sexual abuse of a boy occurs at home, typically by his father or stepfather, the problems of vulnerability and loss of self-esteem are multiplied (Finkelhor, 1994).

Although mothers and other female relatives are less often abusers than fathers and male relatives, they are sometimes guilty—especially with sons when the father is absent—of sexual teasing and fondling. These sexual activities can evoke feelings of confusion and shame (Hunter, 1990). Mothers can be part of the problem in another way: by failing to notice, believe, or

A Thousand Hamburgers per Person per Year
Some teenagers easily reach the thousand mark wolfing down three burgers a day in after-school or midnight snacks, or even breakfast at noon. This Charlotte, North Carolina, basketball star knows that he should avoid high-fat foods and fill up on whole grains, fresh fruits, and various vegetables. However, for him and for most other teenagers, knowledge does not change habits.

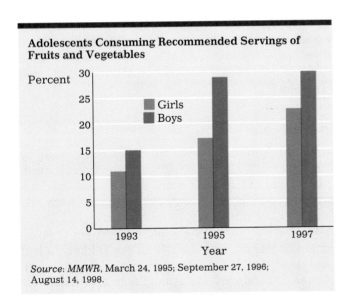

Adolescents Consuming Recommended Servings of Fruits and Vegetables

Source: MMWR, March 24, 1995; September 27, 1996; August 14, 1998.

Figure 14.4 Five a Day. Nutritionists recommend that everyone eat at least five portions of fruits and vegetables a day— more would be better. Unfortunately, less than one-third of high school seniors reach this minimum. Perhaps suprisingly, younger adolescents do better on this measure than seniors do.

report that the child is sexually abused at home, or by failing to support and protect the child when the abuse is reported to authorities. In such circumstances, the child is doubly victimized—first by the perpetrator and then by the parent who fails to intervene.

As with other types of maltreatment, parents who fight with each other or who are immature, socially isolated, alcoholic, or drug abusers are more likely than other parents to sexually abuse their children. They are also more likely to neglect their children to the point where the children become ready prey for the abuse of others. Unlike other forms of maltreatment, however, sexual abuse occurs almost equally in homes of all income and educational levels.

Nutrition

The rapid body changes of puberty require fuel in the form of additional calories, as well as additional vitamins and minerals. In fact, the recommended daily intake of calories is higher for an active adolescent than for anyone else; the greatest calorie requirement occurs at about age 14 years for girls and 17 years for boys (Malina & Bouchard, 1991). During the growth spurt, the need for calcium, iron, and zinc (for both bone and muscle development) is about 50 percent greater than it was only 2 years earlier.

In developed nations, where quality food is sufficiently available, most adolescents meet their basic caloric needs most of the time, typically consuming four or more meals a day even without breakfast. Actually, skipping breakfast is not much of a nutritional problem in adolescence, despite what parents and teachers may think. In one study an experimental group of high school students was kept on very low calorie breakfasts while a control group was allowed full, high-calorie breakfasts. To their surprise, the experimenters found no difference in the groups' performance on a battery of cognitive and psychological tests (Cromer et al., 1990).

Although adolescents in developed nations generally eat enough, they do not always eat right. Only 27 percent of U.S. high school seniors consume the recommended five servings of fruits and vegetables a day, and 33 percent (23 percent of the girls and 41 percent of the boys) eat too many fried or fatty foods (*MMWR,* August 14, 1998). This is an improvement over the early 1990s, but it is far from ideal (see Figure 14.4). It is rare for today's young people to sit down with their families to eat a meal of fresh foods that have been washed, cut, spiced, combined, and cooked by a parent. As a result, teenagers are often unaware of diet requirements. For example:

Christina Green, a 17-year-old high school student in Delaware, Ohio, considers herself old-fashioned when she shops for groceries. Most of her friends buy meals to go, she said—"stuff they can eat right away or zap." She, on the other hand, picks up frozen pot pies and breaded chicken, fishsticks and pizza, boxed macaroni and cheese.

"I like a homemade meal," she said.

To many teen-agers, "homemade" has come to mean nothing more than "home heated." [O'Neill, 1998]

Most teenagers end up getting too much salt, sugar, fat, and preservatives in their diet, and not enough iron. Indeed, fewer than half consume the recommended daily dose of 15 milligrams of iron, a nutrient that is present

● Response for Social Workers (from page 454): Although some sexually abused children are also physically abused or neglected, some seem quite well cared for. Therefore, an unusually devoted or protective father, who wants to keep his daughter away from the boys or who gives her expensive presents, may not be as wonderful as he seems. Similarly, any adolescent girl or boy who is self-destructive, with drugs, mutilation, or suicide attempts, may be a victim of abuse. Finally, most sexually abused adolescents are ashamed, and thus reticent to talk about their family relationships. None of these signs proves abuse, of course, but given the frequency of sexual abuse in early adolescence, further exploration is recommended when any of these signs appears.

mainly in green vegetables, eggs, and meat. Because each menstrual period depletes the body of some iron, females between the ages of 15 and 17 are more likely to suffer from iron-deficiency anemia (low blood hemoglobin) than any other subgroup of the population (Baynes & Bothwell, 1990). This means, for one thing, that if a teenage girl seems apathetic and lazy, she should have her hemoglobin checked before it is assumed that she suffers from a poor attitude or other psychological difficulties.

Serious Problems

A sizable minority of adolescents have one of four serious problems that interfere with normal, healthy eating. Any of these can make a teenager become a shorter and less well proportioned adult:

- Childhood habits of overeating and underexercising often worsen in adolescence, especially if the overweight young person experiences increased social rejection. For this reason, many chubby children become obese adolescents (although some, who suddenly become aware of body image, dramatically slim down).
- Drug use (including cigarettes and alcohol) often begins in adolescence, affecting eating patterns, altering appetites and digestive processes, and depriving young people of energy and growth.
- Food fads and strange diets are particularly attractive, and particularly harmful, during the rapid growth of early adolescence.
- Severe undernourishment slows or even halts all the changes of puberty, including growth and sexual maturation, and it is sometimes undertaken for precisely that reason.

All of these can be serious problems at any age. However, the fourth item deserves special attention because, unlike the case earlier or later in life, when most malnourished people are forced by lack of food to undereat, many adolescents choose self-deprivation, creating a life-threatening disorder for themselves. Puberty itself correlates with poor eating habits of all kinds; the biological changes that should lead to healthier eating often do the opposite (Cauffman & Steinberg, 1996).

Eating Disorders.   For some young and well-educated teenagers, undereating turns into an addiction no less powerful or shameful to the addict than alcoholism or drug abuse. The two main eating disorders emerge any time from about age 10 to about age 30, but the most hazardous periods are at the beginning of adolescence (about age 13) and just after high school (at about age 18).

anorexia nervosa   A serious eating disorder in which a person undereats to the point of emaciation and possible starvation.

   Anorexia nervosa is characterized by self-starvation, sometimes to the point of death. The typical sufferer is a high-achieving girl who restricts her eating so severely that her body mass index goes below 18. She may weigh a bony 80 pounds or less but still be exercising and complaining about being fat. Approximately 1 percent of adolescent and young adult females are anorexic, according to the DSM-IV (American Psychiatric Association, 1994).

bulimia nervosa   An eating disorder in which a person repeatedly overeats and then induces the expulsion of food, either through vomiting or through the abuse of laxatives. (Sometimes called *binge-purge syndrome.*)

   The second major eating disorder, about three times as common as anorexia, is **bulimia nervosa,** a two-step disease that involves, first, compulsive binge-eating and, then, purging by induced vomiting or by massive ingestion of laxatives. Many young women engage in bulimic behavior at some time or another; some studies have found that half of all college women have binged and purged at least once (Fairburn & Wilson, 1993). This behavior becomes seriously destructive, according to DSM-IV, when it occurs more than once a week over 3 months, with uncontrollable urges to overeat accompanied by a distorted self-image.

Distorted Body Image The image in this trick mirror may be closer to the young woman's own sense of her body than what she sees when she views herself in a true mirror. At some point in her development, almost every young woman in today's developed nations considers herself too fat.

By early adulthood, between 1 and 3 percent of American women are severely bulimic according to this definition, most of them beginning innocently enough, by overeating—"pigging out"—during the teen years and feeling guilty about it (American Psychiatric Association, 1994). Those who suffer from bulimia are usually close to normal weight and therefore do not starve to death; however, they can experience a wide range of serious health problems, including damage to the gastrointestinal system and even heart failure from electrolyte imbalance (Hsu, 1990). Female athletes, in both high school and college—who, we might expect, should know most about health and fitness—are more vulnerable to bulimia than others (Cohn & Adler, 1992; Guthrie, 1991; Thompson & Sherman, 1993). Male athletes (especially wrestlers, rowers, and swimmers) are vulnerable as well.

Recently, researchers have learned that the causes of eating disorders may be partly genetic. If one female monozygotic twin is anorexic, the other twin has a 75 percent chance of also being anorexic, compared to a 27 percent chance for dizygotic female twins (Treasure & Holland, 1993). Further, individuals with eating disorders tend to have a family history of depression, and they themselves have a higher-than-normal rate of depression. They also tend to have a family history of alcoholism, drug addiction, or both (Marx, 1993; Miller, 1993).

Why would individuals torture themselves with such a destructive means of relieving emotional distress? Each theory offers an explanation:

- One *psychoanalytic* hypothesis is that women develop eating disorders because of a conflict with their mothers, who provided their first nourishment and from whom the daughters cannot psychically separate.
- *Learning theory* notes that both these eating disorders are typically associated with psychological problems, including low self-esteem and depression. These precipitate extreme dieting and then perpetuate the destructive pattern, thus becoming part of a stimulus-response chain. Fasting, bingeing, and purging "have powerful effects as immediate reinforcers—that is, [as means of] relieving states of emotional distress and tension" (Gordon, 1990).
- One *cognitive* explanation is that as women compete with men in business and industry, they want to project a strong, self-controlled, masculine image antithetical to the buxom, fleshy body of the ideal woman of the past.
- *Sociocultural* explanations include the contemporary cultural pressure to be "slim and trim" and model-like—a pressure that seems to be felt particularly by unmarried young women seeking autonomy from their parents. This would help explain why these eating disorders were once rare: society expected women to be dependent, first on parents and then on a husband, with no need to prove one's selfhood.
- An *epigenetic* explanation notes that girls who are overwhelmed with the stresses of puberty may discover that self-starvation makes their menstrual periods cease, their sexual hormones decrease, and their curves disappear—all of which remove the sexual pressures that normal maturation compels adolescent girls to experience.

No matter what the explanation, however, eating disorders are a serious problem for today's adolescent, a problem that needs to be recognized and treated in the early stages so that it does not become a serious health hazard.

Alcohol, Tobacco, and Other Drugs

drug abuse   The ingestion of a drug to the extent that it impairs the user's well-being.

addiction   A person's dependence on a drug or a behavior in order to feel physically or psychologically at ease.

Let us begin with definitions. **Drug abuse** is the ingestion of a drug to the extent that it impairs the user's well-being. **Addiction** occurs when the person craves more of a drug in order to feel physically or psychologically at ease.

drug use The ingestion of a drug, regardless of the amount or effect of ingestion.

Drug use is simply the ingestion of a drug, regardless of the amount or effect of ingestion.

Note that the *abuse* of any drug, including alcohol and prescribed or off-the-shelf medicines, always upsets physical and psychological development, whether or not that abuse becomes addictive. Addiction and abuse entail many complications, including death, and are much more likely to emerge full-force in early and middle adulthood than during adolescence. The *use* of drugs is another matter—sometimes harmful, sometimes not, depending on the maturation of the drug user as well as on the reason for and consequences of the use (Gerstein & Green, 1993). Thus, abuse of drugs is always harmful, but use is not necessarily bad—it may be legal, even encouraged, as caffeine and alcohol are.

During adolescence the relationship between adolescent drug *use* and *abuse* is complex (see Changing Policy, pages 462–463).

Disquieting Trends

In recent decades, the use of alcohol and other drugs has become a part of many young people's lives in every industrialized nation in the world, as chronicled by many studies (Silbereisen et al., 1995). One of the most notable of these studies is an annual, detailed, confidential survey of nearly 50,000 American eighth-, tenth-, and twelfth-grade students from over 400 high schools throughout the United States. Since its inception in 1975, this survey has consistently shown that more than 8 out of 10 seniors had drunk alcohol (more than a few sips), 2 out of 3 had smoked at least one cigarette, and close to half (ranging from 66 percent in 1981 to 41 percent in 1992) had tried at least one illegal drug (Johnston et al., 1998).

Then and Now This boy is shown at age 13, in 1986 , when he was living in a German home for troubled boys. While developmental researchers have witnessed many young adolescents who defy the odds, this chilling photo includes four ominous portents.
❷ *Observational Quiz (see answer page 461): What are these portents?*

More Frequent Use. The rates just mentioned refer to "lifetime prevalence." They no doubt include instances of one-time-only experimentation. More troubling are data on use "within the past 30 days." The regular (30-day) use of most drugs (except cocaine) declined during the 1980s and then, in the early 1990s, began to increase (see Figure 14.5 on page 460). From 1991 to 1998, for example, the regular use of marijuana rose significantly for all age groups, reaching 24 percent for twelfth-graders in 1997 (with a slight dip to 23 percent in 1998). There were also increases in the regular use of other illegal drugs (hallucinogens, including LSD and PCP, nonprescription stimulants, cocaine, heroin, and so on), from a low of 6 percent in 1992 to a high of 11 percent in 1998.

Younger and Younger. A particularly disquieting feature of the 1998 school survey is the early onset of drug use. About 53 percent of all eighth-graders had already had at least one alcoholic drink; 46 percent had smoked at least one cigarette; and about 22 percent had tried marijuana, more than twice the number who had done so in the 1991 survey. Repeated use of these drugs by age 13 or so is also on the rise. Between 1991 and 1998, the percentage of eighth-graders who had smoked cigarettes within the past 30 days rose from 14 to 19 percent, and the percentage who had smoked marijuana within the past 30 days tripled from 3 to 10 percent (Johnston et al., 1998). Other research confirms that more younger adolescents are using drugs than ever before.

Obviously, drug abuse and addiction are problems at every age, but some developmentalists hesitate to condemn every instance of drug use, especially among high school seniors or college students. However, every developmentalist is alarmed by drug use by very young teenagers. One reason is that tobacco, alcohol, and marijuana act as **gateway drugs,** opening

gateway drugs Drugs—usually tobacco, alcohol, and marijuana—whose use increases the risk that a person will later use harder drugs, such as cocaine and heroin.

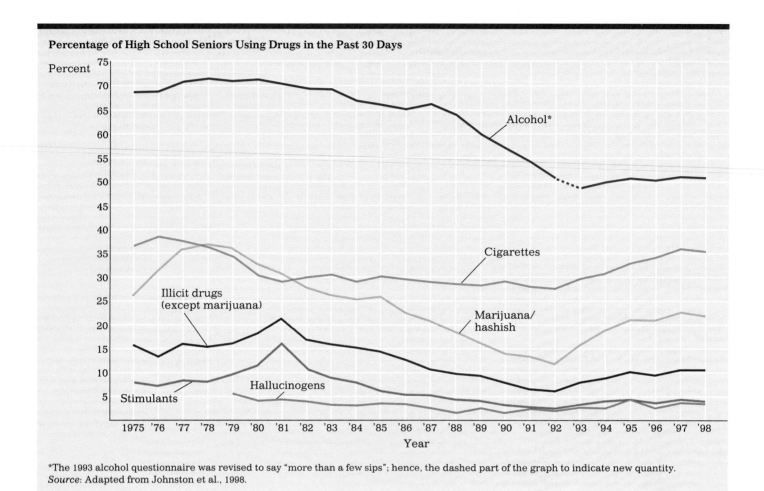

Percentage of High School Seniors Using Drugs in the Past 30 Days

*The 1993 alcohol questionnaire was revised to say "more than a few sips"; hence, the dashed part of the graph to indicate new quantity.
Source: Adapted from Johnston et al., 1998.

Figure 14.5 Drug Use Is Climbing. A decade-long decline in regular drug use among U.S. high school seniors came to an end in 1992. This is so for both legal and illegal drugs; thus, it seems that drinking alcohol and smoking cigarettes are affected by the same cohort conditions as swallowing pills or smoking marijuana (or snorting cocaine or shooting heroin, shown here as part of "other" illicit drugs). The cohort factor that seems most related to the recent upsurge in adolescent drug use is a decline in teenagers' belief that drug use is harmful.

the door to the use of harder drugs (Gerstein & Green, 1993). To be specific, teenagers who begin to use tobacco, alcohol, or marijuana before ninth grade are significantly more likely to use illegal drugs in high school and are also more likely to have serious drug- and alcohol-abuse problems later on.

Indeed, a large longitudinal survey found that early drug use is a gateway to a wide variety of destructive activities and conditions, not only drug abuse but also risky sex, alienation from school, antisocial behavior, poor physical health, and depression (Kandel & Davies, 1996). Similarly, in the 15-year study discussed in Changing Policy (pages 462–463), among children with long-standing personality difficulties, those who had tried marijuana by age 14 were more maladjusted, more unhappy, and more rebellious at age 18 than those with similar problems who remained drug-free until at least high school (Shedler & Block, 1990).

Health Impact of the Gateway Drugs

The early use of gateway drugs makes later drug abuse and addiction more likely, but that outcome is not inevitable. Some early users become early quitters or never become heavy users. However, in addition to increasing the risk of later harm, each of the three gateway drugs has a strong and immediate impact on health and well-being; younger adolescents are particularly vulnerable to their effects.

Figure 14.6 Current Cigarette Use Among Ninth-to Twelfth-Graders. As you can see, cigarette use among U.S. high school students is increasing rapidly. The overall average of 35 percent for females and 38 percent for males is substantially above the average for adults.

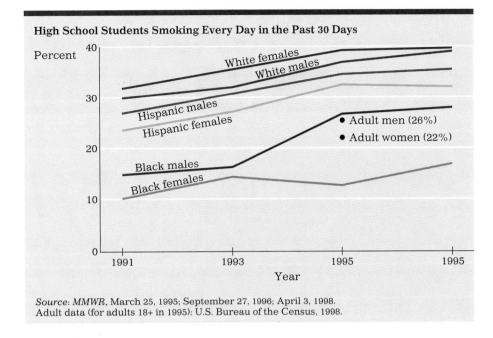

High School Students Smoking Every Day in the Past 30 Days

Source: MMWR, March 25, 1995; September 27, 1996; April 3, 1998.
Adult data (for adults 18+ in 1995): U.S. Bureau of the Census, 1998.

Tobacco.   Tobacco use decreases food consumption and interferes with the absorption of nutrients, both of which can limit the growth spurt, causing young steady smokers to be significantly shorter and smaller than they would have been if they had started smoking when they were fully grown. It also markedly reduces fertility, which means the entire sexual and reproductive maturation process is probably impeded (Fiscella et al., 1998). In addition, nicotine, the toxic chemical found in tobacco, is probably the most physically addictive drug of all (Schilit & Gomberg, 1991), and the great majority of adolescents who become regular smokers are quickly hooked. Proof of this comes from the reports of young people, age 10 to 18 years, who had smoked at least one cigarette a day for the previous 30 days (see Figure 14.6). Most of them (74 percent) said that they smoked partly because "it's really hard to quit" (*MMWR*, October 21, 1994).

Alcohol.   Alcohol consumption can be especially destructive during adolescence. The primary reason is that, even in small doses, alcohol loosens inhibitions and impairs judgment—a dangerous effect in a person who may already be psychologically off balance because of ongoing physical, sexual, and emotional changes. A survey of 46,000 high school students, mostly "middle American" (middle-class, midwestern), compared teenagers who had drunk alcohol six or more times in the previous month with teens who never or rarely drank (Bensen, 1997). It found that the "drinkers" were:

- More than twice as likely to be sexually active (70 percent compared with 32 percent)
- More than twice as likely to engage in antisocial behaviors such as stealing, fighting in groups, and vandalizing property (49 percent compared with 19 percent)
- Almost four times as likely to be excessively absent from school (23 percent compared with 6 percent)
- More likely to ride in a car with a driver who has been drinking (86 percent compared with 56 percent) (Bensen, 1997)

DISTINCTIONS IN ADOLESCENT DRUG USE

In trying to gain a comprehensive understanding of adolescent drug use, psychologists have learned an important lesson: Too simple a view of the problem makes the solution more complicated. One simple view is that all drug use is evil and good teenagers "just say no." Thus, some adults act as if drug addiction and abuse occur the moment a teenager takes one drag, swallow, or snort and as if every drug-using teenager is an uncontrollable threat to self, family, and society. An opposite but equally simple view is that drugs are harmless, a matter of personal preference. Thus, many adolescents take the view that they are just using, only experimenting, and that they are immune to the addictive pull, or destructive impact, of any substance.

The reality is far more complex, as is suggested by the findings of a 15-year longitudinal study that followed children from the age of 3 to young adulthood. By age 18, most had tried marijuana, alcohol, and tobacco. The researchers wondered if such adolescent experimentation was the norm in "psychologically healthy, sociable, and reasonably inquisitive individuals" (Shedler & Block, 1990). To explore this question, the researchers divided their sample into three groups:

- *Abstainers:* those who had never tried any illegal drug
- *Experimenters:* those who may have smoked marijuana, but no more frequently than once a month, and who had tried, at most, one other illegal drug
- *Frequent users:* those who used marijuana once a week or more and who had used at least one other illegal drug

(Subjects who did not fit into any of the groups were omitted from this analysis.)

To no one's surprise, the researchers found the typical "frequent user" to be a "troubled adolescent, an adolescent who is interpersonally alienated, emotionally withdrawn, and manifestly unhappy, and who expresses his or her maladjustment through undercontrolled, overtly antisocial behavior." Somewhat surprisingly, however, the typical "abstainer" was not much better off—a "relatively tense, overcontrolled, emotionally constricted individual who is somewhat socially isolated and lacking in interpersonal skills." The "experimenters," by contrast, were the most outgoing, straightforward, cheerful, charming, and poised of the three groups. Compared to the other two, they were least likely to distrust others or to keep them at a distance.

Remember that this was part of a longitudinal study that began at age 3. The investigators could look back to early patterns. They discovered that the personality patterns of the 18-year-olds were *not* caused by their drug use but, instead, reflected preexisting characteristics. Even as young children, both the frequent drug users and the abstainers tended to be more tense, distressed, and insecure. Those in the third group, the experimenters, were more curious, open, happy, warm, and responsive. Further, the parents of the future frequent users and the future abstainers had much in common. Even with their small children, these parents tended to be cold and unresponsive, pressuring their children to achieve but not encouraging them for what they did. The parents of the experimenters, were, overall, more supportive.

This study by no means suggests that drug use during adolescence should be looked on benignly. The authors emphasize that frequent drug use, especially in early adoles-

Marijuana. The third of the gateway drugs, marijuana, seriously slows down thinking processes, particularly those related to memory and abstract reasoning. Such impairment is a problem at any age but especially in early adolescence, when academic learning requires greater memory and a higher level of abstract thinking. In addition, over time, repeated marijuana "mellowness" may turn into a general lack of motivation and indifference toward the future. The result is apathy at the very time that young people should be focusing their energy on meeting the challenges of growing up.

The last problem may be the most serious. As one research review noted, marijuana users also use alcohol, tobacco, and other drugs, and drug use undermines "the attainment of skills and the mastery of new material, [which are] so important to self-esteem and academic progress, the acquisition of new material, and the type of learning that requires abstract reasoning" (Schilit & Gomberg, 1991). Thus, early drug use impairs the acquisition of knowledge, the ability to reflect on that knowledge, and the growth of mature judgment that leads to reasoned conclusions. The same

Look at Their Expressions As long as these three stay safe at home, they cannot crash a car, and they appear to be at least 16—past the most hazardous time for gateway drugs.

❓ *Observational Quiz (see answer page 464): Is there any long-term harm visible in their activities?*

cence, not only indicates preexisting problems but most likely makes those problems worse, a conclusion found in other research as well (Wilens et al., 1997). For adolescents who are emotionally vulnerable, abstinence is the best choice, because for them, drug use may progress quickly to harmful drug addiction and abuse, not harmless experimentation.

However, the authors of the longitudinal study take strong exception to one form of drug education for teenagers—education that teaches that a single trial will lead to addiction. Such education leads not to abstinence but, rather, to overwhelming anxiety (which might itself lead to drug use) or to the conclusion that adults are hopelessly misguided. Moreover, the study's authors say that many drug education programs

> seem flawed on two counts. First, they are alarmist, pathologizing normative adolescent experimentation and limit-testing, and perhaps frightening parents and educators unnecessarily. Second, and of far greater concern, they trivialize the factors underlying drug abuse, implicitly denying their depth and pervasiveness. [Shedler & Block, 1990]

It seems, then, that the problem of drug abuse during adolescence is really two problems (Dryfoos, 1990; Muisener, 1994). One applies to all adolescents, whose poor judgment about when and how to experiment with drugs and whose behavior when "under the influence" might lead to fatal accidents or other serious consequences. They need to be cautioned, restricted, stalled, controlled, warned, and protected.

The second problem concerns adolescents who use drugs as an attempt to solve, or obliterate, or merely "take the edge off" long-standing personality handicaps or lifelong stresses. For them, drugs may bring temporary relief but, as time goes on, only add to their difficulties and increase the likelihood of addiction. Many of these teenagers have other vulnerabilities as well—with school, with sexual relationships, with the law— that are made worse by drug abuse. They need much more help than a lecture on the evils of addiction.

❓ **Especially for Educators:** How should you teach teenagers to avoid drugs? Specifically, which of the following four strategies would be best to prevent drug abuse in early adolescence: teaching by example, giving informative lectures, having open discussions, or remaining silent on the topic (relying on adolescents to discover lessons through experience)?

cognitive impairment and social ineptness that are caused by early drug *use* play a role later by increasing the chances of drug abuse and addiction. This may help explain why "the longer a person delays initiating drug use, the less likely he or she is to become a chronic user" (Schilit & Gomberg, 1991).

Solutions and Attitudes

What can be done about drug use among adolescents, and particularly among young adolescents? As long as drugs are available and are not perceived as extremely damaging, most young people will try them and many will abuse them. One goal, then, as most developmentalists see it, is to delay drug experimentation as long as possible. This increases the odds that the developing person will be realistically informed and will have the reasoning ability to limit—and perhaps avoid—destructive drugs in dangerous circumstances.

❶ Answer to Observational Quiz (from page 463): *Although many parents rightly fear the physical addiction and thoughtless risk taking that drug abuse can lead to, the faces of this pot-smoking, beer-drinking trio illustrate another danger. Psychoactive drugs suspend the need to engage in meaningful dialogue, while distorting and anesthetizing emotions. Regular drug use brings adolescents into adulthood with diminished self-understanding and immature social responsiveness.*

To this end, a wide array of measures have been tried. Among those that are at least partly effective are:

- Improving health education classes to honestly portray the risks of drug use
- Increasing the punishment for store owners who sell alcohol or cigarettes to minors
- Raising the price of alcohol and cigarettes
- Enforcing drunk-driving laws
- Teaching parents how to communicate with their teenagers

Collectively, these measures do indeed postpone and decrease drug use and prevent or diminish serious consequences when experimentation occurs (Dielman, 1994; Gerstein & Green, 1993; Grossman et al., 1994; Wagenaar & Perry, 1994).

Unfortunately, some social factors work in the opposite direction, tending to encourage drug use—especially among younger adolescents, who are wide open to influences from their peers, the media, and the larger culture. One striking example comes from the cigarette manufacturers themselves. As a result of advertisements and promotions featuring "Joe Camel," a cartoonlike figure that caught the attention of children, the percentage of 10- to 18-year-old smokers who smoked Camel cigarettes leaped from 8 percent in 1989 to more than 13 percent in 1993, a 64 percent increase. During the same period, the percentage of adults who smoked Camels held almost steady (*MMWR*, August 19, 1994). Specially targeted advertising (such as free T-shirts) is another reason for the dramatic increase in smoking, especially among young black males, who experienced the greatest percentage rise in smoking of any group (Feder, 1996) (see Figure 14.6). New laws forbid Joe Camel; we will soon see if adolescent smoking decreases.

Another important factor is parental attitudes. Many parents not only are quiet or poorly informed about the hazards of various drugs but also model the wrong behavior. One extensive New Zealand study found that half of the parents allowed their very young children (age 9 or younger) to have an occasional sip of their alcoholic drinks, and these were the children most likely to become alcoholic by age 18 (Casswell, 1996) (see Figure 14.7).

Given these conflicting forces, what makes a young person choose to use or not use drugs? Young people's likelihood of using drugs is directly related to their peers' attitudes about the acceptability and riskiness of drug use—especially if their parents do not discuss that issue with them (Mounts & Steinberg, 1995).

Figure 14.7 Almost Everybody Drinks. This longitudinal study of Australians found that 80 percent of all 18-year-olds had at least one alcohol-related problem in the past year. Problems ranged from the very serious (one in twenty had a car crash) to the almost-normal (half had had hangovers). Perhaps most disturbing were signs of alcoholism: 44 percent had awakened unable to remember events of the night before, and 14 percent drank first thing in the morning. However, even in a teen culture where almost everyone drank, childhood drinking made a difference, as you can see. A child who had not tasted alcohol at age 9 was was half as likely to have a problem related to alcohol at 18 as a child of 9 who had been given a drink (usually a beer). Most of those who were drinking by age 9 were in trouble by age 18, some of them with many more than three alcohol-related problems.

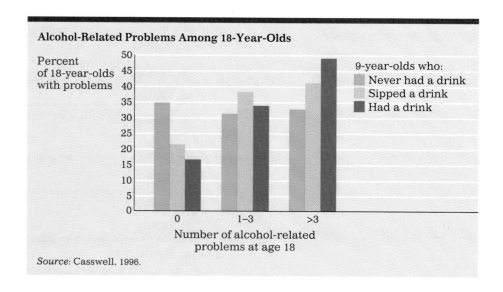

Alcohol-Related Problems Among 18-Year-Olds

Source: Casswell, 1996.

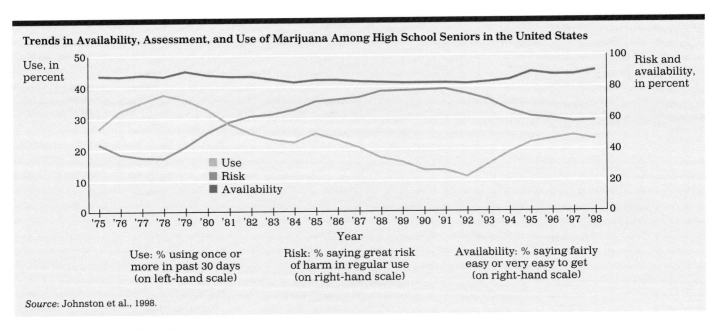

Trends in Availability, Assessment, and Use of Marijuana Among High School Seniors in the United States

Use: % using once or more in past 30 days (on left-hand scale)

Risk: % saying great risk of harm in regular use (on right-hand scale)

Availability: % saying fairly easy or very easy to get (on right-hand scale)

Source: Johnston et al., 1998.

Figure 14.8 Not Supply and Demand, but Attitude and Action. Marijuana has been easily available to almost nine out of ten U.S. high school seniors over the past 25 years, but actual pot smoking is closely related to perception of risk, not to supply. These are patterns for high school seniors, a group most likely to be affected by their peers' attitudes. Adults and addicts are not as vulnerable to shifts in attitudes, except, perhaps, if those changing attitudes are their own.

generational forgetting   The tendency of each new generation to ignore lessons learned by the previous cohort. For example, the hazards of crack were well known a decade ago, but today's teenagers are less aware of them.

❶ **Response for Educators (from page 463):** All of these strategies make some sense, and each of them might backfire. If the "example" smokes or drinks, if the information is alarmist or inaccurate, if the open discussions include popular students defending drug use, or if silence implies consent, the result may be more and earlier drug use. Remember that because adolescents admire honesty, respond to caring, and abhor hypocrisy, any strategy must incorporate these factors. Another tip— sometimes an antidrug peer, a few years older, earns the most respect and trust.

The importance of attitude as a prelude to drug use is indicated in Figure 14.8, which shows that shifts in the actual use of marijuana follow, by about a year, overall shifts in the way young people perceive the dangers of the drug (Johnston et al., 1998). Attitudes, in turn, are powerfully affected by national and local policies, as well as by personal experience. The importance of the macrosystem is indicated by trends in many nations of western Europe, where young people increasingly used drugs throughout the 1980s—the same years when adolescents in the United States were turning away from drugs (Silbereisen et al., 1995).

Unfortunately, antidrug attitudes softened markedly among young Americans during the 1990s, perhaps because each cohort goes through **generational forgetting**—that is, each generation forgets to communicate the hard lessons learned through personal experience. In the case of drugs, generational forgetting renders each generation oblivious to the harm of drug use as directly witnessed by the cohort that preceded it. For example, generational learning is probably the reason heroin was abused less frequently in the 1980s than in the 1970s, and generational forgetting may be the reason heroin seems to be experiencing a comeback. For the same reason, crack, declining markedly in the 1990s (again, unlike other drugs) may be increasing again (Johnston et al., 1998).

The addictive gateway drug of tobacco is the most worrisome here. Despite massive publicity, attitudes have not changed much and older adolescents have a higher smoking rate than any older age group of adults. Many younger adolescents answer "no great risk" when asked, "how much do you think people risk harming themselves (physically or in other ways) if they smoke one or more packs of cigarettes per day?" (See Figure 14.9 on page 466.) The chief investigator of the high school survey comments:

> That's virtually a question with a right-or-wrong answer, and nearly half of these 13- and 14-year-olds get it wrong. By 12th grade, 71 percent of the students see "great risk" in pack-a-day smoking, but by then the horse may already be out of the barn—many are smoking. [Johnston, 1998]

A number of experts believe that if too many adolescents see a certain drug's use as harmless, tomorrow's young adults are going to have "their own epidemic" of drug addiction (Wren, 1996).

Figure 14.9 Slow Progress. The trends are in the right direction, in that with age and time, more adolescents see smoking as harmful. However, since doctors and researchers universally know that tobacco is a leading cause of early death, it is astonishing that even in 1998, one-third of students in the United States deny this reality, with eighth graders particularly willing to ignore possible harm.

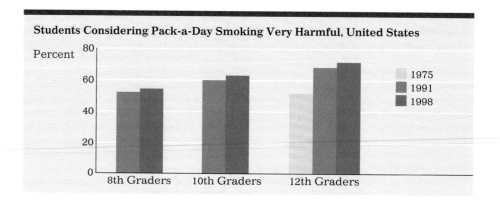

Students Considering Pack-a-Day Smoking Very Harmful, United States

Centuries ago puberty did not occur until the later teens, when the adolescent mind and social context may have been ready for the challenges of sexual awakening and the growth spurt. However, these three health hazards, sexual abuse, malnourishment, and drug use, suggest that when puberty begins at age 11 or 12, today's youths may not be cognitively or socially capable of the autonomy their bodies seek. Fortunately, as you have just learned by looking at trends in drug use, the social context can make a difference in how teenagers respond to their biological growth. Education and social pressures can still guide young people, not only in drug use but in other ways as well. These issues are further explored in the next two chapters, on cognitive and psychosocial development.

SUMMARY

PUBERTY BEGINS

1. The sequence of pubertal events is the same for young people of both sexes and in every culture, but the timing of puberty shows considerable variation. Normal children experience their first body changes some time between the ages of 8 and 14.

2. Puberty is initiated by the production of hormones in the brain. Four of the most important hormones are gonad releasing hormone, growth hormone, testosterone, and estrogen. While performing their biological functions, these hormones can make adolescents' moods more volatile. However, the impact of hormones on emotions depends greatly on personal reactions to the obvious changes in body shape and size, and thus the impact is affected by the social context.

3. The individual's sex, genes, body type, nutrition, and physical and emotional health all determine the age at which puberty begins, with girls and fatter children reaching puberty ahead of boys and leaner children. The secular trend over the past several centuries has resulted in improved nutrition and, consequently, earlier puberty. Emotional stress may also speed the arrival of pubescence.

4. While most teenagers do not have an especially difficult adolescence, early-maturing girls and late-maturing boys are more likely to experience stress because of their off-time physical development. For both sexes, the ecological context—including family interactions, the transition from elementary to junior high or middle school, and cultural values—can ease or intensify the problem.

THE GROWTH SPURT

5. The growth spurt—first in weight, then in height—provides the first obvious evidence of puberty, although some hormonal changes precede it. During the year of fastest growth, an average girl grows about 3½ inches (9 centimeters) and an average boy about 4 inches (10 centimeters).

6. The growth spurt usually affects the extremities first and then proceeds toward the torso. By the end of puberty, the lungs and heart have also increased in size and capacity. During the period of greatest growth, the body often appears misproportioned, since various parts of the body begin growth at different times.

SEXUAL CHARACTERISTICS

7. During puberty, all the sex organs grow larger as the young person becomes sexually mature. Menarche in girls and spermarche in boys are the events usually taken to indicate reproductive potential, although full fertility is reached years after these initial signs of maturation. Both sexes also experience changes in the breasts, voice, and facial and body hair—although there are obvious differences in the typical development of males and females.

8. As the body changes, so must the individual's body image. For many adolescents, this can be a problem, because their actual new shape and appearance are not what they expected or what the cultural ideal promotes.

HEALTH AND HAZARDS

9. Coming at a time when the child is confronted with the physical changes of puberty and their psychological impact, sexual abuse in adolescence can be particularly devastating. The effects of sexual abuse largely depend on the nature of the abuse, its duration, the relationship to the abuser, and the emotional support the victimized adolescent receives when the abuse is reported.

10. To fuel the growth of puberty, adolescents experience increasing nutritional demands for vitamins and minerals as well as for calories—more than at any other period of life. Various nutritional problems, including the destructive effects of overeating, drug use, and overdieting, can slow or even halt normal growth.

11. Many adolescent girls are particularly concerned and unhappy about their changing bodies, and this sets the stage for potentially dangerous eating disorders such as anorexia nervosa (self-starvation) and bulimia nervosa (binge-eating and purging). Boys can also experience these problems.

12. Drug use or experimentation occurs among most adolescents, with almost every teenager knowing how to obtain cigarettes, beer, and other drugs. In the United States, drug use of all kinds is now increasing, after a long period of decline, and drug users are younger. This change accompanies a gradual liberalizing of teenagers' attitudes toward the use of drugs—particularly the gateway drug marijuana—that may foreshadow further increases in both drug use and drug abuse.

13. Addiction, particularly to cigarettes, is a risk that seems to be underestimated by society and by teenagers themselves. However, laws, memories, and attitudes can and do change from generation to generation, and this means drug use by the next cohort may be markedly reduced (or increased) depending on the social context.

KEY TERMS

adolescence (439)
puberty (439)
gonads (440)
menarche (442)
secular trend (442)
growth spurt (445)
primary sex
  characteristics (448)
spermarche (449)
secondary sex
  characteristics (450)

body image (452)
childhood sexual abuse
  (454)
anorexia nervosa (457)
bulimia nervosa (457)
drug abuse (458)
addiction (458)
drug use (459)
gateway drugs (459)
generational forgetting
  (465)

KEY QUESTIONS

1. What is the usual sequence of biological changes during puberty?

2. What is the "secular trend of development," and why does it occur?

3. What factors trigger the onset of puberty?

4. How does the age at which puberty begins affect the adolescent, socially and emotionally?

5. What are the main changes that characterize the growth spurt?

6. How are the sexual maturation of males and that of females similar, and how are they different?

7. How is an adolescent's body image related to the development of self-esteem?

8. What are the potential consequences of sexual abuse in adolescence, and what factors make sexual abuse most damaging?

9. How do the nutritional needs of adolescents differ from those of younger and older individuals?

10. What are the possible causes and consequences of eating disorders?

11. What are the reasons underlying two recent trends among adolescents: increased use of some drugs and use at an earlier age?

12. How might drug use be harmful even if the drug is legal and used only occasionally?

13. *In Your Experience* How did the attitudes of your family, friends, and others affect your experience of puberty?

CRITICAL THINKING EXERCISE

by Richard O. Straub

Take your study of Chapter 14 a step further by working this creative problem-solving exercise:

Puberty can be a difficult time of life. The young people who have the most difficulty are those who must adjust to the physical changes of puberty earlier or later than the majority of their peers. This early or late maturation may be difficult because adolescents do not want to stand out from the crowd in any way that is not admirable.

To help you reason about your own adolescent body image, as well as its impact on your development, we ask you to think back to your physical appearance when you were in the middle of puberty, probably age 13 or 14 and in about eighth grade.

1. What did you (or your friends and parents) consider your "best feature"? What was your "worst feature"—the aspect of your appearance that you felt required the most care or upgrading?

2. Compared to your classmates and friends, were you an average-maturing, early-maturing, or late-maturing individual? What impact do you feel the timing of your puberty had on you at the time?

3. How does the timing of your puberty affect who you are today?

4. Do the ideas you had about your physical appearance reflect your current body image? Why or why not (or to what extent)?

5. What words of advice concerning body image would you offer to a son or daughter at puberty?

Don't bother turning to Appendix B for answers to this exercise because your answers will be uniquely your own. However, you might compare your thoughts with friends, including those of the other sex, to better understand the variable impact of puberty.

Adolescence:
Cognitive Development

CHAPTER 15

Talking with a 16-year-old about international politics, the latest rage in music, or the meaning of life is obviously quite different from conversations on the same topics with an 8-year-old. Thanks to major advances in their cognitive abilities, adolescents are increasingly aware of both world concerns and personal needs—others' as well as their own—and they are more adult in their use of analysis, logic, and reason.

However, as thinking develops and knowledge increases, young people become more vulnerable to ideas, speculations, and insights that are troubling or even dangerous. They may appear tough-minded; at least, their frequent sarcasm, cynicism, and arrogance give this impression. But the opposite is more likely true. Adolescents often are naive, idealistic, troubled by their own introspections, and supersensitive to criticism, real or imagined.

It is important that parents and teachers recognize this peculiar mixture of intellectual bravado and fragile self-centeredness as they try to guide adolescent cognition. When school structure, academic curriculum, or parental advice does not take the adolescent mind-set into account, education is likely to falter and good personal guidance is likely to be resisted. Recognizing the limits of their own reasoning is also crucial for adolescents themselves, lest they be misled by their bravado to take risks that compromise their future.

ADOLESCENT THOUGHT

Every basic skill of thinking, learning, and remembering continues to progress during adolescence (Keating, 1990). Selective attention becomes more skillfully deployed, enabling students to do homework when they are surrounded by peers or blaring music (or both) *if* motivation is high. Expanded memory skills and a growing knowledge base allow adolescents to connect new ideas and concepts to old ones. Metamemory and metacognition help them become better students. This, in turn, deepens adolescents' understanding of calculus and chemistry, fads and friendship, and everything else they set their minds to.

Language mastery continues as well. Vocabulary grows and the nuances of grammar become better understood. Many adolescents develop a personal style in their writing and speech; poets, diarists, and debaters emerge in every high school classroom. However, ongoing maturation of these cognitive skills (already described in Chapter 12) does not capture the essence of adolescent thought. Something new emerges.

formal operational thought   In Piaget's theory, the fourth and final stage of cognitive development; arises from combination of maturation and experience.

Weather Forecasting: Predicting the Possible
Thanks to a satellite feed from high-tech computers and monitors, these students are learning the art and science of weather forecasting. Such education is well suited to the adolescent mind. In their expansive knowledge of relevant factors, ability to remember several interrelated variables, and capacity to imagine possibilities, adolescents' thinking is quite different from that of younger children.

❓ **Especially for Parents:** Suppose your 14-year-old child argues a position you think is completely irrational—that it would be best to leave school at 16, or that all religious leaders are greedy for money, or some such argument. What is the best way to convince him or her otherwise?

New Intellectual Powers

Piaget thought adolescents begin to reach **formal operational thought.** In his theory, formal operational thought is the fourth and final stage of cognitive development, arising from a combination of maturation and experience. Information-processing theorists likewise see a new and higher level of cognition, the result of accumulated improvements in cognitive processing and memory. Similarly, sociocultural theorists point to intellectual advances resulting from the transition from primary school to secondary school, where such things as specialized teachers, changing classes, and long-term homework assignments constitute a new culture of learning. Indeed, almost all developmentalists agree that adolescent thought is qualitatively different from children's thought (Inhelder & Piaget, 1958; Kitchener & Fischer, 1990; Overton, 1990; Siegler, 1991).

For many developmentalists, the single most distinguishing feature of adolescent thought is the capacity to think of *possibility*, not just reality. Adolescents can think "outside the box" of tradition. As John Flavell and his colleagues (1993) explain:

> The elementary school child's characteristic approach to many conceptual problems is . . . an earthbound, concrete, practical-minded sort of problem-solving approach, one that persistently fixates on the perceptible and inferable reality right there in front of him. . . . The child usually begins with reality and moves reluctantly, if at all, to possibility; . . . the adolescent or adult is more apt to begin with possibility and only subsequently proceed to reality. . . . Reality is seen as that particular portion of the much wider world of possibility that happens to exist or hold true in a given problem situation.

This ability to think in terms of possibility allows adolescents to fantasize, speculate, and hypothesize more readily and on a far grander scale than children, who are still tied to the tangible reality of the here and now. Adolescents can, and do, break free from the earthbound, traditional reasoning of the schoolchild, soaring into contradictory notions, rebellious concepts, and ethereal dreams quite apart from conventional wisdom.

Hypothetical Thinking

It may seem paradoxical, but such liberation of thought actually leads to a more logical cast of mind. Consider the following two propositions:

> If elephants are bigger than dogs
> And dogs are bigger than mice
> Then elephants are bigger than mice.
>
> If mice are bigger than dogs
> And dogs are bigger than elephants
> Then mice are bigger than elephants.
> (adapted from Moshman & Franks, 1986)

In evaluating these two propositions, a school-age child is likely to conclude that the first is logical because each part of it is true and it leads to a true conclusion. The same child is likely to consider the second proposition illogical because it conflicts with reality. By contrast, an adolescent is more willing to play with possibilities by imagining a world in which enormous mice tower over minuscule elephants—and to conclude that the second proposition,

hypothetical thought Thought that involves propositions and possibilities that may or may not reflect reality.

while inconsistent with the actual world, is nevertheless perfectly logical because the word "if" opens the way to untold possibilities (Moshman, 1990).

By reasoning this way, adolescents demonstrate a capacity for **hypothetical thought,** that is, thought that involves reasoning about propositions that may or may not reflect reality. For younger children, imagined possibilities (such as in pretend play) are always tied to the everyday world as they know or wish it to be. For adolescents, possibility takes on a life of its own; "here and now" is only one of many alternative possibilities that also include not only "there and then" but also "long, long, ago," "nowhere," "not yet," and "never."

The adolescent's ability to ignore the real and think about the possible is clear in this hypothetical example: If an impoverished college student were offered $50 to argue in favor of the view that government should *never* give

Abstraction Way Beyond Counting on Fingers and Toes This high school student explains a calculus problem, a behavior that requires a level of hypothetical and abstract thought beyond that of any concrete operational child—and beyond that of most adults. At the beginning of concrete operational thought, children need blocks, coins, and other tangible objects to help them understand math. By later adolescence, in the full flower of formal operational thought, such practical and concrete illustrations are irrelevant.

or lend money to impoverished college students, probably he or she could earn the money by providing a convincing (if insincere) argument. This demonstrates that the college student has mastered the skill of hypothetical thought. By contrast, school-age children have great difficulty arguing against their personal beliefs, especially if those personal beliefs arise from their own situation. An 8-year-old would find it almost impossible to explain why parents should *not* give birthday presents to their children, even if the child knew this was "just pretend" (Flavell at al., 1993).

The ability to ignore what one really believes and to argue an opposite or alternative view also makes adolescents quite clever participants in intellectual bull sessions or partners in debate. It also allows them—sometimes unhelpfully—to turn every assumption on its head and to question the logic of every belief.

This is one reason why adolescence can be a time of agonized reflection about the world and one's place in it, because such reflection leads to novel, provocative, and sometimes frightening thoughts. God and religion come up for analysis; the meaning of life is open to question; and the misdeeds and moral failings of national heroes and one's own parents take on heavy significance. For many teenagers, reflection about any serious issue then becomes a complicated and wrenching process. The complications were illustrated on a personal level by one high school student who wanted to keep her friend from making a life-threatening decision but did not want to judge her, because

> to . . . judge [someone] means that whatever you are saying is right and you know what's right. You know it's right for them and you know it's right in every situation. [But] you can't know if you are right. Maybe you are right. But then, right in what way? [quoted in Gilligan et al., 1990]

Although adolescents are not always sure what is "right," they are quick to see what is "wrong." Unlike children, they do not accept current conditions because "that's the way things are." Instead, they criticize what is because they can imagine how things might be in a world in which justice was realized, people were always sincere, and the meaning of human life was truly recognized. This is hypothetical thinking at its best.

Deductive Reasoning

As you saw in Chapter 12, during the school years, children increasingly use their accumulated knowledge of facts, as well as their personal experience, to reach conclusions about their practical experiences. In essence, their

Deductive Reasoning High school chemistry classes, such as the one on the left, first teach students the general principles and then ask them to test the principles with specific substances. There is no way a student could simply be given these materials and told to figure out some generalities, as a teacher of 8-year-olds, with much simpler and safer substances, might do. Younger children think inductively; these students think deductively as well.

Chess is another example of deductive thinking. Unlike simple games of chance, which younger children enjoy, chess requires some general principles, such as protecting your king, focusing on the center, and changing strategies as the game progresses.

❷ *Observational Quiz (see answer page 474): Beyond the intellectual challenge of chemistry or chess, what other type of problem do these adolescents seem to be solving?*

inductive reasoning Reasoning from one or more specific experiences or facts to a general conclusion.

deductive reasoning Reasoning from a general hypothesis, through logical steps, to a specific conclusion.

❶ **Response for Parents (from page 470):** Since adolescents love the game of thinking, and are adept at hypothetical thinking, the first thing to remember is not to take the words too seriously or too personally. Part of the fun of the adolescent years is taking an idea to its hypothetical and deductive extreme—and shocking parents in the process. So listen, provide alternative perspectives and facts, but don't get too upset. Opinions change rapidly during these years.

Figure 15.1 Bottom Up or Top Down? Children are more likely to draw conclusions on the basis of their own experiences and what they have been told, as you might expect from concrete operational thinkers. This is called inductive, or bottom-up, reasoning. Adolescents can think deductively, from the top down. One way to remember this distinction is that *in*ductive reasoning begins *in*side the problem; *de*ductive reasoning begins *de*tached from it. Since adolescents focus on the possible and the hypothetical, they are much more able to detach from reality.

reasoning goes like this: "If it walks like a duck and quacks like a duck, then it must be a duck." Such reasoning from particulars ("walks like" and "quacks like") to a general conclusion ("it's a duck"), is called **inductive reasoning.**

During adolescence, as young people develop their capacity to think hypothetically, they soon become more capable of **deductive reasoning** (Byrnes, 1988). That is, they can begin with a general premise or theory, reason through one or more logical steps to draw a specific conclusion, and then test the validity of that conclusion. Deduction is reasoning from the general to the specific: "If it's a duck, it will walk and quack like a duck" (see Figure 15.1).

Are Dolphins Fish? To see the developmental progression from inductive to deductive reasoning more clearly, let's look at an example of how children of various ages might try to figure out what class of animals dolphins belong to. Preschoolers are quick to believe that dolphins are fish—because dolphins, like fish, live in the water. Moreover, a preschooler might become angry at any suggestion that these obviously fishlike creatures are *not* fish. They center on appearance and stubbornly stick to their conclusion. School-age children might have heard their teachers say

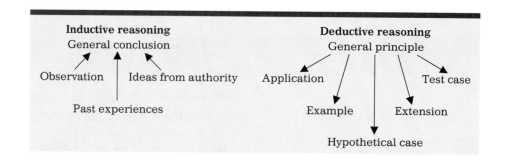

that dolphins are mammals and might have noticed that dolphins breathe air. Accordingly, with those two bits of evidence, they might induce from the two facts they know (that teachers have knowledge and that dolphins breathe air) that dolphins are indeed mammals rather than fish. With the arrogance typical of an absolutist thinker (that is, a thinker who sees things as yes or no, true or false), the schoolchild might lord it over any younger child so foolish as to disagree.

In contrast, adolescents are likely to consider many alternative hypotheses, recognizing that until the evidence is in, things are "maybe," not yes or no, "possible," not true or false. Thus dolphins could be some form of fish, or mammal, or reptile, or even a bizarre type of bird (perhaps a distant relative of the penguin). Acting logically on a teacher's statement that dolphins are mammals, adolescents might search for the general principle that distinguishes mammals from other biological classes—perhaps looking in a dictionary or an encyclopedia. Not only would they question whatever their teacher said; they would actually hope they could prove their teacher wrong. They would find that the root word for mammal is *mamma* (Latin for breast) and that the definition is that mammals suckle their young.

That would lead our adolescents to reason that "if dolphins are mammals, then they nurse their young." And so they would seek evidence that mother dolphins do or do not suckle their pups, and they would ignore irrelevant data (such as that dolphins swim like fish or breathe air or have lateral fins that look like vestigial wings). Their deductive reasoning would have proceeded from the general principle, which may or may not agree with received wisdom or with everyday observation, to the specific application, rather than vice versa.

Illustrating this switch are the results of an experiment testing belief in freedom of religion (Helwig, 1995). When asked, a group of seventh-graders, eleventh-graders, and college students in northern California all endorsed the principle in the Bill of Rights of freedom of religious expression. Then this easy endorsement was put to the test, with questions such as "What if a particular religion refused to allow low-income people to be priests?" Almost all (94 percent) of the seventh-graders abandoned freedom of religion under those circumstances, but almost none (19 percent) of the eleventh graders switched their thinking. They stood their ground—as one might expect for inductive thinkers.

If you are wondering if such firm adherence to principle is always a good thing, you will be interested to know that some psychologists contend that adults can reach a less absolutist stage *after* Piaget's formal operational stage. This fifth stage might be attained in college (Commons & Richards, 1984). In the study just mentioned, the college students were more aware than the high school students of the conflict between two general principles: religious freedom and economic justice. Consequently, 38 percent thought equal opportunity was more important, and 62 percent stuck to freedom of religion as the overriding idea (Helwig, 1995).

Piaget's Balance Experiment

Piaget devised a number of famous tasks involving scientific principles to study the reasoning of children of various ages. In one experiment, shown in Figure 15.2, children were asked to balance a scale with weights that could be hooked onto the scale's arms (Piaget & Inhelder, 1958). Mastering this problem requires realizing that the heaviness of the weights and their distance from the center interact to affect balance. This understanding is

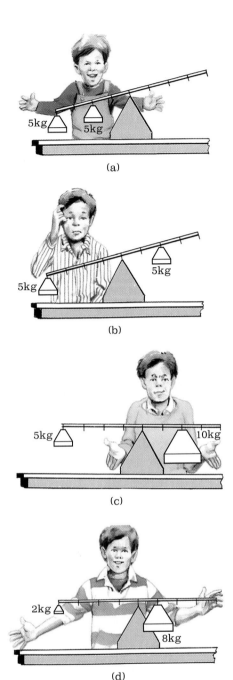

Figure 15.2 How to Balance a Beam. Piaget's balance-scale test of formal reasoning, as it is attempted by *(a)* a 4-year-old, *(b)* a 7-year-old, *(c)* a 10-year-old, and *(d)* a 14-year-old. The key to balancing the scale is to make weight times distance from the center equal on both sides of the center; the realization of that principle requires formal operational thought.

completely beyond the ability of 3- to 5-year-olds, who, in Piaget's research, randomly hung different weights on different hooks.

Piaget found that by age 7 children realized that the scale could be balanced by putting the same amount of weight on both arms but they didn't realize that the distance of the weights from the center of the scale is also important. By age 10, near the end of the concrete operational stage, children often realized the importance of the weights' locations on the arms, but their efforts to coordinate weight and distance from the center to balance the scale involved trial-and-error experimentation, not logical deduction.

Finally, by about age 13 or 14, some children hypothesized that there is a direct relationship between a weight's distance from the center of the scale and the effect it has on a balance. By systematically testing this hypothesis, they correctly formulated the mathematical relation between weight and distance from the center and could solve the balance problem accurately and efficiently. Piaget attributed each of these advances to the intellectual growth from one cognitive stage to the next-higher one.

A Problem with the Theory

Hypothetical thought and deductive reasoning should make the adolescent a more flexible, resourceful thinker. And, in fact, they do—for some adolescents, some of the time. However, researchers find that the growth of formal operational reasoning abilities is far slower and less complete than many—and particularly Piaget—believed it to be (Keating, 1990). Many older adolescents (and adults) do poorly on standard tests of deductive reasoning skills, such as the balance-scale task. The cognitive gains of formal operational thought are not always accomplished during adolescence, nor are they necessarily acquired by all people.

Moreover, a teenager who can easily use deductive reasoning to figure out a mathematics problem may have great difficulty in deducing the solution to a problem in biology, or in assessing the ethics of various approaches to national health insurance, or in determining the most effective way to deal with a complex human dilemma. In other words, adolescents appear to

It's All About Me Personal perceptions cloud judgment at every age. However, egocentrism is particularly apparent in adolescence, when the discovery of self is not yet balanced by a deeper understanding of the breadth of human experience.

apply formal logic to some situations but not to others. It seems that each individual's intellect, experiences, talents, and interests affect his or her thinking at least as much as the ability to reason formally.

Thinking About Me

Adolescents frequently practice their new thinking skills on themselves, a process that makes them lose some of their new detachment. They worry about how they are regarded by others; they try to sort out their own conflicting feelings about parents, school, and close friends; they think deeply but not always realistically about their future possibilities; they reflect, at length, on each day's experiences. Analyzing their private thoughts and feelings, forecasting their future, and reflecting on their experiences underlie the greater reflection and self-awareness—and enhanced capacity for self-centeredness—that distinguish adolescence. (See Children Up Close, pages 476–477.)

All these new ventures in introspection are an essential part of the adolescent's expanding self-awareness. However, they are often distorted by **adolescent egocentrism** (remember, from Chapter 9, that "egocentric" means "self at the center"), a self-view in which adolescents regard themselves as much more socially significant than they actually are (Elkind, 1967, 1984). Younger adolescents tend to hypothesize about what others might be thinking (especially about them) and then egocentrically take their hypotheses to be fact—a kind of deductive reasoning that can lead to very false conclusions.

adolescent egocentrism   A characteristic of adolescent thinking that sometimes leads young people to focus on themselves to the exclusion of others, believing, for example, that their thoughts, feelings, or experiences are unique.

Boys Do It Too   Although it is generally girls who are considered to be overly aware of minor flaws in their complexion or attire, the truth is that boys also pay exaggerated attention to their appearance. The cognitive capacity to think about oneself in egocentric terms makes many young people of both sexes spend hours combing their hair, adjusting their clothing, and searching for blemishes.

According to David Elkind (1978), who first labeled this trait, adolescent egocentrism occurs because adolescents fail to differentiate between the unique and the universal. A young woman who falls in love for the first time is enraptured with the experience, which is entirely new and thrilling. But she fails to differentiate between what is new and thrilling to herself and what is new and thrilling to humankind. It is not surprising, therefore, that this young lady says to her mother, "But, Mother, you don't know how it feels to be in love" (Elkind, 1978).

In a related example described some 20 years later, an 18-year-old young woman rejected her parents' advice to use sexual restraint with her boyfriend. She explains,

> My mother tells me, try to enjoy being young while it lasts . . . look around you a bit more, you'll be old before you know it and where will you be then? But the thing is I simply *love* him. [Ravesloot, 1995]

Once again, the young person uses personal emotions to downplay an adult's general advice.

Many adolescents exhibit this same kind of egocentric thinking, based on two faulty premises: first, that no one else has ever had experiences like theirs; and, second, that their emotions are actually facts from which to induce other logical ideas and actions. A too common example is, "If you love me, then you will . . ." even though parents, religious tradition, or best friends advise otherwise.

A BERGER TEENAGER

Whether they are trying to understand the external world or themselves, adolescents are capable of a type of thinking vastly different from that of elementary school children. However, this new thinking is unpredictable: teenagers' mastery of hypothetical thought and deductive reasoning is not always apparent, and their introspections can cause them to leap in the wrong direction.

This unevenness was well demonstrated by my eldest daughter, Bethany, whose newfound perspectives on art and history made her absolutely certain that she wanted to visit the Metropolitan Museum of Art. It was a humid midsummer afternoon, and all her friends were out of town, so she prevailed on me to go with her. I was ready in 5 minutes but, because she was in her midteens, it took her much longer.

In fact, we left the house so late that I was concerned the museum would close before we finally got there. Hence, I was relieved that our subway train arrived quickly and moved us rapidly to our stop. But when we climbed up to street level from the station, we saw a sudden downpour. Bethany became angry—at *me!*

> *She:* "You didn't bring an umbrella? You should have known."
> *Me:* "It's okay—we'll walk quickly. It's a warm rain."
> *She:* "But we'll get all wet."
> *Me:* "It's okay. We'll dry."
> *She:* "But people will see us with our hair all wet."
> *Me:* "Honey, no one cares what we look like. And we won't see anyone we know."
> *She:* "That's okay for you to say. You're already married."

I was mystified. "Do you think you are going to meet your future husband here?"

"No," she said, with an exasperated scowl that suggested I understood nothing. "People will look at me and think, 'She'll never find a husband looking like that!' "

Bethany's quickness to criticize me, and her egocentric concern with an imaginary audience who might judge her future possibilities, is echoed in almost every other teenager. Another example is reported by a father, himself a therapist:

> The best way I can describe what happens [during adolescence] is to relate how I first noticed the change in my son. He was about 13 years of age. One afternoon he and I were riding in a car on a four-lane highway which circles Boston, Massachusetts. I was driving 65 miles an hour in a 55 mile zone.
>
> He suddenly turned toward me and shouted, *"Dad!"*
>
> I was startled and responded by saying, "What is it, Jim!"
>
> Then there was this pause as he folded his arms and turned slowly in my direction and said, "Dad, do you realize how fast you are driving this car?"
>
> I was obviously embarrassed because after all, I did not want my son to notice that on occasion I break the law! I was able to put this over on him up to this age in his life. But more than that, I was taken back by the new tone in his voice! I had not heard that before. It was a command, not a question!
>
> Anyway, he was asking the question so I simply turned and said, "Oh, I'm doing 65 miles per hour!" (as if I didn't know it).
>
> He then came right back at me and said, *"Dad!* Do you know what the speed limit is on this highway?"
>
> Now my ego was hurt and I wanted to attack! This little voice in the back of my head was saying, "Here comes early adolescent behavior, wipe it out now!"

Mistaken Assumptions

invincibility fable The fiction, fostered by adolescent egocentrism, that one is immune to common dangers, such as those associated with unprotected sex, drug abuse, or high-speed driving.

personal fable The egocentric idea, held by many adolescents, that one is destined for fame and fortune and/or great accomplishments.

As you can see, adolescent egocentrism can lead to false conclusions. Some of these have special names. One is the **invincibility fable,** by which young people feel that they will never fall victim, as others do, to dangerous behavior. Adults find evidence of the invincibility fable in, among other things, teenagers' high rates of smoking (despite awareness of the health risks of tobacco), unsafe sexual behavior (despite risks of pregnancy and of sexually transmitted diseases), and dangerous driving (despite mandated driver education). Invincibility leads to a foolish sense of security, and sometimes to disastrous risks.

Another false conclusion resulting from adolescent egocentrism is the **personal fable,** through which adolescents imagine their own lives as unique, heroic, or even mythical. They perceive themselves as different from others, distinguished by unusual experiences, perspectives, and values. Sometimes adolescents see themselves as destined for honor and glory, perhaps by dis-

Well, he was right, so I kept cool and responded by saying "Yes, Jim, it's 55 miles an hour."

He then said, *Dad!* Do you realize that you are traveling 10 miles over the speed limit! I handled this one with calm because it at least indicated that he could add and subtract!

He continued, *Dad!* Don't you care about my life at all! Do you have any idea of how many thousands of people lose their lives every year on our nation's highways who exceed the speed limit!

Now I was beginning to get angry and I responded by saying, "Look, Jim, I have no idea how many people are killed every year, you were right I shouldn't have been speeding; I promise I won't ever do it again, so let us just forget it!"

Not being satisfied, he continued, *Dad!* Any idea what would happen if the front wheel of this car came off doing 65 miles per hour, how many lives you might jeopardize!

He kept on with this for another 10 minutes until I finally got him quiet for about 20 seconds! Then he came back at me and said, "Dad! I've been thinking about this."

Once he said that, I knew I was in deep trouble! You see, my son was so easy to deal with before he started *to think!* Who told him he had a right to start *thinking!* Before this all happened he would ask, *why,* and I would simply give him the answer and it was good enough! [Garvin, 1994]

Note that both Bethany and Jim were focused on future possibilities, just as one might expect. And both followed an idea, albeit an egocentric one, to a logical conclusion. But don't let these examples leave the wrong impression. Teenagers are not always egocentric and illogical, by any means.

At age 17, Bethany wrote about her art:

Just as the mind, on seeing letters must grab them and process them as words, so I must grab whatever materials are about and process my notions into images . . . struggling to draw certain lines intensifies their loveliness for me, creates a fascination with, say, the line of a dancer's body, a cat's back, a blowing blade of grass. . . . It has always been my sketchbook I grab when I feel too outraged and helpless to do anything but scream. Now I am trying to form a connection with the external world by drawing it. I am experimenting with difficult media, . . . sketching more varied objects and scenes.

Here, Bethany is clearly self-aware and analytic, thinking about the underlying import of her artistic interest and using it to expand her "connection with the external world," far beyond the limits of egocentrism.

In trying to arrive at a balanced view of teenagers' thinking, in which moments of adult insight are juxtaposed with childish reasoning, we cannot expect too much or too little. I would agree that

from early adolescence on, thinking tends to involve abstract rather than merely concrete representation; to become multidimensional rather than limited to a single issue; to become relative rather than absolute in the conception of knowledge; and to become self-reflective and self-aware. . . . [But] it is probably safest to assume that these shifts represent potential accomplishments for most adolescents rather than typical everyday thinking. [Keating, 1990]

covering a cure for cancer, authoring a masterpiece, or influencing the social order. As one high school student expressed it, her goal is to

affect . . . as many people as possible. . . . I see myself in a big way saying big things. I see myself going to school for a long time and learning a lot. I want to write a book that is very, very solid and hard, to say "No, you are wrong." So that I can give it to the President and say, Look, Mr. President, you are wrong and you are going to hurt all these people and you are going to hurt yourself. I want to say something big. I want to change the world. [Gilligan et al., 1990]

Other adolescents hold the personal fable that they are destined for fame and fortune, by becoming a music or movie star, a sports hero, a business tycoon, or whatever else will make millions (sometimes after having already decided that a high school education is a waste of time).

imaginary audience The egocentric idea, held by many adolescents, that others are intensely interested in them, and especially in their appearance and behavior.

The Thrill of the Fast Life These boys ride on top of high-speed trains and risk falling or hitting live electrical wires. Some die every year.

❓ *Observational Quiz (see answer page 480): What culture do you think these boys are from?*

person-environment fit The degree to which a particular environment is conducive to the growth of a particular individual.

A third false conclusion stemming from egocentrism is called the **imaginary audience.** This arises from many adolescents' assumption that other people are as intently interested in them as they themselves are. As a result, they tend to fantasize about how others react to their appearance and behavior. At times, the imaginary audience can cause teenagers to enter a crowded room as if they believe themselves to be the most attractive human beings alive. More often, though, they cringe from any attention, because they view something as trivial as a slight facial blemish or a spot on a shirt as an unbearable embarrassment that everyone will notice and judge.

The acute self-consciousness resulting from the imaginary audience reveals that young people are not relaxed with the broader social world. This is one reason many seem obsessed with their hair, clothing, and so on, before going out in public. It also explains their need to fit in with their peer group, who presumably judge every visible nuance of their appearance and behavior. No wonder, then, that one adolescent explained,

I would like to be able to fly if everyone else did; otherwise it would be rather conspicuous. [quoted in Steinberg, 1993]

Overall, adolescent egocentrism suggests that intense reflection about thoughts, feelings, and motives is a mixed blessing. It enables adolescents to consider their lives more thoughtfully but often at the cost of great self-criticism.

SCHOOLS, LEARNING, AND THE ADOLESCENT MIND

Given the cognitive changes that adolescents typically experience, what kind of school would best foster their intellectual growth? That straightforward question has no single answer. The problem is that the optimum **person-environment fit**—that is, the best setting for an individual's personal growth—depends not only on the individual's developmental stage, cognitive strengths, and learning style but also on the society's traditions, educational objectives, and future needs. These vary substantially from person to person, place to place, and time to time.

The Adolescent Mind in the School Setting

As their ability to think hypothetically and abstractly starts to emerge, adolescents begin to abandon simplistic, concrete thinking and to construct more imaginative, comprehensive, and complex world views, as you have just seen. Consequently, they become increasingly interested in the opinions and judgments of others—adults as well as peers—from a variety of backgrounds. At the same time, they are ready, even eager, to question every idea, sometimes with an egocentrism that is stunning. As one high school student of mine said of the theory of relativity, "That's just Einstein's opinion. I have my own opinion, and I don't agree with him."

Teenagers' self-consciousness makes them highly sensitive to actual or anticipated criticism. This combination of openness and sensitivity puts them in an emotional bind: they are eager for lively intellectual interaction but highly vulnerable to self-doubt. The brash young man who is ready to challenge the ideas of any dead thinker may also avoid coming to class after the teacher has made a wisecrack at his expense.

Similarly, how much students study, and how much they learn, is clearly affected by their attitudes about school. This was shown in a year-long study of high school students of varied ability in eight communities. Those who initially thought achievement depended on others or on fate, rather than on their own ability, tended to have disengaged from class a year later (no longer doing the homework, asking questions, and so on)—a progression from attitude to action that occurred no matter what their actual potential was (Glasgow et al., 1997).

Knowing these teenage tendencies, we might expect high schools to encourage supportive interaction among students and, especially, between teachers and students. Ideally, in offering support, teachers would find ways to build up each student's self-confidence. Too often, however, the opposite is the case.

Instead of an appropriate person-environment fit, a **volatile mismatch** forms between many adolescents and their schools (Carnegie Council, 1989). Compared to elementary schools, most secondary schools have more rigid behavioral demands, intensified competition, and more punitive grading practices, as well as less individualized attention and procedures (Eccles et al., 1996).

The impersonal and bureaucratic nature of many schools is particularly destructive for proper person-environment fit. Many secondary schools attempt to educate more than a thousand students at a time, each of whom is scheduled to travel from teacher to teacher, room to room, topic to topic, every 40 minutes. Some teachers do not know even the names of the hundred or more students they teach, much less their personality traits, intellectual interests, and aspirations (Carnegie Council, 1989). Secondary school teachers tend to consider themselves less effective (and their students tend to see them as less friendly, less caring, and less helpful) than teachers in elementary schools. And they are right: achievement typically drops when a student enters middle school (Eccles et al., 1996). By the end of the high school years, achievement rises again, partly because the lowest achievers have dropped out, partly because the students have become intellectually more mature, and partly because the person-environment fit improves when the older students can choose their courses, lead various clubs, and so on. (See the Research Report on pages 480–481.)

Culture and Schools

Proper person-environment fit requires a good understanding not only of the developmental stage of the person but also of the requirements of the culture. The fact that educational goals (and therefore educational content) differ by culture was convincingly expressed by Native Americans in colonial America in the year 1744. Members of the Council of Five Nations politely declined the offer of scholarships for their young men to William and Mary College, with the following statement:

> You who are wise must know, that different nations have different conceptions of things; and you will therefore not take it amiss if our ideas of this kind of education happen not to be the same with yours. We have had some experience of it; several of our young people were formerly brought up at the college of the northern provinces; they were instructed in all your sciences; but when they came back to us . . . [they were] ignorant of every means of living in the woods . . . neither fit for hunters, warriors, or counselors; they were totally good for nothing. We are, however, not the less obliged by your kind offer . . . and to show our grateful sense of it, if the gentlemen of Virginia will send us a dozen of their sons, we will take great care of their education, instruct them in all we know, and make men of them. [Drake, cited in Rogoff, 1990]

volatile mismatch When teenagers' individual needs—intellectual, emotional, social—do not match the size, routine, and structure of their schools, the result is potentially explosive.

❓ **Especially for Teachers:** How would you use your knowledge of the adolescent mind to teach, say, a foreign language?

UNCARING AND CARELESS STUDENTS

Let us look more closely at a basic general trend: When young people first enter secondary school, academic self-confidence typically dips, with many students feeling less able, less conscientious, and less motivated than they did in elementary school (Eccles, 1993; Hickson et al., 1994; Stipek, 1992). Until and unless they adjust to the school—by making friends, establishing a reputation, getting to know some of the teachers—they feel too anxious to learn as well as they should. They may drift into a kind of fatalism, believing that their grades and their future are determined by something other than their effort or intelligence (Wade, 1996).

Many adolescents in secondary schools seem bored, apathetic, less than half-awake—only partly because they are really tired. (Many secondary schools begin at 8 A.M. or earlier, even though many adolescent bodies are hormonally engineered to be wide awake after midnight and half asleep until noon.) More important, such a cool and uncaring demeanor protects students from the emotional distress of failure. (You can't be considered stupid if you don't try, they think—even though, in the long run, lack of effort leads to failure.)

The attitude of noninvolvement in academic pursuits may also make young people more foolhardy in the halls and

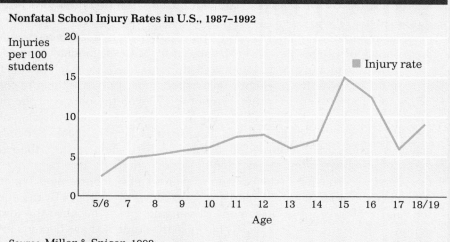

Nonfatal School Injury Rates in U.S., 1987–1992

Injuries per 100 students

Source: Miller & Spicer, 1998.

Figure 15.3 Is School Hazardous to Your Health? Comparison statistics are not shown here, but they reveal that most serious injuries in childhood happen outside of school, by a ratio of 3 to 1. However, when rates are calculated per waking exposure hour, 5- to 10-year-olds are somewhat safer at school and 11- to 19-year-olds are safer outside of school. Fortunately, most school-related injuries are not serious, but about a fourth do involve fractures, dislocations, and brain injuries. In addition, approximately 40 children are killed at school each year, usually in the first years of a large secondary school, about half of those by guns. As chilling as this is, fatalities of children are 400 times more likely not to occur at school, usually on the street or in a car.

❶ Answer to Observational Quiz (from page 478): *Risk taking during adolescence is common in every culture, and it has been a sign of status and independence in every nation and every century, as stories of brave knights fighting fire-breathing dragons attest. Thus, if you thought some cultures are exempt, you are wrong. It is very difficult to deduce from the countryside, the technology, or these teenagers' appearance where they are. The answer is Brazil, where such boys are so common they have a name:* surfistas.

The goals of education in the United States have changed dramatically over the centuries, although "every means of living in the woods" is not yet part of the typical curriculum. Generational differences in goals are quite apparent. At the beginning of the twentieth century, young men needed "vocational training for the sort of employment that likely awaited them" on the assembly line, on the farm, or in the retail store (West, 1996). As the twenty-first century begins, women, as well as men, require computer literacy, scientific understanding, and critical thinking skills.

Further, ethnic diversity in learning goals is widespread and deep. Communities, schools within communities, and even teachers within schools diverge and conflict, as evidenced by the criticism of public schools by those educated in private or parochial schools, and vice versa, and by the always divisive debates on public school funding. "Disagreements over the goals and strategies of education are virtually guaranteed" (West, 1996), perhaps especially within the United States but certainly in other nations as well.

Another Middle School Tragedy These girls are grieving at the deaths of four schoolmates and a teacher who were ambushed by classmates Andrew Golden, 12, and Mitchell Johnson, 14, in Jonesboro, Arkansas. News reports highlighted many causes, including the availability of guns, the violence in the culture, and the absence of the fathers. An additional factor may be the "volatile mismatch" between school culture and adolescent cognition. Note that all the boys who killed other schoolchildren in several areas of the United States in 1998 were in early adolescence, age 12 to 15, and all attended relatively large, impersonal schools.

lunchrooms and on the playing fields. This possibility is suggested by the high rate of injuries at school (see Figure 15.3). Of course, children at every age are more likely to be harmed by an "accident" than by anything else, and violent death and serious injury increase during the teen years. But don't discount this graph as merely showing an increase in injuries with age. Notice, instead, that the injury rate at school increases and dips twice: up at age 11 to 12 years, down at 13, up again at age 15, and down at 16. The two increases occur at just the ages when many American young people enter junior and senior high.

In fact, compared to being at home or on the street attending the first year of middle school is surprisingly hazardous because of sports injuries and injuries caused by "just playing around." The authors of one study estimated the total cost of each childhood injury or death and then noted whether it occurred during school hours or nonschool hours. Younger children were safer at school, but "Middle school students are safer away from school" (Miller & Spicer, 1998). Thus it seems that schools, no less than adolescents, are less caring and careful than they might be to properly protect their students.

Competition and Individual Learning

The emphasis of many high schools is on what some educators refer to as **ego-involvement learning,** that is, learning in which academic grades are based solely on individual test performance and students are ranked against each other from best in the class to worst. This competitive style of education has some drawbacks in elementary school (as you remember from the discussion of norm-referenced testing in Chapter 12), but it gets worse as children grow older and become more self-conscious—painfully aware of how they compare to their peers and almost never happy with themselves.

In an ego-based school, failing students experience embarrassment along with low grades, while exceptionally good students risk being ostracized as "brainiacs," "geeks," or "nerds." In overly competitive conditions, many students—especially girls and students from minority backgrounds—find it easier, and psychologically safer, not to try. They thus avoid the potential pain of

ego-involvement learning An educational strategy that bases academic grades on individual test performance, with students competing against each other.

Lessons Their Ancestors Never Studied
Education today prepares students to think for themselves, not memorize facts. This photo shows a class in prehistory, in contrast to traditional history classes, that began with the first written texts. Note also the "hidden" curriculum—in the way learning occurs. The teacher is acting as a guide rather than as an authority figure. The students are encouraged to draw their own conclusions about the evidence before them, and, most important, this interracial school is in Johannesburg, South Africa. All these features impart lessons that, presumably, will serve these young people well in the twenty-first century.

either success or failure. Within schools, students are tracked; between schools, college acceptances are compared; and among schools and colleges, competition for the "best" students is fierce—with academic and sports scholarships going to the most capable, and the least capable expected to drop out or settle for the form of education without the substance. For example, many students are passed along because of *social promotion,* the practice of promoting and even graduating a student who has not accomplished the basic achievements expected of students.

Standards and Group Learning

task-involvement learning   An educational strategy that bases academic grades on the mastery of certain competencies and knowledge, with students being encouraged to learn cooperatively.

One possible antidote to the stress and competition of ego-involvement learning is **task-involvement learning,** in which achievement is measured only by how well each learning task is done. This educational strategy typically utilizes group learning via team research projects, in-class discussion groups, and after-school study groups—all of which allow students to succeed if they cooperate. Because accomplishing the learning task requires that students assist rather than surpass their peers, the social interaction that teenagers cherish is actually used constructively to enhance education.

In task-involvement learning, one person's success fosters another's success. Grades are based on meeting certain standards of competency and knowledge that everyone, with enough time and effort, is expected to attain. If some students do not reach a standard, instead of receiving an F they are given time, help, and motivation to work harder. This improves their sense of their own efficiency as well as their eventual achievement (Roeser et al., 1996).

❶ Response for Teachers (from page 479):
Immersion, which works well in the early years, might not work so well during adolescence, since self-criticism might make the students too quiet. On the other hand, since deductive thinking is possible, you could teach the general principles of grammar or pronunciation, for instance, much better at this time than during younger years. In any case, you would want to provide high standards and lots of encouragement, as well as many opportunities for the students to help each other.

One of the most remarkable findings to emerge from task-involvement learning is how excited adolescents can become about learning—when conditions foster it. An example comes from science fairs, for which "students become deeply involved in a project of their choosing, conducting research, analyzing results, and presenting findings in a professional manner" (Dreyer, 1994). Other examples include the school play, the school band, the debating, chess, and math teams, and the various athletic teams. All these require—and get—avid participation, extensive practice of various cognitive skills, and an intensity that contrasts dramatically with the apathy ap-

Does This Look Like Your High School?
Probably not, if your diploma is from before 1980.

❷ *Observational Quiz (see answer page 484):* *What four features of this classroom are relatively new, and what four features have been characteristic for decades?*

parent in some classrooms. In all these examples, the goal is to be excellent at the task, not necessarily better than one's classmates, and that goal is reached at least in part through the advancement of abstract, analytic, formal thinking.

Note that the school climate, rather than the adolescent's innate ability, is the prime ingredient for success. Often, the family attitude is equally important. A study of talented teenagers found that predicting which ones would be successful depended on discovering who was willing and able to devote themselves to the *work*, not to the competition. When families and schools made this possible, and when peers did not become distractions, the talented teenagers succeeded. Many times they did not (Csikszentmihalyi et al., 1993). Similarly, a study of Latino 15-year-olds at risk for dropping out found that school practices and family involvement were more significant than the adolescents' ability. Although all the schools and parents said they wanted the youths to graduate, many schools used tracking and testing that make learning difficult and many parents were unaware of the specific impact of class placement on their children (Romo & Falbo, 1996).

Cooperative Learning and Cultural Diversity

Task-involvement learning need not always be done in groups. Individual adolescents sometimes become very involved in their own efforts. However, given the developmental focus of adolescents on social validation and inspiration, especially from peers, *cooperative learning* is particularly useful during the secondary school years. Of course, cooperative learning must be skillfully coordinated within the classroom and within the school to ensure that each individual is challenged and motivated (Johnson & Johnson, 1994).

Once again culture is critical. Reliance on cooperative learning alone may hinder those who are more comfortable with individual learning—especially students from families and cultures that value competition and autonomy much more than cooperation and interdependence. However, when students are socially motivated and personally sensitive, as many adolescents are, the best recipe for academic growth includes social interaction as a main ingredient.

Cooperative learning offers an added benefit when secondary school gives students their first extended exposure to people of differing backgrounds—economic, ethnic, religious, or racial—and thus to ideas, assumptions, and viewpoints that contrast with their own. In a cooperative setting, these differences can expand learning opportunities, bringing new perspectives that are both exciting and enriching.

In a competitive setting, however, these differences can lead to rivalry, social separation, and open hostility. Insecure adolescents may try to protect their own self-concept by exaggerating group differences and rejecting anyone and anything that seems to challenge their identity. Moreover, those on the bottom of the competitive heap are likely to blame others for their failures—suspecting that the other students are cheating, or that the teacher has favorites, or that the curriculum is Eurocentric, multicultural, male-oriented, feminist, irrelevant, unfair, or simply wrong.

The demographics of the future tell us that migration from one nation to another will continue to accelerate and that the United States (and many other nations) will become increasingly multiethnic (see Figure 15.4). Young people will benefit from a better understanding of other groups and from measuring themselves against standards, rather than against their peers. Virtually all developmentalists agree with this ideal, although there is still debate as to what extent our evolutionary history predisposes us to competition or cooperation (Kagen, 1998).

Figure 15.4 Changing Proportions. As the numbers of minority youths rise, the proportions of the population shift, with more Latino and Asian youths than a generation ago. Projections suggest that these trends will continue, so future professionals who work with teenagers will find almost as many "minority" as majority teens. By the year 2040, the "majority" will be one of the minorities.

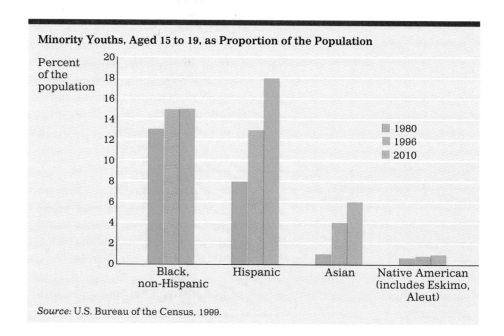

Minority Youths, Aged 15 to 19, as Proportion of the Population

Source: U.S. Bureau of the Census, 1999.

Structuring Education

Too often, poor student achievement is blamed on everything but the schools—on the students' native intelligence, socioeconomic status, minority background, or family disorganization. All these factors are relevant, of course. But many studies over the past 20 years have shown that, beyond these factors, some schools simply educate much more effectively than others. And virtually every study finds that the more effective schools share a central characteristic: educational goals that are high, clearly stated, attainable, and supported by the entire staff, from the principal on down (Kasen et al., 1998; Mortimore, 1995; Reynolds & Cuttance, 1992; Rutter et al., 1979).

Goals and Standards

Initially, it may sound contradictory for goals to be both high *and* attainable by everyone. However, many studies find that this combination is not only possible but also pivotal, particularly for students from whom teachers traditionally demanded little, such as those from minority groups or poor families.

Academic standards and personal warmth can coexist. It is possible to offer, simultaneously, "a curriculum of substance, courses that require students to do serious work . . . [and] teachers who are conveying a sense of caring so that their students feel that their teachers share a stake in their learning" (Commission on the Restructuring of the American High School, 1996). Students themselves agree. One study of 300 tenth-grade students agreed that the best teachers "take pupils seriously," "have confidence in them," "push them to do well," and "make it easier for them to understand" (Tatar, 1998).

Research from a wide assortment of schools finds similar results. For example, a study of 571 unusually effective schools found that their standards of attendance, punctuality, homework, and class performance, and their graduation requirements, were higher than the national norms. In addition, their students were well aware of each standard, knew that their teachers cared about their learning, and proudly "praised their teachers for making them work harder than they might have if left to their [own] devices" (Wilson & Corcoran, 1988). Even more telling, among these particular schools the average dropout rate was about 7 percent, and the college enrollment rate for graduates was about 51 percent; the national averages when the study was undertaken were about 27 and 30 percent, respectively.

The contrast is even more dramatic when effective schools in which poor and minority students predominated are compared with their "ineffective" counterparts. According to the study above, in ineffective minority schools, typically more than half the students did not graduate, and virtually none went on to college (Wilson & Corcoran, 1988). A variety of practices— including serious attendance and homework demands, teacher involvement in curriculum decisions, manageable class size, after-school tutoring, and sports and club activities that foster student involvement—increases the likelihood that teachers will expect and get high achievement from every student.

One final characteristic of effective high schools is that the goals and relevancy of the curriculum must be made explicit. This is not easy. Many young people do not realize the connection between specific coursework and later accomplishment; advanced math, foreign languages, and laboratory science often are disregarded as irrelevant. When students already know they want to attend a competitive college, high school teachers use the threat of college admissions, thus setting the preconditions for a "senior slump" after applications are in. For every student, however, prime motivations include looking good, having fun, and becoming independent—all of which lead students away from schoolwork and toward hanging out with friends and taking a part-time job.

School and Employment

Attitudes and practices regarding jobs and school vary a great deal from country to country (Hamilton & Wolfgang, 1996). In some nations, such as Japan, almost no adolescent is employed or even does significant chores at home, because the family and culture agree that the adolescent's job is to study. In other nations, including several in Europe, many older adolescents have jobs that are an integral part

Laughing on the Job These high school students are working in an automobile factory.

❓ *Observational Quiz (see answer page 486): Where is the likely location?*

❶ *Answer to Observational Quiz (from page 485):* The main clue is that Germany is one of the few nations that has an apprenticeship program that includes manufacturing, in this case, a BMW plant. In some nations (such as Japan), few high school students work, and in others (such as the United States) they work in fast-food or other service-oriented jobs.

of their school curriculum. For example, in Germany most vocations require extensive apprenticeship; adolescents first choose a particular vocation and then are chosen by a particular employer, who trains them in conjunction with their schoolwork, not providing the usual salary but giving extra instruction. In still other nations, including the United States, such school-to-work partnerships are relatively rare. When they are implemented by changing the structure of the school day and increasing the relevance of the school curriculum, they seem successful. Participants are more likely to graduate from high school and continue their education (Stern, 1997).

Even without formal school-to-work arrangements, almost all North Amercian adolescents gain nonacademic experience in the job market—after school, on weekends, or during the summer—earning not only substantial spending money but also status in the eyes of their peers and respect from their parents (Mortimer et al., 1994). Indeed, their parents strongly approve of youth employment, citing increased responsibility, better money management, raised confidence, and work-related skills as benefits.

Sometimes such parents are correct if adolescents' job experience is relevant to adult employment, and their earnings make a real family contribution. Under those circumstances the benefits of employment eventually outweigh the problems. This was apparent for almost every adolescent during the Great Depression of the 1930s; for most low-SES boys who found work in the military during World War II; and for rural youths in Iowa during the 1980s downturn in family farming. It is still true for adolescents living in the poorest enclaves of American cities (Elder, 1974; Shanahan et al., 1996).

However, in today's job market meaningful jobs are rare. Most research finds that, especially when adolescents are employed more than 20 hours a week, having a job means less time for study and lower grades. Adolescents conclude that work is routinely dull and that working hard is "a little bit crazy" (Greenberger & Steinberg, 1986). Moreover, the money earned usually goes to clothes, entertainment, cars, alcohol, and drugs—not to basic household necessities or savings accounts (Bachman & Schulenberg, 1993; Mortimer et al., 1996; Steinberg & Dornbusch, 1991). Provocative international data from European nations show a negative correlation between hours of after-school employment and learning in school (Kelly, 1998). Such correlations do not prove causation, of course, but it is curious that U.S. fourth-graders, who obviously have no jobs, score much closer to their European peers on standardized tests than twelfth-graders do, as shown in Chapter 12.

Solid data come from long-term research within the United States comparing teenagers who work long hours and those who do not. Even from one year to the next, having a job pulls down the grade point average (Steinberg, 1993). As adults, those who were employed extensively when teenagers are more likely to use drugs and less likely to feel connected to their families. There is one possible benefit: If someone had a stable work history (such as the same job and schedules for months or years) during adolescence, he or she is more likely to have a stable work history in adulthood (Mihalic & Elliott, 1997). In general, however, an adolescent's decision to work is made for the wrong reasons, sometimes unwittingly encouraged by parents and teachers (Steinberg, 1996).

ADOLESCENT DECISION MAKING

An understanding of adolescent thinking—formal, hypothetical, and egocentric—is important for a very practical reason (Hamburg, 1991). For the first time in their lives, teenagers are in a position to make personal decisions and independent choices that have far-reaching consequences for their future. They decide, for example, what and how diligently to study, whether and where to go to college, whom to befriend, whether to become sexually active, what job skills to acquire, and whether to use drugs. The question for developmentalists is how the cognitive advances that adolescents experience help them to make good (or bad) decisions on such matters.

Deciding Their Future

Because they think about possibilities, not practicalities, and because egocentricism makes it hard to plan ahead and then choose the current path that will make the plans a reality, many adolescents do not make major decisions about their lives and their communities. For most of the big decisions, such as whether and where to go to college, what vocation to pursue, or even whether to vote for one candidate or another for public office, adolescents do very little choosing.

Specifically, college enrollment usually follows a pattern set years before. Teenagers in the college track at high school usually attend the best colleges they can get into and pay for, and those in the basic courses rarely stay in school long enough, or learn well enough, for further education. Family background, not individual potential, is the main determinant.

Similarly, deliberately selecting a vocation on the basis of interests and values is much less common than taking a job that is available, with the best pay scale and work requirements. Employment is usually found through friends or family—not through a methodical search of career possibilities. Finally, voter turnout is notoriously poor among 18- to 21-year-olds (see Figure 15.5), again suggesting that independent commitments and choices are rarely made in adolescence.

Which College, Where? As a 17-year-old basketball star, high school senior Niesha Butler had a critical decision to make—which of the hundreds of colleges to choose. Her top list included Harvard, Virginia, Notre Dame, and Georgia Tech—although she also thought of skipping college and turning pro because "if the money is there, why not?" That was a decision her parents—who had banned television from their home years before—would not let her make. She chose Georgia Tech, where she has a full scholarship and receives living expenses.

Figure 15.5 Political Apathy and Age. Given who elects Congress, it is no wonder that colleges charge tuition and Social Security is a protected "entitlement."

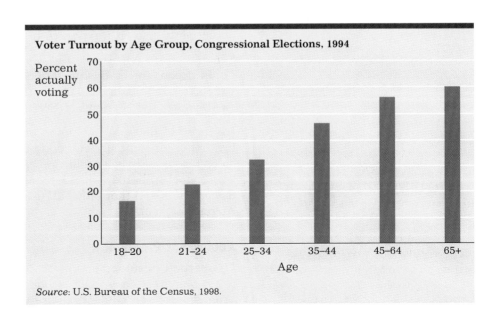

Voter Turnout by Age Group, Congressional Elections, 1994

Percent actually voting (vertical axis, 0 to 70)

Age groups (horizontal axis): 18–20, 21–24, 25–34, 35–44, 45–64, 65+

Source: U.S. Bureau of the Census, 1998.

Better Protection For decades, sex educators have bemoaned the fact that teenage girls have been considered solely responsible for practicing birth control. However, as this poster suggests, the AIDS epidemic has changed advertising and individual practice, with clear results. Almost half of all sexually active boys use condoms regularly, and the rate of teen pregnancy has been decreasing since the late 1980s.

sexually transmitted disease (STD)   A disease spread by sexual contact. Such diseases include syphilis, gonorrhea, herpes, chlamydia, and AIDS.

❷ **Especially for Social Workers:** Suppose you are contacted by a 14-year-old girl who thinks she is pregnant. She asks you to tell her what to do. What should you say?

Thus, until young adulthood, most people do not make major decisions on their own. They are more likely to be moved along by parents, teachers, cultural values, or stuck by inertia. However, when it comes to matters of personal lifestyle, decisions *are* made, though they are not always what adolescents' elders would wish. This is most clearly shown when the decisions involve sex.

THINKING ABOUT SEX

Sexual interest during adolescence is a normal (even essential) part of development. How that interest is expressed depends on a host of factors, including biology and culture, family and friends. In fact, we could easily discuss this topic in Chapter 14, on biosocial development, or in Chapter 16, on psychosocial development. But sexual arousal and activity are not just a biosocial reaction to hormones and drives or a psychosocial reaction to peer pressure. They are also a reaction to mental processes (which is why one wag has said that "the most important sexual organ is between the ears"). Study after study confirm that beliefs, values, and reasoning processes affect what kind of sexual activity adolescents engage in, when they do so, and with whom. For this reason, our major discussion of sex is here, in cognitive development.

The Risks of Sex

The benefits of sexual activity are obvious. Pleasure, intimacy, and sexual release are among the most compelling drives of the human species. However, the risks are not so obvious. There are two apparent risks with sexual behavior—disease and pregnancy—that teenagers seem less aware of than adults.

Sexually Transmitted Diseases

Sexually active teenagers have higher rates of gonorrhea, genital herpes, syphilis, and chlamydia—the most common **sexually transmitted diseases (STDs)**—than any other age group (Centers for Disease Control, 1993). Few cases of STDs are serious if promptly treated, but some untreated STDs can cause lifelong sterility and life-threatening complications. Sexually active adolescents also risk exposure to the HIV virus, a risk that increases if a person:

- Is already infected with other STDs
- Has more than one partner within a year
- Does not use condoms during intercourse

All three of these are common among teenagers and their sex partners (who often are unmarried young adults), making them the most likely to catch the virus. To be specific, recent data reveal that, by their senior year of high school, 21 percent of U.S. teenagers have already had four or more sexual partners and that only half used a condom at last intercourse (*MMWR*, August 14, 1998).

Adolescent Pregnancy

The second developmental risk for adolescents is unwanted pregnancy. Note that pregnancy itself is not the problem. Teenagers have far fewer pregnancies than adults in their twenties and far fewer than teenagers did

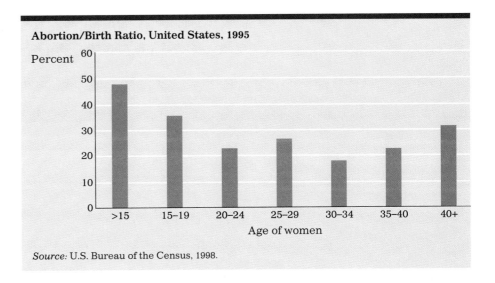

Figure 15.6 Teens More Likely to Choose Abortion. As you can see, almost half of all pregnancies in women under age 15 are aborted, as are only one-sixth of those in women in their early thirties. These age trends are apparent in every nation, although the ratio and rate of teenage abortions in the United States (shown here) are much higher than in nations with better sex education. These figures do not include spontaneous or unrecorded abortions, which would increase the numbers, particularly for younger women.

Source: U.S. Bureau of the Census, 1998.

35 years ago. In the United States, for example, the teenage birth rate was 90 per 1,000 in 1960 compared to 55 per 1,000 in 1996. However, in 1960 few adults considered teen birth a major problem, because about 80 percent of the teen mothers were married and most of them wanted their babies because they expected to be housewives all their lives. Today, the reverse is true: 80 percent of teenage mothers are *unmarried*. Almost no teen mother—married or not—expects to be unemployed while she raises her children, and few wanted to become pregnant (teenagers' abortion rate is twice that of women in their thirties, as shown in Figure 15.6).

Thus, teenage pregnancy has become a problem, especially in the United States, where close to 1 million unmarried teenagers become pregnant every year, more than in any other nation. Very few—perhaps 10 percent—of those pregnancies were intended by both partners (Kost & Forrest, 1995; Marsiglio, 1993). By contrast, 85 percent of births to women age 25 to 40 in 1995 in the United States were intended (U.S. Bureau of the Census, 1998).

About 15 percent of pregnant teens experience spontaneous abortion (also called *miscarriage),* a difficult event, especially if the girl does not have helpful family, friends, and medical care. Another 35 percent of U.S. teen pregnancies are aborted by choice, and that is never easy. The remaining 50 percent are carried to term. That means more than half a million teenage births per year, with both mother and child likely to experience a wealth of problems not only during pregnancy and at birth but for decades beyond (Bachrach et al., 1993).

For the mothers, teenage parenthood slows, and sometimes stops, educational and vocational achievement and restricts social and personal growth. No matter what a teenager's level of family support, income, or intellectual capacity, becoming a mother reduces eventual academic achievement by 3 years, on average (Klepinger et al., 1995). It also reduces the teenager's chances of marriage, and if she marries because she is pregnant, it increases her chance of being abused, abandoned, or divorced (Waite & Lillard, 1991).

The likely consequences for the child are even more troublesome. Babies of teenagers have a higher risk of prenatal and birth complications, including low birthweight and brain damage, than do infants from the same ethnic communities and educational backgrounds whose mothers are older. And, as they develop, children born to young mothers experience more

table **15.1**	When Sexual Intercourse Is Permissible Attitudes of Dutch Adolescents, Ages 16 to 17 Years		
	Boys	Girls	Average
In casual relationship	37%	14%	25%
Only in steady relationship	63	84	74
Only in marriage	0	2	1

Source: Ravesloot, 1995.

❶ Response for Social Workers (from page 488): Remember that at this age people think egocentrically and not very logically. Hence, you need to realize that her biggest worries may be the immediate ones, such as what her parents will say or whether birth will be difficult, not the long-range ones about how she might raise a child or how she can prevent another pregnancy. She might not really *be* pregnant. So your job is not only to provide practical help (get her to a clinic) but to expand her thinking. Be aware that her family is the most likely source of support but that incest or rape is a real possibility. Almost no 14-year-old plans to become pregnant.

mistreatment of all kinds and less educational success of any kind. In adolescence, they are more likely to become drug abusers, delinquents, dropouts, and—against their mothers' advice—parents themselves (Furstenberg et al., 1987; Hoffman et al., 1993).

The Danger of Commitment

Adolescents, boys as well as girls, who engage in early sexual activity face one more risk. To see it, we must first realize that most young people, like adults of every age, believe sex should occur within the context of a committed, loving relationship. This has been found through research in many nations. One such nation is the Netherlands, where a cultural attitude of sexual freedom is combined with extensive sexual education and a social climate that allows scientists to examine a large cross section of adolescent attitudes about sex. Because of this openness, the data on Dutch teenagers probably is accurate. The results are displayed in Tables 15.1 and 15.2.

Most of the teenagers believed that sexual intercourse was permissible *only* in a steady relationship (74 percent) or only in marriage (1 percent); one-fourth said casual coitus can sometimes be okay *if* it is what both persons want. Their own behavior as they approached adulthood was even more conservative: only 11 percent of those age 18 to 19 years were in a casual coital relationship.

The fact that teenagers associate sex with commitment is good from a developmental perspective for many reasons. Commitment reduces both of the risks already described, the spread of STDs and unwanted pregnancy. However, intimate commitment may create a third risk, especially for younger adolescents, because the intensity is difficult to handle. For one thing, breaking up is emotionally draining and is one cause of adolescent depression and suicide (discussed in Chapter 16). Alternatively, intimate re-

table **15.2**	What Kind of Relationship Do You Currently Have? Actual Situations of Dutch Adolescents, Ages 18 to 19 Years
Type of Relationship	Adolescents
No sexual relationship	14%
Casual, no intercourse	10
Steady, no intercourse	15
Casual, includes intercourse	11
Committed, includes intercourse	50

Source: Ravesloot, 1995.

lationships can linger on and on, becoming restrictive of personal growth. Other activities—such as friendships with peers, concentration on academics, and the pursuit of individual interests—are curtailed, with obvious negative consequences.

All this suggests that an early sexual relationship—even with commitment—may cause young people more psychosocial complications than they are developmentally prepared to undertake.

Making Decisions and Taking Action

Some people might be surprised that more than one-third of the older Dutch teens in the study cited in Tables 15.1 and 15.2 were not having sexual intercourse. After all, aren't adolescents sexually interested from the moment puberty begins? Don't most have at least one sexual experience by age 17? Isn't it true that few disapprove of sex outside marriage? Yes, yes, yes.

Imagine the Pleasure As adults try to warn adolescents of the dangers of early sex, they must also recognize the joys of young love. If they don't, their advice is likely to be rejected as either hypocritical or ignorant.

Nevertheless, attitudes do not lead to actions: worldwide, most adolescents under age 16 are still virgins, those who have sex early in adolescence typically are pressured (or even forced) to do so, and rates of intercourse for older teens are lower than those for unmarried adults. Most (80 percent) 19-year-olds have had sex, but even at this ripe old age, the rates of sexual activity are lower than those for young adults.

This raises the question: Why are the rates of STDs and unwanted pregnancy higher among adolescents than among single adults—even though the adults are more active sexually? A logical explanation would be that adolescents are uninformed about sex or that contraception is unavailable to them. But this explanation does not fit current reality. Today, some form of sex education is nearly universal. Specifically, in 1996, 97 percent of all schools in the United States taught HIV prevention and 85 percent taught pregnancy prevention (with a range from 99 and 95 percent in Minnesota down to 76 and 47 percent in Louisiana (*MMWR*, September 11, 1998). In addition, the media are quite open about sexuality—particularly the problems it can cause—and condoms are available in drugstores, in supermarkets, and even in some schools. (In this, the United States is still behind many other nations, but even in the most progressive European nations, sexually active adolescents generally have more unwanted pregnancies than adults.)

Clearly, information about, and protection from, STDs and pregnancy are within reach of today's teenager in every developed nation. The problem, as various studies have found, is that understanding the basic facts of sexuality and knowing where to obtain contraception do not necessarily lead to responsible and cautious sexual behavior (Hanson et al., 1987; Howard & McCabe, 1990). Nor do adolescents always learn from their mistakes: after being treated for an STD, they are two to three times more likely than adults to become reinfected (Bates, 1995).

Reasoning About Sex

Why is it that knowing the sexual facts does not always lead to responsible adolescent sexual behavior? To answer, we must remember how typical younger adolescents think. As you have seen, adolescents of, say, age 11 to 15 are only beginning to acquire the reasoning skills needed for mature decision making.

Thus, they find it difficult to envision all the possible alternatives or scenarios and then choose the best one.

Instead, most sexually naive teenagers tend to focus on immediate considerations (on the immediate difficulty or inconvenience of using contraception, for example) and fail to consider fully future possibilities (such as pregnancy, abortion, and parenthood). This is exactly what we might expect from individuals whose formal logical powers are very new, who reason with adolescent egocentrism, and who have had little personal experience with intimate discussions concerning sexual behavior. Further, the risks of sex—as well as of drugs and alcohol, which often accompany sex (Santelli et al., 1998)—are seen in a positive light by those for whom foolhardy behavior is considered socially bonding and emotionally freeing (Lightfoot, 1997).

When teenagers do consider hypothetical results of proposed actions, they consider only the ones that are most favorable to themselves. Thus, when imagining possible parenthood, they imagine the status and love a baby might bring but ignore the consuming responsibility of caring for an infant. This failure to think through *all the possible consequences* helps explain an interesting finding: Although few teenage girls actually try to become pregnant, most who do not practice contraception believe that having a baby would not be so bad (Hanson et al., 1987; Manlove, 1997). This view is captured in the following response of an eighth-grader who said she did not want to become pregnant but then was asked what her reaction would be if she became a mother in the near future:

> I think having a baby would really make me a little happier because it would make me have something of him, . . . I know I'm young and everything, but I know I could take care of it because my mother had me when she was young. I am just about the same age when she got pregnant. And she did okay, I'm here. [quoted in Taylor et al., 1995]

Unfortunately, in the eleventh grade this girl actually had a baby and dropped out of school. And, in spite of her assurance that she could "take care of it," she was forced to give up custody because she was unable to care for her child properly. Her motherhood did not make her "a little happier"; just the opposite was the result.

In addition, the adolescent sense of personal invincibility makes it hard for teens to be logical about the risk of sexual activity. Many adolescents, particularly those under age 16, seriously underestimate the chance of pregnancy or of contracting a disease from just one episode of unprotected intercourse (Voydanoff & Donnelly, 1990). Although the danger is real, their faith that nothing bad will happen is initially reinforced because the first experience rarely results in pregnancy or an STD, partly because teenagers are actually less fertile and less likely to be diseased in their first encounters. So they do the same thing again, and perhaps again, their "invincibility" now confirmed by past experience. Eventually they suffer the very consequences they assumed would never touch them:

- Regarding the AIDS virus, adolescents generally believe that other teenagers are more likely to contract it than they themselves are. Females are especially likely to underestimate their own risk, despite evidence that females are twice as vulnerable to HIV infection as males (Moore & Rosenthal, 1991; Zierler, 1994).
- Regarding unwanted pregnancy, many teenagers are incredulous when one occurs. Consequently, teenage girls take longer than adults to confirm the pregnancy, to seek advice, to obtain prenatal care, or to have an abortion. Each of the delays increases the actual risk of problems—both with abortion and with birth.

Better Sex Education

How can adolescents be helped to make more rational and timely decisions about their sexual activity? A first step, according to many experts, is for adults to be more rational in *their* thinking. To begin with, adults need to realize that, at some point, almost every adolescent will have some sort of sexual experience—at least an arousing kiss or caress. Such an experience is more powerful in adolescence than later, not only for biological reasons but also for psychological ones: novelty makes the sex drive more compelling. And egocentric adolescents want to experience it for themselves, not hear about it from others.

Thus, given the urgency of the sex drive, adolescents need more than "just the facts" to guide them. They need to develop the attitudes, values, and social skills that will help them refrain from sexual intercourse until they are wise enough to understand, and mature enough to take responsibility for, the consequences of their actions. (See Changing Policy, pages 494–495.)

In addition, adults need to recognize that they themselves are not immune to irrational sexual choices. Many 30- or 40-year-old new mothers are overwhelmed by the unexpected demands a baby brings, and adolescents are quick to notice. As one 18-year-old mother explained:

> I've got an aunt who's 44, and she's got a 3-year-old, so I see a lot of these teenage moms better than her. Because I think teenage moms—we all share energy. We've got a lot more energy than a 30- or 40-year-old woman. She throws her kid in front of the TV and expects that to entertain him because her body's old. She really does not have enough energy to be chasing him. Or going to the grocery store with him kills her. It's just, that's all the energy she'll have for the entire day. The zoo is extremely hard on her. I think we're all very lucky that we have our bodies that are young. [quoted in Higginson, 1998]

Thus the difference between a teen mother and an older mother is not necessarily rational risk assessment but adequate social support. The baby's father and other relatives are understandably more willing and able to help the older mother. Yet teens greatly need such help. For instance, one recent study found that an intensive support system, of caseworkers and parenting programs that worked with (not against) the families of pregnant teenagers, reduced the rates of school dropouts and repeat pregnancy (Soloman & Liefeld, 1998).

Parents as Sex Educators

Ideally, parents should educate their children about sex long before the need to support a pregnant teen arises. Some of that education occurs with explicit conversation. In addition, and probably more important, parents' overall relationship with their children and with each other, as well as their religious convictions and social values regarding sex, health, and each child's future, all have an effect (Hanson et al., 1987).

When it comes to the particulars, few parents are adequate sex educators. For one thing, many parents do not begin discussing sexual issues until long after the children have been informed, or misinformed, by friends, intuition, television, or personal experience. Adolescents who learn about sex at home learn mainly from their older siblings and almost never from their parents (Ansuini et al., 1996). Further, when belatedly trying to talk about sex, parents often close their eyes to the realities and try to set rules, rather than help their children think about options.

One group of researchers summarized parents' typical message to their daughters as "Don't. And if you do, we don't want to hear about it"

SEX CLASSES IN SCHOOL

Traditional in-school sex education may be as unhelpful as parental sex education, especially if the teacher has to fit a bundle of factual information—mostly biology—into a 10-hour course (the usual time allotted). Adolescents are often put off by courses that are merely "organ recitals" or that seem to have little bearing on their actual sexual dilemmas and pressures.

In recognition of these realities, a new form of sex education is emerging (Kirby et al., 1994). It was devised to take into account adolescent thinking—particularly their difficulties:

- Making mature personal choices
- Connecting the immediate lure of sex and the long-term consequences
- Realizing that sex requires thinking about values and relationships
- Moving from the egocentric and personal to the larger social issues

Therefore, the new approach to sex education often uses first-hand accounts instead of textbook examples. Typically, someone with AIDS talks to a class about safe sex; a teenage parent discusses the responsibilities of parenthood; older teenagers explain the social and individual pressures that might push them into becoming sexually active. Intimate topics, such as the proper use of condoms, are discussed candidly and in detail.

Concrete examples are not presented in isolation. Formal thinking is fostered through discussions and exercises that help adolescents weigh alternatives, recognize the rights and needs of others, and analyze risks. Recall that adolescents may develop formal thinking in one domain but not in others and that personally grappling with a problem helps adolescents move from abstract ideas to practical application. For this reason, the new sex education classes make extensive use of role playing, allowing adolescents to "experience" (via acting out) the sexual pressures they might face in the future and then to develop the social skills needed to respond effectively. For example, many adolescents don't know how to say no to sex without hurting the other person's feelings or being emotionally rejected. Role playing can reveal just how difficult a "no" can be to say, or to hear.

The new sex education usually includes the opportunity for students to speak privately with the teacher or a medical practitioner. That allows those who are already experiencing a specific problem, such as sexual abuse or a sexually transmitted disease, to get immediate help. Students are also strongly encouraged to have explicit discussions with their parents (usually, this is one of the first homework assignments) (Freeman & Rickels, 1993).

Taken together, these sex education strategies reflect the realization that, as with other aspects of cognition, the development of mature understanding requires time and opportunity. Furthermore, risks cannot be assessed accurately if adolescents think the adults operate from an anti-youth bias rather than from accurate knowledge. Sex educators need to be straightforward and well-informed in order to be influential.

The Link Between Thinking, Action, and Education

The direct, personal approach to sexual understanding may be working. As an example, one British program that provided 30 hours of social-skills training, as well as factual sexual information, reduced the percentage of high school students who became sexually active during the 2 years following the program from 53 to 42 percent (Mellanby et al., 1995). A review of four programs in the United States that were designed to promote abstinence—or, in the absence of abstinence, contraception—found similar results: three of the four programs were successful in convincing some sexually inexperienced young people to postpone sexual activity and in convincing some who

Will the Lesson Take? Sex education is supposed to help teenagers postpone intercourse, prevent pregnancy, and avoid STDs. Sometimes it is effective, sometimes not—although the fear that education will make sex more attractive has been proved false. This teacher is relatively young, and she is holding a condom—both good signs. However, where are the boys?

were sexually active to use protection (Frost & Forrest, 1995). A study of 1,880 teenage boys likewise found that sex education that combined information with social-skills training succeeded in reducing the incidence of intercourse, the number of partners the boys had, and the practice of unsafe sex (Ku et al., 1992). The author of this study concluded:

> In many communities, concerned parents or community members have feared that education about sex or AIDS may increase sexual activity by condoning contraception; this analysis does not indicate such an association. Education about resisting sexual activity can and does co-exist with education about contraception and condom use. . . . Abstinence and safe sex can be taught together, just as safe driving and using seat belts can be taught together. The point is that people can be taught how to avoid dangerous situations and, at the same time, how to prevent harm in case they are caught in one. [Ku et al., 1992]

Another study found that "abstinence-only" programs were no better or worse at postponing sex then were "safe-sex" programs. However, the safe-sex programs had an advantage once the adolescents did become active, in that sexual experiences were less frequent and were likely to include condoms (Jemmott et al., 1998).

Overall, this new form of sex education is most effective when adolescents have not yet become sexually active. Accurate information and social-skills training help them postpone sex, practice monogamy, and use contraception once they become active. On the other hand, classroom education alone is less likely to change the behavior of teenagers who have already established risky sexual patterns (Kirby et al., 1991).

Notice that although the success rates of sex education are significant, they are not dramatic. As you just read, the 30-hour British program reduced the rate of sexual activity among students from 53 to 42 percent. This means that 21 percent of those who would have said yes said no—a credible achievement, but far from 100 percent. The new sex education does not relieve all the biological and social pressures most young people feel. At least research proves one thing: Contrary to dire predictions, sexual education does not increase sexual activity. When effects are apparent, they not only increase contraception but also decrease sexual experimentation (Grunseit et al., 1997).

The Social Context

The timing and details of sex education programs need to be tailored to fit the specific social context. For example, the age of first sexual activity varies considerably from school to school, state to state, and nation to nation. Accordingly, explicit sex instruction might begin at age 11 in some neighborhoods in Delaware and Mississippi (where sexual activity begins early) and at age 14 in some communities in Iowa and Connecticut (where sexual activity begins later) (MMWR, 1998, August 14). Sex education should begin before a young person is sexually active (earlier than parents believe) but not so early that the instruction seems irrelevant to the students

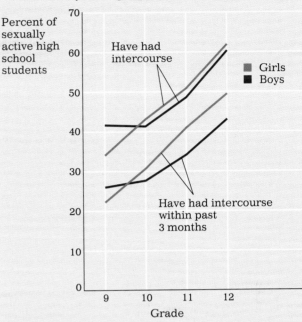

Sexual Activity Among High School Students

Based on a national sample of 16,262 students, surveyed in 1997.
Source: MMWR, August 14, 1998.

Figure 15.7 Sexual Experience. The narrow gender gap in sexual experience has two positive consequences. The first is that the double standard—which dictated that "good girls don't do it," but "real boys score"—is disappearing. The second is that, especially as adolescents grow older, it becomes more likely that those who are sexually active will develop ongoing monogamous relationships rather than engaging in casual sex.

or needlessly provocative to their parents. Similarly, programs need to consider students' religious values and to enlist parents' involvement; both these factors are key to fostering healthy sexual behavior.

Another significant variable is the gender of the participants. Traditionally, sex education was targeted toward girls; they were regarded as the moral gatekeepers who bore the responsibility of saying no to boys' sexual appetites, or at least of ensuring that pregnancy did not occur. Among today's young people, however, sexual decision making is more likely to be shared by both parties, and sexual activity is more apt to be part of a mutual relationship. In fact, girls today are more sexually active than boys are (see Figure 15.7) (*MMWR*, August 14, 1998). Both sexes need the same cautionary messages. Indeed, boys are more likely to postpone intercourse after the new sex education than girls are (Eisen & Zellman, 1992; Frost & Forrest, 1995; Howard & McCabe, 1990), and boys should not be blamed for the high rate of teen pregnancy—since the fathers are often "older men" in their twenties.

(Treboux & Busch-Rossnagel, 1990). Of course, few parents would say this, but most imply it.

For example, the mother in one family confidently explained, "If you spend a lot of time talking with your children . . . they know how we feel about it [premarital intercourse]. As a result, we don't have any major conflict at all." In truth, however, conflicts about sex in this particular family were avoided by silence. Their sexually active daughter never told her parents, because "they simply do not want to know." Consequently, her parents remained ignorant; her father hoped she would not get herself "dishonored," and her mother believed it was still too early for any serious relationship (du Bois-Reymond, 1995).

In another study, mothers were asked to estimate whether their teens had had sex and then the teens were asked for the truth. The difference between the two was astounding (see Figure 15.8), with the gap greater for girls than for boys, and for younger children than for older children.

Figure 15.8   Mother Doesn't Always Know. This graph shows the discrepancy between the answers mothers gave to "Is your child sexually active?" and the answers teenagers gave when asked for the truth. Notice which age group and gender had the largest gap—the younger girls!

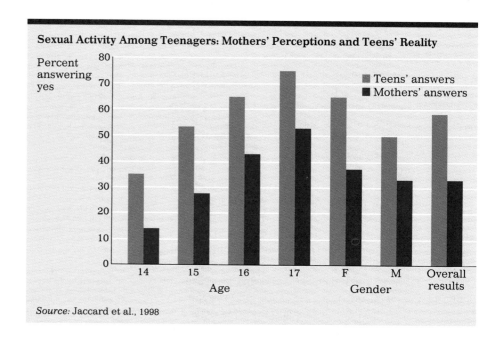

In this study, mothers who were more religious, and more disapproving of teen sex, were *less* likely to know when their children were sexually active (Jaccard et al., 1998). Did these young people avoid the discussion because they already knew their parents' attitudes? No. Few teenagers accurately assessed their mothers' attitudes on a variety of sexual issues—particularly on the practical consequences of pregnancy (such as having to quit school or marry the wrong person).

Sadly, 72 percent of the mothers were firmly convinced that they had talked with their teens at least once about sex, but only 45 percent of the teens agreed (Jaccard et al., 1998). Thus, 27 percent of mother/child pairs do not agree about whether or not they talked about sex. Obviously, even fewer agree about what was said, a generation gap with alarming implications.

An added problem is that many parents are themselves uninformed. This is especially likely if the parents' teenage years occurred

- Before the threat of AIDS
- Before the newer forms of contraception (Implants and injections are now the most common contraception prescriptions among teenagers, and the Pill and the diaphragm are considered old-fashioned.)
- Before "good" girls were sexually interested or "real" boys were sexually careful
- Before sexual activity was an acceptable topic of conversation between partners and generations.

This final item may be the most important. Although many parents were sexually active before marriage, they conducted their activity in secret and shame. This makes it hard for them to discuss the matter openly with their children (Ravesloot, 1995). It should be no surprise, then, that most sex education occurs outside the home.

The Latest Statistics

Many school systems are revising their sex education programs to make them more practical, focused on social interaction. In the United States, 90 percent of schools teach communication regarding health issues, and 48 percent teach the correct use of condoms (*MMWR*, September 11, 1998). These efforts are having an impact, according to many surveys. To be specific, the teen birth rate declined 12 percent between 1991 and 1996; the rate of sexual activity among high school girls fell 6 percent; the abortion rate fell by 30 percent; and the percentage of girls using contraception for their first sexual encounter increased from 65 percent in the late 1980s to 78 percent in 1995. Boys also report less sexual activity and more use of condoms (Donovan, 1997; Kahn et al., 1999; *MMWR*, September 18, 1998).

Sex education deserves part of the credit. One indication is that young women without formal sex education (either because their school doesn't provide it until age 16 or 17 or because they have left school) are more likely to become pregnant than those of the same age, income, and ethnicity who have taken a class on the subject. Another, more telling bit of evidence is seen in condom use. For both sexes, the proportion of sexually active, unmarried teenagers using condoms has increased dramatically over the past 10 years, with rates far surpassing those of teenagers in previous generations and even surpassing those of sexually active, unmarried adults.

Further, although only about half the condom users of any age use them completely correctly, teenagers are more likely to do so than adults, a further indication that the newer forms of sex education have had an impact (Guttmacher Institute, 1994). The increase in condom use parallels a change in attitudes and an increase in sexual communication. For example, in 1988, only 28 percent of young men strongly disagreed that "it would be embarrassing" to discuss using a condom with a girl before having sex. Seven years later the number strongly disagreeing had increased to 47 percent (Murphy & Boggess, 1998).

It would be naive to attribute all these shifts to cognitive advances and even more naive to trumpet sex education. Medical advances in improved contraception and social advances in opportunities and education of young women certainly contribute to the decline of teen births. Nor do the data show that every teenager is thoughtful about sex—far from it. Nonetheless, the thoughts and attitudes adolescents have about sex affect their behavior, and improvement is evident. Facilitating more mature cognition is one way to help teenagers avoid the serious problems that sometimes await.

SUMMARY

ADOLESCENT THOUGHT

1. Unlike younger children, whose thoughts are tied to tangible reality, adolescents can build formal systems and general theories that transcend (and sometimes ignore) practical experience. Their reasoning can be formal and abstract, rather than empirical and concrete. This ability also enables them to consider abstract principles, such as those concerning love, justice, and the meaning of human life.

2. Among the specific characteristics of formal operational thought is the ability to think hypothetically and reason deductively. Adolescents imagine a general principle that might be true, and then deduce specific ideas that follow from that generality. Teenagers do not always think at this advanced level, however.

3. Adolescent thought is marked, and sometimes marred, by egocentrism, exemplified by the invincibility and personal fables. Egocentrism also helps account for the self-consciousness that is typical during this phase of life, when an imaginary audience seems to evaluate the teenager's every move.

SCHOOLS, LEARNING, AND THE ADOLESCENT MIND

4. Adolescence is typically a period of both openness and fear, when adolescents find themselves eager for intellectual stimulation but highly vulnerable to self-doubt. Many students entering secondary school feel less competent, less conscientious, and less motivated than they did in elementary school.

5. Compared with elementary schools, most secondary schools have more rigid behavioral demands, intensified competition, and less individualized attention and procedures. This impedes the proper match between the student's characteristics and the school structure.

6. The culture and the context of the school can support adolescent learning. Schools that have high standards and cooperative, task-involved learning are likely to produce academic growth in all students.

7. Adolescent employment can distract students from their schoolwork, taking time that might be spent on homework. This is especially true if the job is routine, provides easy pocket money, and is not connected to the school program.

ADOLESCENT DECISION MAKING

8. Adolescents have mixed abilities with regard to decision making. On the one hand, adolescence witnesses the growth of many cognitive skills that are essential to good judgment. On the other hand, judgment skills alone do not lead to good decisions.

THINKING ABOUT SEX

9. Cognitive and motivational factors can make it difficult for teenagers to make good judgments about their sexual activity, as reflected in the high rates of sexually transmitted diseases and unwanted pregnancy during adolescence. Adolescents who believe that they are not susceptible to AIDS or pregnancy or who focus exclusively on their own interests and immediate needs may not take appropriate precautions.

10. Family contexts and parental support can reduce the incidence of premature sexual activity, risky sexual behavior, and teen pregnancy. Unfortunately, few parents are timely and informed sex educators.

11. Education that encourages thinking, role playing, and discussion about sexuality appears to be more effective than traditional sex education programs because lack of knowledge is not the primary reason for irresponsible sexuality. New sex education programs may be succeeding, as shown by less sexual activity, more condom use, and fewer births in the past decade.

KEY TERMS

formal operational thought (470)
hypothetical thought (471)
inductive reasoning (472)
deductive reasoning (472)
adolescent egocentrism (475)
invincibility fable (476)
personal fable (476)
imaginary audience (478)

person-environment fit (478)
volatile mismatch (479)
ego-involvement learning (481)
task-involvement learning (482)
sexually transmitted disease (STD) (488)

KEY QUESTIONS

1. What is the crucial difference between concrete operational thought and formal operational thought?

2. What is deductive reasoning, and how does it compare with the inductive reasoning of the younger child?

3. What are some of the characteristics of adolescent egocentrism?

4. Describe ego-involvement learning and some of its consequences for adolescents.

5. Describe task-involvement learning and some of its consequences for adolescents.

6. How should schools be organized to foster better academic success and supportive social interaction among teens?

7. What are the advantages and disadvantages of adolescent employment?

8. What are the risks of sexual activity during adolescence?

9. What are the characteristics of effective sex education?

10. *In Your Experience* Who and where were your worst and best sources of information about sexuality? Discuss your parents, peers, school, books, and any others that were relevant.

CRITICAL THINKING EXERCISE

by Richard O. Straub

Take your study of Chapter 15 a step further by working this scientific reasoning exercise:

In an effort to boost achievement, many schools employ *tracking*, in which students are grouped into classes according to their performance on standardized tests. In theory, each class then contains students of about the same ability level, and teachers can direct their presentation to that level to maximize learning. Critics argue that tracking is divisive and damaging, particularly for lower-level students, who often face a "dumbed-down" curriculum taught by burned-out teachers.

Your task in this exercise is to design an experiment to determine whether or not tracking is effective in boosting academic achievement in high school students of varying abilities. The principal has rounded up 100 student volunteers to serve as subjects. To make sure your study will be valid, she wants answers to the following questions:

1. What might be your hypothesis for this experiment?

2. What would be the independent variable?

3. How would you implement the independent variable, using the 100 volunteers?

4. What would be the dependent variable?

5. How would you perform the actual experiment?

6. What variables would you need to control in order to ensure a valid test of your hypothesis?

Check your answers by comparing them to the sample answers in Appendix B.

Adolescence:
Psychosocial Development

CHAPTER 16

Adolescence starts when the physical changes of puberty transform a childish body into an adult one. Then the cognitive changes of adolescence enable the young person to move beyond concrete thought, to think abstractly and hypothetically. However, the psychosocial changes—relating to parents with new independence, to friends with new intimacy, to society with new commitment, and to oneself with new understanding—are the critical ones that bring the young person to adulthood. Becoming an adult is a matter not of size or intellect but of social maturity.

THE SELF AND IDENTITY

Psychosocial development during adolescence is best understood as a quest for self-understanding. In particular, it is a quest for answers to a question that seldom arises in younger years: "Who am I?" The momentous changes that occur during the teen years—growth spurt, sexual awakening, less personal schools, more intimate friendships, and risk taking—all challenge the adolescent to find his or her **identity,** his or her unique and consistent self-definition (Kroger, 1995; Larson & Ham, 1993).

The first step in the identity process is establishing the integrity of personality, that is, aligning emotions, thinking, and behavior to be consistent no matter what the place, time, circumstances, or social relationship. "Two-faced," "wishy-washy," and "hypocritical" are among the worst accusations one adolescent can throw at another, in part because integrity is fervently sought but is frustratingly elusive.

Multiple Selves

In the process of trying to find their true selves, many adolescents experience **possible selves**—that is, diverse perceptions of who they really are, who they are in different groups or settings, who they might like to become, and who they fear becoming (Markus & Nurius, 1986; Markus et al., 1990). Many teenagers notice how much they are affected by changing settings and circumstances: their behavior switches from reserved to rowdy, from cooperative to antagonistic, from loving to manipulative. Aware of the inconsistencies among these multiple selves, they ask which one, if any, is the "real me." As one teenager put it, "I'd *like* to be friendly and tolerant all of the time. That's the kind of person I *want* to be, and I'm disappointed when I'm not" (Harter, 1990).

Signs of Conformity Adolescents simultaneously develop their own identities and follow the conventions of their society. This young woman seems caught between expressing two quite different selves. The first self seems to flaunt convention, with rings visible in her ears, nose, and lips and with multicolored, beaded, and wired hair. This experimental self actually follows the conventions of many of her peers, although not those of her parents. The second self emerges only when you know more about this photo: she is a good student, at her high school graduation, beside her proud father.

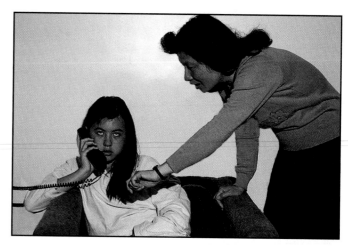

True or False? If this photo is a snapshot of an actual parent-child interaction, both mother and daughter are doing well. Rolling one's eyes to a mother's angry criticism is actually much better than a false self created to win acceptance. Not shown here are dutiful daughters and long-suffering mothers, who may purchase tranquility at the price of mental health.

identity A consistent definition of one's self as a unique individual, in terms of roles, attitudes, beliefs, and aspirations.

possible selves Various intellectual fantasies about what the future might bring if one or another course of action is chosen.

false self A set of behaviors that is adopted by a person to combat rejection, to please others, or to try out as a possible self.

As they try to sort through their possible (and multiple) selves, adolescents frequently take on a **false self**, acting in ways that they know are contrary to their core being—even if they are not sure what that core being is. According to one group of researchers (Harter et al., 1996), adolescents display three distinct types of false selves:

- *The acceptable false self.* This false self arises from the adolescent's perception that the real self is rejected by parents and peers—a perception often colored by the adolescent's own self-hate. Adolescents who adopt a false self in order to be accepted tend to feel worthless, depressed, and hopeless; they engage in self-betrayal to hide their true nature. They also report low levels of real self-understanding.
- *The pleasing false self.* This second type of false self arises from a wish to impress or please others. It is quite common among adolescents. Those who adopt it appear to be less debilitated psychologically, and to have greater self-understanding, than those whose false selves arise from a sense of rejection.
- *The experimental false self.* This type of false self is one that adolescents try out "just to see how it feels." Compared with adolescents who engage in the first two types of false behavior, these adolescents report the highest levels of self-esteem and self-knowledge, partly because although they acknowledge that their experimentation is not their usual, expected behavior, they do not feel it is false.

Identity

As they try to sort through their multiple selves, adolescents know that they are moving toward adult roles and responsibilities and that they are making choices that can have long-term implications. As a consequence, they think of themselves in far more complex ways than they did a few

Who Am I Today? Adolescents seem to be forever arranging and checking out their image, not only in their own mirror in the morning but with spot checks in the windows of stores, cars, and almost any other reflective surface. This narcissism is easier to understand when one realizes that adolescents are not only examining their physical appearance but also trying out various behavior patterns, social roles, and personalities.

identity versus role confusion
Erikson's term for the fifth stage of development, in which the person tries to figure out "Who am I?" but is confused as to which of many roles to adopt.

identity crisis   A condition in which the search for identity becomes so overwhelming and confusing that self-definition is urgently sought.

identity achievement   Erikson's term for attainment of identity. Identity achievement means that a person understands who he or she is as a unique individual, in accord with past experiences and future plans.

years earlier. Younger children describe themselves primarily in terms of their skills in school, with friends, and perhaps on the athletic field. But adolescents distinguish their scholastic competence from other aspects of who they are, and they think, in addition, of their job skills, romantic appeal, moral conduct, and peer acceptance (Harter, 1993). They also begin to ponder career options, political identification, religious commitment, and sexual ethics, questioning how these values fit together with expectations for the future and the beliefs acquired in the past.

As they deal with these increasingly diverse and complex aspects of selfhood, adolescents confront the psychosocial challenge referred to by Erik Erikson as **identity versus role confusion.** For developmentalists like Erikson, the search for identity leads to the primary crisis of adolescence—a crisis in which the young person struggles to reconcile a quest for "a conscious sense of individual uniqueness" with "an unconscious striving for a continuity of experience . . . and a solidarity with a group's ideals" (Erikson, 1968).

In other words, the young person seeks to establish his or her identity as a separate individual while maintaining old connections with the meaningful elements of the past *and* forging new links with the values of a certain group. (The group can be a peer group, an ethnic group, a team, a cult, a gang, or some other group. The critical aspect is that every teenager somehow identifies with a larger body of individuals.) Because the first of these tasks is not easily meshed with the other two—in other words, being a distinct self-determined individual is not always compatible with connections to one's heritage or peers—adolescents experience an **identity crisis.** It is called a crisis because the search for identity can be overwhelming, urgent, disorienting, and troubling, and, like any crisis, it needs to be overcome before a person can move on. Adolescents are much more aware of their thoughts and actions because they seek to be true to themselves, and thus they are confused about what roles they should take. This is a normal, even healthy sign of awareness according to Erikson.

In the process, adolescents attempt to develop sexual, moral, political, and religious identities that are relatively stable and consistent with each other's becoming one self rather than many conflicting ones. Eventually, a newfound identity ushers in adulthood, as it bridges the gap between the experiences of childhood and the goals, values, and decisions that permit each young person to take his or her place in society (Erikson, 1975).

Identity Status

The search for identity is ongoing throughout adolescence. Along the way an adolescent may experience more than one identity status or condition. The ultimate status, called **identity achievement,** is reached through "selective repudiation and mutual assimilation of childhood identifications"

(Erikson, 1968). That is, adolescents ideally establish their own identities by reconsidering the goals and values set by their parents and culture and then accepting some and rejecting others.

Some young people short-circuit this quest for achievement by never reconsidering parental and community values. The result is **foreclosure,** in which an adolescent accepts earlier roles and values wholesale, rather than exploring alternatives and forging a personal identity. A typical example is the young man who has always wanted (or been pressured) to follow in his father's footsteps. If his father was a doctor, the adolescent might diligently study chemistry and biology in high school and take premed courses in college.

foreclosure   Erikson's term for premature identity formation, in which the young person adopts the values of parents, or other significant people, wholesale, without questioning and analysis.

More Similar than Different? Both photos show teenagers in the United States.
❷ Observational Quiz *(see answer page 506): Despite obvious differences, what beyond citizenship do these adolescents have in common?*

Foreclosure prematurely walls out doubt and does not allow for much self-reflection. Foreclosure may suddenly crack and crumble when our doctor discovers, perhaps at age 40, that his success as a surgeon is unfulfilling and that what he really wanted to be was an archaeologist or a poet. One interpretation of the "midlife crisis" is that it is a belated identity crisis.

Other adolescents may decide that the roles their parents and society expect them to fill are unattainable or unappealing, yet they cannot find alternative roles that are truly their own. Adolescents in this position might take on a **negative identity,** that is, an identity opposite to the one they are expected to adopt. The child of a teacher, for instance, might drop out of high school, despite having the capacity to do college-level work. The son of devoutly religious parents might defy his upbringing by stealing or taking drugs. The daughter of a dedicated stay-at-home mom might pursue a career, eschewing marriage and motherhood and perhaps even relationships with men. Choices and actions that are taken with rebellious defiance designed to unnerve the family tradition are characteristic of negative identity.

Still other young people experience **identity diffusion.** They typically have few commitments to goals or values—of parents, peers, or the larger society—and are often apathetic about trying to take on any role. These young people may have difficulty meeting the usual demands of adolescence, such as completing school assignments, finding a job, and thinking about the future. They move from one sexual or platonic relationship to another, never with passion and commitment. They react to the pressure of competition and goal setting by retreating—perhaps smoking marijuana every day and listening to music through headphones whenever they can.

Finally, in the process of finding a mature identity, many young people declare an **identity moratorium,** a kind of time-out during which they exper-

negative identity   An identity that is taken on simply because it is the opposite of whatever parents, or society, prescribe.

identity diffusion   Condition in which a person does not seem to know or care what his or her identity is. Such persons are vague, changeable, erratic, in a fog.

identity moratorium   Erikson's term for a pause in identity formation that allows young people to explore alternatives without making final identity choices.

iment with alternative identities without trying to settle on any one. In some cases, the culture provides formal moratoriums through various institutions. The most obvious example of an institutional moratorium is college, which usually requires that students sample a variety of academic areas before concentrating on any one. Being a full-time student also forestalls pressure from parents and peers to settle down, choose a career, and find a mate. Other institutions that permit a moratorium are the military, the Peace Corps, religious mission work, and various internships; many of these enable older adolescents to travel, acquire valuable skills, and test themselves while delaying lifetime commitments.

Erikson suggested that each of these identity *statuses* or conditions (achieved, foreclosed, negative, diffused, and moratorium) tends to characterize a young person's attitude and values about life issues, and therefore to direct behavior. This means that to understand why someone acts as he or she does, it is helpful to know the person's identity status. For example, all adolescents in foreclosure seem to be afraid of questioning authoritarian values and to fear that someone will discover that they are not the dutiful disciples they seem to be:

> Any change arouses anxiety. Considering this, one can more easily have compassion for those in the foreclosure identity status, who, rather than permit themselves to enter that trough of anxious uncertainty—moratorium—would prefer to bear those ills with which they are familiar . . . even though by so doing, they stunt themselves. [Marcia, 1994]

Research on Identity Status. Many developmentalists have found Erikson's concept of identity status useful in understanding adolescence. Foremost among these is James Marcia, who has defined four major identity statuses (achieved, foreclosed, diffused, and moratorium) in terms precise enough for an interviewer to categorize a research subject (Marcia, 1966, 1980; Marcia et al., 1993). (Not listed is negative identity, since it is a reaction to childhood, and hence one person's negative identity may be quite different from another's.)

Using Marcia's guidelines, dozens of studies have compared identity with cognitive or psychological development (Adams et al., 1992; Archer, 1994). As Table 16.1 on page 506 shows, each identity status is typified by a number of distinct traits. Regarding attitude toward parents, for example, the diffused adolescent is withdrawn, perhaps deliberately avoiding parental contact by sleeping late and answering questions with a shrug; the adolescent in moratorium is independent of parents and busy with his or her own interests; both foreclosed and achieved adolescents are loving, but the foreclosed teen shows more respect and deference, whereas the achieved teen treats parents with more concern, behaving toward them as an equal or even as a caregiver.

Table 16.1 shows some revealing combinations of statuses and traits. Note, for example, that adolescents who have achieved identity and those who have foreclosed their search both have a strong sense of ethnic identification. These teens are proud to be Irish, Italian, Indian, or whatever they may be. However, those who have foreclosed are relatively high in prejudice, perhaps because they have simply seized on their own ethnicity without ever considering the merits of others. By contrast, teens who have achieved identity are relatively low in prejudice, presumably because they are secure enough in their ethnic background that they do not need to denigrate others.

Extensive research, much of it longitudinal, confirms that many adolescents go through a period of foreclosure or diffusion, and then a moratorium,

table 16.1	Attitudes, Relationships, and Emotions Typical of the Major Identity Statuses			
	Identity Status			
Characteristic	Foreclosed	Diffused	Moratorium	Achieved
Degree of anxiety	Tends to repress anxiety	Moderate	High	Moderate
Attitude toward parents	Loving and respectful	Withdrawn	Trying to distance self	Loving and caring
Degree of self-esteem	Low (easily affected by others)	Low ("empty")	High	High
Sense of ethnic identity	Strong	Neutral to ethnicity	Medium	Strong
Degree of prejudice	High	Neutral	Medium	Low
Kohlberg's moral stage	Preconventional or conventional	Preconventional or conventional	Postconventional	Postconventional
Dependence on others	Very dependent	Dependent	Self-directed	Self-directed
Cognitive processes	Simplifies complex issues; refers to others and to social norms for opinions and decisions	Complicates simple issues; defers to others in both personal and ideological choices	Thoughtful; procrastinates, especially in decisions; avoids referring to others' opinions or to social norms	Thoughtful; makes decisions by both seeking new information and considering others' opinions
Attitude about college	Very satisfied as long as guidelines are clear	Variable, indifferent to most subjects unless motivated and "turned on"	Most dissatisfied (likely to change major)	Good; gets high grades
Relations with others	Stereotyped	Stereotyped or isolated	Intimate	Intimate

Source: Adapted from research reviewed by Berzonsky, 1989; Kroger, 1993; Marcia et al., 1993; Streitmatter, 1989.

before they finally achieve a mature identity. The process can take 10 years or more, with many college students still not clear about who they are or what they want to do (Marcia et al., 1993).

Variations in the Identity Search. As individuals search for an identity, many gender, personal, and cultural differences are apparent. Often girls seek their new identities in collaboration or interaction with other people (a best friend, a parent, a romantic relationship), discovering who they are by noting their social relationships. Boys are more self-defining, seeking independence and even isolation from others (Lytle et al., 1997).

Personality differences seem to be more influential than gender in guiding the search for identity. For example, the specific behaviors of someone in diffusion can be either apathetic or alienated, that is, either not caring about anything or rebelling against everything. Both types may seem charming, witty, and shallow—not taking themselves seriously and resenting any adult who says they are "not living up to their potential" (Marcia, 1994).

❶ *Answer to Observational Quiz (from page 504):* Both groups of teenagers are in uniform, parading their postponement of personal identity achievement with body positions and garments that signal their group loyalty.

Similarly, some individuals foreclose by adopting the identities their parents urge on them, whereas other foreclose by aligning themselves with totalitarian groups—such as religious cults or doctrinaire political organizations—that take over all independent decision making (Archer & Waterman, 1990). Also, some adolescents in foreclosure seem to have permanently slammed the door on all other options; others have closed it only temporarily and are likely to reopen it in a few years (Kroger, 1995).

Society and Identity

The ease or difficulty of finding an identity is also affected by forces outside the individual (Grotevant & Cooper, 1998). The surrounding culture can aid identity formation in two major ways: by providing *values* that have stood the test of time and that continue to serve their function, and by providing *social structures and customs* that ease the transition from childhood to adulthood. Whether a given culture actually provides these values and social structures depends primarily on how much the members of the culture agree regarding basic principles and on how stable life circumstances are from one generation to the next.

In a culture where virtually everyone holds the same moral, political, religious, and sexual values and where social change is slow, identity is easy to achieve. Most young people in such traditional societies simply accept the roles and values they grew up with—the only ones they have ever known. (An exception might be the occasional adolescent who possesses some special personality trait—quirky creativity, a rare passion, or an unusual talent—that is contrary to the traditional path within his or her culture. Such individuals become the prophets, the freaks, or the criminals, depending on the place and time.)

In modern industrial and postindustrial societies, by contrast, cultural consensus is rare and continuity is rarer still. Everything is open to question by almost everyone. Rapid social change, a broad diversity of values and goals, and an ever-expanding array of choices characterize such a society and make identity formation difficult. When anything is possible, nothing is easy.

Identity for Minority Adolescents

For members of minority ethnic groups in democratic societies, identity achievement entails additional stress. On the one hand, democratic ideology espouses a color-blind, open society in which background is irrelevant to achievement and in which all citizens develop their potential according to individual merits and personal goals. On the other hand, most minorities take pride in their ethnicity, expecting their teenagers to honor their roots and cherish their heritage.

Hidden beneath both ideologies are instances of prejudice by the majority against the minority, attempts by minority members to mirror majority standards, and stereotypes from both sides. In adolescence, when appearance and mannerisms take on prime importance, coloring, cutting, straightening, or curling one's hair, wearing clothes and jewelry that are or aren't ethnic, and even talking "black" or "white," "Latin" or "Anglo" can become issues. Thus, identity formation requires finding the right balance between transcending one's background and immersing oneself in it. In Erikson's words, during adolescence "each new generation links the actuality of a living past with that of a promising future" (Erikson, 1968). (See Children Up Close, pages 508–509.)

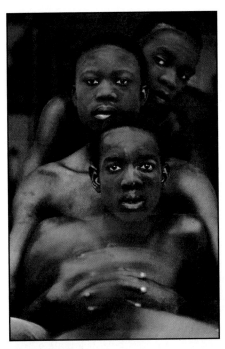

The Rite of Passage These boys are participating in a puberty ritual in the Congo. The blue dye on their faces indicates that they are temporarily dead, to be reborn as men once the ritual is over. Such rites of passage, which are based on strong cultural cohesion regarding social roles and responsibility, make adolescence a quick and distinct transition for all concerned. In technologically sophisticated societies, rites of passage are less obvious, although the events surrounding high school graduation are similar in several ways.

LISTENING TO THEIR VOICES

Erikson's linking of past and future is particularly difficult when one's expectations of living by the democratic ideal are thwarted by social prejudice and institutionalized racism. As a result, "many ethnic minority youth . . . may have to deny large parts of themselves to survive, may internalize negative images of their group, and [because of that] may fail to adopt an ethnic cultural identity" (Hill et al., 1994). In some cases, minority youths adopt a negative identity—rejecting wholesale the traditions of both their ethnic group and the majority culture.

Such resistance to external control may be seen in one 15-year-old's haircut, a decision she made in defiance of her childhood tradition:

> For years, I needed my mom's help to twist my long, thick hair, which fell nearly halfway down my back, into a braid or even a ponytail. I hated that morning ritual because it made me feel helpless. I hated the long hours it took to wash and dry my hair.
>
> I wanted to feel free and independent . . . I wanted a haircut.
>
> But I couldn't make myself do it. A haircut was a big decision. My hair was more than just a bunch of dead cells. It was a symbol of control.
>
> For my parents and relatives, long hair is considered an essential part of being a woman. Especially for "good Indian girls."
>
> Most of my friends didn't want me to go short, either. I'm not sure why. Maybe they were like me, afraid of change. Somewhere inside, I believed that the really beautiful women had long hair. I remembered someone saying that college guys liked women with long hair. (And college is the place where you meet your husband.) [Chikkatur, 1997]

Torn by all these conflicts, one day she decided and—before she told her family or changed her mind—had her hair cut. For the next month, as all her relatives criticized her, she alternated between thinking she had made a "huge mistake" and being "glad I cut my hair." She considered her haircut a symbol of her independence, not only from her family but also from the majority culture's expectations of beauty, marriage, and sexual orientation. She challenged both cultures by finally concluding "that being beautiful has nothing to do with the length of my hair and that a short cut has nothing to do with being gay or straight."

More often than choosing independence, as this young woman did, African American, Native American, Mexican American, and Asian American adolescents choose foreclosed identity, and they do so more readily than European Americans (Phinney, 1990; Rotheram-Borus & Wyche, 1994; Streitmatter, 1988). The searching process itself, with experimental actions, possible identities, and ambivalent judgments, may be too difficult when criticism from one's own group or from the majority group is evoked (or assumed) by every action.

Peers, themselves torn by similar conflicts, can be very critical. Minority-group members may be branded "oreos," "bananas," or "apples"—colorful on the outside but white inside. Whites who associate with blacks may be called "gray," or those who associate with Indians may be said to have "gone native." And these are the kinder comments.

As shown by these examples, the peer group is one possible source of criticism or confirmation for identity questions. Another source is family members, particularly among ethnic groups that revere closeness to family, respect for elders, and self-sacrifice for the sake of kin (Harrison et al., 1990). In many Western societies, this ideal clashes with the majority culture's emphasis on adolescent freedom and self-determination, and that clash lasts for years.

This is potentially problematic for immigrants, because the adolescent's physical and cognitive drives come full-force several years before they would in traditional societies, where puberty occurs later and the age for marriage and adult work follow soon after (Mark Strom-Adams & Spencer, 1994). For many immigrant families, the normal strain between the generations is thus extended for several years longer than it would be in traditional cultures. Some minority adolescents (mostly girls) give in to parental control (perhaps docilely living at home until an early marriage), while others (mostly boys) rebel completely (perhaps leaving home in a mad fury). Some join a gang, typically consisting of other boys from the same ethnic group, who provide an identity complete with codes of behavior, standards of dress, and social bonding experiences. Such gangs are common among immigrant groups living in multiethnic cities (Johnson-Powell & Yamamoto, 1997) and actually make psychological sense as a transition experience.

In a desperate attempt to deal with the severe generation gap that arises in many minority families, the parents send the adolescent back to the grandparents' traditional home, to the original nation, to a more isolated community, or, if those are impossible, to a specialized school, perhaps

Same but Different Traditionally, minority identity in the United States focused on race, with youths "of color" needing to find their place in a white world. Currently, however, the issue has broadened to be seen as ethnic, not racial. These two California high school students look physically similar but are from very different backgrounds: one is from Cambodia and the other from Mexico. Each is finding her own bicultural identity. Their backgrounds differ, but the search is universal; many "white" adolescents also struggle with issues of heritage and self.

only for children of that sex and ethnicity. In all these cases, the teenager's self-actualizing search for identity is sacrificed or at least postponed.

This discussion might imply that minority adolescents must choose between only two identities, their ethnic one and the majority one. Actually, although the U.S. census recognizes five ethnic categories (white non-Hispanic, black non-Hispanic, Hispanic, Asian, Native or Pacific Islander), adolescents acknowledge a hundred or more ethnic identities. There are vast differences within these five groups and even within families, depending on national origin, socioeconomic status, and acculturation (Cooper et al., 1998). For example, the impoverished inner-city African American differs from the middle-class suburban one; the Cuban American is distinct from the Mexican American; the newly arrived Cambodian has little in common with the third-generation Japanese; the Aleut from northern Canada shares almost nothing with the native Hawaiian or the Navajo. Further, the majority category, "white, non-Hispanic," includes Anglo descendants of the Mayflower Pilgrims, Jewish refuseniks from Russia, Iranian Muslims who came as students, and Italian Catholics who immigrated 80 years ago, among many others. And each set of parents established their own ethnic identity several decades earlier with varied degrees of acculturation, so cohort as well as ethnic gaps emerge within every family and neighborhood.

Consequently, in the United States, virtually no adolescent is able to associate only with peers of the same background, even if he or she wanted to, because every individual has a somewhat different background. In the long term, most psychologists would consider this beneficial, because each person's eventual identity becomes truly his or her own. But, obviously, this is not easy. Minority individuals often go to extremes of assimilation and separation before reaching a mature self-affirmation (Cross, 1991). Some take years—even decades—before they can sort through the divergent historical roots, gender roles, vocational aspirations, religious beliefs, and political values of their surrounding cultures (Staples & Johnson, 1993).

Not surprisingly, then, there is "a wide variety among ethnic minority adolescents in the ways in which they identify with their ethnic culture and with the wider society." In the United States, at least, "most combine their sense of being ethnic and American," either defining themselves as bicultural, with two cultural identities, each appropriate in its place, or holding to what they believe is the true democratic ideal: a multicultural, diverse Americanism with appreciation for hundreds of ethnic and other groups (Phinney & Devich-Navarro, 1997).

Gender Identity

Another area to consider concerns the complications of forming gender identity. Each young person obviously develops either a man's body or a woman's body, but what it means to be a man or a woman varies greatly in most large contemporary nations. No longer is the traditional family, with husband as breadwinner and wife as homemaker, the norm. In fact, few young people consider this pattern practical or desirable, except, perhaps, when children are very young.

However, rejecting that traditional pattern does not make it easier to select another. Consequently, many young people temporarily cling to exaggerated gender stereotypes. Some boys wear big boots and black leather and talk in short, gruff obscenities; some girls wear tight or transparent clothes, eye makeup, and perfume to school. In both extremes, perhaps, they are just searching for identity. When they are questioned about the future roles associated with their sexual and gender identities, many teenagers are unsure. For example, a wedding and then motherhood—once the fantasy of every girl with a bride doll—is not necessarily the young woman's goal. Nor does the young man look forward to being a father (East, 1998). Obviously, then, romance triggers confusion and role conflicts because the once straightforward connection between love and marriage has been broken. This is one reason the average age of first marriage in the United States has risen to 25, up from 21 in 1970 (U.S. Bureau of the Census, 1998).

Problems are compounded for those who are gay or lesbian. Trying to figure out what homosexuality means for them, and then trying to explain both their private sexual feelings and their public lifestyle choices, makes many such young people feel socially isolated and rejected. It does not help when people accuse them of being the opposite sex—they know they are not that, but they also know they are not like most people of the same sex.

Other Aspects of Identity

Vocational identity is not simple in modern society, either, because literally thousands of careers are now possible—few of which existed even two decades ago. Political identity is likewise complicated. For example, 40 percent of all 17- to 24-year-old U.S. youths consider themselves politically independent—a higher percentage than that for any other age group. If this simply meant adolescents chose the best candidates, taking on the political role of independent would be no problem. However, role confusion often leads to no voting at all (as you saw in the previous chapter), and even those who identify with a political party typically go to one extreme or the other—unquestioning enthusiasm or studied indifference.

With all types of identity development, when the painful process of identity formation leads to identity achievement, the result is higher self-esteem and self-acceptance, with less interpersonal or intergroup prejudice—all values that are worth the identity struggle. For all kinds of identity, a process of exploration and questioning precedes a state of self-acceptance and certainty, enabling the young person to move on to the next stages of intimacy and generativity.

Choices Her Parents Never Made Many parents complain about various aspects of their teenagers' lives—from their sloppiness and taste in music to their unwillingness to help out around the house—but most parents and their adolescent children are quite supportive of each other. Indeed, many parents accept aspects of their adolescents' lives—such as an unusual vocation, a pregnancy out of wedlock, or, as suggested by the notice on the lower left, a sexual orientation—that the parents never envisioned.

FAMILY AND FRIENDS

The changing seas of development are never sailed alone. At every turn, a voyager's family, friends, and community provide sustenance, provisions, directions, ballast for stability, and a

⊘ Especially for Parents: When should you argue with an adolescent, and when should you let an adolescent have his or her way?

generation gap   The distance between generations in values, behaviors, and knowledge.

generational stake   The need of each generation to view family interactions from its own perspective, because each has a different investment in the family scenario.

Generational Stake This is a family: father, daughter, and mother.
⊘ Observational Quiz (see answer page 512): *From facial expressions and body positions, and from the hypothesis of the generational stake, what can you infer about the relationships among these three?*

safe harbor or at least an anchor when it is time to rest. Through example or insistence, societal forces also provide a reason to move ahead. In adolescence, when the winds of change blow particularly strong, parents and peers become especially powerful influences, for good or ill.

Parents

Adolescence is often characterized as a time of waning adult influence, when the values and behaviors of young people are said to become increasingly distant and detached from those of their parents and other adults. According to all reports, however, the **generation gap,** as the distance between the younger generation and the older one has been called, is not necessarily wide. In fact, younger and older generations have very similar values and aspirations. This is especially true when adolescents are compared not with adults in general but with their own parents (Holmbeck et al., 1995; Steinberg, 1990).

Numerous studies have shown substantial agreement between parents and their teenage children on political, religious, educational, and vocational opinions and values (Coleman & Hendry, 1990; Youniss, 1989). Most parents and offspring favor the same candidate for president or prime minister, follow the same religion, and have similar ethics. Moreover, regardless of academic potential, adolescents who do relatively well in high school and college tend to be the children of parents who most encourage education and were high achievers themselves. The opposite is true as well.

Similarly, whether or not an adolescent experiments with illegal drugs is highly correlated with his or her parents' attitudes and behavior regarding alcohol and legal drugs (Denton & Kampfe, 1994). Indeed, virtually every aspect of adolescent behavior is directly affected by the family.

Harmony and Conflict

The fact that the generation gap is small by objective measures does not mean all is harmonious at home. In fact, each generation has its own distinct **generational stake** (Bengston, 1975). That is, each generation has a natural tendency to see parent-adolescent interactions in a certain way, based on its own position in the family. Parents have a stake in believing that all is well and that their children are basically loyal to the family despite a superficial show of rebellion. Adolescents have a stake in believing their parents are limited, old-fashioned, and out of touch.

As a result, parents' concern about continuity of their own values leads them to minimize whatever friction occurs between the two generations, blaming problems on hormones or peer influences, rather than on anything long-lasting. Adolescents, on the other hand, are concerned with shedding parental restraints and forging their own independent identities, so they are likely to exaggerate intergenerational problems. For example, a conflict about a curfew may be seen by a parent merely as a problem of management, the latest version of trying to get the child to bed on time, but by a teenager as evidence of the parents' outmoded values or a lack of trust. On a deeper level, teenagers may see parental rules as an attempt to control and dominate; parents may see them as an attempt to love and protect.

As long as the parents and the adolescent live under the same roof, a certain amount of conflict occurs in most families, as the young person's drive for independence clashes with the parents' tradition of control.

Talking and Listening One of the biggest issues between adolescents and parents is "You don't listen to me." Unlike when she was a little girl (see photo on mantel), this teenager keeps many of her opinions and experiences from her mother. In fact, she considers herself good when she does not shout, walk away, or cover her ears when her mother talks. Meanwhile, her mother remembers when "listening" meant responding, discussing, and finally obeying.

❶ *Answer to Observational Quiz (from page 511): The father's satisfied smile and his relaxed position, leaning back in his chair, suggest he is proud and happy. The mother also seems content, but she has her eyes on, her arm around, and her body leaning toward her daughter. Meanwhile, the daughter's expression is quizzical, even disbelieving, and her shoulders, arms, and legs all suggest she is keeping to herself, not about to defer to her parents. As a good scientist, you know that nothing can be proved on the basis of one snapshot, but you also know that these gestures and positions are in accord with the generational-stake hypothesis—fathers want to be proud of their families, mothers want to keep their children close, and adolescents want to be independent. Hence, this moment is typical of thousands of other parent-adolescent interactions.*

The extent of the conflict depends on many factors, including parental style, the child's age and gender, and the cultural context.

Parenting Patterns and Conflict. Recall from Chapter 10 that researchers distinguish three broad types of parenting. In the *authoritarian* style, parents expect to be obeyed and show little affection or nurturance; in the *permissive* style, parents are affectionate but nondemanding; in the *authoritative* style, parents set limits but are also nurturant and communicative. As is true for children in earlier stages of development, authoritative parenting is most likely to foster achievement and self-esteem in adolescents (Baumrind, 1991; Coleman & Hendry, 1990; Steinberg, 1990). At least among most European American families, adolescents who have authoritative parents are more self-reliant, perform better in school, and show fewer problem behaviors (such as delinquency or drug and alcohol abuse) compared with other teenagers (Lamborn et al., 1991; Steinberg et al., 1994). Especially harmful are permissive parents who do not seem to care what their children do (a style called *rejecting-neglecting);* their teenagers are likely to lack confidence and to be depressed, low-achieving, and delinquent (Baumrind, 1991; Lamborn et al., 1991; Steinberg et al., 1994).

How do authoritative parents succeed? They are able to ease their authority to accommodate the adolescent's growing desire and capacity for independence, while continuing to provide firm guidance, warmth, and acceptance. Teenagers need to detach emotionally from parents who are either overcontrolling or uninterested, but the offspring of authoritative parents can achieve independence while enjoying a supportive family climate (Furman & Holmbeck, 1995; Lamborn & Steinberg, 1993; Ryan & Lynch, 1989). Notice that good parenting involves give-and-take, rules and exceptions, conversations and compromises, disagreements and disputes. Bickering, as you will now see, is quite normal.

Early Adolescent Bickering. Parent-adolescent conflict typically emerges in early adolescence, and it is particularly notable with daughters who mature early and with mothers more than fathers (Caspi et al., 1993; Montemayor, 1986; Steinberg, 1990). The reason younger adolescents, girls, and mothers are conflict-prone is easy to understand, once you know what the typical issues are. Bickering occurs about habits of daily life—hair, neatness, and clothing issues, for example—that traditionally fall under the mother's supervision. These issues are also ones that girls had been more pressured about and that girls had been more docile about than boys. Thus a daughter's rebellion is more surprising. And it is the relatively young adolescent who feels compelled to make a statement—with green hair or blaring music—to establish in unmistakable terms that a new stage has arrived. Bickering follows.

In addition to the puberty status and gender of the child, another factor in parent-adolescent conflict is birth order. Firstborns have more conflicts with parents than later-borns do, although later-borns may actually be more rebellious (Small et al., 1988; Sulloway, 1996). As my daughter Rachel told her younger sister, Elissa, "You should be grateful to me. I had to break them in, so you have it easy."

Adolescents—both male and female—generally believe that they should be granted the privileges of adult status much earlier, and more extensively, than parents do (Holmbeck & O'Donnell, 1991). This dispute over status and

"Uh oh."

Play It Again, Sam? One of the easiest ways to differentiate one group from another is through music, which is why few adults can sing, understand, or even tolerate the teen top 40 and why few teenagers would recognize the title of this caption. As a cultural protest, the younger generation, whose hearing is most acute, play the loudest music.

❶ Response for Parents (from page 511):
Most arguments are petty, involving disagreements about personal habits, style, and taste. Obviously, these issues are not the most important in the long run; too much bickering might cut off communication when it is really needed. Therefore, wise parents keep careful watch on health and safety issues and leave style alone. For instance, parents might let a son have an earring but not let him have a cigarette, or they might allow a daughter to listen to her own music but make sure she travels with sober girlfriends when she goes out.

age stems from the generational stake. Twelve-year-olds believe that controversies between themselves and their parents involve basic values such as personal privacy and freedom, which ought not to be interfered with by parents. Parents, on the other hand, believe the same issues (sleeping late on weekends, engaging in long telephone conversations, wearing tight or torn clothing, and leaving one's room in a mess) ought to be within their authority, since they have the child's well-being at heart. Few parents can resist making a critical comment about the dirty socks on the floor, and few adolescents can calmly listen to "expressions of concern" without feeling they are unfairly judged (Smetana & Asquith, 1994).

Recurrent squabbling over such matters may seem petty, but the underlying issue—adolescents' freedom to make their own decisions—is far from petty. Moreover, persistent conflict—petty or not—can lower the quality and harmony of family life. And such conflict usually is recurrent: most families can describe about three or four ongoing disputes that each arise about once a week (Smetana et al., 1991).

An ethnic variation is found in the *timing* of parent-child conflict. For Chinese, Korean, and Mexican American teens, stormy relations with parents may not surface until late in adolescence. It may be that because these cultures encourage dependency in children and emphasize family closeness, the typical teenager's quest for autonomy is delayed (Greenberger & Chen, 1996; Molina & Chassin, 1996).

Interesting as these variations are, we should stress that adolescents have *never* been found to benefit from families that are permissive to the point of laxness *or* strict to the point of abuse. The ethnic differences we are discussing occur within the range of normal authoritative and authoritarian parenting, not at the extremes. Families that are high in conflict, or parent-child relationships that are low in support, are almost always hard on the adolescent, no matter what the family structure or culture (Demo & Acock, 1996).

Fortunately, the conflicts that arise in early adolescence usually recede gradually as family members revise their expectations for one another in light of the child's growing maturity (Collins, 1990; Laursen et al., 1998). In many cases, however, parents and offspring do not really see each other as companions until the children have finally attained the trappings of adulthood: independent dwellings, paid employment, and spouses and babies of their own.

Other Family Qualities

Parent-child conflict during adolescence is only one of the dimensions of family functioning that has been studied. Other aspects include:

- Communication (Can they talk openly with one another?)
- Support (Do they rely on one another?)
- Family connectiveness, also called *closeness* or *cohesion* (How close are they?)
- Control (Do they encourage or limit autonomy?)

These four elements vary a great deal from family to family. No one doubts that communication and support are beneficial, if not essential. However, connectiveness seems especially crucial; it is predictive of positive self-esteem and is protective against all potential troubles, including depression, drug abuse, and delinquency (Barber & Olsen 1994). And the degree of control exercised by parents is also important to adolescents' development.

Connectiveness.   Connectiveness takes many forms. As you saw in Chapter 13, minority parents are more inclined than European-American parents to use an authoritarian parenting style, exercising strict control over the daily lives of their adolescent offspring. Their offspring sometimes respond well to this style (Glasgow et al., 1997; Chao, 1994; Chiu, 1987; Dornbusch et al., 1987). Why might this be? According to at least one explanation, connectiveness is the key, and various cultures differ in their expression of this connection. If a child grows up hearing about the importance of family closeness and strong parents, then when he or she is a teenager, that child may perceive such strict parenting as a sign of caring and support rather than as a sign of dominance and rejection.

This explanation makes sense: As you may remember from our discussion of child abuse, a critical issue in determining whether an action is actually maltreatment is its impact on a particular child. The impact on a child, in turn, is affected by the culture. One example comes from a study of 3,000 Zimbabwe adolescents. Those closest to traditional patterns of parental control also had the healthiest development, especially as indicated by the low rate of alcohol use (Eide & Acuda, 1996). This point was forcefully made by the authors of an international study of parenting style and adolescent response:

> Family practices are embedded within a cultural context and are interpreted in light of that culture. For example, consider the case of parents' beating a child because of low school grades. A child from a culture where such behavior was sanctioned, where it occurred frequently, and where this parental behavior was regarded as a sign of parental investment in, and concern over the child's future might interpret this behavior differently than a child from a culture in which such behavior occurred infrequently, and was regarded as deviant and indicative of loss of parental control. Adolescents make social comparisons between their families and other families from within their own culture. It is the perceived departures from the cultural standard of acceptable and good parenting that may be important rather than some absolute set of behavioral practices. [Feldman & Rosenthal, 1994]

Of course this is complex, as you already saw in the discussion of ethnic minorities. The social context keeps shifting; some flexibility is needed in parents as well, especially parents who grew up under different circumstances from those their children experience.

Control.   Another aspect of family functioning is even more tricky: the degree to which the family provides control, restricting the adolescent's autonomy.

On the one hand, some steps to limit freedom are beneficial. A powerful deterrent for delinquency, risky sex, and drug abuse is **parental monitoring**, that is, parental vigilance regarding where one's child is and what he or she is doing and with whom (Fletcher et al., 1995; Patterson et al., 1989; Rogers, 1999; Sampson & Laub, 1993). Such monitoring helps limit access to alcohol, drugs, and guns by keeping the adolescent in places the parent allows.

Other sources of monitoring are the community, neighbors, store owners, and so on. Since many delinquent acts occur in late afternoon, between the closing school bell and the evening meal, after-school programs that include adult supervision, particularly sports leagues or drama workshops that are attractive and available for boys as well as girls, can make a de-

parental monitoring   Parental awareness of what one's children are doing, where, and with whom.

cided difference. Community closeness, allowing neighbors to know which teenagers might be getting into trouble and who their parents are, significantly decreases delinquency (Sampson, 1997).

But, on the other hand, too much interference and parental control is a strong predictor of adolescent depression. Apparently adolescents need some freedom in order to feel good about themselves (Barber et al., 1997). Obviously, parents need to find some middle ground, expressing involvement without interference, concern without restriction. Psychological intrusiveness, in which parents not only want to know where the child is but also to make the child feel guilty and anxious about his or her behavior, may make the child unhappy and sometimes rebellious (Larson & Gillman, 1999). The particulars depend on the culture, on the siblings, and on the inherited personalities of the individuals (Rowe, 1994).

Conclusion

All told, then, parent-teen relationships are typically supportive during adolescence, which is fortunate since family connection underlies psychological functioning. Some conflict is common, typically occurring in early adolescence and centering on day-to-day details like the adolescent's musical tastes, domestic neatness, and sleeping habits, not on world politics or moral issues (Barber, 1994).

Most adolescents report feeling loved and accepted by their parents and perceive them as role models and sources of guidance, a generality found among children of both sexes, adopted and not adopted, in all family types, and in many nations (Hurrelmann, 1994; Larson et al., 1996; Maughan & Pickles, 1990; Montemayor, 1986). Even the adolescents who seem most at risk—because of poverty, family structure, or war or other violence—are often able to function well if their families are protective and supportive (Reynolds, 1998; Richters & Martinez, 1993; Tolen & Gorman-Smith, 1997).

Peers

Friendships, already prominent in middle childhood, become even more influential during early adolescence (Berndt, 1989; Harris, 1998). From hanging out with a large group in the schoolyard or at the mall to whispered phone conversations with a trusted confidant or with a romantic partner, relations with peers are vital to the transition from childhood to adulthood.

Peer Pressure Peers provide each other welcome guidance regarding what to wear, as shown by these two groups of friends. Although there may have been some early-morning phone consultation regarding who was wearing what, the overall fashion mode in both cases—"black with chains" and "casual prep"—was a foregone conclusion.

Adolescents help each other negotiate the tasks and trials of growing up in many ways. As B. Bradford Brown (1990) explains, "Teenagers construct a peer system that reflects their growing psychological, biological, and social-cognitive maturity and helps them adapt to the social ecology of adolescence." Among the special functions performed by peer relationships and close friendships, Brown finds the following four most noteworthy:

- *Pubertal self-help.* Physical changes confront the young person with new feelings, experiences, and challenges to self-esteem. Peers provide both information and the companionship of those who are going through the same changes, able to listen to concerns and provide specific advice as few adults can.
- *Social support.* Friends provide social protection against the turmoil of the social ecology of adolescence, such as the transition to the larger, more impersonal middle and junior high schools, with heterogeneous student populations and fewer nurturant adults. As Brown (1990) observes, "Major changes in peer groups can be seen as efforts to cope with the new school structure thrust on youngsters at adolescence. The depersonalized and complex routine of secondary school increases the young teenager's need for sources of social support and informal exchanges."
- *Identity formation.* The peer group aids the search for self-understanding and identity by functioning as a mirror that reflects dispositions, interests, and capabilities. Superficial identity is often a first step, which explains why many groups watch the same TV shows, wear the same shoes, dance with the same moves to the same music, and so on. As adolescents associate themselves with this or that subgroup (the jocks, the brains, or the druggies, for instance), they are rejecting other subgroups—and the particular self-definitions that would go with them.
- *Value clarification.* Friends are a sounding board for exploring and defining values and aspirations. By experimenting with viewpoints, philosophies, and attitudes toward themselves and the world, with others who are willing to listen, argue, and agree, adolescents begin to discover which values are truest to them.

Because of the nature and importance of these four functions, loyalty and intimacy are the critical elements of peer solidarity (Berndt & Savin-Williams, 1992; Newcomb & Bagwell, 1995). Friends are obligated to stand up for each other, must never speak behind each other's backs, and need to share personal thoughts and feelings without ridicule or betrayal of trust. As one eighth-grader expressed very simply:

> I can tell Karen things and she helps me talk. If we have problems at school, we work them out together. And she doesn't laugh at me if I do something weird—she accepts me for who I am. [from Berndt & Perry, 1990]

Peer Pressure

peer pressure   Social pressure to conform with one's friends or contemporaries in behavior, dress, and attitude; usually considered negative, as when peers encourage each other to defy adult standards.

The four peer functions listed above are constructive ones; for that reason, they are contrary to the notion of **peer pressure,** the idea that peers force adolescents to do things that they otherwise would not do. The idea of peer pressure is not completely false, but it is exaggerated in three ways:

- The social pressure to go along with one's peers—to conform—is strong only for a few years; it rises dramatically in early adolescence, but only until about age 14. Then it declines (Coleman & Hendry, 1990).
- Peer-group conformity can be constructive in some cases. It eases the transition for a young person who is trying to abandon childish modes

of behavior, including dependence on parents, but who is not yet ready for full independence.

■ Peer standards are not necessarily negative. One study of 373 Wisconsin junior and senior high school students found that peer pressure to study hard and get good grades was as apparent as pressure to dress appropriately and that peers were more likely to discourage cigarette smoking than to encourage it (Brown, 1990; Brown et al., 1986). Similarly, peers encourage each other to join sports teams, study for exams, apply to colleges, and so on.

If a young person hangs out with motivated, high-achieving friends, their positive values will be shared and enforced. In fact, one multiethnic study, seeking to determine why Asian Americans generally perform well in high school and many African Americans get into trouble, found that peers and community were pivotal. Among both ethnic groups, parents urged their children to achieve well; if there was any difference, it favored the African-American parents, who were more involved in day-to-day homework and classwork than the Asian parents. However, peers were the deciding influence, especially for practical implementation of academic goals among the Asian students (Steinberg & Darling, 1994). Another study found that, in an inner-city community, many African Americans who did well academically needed to cut themselves off from peer influences (Luthar & McMahon, 1996). Generally, peer-group membership, even more than close friendship, promotes higher grades and prosocial behavior and eases distress and antisocial behavior (Wentzel & Caldwell, 1997).

The reality that peer pressure can be positive does not negate another reality: Young people sometimes lead each other into trouble. When no adults are present, the excitement of being together and the desire to defy adult restrictions can result in risky, forbidden, and destructive behavior (Dishion et al., 1995; Lightfoot, 1997).

However, although parents sometimes blame other teenagers for leading their innocent, self-controlled, law-abiding son or daughter astray, the truth tends to be otherwise. Peers sometimes influence friends who are ambivalent about their values and activities but not those who are already set on a particular path (Vitaro et al., 1997). A young person usually chooses to associate with other teenagers whose values and interests he or she shares, and collectively they may become involved in escapades that none of them would engage in alone. The reason for their behavior is not peer pressure but peer solidarity. As one adolescent described it:

> The idea of peer pressure is a lot of bunk. What I heard about peer pressure all the way through school is that someone is going to walk up to me and say "Here, drink this and you'll be cool." It wasn't like that at all. You go somewhere and everyone else would be doing it and you'd think, "Hey, everyone else is doing it and they seem to be having a good time—now why wouldn't I do this?" In that sense, the preparation of the powers that be, the lessons that they tried to drill into me, they were completely off. They had no idea what we are up against. [Lightfoot, 1997]

Fortunately, most peer-inspired misbehavior is a short-lived experiment rather than a foreshadowing of long-term delinquency. The teenager who argues that he or she must engage in a particular activity, dress a certain way, or hang out in certain parts of town because "everyone else does it" is trying

Bucharest, Romania, 1996 This cement bunker near the main railroad station is sleeping quarters for these three boys, abandoned by their parents. Thievery and glue-sniffing are part of daily life, but so is unexpected loyalty and nurturance, with shared food and warmth. For instance, these two adolescents make sure the younger boy and the dog have a place to sleep. Unfortunately, hundreds of thousands of such children still live in cities worldwide, and millions more grew up in the slums of previous centuries. Most of them died young, but peer protection and luck allowed some to survive, describing strategies and lessons learned from each other that enabled them to become functioning adults.

A Foursome, Not a Twosome When teenagers first start forming couples, they often spend time with other couples to ease the uncertainty about what to say, when to touch, and so on. Interestingly, it is not unusual for a breakup in one couple to trigger a breakup in the other, often with a new alliance between the same individuals.

to lighten the burden of responsibility for some demeanor, style, or philosophy that she or he is trying out. In a way, therefore, "peer pressure" acts as a buffer between the relatively dependent world of childhood and the relatively independent world of young adulthood.

In this light, even the gang or clique fills an important need. When the stresses of adolescence are particularly strong and the usual defense—that is, the family—is unavailable because the parents are too self-absorbed or too distant from the teenage culture, a group of peers takes over. But peer groups are more likely to fill a vacuum than to supersede a well-functioning family.

Boys and Girls Together

During most of early and middle childhood, voluntary segregation of the sexes is common. Then, as puberty begins, boys and girls begin to notice one another in a new way. However, given the diversity of sex roles in today's world, developing a sexual identity and then expressing it with a partner are almost impossible to do without friends. Girls, particularly, may need the intimacy of friendship in order to achieve their own sexual identities.

Usually, the first sign of heterosexual attraction is not an overt, positive interest but a seeming dislike (see Table 16.2). Similar feelings about the other sex have been found in many nations, although the pace of the change depends on several factors. One factor is the biology of puberty, but that is not as powerful as the influence of culture and peers. The final factor in the transformation of attitudes is the availability of someone to arouse sexual feelings in a setting that allows interaction. Quite personal characteristics, such as one's appearance, boldness, and role models, can make some 14-year-olds much more advanced romantically than their classmates.

Typically, friendships within the larger group become a launching pad for romantic involvements, providing individuals with security and role models while sparing any particular teen the embarrassment of being alone with a member of the other sex. The peer group also provides witnesses and

table **16.2**	**Typical Responses to the Opposite Sex***	
	From Girls	From Boys
Age 11	"Boys are a sort of disease."	"Girls are a pin prick in the side."
Age 13	"Boys are stupid although important to us."	"Girls are great enemies."
Age 15	"Boys are strange—they hate you if you're ugly and brainy but love you if you are pretty but dumb."	"Girls are the main objective."
Age 16	"Boys are a pleasant change from the girls."	"Girls have their good and bad points—fortunately, the good outnumber the bad."

*The quotations come from a study of adolescents in New Zealand.
Source: Kroger, 1989.

messengers who will help someone evaluate whether so-and-so (male) is really nice or a nerd, whether so-and-so (female) is cute or stuck up, and—especially important—whether a particular attraction is mutual or not. The role of peers is reflected in the following account of two young adolescent boys working as a team to test the waters of romance:

> We started calling girls we liked on the phone, one at a time. We'd each call the girl the other one liked and ask if she wanted to go with the other one. . . . Usually they wouldn't say too much. So sometimes we would call her best friend to see if she could tell us anything. Then they would call each other and call us back. If we got the feeling after a few calls that she really was serious about No, then we might go on to our next choice, if we had one. [quoted in Adler et al., 1992]

Even if a male and a female in early adolescence manage to set up a date just for the two of them, they are unlikely to be alone for long. Their friends will probably try to find out every detail of their plans and then sit behind them at the movie, hang out near them in the schoolyard, or follow along on the other side of the street as they go from one place to another. As soon as the date is over, the daters are obliged to call their friends, boasting of or bemoaning every detail.

In general, the progression of heterosexual involvement, first described almost 40 years ago (Dunphy, 1963), follows this pattern:

- Groups of friends, exclusively one sex or the other
- A loose association of a girl's group and a boy's group, with all interactions very public
- A smaller, heterosexual group, formed from the more advanced members of the larger association
- A final peeling off of heterosexual couples, with private intimacies

Each of these stages typically lasts several years, with exclusive same-sex groups in elementary school and heterosexual couples in later high school or college.

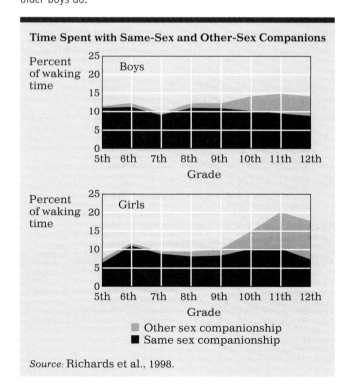

Figure 16.1 We'll Still Be Friends. Through adolescence, young people spend increasing amounts of time with peers of the opposite sex, while almost maintaining the amounts of time spent with same-sex friends. Note, though, that older girls spend much more of their time with opposite-sex friends than older boys do.

Source: Richards et al., 1998.

This overall shift in sexual friendship patterns was documented in a study of students in a large, multiethnic public school outside Chicago (Richards et al., 1998). As they got older, these adolescents gradually spent more time with the opposite sex and enjoyed it more: freshmen were happiest when they were with companions of their own sex or in mixed-sex groups, while juniors and seniors were happiest when they were with one member of the opposite sex.

Interestingly, spending more time with other-sex companions does not usually come at the expense of time and friendship with peers of the same sex. In fact, especially for the girls in the Chicago study, thinking about the other sex made them feel "especially low," but thinking about their relationships and activities with same-sex peers made them feel happier and more excited as they grew older, from age 13 to 18 (Richards et al., 1998).

To get a sense of the time adolescents spend with peers, look at Figure 16.1. In the fifth and sixth grades, when they were on the edge of adolescence, children spent about 1 percent of their waking time (less than an hour a week) with the other sex. (Classroom time was not counted.) By the eleventh grade, however, boys were spending 5 hours a week with girls, and girls about 10 hours with boys. In addition, these older adolescents spent about the same amounts of time thinking

"We slam danced 'til dawn, then we both got tatoos and had our noses pierced. It was so romantic"

Some Enchanted Evening In every generation, shared experiences bring couples closer together. The nature of those experiences varies from cohort to cohort and culture to culture.

❷ Especially for Teachers: Imagine that you teach more than 100 adolescents a semester and that you have no time for intense suicide prevention for everyone. Which of the following students would you be sure to talk privately with: a girl who is discouraged because she keeps getting average grades; a boy whose grade fell from an A to a D; a girl who has a light scratch across her wrist; a boy who plays on the basketball team, which just lost an important game?

about the other sex. Obviously, heterosexual relationships are time-consuming and thought-provoking—something parents do not seem to understand and peers love to discuss.

The need to talk about the other sex is one reason adolescents continue to spend time with same-sex peers even after romantic other-sex relationships develop. For many adolescents, heterosexual intimacy is fraught with problems, especially the likelihood of rejection (Fischer, 1996; Furman & Wehner, 1994). (Indeed, fear of rejection keeps many adolescents from trying to form intimate relationships.) Typically, early romances are intense but soon over (Feiring, 1996). Having supportive friends to cushion the pain, offer reassurance and solace, and validate emotions and self-worth is essential when rejection does occur.

For adolescents who are gay or lesbian, added complications usually slow down romantic attachments. First, there is the problem of finding both romantic partners and friends in whom the adolescent can confide. In addition, feeling at ease with one's sexual identity takes longer, in part because finding an accepting peer network is more difficult.

Especially in homophobic cultures, many young men with homosexual feelings deny these feelings altogether, or they try to change or conceal them by becoming heterosexually involved. Similarly, many young women who will later identify themselves as lesbian spend their teenage years relatively oblivious to, or in denial of, their sexual urges. One difference between the sexes here is that lesbian adolescents find it easier to establish strong friendships with same-sex heterosexual peers than homosexual teenage boys do. The probable reason is that female friendships generally tend to be close and intimate, whereas males are often wary of close friendships with other males, especially if their sexual orientation is in doubt. In many cases, a homosexual boy's best friend is a girl, who is more at ease with his sexuality than a same-sex peer might be (Bell et al., 1981; D'Augelli & Hershberger, 1993; Savin-Williams, 1995).

Overall, then, research suggests that peers aid every major task of adolescence—from adjusting to the physical changes of puberty, to searching for identity, to forming romantic attachments. Peers are more likely to complement the influence of parents during adolescence than to pull in the opposite direction (Brown, 1990) and more likely to moderate the push toward sexual intimacy than to prevent or rush it. The friendless adolescent is much more fragile than the one whose friends dress or talk in ways distinct from the parent's or culture's customs. As you will soon see, both family and friends are crucial in cushioning the serious emotional problems of adolescence, particularly depression and anger, which can lead to suicide or violent crime.

ADOLESCENT SUICIDE

From a life-span perspective, teenagers are just beginning to explore life's possibilities. Even if they experience some troubling event—failing a class, ending a romance, fighting with a parent—surely they must realize that better days lie ahead. Not always. This logical perspective is not shared by suicidal adolescents, who are so overwhelmed with pain or anger that, for a few perilous hours or days, death seems their only solution.

But before discussing this issue, we need to destroy a prejudice: Adolescents under age 20 are much less likely to kill themselves than adults are. This is true now and was true in previous years, in North America and

520

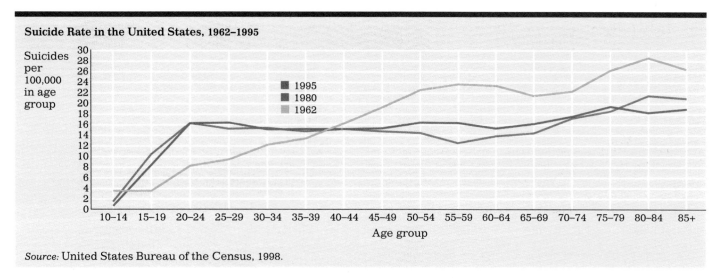

Suicide Rate in the United States, 1962–1995

Suicides per 100,000 in age group

■ 1995
■ 1980
■ 1962

Age group: 10–14, 15–19, 20–24, 25–29, 30–34, 35–39, 40–44, 45–49, 50–54, 55–59, 60–64, 65–69, 70–74, 75–79, 80–84, 85+

Source: United States Bureau of the Census, 1998.

Figure 16.2 So Much to Live For. A historical look at U.S. suicide statistics reveals two trends. First, although their rate is still below that of adults, teenagers are three times as likely to take their own lives as they once were. Second, this increase in teen suicide is part of a life-span trend. Whereas rates used to rise in middle age, recently young adults are more suicidal and older adults less so. Among the possible reasons are that drug abuse, increased parental divorce, and other factors have made adolescence more problematic and that better health care and pension plans have made the later years easier.

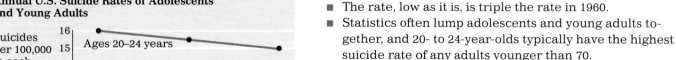

Annual U.S. Suicide Rates of Adolescents and Young Adults

Suicides per 100,000 in each age group

Ages 20–24 years

Overall rate, all ages

Ages 15–19 years

Ages 10–14 years

Year: 1980, 1986, 1992

Source: Kachur et al., 1995.

Figure 16.3 Why? Suicide rates for adolescents have been rising over the past two decades, while rates for older individuals have been decreasing. Note, for example, that the rate for the youngest adolescents has doubled in that time, a cause for great concern.

suicidal ideation Thinking about suicide, usually with some serious emotional and intellectual overtones.

worldwide. Look at data for the United States, where year-by-year records are kept (see Figure 16.2).

These statistics run counter to the popular misconception that teenagers kill themselves at a high rate. Why does this mistaken idea persist? Four reasons:

- The rate, low as it is, is triple the rate in 1960.
- Statistics often lump adolescents and young adults together, and 20- to 24-year-olds typically have the highest suicide rate of any adults younger than 70.
- Every adolescent suicide, particularly of younger adolescents (330 children age 10 to 14 killed themselves in the United States in 1995; see Figure 16.3) is shocking and thus is more likely to be publicized. Suicide in late adulthood, by contrast, rarely attracts public attention, so people do not realize that elder suicide is twice as common as teen suicide.
- Social prejudice tends to consider teenagers as problems, and hence distorts the evidence.(Kachur et al., 1995; Males, 1996)

Suicidal Ideation

Since actual suicide is not common, why focus on this topic? Part of the reason is that adolescents think about suicide often—one of many signs that depression is prevalent during these years. A review of studies from many nations finds that **suicidal ideation,** that is, thinking about committing suicide, is so common among high school students that it might be considered normal (Diekstra, 1995). (See the Research Report, pages 522–523.)

In these studies, the rate of suicidal ideation ranged from 15 to 53 percent. The reason for that wide range seems more related to the specifics of the research—for example, whether adolescents were asked if they had "ever" seriously thought about suicide or if they had done so "in the past year"—rather than to the specifics of the culture. In the United States, when high school students were asked about only one year,

RECOGNIZING SIGNS OF SUICIDE

Suicide is commonly thought of as a response to a specific and immediate psychological blow. However, it usually is the final result of diffuse and long-standing problems within the individual, as well as within the family and social environment (Brent et al., 1994; Diekstra et al., 1995; Shneidman et al., 1994). Some of these problems are:

- Being temperamentally inclined toward fits of rage or bouts of depression
- Having depressed, suicidal, or alcoholic parents
- Experiencing the early loss of an important caregiving parent, grandparent, or older sibling through divorce, abandonment, imprisonment, or death
- Growing up with few steady friends, either because of one's personal traits or because of external circumstances, such as moving frequently
- Experiencing educational pressures, especially if the young person attends a large and impersonal school (Special-education students, recent dropouts, and very high achievers have higher suicide rates than other students.)

For some adolescents, puberty itself may become so difficult that it leads to suicidal ideation and self-destructive acts (Diekstra, 1995). Sexual awakening can be particularly troubling for gay adolescents, whose suicide rate is about three times as high as that of their straight peers (D'Augelli & Dark, 1994). Sexually abused youths, male and female, are also at high risk of suicide—especially those who are blamed by the abuser and feel that no one will believe them if they ask for help (Finkelhor, 1994).

In addition, adolescents are particularly susceptible to **cluster suicide**, in which one suicide—especially of a famous person or a well-known peer—leads other individuals to attempt, and sometimes commit, suicide. Often, it is not the fact of suicide that creates the cluster, but the response of peers, schools, and the media glorifying the death. Large public memorial services with outpourings of praise and grief, or public statements that somehow justify the death or blame it on others, make vulnerable peers imagine that suicide is an attractive, reasonable, and common option.

Because cluster suicides are the result of contagion, some experts suggest that suicides not be reported in the media. However, most believe that factual reports of suicide are necessary to stop gossip and speculation, which themselves excite interest, but that the accounts should avoid emotional overtones (*MMWR*, April 22, 1994). For similar reasons, educational programs aimed at preventing suicide must take care not to glorify it. According to one account, exactly that happened in Germany, where a suicide prevention film shown to adolescents caused an *increase* in the suicide rate (Schmidtke & Häfner, 1988).

Responding to the Cry for Help

Many adolescents have experienced at least one of the five suicide risk factors. Certainly, all teenagers deserve special attention to help them ride out whatever stresses they are experiencing. But how can we recognize those who are in imminent danger and prevent them from making a fatal mistake?

One psychologist, Edwin Shneidman, has devoted his entire career to the study of suicide (Shneidman, 1996). He believes that every suicide is preceded by clues—verbal, behavioral, and situational—that are "not too difficult to recognize" (Shneidman & Mandelkorn, 1994). Beyond the back-

---

the rates were disturbingly high, especially among the younger girls (see Table 16.3 on page 524). Other research also finds that depression suddenly increases at puberty, especially among females.

Parasuicide and Prevention

As you can see from the table, not only is suicidal ideation high in adolescence, but so is **parasuicide** (any deliberate act of self-destruction that does not result in death), with an international rate of between 6 and 20 percent.

Experts prefer the word "parasuicide" over "attempted suicide" or "failed suicide" because this term does not judge severity or intention (Diekstra et al., 1995). Particularly in adolescence, most self-destructive acts are carried out in a state of extreme emotional agitation and confusion. This means that

parasuicide A deliberate act of self-destruction that does not end in death. Parasuicide can be fleeting, such as a small knife mark on the wrist, or potentially lethal, such as swallowing an entire bottle of pills.

Fire Prevention Depression can be an occasional feature of normal adolescence. When it is sustained, or when it is accompanied by loss of interest in social relationships or decline in school achievement, it may be a sign that the adolescent is at risk for suicide. Those around the troubled teen should take this seriously and take preventive action.

ground factors listed above, Shneidman notes the following warning signs that must be taken seriously:

- *A sudden decline in school attendance and achievement, especially in students of better-than-average ability.* About one-third of the young people who attempt suicide had recently failed several subjects or dropped out of school, but most of them had been good students until their grades suddenly fell.

- *Suicidal ideation*. About 80 percent of all those who commit suicide talk about it before they do it, often portraying suicide in idealized, romantic terms.
- *Withdrawal from social relationships*. A depressed adolescent who seems to suddenly brighten up is likely at risk. A cheerful "It's been nice knowing you" or a more direct "Good-bye" from such an individual, followed by a sudden desire to be alone, is a very serious sign.
- *Running away*. The adolescent who literally runs away, or who retreats from normal life through drinking or drugging to oblivion, is at high risk.
- *Parasuicide*. Any attempted suicide, however weak it may seem, must be taken seriously. If nothing changes, a parasuicide becomes practice for the real thing. Virtually all the young adults who die by suicide made their first attempt before age 20.

Attempted suicide is, in fact, a "late clue," usually preceded by other signals that help is needed (Faberow, 1994). As Schneidman explains, reading these clues is everyone's "moral responsibility, something akin to omnipresent fire prevention" (Shneidman & Mandelkorn, 1994). And what should others do when the alarm sounds? Shneidman states it quite clearly:

> The way to save a person's life is . . . put your knowledge of the person's plan to commit suicide into a social network—to let others know about it, to break the secret, to talk to the person, to talk to others, to offer help, to put action around the person, to show response and concern, and, if possible, to offer love. [Shneidman, 1978]

cluster suicide A group of suicides that occur in the same community, school, or time period.

Rank from 1 to 10 the following American ethnic subgroups for suicide rates of their teens ages 15–19. See actual rankings and rates in Table 16.4, page 525.		
	Males	Females
European American		
African American		
Hispanic American		
Asian American		
Native American		

intent may not be clear even to the self-destructive individuals themselves. Many who make a potentially lethal attempt not only are relieved that they did not die but soon wonder what they could possibly have been thinking.

Whether or not suicidal ideation eventually leads to a plan, a parasuicide, and then death depends on a multitude of factors that vary from community to community. In adolescence, five of the most influential are:

- Availability of lethal means, especially guns
- Parental supervision
- Alcohol and other drugs
- Gender
- Attitudes about suicide in the culture

table **16.3**	**Suicidal Ideation and Parasuicide, United States, 1998**			
	Seriously Considered Attempting Suicide	Planned Suicide	Parasuicide (Attempted Suicide)	Actual Suicide (Ages 14–18)
Overall	21%	16%	8%	**Less than .01% (about 9 per 100,000)**
Girls: 9th grade	29	20	15	
10th grade	30	24	14	**About 3 per 100,000**
11th grade	26	21	11	
12th grade	24	15	6	
Boys: 9th grade	16	13	6	
10th grade	15	11	4	**About 15 per 100,000**
11th grade	17	14	4	
12th grade	14	11	4	

Source: MMWR, August 14, 1998, based on a survey of 1,600 students from 23 states; actual suicide estimated from U.S. Bureau of the Census, 1998.

❶ Response for Teachers (from page 520):
The first and the last youngsters are probably fine. Average grades are less worrisome than very high or very low grades, and being on a team is usually protection against isolation and serious drugs. The middle two are more troubling—a sudden drop in grades or change in personality is a worrisome sign, and any form of parasuicide is a cry for help.

The first three factors make clear why the rate of youth suicide in North America and Europe has tripled since 1960: adolescents have more guns, less adult supervision, and more alcohol and drugs because so many parents are divorced, single, or working outside the home. In the United States, accessibility of guns is a major culprit; adolescent gunshot suicide increased by about 50 percent between 1980 and 1995. This accounts for virtually all of the recent increases (Kachur et al., 1995; Sickmund et al., 1997).

Gender and National Differences

At every age, but particularly in adolescence, the parasuicide rate is higher for females than for males. And at every age, but particularly in adolescence, the actual suicide rate is higher for males than for females. One reason is that when males attempt suicide, they use more lethal means—guns rather than pills—and hence it is harder to rescue them from their own destruction.

Adolescent males are more likely to commit suicide, and less likely to attempt it, in every nation of the world, but cultural factors influence the

Figure 16.4 International Suicide Rates.
Comparing international suicide rates for adolescents is very difficult, in part because few nations report separate statistics for age 15 to 19 and in part because rates rise or fall depending on historical factors, so the nations shown as having relatively high rates here may not have high rates in the year 2005. This chart does show, however, that a young man's risk of suicide depends more on his cultural context than on his age and sex.

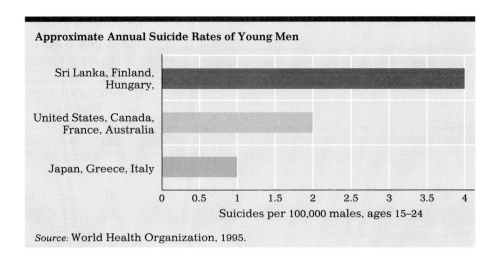

Source: World Health Organization, 1995.

table **16.4**	**Suicide Rates of 15- to 19-Year-Olds, by Ethnic Group**	
Rank	Ethnic Group	Suicides per 100,000
1	Native American males	36.4
2	European American males	19.3
3	Asian American males	12.0
4	African American males	11.5
5	Hispanic American males	10.9
6	Native American females	6.5
7	Asian American females	4.0
8	European American females	4.0
9	Hispanic American females	3.2
10	African American females	1.9

Source: Kachur et al., 1995.

Rank for Teenagers Only Female suicide rates are always lower than male rates in every ethnic and age group, but the male-female ratio varies from six to one for African Americans to three to one for Asian Americans. Not shown here are variations by age, which also can be substantial. For example, among persons age 50 to 80, the Native American rates are lower than those of any other group, and the European American rates are higher.

overall rate of youth suicide. As you can see from Figure 16.4, the data disprove at least one myth about adolescent suicide: The Japanese do not have the highest rate. Japan's teen suicide rate is actually among the lowest.

BREAKING THE LAW

Suicide in thought and deed is one indication of the emotional stress that many adolescents feel. Many psychologists believe that another indication of stress is adolescent crime. Worldwide police statistics on arrests show that arrests are more likely to occur in the second decade of life than at any other time. More specifically, international arrest rates rise rapidly at about age 12, peak at about age 16, and then decline slowly with every passing year (Shoemaker, 1996; Smith, 1995; see Figure 16.5). In the United States, 44 percent of all arrests for serious crimes (crimes of violence, arson, or theft involving thousands of dollars) are of persons between the ages of 10 and 20 (Maguire & Pastore, 1997).

Figure 16.5 We'll Be Seeing You. While these data come from only one group—boys in a Wisconsin town—they exhibit two characteristics that are found no matter where such data are collected. First, the average number of police contacts per individual rises and then falls between ages 10 and 20. Second, almost every American boy has had nearly three police contacts by age 20. Of course, not every transgressor is caught every time: the actual average number of delinquent acts is much higher.

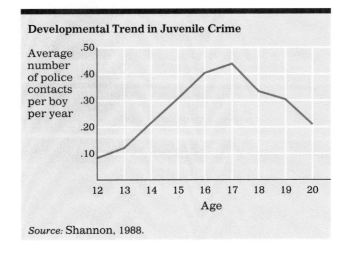

Developmental Trend in Juvenile Crime

Source: Shannon, 1988.

Incidence and Prevalence

The statistics in the preceding paragraph are *incidence* data; they are obtained by determining how all official arrests are distributed among the various age groups of arrestees. They tell us that adolescents have the highest criminal arrest rates, but they cannot tell us the *prevalence* of adolescent crime—that is, how widespread lawbreaking is among adolescents.

Suppose that, as some contend, a small minority of repeat offenders commits a disproportionate share of crimes. In this case, even though the incidence of adolescent crime might be high, the prevalence of lawbreaking would be quite low: many adolescent crimes (high incidence) would then be committed by only a few lawbreakers (low prevalence) (Farrington, 1994). If this were true, and if adolescents on the path to a criminal career could be spotted early and then imprisoned, the *incidence* of adolescent crime would plummet, because the few potential multiple offenders could no longer commit their many crimes. Indeed, this supposition and strategy lead to attempts to "crack down on" and "put away" young criminals.

However, the strategy does not work, because the supposition is false: adolescents are far less often career criminals than adults are. Juveniles are mostly experimenters; they have not yet settled on any career, not even crime. Most have no more than one serious brush with the law, and even chronic offenders typically have a mix of offenses—some minor, some serious, and usually only one violent crime. In fact, of every thousand youths who are arrested at least once, only 13 (1.3 percent) have committed more than one violent offense. In other words, serious adolescent crimes are committed by many one-time offenders rather than by a few multiple offenders. The high incidence of adolescent crime is caused by its high prevalence, not by a few very active delinquents (Snyder, 1997).

Actually, the prevalence of adolescent crime is even greater than official records report, especially if all acts of "juvenile delinquency," (major or minor lawbreaking by youths under age 18) are considered. Many crimes never come to the attention of the police; and many police officers do not arrest a young first-time offender. As an example, according to one confiden-

❷ Especially for Social Scientists: Crime prevention is a hot political issue, but few people understand a developmental perspective. If you had unlimited funds to do research in one small town, with the goal of delinquency prevention, would you begin with police data, school records, parent reports, or interviews with teenagers? Would your study be longitudinal or cross-sectional? Would you have a control group?

Protection or Prejudice? Many question whether adolescent arrest statistics accurately reflect the true ethnic and gender ratios of juvenile delinquents.

❷ Observational Quiz (see answer page 528): *From what you see here, what raised the officers' suspicion, what was the crime, and what is the punishment?*

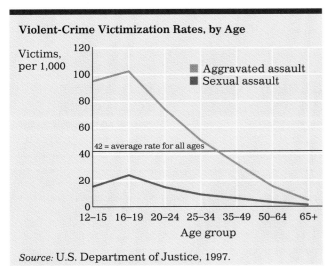

Violent-Crime Victimization Rates, by Age

42 = average rate for all ages

Source: U.S. Department of Justice, 1997.

Figure 16.6 Victims of Violent Crime.
Compared to adults, adolescents are far more often victims of violence, as shown by a survey conducted by the U.S. Department of Justice. This fact is not well known for two reasons. First, adolescents are less likely to report crimes, especially crimes that threaten their self-image, such as aggravated assault and sexual assault. Both of these crimes are experienced by 16- to 19-year-olds three times as often as the overall national average. Second, the general prejudice against teenagers makes society too willing to blame them, not defend them.

Figure 16.7 Homicide Victims in the United States.
As you can see, older adolescents are much more likely to be killed than younger children or older adults. Not shown here is that males are far more likely to be killed than females, and blacks far more than whites. The same age, gender, and trends are apparent in perpetrators (see Appendix A for specifics).

tial survey, only 20 percent of adolescents who were self-admitted repeat offenders had been arrested even once (Henggeler, 1989).

Partly because few young offenders are arrested, law enforcement data on the gender and ethnic prevalences of delinquency are questionable. Official U.S. juvenile arrest statistics show that males are three times as likely to be arrested as females, that African Americans are three times as likely to be arrested as European Americans, and that European Americans are three times as likely to be arrested as Asian Americans (U.S. Department of Justice, 1998). But longitudinal studies that ask teenagers, confidentially, about their own misbehavior find that most admit breaking the law in ways that could have led to arrest. Such confidential studies find much smaller gender and ethnic differences than those reflected in official arrest data.

When all illegal acts—including such minor infractions as underage drinking; disorderly conduct; breaking a community curfew; playing hooky; ticket or fare cheating at a movie, stadium, club, or train; and underage buying of cigarettes—are included, virtually every adolescent is a repeat offender. In addition, most self-report studies (at least in North America, Great Britain, Australia, and New Zealand) reveal that more serious crimes—such as property damage, stealing, causing bodily harm, and buying or selling illegal drugs—are also common, being committed at least once before age 20 by as many as 80 percent of all boys, with lower rates for girls (Binder et al., 1988; Farrington et al., 1990). Thus, again, prevalence seems to be high for both minor infractions and more serious crimes. As one researcher concludes, "Numerous rigorous self-report studies of representative samples have now documented that it is statistically aberrant to refrain from crime during adolescence" (Moffitt, 1997).

The victims of adolescent crime tend to be teenagers—a fact that is much more apparent in confidential surveys than in official statistics. The overall victimization rate of adolescents is two to three times that of adults, and the victimization rate for violent crimes (assault, rape, murder) shows an even greater ratio of teenagers compared to adults (Hashima & Finkelhor, 1997). (See Figures 16.6 and 16.7.)

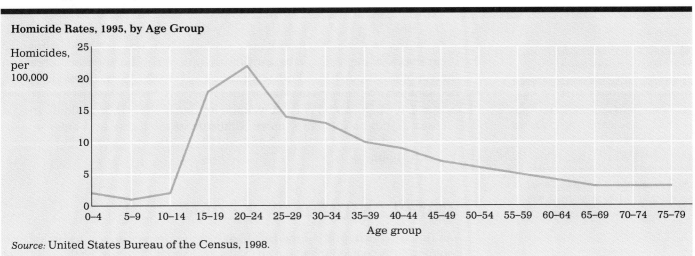

Homicide Rates, 1995, by Age Group

Source: United States Bureau of the Census, 1998.

PREVENTING A LIFE OF CRIME

Given the high victimization rates in adolescence, and the fact that some, but by no means all, adolescent lawbreakers are headed toward repeated, more serious offenses, better efforts to prevent crime and protect victims are needed. A useful distinction can be made between the many who are **adolescent-limited offenders,** whose criminal activity stops by age 21, and the few who are **life-course persistent offenders,** who later become career criminals (Moffitt, 1997).

Most life-course persistent offenders are recognizable long before adulthood. They are among the earliest of their cohort to have sex, drink alcohol, and smoke cigarettes; are among the least involved in school activities and most involved in "hanging out" with older, lawbreaking youths; and are arrested many times for increasingly serious offenses throughout their teen years. They are antisocial in preschool and elementary school. Even earlier, at birth or in the first years of life, they show signs of brain damage—perhaps being slow to express ideas in language, or being hyperactive, or having poor emotional control (Farrington, 1994; Sampson et al., 1997; Moffitt, 1993).

However, while such youngsters are at high risk and while almost all career criminals have this ominous history, not every child with these characteristics becomes a serious criminal. Intervention measures—a particularly cohesive neighborhood, an especially effective school, a supportive peer group, a stable family, or a best friend who discourages crime—can halt the progression in early adolescence (Yoshikawa, 1994). If this fails, or if neighborhood, school, and peers all encourage serious crime, then intensive intervention that teaches life-course persistent teenagers new ways of coping with the biological, cognitive, and psychosocial problems that have plagued them for years, may help.

In general, a developmental perspective always emphasizes earlier recognition and treatment:

Rather than waiting until violence has been learned and practiced, and then devoting increased resources to hiring policemen, building more prisons, and sentencing three-time offenders to life imprisonment, it would be more effective to redirect the resources to early violence prevention programs, particularly for young children and early adolescents. [Slaby & Eron, 1994]

Intensive, residential incarceration in a prison or reform school is needed only for a few. For most delinquents, sending them away from home and neighborhood weakens the protective social bonds that most offenders have (Sampson & Laub, 1993). Prison can actually breed delinquency if it means segregating teenagers with peers who prize possessions more than people and who survive by means of deceit and self-centeredness rather than trust. As this lesson is understood, the crime rate for juveniles is actually falling in the United States. Although this might be surprising to those who look just at demographics (there are about 2 million more teenagers in the United States today than there were a decade ago), it is not surprising given the lower rates of drug abuse, unprotected sex, and school dropouts than a decade ago. Crime is a consequence of other problems, and if those problems are controlled, crime will be also.

Researchers began to look for early signs of risk for life-course persistent delinquency several years ago, but their efforts were stopped because some felt that labeling a particular young boy (maleness was one of the risk factors) "high risk" would stigmatize the innocent and would unfairly target not only boys but also minorities, children of

❶ *Answer to Observational Quiz (from page 526):* If you think the brown bag raised the suspicion, you are wrong, because the same bag carried by a girl, especially a middle-class girl in her suburban neighborhood, would be unnoticed. Even a group of girls, or of middle-class boys, might not attract attention. If you thought the crime was beer purchased underage, you may be partly correct, but how does that explain why the officers seem to be checking everyone's I.D.? And if you thought the punishment is kneeling on the ground, with hands clasped behind the neck and feet crossed, let's hope this is the whole truth.

Before they reach adolescence, most children are neither victims nor aggressors, while a minority are victims, another minority are aggressors, and another minority are both victims and aggressors (Schwartz et al., 1997). At adolescence, fewer are neither, and more are both. Perhaps as a consequence, teenagers who carry a weapon are most likely to view doing so as a defensive, not an offensive, move. Unfortunately, offense and defense usually go hand in hand, making homicide the leading nonaccidental cause of teenage death.

CONCLUSION: A LIFE-SPAN VIEW

As this trio of chapters—and this book—draws to a close, let us look again quickly at the period from age 10 to age 20. Except perhaps for the very first

Who, Where, and When? The sad reality is that this could be young men in almost any place or time. In fact, this photo was taken in southern France on June 14, 1998, the night *before* the World Cup soccer match between England and Tunisia. Street fighting—such as this between supporters of the two teams, which led to 80 arrests, hundreds of wounded, and, fortunately, no deaths—is common among teenage boys in blue jeans, no matter what their ethnicity. The only comforting truth is that most of those rioting young men are adolescent-limited criminals, unlikely to persist in violent crime after they reach adulthood.

single mothers, and the poor (other risk factors). Obviously, such sociological categories are unfair when used to predict the future of individuals. Changing the social structures, not changing the individual who is caught in the structures, makes sense. Nonetheless, many psychologists believe that there are early neurological, genetic, and attachment signs of later violent crime (Moffitt, 1993). The key here is not the research (we can make fairly accurate risk assessments by age 10, if not earlier) but the public attitude. If early diagnosis leads to early punishment, it obviously is wrong. If, instead, it leads to early prevention, it may save what would otherwise be wasted lives.

adolescent-limited offender A juvenile delinquent who is likely to become law-abiding once adulthood is attained.

life-course persistent offender A juvenile delinquent who is likely to continue a pattern of lawbreaking even when adolescence is over. Such individuals usually started their pattern before the teen years.

❶ Response for Social Scientists (from page 526: The answers to the last two questions are easy: Given that life-course persistent and adolescent-limited delinquency look similar, you need a longitudinal study. And given that many solutions have been tried but are unproved, you would need a control group. The first question is harder—where to start. Inaccuracies and omissions would come from all four sources. Perhaps the best way is to begin not with teenagers but with elementary school children.

months of life, no other developmental period is characterized by such multifaceted and compelling biological changes. Nor are developing persons at any other age likely to experience a more fascinating, unnerving, and potentially confusing sequence of intellectual and social transitions. The adolescent's developmental tasks—to reach adult size and sexuality, to adjust to changed educational expectations and intellectual patterns, to develop autonomy from parents and intimacy with friends, to achieve a sense of identity and purpose—are too complex to be accomplished without surprises. No wonder every young person, in every family and culture, experiences disruption of some sort (Schlegal & Barry, 1991).

As you have seen, most adolescents, most families, and most cultures survive this transition fairly well. Parents and children bicker and fight, but they still respect and love each other. Teenagers skip school, eat unwisely, drink too much, experiment with drugs, break laws, feel depressed, rush into sexual activity, conform to peer pressure, disregard their parents' wishes—but all these behaviors typically stay within limits. They do not occur too often or last too long; they do not lead to lifelong or life-threatening harm. For most young people, the teenage years overall are happy ones, during which they escape potentially serious problems and discover the rewards of maturity.

Unfortunately, while all adolescents have some minor difficulties, those with at least one serious problem often have several others as well (Cairns & Cairns, 1994; Dryfoos, 1990). For instance, girls who become mothers by age 16 also tend to be from troubled families, likely to leave school, and likely to experiment with hard drugs. Boys who become chronic criminals also tend to be alienated from their families, failing in school, drug abusing, and brain damaged. Suicidal adolescents typically have been heartbreakingly lonely and seriously depressed for years with inadequate social support from family and friends.

In almost every case, these problems stem from earlier developmental events, beginning with genetic vulnerability and prenatal insults and continuing with family disruptions and discord in early childhood and then with learning disabilities and aggressive or withdrawn behavior in elementary school—all within a community and culture that does not provide adequate intervention. With the inevitable stresses of puberty, problems become worse, more obvious, and more resistant to change. If they are not somehow dealt with, they may persist into adulthood and disrupt the next generation.

Fortunately, an encouraging theme emerges in all three adolescence chapters, as well as in the rest of this book. No developmental path is set in stone by previous events; adolescents are, by nature, innovators, idealists, and risk takers, open to new patterns, goals, and lifestyles. Research on effective schools, on teenage antidrug programs, on the positive role of friendship, and on identity achievement shows that every problem can be adolescent-limited, that young people can find a path that leads them away from the limitations and burdens of their past.

Thus, the final page of this text echoes and elaborates themes sounded in the first chapter. All three domains interact; every day of life builds on the liabilities and strengths of the previous days. Who we were at conception and how we were nurtured prenatally, at birth, and at every previous stage of development somewhat limits who we are today. But these limitations are far from the entire story.

Development is led by people, as if each of us is the conductor of her or his own orchestra. The musicians and their instruments limit what sounds we can evoke, and our own past experiences and preferences make us more likely to produce one kind of music than another, but within those parameters there is a wide range of possibilities. In adult life, while most people follow through on patterns that were set years earlier, most also change the predicted direction of those patterns somewhat. A few of us break the mold—with a career change, a life partner, a new cultural setting, or a conversion of some sort that leaves childhood paths untrod, predictions unfulfilled, early directives ignored.

The interplay of the three domains and of past, present, and future is what makes human development fascinating to study. The ability to place our individual stamp on our journey through time is what makes life even more exciting to live.

SUMMARY

THE SELF AND IDENTITY

1. The growth of self-understanding takes on a new dimension in adolescence, as teenagers begin to recognize and sort through their "possible selves," which reflect different, and sometimes contradictory, aspects of their personality. As they search for their real selves, adolescents often intentionally act out a false self, sometimes to gain acceptance, sometimes to impress others or win approval, and sometimes to test a new role.

2. According to Erikson, the psychosocial crisis of adolescence is identity versus role confusion. Ideally, adolescents resolve this crisis by developing both their own uniqueness and their relationship to the larger society, establishing a sexual, political, moral, and vocational identity in the process.

3. Sometimes the pressure to resolve the identity crisis is too great, and instead of exploring alternative roles, young people foreclose on their options, taking on someone else's values wholesale. They may foreclose the search by seizing their parents' values, or they may choose the values of a cult or hero.

4. Others may take on a negative identity, defying the expectations of family and community. Some teenagers experience identity diffusion, making few commitments to goals, principles, or a particular self-definition. Many young people declare a moratorium, deciding to wait before settling on a mature identity.

5. In industrial and postindustrial societies, social change is rapid, and identity possibilities are endless. Consequently, identity achievement can be more difficult, especially for those—such as members of minority groups—who are caught between divergent cultural patterns.

FAMILY AND FRIENDS

6. Parents are an important influence on adolescents: the generation gap within families is usually not very large, especially with regard to basic values. Children tend not to stray too far from parental beliefs and ideals, and parents have a personal stake in minimizing whatever conflicts there are.

7. Conflict can emerge in parent-adolescent relationships, however, depending partly on the adult's parenting style and the teenager's stage of development. In particular, the onset of puberty forces a change in mutual expectations that can lead parents and adolescents to see their relationship very differently.

8. As at earlier stages of development, authoritative parenting is generally most apt to foster self-esteem and a positive parent-child relationship, in part because it fosters connectiveness and communication. Among some ethnic groups, and in certain conditions, a parental style that is more authoritarian but still nurturing may be beneficial. Immigrant families have a particularly difficult generational gap. In all families, the adolescent needs to feel a balance of support and autonomy.

9. The peer group is a vital source of information and encouragement. The adolescent subculture provides a buffer between the world of children and the world of adults, allowing, for example, a social context for the beginning of heterosexual relationships.

10. While most close friendships in early adolescence are with members of the same sex, by late adolescence friendships typically include members of the opposite sex, as romantic relationships begin to develop. These individuals are in addition to, rather than instead of, same-sex friends.

ADOLESCENT SUICIDE

11. Suicidal ideation is fairly common among high school students, with a small minority engaging in deliberate acts of self-destruction (parasuicide). Wide variation in teenage suicide rates is evident among ethnic and national groups, but, worldwide, girls are more likely to attempt suicide, boys are more likely to complete it, and teenagers are less likely to kill themselves than adults are.

12. Most adolescent suicides are preceded by a long sequence of negative experiences, including family problems, breakdowns in communication, drug and/or alcohol abuse, and sometimes a critical event. Suicide prevention requires heeding the preliminary warning signs and responding quickly to cries for help.

BREAKING THE LAW

13. Lawbreaking is more common in adolescence than in any other period of the life span. Almost all adolescents engage in some delinquency, but relatively few are arrested and even fewer become life-course persistent criminals. Adolescents are often victims of crimes as well.

14. Prevention of adolescent crime includes identifying children at risk, who by age 10 have learning difficulties in school, act aggressively toward other children, and have significant stresses at home. Not all adolescent lawbreakers are equally troubled, and the most effective intervention occurs years before a violent offense is committed.

CONCLUSION: A LIFE-SPAN VIEW

15. Adolescence, even more than other stages of life, offers opportunities for growth as well as destruction. If the groundwork has been well laid, most developing persons become ready for adulthood.

KEY TERMS

identity (501)
possible selves (501)
false self (502)
identity versus role
 confusion (503)
identity crisis (503)
identity achievement
 (503)

foreclosure (504)
negative identity (504)
identity diffusion (504)
identity moratorium (504)
generation gap (511)
generational stake (511)
parental monitoring (514)
peer pressure (516)

suicidal ideation (521)
parasuicide (522)
cluster suicide (522)
adolescent-limited
    offender (528)

life-course persistent
    offender (528)

KEY QUESTIONS

1. How can false selves help an adolescent find an identity?

2. What is the difference between foreclosure and negative identity?

3. What is the difference between identity diffusion and moratorium?

4. In what ways can a society or culture help adolescents form their identities?

5. Why is identity formation especially difficult for minority-group adolescents?

6. Which parenting characteristics are most helpful to adolescents? Why?

7. What factors correlate with parent-adolescent conflict? Why does each lead to disruption?

8. How do peer and friendship groups aid teenagers?

9. What is peer pressure, and how does it affect most adolescents' behavior?

10. What sex differences in suicidal ideation, parasuicide, and completed suicide exist? What might explain these differences?

11. What are the signs that an adolescent might attempt suicide?

12. What do the incidence and prevalence of deliquency tell us about preventing serious crime?

13. How and why do public attitudes about adolescent suicide and adolescent crime differ from the facts?

14. *In Your Experience* Is adolescence difficult, dangerous, and self-destructive? Why or why not?

CRITICAL THINKING EXERCISE

by Richard O. Straub

Take your study of Chapter 16 a step further by working on this pattern-recognition exercise:*

Five identity statuses are described and compared in this chapter—achievement, foreclosure, diffusion, moratorium, and negative. To clarify your understanding of them, and to help you relate them to real life, consider the five cases below. Your job is to decide the identity status of each case and then to explain your reasoning.

1. *Rudy.* Rudy has switched college majors so often that it will take him 6 years to graduate. Since his parents have point-

edly objected to paying the expenses for tuition and room and board, Rudy has cheerfully taken on a variety of jobs, ranging from bartender to shoe salesman. He likes work that allows him time to think and be alone; his few friends are much the same way. Rudy's grades are generally high, though his record is marred by several "incompletes." He has had one very satisfying intimate relationship and is searching rather anxiously for another.

2. *Melissa.* Melissa's parents are both physicians. In college she majored in French and spent a semester in France studying art and culture. Upon graduation she surprised her parents by announcing that she had applied to medical school. A close relationship with a hospice nurse and a summer job as a hospital volunteer helped her arrive at the decision.

3. *Lynn.* Lynn's mother is a professor of women's studies who is deeply involved in feminist issues. Lynn very much admires her mother, a strong woman who, as a single parent, struggled to provide for her daughter while establishing her own career. Lynn believes that she, too, will be a strong and independent woman. She avoids people (especially men) who either don't see her in that light or try to bring out her feminine nature. She certainly steers clear of her paternal grandmother, who (although pleasant) is a very disorganized and "artsy" person. Lynn's college grades are very high, and her course selections reflect an unwavering interest in psychology, politics, and women's studies.

4. *Daniel.* Daniel is a freshman at a college near his old high school. He comes home nearly every weekend but does not enjoy himself once he's there. He avoids talking to his parents or old high school friends, preferring to "surf the web" on the computer in his room. Periodically, he engages in impulsive shopping; after these sprees he comes home and talks excitedly about the latest electronic gadget he's acquired. He gets angry if his parents ask what he considers to be foolish questions, and angrier still if they patronize him. Daniel is enrolled in courses he has been told are easy, and he does not have strong feelings about his studies or his grades.

5. *Casey.* Casey's grandparents, who raised him from childhood, grew up during the Depression. They are extremely conservative in money matters, politics, and social values. They have always had very high goals for Casey, insisting that he get all A's in school, study several languages, and attend an Ivy League law school. Casey, who considers his grandparents' goals for him to be both unattainable and unappealing, is becoming something of a free spirit. He has started spending freely, squandering his savings on gambling and lavish gifts for his friends. He has also become a leader in a left-wing political group at his school. He no longer plans to become an attorney and may not even finish college.

Check your answers by comparing them to the sample answers in Appendix B.

*Adapted from Straub (1998), *Instructor's Resources to Accompany the Developing Person Through the Life Span*, pp. 527, 531–532.

BIOSOCIAL

Physical Growth

Sometime between the ages of 8 and 14, puberty begins with increases in various hormones that trigger a host of changes. Within a year of the hormonal increases, the first perceptible physical changes appear—enlargement of the girl's breasts and the boy's testes. About a year later, a growth spurt begins, when boys and girls gain in height, weight, and musculature.

Sexual Maturation

Toward the end of puberty, menarche in girls and ejaculation in boys signal reproductive potential. On the whole, males become taller than females and develop deeper voices and characteristic patterns of facial and body hair. Females become wider at the hips; breast development continues for several years. The growing bodies of adolescents trigger much stress and confusion, especially if changes occur much earlier or later than one's peers, or if the family and culture are not supportive. Some teenagers, expecially girls, become vulnerable to sexual abuse and/or unhealthy dieting. Others, especially boys, use drugs at an age or dose that is harmful to healthy growth.

COGNITIVE

Adolescent Thinking

Adolescent thought can deal with the possible as well as the actual, thanks to a newly emerging ability to think hypothetically, to reason deductively, and to explain theoretically. At the same time, adolescent egocentrism, along with feelings of uniqueness and invincibility, can cloud teenagers' judgment, as well as make them extraordinarily self-absorbed.

Education

The specific intellectual advancement of each teenager depends greatly on education. Each culture and each school emphasizes different subjects, values, and modes of thinking, a variation that makes some adolescents much more sophisticated in their thoughts and behavior than others. The interplay between education and egocentrism helps explain why some teenagers are at greater risk for STDs, AIDS, and pregnancy than others. Newer forms of sex education that take into account the teenagers' need for social interaction and practical experience have successfully reduced adolescent pregnancy and increased condom use.

PSYCHOSOCIAL

Identity

One of the major goals of adolescence is self-understanding and then identity achievement. Achieving identity can be affected by personal factors—including relationships with family and peers—the nature of the society, and the economic and political circumstances of the times. Identity achievement can be especially problematic for members of a minority group in a multiethnic society.

Peers and Parents

The peer group becomes increasingly important in fostering independence and interaction, particularly with members of the other sex. Parents and young adolescents are often at odds over issues centering on the child's increased assertiveness or lack of self-discipline. These difficulties usually diminish as teenagers become more mature and parents allow more autonomy. Depression and thoughts about suicide are common in adolescence, especially among girls, although boys are more likely to actually complete a suicide. Despite common beliefs to the contrary, teenagers are less likely to commit suicide or, for that matter, abuse drugs or give birth, than young adults are. While most adolescents break the law in some way, the minority who commit serious crimes often come from a troubled family and a debilitating social context. More supportive communities can moderate these problems, and a responsive and aware pattern of child-rearing can prevent serious delinquency.

Appendix A

The following information is designed to give you guidelines and facts to supplement your learning of the main part of the text. The first part of this appendix details some pointers on how to go about gathering more information about child development. The second part of this appendix provides charts and graphs on a wide variety of topics that can be useful, whether it is in your role as a concerned parent or as a researcher looking for trends.

LEARNING MORE

There are many ways to deepen your understanding of human development, including thinking about your own life and watching the children around you with careful attention to details of expression and behavior. Indeed, such thoughts may become second nature, as you realize how much there is to learn through reflection and observation. But we also urge more systematic research, and further book learning, as we will now explain.

Library Research

To read more about a particular topic, you need to focus on readings that are current and scholarly. For instance, if something in a popular magazine or newspaper catches your attention, remember that the writer may have sensationalized, exaggerated, or biased the reporting. You might first check what this text says about the topic, and then look at the references cited.

This is often a good strategy to begin effective library research. Start with current published material and then find material from the bibliographies that can fill you in on the background and historical context of many issues.

In addition, there are two collections of abstracts that review current articles from a variety of developmental journals:

Psychscan: Developmental Psychology is published four times a year by the American Psychological Association and includes abstracts of articles from almost 40 scholarly journals, from *Adolescence* to *Psychological Review*. Volume 20 covers the year 2000.

Child Development Abstracts and Bibliography is published three times a year by the Society for Research in Child Development and is organized topically by author. Included are not only journal articles in biology, cognition, education, personality, and theory, but also reviews of major books in the field. Volume 74 covers the year 2000. The online address is www.scrd.org.

To find the most current research, even before it appears in these abstracts, look at the most recent issues of the many research journals. The two that cover all three domains (biosocial, cognitive, and psychosocial) are *Developmental Psychology*, published by the American Psychological

Association (750 First St., NE, Washington, DC 20002), and *Child Development,* published by Blackwell Publishers for the Society for Research in Child Development. (Blackwell Publishers: 350 Main St., Malden, MA 02138; Society for Research in Child Development: University of Michigan, 505 East Huron St., Suite 301, Ann Arbor, MI 48104-1522.)

These suggestions are only a start. All of us who are professors hope you begin with one topic and soon lose track of time and subject, finding your interest drawn from one journal or book to another.

Learning Through Observation

Much can be learned by becoming more systematic in your observations of the children around you. One way to begin is to collect ten observations of different children, in differing contexts, during the semester. Each profile should be approximately one page and should cover the following four items.

1. *Describe the physical and social context.* You will want to describe where you are, what day and time it is, and how many people you are observing. The weather and age and gender of those who are being observed might also be relevant. For example

    Neighborhood playground on (street), at about 4 P.M. on (day, date), thirty children and ten adults present.
    OR
    Supermarket at (location) on Saturday morning (day, date), about 20 shoppers present.

2. *Describe the specific child who is the focus of your attention.* Estimate age, gender, and so on of the target child and anyone else who interacts with the child. Do not ask the age of the child until after the observation, if at all. Your goal is to conduct a naturalistic observation that is unobtrusive. For example

    Boy, about 7 years old, playing with four other boys, who seem a year or two older. All are dressed warmly (it is a cold day) in similar clothes.
    OR
    Girl, about 18 months old, in supermarket cart pushed by woman, about 30 years old. The cart is half full of groceries.

3. *Write down everything that the child does or says in three minutes.* (Use a watch with a second hand.) Record gestures, facial expressions, movements, and words. Accurate reporting is the goal, and three minutes becomes a surprisingly long time if you write down everything. For example

    Child runs away about 20 feet, returns, and says, "Try to catch me." Two boys look at him, but they do not move. Boy frowns. He runs away and comes back in ten seconds, stands about four feet away from the boys, and says, "Anyone want to play tag?" [And so on.]
    OR
    Child points to a package of Frosted Flakes cereal and makes a noise. (I could not hear if it was a word.) Mother says nothing and pushes the cart past the cereal. Child makes a whining noise, looks at the cereal, and kicks her left foot. Mother puts pacifier in child's mouth. [And so on.]

4. *Interpret what you just observed.* Is the child's behavior typical of children that age? Is the reaction of others helpful or not helpful? What values are being encouraged, and what skills are being mastered? What could have happened differently? This section is your opinion, but it must be based on the particulars you have just observed and on your knowledge of child development, ideally with specific reference to concepts (e.g. the first may be a rejected child, the second may be neglect of early language).

Structuring a Case Study

A case study is more elaborate and detailed than the observation report just described. You need to select one child (ask your instructor if family members can be used) and secure permission from the caregiver and, if the child is old enough, the child him- or herself. Explain that you are not going to report the name of the child, that the material is for your class, that the child or caregiver can stop the project at any time, and that they would be doing you a big favor in helping you learn about child development. Most people are quite happy to help in your education, if you explain this properly.

First, collect the information for your paper by using all the research methods you have learned. See a summary of these methods below.

1. *Naturalistic observation.* Ask the caregiver when the child is likely to be awake and active and observe the child for an hour during this time. Try to be as unobtrusive as possible: you are not there to play with, or care for, the child. If the child wants to play, explain that you must sit and write for now and that you will play later.

    Write down, minute by minute, everything the child does and that others do with the child. Try to be objective, focusing on behavior rather than interpretation. Thus, instead of writing "Jennifer was delighted when her father came home, and he dotes on her," you should write "5:33: Her father opened the door, Jennifer looked up, smiled, said 'dada,' and ran to him. He bent down, stretched out his arms, picked her up, and said 'How's my little angel?' 5:34: He put her on his shoulders, and she said 'Getty up, horsey.'"

After your observation, summarize the data in two ways: (1) Note the percentage of time spent in various activities. For instance, "Playing alone, 15 percent; playing with brother, 20 percent; crying, 3 percent." (2) Note the frequency of various behaviors: "Asked adult for something five times; adult granted request four times. Aggressive acts (punch, kick, etc.) directed at brother, 2; aggressive acts initiated by brother, 6." Making notations like these will help you evaluate and quantify your observations. Also, note any circumstances that might have made your observation atypical (e.g., "Jenny's mother said she hasn't been herself since she had the flu a week ago," or "Jenny kept trying to take my pen, so it was hard to write").

Note: Remember that a percentage can be found by dividing the total number of minutes spent on a specific activity by the total number of minutes you spent observing. For example, if, during your 45-minute observation, the child played by herself for periods of 2 minutes, 4 minutes, and 5 minutes, "playing alone" would total 11 minutes. Dividing 11 by 45 yields .244; thus the child spent 24 percent of the time playing alone.

2. *Informal interaction.* Interact with the child for at least half an hour. Your goal is to observe the child's personality and abilities in a relaxed setting. The particular activities you engage in will depend on the child's age and character. Most children enjoy playing games, reading books, drawing, and talking. Asking a younger child to show you his or her room and favorite toys is a good way to break the ice; asking an older child to show you the neighborhood can provide insights.

3. *Interview adults responsible for the child's care.* Keep these interviews loose and open-ended. Your goals are to learn (1) the child's history, especially any illnesses, stresses, or problems that might affect development; (2) the child's daily routine, including play patterns; (3) current problems that might affect the child; (4) a description of the child's character and personality, including special strengths and weaknesses.

You are just as interested in adult values and attitudes as in the facts; therefore, you might concentrate on conversing during the interview, perhaps writing down a few words. Then write down all you remember as soon as the interview has been completed.

4. *Testing the child.* Assess the child's perceptual, motor, language, and intellectual abilities by using specific test items you have planned in advance. The actual items you use will depend on the age of the child. For instance, you would test object permanence in an infant between 6 and 24 months old; you would test conservation in a child between 3 and 9 years old. Likewise, testing language abilities might involve babbling with an infant, counting words per sentence with a preschooler, and asking a school-age child to make up a story.

Second, write the report, using the following steps.

1. Begin by reporting relevant background information, including the child's birth date and sex, age and sex of siblings, economic and ethnic background of the family, and the educational and marital status of the parents.

2. Describe the child's biosocial, cognitive, and psychosocial development, citing supporting data from your research to substantiate any conclusions you have reached. Do *not* simply transcribe your interview, test, or observation data, although you can attach your notes as an appendix, if you wish.

3. Predict the child's development in the next year, the next five years, and the next ten years. List the strengths in the child, the family, and the community that you think will foster optimal development. Also note whatever potential problems you see (either in the child's current behavior or in the family and community support system) that may lead to future difficulties for the child. Include discussion of the reasons, either methodological or theoretical, that your predictions may not be completely accurate.

Finally, show your report to another classmate (your instructor may assign you to a peer mentor) and ask if you have been clear in your description and predictions. Discuss the child with your classmate to see if you should add more details to your report. Your revised case study should be typed and given to your professor who will evaluate it. If you wish, send Professor Berger a copy at Worth Publishers, 41 Madison Avenue, 36th floor, New York, NY 10010.

CHARTS AND GRAPHS

Often, examining specific data is useful, even fascinating, to developmental researchers. The particular numbers reveal trends and nuances not apparent from a more general view. For instance, many people mistakenly believe that the incidence of Down syndrome babies rises sharply for mothers over 35, or that even the tiniest newborns usually survive. With each chart in the following section you will probably see information not generally known.

A-1 Incidence of Down Syndrome— A Month-by-Month Chart

The odds of any given fetus, at the end of the first trimester, having three chromosomes at the 21st site (trisomy 21) and thus having Down syndrome is shown in the column 10 weeks. Every year of maternal age increases the incidence of trisomy 21. You can also see that, as pregnancy continues, more Down syndrome fetuses are aborted, either spontaneously or by choice, with the number of Down syndrome infants born alive being only half the number who survived the first trimester. Although obviously the least risk is at age 20 (younger is even better), there is some comfort for the older mother. There is no year when the odds suddenly increase (age 35 is an arbitrary cut-off), and even at age 44, less than 4% of all newborns have Down syndrome. Other chromosomal abnormalities in fetuses also increase with mother's age, but the rate of spontaneous abortion is much higher, so births of babies with chromosomal defects is not the norm, even to women over age 40.

Trisomy 21: Estimated Risk by Maternal Age and Gestation

Age (yrs)		Gestation (weeks)			
		10	25	35	Births
20	1:	804	1294	1464	1527
21	1:	793	1277	1445	1507
22	1:	780	1256	1421	1482
23	1:	762	1227	1389	1448
24	1:	740	1191	1348	1406
25	1:	712	1146	1297	1352
26	1:	677	1090	1233	1286
27	1:	635	1022	1157	1206
28	1:	586	943	1068	1113
29	1:	531	855	967	1008
30	1:	471	758	858	895
31	1:	409	658	745	776
32	1:	347	559	632	659
33	1:	288	464	525	547
34	1:	235	378	427	446
35	1:	187	302	342	356
36	1:	148	238	269	280
37	1:	115	185	209	218
38	1:	88	142	160	167
39	1:	67	108	122	128
40	1:	51	82	93	97
41	1:	38	62	70	73
42	1:	29	46	52	55
43	1:	21	35	39	41
44	1:	16	26	29	30

Source: Snijders & Nicolaides.

A-2 Birthweight and Mortality, United States, 1995

Note that, by far, the highest mortality is for those infants under 500 grams (that's 17 ounces, which is slightly more than a pound). Eighty-nine percent of those that live for a few hours (this does not include those who die during birth) die during the neonatal period, which is the first 28 days. Eighty-seven of the 635 tiny survivors in 1995 died between one month and one year. This category of LBW newborns has not benefited from advances in medical care between 1985–1995. Even with the best care, they are simply too immature to survive. By contrast, 1000-gram infants are twice as likely to live as they were ten years ago.

	Live births	Infant deaths (first year)	Neonatal deaths (first 28 days)	Postneonatal deaths (day 29–365)	Infant mortality rate*	Percent decrease in mortality 1985–95
Less than 500 grams	5,703	5,155	5,068	87	903.9	− 1.9
500–749 grams	9,998	5,280	4,674	606	528.1	−31.0
750–999 grams	10,816	1,970	1,516	453	182.1	−55.2
1,000–1,249 grams	12,242	1,047	744	303	85.5	−55.8
1,250–1,499 grams	14,267	779	559	220	54.6	−49.7
1,500–1,999 grams	55,342	1,835	1,164	672	33.2	−39.4
2,000–2,499 grams	177,608	2,406	1,222	1,183	13.5	−35.0
2,500–2,999 grams	640,891	3,484	1,419	2,064	5.4	−30.3
3,000–3,499 grams	1,438,889	4,131	1,389	2,742	2.9	−33.3
3,500–3,999 grams	1,129,470	2,272	770	1,502	2.0	−34.5
4,000–4,499 grams	339,910	618	241	376	1.8	−35.7
4,500–4,999 grams	56,309	122	46	76	2.2	−43.2
5,000 grams or more	6,466	54	36	18	8.4	−42.7

*Rate is per 1,000 live births.
Source: Monthly Vital Statistics Report, 1998.

A-3 Recommended Immunization Chart

Recommended Childhood Immunization Schedule* — United States, January–December 1998

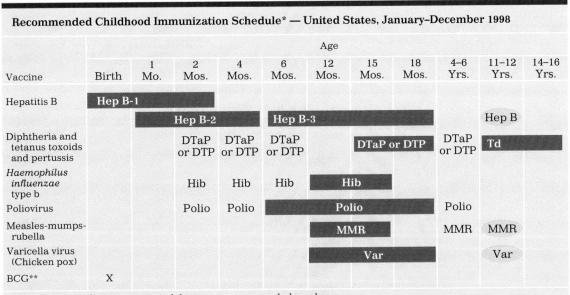

Vaccine	Birth	1 Mo.	2 Mos.	4 Mos.	6 Mos.	12 Mos.	15 Mos.	18 Mos.	4–6 Yrs.	11–12 Yrs.	14–16 Yrs.
Hepatitis B	Hep B-1		Hep B-2		Hep B-3					Hep B	
Diphtheria and tetanus toxoids and pertussis			DTaP or DTP	DTaP or DTP	DTaP or DTP		DTaP or DTP		DTaP or DTP	Td	
Haemophilus influenzae type b			Hib	Hib	Hib	Hib					
Poliovirus			Polio	Polio	Polio				Polio		
Measles-mumps-rubella						MMR			MMR	MMR	
Varicella virus (Chicken pox)						Var				Var	
BCG**	X										

Note: For many diseases, repeated doses are recommended, as shown.
**BCG is highly recommended in most nations. However, it is not required in the United States, because the rate of tuberculosis is low.
Source: *MMWR*, January 16, 1998.

■ Range of acceptable ages for vaccination
⬭ Vaccines to be assessed and administered if necessary

A-4   Height and Weight Gains: First 3 Years

The range of height and weight of American children during their first 3 years. The columns labeled "50th" (the fiftieth percentile) show the average; the columns labeled "90th" (the ninetieth percentile) show the size of children taller and heavier than 90 percent of their contemporaries; and the columns labeled "10th" (the tenth percentile) show the size of children who are taller or heavier than only 10 percent of their peers. Note that girls are slightly shorter and lighter, on the average, than boys.

Also note that these are rough guidelines; a child might differ from these norms and be quite healthy and normal. However, if a particular child shows a discrepancy between height and weight (for instance, at the 90th percentile in height but only the 20th percentile in weight) or is much larger or smaller than most children the same age, a pediatrician should be alerted to see if disease, malnutrition, or genetic abnormality is part of the reason.

Length in Centimeters (and Inches)

AGE	Boys: percentiles			Girls: percentiles		
	10th	50th	90th	10th	50th	90th
Birth	47.5 (18¾)	50.5 (20)	53.5 (21)	46.5 (18¼)	49.9 (19¾)	52.0 (20½)
1 month	51.3 (20¼)	54.6 (21½)	57.7 (22¾)	50.2 (19¾)	53.5 (21)	56.1 (22)
3 months	57.7 (22¾)	61.1 (24)	64.5 (25½)	56.2 (22¼)	59.5 (23½)	62.7 (24¾)
6 months	64.4 (25¼)	67.8 (26¾)	71.3 (28)	62.6 (24¾)	65.9 (26)	69.4 (27¼)
9 months	69.1 (27¼)	72.3 (28½)	75.9 (30)	67.0 (26½)	70.4 (27¾)	74.0 (29¼)
12 months	72.8 (28¾)	76.1 (30)	79.8 (31½)	70.8 (27¾)	74.3 (29¼)	78.0 (30¾)
18 months	78.7 (31)	82.4 (32½)	86.6 (34)	77.2 (30½)	80.9 (31¾)	85.0 (33½)
24 months	83.5 (32¾)	87.6 (34½)	92.2 (36¼)	82.5 (32½)	86.5 (34)	90.8 (35¾)
30 months	88.2 (34¾)	92.3 (36¼)	97.0 (38¼)	87.0 (34¼)	91.3 (36)	95.6 (37¾)
36 months	92.4 (36½)	96.5 (38)	101.4 (40)	91.0 (35¾)	95.6 (37¾)	100.0 (39¼)

Weight in Kilograms (and Pounds)

AGE	Boys: percentiles			Girls: percentiles		
	10th	50th	90th	10th	50th	90th
Birth	2.78 (6¼)	3.27 (7¼)	3.82 (8½)	2.58 (5¾)	3.23 (7)	3.64 (8)
1 month	3.43 (7½)	4.29 (9½)	5.14 (11¼)	3.22 (7)	3.98 (8¾)	4.65 (10¼)
3 months	4.78 (10½)	5.98 (13¼)	7.14 (15¾)	4.47 (9¾)	5.40 (12)	6.39 (14)
6 months	6.61 (14½)	7.85 (17¼)	9.10 (20)	6.12 (13½)	7.21 (16)	8.38 (18½)
9 months	7.95 (17½)	9.18 (20¼)	10.49 (23¼)	7.34 (16¼)	8.56 (18¾)	9.83 (21¾)
12 months	8.84 (19½)	10.15 (22½)	11.54 (25½)	8.19 (18)	9.53 (21)	10.87 (24)
18 months	9.92 (21¾)	11.47 (25¼)	13.05 (28¾)	9.30 (20½)	10.82 (23¾)	12.30 (27)
24 months	10.85 (24)	12.59 (27¾)	14.29 (31½)	10.26 (22½)	11.90 (26¼)	13.57 (30)
30 months	11.80 (26)	13.67 (30¼)	15.47 (34)	11.21 (24¾)	12.93 (28½)	14.81 (32¾)
36 months	12.69 (28)	14.69 (32½)	16.66 (36¾)	12.07 (26½)	13.93 (30¾)	15.97 (35¼)

Source: These data are those of the National Center for Health Statistics (NCHS), Health Resources Administration, DHEW. They were based on studies of The Fels Research Institute, Yellow Springs, Ohio. These data were first made available with the help of William M. Moore, M.D., of Ross Laboratories, who supplied the conversion from metric measurements to approximate inches and pounds. This help is gratefully acknowledged.

A-5 Height and Weight Gains, Boys: Ages 3 to 18

These are rough guidelines; a child might differ from these norms and be quite healthy and normal. However, if a particular child shows a discrepancy between height and weight (for instance, at the 90th percentile in height but only the 20th percentile in weight) or is much larger or smaller than most children the same age, a pediatrician should be alerted to see if disease, malnutrition, or genetic abnormality is part of the reason.

Height in Centimeters (and Inches)
Weight in Kilograms (and Pounds)

	Boys: Percentiles					
	Height			Weight		
Age (Years)	10th	50th	90th	10th	50th	90th
3.0	90.3 (35½)	94.9 (37¼)	100.1 (39½)	12.58 (27¾)	14.62 (32¼)	16.95 (37¼)
4.0	97.3 (38¼)	102.9 (40½)	108.2 (42½)	14.24 (31½)	16.69 (36¾)	19.32 (42½)
5.0	103.7 (40¾)	109.9 (43¼)	115.4 (45½)	15.96 (35¼)	18.67 (41¼)	21.70 (47¾)
6.0	109.6 (43¼)	116.1 (45¾)	121.9 (48)	17.72 (39)	20.69 (45½)	24.31 (53½)
7.0	115.0 (45¼)	121.7 (48)	127.9 (50¼)	19.53 (43)	22.85 (50¼)	27.36 (60¼)
8.0	120.2 (47¼)	127.0 (50)	133.6 (52½)	21.39 (47¼)	25.30 (55¾)	31.06 (68½)
9.0	125.2 (49¼)	132.2 (52)	139.4 (55)	23.33 (51½)	28.13 (62)	35.57 (78½)
10.0	130.1 (51¼)	137.5 (54¼)	145.5 (57¼)	25.52 (56¼)	31.44 (69¼)	40.80 (90)
11.0	135.1 (53¼)	143.33 (56½)	152.1 (60)	28.17 (62)	35.30 (77¾)	46.57 (102¾)
12.0	140.3 (55¼)	149.7 (59)	159.4 (62¾)	31.46 (69¼)	39.78 (87¾)	52.73 (116¼)
13.0	145.8 (57½)	156.5 (61½)	167.0 (65¾)	35.60 (78½)	44.95 (99)	59.12 (130¼)
14.0	151.8 (59¾)	63.1 (64¼)	173.8 (68½)	40.64 (89½)	50.77 (112)	65.57 (144½)
15.0	158.2 (62¼)	169.0 (66½)	178.9 (70½)	46.06 (101½)	56.71 (125)	71.91 (158½)
16.0	163.9 (64½)	173.5 (68¼)	182.4 (71¾)	51.16 (112¾)	62.10 (137)	77.97 (172)
17.0	167.7 (66)	176.2 (69¼)	184.4 (72½)	55.28 (121¾)	66.31 (146¼)	83.58 (184¼)
18.0	168.7 (66½)	176.8 (69½)	185.3 (73)	57.89 (127½)	68.88 (151¾)	88.41 (195)

Source: Data are those of the National Center for Health Statistics, Health Resources Administration, DHEW, collected in its Health Examination Surveys.

A-6 Height and Weight Gains, Girls: Ages 3 to 18

These are rough guidelines; a child might differ from these norms and be quite healthy and normal. However, if a particular child shows a discrepancy between height and weight (for instance, at the 90th percentile in height but only the 20th percentile in weight) or is much larger or smaller than most children the same age, a pediatrician should be alerted to see if disease, malnutrition, or genetic abnormality is part of the reason.

Height in Centimeters (and Inches)
Weight in Kilograms (and Pounds)

	Girls: Percentiles					
	Height			Weight		
Age (Years)	10th	50th	90th	10th	50th	90th
3.0	89.3 (35¼)	94.1 (37)	99.0 (39)	12.26 (27)	14.10 (31)	16.54 (36½)
4.0	96.4 (38)	101.6 (40)	106.6 (42)	13.84 (30½)	15.96 (35¼)	18.93 (41¾)
5.0	102.7 (40½)	108.4 (42¾)	113.8 (44¾)	15.26 (33¾)	17.66 (39)	21.23 (46¾)
6.0	108.4 (42¾)	114.6 (45)	120.8 (47½)	16.72 (36¾)	19.52 (43)	23.89 (52¾)
7.0	113.6 (44¾)	120.6 (47½)	127.6 (50¼)	18.39 (40½)	21.84 (48¼)	27.39 (60½)
8.0	118.7 (46¾)	126.4 (49¾)	134.2 (52¾)	20.45 (45)	24.84 (54¾)	32.04 (70¾)
9.0	123.9 (48¾)	132.2 (52)	140.7 (55½)	22.92 (50½)	28.46 (62¾)	37.60 (83)
10.0	129.5 (51)	138.3 (54½)	147.2 (58)	25.76 (56¾)	32.55 (71¾)	43.70 (96¼)
11.0	135.6 (53½)	144.8 (57)	153.7 (60½)	28.97 (63¾)	36.95 (81½)	49.96 (110¼)
12.0	142.3 (56)	151.5 (59¾)	160.0 (63)	32.53 (71¼)	41.53 (91½)	55.99 (123½)
13.0	148.0 (58¼)	157.1 (61¾)	165.3 (65)	36.35 (80¼)	46.10 (101¾)	61.45 (135½)
14.0	151.5 (59¾)	160.4 (63¼)	168.7 (66½)	40.11 (88½)	50.28 (110¾)	66.04 (145½)
15.0	153.2 (60¼)	161.8 (63¾)	170.5 (67¼)	43.38 (95¾)	53.68 (118¼)	69.64 (153¼)
16.0	154.1 (60¾)	162.4 (64)	171.1 (67¼)	45.78 (101)	55.89 (123¼)	71.68 (158)
17.0	155.1 (61)	163.1 (64¼)	171.2 (67½)	47.04 (103¾)	56.69 (125)	72.38 (159½)
18.0	156.0 (61½)	163.7 (64½)	171.0 (67¼)	47.47 (104¾)	56.62 (124¾)	72.25 (159¼)

A-7 DSM-IV Criteria for Conduct Disorder (CD), Attention-Deficit/Hyperactivity Disorder (ADHD), and Oppositional Defiant Disorder (ODD)

As you'll see below, the specific symptoms for these various disorders overlap. Many other childhood disorders also have some of the same symptoms. Differentiating one problem from another is the main purpose of DSM-IV. That is no easy task, which is one reason the book is now in its fourth major revision and contains 886 pages.

Diagnostic Criteria for Conduct Disorder

A. A repetitive and persistent pattern of behavior in which the basic rights of others or major age-appropriate societal norms or rules are violated, as manifested by the presence of three (or more) of the following criteria in the past 12 months, with at least one criterion present in the past 6 months:

Aggression to people and animals

(1) often bullies, threatens, or intimidates others
(2) often initiates physical fights
(3) has used a weapon that can cause serious physical harm to others (e.g., a bat, brick, broken bottle, knife, gun)
(4) has been physically cruel to people
(5) has been physically cruel to animals
(6) has stolen while confronting a victim (e.g., mugging, purse snatching, extortion, armed robbery)
(7) has forced someone into sexual activity

Destruction of property

(8) has deliberately engaged in fire setting with the intention of causing serious damage
(9) has deliberately destroyed others' property (other than by fire setting)

Deceitfulness or theft

(10) has broken into someone else's house, building, or car
(11) often lies to obtain goods or favors or to avoid obligations (i.e., "cons" others)
(12) has stolen items of nontrivial value without confronting a victim (e.g., shoplifting, but without breaking and entering; forgery)

Serious violations of rules

(13) often stays out at night despite parental prohibitions, beginning before age 13 years
(14) has run away from home overnight at least twice while living in parental or parental surrogate home (or once without returning for a lengthy period)

(15) is often truant from school, beginning before age 13 years

B. The disturbance in behavior causes clinically significant impairment in social, academic, or occupational functioning.

Diagnostic Criteria for Attention-Deficit/Hyperactivity Disorder

A. Either (1) or (2):
(1) six (or more) of the following symptoms of **inattention** have persisted for at least 6 months to a degree that is maladaptive and inconsistent with developmental level:

Inattention
(a) often fails to give close attention to details or makes careless mistakes in schoolwork, work, or other activities
(b) often has difficulty sustaining attention in tasks or play activities
(c) often does not seem to listen when spoken to directly
(d) often does not follow through on instructions and fails to finish schoolwork, chores, or duties in the workplace (not due to oppositional behavior or failure to understand instructions)
(e) often has difficulty organizing tasks and activities
(f) often avoids, dislikes, or is reluctant to engage in tasks that require sustained mental effort (such as schoolwork or homework)
(g) often loses things necessary for tasks or activities (e.g., toys, school assignments, pencils, books, or tools)
(h) is often easily distracted by extraneous stimuli
(i) is often forgetful in daily activities

(2) six (or more) of the following symptoms of **hyperactivity-impulsivity** have persisted for at least 6 months to a degree that is maladaptive and inconsistent with developmental level:

Hyperactivity
(a) often fidgets with hands or feet or squirms in seat
(b) often leaves seat in classroom or in other situations in which remaining seated is expected
(c) often runs about or climbs excessively in situations in which it is inappropriate (in adolescents or adults, may be limited to subjective feelings of restlessness)
(d) often has difficulty playing or engaging in leisure activities quietly
(e) is often "on the go" or often acts as if "driven by a motor"
(f) often talks excessively

Impulsivity

    (g) often blurts out answers before questions have been completed

    (h) often has difficulty awaiting turn

    (i) often interrupts or intrudes on others (e.g., butts into conversations or games)

B.   Some hyperactive-impulsive or inattentive symptoms that caused impairment were present before age 7 years.

C.   Some impairment from the symptoms is present in two or more settings (e.g., at school [or work] and at home).

D.   There must be clear evidence of clinically significant impairment in social, academic, or occupational functioning.

Diagnostic Criteria for 313.81 Oppositional Defiant Disorder

A.   A pattern of negativistic, hostile, and defiant behavior lasting at least 6 months, during which four (or more) of the following are present;

    (1) often loses temper

    (2) often argues with adults

    (3) often actively defies or refuses to comply with adults' requests or rules

    (4) often deliberately annoys people

    (5) often blames others for his or her mistakes or misbehavior

    (6) if often touchy or easily annoyed by others

    (7) is often angry and resentful

    (8) is often spiteful or vindictive

Note: Consider a criterion met only if the behavior occurs more frequently than is typically observed in individuals of comparable age and developmental level.

B.   The disturbance in behavior causes clinically significant impairment in social, academic, or occupational functioning.

A-8   United States Children in Relatives' Care

The number of children living with relatives and no parents grew 59 percent between 1989 and 1996. Notice the big jump between 1993 and 1994. What factors do you think can account for that change? See page 263 for a discussion of kinship care.

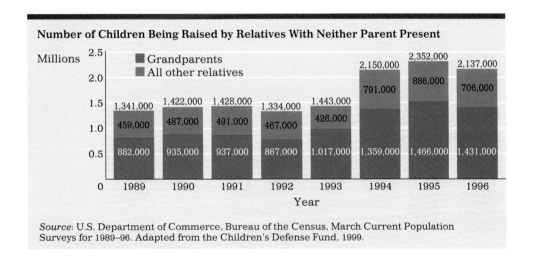

Number of Children Being Raised by Relatives With Neither Parent Present

Source: U.S. Department of Commerce, Bureau of the Census, March Current Population Surveys for 1989–96. Adapted from the Children's Defense Fund, 1999.

A-9 Gap Between Rich and Poor Children in Australia, North America, and Europe

The table shows the after-tax household income of a poor family of four with children and a rich family of four (including food stamps and earned income tax credit). Poor means poorer than 90% and richer than 10% of all households in the country. Rich means richer than 90% and poorer than 10% of households.

Gap Between Rich and Poor Children

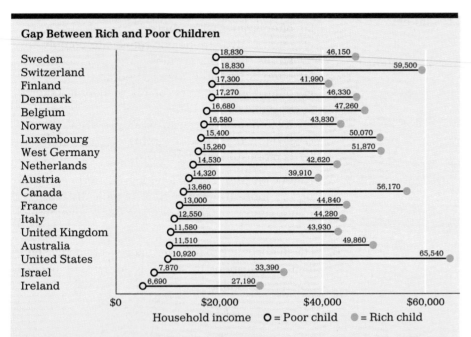

Source: Chart adapted from *The New York Times*, August 14, 1995, citing Luxembourg Income Study data. All figures are in 1991 dollars, with other currencies converted using adjustments for national differences in purchasing power.

A-10 Percentage of Population Under Age 15, by Country

Country or Area	1998 Under 15 Years Old	Country or Area	1998 Under 15 Years Old
World	30.7	Kenya	43.6
Afghanistan	42.9	Korea, North	25.8
Algeria	38.2	Korea, South	22.4
Angola	44.9	Madagascar	44.7
Argentina	27.5	Malaysia	35.7
Australia	21.2	Mali	47.4
Bangladesh	37.4	Mexico	35.6
Belarus	20.0	Morocco	36.4
Belgium	17.3	Mozambique	44.9
Brazil	30.2	Nepal	41.6
Burkina Faso	48.0	Netherlands	18.3
Burma	36.5	Nigeria	44.8
Cambodia	45.4	Pakistan	41.8
Cameroon	45.9	Peru	35.7
Canada	19.8	Philippines	37.6
Chile	28.3	Poland	20.6
China	25.8	Romania	19.0
Colombia	33.2	Russia	19.7
Congo (Kinshasa)	48.2	Saudi Arabia	43.0
Cote d'Ivoire	46.7	Serbia	20.6
Cuba	22.0	South Africa	34.7
Czech Republic	17.2	Spain	15.2
Ecuador	35.9	Sri Lanka	27.6
Egypt	36.1	Sudan	45.4
Ethiopia	46.0	Syria	46.1
France	18.9	Taiwan	22.4
Germany	15.6	Tanzania	44.6
Ghana	42.9	Thailand	24.3
Greece	16.1	Turkey	30.9
Guatemala	42.9	Uganda	51.1
Hungary	17.5	Ukraine	19.0
India	34.5	United Kingdom	19.3
Indonesia	30.8	United States	21.6
Iran	43.3	Uzbekistan	38.0
Iraq	44.1	Venezuela	33.8
Italy	14.4	Vietnam	34.6
Japan	15.2	Yemen	48.1
Kazakhstan	29.1	Zimbabwe	43.8

Covers countries with 10 million or more population in 1998.
Source: U.S. Bureau of the Census, unpublished data from the International Data Base.

A-11 Sexual Behaviors of High School Students

These numbers, as high as they are, are actually lower than what they were in the early 1990s.

Percentage of High School Students Who Reported Engaging in Sexual Behaviors

Category	Ever had sexual intercourse			[1993]† [Total]	First sexual intercourse before age 13			Four or more sex partners during lifetime			[1993]† [Total]	Currently sexually active*			[1993]† [Total]
	Female	Male	Total		Female	Male	Total	Female	Male	Total		Female	Male	Total	
Arkansas	57.5	61.9	**59.7**		5.9	18.7	**12.4**	19.2	29.7	**24.5**		45.4	43.5	**44.4**	
Connecticut	42.3	44.4	**43.5**		3.3	5.9	**4.7**	10.0	13.0	**11.7**		33.4	31.6	**32.7**	
Hawaii	44.8	35.8	**40.3**	[44.3]	4.9	9.1	**7.0**	8.2	9.7	**9.1**	[11.4]	32.6	19.3	**25.8**	[28.7]
Iowa	39.2	46.3	**42.8**		2.0	5.6	**3.8**	13.4	11.9	**12.7**		31.5	34.3	**33.0**	
Kentucky	50.3	56.9	**53.7**		3.4	10.7	**7.2**	12.6	23.1	**18.1**		38.3	40.2	**39.4**	
Maine	50.1	52.9	**51.6**		4.3	9.2	**6.8**	11.9	13.2	**12.5**		38.3	34.0	**36.2**	
Massachusetts	42.4	46.8	**44.7**	[48.7]	4.2	9.8	**7.1**	10.6	14.8	**12.7**	[14.5]	31.8	30.0	**31.0**	[33.4]
Michigan	47.2	50.7	**48.9**		5.0	11.8	**8.3**	14.2	18.5	**16.4**		36.0	32.7	**34.4**	
Mississippi	64.5	74.9	**69.5**	[69.0]	8.5	34.7	**21.2**	19.7	44.1	**31.4**	[28.1]	49.2	55.1	**52.1**	[50.4]
Missouri	52.4	50.4	**51.5**		4.5	11.9	**8.2**	13.1	18.3	**15.8**		41.2	31.9	**36.7**	
Montana	44.4	47.3	**45.9**	[51.0]	4.1	9.0	**6.5**	14.5	16.6	**15.5**	[17.9]	33.1	29.8	**31.5**	[33.7]
Nevada	46.7	47.6	**47.1**	[58.4]	3.9	9.1	**6.5**	12.6	18.0	**15.3**	[23.0]	35.6	31.5	**33.5**	[39.7]
New York	37.0	45.4	**41.2**		3.2	11.7	**7.4**	8.0	17.4	**12.6**		27.9	30.5	**29.2**	
Ohio	47.4	49.9	**48.7**	[55.2]	4.7	14.2	**9.4**	13.0	20.1	**16.6**	[20.6]	35.3	32.9	**34.2**	[39.2]
Rhode Island	42.2	43.1	**42.7**		3.8	7.5	**5.7**	9.8	14.2	**12.1**		33.8	27.9	**31.1**	
South Carolina	59.1	64.0	**61.5**	[65.5]	9.3	22.5	**15.8**	20.1	29.9	**25.0**	[28.3]	43.4	41.0	**42.3**	[46.4]
South Dakota	43.1	39.4	**41.2**	[52.0]	3.9	6.1	**5.0**	14.5	12.9	**13.7**	[16.5]	30.3	26.9	**28.6**	[37.0]
Vermont	NA	NA	**NA**		4.3	9.5	**7.0**	9.8	13.3	**11.6**		31.5	29.6	**30.6**	
West Virginia	53.1	58.0	**55.5**	[63.1]	3.6	11.4	**7.4**	15.1	19.1	**17.0**	[22.4]	40.1	40.7	**40.4**	[45.6]
Wisconsin	38.7	43.7	**41.3**	[47.0]	4.2	6.8	**5.5**	11.4	11.4	**11.4**	[14.3]	30.5	27.0	**28.7**	[32.5]
Wyoming	44.0	45.9	**45.0**		4.3	8.2	**6.2**	16.3	17.5	**16.9**		32.4	28.8	**30.6**	

*Active in 3 months prior to survey
†If available
Source: MMWR, August 14, 1998 (Selected U.S. sites, Youth Risk Behavior Surveys, 1997.)

A-12 Rates of Births to Teenage Mothers, International Comparisons

Note that teens in the United States have far more babies than their counterparts in other developed countries.

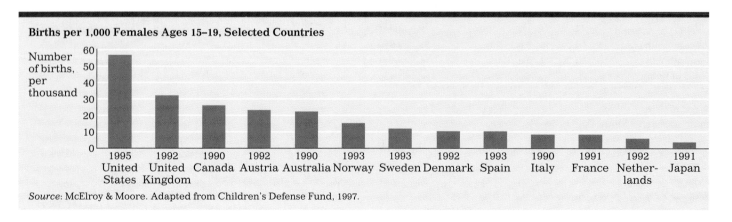

Births per 1,000 Females Ages 15–19, Selected Countries

Source: McElroy & Moore. Adapted from Children's Defense Fund, 1997.

A-13 Homicide Victim and Offender Rates, Adolescents Compared to All Ages

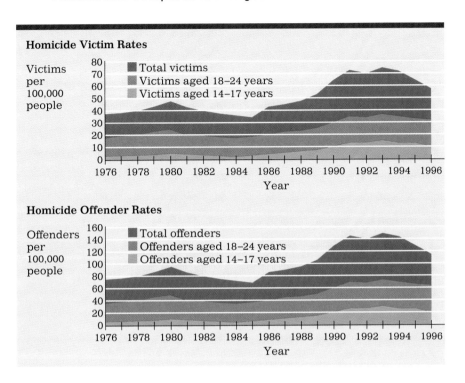

Homicide Victim Rates

Victims per 100,000 people

- Total victims
- Victims aged 18–24 years
- Victims aged 14–17 years

Homicide Offender Rates

Offenders per 100,000 people

- Total offenders
- Offenders aged 18–24 years
- Offenders aged 14–17 years

A-14 Homicide Victim and Offender Rates, by Race and Gender, Ages 14–17

As you can see, teenage boys are almost as often victims as they are violent offenders. Teenage girls are much more often victims than offenders.

Homicide Victimization Rates per 100,000 Population for 14–17-Year-Olds

	Male		Female	
Year	White	Black	White	Black
1976	3.7	24.6	2.2	6.4
1981	4.4	23.6	2.4	6.2
1986	4.2	27.4	2.3	6.6
1991	8.7	73.6	2.6	9.6
1996	8.4	53.3	2.1	8.9

Tabulations based on FBI Supplementary Homicide Reports and Census Bureau, Current Population Reports.

Estimated Homicide Offending Rates per 100,000 Population for 14–17-Year-Olds

	Male		Female	
Year	White	Black	White	Black
1976	10.4	72.4	1.3	10.3
1981	10.9	73.1	1.3	8.6
1986	12.3	72.2	1.1	5.6
1991	21.9	199.1	1.3	12.1
1996	17.4	134.8	1.7	7.8

Tabulations based on FBI Supplementary Homicide Reports and Census Bureau, Current Population Reports. Rates include both known perpetrators and estimated share of unidentified perpetrators.

Appendix B

CHAPTER 1

1. This study tested the hypothesis that breast milk offers a nutritional advantage over formula, resulting in increased intelligence in children, which the researchers defined as performance on an IQ test. The independent variable was the type of food (breast milk or formula) fed to infants in the study. The dependent variable was IQ score, as measured at 8 years of age. The experimental group was the breast-fed group; the control group, the formula-fed group.

2. The hypothesis is tested by research comparing IQ test scores of two groups of children: one that was fed breast milk as prematurely born infants and one that was fed formula. The research seems valid, especially since the researchers attempted to adjust the research for factors other than the independent variable that might have influenced the results, such as the mothers' social and educational status.

3. The researchers argue that the IQ advantage of infants fed breast milk is the result of nutritional factors that promote brain growth and thereby facilitate development of mental abilities. Based on the evidence presented, this explanation does make sense.

4. Because the researchers did not control all possible variables, we can't be sure that breast milk actually causes increased intelligence. The researchers did make an effort to rule out differences in the mothers' social classes and educational levels. However, it is still possible that mothers who nurse their babies are generally more nurturing and produce better-cared-for infants who do better on tests as children. To pinpoint breast milk as the causal factor, researchers might do an experiment using mothers who intend to bottle-feed rather than nurse. Half their infants could be given formula, and half breast milk from a donor.

5. We cannot yet be certain that breast milk is better in this regard, but the evidence suggests that it is not worse. Thus, mothers should be encouraged to breast-feed their babies, and mothers who will not or cannot breast-feed might explore alternative ways to provide breast milk. The nutritional and intellectual advantages of breast milk, if other research confirms them, may be particularly beneficial to premature babies, who are born at a stage of especially rapid brain growth.

CHAPTER 2

1. (a) Psychoanalytic theory might explain the problem of teenage pregnancy as being rooted in unconscious sexual urges or unresolved conflicts from childhood. According to this viewpoint, although they no not realize it, teenagers may have uncontrollable and unconscious drives to have children in order to recover the childhood fantasy of being adored or to get back at their parents for not loving them enough.

(b) A learning theorist would probably explain the teenage birth rate as being the result of powerful environmental forces that condition and reinforce early sexual activity. Through classical conditioning, for example, television programs, advertisements, and other media messages connect sexuality with maturity, success, and happiness. In addition, teens may engage in risky behaviors (such as unprotected sex) because the *immediate* reinforcement associated with these behaviors (physical pleasure, social acceptance, and so on) overshadows the *delayed* consequences (such as having 20 years of increased responsibility).

(c) A cognitive theorist would point out that something in the person's thinking leads him or her to want a baby. For example, a teenager might believe that a real woman or a real man is one who can produce a baby or even that having children gives meaning to life. The disequilibrium produced by being treated as a child might push a teenager into getting one of the signs of adulthood—a baby!

(d) According to sociocultural theory, children follow the social lessons they have learned. Many cultures teach young women that motherhood is their future. For example, almost every little girl receives, as toys, baby dolls to dress and cuddle, as well as dollhouses, toy bottles, fake dishes, and other things with which to "play house" and rehearse motherhood. With these potent cultural messages, no wonder girls grow up wanting their own babies as soon as they can have them.

(e) Epigenetic systems theory emphasizes forces that aid species survival. Perhaps the most powerful of all such forces is the sexual drive—the biological imperative to reproduce. Through most of human history, species survival depended on a high birth rate to replace both adults, who generally died young, and the many children who died from starvation or disease. Survival also required that reproduction begin at the onset of sexual maturity, which was at the time delayed by hunger and sickness until age 16 or so. This combined genetic legacy may now be "instructing" some young women and men to have children soon after they become sexually mature.

2. This answer is, of course, strictly your own.

CHAPTER 3

1. The genes that affect skin color usually interact in an additive fashion. The offspring of a dark-skinned woman (whose parents and grandparents were also dark skinned) and a light-skinned man (whose parents and grandparents were light skinned) would likely be of middling skin tone.

2. This question is a bit trickier. First, you need to realize that the woman must have one recessive gene for red hair (inherited from her red-haired mother), while the man has two recessive red-hair genes. Thus, the chances that their first child will have red hair are two in four. The chances that their first child will have black hair are also two in four.

3. In this example, you must realize not only that both parents have a recessive gene for blue eyes (how else could their child be blue eyed?) but also that heredity "has no memory": the odds of blue eyes for each child born to that couple are one in four, no matter how many previous children already have blue eyes.

4. There is one chance in two that the boy's sister is a carrier and no chance that she will develop the disability herself. Here, you must first realize that the mother is a carrier. Then you need to remember that a woman who is a carrier of an X-linked disorder must have a healthy gene on *one* of her two X chromosomes. Therefore, all her offspring have a 50-50 chance of receiving the defective X chromosome. Because the disorder is recessive, daughters who receive the defective X chromosome will be protected by the normal X from their fathers. Sons will not receive a normal X chromosome from their fathers and therefore will express the disorder if they receive a defective X from their mothers.

CHAPTER 4

1. Your argument might be based on the assumption that a developing fetus has some (or all) of the rights and needs previously reserved for a fully formed, independently breathing newborn. Your strategies might include descriptions of fetuses at that stage—fully formed, brain-functioning, but with a high death rate if they are born without having the proposed surgery.

2. Here your arguments might stress the importance of the woman to her family, especially her husband and her future children, as well as the need for children to have the protection of their own families. You could stress risk analysis: If the mother dies, harm occurs to her and to each member of her family. If the fetus dies, harm occurs to the fetus alone. If she lives and the fetus lives, there is a possibility that she will resent the child who caused her such pain. These are risks that should be decided upon by those most directly involved. Otherwise, a dangerous precedent occurs for a frightening

scenario in which protective-custody laws can cause pregnant women to lose their personal freedom in the face of overzealous doctors, courts, or societal values regarding childbearing.

Conclusion: Critical thinking means truly being able to see both sides of a controversial issue. Ideally, you can argue passionately, and with facts and examples, for both sides.

CHAPTER 5

1. Brain development in early years depends upon both biological maturation and experience. The role of experience is clearly demonstrated by experiments cited in the chapter: Kittens that were temporarily blindfolded for the first several weeks of life never developed normal visual pathways; consequently, their vision was permanently impaired.

The fine-tuning of the visual systems of human babies is much more gradual than for kittens, lasting up to six years. Still, abnormal visual experiences during any of those years can have a damaging effect on sight; the sooner Samantha's disorder is corrected, the smaller the chance of permanent problems.

2. If Samantha's vision is abnormal, it is possible that the rate at which she acquires gross motor skills—such as crawling, creeping, and walking—may lag behind that of other children. This is so because her less-than-optimal vision may distort the perceptual feedback her brain receives as she moves about the environment.

Samantha's fine motor skills may also suffer. For example, as a result of her faulty vision she may find it difficult to learn to coordinate her arm and hand muscles as she reaches out to grasp toys and other small objects. Her ability to "track" moving objects may also be slow to develop.

3. Scientists' understanding of the role of early experiences in cognitive and social development is far from complete. However, without the surgery Samantha may, for example, be slower to learn about color, form, size, and other visual concepts, since her vision is distorted. Distorted vision may also slow down her ability to learn from her visual surroundings, or even to guide her efforts to reach, climb, and run. In the case that her cognitive and motor skills lag behind other children, she may tend to withdraw socially from them. If her visual, cognitive, and motor-skill development do not improve, the impact on social development can become more severe as Samantha gets older and social interaction becomes more important.

Overall, you can reassure Samantha's parents that her brain at 6 months is sufficiently flexible that surgery and even separation from parents will be much less traumatic than they will be a year later. Moreover, most modern hospitals control infant pain very well, and allow parents to be with the child every moment.

4. Nature allows experience to influence development because that allows humans to be more flexible and adaptive. It is that quality that has allowed humans to survive and multiply in many climates and habitats—unlike other species, who are much more limited by their biological destiny.

CHAPTER 6

1. This example implies *learning*. Juwan's uttering of "ma" is reinforced each time by the appearance of his mother, who probably brings him a bottle or a toy or perhaps will hold him for a while. He soon learns the benefits of saying "ma," and he practices it diligently.

2. This example implies *biology* mainly, but perhaps some *learning* as well. The fact that Melissa correctly applies this basic rule of grammar in her first sentences—sentences that she probably never heard from her parents—suggests that she has an inborn facility for acquiring language. However, she must have learned the proper word order by hearing her parents speak short sentences, with the usual noun-verb structure.

3. This example implies *biology*. Hearing infants start to babble verbally at about seven months of age. The fact that deaf children begin manual babbling at approximately the same age implies that at least the babbling stage of language acquisition is a product of brain maturation.

4. This example involves the *interaction* of biology and learning. When Michelle was younger, she had the biologically based ability to distinguish and mimic the sounds of all languages. But as she grew and concentrated on learning French and English, she lost the ability to hear some of the nuances of other languages (as she "learned" that she would not need that ability).

CHAPTER 7

1. Because a single sample of subjects was followed and retested over a period of time, this study is an example of the longitudinal research design. Because the researchers did not directly manipulate an independent variable or employ separate groups of subjects in order to control extraneous variables, the design was correlational rather than experimental. Another feature of the design was naturalistic observation of the children by parents and teachers through the use of behavior checklists. Given the purpose of the study—to uncover aspects of childhood temperament that predict later behavior problems—the research design seems appropriate.

2. Because the evidence is correlational, not based on experimental data, we can't be sure that certain temperamental styles in young children always mature into certain behavior disorders later in life. Although the research seems valid, it makes no attempt to rule out factors other than temperament that might have caused the behavior disorders.

3. One possible alternative explanation is that early-childhood behavioral styles and later behavior problems are, in fact, separate phenomena, both triggered by some aspect of the child's upbringing. Much could have happened before age 3 to explain the seeming cause-and-effect correlation. Another alternative explanation is that temperamental differences cause different children to evoke different responses from others, as well as to react differently to similar environmental experiences. The cumulative effect of this process may be the appearance of certain behavior disorders in some individuals.

CHAPTER 8

The most significant aspect of biosocial development during the play years is the continued maturation of the nervous system and the refinement of the visual, muscular, and cognitive skills that will be necessary for children to function in school. Appropriate toys for 2- to 6-year-old children would therefore not only stimulate the senses but encourage coordination of several senses, help master new gross motor, fine motor, or intellectual skills and provide for healthy physical exercise. Toys that encourage social play (such as some kind of ball) are also good, as long as the designer considers the limited social skills of the child.

Every toy must be safe for a curious child: there must be no pieces small enough to choke on and nothing that might pinch, poke, or bruise the child or a playmate.

CHAPTER 9

1. Though you know it's not possible, you feel as if you caused your relative's death. This is an example of *egocentrism*—contemplating the world exclusively from your own personal perspective.

2. Your susceptibility to deceptive packaging is an example of a failure in *conservation*, the idea that the amount of a substance present is unaffected by changes in its shape or placement.

3. Because your analysis of your friend's circumstances tends to focus on one aspect of her situation to the exclusion of all others, this is an example of *centration*. You also are thinking primarily of the appearance of wealth.

4. Your thinking is *static*, not changing. This makes it difficult for you to reverse your earlier conclusion.

CHAPTER 10

1. *Argument supported:* Cultural learning, because the social and cultural environment in which a child develops does create stereotypes regarding "gender-appropriate" and "gender-inappropriate" occupations, and children tend to aspire to "appropriate" occupations.

Counterargument: Biological differences in girls and boys create differences in abilities and interests, which can influence their choices of occupations. Here, boys' proven ability with spatial representation might lead to their greater choice of these three occupations.

2. *Argument supported:* Cultural learning, here perhaps mostly via observation, plus reinforcement by parents and teachers of "gender-appropriate" behavior.

Counterargument: If gender differences involving play emerge at a young age, before children have a chance to be influenced by learning, those differences may well be—at least partly—biological in nature.

3. *Argument supported:* Biological. If gender distinctions are all learned, children would almost certainly be socialized into adopting the gender roles modeled by their parents. But this

evidence says they don't adopt those roles, so some other, nonenvironmental, variable is a factor in gender development.

Counterargument: The role of the environment cannot be ruled out in this example. Gender roles are not exclusively the individual parent's choice. Such roles are strongly endorsed by the culture, and a child may mirror whatever gender distinctions the culture endorses. Children will notice, for example, that most of their teachers are women while most political leaders are men, and they will take those roles in their play.

CHAPTER 11

Question: How many hours of television does Celine watch each day?

Reason: Excessive TV viewing promotes a lower level of activity and a lowered metabolic state, both of which mean that Celine is burning fewer calories than she would, say, while running and playing outdoors. Celine's television-viewing habit may also encourage her to consume more calories in the form of snack foods.

Recommendation: If Celine does spend much time watching TV, she should be encouraged to reduce her TV time and substitute some sort of physical activity.

Question: Are Celine's biological parents obese?

Reason: Research on adopted children shows that heredity is at least as strong as environment in predisposing a person toward being overweight. Body type, height, bone structure, and individual differences in metabolic rate and activity level are all strongly influenced by heredity.

Recommendation: Knowing Celine's genetic inheritance would be of help in setting a goal for her weight-reduction program.

Question: Does Celine get much exercise? Do her adoptive parents exercise regularly?

Reason: Especially during childhood, inactive people burn fewer calories and are more likely to be overweight than are active people. The best way for children to lose weight is to increase their physical activity.

Recommendation: If Celine is relatively inactive, her parents should help her find exercises to do in which her size would not be a disadvantage, and they should exercise with her.

Question: Is the family diet low fat, and are family attitudes toward food healthy?

Reason: By equating love with food, some parents inadvertently encourage overeating, a problem that might be particularly likely if the parents are seeking to establish a loving relationship with their newly adopted child. Diets high in fat and sugar are also more likely to lead to excess weight gain than are diets that emphasize fruits, vegetables, and grains. Parents may unknowingly encourage unhealthy attitudes toward food by giving sweets to their children as rewards or by taking satisfaction when they eat unnecessarily large portions.

Recommendation: The members of Celine's family should change their eating habits, cutting down on high-fat foods, and they should examine their attitudes toward food.

Question: When did Celine's weight problem begin?

Reason: It is possible that the onset of Celine's obesity coincided with some traumatic experience—such as being adopted or being abused at her earlier home—that created a sense of loss or diminished self-image and a corresponding need for an alternative source of gratification, such as food.

Recommendation: If so, Celine will need emotional support, along with other help, in losing weight.

Question: Is Celine's teacher aware of her self-image problem?

Reason: Teachers can set the tone in a class, allowing or even endorsing teasing or, alternatively, establishing an atmosphere of mutual respect that helps each child feel appreciated.

Recommendation: Celine's parents might talk to her teacher, explaining the need for special support for Celine.

CHAPTER 12

1. Examples of evidence supporting the argument that the school year should be lengthened:

   - Compared with students in Pacific Rim nations, American students tend to score lower on standardized achievement tests, especially in math and science. Since one obvious and dramatic educational difference is length of school year, the United States should try that strategy.
   - Because of differences in the length of the school year, the length of the school day, and time on task in the classroom, there is a wide gap in available learning time between Pacific Rim and American schoolchildren.
   - Children follow the lead of their parents and society. If they see that schoolwork and homework are valued as the most important activities of their lives, they will study harder and learn more.

2. Examples of evidence challenging the argument that the school year should be lengthened:

   - The number of days in school is a superficial indicator. More important is how children spend their classroom time. American children more frequently work alone in class and are engaged in nonacademic activities. Teachers in Japan and China tend to emphasize group instruction, with every child actively participating and with every teacher following a process designed to motivate as well as educate.
   - Education is more of a national priority in Pacific Rim countries than it is in the United States. Asian teachers are held in higher esteem and are better paid and trained. By contrast, if American teachers worked longer hours, they would actually lose esteem and have less time for training.

■ Compared with American parents, Japanese and Chinese parents have higher academic expectations for their children and tend to be more involved in their children's success. Unless parents in the United States develop such expectations and involvement, more school time might actually make American parents less involved in their children's lives.

3. Answers will vary.

CHAPTER 13

Preconventional level: Moral reasoning at this level is self-centered and emphasizes obtaining rewards and avoiding punishments.

Blake: "There's no way I'll be caught. I don't think the teacher even knows there are term papers on the web."

Jennifer: "If I turn Blake in, he'll find some way to get back at me."

Sharon: "If the term papers are graded on a curve, Blake's unearned A will affect my class standing."

Conventional level: Moral reasoning at this level focuses on pleasing other people and obeying the laws and conventions set down by society.

Blake: "Who hasn't cheated at least once in school? If everyone cheats, what's the big deal? My father will be happy if my grades go up."

Jennifer: "If I turn Blake in, everyone will hate me for being a snitch."

Sharon: "Blake broke the rules set by the history department; he should pay the consequences."

Postconventional level: Moral reasoning at this level emphasizes rules of society that are established by mutual agreement, or the principles that are universal (not only in one culture).

Blake: "I'm going to be a computer programmer, not a historian. This assignment has nothing to do with computers. Besides, I've heard that the teacher doesn't even read these papers, so its not fair for him to demand work of us when he doesn't do the work himself."

Jennifer: "My guiding principle is to be true to myself and let others live their own lives. What Blake does is not my business; my only concern is whether I do a good job on the paper."

Sharon: "If people stand by while others cheat, the meaning of grades and an education will be diminished. Integrity is everyone's concern."

CHAPTER 15

1. A viable hypothesis for this experiment would be that the separation of students into tracks based on achievement scores leads to gains in academic performance.

2. The independent variable in an experiment is the factor that is manipulated by the researcher to test the hypothesis. In this case, it would be assigning students to tracks.

3. You would likely use standardized tests to track about half the volunteers and leave the other half untracked. Alternatively, you could randomly assign half of them to the proper track and the other half to a track higher or lower (again randomly) than their scores indicate.

4. The dependent variable in an experiment is always the one that, according to your hypothesis, might be affected by the independent variable. In this case, academic performance after a year or so of your special assignments seems a good choice.

5. You would test the students, assign them to classes, and then retest them.

6. Ideally, the two groups should differ only in the one independent variable—here, tracking, no tracking, or incorrect tracking. Any other variables that might affect the dependent variable you are measuring—here, academic performance—would need to be controlled. These include student motivation, ability (both the tracked and untracked groups should include a full range of abilities), initial achievement levels, study skills, age, and sex. The results should show whether or not one group (tracked, mistracked high, mistracked low, or not tracked) achieved more than the other.

CHAPTER 16

1. *Rudy.* This is an example of identity moratorium. In the United States, the most obvious place to engage in such a moratorium is college, which is allowing Rudy to sample a variety of academic areas before choosing a career.

2. *Melissa.* This is an example of identity achievement. Melissa is self-directed and thoughtful and has established her own career goals by abandoning some of those of her parents and society and accepting others.

3. *Lynn.* This is an example of foreclosure. You might have felt that Lynn's case falls into the identity-achievement category. However, several aspects of the description point toward foreclosure: (1) Lynn avoids exploring alternatives in her social life (she resists the influences of someone who is very different from her and her mother; she avoids men who might bring out other facets of her personality). (2) Her academic interests are "unvarying." (3) Her interests coincide with those of a much-admired parent.

4. *Daniel.* This is an example of identity diffusion. Daniel apparently has few goals and does not care much about finding an identity.

5. *Casey.* This is negative identity. Casey, who finds the roles his grandparents expect him to fill unappealing, is developing an identity that is the opposite of the one he was expected to adopt.

Glossary

abuse Any action that is harmful (either physically or psychologically) to an individual's well-being. The severity of abuse depends on how much and how often it occurs and on the vulnerability of the victim. (p. 255)

achievement tests Tests designed to measure how much a person has learned in a specific subject area. (p. 388)

acquired immune deficiency syndrome (AIDS) The diseases and infections, many of them fatal, that result from the degradation of the immune system by HIV. (p. 111)

addiction A person's dependence on a drug or a behavior in order to feel physically or psychologically at ease. (p. 458)

additive pattern A common pattern of genetic inheritance in which each gene affecting a specific trait makes an active contribution to that trait. Skin color and height are determined by an additive pattern. (p. 76)

adolescence The period of biological, cognitive, and psychosocial transition from childhood to adulthood, usually lasting a decade or so. (p. 439)

adolescent egocentrism A characteristic of adolescent thinking that sometimes leads young people to focus on themselves to the exclusion of others, believing, for example, that their thoughts, feelings, or experiences are unique. (p. 475)

adolescent-limited offender A juvenile delinquent who is likely to become law-abiding once adulthood is attained. (p. 528)

affordance Each of the various opportunities for perception, action, and interaction that an object or place offers to any individual. (p. 174)

age of viability The age (about 22 weeks after conception) at which a fetus can survive outside the mother's uterus if specialized medical care is available. (p. 104)

aggressive-rejected children Children who are actively rejected by their peer group because of their aggressive, confrontational behavior. (p. 411)

anal stage Freud's second stage of psychosexual development, in which the anus becomes the main source of bodily pleasure, and control of defecation and toilet training are therefore important activities. (p. 217)

androgyny A balance, within an individual, of male and female gender characteristics such that the individual feels comfortable in breaking through gender stereotypes; thus, for example, an androgynous male will feel comfortable being nurturant as well as being assertive. (p. 333)

anorexia nervosa A serious eating disorder in which a person undereats to the point of emaciation and possible starvation. (p. 457)

anoxia A lack of oxygen that, if prolonged, can cause brain damage or death. (p. 128)

antisocial behavior An action, such as hitting, insulting, lying about, or taking from another person, that is intended to harm someone else. (p. 310)

Apgar scale A means of quickly assessing a newborn's body functioning. The baby's color, heart rate, reflexes, muscle tone, and respiratory effort are scored (from 0 to 2) 1 minute and 5 minutes after birth and compared with a standard for healthy babies (a perfect 10). (p. 123)

aptitude tests Tests designed to measure potential, rather than actual, accomplishment. (p. 385)

Asperger syndrome A disorder in which a person masters verbal communication (sometimes very well) but has unusual difficulty with social perceptions and skills. (Also called *high-functioning autism*.) (p. 352)

asthma A disorder characterized by chronic inflammation of the airways. (p. 346)

attachment An enduring emotional connection between people that produces a desire for continual contact as well as feelings of distress during separation. (p. 225)

attention-deficit hyperactivity disorder (ADHD) A behavior problem characterized by excessive activity, an inability to concentrate, and impulsive, sometimes aggressive, behavior. (p. 357)

authoritarian parenting A style of child rearing in which standards for proper behavior are high, misconduct is strictly punished, and parent-child communication is low. (p. 318)

authoritative parenting A style of child rearing in which the parents set limits and provide guidance but are willing to listen to the child's ideas and make compromises. (p. 319)

autism A disorder characterized by an inability or unwillingness to communicate with others, poor social skills, and diminished imagination. (p. 352)

automatization The process by which familiar and well-rehearsed mental activities become routine and automatic. (p. 368)

autonomy versus shame and doubt Erikson's second stage of psychosocial development, in which the toddler struggles for self-control but feels shame and doubt about his or her abilities if it is not achieved. (p. 218)

axon The single nerve fiber that extends from a neuron and transmits impulses from that neuron to the dendrites of other neurons. (p. 143)

babbling The extended repetition of certain syllables, such as "ba, ba, ba," that begins at about 6 or 7 months of age. (p. 195)

baby talk The special form of language that adults use when they talk to babies, with shorter, more emphatic sentences and higher, more melodious pitch. (p. 200)

behavioral teratogens Teratogens that tend to harm the prenatal brain, affecting the future child's intellectual and emotional functioning. (p. 106)

big five The five main clusters of personality, found in adults to be extroversion, agreeableness, conscientiousness, neuroticism, and openness. (p. 221)

bilingual education An approach to teaching a second language that also advances knowledge in the first language. Instruction occurs, side by side, in two languages. (p. 381)

bilingual-bicultural education An approach to teaching a second language that adds preservation of nonnative cultural symbols and strategies (such as in the way teaching occurs) to a bilingual program. (p. 381)

binocular vision The ability to use both eyes together to focus on a single object. (p. 145)

biosocial domain The part of human development that includes physical growth and development as well as the family, community, and cultural factors that affect that growth and development. (p. 2)

blended family A family consisting of two parents, at least one with biological children from another union; thus, at least one adult is a stepparent. Blended families may include children of several prior unions as well as children of the current union. (p. 418)

blind The "state" of researchers who are deliberately kept ignorant of the purpose of the research, or of relevant traits of the research subjects, to avoid biasing their data collection. (p. 22)

body image A person's mental concept of how his or her body appears. (p. 452)

body mass index A measure of obesity determined by dividing weight in kilograms by height squared in meters. (p. 342)

breathing reflex A reflex that ensures an adequate supply of oxygen and the discharge of carbon dioxide by causing the individual to inhale and exhale. (p. 149)

bulimia nervosa An eating disorder in which a person repeatedly overeats and then induces the expulsion of food, either through vomiting or through the abuse of laxatives. (Sometimes called *binge-purge syndrome*.) (p. 457)

bullying aggression Aggressive behavior in the form of an unprovoked physical or verbal attack on another person. (p. 315)

bullying Repeated efforts to inflict harm on a particular child through physical, verbal, or social attacks. (p. 412)

carrier A person who has a gene in his or her genotype that is not evident as part of the phenotype. Carriers can pass such a gene on to their offspring. (p. 76)

case study A research method that focuses on the life history, attitudes, behavior, and emotions of a single individual. (p. 28)

centration The tendency to focus on one way of thinking and perceiving, without acknowledging any alternatives. (p. 272)

cephalo-caudal development Growth and maturation of the human body that progresses from the head downward. This sequence is obvious in prenatal development; it continues throughout childhood. (p. 101)

cerebral palsy A disorder that results from damage to the brain's motor centers, usually as a result of events during or before birth. People with cerebral palsy have difficulty with muscle control, which can affect speech or other body movements. (p. 128)

Cesarean section A means of childbirth in which the fetus is taken from the mother surgically, through an incision that extends from the mother's abdomen through the uterus. (p. 125)

child maltreatment Any intentional harm to anyone under age 18. (p. 255)

childhood sexual abuse Any activity in which an adult uses a child for his or her own sexual stimulation or pleasure—even if the use does not involve physical contact. For purposes of defining sexual abuse, childhood ends between ages 14 and 18, depending on state laws. (p. 454)

children with special needs Children for whom learning new skills and developing friendships are hampered by a psychological or physical disorder (p. 351)

chromosome A carrier of genes; one of forty-six segments of DNA that together contains all human genes. (p. 68)

class inclusion The idea that an object may be classified into more than one group, depending on its properties and how the groups are defined. (p. 374)

classification The process of organizing objects into groups on the basis of some common property; also, the result of that process and the understanding that such a process is possible. (p. 374)

cluster suicide A group of suicides that occur in the same community, school, or time period. (p. 522)

code switching A pragmatic communication skill that involves a person's switching from one form of language, such as dialect or slang, to another. (p.378)

cognitive domain The part of human development that includes all the mental processes through which the individual thinks, learns, and communicates, plus the institutions involved in learning and communicating. (p. 2)

cognitive equilibrium A state of mental balance, in which a person's thoughts and assumptions about the world seem (at least to that person) not to clash with each other or with that person's experiences. (p. 47)

cognitive theory A theory that holds that the way people think and understand the world shapes their perceptions, attitudes, and actions. (p. 45)

cohort A group of people who, because they were born within a few years of each other, experience many of the same historical and social conditions. (p. 9)

concrete operational thought In Piaget's theory, the third period of cognitive development, in which a child can reason logically about concrete events and problems but cannot reason about abstract ideas and possibilities. (p. 372)

conditioning Any learning process that occurs according to the laws of behaviorism or learning theory. This can be classical conditioning, in which one stimulus is associated with another, or operant conditioning, in which a response is gradually learned via reinforcement. (p. 42)

conservation The concept that the total quantity, number, or amount of something is the same (preserved) no matter what the shape or configuration. (p. 273)

contact-maintaining behaviors Behaviors that are intended to keep a person near another person to whom he or she is attached. (p. 226)

control group Research subjects who are comparable to those in the experimental group in every relevant dimension except that they do not experience the special condition or treatment that is the key variable of the experiment. (p. 23)

control processes That part of the information-processing system that regulates the analysis and flow of information, including memory and retrieval strategies, selective attention, and rules or strategies for problem solving. (p. 366)

conventional moral reasoning Kohlberg's term for the second level (stages three and four) of moral thinking, in which the individual considers social standards and laws to be the primary arbiters of moral values. (p. 403)

corpus callosum A network of nerves connecting the left and right hemispheres of the brain. (p. 246)

correlation A relation between two variables such that one is likely (or unlikely) to occur when the other occurs or one is likely to increase (or decrease) in value when the other increases (or decreases). (p. 24)

cortex The outer layer of the brain, about an eighth of an inch thick. This area is involved in the voluntary, cognitive aspects of the mind. (p. 144)

critical period In prenatal development, the time when a particular organ or other body part is most susceptible to teratogenic damage. (p. 108)

cross-modal perception The mental ability to translate (or transfer) information obtained through one sensory mode (say, touch) to another (say, vision). (p. 179)

cross-sectional research A research design in which groups of people, each group different from the others in age but similar to them in other important ways, are studied during the same time period. (p. 29)

cross-sequential research A research design in which groups of people of different ages are studied over time, to distinguish differences related to age from differences related to historical period. (Also called *cohort-sequential research* or *time-sequential research.*) (p. 30)

culture The set of shared values, assumptions, customs, and physical objects that are maintained by a group of people in a specific setting (a society) as a design for living daily life. (p. 12)

deductive reasoning Reasoning from a general hypothesis, through logical steps, to a specific conclusion. (p. 472

deferred imitation The ability to witness, remember, and later copy a particular behavior. (p. 185)

dendrites Nerve fibers that extend from a neuron and receive the impulses transmitted from other neurons via their axons. (p. 143)

dependent variable The variable that is being studied in an experiment. (p. 25)

developmental biodynamics Maturation of the developing person's ability to move through, and with, the environment, by means of crawling, running, grasping, and throwing. (p. 148)

developmental psychopathology A field of psychology that applies the insights from studies of normal development to the study and treatment of childhood disorders, and vice versa. (p. 351)

developmental theory A systematic set of principles and generalizations that explains development, generates hypotheses, and provides a framework for future research. (p. 37)

differential response The idea that child maltreatment reports should be separated into those that require immediate investigation, possibly leading to foster care and legal prosecution, and those requiring supportive measures to encourage better parental care. (p. 260)

differential treatment The practice of responding to individuals on the basis of their own real or presumed characteristics. In families, differential treatment means that the parents give praise, permission, and punishment to each of their children in a distinct way. (p. 321)

dizygotic twins Twins formed when two separate ova were fertilized by two separate sperm at roughly the same time. Such twins share about half their genes, like any other siblings. (p. 71)

dominant-recessive pattern A pattern of genetic inheritance in which one member of a gene pair (referred to as *dominant*) hides the influence of the other *(recessive)* gene. Eye color is determined via a dominant-recessive pattern. (p. 76)

drug abuse The ingestion of a drug to the extent that it impairs the user's well-being. (p. 458)

drug use The ingestion of a drug, regardless of the amount or effect of ingestion. (p. 459)

DSM-IV The fourth edition of the *Diagnostic and Statistical Manual of Mental Disorders,* developed by the American Psychiatric Association, which describes and distinguishes the symptoms of various emotional and behavioral disorders. (p. 352)

dynamic perception Perception that arises from the movement of objects and changes in their positions. (p. 178)

dyscalcula A specific learning disability involving unusual difficulty with math. (p. 356)

dyslexia A specific learning disability involving unusual difficulty with reading. (p. 356)

eclectic perspective Perspective choosing what seem to be the best, or most useful, elements from the various theories, instead of adhering to only a single perspective. (p. 61)

ecological approach A perspective on development that takes into account the various physical and social settings in which human development occurs. (p. 4)

ego-involvement learning An educational strategy that bases academic grades on individual test performance, with students competing against each other. (p. 481)

egocentrism The tendency to perceive events and interpret experiences exclusively from one's own, self-centered, perspective. (p. 272)

Electra complex In the phallic stage of psychosexual development, the female version of the Oedipus complex: girls have sexual feelings for their fathers and accompanying hostility toward their mothers. (p. 329)

electroencephalogram (EEG) A graphic recording of the waves of electrical activity that sweep across the brain's surface. (p. 147)

emergent theories Relatively new comprehensive theories formulated within the past 30 years, that bring together information from many disciplines but are not yet a coherent, comprehensive whole. (p. 38)

emotional regulation The ability to direct or modify one's feelings, particularly feelings of fear, frustration, and anger. Because of brain maturation, emotional regulation becomes more possible during the preschool years. (p. 308)

English as a second language (ESL) An approach to teaching English in which English is the only language of instruction for students who speak many other native languages. (p. 381)

environment All the nongenetic factors that can affect development—everything from the impact of the immediate cell environment on the genes themselves to the broader effects of nutrition, medical care, socioeconomic status, family dynamics, and the economic, political, and cultural contexts. (p. 79)

epigenetic systems theory The developmental theory that emphasizes the genetic origins of behavior but also stresses that genes, over time, are directly and systematically affected by many environmental forces. (p. 55)

ethnic group A collection of people who share certain background characteristics, such as national origin, religion, upbringing, and language, and who, as a result, tend to have similar beliefs, values, and cultural experiences. (p. 14)

ethology The study of behavior as it is related to the evolution and survival of a species. (p. 56)

experiment A research method in which the scientist deliberately causes changes in one variable (called the *independent variable*) and then observes and records the resulting changes in some other variable (called the *dependent variable*). (p. 25)

experimental group Research subjects who experience the special condition or treatment that is the crux of the research. (See also **control group.**) (p. 23)

explicit memory Memory that can be recalled and thus demonstrated verbally, such as in response to a written test or an oral question. (p. 186)

extended family A family that includes other relatives in addition to parents (or a parent) and their children. Extended families usually include grandparents and may include aunts, uncles, and cousins as well. (p. 418)

failure-to-thrive Undernutrition; usually applied to a child who lives in an adequately nourished community but is not exhibiting normal childhood weight gain. (p. 167)

false self A set of behaviors that is adopted by a person to combat rejection, to please others, or to try out as a possible self. (p. 502)

family structure The legal and genetic relationships between members of a particular family. (p. 418)

fast mapping Used by children to add words to their vocabulary, the process of hearing a word once or twice and then quickly defining it by categorizing it with other words. (p. 291)

fetal alcohol syndrome (FAS) A cluster of birth defects, including abnormal facial characteristics, slow physical growth, and retarded mental development, that is caused by the mother's drinking excessive quantities of alcohol when pregnant. (p. 113)

fine motor skills Physical skills involving small body movements, especially with the hands and fingers, such as picking up a coin or drawing. (p. 151)

5-to-7 shift The rapid change in intellectual and social competence that many children experience between ages 5 and 7. (p. 400)

foreclosure Erikson's term for premature identity formation, in which the young person adopts the values of parents, or other significant people, wholesale, without questioning and analysis. (p. 504)

formal code A form of speech used by children in school and in other formal situations; characterized by extensive vocabulary, complex syntax, lengthy sentences, and conformity to other middle-class norms for correct language. (Sometimes called *elaborated code*.) (p. 379)

formal operational thought In Piaget's theory, the fourth and final stage of cognitive development; arises from combination of maturation and experience. (p. 470)

foster care A legally sanctioned, publicly supported arrangement in which children are cared for by someone other than their biological parents. (p. 263)

fragile-*X* syndrome A disorder in which part of the X chromosome is attached to the rest by a very slim string of molecules; it is caused by a genetic abnormality and often produces mental deficiency. (p. 87)

gamete A reproductive cell; that is, a cell that can reproduce a new individual if it combines with a gamete from the other sex. (p. 67)

gateway drugs Drugs—usually tobacco, alcohol, and marijuana—whose use increases the risk that a person will later use harder drugs, such as cocaine and heroin. (p. 459)

gender differences Cultural differences in the roles and behavior of the two sexes. (p. 326)

gender-schema theory The theory that children's ideas about gender are based on simple and somewhat stereotyped generalities (scripts) developed from their experience. (p. 332)

gene The basic unit for the transmission of heredity instructions. (p. 68)

generation gap The distance between generations in values, behaviors, and knowledge. (p. 511)

generational forgetting The tendency of each new generation to ignore lessons learned by the previous cohort. For example, the hazards of crack were well known a decade ago, but today's teenagers are less aware of them. (p. 465)

generational stake The need of each generation to view family interactions from its own perspective, because each has a different investment in the family scenario. (p. 511)

genetic code The sequence of chemical compounds (called bases) that is held within DNA molecules and directs development, behavior, and form. (p. 68)

genetic counseling Consultation and testing that enables individuals to learn about their genetic heritage, including conditions that might affect future children. (p. 89)

genetic imprinting The tendency of certain genes to be expressed differently when they are inherited from the mother than when they are inherited from the father. (p. 78)

genotype A person's entire genetic inheritance, including genes that are not expressed in the person. (p. 76)

germinal period The first 2 weeks of development after conception; characterized by rapid cell division and the beginning of cell differentiation. (p. 99)

goal-directed behavior Purposeful action initiated by infants in anticipation of events that will fulfill their needs and wishes. (p. 192)

gonads The pair of sex glands in humans. In girls, these are called ovaries; in boys, these are called testes or testicles. (p. 440)

goodness of fit The degree to which a child's temperament matches the demands of his or her environment. (p. 222)

grand theories Comprehensive theories that have inspired and directed thinking about development for decades but no longer seem as adequate as they once did. (p. 38)

graspability The perception of whether or not an object is of the proper shape, size, texture, and distance to afford grasping or grabbing. (p. 174)

gross motor skills Physical skills involving large body movements such as waving the arms, walking, and jumping. (p. 150)

growth spurt The period of relatively sudden and rapid physical growth of every part of the body that occurs during puberty. (p. 445)

guided participation A learning process in which an individual learns through social interaction with a "tutor" (a parent, a teacher, a more skilled peer) who offers assistance, structures opportunities, models strategies, and provides explicit instruction as needed. (pp. 51, 275)

habituation The process of becoming so familiar with a particular stimulus that it no longer elicits the physiological responses it did when it was originally experienced. (p. 156)

holophrase A single word that expresses a complete thought. (p. 198)

human immunodeficiency virus (HIV) A virus that gradually overwhelms the body's immune responses, leaving the individual defenseless against a host of pathologies that eventually manifest themselves as AIDS. (p. 111)

hypothesis A specific prediction that is stated in such a way that it can be tested and either proved or disproved. (p. 19)

hypothetical thought Thought that involves propositions and possibilities that may or may not reflect reality. (p. 471)

identification A defense mechanism that makes a person take on the role and attitudes of someone more powerful than himself or herself. (p. 329)

identity In Piaget's theory, the logical principle that certain characteristics of an object remain the same when other characteristics are changed. (p. 372)

identity As used by Erikson, a consistent definition of oneself as a unique individual, in terms of roles, attitudes, beliefs, and aspirations. (p. 501)

identity achievement Erikson's term for a person's forming an identity and understanding who he or she is as a unique individual, in accord with past experiences and future plans. (p. 503)

identity crisis A condition in which the search for identity becomes so overwhelming and confusing that self-definition is urgently sought. (p. 503)

identity diffusion Condition in which a person does not seem to know or care what his or her identity is. Such persons are vague, changeable, erratic, in a fog. (p. 504)

identity moratorium Erikson's term for a pause in identity formation that allows young people to explore alternatives without making final identity choices. (p. 504)

identity versus role confusion Erikson's term for the fifth stage of development, in which the person tries to figure out "Who am I?" but is confused as to which of many roles to adopt. (p. 503)

imaginary audience The egocentric idea, held by many adolescents, that others are intensely interested in them, and especially in their appearance and behavior. (p. 478)

immersion An approach to learning a second language in which the learner is placed in an environment where only the second language is spoken. (p. 380)

immunization A process that stimulates the body's own defensive (immune) system to defend against attack by a particular infectious disease. (p. 138)

implantation Beginning about a week after conception, the burrowing of the organism into the lining of the uterus, where it can be nourished and protected during growth. (p. 100)

implicit memory Memory that a person is not able to recall verbally on demand but nonetheless has some recollection of—such as seeing a face and recognizing that it is familiar or being able to ride a bicycle by knowing, in the abstract, what the process is. (p. 186)

in vitro fertilization (IVF) Fertilization of ova by sperm in the laboratory, usually followed by insertion of the resulting cell mass into the uterus in the hope that it will implant and develop as a normal pregnancy and birth. (p. 73)

inadequate families Families that are so impaired by emotional problems and/or cognitive deficiencies that they can never meet their children's needs. (p. 262)

inclusion An approach to educating children with special needs whereby they are included in the regular classroom while also receiving special individualized instruction, typically from a teacher or paraprofessional trained in special education. (p. 360)

independent variable The variable that is manipulated in an experiment. (p. 25)

inductive reasoning Reasoning from one or more specific experiences or facts to a general conclusion. (p. 472)

industry versus inferiority The fourth of Erikson's eight crises of psychosocial development, in which school-age children attempt to master many skills and develop a sense of themselves as either industrious and competent or incompetent and inferior (p. 399).

infertile Unable to conceive a child despite a year of trying to do so. (p. 72)

informal code A form of speech characterized by limited use of vocabulary and syntax. Meaning is communicated by gestures, intonation, and shared understanding. (Sometimes called *restricted code*.) (p. 379)

information-processing theory A theory of learning that focuses on the steps of thinking—such as sorting, categorizing, storing, and retrieving—that are similar to the functions of a computer. (p. 365)

initiative versus guilt The third of Erikson's eight "crises" of psychosocial development, in which the preschool child eagerly begins new projects and activities—and feels guilt when his or her efforts result in failure or criticism. (p. 307)

injury control The practice of limiting the extent of injuries by planning ahead, controlling the circumstances, preventing certain dangerous activities, and adding safety features to others. (p. 248)

insecure attachment A caregiver-infant relationship characterized by the child's overdependence on or lack of interest in the caregiver and by a lack of confidence on the part of the child. (p. 228)

instrumental aggression Aggressive behavior whose purpose is to obtain or retain an object desired by another. (p. 315)

interaction effect The phenomenon in which a teratogen's potential for causing harm increases when it is combined with another teratogen or another risk factor. (p. 109)

intergenerational transmission The assumption that mistreated children grow up to become abusive or neglectful parents themselves. This is less common than is generally supposed. (p. 259)

intermodal perception The ability to connect, simultaneously, information from one sensory mode (such as vision) with information from another (such as hearing). (p. 178)

invincibility fable The fiction, fostered by adolescent egocentrism, that one is immune to common dangers, such as those associated with unprotected sex, drug abuse, or high-speed driving. (p. 476)

IQ tests Aptitude tests designed to measure a person's intelligence (which at one time was defined as mental age divided by chronological age, times 100—hence, intelligence quotient, or IQ). (p. 388)

irreversibility The inability to review the prior steps to whatever the current situation might be, leading to an inability to change things by reversing the process. (p. 273)

kinship care A form of foster care in which a relative of a maltreated child takes over from the abusive or neglectful parents. (p. 263)

knowledge base A body of knowledge in a particular area that has been learned and on which additional learning can be based. (p. 368)

kwashiorkor A disease resulting from a protein deficiency in children. The symptoms include thinning hair and bloating of the legs, face, and abdomen. (p. 166)

language acquisition device (LAD) Chomsky's term to denote the innate ability to acquire language, including the basic aspects of grammar. (p. 200)

language function The primary purpose of language—communication, allowing people to understand, and be understood by, others. (p. 194)

language structure The body of sounds, words, and rules (including grammar, usage, inflection) of a particular language. (p. 194)

launching event Something that seems to start, or trigger, a particular happening. Launching events are used to study understanding of cause-and-effect relationships. (p. 187)

learning disability Difficulty in mastering a specific cognitive skill that is *not* attributable to intellectual slowness, obvious impairment of the senses, lack of education, or family dysfunction. (p. 355)

learning theory A grand theory of development, built on behaviorism, that focuses on the sequences and processes by which behavior is learned. (p. 42)

life-course persistent offender A juvenile delinquent who is likely to continue a pattern of lawbreaking even when adolescence is over. Such individuals usually started their pattern before the teen years. (p. 528)

little scientist Piaget's term for the stage-five toddler (age 12 to 18 months), who actively experiments to learn about the properties of objects. (p. 193)

long-term memory The part of memory that stores information for days, months, or years. (p. 366)

longitudinal research A research design in which the same people are studied over time to measure both change and stability as they age. (p. 30)

low birthweight (LBW) A birthweight of less than 5 1/2 pounds (2,500 grams). (p. 116)

mainstreaming An approach to educating children with special needs by putting them in the same "stream"—the general-education classroom—as all the other children, rather than segregating them. (p. 360)

marasmus A disease that afflicts young infants suffering from severe malnutrition. Growth stops, body tissues waste away, and death may eventually occur. (p. 166)

markers Particular genetic traits, physiological characteristics, or gene clusters that suggest the presence of a genetic disorder. (p. 92)

mastery play Any form of play that leads to a mastering of new skills, including motor skills as well as language and intellectual abilities. (p. 306)

menarche A female's first menstrual period. (p. 442)

mental combinations Sequences of actions developed intellectually, before they are actively performed. Mental combinations are a characteristic of the toddlers at Piaget's stage six of sensorimotor intelligence. (p. 193)

mental retardation Slow learning in all, or almost all, intellectual abilities. The degree of retardation is usually measured by an intelligence test. In young children, mental retardation is often called *pervasive developmental delay*, allowing the possibility that the child will catch up to normal, age-appropriate development. (p. 355)

metacognition The ability to evaluate a cognitive task to determine how best to accomplish it, and then to monitor one's performance—"thinking about thinking." (p. 370)

minitheories Theories that explain some specific area of development, but that are not as general and comprehensive as grand theories. (p. 38)

modeling Part of social learning theory; in particular, the process whereby a person tries to imitate the behavior of someone else. Modeling occurs with minor actions, such as how someone laughs or what shoes he or she wears, but it also occurs in powerful ways, as when a male child identifies with his father as a role model. (p. 44)

monozygotic twins Twins who have identical genes because they were formed from one zygote that split into two identical organisms very early in development. (p. 71)

morality of care Moral thought and behavior based on comparison, nurturance, and concern for the well-being of other people. This morality is said to be more common among girls and women. (p. 404)

morality of justice Moral thought and behavior based on depersonalized standards of right and wrong, with judgments based on abstractions, not relationships. This morality is said to be more common among boys and men. (p. 404)

multifactorial traits Characteristics produced by the interaction of genetic and environmental (or other) influences (rather than by genetic influences alone). (p. 75)

myelination The process in which axons are coated with myelin, a fatty substance that speeds communication between neurons. (p. 144)

negative identity An identity that is taken on simply because it is the opposite of whatever parents, or society, prescribe. (p. 504)

neglect Any inaction that harms or endangers a person. Neglect can involve physical needs (food, warmth) or psychological needs (love, language). (p. 255)

neural tube A fold of outer embryonic cells that appears about 3 weeks after conception and later develops into the central nervous system. (p. 101)

neuron A nerve cell of the central nervous system. Most neurons are in the brain. (p. 143)

nonadditive pattern A pattern of genetic inheritance in which a trait is influenced much more by one gene than by other genes that could also influence the trait. (p. 76)

norm A standard or average, derived or developed for a specified group population. What is "normal" may not be what is ideal. (p. 154)

norm-referenced A test or procedure that is assessed relative to a particular average or norm based on a group already tested. The norm is the average, but soon after a norm is set, performance tends to surpass it. (p. 390)

nuclear family A family consisting of two parents and their mutual biological children. (p. 418)

object constancy The concept that each object is whatever it is, despite changes in appearance or movement caused by shifts in the observer, the object, or the context. (p. 177)

object permanence The realization that objects (including people) still exist even when they cannot be seen, touched, or heard. (p. 181)

Oedipus complex In the phallic stage of psychosexual development, the sexual desire that boys have for their mothers and the related hostility they have toward their fathers. (p. 329)

oral stage Freud's term for the first stage of psychosexual development, in which the infant gains pleasure through sucking and biting. (p. 217)

otitis media A middle ear infection that can impair hearing temporarily and therefore can impede language development and socialization if it continues too long in the first years of life. (p. 161)

overextension The application of a newly learned word to a variety of objects that may share a particular characteristic but are not in the general category described by that word. (p. 197)

overregularization The tendency to make a language more logical and "regular" than it actually is, which leads to mistaken application of the rules of grammar. (p. 295)

ovum A female gamete, or reproductive cell (plural: ova). (p. 67)

parasuicide A deliberate act of self-destruction that does not end in death. Parasuicide can be fleeting, such as a small knife mark on the wrist, or potentially lethal, such as swallowing an entire bottle of pills. (p. 522)

parent-newborn bond The strong feelings of attachment that arise between parents and their newborn infants. (p. 129)

parental monitoring Parental awareness of what one's children are doing, where, and with whom. (p. 514)

peer group A group of individuals of roughly the same age and social status who play, work, or learn together. (p. 407)

peer pressure Social pressure to conform with one's friends or contemporaries in behavior, dress, and attitude; usually considered negative, as when peers encourage each other to defy adult standards. (p. 516)

perception The mental processing of sensory information. (p. 156)

perceptual constancy The fact that the size and shape of an object remain the same despite changes in the object's appearance due to changes in its location. (p. 177)

period of the embryo From approximately the third through the eighth weeks after conception, the period during which the rudimentary forms of all anatomical structures develop. (p. 99)

period of the fetus From the ninth week after conception until birth, the period during which the organs grow in size and complexity. (p. 99)

permissive parenting A style of child rearing in which the parents rarely punish, guide, or control their children but are nurturant and communicate well with their children. (p. 318)

person-environment fit The degree to which a particular environment is conducive to the growth of a particular individual. (p. 478)

personal fable The egocentric idea, held by many adolescents, that one is destined for fame and fortune and/or great accomplishments. (p. 476)

personality The emotions, behaviors, and attitudes that make an individual unique. (p. 216)

phallic stage The third stage of psychosexual development, occurring in early childhood, in which the penis becomes the focus of psychological concerns as well as physiological pleasure. (p. 328)

phenotype All the genetic traits, including physical characteristics and behavioral tendencies, that are expressed in a person. (p. 76)

phobia An irrational fear that is strong enough to make a person try to avoid the fearful object or experience. (p. 305)

physiological states The various levels of an organism's mental and biological activity, such as quiet sleep and alert wakefulness. (p. 147)

pincer grasp The skill of using the thumb and forefinger together, usually mastered between the ages of 9 and 14 months. (p. 153)

placenta The organ that connects the circulatory system of a mother with that of her growing embryo. It allows nourish-

ment to flow to the embryo and wastes to flow away but maintains the separation of the two circulatory systems. (p. 103)

play face A smiling or relaxed facial expression that indicates that a child (or other animal) does not intend to be aggressive; used, for example, during rough-and-tumble play. (p. 312)

polygenic traits Characteristics produced by the interaction of many genes (rather than a single gene). (p. 75)

population The entire group of individuals who are of particular concern in a scientific study, such as all the children of the world or all newborns who weigh less than 3 pounds. (p. 22)

possible selves Various intellectual fantasies about what the future might bring if one or another course of action is chosen. (p. 501)

postconventional moral reasoning Kohlberg's term for the third and highest level (stages five and six) of moral thinking, in which the individual follows moral principles that may supersede the standards of society or the wishes of the individual. (p. 403)

postpartum depression The profound feeling of sadness and inadequacy that sometimes is experienced by new mothers, leading to an inability to eat, sleep, or care normally for their newborns. (p. 131)

preconventional moral reasoning Kohlberg's term for the first level (stages one and two) of moral thinking, in which the individual reasons in terms of his or her own welfare. (p. 403)

preoperational thought Piaget's term for the cognition of children between the ages of about 2 and 6 years, implying that such children have not yet learned to use logical principles in their thinking. (p. 272)

preterm birth Birth that occurs 3 weeks or more before the full term of pregnancy has elapsed, that is, at 35 or fewer weeks past conception rather than at the full term of about 38 weeks. (p. 116)

primary prevention An approach to child maltreatment that is designed to prevent maltreatment (or other harm) from ever occurring. (p. 265)

primary sex characteristics The sex organs—those parts of the body that are directly involved in reproduction, including the vagina, uterus, ovaries, testicles, and penis. (p. 448)

private speech The dialogue that occurs when one talks to oneself, either silently or out loud, to form thoughts and analyze ideas. (p. 277)

Project Headstart A massive preschool education program, developed in the United States in the early 1960s, for children from low-SES families. (p. 297)

prosocial behavior An action, such as sharing, cooperating, or sympathizing, that is performed to benefit other people without the expectation of reward for oneself. (pp. 310, 406)

protein-calorie malnutrition A nutritional problem that results when a person does not consume enough nourishment to thrive. (p. 166)

proximity-seeking behaviors Behaviors that are intended to place a person close to another person to whom he or she is attached. (p. 226)

proximo-distal development Growth and maturation of the human body that progresses from the spine outward. (p. 101)

psychoanalytic theory A grand theory of human development that holds that irrational, unconscious forces, many of them from childhood, underlie human behavior. (p. 38)

psychosocial domain The part of human development that includes emotions, personality characteristics, and relationships with other people, as well as cultural influences. (p. 2)

puberty A period of rapid growth and sexual change that occurs in early adolescence and produces a person of adult size, shape, and sexual potential. (p. 440)

reaction time The time it takes to respond to a particular stimulus. (p. 348)

reactive aggression Aggressive behavior that is an angry retaliation for some intentional or accidental act by another. (p. 315)

reciprocity The logical principle that two objects, quantities, or actions can be mutually related, such that a change in one can be compensated for by a corresponding or opposite change in another. (p. 372)

reflexes Involuntary physical responses to stimuli. (p. 148)

reinforcement The process whereby a particular behavior is strengthened, making it more likely that the behavior will be repeated. (p. 43)

relational aggression Aggressive behavior that takes the form of insults or social rejection. (Also called *social aggression.*) (p. 315)

reminder session An experience that includes some aspect (a sight, a smell, a sound) of something to be remembered, and thus serves to trigger the entire memory. (p. 184)

replicate To repeat a previous scientific study, at a different time and place but with the same research design and procedures, in order to verify that study's conclusions. (p. 19)

representative sample A group of research subjects who reflect the relevant characteristics of the larger population whose attributes are under study. (p. 22)

resource room A designated room, equipped with special material and staffed by a trained teacher, where children with special needs spend part of their school day getting help with basic skills. (p. 360)

response A behavior (either instinctual or learned) that is elicited by a certain stimulus. (p. 42)

restorable families Families that have the potential to provide adequate care but are experiencing a combination of current stresses and past deficits that seriously impairs their parenting abilities. (p. 262)

retrieval strategies Procedures for recalling previously memorized information. (p. 371)

reversibility The logical principle that something that has been changed can be returned to its original state by reversing the process of change. (p. 372)

risk analysis The process of weighing the potential outcomes of a particular event, substance, or experience to determine the likelihood of harm. In teratology, the attempt to evaluate all the factors that can increase or decrease the likelihood that a particular teratogen will cause harm. (p. 106)

rooting reflex A reflex that helps babies find a nipple by causing them to turn their heads toward anything that brushes against their cheeks and to attempt to suck on it. (p. 149)

rough-and-tumble play Play such as wrestling, chasing, and hitting that mimics aggression but actually occurs purely in fun, with no intent to harm. (p. 311)

rubella A viral disease that, if contracted early during pregnancy, can harm the fetus, causing blindness, deafness, and damage to the central nervous system. (Sometimes called *German measles.*) (p. 110)

sample A group of individuals drawn from a specified population. A sample might be the low-birthweight babies born in four particular hospitals that are representative of all hospitals. (p. 22)

sample size The number of individuals who are being studied in a single sample in a research project. (p. 22)

scaffold To structure participation in learning encounters in order to foster a child's emerging capabilities. Scaffolds can be provided in many ways: by a mentor, by the objects or experiences of a culture, or by the child's past learning. (p. 276)

scientific method The principles and procedures used in the systematic pursuit of knowledge (formulating questions, testing hypotheses, and drawing conclusions) designed to reduce subjective reasoning, biased assumptions, and unfounded beliefs. (p. 18)

scientific observation The unobtrusive watching and recording of subjects' behavior in a situation that is being studied, either in the laboratory or in a natural setting. (p. 20)

scientific study of human development A science that seeks to understand how and why people change, and how and why they remain the same, as they grow older. (p. 2)

scripts Skeletal outlines of the usual sequence of events during certain common, recurring experiences. (p. 283)

secondary prevention An approach to child maltreatment that focuses on responding to the first symptoms of maltreatment or risk of maltreatment. Secondary prevention can, and should, begin before the problem becomes severe. (p. 266)

secondary sex characteristics Body characteristics that are not directly involved in reproduction but that indicate sexual maturity, such as a man's beard or a woman's breasts. (p. 450)

secular trend The tendency of successive generations to develop differently as a result of social changes—mainly improved nutrition and medical care. As related to adolescence, the secular trend results in earlier puberty than in previous centuries. (p. 442)

secure attachment A caregiver-infant relationship from which the infant derives enough comfort and confidence to begin exploration of the environment on his or her own. (p. 228)

selective adaptation An aspect of evolution in which, over generations, genes for the traits that are most useful will become more frequent within individuals, making the survival of the species more likely. (p. 58)

selective attention The ability to concentrate on relevant information and ignore distractions. (p. 367)

self-awareness A person's sense of himself or herself as being distinct from other people. (p. 214)

sensation The response of a sensory system when it detects a stimulus. People are not necessarily aware of sensations. (p. 156)

sensorimotor intelligence Piaget's term for the intelligence of infants during the first (sensorimotor) period of cognitive development, when babies think by using the senses and motor skills. (p. 189)

sensory register A memory system that functions for only a fraction of a second, retaining a fleeting impression of a stimulus on a particular sense organ. (p. 366)

separation anxiety An infant's fear of being left by his or her caregiver. (p. 209)

sex differences Biological differences between males and females. (p. 326)

sexually transmitted disease (STD) A disease spread by sexual contact. Such diseases include syphilis, gonorrhea, herpes, chlamydia, and AIDS. (p. 488)

single-parent family A family consisting of a single parent and his or her children—usually the parent's biological children. (p. 418)

sleeper effect Any outcome of a program or experience that is hidden for a while (asleep) but later becomes apparent (awake). (p. 299)

small for gestational age (SGA) A term applied to newborns who weigh substantially less than they should, given how much time has passed since conception. (p. 117)

social cognition A person's awareness and understanding of human personality, motives, emotions, intentions, and interactions. (p. 400)

social comparison The tendency to assess one's abilities, achievements, social status, and the like, by measuring them against those of others, especially those of one's peers. (p. 401)

social construction An idea about the way things are, or should be, that is built more on the shared perceptions of members of a society than on objective reality. (p. 10)

social context All the means—including the people, the customs, the institutions, and the beliefs—by which society influences the developing person. (p. 6)

social learning The theory that learning occurs through observation and imitation of other people. (p. 44)

social mediation In regard to language, the use of speech as a tool to bridge the gap in understanding or knowledge between learner and tutor. (p. 277)

social referencing Looking to trusted adults for cues on how to interpret unfamiliar or ambiguous events. (p. 210)

social smile An infant's smile of pleasure in response to a human face or voice. (p. 208)

society of children The social culture of children, including the games, vocabulary, dress codes, and rules of behavior that characterize their interactions. (p. 408)

sociocultural theory A theory which holds that human development results from the dynamic interaction between developing persons and the surrounding culture, primarily as expressed by the parents and teachers who transmit it. (p. 50)

sociodramatic play Pretend play in which children act out various roles and themes in stories of their own creation. (p. 312)

socioeconomic status (SES) An indicator of social class that is based primarily on income, education, place of residence, and occupation. (p. 11)

sperm A male gamete, or reproductive cell (plural: sperm). (p. 67)

spermarche A male's first ejaculation of live sperm. (p. 449)

standards-based A test or procedure that is assessed relative to a particular criterion or standard set in advance. For example, if the standard for keyboarding speed is set at 100 words a minute, the standard does not change even if everyone, or no one, achieves it. (p. 390)

statistical significance A mathematical measure of the likelihood that a particular research result occurred by chance. (p. 23)

stimulus An action or event that elicits a behavioral response. (p. 42)

storage strategies Procedures for placing and holding information in memory. (p. 371)

Strange Situation An experimental condition devised by Mary Ainsworth to assess an infant's attachment to a caregiver. The infant's behavior is observed in an unfamiliar room while the caregiver (usually the mother) and a stranger move in and out of the room. (p. 228)

stranger wariness A fear of unfamiliar people, exhibited (if at all) by infants over the age of about 6 months. (p. 209)

sucking reflex A reflex that causes newborns to suck anything that touches their lips. (p. 149)

sudden infant death syndrome (SIDS) Death of a seemingly healthy baby who, without apparent cause, stops breathing during sleep. (p. 140)

suicidal ideation Thinking about suicide, usually with some serious emotional and intellectual overtones. (p. 521)

superego The part of the personality that is self-critical and judgmental and that internalizes the moral standards set by parents and society. (p. 329)

supportable families Families that can meet their children's needs only with the help of an extensive array of social services. (p. 262)

survey A research method in which information is collected from a large number of people, either through written questionnaires or through interviews. (p. 27)

symbolic thought Thinking that involves the use of words, gestures, pictures, or actions to represent ideas, things, or behaviors. (p. 272)

synapse The point at which the axon of one neuron meets the dendrites of another neuron. At that point, brain chemicals called neurotransmitters carry the impulse from axon to dendrites. (p. 143)

synchrony Coordinated interaction between infant and parent (or other caregiver) in which each individual responds to and influences the other. (p. 224)

syndrome A cluster of distinct characteristics that tend to occur together in a given disorder. (p. 86)

task-involvement learning An educational strategy that bases academic grades on the mastery of certain competencies and knowledge, with students being encouraged to learn cooperatively. (p. 482)

temperament The set of innate tendencies, or dispositions, that underlie and affect each person's interactions with people, situations, and events. (p. 219)

teratogens Agents and conditions, including viruses, drugs, chemicals, stessors, and malnutrition, that can impair prenatal development and lead to birth defects or even death. (p. 105)

teratology The scientific study of birth defects caused by genetic or prenatal problems or by birth complications. (p. 105)

tertiary prevention An approach to child maltreatment that is aimed at halting maltreatment after it occurs and treating the victim. Removing a child from the home, providing needed hospitalization or psychological counseling, and jailing the perpetrator are all examples of tertiary-prevention measures. (p. 267)

theory of mind An understanding of human mental processes, that is, of one's own and others' emotions, perceptions, intentions, and thoughts. (p. 287)

threshold effect The phenomenon in which a particular teratogen is relatively harmless in small doses but becomes harmful when exposure reaches a certain level (the threshold). (p. 109)

toddler A child, usually between the ages of 1 and 2, who has just begun to master the art of walking. (p. 151)

transient exuberance The great increase in neurons, dendrites, and synapses that occurs in an infant's brain over the first 2 years of life. (p. 144)

trisomy-21 (Down syndrome) A syndrome that includes such symptoms as a rounded head, thick tongue, unusual eyes, heart abnormalities, and mental retardation. It results when there is an extra chromosome at the site of the twenty-first pair. (p. 86)

trust versus mistrust Erikson's first stage of psychosocial development, in which the infant experiences the world either as secure and comfortable or as unpredictable and uncomfortable. (p. 218)

twenty-third pair The chromosome pair that, in humans, determines the zygote's (and hence the person's) sex, among other things. (p. 69)

underextension The use of a word to refer only to certain things, even though the word generally means much more to most people. (p. 197)

undernutrition Inadequate nutrition, but not as severe as in malnutrition. Sometimes called *failure-to-thrive*. Undernutrition in children is indicated by a child who is notably underweight (called *wasted*) or short (called *stunted*) compared to the norms. (p. 167)

variable Any quantity, characteristic, or action that can take on different values within a group of individuals or a single individual. (p. 19)

visual cliff An apparent (but not actual) drop between one surface and another. The illusion of the cliff is created by connecting a transparent glass surface to an opaque patterned one, with the floor below the same pattern as the surface. (p. 175)

volatile mismatch When teenagers' individual needs–intellectual, emotional, social–do not match the size, routine, and structure of their schools, the result is potentially explosive. (p. 479)

vulnerable-to-crisis families Families that are experiencing unusual problems and need temporary help to resolve them. (p. 261)

withdrawn-rejected children Children who are actively rejected by their peer group because of their withdrawn, anxious behavior. (p. 411)

Wobegon effect The tendency to view oneself, one's children, and one's culture as "above-average." Tests that are designed with norms for average scores quickly become ways to prove that some children are better than others. (p. 391)

working memory The part of memory that handles current, conscious mental activity. (Also called *short-term memory*.) (p. 366)

X-linked genes Genes that are carried on the X chromosome. (p. 77)

zone of proximal development The skills, knowledge, and understanding that an individual cannot yet perform or comprehend on his or her own but could master with guidance; this is the arena where learning occurs. (pp. 54, 276)

zygote The single cell formed from the fusing of a sperm and an ovum. (p. 67)

References

Aboud, F.E. (1988). *Children and prejudice*. New York: Blackwell.

Achenbach, Thomas M., Howell, Catherine T., Quay, Herbert C., & Conners, C. Keith. (1991). National survey of problems and competencies among four- to sixteen-year-olds. *Monographs of the Society for Research in Child Development, 56* (Serial No. 225), 3.

Ackerman, Brian P. (1996). Induction of a memory retrieval strategy by young children. *Journal of Experimental Child Psychology, 62,* 243–271.

Ackerman, Brian P., Kogos, Jen, Youngstrom, Eric, Schoff, Kristen, & Izard, Carroll. (1999). Family instability and the problem behaviors of children from economically disadvantaged families. *Developmental Psychology, 35,* 258–268.

Acock, Alan C., & Demo, David H. (1994). *Family diversity and well-being*. Thousand Oaks, CA: Sage.

Adams, G. R., Gullottra, T. P., & Montemayor, R. (1992). *Advances in adolescent development: Adolescent identity formation*. New York: Russell Sage.

Adams, Marilyn Jager. (1990). *Beginning to read: Thinking and learning about print*. Cambridge, MA: MIT Press.

Adams, Russell J. (1989). Newborns' discrimination among mid- and long-wavelength stimuli. *Journal of Experimental Child Psychology, 47,* 130–141.

Adolph, Karen E. (1997). Learning in the development of infant locomotion. With commentary by Bennett I. Bertenthal & Steven M. Boker, by Eugene C. Goldfield and by Eleanor J. Gibson. *Monographs of the Society for Research in Child Development, 62.*

Adolph, K.E., Eppler, M.A., & Gibson, E.J. (1993). Crawling versus walking infants' perception of affordances for locomotion over sloping surfaces. *Child Development, 64,* 1158–1174.

Adolph, K.E., Eppler, M.A., & Gibson, E.J. (1993). Development of perception of affordances. In C. Rovee-Collier & L.P. Lipsitt (Eds.), *Advances in infancy research* (Vol. 8). Norwood, NJ: Ablex.

Ainsworth, Mary D. Salter. (1967). *Infancy in Uganda: Infant care and the growth of love*. Baltimore: Johns Hopkins Press.

Ainsworth, Mary D. Salter. (1973). The development of infant-mother attachment. In Bettye M. Caldwell & Henry N. Ricciuti (Eds.), *Review of child development research* (Vol. 3). Chicago: University of Chicago Press.

Ainsworth, Mary D. Salter. (1993). Attachment as related to mother-infant interaction. In C. Rovee-Collier & L.P. Lipsitt (Eds.), *Advances in infancy research* (Vol. 8). Norwood, NJ: Ablex.

Akhtar, N., Dunham, F., & Dunham, P. (1991). Directive interactions and early vocabulary development: The role of joint attentional focus. *Journal of Child Language, 18,* 41–49.

Aldwin, Carolyn M. (1994). *Stress, coping, and development*. New York: Guilford.

Alessandri, Steven M., Bendersky, Margaret, & Lewis, Michael. (1998). Cognitive functioning in 8- to 18-month-old drug-exposed infants. *Developmental Psychology, 34,* 565–573.

Allen, E.M., Mitchell, E.H., Stewart, A.W., & Ford, R.P.K. (1993). Ethnic differences in mortality from sudden infant death syndrome in New Zealand. *British Medical Journal, 306,* 13–16.

Allen, Stanley E. M., & Crago, Martha B. (1996). Early passive acquisition in Inuktitut. *Journal of Child Language, 23,* 129–155.

Allison, Clara. (1985). Development direction of action programs: Repetitive action to correction loops. In Jane E. Clark & James H. Humphrey (Eds.), *Motor development: Current selected research*. Princeton, NJ: Princeton Book Company.

Allison, Paul D., & Furstenberg, Frank F. (1989). How marital dissolution affects children: Variations by age and sex. *Developmental Psychology, 25,* 540–549.

Altergott, Karen. (1993). *One world, many families*. Minneapolis, MN: National Council on Family Relations.

Alwin, D.F. (1997). Aging, social change, and conservatism: The link between historical and biographical time in the study of political identities. In M. Hardy (Ed.), *Studying aging and social change: Conceptual and methodological issues*. Thousand Oaks, CA: Sage.

Aman, Christine J., Roberts, Ralph J., & Pennington, Bruce F. (1998). A neuropsychological examination of the underlying deficit in attention deficit hyperactivity disorder: Frontal lobe versus right parietal lobe theories. *Developmental Psychology, 34,* 956–969.

Amato, Paul R. (1993). Children's adjustment to divorce: Theories, hypotheses, empirical support. *Journal of Marriage and the Family, 55,* 23–38.

Amato, Paul R., & Booth, Alan. (1996). A prospective study of divorce and parent-child relationships. *Journal of Marriage and the Family, 58,* 356–365.

Amato, Paul R., & Rezac, Sandra J. (1994). Contact with non-resident parents, interparental conflict, and children's behavior. *Journal of Family Issues, 15,* 191–207.

American Association of University Women Foundation. (1993). *Hostile hallways: The AAUW survey on sexual harassment in America's schools.* Washington DC: AAUW Educational.

American Psychiatric Association. (1994). *Diagnostic and Statistical Manual of Mental Disorders—DSM-IV.* Washington, DC.

Anderson, Arnold E. (1998). The self—bridging the gap between brain and mind. *Contemporary Psychology, 43,* 361–362.

Anderson, W. French. (1995). Gene therapy. *Scientific American, 273,* 124–128.

Angel, Ronald J., & Angel, Jacqueline L. (1994). *Painful inheritance: Health and the new generation of fatherless families.* Madison: University of Wisconsin Press.

Angier, Natalie. (1994, May 24). Mother's milk found to be potent cocktail of hormones. *New York Times,* C1.

Anglin, Jeremy M. (1993). Vocabulary development: A morphological analysis. *Monographs of the Society for Research in Child Development, 58* (Serial No. 238), 10.

Ansuini, C.G., Fiddler-Woite, J., & Woite, R.S. (1996). The source, accuracy, and impact of initial sexuality information on lifetime wellness. *Adolescence, 31,* 283–289.

Apgar, Virginia. (1953). A proposal for a new method of evaluation in the newborn infant. *Current Research in Anesthesia and Analgesia, 32,* 260.

Archer, Sally. (1994). *Interventions for adolescent identity development.* Thousand Oaks, CA: Sage.

Archer, Sally L., & Waterman, Alan S. (1990). Varieties of identity diffusions and foreclosures: An exploration of the subcategories of the identity statuses. *Journal of Adolescent Research, 5,* 96–111.

Arendell, Terry. (1997). A social constructionist approach to parenting. In Terry Arendell (Ed.), *Contemporary parenting: Challenges and issues.* Thousand Oaks, CA: Sage.

Armistead, Lisa, Kempton, Tracy, Lynch, Sean, Forehand, Rex, Nousiainen, Sarah, Neighbors, Bryan, & Tannenbaum, Lynne. (1992). Early retention: Are there long-term beneficial effects? *Psychology in the Schools, 29,* 342–347.

Armstrong, Neil, & Welsman, Joanne. (1997). *Young people and physical activity.* Oxford, England: Oxford University Press.

Arnold, Georgianne. (1997). Solvent abuse and developmental toxicity. In Sam Kacew & George H. Lambert (Eds.), *Environmental toxicology and pharmacology of human development.* Washington, DC: Taylor & Francis.

Arsenio, W.F., & Kramer, R. (1992). Victimizers and their victims: Children's conceptions of the mixed emotional consequences of moral transgressions. *Child Development, 63,* 915–927.

Asch, David A., Hershey, John C., Pauly, Mark V., Patton, James P., Jedriziewski, Kathryn M., & Mennuti, Michael T. (1996). Genetic screening for reproductive planning: Methodological and conceptual issues in policy analysis. *American Journal of Public Health, 86,* 684–690.

Aslin, Richard N. (1987). Visual and auditory development in infancy. In Joy Doniger Osofsky (Ed.), *Handbook of infant development* (2nd ed.). New York: Wiley.

Aslin, Richard N. (1988). Visual perception in early infancy. In Albert Yonas (Ed.), *Perceptual development in infancy.* Hillsdale, NJ: Erlbaum.

Associated Press. (1996). *Texas driver convicted of manslaughter,* October 23, 1996.

Astington, Janet Wilde. (1993). *The child's discovery of the mind.* Cambridge, MA: Harvard University Press.

Astington, Janet Wilde, & Gopnik, A. (1988). Knowing you've changed your mind: Children's understanding of representational change. In J.W. Astington, P.L. Harris, & D.R. Olson (Eds.), *Developing theories of mind.* Cambridge, England: Cambridge University Press.

Aureli, Tiziana & Colecchia, Nicola. (1996). Day care experience and free play behavior in preschool children. *Journal of Applied Developmental Psychology, 17,* 1–17.

Axia, Giovanna, & Baroni, Rosa. (1985). Linguistic politeness at different age levels. *Child Development, 56,* 918–927.

Bachman, J.G., & Schulenberg, J. (1993). How part-time work intensity relates to drug use, problem behavior, time use, and satisfaction among high school seniors: Are these consequences or merely correlates? *Developmental Psychology, 29,* 220–235.

Bachrach, C.A., Clogg, C.C., & Carver, K. (1993). Outcomes of early childbearing: Summary of a conference. *Journal of Research on Adolescence, 3,* 337–348.

Bahrick, L.E. (1983). Infants' perception of substance and temporal synchrony in multimodal events. *Infant Behavior and Development, 6,* 429–451.

Bailey, J. Michael. (1995). Biological perspectives on sexual orientation. In Anthony R. D'Augelli & Charlotte J. Patterson (Eds.), *Lesbian, gay, and bisexual identities over the lifespan.* New York: Oxford University Press.

Bailey, J. Michael, Pillard, Richard C., & Knight, Robert. (1993). At issue: Is sexual orientation biologically determined? *CQ Researcher, 3,* 209.

Bailey, William T. (1994). Fathers' involvement and responding to infants: "More" may not be "better". *Psychological Reports, 74,* 92–94.

Baillargeon, R. (1987). Object permanence in 3.5- and 4.5-month-old infants. *Developmental Psychology, 23,* 655–664.

Baillargeon, R. (1991). Reasoning about the height and location of a hidden object in 4.5- and 6.5-month-old infants. *Cognition, 38,* 13–42.

Baillargeon, R., & DeVos, J. (1992). Object permanence in young infants: Further evidence. *Child Development, 62,* 1227–1246.

Bakeman, Roger, Adamson, Lauren B., Konner, Melvin, & Barr, Ronald G. (1990). !Kung infancy: The social context of object exploration. *Child Development, 61,* 794–809.

Baker, Colin. (1993). *Foundation of bilingual education and bilingualism.* Clevedon, England: Multilingual Matters.

Baker-Ward, Lynne, Gordon, Betty N., Ornstein, Peter A., Larus, Deanna M., & Clubb, Patricia A. (1993). Young children's long-term retention of a pediatric examination. *Child Development, 64,* 1519–1533.

Bakken, B. (1993). Prejudice and danger: The only child in China. *Childhood, 1,* 46–61.

Balaban, Marie T. (1995). Affective influences on startle in five-month-old infants: Reactions to facial expressions of emotion. *Child Development, 66,* 28–36.

Bamford, F.N., Bannister, R., Benjamin, C.M., Hillier, V.F., Ward, B.S., & Moore, W.M.O. (1990). Sleep in the first year of life. *Developmental and Child Neurology, 32,* 718–734.

Bandura, Albert. (1977). *Social learning theory.* Englewood Cliffs, NJ: Prentice-Hall.

Bandura, Albert. (1986). *Social foundations of thought and action: A social cognitive theory.* Englewood Cliffs, NJ: Prentice-Hall.

Bandura, Albert. (1989). Social cognitive theory. In R. Vasta (Ed.), *Annals of child development* (Vol. 6). Greenwich, CT: JAI Press.

Bandura, Albert, Barbaranelli, Claudio, Caprara, Gian Vittorio, & Pastorelli, Concetta. (1996). Multifaceted impact of self-efficacy beliefs on academic functioning. *Child Development, 67,* 1206–1222.

Banerji, Madhabi & Dailey, Ronald A. (1995). A study of the effects of the inclusion model on students with specific learning disabilities. *Journal of Learning Disabilities, 28,* 511–522.

Barabasz, Marianne & Barabasz, Arreed. (1996). Attention deficit disorder: Diagnosis, etiology and treatment. *Child Study Journal, 26,* 1–37.

Barber, B.K. (1994). Cultural, family, and personal contexts of parent-adolescent conflict. *Journal of Marriage and the Family, 56,* 375–386.

Barber, Brian K., & Olsen, Joseph A. (1996). Socialization in context: Connection, regulation and autonomy in the family, school, and neighborhood with peers. *Journal of Adolescent Research, 12,* 287–315.

Barinaga, Marcia. (1994). Surprises across the cultural divide. *Science, 263,* 1468–1472.

Barkow, Jerome H., Cosmides, Leda, & Tooby, John. (Eds.). (1992). *The adapted mind: Evolutionary psychology and the generation of culture.* New York: Oxford University Press.

Barling, Julian, & MacEwan, Karyl. (1992). Linking work experiences to facets of marital functioning. *Journal of Organizational Behavior, 13,* 573–583.

Barnard, Kathryn E. & Martell, Louise K. (1995). Mothering. In Marc H. Bornstein (Ed.), *Handbook of parenting: Status and social conditions of parenting.* New Jersey: Erlbaum.

Barnett, Mark A. (1986). Sex bias in the helping behavior presented in children's picture books. *Journal of Genetic Psychology, 147,* 343–351.

Barnett, Rosalind C., & Rivers, Caryl. (1996). The new dad works the "second shift," too. *Radcliff Quarterly, 82,* 9.

Barr, Rachel, Dowden, Anne, & Hayne, Harlene. (1996). Developmental changes in deferred imitation by 6- to 24-month-old infants. *Infant Behavior & Development, 19,* 159–170.

Barrett, Martyn D. (1986). Early semantic representations and early word-usage. In Stan A. Kuczaj & Martyn D. Barrett (Eds.), *The development of word meaning: Progress in cognitive developmental research.* New York: Springer-Verlag.

Barth, R.P., Courtney, M., Berrick, J.D., & Albert, V. (1994). *From child abuse to permanency planning: Child welfare services, pathways, and placements.* New York: Aldine de Gruyter.

Bassuk, E.L., & Rosenberg, L. (1990). Psychosocial characteristics of homeless children and children with homes. *Pediatrics, 85,* 257–261.

Bateman, David A., Ng, Stephen K.C., Hansen, Catherine A., & Heagarty, Margaret C. (1993). The effects of intrauterine cocaine exposure in newborns. *American Journal of Public Health, 83,* 190–193.

Bates, Betsy. (1995). STD reinfection greatest in teens. *Pediatric News, 29* (12), 8.

Bates, Elizabeth, & Carnevale, George F. (1994). Developmental psychology in the 1990s: Research on language development. *Developmental Review, 13,* 436–470.

Bauer, H.H. (1992). *Scientific literacy and the myth of the scientific method.* Urbana: University of Illinois Press.

Bauer, Patricia J., & Dow, Gina. (1994). Episodic memory in 16- and 20-month-old children. Specifics are generalized but not forgotten. *Developmental Psychology, 30,* 403–417.

Bauer, Patricia J., & Mandler, J.M. (1990). Remembering what happened next: Very young children's recall of event sequences. In R. Fivush & J.A. Hudson (Eds.), *Knowing and remembering in young children.* Cambridge, England: Cambridge University Press.

Bauer, Patricia J., & Mandler, J.M. (1992). Putting the horse before the cart: The use of temporal order in recall of events by one-year-old children. *Developmental Psychology, 28,* 441–452.

Baumrind, Diana. (1967). Child-care practices anteceding three patterns of preschool behavior. *Genetic Psychology Monographs, 75,* 43–88.

Baumrind, Diana. (1971). Current patterns of parental authority. *Developmental Psychology, 4* (Monograph 1), 1–103.

Baumrind, Diana. (1989). Rearing competent children. In William Damon (Ed.), *New directions for child development: Adolescent health and human behavior.* San Francisco: Jossey-Bass.

Baumrind, Diana. (1991). Effective parenting during the early adolescent transition. In P.A. Cowan & E.M. Hetherington (Eds.), *Advances in family research* (Vol. 2). Hillsdale, NJ: Erlbaum.

Baumrind, Diana. (1991). Parenting styles and adolescent development. In Jeanne Brooks-Gunn, Richard Lerner, & Anne C. Petersen (Eds.), *The encyclopedia of adolescence.* New York: Garland.

Baumrind, Diana. (1991). The influence of parenting style on adolescent competence and substance use. *Journal of Early Adolescence, 11,* 56–95.

Baumrind, Diana. (1993). The average expectable environment is not good enough: A response to Scarr. *Child Development, 64,* 1299–1317.

Baumwell, Lisa, Tamis-LeMonda, Catherine S. & Bornstein, Marc H. (1997). Maternal verbal sensitivity and child language comprehension. *Infant Behavior & Development, 20,* 247–258.

Baynes, R.D., & Bothwell, T.H. (1990). Iron deficiency. *Annual Review of Nutrition, 10,* (Palo Alto: Annual Reviews), 133.

Beal, Carole R. (1994). *Boys and girls: The development of gender roles.* New York: McGraw-Hill.

Beal, S.M., & Porter, C. (1991). Sudden infant death syndrome related to climate. *Acta Paediatrica Scandinavica, 80,* 278–287.

Beaudry, Micheline, Dufour, R., & Marcoux, Sylvie. (1995). Relation between infant feeding and infections during the first six months of life. *Journal of Pediatrics, 126,* 191–197.

Behrman, Richard E. (1992). *Nelson textbook of pediatrics.* Philadelphia: W.B. Saunders.

Beilin, H. (1992). Piaget's enduring contribution to developmental psychology. *Developmental Psychology, 28,* 191–204.

Bell, A.P., Weinberg, M.S., & Mammersmith, S. (1981). *Sexual preference: Its development in men and women.* Bloomington: University of Indiana Press.

Bell, M.A., & Fox, N.A. (1992). The relations between frontal brain electrical activity and cognitive development during infancy. *Child Development, 63,* 1142–1163.

Beller, Michal, & Gafni, Naomi. (1996). International assessment of educational progress in mathematics and sciences: The gender differences perspective. *Journal of Educational Psychology, 88,* 365–377.

Belsky, Jay. (1986). Infant day care: A cause for concern? *Zero to Three, 6,* 1–7.

Belsky, Jay. (1990). Infant day care, child development, and family policy. *Society, 27* (5), 10–12.

Belsky, Jay. (1996). Parent, infant, and social-contextual antecedents of father-son attachment security. *Developmental Psychology, 32,* 905–913.

Belsky, Jay. (1997). Theory testing, effect-size evaluation, and differential susceptibility to rearing influence: The case of mothering and attachment. *Child Development, 64,* 598–600.

Belsky, Jay, & Cassidy, J. (1995). Attachment theory and evidence. In M. Rutter, D. Hay, & S. Baron-Cohen (Eds.), *Developmental principles and clinical issues in psychology and psychiatry.* Oxford, England: Blackwell.

Bem, Sandra L. (1989). Genital knowledge and gender constancy in preschool children. *Child Development, 60,* 649–662.

Bem, Sandra L. (1993). *The lenses of gender.* New Haven, CT: Yale University Press.

Benbow, Camilla P., & Lubinski, David. (1996). *Intellectual talents: Psychometric and social issues.* Baltimore: Johns Hopkins.

Bendersky, M., & Lewis, M. (1995). Effects of intraventricular hemorrhage and other medical and environmental risks on multiple outcomes at age three years. *Developmental and Behavioral Pediatrics, 16,* 89–96.

Bengston, Vern L. (1975). Generation and family effects in value socialization. *American Sociological Review, 40,* 358–371.

Bensen, Peter L. (1997). *All kids are our kids: What communities must do to raise caring and responsible children and adolescents.* San Francisco: Jossey Bass.

Benoit, Diane, & Parker, Kevin C. (1994). Stability and transmission of attachment across three generations. *Child Development, 65,* 1444–1456.

Bensur, Barbara, & Eliot, John. (1993). Case's developmental model and children's drawings. *Perceptual and Motor Skills, 76,* 371–375.

Berenbaum, Sheri, & Snyder, Elizabeth. (1995). Early hormonal influences on childhood sex-typed activity and playmate preferences: Implications for the development of sexual orientation. *Developmental Psychology, 31,* 31–42.

Bergman, Abraham B., & Rivara, Fred P. (1991). Sweden's experience in reducing childhood injuries. *Pediatrics, 88,* 69–74.

Berkson, Gershon. (1993). *Children with handicaps: A review of behavioral research.* Hillsdale, NJ: Erlbaum.

Berndt, Thomas J. (1981). Relations between social cognition, nonsocial cognition, and social behavior. In John H. Flavell & Lee Ross (Eds.), *Social cognitive development: Frontiers and possible futures.* Cambridge, England: Cambridge University Press.

Berndt, Thomas J. (1989). Friendships in childhood and adolescence. In William Damon (Ed.), *Child development today and tomorrow.* San Francisco: Jossey-Bass.

Berndt, Thomas J., & Perry, T.B. (1990). Distinguishing features of early adolescent friendship. In Raymond Montemeyer, Gerald R. Adams, & Thomas P. Gullota (Eds.), *From childhood to adolescence: A transitional period?* Newbury Park, CA: Sage.

Berndt, Thomas J., & Savin-Williams, R.C. (1992). Peer relations and friendships. In P.H. Tolan & B.J. Kohler (Eds.), *Handbook of clinical research and practice with adolescents.* New York: Wiley.

Berrick, Jill Duerr. (1998). When children cannot remain home: Foster family care and kinship care. *The Future of Children: Protecting children from abuse and neglect, 8,* 4–22.

Bertenthal, Bennett I., & Campos, Joseph J. (1990). A systems approach to the organizing effect of self-produced locomotion during infancy. In Carolyn Rovee-Collier & Lewis P. Lipsitt (Eds.), *Advances in infancy research* (Vol. 6). Norwood, NJ: Ablex.

Berzonsky, Michael D. (1989). Identity style: Conceptualization and measurement. *Journal of Adolescent Research, 4,* 268–282.

Besharov, Douglas J. (1998). Commentary 1: How we can better protect children from abuse and neglect. *The future of children: Protecting Children from Abuse and Neglect, 8,* 120–123.

Best, Deborah L. (1993). Inducing children to generate mnemonic organizational strategies: An examination of long term retention and materials. *Developmental Psychology, 29,* 324–336.

Bettes, Barbara A. (1988). Maternal depression and motherese: Temporal and intonational features. *Child Development, 59,* 1089–1096.

Beunen, G.P., Malina, R.M., Van't Hof, M.A., Simons, J., Ostyn, M., Renson, R., & Van Gerven, D. (1988). *Adolescent growth and motor performance: A longitudinal study of Belgian boys.* Champaign, IL: Human Kinetics Books.

Bhatia, M.S., Nigam, V.R., Bohra, N., & Malik, S.C. (1991). Attention deficit disorder with hyperactivity among paediatric outpatients. *Journal of Child Psychology and Psychiatry and Allied Disciplines, 32,* 297–306.

Bialystok, Ellen. (1997). Effects of bilingualism and biliteracy on children's emerging concepts of print. *Developmental Psychology, 33,* 429–440.

Bierman, Karen Lynn, Smoot, D.L., & Aumiller, K. (1993). Characteristics of aggressive-rejected, aggressive (nonrejected), and rejected (nonaggressive) boys. *Child Development, 64,* 139–151.

Bigsby, Rosemarie, Coster, Wendy, Lester, Barry M., & Peucker, Mark R. (1996). Motor behavioral cues of term and preterm infants at 3 months. *Infant Behavior & Development, 19,* 295–307.

Binder, Arnold, Geis, Gilbert, & Bruce, Dickson. (1988). *Juvenile delinquency: Historical, cultural and legal perspectives.* New York: Macmillan.

Birch, Leann L. (1990). Development of food acceptance patterns. *Developmental Psychology, 26,* 515–519.

Biringen, Zeynep, Emde, Robert N., & Pipp-Siegel, Sandra. (1997). Dyssynchrony, conflict, and resolution: Positive contributions in infant development. *American Journal of Orthopsychiatry, 67,* 4–19.

Bishop, Virginia E. (1993). Peter and the watermelon seeds. In P.J. McWilliam & Donald B. Bailey, Jr. (Eds.), *Working together with children & families.* Baltimore: Brookes.

Bitto, Adenike, Gray, Ronald H., Simpson, Joe L., Queenan, John T., Kambic, Robert T., Perez, Alfredo, Mena, Patricio, Barbato, Michele, Li, Chuanjun, & Jennings, Victoria. (1997). Adverse outcomes of planned and unplanned pregnancies among users of natural family planning: A prospective study. *American Journal of Public Health, 87,* 338–343.

Bjorklund, D.F. (Ed.). (1990). *Children's strategies: Contemporary views of cognitive development.* Hillsdale, NJ: Erlbaum.

Bjorklund, David F. (1997). In search of a metatheory for cognitive development (or, Piaget is dead and I don't feel so good myself). *Child Development, 68,* 144–148.

Bjorklund, D.F., & Bjorklund, B.R. (1992, August). "I forget." *Parents,* 62–68.

Bjorklund, D.F., & Harnishfeger, K.K. (1990). The resources construct in cognitive development: Diverse sources of evidence and a theory of inefficient inhibition. *Developmental Review, 10,* 48–71.

Blachman, Benita. (1997). *Foundations of reading acquisition and dyslexia: Implications for early intervention.* Mahwah, NJ: Erlbaum.

Blake, Judith. (1989). *Family size and achievement.* Berkeley: University of California Press.

Blankenhorn, David. (1995). *Fatherless America: Confronting our most urgent social problem.* New York: Basic Books.

Bloom, L. (1991). *Language development from two to three.* New York: Cambridge University Press.

Bloom, L. (1993). *The transition from infancy to language: Acquiring the power of expression.* New York: Cambridge University Press.

Bloom, L., Merkin, S., & Wootten, Janet. (1982). Wh- questions: Linguistic factors that contribute to the sequence of acquisition. *Child Development, 53,* 1084–1092.

Bloomfield, L. (1933). *Language.* New York: Henry Holt.

Bogin, Barry. (1996). Human growth and development from an evolutionary perspective. In C.J.K. Henry & S.J. Uliajaszel (Eds.), *Long-term consequences of early environment: Growth, development and the lifespan developmental perspective.* Cambridge, England: Cambridge University Press.

Bogin, Barry. (1995). Plasticity in the growth of Mayan refugee children living in the United States. In C.G.N. Mascie-Taylor & B. Bogin (Eds.), *Human variability and plasticity.* Cambridge: Cambridge University Press.

Bolger, Kerry E., Patterson, Charlotte J., Thompson, William W., & Kupersmidt, Janis B. (1995). Psychosocial adjustment among children experiencing persistent and intermittent family economic hardship. *Child Development, 66,* 1107–1129.

Bolger, K.E., Patterson, C.J., & Kupersmidt, J.B. (1998). Peer relationships and self-esteem among children who have been maltreated. *Child Development, 69,* 1171–1197.

Bolton, Frank G., Morris, Larry A., & MacEacheron, Ann E. (1989). *Males at risk: The other side of child sexual abuse.* Newbury Park, CA: Sage.

Borgaonkar, Digamber S. (1994). *Chromosomal variation in man.* New York: Wiley.

Bornstein, Marc H. (Ed.). (1995). *Handbook of parenting (Vol. 4): Applied and practical parenting.* Mahwah, NJ: Erlbaum.

Bornstein, Marc H. (1995). Parenting infants. In Marc H. Bornstein (Ed.), *Handbook of parenting: Childhood and parenting.* New Jersey: Erlbaum.

Bornstein, Marc H., & Lamb, M.E. (1992). *Development in infancy* (3rd ed.). New York: McGraw-Hill.

Bornstein, Marc H., Tamis-LeMonda, C.S., Tal, J., Ludemann, P., Toda, S., Rahn, C.W., Pecheux, M.-G., Azuma, H., & Vardi, D. (1992). Maternal responsiveness to infants in three societies: The United States, France, and Japan. *Child Development, 63,* 808–821.

Borovsky, D., & Rovee-Collier, C. (1990). Contextual constraints on memory retrieval at six months. *Child Development, 61*, 1569–1583.

Borsting, Eric. (1994). Overview of vision and visual processing development. In Mitchell Scheiman & Michael Rouse (Eds.), *Optimetric management of learning-related vision problems*. St. Louis, MO: Mosby.

Bouchard, Thomas J. (1994). Genes, environment, and personality. *Science, 264*, 1700–1701.

Bouchard, Thomas J., Lykken, David T., McGue, Matthew, Segal, Nancy L., & Tellegen, Auke. (1990). Sources of human psychological differences: The Minnesota study of twins reared apart. *Science, 250*, 223–228.

Boulton, Michael, & Smith, Peter K. (1989). Issues in the study of children's rough-and-tumble play. In Marianne N. Bloch & Anthony D. Pellegrini (Eds.), *The ecological context of children's play*. Norwood, NJ: Ablex.

Boulton, M.J. & Underwood, K. (1992). Bully/victim problems among middle school children. *British Journal of Educational Psychology, 62*, 73–87.

Bower, Bruce. (1996). Alcohol-loving mice spur gene search. *Science News, 149*, 340.

Bower, T.G.R. (1989). *The rational infant: Learning in infancy*. New York: Freeman.

Bowerman, Melissa. (1982). Reorganizational processes in lexical and syntactic development. In Eric Wanner & Lila R. Gleitman (Eds.), *Language acquisition: The state of the art*. Cambridge, England: Cambridge University Press.

Bowman, James E., and Murray, Robert F. (1990). *Genetic variation and disorders in peoples of African origin*. Baltimore, MD: Johns Hopkins University Press.

Boyer, Debra, & Fine, David. (1992). Sexual abuse as a factor in adolescent pregnancy and child maltreatment. *Family Planning Perspectives, 24*, 4–11, 19.

Boysson-Bardies, B., Halle, P., Sagart, L., & Durand, C. (1989). A crosslinguistic investigation of vowel formants in babbling. *Journal of Child Language, 16*, 1–17.

Brackbill, Yvonne, McManus, Karen, & Woodward, Lynn. (1988). *Medication in maternity: Infant exposure and maternal information*. Ann Arbor: University of Michigan Press.

Braddick, Oliver, & Atkinson, Janette. (1988). Sensory selectivity, attentional control, and cross-channel integration in early visual development. In Albert Yonas (Ed.), *Perceptual development in infancy*. Hillsdale, NJ: Erlbaum.

Bradley, Robert H. (1995). Environment and parenting. In Marc H. Bronstein (Ed.), *Handbook of parenting (Vol. 2): Biology and ecology of parenting*. Mahwah, NJ: Erlbaum.

Brainerd, C. J., & Reyna, V. F. (1995). Learning rate, learning opportunities, and the development of forgetting. *Developmental Psychology, 31*, 251–262.

Bray, G.A. (1989). Obesity: Basic considerations and clinical approaches. *Disease a Month, 35*, 449–537.

Breakey, G., & Pratt, B. (1991). Healthy growth for Hawaii's "Healthy Start": Toward a systematic statewide approach to the prevention of child abuse and neglect. *Zero to Three* (Bulletin of the National Center for Clinical Infant Programs), *11*, 16–22.

Bremner, J. Gavin. (1988). *Infancy*. Oxford, England: Basil Blackwell.

Brent, David A., Johnson, Barbara A., Perper, Joshua, Connolly, John, Bridge, Jeff, Bartle, Sylvia, & Rather, Chris. (1994). Personality disorder, personality traits, impulsive violence, and complete suicide in adolescents. *Journal of the American Academy of Child and Adolescent Psychiatry, 33*, 1080–1086.

Bretherton, Inge. (1992). The origins of attachment theory: John Bowlby and Mary Ainsworth. *Developmental Psychology, 28*, 759–775.

Bretherton, Inge. (1995). The origins of attachment theory: John Bowlby and Mary Ainsworth. In Ross D. Parke, Peter A. Ornstein, John J. Rieser, & Carolyn Zahn-Waxler (Eds.), *A century of developmental psychology*. Washington, DC: American Psychological Association.

Brett, Doris. (1988). *Annie stories: A special kind of storytelling*. New York: Workman Publishing.

Bril, B. (1986). Motor development and cultural attitudes. In H.T.A. Whiting & M.G. Wade (Eds.), *Themes in motor development*. Dordrecht, Netherlands: Martinus Nijhoff Publishers.

Bristol, M.M., Cohen, D.J., Costello, E.J., Denckla, M., Eckberg, T.J., Kallen, R., Kraemer, H.C., Lord, C., Maurer, R., Milvane, W.J., Minshew, N., Sigman, M., & Spence, M.A. (1996). State of the science in autism: Report to the National Institutes of Health. *Journal of Autism & Developmental Disorders, 26*, 121–154.

Bronfenbrenner, Urie. (1977). Toward an experimental ecology of human development. *American Psychologist, 32*, 513–531.

Bronfenbrenner, Urie. (1979). *The ecology of human development: Experiments by nature and design*. Cambridge, MA: Harvard University Press.

Bronfenbrenner, Urie. (1986). Ecology of the family as a context for human development research perspectives. *Developmental Psychology, 22*, 723–742.

Bronfenbrenner, Urie. (1993). The ecology of cognitive development: Research models and fugitive findings. In Robert H. Wozniak & Kurt W. Fischer (Eds.), *Development in context: Acting and thinking in specific environments*. Hillsdale, NJ: Erlbaum.

Bronfenbrenner, Urie, & Ceci, Stephen J. (1994). Nature-nurture reconceptualized in developmental perspective: A bioecological model. *Psychological Review, 10*, 568–586.

Bronson, Gordon W. (1990). Changes in infants' visual scanning across the 2- to 14-week age period. *Journal of Experimental Child Psychology, 49*, 101–125.

Bronstein, Phyllis. (1984). Differences in mothers' and fathers' behaviors toward children: A cross-cultural comparison. *Developmental Psychology, 20*, 995–1003.

Brooks-Gunn, Jeanne. (1991). Maturational timing variations in adolescent girls, antecedents of. In Richard M. Lerner, Ann C. Petersen, & Jeanne Brooks-Gunn (Eds.), *Encyclopedia of adolescence* (Vol. 2). New York: Garland.

Brooks-Gunn, Jeanne. (1991). Maturational timing variations in adolescent girls, consequences of. In Richard M. Lerner, Ann C. Petersen, & Jeanne Brooks-Gunn (Eds.), *Encyclopedia of adolescence* (Vol. 2). New York: Garland.

Brooks-Gunn, Jeanne, & Reiter, Edward O. (1990). The role of pubertal processes. In Shirley S. Feldman & Glenn R. Elliott (Eds.), *At the threshold: The developing adolescent.* Cambridge, MA: Harvard University Press.

Brooks-Gunn, Jeanne, Warren, M.P., Samelson, M., & Fox, R. (1986). Physical similarity of and disclosure of menarchal status to friends: Effects of grade and pubertal status. *Journal of Early Adolescence, 6,* 3–14.

Brooks-Gunn, Jeanne, Attie, I., Burrow, C., Rosso, J.T., & Warren, M.P. (1989). The impact of puberty on body and eating concerns in athletic and nonathletic contexts. *Journal of Early Adolescence, 9,* 269–290.

Brooks-Gunn, Jeanne, Klebanov, P.K., Liaw, F., & Spiker, D. (1993). Enhancing the development of low-birthweight, premature infants: Changes in cognition and behavior over the first three years. *Child Development, 64,* 736–753.

Brown, B.B. (1990). Peer groups and peer cultures. In S.S. Feldman & G.R. Elliott (Eds.), *At the threshold: The developing adolescent.* Cambridge, MA: Harvard University Press.

Brown, B.B., Lohr, Mary Jane, & McClenahan, Eben L. (1986). Early adolescents' perception of peer pressure. *Journal of Early Adolescence, 6,* 139–154.

Brown, J.L., & Sherman, L.P. (1995). Policy implications of new scientific knowledge. *Journal of Nutrition,* 2281S–2284S.

Brown, Josephine V., Bakeman, Roger, Coles, Clair D., Sexson, William R., & Demi, Alice S. (1998). Maternal drug use during pregnancy: Are preterm and full-term infants affected differently? *Developmental Psychology, 34,* 540–554.

Bruck, Maggie, Ceci, Stephen J., Francoeur, Emmett, & Barr, Ronald. (1995). "I hardly cried when I got my shot!": Influencing children's reports about a visit to their pediatrician. *Child Development, 66,* 193–208.

Bruck, Maggie, Ceci, Stephen J., & Melnyk, Laura. (1997). External and internal sources of variation in the creation of false reports in children. *Learning and Individual Differences, 9,* 289–319.

Bruner, Jerome S. (1982). The organization of action and the nature of adult-infant transaction. In M. von Cranach & R. Harre (Eds.), *The analysis of action.* Cambridge, England: Cambridge University Press.

Brunn, Ruth Dowling, & Brunn, Bertel. (1994). *A mind of its own: Tourette's syndrome—a story and a guide.* New York: Oxford University Press.

Buchanan, Ann. (1996). *Cycles of child maltreatment: Facts, fallacies and interventions.* Chichester, England: John Wiley & Sons.

Buchanan, Christy M., Maccoby, Eleanor E., & Dornbusch, Sanford M. (1996). *Adolescents after divorce.* Cambridge, MA: Harvard University Press.

Buckner, John C., Bassuk, Ellen L., Weinreb, Linda F., & Brooks, Margaret G. (1999). Homelessness and its relation to the mental health and behavior of low-income school-age children. *Developmental Psychology, 35,* 246–257.

Buekens, Pierre, Masury-Stroobant, Godelieve, & Delvaux, Therese. (1998). High birthweights among infants of North Africa, immigrants in Belgium. *American Journal of Public Health, 88,* 808–811.

Bukowski, W.M., Newcomb, A.F., & Hartup, W.W. (Eds.). (1996). *The company they keep: Friendship in childhood and adolescence.* New York: Cambridge University Press.

Bumpass, L.L., & Raley, R.K. (1995). Redefining single-parent families: Cohabitation and changing family reality. *Demography, 32,* 97–109.

Burns, Ailsa, & Scott, Cath. (1994). *Mother-headed families and why they have increased.* Hillsdale, NJ: Erlbaum.

Burton, Linda M. (1995). Intergenerational patterns of providing care in African-American families with teenage childbearers: Emergent patterns in an ethnographic study. In Vern L. Bengtson, K. Warner Schaie, & Linda M. Burton (Eds.), *Adult intergenerational relations: Effects of societal change.* New York: Springer.

Bushnell, E.W., & Boudreau, J.P. (1993). Motor development and the mind: The potential role of motor abilities as a determinant of aspects of perceptual development. *Child Development, 64,* 1005–1021.

Buss, A.H. (1991). The EAS theory of temperament. In J. Strelau & A. Angleitner (Eds.), *Explorations of temperament.* New York: Plenum Press.

Buss, David M. (1994). *The evolution of desire: Strategies of human mating.* New York: Basic Books.

Buss, David M., Haselton, Martie G., Shackelford, Todd K., Bleske, April L., & Wakefield, Jerome C. (1998). Adaptations, exaptations, and spandrels. *American Psychologist, 53,* 533–548.

Bussey, K., & Bandura, A. (1992). Self-regulatory mechanisms governing gender development. *Child Development, 63,* 1236–1250.

Bustan, Muhammad N., & Coker, Ann L. (1994). Maternal attitude toward pregnancy and the risk of neonatal death. *American Journal of Public Health, 84,* 411–414.

Butler, J., & Rovee-Collier, Carolyn K. (1989). Contextual gating of memory retrieval. *Developmental Psychobiology, 22,* 533–552.

Butler, Ruth. (1998). Age trends in the use of social and temporal comparison for self-evaluation: Examination of a novel developmental hypothesis. *Child Development, 69,* 1054–1073.

Byrne, J., Ellsworth, C., Bowering, E., & Vincer, M. (1993). Language development in low birth weight infants: The first two years of life. *Journal of Developmental and Behavioral Pediatrics, 14,* 21–27.

Byrnes, J.P. (1988). Formal operations: A systematic reformulation. *Developmental Review, 8,* 66–87.

Cai, Wen-Wei, Marks, James S., Chen, Charles H.C., Zhuang, You-Xien, Morris, Leo, & Harris, Jeffrey R. (1998) Increased cesarean section rates and emerging patterns of health insurance in Shanghai, China. *American Journal of Public Health, 88,* 777–780.

Cairns, Robert B. (1994). The making of a developmental science: The contributions and intellectual heritage of James Mark Baldwin. In Ross D. Parke, Peter A. Ornstein, John J. Rieser, & Carolyn Zahn-Waxler (Eds.), *A century of developmental psychology.* Washington, DC: American Psychological Association.

Cairns, Robert B., & Cairns, Beverly D. (1994). *Lifelines and risks: Pathways of youth in our time.* Cambridge, England: Cambridge University Press.

Calkins, Susan D. (1994). Origins and outcomes of individual differences in emotional regulation. *Monographs of the Society for Research in Child Development, 59* (2–3, Serial No. 240), 53–72.

Calkins, Susan D., Fox, Nathan A., & Marshall, Timothy R. (1996). Behavioral and physiological antecedents of inhibited and uninhibited behavior. *Child Development, 67,* 523–540.

Campos, Joseph J., Hiatt, Susan, Ramsay, Douglas, Henderson, Charlotte, & Svejda, Marilyn. (1978). The emergence of fear on the visual cliff. In Michael Lewis & Leonard A. Rosenblum (Eds.), *The development of affect.* New York: Plenum.

Campos, J.J., Campos, R.G., & Barrett, K.C. (1989). Emergent themes in the study of emotional development and emotion regulation. *Developmental Psychology, 25,* 394–402.

Cappelleri, J.C., Eckenrode, J., & Powers, J.L. (1993). The epidemiology of child abuse: Findings from the Second National Incidence and Prevalence Study of Child Abuse and Neglect. *American Journal of Public Health, 83,* 1622–1624.

Cardon, L.R., Smity, S.D., Fulker, D.W., Kimberling, W.J., Pennington, B.R., & DeFries, J.C. (1994). Quantitative trait locus for reading disability on chromosome 6. *Science, 266,* 276–279.

Carey, William B., & McDevitt, Sean C. (1978). Stability and change in individual temperament diagnoses from infancy to early childhood. *Journal of the American Academy of Child Psychiatry, 17,* 331–337.

Carlson, Bruce M. (1994). *Human embryology and developmental biology.* St. Louis, MO: Mosby.

Carmen, Elaine. (1989). Family violence and the victim-to-patient process. In Leah J. Dickstein & Carol C. Nadelson (Eds.), *Family violence: Emerging issues of national crisis.* Washington, DC: American Psychiatric Press.

Carmichael, S.L., Pollitt, E., Gorman, K.S., & Martorell, R. (1994). Determinants of participation in a nutritional supplementation project in rural Guatemala. *Nutrition Research, 14* (2), 163–173.

Carnegie Council on Adolescent Development. (1989). *Turning points: Preparing American youth for the 21st century.* New York: Carnegie Corporation.

Caron, Albert J., & Caron, Rose F. (1981). Processing of relational information as an index of infant risk. In S.L. Friedman & M. Sigman (Eds.), *Preterm birth and psychological development.* New York: Academic Press.

Carr, Janet. (1995). *Down's Syndrome: Children growing up: A longitudinal perspective.* Cambridge, England: Cambridge University Press.

Carraher, T.N., Carraher, D.W., & Schliemann, A.D. (1985). Mathematics in the streets and in schools. *British Journal of Developmental Psychology, 3,* 21–29.

Carraher, T.N., Schliemann, A.D., & Carraher, D.W. (1988). Mathematical concepts in everyday life. In G.B. Saxe & M. Gearhart (Eds.), *New directions for child development: Vol. 41. Children's mathematics.* San Francisco: Jossey-Bass.

Carter, D.B., & Middlemiss, W.A. (1992). The socialization of instrumental competence in families in the United States. In J.L. Roopnarine & D.B. Carter (Eds.), *Annual advances in applied developmental psychology: Vol. 5. Parent-child socialization in diverse cultures.* Norwood, NJ: Ablex.

Casey, Rita J. (1996). Emotional competence in children. In Michael Lewis & Margaret Wolan Sullivan (Eds.), *Emotional development in atypical children.* Mahwah, NJ: Erlbaum.

Caskey, C.T. (1992). DNA-based medicine: Prevention and therapy. In D.J. Kevles & L. Hood (Eds.), *The code of codes: Scientific and social issues in the Human Genome Project.* Cambridge, MA: Harvard University Press.

Caspi, A., Elder, G.H., Jr., & Bem, D.J. (1988). Moving away from the world: Life-course patterns of shy children. *Developmental Psychology, 24,* 824–831.

Caspi, Avshalom, & Moffitt, Terrie. (1991). Individual differences are accentuated during periods of social change: The sample case of girls at puberty. *Journal of Personality and Social Psychology, 61,* 157–168.

Caspi, Avshalom, & Silva, Phil A. (1995). Temperamental qualities at age three predict personality traits in young adulthood: Longitudinal evidence from a birth cohort. *Child Development, 66,* 486–498.

Caspi, Avshalom, Lynam, Donald, Moffit, Terrie, & Silva, Phil A. (1993). Unraveling girls' delinquency: Biological, dispositional, and contextual contributions to adolescent misbehavior. *Developmental Psychology, 29,* 19–30.

Caspi, A., Begg, D., Dickson, N., Harrington, H., Langley, J., Moffitt, T.E., & Silva, P.A. (1997). Personality differences predict health-risk behaviors in young adulthood: Evidence from a longitudinal study. *Journal of Personality and Social Psychology, 73,* 1052–1063.

Cassel, W.W., Roebers, C.E.M., & Bjorklund, D.F. (1996). Developmental patterns of eyewitness responses to repeated and increasingly suggestive questions. *Journal of Experimental Child Psychology, 61,* 116–133.

Casswell, Sally. (1996). Alcohol use: Growing up and learning about drinking—Children in Dunedin in the 1980s. In Phil A. Silva & Warren R. Stanton (Eds.), *From child to adult: The Dunedin multidisciplinary health and development study.* Auckland: Oxford University Press.

Cauffman, Elizabeth, & Steinberg, Laurence. (1996). Interactive effects of menarcheal status and dating on dieting and disordered eating among adolescent girls. *Developmental Psychology, 32,* 631–635.

Ceci, Stephen J., & Bruck, M. (1993). Child witnesses: Translating research into policy. *Social Policy Report of the Society for Research in Child Development, 7,* 1–30.

Ceci, Stephen J., & Bruck, M. (1993). The suggestibility of the child witness. *Psychological Bulletin, 113,* 403–439.

Ceci, Stephen J., & Huffman, Mary Lyn Crotteau. (1997) How suggestible are preschool children? Cognitive and social factors. *Journal of the American Academy of Child & Adolescent Psychiatry, 36,* 948–958.

Centers for Disease Control, (1993). *1992 Annual Report.* Division of STD/HIV prevention. Atlanta: GA.

Centers for Disease Control and Prevention. (1994, April 22). Programs for the prevention of suicide among adolescents and young adults. *Morbidity and Mortality Recommendations and Reports, 43,* 1–7.

Centers for Disease Control and Prevention. (1994, April 22). Suicide contagion and the reporting of suicide. *Morbidity and Mortality Weekly Report, 43,* (No. RR–6), 13–18.

Centers for Disease Control and Prevention. (1994, April 29). Zidovudine for the prevention of HIV transmission from mother to infant. *Morbidity and Mortality Weekly Report, 43,* 285–287.

Centers for Disease Control and Prevention. (1994, August 19). Changes in the cigarette brand preferences of adolescent smokers—United States, 1989–1993. *Morbidity and Mortality Weekly Report, 43,* 577–581.

Centers for Disease Control and Prevention. (1994, October 21). Reasons for tobacco use and symptoms of nicotine withdrawal among adolescent and young adult tobacco users—United States, 1993. *Morbidity and Mortality Weekly Report, 43,* 745–750.

Centers for Disease Control and Prevention. (1995, March 24). Youth risk behavior surveillance—United States, 1993. *Morbidity and Mortality Weekly Report, 44,* (No. SS–1), 1–56.

Centers for Disease Control and Prevention. (1996, September 27). Youth risk behavior survellance—United States, 1995. *Morbidity and Mortality Weekly Report, 45,* 20.

Centers for Disease Control and Prevention. (1996, October 11). Sudden Infant Death Syndrome—1983–1994. *Morbidity and Mortality Weekly Report, 45,* 859–865.

Centers for Disease Control and Prevention. (1997, February 28). Update: Trends in AIDS incidence, deaths, and prevalence—United States, 1996. *Morbidity and Mortality Weekly Report, 46,* 165–173.

Centers for Disease Control and Prevention. (1997, April 25). Alcohol consumption among pregnant and childbearing-aged women—United States, 1991–1995. *Morbidity and Mortality Weekly Report, 46,* 346–350.

Centers for Disease Control and Prevention. (1997, May 16). Varicella-related deaths among adults—United States, 1997. *Morbidity and Mortality Weekly Report, 46,* 409–412.

Centers for Disease Control and Prevention. (1998, April 3). Youth risk behavior surveillance—United States, 1997. Tobacco use among high school students. *Morbidity and Mortality Weekly Report, 47,* 229–233.

Centers for Disease Control and Prevention. (1998, April 17). Measles—United States, 1997. *Morbidity and Mortality Weekly Report, 47,* 273–276.

Centers for Disease Control and Prevention. (1998, August 14). Youth risk behavior surveillance—United States, 1997. *Morbidity and Mortality Weekly Report, 47.*

Centers for Disease Control and Prevention. (1998, September 11). Characteristics of health education among secondary schools—School health education profiles, 1996. *Morbidity and Mortality Weekly Report, 47,* 1–31.

Centers for Disease Control and Prevention. (1998, September 18). Trends in sexual risk behaviors among high school students—United States, 1991–1997. *Morbidity and Mortality Weekly Report, 47,* 1–31.

Ceron-Mireles, Prudencia, Harlow, Sioban D., & Sanchez-Carrillo, Constanza I. (1996). The risk of prematurity and small-for-gestational-age birth in Mexico City: The effects of working conditions and antenatal leave. *American Journal of Public Health, 86,* 825–831.

Chalfant, J.C. (1989). Learning disabilities: Policy issues and promising approaches. *American Psychologist, 44,* 392–398.

Chandler, Lynette A. (1990). Neuromotor assessment. In Elizabeth D. Gibbs & Douglas M. Teti (Eds.), *Interdisciplinary assessment of infants.* Baltimore: Brookes.

Chandler, Michael. (1997). Stumping for progress in a post-modern world. In Eric Amsel & K. Ann Renninger (Eds.), *Change and development: Issues of theory, method, & application.* Mahwah, NJ: Erlbaum.

Chandler, Michael, Fritz, Anna S., & Hala, Suzanne. (1989). Small scale deceit: Deception as a marker of two, three, and four-year-olds' early theories of mind. *Child Development, 60,* 1263–1277.

Chao, Ruth K. (1994). Beyond parental control and authoritarian parenting style: Understanding Chinese parenting through the cultural notion of training. *Child Development, 65,* 1111–1119.

Chappell, Patricia A., & Steitz, Jean A. (1993). Young children's human figure drawings and cognitive development. *Perceptual and Motor Skills, 76,* 611–617.

Chen, Shing-Jen. (1996). Positive childishness: Images of childhood in Japan. In C. Philip Hwang, Michael E. Lamb, & Irving E. Sigell (Eds.), *Images of childhood.* Mahwah, NJ: Erlbaum.

Chen, Zhe, Sanchez, Rebecca Polley, & Campbell, Tammy. (1997). From beyond to within their grasp: The rudiments of analogical problem solving in 10- and 13-month-olds. *Developmental Psychology, 33,* 790–801.

Cherlin, Andrew. (1992). *Marriage, divorce, remarriage.* Cambridge, MA: Harvard University Press.

Chess, Stella, & Thomas, Alexander. (1990). Continuities and discontinuities in development. In Lee N. Robins & Michael

Rutter (Ed.), *Straight and devious pathways from childhood to adulthood.* New York: Cambridge University Press.

Chess, Stella, Thomas, Alexander, & Birch, Herbert. (1965). *If your child is a person.* New York: Viking Press.

Chi, Micheline T.H. (1978). Knowledge structures and memory development. In R.S. Siegler (Ed.), *Children's thinking: What develops?* Hillsdale, NJ: Erlbaum.

Chi, Micheline T.H., Hutchinson, J.E., & Robin, A.F. (1989). How inferences about novel domain-related concepts can be constrained by structured knowledge. *Merrill-Palmer Quarterly, 35,* 27–62.

Chikkatur, Anita. (1997). A shortcut to independence. In Andrea Estepa & Philip Kay (Eds.) *Starting with I: Personal essays by teenagers.* New York: Persea Books.

Children's Defense Fund. (1998). *The state of America's children, yearbook 1998.* Washington, DC: Publications Department.

Child Welfare League of America. (1996). Family Preservation Programs: State agency survey. In Michael R. Petit & Patrick A. Curtis, *Child abuse and neglect: A look at the states: The CWLA stat book.* Washington, DC: Child Welfare League of America.

Chisolm, Kim. (1998). A three year follow-up of attachment and indiscriminate friendliness in children adopted from Romanian orphanages. *Child Development, 69,* 1092–1106.

Chiu, L.H. (1987). Child-rearing attitudes of Chinese, Chinese-American, and Anglo-American mothers. *International Journal of Psychology, 22,* 409–419.

Chomitz, Virginia Rall, Cheung, Lilian W.Y., & Lieberman, Ellice. (1995). The role of lifestyle in preventing low birth weight. *The Future of Children: Low Birth Weight, 5,* 121–138.

Chomsky, Noam. (1968). *Language and mind.* New York: Harcourt, Brace, World.

Chomsky, Noam. (1980). *Rules and representations.* New York: Columbia University Press.

Chorney, M.J., Adolph, Karen E., Eppler, M.A., & Gibson, Eleanor J. (1993). Crawling versus walking infants' perception of affordances for locomotion over sloping surfaces. *Child Development, 64,* 1158–1174.

Chorney, M.J., Chorney, K., Seese, N., Owen, M.J., Daniels, J., McGuffin, P., Thompson, L.A., Detterman, D.K., Benbow, C., Lubinski, D., Eley, T., & Plomin, R. (1998). A quantitative trait locus associated with cognitive ability in children. *Psychological Science, 3,* 159–166.

Cicchetti, Dante. (1990). The organization and coherence of socioemotional, cognitive, and representational development: Illustrations through a developmental psychopathology perspective on Down syndrome and child maltreatment. In R.A. Thompson (Ed.), *Nebraska symposium on motivation: Vol. 36. Socioemotional development.* Lincoln: University of Nebraska Press.

Cicchetti, Dante, & Beeghly, Marjorie. (1990). *Children with Down Syndrome: A developmental perspective.* Cambridge, England: Cambridge University Press.

Cicchetti, Dante, & Carlson, Vicki. (Eds.). (1989). *Child maltreatment: Theory and research on the causes and consequences of child abuse and neglect.* Cambridge, England: Cambridge University Press.

Cicchetti, Dante, Toth, S.L., & Hennessy, K. (1993). Child maltreatment and school adaptation: Problems and promises. In Dante Cicchetti & S.L. Toth (Eds.), *Advances in applied developmental psychology series: Vol. 8. Child abuse, child development, and social policy.* Norwood, NJ: Ablex.

Cicirelli, Victor G. (1995). *Sibling relationships across the life span.* New York: Plenum Press.

Cillessen, A.H.N., van Ijzendoorn, H.W., van Lieshout, C.F.M., & Hartup, W.W. (1992). Heterogeneity among peer-rejected boys: Subtypes and stabilities. *Child Development, 63,* 893–905.

Clark, Eve V. (1982). The young word maker: A case study of innovation in the child's lexicon. In Eric Wanner & Lila R. Gleitman (Eds.), *Language acquisition: The state of the art.* Cambridge, England: Cambridge University Press.

Clark, Eve V. (1990). On the pragmatics of contrast. *Journal of Child Language, 17,* 417–431.

Clark, Tim, & Rees, John. (1996). *Practical management of asthma.* London: Martin Dunitz.

Clarke-Stewart, K. Alison. (1989). Infant day care: Maligned or malignant? *American Psychologist, 44,* 266–273.

Cnattingius, Sven, & Haglund, Bengt. (1997). Decreasing smoking prevalence during pregnancy in Sweden: The effect on small-for-gestational-age births. *American Journal of Public Health, 87,* 410–413.

Cobb, Paul, Wood, Terry, & Yackel, Erna. (1993). Discourse, mathematical thinking and classroom practice. In Ellice A. Forman, Norris Minick, & C. Addison Stone (Eds.), *Contexts for learning.* New York: Oxford University Press.

Coelho, Elizabeth. (1991). Social integration of immigrant and refugee children. In J. Porter (Ed.), *New Canadian voices.* Toronto: Wall & Emerson.

Cohen, L.B., & Oakes, L.M. (1993). How infants perceive a simple causal event. *Developmental Psychology, 29,* 421–433.

Cohn, Jeffrey F., & Tronick, Edward Z. (1983). Three-month-old infants' reaction to stimulated maternal depression. *Child Development, 54,* 185–193.

Cohn, Lawrence D.S., & Adler, Nancy E. (1992). Female and male perception of ideal body shapes. *Psychology of Women Quarterly, 16,* 69–79.

Coie, John D., & Cillessen, A.H.N. (1993). Peer rejection: Origins and effects on children's development. *Current Directions in Psychological Science, 2,* 89–92.

Cole, Michael. (1996). *Cultural psychology: A once and future discipline.* Cambridge, MA: Belknap Press.

Cole, M., Gay, J., Glick, J., & Sharp, C.W. (1971). *The cultural context of learning and thinking.* New York: Basic Books.

Cole, Pamela M., Barrett, Karen C., & Zahn-Waxler, Carolyn. (1992). Emotion displays in two-year-olds during mishaps. *Child Development, 63,* 314–324.

Coleman, J.C., & Hendry, L. (1990). *The nature of adolescence* (2nd ed.). London: Routledge.

Coles, Robert. (1990). *The spiritual life of children.* Boston: Houghton Mifflin.

Coles, Robert. (1997). *How to raise a moral child: The moral intelligence of children.* New York: Random House.

Colin, Virginia L. (1996). *Human attachment.* Philadelphia: Temple University Press.

Coll, Cyntich T. Garcia, Meyer, Elaine C., & Brillon, Lisa. (1995). Ethnic and minority parenting. In Marc H. Bronstein (Ed.), *Handbook of parenting (Vol. 2): Biology and ecology of parenting.* Mahwah, NJ: Erlbaum.

Collins, W. Andrew. (1990). Parent-child relationships in the transition to adolescence: Continuity and change in interaction, affect, and cognition. In R. Montemayor, G. Adams, & T. Gullotta (Eds.), *From childhood to adolescence: A transitional period? Advances in adolescent development: Vol. 2. The transition from childhood to adolescence.* Beverly Hills, CA: Sage.

Commission on the Restructuring of the American High School. (1996). *Breaking ranks: Changing an American institution.* Reston, VA: National Association of Secondary School Principles.

Commons, Michael L., & Richards, Francis A. (1984). A general model of stage theory. In Michael L. Commons, Francis A. Richards, & Cheryl Armon (Eds.), *Beyond formal operations.* New York: Praeger.

Compas, Bruce E., Banez, Gerard A., Malcarne, Vanessa, & Worsham, Nancy. (1991). Perceived control and coping with stress: A developmental perspective. *Journal of Social Issues, 47,* 23–34.

Connor, J.M., & Ferguson-Smith, M.A. (1991). *Essential medical genetics.* Oxford, England: Blackwell Scientific Publications.

Conrad, Marilyn, & Hammen, Constance. (1993). Protective and resource factors in high- and low-risk children: A comparison of children with unipolar, bipolar, medically ill, and normal mothers. *Development and Psychopathology, 5,* 593–607.

Constable, Catherine. (1987). Talking with teachers. Increasing our relevance as language interventionists in the schools. *Seminars in Speech & Lanugage, 8,* 345–356.

Constantine, L.L. (1986). *Family paradigms: The practice of theory in family therapy.* New York: Guilford.

Constantine, L.L. (1993). The structure of family paradigms: An analytical model of family variation. *Journal of Marital and Family Therapy, 19,* 39–70.

Cooksey, Elizabeth C. (1997). Consequences of young mothers' marital histories for children's cognitive development. *Journal of Marriage and the Family, 57,* 245–262.

Cookson, William O.C.M., & Moffatt, Miriam F. (1997). Asthma: An epidemic in the absence of infection? *Science, 275,* 41–42.

Coontz, Stephanie. (1992). *The way we never were: American families and the nostalgia trap.* New York: Basic Books.

Cooper, M. Lynne, Shaver, Phillip R., & Collins, Nancy L. (1998). Attachment styles, emotion regulation, and adjustment in ado-lescence. *Journal of Personality and Social Psychology, 74,* 1380–1397.

Cooper, R.O. (1993). The effect of prosody on young infants' speech perception. In C. Rovee-Collier & L.P. Lipsitt (Eds.), *Advances in infancy research* (Vol. 8). Norwood, NJ: Ablex.

Corter, Carl M., & Fleming, Alison S. (1995). Psychobiology of maternal behavior in human beings. In Marc H. Bornstein (Ed.), *Handbook of parenting: Biology and ecology of parenting.* Mahwah, NJ: Erlbaum.

Cosby, Ennis, quoted in Chua-Eoan, Howard. (1997, January 27.) He was my hero. *Time Magazine, 149.*

Courchesne, Eric, Chisum, Heather, & Tounsend, Jeanne. (1994). Neural activity-dependent brain changes in development: Implications for psychopathology. *Development and Psychopathology, 6,* 697–722.

Courtney, Mark E. (1998) The costs of child protection in the context of welfare reform. *The Future of Children: Protecting Children from Abuse and Neglect, 8,* 88–103.

Cowan, Nelson. (Ed.). (1997). *The development of memory in childhood.* Hove, East Sussex, UK: Psychology Press.

Cowen, Emory I., Wyman, Peter A., & Work, William C. (1992). The relationship between retrospective reports of early child temperament and adjustment at ages 10–12. *Journal of Abnormal Child Psychology, 20,* 39–50.

Crabb, Peter B., & Bielawski, Dawn. (1994). The social representation of material culture and gender in children's books. *Sex Roles, 30,* 69–70.

Cramer, Phebe, & Skidd, Jody E. (1992). Correlates of self-worth in preschoolers: The role of gender-stereotyped styles of behavior. *Sex Roles, 26,* 369–390.

Creasy, Robert K. (Ed.). (1997). *Management of labor and delivery.* Malden, MA: Blackwell Science.

Crick, N.R., & Grotpeter, J.K. (1996). Children's treatment by peers: Victims of relational and overt aggression. *Development and Psychopathology, 8,* 367–380.

Crick, Nicki R., Casas, Juan F., & Mosher, Monique. (1997). Relational and overt aggression in preschool. *Developmental Psychology, 33,* 579–588.

Crittenden, Patricia M. (1992). The social ecology of treatment: Case study of a service system for maltreated children. *American Journal of Orthopsychiatry, 62,* 22–34.

Crittenden, Patricia McKinsey. (1995). Attachment and psychopathology. In Susan Goldberg, Roy Muir, & John Kerr (Eds.), *Attachment theory: social, developmental, and clinical perspectives.* Hillsdale, NJ: Analytic Press.

Crittenden, Patricia M., Claussen, Angelika H., & Sugarman, David B. (1994). Physical and psychological maltreatment in middle childhood and adolescence. *Development and Psychopathology, 6,* 145–164.

Crockenberg, S., & Litman, C. (1990). Autonomy as competence in 2-year-olds: Maternal correlates of child defiance, compliance, and self-assertion. *Developmental Psychology, 26,* 961–971.

Cromer, B.A., Tarnowski, K.J., Stein, A.M., Harton, P., & Thornton, D.J. (1990). The school breakfast program and cognition in adolescents. *Journal of Developmental and Behavioral Pediatrics, 11*, 295–300.

Cromwell, Rue L. (1993). Searching for the origins of schizophrenia. *Psychological Science, 4*, 276–279.

Cross, W.W., Jr. (1991). *Shades of black: Diversity in African-American identity*. Philadelphia: Temple University Press.

Crowell, Judith A., Waters, Everett, Treboux, Dominique, O'Connor, Elizabeth, Colon-Downs, Christina, Feider, Olga, Golby, Barbara, & Posada, German. (1996). Discriminant validity of the adult attachment interview. *Child Development, 67*, 2584–2599.

Crystal, Ronald. (1995). Transfer of genes to humans: Early lessons and obstacles to success. *Science, 270*, 404–409.

Crystal, Stephen. (1996). Economic status of the elderly. In Robert H. Binstock & Linda K. George (Eds.), *Handbook of aging and the social sciences*. San Diego, CA: Academic Press.

Csikszentmihalyi, M., Rathunde, K., & Whalen, S. (1993). *Talented teenagers: The roots of success and failure*. Cambridge: Cambridge University Press.

Cummings, E.M., & Davies, P. (1994). *Children and marital conflict: The impact of family dispute and resolution*. New York: Guilford.

Cummings, E.M., Hennessy, K.D., Rabideau, G.J., & Cicchetti, D. (1994). Responses of physically abused boys to interadult anger involving their mothers. *Development and Psychopathology, 6*, 31–41.

Curtis, P.A., Boyd, J.D., Liepold, M., et al. (1995). *Child abuse and neglect: A look at the states: The CWLA stat book*. Washington, DC: Child Welfare League of America.

Daly, M., Singh, L., & Wilson, M. (1993). Children fathered by previous partners: A risk factor for violence against women. *Canadian Journal of Public Health, 84*, 209–210.

Daniels, C.R. (1993). *At women's expense: State power and the politics of fetal rights*. Cambridge, MA: Harvard University Press.

Darling, N., & Steinberg, L. (1993). Parenting style as context: An integrative model. *Psychological Bulletin, 113*, 487–496.

Dash, L. (1986, January 26). Children's children: The crisis up close. *The Washington Post*, A1, A12.

Datan, Nancy. (1986). Oedipal conflict, platonic love: Centrifugal forces in intergenerational relations. In Nancy Datan, Anita L. Greene, & Hayne W. Reese (Eds.), *Life-span developmental psychology: Intergenerational relations*. Hillsdale, NJ: Erlbaum.

D'Augelli, A.R., & Hershberger, S.L. (1993). Lesbian, gay and bisexual youth in community settings: Personal challenges and mental health problems. *American Journal of Community Psychology, 21*, 421–448.

D'Augelli, Anthony R., & Dark, Lawrence J. (1994). Lesbian, gay, and bisexual youths. In Leonard D. Eron, Jacquelyn H. Gentry, & Peggy Schlegel (Eds.), *Reason to hope: A psychosocial per-spective on violence and youth*. Washington, DC: American Psychological Association.

Davidson, Philip W., Cain, Nancy N., Sloane-Reeves, Jean E., & Van Speybroech, Alec. (1994). Characteristics of community-based individuals with mental retardation and aggressive behavioral disorders. *American Journal of Mental Retardation, 98*, 704–716.

Davies, Bronwyn. (1982). *Life in the classroom and playground*. London: Routledge and Kegan Paul.

Davies, D.P., & Gantley, M. (1994). Ethnicity and the aetiology of sudden infant death syndrome. *Archives of Disease in Childhood, 70*, 349–353.

Davies, Lorraine, Avison, William R., & McAlpine, Donna D. (1997). Significant life experiences and depression among single and married mothers. *Journal of Marriage and the Family, 59*, 294–308.

Davis-Floyd, Robbie E. (1992). *Birth as an American rite of passage*. Berkeley: University of California Press.

Dawson, Deborah A. (1991). Family structure and children's health and well-being: Data from the 1988 national health interview study on child health. *Journal of Marriage and the Family, 53*, 573–584.

Dawson, Geraldine. (1994). Frontal electroencephalographic correlates of individual differences in emotional expression in infants. In N. Fox (Ed.), Emotion regulation: Behavioral and biological considerations. *Monographs of the Society for Research in Child Development, 59* (Serial No. 240).

Deater-Deckard, Kirby, Dodge, Kenneth A., Bates, John E., & Pettit, Gregory S. (1996). Physical discipline among African American and European American mothers: Links to children's externalizing behaviors. *Developmental Psychology, 32*, 1065–1072.

DeFries, John C., Plomin, Robert, & Fulker, David W. (Eds.). (1994). *Nature and nurture during middle childhood*. Cambridge, MA: Blackwell.

Delpit, Lisa. (1995). *Other people's children: Cultural conflict in the classroom*. New York: New Press.

Demo, D.H., & Acock, A.C. (1986). Family structure, family process, and adolescent well-being. *Journal of Research on Adolescence, 6*, 457–488.

Dempster, Frank N. (1993). Resistance to interference: Developmental changes in a basic processing mechanism. In M. L. Howe and R. Pasnak (Eds.), *Emerging themes in cognitive development: Vol I. Foundations*. New York: Springer-Verlag.

Denton, Rhonda, & Kampfe, Charlene M. (1994). The relationship between family variables and adolescent substance abuse: A literature review. *Adolescence, 29*, 475–495.

Dent-Read, Cathy, & Zukow-Goldring, Patricia. (1997). Introduction: Ecological realism, dynamic systems, and epigenetic systems approaches to development. In Cathy Dent-Read & Patricia Zukow-Goldring (Eds.), *Evolving explanations of development*. Washington, DC: American Psychological Association.

de Quirós, Gullermo Bernaldo, Kinsbourne, Marcel, Palmer, Roland L., & Rufo, Dolores Tocci. (1994). Attention deficit disorder in children: Three clinical variants. *Journal of Developmental and Behavioral Pediatrics, 15,* 311–319.

Derochers, Stephen, Ricard, Marcelle, Dexarie, Therese Gouin, & Allard, Louise. (1994). Developmental syncronicity between social referencing and Piagetian sensorimotor causality. *Infant Behavior and Development, 17,* 303–309.

de Róiste, A. & Bushnell, I.W.R. (1996). Tactile stimulation: Short- and long-term benefits for pre-term infants. *British Journal of Developmental Psychology, 14,* 41–53.

DeRosier, Melissa E., Cillessen, Antonius H.N., Coie, John D., & Dodge, Kenneth. (1994). Group social context and children's aggressive behavior. *Child Development, 65,* 1068–1079.

de Villiers, Jill G., & de Villiers, Peter A. (1978). *Language acquisition.* Cambridge, MA: Harvard University Press.

de Villiers, Peter A., & de Villiers, Jill G. (1992). Language development. In M.H. Bornstein & M.E. Lamb (Eds.), *Developmental psychology: An advanced textbook* (3rd ed.). Hillsdale, NJ: Erlbaum.

Dewey, Kathryn G., Heinig, M. Jane, & Nommsen-Rivers, Laurie A. (1995). Differences in morbidity between breast-fed and formula-fed infants. *Journal of Pediatrics, 126,* 696–702.

DeWolff, Marianne S. & van Ijzendoorn, Mariuns H. (1997). Sensitivity and attachment: A meta-analysis on parental antecedents of infant attachment. *Child Development, 68,* 571–591.

Diamond, A. (1990). Neuropsychological insights into the meaning of object concept development. In S. Carey & R. Gelman (Eds.), *The epigenesis of mind: Essays on biology and cognition.* Hillsdale, NJ: Erlbaum.

Diamond, Adele, Prevor, Meredith B., Callender, Glenda, & Druin, Donald P. (1997). Prefrontal cortex cognitive deficits in children treated early and continuously for PKU. *Monographs of the Society for Research in Child Development, 62* (Serial No. 252).

Diaz, Rafael M. (1987). The private speech of young children at risk: A test of three deficit hypotheses. *Early Childhood Research Quarterly, 2,* 181–197.

Dickerson, Leah J., & Nadelson, Carol (Eds.). (1989). *Family violence: Emerging issues of national crisis.* Washington, DC: American Psychiatric Press.

Diekstra, Rene. (1995). Depression and suicidal behaviors in adolescence: Sociocultural and time trends. The positive effects of schooling. In Michael Rutter (Ed.), *Psychosocial disturbances in young people: Challenges for prevention.* Cambridge, England: Cambridge University Press.

Diekstra, Rene F.W., Kienhorst, C.W.M., & Witde, E.J. (1995). Suicide and suicidal behavior among adolescents. In Michael Rutter & David J. Smith (Eds.), *Psychosocial disorders in young people: Time trends and their causes.* New York: Published for Academia Europaea by J. Wiley.

Dielman, T.E. (1994). School-based research on the prevention of adolescent alcohol use and misuse: Methodological issues and advances. *Journal of Research on Adolescence, 4,* 271–294.

Dietz, William H. (1995). Childhood obesity. In Lilian W.Y. Cheung & Julius B. Richmond (Eds.), *Child health, nutrition, and physical activity.* Champaign, IL: Human Kinetics.

Digman, J.M. (1990). Personality structure: Emergence of the five-factor model. *Annual Review of Psychology, 41,* 417–440.

DiMatteo, M. Rubin, Morton, Sally C., Lepper, Heidi S., Damush, Teresa M., Carney, Maureen F., Pearson, Marjorie, & Kahn, Katherine L. (1996). Cesarean childbirth and psychosocial outcomes: A meta-analysis. *Health Psychology, 15,* 303–314.

DiPietro, Janet A., Hodgson, Denice M., Costigan, Kathleen A., & Hilton, Sterling C. (1996). Fetal neurobehavioral development. *Child Development, 67,* 2553–2567.

Dishion, Thomas J., Andrews, David W., & Crosby, Lynn. (1995). Antisocial boys and their friends in early adolescence: Relationship characteristics, quality, and interactional processes. *Child Development, 66,* 139–151.

Dix, T. (1991). The affective organization of parenting: Adaptive and maladaptive processes. *Psychological Bulletin, 110,* 3–25.

Dixon, Wallace E., Jr., & Shore, Cecilia. (1997). Temperamental predictors of linguistic style during multiword acquisition. *Infant Behavior & Development, 20,* 93–98.

Dodge, Kenneth A., Coie, J.D., Pettit, G.S., & Price, J.M. (1990). Peer status and aggression in boys' groups: Developmental and contextual analyses. *Child Development, 61,* 1289–1309.

Dodge, Kenneth A., Pettit, Gregory S., & Bates, John E. (1994). Effects of physical maltreatment on the development of peer relations. *Development and Psychopathology, 6,* 43–55.

Doherty, William J., Kouneski, Edward F., & Erickson, Martha F. (1998) Responsible fathering: An overview and conceptual framework. *Journal of Marriage and the Family, 60,* 277–292.

Donaldson, Margaret. (1978). *Children's minds.* New York: Norton.

Donovan, Patricia. (1997). Can statutory rape laws be effective in preventing adolescent pregnancy? *Family Planning Perspectives, 29,* 30–34, 40.

Dornbusch, S.M., Ritter, P.L., Leiderman, P.H., Roberts, D.F., & Fraleigh, M.J. (1987). The relation of parenting style to adolescent school performance. *Child Development, 58,* 1244–1257.

Doussard-Roosevelt, Jane A., Porges, Stephen W., Scanlon, John W., Alemi, Behjat, & Scanlon, Kathleen B. (1997). Vagal regulation heart rate in the prediction of developmental outcome for very low birth weight preterm infants. *Child Development, 68,* 173–186.

Downs, A. Chris. (1990). The social biological constraints of social competency. In Thomas P. Gullotta, Gerald R. Adams, & Raymond R. Montemayor (Eds.), *Developing social competency in adolescence.* Newbury Park, CA: Sage.

Drake, Brett, & Zuravin, Susan. (1998). Bias in child maltreatment reporting: Revisiting the myth of classlessness. *American Journal of Orthopsychiatry, 68,* 295–304.

Dreyer, Philip H. (1994). Designing curricular identity interventions. In Sally L. Archer (Ed.), *Interventions for adolescent identity development.* Thousand Oaks, CA: Sage.

Drotar, Dennis, Eckerle, Debby, Satola, Jackie, Pallotta, John, & Wyatt, Betsy. (1990). Maternal interactional behavior with nonorganic failure-to-thrive infants: A case comparison study. *Child Abuse and Neglect, 14,* 41–51.

Drotar, Dennis, Pallotta, John, & Eckerle, Debbie. (1994). A prospective study of family environments of children hospitalized for nonorganic failure-to-thrive. *Developmental and Behavioral Pediatrics, 15,* 78–85.

Dryfoos, Joy. (1990). *Adolescents at risk: Prevalence and prevention.* New York: Oxford University Press.

Dubas, Judith Semon, Graber, Julia A., & Petersen, Anne C. (1991). A longitudinal investigation of adolescents' changing perceptions of pubertal timing. *Developmental Psychology, 27,* 580–586.

du Bois-Reymond, Manuela. (1995). The role of parents in the transition period of young people. In Manuel du Bois-Reymond, Rene Diekstra, Klaus Hurrelmann, & Els Peters (Eds.), *Childhood and youth in Germany and the Netherlands: Transitions and coping strategies of adolescents.* Berlin: Mouton de Gruyter.

Dudek, Stephanie Z., Strobel, M.G., & Runco, Mark A. (1994). Cumulative and proximal influences on the social environment and children's creative potential. *Journal of Genetic Psychology, 154,* 487–499.

Duncan, Greg J., & Brooks-Gunn, Jeanne. (Eds). (1997). *Consequences of growing up poor.* New York: Russell Sage Foundation.

Dunn, Judy, Bretherton, I., & Munn, P. (1987). Conversations about feeling states between mothers and their young children. *Developmental Psychology, 23,* 132–139.

Dunphy, Dexter C. (1963). The social structure of urban adolescent peer groups. *Sociometry, 26,* 230–246.

Durrant, Joan E. (1996). Public attitudes toward corporal punishment in Canada. In Detlev Frehsee, Wiebke Horn, & Kai-D. Bussmann (Eds.), *Family violence against children: A challenge for society.* Berlin: De Gruyter.

Dykens, Elisabeth M., Hodapp, Robert M., & Leckman, James F. (1994). *Behavior and development in fragile X syndrome.* Thousand Oaks, CA: Sage.

Dykman, Roscoe, & Ackerman, Peggy T. (1993). Behavioral subtypes of attention deficit disorder. *Exceptional Children, 60,* 132–141.

East, Patricia L. (1998). Racial and ethnic differences in girls' sexual, marital, and birth expectations. *Journal of Marriage and the Family, 60,* 150–162.

Ebrahim, S. H., Suman, E.T., Floyd, R.L., Murphy, C.C., Bennett, E.M., & Boyle, C.A. (1998). Alcohol consumption by pregnant women in the United States during 1988–1995. *Obstetrics and Gynecology, 92,* 187–192.

Eccles, J.S. (1993). School and family effects on the ontogeny of children's interests, self-perceptions, and activity choices. In J.E. Jacobs (Ed.), *Nebraska symposium on motivation: Vol. 40. Developmental perspectives on motivation.* Lincoln: University of Nebraska Press.

Eccles, Jacquelynne S., Lord, Sarah, & Buchanan, Christy Miller. (1996). School transitions in early adolescence: What are we doing to our young people? In Julia A. Graber, Jeanne Brooks-Gunn, & Anne C. Pattersen (Eds.), *Transitions through adolescence: Interpersonal domains and context.* Mahwah, NJ: Erlbaum.

Eckenrode, J., Laird, M., & Doris, J. (1993). School performance and disciplinary problems among abused and neglected children. *Developmental Psychology, 29,* 53–62.

Eder, R.A. (1989). The emergent personologist: The structure and content of 3.5-, 5.5-, and 7.5-year-olds' concepts of themselves and other persons. *Child Development, 60,* 1218–1228.

Eder, R.A. (1990). Uncovering young children's psychological selves: Individual and developmental differences. *Child Development, 61,* 849–863.

Edwards, John R. (1994). *Multilingualism.* London: Routledge.

Egeland, Byron. (1991). A longitudinal study of high risk families: Issues and findings. In Raymond H. Starr & Davia A. Wolfe (Eds.), *The effects of child abuse and neglect.* New York: Guilford.

Egeland, Byron. (1993). A history of abuse is a major risk factor for abusing the next generation. In Richard J. Gelles & Donileen R. Loseke (Eds.), *Current controversies in family violence.* Newbury Park, CA: Sage.

Eide, A.H. & Acuda, S.W. (1996). Cultural orientation and adolescents' alcohol use in Zimbabwe. *Addiction, 92,* 807–814.

Eimas, Peter D., Sigueland, Einar R., Jusczyk, Peter, & Vigorito, James. (1971). Speech perception in infants. *Science, 171,* 303–306.

Eisen, M., & Zellman, G. L. (1992). A health beliefs field experiment: Teen talk. In B.C. Miller et al. (Eds.), *Preventing adolescent pregnancy.* Newbury Park, CA: Sage.

Eisenberg, N. (1986). *Altruistic emotion, cognition, and behavior.* Hillsdale, NJ: Erlbaum.

Eisenberg, Nancy, & Fabes, Richard A. (1992). Emotion, self-regulation, and the development of social competence. In M. S. Clark (Ed.), *Emotions and social behavior: Vol. 14, Review of personality and social psychology.* Newbury Park, CA: Sage.

Eisenberg, Nancy & Murphy, Bridget. (1995). Parenting and children's moral development. In Marc H. Bronstein (Ed.), *Handbook of parenting (Vol. 4): Applied and practical parenting.* Mahwah, NJ: Erlbaum.

Eisenberg, Nancy, Fabes, Richard A., & Murphy, Bridget C. (1996). Parents' reactions to children's negative emotions: Relations to children's social competence and comforting behavior. *Child Development, 67,* 2227–2247.

Eisenberg, Nancy, Fabes, Richard A., Shepard, Stephanie A., Murphy, Bridget C., Guthrie, Ivanna K., Jones, Sarah, Friedman, Jo, Poulin, Rick, & Maszk, Pat. (1997). Contemporaneous and longitudinal prediction of children's social functioning from regulation and emotionality. *Child Development, 68,* 642–664.

Elder, Glen H. (1974). *Children of the great depression: Social change in life experience.* Chicago: University of Chicago Press.

Elder, Glen H., Jr. (1998). Life course theory and human development. *Sociological Analysis, 1* (2), 1–12.

Elder, Glen H., Jr., Rudkin, Laura, & Conger, Rand D. (1995). Intergenerational continuity and change in rural America. In Vern L. Bengtson, K. Warner Schaie, & Linda M. Burton (Eds.), *Adult intergenerational relations: Effects of societal change.* New York: Springer.

Elias, Gordan, & Broerse, Jack. (1996). Developmental changes in the incidence and likelihood of simultaneous talk during the first two years: A question of function. *Journal of Child Language, 23,* 201–217.

Elkind, David. (1967). Egocentrism in adolescence. *Child Development, 38,* 1025–1034.

Elkind, David. (1978). *The child's reality: Three developmental themes.* Hillsdale, NJ: Erlbaum.

Elkind, David. (1984). *All grown up and no place to go.* Reading, MA: Addison-Wesley.

Ellsworth, C.P., Muir, D.W., & Hains, S.M.J. (1993). Social competence and person-object differentiation: An analysis of the still-face effect. *Developmental Psychology, 29,* 63–73.

Elo, Irma T., King, Rosalind Berkowitz, & Furstenberg, Frank F., Jr. (1999). Adolescent females: Their sexual partners and the fathers of their children. *Journal of Marriage and the Family, 61,* 74–84.

Emde, Robert N. (1994). Individual meaning and increasing complexity: Contributions of Sigmund Freud and Rene Spitz to developmental psychology. In Ross D. Parke, Peter A. Ornstein, John J. Rieser, & Carolyn Zahn-Waxler (Eds.), *A century of developmental psychology.* Washington, DC: American Psychological Association.

Emde, Robert N., Biringen, Z., Clyman, R.B., & Oppenheim, D. (1991). The moral self of infancy: Affective core and procedural knowledge. *Developmental Review, 11,* 251–270.

Emory, Eugene K., Schlackman, Lisa J., & Fiano, Kristin. (1996). Drug-hormone interactions on neurobehavioral responses in human neonates. *Infant Behavior & Development, 19,* 213–220.

Enkin, Murray, Keirse, Marc J.N.C., & Chalmers, Iain. (1989). *Effective care in pregnancy and childbirth.* Oxford, England: Oxford University Press.

Entwisle, Doris R., & Alexander, Karl L. (1996). Family type and children's growth in reading and math over the primary grades. *Journal of Marriage and the Family, 58,* 341–355.

Epstein, M.A., Shaywitz, S.E., Shaywitz, B.A., & Woolston, J.L. (1991). The boundaries of attention deficit disorder. *Journal of Learning Disabilities, 2,* 78–86.

Erdley, Cynthia A., & Asher, Steven R. (1996). Children's social goals and self-efficacy perceptions as influences on their responses to ambiguous provocation. *Child Development, 67,* 1329–1344.

Erikson, Erik H. (1963). *Childhood and society* (2nd ed.). New York: Norton.

Erikson, Erik H. (1968). *Identity, youth, and crisis.* New York: Norton.

Erikson, Erik H. (1975). *Life history and the historical moment.* New York: Norton.

Eskenazi, Brenda, Prehn, Angela W., & Christianson, Roberta E. (1995). Passive and active maternal smoking as measured by serum cotinine: The effect on birthweight. *American Journal of Public Health, 85,* 395–398.

Etaugh, Claire, & Liss, Marsha B. (1992). Home, school, and playroom: Training ground for adult gender roles. *Sex Roles, 26,* 129–147.

Evans, David W., Leckman, James F., Carter, Alice, Reznick, J. Steven, Henshaw, Desiree, King, Robert A., & Pauls, David. (1997). Ritual, habit, and perfectionism: The prevalence and development of compulsive-like behavior in normal young children. *Child Development, 68,* 58–68.

Evans, Mark I., Belsky, Robin L., Greb, Anne, Clementino, Nancy, & Snyder, Frank N. (1989). Prenatal diagnosis of congenital malformation. In Mark I. Evans, Alan O. Dixler, John C. Fletcher, & Joseph D. Schulman (Eds.), *Fetal diagnosis and therapy: Science, ethics, and the law.* Philadelphia: Lippincott.

Eveleth, Phyllis B., & Tanner, James M. (1976). *Worldwide variation in human growth.* Cambridge, England: Cambridge University Press.

Eveleth, Phyllis B. & Tanner, James M. (1991). *Worldwide variation in human growth* (2nd ed.). Cambridge, England: Cambridge University Press.

Ewing, Charles Patrick. (1990). *Kids who kill.* Lexington, MA: Lexington Books.

Eyberg, Sheila M., Schulmann, Elena M., & Rey, Jannette. (1998). Child and adolescent psychotherapy research: Developmental issues. *Journal of Abnormal Child Psychology, 26,* 71–82.

Eyer, D. (1992). *Maternal-infant bondings: A scientific fiction.* New Haven, CT: Yale University Press.

Faberow, Norman L. (1994). Preparatory and prior suicidal behavior factors. In Edwin S. Schneidman, Norman L. Faberow, & Robert E. Litman (Eds.), *The psychology of suicide* (rev. ed.). Northwale, NJ: Aronson.

Fabes, R.A. (1994). Physiological, emotional, and behavioral correlates of gender segregation. In C. Leaper (Ed.), *Childhood gender segregation: Causes and consequences.* San Francisco: Jossey-Bass.

Fadiman, Ann. (1997). *The spirit catches you and you fall down: A Hmong child, her American doctors, and the collision of two cultures.* New York: Farrar, Straus, and Giroux.

Fagen, Jeffrey, Prigot, Joyce, Carroll, Marjorie, Pioli, Liane, Stein, Adam, & Franco, Adriana. (1997). Auditory context and memory retrieval in young infants. *Child Development, 68,* 1057–1066.

Fagot, Beverly. (1995). Parenting boys and girls. In Marc H. Bronstein (Ed.), *Handbook of parenting (Vol. 1): Children and parenting.* Mahwah, NJ: Erlbaum.

Fagot, Beverly. (1997). Attachment, parenting, and peer interactions of toddler children. *Developmental Psychology, 33,* 489–499.

Fagot, Beverly I., & Leinbach, M.D. (1993). Gender-role development in young children: From discriminating to labeling. *Developmental Review, 13*, 205–224.

Fagot, Beverly I., Leinbach, Mary D., & O'Boyle, C. (1992). Gender labeling, gender stereotyping, and parenting behaviors. *Developmental Psychology, 28*, 225–230.

Fairburn, Christopher G., & Wilson, G. Terence. (Eds). (1993). *Binge eating: Nature, assessment and treatment.* New York: Guilford.

Falbo, T., & Poston, D.L. (1993). The academic, personality, and physical outcomes of only children in China. *Child Development, 64*, 18–35.

Fantuzzo, J., DePaola, L., Lambert, L., Martino, T., Anderson, G., & Sutton, S. (1991). Effects of inter-parental violence on the psychological adjustment and competencies of young children. *Journal of Consulting and Clinical Psychology, 59*, 258–265.

Farooqi, S., Perry, I.J., & Beevers, D.G. (1994). Ethnic differences in infants. *Pediatric and Prenatal Epidemiology, 7*, 245–252.

Farrar, J., & Goodman, G.S. (1992). Developmental changes in event memory. *Child Development, 63*, 173–187.

Farrar, M.J. (1992). Negative evidence and grammatical morpheme acquisition. *Developmental Psychology, 28*, 90–98.

Farrington, David P. (1994). Interactions between individual and contextual factors in the development of offending. In Rainer K. Silbereisen and Eberhard Todt (Eds.), *Adolescence in context: The interplay of family, school, peers, and work in adjustment.* New York: Springer-Verlag.

Farrington, David P., Loeber, Rolf, Elliot, Delbert S., Hawkins, J. David, Kendell, Denise B., Klein, Malcolm W., McCord, Joan, Rowe, David C., & Tremblay, Richard E. (1990). Advancing knowledge about the onset of delinquency and crime. In *Advances in clinical child psychology* (Vol. 13). New York: Plenum Press.

Farver, Jo Ann M., & Frosch, Dominick L. (1996). L.A. stories: Aggression in preschoolers' spontaneous narratives after the riots of 1992. *Child Development, 67*, 19–32.

Feder, Barnaby J. (1996, September 7). Liggett's tobacco settlement in danger of coming undone. *The New York Times, 38.*

Feeny, Norah C., Eder, Rebecca A., & Rescorla, Leslie. (1996). Conversations with preschoolers: The feeling state content of children's narratives. *Early Education and Development, 7*, 79–97.

Feiring, Candice. (1996). Concepts of romance in 15-year-old adolescents. *Journal of Research on Adolescence, 6*, 181–200.

Feiring, Candice, & Lewis, Michael. (1989). The social network of girls and boys from early through middle childhood. In Deborah Belle (Ed.), *Children's social networks and social supports.* New York: Wiley.

Feldman, David Henry, & Piirto, Jane. (1996). Parenting talented children. In Marc H. Bornstein (Ed.), *Handbook of Parenting: Children and Parenting.* Mahwah, NJ: Erlbaum.

Feldman, Ruth, Greenbaum, Charles W., Mayes, Linda C., & Erlich, Samuel H. (1997). Change in mother-infant interactive behavior: Relations to change in the mother, the infant, and the social context. *Infant Behavior & Development, 20*, 151–163.

Feldman, Ruth, Greenbaum, Charles W., & Yirmiya, Nurit. (1999). Mother-infant affect synchrony as an antecedent of the emergence of self-control. *Developmental Psychology, 35*, 3–19.

Feldman, Shirley & Rosenthal, Doreen A. (1994). Culture makes a difference . . . or does it? A comparison of adolescents in Hong Kong, Australia, and the United States. In Rainer K. Silbereisen and Eberhard Todt (Eds.), *Adolescence in context: The interplay of family, school, peers, and work in adjustment.* Berlin: Springer-Verlag.

Fenson, Larry, Dale, Philip S., Resnick, J. Steven, Bates, Elizabeth, Thal, Donna J., & Petchick, Stephen J. (1994). Variability in early communicative development. *Monographs of the Society for Research in Child Development, 59* (Serial No. 242).

Ferguson, Charles A. (1977). Baby talk as a simplified register. In Catherine E. Snow & Charles A. Ferguson (Eds.), *Talking to children: Language input and requisition.* Cambridge, England: Cambridge University Press.

Ferguson, William G. L. (1997). Normal labor and delivery. In Robert K. Creasy (Ed.), *Management of labor and delivery.* Malden, MA: Blackwell Science.

Fergusson, David M., & Lynskey, Michael. (1997). Early reading difficulties and later conduct problems. *Journal of Child Psychology and Psychiatry, 38*, 899–907.

Fergusson, David M., Horwood, L. John, Caspi, Avshalom, Moffitt, Terrie E., et al. (1996). The artefactual remission of reading disability: Psychometric lessons in the study of stability and change in behavioral development. *Developmental Psychology, 32*, 132–140.

Fernald, Anne. (1985). Four-month-old infants prefer to listen to motherese. *Infant Behavior and Development, 8*, 181–195.

Fernald, Anne. (1993). Approval and disapproval: Infant responsiveness to vocal affect in familiar and unfamiliar languages. *Child Development, 64*, 657–674.

Fernald, Anne, & Mazzie, Claudia. (1991). Prosody and focus in speech to infants and adults. *Developmental Psychology, 27*, 209–221.

Fernald, Anne, & Morikawa, Hiromi. (1993). Common themes and cultural variations in Japanese and American mothers' speech to infants. *Child Development, 64*, 657–674.

Ferron, Christine. (1997). Body image in adolescence: Cross-cultural research. *Adolescence, 32*, 735–745.

Field, Tiffany M. (1987). Affective and interactive disturbances in infants. In Joy Doniger Osofsky (Ed.), *Handbook of infant development* (2nd ed.). New York: Wiley.

Field, Tiffany M. (1991). Quality infant day-care and grade school behavior and performance. *Child Development, 62*, 863–870.

Field, Tiffany M. (1995). Infants of depressed mothers. *Infant Behavior and Development, 18*, 1–13.

Fifer, William P. & Moon, Chris M. (1995). The effects of fetal experience with sound. In Jean-Pierre Lecanuet, William P. Fifer, Norman A. Krasnegor, & William P. Smotherman (Eds.), *Fetal development: A psychobiological perspective.* Hillsdale, NJ: Erlbaum

Finch, Caleb E., & Tanzi, Rudolph E. (1997). Genetics of aging. *Science, 278,* 407–424.

Finkel, D., Pedersen, N.L., McGue, M., & McClearn, G.E. (1995). Heritability of cognitive abilities in adult twins: Comparison of Minnesota and Swedish data. *Behavior Genetics, 25,* 421–432.

Finkelhor, David. (1993). The main problem is still underreporting, not overreporting. In Richard J. Gelles & Donileen R. Loseke (Eds.), *Current controversies in family violence.* Newbury Park, CA: Sage.

Finkelhor, David. (1994). Current information on the scope and nature of child sexual abuse. *The Future of Children, 4,* 31–53.

Fiscella, K., Kitzman, H.J., Cole, R.E., Sidora, K., & Olds, D. (1998). Delayed first pregnancy among African-American adolescent smokers. *Journal of Adolescent Health, 23,* 232–237.

Fischer, Kurt W., & Rose, Samuel P. (1994). Dynamic development of coordination of components in brain and behavior: A framework for theory and research. In G. Dawson & Kurt W. Fischer (Eds.), *Human behavior and the developing brain.* New York: Guilford.

Fischer, Kurt W., Ayoub, Catherine, Sigh, Ilina, Noam, Gil, Maraganore, Andronicki, & Raya, Pamela. (1997). Psychopathology as adaptive development along distinctive pathways. *Development and Psychopathology, 9,* 749–779.

Fisher, Celia B. (1993). Integrating science and ethics in research with high-risk children and youth. *Society for Research in Child Development: Social Policy Report, 7* (4), 1–26.

Fivush, R., & Hamond, N.R. (1990). Autobiographical memory across the preschool years: Toward reconceptualizing childhood amnesia. In R. Fivush & J.A. Hudson (Eds.), *Knowing and remembering in young children.* Cambridge, England: Cambridge University Press.

Fivush, R., & Shukat, J.R. (1995). Content, consistency, and coherence of early autobiographical recall. In M.S. Zaragoza, J.R. Graham, G.C.N. Hall, R. Hirschman, & Y.S. Ben-Porath (Eds.), *Memory and testimony in the child witness.* Newbury Park, CA: Sage.

Flavell, John H. (1985). *Cognitive development* (2nd ed.). Englewood Cliffs, NJ: Prentice Hall.

Flavell, John H., Miller, P.H., & Miller, S.A. (1993). *Cognitive development* (3rd ed.). Englewood Cliffs, NJ: Prentice-Hall.

Flavell, John H., Green, Frances L., & Flavell, Eleanor R. (1995). Young children's knowledge about thinking. *Monographs of the Society for Research in Child Development, 60* (Serial no. 243).

Flavell, John H., Green, Frances L., Flavell, Eleanor R., & Grossman, James B. (1997). The development of children's knowledge about inner speech. *Child Development, 68,* 39–47.

Fletcher, Anne C., Darling, Nancy, & Steinberg, Laurence. (1995). Parental monitoring and peer influences on adolescent substance use. In Joan McCord (Ed.), *Coercion and punishment in long-term perspectives.* New York: Cambridge University Press.

Fleming, Alison S., & Corter, Carl M. (1995). Psychobiology of maternal behavior in nonhuman mammals. In Marc H. Bornstein (Ed.), *Handbook of parenting: Biology and ecology of parenting.* Mahwah, NJ: Erlbaum.

Fonagy, Miriam Steele, Steele, Howard, Leigh, Tom, Kennedy, Roger, Mattoon, Gretta, & Target, Mary. (1995). The predictive specificity of the adult attachment interview and pathological emotional development. In Susan Goldberg, Roy Muir, & John Kerr (Eds.), *Attachment theory: Social, developmental, and clinical perspectives.* Hillsdale, NJ: Analytic Press.

Foster, Sharon, Martinez, Charles, & Kulberg, Andrea. (1996). Race, ethnicity, and children's peer relations. In Thomas H. Ollendick & Ronald J. Prinz (Eds.), *Advances in clinical child psychology* (Vol. 18). New York: Plenum Press.

Fox, Nathan A. (1991). If it's not left, it's right: Electroencephalograph asymmetry and the development of emotion. *American Psychologist, 46,* 863–872.

Fox, Nathan A., Calkins, Susan D., & Bel, Martha Ann. (1994). Neural plasticity and development in the first two years of life: Evidence for cognitive and socioemotional domains of research. *Development and Psychopathology, 6,* 677–696.

Fox, Nathan A., Sobel, Ana, Calkins, Susan, & Cole, Pamela. (1996). Inhibited children talk about themselves: Self-reflection on personality development and change in 7-year-olds. In Michael Lewis & Margaret Wolan Sullivan (Eds.), *Emotional development in atypical children.* Mahwah, NJ: Erlbaum.

Fox, Nathan A., & Fein, Greta G. (1990). *Infant day care: The current debate.* Norwood, NJ: Ablex.

Frankenburg, W.K., Frandel, A., Sciarillo, W., & Burgess, D. (1981). The newly abbreviated and revised Denver Developmental Screening Test. *Journal of Pediatrics, 99,* 995–999.

Franklin, Deborah. (1984). Rubella threatens unborn in vaccine gap. *Science News, 125,* 186.

Freda, B. (1997). *Personal communication.*

Freeman, Ellen W., & Rickels, Karl. (1993). *Early childbearing: Perspectives on black adolescents and pregnancy.* Newbury Park, CA: Sage.

Frehsee, Detlev. (1996). Violence toward children in the family and the role of law. In Detlev Frehsee, Wiebke Horn, & Kai-D. Bussmann (Eds.), *Family violence against children: A challenge for society.* Berlin: de Gruyter.

Freud, Sigmund. (1935). *A general introduction to psychoanalysis* (Joan Riviare, Trans.). New York: Modern Library.

Freud, Sigmund. (1938). *The basic writings of Sigmund Freud.* A.A. Brill (Ed. and Trans.). New York: Modern Library.

Freud, Sigmund. (1963). *Three case histories.* New York: Collier. (Original work published 1918).

Freud, Sigmund. (1964). *An outline of psychoanalysis: Vol. 23. The standard edition of the complete psychological works of Sigmund Freud.* James Strachey (Ed. and Trans.). London: Hogarth Press. (Original work published 1940).

Freud, Sigmund. (1965). *New introductory lectures on psychoanalysis.* James Strachey (Ed. and Trans.). New York: Norton. (Original work published 1933).

Frost, Jennifer J., & Forrest, Jacqueline Darroch. (1995). Understanding the impact of effective teenage pregnancy prevention programs. *Family Planning Perspectives, 27,* 188–195.

Frye, Douglas, & Moore, Chris. (Eds.). (1991). *Children's theories of mind: Mental states and social understanding.* Hillsdale, NJ: Erlbaum.

Fuligni, Andrew J. (1997). The academic achievement of adolescents from immigrant families: The roles of family background, attitudes, and behavior. *Child Development, 68,* 351–363.

Fuhrman, Teresa, & Holmbeck, Grayson N. (1995). A contextual-moderator analysis of emotional autonomy and adjustment in adolescence. *Child Development, 66,* 763–811.

Furman, Wyndol. (1995). Parenting siblings. In Marc H. Bronstein (Ed.), *Handbook of parenting (Vol. 1): Children and parenting.* Mahwah, NJ: Erlbaum.

Furman, Wyndol, & Buhrmester, D. (1992). Age and sex differences in perceptions of networks of personal relationships. *Child Development, 63,* 103–115.

Furman, W., & Wehner, E.A. (1994). Romantic views: Toward a theory of adolescent romantic relationships. In R. Montemayer, G.M. Adams, & C.T. Fullotta (Eds.), *Personal relationships during adolescence.* Thousand Oaks, CA: Sage.

Furstenberg, Frank F., & Cherlin, Andrew J. (1991). *Divided families: What happens to children when parents part.* Cambridge, MA: Harvard University Press.

Furstenberg, Frank F., Jr., Brooks-Gunn, Jeanne, & Morgan, Philip S. (1987). *Adolescent mothers in later life.* New York: Cambridge University Press.

Furth, Hans G. (1996). *Desire for society: Children's knowledge as social imagination.* New York: Plenum.

Fuson, Karen C., & Kwon, Youngshim. (1992). Korean children's understanding of multidigit addition and subtraction. *Child Development, 63,* 491–506.

Gabennesch, H. (1990). The perception of social conventionality by children and adults. *Child Development, 61,* 2047–2059.

Gaddis, Alan, & Brooks-Gunn, Jeanne. (1985). The male experience of pubertal change. *Journal of Youth and Adolescence, 14,* 61.

Galen, Britt Rachelle & Underwood, Marion K. (1997). A developmental investigation of social aggression among children. *Developmental Psychology, 33,* 589–600.

Gall, Stanley A. (1996). *Multiple pregnancy and delivery.* St. Louis: Mosby.

Gallagher, James J. (1990). The family as a focus for intervention. In Samuel J. Meisels & Jack P. Shonkoff (Eds.), *Handbook of early childhood intervention.* Cambridge, England: Cambridge University Press.

The Gallup Organization. (1995). *Disciplining children in America: A Gallup Poll report.* Princeton, NJ: The Gallup Organization.

Ganong, Lawrence H., & Coleman, Marilyn. (1994). *Remarried family relationships.* Thousand Oaks, CA: Sage

Gantley, M., Davies, D.P., & Murcett, A. (1993). Sudden infant death syndrome: Links with infant care practices. *British Medical Journal, 306,* 16–20.

Garbarino, James. (1988). Preventing childhood injury: Developmental and mental health issues. *American Journal of Orthopsychiatry, 58,* 25–45.

Garbarino, James, Guttmann, Edna, & Seeley, James Wilson. (1986). *The psychologically battered child.* San Francisco: Jossey-Bass.

Garbarino, James, Dubrow, N., Kostelny, K., & Pardo, C. (1992). *Children in danger: Coping with the consequences of community violence.* San Francisco: Jossey-Bass.

Garbarino, James, Kostelny, Kathleen, & Barry, Frank. (1997). Value transmission in an ecological context: The high-risk neighborhood. In Joan E. Grusec & Leon Kuczynski (Eds.), *Parenting and children's internalization of values: A handbook of contemporary theory.* New York: John Wiley & Sons.

Gardner, Howard. (1980). *Artful scribbles: The significance of children's drawings.* New York: Basic Books.

Gardner, Howard. (1983). *Frames of mind: The theory of multiple intelligences.* New York: Basic Books.

Gardner, Howard. (1987). *The mind's new science: A history of cognitive revolution.* New York: Basic Books.

Gardner, Howard. (1991). *The unschooled mind: How children think and how schools should teach.* New York: Basic Books.

Gardner, William P. (1991). A theory of adolescent risk taking. In N. Bell (Ed.), *Adolescent and adult risk taking. The eighth Texas Tech symposium on interfaces in psychology.* Lubbock: Texas Tech University Press.

Garmezy, Norman. (1985). Stress-resistant children: The search for protective factors. In J. E. Stevenson (Ed.), *Recent research in developmental psychopathology.* Oxford, England: Pergamon.

Garmezy, Norman. (1993). Vulnerability and resilience. In David C. Funder, Ross D. Parke, Carol Tomlinson-Keasy, & Keith Widaman (Eds.), *Studying lives through time.* Washington, DC: American Psychological Association.

Garrity, Carla & Baris, Mitchell A. (1996). Bullies and victims. *Contemporary Pediatrics, 13,* 90–114.

Garrod, Andrew. (Ed.). (1993). *Approaches to moral development: New research and emerging themes.* New York: Teachers College Press.

Garrod, A., & Beal, C.R. (1993). Voices of care and justice in children's responses to fable dilemmas. In A. Garrod (Ed.), *Approaches to moral development: New research and emerging themes.* New York: Teachers College Press.

Garvin, James P. (1994). *Learning how to kiss a frog: Advice for those who work with pre- and early adolescents.* Newburyport, MA: Garvin Consultant Association.

Gaulin, S.J.C. (1993). How and why sex differences evolve, with spatial ability as a paradigm example. In Marc Haug, Richard Whalen, Claude Aron, & Kathie Olsen (Eds.), *The development of sex differences and similarities in behavior.* Boston: Kluwer.

Gauvain, Mary. (1990). Review of Kathleen Berger's *The developing person through childhood and adolescence* (3rd ed.). New York.

Geiger, Brenda. (1996). *Fathers as primary caregivers.* Westport, CT: Greenwood Press.

Gelman, Rochel, & Massey, Christine M. (1987). Commentary. In Geoffrey B. Saxe, Stephen R. Guberman, & Maryl Gearhart, Social processes in early number development. *Monographs of the Society for Research in Child Development, 52* (Serial No. 216).

Genesee, Fred. (1994). *Educating second-language children: The whole child, the whole curriculum, the whole community.* Cambridge, England: Cambridge University Press.

Gerber, Adele. (1993). *Language-related learning disabilities.* Baltimore: Brookes.

Gerstein, Dean R., & Green, Lawrence W. (Eds.). (1993). *Preventing drug abuse.* Washington, DC: National Academy of Science.

Gesell, Arnold. (1926). *The mental growth of the pre-school child: A psychological outline of normal development from birth to the sixth year including a system of developmental diagnosis.* New York: Macmillan.

Giardino, Angelo P., Christian, Cindy W., & Giardino, Eileen R. (1997). *A practical guide to the evaluation of child physical abuse & neglect.* Thousand Oaks, CA: Sage.

Gibbons, Ann. (1998). Which of our genes makes us human? *Science, 281,* 1432–1434.

Gibson, Eleanor. (1969). *Principles of perceptual learning and development.* New York: Appleton-Century-Crofts.

Gibson, Eleanor. (1988). Levels of description and constraints on perceptual development. In Albert Yonas (Ed.), *Perceptual development in infancy.* Hillsdale, NJ: Erlbaum.

Gibson, Eleanor Jack. (1997). An ecological psychologist's prolegomena for perceptual development: A functional approach. In Cathy Dent-Read & Patricia Zukow-Goldring (Eds.), *Evolving explanations of development: Ecological approaches to organism-environment systems.* Washington, DC: American Psychological Association.

Gibson, Eleanor Jack, & Walk, Richard D. (1960). The visual cliff. *Scientific American, 202,* 64–72.

Gibson, James J. (1979). *The ecological approach to visual perception.* Boston: Houghton Mifflin.

Gilbert, Enid F., Arya, Sunita, Loxova, Renata, & Opitz, John M. (1987). Pathology of chromosome abnormalities in the fetus: Pathological markers. In Enid F. Gilbert & John M. Opitz (Eds.), *Genetic aspects of developmental pathology.* New York: Liss.

Gilbert, Scott F., & Borish, Steven. (1997). How cells learn, how cells teach: Education in the body. In Eric Amsel & K. Ann Renninger (Eds.), *Change and development: Issues of theory, method, and application.* Mahwah, NJ: Erlbaum.

Gillberg, Christopher. (1991). Clinical and neurobiological aspects of Asperger syndrome in six family studies. In Uta Frith (Ed.), *Autism and Asperger syndrome.* Cambridge, England: Cambridge University Press.

Gilligan, Carol. (1982). *In a different voice: Psychological theory and women's development.* Cambridge, MA: Harvard University Press.

Gilligan, Carol, Murphy, John M., & Tappan, Mark B. (1990). Moral development beyond adolescence. In Charles N. Alexander & Ellen J. Langer (Eds.), *Higher stages of human development.* New York: Oxford University Press.

Gjessing, Hans-Jorgen, & Karlsen, Bjorn. (1989). *A longitudinal study of dyslexia.* New York: Springer-Verlag.

Glasgow, Kristin L., Dornbusch, Sanford M., Troyer, Lisa, Steinberg, Laurence, & Ritter, Philip L. (1997). Parenting styles, adolescents' attributions, and educational outcomes in nine heterogeneous high schools. *Child Development, 68,* 507–529.

Gleason, Jean Berko. (1967). Do children imitate? *Proceedings of the International Conference on Oral Education of the Deaf, 2,* 1441–1448.

Glick, J. (1968, February). *Cognitive style among the Kpelle of Liberia.* Paper presented at the meeting on Cross-Cultural Cognitive Studies, American Educational Research Association, Chicago.

Gnepp, Jackie, & Chilamkurti, Chinni. (1988). Children's use of personality attributions to predict other people's emotional and behavioral reactions. *Child Development, 59,* 743–754.

Goldberg, Margaret, Lex, Barbara W., Mello, Nancy K., Mendelson, Jack H., & Bower, Tommie A. (1996). Impact of maternal alcoholism on separation of children from their mothers: Findings from a sample of incarcerated women. *American Journal of Orthopsychiatry, 66,* 228–238.

Goldberg, Susan, & Divitto, Barbara. (1995). Parenting children from preterm. In Marc H. Bornstein (Ed.), *Handbook of parenting: Children and parenting.* Mahwah, NJ: Erlbaum.

Goldberg, Susan, Muir, Roy, & Kerr, John. (Eds.) (1995) *Attachment theory: social, developmental, and clinical perspectives.* Hillsdale, NJ: Analytic Press.

Goldberg-Reitman, Jill. (1992). Young girls' conception of their mother's role: A neo-structural analysis. In Robbie Case (Ed.), *The mind's staircase: Exploring the conceptual underpinning of children's thought and knowledge.* Hillsdale, NJ: Erlbaum.

Golden, Michael H.N. (1996). The effect of early nutrition on later growth. In C.J.K. Henry & S.J. Uliajaszel (Eds.), *Long-term consequences of early environment: Growth, development and the lifespan developmental perspective.* Cambridge, England: Cambridge University Press.

Goldenberg, Robert L., Iams, Jay D., Mercer, Brian M., et al. (1998). The preterm prediction study: The value of new vs. standard risk factors in predicting early and all spontaneous preterm births. *American Journal of Public Health, 88,* 233–238.

Goldfield, E.G., Kay, B.A., & Warren, W.H., Jr. (1993). Infant bouncing: The assembly and tuning of action systems. *Child Development, 64,* 1128–1142.

Goldman, Gail, Pineault, Raynald, Potvin, Louise, Blais, Regis, & Bilodeau, Henriette. (1993). Factors influencing the practice of vaginal birth after Cesarean section. *American Journal of Public Health, 83,* 1104–1108.

Goldsmith, H. Hill, Buss, A.H., Plomin, R., Rothbart, M. Klevjord, Thomas, A., Chess, S., Hinde, R.A., & McCall, R.B. (1987). Roundtable: What is temperament? Four approaches. *Child Development, 58,* 505–529.

Goldsmith, H.H., Gottesman, I.I., & Lemery, K.S. (1997). Epigenetic approaches to developmental psychopathology. *Development and Psychopathology, 9,* 365–387.

Goleman, Daniel. (1998). *Building emotional intelligence.* APA Convention, San Francisco.

Golinkoff, Roberta Michnick, & Hirsh-Pasek, Kathy. (1990). Let the mute speak: What infants can tell us about language acquisition. *Merrill-Palmer Quarterly, 36,* 67–91.

Golinkoff, Roberta Michnick, Hirsh-Pasek, Kathy, Bailey, Leslie M., & Wenger, Neill R. (1992). Young children and adult use lexical principles to learn new nouns. *Developmental Psychology, 28,* 99–108.

Golombok, Susan, & Tasker, Fiona. (1996). Do parents influence the sexual orientation of their children? Findings from a longitudinal study of lesbian families. *Developmental Psychology, 32,* 3–11.

Golub, S. (1992). *Periods: From menarche to menopause.* Newbury Park, CA: Sage.

Golumb, C., & McLean, L. (1984). Assessing cognitive skills in pre-school children of middle and low income families. *Perceptual and Motor Skills, 58,* 119–125.

Goncu, A. (1993). Development of intersubjectivity in social pretend play. *Human Development, 36,* 185–198.

Goodman, G.S., Rudy, L., Bottoms, B.L., & Aman, C. (1990). Children's concerns and memory: Issues of ecological validity in the study of children's eyewitness testimony. In Robyn Fivush & Judith A. Hudson (Eds.), *Knowing and remembering in young children.* Cambridge, England: Cambridge University Press.

Goodnow, Jacqueline J. (1993). Direction of post-Vygotsky research. In Ellice A. Foreman, Norris Minick, & C. Addison Stone (Eds.), *Contexts for learning: Sociocultural dynamics in children's development.* New York: Oxford Press.

Goodnow, Jacqueline J. (1997). Parenting and the transmission and internalization of values: From social-cultural perspectives to within-family analyses. In Joan E. Grusec & Leon Kuczynski (Eds.), *Parenting and children's internalization of values: A handbook of contemporary theory.* New York: John Wiley & Sons.

Goodnow, Jacqueline J., & Collins, W. Andrew. (1990). *Development according to parents: The nature, sources, and consequences of parents' ideas.* Hillsdale, NJ: Erlbaum.

Goodwin, M.H. (1990). *He-said-she-said: Talk as social organization among black children.* Bloomington: Indiana University Press.

Gordon, Debra Ellen. (1990). Formal operational thinking: The role of cognitive-developmental processes in adolescent decision-making about pregnancy and contraception. *American Journal of Orthopsychiatry, 60,* 346–356.

Gottesman, Irving I. (1991). *Schizophrenia genesis: The origins of madness.* New York: Freeman.

Gottesman, Irving I., and Goldsmith, H.H. (1993). Developmental psychopathology of antisocial behavior: Inserting genes into its ontogenesis and epigenesis. In C.A. Nelson (Ed.), *Minnesota Symposia on Child Psychology: Vol. 27. Threats to optimal development: Integrating biological, psychological, and social risk factors.* Hillsdale, NJ: Erlbaum.

Gottlieb, Diane, & Bronstein, Phyllis. (1996). Parents' perceptions of children's worries in a changing world. *Journal of Genetic Psychology, 157,* 104–118.

Gozal, D. (1998). Sleep-disordered breathing and school performance in children. *Pediatrics, 102,* 616–620.

Graber, Julia A., Brooks-Gunn, Jeanne, Paikoff, Roberta L., & Warren, Michelle P. (1994). Prediction of eating problems: An 8-year study of adolescent girls. *Developmental Psychology, 30,* 823–834.

Graham, Sandra, & Hoehn, Susan. (1995). Children's understanding of aggression and withdrawal as social stigmas: An attributional analysis. *Child Development, 66,* 1143–1161.

Graham, Sandra, & Juvonen, Jaana. (1998). Self-blame and peer victimization in middle school: An attributional analysis. *Developmental Psychology, 34,* 587–599.

Grandin, Temple. (1995). *Thinking in pictures: And other reports from my life with autism.* New York: Vintage.

Grant, James P. (1986). *The state of the world's children.* Oxford, England: Oxford University Press.

Gratch, Gerald, & Schatz, Joseph. (1987). Cognitive development: The relevance of Piaget's infancy books. In Joy Doniger Osofsky (Ed.), *Handbook of infant development* (2nd ed.). New York: Wiley.

Greenberger, E., & Steinberg, L. (1986). *When teenagers work.* New York: Basic Books.

Greenberger, Ellen, & Chen, Chuansheng. (1996). Perceived family relationships and depressed mood in early and late adolescence: A comparison of European and Asian Americans. *Developmental Psychology, 32,* 707–716.

Greene, Sheila. (1997). Child development: Old themes and new directions. In Ray Fuller, Patricia Noonan Walsh, & Patrick McGinley (Eds.), *A century of psychology: Progress, paradigms and prospects for the new millennium.* London: Routledge.

Greenfield, Patricia M. (1997). You can't take it with you: Why ability assessments don't cross cultures. *American Psychologist, 52,* 1115–1124.

Greif, Geoffrey. (1995). Single fathers with custody following separation and divorce. *Marriage and Family Review, 20,* 213–232.

Greif, Geoffrey L., DeMaris, Alfred, & Hood, Jane C. (1993). Balancing work and single fatherhood. In Jane C. Hood (Ed.), *Men, work, and family.* Newbury Park, CA: Sage.

Gresham, Frank M., & MacMillan, Donald L. (1998). Early intervention project: Can its claims be substantiated and its effects replicated? *Journal of Autism & Developmental Disorders, 28,* 5–13.

Greydanus, Donald Everett. (1997). Neurological disorders. In Adele Dellenbaugh Hofmann & Donald Everett Greydanus (Eds.), *Adolescent medicine* (3rd Ed.). Stamford, CT: Appleton and Lange.

Greydanus, Donald Everett. (1997). Disorders of the skin. In Adele Dellenbaugh Hofmann & Donald Everett Greydanus (Eds.), *Adolescent medicine* (3rd ed.). Stamford, CT: Appleton and Lange.

Grolnick, Wendy S., Deci, Edward L., & Ryan, Richard M. (1997). Internalization within the family: The self-determination theory perspective. In Joan E. Grusec & Leon Kuczynski (Eds.), *Parenting and children's internalization of values: A handbook of contemporary theory.* New York: John Wiley & Sons.

Grossman, Herbert. (1995). *Special education in a diverse society.* Needham, MA: Allyn and Bacon.

Grossman, K., Thane, K., & Grossman, K.E. (1981). Maternal tactile contact of the newborn after various postpartum conditions of mother-infant contact. *Developmental Psychology, 17,* 159–169.

Grossman, Michael, Chaloupka, Frank J., Saffer, Henry, & Laixuthai, Adit. (1994). Effects of alcohol price policy on youth: A summary of economic research. *Journal of Research on Adolescence, 4,* 347–364.

Grotevant, H. & Cooper, C.R. (1998). Individuality and connectedness in adolescent development. In E. Skoe & A. von der Lippe (Eds.), *Personality development in adolescence: A cross-national and life span perspective.* London: Routledge.

Gruber, H., Reykl, A., & Schneider, W. (1994). Expertise and memory development: Longitudinal findings from the chess domain. *Zeitschrift für Entwicklungs Psychologie und Pädagogische Psychologie, 26,* 53–70.

Grubman, Samuel, Gross, Elaine, Lerner-Weiss, Nancy, & Hernadez, Miriam. (1995). Older children and adolescents living with perinatally acquired human immuno-deficiency virus infection. *Pediatrics, 95,* 657–663.

Grunseit, Anne, Kippaz, Susan, Aggleton, Peter, Baldo, Mariella, & Shutkin, Gary. (1997). Sexuality education and young people's sexual behavior: A review of studies. *Journal of Adolescence Research, 12.*

Grusec, Joan E. (1992). Social learning theory and developmental psychology: The legacies of Robert Sears and Albert Bandura. *Developmental Psychology, 28,* 776–786.

Guberman, Steven R. (1996). The development of everyday mathematics in Brazilian children with limited formal education. *Child Development, 67,* 1609–1623.

Guerin, Diana Wright, & Gottfried, Allen W. (1994). Temperamental consequences of infant difficultness. *Infant Behavior and Development, 17,* 413–421.

Guilleminault, C., Boeddiker, Margaret Owen, & Schwab, Deborah. (1982). Detection of risk factors for "near miss SIDS" events in full-term infants. *Neuropediatrics, 13,* 29–35.

Gustafson, G.E., & Green, J.A. (1991). Developmental coordination of cry sounds with visual regard and gestures. *Infant Behavior and Development, 14,* 51–57.

Guthrie, Sharon R. (1991). Prevalence of eating disorders among intercollegiate athletes: Contributing factors and preventative measures. In David R. Black (Ed.), *Eating disorders among athletes.* Reston, VA: American Alliance for Health, Physical Education, Recreation and Dance.

Guttmacher Institute. (1994). *Sex and America's teenagers.* New York: Alan Guttmacher Institute.

Haas, Joel E., Taylor, James S., Bergman, Abraham B., & van Belle, Gerald. (1993). Relationship between epidemiologic risk factors and clinicopathologic findings in sudden infant death syndrome. *Pediatrics, 91,* 106–112.

Hack, Maureen, Klein, Nancy, & Taylor, H. Gerry. (1995). Long-term developmental outcomes of low birth weight infants. *The Future of Children: Low Birth Weight, 5,* 176–196.

Hagerman, Randi J. (1996). Biomedical advances in developmental psychology: The case of Fragile X syndrome. *Developmental Psychology, 32,* 416–424.

Haig, David. (1995). Prenatal power plays. *Natural History, 104,* 39.

Haith, M. (1980). Progress in the understanding of sensory and perceptual processes in early infancy. *Merrill-Palmer Quarterly, 26,* 1–20.

Haith, Marshall M. (1980). *Rules that babies look by.* Hillsdale, NJ: Erlbaum.

Haith, Marshall M. (1990). Perceptual and sensory processes in early infancy. *Merrill-Palmer Quarterly, 36,* 1–26.

Haith, Marshall M. (1993). Preparing for the 21st century: Some goals and challenges for studies of infant sensory and perceptual development. *Developmental Review, 13,* 354–371.

Haith, Marshall M., Wentworth, N., & Canfield, R.L. (1993). The formation of expectations in early infancy. In C. Rovee-Collier & L.P. Lipsitt (Eds.), *Advances in infancy research, 8.* Norwood, NJ: Ablex.

Hakuta, K., & Garcia, E. (1989). Bilingualism and education. *American Psychologist, 44,* 374–379.

Halliday, M.A.K. (1979). One child's protolanguage. In Margaret Bullowa (Ed.), *Before speech: The beginning of interpersonal communication.* Cambridge, England: Cambridge University Press.

Hamburg, B. (1991). Developmental factors and stress in risk-taking behavior of early adolescents. In L.P. Lipsitt & L.L. Mitnick (Eds.), *Self-regulatory behavior and risk taking: Causes and consequences.* Norwood, NJ: Ablex.

Hamer, Dean H., Hu, Stella, Magnuson, Victoria L., Hu, Nan, & Pattatucci, Angela M.L. (1993). A linkage between DNA markers on the X chromosome and male sexual orientation. *Science, 261,* 321–327.

Hamilton, Stephen A., & Wolfgang, Lempert. (1996). The impact of apprenticeship on youth: A prospective analysis. *Journal of Research on Adolescence, 6,* 427–455.

Hamond, Nina R., & Fivush, Robyn. (1991). Memories of Mickey Mouse: Young children recount their trip to Disneyworld. *Cognitive Development, 6,* 433–448.

Hanson, Sandra L., Myers, David E., & Ginsberg, Alan L. (1987). The role of responsibility and knowledge in reducing teenage out-of-wedlock childbearing. *Journal of Marriage and the Family, 49,* 241–256.

Harkness, Sara, & Super, Charles, M. (1995). Culture & parenting. In Marc H. Bornstein (Ed.), *Handbook of parenting: Biology and ecology of parenting*. Mahwah, NJ: Lawrence Erlbaum.

Harkness, Sara, & Super, Charles, M. (1996). *Parents' cultural belief systems: Their origins, expressions, and consequences*. New York: Guilford.

Harrington, Donna, Black, Maureen M., Starr, Raymond H., Jr., & Dubowitz, Howard. (1998). Child neglect: Relation to child temperament and family context. *American Journal of Orthopsychiatry, 68*, 108–115.

Harris, Judith Rich. (1998). *The nurture assumption: Why children turn out the way they do*. New York: Free Press.

Harris, P.L. (1987). The development of search. In Philip Salapatek & Leslie Cohen (Eds.), *Handbook of infant perception: Vol. 2. From perception to cognition*. Orlando, FL: Academic Press.

Harris, P.L., & Kavanaugh, R.D. (1993). Young children's understanding of pretense. *Monographs of the Society for Research in Child Development, 58* (Serial No. 231).

Harrison, Algea O., Wilson, Melvin N., Pine, Charles J., Chan, Samuel Q., & Buriel, Raymond. (1990). Family ecologies of ethnic minority children. *Child Development, 61*, 347–362.

Harter, Susan. (1990). Causes, correlates, and the functional role of global self-worth: A life-span perspective. In R.J. Sternberg & J. Kolligian, Jr. (Eds.), *Competence considered*. New Haven: Yale University Press.

Harter, Susan. (1990). Processes underlying adolescent self-concept formation. In Raymond Montemayor, Gerald R. Adams, & Thomas P. Gullotta (Eds.), *From childhood to adolescence: A transitional period?* Newbury Park, CA: Sage.

Harter, Susan. (1990). Self and identity development. In S.S. Feldman & G.R. Elliott (Eds.), *At the threshold: The developing adolescent*. Cambridge, MA: Harvard University Press.

Harter, Susan. (1993). Visions of self: Beyond the me in the mirror. In J.E. Jacobs (Ed.), *Nebraska symposium on motivation: Vol. 40. Developmental perspectives on motivation*. Lincoln: University of Nebraska Press.

Harter, Susan. (1996). Developmental changes in self-understanding. In Arnold J. Sameroff & Marshall M. Haith (Eds.), *The five to seven year shift: The age of reason and responsibility*. Chicago: The University of Chicago Press.

Harter, Susan, Marold, Donna B., Whitesell, Nancy R., & Cobbs, Gabrielle. (1996). A model of the effects of perceived parent and peer support on adolescent false self behavior. *Child Development, 67*, 360–374.

Hartup, Willard W. (1996). The company they keep: Friendships and their developmental significance. *Child Development, 67*, 1–13.

Harwood, Robin L., Schoelmerich, Axel, Ventura-Cook, Elizabeth, Schulze, Pamela A., & Wilson, Stephanie P. (1996). Culture and class influences on Anglo and Puerto Rican mothers' beliefs regarding long-term socialization goals and child behavior. *Child Development, 67*, 2446–2461.

Hashima, Patricia, & Finkelhor, David. (1997). *Violent victimization of youth versus adults in the National Crime Victimization Survey*. Paper accepted for presentation at the Fifth International Family Violence Research Conference, Durham, NH.

Haskins, Ron. (1989). Beyond metaphor: The efficacy of early childhood education. *American Psychologist, 44*, 274–282.

Hawaii Department of Health. (1992). *Healthy Start: Hawaii's system of family support services*. Honolulu: Hawaii Department of Health.

Hawkins, Alan J., & Eggebeen, David J. (1991). Are fathers fungible? *Journal of Marriage and the Family, 53*, 958–972.

Hayes, C.D., Palmer, J.L., & Zaslow, M.J. (Eds.). (1990). *Child care choices*. Washington, DC: National Academy Press.

Hayne, Harlene, & Rovee-Collier, Carolyn K. (1995). The organization of reactivated memory in infancy. *Child Development, 66*, 893–906.

Heimann, Mikael, & Meltzoff, Andrew N. (1996). Deferred imitation in 9- and 14-month- old infants: A longitudinal study of a Swedish sample. *British Journal of Developmental Psychology, 14*, 55–64.

Held, Richard. (1995). Binocular vision. In P.D. Gluckman and M.A. Heymann (Eds.), *Developmental physiology: A pediatric perspective* (2nd ed.). London: Edward Arnold Publishers.

Hellerstedt, Wendy L., Himes, John H., Story, Mary, Alton, Irene R., & Edwards, Laura E. (1997). The effects of cigarette smoking and gestational weight change on birth outcomes in obese and normal-weight women. *American Journal of Public Health, 87*, 591–596.

Helwig, Charles C. (1995). Adolescents' and young adults' conceptions of civil liberties: Freedom of speech and religion. *Child Development, 66*, 152–166.

Henggeler, S.W. (1989). *Delinquency in adolescence*. Newbury Park, CA: Sage.

Henke, Robin, Choy, Susan P., Geis, Sonya, & Broughman, Stephen. (1996). *Schools and staffing in the United States*. Washington, DC: U.S. Department of Education, National Center for Education Statistics.

Henry, C.J.K. (1996). Early environmental and later nutritional needs. In C.J.K. Henry & S.J. Uliajaszel (Eds.), *Long-term consequences of early environment: Growth, development and the lifespan developmental perspective*. Cambridge, England: Cambridge University Press.

Hensch, Takao K., & Stryker, Michael P. (1996). Ocular dominance plasticity under metabotropic glutamate receptor blockade. *Science, 272*, 554–557.

Hetherington, E. Mavis. (1998). Relevant issues in developmental science. *American Psychologist, 53*, 93–94.

Hetherington, E. Mavis, & Clingempeel, W. Glenn. (1992). Coping with marital transitions. *Monographs of the Society for Research in Child Development, 57* (2–3, Serial No. 227).

Hetherington, E.M., & Jodl, K.M. (1994). Stepfamilies as settings for child development. In A. Booth & J. Dunn (Eds.), *Stepfamilies: Who benefits? Who does not?* Hillsdale, NJ: Erlbaum.

Hetherington, E. Mavis, Bridges, Margaret, & Insabella, Glendessa M. (1998). What matters? What does not? Five perspectives on the association between marital transitions and children's adjustment. *American Psychologist, 53,* 167–184.

Hetheringon, E. M., & Stanley-Hagan, M.S. (1999). Divorce and the adjustment of children: A risk and resiliency perspective. *The Journal of Child Psychology and Psychiatry, 40,* 129–140.

Hickok, G., Bellugi, U., & Klima, E.S. (1996). The neurobiology of sign language and its implications for the neural basis of language. *Nature, 381,* 699–702.

Hickson, Joyce, Land, Arthur J., & Aikman, Grace. (1994). Learning style differences in middle school pupils from four ethnic backgrounds. *School Psychology International, 15,* 349–359.

Higgins, Carol I., Campos, Joseph J., & Kermoian, Rosanne. (1996). Effect of self-produced locomotion on infant postural compensation to optic flow. *Developmental Psychology, 32,* 836–841.

Higginson, Joanna Gregson. (1998). Competitive parenting: The culture of teen mothers. *Journal of Marriage and the Family, 60,* 135–149.

Hill, Hope M., Soriano, Fernando I., Chen, S. Andrew, & LaFromboise, Teresa D. (1994). Sociocultural factors in the etiology and prevention of violence among ethnic minority youth. In Leonard D. Eron, Jacquelyn H. Gentry, & Peggy Schlegel (Eds.), *Reason to hope: A psychosocial perspective on violence and youth.* Washington, DC: American Psychological Association.

Hill, Roslyn, Collis, Glyn M., & Lewis, Vicky A. (1997). Young children's understanding of the cognitive verb forget. *Journal of Child Language, 24,* 57–79.

Hills, Andrew P. (1992). Locomotor characteristics of obese children. *Child: Care, Health and Development, 18,* 29–34.

Hinde, Robert A. (Ed.). (1983). *Primate social relationships.* Oxford, England: Blackwell.

Hinde, Robert A. (1989). Ethological and relationships approaches. In R. Vasta (Ed.), *Annals of Child Development* (Vol. 6). Greenwich, CT: JAI Press.

Hinde, Robert A. (1995). Foreward. In Marc H. Bornstein (Ed.), *Handbook of Parenting (Vol. 4): Applied and practical parenting.* Mahwah, NJ: Erlbaum.

Hinde, R.A., Titmus, G., Easton, D., & Tamplin, A. (1985). Incidence of "friendship" and behavior toward strong associates versus nonassociates in preschoolers. *Child Development, 56,* 234–245.

Hines, Marc. (1993). Hormonal and neural correlates of sex-typed behavioral development in human beings. In Marc Haug, Richard Whalen, Claude Aron, & Kathie Olsen (Eds.), *The development of sex differences and similarities in behavior.* Boston: Kluwer.

Hinshaw, Stephen P. (1994). *Attention deficits and hyperactivity in children.* Thousand Oaks, CA: Sage.

Hitchens, Christopher. (1998). Goodbye to all that: Why Americans are not taught history. *Harper's, 297* (1782), 37–47.

Hochschild, Arlie. (1989). *The second shift: Working parents and the revolution at home.* New York: Viking.

Hodder, Harbour Fraser. (1997). The new fertility: The promise– and perils–of human reproductive technologies. *Harvard Magazine,* 54–64, 97–99.

Hodges, Ernest V.E., Boivin, Michel, Vitaro, Frank, & Bukowski, William M. (1999). The power of friendship: Protection against an escalating cycle of peer victimization. *Developmental Psychology, 35,* 258–268.

Hofer, Myron A. (1995) Hidden regulators: Implications for a new understanding of attachment, separation and loss. In Susan Goldberg, Roy Muir, & John Kerr (Eds.), *Attachment theory: Social, developmental and clinical perspectives.* Hillsdale, NJ: The Analytic Press.

Hoff-Ginsberg, E. (1986). Function and structure in maternal speech: Their relation to the child's development of syntax. *Developmental Psychology, 22,* 155–163.

Hoff-Ginsberg, Erika, & Tardif, Twila. (1995). Socioeconomic status and parenting. In Marc H. Bornstein (Ed.), *Handbook of parenting (Vol. 2): Biology and ecology of parenting.* Mahwah, NJ: Erlbaum.

Hoffman, Michelle. (1991). How parents make their mark on genes. *Science, 252,* 1250–1251.

Hoffman, S.D., Foster, E.M., & Furstenberg, F.F. (1993). Reevaluating the costs of teenage childbearing. *Demography, 30,* 1–13.

Hofman, Adele Dellenbaugh. (1997). Adolescent growth and development. In Adele Dellenbaugh Hofmann & Donald Everett Greydanus (Eds.), *Adolescent medicine* (3rd ed.). Stamford, CT: Appleton and Lange.

Holden, Constance. (1980). Identical twins reared apart. *Science, 207,* 1323–1328.

Holmbeck, Grayson N., & O'Donnell, K. (1991). Discrepancies between perceptions of decision making and behavioral autonomy. In R.L. Paikoff (Ed.), *New directions for child development: No. 51. Shared views in the family during adolescence.* San Francisco: Jossey-Bass.

Holmbeck, Grayson N., Paikoff, Roberta L., & Brooks-Gunn, Jeanne. (1995). Parenting adolescents. In Marc H. Bornstein (Ed.), *Handbook of parenting: Vol. 1. Children and parenting.* Mahwah, NJ: Erlbaum.

Holroyd, Sarah, & Baron-Cohen, Simon. (1993). Brief report: How far can people with autism go in developing a theory of mind? *Journal of Autism and Developmental Disorders, 23,* 379–385.

Horney, Karen. (1967). *Feminine psychology.* Harold Kelman (Ed.). New York: Norton.

Hornick, R., Risenhoover, N., & Gunnar, M. (1987). The effects of maternal positive, neutral, and negative affective communications on infant responses to new toys. *Child Development, 58,* 937–944.

Horowitz, Frances Degen. (1994). John B. Watson's legacy: Learning and environment. In Ross D. Parke, Peter A. Ornstein, John J. Rieser, & Carolyn Zahn-Waxler (Eds.), *A century of developmental psychology.* Washington, DC: American Psychological Association.

Hossain, Z., & Roopnarine, J.L. (1994). African-American fathers with infants: Relationship to their functional style, support, education, and income. *Infant Behavior and Development, 17,* 175–184.

Howard, Marion, & McCabe, Judith Blamey. (1990). Helping teenagers postpone sexual involvement. *Family Planning Perspectives, 22,* 21–26.

Howard, Robert W. (1996). Asking nature the right questions. *Genetic, Social & General Psychology Monographs, 122,* 161–178.

Howe, Mark L. (1997). Children's memory for traumatic experiences. *Learning and Individual Differences, 9,* 153–174.

Howes, Carollee. (1983). Patterns of friendship. *Child Development, 54,* 1041–1053.

Hsu, L.K. George. (1990). *Eating disorders.* New York: Guilford.

Hubbard, Van S. (1995). Future directions in obesity research. In Lilian W.Y. Cheung & Julius B. Richmond (Eds.), *Child health, nutrition, and physical activity.* Champaign, IL: Human Kinetics.

Hubel, David H. (1988). *Eye, brain, and vision.* New York: Scientific American Library.

Hudson, J.A. (1990). The emergence of autobiographical memory in mother-child conversation. In R. Fivush & J.A. Hudson (Eds.), *Knowing and remembering in young children.* Cambridge, England: Cambridge University Press.

Huffman, Lynne C., Bryan, Yvonne E., del Carmen, Rebecca, Pedersen, Frank A., Doussard-Roosevelt, Jane A., & Porges, Stephen W. (1998). Infant temperament and cardiac vagal tone: Assessments at twelve weeks of age. *Child Development, 69,* 624–635.

Hughes, Dana, & Simpson, Lisa. (1995). The role of social change in preventing low birth weight. *The Future of Children: Low Birth Weight, 5,* 87–102.

Hughes, Jan N., Cavell, Timothy A., & Grossman, Pamela B. (1997). A positive view of self: Risk or protection for aggressive children? *Development and Psychopathology, 9,* 75–94.

Hull, Harry F., & Aylward, R. Bruce. (1997). Ending polio immunization. *Science, 277,* 780.

Hunter, M. (1990). *Abused boys: The neglected victims of sexual abuse.* Lexington, MA: Lexington Books.

Hurrelmann, K. (1994). *International handbook on adolescence.* Westport, CT: Greenwood.

Hurt, Hallam, Brodsky, Nancy L., Betanourt, Laura, Braitman, Leonard E., et al. (1996). Play behavior in toddler with in utero cocaine exposure: A prospective, masked, controlled study. *Journal of Developmental & Behavioral Pediatrics, 17,* 373–379.

Huston, Aletha C. (1983). Sex-typing. In P.H. Mussen (Ed.), *Handbook of child psychology: Vol. 4. Socialization, personality and social development.* New York: Wiley.

Huston, Aletha C., Watkins, Bruce A., & Kunkel, Dale. (1989). Public policy and children's television. *American Psychologist, 44,* 424–433.

Huston, Aletha C., McLoyd, Vonnie C., & Coll, Cynthia Garcia. (1994). Children and poverty: Issues in contemporary research. *Child Development, 65,* 275–282.

Huth, Mary Jo. (1997). America's new homeless: Single-parent families. In Mary Jo Huth & Talmadge Wright (Eds.), *International critical perspectives on homelessness.* Westport, CT: Praeger.

Huttenlocher, Janellen, Levine, Susan, & Vevea, Jack. (1998). Environmental input and cognitive growth: A study using time-period comparisons. *Child Development, 69,* 1012–1029.

Huttenlocher, Peter R. (1994). Synaptogenesis in human cerebral cortex. In Geraldine Dawson & Kurt W. Fischer (Eds.), *Human behavior and the developing brain.* New York: Guilford.

Hwang, C. Philip, Lamb, Michael E., & Sigel, Irving E. (Eds.). (1996). *Images of childhood.* Mahwah, NJ: Erlbaum.

Hyde, Kenneth E. (1990). *Religion in childhood and adolescence: A comprehensive review of the research.* Birmingham, AL: Religious Education Press.

Hymel, S., Bowker, A., & Woody, E. (1993). Aggressive versus withdrawn unpopular children: Variations in peer and self-perceptions in multiple domains. *Child Development, 64,* 879–896.

Inhelder, Bärbel, & Piaget, Jean. (1958). *The growth of logical thinking from childhood to adolescence.* New York: Basic Books.

Institute for Social Research. (1997) *Healthy environments, healthy children.* Child development supplement: Panel study of income dynamics. Ann Arbor, MI: University of Michigan Institute for Social Research.

Irazuzta, José E., McJunkin, James E., Danadian, Kapriel, Arnold, Forest, & Zhang, Jianliang. (1997). Outcome and cost of child abuse. *Child Abuse and Neglect, 21,* 751–757.

Isabella, R.A. (1993). Origins of attachment: Maternal interactive behavior across the first year. *Child Development, 64,* 605–621.

Isabella, R.A., & Belsky, J. (1991). Interactional synchrony and the origins of infant-mother attachment: A replication study. *Child Development, 62,* 373–384.

ISLAT Working Group. (1998, July 31). Art into science: Regulation of fertility techniques. *Science, 281,* 651–652.

Isolauri, E., Sutas, Y., Salo, M.K., Isosonppi, R., & Kaila, M. (1998). Elimination diet in cow's milk allergy: Risk for impaired growth in young children. *Journal of Pediatrics, 132,* 1004–1009.

Itoigawa, Naosuke, Minami, T., Kondo-Ikemujra, K., Tachibana, H., et al. (1996). Parenting and family support in Japan for 6- to 8-year-old children weighing under 1000 grams at birth. *International Journal of Behavioral Development, 19,* 477–490.

Izard, Carroll E., Hembree, E.A., & Huebner, R.R. (1987). Infants' emotional expressions to acute pain: Developmental change and stability of individual differences. *Developmental Psychology, 23,* 105–113.

Jaccard, James, Dittus, Patricia J., & Gordon, Vivian V. (1998). Parent-adolescent congruency in reports of adolescent sexual behavior and in communications about sexual behavior. *Child Development, 69,* 247–261.

Jacklin, Carol Nagy, Wilcox, K.T., & Maccoby, Eleanor E. (1988). Neonatal sex-steroid hormone and intellectual abilities of six-year-old boys and girls. *Developmental Psychobiology, 21,* 567–574.

Jackson, Jacquelyne Faye. (1993). Human behavioral genetics, Scarr's theory, and her views on interventions: A critical review and commentary on their implications for African American children. *Child Development, 64,* 1318–1332.

Jacob's Father. (1997). Jacob's story: A miracle of the heart. *Zero to Three, 17,* 59–64.

Jacobson, Joseph L. & Jacobson, Sandra W. (1996). Methodological considerations in behavioral toxicology in infants and children. *Developmental Psychology, 32,* 390–403.

James, William. (1950). *The principles of psychology* (Vol. 1). New York: Dover. (Original work published 1890.

Janowsky, Jeri S., & Carper, Ruth. (1996). Is there a neural basis for cognitive transitions in school-age children? In Arnold J. Sameroff & Marshall M. Haith, *The five to seven year shift: The age of reason and responsibility.* Chicago & London: The University of Chicago Press.

Jemmott, John B., III, Jemmott, Loretta Sweet, & Fong, Geoffrey T. (1998). Abstinence and safer sex HIV risk-reduction interventions for African American adolescents. *Journal of the American Medical Association, 279,* 1529–1536.

Jencks, Christopher. (1994). *The homeless.* Cambridge, MA: Harvard University Press.

Jenkins, Jennifer M., & Astington, Janet Wilde. (1996). Cognitive factors and family structure associated with theory of mind development in young children. *Developmental Psychology, 32,* 70–78.

Jensen, Peter S., & Hoagwood, Kimberly. (1997). The book of names: DSM-IV in context. *Development and Psychopathology, 9,* 231–249.

Johnson, David W., & Johnson, Roger T. (1994). *Learning together and alone: Cooperative, competitive, and individualistic learning* (4th ed.). Boston: Allyn & Bacon.

Johnson, Edward S., & Meade, Ann C. (1987). Developmental patterns of spatial ability: An early sex difference. *Child Development, 58,* 725–740.

Johnson-Powell, Gloria, & Yamamoto, Joe. (1997). *Transcultural child development: Psychological assessment and treatment.* New York: Wiley.

Johnston, Lloyd D., O'Malley, Patrick M., & Bachman, Jerald G. (1989). *Drug use, drinking, and smoking: National survey results from high school, college, and young adult populations, 1975–1988.* Rockville, MD: National Institute for Drug Abuse.

Johnston, Lloyd D., O'Malley, Patrick M., & Bachman, Jerald G. (1997). *Monitoring the future study: Drug use among American teens shows some signs of leveling after a long rise.* (University of Michigan News and Information Services Press Release, December 18, 1997). Ann Arbor: University of Michigan.

Johnston, Lloyd D., O'Malley, Patrick M., & Bachman, Jerald G. (1998). *Drug use by American young people begins to turn downward.* (University of Michigan News and Information Services Press Release, December, 1998). Ann Arbor: University of Michigan.

Johnston, Lloyd D., O'Malley, Patrick M., & Bachman, Jerald G. (1998). *Monitoring the future study: Drug use among American teens shows some signs of leveling after a long rise.* (University of Michigan News and Information Services Press Release, December, 1998). Ann Arbor: University of Michigan.

Johnston, Lloyd D., O'Malley, Patrick M., & Bachman, Jerald G. (1998). *Smoking among American teens declines some.* (University of Michigan News and Information Services Press Release, December, 1998). Ann Arbor: University of Michigan.

Jones, Elizabeth, & Reynolds, Gretchen. (1992). *The play's the thing: Teachers' roles in children's play.* New York: Teacher's College Press.

Jones, Nancy Aaron, Field, Tiffany, Fox, Nathan A., Lunedy, Brenda, & Davalos, Marisabel. (1997). EEG activation in 1-month-old infants of depressed mothers. *Development and Psychopathology, 9,* 491–505.

Jones, N. Burton. (1976). Rough-and-tumble play among nursery school children. In Jerome S. Bruner, Alison Jolly, & Kathy Sylva (Eds.), *Play.* New York: Basic Books.

Jones, Susan S., Smith, Linda B., & Landau, Barbara. (1991). Object properties and knowledge in early lexical learning. *Child Development, 62,* 499–516.

Junger-Tas, J., Terlouw, G. J., & Klein, M. W. (1994). *Delinquent behavior among young people in the Western World.* New York: Kugler.

Jusczyk, Peter W. (1995). Language acquisition: Speech sounds and the beginnings of phonology. In J.L. Miller & P.D. Eimas (Eds.), *Speech, language and communication.* New York: Academic Press.

Jusczyk, Peter W. (1997). *The discovery of spoken language.* Cambridge, Mass.: MIT Press.

Jusczyk, Peter W., & Hohue, Elizabeth A. (1997). Infants' memory for spoken words. *Science, 277,* 1984–1986.

Kachur, S. Patrick, Potter, Lloyd B., James, Stephen P., & Powell, Kenneth E. (1995). *Suicide in the United States: 1980–1992* (Violence Surveillance Summary Series No. 1). Atlanta, GA: National Center for Injury Prevention and Control.

Kagen, Jerome. (1994). *Galen's prophecy.* New York: Basic Books.

Kagen, Jerome. (1998). *Three seductive ideas.* Cambridge, MA: Harvard University Press.

Kahn, James G., Brindis, Claire D., & Glei, Dana A. (1999). Pregnancies averted among U.S. teenagers by the use of contraceptives. *Family Planning Perspectives, 31,* 29–34.

Kail, R. (1990). *The development of memory in children* (3rd ed.). New York: Freeman.

Kail, R. (1991). Developmental changes in speed of processing during childhood and adolescence. *Psychological Bulletin, 109,* 490–501.

Kail, R. (1991). Processing time declines exponentially during childhood and adolescence. *Developmental Psychology, 27,* 259–266.

Kallen, Karin. (1997). Maternal smoking during pregnancy and limb reduction malformations in Sweden. *American Journal of Public Health, 87,* 29–32.

Kalmar, Magda. (1996) The course of intellectual development in preterm and full-term children: An 8-year longitudinal study. *International Journal of Behavioral Development, 19,* 491–516.

Kamerman, S.B., & Kahn, A.J. (1993). Home health visiting in Europe. *The Future of Children, 3,* 39–52.

Kandel, Denise B., & Davies, Mark. (1996). High school students who use crack and other drugs. *Archives of General Psychiatry, 53,* 71–80.

Kandel, Denise B., Wu, Ping, & Davies, Mark. (1994). Maternal smoking during pregnancy and smoking by adolescent daughters. *American Journal of Public Health, 84,* 1407–1413.

Kanner, Leo. (1943). Autistic disturbances of affective contact. *Nervous Child, 2,* 217–250.

Kaplan, Elaine Bell. (1997). Adolescent sexual abuse, sexual assault, and rape. *Adolescence, 32,* 713–734.

Karpov, Yuriy, & Haywood, H. Carl. (1998). Two ways to elaborate Vygotsky's concept of mediation: Implications for instruction. *American Psychologist, 53,* 27–36.

Kasen, Stephanie, Cohen, Patricia, & Brook, Judith S. (1998). Adolescent school experiences and dropout, adolescent pregnancy, and young adult deviant behavior. *Journal of Adolescent Research, 13,* 49–72.

Kaufman, Joan, & Zigler, Edward. (1989). The intergenerational transmission of child abuse. In Dante Cicchetti & Vicki Carlson (Eds.), *Child maltreatment: Theory and research on the causes and consequences of child abuse and neglect.* Cambridge, England: Cambridge University Press.

Kaufman, Joan, & Zigler, Edward. (1993). The intergenerational hypothesis is overstated. In Richard J. Gelles & Donileen R. Loseke (Eds.), *Current controversies in family violence.* Newbury Park, CA: Sage.

Kaye, Kenneth. (1982). *The mental and social life of babies: How parents create persons.* Chicago: University of Chicago Press.

Keating, D.P. (1990). Adolescent thinking. In S.S. Feldman & G.R. Elliott (Eds.), *At the threshold: The developing adolescent.* Cambridge, MA: Harvard University Press.

Kelly, Karen. (1998). Working teenagers: Do after-school jobs hurt? *The Harvard Education Letter, 14,* 1–3.

Kerr, Margaret, Lambert, William W., & Bem, Daryl J. (1996). Life course sequelae of childhood shyness in Sweden: Comparison with the United States. *Developmental Psychology, 32,* 1100–1105.

Kessen, W. (1990). *The rise and fall of development.* Worcester, MA: Clark University Press.

King, Valerie. (1994). Non-resident father involvement and child well-being: Can dads make a difference? *Journal of Family Issues, 15,* 78–96.

Kinney, Hannah C., Filiano, James J., Sleeper, Lynn A., Mandell, Frederick, Valdes-Dapena, Marie, & White, W. Frost. (1995). Decreased muscarinic receptor binding in the arcuate nucleus in sudden infant death syndrome. *Science, 269,* 1446–1450.

Kirby, Douglas, Barth, Richard P., Leland, Nancy, & Fetro, Joyce V. (1991). Reducing the risk: Impact of a new curriculum on sexual risk-taking. *Family Planning Perspectives, 21,* 253–263.

Kirby, D., Short, L., Collins, J., Rugg, D., Kolbe, L., Howard, M., Miller, B., Sonenstein, F., & Zabin, L.S. (1994). School-based programs to reduce sexual risk behaviour: A review of effectiveness. *Public Health Reports, 109,* 339–360.

Kisilevsky, B.S., & Low, J.A. (1998). Human fetal behavior: 100 years of study. *Developmental Review, 18,* 1–29.

Kisilevsky, Barbara S., Hains, Sylvia M. J., Lee, Kang, Muir, Darwin W., Xu, Fen, Fu, Genyao, Zhao, Zneng Y., & Yang, Ru L. (1998). The still-face effect in Chinese and Canadian 3- to 6-month-old infants. *Developmental Psychology, 34,* 629–640.

Kitchener, Karen S., & Fischer, Kurt S. (1990). A skill approach to the development of reflective thinking. In D. Kuhn (Ed.), *Developmental aspects of teaching and learning thinking skills: Vol. 21. Contributions to human development.* Basel, Switzerland: Karger.

Kitzinger, Sheila. (1989). *The complete book of pregnancy and childbirth.* New York: Knopf.

Klahr, David. (1989). Information-processing approaches. In R. Vasta (Ed.), *Annals of child development* (Vol. 6). Greenwich, CT: JAI Press.

Klahr, David. (1992). Information-processing approaches to cognitive development. In M.H. Bornstein & M.E. Lamb (Eds.), *Developmental psychology: An advanced textbook* (3rd ed.). Hillsdale, NJ: Erlbaum.

Klaus, Marshall H., & Kennell, John H. (1976). *Maternal-infant bonding: The impact of early separation or loss on family development.* St. Louis: Mosby.

Klee, Linnea, Kronstadt, Diana, & Zlotnic, Cheryl. (1997). Foster care's youngest: A preliminary report. *America Orthopsychiatric Association, Inc., 67,* 290–299.

Klein, Melanie. (1957). *Envy and gratitude.* New York: Basic Books.

Klein, T.W. (1988). *Program evaluation of the Kaemhameha Elementary Education Program's reading curriculum in Hawaii public schools: The cohort analysis 1978–1986.* Honolulu: Center for Development of Early Education.

Klepinger, Daniel H., Lundberg, Shelly, & Plotnick, Robert D. (1995). Adolescent fertility and the educational attainment of young women. *Family Practice Perspectives, 27,* 23–28.

Klerman, Lorraine V., Cliver, Suzanne P., & Goldenberg, Robert L. (1998) The impact of short interpregnancy intervals on pregnancy outcomes in a low-income population. *American Journal of Public Health, 88,* 1182–1185.

Klesges, Robert. (1993). Effects of television on metabolic rate: Potential implications for childhood obesity. *Pediatrics, 91,* 281–286.

Klopfer, P. (1971). Mother love: What turns it on? *American Scientist, 49*, 404–407.

Kochanska, Grazyna. (1991). Socialization and temperament in the development of guilt and conscience. *Child Development, 62*, 1379–1392.

Kochanska, Grazyna. (1993). Toward a synthesis of parental socializations and child temperament in early development of conscience. *Child Development, 64*, 325–347.

Kochanska, Grazyna, Coy, Katherine C., Tjebkes, Terri L., & Husarek, Susan J. (1998). Individual differences in emotionality in infancy. *Child Development, 64*, 375–390.

Kochenderfer, Becky J., & Ladd, Gary W. (1997). Victimized children's responses to peers' aggression: Behaviors associated with reduced versus continued victimization. Development and Psychopathology, 9, 59–73.

Koepke, Jean E., & Bigelow, Ann E. (1997). Observations of newborn suckling behavior. *Infant Behavior & Development, 20*, 93–98.

Koff, E., & Rierdan, Jill. (1995). Preparing girls for menstruation: Recommendations from adolescent girls. *Adolescence, 30*, 795–811.

Kohlberg, Lawrence. (1963). Development of children's orientation towards a moral order (Part I). Sequencing in the development of moral thought. *Vita Humana, 6*, 11–36.

Kohlberg, Lawrence. (1981). *Essays on moral development* (Vol. 1). New York: Harper & Row.

Kohlberg, Lawrence. (1981). *The philosophy of moral development*. New York: Harper & Row.

Kohnstamm, Geldoph A., Halverson, Charles F., Havil, Valeri L., & Mervielde, Ivan. (1996). Parents' free descriptions of child characteristics: A cross cultural search for the developmental antecedents of the big five. In Sara Harkness & Charles M. Super (Eds.), *Parents' cultural belief systems: The origins, expressions, and consequences*. New York: Guilford.

Kolata, Gina. (1995, May 23). Molecular tools may offer clues to reducing risks of birth defects. *The New York Times*.

Kools, Susan M. (1997). Adolescent identity development in foster care. *Family Relations, 46*, 263–271.

Koop, C. Everett. (1997). The tiniest patients. *Newsweek, Special Edition, 51*.

Koopman, Peter, Gubbay, John, Vivian, Nigel, Goodfellow, Peter, & Lovell-Badge, Robin. (1991). Male development of chromosomally female mice transgenic for Sry. *Nature, 351*, 117–122.

Korbin, Jill E. (1994). Sociocultural factors in child maltreatment. In G.B. Melton & F. Barry (Eds.), *Safe neighborhoods: Foundations for a new national strategy on child abuse and neglect*. New York: Guilford.

Korbin, Jill E., Coulton, Claudia J., Chard, Sarah, Platt-Houston, Candis & Su, Marilyn. (1998). Impoverishment and child maltreatment in African American and European American neighborhoods. *Development and Psychopathology, 10*, 215–233.

Kost, Kathryn, & Forrest, Jacqueline Darroch. (1995). Intention status of United States births in 1988: Differences by mother's socioeconomic and demographic characteristics. *Family Planning Perspectives, 27*, 11–17.

Kovacs, Donna M., Parker, Jeffrey G., & Hoffman, Lois W. (1996). Behavioral affective, and social correlates of involvement in cross-sex friendship in elementary school. *Child Development, 67*, 2269–2286.

Kozol, Jonathan. (1991). *Savage inequalities*. New York: Crown.

Kraft, Joan Creech & Willhite, Calvin C. (1997). Retinoids in abnormal and normal embryonic development. In Sam Kacew & George H. Lambert (Eds.), *Environmental toxicology and human development*. Washington DC: Taylor & Francis.

Kranichfeld, Marion L. (1987). Rethinking family power. *Journal of Family Issues, 8*, 42–56.

Kroger, Jane. (1989). *Identity in adolescence: The balance between self and other*. London: Routledge.

Kroger, Jane. (1993). Ego identity: an overview. In J. Kroger (Ed.), *Discussions on ego identity*. Hillsdale, NJ: Erlbaum.

Kroger, Jane. (1995). *Identity in adolescence: The balance between self and other*. London: Routledge.

Kroger, Jane. (1995). The differentiation of "firm" and "developmental" foreclosure identity statuses: A longitudinal study. *Journal of Adolescent Research, 10*, 317–337.

Kromelow, Susan, Harding, Carol, & Touris, Margot. (1990). The role of the father in the development of stranger sociability during the second year. *American Journal of Orthopsychiatry, 6*, 521–530.

Krusch, D.A., Klorman, R., Brumaghim, J.T., Fitzpatrick, P.A., Borgstedt, A.D., & Strauss, J. (1996). Methylphenidate slows reactions of children with attention deficit disorder during and after an error. *Journal of Abnormal Child Psychology, 24*, 633–650.

Ku, Leighton C., Sonenstein, Freya L., &Pleck, Joseph H. (1992). The association of AIDS education and sex education with sexual behavior and condom use among teenage men. *Family Planning Perspectives, 24*, 100–106.

Kuczaj, Stan A. (1986). Thoughts on the intentional basis of early object word extension: Evidence from comprehension and production. In Stan A. Kuczaj & Martyn D. Barrett (Eds.), *The development of word meaning: Progress in cognitive developmental research*. New York: Springer-Verlag.

Kuczynski, L., & Kochanska, G. (1990). Development of children's noncompliance strategies from toddlerhood to age 5. *Developmental Psychology, 26*, 398–408.

Kuhl, P.K., & Meltzoff, A.N. (1988). Speech as an intermodal object of perception. In A. Yonas (Ed.), *Minnesota symposia on child psychology: Vol. 20. Perceptual development in infancy*. Hillsdale, NJ: Erlbaum.

Kuhn, Deanna, Garcia-Mita, Merce, Zohar, Arat, & Anderson, Christopher. (1995). Strategies of knowledge acquisition. *Monographs of the Society for Research in Child Development, 60* (Serial No. 245).

Kulin, H.E. (1993). Editorial: Puberty: When? *Journal of Clinical Endocrinology and Metabolism, 76*, 24–25.

Lagerspetz, Kirsti & Bjorkquist, Kaj. (1994). In L. Rowell Huesmann (Ed.) *Aggressive Behavior*. New York: Plenum.

Lahey, Benjamin B., & Loeber, Rolf. (1994). Framework for a developmental model of oppositional defiant disorder and conduct disorder. In Donald K. Routh (Ed.), *Disruptive behavior disorders in childhood*. New York: Plenum Press.

La Leche League International. (1997). *The womanly art of breastfeeding*. New York: Plume.

Lamb, Michael E. (1982). Maternal employment and child development: A review. In Michael E. Lamb (Ed.), *Nontraditional families: Parenting and child development*. Hillsdale, NJ: Erlbaum.

Lamb, Michael E. (1987). *The father's role: Cross-cultural perspectives*. Hillsdale, NJ: Erlbaum.

Lamb, Michael E. (1997). The development of father-infant relationships. In M.E. Lamb (Ed.), *The role of the father in child development*. New York: Wiley.

Lamb, Michael E., & Sternberg, Kathleen J. (1990). Do we really know how day care affects children? *Journal of Applied Developmental Psychology, 11*, 351–379.

Lamb, Wally. (1993). *She's come undone*. New York: Washington Square Press.

Lambert, Wallace E., Genesee, Fred, Holobow, Naomi & Chartrand, Louise. (1993). Bilingual education for majority English-speaking children. *European Journal of Psychology of Education, 8*, 3–22.

Lamborn, Susie D., & Steinberg, Laurence. (1993). Emotional autonomy redux: Revisiting Ryan and Lynch. *Child Development, 64*, 483–499.

Lamborn, Susie D., Mounts, Nina S., Steinberg, Laurence, & Dornbusch, Sanford M. (1991). Patterns of competence and adjustment among adolescents from authoritarian, authoritative, indulgent, and neglectful families. *Child Development, 62*, 1049–1065.

Lamborn, Susie D., Dornbusch, Sanford M., & Steinberg, Laurence. (1996). Ethnicity and community context as moderators of the relations between family decision making and adolescent adjustment. *Child Development, 67*, 283–301.

Lansing, L. Stephen. (1983). *The three worlds of Bali*. New York: Praeger.

Laosa, Luis M. (1996). Intelligence testing and social policy. *Journal of Applied Developmental Psychology, 17*, 155–173.

LaPointe, A.E., Mead, N.A., & Askew, J.M. (1992). *Learning mathematics*. Princeton, NJ: Educational Testing Service.

Larner, M.B., Stevenson, C.S., & Behrman, R.E. (1998). Protecting children from abuse and neglect: Analysis and recommendations. *Future Child, 8*, 4–22.

LaRossa, R. (1997). *The modernization of fatherhood: A social and political history*. Chicago: University of Chicago Press.

Larsen, William J. (1998). *Essentials of human embryology*. New York: Churchill Livingstone.

Larson, Reed W. & Gillman, Sally. (1999). Transmission of emotions in the daily interactions of single-mother families. *Journal of Marriage and the Family, 61*, 21–37.

Larson, Reed W., & Ham, Mark. (1993). Stress and "storm and stress" in early adolescence: The relationship of negative events with dysphoric affect. *Developmental Psychology, 29*, 130–140.

Laursen, Brett, Coy, Katherine C., & Collins, W. Andrew. (1998). Reconsidering changes in parent-child conflict across adolescence: A meta-analysis. *Child Development, 69*, 817–832.

Lawrence, Ruth A. (1998). *Breastfeeding: A guide for the medical profession* (5th ed.). St. Louis: Mosby.

Leach, Penelope. (1989). *Babyhood* (2nd ed.). New York: Knopf.

Leach, Penelope. (1997). *Your baby & child: From birth to age 5*. New York: Knopf.

Leaper, Campbell, Anderson, Kristin J., & Sanders, Paul. (1998). Moderators of gender effects on parents' talk to their children: A meta-analysis. *Developmental Psychology, 34*, 3–27.

Leavitt, L., & Fox, N. (1993). *The psychological effects of war and violence on children*. Hillsdale, NJ: Erlbaum.

Lee, Thomas F. (1993). *Gene future: The promise and perils of the new biology*. New York: Plenum.

Leffert, Nancy, & Petersen, Anne C. (1995). Patterns of development during adolescence. In Michael Rutter & David J. Smith (Eds.), *Psychosocial disorders in young people: Time trends and their causes*. Chichester: John Wiley & Sons.

Leifer, A.D., Leiderman, P.H., Barnett, C.R., & Williams, J.A. (1972). Effects of mother-infant separation on maternal attachment behavior. *Child Development, 43*, 1203–1218.

Lemery, Kathryn S., Goldsmith, H. Hill, Klinnert, Mary D., & Mrazel, David A. (1999). Developmental models of infant and childhood temperament. *Developmental Psychology, 35*, 189–204.

Lenneberg, Eric H. (1967). *Biological foundations of language*. New York: Wiley.

Lerner, H.E. (1978). Adaptive and pathogenic aspects of sex-role stereotypes: Implications for parenting and psychotherapy. *American Journal of Psychiatry, 135*, 48–52.

Lerner, Richard A., Delaney, Mary, Hess, Laura E., Jovanovic, Jasna, & von Eye, Alexander. (1990). Adolescent physical attractiveness and academic competence. *Journal of Early Adolescence, 10*, 4–20.

Lerner, Richard M., Castellino, Domini R., Terry, Patterson A., Villarruel, Francisco A., & McKinney, Marvin H. (1995). Developmental contextual perspective on parenting. In Marc H. Bornstein (Ed.), *Handbook of parenting: Biology and ecology of parenting*. Mahwah, NJ: Erlbaum.

Leslie, A.M., & Frith, U. (1988). Autistic children's understanding of seeing, knowing, and believing. *British Journal of Developmental Psychology, 6*, 315–324.

Leslie, A.M., & Keeble, S. (1987). Do six-month-olds perceive causality? *Cognition, 25*, 265–288.

Lester, Barry M., & Dreher, Melanie. (1989). Effects of marijuana use during pregnancy on newborn cry. *Child Development, 60*, 765–771.

Lester, Barry M., Hoffman, Joel, & Brazelton, T. Berry. (1985). The rhythmic structure of mother-infant interaction in term and preterm infants. *Child Development, 56,* 15–27.

Levine, Murray, & Doueck, Howard J. (1995). *The impact of mandated reporting on the therapeutic process: Picking up the pieces.* Thousand Oaks: Sage.

LeVine, Robert A. (1988). Human parental care: Universal goals, cultural strategies, individual behavior. In R.A. LeVine, P.M. Miller, & M.M. West (Eds.), *Parental behavior in diverse societies.* San Francisco: Jossey-Bass.

LeVine, Robert A., Dixon, Suzanne, LeVine, Sarah, Richman, Ay, Leiderman, P. Herbert, Keeferk Constance H. & Brazelton, Berry. (1994). *Child care and culture: Lessons from Africa.* New York: Cambridge University Press.

Levine, Sarah & Osbourne, Sally. (1989). Living and learning with Sally. *Phi Delta Kappan, 70,* 594–598.

Levinson, D. (1989). Physical punishment of children and wife beating in cross-cultural perspective. *Child Abuse & Neglect, 5,* 193–195.

Levy, Gary D. (1994). Aspects of preschoolers' comprehension of indoor and outdoor gender-typed toys. *Sex Roles, 30,* 391–405.

Levy, G.D., & Fivush, R. (1993). Scripts and gender: A new approach for examining gender role development. *Developmental Review, 13,* 126–146.

Lewis, Catherine C. (1996). Fostering social and intellectual development: The roots of Japan's educational success. In Thomas P. Rohlen & Gerald K. LeTendre (Eds.), *Teaching and learning in Japan.* Cambridge, England: Cambridge University Press.

Lewis, Lawrence B., Antone, Carol, & Johnson, Jacqueline S. (1999). Effects of prosodic stress and serial position on syllable omission in first words. *Developmental Psychology, 35,* 45–59.

Lewis, M. (1990). Social knowledge and social development. *Merrill-Palmer Quarterly, 36,* 93–116.

Lewis, M., & Brooks, J. (1978). Self-knowledge and emotional development. In M. Lewis & L.A. Rosenblum (Eds.), *The development of affect.* New York: Plenum.

Lewis, M., Sullivan, M.W., Stanger, C., & Weiss, M. (1989). Self development and self-conscious emotions. *Child Development, 60,* 146–156.

Lewis, M., Alessandri, S.M., & Sullivan, M.W. (1990). Violation of expectancy, loss of control, and anger expressions in young infants. *Developmental Psychology, 26,* 745–751.

Lewis, M., Alessandri, S.M., & Sullivan, M.W. (1992). Differences in shame and pride as a function of children's gender and task difficulty. *Child Development, 63,* 630–638.

Lewit, Eugene M. & Kerrebrock, Nancy. (1998). Child indicators: Dental health. *The Future of Children: Protecting Children from Abuse and Neglect, 8,* 4–22.

Li, De-Kun, Mueller, Beth A., Hickok, Durlin E., Daling, Janet R., Fantel, Alan G., Checkoway, Harvey, & Weiss, Noel S. (1996). Maternal smoking during pregnancy and the risk of congential urinary tract anomalies. *American Journal of Public Health, 86,* 249–253.

Lidz, Theodore. (1976). *The person: His and her development throughout the life cycle* (rev. ed.). New York: Basic Books.

Lieberman, A.F. (1993). *The emotional life of the toddler.* New York: Free Press.

Lieberman, Alicia F., Weston, Donna R., & Pawl, Jeree H. (1991). Preventive intervention and outcome with anxiously attached dyads. *Child Development, 62,* 199–209.

Lightfoot, Cynthia. (1997). *The culture of adolsecent risk-taking.* New York: Guilford Press.

Lillard, A.S. (1993). Pretend play skills and the child's theory of mind. *Child Development, 64,* 348–371.

Lillard, A.S. (1993). Young children's conceptualization of pretense: Action or mental representational state? *Child Development, 64,* 372–386.

Lillard, A.S. (1994). Making sense of pretense. In C. Lewis & P. Mitchell (Eds.), *Children's early understanding of mind.* Hillsdale, NJ: Erlbaum.

Lobel, T.E., & Menashri, J. (1993). Relations of conceptions of gender-role transgressions and gender constancy to gender-typed toy preferences. *Developmental Psychology, 29,* 150–155.

Locke, J.L. (1993). *The child's path to spoken language.* Cambridge, MA: Harvard University Press.

Lockman, J.J., & Thelen, E. (1993). Developmental biodynamics: Brain, body, behavior connections. *Child Development, 64,* 953–959.

Loehlin, John C. (1992). *Genes and environment in personality development.* Newbury Park, CA: Sage.

Loftus, Elizabeth F. (1997, September). Creating false memories. *Scientific American,* 70–75.

Loscocco, Karyn, & Roschlee, Anne R. (1991). Influences on the quality of work and nonwork life: Two decades in review. *Journal of Vocational Behavior, 39,* 182–225.

Losoya, Sandra H., Goldsmith, H. Hill, Callor, Suzanne, & Rowe, David C. (1997). Origins of familial similarity in parenting: A study of twins and adoptive siblings. *Developmental Psychology, 33,* 1012–1023.

Lott, I.T., & McCoy, E.E. (1992). *Down syndrome: Advances in medical care.* New York: Wiley-Liss.

Lowrey, George H. (1986). *Growth and development of children* (8th ed.). Chicago: Year Book Medical Publishers.

Lozoff, Betsy, Klein, Nancy K., Nelson, Edward C., McClish, Donna K., Manuel, Martin & Chacon, Maria Elena. (1998). Behavior of infants with iron-deficiency anemia. *Child Development, 69,* 24–36.

Lucas, A., Morley, R., Lister, G., & Leeson-Payne, C. (1992). Effect of very low birth weight on cognitive abilities at school age. *New England Journal of Medicine, 326* (3), 202–203.

Lucas, Tamara, Hense, Rosemary, & Donato, Ruben. (1990). Promoting the success of Latino language-minority students: An exploratory study of six high schools. *Harvard Educational Review, 60,* 315–340.

Luke, Barbara. (1993). Nutrition and prematurity. In Frank R. Witter & Louis G. Keith (Eds.), *Textbook of prematurity: Antecedents, treatment, and outcome.* Boston: Little, Brown.

Lukeman, Diane, & Melvin, Diane. (1993). Annotation: The preterm infant: Psychological issues in childhood. *Journal of Child Psychology and Psychiatry, 34,* 837–849.

Luria, A.R. (1976). *Cognitive development: Its cultural and social foundations.* Cambridge, MA: Harvard University Press.

Luria, A.R. (1979). *The making of mind.* Cambridge, MA: Harvard University Press.

Luthar, Suniya S., & McMahon, Thomas J. (1996). Peer reputation among inner city adolescents: Structure and correlates. *Journal of Adolescent Research, 12,* 581–603.

Luthar, Suniya S., & Zigler, Edward. (1991). Vulnerability and competence: A review of research on resilience in childhood. *American Journal of Orthopsychiatry, 61,* 6–22.

Lykken, D.T., McGue, M., Tellegen, A., & Bouchard, T.J., Jr. (1992). Emergenesis: Genetic traits that may not run in families. *American Psychologist, 47,* 1565–1577.

Lyon, Jeff, & Gorner, Peter. (1995). *Altered fates: Gene therapy and the retooling of human life.* New York: Norton.

Lyons, Peter & Rittner, Barbara. (1998). The construction of the crack babies phenomenon as a social problem. *American Journal of Orthopsychiatry, 68.* 313–320.

Lytle, L. Jean, Bakken, Linda, & Roming, Charles. (1997). Adolescent female identity development. *Sex Roles, 37,* 175–185.

Lytton, Hugh, & Romney, D.M. (1991). Parents' differential socialization of boys and girls: A meta-analysis. *Psychological Bulletin, 109,* 267–296.

MacArdle, Paul, O'Brien, Gregory, & Kolvin, Israel. (1995). Hyperactivity: Prevalence and relationship with conduct disorder. *Journal of Child Psychology and Psychiatry and Allied Disciplines, 36,* 279–303.

Maccoby, Eleanor Emmons. (1980). *Social development: Psychological growth and the parent-child relationship.* New York: Harcourt Brace Jovanovich.

Maccoby, Eleanor Emmons. (1992). The role of parents in the socialization of children: An historical overview. *Developmental Psychology, 28,* 1006–1017.

Maccoby, Eleanor Emmons, & Mnookin, R.H. (1992). *Dividing the child: Social and legal dilemmas of custody.* Cambridge, MA: Harvard University Press.

MacDonald, Kevin, & Parke, Ross D. (1986). Parent-child physical play: The effect of sex and age of children and parents. *Sex Roles, 15,* 367–378.

MacDonald, Shelley, & Hayne, Harlene. (1996). Child-initiated conversations about the past and memory performance by preschoolers. *Cognitive Development, 11,* 421–442.

Mackey, Wade C. (1996). *The American father: Biocultural and developmental aspects.* New York: Plenum.

Maddox, John. (1993). Wilful public misunderstanding of genetics. *Nature, 364,* 281.

Maguire, Kathleen, & Pastore, Ann L. (Eds.). (1998). *Sourcebook of criminal justice statistics, 1997.* Washington, DC: U.S. Government Printing Office.

Maier, Susan E., Chen, Wei-Jung A., & West, James R. (1996). The effects of timing and duration of alcohol exposure on development of the fetal brain. In Ernest L. Abel (Ed.), *Fetal alcohol syndrome: From mechanism to prevention.* Boca Raton: CRC Press.

Main, Mary. (1995). Recent studies in attachment. In Susan Goldberg, Roy Muir, & John Kerr (Eds.), *Attachment theory: social, developmental, and clinical perspectives.* Hillsdale, NJ: Analytic Press.

Malatesta, C.Z., Culver, C., Tesman, J.R., & Shepard, B. (1989). The development of emotional expression during the first two years of life. *Monographs of the Society for Research in Child Development, 54* (1–2), (Serial No. 219).

Males, Mike A. (1996). *The scapegoat generation: America's war on adolescents.* Monroe, ME: Common Courage Press.

Malina, Robert M. (1990). Physical growth and performance during the transitional years (9–16). In Raymond Montemayor, Gerald R. Adams, & Thomas P. Gullotta (Eds.), *From childhood to adolescence: A transitional period?* Newbury Park, CA: Sage.

Malina, Robert M. (1991). Growth spurt, adolescent. In Richard M. Lerner, Ann C. Petersen, & Jeanne Brooks-Gunn (Eds.), *Encyclopedia of adolescence* (Vol. 1). New York: Garland.

Malina, Robert M., & Bouchard, Claude. (1991). *Growth, maturation, and physical activity.* Champaign, IL: Human Kinetics Books.

Malina, Robert M., Bouchard, Claude, & Beunen, G. (1988). Human growth: Selected aspects of current research on well-nourished children. *Annual Review of Anthropology, 17,* 187–219.

Mallory, B.L., & New, R.S. (1994). *Diversity and developmentally appropriate practice: Challenges for early childhood education.* New York: Teachers College Press.

Mangelsdorf, S., Gunnar, M., Kestenbaum, R., Lang, S., & Andreas, D. (1990). Infant proneness-to-distress temperament, maternal personality, and mother-infant attachment: Associations and goodness of fit. *Child Development, 61,* 820–831.

Manlove, Jennifer. (1997). Early motherhood in an intergenerational perspective: The experiences of a British cohort. *Journal of Marriage and the Family, 59,* 263–280.

Manteuffel, Mary Druse. (1996). Neurotransmitter function: Changes associated with *in utero* alcohol exposure. In Ernest L. Abel (Ed.), *Fetal alcohol syndrome: From mechanism to prevention.* Boca Raton: CRC Press.

Marcia, James E. (1966). Development and validation of ego identity status. *Journal of Personality and Social Psychology, 3,* 551–558.

Marcia, James E. (1980). Identity in adolescence. In J. Adelson (Ed.), *Handbook of adolescent psychology.* New York: Wiley.

Marcia, J.E. (1994). In Rainer K. Silbereisen & Eberhard Todt (Eds.), *Adolescence in context: The interplay of family, school, peers, and work in adjustment.* New York: Springer-Verlag.

Marcia, J.E., Waterman, A.S., Matteson, D.R., Archer, S.L., & Orlofsky, J.L. (Eds.). (1993). *Ego identity: A handbook for psychosocial research*. New York: Springer-Verlag.

Markman, E.M. (1991). The whole object, taxonomic, and mutual exclusivity assumptions as initial constraints on word meanings. In J.P. Byrnes & S.A. Gelman (Eds.), *Perspectives on language and cognition*. Cambridge, England: Cambridge University Press.

Markus, H., & Nurius, P. (1986). Possible selves. *American Psychologist, 41*, 954–969.

Marsiglio, W. (1993). Adolescent males' orientation toward paternity and contraception. *Family Planning Perspectives, 25*, 22–31.

Martin, C.L. (1993). New directions for investigating children's gender knowledge. *Developmental Review, 13*, 184–204.

Martin, C.L., & Little, J.K. (1990). The relation of gender understanding to children's sex-typed preferences and gender stereotypes. *Child Development, 61*, 1427–1439.

Martin, Carol Lynn, Eisenbud, Lisa, & Rose, Hilary. (1995). Children's gender-based reasoning about toys. *Child Development, 66*, 1453–1471.

Martin, Sandra L., English, Kathleen T., Clark, Kathryn Andersen, Cilenti, Dorothy, & Kupper, Lawrence L. (1996). Violence and substance use among North Carolina pregnant women. *American Journal of Public Health, 86*, 991–998.

Martin, Sandra L., Kim, Haesook, Kupper, Lawrence I., Meyer, Robert E., & Hays, Melissa. (1997). Is incarceration during pregnancy associated with infant birthweight? *American Journal of Public Health, 87*, 1526–1531.

Marvin, Robert S. (1997). Ethological and general systems perspectives on child-parent attachment during the toddler and preschool years. In Nancy L. Segal, Glenn E. Weisfeld, & Carol C. Weisfeld (Eds.), *Uniting psychology and biology: Integrative perspectives on human development*. Washington, DC: American Psychological Association.

Marx, Russell D. (1993). Depression and eating disorders. In A. James Giannini and Andrew E. Slaby (Eds.), *The eating disorders*. New York: Springer-Verlag.

Masataka, Nobuo. (1992). Early ontogeny of vocal behavior of Japanese infants in response to maternal speech. *Child Development, 63*, 1177–1185.

Masataka, Nobuo. (1996). Perception of motherese in a signed language by 6-month-old deaf infants. *Developmental Psychology, 32*, 874–879.

Mason, J.A., & Herrmann, K.R. (1998). Universal infant bearing screening by automated auditory brainstem response measurement. *Pediatrics, 101*, 221–228.

Masten, Ann S. (1992). Homeless children in the United States: Mark of a nation at risk. *Current Directions in Psychological Science, 1*, 41–43.

Masten, Ann S., & Coatsworth, J. Douglas. (1998). The development of competence in favorable and unfavorable environments: Lessons from research on successful children. *American Psychologist, 53*, 205–220.

Masterpasqua, Frank. (1997). Toward a dynamic developmental understanding of disorder. In Frank Masterpasqua & Phyllis A. Perna (Eds.), *The psychological meaning of chaos: Translating theory into practice*. Washington, DC: American Psychological Association.

Maughan, Barbara, & Pickles, Andres. (1990). Adopted and illegitimate children growing up. In Lee N. Robins & Michael Rutter (Eds.), *Straight and devious pathways from childhood to adulthood*. Cambridge, England: Cambridge University Press.

Mayes, L.C., Granger, R.H., Bornstein, M.H., & Zuckerman, B. (1992). The problem of prenatal cocaine exposure: A rush to judgment. *Journal of the American Medical Association, 267*, 406–408.

McCalla, Sandra, Feldman, Joseph, Webbeh, Hassan, Ahmadi, Ramin, & Minkoff, Howard L. (1995). Changes in perinatal cocaine use in an inner-city hospital, 1988 to 1992. *American Journal of Public Health, 85*, 1695–1697.

McCauley, Elizabeth, Kay, Thomas, Ito, Joanne, & Treder, Robert. (1987). The Turner Syndrome: Cognitive deficits, affective discrimination, and behavior problems. *Child Development, 58*, 464–473.

McCrae, Robert R., Costa, Paul T. Jr., de Lima, Margarida Pedroso, Simões, António, Ostendorf, Fritz, Angleitner, Alois, Marusic, Iris, Bratko, Denis, Caprara, Gian Vittorio, Barbaranelli, Claudio, Chae, Joon-Ho, & Piedmont, Ralph L. (1999). Age differences in personality across the adult life span: Parallels in five cultures. *Developmental Psychology, 35*, 466–477.

McCourt, Frank. (1996). *Angela's ashes*. New York: Scribner.

McDonough, Laraine, & Mandler, Jean M. (1994). Very long term recall in infants: Infantile amnesia reconsidered. In Robyn Fivush (Ed.), *Long-term retention of infant memories*. Hove, England: Erlbaum.

McEachin, John J., Smith, Tristram, & Lovaas, O. Ivaf. (1993). Long-term outcome for children with autism who received early intensive behavioral treatment. *American Journal on Mental Retardation, 97*, 359–372.

McElroy, Susan Williams, & Moore, Kristin Anderson. (1997). Trends over time in teenage pregnancy and childbearing: The Critical Changes. In Rebecca A. Maynard (Ed.), *Kids having kids: Economic costs and social consequences of teen pregnany*. Urban Institute Press.

McGue, Matthew. (1993). From proteins to cognitions: The behavioral genetics of alcoholism. In Robert Plomin &Gerald E. McClearin (Eds.), *Nature, nurture, and psychology*. Washington, DC: American Psychological Association.

McGue, Matthew. (1995). Mediators and moderators of alcoholism inheritance. In J.R. Turner, L.R. Cardon, & J. K. Hewitt (Eds.), *Behavior genetic approaches to behavioral medicine*. New York: Plenum Press.

McGue, Matthew, Bouchard, Thomas J., Jr., Iacono, William G., & Lykken, David T. (1993). Behavioral genetics of cognitive ability: A life-span perspective. In Robert Plomin & Gerald E. McClearin (Eds.), *Nature, nurture, and psychology*. Washington, DC: American Psychological Association.

McGuire, Judith, & Bundy, Donald. (1996). Nutrition, cognitive development, and economic progress. *Social Policy Report: Society for Research in Child Development, 10*, 26–28.

McGuire, Shirley, Dunn, Judy, & Plomin, Robert. (1995). Maternal differential treatment of siblings and children's behavioral problems: A longitudinal study. *Development and Psychopathology, 7,* 515–528.

McKenzie, Lisa, & Stephenson, Patricia A. (1993). Variation in Cesarean section rates among hospitals in Washington state. *American Journal of Public Health, 83,* 1109–1112.

McKeon, Denise. (1994). Language, culture, and schooling. In Fred Genesee (Ed.), *Educating second-language children: The whole child, the whole curriculum, the whole community.* Cambridge, England: Cambridge University Press.

McKeough, Anne. (1992). A neo-structural analysis of children's narrative and its development. In Robbie Case (Ed.), *The mind's staircase: Exploring the conceptual underpinning of children's thought and knowledge.* Hillsdale, NJ: Erlbaum.

McKusick, Victor A. (1994). *Mendelian inheritance in humans* (10th ed.). Baltimore: Johns Hopkins University Press.

McLanahan, Sara S. (1997). Parent absence or poverty: Which matters more? In Greg J. Duncan & Jeanne Brooks-Gunn (Eds), *Consequences of growing up poor.* New York: Russell Sage Foundation.

McLanahan, Sara S., & Sandefur, G. (1994). *Growing up with a single parent: What hurts, what helps.* Cambridge, MA: Harvard University Press.

McLoyd, Vonnie C. (1998). Socioeconomic disadvantage and child development. *American Psychologist, 2,* 185–204.

Meacham, Jack. (1997). Autobiography, voice, and developmental theory. In Eric Amsel & K. Ann Renninger (Eds.), *Change and development: Issues of theory, method, and application.* Mahwah, NJ: Erlbaum.

Mehler, Jacques, & Fox, Robin. (Eds.). (1985). *Neonate cognition: Beyond the blooming buzzing confusion.* Hillsdale, NJ: Erlbaum.

Meis, Paul J., Goldenberg, Brian, Mercer, Brian M., Moawad, Atef, Das, Anita, McNellis, Donald, Johnson, Francee, Iams, Jay D., Thom, Elizabeth, & Andrews, William W. (1995). The preterm prediction study: Significance of vaginal infections. *American Journal of Obstetrics and Gynecology, 173,* 1231–1235.

Mellanby, Alex R., Phelps, Fran A., Chrichton, Nicola J., & Tripp, John H. (1995). School sex education: An experimental programme with educational and medical benefit. *British Medical Journal, 311,* 414–417.

Mellor, Steven. (1990). How do only children differ from other children. *Journal of Genetic Psychology, 151,* 221–230.

Meny, Robert G., Carroll, John L., Carbone, Mary Terese, & Kelly, Dorothy H. (1994). Cardiorespiratory recordings from infants dying suddenly and unexpectedly at home. *Pediatrics, 93,* 44–49.

Meredith, Howard V. (1978). Research between 1960 and 1970 on the standing height of young children in different parts of the world. In Hayne W. Reese & Lewis P. Lipsitt (Eds.), *Advances in child development and behavior* (Vol. 12). New York: Academic Press.

Merrell, Kenneth W., & Gimpel, Gretchen A. (1998). *Social skills of children and adolescents: Conceptualization, assessment, treatment.* Mahwah, NJ: Erlbaum.

Merriman, W. E. (1998). Competition, attention, and young children's lexical processing. In B. MacWhinney (Ed.), *The emergence of language.* Hillsdale, NJ: Erlbaum.

Messer, David J. (1994). *The development of communication.* New York: Wiley.

Michelsson, Katarina, Rinne, Arto, & Paajanen, Sonja. (1990). Crying, feeding and sleeping patterns in 1- to 12-month-old infants. *Child: Care, Health, and Development, 116,* 99–111.

Mihalic, Sharon Wofford & Elliott, Delbert. (1997). Short- and long-term consequences of adolescent work. *Youth & Society, 28,* 464–498.

Miller, Jane E., & Davis, Diane. (1997). Poverty history, marital history, and quality of children's home environments. *Journal of Marriage and the Family, 59,* 996–1007.

Miller, Norman S. (1993). Eating disorders and drug and alcohol dependency. In A. James Giannini and Andrew E. Slaby (Eds.) *The eating disorders.* New York: Spinger-Verlag.

Miller, Patricia H. (1993). *Theories of developmental psychology.* New York: Freeman.

Miller, Ted R., & Spicer, Rebecca S. (1998). How safe are our schools? *American Journal of Public Health, 88,* 413–418.

Mills, James L., McPartlin, Joseph M., Kirke, Peadar N., & Lee, Young J. (1995). Homocysteine metabolism in pregnancies complicated by neural-tube defects. *Lancet, 345,* 149–151.

Mills, Jon K., & Andrianopoulos, Georgia D. (1993). The relationship between childhood onset obesity and psychopathology in adulthood. *Journal of Psychology, 127,* 547–551.

Minuchin, Salvador, & Nichols, Michael P. (1993). *Family healing: Tales of hope and renewal from family therapy.* New York: Free Press.

Mitchell, E.A., Ford, R.P.K., Steward, A.W., & Taylor, B.J. (1993). Smoking and the sudden infant death syndrome. *Pediatrics, 91,* 893–896.

Mitchell, Peter. (1997). *Introduction to theory of mind: Children, autism and apes.* New York: St. Martin's Press.

***MMWR** (Morbidity and Mortality Weekley Report)*. See **Centers for Disease Control and Prevention.**

Moerk, Ernst L. (1996). First language acquisition. In W. Reese Hayne (Ed), *Advances in child development and behavior* (Vol. 26). San Diego: Academic Press.

Moffitt, Terrie E. (1993). The neuropsychology of conduct disorder. *Development and Psychopathology, 5,* 135–151.

Moffitt, Terrie E. (1997). Adolescence—Limited and life-course-persistent offending: A complementary pair of developmental theories. In Terence P. Thornberry (Ed.), *Development theories of crime and delinquency.* New Brunswick, NJ: Transaction.

Moffitt, Terrie E. (1997). Helping poor mothers and children. *Journal of the American Medical Association, 278,* 680–682.

Moffitt, Terrie E., Caspi, Avshalom, Belsky, Jay, & Silva, Paul A. (1992). Childhood experience and the onset of menarche. *Child Development, 63,* 47–58.

Molina, Brooke S.G., & Chassin, Laurie. (1996). The parent-adolescent relationship at puberty: Hispanic ethnicity and parent alcoholism as moderators. *Developmental Psychology, 32,* 675–686.

Moller, Lora C. & Serbin, Lisa A. (1996). Antecedents of toddler gender segregation: Cognitive consonance, gender-typed toy preferences and behavioral compatibility. *Sex Roles, 35,* 445–460.

Montemayor, Raymond. (1986). Family variation in parent-adolescent storm and stress. *Journal of Adolescent Research, 1,* 15–31.

Montgomery, Laura E., Kiely, John L., & Pappas, Gregory. (1996). The effects of poverty, race, and family structure on US children's health: Data from the NHIS, 1978 through 1980 and 1989 through 1991. *American Journal of Public Health, 86,* 1401–1405.

Monthly Vital Statistics Report. (1998, September 4). *Births and Deaths: United States, July 1996–1998.* Atlanta, GA: Centers for Disease Control.

Moon, Christine, Cooper, Robin Panneton, & Fifer, William P. (1993). Two-day olds prefer their native language. *Infant Behavior and Development, 16,* 495–500.

Moore, Keith L., & Persaud, T.V.N. (1998). *The developing human: Clinically oriented embryology.* Philadelphia: W. B. Saunders.

Moore, Susan, & Rosenthal, Doreen. (1991). Adolescent invulnerability and perceptions of AIDS risk. *Journal of Adolescent Research, 6,* 164–180.

Moore, Chris, Pure, K., & Furrow, D. (1990). Children's understanding of the modal expression of certainty and uncertainty and its relation to the development of a representational theory of mind. *Child Development, 61,* 722–730.

Morrongiello, B.A., & Rocca, P.T. (1990). Infants' localization of sounds within hemifields: Estimates of minimum audible angle. *Child Development, 61,* 1258–1270.

Mortimer, David. (1994). *Practical laboratory andrology.* New York: Oxford University Press.

Mortimer, Jeylan T., Finch, Michael D., Dennehy, Katherine, Lee, Chaimun, & Beebe, Timothy. (1994). Work experience in adolescence. *Journal of Vocational Education Research, 19,* 39–70.

Mortimer, Jeylan T., Finch, Michael D., Ryu, Seongryeol, Shanahan, Michael J., & Call, Kathleen T. (1996). The effects of work intensity on adolescent mental health, achievement, and behavioral adjustment: New evidence from a prospective study. *Child Development, 67,* 1243–1261.

Mortimore, Peter. (1995). The positive effects of schooling. In Michael Rutter (Ed.), *Psychosocial disturbances in young people: Challenges for prevention.* Cambridge, England: Cambridge University Press.

Moshman, D. (1990). The development of metalogical understanding. In W.F. Overton (Ed.), *Reasoning, necessity, and logic: Developmental perspectives.* Hillsdale, NJ: Erlbaum.

Moshman, D., & Franks, B.A. (1986). Development of the concept of inferential validity. *Child Development, 57,* 153–165.

Mott, Frank L., Kowaleski-Jones, Lori, & Menaghan, Elizabeth G. (1997). Paternal absence and child behavior: Does a child's gender make a difference? *Journal of Marriage and the Family, 59,* 103–118.

Mounts, Nina S., & Steinberg, Laurence. (1995). An ecological analysis of peer influence on adolescent grade point average and drug use. *Developmental Psychology, 31,* 915–922.

Muisener, Philip P. (1994). *Understanding and treating adolescent substance abuse.* Thousand Oaks, CA: Sage.

Muller, J., Nielson, C. Thoger, & Skakkebaek, N.E. (1989). Testicular maturation and pubertal growth in normal boys. In I.M. Tanner & M.A. Preece (Eds.), *The physiology of human growth.* Cambridge, England: Cambridge University Press.

Murphey, D.A. (1992). Constructing the child: Relations between parents' beliefs and child outcomes. *Developmental Review, 12,* 199–232.

Murphy, J.J., & Boggess, S. (1998). Increased condom use among teenage males, 1988–1995: The role of attitudes. *Family Planning Perspective, 30,* 276–280..

Myers, B.J. (1987). Mother-infant bonding as a critical period. In M.H. Bornstein (Ed.), *Sensitive periods in development: Interdisciplinary perspectives.* Hillsdale, NJ: Erlbaum.

Myers, N.A., Clifton, R.K., & Clarkson, M.H. (1987). When they were very young: Almost-threes remember two years ago. *Infant Behavior and Development, 10,* 123–132.

Nation, Kate, & Snowling, Margaret J. (1998). Individual differences in contextual facilitation: Evidence from dyslexia and poor reading comprehension. *Child Development, 69,* 996–1011.

National Academy of Sciences. (1994). *Assessing genetic risks: Implications for health and social policy.* Washington DC: National Academy Press.

National Center for Health Statistics. (1995). *Health, United States, 1994.* Hyattsville, MD: Public Health Service.

National Center for Injury Prevention and Control. (1992). *Position papers from the third National Injury Control Conference.* Atlanta, GA: Centers for Disease Control.

National Center for Injury Prevention and Control. (1993). *Injury control in the 1990s: A national plan for action.* Atlanta, GA: Centers for Disease Control and Prevention, U.S. Department of Health and Human Services.

National Child Abuse and Neglect Data System. (1997). *U.S. Department of Health and Human Services, Child Maltreatment 1995: Reports from the states to the National Child Abuse and Neglect Data System.* Washington, D.C.: U.S. Government Printing Office.

National Coalition on Television Violence. (1993). *In television cartoons designed primarily for young children, physical violence occurs an average of twenty-five times an hour.* 5132 Newport Avenue, Bethesda, MD 20816.

National Education Goals Panel. (1997). *The national education goals report summary, 1997: Mathematics and science achievement for the 21st century.* Washington, DC: National Education Goals Panel.

National Institute of Child Health and Development, Early Child Care Research Network. (1997). The effects of infant child care on infant-mother attachment security: Results of the NICHD study of early child care. *Child Development, 68,* 860–879.

Neilson Media Research. (1997). Neilson Media Research.

Neisser, Ulric, Boodoo, Gwyneth, Bouchard, Thomas J., Boykin, A. Wade, Brody, Nathan, Ceci, Stephen J., Halpern, Diane F., Loehlin, John C., Perloff, Robert, Sternberg, Robert J., & Urbina, Susana. (1996). Intelligence: Knowns and unknowns. *American Psychologist, 51,* 77–101.

Nelson, Charles A. (1997). The neurobiological basis of early memory development. In Nelson Cowan & Charles Hulme (Eds.), *The development of memory in childhood: Studies in developmental psychology.* Hove, East Sussex, UK: Psychology Press.

Nelson, Charles A., & Bloom, Floyd E. (1997). Child development and neuroscience. *Child Development, 69,* 970–987.

Nelson, Charles A., & Horowitz, Frances Degen. (1987). Visual motion perception in infancy: A review and synthesis. In Philip Salapatek & Leslie Cohen (Eds.), *Handbook of infant perception: Vol. 2. From perception to cognition.* New York: Academic Press.

Nelson, Katherine. (1981). Individual differences in language development: Implications for development and language. *Developmental Psychology, 17,* 171–187.

Nelson, Katherine. (Ed.). (1986). *Event knowledge: Structure and function in development.* Hillsdale, NJ: Erlbaum.

Nelson, Katherine. (1993). Events, narrative, and memory: What develops? In C.A. Nelson (Ed.), *Memory and affect in development: Minnesota symposium on child psychology.* Hillsdale, NJ: Erlbaum.

Nelson, Melvin D. (1992). Socioeconomic status and childhood mortality in North Carolina. *American Journal of Public Health, 82,* 1131–1133.

Neumann, C.G. (1983). Obesity in childhood. In M.D. Levine, W.B. Carey, A.C. Crocker, & R.T. Gross (Eds.), *Developmental-behavioral pediatrics.* Philadelphia: Saunders.

Neuspiel, Daniel R., Markowitz, Morri, & Drucker, Ernest. (1994). Intrauterine cocaine, lead and nicotine exposure and fetal growth. *American Journal of Public Health, 84,* 1492–1495.

Newcomb, A.F. & Bagwell, C.L. (1995). Children's friendship relations: A meta-analytic review. *Psychological Bulletin, 117,* 306–347.

The New York Times. (1997, August 18). Keeping track: Adoptions of foreign children.

Neysmith-Roy, J.M. (1994). Constructing toys to integrate knowledge about child development. *Teaching of Psychology, 21* (2), 101–103.

Nichols, Francine & Zwelling, Elaine. (1997) *Maternal newborn nursing.* Philadelphia: Saunders.

Nordentoft, Merete, Lou, Hans C., Hanson, Dorthe, Nim, J., Pryds, Ole, Rubin, Pia, & Hemmingsen, Ralf (1996). Intrauterine growth retardation and premature delivery: The influence of maternal smoking and psychosocial factors. *American Journal of Public Health, 86,* 347–354.

Nottelmann, Edith D., Inoff-Germain, Gale, Susman, Elizabeth J., & Chrousos, George P. (1990). Hormones and behavior at puberty. In John Bancroft & June Machover Reinisch (Eds.), *Adolescence in puberty.* New York: Oxford University Press.

Nowak, Rachel. (1995). New push to reduce maternal mortality in poor countries. *Science, 269,* 780–782.

Nowakowski, R.S. (1987). Basic concepts of CNS development. *Child Development, 58,* 598–595.

Nugent, J. Kevin. (1991). Cultural and psychological influences on the father's role in infant development. *Journal of Marriage and the Family, 53,* 475–485.

Nugent, J. Kevin, Lester, Barry M., Greene, Sheila M., Wieczorek-Deering, Dorith, & O'Mahony, Paul. (1996). The effects of maternal alcohol consumption and cigarette smoking during pregnancy on acoustic cry analysis. *Child Development, 67,* 1806–1815.

Nunez, Ralph. (1996). *The new poverty: Homeless families in America.* New York: Plenum Press.

Oakes, L.M., & Cohen, L.B. (1990). Infant perception of a causal event. *Cognitive Development, 5,* 193–207.

Offenbacher, S., Katz, V., Fertik, G., Connins, J., Boyd, D., Maynor, G., McKaig, R., & Beck, J. (1996). Periodontal infection as a possible risk factor for preterm low birth weight. *Journal of Periodontology, 67,* 1103–1113.

Ogilvy, C.M. (1994). Social skills training with children and adolescents: A review of the evidence of effectiveness. *Educational Psychology, 14,* 73–83.

Ogletree, Shirley M., Williams, Sue W., Raffeld, Paul, Mason, Bradley, & Fricke, Kris. (1990). Female attractiveness and eating disorders: Do children's television commercials play a role? *Sex Roles, 22,* 791–797.

Ogletree, Shirley Matile, Denton, Larry, & Williams, Sue Winkle. (1993). Age and gender differences in children's Halloween costumes. *Journal of Psychology, 127,* 633–637.

O'Hara, Michael W. (1997). The nature of postpartum depressive disorders. In Lynne Murray & Peter J. Cooper (Eds.), *Postpartum depression and child development.* New York: Guilford.

Oller, D. Kimbrough, & Eilers, Rebecca. (1988). The role of audition in infant babbling. *Child Development, 59,* 441–449.

Olsho, Lynn Werner, Koch, E.G., Carter, E.A., Halpin, C.F., & Spetner, N.B. (1988). Pure tone sensitivity in human infants. *Journal of the Acoustical Society of America, 84,* 1316–1324.

Olweus, Dan. (1992). Bullying among schoolchildren: Intervention and prevention. In Peters, R.D., McMahon, R.J. &Quincy, V.L. (Eds.). *Aggression and violence throughout the life span.* Newbury Park, CA: Sage.

Olweus, Dan. (1993). *Bullying at school: What we know and what we can do.* Oxford, England; Blackwell.

Olweus, Dan. (1993). Victimization by peers: Antecedents and long-term outcomes. In K.H. Rubin & J.B. Asendorf (Eds.),

Social withdrawal, inhibition, and shyness in childhood. Hillsdale, N.J.: Erlbaum.

Olweus, Dan. (1994). Bullying at school: Basic facts and effects of a school based intervention program. *Journal of Child Psychology and Psychiatry, 35,* 1171–1190.

O'Neill, Molly. (1998, March 14). Feeding the next generation: Food industry caters to teen-age eating habits. *The New York Times,* D1.

Oosterlaan, Jaap, Logan, Gordon D., & Sergeant, Joseph A. (1998). Response inhibition in AD/HD, CD, comorbid AD/HD + CD, anxious, and control children: A meta-analysis of studies with the stop task. *Journal of Child Psychology & Psychiatry & Allied Disciplines, 39,* 411–425.

Overton, William F. (1990). *Reasoning, necessity, and logic: Developmental perspectives.* Hillsdale, NJ: Erlbaum.

Owen, M.T., & Cox, M.J. (1997). Marital conflict and the development of infant-parent attachment relationships. *Journal of Family Psychology, 11,* 152–164.

Paley, V.G. (1984). *Boys and girls: Superheros in the doll corner.* Chicago: University of Chicago Press.

Palmer, Carolyn F. (1989). The discriminating nature of infants' exploratory actions. *Developmental Psychology, 25,* 885–893.

Panel on Research on Child Abuse and Neglect, National Research Council. (1993). *Understanding child abuse and neglect.* Washington, DC: National Academy Press.

Parcel, Toby L., & Menaghan, Elizabeth G. (1997). Effects of low-wage employment on family well-being. *The Future of Children (Special Issue on Welfare to Work), 7,* 116–121.

Park, K.A., Lay, K. L., & Ramsay, L. (1993). Individual differences and developmental changes in preschoolers' friendships. *Developmental Psychology, 29,* 264–270.

Parke, Ross D. (1995). Fathers and families. In Marc H. Bornstein (Ed.) *Handbook of parenting: Status and social conditions of parenting.* New Jersey: Erlbaum.

Parke, Ross D., Ornstein, Peter A., Rieser, John J., & Zahn-Waxler, Carolyn. (1994). The past as prologue: An overview of a century of developmental psychology. In Ross D. Parke, Peter A. Ornstein, John J. Rieser, & Carolyn Zahn-Waxler (Eds.), *A century of developmental psychology.* Washington, DC: American Psychological Association.

Parker, Jeffrey G., & Asher, Steven R. (1993). Friendship and friendship quality in middle childhood: Links with peer group acceptance and feelings of loneliness and social dissatisfaction. *Developmental Psychology, 29,* 611–621.

Parker, Jeffrey G., & Gottman, J.M. (1989). Social and emotional development in a relational context. In T.J. Berndt & G.W. Ladd (Eds.), *Peer relationships in child development.* New York: Wiley.

Parkhurst, J.T., & Asher, S.R. (1992). Peer rejection in middle school: Subgroup differences in behavior, loneliness, and interpersonal concerns. *Developmental Psychology, 28,* 231–241.

Parkin, Alan J. (1993). *Memory: Phenomena, experiment and theory.* Oxford: Blackwell.

Parritz, Robin Hornik. (1996). A descriptive analysis of toddlers coping in challenging circumstances. *Infant Behavior & Development, 19,* 171–180.

Parten, Mildred B. (1932). Social participation among preschool children. *Journal of Abnormal and Social Psychology, 27,* 243–269.

Patterson, Charlotte J. (1995). Lesbian mothers, gay fathers, and their fathers. In Anthony R. D'Augelli and Charlotte J. Patterson (Eds.), *Lesbian, gay, and bisexual identities over the lifespan: Psychological perspectives.* New York: Oxford University Press.

Patterson, C.J., Kupersmidt, J.B., & Griesler, P.C. (1990). Children's perceptions of self and of relationships with others as a function of sociometric status. *Child Development, 61,* 1335–1349.

Patterson, Gerald R. (1982). *Coercive family processes.* Eugene, OR: Castalia Press.

Patterson, Gerald R. (1998). Continuities—A search for causal mechanisms: Comment on the special section. *Developmental Psychology, 34,* 1263–1268.

Patterson, Gerald R., & Capaldi, D. (1991). Antisocial parents: Unskilled and vulnerable. In Paul E. Cowan & Mavis Hetherington (Eds.), *Family transitions.* Hillsdale, NJ: Erlbaum.

Patterson, Gerald R., DeBaryshe, Barbara D., & Ramsey, Elizabeth. (1989). A developmental perspective on antisocial behavior. *American Psychologist, 44,* 329–335.

Patterson, Gerald R., Reid, J.B., & Dishion, T.J. (1992). *Antisocial boys.* Eugene, OR: Castalia Press.

Peak, L. (1991). *Learning to go to school in Japan: The transition from home to preschool life.* Berkeley: University of California Press.

Pecheux, Marie Germaine, & Labrell, Florence. (1994). Parent-infant interactions and early cognitive development. In Andre Vyt, Henriette Bloch, & Marc H. Bornstein (Eds.), *Early child development in the French tradition:* Contributions from current research. Hillsdale, NJ: Erlbaum.

Pelham, William E. Jr., Wheeler, Trilby, & Chronis, Andrea. (1998). Empirically supported psychosocial treatments for attention deficit hyperactivity disorder. *Journal of Clinical Child Psychology, 27,* 190–205.

Pellegrini, A.D. & Smith, Peter K. (1998). Physical activity play: The nature and function of a neglected aspect of play. *Child Development, 69,* 577–598.

Pelton, Leroy H. (1994). The role of material factors in child abuse and neglect. In G.B. Melton & F. Barry (Eds.), *Safe neighborhoods: Foundations for a new national strategy on child abuse and neglect.* New York: Guilford.

Pelton, Leroy H. (1998). Commentary. *The Future of Children: Protecting Children from Abuse and Neglect, 8,* 126–132.

Pennisi, Elizabeth, & Roush, Wade. (1997). Developing a new view of evolution. *Science, 277,* 34–37.

Perkins, D., Goodrich, H., Tishman, S., & Mirman, Owen J. (1994). *Thinking connections: Learning to think and thinking to learn.* Menlo Park, CA: Addison-Wesley.

Perris, Eve Emmanuel, Myers, Nancy Angrist, & Clifton, Rachel Kern. (1990). Long-term memory for a single infancy experience. *Child Development, 61,* 1796–1807.

Perry, David G., Kusel, Sara J., & Perry, Louise C. (1988). Victims of peer aggression. *Developmental Psychology, 24,* 807–814.

Perry, D.G., Perry, L.C., & Kennedy, E. (1993). Conflict and the development of antisocial behavior. In C. Shantz and W.W. Hartup (Eds.), *Conflict in child and adolescent development.* Cambridge: Cambridge.

Peterson, Lizette, Ewigman, Bernard, & Kivlahan, Coleen. (1993). Judgments regarding appropriate child supervision to prevent injury: The role of environmental risk and child age. *Child Development, 64,* 934–950.

Petitto, Anne, & Marentette, Paula F. (1991). Babbling in the manual mode: Evidence for the ontogeny of language. *Science, 251,* 1493–1496.

Phinney, J. (1990). Ethnic identity in adolescents and adults: A review of the literature. *Psychological Bulletin, 108,* 499–514.

Phinney, J., & Devich-Navarro, M. (1997). Variations in bicultural identification among African American and Mexican American adolescents. *Journal of Research on Adolescence, 7,* 3–32.

Piaget, Jean. (1952). *The child's conception of number.* London: Routledge and Kegan Paul.

Piaget, Jean. (1952). *The origins of intelligence in children.* Margaret Cook (Trans.). New York: International Universities Press.

Piaget, Jean. (1970). *The child's conception of movement and speed.* G.E.T. Holloway & M.J. Mackenzie (Trans.). New York: Basic Books.

Piaget, Jean. (1970). *The child's conception of time.* A.J. Pomerans (Trans.). New York: Basic Books.

Pierce, Karen A. & Cohen, Robert. (1995). Aggressors and their victims: Toward a contextual framework for understanding children's aggressor-victim relationships. *Developmental Review, 15,* 292–310.

Pipp, S., Fischer, K.W., & Jennings, S. (1987). Acquisition of self- and mother knowledge in infancy. *Developmental Psychology, 23,* 86–96.

Pleck, Elizabeth H., & Pleck, Joseph H. (1997). Fatherhood ideals in the United States: Historical dimensions. In M.E. Lamb (Ed.) *The role of the father in child development.* New York: Wiley.

Pleck, Joseph H. (1997). Paternal involvement: Levels, sources, and consequence. In M.E. Lamb (Ed.), *The role of the father in child development.* New York: Wiley.

Plomin, Robert. (1995). Molecular genetics and psychology. *Current Directions in Psychological Science, 4,* 114–117.

Plomin, Robert, & Rutter, Michael. (1998). Child development, molecular genetics, and what to do with genes once they are found. *Child Development, 69,* 1223–1242.

Plomin, Robert, Emde, R.N., Braungart, J.M., Campos, J., Corley, R., Fulker, D.W., Kagan, J., Reznick, J.S., Robinson, J.,

Zahn-Waxler, C., & DeFries, J.C. (1993). Genetic change and continuity from fourteen to twenty months: The MacArthur Longitudinal Twin Study. *Child Development, 64,* 1354–1376.

Plomin, Robert, DeFries, J.C., McClearn, G.E., & Rutter, M. (1997). *Behavioral genetics.* New York: Freeman.

Pollack, William S., & Grossman, Frances K. (1985). Parent-child interaction. In L. L'Abate (Ed.), *The handbook of family psychology and therapy* (Vol. I). Homewood, IL: Dorsey Press.

Pollitt, Ernesto, Gorman, Kathleen S., Engle, P., Martorell, R., & Rivera, J. (1993). Early supplementary feeding and cognition: Effects over two decades. *Monographs of the Society for Research in Child Development, 58.*

Pollitt, Ernesto, Golub, Mari, Gorman, Kathleen, Grantham-McGregor, Sally, Levitsky, David, Schurch, Beat, Strupp, Barbara, & Wachs, Theodore. (1996). A reconceptualization of the effects of undernutrition on children's biological, psychosocial, and behavioral development. *Social policy report: Society for Research in Child Development, 10,* 1–21.

Pomerantz, Eva M., Ruble, Diane N., Frey, Karin S., & Greulich, Faith. (1995). Meeting goals and confronting conflicts: Children's changing perceptions of social comparison. *Child Development, 66,* 723–738.

Pong, Suet-Long. (1997). Family structure, school context, and eighth grade math and reading achievement. *Journal of Marriage and the Family, 59,* 734–746.

Ponsoby, Anne-Louise, Dwyer, Terence, Gibbins, Laura E., Cochrane, Jennifer A., & Wang, Yon-Gan. (1993). Factors potentiating the risk of sudden infant death syndrome associated with the prone position. *New England Journal of Medicine, 329,* 377–382.

Pool, Robert. (1993). Evidence for the homosexuality gene. *Science, 261,* 291–292.

Porter, R.H., Makin, J.W., Davis, L.B., & Christensen, K.M. (1992). Breast-fed infants respond to olfactory cues from their own mother and unfamiliar lactating females. *Infant Behavior and Development, 15,* 85–93.

Porter, Richard, Varendi, H., Christensson, K., Porter, R.H. and Winberg, J. (1998). Soothing effect of amniotic fluid smell in newborn infants. *Early Human Development, 51,* 47–55.

Poussaint, Alvin F. (1990). Introduction. In Bill Cosby, *Fatherhood.* New York: Berkley Books.

Proos, L.A., Hofvander, Y., & Tuvemo, T. (1991). Menarcheal age and growth pattern of Indian girls adopted in Sweden. *Acta Paediatrica Scandinavica, 80,* 852–858.

Quinn, Paul C., Cummins, Maggie, Kase, Jennifer, Martin, Erin, & Weissman, Sheri. (1996). Development of categorical representations for above and below spatial relations in 3- to 7-month-old infants. *Developmental Psychology, 32,* 942–950.

Ramey, C.T., Bryant, D.B., Wasik, B.H., Sparling, J.J., Fendt, K.H., & Levange, L.M. (1992). The Infant Health and Development Program for low birth weight, premature infants: Program elements, family participation, and child intelligence. *Pediatrics, 89,* 454–465.

Rasmussen, Dianne E., & Sobsey, Dick. (1994). Age, adaptive behavior, and Alzheimer disease in Down syndrome: Cross-sectional and longitudinal analyses. *American Journal on Mental Retardation, 99,* 151–165.

Ratner, H.H., Smith, B.S., & Padgett, R.J. (1990). Children's organization of events and event memories. In R. Fivush & J.A. Hudson (Eds.), *Knowing and remembering in young children.* Cambridge, England: Cambridge University Press.

Rauste-von Wright, Maijaliisa. (1989). Body image satisfaction in adolescent girls and boys: A longitudinal study. *Journal of Youth and Adolescence, 18,* 71–83.

Ravesloot, Janita. (1995). Courtship and sexuality in the youth phase. In Manuel du Bois-Reymond, Rene Diekstra, Klaus Hurrelmann, & Els Peters (Eds.), *Childhood and youth in Germany and the Netherlands: Transitions and coping strategies of adolescents.* Berlin: Mouton de Gruyter.

Rawlins, William K. (1992). *Friendship matters.* Hawthorne, NY: Aldine de Gruyter.

Reed, Edward S. (1993). The intention to use a specific affordance: A conceptual framework for psychology. In Robert H. Wozniak & Kurt W. Fischer (Eds.), *Development in context: Acting and thinking in specific environments.* Hillsdale, NJ: Erlbaum.

Reich, Peter A. (1986). *Language development.* Englewood Cliffs, NJ: Prentice-Hall.

Reiss, David. (1997). Mechanisms linking genetic and social influences in adolescent development: Beginning a collaborative search. *Current Directions in Psychological Science, 6,* 100–105.

Reiss, David, Neiderhiser, Jenae, Hetherington, E. Mavis, & Plomin, Robert. (1999). *The relationship code: Deciphering genetic and social patterns in adolescent development.* Cambridge, MA: Harvard University Press.

Renninger, K. Ann, & Amsel, Eric. (1997). Change and development: An introduction. In Eric Amsel & K. Ann Renninger (Eds.), *Change and development: Issues of theory, method, & application.* Mahwah, NJ: Erlbaum.

Rest, James R. (1983). Morality. In Paul H. Mussen (Ed.), *Handbook of child psychology: Vol. 3. Cognitive development.* New York: Wiley.

Reuss, M. Lynne, & Gordon, Howard R. (1995). Obstetrical judgments of viability and perinatal survival of extremely low birthweight infants. *American Journal of Public Health, 85,* 362–366.

Reynolds, Arthur J. (1998). Resilience among black urban youth: Prevalence, intervention effects, and mechanisms of influence. *American Journal of Orthopsychiatry, 68,* 84–100.

Reynolds, D., & Cuttance, P. (Eds.). (1992). *School effectiveness: Research, policy, and practice.* London: Cassell.

Ricciuti, Henry N. (1991). Malnutrition and cognitive development: Research policy linkages and current research directions. In Lynn Okagaki & Robert J. Sternberg (Eds.), *Directors of development.* Hillsdale, NJ: Erlbaum.

Ricciuti, H.N. (1993). Nutrition and mental development. *Current Directions in Psychological Science, 2,* 43–46.

Richards, M.P.M. (1996). The childhood environment and the development of sexuality. In C.J.K. Henry & S.J. Ulijaszek (Eds.), *Long-term consequences of early environment: Growth, development and the lifespan developmental perspective.* Cambridge: Cambridge University Press.

Richards, M.P.M., & Elliott, B.J. (1993). Unpublished observations.

Richards, Maryse, Crowe, Paul A., Larson, Reed, & Swarr, Amy. (1998). Developmental patterns and gender differences in the experience of peer companionship during adolescence. *Child Development, 69,* 154–163.

Richardson, Gale A., & Day, Nancy L. (1994). Detrimental effects of prenatal cocaine exposure: Illusion or reality? *Journal of the American Academy of Child and Adolescent Psychiatry, 33,* 28–34.

Richman, Amy L., Miller, Patrice M., & LeVine, Robert A. (1992). Cultural and educational variations in maternal responsiveness. *Developmental Psychology, 28,* 614–621.

Richters, J.E. & Martinez, P. (1993). Violent communities, family choices, and children's chances: An algorithm for improving the odds. *Development and Psychopathology, 5,* 609–627/

Rieck, Miriam, Arad, Ilan, & Netzer, Dvorah. (1996). Developmental evaluation of very-low-birthweight infants: Longitudinal and cross-sectional studies. *Journal of Behavioral Development, 19,* 549–562.

Rivara, Fred P. (1994). Unintentional injuries. In Ivan Barry Pless (Ed.), *The epidemiology of childhood disorders.* New York: Oxford University Press.

Robert, Elizabeth. (1996). Treating depression in pregnancy, editorial. *New England Journal of Medicine, 335,* 1056–1058.

Roberts, J.E., Sanyal, M.A., Burchinal, M.R., Collier, A.M., Ramey, C.T., & Henderson, F.W. (1986). Otitis media in early childhood and its relationship to later verbal and academic performance. *Pediatrics, 78,* 432–440.

Roberts, K. (1988). Retrieval of a basic-level category in prelinguistic infants. *Developmental Psychology, 24,* 21–27.

Robin, Daniel J., Berthier, Neil E., & Clifton, Rachel K. (1996). Infants' predictive reaching for moving objects in the dark. *Developmental Psychology, 32,* 824–835.

Robins, Lee N., & Mills, James L. (1993). Effects of in utero exposure to street drugs. *American Journal of Public Health, 83* (Suppl.), 1–32.

Rochat, Philipe. (1989). Object manipulation and exploration in 2- to 5-month-old infants. *Developmental Psychology, 25,* 871–884.

Rochat, Philippe, & Bullinger, Andre. (1994). Posture and functional action in infancy. In Andre Vyt, Henriette Bloch, & Marc H. Bornstein (Eds.), *Early child development in the French tradition: Contributions from current research.* Hillsdale, NJ: Erlbaum.

Rochat, Philippe, & Goubet, Nathalie. (1995). Development of sitting and reaching in 5- to 6-month-old infants. *Infant Behavior and Development, 18,* 53–68.

Rodriguez, Richard. (1983). *Hunger of memory.* New York: Bantam.

Roeser, Robert W., Midgley, Carol, & Urdan, Timothy C. (1996). Perceptions of the school psychological and behavioral functioning in school: The mediating role of goals and belonging. *Journal of Educational Psychology, 88*, 408–422.

Rogers, Kathleen Boyce. (1999). Parenting processes related to sexual risk-taking behaviors of adolescent males and females. *Journal of Marriage and the Family, 61*, 99–109.

Roggman, Lori A., Langlois, Judith H., Hubbs-Tait, Laura, & Rieser-Danner, Loretta A. (1994). Infant day-care, attachment, and the "filedrawer problem". *Child Development, 65*, 1429–1443.

Rogoff, Barbara. (1990). *Apprenticeship in thinking: Cognitive development in social context.* New York: Oxford University Press.

Rogoff, Barbara. (1997). Evaluating development in the process of participation: Theory, methods, and practice building on each other. In Eric Amsel & K. Ann Renninger (Eds.), *Change and development: Issues of theory, method, & application.* Mahwah, NJ: Erlbaum.

Rogoff, Barbara, & Mistry, Jayanthi. (1990). The social and functional context of children's remembering. In Robyn Fivush & Judith A. Hudson (Eds.), *Knowing and remembering in young children.* Cambridge, England: Cambridge University Press.

Rogoff, Barbara, Mistry, Jayanthi, Goncu, Artin, & Mosier, Christine. (1993). Guided participation in cultural activity by toddlers and caregivers. *Monographs of the Society for Research in Child Development, 58* (Serial No. 236).

Rohlen, Thomas P., & LeTendre, Gerald K. (1996). *Teaching and learning in Japan.* Cambridge, England: Cambridge University Press.

Romaine, Suzanne. (1984). *The language of children and adolescents: The acquisition of communication competence.* Oxford, England: Blackwell.

Romaine, Suzanne. (1995). *Bilingualism,* second edition. New York and Oxford: Basil Blackwell.

Romo, Harriett D., & Falbo, Toni. (1996). *Latino high school graduation: Defying the odds.* Austin: University of Texas Press.

Ronca, April E. & Alberts, Jeffrey R. (1995). Maternal contributions to fetal experience and the transition from prenatal to postnatal life. In Jean-Pierre Lecanuet, William P. Fifer, Norman A. Krasnegor, & William P. Smotherman (Eds.), *Fetal development: A psychobiological perspective.* New Jersey: Erlbaum.

Rose, Susan A., Feldman, Judith F., Futterweit, Lorelle R., & Jankowski, Jeffery J. (1998). Continuity in tactual–visual cross-modal transfer: Infancy to 11 years. *Developmental Psychology, 34*, 435–440.

Rose, Susan A., & Ruff, Holly A. (1987). Cross-modal abilities in infants. In J. Doniger Osofsky (Ed.), *Handbook of infant development* (2nd ed.). New York: Wiley.

Rosenblith, Judy F. (1992). *In the beginning: Development from conception to age two* (2nd ed.). California: Sage Newbury Park.

Rosenstein, Diana, & Oster, Harriet. (1988). Differential facial responses to four basic tastes. *Child Development, 59*, 1555–1568.

Rosenthal, M. Sara. (1996). *The fertility sourcebook.* Anodyne: Lowell House.

Rosenthal, Robert. (1996). *Pygmalion in the classroom.* New York: Irvington.

Ross, Gail, Lipper, Evelyn, & Auld, Peter A.M. (1996). Cognitive abilities and early precursors of learning disabilities in very-low-birthweight children with normal intelligence and normal neurological status. *International Journal of Behavioral Development, 19*, 563–580.

Ross, J.G., Pate, R.R., Casperson, C.J., Domberg, C.L., & Svilar, M. (1987). Home and community in children's exercise habits. *Journal of Physical Education, Recreation and Dance, 58*, 85–92.

Rosser, Pearl L., & Randolph, Suzanne M. (1989). Black American infants: The Howard University normative study. In J. Kevin Nuegent, Barry M. Lester, & T. Berry Brazelton (Eds.), *The cultural context of infancy: Vol I. Biology, culture, and infant development.* Norwood, NJ: Ablex.

Rotenberg, Ken J., & Sliz, Dave. (1988). Children's restrictive disclosure to friends. *Merrill-Palmer Quarterly, 34*, 203–215.

Rothbart, M.K. & Bates, J.E. (1998). Temperament. In W. Damon (Series Ed.), N. Eisenberg (Volume Ed.), *Handbook of child psychology: Vol. 3. Social, emotional, and personality development* (5th ed.). New York: Wiley.

Rothbart, M.K., Derryberry, D., & Posner, M.I. (1994). A psychobiological approach to the development of temperament. In J.E. Bates & T.D. Wachs (Eds.), *Temperament: Individual differences at the interface of biology and behavior.* Washington, DC: American Psychological Association.

Rotheram-Borus, Mary Jane, & Wyche, Karen Fraser. (1994). Ethnic differences in identity development in the United States. In Sally L. Archer (Ed.), *Interventions for adolescent identity development.* Thousand Oaks, CA: Sage.

Rourke, B.P. (1989). *Non-verbal learning disabilities: The syndrome and the model.* New York: Guilford.

Rovee-Collier, Carolyn K. (1987). Learning and memory in infancy. In J. Doniger Osofsky (Ed.), *Handbook of infant development* (2nd ed.). New York: Wiley.

Rovee-Collier, Carolyn K. (1990). The "memory system" of prelinguistic infants. In A. Diamond (Ed.), *The development and neural bases of higher cognitive functions.* New York: New York Academy of Sciences.

Rovee-Collier, Carolyn K. (1995). Time windows in cognitive development. *Developmental Psychology, 31*, 147–169.

Rovee-Collier, Carolyn K., & Gerhardstein, Peter. (1997). The development of infant memory. In Nelson Cowan & Charles Hulme (Eds.), *The development of memory in childhood: Studies in developmental psychology.* Hove, East Sussex, UK: Psychology Press.

Rovee-Collier, Carolyn K., & Hayne, H. (1987). Reactivation of infant memory: Implications for cognitive development. In H.W. Reese (Ed.), *Advances in child development and behavior* (Vol. 20). New York: Academic Press.

Rovet, Joanne, Netley, Charles, Keenan, Maureen, Bailey, Jon, & Steward, Donald. (1996). The psychoeducational profile of boys with Klinefelter syndrome. *Journal of Learning Disabilities, 29,* 180–196.

Rowe, David C. (1994). *The limits of family influence: Genes, experience, and behavior.* New York: Guilford Press.

Ruffman, Ted, Perner, Josef, Olson, David R., & Doherty, Martin. (1993). Reflecting on scientific thinking: Children's understanding of the hypothesis-evidence relation. *Child Development, 64,* 1617–1636.

Rutter, Michael. (1979). Protective factors in children's responses to stress and disadvantage. In Martha Whalen Kent & Jon E. Rolf (Eds.), *Primary prevention of psychopathology: Vol. 3. Social competence in children.* Hanover, NH: University Press of New England.

Rutter, Michael. (1980). *Changing youth in a changing society: Patterns of development and disorder.* Cambridge, MA: Harvard University Press.

Rutter, Michael. (1987). Psychosocial resilience and protective mechanisms. *American Journal of Orthopsychiatry, 57,* 316–331.

Rutter, Michael, Maughan, Barbara, Mortimore, Peter, & Ouston, Janet. (1979). *Fifteen thousand hours: Secondary schools and their effects on children.* Cambridge, MA: Harvard University Press.

Rutter, Michael, Bailey, A., Simonoff, Emily, & Pickles, Andrew. (1997). Genetic influences and autism. In Donald Cohen & Fred R. Volkmar (Eds.), *Handbook of autism and pervasive developmental disorders.* New York: Wiley.

Rutter, Michael, Dunn, Judy, Plomin, Robert, Simonoff, Emily, Pickles, Andrew, Maughan, Barbara, Ormel, Johan, Meyer, Joanne, & Eaves, Lindon. (1997). Integrating nature and nurture: Implications of person-environment correlations and interactions for developmental psychopathology. *Development and Psychopathology, 9,* 335–364.

Ryan, R.M., & Lynch, J.H. (1989). Emotional autonomy versus detachment: Revisiting the vicissitudes of adolescence and young adulthood. *Child Development, 60,* 340–356.

Rys, Gail S., & Bear, George G. (1997). Relational aggression and peer relations: Gender and developmental issues. *Merrill-Palmer Quarterly, 43,* 87–106.

Sabatier, Colette. (1994). Parental conceptions of early development and developmental stimulation. In Andre Vyt, Henriette Bloch, & Marc H. Bornstein (Eds.), *Early child development in the French tradition: Contributions from current research.* Hillsdale, NJ: Erlbaum.

Sagi, Abraham, van Ijzendoorn, Marinus H., & Koren-Karie, Nina. (1991). Primary appraisal of the Strange Situation: A cross-cultural analysis of preseparation episodes. *Developmental Psychology, 27,* 587–596.

Salmi, L.R., Weiss, H.B., Peterson, P.L., Spengler, R.F., Sattin, R.W., & Anderson, H.A. (1989). Fatal farm injuries among young children. *Pediatrics, 83,* 267–271.

Sameroff, Arnold J., & Haith, Marshall M. (1996). *The five to seven year shift: The age of reason and responsibility.* Chicago: University of Chicago Press.

Sampson, P.D., Streissguth, A.P., Bookstein, F.L., Little, R.E., Clarren, S.K., Dehaene, P., Hanson, J.W., & Graham, J.M., Jr. (1997). Incidence of fetal alcohol syndrome and prevalence of alcohol-related neurodevelopmental disorder. *Teratology, 56,* 317–326.

Sampson, Robert J. (1997). Collective regulation of adolescent misbehavior. *Journal of Adolescence Research, 12,* 227–244.

Sampson, Robert J., & Laub, John. (1993). *Crime in the making: Pathways and turning points through life.* Cambridge, MA: Harvard University Press.

Sampson, Robert J., & Laub, John. (1996) Socioeconomic achievement in the life course of disadvantaged men: Military service as a turning point, circa 1945–1965. *American Sociological Review, 61,* 347–367.

Sampson, Robert J., Raudenbush, Stephen W., & Earls, Felton. (1997). Neighborhoods and violent crime: A multilevel study of collective efficacy. *Science, 277,* 918–924.

Sandelowski, Margarete. (1993). *With child in mind: Studies of the personal encounter with infertility.* Philadelphia: University of Pennsylvania Press.

Sansavini, Alessandra, Bertoncini, Josiane, & Giovanelli, Fiuliana. (1997). Newborns discriminate the rhythm of multi-syllabic stressed words. *Developmental Psychology, 33,* 3–11.

Sansavini, Alessandra, Rizzardi, Mario, Alessandroni, Rosina, & Giovanelli, Giuliana. (1996). The development of Italian low- and very-low- birthweight infants from birth to 5 years: The role of biological and social risks. *International Journal of Behavioral Development, 19,* 533–547.

Sanson, Ann, & Rothbart, Mary K. (1995). Child temperament and parenting. In Marc H. Bornstein (Ed.), *Handbook of parenting: Applied and practical parenting.* Mahwah, NJ: Erlbaum.

Santelli, J.S., Brener, N.D., Lowry, R., Bhatt, A., & Zubin, L.S. (1998). Multiple sexual partners among U.S. adolescents and young adults. *Family Planning Perspectives, 30,* 271–275.

Sapolsky, Robert M. (1997). The importance of a well-groomed child. *Science, 277,* 1620–1621.

Sargent, James D., Stukel, Therese A., Dalton, Madeline A., Freeman, Jean L., & Brown, Mary Jean. (1996). Iron deficiency in Massachusetts communities: Socioeconomic and demographic risk factors among children. *American Journal of Public Health, 86,* 544–550.

Savin-Williams, Ritch C. (1995). An exploratory study of pubertal maturation timing and self-esteem among gay and bisexual male youths. *Developmental Psychology, 31,* 56–64.

Savin-Williams, Ritch C., & Diamond, Lisa M. (1997). Sexual orientation as a developmental context for lesbians, gays, and bisexuals: Biological perspectives. In Nancy L. Segal, Glenn E. Weisfeld, & Carol C. Weisfeld (Eds.), *Uniting psychology and biology: Integrative perspectives on human development.* Washington, DC: American Psychological Association.

Savitz, David A., Whelan, Elizabeth A., & Kleckner, Robert C. (1989). Self-reported exposure to pesticides and radiation related to pregnancy outcome: Results from National Natality and Fetal Mortality Surveys. *Public Health Reports, 104,* 473–477.

Saxe, Geoffrey, Guberman, Steven R., & Gearhart, Maryl. (1987). Social processes in early number development. *Monographs of the Society for Research in Child Development, 52* (Serial No. 216).

Scafidi, Frank A., Field, Tiffany, & Schanberg, Saul M. (1993). Factors that predict which preterm infants benefit most from massage therapy. *Journal of Developmental and Behavioral Pediatrics, 14,* 176–180.

Scarr, Sandra. (1992). Developmental theories for the 1990s: Development and individual differences. *Child Development, 63,* 1–19.

Scarr, Sandra. (1996). Families and day care: Both matter for children. *Contemporary Psychology, 41,* 330–331.

Scarr, Sandra. (1998). American child care today. *American Psychologist, 53,* 95–108.

Schaal, B. (1986). Presumed olfactory exchanges between mother and neonate in humans. In J. Le Camus & J. Cosnier (Eds.), *Ethology and psychology.* Toulouse, France: Private, I.E.C.

Schaie, K. Warner. (1996). *Intellectual development in adulthood: The Seattle Longitudinal Study.* Cambridge, England: Cambridge University Press.

Schene, P.A. (1998). Past, present, and future roles of child protective services. *Future Child, 8,* 23–38.

Scher, Anat & Mayseless, Ofra. (1997). Changes in negative emotionality in infancy: The role of mother's attachment concerns. *British Journal of Developmental Psychology, 15,* 311–321.

Schilit, Rebecca, & Gomberg, Edith S. Lisansky. (1991). *Drugs and behavior: A sourcebook for the helping professions.* Newbury Park, CA: Sage.

Schlegal, Alice, & Barry, Herbert. (1991). *Adolescence: An anthropological inquiry.* New York: Free Press.

Schmidtke, A., & Häfner, H. (1988). The Werther effect after television films: New evidence for an old hypothesis. *Psychological Medicine, 18,* 665–676.

Schneider, Jane W., & Hans, Sydney L. (1996). Effects of prenatal exposure to epodes on focused attention in toddlers during free play. *Journal of Developmental & Behavioral Pediatrics, 17,* 240–247.

Schneider, Wolfgang, Bjorklund, David F., & Maier-Bruckner, Wolfgang. (1996). The effects of expertise and IQ on children's memory: When knowledge is, and when it is not enough. *International Journal of Behavioral Development, 19,* 773–796.

Schneider, Wolfgang, & Pressly, Michael. (1997). *Memory development: Between two and twenty.* Mahwah, NJ: Erlbaum.

Schneider-Rosen, Karen, & Cicchetti, Dante. (1991). Early self-knowledge and emotional development: Visual self-recognition and affect reactions to mirror self-images in mal-treated and non-maltreated toddlers. *Developmental Psychology, 27,* 471–478.

Scholl, Theresa O., Hediger, Mary L., Schall, Joan I., Khoo, Chor-San, & Fischer, Richard L. (1996). Dietary and serum folate: Their influence on the outcome of pregnancy. *American Journal of Clinical Nutrition, 63,* 520–525.

Schore, Allan N. (1994). *Affect regulation and the origin of the self: The neurobiology of emotional development.* Hillsdale, NJ: Erlbaum.

Schore, Allan N. (1996). The experience-dependent maturation of a regulatory system in the orbial prefrontal cortex and the origin of developmental psychopathology. *Development and Psychopathology, 8,* 59–88.

Schwartz, David, Dodge, Kenneth A., Pettit, Gregory S., & Bates, John E. (1997). The early socialization of aggressive victims of bullying. *Child Development, 68,* 665–675.

Schwartz, Peter John, Stramba-Badiale, Marco, Segantini, Alessandro, et al. (1998). Prolongation of the QT interval and the sudden infant death syndrome. *New England Journal of Medicine, 338,* 1709–1714.

Schweder, R.A. (1990). In defense of moral realism: Reply to Gabennesch. *Child Development, 61,* 2060–2067.

Schweder, R.A., Mahapatra, M., & Miller, J.G. (1990). Culture and moral development. In J.W. Stigler, R.A. Schweder, & G. Herdt (Eds.), *Cultural psychology: Essays on comparative human development.* Cambridge, England: Cambridge University Press.

Schweinhart, Laurence J., & Weikart, David (Eds.). (1993). *Significant benefits: High/Scope Perry preschool study through age 27.* Ypsilanti, MI: High/Scope Press.

Scott, Fiona J., & Baron-Cohen, Simon. (1996) Logical, analogical, and psychological reasoning in autism: A test of the Cosmides theory. *Development and Psychopathology, 8,* 235–245.

Sedlak, A.J. & Broadhurst, D.D. (1996). *Third national study of child abuse and neglect: Final report.* Washington DC: US Department of Health and Human Services.

Seibel, Machelle M. (1993). Medical evaluation and treatment of the infertile couple. In Machelle M. Seibel, Ann A. Kiessling, Judith Bernstein, & Susan R. Levin (Eds.), *Technology and infertility: Clinical, psychosocial, legal and ethical aspects.* New York: Springer-Verlag.

Seibel, Machelle M. (moderator). (1993). Panel discussion: Ethical issues in fertility. In Machelle M. Seibel, Ann A. Kiessling, Judith Bernstein, and Susan R. Levin (Eds.), *Technology and infertility: Clinical, psychosocial, legal and ethical aspects.* New York: Springer-Verlag.

Seltser, Barry Jay, & Miller, Donald E. (1993). *Homeless families: The struggle for dignity.* Urbana, Illinois: University of Illinois Press.

Seltzer, Judith A. (1991). Legal custody arrangements and children's economic welfare. *American Journal of Sociology, 96,* 895–929.

Seltzer, Judith A. (1991). Relationships between fathers and children who live apart: The father's role after separation. *Journal of Marriage and the Family, 53,* 79–102.

Sena, Rhonda, & Smith, Linda B. (1990). New evidence on the development of the word Big. *Child Development, 61,* 1034–1052.

Serbin, Lisa A. (1997). Research on international adoption: Implications for developmental theory and social policy. *International Journal of Behavioral Development, 20,* 83–92.

Serra-Prat, Mateu, Gallo, Pedro, Jovell, Albert J., Aymerich, Marta, & Estrada, M. Dolors. (1998). Public health policy forum: Trade-offs in prenatal detection of Down syndrome. *American Journal of Public Health, 88,* 551–557.

Shanahan, M.J., Elder, G.H., Jr., Burchinal, M., & Conger, R.D. (1996). Adolescent paid labor and relationships with parents: Early work-family linkages. *Child Development, 67,* 2183–2200.

Shannon, R.J. (1988). *Criminal career continuity: Its social context.* New York: Human Sciences Press.

Shatz, Marilyn. (1994). *A toddler's life.* New York: Oxford University Press.

Shaw, Daniel S., Vondra, Joan I., Hommerding, Katherine Dowdell, Keenan, Kate & Dunn, Marija. (1994). Chronic family adversity and early child behavior problems. A longitudinal study of low income families. *Journal of Child Psychology and Psychiatry, 35,* 1109–1122.

Shaw, Gary M., Velie, Ellen M. & Wasserman, Cathy R. (1997). Risk for neural tube defect—affected pregnancies among women of Mexican descent and white women in California. *American Journal of Public Health, 87,* 1467–1471.

Shaywitz, Sally E., Excobar, M.D., Shaywitz, Bennett A., Fletcher, J.M., & Makuch, R. (1992). Evidence that dyslexia may represent the lower tail of a normal distribution of reading disability. *New England Journal of Medicine, 326,* 145–151.

Shedler, Jonathan, & Block, Jack. (1990). Adolescent drug use and psychological health: A longitudinal inquiry. *American Psychologist, 45,* 612–630

Sherman, T. (1985). Categorization skills in infants. *Child Development, 53,* 183–188.

Shiffrin, R.M., & Atkinson, R.C. (1969). Storage and retrieval processes in long-term memory. *Psychological Review, 76,* 179–193.

Shiono, Patricia H., Rauh, Virginia A., Park, Mikyung, Lederman, Sally A., & Zuskar, Deborah. (1997). Ethnic differences in birthweight: The role of lifestyle and other factors. *American Journal of Public Health, 87,* 787–793.

Shirley, Mary M. (1933). *The first two years: A study of twenty-five babies.* Institute of Child Welfare Monograph No. 8. Minneapolis: University of Minnesota Press.

Shneidman, Edwin S. (1978). Suicide. In Gardner Lindzey, Calvin S. Hall, & Richard F. Thompson, *Psychology* (2nd ed.). New York: Worth.

Shneidman, Edwin S. (1996). *The suicidal mind.* New York: Oxford.

Shneidman, Edwin S., & Mandelkorn, Philip. (1994). Some facts and fables of suicide. In Edwin S. Shneidman, Norman L. Faberow, & Robert E. Litman (Eds.), *The psychology of suicide* (rev. ed.). Northwale, NJ: Aronson.

Shneidman, Edwin S., Faberow, Norman L., & Litman, Robert E. (1994). *The psychology of suicide* (rev. ed.). Northwale, NJ: Aronson.

Shoemaker, Donald J. (1996). *Theories of delinquency: An examination of explanations of delinquent behavior* (3rd ed.). New York: Oxford University Press.

Shore, R. Jerald, & Hayslip, Bert, Jr. (1994). Custodial grandparenting: Implications for children's development. In Adele Eskeles Gottfried & Allen W. Gottfried (Eds.), *Redefining families: Implications for children's development.* New York: Plenum Press.

Sickmund, Melissa, Snyder, Howard N., & Poe-Yamagata, Eileen. (1997). *Juvenile offenders and victims: 1997 update on violence.* Washington DC: Office of Juvenile Justice and Delinquency Prevention.

Siegler, Robert. (1983). Five generalizations about cognitive development. *American Psychologist, 38,* 263–277.

Siegler, Robert. (1983). Information processing approaches to development. In Paul H. Mussen (Ed.), *Handbook of child psychology: Vol. 1. History, theory, and methods.* W. Kessen (Vol. Ed.). New York: Wiley.

Siegler, Robert. (1991). *Children's thinking* (2nd ed.). Englewood Cliffs, NJ: Prentice-Hall.

Siegler, Robert. (1996). A grand theory of development. *Monographs of the Society for Research in Child Development, 61,* 266–275.

Siegler, Robert S., & Thompson, Douglas R. (1998). "Hey, would you like a nice cold cup of lemonade on this hot day?": Children's understanding of economic causation. *Developmental Psychology, 34,* 146–160.

Sigel, I.E., McGillicuddy-DeLisi, A.V., & Goodnow, J.J. (Eds.). (1992). *Parent belief systems* (2nd ed.). Hillsdale, NJ: Erlbaum.

Sigler, Robert T. (1989). *Domestic violence: An assessment of community attitudes.* Lexington, MA: Lexington Books.

Silbereisen, Rainer K., & Kracke, Barbel. (1993). Variation in maturational timing and adjustment in adolescence. In Sandy Jackson & Hector Rodriguez-Tome (Eds.), *Adolescence and its social worlds.* Hove, England: Erlbaum.

Silbereisen, Rainer K., Robins, Lee, & Rutter, Michael. (1995). Secular trends in substance use. In Michael Rutter & David J. Smith (Eds.), *Psychosocial disorders in young people: Time trends and their causes.* West Sussex, England: Wiley.

Silva, Phil A. (1996). Health and development in the early years. In Phil A. Silva & Warren R. Stanton (Eds.), *From child to adult: The Dunedin multidisciplinary health and development study.* New Zealand: Oxford University Press.

Silver, L.B. (1991). Developmental learning disorders. In M. Lewis (Ed.), *Child and adolescent psychiatry: A comprehensive textbook.* Baltimore: Williams and Wilkins.

Simmons, Roberta G., & Blyth, Dale A. (1987). *Moving into adolescence: The impact of pubertal change and school context.* New York: Aldine de Gruyter.

Simonoff, Emily, Bolton, Patrick, & Rutter, Michael. (1996). Mental retardation: Genetic findings, clinical implications and research agenda. *Journal of Child Psychology & Psychiatry & Allied Disciplines, 37,* 259–280.

Simons, Ronald L. (1996). *Understanding differences between divorced and intact families.* Thousand Oaks, CA: Sage.

Simonton, Dean Keith. (1988). *Scientific genius: A psychology of science.* Cambridge: Cambridge University Press.

Singh, Gopal K., & Yu, Stella M. (1996). Adverse pregnancy outcomes differences between US- and foreign-born women in major US racial and ethnic groups. *American Journal of Public Health, 86,* 837–843.

Siperstein, Gary N., Leffert, James S., & Wenz-Gross, Melodie. (1997). The quality of friendships between children with and without learning problems. *American Journal on Mental Retardation, 102,* 111–125.

Skinner, B.F. (1953). *Science and human behavior.* New York: Macmillan.

Skinner, B.F. (1957). *Verbal behavior.* New York: Appleton-Century-Crofts.

Slaby, Ronald J., & Eron, Leonard D. (1994). Afterword. In Leonard D. Eron, Jacquelyn H. Gentry, & Peggy Schlegel (Eds.), *Reason to hope: A psychosocial perspective on violence and youth.* Washington, D.C: American Psychological Association.

Small, Stephen A., Eastman, Gay, & Cornelius, Steven. (1988). Adolescent autommy and parental stress. *Journal of Youth and Adolescence, 17,* 377–391.

Smetana, Judith G., & Asquith, P. (1994). Adolescents' and parents' conceptions of parental authority and adolescent autonomy. *Child Development, 65,* 1147–1162.

Smetana, Judith G., Killen, M., & Turiel, E. (1991). Children's reasoning about interpersonal and moral conflicts. *Child Development, 62,* 629–644.

Smetana, Judith G., Yau, Jenny, Restrepo, Angela, & Braeges, Judith L. (1991). Adolescent-parent conflict in married and divorced families. *Developmental Psychology, 27,* 1000–1010.

Smith, David J. (1995). Youth crime and conduct disorders: Trends, patterns and causal explanations. In Michael Rutter & David J. Smith (Eds.), *Psychosocial disorders in young people: Time trends and their causes.* New York: Wiley.

Smith-Hefner, N. J. (1993). Education, gender, and generational conflict among Khmer refugees. *Anthropology and Education Quarterly, 24,* 135–158.

Snarey, John R. (1993). *How fathers care for the next generation: A four-decade study.* Cambridge, MA: Harvard University Press.

Snijders, R.J.M., & Nicolaides, K.H. (1996). *Ultrasound markers for fetal chromosomal defects.* New York: Parthenon.

Snow, Catherine E. (1984). Parent-child interaction and the development of communicative ability. In Richard L. Schiefelbusch & Joanne Pickar (Eds.), *The acquisition of communicative competence.* Baltimore: University Park Press.

Snyder, Dona J. (1985). Psychosocial effects of long-term antepartal hospitalization. In Manohar Rathi (Ed.), *Clinical aspects of perinatal medicine.* New York: Macmillan.

Snyder, Howard N. (1997). *Serious, violent, and chronic juvenile offenders: An assessment of the extent of and trends in officially-recognized serious criminal behavior in a delinquent population.* Pittsburgh, PA: National Center for Juvenile Justice.

Society for Research in Child Development. (1996). Ethical standards for research with children. *SCRD Directory of Members,* 337–339.

Sodain, Beate. (1991). The development of deception in young children. *British Journal of Developmental Psychology, 9,* 173–188.

Solomon, Richard, & Liefeld, Cynthia Pierce. (1998). Effectiveness of a family support center approach to adolescent mothers: Repeat pregnancy and school drop-out rates. *Family Relations, 47,* 139–144.

Spelke, Elizabeth. (1991). Physical knowledge in infancy: Reflections on Piaget's theory. In S. Carey & R. Gelman (Eds.), *The epigenesis of mind: Essays on biology and cognition.* Hillsdale, NJ: Erlbaum.

Spence, Melanie J., & Freeman, Mark S. (1996). Newborn infants prefer the maternal low-pass filtered voice, but not the maternal whispered voice. *Infant Behavior & Development, 19,* 199–212.

Spock, Benjamin. (1976). *Baby and child care.* New York: Pocket Books.

Sroufe, L. Alan. (1996). *Emotional development: The organization of emotional lie in the early years.* Cambridge: Cambridge University Press.

Stanger, Catherine, Achenbach, Thomas M., & Verhulst, Frank C. (1997). Accelerated longitudinal comparisons of aggressive versus delinquent syndromes. *Development and Psychopathology, 9,* 43–58.

Stanley, B., & Sieber, J.E. (Eds.). (1992). *Social research on children and adolescents: Ethical issues.* Newbury Park, CA: Sage.

Staples, Robert, & Johnson, Leanor B. (1993). *Black families at the crossroads.* San Francisco: Jossey-Bass.

Starfield, B., Shapiro, S., Weiss, J., Liang, K.Y., Ra, K, Paige, D., & Wang, X.B. (1991). Race, family income and low birthweight. *American Journal of Epidemiology, 134,* 1167–1174.

Steffenburg, S. (1991). Neuropsychiatric assessment of children with autism: a population-based study. *Dev Med Child Neurol, 33,* 495–511.

Stein, N.L., & Levine, L.J. (1989). The causal organization of emotional knowledge: A developmental study. *Cognition and Emotion, 3,* 343–378.

Steinberg, Adria. (1993). Adolescents and schools: Improving the fit. *The Harvard Education Letter.*

Steinberg, Lawrence. (1988). Reciprocal relation between parent-child distance and pubertal maturation. *Developmental Psychology, 24,* 122–128.

Steinberg, Lawrence. (1990). Interdependency in the family: Autonomy, conflict, and harmony in the parent-adolescent relationship. In Shirley S. Feldman & G.R. Elliot (Eds.), *At the threshold: The developing adolescent.* Cambridge, MA: Harvard University Press.

Steinberg, Lawrence. (1996). *Beyond the classroom: Why school reform has failed and what parents need to do.* New York: Simon & Schuster.

Steinberg, Lawrence & Darling, Nancy. (1994). The broader context of social influence in adolescence. In Rainer K. Silbereisen and Eberhard Todt (Eds.), *Adolescence in context: The interplay of family, school, peers, and work in adjustment.* Berlin: Springer-Verlag.

Steinberg, Lawrence, & Dornbusch, Sanford M. (1991). Negative correlates of part-time employment during adolescence: Replication and elaboration. *Developmental Psychology, 27,* 304–313.

Steinberg, Lawrence, Elmen, J.D. & Mounts, N.S. (1989). Authoritative parenting, psychosocial maturity and academic success among adolescents. *Child Development, 60,* 1424–1436.

Steinberg, Lawrence, Lamborn, Susie D., Darling, Nancy, Mounts, Nina A., & Dornbusch, Sanford M. (1994). Over-time changes in adjustment and competence among adolescents from authoritative, authoritarian, indulgent, and neglectful families. *Child Development, 65,* 754–770.

Stenberg, C.R., & Campos, J.J. (1983). The development of anger expressions in infancy. In N.L. Stein, B. Leventhal, & T. Trabasso (Eds.), *Psychological and biological approaches to emotion.* Hillsdale, NJ: Erlbaum.

Stenberg, Gunilla & Hagekull, Berit. (1997). Social referencing and mood modification in 1-year-olds. *Infant Behavior and Development, 19,* 209–232.

Stern, Daniel N. (1977). *The first relationship: Mother and infant.* Cambridge, MA: Harvard University Press.

Stern, Daniel N. (1985). *The interpersonal world of the infant.* New York: Basic Books.

Stern, David. (1997). What difference does it make if school and work are connected? Evidence on cooperative education in the United States. *Economics of Education Review, 16,* 213–229.

Sternberg, R.J. (1996). *Successful intelligence.* New York: Simon & Schuster.

Stevenson, Harold W., & Lee, Shin-ying. (1990). Contexts of achievement: A study of American, Chinese, and Japanese children. *Monographs of the Society for Research in Child Development, 55* (1–2, Serial No. 221).

Stevenson, Harold W., & Stigler, Robert W. (1992). *The learning gap: Why our schools are failing and what we can learn from Japanese and Chinese education.* New York: Summit Books.

Stevenson, Harold W., Chen, Chuansheng, & Lee, Shin-Ying. (1993). Mathematics achievement of Chinese, Japanese, and American children: Ten years later. *Science, 259,* 53–58.

Stewart, Deborah A. (1997). Adolescent sexual abuse, sexual assault, and rape. In Adele Dellenbaugh Hofmann & Donald Everett Greydanus (Eds.), *Adolescent medicine* (3rd ed.). Stanford, CT: Appleton and Lange.

Stifter, Cynthia, & Braungart, Julia M. (1995). The regulation of negative reactivity in infancy: Function and development. *Developmental Psychology, 31,* 448–455.

Stiles, Deborah A., Gibbons, Judith L., Hardardottir, Sara, & Schnellmann, Jo. (1987). The ideal man or woman as described by young adolescents in Iceland and the United States. *Sex Roles, 17,* 313–320.

Stipek, Deborah J. (1992). The child at school. In M.H. Bornstein & M.E. Lamb (Eds.), *Developmental psychology: An advanced textbook* (3rd ed.). Hillsdale, NJ: Erlbaum.

Stipek, Deborah J., Feiler, Rachell, Daniels, Denise & Milburn, Sharon. (1995). Effects of different instructional approaches on young children's achievement and motivation. *Child Development, 66,* 209–223.

Stipek, Deborah J., Recchia, Susan, & McClintic, Susan. (1992). Self-evaluation in young children. *Monographs of the Society for Research in Child Development, 57* (Serial No. 226), 1–79.

Stolberg, Sheryl Gay. (1997, September 6). Thalidomide, long banned, wins support: Possible use in leprosy, AIDS, and cancer but with tight controls. *New York Times,* C13.

Stone, C. Addison. (1993). What is missing in the metaphor of scaffolding. In Ellice A. Foreman, Norris Minick, & C. Addison Stone (Eds.), *Contexts for learning: Sociocultural dynamics in children's development.* New York: Oxford Press.

Stormshak, Elizabeth, Bierman, Karen, & The Conduct Problems Prevention Research Group. (1998). The implications of different developmental patterns of disruptive behavior problems for school adjustment. *Development and Psychopathology, 10,* 451–468.

Strassberg, Zvi, Dodge, Kenneth A., Pettit, Gregory S., & Bates, John E. (1994). Spanking in the home and children's subsequent aggression toward kindergarten peers. *Development and Psychopathology, 6,* 445–462.

Straub, Richard O. (1998). *Instructor's resource manual to accompany: The developing person through the life span.* New York: Worth.

Straus, Murray A. (1994). *Beating the devil out of them: Corporal punishment in American families.* Lexington, MA: Lexington Books.

Strauss, David, & Eyman, Richard K. (1996). Mortality of people with mental retardation in California with and without Down syndrome, 1986–1991. *American Journal on Mental Retardation, 100,* 643–653.

Streissguth, Ann P., Bookstein, Fred L., Sampson, Paul D., & Barr, Helen M. (1993). *The enduring effects of prenatal alcohol exposure on child development: Birth through seven years, a partial least squares solution.* Ann Arbor: University of Michigan Press.

Streitmatter, Janice L. (1988). Ethnicity as a mediating variable of early adolescent identity development. *Journal of Adolescence, 11,* 335–346.

Streitmatter, Janice L. (1989). Identity status development and cognitive prejudice in early adolescents. *Journal of Early Adolescence, 11*, 335–346.

Streri, A. (1987). Tactile discrimination of shape and intermodal transfer in 2- to 3-month-old infants. *British Journal of Developmental Psychology, 5*, 213–220.

Sullivan, Kate, & Winner, Ellen. (1993). Three-year-olds' understanding of mental states: The influence of trickery. *Journal of Experimental Child Psychology, 56*, 135–148

Sulloway, Frank. (1996). *Born to rebel: Radical thinking in science and social thought.* New York: McKay.

Surbey, M. (1990). Family composition, stress, and human menarche. In F. Bercovitch & T. Zeigler (Eds.), *The socioendocrinology of primate reproduction.* New York: Liss.

Susman, Elizabeth J. (1997). Modeling development complexity in adolescence: Hormones and behavior in context. *Journal of Research on Adolescence, 7*, 283–306.

Swanson, James M., McBurnett, Keith, Wigal, Tim, & Pfiffner, Linda J. (1993). Effect of stimulant medication on children with attention deficit disorder: "A review of reviews." *Exceptional Children, 60*, 154–161.

Szatmari, Peter. (1992). The validity of autistic spectrum disorders: A literature review. *Journal of Autism and Developmental Disorders, 22*, 583–600.

Tallal, Paula, Miller, S., & Fitch, R.H. (1993). Neurological basis of speech: A case for the preeminence of temporal processing. In Paula Tallal (Ed.), *Annals of the New York Academy of Sciences: Vol. 682. Temporal information processing in the nervous system: Special reference to dyslexia and aphasia.* New York: New York Academy of Sciences.

Tangney, J.P., & Fischer, K.W. (1995). *The self-conscious emotions: The psychology of shame, guilt, embarrassment, and pride.* New York: Guilford Press.

Tanner, James M. (1971). Sequence, tempo, and individual variation in the growth and development of boys and girls aged twelve to sixteen. *Daedalus, 100*, 907–930.

Tanner, James M. (1991). Growth spurt, adolescent. In Richard M. Lerner, Ann C. Petersen, & Jeanne Brooks-Gunn (Eds.), *Encyclopedia of adolescence* (Vol. 1). New York: Garland.

Tanner, James M. (1991). Menarche, secular trend in age of. In Richard M. Lerner, Ann C. Petersen, & Jeanne Brooks-Gunn (Eds.), *Encyclopedia of adolescence* (Vol. 2). New York: Garland.

Tanzer, Deborah, & Block, Jean Libman. (1976). *Why natural childbirth? A psychologist's report on the benefits to mothers, fathers and babies.* New York: Schocken.

Tardif, Twila. (1996). Nouns are not always learned before verbs: Evidence from Mandarin speakers' early vocabularies. *Developmental Psychology, 32*, 492–504.

Tatar, Moshe. (1998). Teachers as significant others: Gender differences to secondary school pupils' perceptions. *British Journal of Educational Psychology, 68*, 217–227.

Taylor, Jill McLean, Gilligan, Carol, & Sullivan, Amy M. (1995). *Between voice and silence: Women and girls, race and relationship.* Cambridge, MA: Harvard University Press.

Taylor, Ronald D., Casten, Robin, & Flickinger, Susan M. (1993). Influence of kinship social support on the parenting experiences and psychosocial adjustment of African-American adolescents. *Developmental Psychology, 29*, 382–388.

Taylor, Ronald L. (1997). Who's parenting? Trends and patterns. In Terry Arendell (Ed.), *Contemporary parenting: Challenges and issues.* Thousand Oaks, California: Sage.

Teitelbaum, Philip, Teitelbaum, Osnat, Nye, Jennifer, Fryman, Joshua, & Maurer, Ralph G. (1998). Movement analysis in infancy may be useful for early diagnosis of autism. *Proceedings of the National Academy of Sciences, 23*, 13982–13987.

Teller, Davida Y. (1997). First glances: The vision of infants. *Investigative Ophthalmology & Visual Sicence, 38*, 2183–2203.

Tharp, Roland G., & Gallimore, Ronald. (1988). *Rousing minds to life: Teaching, learning, and schooling in social context.* Cambridge, England: Cambridge University Press.

Thatcher, Robert W. (1994). Cyclic cortical reorganization: Origins of human cognitive development. In Geraldine Dawson & Kurt W. Fischer (Eds.), *Human behavior and the developing brain.* New York: Guilford.

Thelen, Esther. (1987). The role of motor development in developmental psychology: A view of the past and an agenda for the future. In Nancy Eisenberg (Ed.), *Contemporary topics in developmental psychology.* New York: Wiley.

Thelen, Esther, & Ulrich, Beverly D. (1991). Hidden skills. *Monographs of the Society for Research in Child Development, 56* (Serial No. 223).

Thelen, Esther, Corbetta, D., Kamm, K., Spencer, J.P., Schneider, K., & Zernicke, R.F. (1993). The transition to reaching: Mapping intention and intrinsic dynamics. *Child Development, 64*, 1058–1098.

Thoman, E.B., & Whitney, M.P. (1990). Behavioral states in infants: Individual differences and individual analyses. In J. Colombo & J. Fagen (Eds.), *Individual differences in infancy.* Hillsdale, NJ: Erlbaum.

Thomas, Alexander, & Chess, Stella. (1977). *Temperament and development.* New York: Brunner/Mazel.

Thomas, Alexander, Chess, Stella, & Birch, Herbert G. (1963). *Behavioral individuality in early childhood.* New York: New York University Press.

Thomas, Alexander, Chess, Stella, & Birch, Herbert G. (1968). *Temperament and behavior disorders in children.* New York: New York University Press.

Thompson, Frances E., & Dennison, Barbara. (1994). Dietary sources of fats and cholesterol in U.S. children aged 2 through 5 years. *American Journal of Public Health, 84*, 799–806.

Thompson, Larry W. (1994). *Correcting the code.* New York: Simon & Schuster.

Thompson, Linda, & Walker, Alexis J. (1989). Gender in families: Women and men in marriage, work, and parenthood. *Journal of Marriage and the Family, 5*, 845–871.

Thompson, Richard F. (1993). *The brain: A neuroscience primer.* New York: W.H. Freeman.

Thompson, Ron A., & Sherman, Roberta. (1993). *Helping athletes with eating disorders.* Bloomington, IN: Human Kinetics Books.

Thompson, Ross A. (1992). Developmental changes in research risk and benefit: A changing calculus of concerns. In B. Stanley & J.E. Sieber (Eds.), *Social research on children and adolescents: Ethical issues.* Newbury Park, CA: Sage.

Thompson, Ross A. (1994). Emotional regulation: A theme in search of definition. In Nathan A. Fox (Ed.), The development of emotional regulation: Biological and behavioral considerations. *Monographs of the Society for Research in Child Development.* (Serial no. 240.)

Thompson, Ross A. (1994). Fatherhood and divorce. *The Future of Children, 4.*

Thompson, Ross A. (1995). *Personal communication from one of Professor Thompson's students.*

Thompson, Ross A. (1997). Early sociopersonality development. In William Damon (Ed.), *Handbook of child psychology* (5th ed., Vol. 3). New York: Wiley.

Thompson, Ross A., & Frodi, A.M. (1984). The sociophysiology of infants and their caregivers. In W.M. Waid (Ed.), *Sociophysiology.* New York: Springer-Verlag.

Thompson, Ross A., & Limber, S.P. (1990). "Social anxiety" in infancy: Stranger and separation anxiety. In H. Leitenberg (Ed.), *Handbook of social anxiety.* New York: Plenum Press.

Tisi, Gennaro M. (1988). Pulmonary problems: Smoking, obstructive lung disease, and other lung disorders. In Dorothy Reycroft Hollingsworth & Robert Resnik (Eds.), *Medical counseling before pregnancy.* New York: Churchill-Livingstone.

Tobin, J.D., Wu, D.Y.H., & Davidson, D. (1989). *Preschool in three cultures.* New Haven: Yale University Press.

Toch, Thomas. (1991). *In the name of excellence: The struggle to reform the nation's schools, why it's failing, and what should be done.* New York: Oxford University Press.

Tolan, P.H., & Gorman-Smith, D. (1997) Families and the development of urban children. In H.J. Walberg, O. Reyes, & R.P. Weissberg (Eds.), *Interdisciplinary perspectives on children and youth.* Newberry Park, CA: Sage.

Tomasello, Michael. (1992). The social bases of language acquisition. *Social Development, 1,* 67–87.

Tomasello, Michael. (1995). Joint attention as social cognition. In C. Moore & P.J. Dunham (Eds.), *Joint attention: Its origins and role in development.* Hillsdale, NJ: Erlbaum.

Tomasello, Michael. (1996). Piagetian and Vygotskian approaches to language acquisition. *Human Development, 39,* 269–276.

Tovey, Robert. (1997). Rethinking homework. *The Harvard Education Letter, 13,* 6–8.

Treasure, J.L., & Holland, A.J. (1993). What discordant twins tell us about the etiology of anorexia nervosa. In E. Ferrari, F. Branbilla, & S.B. Solerte (Eds.), *Primary and secondary eating disorders.* Oxford, England: Pergamon Press.

Treboux, Dominique, & Busch-Rossnagel, Nancy. (1990). Social network influences on adolescent sexual attitudes and behaviors. *Journal of Adolescent Research, 5,* 175–189.

Trehub, S.E., Schneider, B.A., Thorpe, L.A., & Judge, P. (1991). Observational measures of auditory sensitivity in early infancy. *Developmental Psychology, 27,* 40–49.

Trehub, Sandra E., Unyk, Anna M., Kamenetsky, Stuart B., et al. (1997). Mothers' and fathers' singing to infants. *Developmental Psychology, 33,* 500–507.

Tronick, Edward Z., Cohn, Jeffrey, & Shea, E. (1986). The transfer of affect between mothers and infants. In T. Berry Brazelton & M.W. Yogman (Eds.), *Affective development in infancy.* Norwood, NJ: Ablex.

Tronick, Edward Z., Morelli, G.A., & Ivey, P.K. (1992). The Efe forager infant and toddler's pattern of social relationships: Multiple and simultaneous. *Developmental Psychology, 28,* 568–577.

Tucker, C.M., Harris, Y.R., Brady, B.A., & Herman, K.C. (1996). The association of selected parent behaviors with the academic achievement of African American children and European American children. *Child Study Journal, 26,* 253–277.

Turiel, Elliot. (1983). *The development of social knowledge: Morality and convention.* Cambridge, England: Cambridge University Press.

Turiel, Elliot, Smetana, Judith G., & Killen, Melanie. (1991). Social context in social cognitive development. In William M. Kurtines & Jacob L. Gewirtz (Eds.), *Handbook of moral behavior and development: Vol. 2. Research.* Hillsdale, NJ: Erlbaum.

Turner, Patricia J. (1991). Relations between attachment, gender, and behavior with peers in preschool. *Child Development, 62,* 1475–1488.

Turner, Patricia J. (1993). Attachment to mother and behavior with adults in preschool. *British Journal of Developmental Psychology, 11,* 75–89.

UNICEF. (1990). *Children and development in the 1990s: A UNICEF sourcebook.* New York: United Nations.

UNICEF. (1994). *The state of the world's children, 1994.* New York: Oxford University Press.

UNICEF. (1995). *The state of the world's children, 1995.* New York: United Nations.

UNICEF. (1996). *The state of the world's children, 1996.* New York: Oxford University Press.

UNICEF. (1996). *Statistical yearbook, 1996.* Lanham, MD: Bernan Press.

UNICEF. (1998). *The state of the world's children, 1998.* New York: Oxford University Press.

United Nations. (1994). *The state of the world's children, 1994.* New York: Oxford University Press.

United Nations Department of Economic and Social Affairs. (1996). *World population prospects: The 1996 revision.*

United States Bureau of the Census. (1992). *Statistical abstract of the United States, 1992* (112th ed.). Washington, DC: U.S. Department of Commerce.

United States Bureau of the Census. (1996). *Statistical abstract of the United States, 1996* (116th ed.). Washington, DC: U.S. Department of Commerce.

United States Bureau of the Census. (1997). *Statistical abstract of the United States, 1997* (117th ed.). Washington, DC: U.S. Department of Commerce.

United States Bureau of the Census. (1998) March current population survey. Washington, DC: U.S. Department of Commerce.

United States Bureau of the Census. (1998). *Statistical abstract of the United States, 1998* (118th ed.). Washington, DC: U.S. Department of Commerce.

United States Bureau of the Census. (1999). *Statistical abstract of the United States, 1999* (119th ed.). Washington, DC: U.S. Department of Commerce.

United States Bureau of Labor Statistics. (1990). Washington, DC: U.S. Department of Labor.

United States Department of Education. (1991). *The condition of education, 1991: Vol 1. Elementary and secondary education.* Washington, DC: National Center for Educational Statistics.

United States Department of Education. (1998). *Digest of education statistics.* Washington DC: National Center for Education Statistics.

United States Department of Education, National Center for Education Statistics. (1997) *Third international math and science study, 1997.* Washington DC.

Vallee, Bert L. (1998). Alcohol in the western world. *Scientific American, 278,* 80–85.

Valsiner, Jaan. (1997). Constructing the personal through the cultural redundant organization of psychological development. In Eric Amsel & K. Ann Renninger (Eds.), *Change and development: Issues of theory, method, & application.* Mahwah, NJ: Erlbaum

Van Biema, David. (1995, December 11). A shameful death. *Time,* 33–36.

Vandell, Deborah Lowe, & Hembree, Sheri E. (1994). Peer social status and friendship: Independent contributors to children's social and academic adjustment. *Merrill Palmer Quarterly, 40,* 461–477.

Van den Boom, Dymphna C. (1995). Do first-year intercention effects endure? Follow-up during toddlerhood of a sample of Dutch irritable infants. *Child Development, 66,* 1798–1816.

Van Ijzendoorn, M.H., & Kroonenberg, P.M. (1988). Cross-cultural patterns of attachment: A meta-analysis of the Strange Situation. *Child Development, 59,* 147–156.

Van Ijzendoorn, M.H., & De Wolff, M.S. (1997). In search of the absent father—meta-analyses of infant-father attachment: a rejoinder to our discussants. *Child Development, 68,* 604–609.

Van Loosbroek, E., & Smitsman, A.W. (1990). Visual perception of numerosity in infancy. *Developmental Psychology, 26,* 916–922.

Vernon-Feagens, Lynne, & Manlove, Elizabeth E. (1996). Otitis media and the social behavior of day-care-attending children. *Child Development, 67,* 1528–1539.

Vinden, Penelope. (1996). Junin Quechua Children's understanding of the mind. *Child Development, 67,* 1707–1716.

Vitaro, Frank, Tremblay, Richard E., Kerr, Margaret, Pagani, Linda, & Bukowski, William M. (1997). Disruptiveness, friends' characteristics, and delinquency in early adolescence: A test of two competing models of development. *Child Development, 68,* 676–689.

Vogel, Gretchen. (1997). New clues to asthma therapies. *Science, 276,* 1643–1646.

von Hofsten, Claes. (1983). Catching skills in infancy. *Journal of Experimental Psychology: Human Perception and Performance, 9,* 75–85.

Voydanoff, P., & Donnelly, B.W. (1990). *Adolescent sexuality and pregnancy.* Newbury Park, CA: Sage.

Vuchinich, S., Hetherington, E.M., Vuchinich, R.A., & Clingempeel, W.G. (1991). Parent-child interaction and gender differences in early adolescents' adaptation to stepfamilies. *Developmental Psychology, 27,* 618–626.

Vygotsky, Lev S. (1978). *Mind in society: The development of higher psychological processes.* Cambridge, MA: Harvard University Press.

Vygotsky, Lev S. (1986). *Thought and language.* Cambridge, MA: MIT Press. (Original work published 1934)

Vygotsky, Lev S. (1987). *Thinking and speech* (N. Minick, Trans.). New York: Plenum Press.

Wachs, Theodore D. (1995). Relation of mild-to-moderate malnutrition of human development: correlational studies. *Journal of Nutrition Supplement, 125,* 2245S–2254S.

Wade, T. Joel. (1996). An examination of locus of control/fatalism for blacks, whites, boys, and girls over a two year period of adolescence. *Social Behavior and Personality, 24,* 239–248.

Wagenaar, Alexander, & Perry, Cheryl L. (1994). Community strategies for the reduction of youth drinking: Theory and application. *Journal of Research on Adolescence, 4,* 319–346.

Waggoner, J.E., & Palermo, D.S. (1989). Betty is a bouncing bubble: Children's comprehension of emotion-descriptive metaphors. *Developmental Psychology, 25,* 152–163.

Wainryb, Cecilia, & Turiel, Elliot. (1995). Diversity in social development: Between or within cultures? In Melanie Killen & Daniel Hart (Eds.), *Morality in everyday life: Developmental perspectives.* Cambridge, England: Cambridge University Press.

Waite, L. J., & Lillard, L. A. (1991). Children and marital disruption. *American Journal of Sociology, 96,* 930–953.

Waldfogel, Jane. (1998). Rethinking the paradigm for child protection. *The Future of Children: Protecting children from abuse and neglect, 8,* 4–22.

Walker, Arlene S. (1982). Intermodal perception of expressive behaviors by human infants. *Journal of Experimental Child Psychology, 33,* 514–535.

Walker, Lawrence J. (1988). The development of moral reasoning. *Annals of Child Development, 55,* 677–691.

Walker, Lawrence J., Pitts, Russell C., Hennig, Karl H., & Matsuba, M. Kyle. (1995). Reasoning about morality and real-life moral problems. In Melanie Killen & Daniel Hart (Eds.), *Morality in everyday life: Developmental perspectives.* Cambridge, England: Cambridge University Press.

Walker-Andrews, A.S., Bahrick, L.E., Raglioni, S.S., & Diaz, I. (1991). Infants' bimodal perception of gender. *Ecological Psychology, 3,* 55–75.

Wallace, Ina F., Gravel, Judith S., Schwartz, Richard G., & Ruben, Robert J. (1996). Otitis media, communication style of primary caregivers, and language skills of 2 year olds: A preliminary report. *Journal of Developmental & Behavioral Pediatrics, 17,* 27–35.

Walton, Irene, & Hamilton, Mary. (1998). *Midwives and changing childbirth.* Books for Midwives Press: Cheshire, England.

Wang, Ching-Tung, & Daro, Deborah. (1998). *Current trends in child abuse reporting and fatalities: The results of the 1997 annual fifty-state survey.* Chicago: National Committee to Prevent Child Abuse.

Wanner, Eric, & Gleitman, Lila R. (Eds.). (1982). *Language acquisition: The state of the art.* Cambridge, England: Cambridge University Press.

Ward, Margaret. (1997). Family paradigms and older-child adoption: A proposal for matching parents' strengths to children's needs. *Family Relations, 46,* 257–262.

Waterhouse, Lynn, Fein, Deborah, & Modahl, Charlotte. (1996). Neurofunctional mechanisms in autism. *Psychological Review, 103,* 457–489.

Waterson, E.J., & Murray-Lyon, Iain M. (1990). Preventing alcohol related birth damage: A review. *Social Science and Medicine, 30,* 349–364.

Watson, John B. (1927, March). What to do when your child is afraid (interview with Beatrice Black). *Children,* 25–27.

Watson, John B. (1928). *Psychological care of the infant and child.* New York: Norton.

Watson, John B. (1930). *Behaviorism.* New York: Norton.

Watson, John B. (1967). *Behaviorism* (rev. ed.). Chicago: University of Chicago Press. (Original work published 1930).

Wattenberg, E. (1993). Paternity actions and young fathers. In R.I. Lehman & T.J. Ooms (Eds.), *Young unwed fathers: Changing roles and emerging policies.* Philadelphia: Temple University Press.

Weinberg, M. Katherine, Tronick, Edward Z., Cohn, Jeffrey F., & Olson, Karen L. (1999). Gender differences in emotional expressivity and self-regulation during early infancy. *Developmental Psychology, 35,* 175–188.

Weinraub, Marsha, & Gringlas, Marcy B. (1995). Single parenthood. In Marc H. Bornstein (Ed.), *Handbook of parenting: Status and social conditions of parenting.* Mahwah, NJ: Erlbaum.

Weiss, Gabrielle. (1991). Attention deficit hyperactivity disorder. In M. Lewis (Ed.), *Child and adolescent psychiatry: A comprehensive textbook.* Baltimore: Williams & Wilkins.

Wellman, H.M. (1990). *The child's theory of mind.* Cambridge, MA: MIT Press.

Wellman, H.M., & Gelman, S.A. (1992). Cognitive development: Foundational theories of core domains. *Annual Review of Psychology, 43,* 337–375.

Wentzel, Kathryn R. & Caldwell, Kathryn. (1997). Friendships, peer acceptance, and group membership: Relations to academic achievement in middle school. *Child Development, 68,* 1198–1209.

Werker, J.F. (1989). Becoming a native listener. *American Scientist, 77,* 54–59.

Werner, Emmy E., & Smith, Ruth S. (1992). *Overcoming the odds: High risk children from birth to adulthood.* Ithaca, NY: Cornell University Press.

Werner, Lynne A., & Ward, Jeffrey H. (1997). The effect of otitis media with effusion on infants' detection of sound. *Infant Behavior & Development, 20,* 275–279.

Wertsch, J.V. (1985). *Vygotsky and the social formation of mind.* Cambridge, MA: Harvard University Press.

Wertsch, J.V., & Tulviste, P. (1992). L.S. Vygotsky and contemporary developmental psychology. *Developmental Psychology, 28,* 548–557.

West, Elliott. (1996). *Growing up in twentieth-century America: A history and reference guide.* Westport, Conn.: Greenwood Press.

Westinghouse Learning Corporation. (1969). *The impact of Head Start: An evaluation of the Head Start experience on children's cognitive and affective development.* Athens, OH: Ohio University Press.

Wharton, Brian. (1996). Nutritional deficiency in the breast-fed infant. In J.G. Bindels, A.C. Goedhart, & H.K.A. Visser (Eds.), *Recent developments in infant nutrition.* Dordrecht: Kluwer Academic Publishers.

Whitaker, Robert C., Wright, Jeffrey A., Pepe, Margaret S., Seidel, Kristy D., & Dietz, William H. (1997). Predicting obesity in young adulthood from childhood and parental obesity. *New England Journal of Medicine, 337,* 869–873.

Whitam, Frederick L., Diamond, Milton, Martin, James. (1993). Homosexual orientation in twins: A report on 61 pairs and three triplet sets. *Archives of Sexual Behavior, 22,* 187–206.

Whiting, Beatrice Blyth, & Edwards, Carolyn Pope. (1988). *Children of different worlds: The formation of social behavior.* Cambridge, MA: Harvard University Press.

Wierson, M., Long, P.J., & Forehand, R. L. (1993). Toward a new understanding of early menarche: The role of environmental stress in pubertal timing. *Adolescence, 28,* 913–924.

Wilcox, Teresa, Nadel, Lynn, & Rosser, Rosemary. (1996). Location memory in healthy preterm and full-term infants. *Infant Behavior & Development, 19,* 309–323.

Wilens, Timothy E., Biderman, Joseph, Abrantes, Ana M., & Spencer, Thomas J. (1997). Clinical characteristics of psychiatrically referred adolescent outpatients with substance use disorder. *Journal of the American Academy of Child & Adolescent Psychiatry, 36,* 941–947.

Wilfert, C.M., & McKinney, R.E., Jr. (1998). When children harbor HIV. *Scientific American, 279,* 94–95.

Wilkinson, Krista M., Dube, William V., & McIlvane, William J. (1996). A crossdisciplinary perspective on studies of rapid word mapping in psycholinguistics and behavior analysis. *Developmental Review, 16,* 125–148.

Willatts, P. (1989). Development of problem-solving in infancy. In A. Slater & G. Bremner (Eds.), *Infant development.* Hove, United Kingdom: Erlbaum.

Willinger, M., Hoffman, H.J., & Hartford, R.B. (1994). Infant sleep position and risk for sudden infant death syndrome. *Pediatrics, 93,* 814–819.

Willinger, M., Hoffman, H.J., Wu, K.-T., Hou, J.-R., Kessler, R.C., Ward, S.L., Keens, T.G., & Corwin, M.J. (1998). Factors associated with the transition to nonprone sleep positions of infants in the United States: The national infant sleep position study. *Journal of the American Medical Association, 280,* 329–335.

Willis, D.J., Holden, E.W., & Rosenberg, M. (Eds.). (1992). *Prevention of child maltreatment: Developmental and ecological perspectives.* New York: Wiley.

Wilson, B.L., & Corcoran, T.B. (1988). *Successful secondary schools.* New York: Falmer Press.

Wing, R.R. (1992). Weight cycling in humans: A review of the literature. *Annals of Behavioral Medicine, 14,* 113–119.

Winner, Ellen. (1996). *Gifted children: Myths and realities.* New York: Basic Books.

Wolfner, Glenn D., & Gelles, Richard J. (1993). A profile of violence toward children: A national study. *Child Abuse and Neglect, 17,* 197–212.

Wolfson, Amy R. & Carskadon, Mary A. (1998). Sleep schedules and daytime functioning in adolescents. *Child Development, 69,* 875–887.

Wolraich, Mark L., Hannah, Jane N., Baumgaertel, Anna, & Feurer, Irene D. (1998). Examination of DSM-IV criteria for attention deficit hyperactivity disorder in a county-side sample. *Journal of Developmental & Behavioral Pediatrics, 19,* 162–168.

Wong Fillmore, Lily. (1991). Second-language learning in children: A model of language learning in social context. In Ellen Bialystok (Ed.), *Language processing in bilingual children.* Cambridge, England: Cambridge University Press.

Wood, D., Bruner, Jerome S., & Ross, G. (1976). The role of tutoring in problem solving. *Journal of Child Psychology and Psychiatry, 17,* 89–100.

World Health Organization (WHO). (1995). *World Health Statistics Quarterly, 48,* No. 1.

Wren, Christopher S. (1996, February 20). Marijuana use by youths continues to rise. *The New York Times,* A11.

Wright, C.M., & Talbot, E. (1996). Screening for failure to thrive: What are we looking for? *Child: Care, Health & Development, 22,* 223–234.

Wynn, K. (1992). Addition and subtraction by human infants. *Nature (London), 358,* 749–750.

Yang, Bin, Ollendick, Thomas, Dong, Qi, Xia, Yong, & Lin, Lei. (1995). Only children and children with siblings in the People's Republic of China: Levels of fear, anxiety, and depression. *Child Development, 66,* 1301–1311.

Yeung-Courchesne, Rachel & Courchesne, Eric. (1997). From impasse to insight in autism research: From behavioral symptoms to biological explanations. *Development and Psychopathology, 9,* 389–420.

Yoon, Keumsil Kim. (1992). New perspective on intrasentential code-switching: A study of Korean-English switching. *Applied Psycholinguistics, 13,* 433–449.

Yoshikawa, H. (1994). Prevention as cumulative protection: Effects of early family support and education on chronic delinquency and its risks. *Psychological Bulletin, 115,* 28–54.

Younger, B.A. (1990). Infant categorization: Memory for category-level and specific item information. *Journal of Experimental Child Psychology, 50,* 131–155.

Younger, B.A. (1993). Understanding category members as "the same sort of thing": Explicit categorization in ten-month-old infants. *Child Development, 64,* 309–320.

Youniss, James. (1989). Parent-adolescent relationships. In William Damon (Ed.), *Child development today and tomorrow.* San Francisco: Jossey-Bass.

Zahn-Waxler, Carolyn, Cole, Pamela M., Welsh, Jean Darby, & Fox, Nathan A. (1995). Psychophysiological correlates of empathy and prosocial behaviors in preschool children with behavior problems. *Development and Psychopatholgy, 7,* 27–48.

Zahn-Waxler, Carolyn, Radke-Yarrow, M., Wagner, E., & Chapman, M. (1992). Development of concern for others. *Child Development, 28,* 126–136.

Zahn-Waxler, Carolyn, Schmitz, Stephanie, Fulker, David, Robinson, Joann, & Emde, Robert. (1996). Behavior problems in 5-year-old monozygotic and dyzygotic twins: Genetic and environmental influences, patterns of regulation, and internalization of control. *Development and Psychopathology, 8,* 103–122.

Zajonc, Robert B., & Mullally, Patricia R. (1997). Birth order: Reconciling conflicting effects. *American Psychologist, 52,* 685–699.

Zambrana, Ruthe E., Scrimshaw., Susan C.M., Collins, Nancy, & Dunkel-Schetter, Christine. (1997). Prenatal health behaviors and psychosocial risk factors in pregnant women of Mexican origin: The role of acculturation. *American Journal of Public Health, 87,* 1022–1026.

Zarbatany, L., Hartmann, D.P., & Rankin, D.B. (1990). The psychological functions of preadolescent peer activities. *Child Development, 61,* 1067–1080.

Zaslow, Martha J. (1991). Variation in child care quality and its implications for children. *Journal of Social Issues, 47,* 125–138.

Zeanah, C.H., Benoit, D., Barton, M. Regan, C., Hirshberg, L.M., & Lipsitt, L.P. (1993). Representations of attachment in mothers and their one-year-old infants. *Journal of the American Academy of Child and Adolescent Psychiatry, 32,* 278–286.

Zedeck, Sheldon. (Ed.). (1992). *Work, families, and organizations.* San Francisco: Jossey-Bass.

Zeifman, Debra, Delaney, Sarah, & Blass, Elliott. (1996). Sweet taste, looking, and calm in two- and four-week-old infants: The eyes have it. *Developmental Psychology, 32,* 1090–1099.

Zeskind, Philip Sanford & Barr, Ronald G. (1997) Acoustic characteristics of naturally occurring cries of infants with "Colic." *Child Development, 68,* 394–403.

Zierler, Sally. (1994). Women, sex, and HIV. *Epidemiology, 5,* 565–567.

Zigler, Edward, & Berman, Winnie. (1983). Discerning the future of early childhood intervention. *American Psychologist, 38,* 894–906.

Zigler, Edward, & Lang, M.E. (1990). *Child care choices.* New York: Free Press.

Zigler, Edward, Styfco, Sally, & Gilman, Elizabeth. (1993). National Head Start program for disadvantaged preschoolers. In E. Zigler & S. Styfco (Eds.), *Head Start and beyond: A national plan for extended childhood intervention.* New Haven, CT: Yale University Press.

Zimmerman, Marc A., Salem, Deborah A., Maton, Kenneth I. (1995). Family structure and psychosocial correlates among urban African-American adolescent males. *Child Development, 66,* 1598–1613.

Zukow-Goldring, Patricia. (1995). Sibling caregiving. In Marc H. Bornstein (Ed.), *Handbook of Parenting: Status and social conditions of parenting.* New Jersey: Erlbaum.

Illustration Credits

Author Photo, p. v Siva Bonatti

PART OPENERS

Preface p. vii Corbis/Laura Dwight; **Part I pp. viii, 64** Laura Dwight; **Part II pp. ix, 134** Myrleen Ferguson/PhotoEdit; **Part III pp. xi, 240** Dreyfuss/Monkmeyer; **Part IV pp. xiii, 338** Tom and Deann McCarthy/The Stock Market; **Part V pp. xxiv, 436** John Henley/The Stock Market.

CHAPTER 1

Chapter Opener p. xxvi Jeffrey W. Myers/Stock, Boston; **p. 3** Tony Freeman/PhotoEdit; **p. 4** Ira Kirschenbaum/Stock, Boston; **p. 7** Ida Wyman/Monkmeyer; **p. 11** Library of Congress; **p. 13** *(top)* Joan Lebold Cohen/Photo Researchers, Inc.; *(bottom)* Philippe Maille/Photo Researchers, Inc.; **p. 14** Elizabeth Crews/The Image Works; **p. 17** Bob Daemmrich/The Image Works; **p. 18** Joe Sohm/Chromosohm/The Stock Market; **p. 20** Richard T. Nowitz/Photo Researchers, Inc.; **p. 21** **(Table 1.1)** Jo Ann M. Farver and Dominick L. Frosch. (1996). L.A. stories: Aggression in preschoolers' spontaneous narratives after the riots of 1992. *Child Development, 67,* 19–32. **p. 24** Lawrence Manning/Woodfin Camp & Associates; **p. 25** Alon Reininger/Woodfin Camp & Associates; **p. 29** *(left)* Bob Daemmrich/The Image Works; *(right)* Ulrich Tutsch; **p. 31** *(all photos)* George Goodwin/Monkmeyer; **p. 33** Courtesy of Kathleen Berger.

CHAPTER 2

Chapter Opener p. 36 Corbis/Laura Dwight; **p. 38** Corbis/Kevin R. Morris; **p. 39** *(top)* AKG/Photo Researchers, Inc.; *(bottom)* Susan Lapides/Design Conceptions; **p. 40** *(top)* Corbis; *(bottom)* Sylvain Grandadam/Photo Researchers, Inc.; **p. 42** Sovfoto; **p. 43** Sam Falk/Monkmeyer; **p. 44** Cindy Roesinger/Photo Researchers, Inc.; **p. 45** *(left)* Elizabeth Crews; *(right)* Richard Hutchin/PhotoEdit; *(bottom)* Yves Debraine/Black Star; **p. 46** *(left)* Sally Cassidy/The Picture Cube/Index Stock; *(center)* David Austen/Stock, Boston; *(right)* Lew Merrim/Monkmeyer; **p. 48** Bob Daemmrich/The Image Works; **p. 50** Courtesy of Dr. Michael Cole, Laboratory of Comparative Human Cognition, University of California, San Diego; **p. 51** Rick Smolan/Stock, Boston; **p. 53 (Figure 2.1)** Marcia Barinaga. (1994). Surprises across the cultural divide. *Science, 263,* 1468–1472. Used by permission; **p. 54** Mark Antman/The Image Works; **p. 57** *(top)* Gregory K. Scott/The Picture Cube/Index Stock; *(bottom)* Laura Dwight.

CHAPTER 3

Chapter Opener p. 66 David M. Phillips/The Population Council/Photo Researchers, Inc.; **p. 68** From Lennart Nilsson, *A child is born,* 2nd ed., Delacourt Press, © 1990. Photograph courtesy Lennart Nilsson/Bonnier Fakta/Stockholm; **p. 69** Omikron/Photo Researchers, Inc.; **p. 71** *(top)* Ulrike Welsch/PhotoEdit; *(bottom)* John Ficara/Woodfin Camp & Associates; **p. 72** AP/Wide World Photos; **p. 73** *(top left and right)* Mark Richards/PhotoEdit; *(bottom)* Courtesy of Thomas M. Pinkerton, Attorney at Law; **p. 76** Thomas Digory/Stockphotos/The Image Bank; **p. 81** Robert Burroughs; **p. 83** Corbis/The Purcell Team; **p. 84** **(Figure 3.5)** Data from I. I. Gottesman. (1991). *Schizophrenia genesis: The origins of madness.* Copyright © 1991 by W.H. Freeman and Company; **p. 86** Laura Dwight; **p. 88** Laura Dwight; **p. 89** Will and Deni McIntyre/Photo Researchers, Inc.; **p. 92** DPA/The Image Works; **p. 95** Ted Thai/Time Magazine.

CHAPTER 4

Chapter Opener p. 98 Corbis/Phil Schermeister; **p. 100** *(all photos)* Petit Format/Nestle/Science Source/Photo Researchers, Inc.; **p. 102** *(left, center left, and center right)* Petit Format/Nestle/Science Source/Photo Researchers, Inc.; *(right)* National Medical Slide/Custom Medical Stock Photo; **p. 104** S.J. Allen/International Stock Photo; **p. 107** Peter Byron/Monkmeyer; **p. 108 (Figure 4.1)** From K.L. Moore and T.V.N. Persaud. (1998) *The developing human: Clinically oriented embryology.* Philadelphia: W.B. Saunders. © 1998 by W.B. Saunders. Used by permission; **p. 109** *(all photos)* Carnegie Institute of Washington, Department of Embryology, David Division; **p. 111** Scott McKiernan/The Gamma Liaison Network; **p. 112** *(top)* John Maier, Jr./The Image Works; *(bottom left and right)* George Steinmetz; **p. 115** Bob Daemmrich/The Image Works; **p. 117** Dan McCoy/Rainbow; **p. 119 (Table 4.4)** From Barbara Luke. (1993). Nutrition and prematurity. In Frank R. Witter & Louis G. Keith (Eds.) *Textbook of prematurity: Antecedents, treatment, and outcome.* Boston: Little, Brown; **p. 120** Andrew Brilliant/The Picture Cube/Index Stock; **p. 123** Henry Schleichkorn/Custom Medical Stock Photo; **p. 124** Laura Dwight; **p. 125** *(left)* William Hubbell/Woodfin Camp & Associates; *(right)* Viviane Moos; **p. 126** J.T. Miller/The Stock Market; **p. 128** Mark Richards/PhotoEdit; **p. 129** Gregory Dimijian/Photo Researchers, Inc.

CHAPTER 5

Chapter Opener p. 136 Lisl Dennis/The Image Bank; **p. 138** Simon Fraser/Photo Researchers, Inc.; **p. 142** Jeff Greenberg/MRP/Photo Researchers, Inc.; **p. 143** CNRI/Science Source/Photo Researchers, Inc.; **p. 146** Laura Dwight; **p. 149** *(left and center)* Elizabeth Crews; *(right)* Petit Format/Photo Researchers, Inc.; **p. 150** *(all photos)* Laura Dwight; **p. 151** Brady/Monkmeyer; **p. 152** Corbis/Laura Dwight; **p. 153 (Table 5.2)** From W.K. Frankenburg, et al. (1981). The newly abbreviated and revised Denver Developmental Screening Test. *Journal of Pediatrics, 99,* 995–999; **p. 154** Rick Browne/Stock, Boston; **p. 155** Hazel Hankin; **p. 157** From "First Glances" by Davida Y. Teller, *Journal Of Investigative Opthalmology And Visual Science*, Vol. 38, 1997, pp. 2183-2203. Photographs copyright of Anthony Young; **p. 158** Peter Menzel; **p. 160** *(both photos)* Peter McLeod/Acadia University; **p. 162 (Figure 5.7)** From Lynne Vernon-Feagens & Elizabeth E. Manlove. (1996). Otitis media and the social behavior of day-care-attending children. *Child Development, 67,* 1528–1539; **p. 164** Barbara Alper/Stock, Boston; **p. 166** *(top)* Eric Feferberg/Agence France-Presse; *(bottom)* AP/Wide World Photos.

CHAPTER 6

Chapter Opener p. 172 Bob Daemmrich/Stock, Boston; **p. 174** Catherine Ursillo/Photo Researchers, Inc.; **p. 175** Joe Epstein/Design Conceptions; **p. 176** *(top)* Innervisions; *(all bottom photos)* Courtesy of Karen Adolph; **p. 178** Ulli Seer/Image Bank; **p. 180** Corbis/Laura Dwight; **p. 181** Laura Dwight; **p. 182** Laura Dwight; **p. 184** Michael Newman/PhotoEdit; **p. 185** Renate Hiller/Monkmeyer; **p. 190** Robert Ullman/Monkmeyer; **p. 191** Laura Dwight; **p. 192** Laura Dwight; **p. 196** *(top)* Corbis/Anthony Bannister; *(bottom)* Laura Dwight; **p. 197** Elliott Varner Smith; **p. 200** Hazel Hankin/Stock, Boston; **p. 203** Betty Press/Woodfin Camp & Associates.

CHAPTER 7

Chapter Opener p. 206 Young-Wolff/PhotoEdit; **p. 208** Laura Dwight; **p. 209** Susan Lapides/Design Conceptions; **p. 210** Corbis/Michael S. Yamashita; **p. 213** Bob Daemmrich/Stock, Boston; **p. 214** Peter Southwick/Stock, Boston; **p. 215** Laura Dwight; **p. 218** Tom McCarthy/The Picture Cube/Index Stock; **p. 219** Nancy Sheehan/The Picture Cube/Index Stock; **p. 220** Corroon and Company/Monkmeyer; **p. 222** Leong Ka Tai/Material World; **pp. 222–223** Excerpt from S. Chess & A. Thomas. (1990). Continuities and discontinuities in development. In Lee N. Robbins & Michael Rutter (Eds.), *Straight and devious pathways from childhood to adulthood.* New York: Cambridge University Press. Reprinted with permission of Cambridge University Press; **p. 224** *(left)* Elizabeth Crews; *(right)* Bruce Plotkin/The Image Works; **p. 225** Betts Anderson/Unicorn Stock; **p. 227** Excerpts in box from Jacob's Father. (1997). Jacob's story: A miracle of the heart. *Zero to Three, 17,* 59–64; **p. 229** *(all photos)* Courtesy of Mary Ainsworth; **p. 231** James Nachtwey/Magnum Photos, Inc.; **p. 232** Corbis/Laura Dwight; **p. 233 (Figure 7.1)** From D. Benoit & K.C. Parker. (1994). Stability and transmission of attachment across three generations. *Child Development, 65,* 1444–1456. Copyright © 1994 Society for Research in Child Development; **p. 235** Richard Frieman/Photo Researchers, Inc.; **p. 239** *(left)* Brady/Monkmeyer; *(center)* Corbis/Laura Dwight; *(right)* Bob Daemmrich/Stock, Boston.

CHAPTER 8

Chapter Opener p. 242 Cathy McLaughlin/The Image Works; **p. 245** Laura Dwight; **p. 249** *(left)* Tony Freeman/PhotoEdit; *(right)* Adam Woolfitt/Woodfin Camp & Associates; **p. 250** *(left)* Lew Merrim/Monkmeyer; *(right)* Myrleen Ferguson/PhotoEdit; *(bottom)* Carol Palmer/The Picture Cube/Index Stock; **p. 252** Royce Bair/Monkmeyer; **p. 253** *(top left)* Ken Cavanagh/Photo Researchers, Inc.; *(top right)* Ellen Senisi/The Image Works; *(bottom left)* Laura Dwight/PhotoEdit; *(bottom right)* F.B. Grunzweig/Photo Researchers, Inc.; **p. 254** AP/Wide World Photos; **p. 256** James Nachtwey/Magnum Photos; **p. 257** Margot Granitsas/The Image Works; **p. 258** Joan Lebold Cohen/Photo Researchers, Inc.; **p. 264** Corbis/Stephane Maze; **p. 266** Inge King.

CHAPTER 9

Chapter Opener p. 270 Hinton/Monkmeyer; **p. 273** *(both photos)* Hazel Hankin; **p. 275** Dave Bartruff/Stock, Boston; **p. 276** Laura Dwight; **p. 280** John Lei/Stock, Boston; **p. 280 (Figure 9.2)** From G. Saxe, S.R. Guberman, & M. Gearhart. (1987). Social processes in early number development. *Monographs of the Society for Research in Child Development,* 52 (Serial No. 216). Copyright © 1987 Society for Research in Child Development; **p. 282** Elizabeth Crews; **p. 283** Trinceri/Monkmeyer; **p. 285** James Kamp/LIFE Magazine; **p. 286 (Figure 9.3)** From N.R. Hamond, & R. Fivush. (1991). Memories of Mickey Mouse: Young children recount their trip to Disney World. *Cognitive Development, 6,* 433–448; **p. 287** Corbis/Laura Dwight; **p. 288** PhotoWorks/Monkmeyer; **p. 290** Laura Dwight; **p. 293** Elizabeth Crews; **p. 297** *(left)* Tom Prettyman/PhotoEdit; *(right)* Fujiphotos/The Image Works.

CHAPTER 10

Chapter Opener p. 302 Corbis/Laura Dwight; **p. 304** Laura Dwight; **p. 306** Mel Digiacomo/The Image Bank; **p. 307** Jim Harrison/Stock, Boston; **p. 309** Margaret Miller/Photo Researchers, Inc.; **p. 312** Myrleen Ferguson/PhotoEdit; **p. 313** Laura Dwight; **p. 314** Kopstein/Monkmeyer; **pp. 316–317** Excerpts from Hans G. Furth. (1996). *Desire for society: Children's knowledge as social imagination.* New York: Plenum. Copyright © 1996 by Hans G. Furth. Used by permission; **p. 320** Robert Brenner/PhotoEdit; **p. 322** David Strickler/Monkmeyer; **p. 323 (graph)** From Zvi Strassberg, Kenneth A. Dodge, Gregory S. Pettit, & John E. Bates. (1994). Spanking in the home and children's subsequent aggression toward kindergarten peers. *Development and Psychopathology, 6,* 445–462. Used by permission; **p. 324** Sybil Shackman/Monkmeyer; **p. 325** Jerry Cooke/Photo Researchers, Inc.; **p. 326** George Gerster/Photo Researchers, Inc.; **p. 327** *(both photos)* Brady/Monkmeyer; **p. 328** *(left)* Erika Stone; *(right)* John Coletti/Stock, Boston; **p. 330** Courtesy of Kathleen Berger; **p. 331** Grantpix/Monkmeyer; **p. 333** Sybil Shackman/Monkmeyer; **p. 337** *(left)* Royce Bair/Monkmeyer; *(center)* Elizabeth Crews; *(right)* Laura Dwight.

CHAPTER 11

Chapter Opener p. 340 J. Gerard Smith/Photo Researchers, Inc.; **p. 342** Jeff Greenberg/Photo Researchers, Inc.; **p. 344** Bob Daemmrich/Stock, Boston; **p. 348** *(both photos)* Bob Daemmrich/Stock, Boston; **p. 349** Bob Daemmrich/Stock, Boston; **p. 354** Alan Carey/The Image Works; **p. 355** Bob

Daemmrich/Stock, Boston; **p. 358** Nancy Acevedo/
Monkmeyer; **p. 359** Jose Azel/Aurora; **p. 361** Robin L.
Sachs/PhotoEdit.

CHAPTER 12

Chapter Opener   p. 364 Bachmann/Photo Researchers, Inc.;
p. 367 Will & Deni McIntyre/Photo Researchers, Inc.; **p. 368**
Kaz Mori/The Image Bank; **p. 369 (figure)** From M.T.H. Chi.
(1978). Knowledge structures and memory development. In
R. S. Siegler (Ed.), *Children's thinking: What develops?* Hillsdale,
NJ: Erlbaum; **p. 370** Bachmann/Photo Researchers, Inc.;
p. 371 Elizabeth Crews; **p. 372** Richard Hutchings/Photo
Researchers, Inc.; **p. 373** Leif Skoogfors/Woodfin Camp &
Associates; **p. 374 (Figure 12.2)** From Robert S. Siegler &
Douglas R. Thompson. (1998). "Hey, would you like a nice cold
cup of lemonade on this hot day?": Children's understanding
of economic causation. *Developmental Psychology, 34,* 146–160.
Used by permission; **p. 375** *(left)* Laura Dwight; *(right)*
Eastcott-Momatiuk/Stock, Boston; **p. 378** Jeff Isaac Greenberg/
Photo Researchers, Inc.; **p. 379** Hazel Hankin ; **p. 380** Bob
Daemmrich/The Image Works; **p. 382** John O'Brian/Canada
in Stock Inc.; **p. 384** *(left)* Allison Wright/Photo Researchers,
Inc.; *(right)* Michael Yamashita/Woodfin Camp & Associates;
p. 385 Lew Merrim/Monkmeyer; **p. 386** Russell D. Curtis/
Photo Researchers, Inc.; **p. 390** Owen Franken/Stock, Boston;
p. 391 Bob Daemmrich/Stock, Boston; **p. 393** George
Ancona/International Stock.

CHAPTER 13

Chapter Opener p. 398 Rashid/Monkmeyer; **p. 400** Lindsay
Hebberd/Woodfin Camp & Associates; **p. 401** Ellis Herwig/
Stock, Boston; **p. 402** Lisa Law/The Image Works; **p. 405**
(left) Bob Daemmrich/Stock, Boston; *(right)* Joel Gordon;
p. 406 Gary Langley; **p. 408** *(left)* Joel Gordon; *(right)* Peter
Miller/Photo Researchers, Inc.; **p. 409** Jim Weiner/Photo
Researchers, Inc.; **p. 410** Bob Daemmrich/The Image Works;
p. 411 Ellen Senisi/The Image Works; **p. 412** George White
Location Photography; **p. 415** *(both photos)* Frank
Fournier/Woodfin Camp & Associates; **p. 417** Linda
Phillips/Photo Researchers, Inc.; **p. 419** Corbis/Earl Kowall;
p. 422 Bob Daemmrich/The Image Works; **p. 424** Steven
Rubin/The Image Works; **p. 426** Michael Newman/PhotoEdit;
p. 429 Katherine McGlynn/The Image Works; **p. 431** Bob
Daemmrich/The Image Works; p. 435 *(left)* Bob Daemmrich/
Stock, Boston; *(center)* Lew Merrim/Monkmeyer; *(right)* Bob
Daemmrich/The Image Works.

CHAPTER 14

Chapter Opener   p. 438 Tom & Dee Ann McCarthy/The Stock
Market; **p. 441** Richard Hutchings/Photo Researchers, Inc.;
p. 442 Bob Daemmrich/Stock, Boston; **p. 443** Rick
Kopstein/Monkmeyer; **p. 444** Joel Gordon; **p. 445** Sybil
Shackman/Monkmeyer; **p. 446** *(top)* Stephen Wilkes/The
Image Bank; *(bottom)* Henley & Savage/The Stock Market;
p. 448 Bill Gillette/Stock, Boston; **p. 450** Arlene
Collins/Monkmeyer ; **p. 451** *(top)* AP/Wide World Photos;
(bottom) Janeart/The Image Bank; **p. 452** *(top)* Fran Heyl &
Associates; *(bottom)* Michael Newman/PhotoEdit; **p. 456**
Nancy J. Pierce/Photo Researchers, Inc.; **p. 458** Tony
Freeman/PhotoEdit; **p. 459** Margot Granitsas/The Image
Works; **p. 463** Mark M. Walker/The Picture Cube/Index

Stock; **p. 464 (Figure 14.7)** From Sally Casswell. (1996). Alcohol
use: Growing up and learning about drinking—Children in
Dunedin in the 1980s. In Phil A. Silva & Warren R. Stanton
(Eds.), *From child to adult: The Dunedin multidisciplinary
health and development study.* Auckland: Oxford University
Press.

CHAPTER 15

Chapter Opener   p. 468 Mug Shots/The Stock Market; **p. 470**
Jim Pickerell/The Image Works; **p. 471** Will McIntyre/Photo
Researchers, Inc.; **p. 472** *(left)* Doug Martin/Photo
Researchers, Inc.; *(right)* Richard Hutchings/Photo
Researchers, Inc.; **p. 475** Sybil Shackman/Monkmeyer;
p. 478 Miguel L. Fairbanks; **p. 480 (Figure 15.3)** From Ted R.
Miller & Rebecca S. Spicer. (1998). How safe are our schools?
American Journal of Public Health, 88, 413–418; **p. 481**
AP/Wide World Photos; **p. 482** H. Marais-Barrit/The Gamma
Liaison Network; **p. 483** Bonnie Kamin/PhotoEdit; **p. 485**
Corbis/Michael S. Yamashita; **p. 487** Michelle Agins/NYT
Pictures; **p. 488** Rhoda Sidney/Stock, Boston; **p. 491** Richard
Hutchin/Photo Researchers, Inc.; **p. 494** Mary Kate
Denny/PhotoEdit.

CHAPTER 16

Chapter Opener   p. 500 Tom & Dee Ann McCarthy/The Stock
Market; **p. 502** *(left)* Eastcott-Momatiuk/The Image Works;
(right) Robert Clay/Monkmeyer; **p. 503** Jeffrey W.
Myers/Stock, Boston; **p. 504** *(left)* Renato Rotolo/The Gamma
Liaison Network; *(right)* Elizabeth Crews; **p. 507** Lester
Sloan/Woodfin Camp & Associates; **p. 509** *(top)* Lester
Sloan/Woodfin Camp & Associates; *(bottom)* Charles
Gupton/The Stock Market; **p. 510** Christopher Smith/Impact
Visuals; **p. 511** Rhoda Sidney/Monkmeyer; **p. 512** Paula
Lerner/The Picture Cube/Index Stock; **p. 515** *(left)* Joel
Gordon; *(right)* Dan Walsh/The Picture Cube/Index Stock;
p. 517 Eileen Kovchok; **p. 518** Butch Martin/The Image Bank;
p. 519 (Figure 16.1) From Maryse Richards, Paul A. Crowe,
Reed Larson, & Amy Swarr. (1998). Developmental patterns
and gender differences in the experience of peer companion-
ship during adolescence. *Child Development, 69,* 154–163;
p. 523 Joel Gordon; **p. 525 (Figure 16.5)** Adapted from Lyle W.
Shannon. (1988). *Criminal career continuity: Its social context.*
New York: Human Sciences Press. Reprinted with permission
of Plenum Publishing Corp.; **p. 526** Alon Reininger/Woodfin
Camp & Associates; **p. 529** AP/Wide World Photos; **p. 533**
(left) Stephen Wilkes/The Image Bank; *(center)* Charles
Gupton/The Stock Market; *(right)* Jeffrey W. Myers/Stock,
Boston.

APPENDIX A

p. A-4 (Figure A-1) From R.J.M. Snijders & K.H. Nicolaides.
(1996). *Ultrasound markers for fetal chromosomal defects.*
New York: Parthenon **p. A-10 (Figure A-9)** From *The New
York Times,* August 14, 1995. Gap between rich and poor chil-
dren. Used by permission. **p. A-12 (Figure A-12)** From Susan
Williams McElroy & Kristin Anderson Moore. (1997). Trends
over time in teenage pregnancy and childbearing: The critical
changes. In Rebecca A. Maynard (Ed.), *Kids having kids:
Economic costs and social consequences of teen pregnancy.*
Urban Institute Press.

Name Index

Page references in *italic* type indicate illustrations.

Subject Index

Page references in *italic* type refer to illustrations. Page numbers followed by italic *t* indicate tables. A selected number of key names are included in the Subject Index. See the Name Index for additional names.